Monetary Economics

Jagdish Handa

LONDON & NEW YORK

First published 2000
by Routledge
11 New Fetter Lane, London EC4P 4EE

Simultaneously published in the USA and Canada
by Routledge
29 West 35th Street, New York, NY 10001

Routledge is an imprint of the Taylor & Francis Group

Typeset in Plantin and Rockwell by
Keystroke, Jacaranda Lodge, Wolverhampton
Printed and bound in Great Britain by
TJ International Ltd, Padstow, Cornwall

British Library Cataloguing in Publication Data
A catalogue record for this book is available from the British Library

Library of Congress Cataloging in Publication Data
A catalogue record for this book has been requested

ISBN 0–415–19925–5 (hbk)
ISBN 0–415–19926–3 (pbk)

Contents

Preface

This book represents a comprehensive presentation of monetary economics. It integrates the presentation of monetary theory with its heritage, its empirical formulations and their econometric tests. While its main focus is on monetary theory and its empirical tests rather than on the institutional monetary and financial structure of the economy, the latter is brought in wherever needed for elucidating a theory or showing the limitations to its applicability. The illustrations for this purpose, as well as the empirical studies cited, are taken from the United States, Canada and the United Kingdom. We also attempt to take some account of the significant differences between the financially developed economies and the less-developed or developing ones.

In addition, our presentation also provides an introduction to the main historical patterns of monetary thought and the diversity of ideas in monetary economics, especially on the effectiveness of monetary policy and the contending schools in monetary theory and policy.

Our presentation of the theoretical aspects of monetary economics is tempered by the goals of empirical relevance and intuitive understanding. The derivation of the theoretical implications is followed by a discussion of their simplifications and modifications made in the process of econometric testing, and the empirical results from some empirical studies.

Part One of the book consists of the introduction to monetary economics and its heritage. The latter is not meant to be exhaustive but is intended to illustrate the evolution of monetary thought and to provide the reader with a flavour of the earlier literature on this subject.

Part Two places monetary microeconomics in the context of the Walrasian general equilibrium model. This chapter captures the foundations of money in the economy to the extent that these are reflected in the rational economic behaviour of households and firms in competitive markets.

Part Three focuses on the demand for money. Besides the usual treatment of the transactions and speculative demands, this part also presents recent models of the precautionary demand for money. It further introduces the reader to the more recent contributions on the buffer stock demand for money. The three theoretical chapters on the components of money demand are followed by three chapters on its empirical aspects, including a separate chapter on the criteria and tests underlying monetary aggregation.

Part Four deals with the supply of money and the role of the central bank in determining the money supply. Besides presenting the main approaches to the money supply process, this part also examines the important policy issues of the potential conflicts among policy makers, central bank independence, discretionary monetary policy versus simple decision rules, and credibility of monetary policy.

No presentation of monetary economics can be complete without adequate coverage of monetary policy and its impact on the macroeconomy. Proper treatment of this topic requires knowledge of the underlying macroeconomic models and their implications for monetary policy. Parts Five and Six of the book focus on money and monetary policy in the macroeconomy. The five chapters of Part Five present the main macroeconomic models of both the classical and Keynesian paradigms and their monetary implications for the closed economy. Part Six presents the open economy models.

The remaining parts of the book deal with special topics. Part Seven deals with the theories of the rate of interest and of the term and risk structures of interest rates. Part Eight presents the newer overlapping generations models of fiat money and compares their implications and empirical validity with those of the theories based on money in the utility function and money in the production function. Part Nine addresses monetary growth theory, and assesses the contributions of both the quantity of money and those of financial institutions to output growth. To do so, it covers the neoclassical growth theory, as well as the newer endogenous growth theories.

Level and patterns of use of this book

This book is at the level of the advanced undergraduate and graduate courses in monetary economics. It requires that the students have had at least one prior course in macro-economics and/or money and banking. It also assumes some knowledge of differential calculus and statistics.

Given the large number of topics covered and the number of chapters, this book can be used over one semester on a selective basis or over two semesters on a fairly complete basis. It also offers considerable scope for the instructors to adapt the material to their specific interests and to the levels of their courses by exercising selectivity in the chapters covered and the sequence of topics.

The full coverage of this book requires courses over at least a full academic year. Some suggested patterns for one-term courses are:

1. Courses on the demand and supply of money and including central banking: Chapters 1, 2, 4, 5, 7–12.
2. Courses on monetary macroeconomics: Chapters 1, 2, 13–20.
3. Courses on monetary macroeconomics and central bank policies: Chapters 1, 2, 11–16, 18, 19.
4. Courses on advanced topics in monetary economics: Chapters 3, 6, 15–26.
   A first course along the lines of 1, 2 or 3 can be followed by a second course based on 4.

McGill offers a tandem set of two one-term graduate courses covering money and banking and monetary economics. The first term of these is also open to senior honours students. This book came out of my lectures for these courses.

My students in the first one of the two courses almost invariably have shown a strong interest in monetary policy issues and want its analysis to be covered at an early stage, while I want to also cover the main material on the demand and supply of money. I allow the students a wide degree of latitude in selecting the pattern in which these topics are covered. The mutually satisfactory combination in our case has often been to do the introductory Chapters 1 and 2, followed by the monetary macroeconomics Chapters 13 to 16 and then money demand and supply Chapters 4 to 12 (excluding Chapter 6 on the precautionary and buffer stock demands for money). However, we have in some years chosen to do the money demand and supply chapters before the monetary macroeconomics ones. These patterns left the more theoretical, advanced or special topics Chapters 3, 6 and 17–26 for the following second course in monetary theory.

Acknowledgments

I am indebted to my students in monetary economics who suffered – and hopefully benefited – from several drafts of this manuscript. Many helped to improve it.

I owe a special debt to Ossama Mikhail. He not only offered me suggestions on the analysis and helped in drawing the figures but also came to my rescue in innumerable struggles with the mulish waywardness of my computer. I am also indebted to several referees who had to plough through this rather large manuscript. Their suggestions have definitely led to its improvement.

It is, as always, a pleasure to acknowledge the love and support of my wife, Sushma, and sons, Sunny and Rishi, as well as of other family members, especially my brother Subash.

Professor Jagdish Handa
Handa@Leacock.lan.mcgill.ca

part one

INTRODUCTION AND HERITAGE

chapter
one

INTRODUCTION

Monetary economics has both a microeconomics component and a macroeconomics one.

The fundamental questions of monetary economics concern the proper definition of money, its demand and supply, and its impact on the economy.

The financial assets that can serve the medium of payments role of money have changed over time so that the proper definition of money has also kept changing.

Commercial banks are only one type of financial intermediaries. The distinction between banks and other financial institutions has increasingly become blurred in recent decades as the barriers between them have been reduced or eliminated and the competition between them for the public's deposits has increased.

At the level of the overall economy, monetary economics is a central part of macroeconomics. The main paradigms of macroeconomics are the classical and the Keynesian ones. The former studies the competitive economy at its full employment equilibrium, while the latter studies its deviations away from this equilibrium.

Monetary policy has to be studied in the context of macroeconomics.

---

key concepts introduced in this chapter

- The functions of money
- Money supply versus money stock
- The definition of money
- M1, M2 and broader definitions of money
- Financial intermediaries
- The creation of money by banks
- The classical paradigm for macroeconomics
- The Walrasian general equilibrium model
- Neoclassical, traditional classical, modern classical and new classical models
- The Keynesian paradigm for macroeconomics

Monetary economics is the economics of the money stock and of its repercussions on the economy. It studies the money and financial markets, the extent to which money and its substitutes influence the behaviour of the economic units in their decisions and the implications of that influence in the macroeconomic context.

In a monetary economy, virtually all exchanges of commodities among distinct economic agents are against money and virtually all loans are made in money and not in commodities, so that virtually all market transactions in a modern monetary economy involve money.[1] Therefore, the scope of monetary economics is a very wide one. Few aspects of a monetary economy are totally divorced from the role of money and the efficiency of its provision and usage.

Monetary economics has both a microeconomics and a macroeconomics part.

The microeconomics part of monetary economics

The microeconomics part of monetary economics focuses on the study of the demand and supply of money and their equilibrium. No study of monetary economics can be even minimally adequate without a study of the behaviour of those financial institutions whose behaviour determines the money stock and its close substitutes. The institutions supplying the main components of the money stock are the monetary authorities – often a euphemism for the central banking system of the country[2] – and the commercial banks. The commercial banks are themselves part of the wider system of financial intermediaries which determine the supply of some of the components of money as well as the substitutes for money, also known as near-monies.

The three major components of the microeconomics part of monetary economics are the demand for money, covered in Chapters 4 to 9, the supply of money, covered in Chapter 10, and the central bank and financial institutions, covered in Chapters 11 and 12.

The macroeconomics part of monetary economics: money in the macroeconomy

The macroeconomics part of monetary economics is closely integrated into the standard short-run macroeconomic theory. The reason for such closeness in short-run analysis is that monetary phenomena are pervasive in their influence on virtually all the major macro-economic variables in the short run. Among variables influenced by the shifts in the supply and demand for money are national output and employment, the rate of unemployment, interest rates, exports and imports, exchange rates and the balance of payments. And among the most important questions in macroeconomic analysis are whether – to what extent and how – the changes in the money supply, prices and inflation affect the above variables, especially national output and employment. This part of monetary economics is presented in Chapters 13 to 21.

A departure from the traditional treatment of money in economic analysis has been provided in the last couple of decades by the overlapping generations models of money. These have different implications for monetary policy and its impact on the economy than the standard short-run macroeconomic models. While most textbooks on monetary economics exclude the overlapping generations models of money, they are an important new development in monetary economics. They are presented in Chapters 22 to 24.

The long-run analysis of monetary economics is less extensive and while macroeconomic growth theory is sometimes extended to include money, the resulting monetary growth theory is only a small element of monetary economics. It is also omitted from the usual textbook presentation of monetary economics. However, there is increasing emphasis on growth theory within macroeconomics and there are still unresolved questions about the role of money in growth. To investigate these issues, monetary growth theory is covered in Chapter 26, with Chapter 25 acting as a prelude to it by introducing the standard growth theory analysis without money.

There are different approaches to the macroeconomics of monetary policy. These include the Walrasian model, the classical group of models and the Keynesian group of models. We elucidate their differences at an introductory level towards the end of this chapter. Their detailed exposition is given in Chapters 13 to 17.

1.1 WHAT IS MONEY AND WHAT DOES IT DO?

1.1.1 The functions of money

Money is not itself the name of a particular asset and is best defined independently of the particular assets that may exist in the economy at any one time, since the assets which function as money tend to change over time in any given country and among countries. At a theoretical level, money is defined in terms of the functions that it performs. The traditional specification of these functions is:

(i)   medium of exchange/payments;
(ii) store of value, sometimes specified as a temporary store of value or temporary abode of purchasing power;
(iii) standard of deferred payments;
(iv) unit of account.

Of these functions, the medium of payments is the absolutely essential function of money. Any asset that does not directly perform this function – or cannot indirectly perform it through a quick and costless transfer into a medium of exchange – cannot be designated as money. A developed economy usually has many assets which can perform such a role, though some do so better than others. The particular assets that perform this role vary over time, with currency being the only or main medium of exchange early in the evolution of monetary economies. It is complemented by demand deposits with the arrival of the banking system and then by an increasing array of financial assets as other financial intermediaries become established.

1.1.2 The definitions of money

Historically, the definitions of money have measured the quantity of money in the economy as the sum of those items that serve as media of exchange in the economy. However, at any time in a developed monetary economy, there may be other items that do not directly serve as a medium of exchange but are readily convertible into the medium of exchange at little cost and trouble and can simultaneously be a store of value. Such items are close substitutes for the medium of exchange itself. Consequently, there is a considerable measure of controversy and disagreement about whether to confine the definition of money to the narrow role of the medium of exchange or to include in this definition those items that are close substitutes for the medium of exchange.[3]

A theoretically oriented answer to this question would aim at a *pure* definition: money is that good which serves directly as a medium of exchange or payments. This approximates the *narrow definition of money* and is given the symbol M1. Close substitutes to money defined as the medium of payments are referred to as *near-monies*. The narrow definition of money – in common usage at the present time – is that money in the economy is the sum of the currency in the hands of the public and the public's demand deposits in commercial banks, since the payments for commodities are only made by transfers of these from the buyer to the seller.

An empirical answer to the definition of the money stock is much more eclectic than its theoretical counterpart. It could define money narrowly or broadly, depending upon what substitutes to the medium of exchange are included or excluded. The broad definition that has won the widest acceptance among economists is known as (Milton) *Friedman's definition of money*. It defines money as the sum of currency in the hands of the public plus all of the public's deposits in commercial banks. The latter include demand deposits as well as time and savings deposits in commercial banks. Friedman's definition of money is often symbolized as M2. It is also sometimes referred to as 'the broad definition of money'. However, there are now in usage many still broader definitions, usually designated as M3, M4, etc., so that it has become inappropriate to refer only to M2 as the broad definition of money. We will, therefore, refer to it as the Friedman definition or as M2.

A still broader definition of money is M2 plus deposits in near-banks – i.e., those financial institutions in which the deposits perform almost the same role for depositors as similar deposits in commercial banks. Examples of such institutions are savings and loan associations and mutual savings banks in the United States; credit unions, trust companies and mortgage loan companies in Canada; and building societies in the United Kingdom. The incorporation of such deposits into the measurement of money is designated by the symbols M3, M4, etc., or by M2A, M2B, etc. However, the definitions of these symbols have not become standardized, so that their definitions remain country specific. Their specification and the basis for choosing among them is given briefly later in this chapter and discussed more fully in Chapter 8.

1.2 MONEY SUPPLY AND MONEY STOCK

Money is a good which, just like other goods, is demanded and supplied by the various participants in the economy. There are a number of determinants of the demand and supply of money. The most important of the determinants of money demand are national income, the price level and interest rates, while that of money supply is the behaviour of the central bank of the country which is given the power to control the money supply and bring about changes in it.

The *equilibrium amount* in the market for money specifies the *money stock*, as opposed to the *money supply*, which is a behavioural function. These are depicted in Figure 1.1a with money M on the horizontal axis and the interest rate r on the vertical axis. The money supply curve is designated as M^s and the money demand curve is designated as M^d. The equilibrium point is M_0 and shows the money stock. It equals the quantity of money supplied at the existing interest rates. It is not the supply of money, which is a curve or a function.

The money supply and the money stock are identical in the case where the money supply is exogenously determined, usually by the policies of the central bank. In such a case, it is independent of the interest rate and other economic variables, though it may influence them. In this case, the money supply curve will be a vertical line, as shown by the line M^s in Figure 1.1b. Much of the monetary and macroeconomic reasoning of a theoretical nature

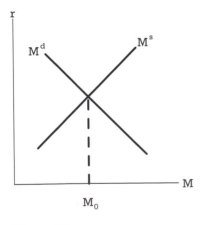

Figure 1.1a

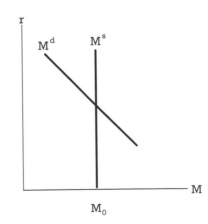

Figure 1.1b

assumes this case, so that the terms 'money stock' and 'money supply' are used synony-mously. One has to judge from the context whether the two concepts are being used as distinct or as identical ones.

The control of the money supply rests with the monetary authorities. Their policy with respect to changes in the money supply is known as monetary policy.

1.3 THE NOMINAL VERSUS THE REAL VALUE OF THE MONEY SUPPLY

It is important to distinguish between the nominal and the real value of the money stock. The *nominal value of money* is in terms of money itself as the measuring unit. The *real value of money* is in terms of its purchasing power. Thus, the nominal value of a $1 note is 1 – and that of a $20 note is 20. The real value of money is the amount of goods and services one unit of money can buy and is the reciprocal of the price level of commodities traded in the economy. It equals $1/P$ where P is the price level in the economy. The real value of money is what we usually mean when we use the term 'the value of money'.

The demand and supply functions of money are often stated in nominal terms in a general analysis involving *both* of them. However, the demand for money is mainly by the public, which is concerned not so much with its nominal as with its real value. Therefore, the demand for money is usually investigated in real terms. However, the supply of money is mainly determined by the central bank in nominal terms.[4]

1.4 THE MONEY MARKET IN MONETARY AND MACROECONOMICS

The money market in monetary and macroeconomics is defined as the market in which the demand and supply of money (M1, M2 or a broader money measure) interact, with equilibrium representing its clearance. However, the common English language usage of this term refers to the market for short-term bonds, especially that of Treasury bills. To illustrate this common usage, this definition is embodied in the term, money market mutual funds, which are mutual funds with holdings of short-term bonds. It is important to note that our usage of the term 'the money market' in this book will follow that of macroeconomics. To reiterate, we will mean by it the market for money, not the market for short-term bonds.

1.5 A BRIEF HISTORY OF THE DEFINITION OF MONEY

The multiplicity of the functions performed by money does not aid in the task of unambiguously identifying particular assets with money and often poses severe problems for such identification since different assets perform these functions to varying degrees. Problems with an empirical measure of money are not new nor have they necessarily taken their most acute form only recently.

Early stages in the evolution from a barter economy to a monetary economy usually have a commodity money. One form of these is currency in the form of coins made of a precious metal, with an exchange value which is at least roughly equal to the value of the metal in the coin. These coins were usually minted with the monarch's authority and were made legal tender, so that the seller or creditor could not refuse to accept them in payment.

Legal tender was in certain circumstances supplemented as a means of payment by the promissory notes of trustworthy persons or institutions and in the eighteenth and nineteenth centuries by bills of exchange in Britain. However, they never became a generally accepted medium of payment. The emergence of private commercial banks after the eighteenth century in Britain led to note issues by them and eventually also led to orders of withdrawal – i.e., cheques – drawn upon these banks by those holding demand deposits with them. However, while the keeping of demand deposits with banks had become common among firms and richer individuals by the beginning of the twentieth century, the popularity of such deposits among the ordinary person came only in the twentieth century. With this popularity, demand deposits became a component of the medium of exchange in the economy, with their amount eventually becoming larger than that of currency.

In Britain, in the mid-nineteenth century, economists and bankers faced the problem of whether to treat the demand liabilities of commercial banks, in addition to currency, as money or not. Commercial banking was still in its infancy and was confined to richer individuals and larger firms. While it functioned as a medium for payments among these groups, most of the population did not use it. In such a context, there was considerable controversy on the proper definition of money and the appropriate monetary policies and regulations in mid-nineteenth-century England. These disputes revolved around the emergence of bank demand deposits as a substitute, though yet quite imperfect, for currency and whether or not the former were a part of the money supply. Further evolution of demand deposits and of banks in the nineteenth and the first half of the twentieth century in Britain, Canada and the USA, led to the relative security and common usage of demand deposits and established their close substitutability for currency. Consequently, the accepted definition of money by the second quarter of the twentieth century had become currency in the hands of the public plus demand deposits in commercial banks. As we have indicated above, this definition is known as the narrow definition of money and is denoted as M1.

Until the mid-twentieth century, demand deposits did not pay interest but savings deposits in commercial banks did do so, though subject to legal or customary ceilings on their interest rates. During the 1950s, changes in banking practices caused these savings deposits to increasingly become closer substitutes for demand deposits so that the major dispute of the 1950s on the definition of money was whether savings deposits should or should not be included in the definition of money. However, by the early 1960s, most economists had come to measure the supply of money by M2 – that is, as M1 plus savings deposits in commercial banks – which does not include any types of deposits in other financial institutions. M2 is known as the Friedman definition (measure) of money, since Milton Friedman had been one of its main proponents in the 1950s and 1960s.

In the USA, during the 1960s, market interest rates on bonds and Treasury bills rose significantly above the ceilings set by the regulatory authorities on the interest rates which could be paid on savings deposits in commercial banks. Competition in the unregulated sphere led to changes in the characteristics of existing near-monies in non-bank financial intermediaries which made them closer to demand deposits and also led to the creation of a range of other assets in the unregulated sphere. Such liabilities of non-bank financial intermediaries were substitutes – some closer than others but mostly still quite imperfect ones – for currency and demand deposits. Their increasing closeness raised the same sort of controversy that had existed during the nineteenth century about the role of demand deposits and in the 1950s occurred about savings deposits in commercial banks. Similar evolution and controversies occurred in Canada and the UK. The critical question in these controversies was – and still is – how close an asset has to be to M1 to be included in the measure of money.

Financial innovation has been extremely rapid in the last few decades. It has included technical changes in the servicing of various kinds of deposits, such as the introduction of automatic teller machines, banking from home through the use of computers, etc. It has also included the creation of new assets such as the NOW (negotiable orders of deposit), money market mutual funds, etc. There has also been the spread first of credit cards, then of debit or bank cards, followed still more recently by the attempts to create and market electronic money cards – sometimes also known as electronic purses or smart cards. Further, competition among the different types of financial intermediaries in the provision of liabilities that are close to demand deposits or readily convertible into the latter, has increased considerably in recent decades. Many of these innovations served to further blur the distinction between demand and savings deposits to the point of its being only in name rather than in effect, and also blurred the distinction between banks and some of the other types of financial intermediaries as providers of liquid liabilities. This process of innovation and the evolution of financial institutions into an overlapping pattern in the provision of financial services is still continuing.

The evolution of money and near-monies since 1945

To summarize the developments on the definition of money in the period since 1945, this period opened with the widely accepted definition of money as being currency in the hands of the public plus demand deposits in commercial banks (M1). This definition emphasized the medium of exchange role of money. Demand deposits were regulated in several respects, interest could not be legally – or was not customarily – paid on them and certain amounts of reserves had to be legally – or were customarily – maintained against them in the banks. Against this background, a variety of developments led to the widespread creation and acceptance of new substitutes for demand deposits and the increasing closeness of savings and time deposits to demand deposits. In Canada, this evolution increased the liquidity of notice and time deposits with the chartered banks which dominated this end of the financial sector, with also some increase in the liquidity of the liabilities of trust companies, credit associations and *caisses populaires*, and mortgage and loan associations. In the United States until the 1970s, the changes increased the liquidity primarily of time deposits in the commercial banks, and to some extent of deposits in mutual savings banks, and shares in savings and loan associations. In the United Kingdom, the increase in liquidity occurred for interest-bearing deposits in retail banks and building societies. Given this evolution in the 1960s and 1970s, a variety of studies established these assets to be fairly close – but not perfect – substitutes for demand deposits.

This evolution of close substitutes for M1 led in the 1950s to a renewal of controversy, almost dormant in the first half of this century, on the proper definition of money. In particular, in the third quarter of the twentieth century, there was rapid growth of savings deposits in commercial banks and in non-bank financial intermediaries, with their liabilities becoming increasingly closer substitutes for demand deposits, without becoming direct media of exchange. This led to the acceptance of M2 as the appropriate definition of money, though not without some disputes. In the fourth quarter, as mentioned above, there have been numerous innovations that have made many liabilities of financial intermediaries increasingly indistinguishable from demand deposits. This has led to the adoption or at least espousal of still wider definitions under the symbols M3, M4, etc.

Theoretical and econometric developments on the definition of money

Keynes in 1936 had already stressed the speculative demand for money as a major motive for holding money and Milton Friedman in 1956 had reinterpreted the quantity theory of money to stress the role of money as a temporary abode of purchasing power, similar to a durable consumer good or a capital good. Other authors had pointed out the development of close substitutes for money as an aspect of the evolution of economies. These developments led to a realignment of the functional definition of money to stress its store of value aspect relative to its medium of exchange one. The result of this shift in focus was to further stress the closeness of substitution between the liabilities of banks and those of other financial intermediaries.

Such shifts in the definition of money have been supported by shifts in both the analysis of the demand for money, suited to the stress on the store of value function, and by a large number of empirical studies. However, in the presence of a variety of assets performing the functions of money to varying degrees, purely theoretical analysis has not proved to be a clear guide to the empirical definition or measurement of money. As a result, research on measuring the money stock for empirical and policy purposes has taken a variety of routes since the 1960s. Two broad routes may be distinguished in this empirical work, which are as follows.

(i) One of the routes was to measure money as the sum of M1 and those assets that are close substitutes for demand deposits. Closeness of substitution was determined on the basis of the *price elasticities* in the money demand functions or the *elasticities of substitution* between M1 and various non-money assets. Such studies generally reported relatively high degrees of substitution among M1, savings deposits in commercial banks, and deposits in near-bank financial intermediaries and therefore supported a definition of money that is broader than M1 and in many studies even broader than M2.

(ii) The second major mode of defining money was to examine its appropriateness in a macroeconomic framework. In this approach, the definition of money was specified as that which would 'best' explain or predict the course of nominal national income and of other relevant macroeconomic variables over time. But there proved to be little agreement on what these other relevant variables should be. The quantity theory tradition (in the work of Milton Friedman, most of his associates and many other economists) took nominal national income as the only relevant variable. For the 1950s and 1960s, this approach found that the 'best' definition of money, as shown by examining the correlation coefficients between various definitions of money and nominal national income, was currency in the hands of the public plus deposits (including time) in the commercial banks. This was the Friedman definition of money and was widely used in the 1960s. However, it should be obvious that the appropriate definition of money under Friedman's procedure could vary between periods and countries, as it did in the 1970s and 1980s.

Further, in the disputes on this issue in the 1960s, many researchers in the Keynesian tradition took the appropriate macroeconomic variables related to money as being nominal national income and an interest rate, and defined money much more broadly than M2 to include deposits in several types of non-bank financial intermediaries and various types of Treasury bills and government bonds. The latter types of assets do not possess the same degree of liquidity as money narrowly defined and the evaluation of their degrees of moneyness or liquidity became an important and disputed issue.[5]

Up to the 1970s, empirical work along the above lines brought out an array of results, conflicting in detail though often in agreement that a definition of money wider than currency plus demand deposits does better in explaining the relevant macroeconomic variables than money narrowly defined. This consensus vanished in the 1970s and 1980s in the face of increasing empirical evidence that none of the simple-sum aggregates of money – whether M1, M2 or a still broader one – had a stable relationship with nominal national income. Research on the 1970s and 1980s data showed that the demand functions for the various simple-sum monetary aggregates were unstable. Further, they did not possess a stable relationship with nominal income.

The above findings prompted the espousal of several new functional forms for the definition of money. Among these are the Divisia aggregates. It also led to the use of new econometric techniques, such as cointegration analysis and error-correction models, for estimating the money function and the derivation of long-run and short-run demand functions for money. These issues are further investigated in Chapters 7 to 9.

1.6　THE PRACTICAL DEFINITIONS OF MONEY AND RELATED CONCEPTS

We have already referred to several definitions of money. These definitions are fairly, though not completely, standardized across countries for M1 and M2 but tend to differ for broader designations. Note that these definitions have usually broadened over time. The following gives their current usage in the USA.

M1   = currency in circulation among the public (i.e., excluding the Fed, the US Treasury and commercial banks) + demand deposits in commercial banks[6] (excluding interbank and US government deposits and those of foreign banks) + other checkable deposits including negotiable orders of withdrawal (NOW) + credit union (such as savings and loan associations) share draft accounts + demand deposits at thrift institutions (such as mutual savings banks) – cash items in the process of collection and Federal reserve float.

M2   = M1 + savings deposits, including money market deposit accounts + small time deposits under $100,000 + balances in retail money market mutual funds.

M3   = M2 + time deposits over $100,000 + Eurodollars held by US residents at foreign branches of US banks and at all banks in the UK and Canada + money market mutual funds held by institutions.

Note that M1, M2 and M3 exclude amounts held by US commercial banks, the US government, money market funds, foreign banks and official institutions.

The above detailed descriptions for the United States of M1 and M2 are more complex than our usual modes of defining them. However, our usual definitions are reasonable proxies. Under our proxy definitions, M1 is defined as currency in the hands of the public plus checkable deposits in deposit-taking financial institutions. M2 is defined as M1 plus (small or retail) time and savings deposits in these institutions.

For Canada, the monetary aggregates are measured as:

M1   = currency in the hands of the public and demand deposits in chartered banks.[7]

M2   = M1 plus personal savings deposits and non-personal notice deposits at chartered banks.

M2+   = M2 plus deposits at trust and mortgage loan companies and credit unions (including *caisses populaires*[8]).

'Adjusted M2+' = M2+ plus Canada Savings Bonds and mutual funds at financial institutions.

M3   = M2 plus non-personal fixed-term deposits at chartered banks and foreign currency deposits of residents booked in Canada.

For the United Kingdom, the definitions of the symbols in common usage are:

M1   = currency plus current account (checking) sterling deposits in retail banks and building societies, held by 'UK residents'.[9]

M2   = currency plus sterling deposits in retail banks[10] and building societies, held by UK residents.

M4   = currency plus sterling deposits at the central bank, other banks and building societies, held by UK residents.

Note that the definitions of the monetary aggregates beyond M2, e.g., M3 and M4, differ more radically among countries than of M1 and M2. For M3 and M4, the only common denominator is that they are broader than M2 and include, besides M2, other highly liquid assets held at financial institutions. The reliance on these specific wider aggregates usually reflects the peculiarities of the country's financial structure.

As Chapters 8 and 9 show, the relative merits of using M1, M2 and still broader aggregates depend upon the period, the country and the function being estimated.

Note that currency holdings and M1 are becoming increasingly smaller proportions of M2 and wider aggregates. In the USA, at the end of 1995, the amount of currency in the economy was $379b,[11] M1 was $1,150b, M2 was $3,680b and M3 was $4,954b. The ratio of M1 to M2 was only 31% and to M3 was 23%. For Canada in 1995, the currency in the economy was $26.8b, M1 was $62.7b while M2+ was $618.4b. The ratio of M1 to M2+ was only 10%. For the UK in 1995, currency holdings were £20.8b, M2 was £439.4b, M4 was £682.5b.[12]

The monetary base

The money supply is related to the monetary base – sometimes also called the *reserve base* – by the monetary base multiplier, which is greater than one. Consequently, the monetary base is also known as *high-powered money*. We will use the symbol B for it. It is specified for the USA as:

B = Currency outside the Federal Reserve System (or alternatively stated as, currency in the hands of the non-bank public and vault cash held by banks) + reserves held by the commercial banks at the Federal Reserve Banks.

This is a fairly standard definition of the monetary base. For the United Kingdom, M0 is often used as the symbol for the monetary base. It is defined as currency in the hands of the public plus banks' operational deposits with the Bank of England. This symbol is usually not used in Canada and the USA.

1.7 FINANCIAL INTERMEDIARIES AND THE CREATION OF FINANCIAL ASSETS

Asset transmutation by financial intermediaries

Financial intermediaries are institutions that *intermediate* in the financial process between ultimate borrowers and ultimate lenders in the economy. The *ultimate borrowers* include consumers who need to borrow to finance part or all of their consumption, firms that borrow to invest in physical capital and the government which borrows to finance its deficits. The *ultimate lenders* are the economic units that save part of their current income by spending less than their current income on their purchases of commodities and want to lend some or all of these savings to others for some duration. Householders form the major bulk of the ultimate lenders, saving part of their current income. Some of the firms engaged in production also do not spend all of their current income on immediate purchases of inputs and save part of it, and are willing to lend these to others. The government does the same on a net basis when it runs a surplus.

Financial intermediaries borrow from the ultimate lenders or from other intermediaries by issuing their own liabilities in exchange and re-lend to others by accepting the latter's liabilities. In the modern economy, only a small proportion of the savings is directly transferred from the savers to the ultimate borrowers. Most of the savings are directed by the savers to financial intermediaries such as banks, mutual funds, pension funds, insurance companies etc., which re-channel the funds thus obtained to firms and the government, directly by buying their shares and bonds or indirectly through other financial intermediaries such as investment banks.

The basic reason for this intermediation is the differences in the preferences of the savers for asset characteristics, such as liquidity and security, and those attaching to the instruments issued by the firms and the government. Consequently, there is in general a considerable difference in the characteristics of the liabilities sold to the savers by a financial intermediary and those of the assets bought by it, resulting in what is sometimes called the *asset-transmutation process*.

The multiple creation of financial assets

All financial assets are 'created' and have no intrinsic physical existence, but are the liabilities of some economic unit or other. They may be examined in terms of their characteristics, especially in terms of their yield or expected yield, risk of loss, marketability, maturity and so on. Anyone purchasing a financial asset may be thought of as purchasing a particular set of characteristics such as risk and marketability etc., in exchange for a specified expected yield on the asset. Financial intermediaries cater to this demand through the creation of assets with differing combinations of characteristics. For many pairs of assets, it is feasible for some intermediary to create a third asset that offers a mix of the characteristics of the original two assets, so that the multiplicity of differentiated assets is a common outcome of unregulated financial intermediation.

Financial intermediaries typically issue assets with more desirable characteristics for lenders than do the ultimate borrowers, persuading the latter to hold the liabilities of the intermediaries. In turn, the intermediaries use the funds obtained from the sale of their liabilities to purchase the liabilities of other borrowers which pay a higher expected net yield, thus covering the expenses of intermediation and making a profit in the process.

Banks are financial intermediaries that borrow from the public by inviting demand and time deposits or issuing their own securities and hold the liabilities issued by others. Their existence is a superb example of the asset transmutation through financial intermediation. The main liabilities of banks are deposits which are virtually riskless to the depositors since they are payable on demand or after a short specified notice. In short, they are highly liquid. By contrast, the assets held by the banks are government securities, loans to the public, etc., possessing some risk of loss and, as with loans, a limited degree of marketability or encashment at short notice. Therefore, the assets issued by the banks are much more liquid than the assets held by them. Conversely, the return paid by the banks on the former is less than the return that the banks earn on the latter.

Financial intermediaries permeating an unregulated economy lead to a multiplicative creation of their liabilities. To illustrate, consider an economy in which everyone is willing to hold the asset A issued by a given intermediary.[13] Now assume that an ultimate lender saves $100 and exchanges it for the asset A. The intermediary transfers (lends) the $100 to another individual B, who transfers them in some way, such as through consumption or investment expenditures, to a third individual C. The last individual again exchanges the $100 of funds for the assets issued by the intermediary. Suppose these are the only transactions that take place in a given period and there are no leakages at any point. Then, the intermediary, for an initial $100 lent to it, has created $100 of its liabilities. The amount created over n periods will be $100n$ and will approach infinity over time. The implication of this example is clear: the multiplicative creation of the liabilities of financial intermediaries is inherent in an economy in which these liabilities are widely held. The extent of this creation is limited by the leakages out of the recycling process. Thus, if individual C had only deposited $50 of resources with the intermediary and retained the remainder in his storage, the recycling process would have had a leakage of $50 (or 50%). The total assets created by the intermediary in the period would be worth only $50 and only $100 over time.

Banks conform to the above pattern. The funds they receive are deposits of currency and are part of their reserve base. They lend these out, after keeping some of this currency to meet their own demand for reserves, part of which they may be legally required to keep. The public receiving the funds may, after some transfers within its own members or even without any transfers, redeposit the funds in the banks. It may also retain some currency to meet its own demand for it. The remainder returns to the banks and starts the next cycle of the asset-creation process. The leakages in the form of the currency demand of the public and of the banks against their deposits prevent an infinite creation of deposits over time but nevertheless lead to some multiple expansion of the bank's liabilities, unless the leakages were 100% in the first cycle.

Since financial assets are created, it is natural to expect that in an unregulated system a variety of financial assets differing only slightly in their characteristics and with varying degrees of closeness of substitution will come into existence. Such variety and closeness of substitution is also evident in commodity markets, as, for instance, in the case of cars. This innovation and the multiplicity of financial assets introduce severe problems in defining money and in its regulation. Further, the regulation of existing assets tends to increase the profitability of unregulated potential substitutes and usually leads to their creation. Consequently, questions on the proper definition of money never seem to die out.

The distinctive role of banks as financial intermediaries

Banks are not the only financial intermediaries in the economy. But they are the most widespread and their liabilities are so widely demanded that the multiple creation of their liabilities is both the greatest and the most widely recognized. Banks, accepting demand and time deposits, differ from other financial intermediaries in that their liabilities are readily acceptable and are liquid since demand deposits are a medium of exchange and hence a form of money. Further, another of their liabilities, time deposits, is a very close substitute for currency and demand deposits. By comparison, the liabilities of non-bank financial intermediaries are not directly a medium of exchange, nor are they perfect substitutes for it. This special role of the liabilities of banks in the economy makes the banks a rather distinctive type of financial intermediary and makes a study of their behaviour and reaction to monetary policy especially important.

1.8 DIFFERENT MODES OF ANALYSING THE ECONOMY

Since the money market is only one of the markets in the economy, monetary economics is closely intertwined with the analysis of the other markets in the economy. This unified analysis of money and all other markets in the economy can be conducted in one of two ways:

(a) *A microeconomic analysis* of the market for each of the goods in the economy. While there can be different types of such models, many of them are made analytically tractable by the assumption of perfect competition in all markets. Microeconomic models of the economy assuming perfect competition are called *Walrasian models.*

Microeconomic models of the economy are also difficult to manage unless the assumption of equilibrium in all markets is imposed on them. The (subsidiary) group of Walrasian models that do so provide microeconomic models of the economy known as:

(a′) *The Walrasian general equilibrium models.*

A one-period version of a Walrasian general equilibrium model is presented in Chapter 3. To show its relevance to monetary economics, its implications for the relationship between the money supply and the price level are derived in that chapter.

(b) *A macroeconomic analysis* where the goods are classified into a small number of categories and the analysis is performed at this composite level. Although many different ways of categorizing goods are possible, the generally used one in short-run macroeconomics is that of classifying goods into the four categories of commodities, money, bonds (non-monetary financial assets) and labour.

The relationship between the microeconomic and the macroeconomic varieties of models can be either:

(i) (b) is merely a compact form of (a). In this case, the assumptions and implications of macroeconomic analysis must be consistent with the microeconomic analysis of markets. This approach seeks to set the foundations of macroeconomics in micro-economic theory.

(ii) (b) is different from, and possibly more than, being a compact form of (a). In this case, macroeconomics can have assumptions that deal with group behaviour[14] and inter-actions among markets[15] and groups[16] that is not visible in microeconomic analysis. Further, such models can be used to study the properties of the economy in disequilibrium, so that they can further differ from (a').

Each of these types of analysis has its advantages and disadvantages. The advantage of (i) is that it roots macroeconomic behaviour in the microeconomic analysis of the household and firm. This confers on it the highly desirable property of being based on the fundamental assumption of the rationality of individual economic agents, which implies that households maximize utility while firms maximize profits. Such rationality also implies that economic agents form their expectations rationally by basing them on all available information.

However, there are two major disadvantages to using (i). One of these is that it extends the assumption of equilibrium to all markets, thereby usually assuming that all markets are simultaneously and always in equilibrium. While such an assumption seems quite sensible and maybe relatively innocuous at the level of one market, it is not clear to the profession as a whole that it is a sufficiently valid assumption for the whole economy. In particular, the assumption of simultaneous and instantaneous equilibrium prevents the study of the pathology of the system, i.e., when some part of it breaks down, so that the overall system does not possess general equilibrium, possibly not even the ability to return to it soon.[17] The other major disadvantage of purely microeconomic analysis is, as mentioned above, that it tends to ignore behaviour which is applicable only in the mass or in groups but not in individual economic units studied in isolation.[18]

The Walrasian general equilibrium system provides the benchmark of the well-functioning, healthy economy. It is extremely useful in this respect and must remain central to the study of macroeconomics. Among the major components of this system are: a complete set of markets for all possible goods, utility maximization by consumers and workers and profit maximization by firms,[19] perfectly competitive and efficient markets, absence of barriers to the attainment of equilibrium, absence of lags and false trading, and the availability of a mechanism for reaching the general equilibrium for the economy.[20] This is indeed a tall set of assumptions and many economists harbour doubts about the validity of one or several of them for an organism as complex as the economy.

The Walrasian general equilibrium system, by its very nature, does not provide an appropriate platform for studying the pathology of the economy when it is not functioning well in the whole or in some of its parts.[21] The reason for this deficiency partly flows from its assumption of equilibrium in all markets. But it is also partly due to its elaborate – ponderous – nature. The Walrasian analysis is made more tractable by compressing it to a macroeconomic model with only a few composite goods.

Macroeconomic models consistent with the Walrasian analysis are the 'classical' group of models. They belong to category (i) above. Their main rival is the Keynesian group of models. The Keynesian models belong to category (ii) above.

1.9 THE CLASSICAL PARADIGM AND THE CLASSICAL SET OF MACROECONOMIC MODELS

This group of models is consistent with the Walrasian general equilibrium framework and assumes that the market for each of the goods clears, so that the demand and the supply will be in equilibrium. Since one of the markets is labour, its clearance implies that every worker who wishes to supply labour at the existing wage will have a job and each firm will be able to employ all the workers that it wants to at the existing wage. This state is known as full employment, so that a hallmark of the classical models is that, in equilibrium, they imply full employment. However, in view of their emphasis on labour market clearance, this implication of equilibrium is often turned around and stated as if it was an assumption. The literature, therefore, abounds with the statement that 'the classical models assume full employment', which is not strictly correct.[22]

While there is no consensus on the division of the classical group into individual models, we adopt the following taxonomy for this book.

I. The traditional classical ideas

'The traditional classical ideas' is being proposed as the name for the somewhat disparate ideas on the macro-structure of the economy from the middle of the eighteenth century to the publication of Keynes' *The General Theory* in 1936. To quite a considerable extent, these ideas were diffuse, varied among authors and changed over time. In any case, there was no single compact version of the overall exposition, though we do now treat them as if there was a compact model. We will call this compact statement of the traditional classical ideas as the traditional classical model. Since, during its heyday, it was never stated as a compact model, it is nowhere to be found in a compact form in this book but its ideas permeate Chapters 13, 15 and 16 on the classical paradigm.

The two components of the traditional classical model relevant to monetary economics were the *quantity theory* for the determination of prices (Chapter 2) and the *loanable funds theory* for the determination of interest rates (Chapter 20).

II. The neoclassical model

This name was given to the restatement of the traditional classical ideas rebottled and re-flavoured in the post-*General Theory* period in a new compact framework. The new bottle was the IS–LM framework of analysis; the re-flavouring included the elucidation of some of the nuances of the traditional classical ideas, and the addition of new elements such as the wealth and real balance effects on commodity demand. Further, certain elements of the traditional ideas such as the quantity theory, Say's law and the dichotomy between the real and the monetary sectors of the economy were discarded in the rebottling process.

The classical paradigm was, in general, rejected by the majority of the economics profession from the 1940s to the 1970s, though it continued to exist as an outcast. However, refinements and additions to it continued to be made during these decades. The dominant paradigm in these decades was the Keynesian one. The classical paradigm roared back in the 1970s and has since then taken various forms. These are the 1970s monetarism, the modern classical model and the new classical model.

III. The 1970s monetarism

This approach is also known as the St Louis school, since its empirical and theoretical exposition was by the economists at the Federal Reserve Bank of St Louis. The short-run version of their model did not assume full employment and did not imply continuous full employment in the economy. It was relatively close to the then Keynesian models in terms of the impact of monetary policy on output and employment but denied on empirical grounds the Keynesian claim of the efficacy of fiscal policy. In its long-run version, it belonged in the classical paradigm.

Therefore, the 1970s monetarism was a hybrid between the classical and the Keynesian paradigms, and made the switch away from Keynesianism palatable for many economists. However, it had a short life and was replaced in the early 1980s by ideas truer to the classical paradigm, which eventually took the form of the modern classical paradigm.

IV. The modern classical model

This model is a statement of the classical paradigm under the assumptions of *continuous* labour market clearance and rational expectations. Because of the former assumption, it has continuous full employment. Given full employment as the equilibrium state, the latter assumption implies that systematic monetary policy will not be able to change real output and unemployment in the economy, though random changes in the money supply can affect them.

The modern classical model differs from the neoclassical one since it assumes continuous labour market clearance and rational expectations while the neoclassical one does not.

The modern classical model is a compact form of the Walrasian general equilibrium one, so that its implications are consistent with those of the latter. Intuitively, both focus on the economy in good health (functioning at peak performance) and serve to provide the benchmark of what the economy can do. Both imply that there is no need for governmental policies, either monetary or fiscal ones, to try to improve on this level of performance. In fact, they point to the potential danger of trying to do so.

V. The new classical model

The new classical model imposes the assumption of Ricardian equivalence on the modern classical model. This assumption is an aspect of intertemporal rationality and the Jeffersonian (democratic) notion that the government is nothing more than a representative of its electorate and is regarded as such by the public in making the decisions on its own consumption. This government provides just the goods that the population wants and its bonds, held by the public, are regarded by it (the public) as a debt owed by the public to itself. Its implications are that the public debt is not part of the net worth of the public and that the public increases private savings by the amount of a bond-financed government deficit. The latter implies that such deficits do not affect aggregate demand in the economy, and, therefore, do not change nominal GDP let alone the real value of the economy's output.

Of all the macroeconomic models in the classical paradigm, the new classical model is the most restrictive one. It is a subset of, and more restrictive than, the modern classical one because of its assumption of Ricardian equivalence. While the modern classical model implies that changes in both the money supply and fiscal deficits will change nominal national expenditures, the new classical model implies that only the money supply changes will do so. The new classical model is more restrictive than the neoclassical one because of its assumptions of continuous full employment, rational expectations and Ricardian equivalence, which are not in the neoclassical model.

The major alternative to the neoclassical paradigm is the Keynesian one, which has its own set of models. The Keynesian paradigm is introduced in the next section. Its models are presented in Chapter 14.

1.10 THE KEYNESIAN PARADIGM AND THE KEYNESIAN SET OF MACROECONOMIC MODELS

Using the analogy between the economy and human body

The fundamental difference between the classical and Keynesian paradigms is that while the former focuses on the healthy state of the economy,[23] the latter focuses on the pathology – especially the system-wide pathology – of the economy,[24] which may not fully or soon recover[25] from a shock to it (Solow, 1980, 1991). The Keynesian paradigm recognizes that the economy may sometimes have equilibrium in all markets, but does not assert that this occurs always or most of the time. Further, even if there is equilibrium, it may not be the competitive equilibrium of the Walrasian general equilibrium model because the economy may have a different structure or because of group behaviour. As a consequence, the Keynesian paradigm implies that when the economy is outside the Walrasian general equilibrium, the government and the central bank may be able to improve on its actual performance through their policies.

We have at various places drawn an analogy between the equilibrium state of the economy and the healthy state of the human body, and that between the deviations from equilibrium with the pathology of the human body. We have made this analogy because we believe that it provides insights into the study of the economy by reference to our personal experiences and knowledge on the performance of the human body. Rather than leave this analogy at an implicit and seemingly underhanded level, we have tried in these paragraphs to make it explicit, so that it can be properly evaluated within the boundaries we intend for it.

For this analogy, we assume that the human body sometimes functions in perfect health and sometimes suffers minor illnesses of a brief expected duration and without any need for the help of a professional (doctor). But it could sometimes suffer from serious illnesses from which the recovery may occur but be slow and be speeded up by the help of a doctor, or suffer ones from which there is no recovery without the intervention of a specialist. There may also be illnesses from which there is no cure and no recovery, but we do not include this limiting state within our analogy. Among the serious illnesses, note there can be many possibilities: infection with bacterium A rather than B, infection by a bacterium versus a virus, an infection versus a collapse of a lung, a collapse of a lung rather than a heart attack, etc. The list of the possible sources of the deviations from the healthy state can be endless.

Comparing the approach of the two paradigms to the pathology of the economy and applying our analogy, when the classical paradigm does envisage deviations away from the healthy state of the economy, they are supposed to be minor, transitory and self-correcting. Under it, while the economic body may become ill, the illnesses are never serious or long lasting, so that a trip to a doctor never becomes necessary or will not really be worth the hassle and the cost. By comparison, the Keynesian paradigm envisages the possibility of more serious departures from the general equilibrium (healthy) state of the economy. Its deviations from equilibrium can be due to different pathogens or breakdowns of the different components of the economy. It, further, allows for the possibilities that the recovery may be slow and could be speeded up with expert help (from the government and the central bank), or that it may never occur without such help.

Using the analogy with the human body, we offer the following two fundamental – and highly plausible – axioms on the performance of the macroeconomy.

(α) *The economy, like the human body, may sometimes function well and sometimes not.*

Hence, it is essential to study both states, with the former serving as the benchmark for the treatment of the latter.

(β) *When the economy, just like the human body, is not functioning properly, the causes, symptoms and effective treatments of the malfunction can be quite varied.*

The justification for the β axiom is that one cannot plausibly attribute all possible illnesses to a single underlying cause or attribute all potential causes to an overarching single source. An implication of the β axiom is that since the Keynesian paradigm focuses on the pathology of the economy, it cannot properly be encapsulated within one model with one root pathogen. Hence, more than the classical paradigm and its models, which are almost linear or hierarchical in their relationship, the Keynesian paradigm, if it is to do its job properly, has to be a disparate and, at best, a rather loose collection of models.

To reiterate, by the nature of their attempts to deal with the pathology of the economy, the Keynesian models have to be, and are, quite varied. If they are to do their job properly of dealing with the different types of deviations, such models need not – in fact, must not – all focus on the same types of deviations from the overall equilibrium state or make the same recommendations for policies to address these deviations. Unfortunately, this aspect of the Keynesian paradigm is often not recognized. Frequently, the presentations and discussions of the Keynesian models miss this requirement for variety within the Keynesian paradigm and seek to force the various Keynesian models into a single format or view it as one unified model. The danger in doing so is that a single prescription could be given as a cure-all for very disparate causes and be inappropriate for many.[26]

Frequent themes in the Keynesian models

A common concern of the Keynesian models is with the potential for involuntary unemployment, which is the deviation of actual employment in the economy from its full employment level. Consequently, these models tend to pay special attention to the structure of the labour market: its demand and supply functions and whether or not equilibrium holds between them. Within this focus, many Keynesian models assume nominal wage rigidity, often justified by theories of nominal wage contracts between the workers and the firms. However, there is also a place for Keynesian models that consider the deviations from general equilibrium that could occur even when the nominal wage is fully flexible.

The assumption of the rigidity or stickiness of prices in the economy is often regarded as another common theme of Keynesian models. While this assumption can impose deviations from a general equilibrium, it need not be the only cause or reason for potential deviations. Therefore, models within the Keynesian paradigm need not, and should not, all be based on price rigidity. There is, consequently, also a place for Keynesian models that consider the deviations from general equilibrium that could occur even when the prices are fully flexible.

Chapter 14 provides a look at some of the Keynesian models. While some of the models presented there assume equilibrium in the macroeconomic models, others do not do so. While some assume a special form of the labour supply function, others assume a different form. While some assume nominal wage rigidity of some form, others do not do so. Similarly, while some models assume price-level stickiness or rigidity, others do not do so. This variety in modelling within the Keynesian paradigm becomes even more evident when the Keynesian and the neo-Keynesian models are compared.

To reiterate, the variety of modelling, though perplexing and sometimes seemingly contradictory, in the Keynesian paradigm is essential to the proper study of the pathology of the economy. It would be a mistake to force the Keynesian models into a single straitjacket, even though this would provide an attractive means of comparing the classical and Keynesian paradigms as a whole.

1.11 WHICH MACRO-PARADIGM OR MODEL MUST ONE BELIEVE IN?

While most textbooks and economists would consider this a legitimate question, our remarks above suggest that it is an improper, and quite likely dangerous, one for the formulation of economic policies. The proper study of the economy requires the study of both its healthy state and its diseases. Since we cannot be sanguine that the economy will always operate in general equilibrium, the models of the Keynesian paradigm must not be neglected. Since we cannot be sure that the economy will never be in general equilibrium, the models of the classical paradigm must also not be neglected. Both paradigms have their relevance and usefulness. Neglecting either of them can lead to erroneous policies that impose high costs on the economy and its citizens.

For the practical formulation of monetary policy, the relevant and 'interesting' question is not the *a priori* choice between the classical and the Keynesian models, but rather the perpetually topical one: *what is the current state of the economy like and which model is most applicable to it?* There is rarely a sure answer to this question. Consequently, the judgement on this question and the formulation of the proper monetary policy are an art, not a science – and very often rest on faith in one's prior beliefs about the nature of the economy.

While one cannot dispense with one's beliefs and economists rarely give up their conception of the nature of the economy, the fundamental role of economics must be kept in mind. This is that economics is a positivist science, with the objective of explaining the real world. This is done through its theories, which, by their very nature, must be simplifications – more like caricatures – of reality. As such, they may be valid or not, or better for explaining some aspects of reality rather than others. Intuition and econometrics are both needed and useful in judging their validity and relative value.

A side implication of the positivist objective of economics is the normative one – i.e., the ability to offer policy prescriptions to improve on the performance of the economy, hopefully as a means of increasing the welfare of its citizens. Both the Keynesian and the classical paradigms are essential to these roles.

1.12 THE PARAMETERS OF THE IS–LM EXPOSITIONS OF MACROECONOMIC MODELS

Our purpose in this section is not to present the so-called 'IS–LM model'. We assume that the student already has some familiarity with it. It will be covered in Chapters 13 and 14 for the closed economy and Chapter 19 for the open economy. We mention our overall perspective on this issue at this point.

The IS–LM models represent the currently dominant *technique* for the expositions of the classical and Keynesian paradigms. It is not a paradigm or a theory, but rather a mode of exposition. It encapsulates the information assumed on the macro-markets or sectors of the economies into compact relationships, or curves in diagrammatic analysis, and studies the equilibrium properties of the assumed model.

For the closed economy, the standard models of the two paradigms assume four goods, commodities, money, bonds (i.e., non-monetary financial assets) and labour. Therefore, there should be four equilibrium statements, one for each of the four goods, and the corresponding four curves in the diagrammatic expositions. However, Walras' law (Chapter 17) ensures that equilibrium in any of the three out of the four markets implies equilibrium in the fourth one, so that one of the markets need not be explicitly studied. This allows the diagrammatic exposition to work with only three curves. These are usually those of the commodity market (the IS curve), the money market (the LM curve) and the labour market (designated as the y–n curve in this book, as in Chapters 13 and 14). In doing so, the bond market is the one excluded from explicit analysis, so that the bond market curve is not usually drawn. It does, however, remain implicitly in the exposition and can be deduced from the other curves.[27]

Note that this mode of exposition involves three equilibrium relationships or three curves,[28] not two, even though it is known as the IS–LM analysis. The reason for this misnomer is a continuation of the name from the early development of this technique by Hicks (1937),[29] who used the IS and LM curves to study aggregate demand in the economy, for which only these two curves are needed. The complete macroeconomic models nowadays include both aggregate demand and supply, so that their proper expositions require the three curves (IS, LM and y–n), even though the name for this mode of exposition continues to be the IS–LM analysis. The y–n curve must be included in the analysis in order to capture the relationship between aggregate demand and supply – and the determination of the price level.

Note that even in the limiting case for which continuous full employment is assumed, as in the modern classical approach, the IS–LM analysis must still include the three curves.

1.13 MONETARY AND FISCAL POLICIES

The major policy concern of monetary economics is with the impact of monetary policies on the economy. These policies include changes in the money supply or in interest rates brought about by the central bank of the country. The Walrasian general equilibrium model implies that there is no positive benefit in terms of higher output or lower unemployment from their systematic or anticipated operation (Friedman, 1977; Lucas, 1996). The Keynesian models usually imply that there are such benefits (Solow, 1980).

Fiscal policy is the use of government expenditures, taxes and deficits (or surpluses) as a policy to change the economy. While government deficits can be financed through increases in the money supply (and surpluses be accompanied by decreases in it), macroeconomics defines fiscal policy as one in which the money supply is held constant, so that the deficits must be financed by government borrowing through increases in its bonds sold to the public.

In the real world, fiscal and monetary policies are intertwined, more so in some countries than in others. However, we will treat them as conceptually independent ones and perform their analyses under this assumption.

CONCLUSIONS

Money performs the two main functions of medium of exchange and the store of value, with the former being absolutely critical to the transactions role of money in the economy. These functions are performed by a variety of assets, with their liquidity characteristics and substitutability among them changing over time. Innovations in the types of assets and the changing characteristics of existing financial assets mean that the financial assets which meet the role of money keep changing over time.

While currency was considered to be the only form of money at one time, currency and demand deposits were taken to be the only components of money early in the twentieth century, so that the appropriate measure of money was considered to be M1. By 1960, the measure of money had expanded to include time and savings deposits in commercial banks, and therefore had become M2. In subsequent decades, as the liabilities of near-banks became more and more similar to the demand and time deposits of banks, the measures of money were broadened to include the deposits in near-bank financial intermediaries.

The recent incursion of electronics into banking in the form of automatic tellers, banking from home through one's computer or telephone, and the use of electronic purses for payments, etc., represent a very fast pace of technical change in the banking industry. It is a safe bet that the empirically appropriate measure of money is changing and will keep changing in the future. During this period of change, the demand functions for money tended to become unstable, more so for some definitions than others, so that disputes about the proper measure of money have expanded beyond the simple sum aggregates of M1 and M2 to encompass more complex forms.

This chapter has also provided an introduction to the major paradigms in macro-economics. The two main ones are the classical and the Keynesian ones. Each consists of several models. The classical paradigm usually focuses on the general equilibrium of the economy and its models are closely related to each other. The Keynesian one focuses on the deviations from the general equilibrium of the economy. Since there can be many different causes of such deviations in the real-world economies, the Keynesian models are a much more diverse group than the classical ones. Knowledge of both paradigms is essential for the proper understanding of the economy and for the appropriate formulation of monetary policies.

SUMMARY OF CRITICAL CONCLUSIONS

- The appropriate definition of money keeps changing. There are currently several definitions of money in common usage. These include M1, M2 and broader monetary aggregates.
- All definitions of money include currency in the hands of the public and demand/checking deposits in commercial banks.
- Banks are one type of financial intermediaries but are different from others in that their liabilities in the form of checking and savings deposits are the most liquid of all assets in the economy.
- Financial assets are created, so that an unregulated financial system tends to create a multiplicity of differentiated assets.
- Monetary policy has to be studied in the context of a macroeconomic model.
- The two main paradigms for macroeconomics are the classical and the Keynesian paradigms.
- The classical paradigm focuses on the general equilibrium of the competitive economy.
- The Keynesian paradigm focuses on the deviations from the general equilibrium of the competitive economy. There can be a variety of reasons for such deviations, requiring different models for their explanations.

---

review and discussion questions

1 What is the distinction between the money stock and the money supply? Under what assumptions would they be identical?

2 What are the different ways of defining money in your economy? Compare these with the monetary aggregates commonly used in another selected country. Explain their differences and the reasons for such differentiation.

3 Can banks create money? How and under what conditions?

4 Why do we observe a wide variety of checking and savings accounts, rather than just one of each type?

5 What are the underlying themes (or theme, if only one) of the classical paradigm? How are they represented in the different models within this paradigm?

6 Explain the various models within the classical approach and compare them. Which would you accept for your economy?

7 What are the underlying themes of the Keynesian paradigm? Do they justify the study of just one model, one variety of models, or several different varieties of models? Why?

8 In order to explain the performance of the economy through the business cycle and the formulation of the appropriate monetary policy, would you rely on either the classical paradigm or the Keynesian one, or sometimes on one and sometimes on the other? Explain your answer with reference to the different phases of the business cycle.

NOTES

1 Even an economy which starts out without money soon discovers its usefulness and creates it in some form or other. Radford (1945) provides an illustration of this from a prisoner-of-war camp in Germany during the Second World War.

2 In the United States and Canada, the control of monetary policy rests solely with the central bank, so that the central bank alone constitutes the monetary authority. In the United

Kingdom, control over the goals of monetary policy rests with the government while its implementation rests with the Bank of England (the central bank), so that the 'monetary authority' in the UK is composed of the government in the exercise of its powers over monetary policy and the central bank.

3 Goodhart (1984).

4 Note that in the equilibrium equation setting money demand equal to money supply, the dimensions – which can be either real or nominal – of both the money supply and demand must be identical.

5 That is, if the units of currency and demand deposits were taken to have a liquidity weight of unity, the weights to be attached to the lower liquidity of near-money assets would be less than one.

6 Our usage of the term 'commercial banks' refers to 'depository institutions' in the USA.

7 The chartered banks in Canada correspond to the commercial banks in our discussions.

8 These are essentially credit unions in Quebec.

9 'UK residents' is meant to exclude the public sector and the financial institutions.

10 Since 1993, these deposits include both non-interest-bearing and interest-bearing deposits.

11 b stands for billion defined as 1,000 million.

12 These figures are taken from *Statistics on Payment Systems in the Group of Ten Countries*, published by the Bank for International Settlements, various years.

13 For example, deposits in a bank.

14 For example, 'herd instinct' (such as panics and in forming expectations) may be important when studying macroeconomics but not important when studying the market for each good separately.

15 For example, spillovers between markets can be quite important between the labour market and the commodity market – such as the fact that unemployed workers reduce their consumption of commodities – while they tend to be ignored in microeconomic analysis of individual markets.

16 For example, labour unions and firms' cartels.

17 A comparison of the economy with the human body can illustrate this point. The human body does not always stay healthy. Further, if it gets sick, it may be able to recover back to good health but may not do so soon. Further, modelling (studying) only the properties of the healthy body may provide poor or disastrous recommendations of what treatment to administer when it does become ill.

18 Note that neither of these disadvantages resorts to an appeal to irrational economic behaviour. Additionally, if behaviour is, in fact, non-rational, then a model which excludes such behaviour would not capture reality.

19 Under uncertainty, these would become expected utility maximization by both households and firms.

20 These are often presented under the rubric of the Arrow–Debreu model, which is a rigorous statement of the Walrasian general equilibrium model.

21 This is not meant to deny that this approach does sometimes provide for the possibility of some types of deviations away from equilibrium. However, such deviations are never meant to be serious or of more than a transitory nature. Using our analogy with the human body, the illnesses are minor in nature and an early recovery from them is guaranteed, so that the patient does not need to think of going to the doctor for either a recovery or a speedier recovery.

22 The difference between an assumption of full employment and one which is an implication of the equilibrium state is that the former rules out the derivation of the properties of the system when it is in disequilibrium; the latter does not necessarily do so.

23 That is, with clearance of all markets.

24 That is, when the economy is thrown out of equilibrium.

25 That is, return to equilibrium in all markets.

26 An example of this is the economists' inappropriate policy prescriptions, based mainly on the traditional classical ideas, during the early stages of the Great Depression in the 1930s. These

worsened the depth of the fall in GDP and lengthened the depression – and contributed to the demise of faith in the traditional classical ideas. Another example of inappropriate policies, based on the aggregate demand management approach in the Keynesian paradigm, occurred in response to the supply shocks of 1973 and 1974. This led to stagflation and contributed to the demise of faith in the Keynesian paradigm.

27 This is done in Chapters 17 and 18.
28 It is, therefore, sometimes called the three-curve analysis, but such a name is not in common usage or very informative.
29 Also see Samuelson (1946). This article is also a fascinating one on the enthusiasm with which Keynes' *General Theory* was greeted.

REFERENCES

Friedman, Milton. 'Nobel Prize Lecture: Inflation and Unemployment'. *Journal of Political Economy*, 85, June 1977, pp. 451–73.
Goodhart, C. A. E. *Monetary Theory and Practice: The UK Experience*. London: Macmillan, 1984.
Hicks, J. R. 'Mr. Keynes and the "Classics"; A Suggested Interpretation'. *Econometrica*, 5, April 1937, pp. 147–59.
Lucas, Robert E. Jr. 'Nobel Lecture: Monetary Neutrality'. *Journal of Political Economy*, 104, August 1996, pp. 661–82.
Radford, R. A. 'The Economic Organisation of a POW Camp'. *Economica*, 12, 1945, pp. 189–201.
Samuelson, Paul A. 'Lord Keynes and the General Theory'. *Econometrica*, 14, July 1946, pp. 187–200.
Solow, Robert M. 'On Theories of Unemployment'. *American Economic Review*, 70, March 1980, pp. 1–11.
——. 'Cowles and the Tradition of Economics'. In *Cowles Fiftieth Anniversary, Four Essays and an Index of Publications*, Cowles Foundation, 1991, pp. 81–104.

chapter
two

THE ANALYSIS OF MONEY AND PRICES: THE HERITAGE

Current monetary theory has evolved from two different streams: the quantity theory one, which was a part of the classical set of ideas, and the Keynesian one. This heritage includes both the microeconomic and macroeconomic aspects of monetary economics.

The quantity theory is the name given to the ideas on the determination of the price level from the middle of the eighteenth century to the publication of Keynes' The General Theory in 1936. This was an evolutionary tradition with several – at least three – distinct approaches to the role of money in the economy. These quite diverse approaches shared the common conclusion that, in equilibrium, the changes in the money supply caused proportionate changes in the price level but did not change output and unemployment in the economy.

The Keynesian approach discarded certain aspects of the quantity theory ideas and developed others in a new and distinctive format. In particular, it elaborated on the motives for holding money, eventually leading to considerable microeconomic sophistication of the analysis of the demand for money. It also integrated the analysis of the monetary sector into the complete macroeconomic model for the economy.

key concepts introduced in this chapter

- An identity versus a theory
- The quantity equation
- The quantity theory
- Wicksell's pure credit economy
- Transactions demand for money
- Speculative demand for money
- Precautionary demand for money
- Transmission mechanism
- Direct transmission mechanism
- Indirect transmission mechanism
- Lending channel
- Permanent income

The discussion of the role of money in the determination of prices and nominal national income in the economy has chronologically an extremely long heritage, extending back to Aristotle in ancient Greece, with explicit formulation of theories on it emerging in the mid-seventeenth century. The present very brief review of this heritage covers the contributions of David Hume, Irving Fisher, A. C. Pigou and Knut Wicksell for the classical period in economics and of John Maynard Keynes and Milton Friedman for the modern period. In the evolution of ideas and emphasis in monetary economics, the theoretical and empirical analysis of the demand for money emerged during the twentieth century as a major element of monetary economics.

This chapter starts with the review of the quantity equation and the quantity theory which deal with the determination of the price level, and ends with the ideas of Keynes and Friedman on the demand for money.

2.1 THE QUANTITY EQUATION

Any exchange of goods in the market between a buyer and a seller involves an expenditure that can be specified in two different ways.

A. Expenditures by a buyer must *always* equal the amount of money handed over to the sellers, and expenditures by the members of a group which includes both buyers and sellers must *always* equal the amount of money used by the group multiplied by the number of times it has been used over and over again.[1] Designating the average number of times money turns over in financing transactions as its velocity of circulation V, expenditures as $\$Y$ and the money stock in use as $\$M$, we have $\$Y \equiv \$MV$, where $\equiv$ indicates an *identity* rather than merely an equilibrium condition.

B. Expenditures on the goods bought can also be measured as the quantity of physical goods traded times the average price of these commodities.[2] Expenditures Y then always equal the quantity y of the goods bought times their price level P, so that, $\$Y \equiv \$Py$.

Obviously, these two different ways of measuring expenditures must yield the identical amount. These two measures are,

$$Y \equiv MV$$
$$Y \equiv Py$$

Hence,

$$MV \equiv Py \qquad (1)$$

Equation (1) is an identity since it is derived solely from identities. It is valid under any set of circumstances whatever since it can be reduced to the statement: in a given period by a given group of people, expenditures equal expenditures, with only a difference in the computational method between them. Equation (1) is *true* for any person or group of persons.[3] If it is applied, as it usually is, to the aggregate level for the whole economy, the two sides of the identity and its four variables refer to all expenditures in the economy. But if it is applied to the world economy as a whole, its total expenditures and the four variables will be for the world economy.

Equation (1) is called the *quantity equation*, the word 'equation' in this expression serving to distinguish it from the *quantity theory* which is vitally different in spirit and purpose from the quantity equation. As we shall see later, the *quantity theory* is not an identity while the *quantity equation* is not a *theory* for the determination of prices, incomes or even of the velocity of circulation in the economy.

Note that a relationship or statement that is *always* valid under *any* circumstances is said to be an *identity* or *tautology*. Identities generally arise by the way the terms in the relationship are defined or measured. Thus, (1) defined (measured) expenditures in two different ways, once as MV and then as Py, so that (1) is an identity. An identity is different from an equilibrium condition that holds only if there is equilibrium but not otherwise – i.e., if there is disequilibrium. Further, a *theory* may or may not apply to any particular economy in the real world or it may be valid for some states – for example, equilibrium ones – but not for others, while an *identity* is true (or false) by virtue of the definitions of its variables and its logic so that its truth or falsity cannot be checked by reference to the real world. A theory usually includes some identities but must also include behavioural conditions – which are statements about the behaviour of the economy or its agents – and often also equilibrium conditions on its markets.

2.1.1 Some variants of the quantity equation

There are several major variants of the quantity equation. One set of variants focuses attention on the goods traded or the transactions in which they are traded, so that they modify the right-hand side of (1). The second set of variants imposes disaggregation on the media of payments and modifies the left-hand side of (1). We present two forms of each of these variants. The first set of these variants is (i) and (ii) below. The second set is given by (iii) and (iv).

(i) The commodities approach to the quantity equation

One way of measuring expenditures is as the multiple of the amount y of marketable goods produced in the economy in the current period times their average price level P. Therefore, the quantity equation can be written as:

$$M \cdot V_{My} \equiv P_y \cdot y \tag{2}$$

where:

V_{My} the income-velocity of circulation per period of money balances M in the financing of y
P_y the average price level of currently produced goods in the economy
y real aggregate income in the economy

Equation (2) is often also stated as:

$$M \cdot V_{My} \equiv Y \tag{3}$$

Equation (3) yields velocity V_{My} as equalling the ratio Y/M.

(ii) The transactions approach to the quantity equation

If the focus of the analysis is intended to be the number of *transactions* in the economy rather than on the quantity of goods, expenditures can be viewed as the number of transactions T of all goods, whether currently produced or not, in the economy times the average price P_T paid *per transaction*. The concept of velocity relevant here would be the rate of turnover per period of money balances in financing all such transactions. The quantity equation then becomes,

$$M \cdot V_{MT} \equiv P_T \cdot T \tag{4}$$

where:

V_{MT} the transactions-velocity of circulation per period of money balances M in financing transactions T

P_T the average price of transactions
T the number of transactions during the period.

To illustrate the differences between y and T and between P_y and P_T, assume that we are dealing with a single transaction involving the purchase of ten shirts at a price of $10 each. The total cost of the transaction is $100. Here, the quantity y of goods is 10 and their average price P_y is $10, while the number of transactions T is 1 and their average price P_T is $100.

(iii) Disaggregation among the components of money

Another variant of the quantity equation disaggregates the money stock into two or more of its components and studies the velocity of circulation of each component separately. To illustrate, if the contribution to expenditures of currency and demand deposits needed to be separately studied, the quantity equation would be reformulated as:

$$D \cdot V_{Dy} + C \cdot V_{Cy} \equiv P_y \cdot y \tag{5}$$

where:

D quantity of demand deposits
V_{Dy} income velocity of circulation per period of demand deposits
C quantity of currency in the hands of the public
V_{Cy} income velocity of circulation of currency
P_y average price of current output

In the preceding form of the quantity equation, total expenditures are the sum of the expenditures financed by the use of the demand deposits and those financed by the use of currency.

(iv) The quantity equation in terms of the monetary base

The monetary base[4] consists of the currency in the hands of the public (households and firms), the currency held by the financial intermediaries and the deposits of the latter with the central bank. The velocity of circulation V_{By} of the monetary base depends not only upon the behaviour of the non-banking public but also upon the behaviour of firms and financial intermediaries. The quantity equation in terms of the monetary base is:

$$B \cdot V_{By} \equiv P_y \cdot y \tag{6}$$

where:

B quantity of the monetary base
V_{By} income-velocity of circulation per period of the monetary base

The quantity equation is thus a versatile tool. Note that all versions of it are identities. The form in which it is stated should depend upon the analysis which is to be performed. Examples of such interaction between the intended use and the actual variant of the quantity equation employed occur often in monetary economics.

2.2 THE QUANTITY THEORY

The quantity theory had a rich and varied tradition, going as far back as the eighteenth century. It is the proposition that *a change in the money supply in the economy causes a proportionate change in the price level.*

The quantity theory was dominant in its field through the nineteenth century, though more as an approach than a rigorous theory and varied considerably among writers and periods. Two versions of the form that it had achieved by the beginning of the twentieth century are presented below from the works of Irving Fisher and A. C. Pigou. A third version, radically different from those of these writers, is presented later from the writings of Knut Wicksell.

2.2.1 The transactions approach to the quantity theory

Irving Fisher in his book *The Purchasing Power of Money* (1911) sought to provide a firm and rigorous basis for the quantity theory by approaching it from the quantity equation. He recognized the latter as an identity and added assumptions to it to transform it into a theory for the determination of prices. A considerable part of his argument was concerned with providing a clear and relevant exposition of the quantity equation and one of his versions of this equation is first presented below.

Fisher recognized that goods were sometimes paid for by currency, which he called 'money', and sometimes by demand deposits in the banks. If C is designated as the amount of currency and V_C its rate of turnover in meeting the expenditures, it would finance CV_C of expenditures. Similarly, if D is the amount of demand deposits and V_D is its rate of turnover, DV_D would be the amount of expenditures paid for through the use of cheques. Total expenditures would then be $(CV_C + DV_D)$. The alternative way of measuring expenditures is as PQ where P is the average price level and Q is the aggregate quantity of all goods traded in the economy.

The relevant version of the quantity equation equates these two measures of total expenditures and has the form:

$$CV_C + DV_D \equiv PQ \tag{7}$$

In (7), Fisher maintained 'that bank reserves are kept in a more or less definite ratio to bank deposits' and 'that individuals, firms and corporations maintain more or less definite relations between their money [currency] and deposit balances'. Hence C and D will always change in proportion.

To transform the quantity equation into the quantity theory, Fisher put forth two propositions about economic behaviour. These are:

[i] The velocities of circulation of 'money' [currency] and deposits depend . . . on technical conditions and bear no discoverable relation to the quantity of money in circulation. Velocity of circulation is the average rate of 'turnover' and depends on countless individual rates of turnover. These . . . depend on individual habits. . . . The average rate of turnover . . . will depend on density of population, commercial customs, rapidity of transport, and other technical conditions, but *not on the quantity of money and deposits nor on the price level.*

[ii] [*except during transition periods*] the volume of trade, like the velocity of circulation of money, is *independent of the quantity of money.* An inflation of the currency cannot increase the product of farms and factories, nor the speed of freight trains or ships. The stream of business depends on natural resources and technical conditions, not on the quantity of money. The whole machinery of production, transportation and sale is a matter of physical capacities and technique, none of which depend on the quantity of money. . . .

(Fisher, 1911)

Therefore, Fisher's conclusion was that:

> while the equation of exchange is, if we choose, a mere '*truism*' based on the equivalence, in all purchases, of the money or checks expended, on the one hand, and what they buy on the other, yet *in view of supplementary knowledge as to the relation of C to D, and the non-relation of C to V_C, V_D and Q*, this equation is the means of demonstrating the fact that normally the prices vary directly as M, that is, demonstrating the quantity theory.
>
> (Fisher, 1911, italics added)[5]

Fisher was certainly right in specifying that the transformation from his version of the quantity equation to the quantity theory *requires* that, as the monetary authorities increase the amount of currency in the economy, bank deposits must increase in the same proportion while the velocities of circulation and the quantities of goods remain unchanged. This assumption, as well as (i) and (ii) above, are economic ones, resting on assumptions about human behaviour, and may or may not be valid. In symbols, these assumptions are that: $D = \alpha C$ with $M \equiv D + C$, $\partial Q/\partial M = 0$, $\partial V/\partial M = 0$, $\partial Q/\partial P = 0$ and $\partial V/\partial P = 0$.

On assumption (ii) of Fisher, the dominant theory – which was part of Fisher's own views of the economy – of the early twentieth century on output and employment in the economy was the classical one in macroeconomic analysis and Walrasian in microeconomic analysis. It implied that the labour market would clear, there would be full employment and output would tend to stay at the full employment level except in temporary disequilibria. This full employment output was independent of money supply and prices. Therefore, consistent with the real economic theory of the time, Fisher assumed that changes in the money supply would not affect the output of goods. However, this assumption was to be later challenged by Keynes and the Keynesians for demand-deficient economies – but later still (in the 1980s and 1990s) to be reaffirmed by the modern classical economists.[6]

Fisher's assumption (i) on the independence of velocities from changes in the money supply is also questionable. The velocity of circulation of money is not directly related to the behaviour of firms and households and if one thinks solely in terms of velocity, Fisher's simplistic argument on this point seems reasonable. Since velocity is a ratio of expenditures to money holdings, Fisher's assertion becomes more easily subject to doubt if the determinants of velocity are approached from the determinants of expenditures and the demand for money, as Keynesians do, and if the economy is not continuously in general equilibrium at full employment.

However, velocity is a real variable since it can be defined as equal to real income divided by the real money stock in the economy. Modern classical economists focus on velocity as a real variable, as Fisher had done, and, along with other real variables, take it to be independent of money supply and the price level in the full employment state of the economy.

Hence, modern classical economists agree with both of Fisher's assumptions for the general equilibrium – that is, with all markets clearing – state of the economy. Keynesians question the validity of the assumption of general equilibrium with full employment and of both of Fisher's assumptions. Modern classical economists, therefore, assuming continuous full employment, still maintain Fisher's quantity theory assertion that an increase in the money supply will cause a proportionate increase in the price level, with velocity remaining unchanged. Keynesians deny these propositions for the real world since they maintain that continuous full employment does not exist.

The constancy of velocity versus the stability of the velocity function

Many textbooks assert that Fisher had assumed the constancy of velocity. Even if meant as a simplification, this assertion is so simplistic as to be erroneous. In our interpretation of

Fisher's analysis, we have not attributed to him the constancy of velocity but, by direct quotes from his writings, shown that his assumption was the independence of velocity – a real variable – from that of money supply and price level changes. We have also shown that this assumption is brought into his partial analysis by the assumption of general equilibrium with full employment for the real sectors of the economy.

From a theoretical perspective, velocity is not a constant either in the short run or the long run in economic analysis. As Chapter 9 on money demand shows, the income elasticity of real money balances is less than unity, around 0.7. Since velocity is the ratio of real income to real money balances, velocity increases as income increases. Therefore, as income changes over the business cycle and over the long run of growth theory, velocity changes. Further, the interest elasticity of money demand is negative, so that an increase in the rate of interest increases velocity. There are also other reasons, such as innovations, for changes in velocity both over the short and the long term. Hence, from a realistic perspective, velocity is continuously changing in the economy. Estimates of the annual fluctuation in velocity for the USA are about 3% to 4%. To conclude, neither Fisher nor economic theory assumes velocity to be a constant, nor is it constant in the real economy. Rather, both take it to be an economic variable, determined in the economy by other economic variables.

Fisher's direct transmission mechanism

For the transmission mechanism from exogenous money supply changes to the endogenous changes in aggregate demand and prices, Fisher argued that *in equilibrium (though not in disequilibirum or transition stages)*, an increase in the money supply leads to a proportionate increase in prices through higher expenditures. Fisher's version of the disequilibrium chain of causation from changes in the money supply to changes in the nominal value of aggregate expenditures is given in the following quotation. Fisher starts by assuming that an individual's money holdings are doubled, and continues as:

> Prices being unchanged, he now has double the amount of money and deposits which his convenience had taught him to keep on hand. He will then try to get rid of the surplus money and deposits *by buying goods*. But as somebody else must be found to take the money off his hands, its mere transfer will not diminish the amount in the community. It will simply increase somebody else's surplus. . . . Everybody will want to exchange this relatively useless extra money for goods, and the desire so to do must surely drive up the price of goods.

(Fisher, 1911, italics added)

This process will continue until prices double and equilibrium is restored at the initial levels of output and velocity.

Fisher's mechanism by which changes in the money supply induce changes in aggregate expenditures has come to be known as the *direct transmission mechanism* of monetary policy, as compared with the *indirect transmission mechanism* which relies upon the changes in the money supply inducing changes in interest rates, which induce changes in investment, which then cause changes in aggregate expenditures. The latter was incorporated in the 1930s into the Keynesian and neoclassical macroeconomic models but the former was revived in the monetarist models of the 1970s. The modern classical models generally incorporate the indirect transmission mechanism.

2.2.2 The cash balances (Cambridge) approach to the quantity theory

Another popular approach to the quantity theory examined the determination of prices from the perspective of the demand and supply of money. Some of the best known exponents of this approach were at Cambridge University in England and included, among others, Alfred

Marshall, the early writings (that is, pre-1936) of John Maynard Keynes and A. C. Pigou. Our exposition of this approach will follow that of Pigou in his article, *The Value of Money* (1917).

Pigou, like Fisher, defined currency or *legal tender* as money but was, in general, concerned with what he called '*the titles to legal tender*'. He defined these titles as including currency and demand deposits in banks, which correspond to the modern concept of M1. He argued that a person held currency and demand deposits:

> to enable him to effect the ordinary transactions of life without trouble, and to secure him against unexpected demands due to a sudden need, or to a rise in the price of something that he cannot easily dispense with. For these two *objects*, the *provision of convenience* and the *provision of security*, people in general elect to hold currency and demand deposits.
>
> (Pigou, 1917, italics added)

The actual demand for currency and demand deposits is:

> determined by the *proportion* of his resources that the average man chooses to keep in that form. This proportion depends upon the convenience obtained and the risk avoided through the possession of such titles, by the loss of real income involved through the provision to this use of resources that might have been devoted to the production of future commodities, and by the satisfaction that might be obtained by consuming resources immediately and not investing at all.
>
> (Pigou, 1917)

Pigou thus claimed that the individual is not directly concerned with the demand for currency and demand deposits but with their relation to his total resources. These resources can be interpreted as wealth in stock terms or as income/expenditures in flow terms. We will use the latter, so that income will be the proxy for Pigou's 'resources'. Further, according to Pigou, this ratio of money demand to resources is a function of the internal rate of return on investments and of the marginal satisfaction forgone from less consumption. Representing the internal rate of return on investment as r and assuming it to be an approximate measure, in equilibrium, of satisfaction forgone, the ratio of money balances demanded (M^d) to total nominal expenditures (Y) is given by

$$M^d/Y = k(r) \quad k'(r) < 0 \tag{8}$$

where k is a functional symbol. M^d/Y decreases with r, or, in Pigou's words, 'the variable k will be larger the less attractive is the production use and the more attractive is the rival money use of resources'. Hence, $\partial k/\partial r < 0$. Therefore, the demand for money balances, M^d, is:

$$M^d = k(r)Y \tag{9}$$

The determination of the price level in the cash balance approach

Assuming a given money supply M, equilibrium in the money market with (9) requires that:

$$M = k(r)Y \tag{10}$$

Writing Py for Y, with P as the price level and y as the real amount of goods,

$$M = k(r)Py \tag{11}$$

Assuming that output y is at its full employment level y^f in equilibrium, $y = y^f$, so that (11) becomes:

$$M = k(r)Py^f$$

where $\partial y^f / \partial P = 0$ and $\partial y^f / \partial M = 0$. Further, Pigou assumed[7] that the equilibrium rate of return (r^*) was determined by the marginal productivity of capital (MPK) which was independent of the supply of money and the price level, so that $\partial r^* / \partial P = 0$ and $\partial r^* / \partial M = 0$. Therefore, in equilibrium,

$$M = k(r^*)Py^f \tag{12}$$

so that, in equilibrium,

$$P = M/[k(r^*) \cdot y^f] \tag{13}$$

which implies that:

$$\partial P / \partial M = 1/[k(r^*) \cdot y^f]$$
$$E_{P \cdot M} = (M/P) \cdot (\partial P / \partial M) = 1$$

where $E_{P \cdot M}$ is the elasticity of P with respect to M. Since this elasticity equals unity, the price level will, in comparative statics equilibria, vary proportionately with the supply of money. Therefore, (13) establishes Pigou's version of the quantity theory proposition.

This analysis views the quantity theory as a theory of equilibrium in the money market. Note that from a rigorous standpoint, it does not become a theory of the price level until the complete model – which includes the determination of output and interest rates – is specified. On the latter variables, Pigou and his colleagues in the quantity theory tradition had in mind the generally accepted traditional classical ideas for the determination of output and interest rates. These ideas implied the independence of both these variables from the demand and supply for money and turned the money market equilibrium equation (11) into a statement of the quantity theory.

Velocity in the cash balance approach

On the velocity of circulation V in Pigou's analysis, we have found from (11) that:

$$V = Y/M$$
$$= 1/[k(r)] \tag{14}$$

In (14), since velocity depends upon the rate of interest, it is not a constant in the context of Pigou's money market analysis. However, given the independence of the equilibrium rate of interest and the marginal productivity of capital from the supply of money, the *equilibrium* level of velocity equals $[1/k(r^*)]$ which is independent of the supply of money. This confirms the quantity theory's proposition on velocity. This independence of velocity with respect to the money supply does not mean its constancy over time, since velocity could still depend upon other variables, such as banking practices and payment habits, and these often change over time. Further, the independence of velocity from the money supply was asserted only for equilibrium but not for disequilibrium. However, Pigou and other economists in the Cambridge School often fell into the habit of treating k as a constant even though it was a functional symbol with $k'(r) < 0$, so that velocity also became a constant both in and out of equilibrium.

The legacy of the cash balance approach for the analysis of the demand for money

Further developments in monetary theory make it necessary to note another part of the nineteenth- and early twentieth-century monetary theory. This was that the demand for money was viewed as a demand for its characteristics or functions, with the main emphasis on these being placed on the medium of exchange and the store of value functions. Pigou's classification of the reasons for holding money balances should also be noted. These were:

(i) *the provision of convenience in transactions;*
(ii) *the provision of security against unexpected demands due to a sudden need or to a rise in the prices.*

The former was related to the demand for the medium of exchange function of money and the latter to its store of value function. These reasons for holding money were expanded by Keynes into three motives for doing so. These motives are now a standard part of modern monetary economics.

2.3 WICKSELL'S PURE CREDIT ECONOMY

Knut Wicksell was a Swedish monetary economist writing within the classical tradition in the last decades of the nineteenth and the first quarter of the twentieth century and was an exponent of the quantity theory. His treatment of the quantity theory was very distinctive and quite different from the English and American traditions of the time, as represented in the works of Fisher and Pigou. Further, elements of Wicksell's analysis led to the formulation of modern macroeconomic analysis and have relevance even in modern economies.

Wicksell sought to defend the quantity theory as the appropriate theory for the determination of prices against its alternative, the *full cost pricing* theory. The latter argued that each firm sets the prices of its products on the basis of its cost of production, including a margin for profit, with the aggregate price level being merely the average of the individual prices set by firms. The amount of money supply in the economy adjusts to accommodate this price level and is therefore determined by the price level, rather than determining it. Wicksell considered this full cost pricing theory as erroneous and argued that such pricing by firms determined the relative prices of commodities, rather than the price level. In his analysis, the latter was determined by the quantity of money in the economy relative to national output since commodities exchange against money and not against each other.

Within the realm of the quantity theory, Wicksell sought to shift the focus of attention to the transmission mechanism relating changes in the money supply to changes in the price level. He specified this mechanism for economies using either metallic or fiat money and for a *pure credit* economy. The latter analysis is the more distinctive one and illustrates Wicksell's transmission mechanism more clearly. It is also the one likely to be more relevant to the future evolution of our present-day economies and, therefore, is the one presented below.

Wicksell's analysis of the pure credit economy is essentially short run, and assumes a fixed capital stock. The economy is a pure credit one in the sense that the public does not hold currency and all transactions are paid by cheque drawn on checking accounts with banks, which do not hold any reserves against their demand deposits. Since the banks do not hold reserves and any loans made by them are redeposited by the borrowers or their suppliers in the banks, the banks can lend any amount that they desire without risking insolvency. Wicksell calls the rate of interest at which they lend to the public the 'money' or *market rate of interest*. The amount of money supply in this economy is precisely equal to the amount of credit extended by the banks so that changes in the money supply occur when the banks alter the amount of credit to the economy. Banks are assumed to be willing to lend any amount that the firms wish to borrow at the specified market rate of interest set by the banks.

A critical element of Wicksell's theory is the emphasis on saving and investment in the economy. Funds for investment come from savings and changes in the amount of credit provided by banks. The rate of interest which equates saving and investment was labelled by Wicksell as the *normal rate of interest*. For a stable amount of credit and money supply in the economy, the nominal rate of interest is the equilibrium rate. With equilibrium in the product market and with a stable output and money supply, this normal rate of interest will be accompanied by a stable price level.

Firms borrow to finance additions to their physical capital. The marginal productivity of capital specifies the internal rate of return to the firm's investments and was referred to by Wicksell as the *natural rate of interest*. The firm's production function has diminishing marginal productivity of capital, so that the natural rate decreases as capital increases in the economy.

To see the mechanics of this model, start from an initial position of equilibrium in the economy, with a stable money supply and prices, and with the equality of the market/loan and natural rates of interest at the normal/equilibrium rate of interest. Now suppose that while the market rate of interest is held constant by the banks, the marginal productivity of capital rises. This could occur because of technological change, discovery of new mines, a fall in the real wage rate, etc. Firms can now increase their profits by increasing their capital stock and production. To do so, they increase their investments in physical capital and finance these by increased borrowing from the banks. This causes the amount of credit and money supply in the economy to expand.

Wicksell appended to this analysis the disaggregation of production in the economy between the capital goods industries and the consumer goods industries. As the demand for investment in physical capital increases, factors of production are drawn into such industries from the consumer goods industries, so that the output of the latter falls. At the same time, the competition for labour and the other factors of production will drive up their incomes, leading to an increase in the demand for consumer goods, thereby pushing up prices. Consequently, the price level will rise.

The cumulative price increase or the inflationary process

In the above process, initiated by an increase in the natural rate above the market rate set by the banks, the price rise will continue as long as the market rate of interest is below the natural rate, since the firms will then continue to finance further increases in investment through increased borrowing from the banks. This constitutes a process of cumulative price increases. These increases can only come to an end once the banks put an end to further increases in their loans or credit to firms. A closed pure credit economy does not provide a mechanism that will compel the banks to do this.

However, in an open economy where the banking system keeps gold reserves out of which deficits in the balance of payments have to be settled, gold outflows provide a limit to the cumulative price increases. In such a context, as prices continue to increase, foreign trade deficits develop, the gold reserves of banks fall and the banks raise their loan rate of interest to the natural rate to stem the outflow of gold. This is especially so if the banks hold the gold as part of their reserves and the public holds gold coins circulating as currency for some transactions. In the latter case, as prices rise, the public's demand for currency will also increase and gold will flow out of the banks' reserves to the public. Such losses of the gold reserves to the public and abroad forces banks to restrict their lending to the firms by raising their loan rate to match the natural rate. This puts an end to the cumulative credit and money supply increases and therefore to the cumulative price increases.

This cumulative process can also be initiated by banks arbitrarily lowering the market rate below the natural rate, with the resultant adjustments being similar to those specified above for an exogenous increase in the natural rate. However, Wicksell viewed the bankers as being conservative enough not to change the market rate except in response to changes in their gold holdings or an exogenous change in the normal rate. Therefore, in Wicksell's view, the cumulative process was usually a result of exogenous changes in the marginal productivity of capital impinging on an economy whose credit structure responds with gradual and possibly oscillatory adjustments – for example, if the banks sometimes overdo the adjustment of the market rate.

The determination of output and the re-orientation of the quantity theory to modern macroeconomics

Wicksell, just as Fisher and Pigou, did not pay particular attention to the changes in the national output that might occur in the cumulative process. While disequilibrium and transient changes in national output are discussed, his overall discussion was usually within the context of an implicitly unchanged equilibrium level of output. Given this level, Wicksell claimed that increases in the money supply are accompanied sooner or later by proportionate price increases. Keynes in 1936 was to question the implicit assumption of an unchanged level of output and allow for changes in output and unemployment. Merging this into Wicksell's cumulative process would mean that this process will possess both output and price increases.

Wicksell was a proponent of the quantity theory of money, but shifted its focus away from exclusive attention on the monetary sector of the economy to the saving–investment process, and to the role of interest rates and financial institutions in the propagation of economic disturbances. In doing so, he led the way to the formulation of current macroeconomics, with the treatment of the commodities market at its core. This was to appear later as the IS relationship of the modern IS–LM analysis.

Further, Wicksell introduced into the analysis a fundamental aspect of the modern monetary economies: loans are made in money, not in physical capital, so that the rate of interest on loans is conceptually different from the productivity of physical capital. Even if they are equal in equilibrium, they will not be equal in disequilibrium. These ideas led the way to the analysis of the impact that the financial institutions and especially central bank can have on the interest rates in the economy.

In many ways, Wicksell was a precursor of Keynes' macroeconomic analysis, though not of Keynes' contributions to the demand for money.

2.4 KEYNES' CONTRIBUTIONS ON THE DEMAND FOR MONEY

Keynes in his earlier writings had proved to be an able and innovative exponent of the heritage of the quantity theory in its Cambridge school version. He had extensively explored the effects of changes in the money stock, though still mainly within the quantity theory tradition, in his book *The Treatise on Money* published in 1930. He was to extend this tradition or depart from it – depending upon how one chooses to look at it – considerably in *The General Theory*, published in 1936. The latter book represents a milestone in the development of macroeconomics and monetary thought. Among other departures from the nineteenth-century classical tradition, it rejected the validity of the quantity theory. Contrary to the assumptions of the quantity theory, *The General Theory* asserted the usual absence of full employment in the economy and argued that output and velocity in the economy depended upon the money supply. These contributions are fundamental to monetary theory and will be examined in Chapter 13 on the Keynesian macroeconomic models.

This section only examines Keynes' contributions on the demand for money in *The General Theory*. As a prelude to these, remember that Pigou's basic reasons for the demand for money balances were the 'objects' of the provision of convenience and the provision of security. Keynes re-labelled 'objects' as 'motives' for holding money balances and categorized them as the transactions, precautionary and speculative motives. Of these, the transactions motive corresponded basically to the provision of convenience 'object' of Pigou and the precautionary motive corresponded basically to the provision of security 'object' of Pigou. Keynes was more original with respect to his speculative motive and his analysis of the demand for money balances arising from this motive.

2.4.1 Keynes' transactions demand for money

Keynes defined the transactions motive as:

> *The transactions-motive*, i.e. the need of cash for the current transaction of personal and business exchanges.
>
> (Keynes, 1936, Ch. 13 , p. 170)

The transactions motive was further separated into an 'income-motive' to bridge the interval between the receipt of income and its disbursement by households, and a 'business-motive' to bridge the interval between payments by firms and their receipts from the sale of their products (Keynes, 1936, Ch. 15, pp. 195–96). Keynes did not present a rigorous analysis of the transactions and precautionary motives but 'assumed [them] to absorb a quantity of cash which is not very sensitive to changes in the rate of interest as such . . . apart from its reactions on the level of income' (Keynes, 1936, p. 171). This assumption of Keynes was in fact somewhat more restrictive than that of Pigou where the demand for money due to the objects of the provision of convenience and of the provision of security was dependent upon the return on investments and the utility forgone in abstaining from consumption. Designating the *joint* transactions and precautionary demand for money balances as M^{tr} and nominal income as Y, Keynes assumed that:

$$M^{tr} = M^{tr}(Y) \qquad\qquad (15)$$

where M^{tr} increases as Y increases.

Now consider the ratio (Y/M^{tr}) which is the velocity of circulation of transactions balances alone in the preceding equation. Keynes followed the simplistic pattern of Pigou's reasoning in stating that,

> There is, of course, no reason for supposing that $V (=Y/M^T)$ is constant. Its value will depend on the character of banking and industrial organization, on social habits, on the distribution of income between different classes and on the effective cost of holding idle cash. Nevertheless, if we have a short period of time in view and can safely assume no material change in any of these factors, we can treat V as nearly enough constant.
>
> (Keynes, 1936, p. 201)

This reasoning implies that Y/M^{tr} is a constant $\frac{1}{k}$, independent of income and interest rates, so that Keynes' transactions demand for money was:

$$M^{tr} = kY \qquad\qquad (16)$$

2.4.2 Keynes' precautionary demand for money

Keynes' second motive for holding money was the precautionary one, defined by him as:

> *The precautionary-motive*, i.e., the desire for security as to the future cash equivalent of a certain proportion of total resources.
>
> (Keynes, 1936, Ch. 13, p. 170)

Another definition of this motive was given later in Chapter 15 of the *General Theory* as,

> To provide for contingencies requiring sudden expenditure and for unforeseen opportunities of advantageous purchases, and also to hold an asset of which the value is fixed in terms of money. . . .
>
> (Keynes, 1936, Ch. 15, p. 196)

Keynes amplified his definitions in:

> if a need for liquid cash may conceivably arise before the expiry of *n* years [that is, the time when long-term debt matures], there is a risk of loss being incurred in purchasing a long-term debt and subsequently turning it into cash, as compared with holding cash. [For the individual to hold such debt], the actuarial profit or mathematical expectation of gain calculated in accordance with the existing probabilities – if it can be so calculated, which is doubtful – must be sufficient to compensate for the risk of disappointment.
>
> (Keynes, 1936, Ch. 13, p. 169)

Keynes' two definitions of the precautionary motive are clearly not identical. Out of their possible interpretations, the one that has been incorporated into modern analysis is that the precautionary motive for holding money arises because of the uncertainty of future income and consumption needs and purchases. These purchases will have to be met by payments in money; so that if the individual only holds non-monetary assets, he will first have to sell them to obtain the money needed for his payments. He will have formed subjective expectations as to the dates and amounts required for his payments and income receipts, and will decide on the optimal amounts of his money balances and other assets in the light of these expectations. The further ahead are the dates of anticipated expenditures and the greater is the yield from investments, the more likely is the individual to invest his temporarily spare funds in bonds and decrease his money holdings. Conversely, an increase in the probability of requirement in the near future will lead him to increase his money holdings and decrease his bond holdings.

2.4.3 Keynes' speculative demand for money

Keynes' third motive for holding money was:

> [3] *The speculative-motive*, i.e. the object of securing profit from knowing better than the market what the future will bring forth.
>
> (Keynes, 1936, Ch. 13, p. 170)

Keynes had earlier explained this motive as resulting:

> from the existence of uncertainty as to the future of the rate of interest, provided that there is an organized market for dealing in debts. For different people will estimate the prospects differently and anyone who differs from the predominant opinion as expressed in market quotations may have a good reason for keeping liquid resources in order to profit, if he is right . . . the individual who believes that future rates of interest will be above the rates assumed by the market, has a reason for keeping liquid cash, whilst the individual who differs from the market in the other direction will have a motive for borrowing money for short periods in order to purchase debts of longer term. The market price will be fixed, at the point at which the sales of the 'bears' and the purchases of the 'bulls' are balanced.
>
> (Keynes, 1936, Ch. 13, pp. 169–70)

In this motive, the individual, with a given amount to invest in bonds or hold in money balances, is concerned with the maturity value – equal to the capital invested plus accumulated interest – of his portfolio at the beginning of the next decision period. Assuming such a value to be uncertain, Keynes postulated a rather simple form of the expectations function: the individual anticipates a particular rate of interest to exist at the beginning of his next decision period, thereby implying a particular expected price, without dispersion,[8] for each type of bond. If these expected bond prices plus the accumulated interest are higher than the current prices, he expects a net gain from holding bonds, so that he will put all his funds in bonds rather than in money which was assumed not to pay interest and therefore to have zero net gain. If he expects a lower price for bonds in the future than at present, a net loss from holding bonds would be expected, so that he will put all his funds into money balances since there is no loss from holding these. Consequently, a particular individual will hold either bonds or money but not both simultaneously.

Since individuals tend to differ in their views on the future of the rate of interest, some would expect an increase in bond prices and are labelled as *bulls* in bond market parlance, choosing to increase their bond holdings, while others would expect a decrease in bond prices and are labelled as *bears*, choosing to reduce their bond holdings. Any increase in bond prices will exceed the expectations of some bulls – that is, convince them that bond prices have gone up too far and convert them into bears. A preponderance of bulls in the bond market pushes up the prices of the bonds and pushes down the rate of interest. This movement converts an increasing number of bulls (who want to buy and hold bonds) into bears (who want to sell bonds and hold money), until an equilibrium price of bonds is reached where the demand for bonds just equals their supply. Therefore, the demand for speculative money balances – by bears – increases as the prices of bonds rise, or conversely, as the interest rate falls, so that the aggregate speculative demand for money is inversely related to the rate of interest.

2.4.4 Tobin's formalization of Keynes' version of the speculative demand for money

Tobin's (1958)[9] formalization of Keynes' speculative demand analysis has become a classic and is presented in the following.

As with Keynes' analysis, Tobin assumes that there are only two assets, money and bonds, in which the individual can invest the amount of funds in his portfolio. Money is assumed to have a known yield of zero and is therefore riskless in the sense of possessing a zero standard deviation of yield. The bond is a consol, also known as a 'perpetuity' in the United States, and has the characteristic that it does not have a redemption date, so that the issuer need never redeem it, but continue to make the coupon on it indefinitely. The current return on consols is assumed to be r per year so that a dollar invested in consols will yield $\$r$ per year in perpetuity.

In perfect capital markets, the market price of a consol will equal its present discounted value. Therefore, the price p_b of a consol which has a coupon payment c per period and is discounted at a market rate of interest x on loans, is given by:[10]

$$p_b = \frac{c}{1+x} + \frac{c}{\left(1+x\right)^2} + \cdots$$

$$= c\left(\sum_{t=1}^{\infty} \frac{1}{\left(1+x\right)^t}\right)$$

$$= c\left(\frac{1}{x}\right) = \frac{c}{x}$$

If $c = x$, $p_b = 1$. Since the consol has been assumed to yield a coupon payment r in perpetuity, its present value at the rate of interest r would be 1.

Now assume that the individual expects the market rate of return on consols to be r^e for the future, with this expectation held with certainty and independent of the current yield r. With r treated as the coupon payment and the rate of discount expected to be r^e in perpetuity, the expected value of the consol next year will be r/r^e. Therefore, the expected capital gain or loss g on the consol will be:

$$g = r/r^e - 1$$

The expected yield $(r + g)$ from holding the consol is the sum of the coupon r and the capital gain g, and is given by:

$$r + g = r + r/r^e - 1$$

If the yield $(r + g)$ were greater than zero, the rational individual will buy only consols, since they would then have a yield greater than on money which was assumed above to have a zero yield.[11] Conversely, if the yield on consols were negative, the individual will hold only money since money would be the asset with the higher yield.

The switch from holding bonds to money occurs at $r + g = 0$. This condition can be used to derive the *critical level* r^c of the current return r such that:

$$r^c + r^c/r^e - 1 = 0$$

which implies that,

$$r^c = r^e/[1 + r^e]$$

For a given r^e, if the current interest rate r is above r^c, only consols will be bought; if it is below r^c, only money will be held. Therefore, in Figure 2.1, the individual's demand for money is the discontinuous step function (AB, CW): above r^c, the rational *individual's* whole portfolio W is held in consols and the demand for money along AB is zero; below r^c, all of W is held in money balances and the demand function is CW.

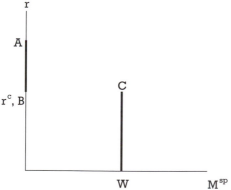

Figure 2.1   *Figure 2.2*

For the aggregate demand function for money, Keynes had argued that the bond market has a large number of investors who differ in their expectations such that the lower the rate of interest, the greater will be the number of investors who expect it to rise, and vice versa. Therefore, at high rates of interest, more investors will expect them to fall and few will hold cash. At a somewhat lower rate of interest, a smaller number of the investors will expect the interest rates to fall and more will hold cash. Hence, the aggregate demand for cash will rise as the interest rate falls, and is shown as the continuous downward sloping curve M^{sp} in Figure 2.2. Therefore, Keynes' analysis implies that the speculative demand for money depends inversely upon the rate of interest, so that the speculative demand function for money can be written as:

$$M^{sp} = L(r) \qquad\qquad (17)$$

where:

     M^{sp} speculative demand for money
     r market rate of interest

Keynes called $L(r)$ as the degree of *liquidity preference*, with L standing for liquidity.

2.4.5 Keynes' overall demand for money

Keynes argued that:

> Money held for each of the three purposes forms . . . a single pool, which the holder is under no necessity to segregate into three water-tight compartments; for they need not be sharply divided even in his own mind, and the same sum can be held primarily for one purpose and secondarily for another. Thus we can – equally well, and, perhaps, better – consider the individual's aggregate demand for money in given circumstances as a single decision, though the composite result of a number of different motives.
>
> (Keynes, 1936, p. 195)

Hence, the aggregate demand for money, M, depends positively upon the level of income Y due to the transactions and precautionary motives and negatively upon the rate of interest r due to the speculative motive. In symbols,

$$M^d = M^{tr} + M^{sp} = M(Y, r)$$

However,

> whilst the amount of cash which an individual decides to hold to satisfy the transactions-motive and the precautionary-motive is not entirely independent of what he is holding to satisfy the speculative motive, it is a safe first approximation to regard the amounts of these two sets of cash-holdings as being largely independent of one another.
>
> (Keynes, 1936, p. 199)

Hence, as an *approximation*, the demand function for money balances M^d is given by:

$$
\begin{aligned}
M^d &= M^{tr} + M^{sp} \\
&= kY + L(r) = kPy + L(r)
\end{aligned}
\qquad\qquad (18)
$$

where $k > 0$ and $L'(r) < 0$.

2.4.6 The liquidity trap

Keynes argued that the speculative demand for money would become 'absolute' (infinitely elastic) at that rate of interest at which the bond market participants would prefer holding cash to bonds, so that they would be willing to sell rather than buy bonds at the existing bond prices. Following Keynes' reasoning, the liquidity trap occurs at the rate of interest at which a generally unanimous opinion comes into being that the rate of interest will not fall further but may rise. At this rate, there would be a unanimous opinion that bond prices will not rise but could fall, thereby causing capital losses to bondholders, with the existing rate of interest merely compensating for the risk of such a capital loss. In such circumstances, the public would be willing to sell all its bond holdings for money balances at their existing prices, so that the monetary authorities could buy any amount of the bonds from the public and, conversely, increase the money holdings of the public by any amount, at the existing bond prices and rate of interest. Therefore, once the economy is in the liquidity trap, the monetary authorities cannot use expansionary monetary policy to lower the rate of interest.

Keynes asserts, however, that 'whilst this limiting case might become practically important in future, I know of no example of it hitherto' (Keynes, 1936, p. 207). This statement is incorrect under Keynes' own reasoning behind the speculative demand for money. The liquidity trap will come into existence whenever the dominant opinion in the bond market is that the market interest rates are going to rise, not decline. Such an opinion does quite frequently come into existence in the bond markets, so that the liquidity trap is not unknown in them. Further, such an opinion can exist at any level of the rate of interest and not merely at low or even single-digit rates. Furthermore, the liquidity trap will continue to exist until the dominant market opinion changes to envision possible decreases in the rate of interest. This would happen once the interest rates have adjusted to the market opinion, so that the liquidity trap would usually exist for short periods, which may not be long enough to affect investment and the macroeconomy. Therefore, while liquidity traps may often come into existence in the normal day-to-day functioning of bond markets, their existence for macroeconomics could be quite insignificant.

2.4.7 The volatility of money demand

Keynes' analysis of the speculative demand for money made it a function of the expectations of the bulls and the bears in the bond and stock markets. Such expectations were quite volatile in the 1930s and can be quite volatile even nowadays, as one can observe in the day-to-day volatility of the stock markets and the periodic 'collapse' or sharp run-ups of prices in them. Given this volatility, Keynes asserted that the speculative demand function for money was very volatile – that is, this function shifts often. Since Keynes believed that the speculative demand for money was a significant part of the overall demand for money, the latter would also be quite volatile. This would introduce a considerable degree of instability into the aggregate demand, prices and output in the economy, and also make the pursuit of monetary policy, which could trigger changes in the investors' expectations, very risky. Keynes, therefore, was more supportive of fiscal policy than of monetary policy as the major stabilization policy in the economy.

This was the general attitude of the Keynesians into the late 1950s. It was reinforced by the Radcliffe Report[12] in Britain, which argued that money was one liquid asset among many, of which trade credit was a major part, and that the economy was 'awash in liquidity', so that the changes in the money supply could not be used as an effective policy tool for changing aggregate demand in the economy. Therefore, Keynes' belief in the unreliability of the effects of monetary policy because of the instability of the money demand function, was buttressed by the Radcliffe Report that the money supply was only a small part of the total supply of liquidity which was the proper determinant of aggregate demand but could not be changed by monetary policy.[13] Both arguments were discarded during the 1960s, during which both the Keynesians and the neoclassicists and later the monetarists came to the conclusion that monetary policy and changes in M1 or M2 had a strong impact on the economy. Part of this achievement was due to the contributions of Milton Friedman. Among his numerous contributions was his article on the restatement of the quantity theory.

2.5 FRIEDMAN AND THE 'RESTATEMENT' OF THE QUANTITY THEORY OF MONEY

Milton Friedman (1956) in his article 'The Quantity Theory of Money: A Restatement' sought to shift the focus of the quantity theory and bring it into closer proximity with the developments in monetary theory up to the mid-1950s. Three strands of these developments are important to note. One of these was the development of Keynesian macroeconomics which placed the determination of the price level in a broad-based macroeconomic model with product, money and labour markets, and restricted the analysis of the money market to the specification of the demand, supply and equilibrium in the money market. This development had argued that the price level can be affected by changes in the product markets such as induced by investment, and that changes in the money supply could affect output, and not merely prices, in an economy operating at less than full employment. The second development was Keynes' emphasis on the speculative demand for money and therefore on the role of money as a temporary store of value for the individual's wealth. The third development was the integration of the theory of the demand for money into that of goods generally by treating money as a consumer good in the consumer's utility function and as an input in the firm's production function (Patinkin, 1965).

Friedman argued that the quantity theory was merely the proposition that *money matters*, not the more specific statement that changes in it will cause proportional changes in the price level. The term 'money matters' meant that changes in the money supply could cause changes in nominal variables and sometimes even in real ones, such as output and employment in the economy.

Friedman restated the quantity theory to limit its main role to that of a theory of the demand for money. For consumers, the demand for money was made identical to that of other consumer goods, with real balances being one of the goods in the consumer's utility function. In this role, Friedman viewed real balances as an asset, with money stocks, bonds and physical assets being alternative forms of holding wealth. For firms, the demand for money was made identical with that of physical capital goods, with money appearing as an input in the firm's production function.

Individuals may hold money as a medium of exchange for financing transactions or purely as a store of value. However, in the former case, its durability ensures that it serves as a store of value even when it is being basically held for its medium of exchange characteristic. Similarly, an individual holding money balances as a store of value cannot but benefit from their medium of exchange characteristic if the need arises. Friedman, therefore, concluded that it is best to view cash balances held for either purpose as being an asset, among many, for consumers, so that it was one form of holding wealth. For firms, it was a durable good, similar to physical capital. Friedman, therefore, concluded that the analysis of the demand for money was a special topic in the theory of the demand for consumer and capital goods.

Further, Friedman argued that a unit of money is not desired for its own sake but for its purchasing power over goods, so that it is a good in terms of its real and not its nominal value. This real purchasing power of money over commodities is reduced by the rate of inflation so that the rate of inflation is the cost of holding real balances as against holding commodities.

Since a unit of money yields services in the present, it is like a consumer good and the demand for it is affected by the prices of consumer goods. Since it is also a store of value, it is like other assets and the demand for it must also depend upon the yield on other assets. These yields, to reflect the concern of the individual with his purchasing power, must be taken to be in their real and not their nominal value. Thus, in periods of inflation, the individual would discount the nominal yields on assets by the rate of inflation.

Friedman further argued, as in his consumption theory, that the individual will allocate his lifetime wealth over commodities and over the liquidity services of real balances, with this wealth being the sum of his human and non-human wealth. Human wealth (HW) is defined as the present discounted value of labour income while non-human wealth (NHW) consists of the individual's financial and physical assets. Since the value of these assets is known in the present, while future labour income is uncertain, the degrees of uncertainty affecting human and non-human wealth are quite different, so that their effects on the demands for commodities and money would also be different. Friedman proxied the individual's degree of uncertainty of wealth by the ratio of his human to non-human wealth.

Therefore, according to Friedman, the main determinants of the individual's demand for real balances were the real yields on other assets (bonds, equities and physical assets), the rate of inflation, real wealth and the ratio of human to non-human wealth. Writing this demand function in symbols,

$$m^d = M^d/P = m^d(r_1, ..., r_n, \pi, w, \omega) \tag{19}$$

where:

m^d demand for money balances in real terms
M^d demand for money balances in nominal terms
P price level
r_i yield in real terms on the ith asset
π rate of inflation
w wealth in real terms
ω ratio of human to non-human wealth ($=HW/NHW$)

Permanent income instead of current income as the scale determinant of money demand

Since data on human and total wealth was not available, Friedman proxied total wealth by permanent income y^p. At the theoretical level, the relationship between these variables is specified by:

$$y^p = rw \tag{20}$$

where r is the expected average interest rate over the future and permanent income y^p can be interpreted as the average expected income over the future. In line with Friedman's work on the consumption function, Friedman employed adaptive expectations – which uses a geometric lag of past incomes – to estimate y^p. This procedure will be covered in Chapter 7.

Since the demand function is derived from the consumer's utility function, which represents the individuals' tastes, shifts in these tastes will shift the demand function. Friedman sought to take account of such shifts by incorporating a variable u for tastes in the demand function.

Substituting y^p instead of w and adding a new variable u, in the manner of Friedman's article, the demand function for real balances becomes:

$$m^d = M^d/P = m^d(r_1, ..., r_n, \pi, y^p, \omega, u) \tag{21}$$

The velocity of money

Since the velocity of circulation V equals Y/M, and M in equilibrium equals M^d, we have:

$$V = \frac{y}{m^d\left(r_1, \cdots, r_n, \pi, y^p, HW/NHW, u\right)} \tag{22}$$

Therefore, for Friedman, velocity was not a constant but a real variable that depended upon the yields on alternative assets and other variables. Again, except for the introduction of permanent income as a determinant on the right-hand side, (22) was consistent with the Keynesian tradition.

Friedman versus Keynes

In comparison with Keynes' analysis, Friedman's main concern in deriving his demand function was with money as an asset held as an alternative to other forms of holding wealth. This was narrower than Keynes' analysis – and also differed from the classical and quantity theory approach[14] – which had included the transactions and precautionary motives/objects for holding money.

However, Friedman did quite correctly point out that money balances could not be separated by the function they performed, as Keynes had done, since each dollar held performed a variety of functions. Hence, (21) could not be separated into three separate components corresponding to Keynes' three motives for holding money. Further, Friedman believed that the demand for money does not become infinitely elastic – i.e., in the absence of a liquidity trap. As we have mentioned earlier, Keynes had also downplayed its practical importance.

Friedman's specification of the money demand function, except for its replacement of current income by wealth or permanent income, was hardly new or distinct from the Keynesian tradition. In many ways, it was an elaboration and restatement of the Keynesian money demand function, modified to take account of the contributions in the literature, especially by Patinkin, since Keynes' writings. It was not an elaboration or restatement of the quantity theory, despite Friedman's claim for it, and could more appropriately have been labelled as a statement of the Keynesian money demand function or of the portfolio approach – as in Tobin (1958) – to money demand topical in the 1950s (Patinkin, 1969).[15]

Friedman on the money supply

Friedman also asserted that the supply function of money was independent of the money demand function. Some of the important determinants of the former, including political and psychological factors, were not in the latter. Hence, the money demand and supply functions were separate and could be identified in the data.

Friedman versus Keynes on the stability of the money demand and velocity functions

It was Friedman's additional remarks on his money demand and velocity functions that set him apart from Keynes and the early Keynesians and came from his traditional classical heritage. Among these was his assertion that both the money demand and velocity functions were highly stable. This differed from the viewpoints of many, though not all, Keynesians during the 1940s to the 1960s that these functions were volatile[16] and, therefore, essentially unpredictable. This had led them to the implication that monetary policy could not be a reliable stabilization policy, so that fiscal policy was to be the strongly preferred policy tool.

Friedman further asserted that the money demand and velocity functions were even more stable than the consumption function.[17] The stability of the latter was the linchpin of the Keynesian analysis and enthusiastic support for fiscal policy at the time. Friedman's assertion meant that monetary policy would, at least, also have a strong impact on the economy. The success of Friedman's agenda was such that the Keynesians by the early 1960s had accepted monetary policy as having a strong and fairly reliable impact on aggregate demand, so that a synthesis – known as the neoclassical– Keynesian synthesis – emerged in the 1960s. This synthesis was reflected in the common usage of the IS–LM model for the macroeconomic analysis of the impact of monetary policy on aggregate demand. The divisions among these schools were henceforth confined to questions of the further impact of aggregate demand changes on output and unemployment.

These policy issues and some other aspects of Friedman's contributions to monetary theory and policy will be discussed at greater length in the macroeconomic Chapters 13 to 17.

2.6 THE TRANSMISSION MECHANISMS FOR THE IMPACT OF MONEY SUPPLY CHANGES ON NATIONAL INCOME

The standard short-run macroeconomic models establish the importance of the money supply in determining nominal national income. As we have seen in this chapter, the dominant theory on this subject in the nineteenth and early twentieth centuries was the quantity theory. It had implicit in its acceptance the classical theories on the determination of output and interest rates, both of which were outside the influence of the demand and supply of money in *equilibrium*. However, as Hume and other economists in the eighteenth and nineteenth centuries had argued, the money supply did significantly affect output and other real variables in the disequilibrium process through the greater availability of funds for consumption, investment and loans.

The impact of Keynes' *General Theory* and the Great Depression led to the recognition that output may not always be at its full employment level. This meant that one of the critical background assumptions of the quantity theory and classical economics had to be abandoned. This is the assumption that labour markets work in such a manner as to ensure *continuous* full employment of resources and hence ensure that output is *always* at its full employment level. Keynesian analysis showed that in the presence of less than full employment, real output and unemployment can be influenced by the policy makers through money supply changes. This proposition became part of the Keynesian–neoclassical synthesis of the 1960s, before it – and the existence of a persistent state of less than full employment – was questioned by the emerging new classical school of macroeconomics in the 1970s. In any case, the impact of increases in the money supply on *nominal* national income has remained undisputed.

The mechanism which causes increases in the money supply to affect nominal national income has historically been a matter of considerable dispute. Hume had specified this mechanism as being of a dual nature. He started with the supposition that there is a sudden increase in everyone's money holdings and analysed the transmission channel of its effects on national income and expenditures in the following terms:

> The prodigal landlord dissipates it as fast as he receives it and the beggarly peasant has no means, nor view, nor ambition of obtaining above a bare livelihood. The overplus of borrowers above that of lenders continuing still the same, there will follow no reduction on interest.
>
> (Hume, *Of Interest*, 1752)

However, if the increase in the money supply falls into a few hands and is:

> gathered into large sums, which seek a secure revenue either by the purchase of land or by interest . . . the increase of lenders above the borrowers sinks the interest. . . . But after this new mass of gold and silver has been digested and has circulated through the entire state . . . the rate of interest will return to its former level.
>
> (Hume, *Of Interest*, 1752)

Hume thus emphasized two channels of influence of increases in the money supply. One of these was through increased spending, mainly by those who are not habitually lenders. The other channel was through the increased availability of loanable funds. The second channel operated mainly if the initial increase in the money supply ended up in lump sums in the hands of lenders, whose modern counterpart is mainly financial institutions. The relative strength of each channel depended upon the structure of the economy and the diffusion of the new money balances. Fisher mainly emphasized the former channel, as in:

Suppose that an individual's money holdings are doubled. Prices being unchanged, he now has double the amount of money and deposits which his convenience had taught him to keep on hand. He will then try to get rid of the surplus money and deposits by buying goods. Everybody in the community will want to exchange this relatively useful extra money for goods, and the desire to do so must surely drive up the price of goods.

(Fisher, 1911)

The direct transmission channel

This transmission channel whereby increases in the money supply cause undesired money balances which are then directly spent on commodities, with these increased expenditures on commodities inducing an increase in national expenditure and income, is called the *direct transmission channel* and is associated with the followers of the quantity theory. Among these was the *monetarist* school of the 1970s. However, the modern classical school has not followed the monetarists in this respect and has stayed with the indirect transmission mechanism in their models. Part of the reason for this lies in the nature of the modern economy in which changes in the money supply are not disbursed directly to households but initially enter the financial markets.

The indirect transmission channel

The Keynesian tradition and the IS–LM macroeconomic models ignore the direct transmission channel. The closed economy versions of these models assume that total expenditures are composed of consumption, investment and government expenditures. In these models, consumption depends upon real income, investment depends upon the rate of interest and government expenditures are exogenously determined. None of these major components of total expenditures depend *directly* upon the availability of money, so that increases in the latter are not directly spent on any of those components. Money supply increases affect the economy by lowering interest rates which increase investment, which in turn pushes up nominal national income through the multiplier in the product markets. This mode of transmission of money supply increases to national expenditure and income increases is known as the *indirect transmission channel*.

Wicksell had based his analysis of the pure credit economy on the indirect transmission channel, as did Keynes and the Keynesians for their models. The neoclassical and modern classical schools have continued with this practice. Therefore, most macroeconomic models nowadays incorporate the indirect transmission channel but not the direct transmission mechanism.

The lending channel

Hume had specified two transmission channels for the effects of increases in the money supply on nominal income: the direct one emphasized by the quantity theorists and the indirect encoded in the Keynesian–neoclassical synthesis in the form of the IS–LM short-run macroeconomic models. However, a great deal of lending in Hume's times (mid-eighteenth century) was through direct lending by savers to borrowers. This occurred through loans made by the relatives and friends of the borrowers and never passed through the organized financial markets or financial institutions operating in these markets. Such lending through the *informal* (unorganized) sector still occurs in the modern economy but is now of relatively little significance, except in the LDCs where it can still be a major proportion of investment in the economy.

However, even in the modern economy, some of the total borrowing in the financially developed economy continues to occur in the form of loans by banks to their customers, by suppliers to the buying firms in the form of trade credit, and from households to small firms. In these loans, the interest rate is usually one of the elements of the loans. Another is the lender's belief in the creditworthiness of the borrower. Given the existence of uncertainty and moral hazard, lenders can reduce their risks by rationing the amounts lent or making the loans only to certain categories of borrowers. In view of this aspect of direct loans, some economists distinguish between the flows of funds through the bond (and equity) market and those through loans, thereby creating a distinction between bonds and loans as distinctive assets, with less than perfect substitution between them (Kashyap and Stein, 1994). Given the special aspects of loans, loans usually offer a higher return than bonds to the lender while enabling borrowers, who may not have access to the bond market, to obtain funds.

A decrease in the money supply by the central bank not only increases the interest rate on bonds but also makes the banks raise the barriers for their loans. The latter has a different effect on investment and expenditures than that captured by the interest elasticity of investment in the indirect transmission mechanism, so that the overall impact of the decreases in the money supply on aggregate demand will partly depend on the distinctive elements of the loan market. For the financially developed economy, while some economists believe the lending channel to be a significant and distinct one in the effects of monetary policy (Kashyap and Stein, 1994), most of the profession remains sceptical about its relative significance (Miron, Romer and Weil, 1994).

CONCLUSIONS

Milton Friedman in the 1950s argued that the quantity theory should be viewed not as the ideas of one writer or a group of writers on the subject but as a 'living tradition' which is subject to change and refinement as the economy changes and economic theory advances. This tradition was the result of the thinking of many great economists over more than a century and its postulates were the postulates of economics generally in the nineteenth and early twentieth centuries. The writings of Hume, Fisher, Pigou and Wicksell, among others, illustrate that there was a great deal of variation around the central theme of the quantity theory that changes in the money supply cause proportional changes in prices and nominal national income in equilibrium. These writings left open the possibility that the money supply increases and decreases could change national output in disequilibrium and also allowed the possibility that equilibrium was not a continuous state of the economy. However, they also asserted or implied that such disequilibrium was not a permanent or long run state. This was the gist of Friedman's own beliefs on the impact of the money supply on the economy. While Friedman was right that the quantity theory was a living tradition and not a rigid doctrine through the traditional classical period (until Keynes), the profession – including the neoclassical and the modern classical schools – have not followed him in viewing their monetary theory as an aspect of the quantity theory. Therefore, the quantity theory should now be viewed as an historical but not a modern doctrine: it is not a living tradition now.

Some aspects of the tradition of the quantity theory are worth noting. One, its central proposition that, in equilibrium, the changes in the money supply cause proportionate increases in the price level but do not affect output and employment is also an implication of the equilibrium properties of the neoclassical and modern classical approaches to macroeconomics. Two, the Cambridge version of the quantity theory had viewed money as a subject for demand and supply analysis, just as for any commodity, while postulating that money was not desired for its direct contribution to consumption or production but for financing the purchase or sale of commodities. As such, the individual's demand was for the real value of money balances. This approach had further postulated economic rationality – that is, constrained utility maximization by individuals and profit maximization by firms in their demand for money balances. This implied that the demand for money was to be analysed in real terms, just as for any commodity, and must depend upon the opportunity cost of real balances. This cost would be the return on alternative investments or the forgone satisfaction from extra consumption. Keynes' motives for holding money and their analyses were a continuation and elaboration of these ideas of the Cambridge School.

In many ways, Friedman's (1956) statement of the demand for money function was not a statement of the historical doctrine of the quantity theory but rather a topical synopsis of the ideas and developments in monetary theory up to the 1950s. These consisted of the Keynesian approach to the demand for money and Patinkin's contributions (1965) on the general form of the money demand function. In particular, Friedman followed the Keynesians in their emphasis on money as an asset acting as a temporary store of value – and therefore an asset among many. This represented an undue emphasis on the speculative component of Keynes' analysis, to the unwarranted downplaying of the transactions role of money. His integration of money demand analysis into that of goods was also a continuation of an agenda already laid out by Hicks and others during the 1930s, and already followed by Patinkin.

Notwithstanding Friedman's claim to the contrary, his exposition was really not a restatement of the quantity theory,[18] which had been a theory of prices and not of money demand. However, on the restricted topic of the money demand function, it is better to view both Keynes' and Friedman's contributions as belonging within a continuous evolution of money demand analysis.

The distinctive aspects of Friedman's 1956 article were his assertions that the money demand function and the velocity function are stable and have few arguments. This was a radical departure from the Keynesian viewpoints (of the 1950s) which viewed money as merely one liquid asset among many and considered the money demand function as volatile. His further assertion that the money multiplier was more stable than the investment multiplier represented an even greater challenge to the Keynesian strong preference for fiscal over monetary policy. While his success in this tournament was not unanimously accepted, it was sufficient to lead the profession – including the Keynesians – to accept by the 1960s that money matters and so does monetary policy. The acceptance of these propositions was to take the debate to another level: money matters but is it advisable to pursue a discretionary monetary policy? Chapters 13 to 16 will look at this issue.

Knut Wicksell's contributions were seminal in making the saving–investment process central to the analysis of the impact of money supply changes on the economy. Unlike some of the traditional versions of the quantity theory – which had kept the monetary analysis separate or used a dichotomy between the real and the monetary sectors – Wicksell integrated the monetary analysis with that of the commodity and bond markets. This approach led the way to the later Keynesian and neoclassical macroeconomic models.

Returning to the analysis of the demand for money, this analysis has developed considerably since Keynes' *General Theory* (1936), basically reaching a synthesis on some of the controversial issues raised by Keynes and opening new issues of controversy at a somewhat more advanced level of analysis. These further developments have focused on separate models of the three motives specified by Keynes and are presented in the next three chapters.

Keynes had left the quantity theory's representation of the transactions demand for money essentially unchallenged. As an asset not itself used for consumption or production but held for financing transactions, money balances held by an individual have all the characteristics of inventories of goods held for production or sale. Baumol (1952) and Tobin (1956) later formulated the transactions demand for money balances by applying to it the basic inventory theory of operations research to it. It is the subject of Chapter 4.

The fervent in monetary theory raised by Keynes' emphasis on the speculative demand for money was, as seen above, essentially a formalization of some aspects of the store of value function of money; that is, of money as an asset among many forms of holding wealth. Friedman (1956) presented a compact statement of the further developments of this approach. Formal and rigorous analysis of risk taking in the demand for money and other financial assets was subsequently developed by the application of the expected utility theory of portfolio selection. This analysis is presented in Chapter 5.

The analyses of the precautionary demand and the buffer stock for money have been receiving increasing attention in recent decades. Keynes himself had simply lumped the former in the transactions demand and did not present any analysis of it. While there is still no single generally accepted treatment of these two elements of the demand for money, there are several promising lines of further development. These are explored in Chapter 6.

There are, therefore, two different routes after this chapter. One is the microeconomics one to the demand and supply of money and runs through Chapters 3 to 12. The other is the macroeconomics one and runs through Chapters 13 to 17.

SUMMARY OF CRITICAL CONCLUSIONS

- The quantity theory consisted of several approaches in its evolutionary history. They asserted that, in equilibrium, a change in the money supply will cause a proportionate change in the price level but will not affect output and unemployment. These assertions are also implied by the neoclassical and the modern classical approaches – currently the dominant approaches in macroeconomics.
- The quantity theory allowed that the changes in the money supply would affect output and employment in disequilibrium. This is consistent with the neoclassical approach. It is a fundamental aspect of Keynesian ideas.
- Wicksell shifted the transmission mechanism (from money to aggregate demand) from the direct transmission one to the indirect one.
- Keynes expanded the reasons for holding money to encompass the transactions motive, the precautionary motive and the speculative motive. Keynesians subsequently provided distinctive analyses for each of these motives.
- Friedman, although ostensibly claiming to provide a 'restatement' of the quantity theory, in fact provided an integrated version of the neoclassical and the Keynesian ideas on the demand for money. However, his replacement of current income by permanent income as the scale determinant of money demand belonged in neither the quantity theory nor the Keynesian traditions.
- Keynes and the Keynesians integrated the analysis of the money market and the price level into the general macroeconomic model, rather than leaving it as an appendage to the analysis of the commodity markets. They also introduced bonds as an alternative asset to money in the demand for money and made the bond market a component of the macroeconomic analysis.
- There are three potential transmission mechanisms through which the changes in the money supply impact on aggregate demand. These are the direct transmission mechanism, the indirect one and the lending one. The Keynesians and the modern classical macroeconomic schools, following Wicksell and Keynes, have based their IS–LM analysis on the indirect mechanism, with the direct one being ignored for the modern financially developed economies.
- The lending channel has been proposed by some economists. Whether it is distinctive from the indirect one and whether it is also significant for the modern financially developed economies is not generally accepted. Its role for financing investment in financially under-developed economies is likely to be much greater.

review and discussion questions

1 Discuss the statement: the quantity theory and the quantity equation are one and the same in the sense that each implies the other.

2 Compare Fisher's transactions and Pigou's cash balances approaches to the quantity theory. Are there any similarities between them? If so, which ones? Or should they be treated as different approaches altogether?

3 Given Pigou's elucidation of his two 'provisions' for holding money, was Keynes' exposition of his three 'motives' a revolutionary change or merely an extension of the money demand analysis to an economy in which the bond and stock markets were becoming increasingly visible and significant for the macroeconomy? Discuss.

4 Compare the contributions of Pigou, Keynes and Friedman on the interest elasticity of the demand for money.

5 Discuss the following statement: Wicksell's analysis of the pure credit economy belongs in the Keynesian rather than the quantity theory tradition, so that Wicksell's analysis should be taken as the precursor of Keynesianism in monetary economics.

6 Discuss the following statement: Friedman's analysis of the demand for money belongs in the Keynesian rather than the quantity theory tradition, so that his analysis should be taken as a statement or modification of Keynesian ideas in monetary economics.

7 For Keynes, the speculative component of money demand was volatile. This made the demand for money and the money multiplier volatile, so that monetary policy became an unreliable tool for stabilization. What were Keynes' reasons for his assertion on volatility? Do you think such volatility exists in the modern economy? Has it increased or decreased over time?

8 For Friedman, the money demand function was highly stable. This made the money-income multiplier highly stable, so that changes in the money supply had a strong impact on nominal national income. What were Friedman's reasons for his assertion on the stability of money demand?

   Has the money demand function in recent years been stable in the sense of not possessing the type of volatility asserted by Keynes? Discuss.

   In many economies in recent decades, the money demand function has shifted over time due to financial innovations. Have these shifts destroyed Friedman's assertion, or is this instability of a different kind from what Friedman and Keynes had in mind?

9 What were the similarities and differences between Keynes' and Friedman's demand functions for money? In which tradition (Keynesian, quantity theory or traditional classical) did Friedman's analysis belong?

10 Discuss the following statement: Friedman's critique of Keynesian liquidity preference theory and especially of the Keynesian speculative motive, is more concerned with the stability rather than with the interest elasticity of money demand.

11 On what does the demand for money depend: current income or permanent income? Or does it directly depend upon neither of them but on the consumption expenditures of households and the output of firms? If so, why is money demand usually specified as a function of income?

NOTES

1 Thus a person buying $100 of goods pays $100 to seller 1. Suppose the latter in turn buys $100 worth of goods from another seller (seller 2) of goods. The total expenditure was thus $200, the amount of money used was only $100 and it was paid over twice in financing the expenditures. Suppose now that the initial seller had bought only $50 worth of goods from seller 2. Total expenditures would now be $150, the amount of money in use remains at $100 but it has been paid over only 1.5 times on average.

2 Since the goods traded are generally of different kinds, there are obviously problems in thinking of an aggregate measure of goods in physical terms and of the price level to be associated with a unit of such a conglomerate or composite good. Both the 'quantity' or 'output' y of this good and its average price P must then be thought of as indices.

3 Identities are said to be true or false. By comparison, propositions or relationships about the real world are said to be valid or invalid.

4 The monetary base is also sometimes called the reserve base or high-powered money.

5 The symbols have been changed and italicized in the above quotation as well as in following ones.

6 See Chapters 13 to 17 for more information on these schools.

7 Pigou implicitly did so in *The Value of Money*. This was consistent with his ideas on the determination of the equilibrium rate of return in the economy by the marginal productivity of capital.

8 This simplification was subsequently abandoned in the 1950s by monetary economics in the application of portfolio selection analysis to the speculative demand for money, presented in Chapter 5 below.

9 Parts of the analysis of this article are presented later in Chapter 5 on the speculative demand for money.

10 The proof uses the mathematical formula that for $x > 0$,

$$\sum_{t=1}^{\infty} \frac{1}{\left(1 + x\right)^t} = \frac{1}{x}$$

Many bonds have a finite redemption date, say n. For this, the relevant formula is:

$$\sum_{t=1}^{n} D^t = \sum_{t=0}^{n} D^t - 1 = \frac{1 - D^{n+1}}{1 - D} - 1$$

where $D = 1/(1 + x)$. Since $x > 0$, $D^{n+1} \to 0$ as $t \to \infty$.

11 Risk does not enter this choice since the individual's expectations are so firm that the subjective standard deviation of expected yields is zero. Since risk is taken to be measured by the standard deviation of expected yields, the zero standard deviation means that the individual does not believe there to be any risk in holding consols.

12 This was the report of a parliamentary committee in Britain in the late 1950s. It reflected the then dominant Keynesian ideas on monetary policy. Its ideas were eventually not borne out empirically.

13 Monetary analysis and empirical research in subsequent decades did not support the conclusions of the Radcliffe Report.

14 By comparison, the primary emphasis of the quantity theorists was on the relationship between money and current expenditures on goods and services.

15 Patinkin, another economist at the University of Chicago in the 1950s, presented a clearer and more accurate representation of the Chicago tradition and argued that Friedman was closer to the Keynesian tradition than the quantity theory one. He points out the strong influence of Keynesian monetary ideas on the Chicago school during the 1940s and 1950s, especially in terms of the emphasis on the portfolio demand for money, and on Friedman's own analysis.

16 Remember that Keynes' speculative demand was dependent on subjective market expectations and, therefore, could be highly volatile.
17 Friedman sought to establish this in his later publications, jointly with David Meiselman.
18 Patinkin (1969) cogently argued that Friedman (1956) 'provided us with a most elegant and sophisticated statement of modern Keynesian monetary theory – misleadingly entitled "The Quantity Theory: A Restatement" (Patinkin, 1969, p. 61).

REFERENCES

Baumol, William J. 'The Transactions Demand for Cash: An Inventory Theoretic Approach'. *Quarterly Journal of Economics*, 66, November 1952, pp. 453–556.

Fisher, Irving. *The Purchasing Power of Money*. New York: Macmillan, 1911, Chs. 1–4, 8.

Friedman, Milton. 'The Quantity Theory of Money: A Restatement.' In M. Friedman, ed., *Studies in the Quantity Theory of Money*. Chicago, 1956, pp. 3–21.

Hume, David. *Of Money* and *Of Interest*, 1752.

Kashyap, Anil K., and Jeremy C. Stein. 'Monetary Policy and Bank Lending'. In Mankiw (1994).

Keynes, John Maynard. *The General Theory of Employment, Interest and Money*. London and New York, 1936, Chs 13, 15.

Laidler, David. 'British Monetary Orthodoxy in the 1870s'. *Oxford Economic Papers*, 40, March 1988, pp. 74–109.

Mankiw, N. Gregory, ed. *Monetary Policy*. Chicago: University of Chicago Press, 1994.

Miron, Jeffrey A., Christina D. Romer and David N. Weil. 'Historical Perspectives on the Monetary Transmission Mechanism'. In Mankiw (1994).

Patinkin, Don. *Money, Interest and Prices*, 2nd edn. New York: Harper & Row, 1965, Chs 2, 5–8.

——. 'The Chicago Tradition, The Quantity Theory, and Friedman'. *Journal of Money, Credit and Banking*, 1, February 1969, pp. 46–70.

Pigou, A. C. 'The Value of Money'. *Quarterly Journal of Economics*, 32, November 1917, pp. 38–65.

Robinson, Joan. 'The Theory of Money and the Analysis of Output'. In Joan Robinson, ed., *Collected Economic Papers*. Oxford, 1951, pp. 52–58.

Tobin, James. 'The Interest-Elasticity of Transactions Demand for Cash'. *Review of Economics and Statistics*, 28, August 1956, pp. 241–47.

——. 'Liquidity Preference as Behavior towards Risk'. *Review of Economic Studies*, 25, February 1958, pp. 65–86.

Wicksell, Knut. 'The Influence of the Rate of Interest on Prices'. *Economic Journal*, 17, June 1907, pp. 213–20.

part two

MONEY IN THE ECONOMY

chapter
three

MONEY IN THE ECONOMY: GENERAL EQUILIBRIUM ANALYSIS

This is a core analytical chapter from a microeconomic perspective on money in the economy. It treats real balances as a good like other goods such as commodities and labour in the economy and derives their demand in the overall context of the demands and supplies for all goods in the economy. It uses these in a Walrasian general equilibrium model to determine the relative and absolute prices of goods and examines their properties. In particular, it addresses rigorously the controversial and important questions of the neutrality and super-neutrality of money.

While the analysis of this chapter is based in microeconomics, its conclusions apply to both the microeconomics and macroeconomics of money. Therefore, this chapter can be covered immediately after Chapter 2 as a continuation of the heritage of monetary economics to the Walrasian model. Alternatively, it can be covered after Chapter 12 and thereby be a precursor to the macroeconomics chapters 13 to 17 on money in the macroeconomy.

The analysis of this chapter is fundamental to a rigorous consideration of the foundations of monetary theory.

---

key concepts introduced in this chapter

- The definition of a good in economics
- Money as a good
- The demand for real balances
- Numeraire
- User cost of money
- Money in the utility function (MIUF)
- Money in the production function (MIPF)
- Relative versus absolute prices
- Homogeneity of degree zero
- Neutrality of money
- Super-neutrality of money
- Dichotomy between the real and monetary sectors
- The real balance effect

This chapter considers real balances as a 'good' in economics and presents its analysis as an element of the Walrasian (general equilibrium) model. This model forms the foundation of the microeconomic analysis of the markets of the economy and the determination of individual prices. It also forms the basis of the modern classical and neoclassical macro-economic models, and the standard against which Keynesian macroeconomics lays out its differences. Therefore, this chapter serves as the prelude to Chapters 4 to 12 on the microeconomic aspects of monetary analysis – that is, the demand and supply of money. It also serves as a prelude to Chapters 13 to 19 on the macroeconomic aspects of monetary economics – that is, money and monetary policy in macroeconomic models. The reader more interested in these macroeconomic aspects can, therefore, proceed after this chapter directly to Chapters 13 to 19.

3.1 MONEY AND OTHER GOODS IN THE ECONOMY

The definition of a good

To consider money as a good, we need a definition of 'goods'. From the analysis of the behaviour of individuals or households, define a *good* as something of which an individual desires more rather than less, or less rather than more, *ceteris paribus*. A particular good may or may not be marketed: thus silence may be a good in the midst of overwhelming noise and yet may not be marketed.[1] From the point of view of the relevance to a market economy, only those goods that are marketed at some price or other need to be considered. Further, note that economic analysis does not ask why more of a good is desired to less of it. Therefore, it does not need to consider whether the good is in some sense beneficial or injurious for the individual, or whether there is something innate to the individual as a biological entity or something in the social or physical environment, or any other factor, which affects the individual's desire for its acquisition. To take some odd examples, cigarettes, drugs, labour time spent in a criminal activity, guns and bombs, etc., are all treated as goods in microeconomic analysis. So is money, though it is not directly consumed and even though its components (such as currency of a particular country and the demand deposits in it) only constitute money by virtue of the social and economic environment which make them acceptable as a medium of exchange. The desire of an individual to hold real balances constitutes adequate reason for treating it as a good in his utility function. The fact that money can only be held and used at a cost only adds confirmation to the treatment of money as a good for individuals but is strictly not necessary to this treatment.

From the point of view of firms, goods are anything of which more rather than less increases (or decreases) its production. Again, economic theory does not ask why it does so and, therefore, does not consider whether a good directly enters production or by virtue of the environment in which the firms function. The desire of firms to hold real balances constitutes an adequate reason for treating money as a good for them.

Money and other goods in macroeconomic analysis

For macroeconomic modelling, *goods* are subdivided into the categories of *commodities or products, labour or its converse as leisure, money* and *bonds*, where the term 'bonds' is defined to encompass all *non-monetary financial assets*.[2] Compared with other goods, *money* is the most liquid one and serves as the medium of payments. This chapter assumes that commodities, labour and bonds are relatively illiquid goods and cannot be used directly for exchanges against goods other than money.

One general trend of thought through the nineteenth century, and increasingly since the 1930s, argued that the demand for money should be analysed as that of a choice of one good among many. This approach claimed that the analytical framework for determining the demand for real balances to hold by an individual or firm is the same as that for determining the demand for commodities in general and that this framework is that of utility maximization for the individual or household and profit maximization for the firm. This approach is at present the dominant one in monetary theory. It can be formulated in terms of a timeless analysis, a single-period one or an intertemporal one. The former is presented in this chapter.

Money in the utility function and the production function

The approach to money in this chapter puts it in the individual's utility function and the firm's production function. This approach is known as the money in the utility function (MIUF) and the money in the production function (MIPF) approach. Many economists object to this approach on the grounds that real balances do not directly yield satisfaction or increase production. A modification of this approach would be that real balances allow the consumer to save shopping and transactions time and therefore to increase leisure, and allow the firm to save on its labour resources. These arguments lead to the *indirect* utility and production functions and are briefly presented in sections 3.2.2 and 3.3.2 of this chapter.

However, many economists prefer to completely eschew the above lines of analyses, with some of them opting for money in an overlapping generations framework. This approach is presented in Chapters 22 to 24.

Money as a durable good

Financial assets are durable goods in an economic sense. The concept of the economic durability of money can be quite confusing and needs clarification.

The demand for money is taken to be a demand for the *average money balances held by the individual in a period* and is often designated as *the demand for nominal balances to hold*. This demand differs from the amounts that the individual would hold at various points in time during the period but is a weighted average of the latter amounts, with the weights being the duration a particular amount is held.[3]

However, an individual may or may not hold a durable good for its transactions services. He may instead use it as a means of transferring his wealth or real purchasing power from one week to the next.[4] Such a usage would be one of a *store of value*.[5] For convenience, monetary theory has generally treated the demand for money as a medium of payments under the category of the transactions demand for money and the demand for money as a store of value (relative to other assets) as the speculative or portfolio demand for money. But any particular unit of money balances can be used for either function, and the division into the transactions and speculative balances must be taken to be analytical division and not necessarily applicable to the real world. This chapter confines itself to general propositions on the total demand for money.

3.2 INSERTING MONEY INTO THE INDIVIDUAL'S UTILITY FUNCTION

As discussed in the introduction to this chapter, money balances can be inserted as a variable in the utility function or in the indirect utility function. Since doing so is a matter of some dispute in the literature, this section presents the justifications for doing so at somewhat greater length than normally done in monetary economics textbooks.

We will use one-period analysis. Further, our introduction of money in the utility function is at its core the introduction of money's liquidity services, a real good, into the utility function, with these services proxied by the amount of real balances held. Consequently, the assets that do not yield liquidity services in facilitating transactions during the current period will be excluded from the utility function. Stocks and long-term bonds are among such assets. However, short-term bonds and savings and term deposits do possess some liquidity in modern economies and are often taken to be near-monies. This leads to questions about the definition of money. This was partly addressed in Chapter 1 and will be more fully dealt with in Chapter 8 on monetary aggregation. For the time being, 'money' will be understood to include financial assets possessing liquidity and, with further simplification, will be taken to be M1.

3.2.1 Money in the utility function (MIUF)

This subsection presents the axiomatic basis for including money in the utility function. Individuals differ in their tastes or preferences over goods and in their income or wealth. Microeconomic theory defines the 'rational' individual as one whose preferences are consistent and transitive.[6] The definitions of these terms are specified by the following axioms of utility theory:

Axiom (1): Consistent preferences
If the individual prefers a bundle of goods A to another bundle B, then he will always choose A over B.

Axiom (2): Transitive preferences
If the individual prefers A to B and B to a third bundle of goods C, then he prefers A to C.

To these axioms in the theory of the demand for commodities, monetary theory usually adds the following one.

Axiom (3): Real balances as a good
In the case of financial goods which are not used directly in consumption or production but are held for exchange for other goods in the present or the future, the individual is concerned with the former's exchange value into commodities – that is, their real purchasing power over commodities and not with their nominal quantity.[7]

The axioms of consistency and transitivity ensure that the individual's preferences among goods can be ordered monotonically and represented by a utility or preference function. Axiom (3) ensures that financial assets when considered as goods in such a utility function, should be measured in terms of their *purchasing power and not their nominal quantity*. The inclusion of money – and other financial assets – directly into the utility function can be justified on the grounds that the utility function expresses preferences and that since more of financial assets is demanded to less, they should be included in the utility function just like other goods.

Given these axioms, let the individual's period utility function be specified as:

$$U(\cdot) = U(x_1, \ldots, x_K, n, m^h) \tag{1}$$

where:

x_k quantity of the kth commodity, $k = 1, \ldots, K$

n labour supplied, in hours

m^h average amount of real balances held by the individual/household for their liquidity services

Note that (1) has $K + 2$ goods, consisting of K commodities, labour and real balances.

Axioms (1) to (3) only specify $U(\cdot)$ an ordinal utility function.[8] $U_k = \partial U/\partial x_k > 0$ for all k, $U_n = \partial U/\partial n < 0$, $U_m = \partial U/\partial m^h > 0$. All second-order partial derivatives of $U(\cdot)$ are assumed to be negative. That is, each of the commodities and real balances yields positive marginal utility and hours worked have negative marginal utility.

3.2.2 Money in the indirect utility function

It is sometimes asserted that money does not directly yield consumption services to the individual, but that its usage saves on the time spent in making transactions. This first part of this assertion implies that the first two axioms of preferences in the preceding subsection are not applied to real balances but only to commodities and leisure.

A model that leaves real balances out of the direct utility function but embodies their usage for facilitating purchases and sales of commodities is briefly specified in this subsection. For this model, assume that only consumer goods and leisure directly yield utility. Hence, the one-period utility function $U(\cdot)$ is:

$$U(\cdot) = U(c, \Theta) \tag{2}$$

where:

    c consumption
    Θ leisure

and U_c, $U_\Theta > 0$. Assume that consumption requires purchases of consumer goods which necessitate 'shopping time', so that leisure is the time remaining in the day after deducting the time spent on a job and in shopping. Hence,

$$\Theta = h_0 - n - n^\sigma \tag{3}$$

where:

    h_0 maximum available time for leisure, work and shopping
    n time spent working
    n^σ time spent shopping[9]

The transactions and financial environment is assumed to be such that the '*shopping time function*' is,

$$n^\sigma = n^\sigma(m^h, c) \tag{4}$$

where $\partial n^\sigma/\partial c > 0$ and $\partial n^\sigma/\partial m^h \le 0$. From (2) and (4), $\partial U/\partial n^\sigma = (\partial U/\partial \Theta)(\partial \Theta/\partial n^\sigma) < 0$. That is, an increase in shopping time decreases leisure and, therefore, decreases utility. But, since an increase in the amount held and utilized of real balances decreases shopping time, $\partial U/\partial m^h = (\partial U/\partial n^\sigma)(\partial n^\sigma/\partial m^h) > 0$.

Equation (4) specifies the time it takes to purchase an amount c of commodities while utilizing an average amount m^h of real balances. In a monetary economy in which the shops would only sell against money, the time required to purchase any positive level of commodities would become infinitely large as the individual tries to do without money. That is, as $m^h \to 0$, $n^\sigma \to \infty$. For positive levels of real balances, $\partial n^\sigma/\partial m^h \le 0$. The reason for this is that, in a monetary economy, money is the most widely accepted medium of payments, so that trying to pay in any other way may mean searching for special suppliers which would increase the shopping time.[10] However, beyond some limit, say for $m^h \ge c$, there is unlikely to be any further decrease in shopping time from additional real balances, so that, beyond this limit, $\partial n^\sigma/\partial m^h = 0$.

A proportional form of the shopping time function is:

$$n^\sigma/c = \phi(m^h/c) \tag{5}$$

where $-\infty < \phi' \le 0$, with ϕ' as the first-order derivative of ϕ with respect to m^h/c. The satiation in real balances occurs as $\phi' \to 0$. Equation (5) implies that $\partial \phi/\partial m^h \le 0$. Incorporating this shopping time function into the utility function above, we have,

$$U(\cdot) = U(c, h_0 - n - c\phi(m/c)) \tag{6}$$

Equation (6) can be rewritten as the indirect utility function:

$$V(\cdot) = V(c, n, m^h) \tag{7}$$

where

$$\frac{\partial V}{\partial m^h} = \frac{\partial U}{\partial \Theta}\left[-c\frac{\partial \phi}{\partial m^h}\right]$$

Since

$$\frac{\partial U}{\partial \Theta} > 0 \text{ but } \frac{\partial \phi}{\partial m^h} \le 0, \frac{\partial V}{\partial m^h} \ge 0$$

The generic form and properties of the indirect utility function (7), which has real balances as a variable, are similar (though not identical[11]) to those of the direct one used earlier in this chapter. Therefore, economists who prefer its shopping-time justification for putting money in the utility function substitute this justification for the one given earlier for the direct MIUF, which was simply that money is in the utility function because the individual prefers more of it to less, *ceteris paribus*. Both justifications are acceptable. However, given the similarity of the direct and the indirect utility functions, and the relative simplicity of using the former, we revert for convenience to the direct utility function.

3.3 THE DIFFERENT CONCEPTS OF PRICES

Prices, like temperature, distance, etc., have to be measured in terms of a scale. Such a scale for measuring prices is called a *unit of account*. The goods which serve as a medium of payments in a certain society may or may not be actually used as a unit of account in those societies or may only do so for certain purposes.[12]

The prices of individual goods measured in terms of a unit of account are referred to as *accounting prices*.[13] If the unit of account is money, then the prices are implicitly in terms of money but are sometimes more explicitly referred to as '*money prices*', '*monetary prices*', '*absolute prices*' or '*prices in terms of money*'.

If prices are measured in terms of money, then the price of a nominal unit of money itself must be unity, since a dollar note has a price of one in terms of itself. Hence, the *price of nominal balances* is a constant at unity and cannot change. However, the *price (of a unit of) of real balances* is the price level itself.

The term '*price level*' or the '*general price level*' is the weighted average of the prices of a representative bundle of the commodities in the economy. The price level is, in practice, measured by an index whose mode of calculation is specified later by equation (18).

3.4 THE USER COST OF MONEY

For one-period analysis, the cost of using the services of a durable good or asset is its rental or user cost during the period. This cost is the sum of the interest cost and depreciation less the increase in the capital value of the good during the period. This is also the relevant concept for using the services of money in facilitating the exchanges among commodities.

The user cost of real balances is specified as the *interest forgone from holding real balances* relative to holding a totally illiquid asset.[14] That is, the user cost ρ_m of *real* balances[15] is:

$$\rho_m = (r - r_m)P \tag{8}$$

and the user cost ρ'_M per unit of *nominal* balances is:

$$\rho'_M = (r - r_m) \tag{8'}$$

where:

    ρ_m nominal user cost per unit of real balances
    r market interest rate on the illiquid asset
    r_m interest rate paid on nominal balances
    P price level
    m real balances

In (8) and (8'), $(r - r_m)$ is the interest forgone from holding a dollar of nominal balances. On an amount m of real balances, Pm is the nominal value of the m real balances and $(r - r_m)Pm$ would be the total rental cost of these balances.

3.5 THE INDIVIDUAL'S DEMAND FOR AND SUPPLY OF MONEY AND OTHER GOODS

3.5.1 Deriving the demand and supply functions

To derive the individual's demand and supply functions for all goods, maximize:

$$U(x_1, ..., x_K, n, m^h) \tag{9}$$

subject to:

$$\sum_k p_k x_k + (r - r_m)Pm^h = A_0 + Wn \quad k = 1, ..., K \tag{10}$$

where:

    p_k price of kth commodity
    P price level
    W nominal wage rate
    A_0 nominal value of initial endowments of commodities and financial assets

Maximizing (9) subject to (10) gives the first-order maximizing conditions as:

$$U_k - \lambda p_k = 0 \quad k = 1, ..., K \tag{11}$$

$$U_n + \lambda W = 0 \tag{12}$$

$$U_m - \lambda(r - r_m)P = 0 \tag{13}$$

$$\sum_k p_k x_k + (r - r_m)Pm^h = A_0 + Wn \tag{14}$$

where λ is the Lagrangian multiplier. Equations (11) to (14) constitute a system of $K + 3$ equations in the $K + 3$ endogenous variables $x_1, ..., x_K, n, m^h$ and λ. The exogenous variables are: $p_1, ..., p_K, W, r, r_m$ and P.

Assuming that a unique solution exists for the set of equations (11) to (15) and that the sufficiency conditions for a maximum are satisfied, the solution for the $K + 3$ endogenous variables will have the general form:

$$x_k^{dh} = x_k^{dh} (p_1, ..., p_K, W, (r - r_m)P, A_0) \quad k = 1, ..., K \tag{15}$$

$$n^s = n^s(p_1, ..., p_K, W, (r - r_m)P, A_0) \tag{16}$$

$$m^{dh} = m^{dh}(p_1, ..., p_K, W, (r - r_m)P, A_0) \tag{17}$$

where the superscripts d and s stand for the demand and supply functions respectively, and the superscript h stands for households.

3.5.2 The price level

The price level P is related to $p_1, ..., p_K$ by the index number formula:

$$P_t = [\sum_k p_{kt} x_{k0}]/[\sum_k p_{k0} x_{k0}] \tag{18}$$

where the subscript t refers to the period t and the subscript 0 refers to the base period for the construction of the price index. x_{k0}, $k = 1, ..., K$, is the weight attached to the kth commodity used in constructing the price index and is usually specified as the amount of it purchased in the base period.

A common example of a price index constructed according to (18) is the consumer price index (CPI). For such an index, x_{k0} is the amount of commodities bought for consumption in the economy during the base year.

Another popular price index is the GDP deflator. The latter takes the composite bundle of commodities to be used for (18) as the commodities included in GDP, with their weights specified by their weight in GDP. The GDP deflator includes both capital and consumer goods, while the CPI excludes capital goods. Since our concern will usually be with the total output of the economy, for our purposes the GDP deflator will be the more appropriate proxy for the theoretical concept of the price level.[16]

Our main concern with the price index is going to be with its homogeneity properties. Equation (18) has the property that the price level is homogeneous of degree one in all prices, so that a doubling of the latter will also double the former. That is,

$$\alpha P_t = (\alpha p_{1t}, ..., \alpha p_{Kt}) \quad \text{for } \alpha > 0 \tag{19}$$

3.5.3 The homogeneity of degree zero of the demand and supply functions

We can now determine the effects on the individual's demand and supply functions of increasing the nominal variables $p_1, ..., p_K$, W and A_0 by an identical proportion, such that these values are replaced respectively by $\alpha p_1, ..., \alpha p_K$, αW and αA_0. First, note that doing so in (19) will mean that P will also be replaced by αP. Second, doing so in the budget constraint (10) will multiply each of the terms in it by α. This yields:

$$\sum_k \alpha p_k x_k + (r - r_m)\alpha Pm = \alpha A_0 + \alpha Wn \tag{10'}$$

But cancelling out α from both sides of (10') returns us to (10), so that the first-order conditions (11) to (14) and the solutions given by (15) to (17) for the values of the endogenous variables must be the same for (9) subject to (10') as for (9) subject to (10). Hence, the quantities demanded of the commodities and real balances and the supply of labour are not affected by a proportionate increase from $(p_1, ..., p_K$, W and $A_0)$ to $(\alpha p_1, ..., \alpha p_K$, αW, and $\alpha A_0)$. Formally stated, *the demand and supply functions in (15) to (17) are homogeneous of degree zero in $p_1, ..., p_K$, W, A_0.*[17] This property is incorporated in the following set of equations.

$$x_k^{dh} = x_k^{dh}(\alpha p_1, ..., \alpha p_K, \alpha W, (r - r_m)\alpha P, \alpha A_0) \quad k = 1, ..., K \tag{20}$$

$$n^s = n^s(\alpha p_1, ..., \alpha p_K, \alpha W, (r - r_m)\alpha P, \alpha A_0) \tag{21}$$

$$m^{dh} = m^{dh}(\alpha p_1, ..., \alpha p_K, \alpha W, (r - r_m)\alpha P, \alpha A_0) \tag{22}$$

for any $\alpha > 0$. The superscript h in (22) differentiates the household demand for real balances given by (22) from the firm's demand (m^{df}) for them derived later in this chapter.

3.5.4 Relative prices and the numeraire

If we let $\alpha = 1/P$, (15) to (17) yield,

$$x_k^{dh} = x_k^{dh}(p_1/P, ..., p_K/P, W/P, (r - r_m), A_0/P) \quad k = 1, ..., K \tag{23}$$

$$n^s = n^s(p_1/P, ..., p_K/P, W/P, (r - r_m), A_0/P) \tag{24}$$

$$m^{dh} = m^{dh}(p_1/P, ..., p_K/P, W/P, (r - r_m), A_0/P) \tag{25}$$

where:

x_k	relative price of the kth commodity
W/P	relative price of labour (real wage rate)
A_0/P	real value of initial endowments

Equations (23) to (25) assert that the demands for commodities and real balances and the supply of labour depend only upon relative prices – but not on absolute prices – and the real value of initial endowments. These relative prices have been defined in terms of the composite bundle of commodities used in calculating the price level. This composite bundle is here being used as a *numbering device* or *numeraire* for measuring the real cost of the various goods.

In (23) to (25), if we had specified α to equal $1/p_i$ rather than $1/P$, where p_i is the price of a specific good i, good i would have served as the *numeraire*. In this case, the resulting relative prices p_k/p_i and W/p_i would have been in terms of the numeraire good i rather than of the composite bundle of commodities in the price index.

If we had wanted to express the cost of buying goods in terms of *labour units* – i.e., the hours of work (of the worker with the average wage W) required to buy one unit of a good – we would set $\alpha = 1/W$. Doing so would make the relative price of the kth good p_k/W. Labour would become the numeraire. Many classical economists in the nineteenth and early twentieth centuries, as well as Keynes in *The General Theory*, had used this mode for expressing relative prices. This was partly because the construction, availability and use of the price indices were not common until the 1930s. But it was also partly to allow the traditional classical economists to conduct their analysis of the commodities and labour markets completely in real rather than nominal terms, with monetary factors thereby kept out of their analysis. However, the use of labour as a numeraire for analytical purposes has gone into disuse since the 1940s, and the standard practice now is to express relative prices using the CPI or the GDP deflator in the denominator.

3.6 THE FIRM'S DEMAND AND SUPPLY FUNCTIONS FOR MONEY AND OTHER GOODS

Corresponding to the two ways of introducing real balances into the utility function, real balances can also be introduced directly or indirectly into the production function.

3.6.1 Money in the production function (MIPF)

Assume that the representative firm produces the commodity x_k and has a production function specified by:

$$x_k = F(n, \kappa, m^f) \tag{26}$$

where:

x_k quantity of the kth good, $k = 1, ..., K$, produced by the kth firm
n number of workers
κ variable physical capital stock
m^f real balances held by the firm

The rationale for putting the firm's real balances as an input in its production function is that holding them allows the firm to produce greater output with given amounts of labour and capital. If it did not hold any real balances, it would have great difficulty in paying its employees and suppliers or selling its output. To avoid handling payments and receipts in money, the firm would have to divert part of its labour and capital to somehow arrange for payments and receipts directly in commodities, with such diversion reducing the amounts of labour and capital allocated to the production of output and thereby reducing the firm's output. Further, the greater the real balances held by the firm, the easier it is for the firm to handle its payments and receipts and the less the need for diverting labour and capital to the exchange processes and away from production. Therefore, in an economy requiring the exchange of goods against money, real balances function as an input in the firm's production function, with higher real balances leading to higher output, so that the marginal productivity of real balances is positive. We will assume that this marginal productivity is diminishing, just as for labour and capital.

Therefore, in equation (26), the first-order partial derivatives, F_n, F_κ and F_m, are assumed to be all positive, and the second-order ones, F_{nn}, $F_{\kappa\kappa}$, F_{mm}, are all negative. The firm may also have a fixed capital stock, implying that it also has some fixed costs of production.

3.6.2 Money in the indirect production function

It is sometimes argued that money does not directly increase the productive capacity of the firm and should not be put in the production function. However, just as with the indirect utility function, we can specify a production function in which money does not appear directly but does so indirectly. This is done in the following.

We assume that the firm's output depends on its capital and that part of its employment which it uses directly as an input in production. However, it has to divert some of its workers to carrying out transactions involving the purchase of inputs – that is, labour and purchases of raw materials and intermediate inputs – and the sale of its output. In the extreme case where the firm does not hold any balances in a monetary economy, it would have to persuade workers and other input suppliers to accept the commodity it produces as payment. It would also have to pay profits to its owners in the same commodity. If it is a corporation, its distributed profits would have to be in this commodity and, for retained profits diverted to investment, it would have to exchange for investment goods some of the commodity it produces. Any such attempt would prevent the firm from existing in the modern economy. In a less extreme case, if the firm held only a small and relatively inadequate amount of money, it would have to employ workers in juggling its money holdings to carry out the required transactions of purchase and sale. Holding real balances, therefore, allows the firm to economize on the workers it has to divert to carrying out transactions.

These arguments imply the production function to be:

$$x_k = x_k(\kappa, n_1) \tag{27}$$

where both partial derivatives are positive and:

x_k output of the kth commodity
κ physical capital stock
n_1 labour directly involved in production

Total employment by the firm is n where $n = (n_1 + n_2)$, so that:

$$n_1 = n - n_2 \tag{28'}$$

where n_2 is the amount of the firm's employment used in performing transactions. Therefore, $\partial n_1/\partial n_2 < 0$.

For the labour used in carrying out transactions, and using the firm's output x_k as a proxy for the number of transactions involved in purchasing inputs and selling output, the general form of the 'transactions technology function' for a monetary economy would be:

$$n_2 = n_2(m^f, x_k) \tag{28''}$$

where m^f are the real balances held by the firm, $\partial n_2/\partial m^f \le 0$ and $\partial n_2/\partial x_k > 0$. The specific form of $n_2(\cdot)$ would depend on the trading and payments technology of the economy and would shift with that technology. Innovations in the financial system, such as the use of direct deposit of salaries into the workers' accounts, payments to suppliers by electronic transfers, would reduce the demand for real balances for transactions associated with a given level of output and shift the transactions technology function.

From (27), (28') and (28''),

$$\frac{\partial x_k}{\partial m^f} = \frac{\partial x_k}{\partial n_1} \frac{\partial n_1}{\partial n_2} \frac{\partial n_2}{\partial m^f} \ge 0$$

A specific form of (28'') is:

$$n_2/x_k = \phi(m^f/x_k) \tag{29}$$

where $\phi' = \partial \phi/\partial(m^f/x_k) \le 0$. For this function, the firm reaches 'saturation' in real balances relative to its output when $\phi' = 0$. From (27) to (29),

$$x_k = x_k(\kappa, n - x_k \cdot \phi(m^f/x_k)) \tag{30}$$

which can be rewritten as the indirect production function,

$$x_k = f(\kappa, n, m^f) \tag{31}$$

where, as shown earlier, $\partial x_k/\partial m^f \ge 0$. Hence, the use of money by the firm increases its output, with its marginal product being positive up to the saturation point. Up to this point, the usage of money allows the firm to reduce the labour allocated to transactions, thereby increasing the labour allocated directly to production. This increases the firm's output produced with a given amount of employment.

The preceding analysis provides a rationale for putting money in the production function, even though real balances were not assumed to directly increase output for the firm. Given this result, we will revert in further analysis to the direct production function (26).

3.6.3 Maximization of profits by the firm

The firm is assumed to operate in perfect competition in all (output and input) markets and to maximize profits. Its profits are given by:

$$\Pi = p_k F(n, \kappa, m^f) - Wn - \rho_\kappa \kappa - \rho_m m^f - F_0 \tag{32}$$

where:

Π profits
ρ_κ nominal user cost of variable physical capital
F_0 fixed cost of production

The nominal user cost ρ_m of real balances was derived above as $(r - r_m)P$. The *user cost of capital* is similarly the rental value of a unit of physical capital (such as a machine) per period. The nominal user cost of physical capital in perfect markets is given by:

$$\rho_\kappa = (r + \delta_\kappa - \pi_\kappa) \, p_\kappa \tag{33}$$

where:

δ_κ rate of depreciation of the capital good
π_κ rate of increase in the price of the capital good
p_κ price of the capital good

Since the rate of depreciation of capital does not play any particular role in our further analysis, let $\delta_\kappa = 0$. Therefore, the nominal user cost of capital in our analysis would be:

$$\rho_\kappa = (r - \pi_\kappa) p_\kappa$$

Hence,

$$\Pi = p_k F(n, \kappa, m^f) - Wn - (r - \pi_\kappa) p_\kappa \kappa - (r - r_m) Pm - F_0 \tag{34}$$

The first-order conditions for maximizing profits with respect to n, κ, m^f, are:

$$p_k F_n - W = 0 \tag{35}$$

$$p_k F_\kappa - (r - \pi_\kappa) p_\kappa = 0 \tag{36}$$

$$p_k F_m - (r - r_m)P = 0 \tag{37}$$

3.6.4 The firm's demand and supply functions for money and other goods

Dividing each term in the first-order conditions (35) to (37) by the price level P, these conditions become:

$$(p_k/P)F_n = W/P \tag{38}$$

$$(p_k/P)F_\kappa = (r - \pi_\kappa)(p_\kappa/P)\kappa \tag{39}$$

$$(p_k/P)F_m = (r - r_m)m^f \tag{40}$$

Solving the set of equations (38) to (40) yields:

$$n^d = n^d(p_k/P, w, (r-\pi_\kappa)(p_\kappa/P), (r-r_m)) \tag{41}$$

$$\kappa^d = K^d(p_k/P, w, (r-\pi_\kappa)(p_\kappa/P), (r-r_m)) \tag{42}$$

$$m^{df} = m^{df}(p_k/P, w, (r-\pi_\kappa)(p_\kappa/P), (r-r_m)) \tag{43}$$

where w is the real wage rate W/P. The superscript d indicates demand and the superscript f indicates the representative firm. To be added to (41) to (43) is the supply function for commodities, obtained by substituting (41) to (43) in (26). These yield:

$$x^s = x^s(p_1/P, ..., p_K/P, w, (r-\pi_\kappa)(p_\kappa/P), (r-r_m)) \tag{44}$$

The first-order conditions (38) to (40) imply that (41) to (44) are *homogeneous of degree zero* in p_k, $k = 1, ..., K$, W and P. That is, proportionate increases in these variables will not alter the inputs demanded and the output supplied by the firm. Note that this result requires constancy of the user costs $(r-\pi_\kappa)$ and $(r-r_m)$, so that a proportional increase in these would change the demand for inputs and the supply of output.

Since physical capital is a commodity, though both used and produced by firms, the general properties of its demand and supply functions are identical to those of commodities.

3.7 THE AGGREGATE DEMAND AND SUPPLY FUNCTIONS FOR MONEY AND OTHER GOODS IN THE ECONOMY

Equations (23) to (25) had specified the demand and supply functions of a representative consumer. Aggregating these over all consumers, with the relevant symbols now taken to refer to the respective aggregate, we have from (23) to (25):

$$x_k^d = x_k^d(p_1/P, ..., p_K/P, W/P, (r-r_m), A_0/P) \quad k = 1, ..., K \tag{45}$$

$$n^s = n^s(p_1/P, ..., p_K/P, W/P, (r-r_m), A_0/P) \tag{46}$$

$$m^{dh} = m^{dh}(p_1/P, ..., p_K/P, W/P, (r-r_m), A_0/P) \tag{47}$$

where:

x_k^d aggregate demand for the kth commodity

n^s aggregate supply of labour

m^{dh} households' demand for real balances

A_0 aggregate initial endowment of all consumers

Also aggregate (41) to (43) over all firms in the economy, again adopting the convention that the relevant symbols will now refer to the respective aggregates. These yield the supply functions for commodities and the demand functions for labour and the real balances of firms as:

$$x_k^s = x^s(p_1/P, ..., p_K/P, W/P, (r-\pi_\kappa)(p_\kappa/P), (r-r_m)) \quad k = 1, ..., K \tag{48}$$

$$x_\kappa^s = x_\kappa^s(p_1/P, ..., p_K/P, W/P, (r-\pi_\kappa)(p_\kappa/P), (r-r_m)) \tag{49}$$

$$x_\kappa^d = x_\kappa^d(p_1/P, ..., p_K/P, W/P, (r-\pi_\kappa)(p_\kappa/P), (r-r_m)) \tag{50}$$

$$n^d = n^d(p_1/P, ..., p_K/P, W/P, (r-\pi_\kappa)(p_\kappa/P), (r-r_m)) \tag{51}$$

$$m^{df} = m^{df}(p_1/P, ..., p_K/P, W/P, (r-\pi_\kappa)(p_\kappa/P), (r-r_m)) \tag{52}$$

Adding equations (47) and (52) yields the economy's aggregate demand for real balances m^d as:

$$m^d = m^d(p_1/P, \ldots, p_K/P, W/P, (r - \pi_\kappa)(p_\kappa/P), (r - r_m), A_0/P) \tag{53}$$

Equations (45) and (48) are respectively the economy's demand and supply functions for commodities, (51) and (46) are respectively the demand and supply functions for labour, and (53) is the economy's demand for real balances. For a complete model of the economy, we are still missing an equation for the supply of real balances to the economy.

3.8 THE SUPPLY OF NOMINAL AND REAL BALANCES

The supply of nominal balances to the economy can be endogenous – that is, be a function of some of the other variables in the model – or exogenous. Which of these is the pertinent one to a given economy will depend upon the degree of control the central bank has over the nominal money supply and upon its preferences. This issue requires discussion of the determination of the money supply by the central bank. This is done in Chapters 10 to 12.

In a developed financial system with a central bank, the central bank is allocated the task of controlling the nominal money supply M^s to the economy. It is standard practice in macroeconomics to assume that the central bank determines the nominal money supply independently of the current values of the (other) endogenous macroeconomic variables. We adopt this assumption in this chapter, as in most of this book. Designating M as the exogenously supplied money stock, this assumption implies that:

$$M^s = M \tag{54}$$

Therefore, the amount of real balances m^s supplied to the economy is given by:

$$m^s = M/P$$

Since the price level P is determined endogenously by the model, the supply of real balances m^s is an endogenous variable even though the nominal money supply M was assumed to be exogenously determined. That is, while the central bank controls the nominal supply, the economy determines the real balances in the economy.

3.9 GENERAL EQUILIBRIUM IN THE ECONOMY

The preceding analysis specifies the equilibrium conditions for all markets as:

The markets for consumer commodities, with k = 1, ..., K:
$$x_k^d(p_1/P, \ldots, p_K/P, W/P, (r - r_m), A_0/P) = x_k^s(p_1/P, \ldots, p_K/P, w, (r - \pi_\kappa)(p_\kappa/P), (r - r_m)) \tag{55}$$

The market for physical capital:
$$x_\kappa^d(p_1/P, \ldots, p_K/P, W/P, (r - \pi_\kappa)(p_\kappa/P), (r - r_m)) = x_\kappa^s(p_1/P, \ldots, p_K/P, W/P, (r - \pi_\kappa)(p_\kappa/P), (r - r_m)) \tag{56}$$

The labour market:
$$n^d(p_1/P, \ldots, p_K/P, W/P, (r - \pi_\kappa)(p_\kappa/P), (r - r_m)) = n^s(p_1/P, \ldots, p_K/P, W/P, (r - r_m), A_0/P) \tag{57}$$

The money market:
$$m^d(p_1/P, \ldots, p_K/P, W/P, (r - \pi_\kappa)(p_\kappa/P), (r - r_m), A_0/P) = M^s/P \tag{58}$$

In addition, the definition of the price level from (18) is:

$$P_t = [\textstyle\sum_k p_{kt} x_{k0}]/[\textstyle\sum_\kappa p_{k0} x_{k0}] \tag{59}$$

Equations (55) to (59) constitute a set of $(K + 4)$ equations in the $(K + 4)$ endogenous variables $p_1, ..., p_K$, W, ρ_κ $(= r - r_\kappa)$, P and ρ_m $(= r - r_m)$. We follow the usual assumption that since the number of equations equals the number of endogenous variables, a unique solution exists for this system.

The above equilibrium equations (55) to (58) are homogeneous of degree zero in $p_1, ...,$ p_K, W, A_0 and M^s. Therefore, a once-for-all proportionate increase in all prices and therefore in P, provided the real values of the initial endowments and real balances are held constant, would not change the quantities demanded, supplied and traded in the economy. The real values of the variables would not be affected and neither consumers nor firms will be better or worse off under these changes.

Therefore, a *once-for-all increase in the money supply which results in a once-for-all proportionate increase in all prices* – so that the growth rate of the money supply does not change – will not have any real effects on the economy as long as these do not change the real value of initial endowments and do not induce expectations of inflation.[18]

The role of initial endowments in general equilibrium analysis

Initial endowments can be in the form of commodities, money or other financial assets (bonds), so that:

$$A_0 = \textstyle\sum_k p_k \bar{x}_{k,0} + \bar{M}_0 + p_b \bar{b}_0 \tag{60}$$

where $\bar{x}_{k,0}$ is the initial endowment of the kth commodity, $\bar{M}_0$ is the carryover of nominal balances and $\bar{b}_0$ is the carryover of real bonds at a market price of p_b. The real value a_0 of endowments is given by:

$$a_0 = A_0/P = \textstyle\sum_\kappa (p_k/P)\bar{x}_{k,0} + \bar{M}_0/P + (p_b/P)\bar{b}_0 \tag{60'}$$

A change in the prices of all commodities does not necessarily imply a proportionate change in the nominal balances carried over from the preceding period or a proportionate change in the price of bonds. If these do not change proportionately, a change in the commodity price level will change the real value of endowments.

The real balance effect

If the money supply is held constant, an increase in P will reduce the initial endowments of real balances, making the individual poorer and causing an income effect on the demands for goods. This income effect, in the normal case, would reduce the demands for commodities and real balances, and will increase the supply of labour. The name given to this effect of changes in the real money stock on the aggregate demand for commodities, and other goods, is the real balance effect. Note that it can occur through a change in the price level or a change in the money supply, but it does not come into play if both the money supply and the price level change in the same proportion.

The real balance effect is an important analytical mechanism connecting the commodity sector to the monetary one. To illustrate, suppose that the money supply increases. Until prices change, the money supply increases the real value of real balances and, therefore, of endowments. This will increase the demand for commodities, creating an excess demand in the commodity markets and pushing up their prices. The real balance effect, therefore, provides a mechanism by which the money supply changes bring about changes in the price level.

Alternatively, suppose the economy is in general equilibrium. A shock to the economy which reduces the aggregate demand for commodities will lower the price level and might also raise unemployment. But this price decrease will increase real balances, which, in turn, will serve to increase the demand for commodities. This increase in commodity demand will continue until real balances return to their original equilibrium level. This will require that the price level return to its original level. Hence, the real balance effect functioned as an equilibrating mechanism and a link between the monetary and the commodity markets. As such, it rejects any assertions about the dichotomy, discussed later in this chapter, between the real and the monetary sectors.

The real balance effect is more appropriately treated in Chapter 17.

The market for bonds and the interest rate

Initial endowments also include all non-monetary assets which we have termed 'bonds'. The relationship of the prices of bonds (including equities) with the commodity price level and the inflation rate is still not well understood in macroeconomics. The usual assumption is that their real value is homogeneous of degree zero in the price level P. However, this is more of a convenient assumption rather than one whose validity is generally accepted. Consequently, besides the real balance effect, there may also be a 'bonds effect' – that is, an income effect from changes in the real value of bonds (for example, induced by changes in the price level) on the demand for commodities.

The preceding general equilibrium analysis does not incorporate the market for bonds. Bonds, which were assumed to be illiquid, are a mechanism for transferring purchasing power from the present to the future. Their proper analysis requires an intertemporal framework, so that the preceding one-period analysis is unsuitable for the analysis of the demand for and supply of bonds. Since the return on bonds is the interest rate r, this rate is not determined in the above static model and has to be taken to be exogenously set, as is the quantity of bonds traded in the economy. However, the above model does determine the user costs of physical capital and real balances.

Further consideration of the market for bonds in the macroeconomic context is presented in Chapters 17 and 20.

3.10 THE NEUTRALITY AND SUPER-NEUTRALITY OF MONEY

3.10.1 The neutrality of money

The *neutrality of money* is said to exist if *once-for-all* changes in the money supply do not affect the real values of the variables – including real balances – in the economy. Another way of expressing this neutrality is to say that money is a *veil*: while its presence – as against its absence in a barter economy – makes a vital difference, changes in it do not have any real effects. The preceding section proves the neutrality of change in the money supply in general equilibrium *if*:

(i)   all prices increase in the same proportion;
(ii) the real value of the initial endowments does not change;
(iii) r_m is paid on *all* money balances; and
(iv) there is no anticipation of further price changes.

Hence, under these conditions, a once-for-all increase in the money supply, no matter how large, can be ignored for all real purposes since it would have no real effects.

3.10.2 The super-neutrality of money

The *super-neutrality of money* is said to exist if continuous changes in the money supply do not have any real effects.

Continuous increases in the money supply usually result in continuous inflation and such inflation is bound to be wholly or mostly expected. Lenders want the rates of interest to rise by the expected rate of inflation, so as to compensate them for the loss through inflation of the purchasing power of the funds that are lent. Therefore, in perfect money and capital markets, the (Fisher) relationship between the interest rates and expected inflation is:

$$r = r^r + \pi^e \tag{61}$$

$$r_m = r_m^r + \pi^e \tag{62}$$

where:

$\quad \pi$ rate of inflation

$\quad \pi^e$ expected rate of inflation

$\quad r^r$ real rate of interest (paid by bonds)

$\quad r_m^r$ real rate of interest on real balances

where,

$$(r - r_m) = (r^r - r_m^r)$$

so that even continuous anticipated inflation does not affect the real user cost of real balances.

Assuming $\pi^e = \pi$ (that is, inflation is fully anticipated) for a period of continuous *systematic* inflation,[19] we have,

$$r = r^r + \pi$$
$$r_m = r_m^r + \pi$$

Further, since capital goods are also commodities, assume that the inflation in the capital goods price is the same as on all the other goods in the economy, so that $\pi_\kappa = \pi$. This implies that $(r - \pi_\kappa)$ can be replaced by r^r in all relevant equations. Under these assumptions, $(r - r_m)$ can be replaced by $(r^r - r_m^r)$ and $(r - \pi_\kappa)$ can be replaced by r^r in (55) to (59).

Consequently, *if the nominal value of the initial endowments increases by the rate of inflation,* the identical rates of inflation in all prices (including wages) would not change the general equilibrium solution. Therefore, continuous money supply increases which induce continuous inflation and simultaneously change the nominal value of the initial endowments by the rate of inflation would not change the demands and supplies in the economy, and, therefore, would not change output, employment, the real rate of interest and real balances. Hence, the super-neutrality of money will hold in general equilibrium under the assumptions:

(i)   all prices increase in the same proportion;
(ii) the real value of the initial endowments does not change;
(iii) r_m is paid on *all* money balances; and
(iv) the expected inflation rate equals the actual one so that there are no errors in inflationary expectations.

3.10.3 Some of the reasons for deviations from neutrality and super-neutrality

Monetary non-neutrality if some components of money do not pay interest

M1 and broader money concepts include currency and demand deposits, of which currency does not pay interest to the holder and many forms of demand deposits also do not do so. Therefore, consider the alternative extreme assumption that all forms of money do not pay interest, so that $r_m = 0$. This implies replacing the rental cost of money $(r - r_m)$ in the equations above by r, so that the real user cost $(r - \pi)$ of money will depend on the rate of inflation. Consequently, changes in the inflation rate will change the cost of using money and, therefore, change its demand. Therefore, continuous inflation will change the solution to the set of equations (55) to (59), so that the real output, employment, the real rate of interest and the real values of the other endogenous variables determined by (55) to (59) will be altered by continuous inflation. That is, if some or all of the components of the money supply do not pay interest, the super-neutrality of money will no longer apply and continuous increases in the money supply will have real effects on the economy.

Monetary non-neutrality if the real value of initial endowments changes

The neutrality of money required that the real value of initial endowments does not change. But this value tends to change in disequilibrium. Whether the increases in the money supply and the inflation change the real value of endowments or not, will depend upon how money is introduced into the economy and the structure of the economy.

If the money supply is introduced through open market operations, the increase in the money supply will be counterbalanced by the decrease in the nominal value of the bonds in the hands of the public, so that the nominal value of the initial endowments (which include both bonds and nominal balances) will remain unchanged while their real value will fall. This implies that the super-neutrality of money will not hold.

Further, as equation (60′) specifies, the constancy of the real value of initial endowments requires that the ratio of bond prices to the price level (of commodities) remains invariant to changes in the money supply and the other economic adjustments to it. Note that 'bonds' cover all non-financial assets so that 'bond prices' include stock market prices. Economics has no generally accepted theory that the required invariance of the relative prices of bonds and equities to money supply changes does hold. It is highly plausible on the basis of everyday experience that it does not hold for the impact period and the short run.

Further, we will also need the invariance of the prices of physical capital and durable consumer goods, including housing, relative to the price level to ensure the neutrality of money. This is also highly questionable for the impact period and the short run.

Hence, the invariance of the real value of initial endowments – the wealth of the economy – to money supply changes is highly doubtful for the short run. It may hold for the long run.

Monetary non-neutrality if there exist rigidities or stickiness in the economy

The specified conditions for the neutrality of a once-for-all increase in the money supply and for the super-neutrality of continuous money supply increases require that prices and income receipts of various types be fully flexible, rather than rigid or sticky for some time. However, rigidities of some form or other are pervasive elements of every real-world economy. Some examples of these are:

(i) Some of the prices, incomes or wages may be rigid or sticky. For instance, the suppliers of commodities put out price lists which are costly to change on a continuing basis so that certain delays in changing them are profit maximizing.

(ii) Many types of incomes such as pensions, social security payments, unemployment insurance benefits, etc., are changed at infrequent intervals or not changed to match the rate of inflation.

(iii) Firms and workers find it optimal to enter into explicit or implicit long-term contracts for durations over which nominal wages are kept fixed or do not keep pace with the rate of inflation.

(iv) In addition, in economies with pervasive uncertainty especially about the values of the variables – such as the rate of return on investment – influenced by events far in the future, the expected real values of the variables may not be invariant to the rate of inflation.

These topics are discussed at greater length in Chapter 14 on Keynesian economics.

Monetary non-neutrality in disequilibrium

In the adjustment or disequilibrium phase while the money supply increase has not yet resulted in equi-proportionate increases in the absolute prices of all the commodities and in the nominal wage rates, the relative prices of commodities and the real value of initial endowments would change, causing real changes in the economy. Hence, money is not neutral in the disequilibrium state of the economy. On a practical note, it is difficult to determine whether disequilibrium is a transitory state, with rapid adjustment to equilibrium, so that its consequences are minimal and can be ignored. The modern classical school assumes that the economy tends to equilibrium rapidly enough to focus on the equilibrium states only. The Keynesian school believes that the economy can persist in less than full employment disequilibrium for long periods, so that the disequilibrium phases cannot be ignored and may well be designated as under-employment equilibria. Money is not neutral in these states.

In the analyses of disequilibrium and the business cycle, the nineteenth-century classical economists had argued that the capital goods prices and the consumer goods prices did not always change in the same proportion. To illustrate their ideas, consider Wicksell's analysis of the effects of a money supply increase in the pure credit economy, as presented in Chapter 2 above. Suppose the banks lower the market rate of interest. This makes it profitable for the firms to increase their borrowings from the banks for the purpose of increasing their investment. The increase in investment increases the demand for capital goods and increases their price, while there is yet no effect on consumer goods prices. That is, in this phase, p_K/P increases. Further, the increased production of capital goods would require increased employment in this industry, changing the structure of output and employment between the consumer and capital goods industries. Once the increase in investment has been accomplished and workers are spending their increased earnings, consumer goods prices will rise, so that in the later phases of the fluctuation, p_K/P will fall to go back to its equilibrium value. Hence, the fluctuations in p_K/P were a fundamental part of the adjustment process by which money affects the economy, and these fluctuations caused fluctuations in the output of different industries and overall employment. Such an analysis was not confined to Wicksell but was a part of traditional classical economics generally, and played an important role in the nineteenth- and the early twentieth-century studies of the business cycle. It disappeared from the macroeconomics based on the IS–LM models since such models do not distinguish between the consumer and capital goods industries.

Overall assessment of the departures from the neutrality and the super-neutrality of money

The preceding arguments provide a very extensive list of reasons why monetary neutrality may not hold, at least in the short run. Hence, at least in the short run, money is not likely to be neutral in the disequilibrium and even the equilibrium phases of the economy in which there is a once-for-all increase in the money supply. It is even less likely to be neutral if there are continuous and variable increases in the money supply.[20]

Therefore, on a practical basis in real-world economies, money supply increases and inflation do have real effects, so that money is not really neutral, at least in the short run during which the rigidities and disequilibrium operate in the economy. It is, however, difficult to determine whether these departures from neutrality are relatively unimportant and transient – as the neoclassical and modern classical schools claim – or very important – as the Keynesian school claims. What does seem to happen is that any economy with persistently high rates of anticipated inflation does adjust its contractual and institutional arrangements to minimize the impact of inflation on the real variables – including the relative prices of commodities, real wages etc. – in the economy, so that the departures from the neutrality of money are reduced. The larger departures from the neutrality of money occur when a significant part of the inflation rate is unanticipated and this tends to occur in periods of fluctuating money supply growth rates and inflation rates. Further, even under fully anticipated inflation, the super-neutrality of money does not hold if an adequate rate of interest is not paid on part or whole of the nominal balances of the public.

Further, as argued above, the method by which money is introduced into the economy could alter the real value of endowments, even in general equilibrium. The general equilibrium equations do not disclose the adjustment path once money is introduced in the economy. This topic will be studied in Chapter 17 in the context of the *real balance effect*.

3.11 THE DICHOTOMY BETWEEN THE REAL AND THE MONETARY SECTORS

The *neutrality of money* in general equilibrium is, as shown above, related to the homogeneity of degree zero of all demand and supply functions, with respect to changes in all absolute prices and initial endowments. The traditional classical economists sometimes extended their arguments to assert the *dichotomy between the real and the monetary sectors*. This dichotomy is the statement that the real values of the endogenous variables in the economy are independent of the nominal money supply and the price level, so that these real values of the variables can be determined independently of the latter.

We can define the *weak* form of the dichotomy as one when the preceding statement holds only in equilibrium and the *strong* form of it as one when that statement holds both in equilibrium and in disequilibrium. The following modifies the Walrasian general equilibrium set of equations to produce the strong form of the dichotomy of the real sector from the monetary one.

The strong dichotomy and the independence of the real sector from the monetary one

The general equilibrium system of equations (55) to (57) for the real sector of the economy has the money stock as a component of the initial endowments, as well as the price level as a variable. Modifying these equations to show the complete independence of the real variables from the money supply and the price level requires exclusion of the financial part of the endowments from these equations and the elimination of the price level from them. On the former, assume that the endowments are only of commodities. That is, rather than assuming (60) as describing the initial endowments, let:

$$A_0 = \sum_k p_k x_{k,0} \tag{63}$$

where $x_{k,0}$ is the initial endowment of the kth commodity, so that there are no carryover money balances and bonds in this system.

To eliminate the price level from the relevant equations, let the numeraire be the first commodity, so that all prices in the economy will be measured in terms of this commodity.

This means dividing all absolute prices by p_1 rather than P, which is permitted by the homogeneity of degree zero of equations (55) to (58). Before doing so, restate (63) as:

$$a_0 = A_0/p_1 = \sum_k (p_k/p_1)x_{k,0} \tag{63'}$$

Using the first commodity as a numeraire means that $p_1 = 1$, so that p_1 (the price of the numeraire commodity in terms of money) cannot be determined in this model. We correspondingly omit the equilibrium condition for the numeraire commodity by virtue of Walras' law (see Chapter 17) which implies that if equilibrium exists in all markets except one, it must also exist in the remaining market. We also delete the user cost of real balances $\rho_m\ (= r - r_m)$ as a variable from our system for reasons of consistency with the historical debates on this topic which excluded any variables related to money from the specified system. The resulting system is:

Modified commodities markets equations for k = 2, ..., K:
$$x_k^d(p_2/p_1, ..., p_K/p_1, W/p_1, a_0) = c^s(p_2/p_1, ..., p_K/p_1, W/p_1, \rho_K/p_1) \tag{64}$$

Modified physical capital market equation:
$$x_K^d(p_2/p_1, ..., p_K/p_1, W/p_1, \rho_K/p_1) = x_K^s(p_2/p_1, ..., p_K/p_1, W/p_1, \rho_K/p_1) \tag{65}$$

Modified labour market equation:
$$n^d(p_2/p_1, ..., p_K/p_1, W/p_1, \rho_K/p_1) = n^s(p_2/p_1, ..., p_K/p_1, W/p_1, a_0) \tag{66}$$

Note that (64) to (66) assume that there are no carryover money balances or bonds, so that they are not valid for an economy with initial endowments of money and bonds. These are $(K + 1)$ equations in the $(K + 1)$ endogenous real variables $(p_2/p_1, ..., p_K/p_1, W/p_1, \rho_K/p_1)$. As in earlier analysis, since this is a one-period and not an intertemporal analysis, the interest rate r on bonds is given to this model. The money supply and the price level are not in these equations. Assuming a solution, (64) to (66) can be solved for the real values of the endogenous variables, even without knowing the amount of nominal balances in the economy or knowing the price level. Hence, these equations represent a strong form of the dichotomy. In it, the real sector determines its relative prices, quantities demanded and supplied, and output of commodities, as well employment in the economy. This determination is independent of the economy's money supply or the price level, so that changes in these cannot affect the real sector of the economy.

The strong dichotomy and the determination of the price level
The relative prices determined from (64) to (66) could be substituted in the money market equation, which – with a_0 replacing A_0/p_1 and omitting P_m – would be given by:

Modified money market equation:
$$m^d(p_1/p_1, ..., p_K/p_1, W/p_1, p_K/p_1\ a_0) = M^s/P \tag{67}$$

Since the real values of all the arguments of the m^d function on the left-hand side are determined by equations (64) to (66) independently of the money supply and the price level, (67) can be rewritten as:

$$P = [1/m^d(\cdot)]M^s \tag{68}$$

Equation (68) determines the price level, so that the money market equilibrium is needed for the determination of the price level but not for the determination of the values of the real variables.

The traditional classical economists had, in fact, used the quantity theory of money instead of the more general money demand function in (67). Therefore, their version of (67) was:

$$M^s = m_y Y = m_y P y^*$$

where y^* was predetermined by the real sector of the economy and M^s was exogenous, so that the quantity theory determined the price level for the economy.

Equation (68) implies that the price level will change in proportion to the money supply. This was the central proposition of the quantity theory, so that the quantity theory and the traditional classical notion of the dichotomy between the real and monetary sectors were consistent with each other, and supported each other in economists' thinking.[21]

The strong dichotomy and the determination of the velocity of money

Note that, for this dichotomous Walrasian system, the velocity v of circulation of money is given by:

$$
\begin{aligned}
v &= Y/M = y/m \\
&= y/m^d(\cdot) \quad\quad\quad\quad\quad\quad\quad\quad\quad\quad\quad\quad\quad\quad\quad (69)
\end{aligned}
$$

Since the dichotomized Walrasian system determines both y and m^d as real variables, independently of the money supply and the price level, the equilibrium velocity of circulation in this system is also a real variable and is independent of the money supply and the price level, as Irving Fisher had claimed (see Chapter 2 above).

The strong dichotomy and the indeterminacy of the price level

It is important to note that a strongly dichotomized system produces indeterminacy of prices: a change in the demands and/or supplies of commodities does not compel the markets for these commodities to change the absolute prices of these commodities, since absolute prices are not variables in these functions. Conversely, an arbitrary change in the price level does not change any demands or supplies in real terms and does not change their equilibrium solutions. Therefore, any arbitrarily specified price level is consistent with the real sector of such an economy. Further, an increase in the money supply will not increase the demand for individual commodities or the aggregate demand for commodities and, therefore, will not put pressure on the individual prices and the price level to rise, so that we are left without a mechanism for increases in prices.

The real balance effect and overall assessment of the strong dichotomy

Since money balances by their nature act as a store of value that must be carried over from one period to the next, they must form part of the initial endowments of the individuals in the economy and of the whole economy. That is, it is not legitimate to rewrite the set of equations (55) to (57) as the set (64) to (66). Hence, the monetary economy does not possess dichotomy between the real and the monetary sectors, and the conclusions based on the dichotomy have to be rejected.

The critical element in the link from the monetary to the real sector is the real balance effect. This link operates in the disequilibrium phase, and operates through changes in the real balances impacting on the demand for commodities. It is primarily a mechanism operating in the disequilibrium phase of the Walrasian system and will not be noticeable in the static equilibrium description of such a system, so that the latter may seem to indicate the dichotomy, even when one does not really exist.

We will return to this issue again in Chapter 17 on Walras' law and the interactions among the sectors of the economy.

3.12 SIMPLIFYING THE AGGREGATE DEMAND FUNCTION FOR MONEY FOR MACROECONOMIC ANALYSIS

We now return to the original, non-dichotomized Walrasian system and single out the demand function for money for adaptation to macroeconomic analysis. The household's demand for real balances was derived in (47) as:

$$m^{dh} = m^{dh}(p_1/P, \ldots, p_K/P, W/P, (r-r_m), A_0/P) \tag{70}$$

Macroeconomics simplifies (70) by ignoring the heterogeneity of commodities and their individual prices, even though they are fundamental to understanding why households and firms will hold money to facilitate transactions among commodities. Eliminating the individual prices $p_1, \ldots, p_K$ by assuming the constancy of the relative prices (which are $p_1/P, \ldots, p_K/P, p_\kappa/P$) of commodities, (70) becomes:

$$m^{dh} = m^{dh}(W/P, (r-r_m), A_0/P) \tag{71}$$

Further, economists rarely want to study the interaction between the demand for money and the supply of labour, but rather focus on the national income in the economy, of which labour income constitutes one of the elements of the constraint on the households' expenditures on commodities and real balances. To focus on labour income rather than the wage rate, rewrite (71) with real labour income y^L instead of W/P. This modifies the money demand function to:

$$m^{dh} = m^{dh}((r-r_m), y^L, A_0/P) \tag{72}$$

That is, the household's demand for real balances now depends on its user cost, real labour income and the real value of existing (physical and financial) wealth.

Turning now to the demand for money by firms, this was derived above as:

$$m^{df} = m^{df}(p_1/P, \ldots, p_K/P, W/P, (r-\pi_\kappa)(p_\kappa/P), (r-r_m)) \tag{73}$$

Simplify (73) under the above assumption of the constancy of the relative prices of commodities, and the assumption that the rate of inflation of capital goods is identical to the rate of inflation (π) given by the price index of all commodities. Further, replacing W/P by real labour income, (73) simplifies to:

$$m^{df} = m^{df}((r-\pi), (r-r_m), y^L) \tag{74}$$

Combining (72) and (74) gives the aggregate demand for real balances as:

$$m^d = m^d((r-\pi), (r-r_m), y^L, A_0/P) \tag{75}$$

where $(r - \pi)$ is the user cost of the alternative asset, physical capital, while $(r - r_m)$ is the user cost of holding money rather than the illiquid bond, which has the return r.

Monetary economics often further simplifies (75) to replace the two variables of real labour income y^L and initial wealth A_0/P sometimes by current real income y (which is the sum of labour income and the return on wealth) alone and sometimes by real wealth alone. Monetary economics, therefore, further modifies (75) to one of the following alternative forms.

3.12.1 The Keynesian money demand function

$$m^d = m^d((r - \pi), (r - r_m), y) \tag{76}$$

Equation (76) is the demand function for money in the Keynesian tradition, with its emphasis on income y rather than wealth. Assuming real balances to be a normal good, $\partial m^d / \partial (r - \pi) < 0$, $\partial m^d / \partial (r - r_m) < 0$ and $\partial m^d / \partial y > 0$.

3.12.2 The life cycle version of the money demand function

If our framework had been an intertemporal one taking account of current and future labour income, the constraining variables would have been the present value of labour income – or *human wealth,* as in Friedman's restatement of the quantity theory set out in Chapter 2 above – and inherited wealth – or *non-human wealth* in Friedman's terminology. In line with this, replacing y^L in (75) by y^{Lae} as the average expected labour income from the presented discounted value (HW) of real labour income in the future, (75) can be transformed to:

$$m^d = m^d((r - \pi), (r - r_m), y^{Lae}, NHW) \tag{77}$$

where:

y^{Lae} average expected labour income over one's lifetime
HW human wealth (= present discounted value of labour income) in real terms
NHW non-human wealth in real terms

and $\partial m^d / \partial (r - \pi) < 0$, $\partial m^d / \partial (r - r_m) < 0$, $\partial m^d / \partial y^{Lae} > 0$ and $\partial m^d / \partial NHW > 0$. Equation (77) is in the spirit of the life cycle consumption hypothesis of Modigliani *et al.*

3.12.3 Friedman's money demand function

It is more usual to proceed to Friedman's demand function for money, as in Chapter 2 above. Proceeding in this spirit, define the individual's permanent income y^p as the average expected income from the sum of his human and non-human wealth and rewrite (77) as:

$$m^d = m^d((r - \pi), (r - r_m), y^p, HW/NHW) \tag{78}$$

which represents a form of Friedman's demand function for money. Comparing (76) and (78), the Keynesian demand function (76) for real balances uses income, while the Friedman demand function (78) uses permanent income, as the relevant constraining argument.

The variations (76), (77) and (78) illustrate that the aggregate demand function for real balances can be represented by several different simplified versions. We will return to some of these in Chapters 7 to 9 on the functions used in estimating the demand for money.

Money has been defined above as a financial asset held for its liquidity services in facilitating transactions. Many assets can provide such services, each with its own user cost: $(r - r_m)$ would then be a vector of these user costs. Further, the user costs encompass both the interest payments and any brokerage costs in obtaining, holding and using real balances.

The latter include monetary and non-monetary components. Among the latter are the amount of time spent by the holder in using the money. These factors are further considered in Chapters 4 and 8.

CONCLUSIONS

This chapter has provided a basis for both the microeconomic analysis of the demand for and supply of money, and the macroeconomic analysis of the role of money in the macro-economy. The former is further developed in Chapters 4 to 12 and the latter in Chapters 13 to 17.

The analysis of this chapter is in the tradition of the MIUF and MIPF models. This approach treats money as a good like other goods in the utility function and as an input like other inputs in the production function. It puts real balances in the utility function since, for the given individual in a monetary economy, more real balances are preferred to less. The basis of this preference is not considered relevant to the issue of putting money in the utility function, just as the basis of including cigarettes and other presumably harmful products which are bought is not considered relevant in deciding whether to include them in the utility function. Further, the question of whether money balances directly yield utility or not is also not considered to be relevant, just as that of whether cigarettes directly yield utility – or do so indirectly through their smoke entering the human body while cigarettes themselves are only held at the lips – is an aspect which has little relevance to their utility and demand analysis. Similar considerations apply to placing real balances in the production function. In any case, this chapter also presented the indirect approach to putting real balances in the utility and production functions. A more distinctive approach which would keep them out of both the direct and indirect utility and production functions is offered by the overlapping generations models presented in Chapters 22 to 24 below.

The representative individual's demand and supply functions for the real values of all goods are homogeneous of degree zero in the nominal prices and the nominal value of the initial endowment. That is, *a change in all prices with the real value of wealth held constant does not change the individual's demand and supply functions.* But a change in the absolute prices which changes the individual's real wealth because part of it is held in money and other financial assets, brings about a wealth effect on the quantities demanded of goods by the individual and in the economy, and changes the relative prices of goods, including commodities.

A change in the *relative prices* of the individual commodities would change the demand for real balances and also the absolute price level, through both substitution and income effects. For the individual, the major determinant of the demand for real balances, as for all commodities collectively, is the scale variable, whether this is taken to be income or wealth.

The demand for real balances by the representative firm depends upon the relative prices of the other inputs in the production function. In the general context, there is no scale variable in the firm's demand and supply functions, as there is for the individual's analysis. The firm's demand for real balances is homogeneous of degree zero in the firm's output and input prices.

Money is neutral in the neoclassical model derived in this chapter for a once-only increase in prices provided that there is a proportionate increase in all prices (including wages), the real value of initial endowments remains unchanged and the expected rate of inflation remains unchanged. In this model, money is also super-neutral for continuous increases in the price level, provided that all prices rise in the same proportion, the real endowments do not change, the expected inflation rate is identically equal to the actual rate of inflation, and the nominal rates of return on bonds, physical capital and *money* all increase by the rate of inflation. These are fairly stringent conditions. Whether the deviations from neutrality and super-neutrality for a given real world economy are significant or not would depend upon the particular characteristics of the economy.

Modern classical economists tend towards acceptance of neutrality and sometimes even of super-neutrality, as an acceptable though rough approximation to reality. Keynesian economists tend to consider these as poor and unacceptable approximations and believe that money is not neutral in the real-world economies. Their reasons for this are discussed in Chapter 14 and include their belief that the commodity and labour markets do not clear fast enough.[22] This discussion and its implications for monetary policy are pursued further in the macroeconomics chapters 12 to 17.

The property of neutrality is different from that of the dichotomy between the real and the monetary sectors. The strong form of the latter makes the real sector independent of the monetary one even in disequilibrium, so that changes in the money supply do not affect relative prices and employment even in disequilibrium. While we consider the neutrality and super-neutrality of money to be moot points, open to discussion and without a uniform answer for all economies, we have rejected the strong form of the dichotomy for monetary economies. The link from the monetary sector to the real one is the real balance effect. The link from the financial sector to the real one would also include a wealth effect operating through changes in the real value of bonds.

The Walrasian general equilibrium model – derived in this chapter as well as its neoclassical macroeconomic version in Chapter 13 – does *not* possess the strong form of the dichotomy between the monetary and the real sectors since it does not assume that the real value of initial endowments, which include money and bonds, is invariant to changes in the current prices of commodities. However, imposing such invariance as an additional assumption would create a dichotomized Walrasian system, with the independence of the commodity and labour markets from the money supply and the price level. This subject is again discussed in Chapter 17 on Walras' law, Say's law and the interrelationship between the sectors.

This chapter has also derived the general demand function for real balances as part of the Walrasian system and examined its properties. The following three chapters use Keynes' motives for holding money to present further analytical developments specific to each motive.

SUMMARY OF CRITICAL CONCLUSIONS

- Money can be an argument of the individual's utility function either directly or indirectly, because its usage reduces the transactions time spent in selling its labour and making its purchases, thereby increasing the individual's leisure and labour supply.
- Money can be an argument of the firm's production function either directly or indirectly because its usage reduces the transactions time spent in hiring its inputs and selling its output and thereby increases the proportion of the firm's labour force and capital engaged directly in production.
- Any good can be a numeraire. If money balances are the numeraire, its own price is one.
- The user cost of money balances as a medium of payments is not the price level but their rental cost and is represented by the interest forgone from holding them.
- The demand for real balances and the demand and supply functions for all other goods are homogeneous of degree zero in all prices *and* (the nominal value of) each individual's initial endowments. The latter requires the homogeneity of degree one of the nominal value of initial endowments in all prices.
- Omitting initial endowments from the preceding conclusion creates a dichotomy between the real and monetary sectors of the Walrasian general equilibrium model.
- Keeping initial endowments in the analysis introduces the real balance effect as a connecting link from the monetary sector to the real one. One cannot also be sanguine that bond and equity prices will rise in proportion to the commodity prices, or that an increase in the money supply will cause a proportionate increase in them, so that the financial and the real sectors are intertwined in disequilibrium.

- Money is neutral – and could be even super-neutral – under rather strict assumptions that do not hold in practice. In particular, changes in all prices are usually not accompanied by a proportionate increase in the nominal value of initial endowments.
- Among the components of initial endowments that, in practice, tend not to be homogeneous of degree one in all prices are money balances, minimum wage rates, pensions, and bond and equity prices.
- Among the assumptions needed for money neutrality is the flexibility of all prices, including wages. However, the existence of long-term explicit or implicit labour contracts and, in some cases, the reluctance of firms to adjust prices, etc., violate this assumption.
- Money is not neutral in the economy, but the real question for monetary economics is not a black or white one but rather the degree and duration of the deviations from neutrality for the economy and the period in question. On this practical issue (within the realm of the short run), there is almost always considerable disagreement among economists.

review and discussion questions

1 Define neutrality of money.

Provide at least a rough proof that the neutrality of money exists in a Walrasian general equilibrium.

Can disequilibrium occur in the Walrasian model? If it can, would money neutrality also exist in disequilibrium in the Walrasian model? If it does not, why is money neutrality usually identified with the Walrasian model?

2 For the Walrasian model, discuss the statement: if nominal wages and prices are fully flexible, then neither a one-time increase in the money supply nor an increase in the rate of monetary growth will have any effect on the level of output in general equilibrium.

3 Discuss the relationship in Walrasian general equilibrium analysis between the neutrality and super-neutrality of money and the classical dichotomy. Does either of them imply the other?

4 Discuss the relationship between the neutrality (and super-neutrality) of money and the quantity theory of money. Does either of them imply the other?

5 How important are the deviations from the neutrality of money likely to be at single-digit but constant rates of inflation? How important are the deviations from the neutrality of money likely to be at single-digit but variable and highly uncertain rates of inflation?

6 Does the neutrality of money hold in hyperinflation? Discuss.

7 Discuss: if all prices, including nominal wages, are flexible, money must be neutral.

8 Why is such a big deal being made of initial endowments in the individual's utility analysis? Suppose that initial endowments were left out of such analysis. What analytical consequences would this imply for neutrality and dichotomy, and for the role of money in the macroeconomy?

9 Assume that the representative individual has the specific utility function:

$$U(c, n, m^h) = U(c + m^h - h(n))$$

where $\partial h/\partial n > 0$ and $\partial^2 h/\partial n^2 < 0$, c is the purchase of commodities, n is the supply of labour and m^h is real balances held by the individual. Also assume that, each period, he or she receives an exogenously specified pension in nominal terms and also earns labour income from his or her labour supply. Derive the relevant demand and supply functions for the individual. (State any assumptions that you need to make.) Are these functions invariant with respect to a proportionate increase in all prices? If not, what is required to make them invariant?

10 Assume that the specific production function of the representative firm is:

$$F(K, L, m^f) = AK^\alpha L^\beta m^{f\gamma}$$

where $F(\cdot)$ is the firm's production function, K is its capital stock, L is its employment and m is its holdings of real balances. Derive the relevant demand and supply functions for the firm. (State any assumptions that you need to make.) Define the user cost of money. Show the dependence of the marginal productivities of labour and capital on the user cost of real balances.

Suppose that a financial innovation multiplies the firm's marginal productivity of real balances by λ. What would be its impact on the firm's demand functions for labour and capital?

11 'Putting money into the utility and production functions is difficult to reconcile with the Walrasian general equilibrium model.' 'Putting money in the utility and production functions does provide a way of theorizing about the benefits from the medium of payments role that money plays in the real-world economy with heterogeneous goods, specialization in production and trade, and absence of the double coincidence of wants.' Discuss these statements.

NOTES

1 It is, however, marketed in some cases as in the case of 'soundproof apartments' commanding higher rents than other apartments.

2 Intuitively, commodities are goods directly used in consumption or production. Financial assets are paper or bookkeeping claims to commodities and are used for their liquidity services or to transfer purchasing power from the present to the future.

3 To consider an example, assume that an individual holds $100 at the beginning of a week and spends it at a *continuous* even rate over the week. His average money balances – designated as his demand for money – held over the month are $50 (=100/2) which clearly differ from his money balance of $100 at the beginning of the week and his money balance of zero dollars at the end of the week. For comparable period analysis, assume that he spent $100/7 (=$14.29) per day of the week. He would then hold $85.71 (=100 – 14.29) for 6 days, $71.42 (= 85.71 – 14.29) for 5 days, and so on. The weighted average (i.e., weighted by the number of days held) of these amounts would be $42.86, so that there is a slight difference between the continuous and the discrete cases for the average calculation. We will proceed with the continuous even expenditure assumption, which implied the weighted average balance to be $50. Under this assumption, the individual would be taken to have had an average demand for $50 of money balances, a durable good, and to have used its services in financing his purchases during the week. Also see Chapter 4 on this point.

4 A pure store of value without any transactions usage would occur if the individual held $50 consistently – and never spent any of it – from the beginning of the week to the end of the week. He would then have bequeathed this amount to the beginning of the following week, much in the manner of a durable consumer good such as a refrigerator, which outlasts the current week of usage and is still available to the individual at the beginning of the following week. Thus, for the pure store of value function, the individual could store the unplugged refrigerator or the $50 of money balances through the week without any intention of using

their services for refrigeration or financing payments, respectively. In practice, both the refrigerator and the money balances will see some usage – the latter for financing transactions – during the week and still act as stores of value. Chapter 4 presents the analysis of the transactions usage combined with the store of value role of money.

5   Friedman called the temporary store of value for which money is used as an *abode of purchasing power*.

6   To these two axioms, a third is sometimes added for analytical convenience. This is that the individual never reaches satiation for any good. That is, he continues to prefer more of each good to less of it. In view of the definition of goods above, this axiom implies that a good never ceases to be a good for the individual, no matter how much or how little he possesses of it.

7   Thus, 100 bank notes with a face value of $1 each have a nominal quantity or value of $100. Assume that the individual wishes to hold a certain amount of real purchasing power in money balances and this demand of his equals $100 at a certain set of prices. If prices of commodities were to double, the individual would no longer demand $100 but $200 of money balances in order to keep his demand in terms of their real purchasing power constant.

8   A utility function which gives a consistent and transitive ranking of preferences, without any other characteristics of measurability, is said to be ordinal or unique up to an increasing monotonic transformation. That is, if $U(x_1, ..., x_s)$ is the individual's utility function, then $F[U(x_1, ..., x_s)]$, where $\partial F/\partial U > 0$ is also an admissible utility function with identical demand functions for x_i, $i = 1, ..., s$.

9   Since this shopping time reduces leisure and leisure has positive marginal utility, such shopping time in this model has negative marginal utility. This is quite reasonable since we are considering the shopping time made necessary by not having adequate money to pay for one's purchases, rather than shopping with enough money in hand to pay for the desired level of purchases. The latter may be enjoyable, while the former is likely to be the chore of finding sellers who will transfer their goods in some form of barter.

10 One can here adapt Lucas's island parable (for which see Lucas, 1980, in the references to Chapter 15) with each supplier on a separate island. To do so, assume that all suppliers are willing to accept money in exchange for commodities while only some suppliers are willing to sell their commodities in exchange for some other means of payments (transfer of bonds, IOUs or other commodities). Further, assume that the given buyer needs to buy c units of commodities but does not know the locations of the different types of suppliers and must search on a random basis among all suppliers. This buyer needs to visit c islands (since only one unit of consumption can be bought on each island) with suppliers who will accept the means of payment carried by the buyer. A buyer who carries enough balances will have to visit c islands, while other buyers with less than c units of money balances will have to visit more islands and spend more time in the search process.

11 For example, the direct utility function has the property $\partial U/\partial m \to \infty$ as $m \to 0$, while this need not occur in the indirect utility function. However, such conditions can be derived from the latter and imposed on the former. For an example of such a condition, let the shopping time without money reach a finite constant ck, so that we have $\partial \phi/\partial m \to ck$ as $m \to 0$. Then, we do not have $\partial V/\partial m \to \infty$ as $m \to 0$.

12 In economies with hyperinflation in terms of the domestic currency, one or more foreign currencies or gold are often used as unit of account.

13 From a rigorous viewpoint, money prices are accounting prices. However, the convention has grown up in economics that only prices measured in terms of a unit which is not one of the goods in the economic system itself are called accounting prices and only the non-good unit is called a unit of account. Such a unit of account is, for example, the guinea in England. The guinea has no physical counterpart in the real world. Traditionally, it had the value of £1.05 – which used to correspond to the old 21 shillings, while the pound was worth 20 shillings. Assume, however, that its value was halved by a decree or fiat to £0.0525.

Since the guinea has no real existence and is not demanded or supplied in the economy, the halving of the value of the guinea in terms of the monetary units of £s would not affect behaviour in the economy. Each money price – that is, the price of a good in terms of money – would remain the same. However, each accounting price calculated in terms of the guinea would double. Such a change in all accounting prices – or as expressed alternatively, a change in the value of the non-good unit of account – does not affect the quantities demanded or supplied or the monetary prices of goods. This is hardly surprising since non-good units of account are bookkeeping devices and do not affect economic behaviour.

14 This is the usual way of specifying the user cost of money. However, in the real world, the user cost of money often does have additional components such as the time taken to obtain cash balances, etc. These are more explicitly considered in Chapter 4 on the transactions demand for money.

15 The user cost over a period of a unit of the ith durable commodity is $(r + d - \pi_i)p_i$ where r is the market rate of interest, d is the rate of depreciation of the commodity, π_i is the rate of increase in the price of the ith commodity and p_i is its price. Applying this formula to the case of money, d is zero; in perfect financial markets, the rate of interest r incorporates the rate of inflation π for all commodities and the price of nominal balances is unity.

16 Both the CPI and the GDP deflator suffer from certain limitations and imperfections. Descriptions of these can be found in many macroeconomics textbooks.

17 This can also be proved directly from the first-order conditions. To do this, divide (11) and (13) by (12). In the resulting set of equations, replacing $(p_1, ..., p_K, W$ and $A_0)$ by $(\alpha p_1, ..., \alpha p_K, \alpha W$ and $\alpha A_0)$ does not induce any change. Further, as discussed above in the text, this replacement does not alter (14), which is the budget constraint itself. Hence, the first-order conditions (11) to (14) and their solution (15) to (17) will remain unchanged.

18 It is generally assumed in macroeconomic theory that once-for-all increases do not lead to anticipations of inflation and therefore do not change the rates of interest r and r_m.

19 This follows from rational expectations. The theory of rational expectations is presented in Chapter 9.

20 We will return to this topic again in the macroeconomics chapters 13 to 17.

21 However, neither alone was sufficient to imply the other.

22 There is an even more fundamental basis for divergence between the neoclassical and Keynesian schools on these issues. Neoclassical economics assumes that all markets tend to clear rapidly so that the analysis can be conducted under the assumption of equilibrium in all markets. This assumption is at the core of the demand and supply functions derived in this chapter. The proper name for such functions is 'notional'. The alternatives to such functions are the 'effective' or 'quantity-constrained' demand and supply functions which do not assume market clearance in other markets. Such functions have not been derived or presented in this chapter. They belong in the Keynesian tradition and some discussion of them is presented in Chapter 14 on Keynesian economics.

REFERENCES

Burstein, M. L. *Modern Monetary Theory*. London: St Martin's Press, 1986.

Cuthbertson, Keith. *The Supply and Demand for Money*. London: Basil Blackwell, 1985, Ch. 2.

Niehans, J. *The Theory of Money*. Baltimore, Md.: Johns Hopkins University Press, 1978, Ch. 1.

Patinkin, Don. *Money, Interest and Prices*, 2nd edn. New York: Harper & Row, 1965, Chs 2, 5–8.

Pesek, Boris P., and Thomas R. Saving. *Money, Wealth and Economic Theory*. New York: Macmillan, 1967.

Sargent, Thomas J. *Macroeconomic Theory*. New York: Academic Press, 1979.

part three

THE DEMAND FOR MONEY

chapter four

THE TRANSACTIONS DEMAND FOR MONEY

Keynes had designated the transactions demand for money as due to the transactions motive but had not provided a theory for its determination. In particular, he had assumed that this demand depended linearly on current income but did not depend on interest rates.

Subsequent contributions by Baumol and Tobin in the 1950s established the theory of the transactions demand for money. These showed that this demand depends not only on income but also on the interest rate on bonds. Further, there are economies of scale in money holdings.

The transactions demand for money is derived under the assumptions of certainty about the yields on bonds, as well as the amounts and the time patterns of income and expenditures.

---

key concepts introduced in this chapter

- The transactions demand for money
- Economies of scale in money demand
- The elasticity of the demand for real balances with respect to the price level
- The elasticity of the demand for real balances with respect to income
- The elasticity of the demand for real balances with respect to the interest rate
- The elasticity of the demand for real balances with respect to their user cost
- Efficient funds management

This chapter presents the main elements of the theory of the demand for transactions balances and derives the *transactions demand for money*. In doing so, it follows Keynes in assuming that the individual's money holdings can be validly subdivided into several components, one of which is purely for meeting transactions.

Chapter 2 had pointed out that many of the classical economists and Keynes had made the simple assumption of the unit elasticity of demand for transactions balances with respect to nominal income. In particular, the demand for transactions balances was taken to double if either the price level or real income/expenditures – but not both – doubled. Hardly any analysis was presented in support of such a statement and it remained very much in the realm of an assumption.

Developments during the 1950s analysed the demand for transactions balances rigorously from the standpoint of an individual who minimizes the costs of financing transactions by holding money balances and other assets. This analysis showed that the transactions demand for money depends negatively upon the rate of interest and that its elasticity with respect to the real level of expenditures is less than unity. The original analyses along these lines were presented by Baumol (1952) and Tobin (1956). The following presentation draws heavily upon Baumol's treatment of the subject.

Developments since the 1950s have extended and broadened the Baumol–Tobin transactions demand analysis, without rejecting it. The most significant extension of this analysis has been to the case where there is uncertainty in the timings of the receipts and payments. The demand for money under this type of uncertainty is usually labelled as the precautionary demand for money and is the subject of Chapter 6.

4.1 THE BASIC INVENTORY ANALYSIS OF THE TRANSACTIONS DEMAND FOR MONEY

This section presents the analysis in Baumol (1952). Baumol's basic assumptions are:

(i) There is no uncertainty in the timing or amount of the individual's receipts and expenditures.

(ii) The individual intends to finance an amount of Y of expenditures, being spent in a steady stream through the given period, and already possesses the funds to meet these expenditures. All payments are made in money.

(iii) There are only two assets, money and bonds. Money holdings do not pay interest. Bond holdings do so at the rate r. There are no own service costs of using money or bonds, but there are transfer costs from one to the other, as outlined in the next point. Bonds can be savings deposits or other financial assets, even though much of the following discussion is as if they were savings deposits in banks.

(iv) The individual intends to withdraw cash from his bonds in lots of W spaced evenly through the period. Each time he makes a withdrawal, he must incur a 'brokerage (bonds–money transfer) cost' that has two components: a fixed cost of B_0 per withdrawal and a variable cost of B_1 per dollar withdrawn. Examples of such brokerage costs are brokers' commission, banking charges and own (or personal) costs in terms of time and convenience for withdrawals from bonds. The overall cost per withdrawal of W is $(B_0 + B_1 W)$.

Since the individual starts with $\$Y$ and spends it in a continuous even stream over the period, his average holdings, over the period, of funds in bonds B and cash M are only $Y/2$. Hence, $M + B = \frac{1}{2}Y$. Further, since the individual withdraws W each time and spends it in a continuous steady stream, and draws out a similar amount the moment it is spent, his average transactions balances M are $\frac{1}{2}W$. These propositions are shown in Figures 4.1 and 4.2. In Figure 4.1 for expenditures over one period, $0Y1$ represents the amount of income that has not been spent at the various points of time within the period and $1YA$ is the amount that has been spent. $0Y1$ equals $\frac{1}{2}Y$ over the period and would be held in either money or bonds. Figure 4.2 focuses on money holdings. Assuming that the period (4 weeks) is divided into 4 weeks, the amount $\$W$ is withdrawn at the beginning of each week and spent evenly through the week. The average cash balances over the period are only $\frac{1}{2}W$. Therefore, from Figures 4.1 and 4.2, the average bond holdings over the period are $(\frac{1}{2}Y - \frac{1}{2}W)$.[1]

Since the total expenditures of Y are withdrawn from bonds in lots of W, the number n of withdrawals is (Y/W). The cost of withdrawing Y from bonds is the cost per withdrawal times the number of withdrawals and is given by $[(B_0 + B_1 W)(Y/W)]$. In addition, the

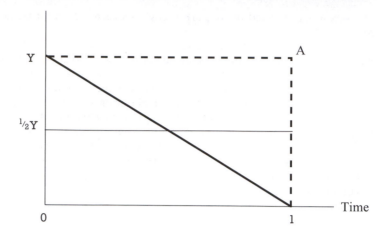

Figure 4.1

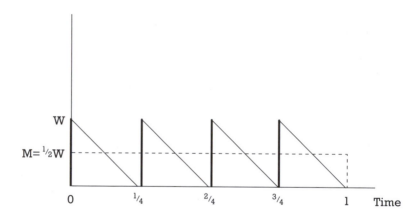

Figure 4.2

interest forgone by holding cash rather than bonds is rM. Since $M = \frac{1}{2}W$, this interest cost equals $rW/2$. The total opportunity cost C of financing Y of expenditures in this manner is the sum of the cost of withdrawing Y from investments and the interest forgone in holding average money balances of $(W/2)$. Hence,

$$C = rW/2 + B_0 \cdot Y/W + B_1 Y \tag{1}$$

If the individual acts rationally in trying to meet his payments Y at minimum cost, he will minimize the cost C of holding transactions balances. To do so, set the derivative of (1) with respect to W equal to zero. This yields,

$$r/2 - B_0 \cdot Y/W^2 = 0 \tag{2}$$

so that,

$$W = [2B_0 \cdot Y/r]^{1/2} \tag{3}$$

and

$$M^{tr} = \frac{1}{2}W = (\frac{1}{2}B_0)^{1/2} Y^{1/2} r^{-1/2} \tag{4}$$

where we have inserted the superscript *tr* to emphasize that (4) specifies only the transactions demand for money and does not include the money demand that would arise for the speculative and other motives. Equation (4) is called the *square root formula* in inventory analysis and has the easily identifiable form of a Cobb–Douglas function. In the present analysis, it specifies the demand for transactions balances for a cost minimizing individual. The preceding demand function is clearly different from the classical and Keynesian demand functions for transactions balances and, among other things, indicates that *the demand for transactions balances depends upon the rate of interest*. The properties of this demand function, showing its response to changes in the real levels of expenditures, interest rates and prices, are discussed below.

To consider the effect of changes in prices, suppose that all prices in the economy were to double. Brokerage costs are the prices charged for brokerage services so that let $B_0 = P \cdot b_0$, and $B_1 = P \cdot b_1$, where b_0 and b_1 are the elements of the brokerage charge *in real terms*, while B_0 and B_1 were nominal brokerage charges and P is the price level. The reason for expressing brokerage costs in this way is that the brokerage services related to cash withdrawals from earning assets are themselves goods and, from a rigorous viewpoint, their cost must also double when the prices of *all* goods double. Hence B_0 and B_1 must both be taken to increase in the same proportion as P.

Therefore, equation (4) can be re-written as:

$$M^d/P = m^{tr} = (\tfrac{1}{2}b_0)^{1/2} y^{1/2} r^{-1/2} \tag{5}$$

The elasticities of the transactions demand for money with respect to y, r and P are:[2]

$$
\begin{aligned}
E_{m \cdot y} &= \tfrac{1}{2}\\
E_{m \cdot r} &= -\tfrac{1}{2}\\
E_{M \cdot P} &= 1\\
E_{m \cdot P} &= 0
\end{aligned}
$$

In (5), since the elasticity of demand for real transactions balances with respect to real income is only $\tfrac{1}{2}$, the demand for real transactions balances increases less than proportionately with the individual's real income due to the economies of scale in the cost of cash withdrawals from bonds. The elasticity of the transactions demand for money with respect to the rate of interest is $-\tfrac{1}{2}$: the higher the rate of interest, the higher is the cost of holding funds in transactions balances and the lower is the demand for such balances. The elasticity ($E_{m \cdot P}$) of the transactions demand for real balances with respect to an increase in all prices is zero, consistent with that derived for the general demand for money in Chapter 3. By implication, from (5), the elasticity ($E_{M \cdot P}$) of the transactions demand for nominal balances is 1.

The elasticity of the demand for nominal balances with respect to nominal income

We can now refine the implications of this analysis for the elasticity ($E_{M \cdot Y}$) of the demand for nominal balances with respect to nominal income Y. Since $Y = Py$, nominal income changes if either real income y or prices P change. Consequently, at rates of inflation close to zero, $E_{M \cdot Y}$ will be approximated by $E_{m \cdot y}$, which is $\tfrac{1}{2}$ in the above analysis. The higher the rate of inflation, the more significant will be the influence of $E_{M \cdot P}$, which is unity, so that in hyperinflation, $E_{M \cdot Y}$ will approximate unity. Therefore, $E_{M \cdot Y}$ will not be a constant over time but will vary between zero and one, depending on real income growth relative to the rate of inflation during the period under study. In a normal context, both output and the price level change each period, so that it is not unusual to find estimates of this elasticity somewhere near the middle (0.75) of the potential range.

4.2 SOME SPECIAL CASES OF THE DEMAND FOR TRANSACTIONS BALANCES

The above analysis incorporates the choice between holding money and the income-earning asset – 'bonds' – to finance transactions. In exercising this choice, the individual will buy only bonds if he can make a profit from holding them; if he cannot, he will only hold money and equation (5) for the demand for real balances will not apply to him. For an analysis of this possibility, we need to derive the profit function from holding money and/or bonds.

As we have shown earlier through Figure 4.1, under Baumol's assumptions, the individual spends his income Y in an even stream over the period and, therefore, holds $\frac{1}{2}Y$ on average in either money or bonds.[3] His average nominal holdings B of bonds are, therefore, equal to $(\frac{1}{2}Y - M)$, where, as before, M equals $\frac{1}{2}W$. The individual earns interest at the rate r on these bond holdings. The profit from holding either money or bonds equals this interest income from holding bonds less the brokerage cost of cash withdrawals from bonds.[4] That is, the profit π from using the combinations of money and bonds is given by:

$$\pi = \text{interest income from bonds} - \text{brokerage expenses}$$
$$= r\{\tfrac{1}{2}Y - M\} - \{\tfrac{1}{2}B_0 Y/M + B_1 Y\} \tag{6}$$

Maximizing (6) with respect to M yields the first-order maximizing condition as:

$$\partial\pi/\partial M = -r + \tfrac{1}{2}B_0 Y/M^2 = 0 \tag{7}$$

Hence, as in (4),

$$M^{tr} = (\tfrac{1}{2}B_0)^{1/2} Y^{1/2} r^{-1/2} \tag{4'}$$

Further,

$$B^{tr} = \tfrac{1}{2}Y - (\tfrac{1}{2}B_0)^{1/2} Y^{1/2} r^{-1/2} \tag{8}$$

where the superscript tr on B emphasizes that this demand for bonds is for transactions purposes and not for speculative or portfolio holdings. Hence,

$$\pi = r\{\tfrac{1}{2}Y - (\tfrac{1}{2}B_0)^{1/2}Y^{1/2}r^{-1/2}\} - \{(\tfrac{1}{2}B_0)^{1/2}Y^{1/2}r^{-1/2} + B_1 Y\} \tag{6'}$$

In equation (6'), π is non-positive if $r = 0$ or if the total brokerage charges exceed the income from holding bonds. The latter would occur if the brokerage costs are relatively high. Note in this regard that the brokerage costs include both the charges explicitly levied by financial institutions and any other costs of conversion from bonds to cash. The latter include the time and inconvenience etc. – sometimes referred to as the 'shoe-leather costs' – of trips to the banks and other relevant financial institutions. These costs can be quite high in areas poorly served by financial institutions, as is common in the rural areas of developing economies and even sometimes of developed ones. They are dominant for individuals for whom the banks refuse to open accounts or for ones who cannot meet the conditions – for example, acceptable references or minimum deposit balances – set by banks for opening or holding such accounts. In these cases, the individual will not find it profitable to hold bonds and will only hold money.

The profit from holding bonds in the transactions process is also non-positive if either income and/or interest rates are sufficiently low. Such considerations are relevant to relatively poor individuals or where the financial system and its regulation limits the interest rates that can be paid on bonds. In these cases, the individual's demand for bonds would again be zero.

In cases of non-positive profits from holding bonds, i.e., $\pi \leq 0$, the demand for bonds would be zero and the optimal transactions demand for nominal balances would be:

$$M^{tr} = \tfrac{1}{2}Y \tag{9}$$

which has a unit income elasticity and a zero interest elasticity.

From (9), the transactions demand function for real balances m^{tr} is,

$$m^{tr} = \tfrac{1}{2}y \tag{10}$$

so that $E_{m \cdot y} = 1$ and $E_{m \cdot r} = 0$. Almost all economies have some individuals – usually those with lower incomes – with such a demand function. The more underdeveloped the financial system of the country or the local area, and the lower the incomes of the people, the more significant would be this case. The inventory demand formula (5) thus tends to have limited validity for many less-developed economies and rural areas, and even for some segments of the population in the developed economies.

4.3 THE DEMAND FOR CURRENCY VERSUS DEMAND DEPOSITS

The above analysis does not really address the interesting question of the relative demands for currency, which is notes and coins, as against that for demand deposits. For this, we need to consider the cost, convenience and safety of holding and using currency versus demand deposits in making payments, rather than the costs of conversion from 'bonds' into these two forms of money. In the choice between using currency or demand deposits, demand deposits do have positive own costs of usage since they require some trips to the bank for making deposits and the banks often levy deposit and withdrawal charges on cheques, while currency holdings do not involve any such charges for making payments from them. Further, the most common types of demand deposits do not pay interest. Consequently, currency involves lower own costs of usage, so that the optimizing individual will only hold currency and not hold demand deposits. This seems to be the case in many less-developed economies and especially in those rural areas poorly served by banks.

However, it is patently not the case in most developed economies or the urban sectors of developing economies, that most individuals do not hold demand deposits, so that there must be other considerations which must be relevant to the choice between currency and demand deposits. The major one here for most individuals seems to be the relative safety of holding demand deposits as against that of holding currency.[5] The concern with theft and robbery if large sums were kept or carried in currency, was a major reason for the origin and spread of deposit banking in eighteenth- and nineteenth-century Europe and continues to be a major determinant of the relative demand for demand deposits versus currency. The greater the concern with the safety and convenience of currency holdings, the lower will be the relative demand for currency balances. To illustrate, Japan, with an extremely low theft and robbery rate, is an economy in which ordinary persons do not normally hold demand deposit accounts but pay for most transactions in cash. Conversely, persons carrying large sums in currency in the United States would be very concerned about their personal safety and the safety of these sums, and tend to prefer to hold demand deposits for meeting most of their transactions needs.

4.4 ECONOMIES OF SCALE AND THE DISTRIBUTION OF INCOME

Consider the following two cases:

(A) an economy with n individuals, but with one having the whole of the national income Y and the rest with zero income;

(B)   an economy with n identical individuals, each having an identical income Y/n.

From (5), the nominal demands for transactions balances are:

For (A):

$$M_A^{tr} = (\tfrac{1}{2}B_0)^{1/2} \, Y^{1/2} \, r^{-1/2} \tag{11}$$

For (B):

$$\begin{aligned} M_B^{tr} &= n\{(\tfrac{1}{2}B_0)^{1/2} \, (Y/n)^{1/2} \, r^{-1/2}\} \\ &= n^{1/2} M_A^{tr} \end{aligned} \tag{12}$$

Since $n \geq 2$, $m_B^{tr} > m_A^{tr}$. Hence, the equal distribution of incomes leads to a higher demand for real balances. In general, Baumol's model implies that the more unequal the distribution of incomes in the economy, the smaller will be the demand for real balances.

4.5 EFFICIENT FUNDS MANAGEMENT IN A FIRM WITH MULTIPLE BRANCHES

The preceding analysis was couched in terms of an individual but it can also be applied to firms. In the case of a firm with many branches, is it optimal for the firm to have centralized or decentralized money management? Centralized money management is here taken to mean a single account held by the firm as a whole, with the central financial department treating all the branches as one unit for its decisions on the amounts to be withdrawn each time. The amount withdrawn is then allocated among the branches. Decentralized money management means separate accounts and separate decisions on the amounts to be withdrawn at any one time.

Consider the case of a firm with total income or receipts equal to y and having n identical branches, each with income/receipts equal to y/n. If it has centralized funds management, with a single demand deposit account and investments from it into bonds, its cost-minimizing transactions balances would be as specified by (11). If it has decentralized funds management, with each branch holding its own demand deposit account and bonds, its transactions balances will be as specified by (12). The latter is larger the larger is the number of branches.

Since centralized funds management implies lower transactions balances, it also implies higher profits. The efficient firm would, therefore, choose to centralize its fund management, all other things being the same. However, there are other factors that make at least partial decentralization of bank accounts desirable for firms. Among these are the convenience, bookkeeping and security aspects. Many firms consider these sufficiently significant to retain decentralized banking arrangements, with the balances being transmitted from the branches to a main account at periodical intervals or when they reach pre-specified levels. Hence, convenience and security reasons play important roles in the choice on the extent of centralization of deposits, as they did in the use of currency versus demand deposits. In recent decades, innovations in electronic transfers between the head office and branches and between branches and banks have reduced the inconvenience connected with centralization and have, therefore, promoted greater centralization of money management. As a consequence, the transactions balances held by firms relative to their revenue have fallen.

4.6 THE DEMAND FOR MONEY AND THE PAYMENT OF INTEREST ON DEMAND DEPOSITS

Many types of demand deposit accounts now pay interest. In order to properly consider these, assume that there are two assets, demand deposits and bonds, with each paying interest. Since currency does not pay interest, we exclude it from the definition of money in this section, so that money will equal demand deposits. The other assumptions of the model are as originally specified, including that the purchases of commodities can only be paid for by cheque drawn on a demand deposit account. As before, bonds are assumed to pay interest at the rate r, while demand deposits are now assumed to pay the rate r_D.

As in the preceding analysis, the average amount of demand deposits D is $W/2$ and that of bonds is $(\frac{1}{2}Y - D)$. The profit π from the use of money and bonds is:

$$\pi = r\{\tfrac{1}{2}Y - D\} + r_D D - \{\tfrac{1}{2}B_0 Y/D + B_1 Y\} \tag{13}$$

which yields the first-order maximizing condition as:

$$\partial\pi/\partial D = -r + r_D + \tfrac{1}{2}B_0 Y/D^2 = 0 \tag{14}$$

Hence,

$$D^{tr} = (\tfrac{1}{2}B_0)^{1/2} Y^{1/2}(r - r_D)^{-1/2} \tag{15}$$

$$B = \tfrac{1}{2}Y - (\tfrac{1}{2}B_0)^{1/2} Y^{1/2}(r - r_D)^{-1/2} \tag{16}$$

where:

$$E_{D\cdot(r-rD)} = -\tfrac{1}{2} \tag{17}$$

$$E_{D\cdot r} = -\tfrac{1}{2}\{r/(r - r_D)\} \tag{18}$$

The demand for transactions balances now depends upon the interest rate *differential* $(r - r_D)$, and the elasticity of the transactions demand for demand deposits with respect to the *differential in the interest rates* is $-\frac{1}{2}$. However, this elasticity with respect to the bond rate of interest alone – that is, if the bond rate rises but the interest rate on demand deposits stays unchanged – is now $[-\frac{1}{2}\{r/(r - r_D)\}]$: the higher is the interest rate on demand deposits, the higher is the elasticity of the demand for such balances. Since these elasticities are different, the impact on the demand for money of changes in bond yields will depend upon whether the interest rate on demand deposits is also changing or not.

4.7 TECHNICAL INNOVATIONS AND THE DEMAND FOR CURRENCY, AND FOR DEMAND AND SAVINGS DEPOSITS

Recent decades have seen a considerable variety of innovations in the financial sector. The broad categories of these have been as follows.

(i) The creation of new types of financial assets and the increasing liquidity of some of the existing assets. These encompass institutional innovations such as interest-bearing demand deposits and checkable savings deposits, which did not become prevalent until the 1970s. They also include the issuance by banks of money market and other mutual funds, without a significant monetary brokerage charge for buying and selling such funds and their divestiture into demand deposits at short notice. Such money market mutual funds became common only in the 1990s. Such innovations have shifted the transactions demand functions for currency, demand deposits and savings deposits.

(ii) Technical innovations in the deposit and withdrawal mechanisms and practices for various types of assets. These encompass the introduction of automatic teller machines (mainly in the 1980s) and telephonic and computer-based transfers of funds between accounts, beginning in the late 1990s but likely to come into common usage in the twenty-first century.

(iii) The development of 'electronic purses' or 'smart cards', which store nominal amounts, just as a banknote or one's account at a bank does, and which allow the transfer of all or part of this amount to others at the point of the transaction without involving a third party such as a bank or a credit card company. Examples of these are certain types of telephone cards. Leaving aside the differences in technology and focusing on the economic nature, such cards are similar to coins and notes which also embody value and allow the transfer of the whole or part of this value by the bearer to another person and allow this to be done with anonymity with respect to other parties. A rather insignificant difference is that paying with a larger note than necessary involves a reverse payment of the 'change', while the smart card allows the transfer of the exact amount. The more important difference would be that a smart card with owner-authentication procedures built into it would prevent its theft to a much greater extent than is possible with currency which can be used by the bearer without any authentication of proper ownership, so that the smart card would be more secure. This feature would make smart cards more attractive, and their use could replace that of both currency and checking accounts to a significant extent. In so far as both currency and smart cards constitute value-carrying purses, the former being a non-electronic one and the latter an electronic one, it would be appropriate to lump them together in the total demand for purses, as against the demand for demand deposits, savings deposits etc. We expect the demand for purses to grow relative to demand deposits.

(iv) The development of digital cards, payments with which require the intervention of a third party such as a bank to verify, authorize and clear transactions over a network connection. These are more like cheques or debit cards – while electronic purses are more like currency – and combine the advantages of cheques with those of a credit or debit card. They leave a trail of transactions, which can be valuable for bookkeeping and security reasons.

4.8 DEMAND DEPOSITS VERSUS SAVINGS DEPOSITS

As explained at the beginning of this chapter, savings deposits can be viewed as a 'bond' which pays interest but which cannot be directly used to make payments to others,[6] so that funds have to be transferred from savings accounts to checking accounts before a payment from them can be made by cheque. Prior to the advent of automatic banking machines and of telephonic and electronic transfers, a trip had to be made to a bank branch to transfer funds from savings accounts to a checking account or to obtain currency. Such a trip involved time and inconvenience, which are elements of the brokerage cost in the Baumol model. The proliferation of automatic banking machines and the general reduction in the banks' conditions and charges for such transfers, has reduced this element of brokerage cost very considerably. The electronic transfer of funds among accounts handled through one's home computer has made this cost relatively insignificant. Up to the 1960s, commercial banks also often imposed other costs, sometimes including a period of prior notice for withdrawal from savings accounts, for handling such transfers. The imposition of such notice has virtually disappeared. The result is that payments from savings deposits are now not very different in terms of costs and delays than from demand deposits.

For the following analysis, assume that savings deposits are the only kind of bond and the amount of savings deposits is designated as S. Since S replaces B in the analysis of section 4.2, the optimal ratio D/S in the context of section 4.2 is given by:

$$D/S \;=\; 1/\{\tfrac{1}{2}Y/D - 1\} \tag{19}$$

$$=\; 1/\{\tfrac{1}{2}(\tfrac{1}{2}B_0)^{-1/2}Y'^{1/2}r^{-1/2} - 1\} \tag{20}$$

so that transactions balances fall with the decrease in brokerage costs. In the limit, $D/S \to 0$ as $B_0 \to 0$.

Historically, as the brokerage costs between demand deposits and savings accounts decreased, the proportion of balances held in demand deposits fell, so that this proportion is currently less than 10% in the United States and Canada. The increasing familiarity in the handling of transfers between bank accounts from telephones and home computers is likely to further reduce this proportion.

The proliferation of automatic banking machines has also reduced the brokerage costs of transfers between currency and demand deposits, and also between currency and savings accounts. Therefore, as implied by Baumol's model, these banking facilities have allowed individuals to reduce their holdings of currency as against holding demand deposits and saving deposits. These banking facilities have therefore led to a decrease in both currency and demand deposits, so that the amounts held in M1 have fallen sharply.

4.9 IMPENDING FINANCIAL INNOVATIONS

The above arguments can also be extended to the choices between holding bank deposits (demand plus savings deposits) versus other financial assets. One of the developments in the 1990s has been the dilution or elimination of the traditional division of financial services between banks and other types of financial intermediaries, with each offering services which were earlier offered by others. This has not only increased competition in the financial sector, it has also changed the degree of substitutability among demand deposits, savings deposits and other financial instruments. In particular, the 1990s have witnessed the increasing availability of mutual funds, as well as the purchase of stocks and bonds, by individuals through the commercial banks. The banks' mutual funds can be bought and sold at short notice, and some of them – especially money market mutual funds – are virtually riskless and pay higher interest rates than savings deposits.

Further, the advent of electronic transfers between bank deposits and banks' mutual funds has also decreased the inconvenience and other personal costs of visiting the banks in person since transfers between them can be made through one's computer. That is, the brokerage cost of transfers, from demand deposits and savings deposits to mutual funds etc., per withdrawal have become fairly insignificant. This implies in the context of Baumol's model that such economic units will not hold significant amounts of demand and savings deposits for transactions purposes, so that we can expect some erosion of the amounts held in M2 relative to those held in other bank-provided financial instruments.

Hence, the very considerable – and continuing pace of – innovations in the financial industry in the past few decades have shifted the demand functions for currency, demand deposits, savings deposits, money market mutual funds, etc., and have, therefore, shifted the demand functions for M1, M2 and the wider definitions of money. Estimates of these demand functions must capture these shifts, for the estimated functions to be valid for calculating the demand elasticities with respect to income and interest rate changes. The impending introduction of electronic purses and other types of smart cards, secure electronic banking from one's home or office, and secure transfers of funds from one party directly to another through computers, are likely to continue to shift the demand functions for money and near-monies.

CONCLUSIONS

Looking at the demand for transactions funds by households, the preceding analyses imply that there will definitely be some individuals with low incomes or inaccessibility to financial institutions who will find it unprofitable to hold bonds and will hold *only* money. In developed economies, with relatively high incomes on average and with extensive and easily accessible banking facilities, the proportion of such individuals in the population can be quite small, and their share of money holdings in the economy even smaller. However, in economies with underdeveloped financial markets, this segment of the population can be quite significant. Further, in such cases, this part of the population may mainly hold currency rather than demand deposits or other types of deposits for transactions purposes.

Assuming positive profits from holding some bonds (including savings deposits) as part of the transactions portfolio, households will have economies of scale in holding demand deposits, and a negative interest elasticity with respect to the interest rate. This elasticity will differ depending upon whether interest is paid on demand deposits or not and upon the interest rate differential.

Some firms may also find that holding savings deposits and bonds as part of the transactions portfolio does not yield positive profits because the brokerage costs are too high relative to the interest income from bonds. However, their number is likely to be relatively insignificant in developed economies. In the opposite limiting case, as the brokerage costs per transaction at the margin tend to zero, the firm's demand for demand deposits would tend to zero. The increasingly efficient electronic transfer and investment of funds have made it profitable for large firms to invest their surplus funds for periods as short as a day. Their end-of-the day holdings of demand deposits may then be zero in desired terms. Unpredictable withdrawals or deposits of funds can still occur but these may be covered through overdraft facilities prearranged with the banks. In such a context, the actual holdings of demand deposits would be largely random. Such firms could still have positive currency demand but this would be largely in the nature of working or petty cash and depend upon considerations – for example, the unpredictable and uneven pattern of receipts and expenditures – other than those incorporated in the Baumol model.

Another consideration that may lead to positive demand deposits being held are minimum compensating balances sometimes required by banks. Such banking practices, as well as the number and sizes of branches, would be among the major factors determining the minimum holdings of money balances by firms. Variations in these balances may be largely dominated by random factors in the case of large firms with efficient funds management in well-developed financial markets.

The above discussion implies that the aggregate demand for transactions balances in the economy has *three components*. These are:

(i)   The demand by households and firms who do not find fund management with some investment in bonds profitable and hold only money. Such a component will exist in virtually any economy but may only be a significant part of the whole in economies with undeveloped banking and other financial facilities.

(ii) The transactions balances of those households and firms which find such financial management profitable and for these the Baumol model would be applicable.

(iii) The demand by optimizing wealthy individuals and large firms for whom the variable part of the brokerage costs are almost zero. For these, the transactions balances are determined by factors not in the Baumol model. The relevant factors could be the requirement for payments in cash to individuals in category (i) or for transactions for which the requirement is to pay in currency (for example, for bus fares), or minimum balances required by banks to keep a demand deposit account.

In applying the above inventory analysis to the data collected on money balances, note that while the theory specifies average money balances held, the data is often collected as end-of-day (or other period) data. Further, for sweep accounts, the banks themselves monitor the state of their customers' accounts at the end of each day and *sweep* the accounts of excess balances, investing them in overnight money market funds. In such a case, the customers need to ensure that they have the minimum desired balances; any amounts above or below these are borrowed or lent in the overnight or day-to-day loan markets or through loan arrangements such as overdrafts with their own bank. For customers with large balances and low transactions costs, the desired minimum balances would be zero under the simpler versions of the inventory analysis. In a more realistic context, the customer would hold positive balances but these would be determined by institutional arrangements such as the minimum balances the bank requires its customers to maintain, and are not encompassed under the preceding inventory analysis. The electronic, regulatory and institutional innovations in recent years have blurred the distinction between demand deposits and various near-monies, and thereby shifted the transactions demand for the former. The invention and use of devices such as electronic or smart purses is reducing the need to hold notes and coins for small expenditures, and thereby reducing the demand for currency.

The demand function (5) is the core implication of the Baumol model. It was derived under rather special and restrictive assumptions. As this chapter has shown, relaxing these assumptions tends to change the implied elasticities of demand. However, in general, the qualitative conclusions remain: in the aggregate, the demand for real transactions balances increases less than proportionately with real expenditures, decreases with the yield on alternative assets; and does not change if all prices change proportionately.

SUMMARY OF CRITICAL CONCLUSIONS

- The transactions demand for real balances has an elasticity of one-half with respect to real income.
- The transactions demand for real balances has an elasticity of zero with respect to the price level while that of nominal balances has a unit elasticity.
- The transactions demand for real balances has an elasticity between one-half and unity with respect to nominal income.
- The transactions demand for nominal balances has an elasticity of one-half with respect to the rate of return on bonds if interest is not paid on money balances.
- If interest is paid on money balances, the transactions demand for real balances has an elasticity of one-half with respect to their user cost (that is, the difference between the return on bonds and the interest rate paid on money balances), but not with respect to the return on bonds.
- Efficient and centralized cash management reduces the transactions demand for money.

review and discussion questions

1 Compare the cost minimization and the profit maximization approaches to the derivation of the transactions demand for money. Do they yield identical or different results?
2 What insights do we get from using the profit maximization approach that are not apparent from the cost minimization one?
3 Explain why there are always a certain percentage of households that do not hold checking accounts even though they do use currency for transactions.
4 Present Baumol's inventory analysis for the transactions demand for money.
5 Derive the income and interest rate elasticities in this model if interest is paid on demand deposits.
6 Assuming that a firm has 25 branches, derive its demand for transactions balances and the income and interest rate elasticities if (a) each branch manages its funds separately, (b) there is central cash management at the head office.

7 How would you incorporate security considerations/costs into the transactions demand model? What would this imply for the demand for currency in a relatively insecure urban environment (a) compared with a relatively safe one, (b) when owner-identified smart cards become available? Do these factors affect the demand for demand deposits? How would the proportion of currency to demand deposits be affected in these cases?

8 Can the transactions demand model be used to explain why financial innovations in recent decades have reduced the transactions demand for M1?

9 Are transactions demand models useless, as Sprenkle (1969) argued? If they are, how would you explain the demand for M1 or just for demand deposits in the economy?

NOTES

1 This amount, and our subsequent calculations of interest on the bonds held, implicitly assume that the withdrawals from bonds are continuous or almost continuous.

2 The elasticity of a variable y with respect to x is defined as:

$$E_{y \cdot x} = (x/y) \cdot (dy/dx)$$

3 The difference between these amounts (Y and $\frac{1}{2}Y$) represents the *average* amount ($\frac{1}{2}Y$) disbursed to other individuals in payments during the period. The total amount disbursed is, by assumption, Y.

4 Since the brokerage cost, as explained earlier, was $(B_0Y/W + B_1Y)$ and $M = \frac{1}{2}W$, the brokerage cost in terms of M is $(\frac{1}{2}B_0Y/M + B_1Y)$ in the following equation (6) for π

5 Another reason is the availability of very large denominations of notes. In the absence of these, it can be quite cumbersome to pay large sums in notes, implying high brokerage costs of using notes in such transactions. The central bank may not be willing to print very large value notes to control illegal transactions and out of concern for the safety of the holders.

6 There are now many types of savings accounts that pay interest and on which cheques can be written. The difference between these and demand deposit accounts is not significant for our analysis since payments from both can be made by cheques. These can be treated as if they were demand deposit accounts.

REFERENCES

Bar-Ilan, A. 'Overdrafts and the Demand for Money'. *American Economic Review*, 80, December 1990, pp. 1201–16.

Baumol, William J. 'The Transactions Demand for Cash: An Inventory Theoretic Approach'. *Quarterly Journal of Economics*, 66, November 1952, pp. 453–556.

Clower, Robert L., and Peter W. Howitt. 'The Transactions Theory of the Demand for Money: A Reconsideration'. *Journal of Political Economy*, 86, June 1978, pp. 449–66.

Sprenkle, Case M. 'The Uselessness of Transactions Demand Models'. *Journal of Finance*, 24, December 1969, pp. 835–47.

Tobin, James. 'The Interest-Elasticity of Transactions Demand for Cash'. *Review of Economics and Statistics*, 28 August 1956, pp. 241–47.

chapter five

PORTFOLIO SELECTION AND THE SPECULATIVE DEMAND FOR MONEY

This chapter presents the demand for money as a component of a portfolio in which the alternatives to holding money are bonds and equities with uncertain rates of return. This topic initially arose from Keynes' contributions on the speculative demand for money but is now treated as part of portfolio selection analysis, with significant differences between these two approaches. Keynes' own approach was presented in Chapter 2 and has been superseded by the portfolio selection approach presented in this chapter.

While Keynes had attached a great deal of importance to the speculative demand for money as part of the overall money demand, the financial sectors have evolved considerably since Keynes' writings and there is increasing doubt about the empirical significance of this demand.

---

key concepts introduced in this chapter

- Portfolio selection
- Money as a riskless asset
- Normal probability distribution and its moments
- Expected utility hypothesis
- St Petersburg paradox
- Von Neumann–Morgenstern utility function
- Risk aversion
- Efficient opportunity locus
- Constant absolute risk aversion
- Constant relative risk aversion

Keynes had introduced the speculative demand for money into the literature. This is a demand for money as an asset for holding wealth, rather than for transactions or precautionary purposes. In modern terminology, it would more appropriately be called the asset or portfolio demand for money. However, we will continue to use the usual terminology and refer to it as the speculative demand for money.

The speculative demand for money arises because of the uncertainty of the yields on alternative assets. However, the speculative demand for money is not the only part of money demand that is related to economic uncertainty. Another part is the precautionary demand for money. The latter is related to the uncertainty of incomes and consumption needs. The precautionary demand analysis will be presented in the next chapter.

The assets considered in this chapter are money and bonds, with the term 'bonds', as usual, referring to financial assets and, therefore, encompassing the shares of corporations as well as other investments, whether in a financial or physical form. However, the focus will be on financial assets. Such assets are usually an uncertain vehicle for transferring purchasing power from the present to the future. The yield on few, if any, assets is known in advance in a world beset, among other things, with the loss of purchasing power through inflation. This uncertainty of yields is not the only property or characteristic of financial assets. Financial assets vary widely with respect to their acceptability in exchange, their maturity or marketability, their reversibility, their divisibility and the costs of their exchange into money.[1] Even in a world of uncertainty, the dominant determinants of the demand for financial assets by a small investor with very limited wealth may well be other than those related to the uncertainty of the yields on assets. Students themselves often fall into these categories, opting very often for a narrowly based portfolio of money balances and savings deposits, rather than opting for risky assets with their higher yields.

A significant factor in the choice among risky assets is the degree of lack of information about the factors determining their past and future yields and the costs of acquiring this information. These costs may be high in terms of time, effort and money, relative to the increase in yields expected from better information. While the analysis presented in this chapter does not take account of the extent of the information available in forming expectations on asset returns, there is no reason to assume that the individual's choices among financial assets are not seriously affected by the extent of reliable information that he has on each asset and on the average on all assets.

However, the managers of large portfolios, whether of individuals, firms or financial institutions, do keep abreast of pertinent available information as a routine matter. For them, the problems of the indivisibility of assets are also less serious since the cost per unit of a financial asset will be relatively small in relation to the size of the portfolio. In large firms engaged in production or trade and in financial institutions, the transfer into and out of a given asset and information-gathering are handled by the employees of the firm so that they are in the nature of fixed costs, while the variable transfer costs among assets tend to be relatively small. Therefore, the dominant considerations determining the short-run structure of the large portfolios are the expected yields on the available assets rather than those imposed by indivisibilities, lack of information or significant variable transfer costs among assets.

The theories of portfolio selection explain the relationship between the yields of assets and the investor's optimal portfolio. There are several types of theories of portfolio selection. The most common among these use portfolio selection analysis based on the expected utility hypothesis (EUH). The analysis of this chapter is based on this hypothesis.

Section 5.1 reviews the statistical relationships between the means and variances of the yields on the individual assets and those of the overall yield to the portfolio as a whole. Section 5.2 examines the individual's objectives for portfolio selection under uncertainty. Section 5.3 presents the concepts of risk aversion, indifference and preference. Section 5.4 presents the implications of expected utility maximization for the attitudes to risk.

Section 5.5 derives the efficient opportunity locus relevant to portfolio selection. This locus corresponds to the budget line in the microeconomic theory of the consumer. Section 5.6 presents Tobin's famous analysis of the portfolio demand for money as an alternative to bonds using the general utility analysis. Section 5.7 extends our analysis to three common specific forms of the expected utility function: the constant absolute risk-aversion one, the constant relative risk-aversion one and the quadratic one.

While this chapter is devoted to the derivation of a portfolio demand for money, sections 5.8 and 5.9 add somewhat heretical notes by asking the questions whether there really does exist a stable demand function – or even positive portfolio demand – for money in the modern economy with well-developed financial markets. This is a legitimate question to ask since Keynes had proposed this demand for a less-developed financial system. The significance of such a demand component in M1 in our developed economies is now doubtful, though M2 and broader definitions of money still seem to include it.

5.1 PROBABILITIES, MEANS AND VARIANCES

Investors in financial assets possess information on the past yield performance of their assets and also have some pertinent knowledge on their current and likely future performance, on the issuer of these assets and the performance of the economy, etc. The rational individual uses any such knowledge and intuition to form estimates of the likelihood of occurrence of each of these possible yields[2] so that the individual's subjective probability distribution of the yields on the available assets can be specified.[3]

Basing the individual's choices on the probability distribution would be analytically cumbersome unless the distribution could be represented by a small number of variables. For many distributions, the distribution can be described by the moments of the distribution: the expected yield, the standard deviation or variance, skewness, etc. For *normal* distributions, it is necessary to know only the expected return and standard deviation to describe the whole distribution. Hence, the individual whose choice is only among assets with the normal distributions of outcomes need not consider the probability of each of their outcomes separately but only their expected return and standard deviation in his decisions. This is not necessarily true for other distributions and the individual may need knowledge of the other moments as well.

Our analysis will only consider the first two moments – that is, the expected value and the standard deviation – of the yields on the assets and the portfolio. Analysis limited to these two moments is also known as the mean-variance analysis. For any asset i, designate the anticipated yields as r_{ki} and the associated probabilities as p_{ki}. The first two moments of the distribution (r_{ki}, p_{ki}) of the yields on *asset i* are:

$$\mu_i = \sum_k p_{ki} r_{ki} \tag{1}$$

$$\sigma_i^2 = \sum_k p_{ki} (r_{ki} - \mu_i)^2 \tag{2}$$

where:

p_{ki} subjective probability of outcome k of asset i

r_{ki} outcome k of asset i

μ_i mathematical expectation of the outcomes – that is, the expected yield – of asset i

σ_i^2 variance of the outcomes of asset i $(= \sigma_{ii})$

σ_i standard deviation of the outcomes of asset i

The expected yield and the standard deviation of the yield to the *portfolio* can be calculated as follows:

$$\mu = \sum_i \mu_i x_i \tag{3}$$

$$\sigma^2 = \sum_i \sum_j \sigma_{ij} x_i x_j \tag{4}$$

$$= \sum_i \sum_j \rho_{ij} \sigma_i \sigma_j x_i x_j$$

where:

μ expected value of the outcomes to the portfolio

σ standard deviation of outcomes to the portfolio

ρ_{ij} correlation coefficient of outcomes between the ith and jth assets

σ_{ij} covariance of the outcomes to assets i and j

x_i quantity of the ith asset

$\sigma_{ij} = \rho_{ij}\sigma_i\sigma_j$

$\sigma_{ii} = \sigma_i^2$

$\rho_{ii} = 1$

5.2 WEALTH MAXIMIZATION VERSUS EXPECTED UTILITY MAXIMIZATION

Suppose the individual knows his subjective probability distribution of the yield on each asset and, by inference, on each possible combination of the assets he can hold in his portfolio. Two hypotheses on his objectives with respect to his portfolio are:

Hypothesis 1: maximization of expected wealth:

The individual maximizes the expected value of his terminal wealth (or the utility of expected terminal wealth).[4]

The argument in favour of this rule is that it would maximize the net worth of the portfolio in an infinite number of experiments or periods under unchanged conditions. It would then seem reasonable to accept such a hypothesis for an individual holding the same assets for an indefinitely long period. However, most investors seem to be concerned with the value of the assets over the current period or over a relatively small number of periods. Expectations of the values of the assets also constantly keep changing so that the main justification for this rule becomes inapplicable.

There are other arguments and counter-examples to the application of this rule, the most famous among these being the counter-example of the *St Petersburg paradox*.[5] Historically, this paradox was used to discount the validity of the expected wealth hypothesis for the case where the deviation around the mean is important. Another argument against it can be formulated as an aspect of rationality, or of the modern rational expectations hypothesis. This hypothesis is that the individual considers all the available information at his disposal where such information affects the future amount of his wealth. Therefore, if the probability distribution of future wealth has a non-zero standard deviation, the rational individual would consider it in his decisions and not follow the maximization of expected wealth (Hypothesis 1 above) since this would mean ignoring information on the standard deviation.[6]

Note that the maximization of expected wealth – that is, of EW – is identical for analytical purposes with the maximization of the utility of expected wealth – that is, of $U(EW)$ – since EW is an admissible monotonic transformation of $U(EW)$. Hence, objections to the former also apply to the latter.

Given the various arguments against this hypothesis, it is rarely, if ever, used in portfolio selection theory and we will not pursue it further.

Hypothesis 2: the expected utility hypothesis (EUH):[7]

The individual maximizes the expected utility of his terminal wealth.

This hypothesis is now based on the *von Neumann–Morgenstern set of axioms*. These axioms ensure that the utility functions would be '*cardinal*'[8] and the individual will maximize the expected value, $EU(W)$, of the N–M (Neumann–Morgenstern) utility function $U(W)$, rather than maximize the utility function itself. These axioms and the expected utility theorem are not presented in this book but can be found in many advanced microeconomics textbooks.

Under the EUH, the individual will base his choices among assets on the probability distribution of his terminal wealth W rather than on only its first moment (expected wealth). We proceed further with this hypothesis.

5.3 RISK PREFERENCE, INDIFFERENCE AND AVERSION

The theories of portfolio selection generally measure the risk of holding assets by the standard deviation or variance of their yields, or of some function of one of these variables.

An individual's attitude to risk can be categorized into the following groups.

(i) Risk aversion

An individual is a risk averter if he wants more than the expected value of a risky prospect before he would be willing to purchase it. Conversely, if the individual already owns a risky prospect, he would be willing to sell it for less than its expected value. Briefly, such individuals like an increase in net worth but dislike an increase in risk, *ceteris paribus*.

A risk averter can have increasing, decreasing or constant degree of risk aversion. These terms will be discussed later in this chapter.

(ii) Risk preference

An individual is a risk preferrer if he is willing to accept less than the expected value of a risky prospect to buy it and, if he already owns it, wants more than the expected value to be persuaded to sell it. Such an individual likes increases in both expected return and risk. The purchase of lottery tickets in the market place, if it is based only on the evaluations of the expected return and risk but does not include the joy and excitement of gambling, can be analysed as a case of risk preference since their expected return is usually less than the cost of the lottery ticket.

(iii) Risk indifference

An individual is risk indifferent if he wants exactly the expected value of the prospect to be persuaded to buy it or sell it.

The rest of this chapter assumes risk aversion.

5.3.1 Indifference loci for a risk averter

It is a fairly safe hypothesis that *investors* in managing their portfolios prefer, *ceteris paribus*, an increase in the expected net worth of their investments and a decrease in its riskiness. Other individuals, and sometimes the same individuals in their gambling activities, prefer an increase in the standard deviation of their expected net worth. Since our concern is with *individuals as investors*, we assume that the individual is a risk averter. This is the general assumption of the theories of portfolio selection, and is the assumption used in this chapter for analysing the speculative demand for money.

Assume that a risk averter has chosen a portfolio with a particular combination of expected net worth and standard deviation of net worth. Suppose now that he is offered, *ceteris paribus*, an increase in the standard deviation of his net worth. Since he dislikes risk, he finds himself worse off by such an increase in risk. Therefore, if he is to remain indifferent between his initially chosen combination and one involving a higher risk, the expected value of his net worth must be simultaneously increased. Hence, indifference curves – the loci of (μ, σ) points between which he is indifferent – must be upward sloping, as in Figures 5.1a, 5.1b and 5.1c, showing an increase in both expected net worth and risk along every indifference curve. The indifference curves shown in Figure 5.1a show increasing risk aversion as risk increases; those in Figure 5.1b show decreasing risk aversion as risk increases; and those in Figure 5.1c show constant risk aversion.[9] The assumption of increasing risk aversion, as the risk to the portfolio increases, seems to be the most realistic one for investment behaviour and is used further in this chapter.

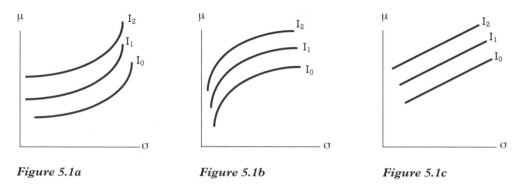

Figure 5.1a   *Figure 5.1b*   *Figure 5.1c*

The risk-averting individual prefers a higher level of expected net worth to a lower level, at any given risk. Hence, the individual prefers being on a higher rather than on a lower indifference curve, so that, for example, being on I_1 is preferred to being on I_0.

5.4 THE EXPECTED UTILITY HYPOTHESIS OF PORTFOLIO SELECTION

The individual may be concerned with the *yields* on his portfolio or with his undiscounted *terminal wealth* at the end of the investment period. Emphasis on Keynes' contributions to this field and especially on his speculative motive which is concerned with the yield on the assets in the portfolio rather than with their terminal net worth, would base the theory of portfolio selection on the yields of assets. Earlier treatments of this subject – for example, Tobin (1958, 1965) – generally followed this approach.[10] However, the classical concept of assets as stores of value would emphasize their terminal net worth, which is the sum of the initial wealth and the yield on the assets. Further, writers concerned with explaining the general behaviour of the individual in buying insurance or gambling (for example, Friedman and Savage, 1948; Arrow, 1971) focus on the individual's terminal wealth, i.e., on the terminal net worth of assets. This is now the general pattern of analysis and we will follow this pattern.

The expected utility hypothesis and the response to risk

Designate the individual's N–M utility function over terminal wealth W as $U(W)$. Assuming that the marginal utility of wealth $U'(W)$ is positive but decreasing at all levels of wealth, $U'(W) > 0$ and $U''(W) < 0$, where $U'(W) = \partial U/\partial W$ and $U''(W) = \partial^2 U/\partial W^2$. Such a utility function is shown by the curve marked $U(W)$ in Figure 5.2 and is concave to the origin. Wealth W is measured on the horizontal axis and the N–M utility of wealth is measured on the vertical one. The individual has an initial wealth of W_0.

Suppose that this individual is offered an uncertain prospect L (where L stands for 'lottery') which has two outcomes of W_1 and W_2, each equi-distant from W_0 and each with

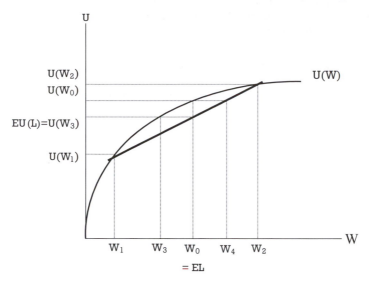

Figure 5.2

a probability of ½. If he accepts the lottery in exchange for W_0, he may win $(W_2 - W_0)$ or lose $(W_0 - W_1)$ which are equal in absolute terms. The expected value of the lottery is EL, where:

$$EL = [½W_1 + ½W_2]$$

and its expected utility $EU(L)$ is:

$$EU(L) = [½U(W_1) + ½U(W_2)]$$

Figure 5.2 shows that $U(W_0) > EU(L)$, so that the individual will prefer the certain wealth W_0 to the risky lottery L, even though EL equals W_0. Hence, this individual is a risk averter. This result will hold if the individual has decreasing marginal utility over the relevant range of the lottery's outcomes.

Figure 5.2 also shows the maximum amount the individual will be willing to pay to buy the lottery. His initial utility is $U(W_0)$ for his initially certain wealth W_0. To persuade him to just buy a lottery with this wealth, the lottery must have an expected value EL such that $EU(L)$ = $U(W_0)$. In Figure 5.2, this will be the lottery with $E(L) = W_4$. Hence, $(W_4 - W_0)$ can be designated as the *risk premium* the individual – who does not yet own the lottery – will want to be paid to just accept the risk of the lottery. Alternatively, if the individual already owns a lottery having $EL = W_0$, he will be willing to sell it for the minimum sure amount of W_3 since $EU(L) = U(W_3)$ – thereby paying an *insurance premium* of $(W_0 - W_3)$ to get rid of the risk associated with his lottery.[11]

Therefore, the individual with decreasing marginal utility over a given range of wealth will be a risk averter for lotteries or uncertain prospects involving outcomes within that range. It can similarly be shown that the individual with increasing marginal utility over a given range of wealth will be a risk preferrer for uncertain prospects involving outcomes within that range. Further, the individual with constant marginal utility over a given range of wealth will be risk indifferent towards uncertain prospects involving outcomes within that range. These considerations led Friedman and Savage (1948) to argue that the individual who buys both insurance for some risks and buys lotteries with very large outcomes having a very small probability must have a segment with decreasing marginal utility, followed by a segment with increasing marginal utility at higher levels of wealth. Subsequent contributions modified this to the assertion that the utility function should be defined over $(W - W_0)$, where W is terminal wealth and W_0 is his existing or customary level of wealth.

5.5 THE EFFICIENT OPPORTUNITY LOCUS

5.5.1 The expected value and standard deviation of the portfolio

For simplification, assume that the probability distributions are normal and, therefore, only the expected net worth and its standard deviation are relevant to the individual's decision. Further, assume that the individual can only hold combinations of two assets, X_1 and X_2, in his portfolio. Then, the first two moments of the frequency distribution of his terminal wealth, which is the value of the portfolio at the end of the relevant period, are:

$$\mu = \mu_1 x_1 + \mu_2 x_2 \tag{3$'$}$$

$$\sigma^2 = \sigma_1^2 x_1^2 + 2\rho_{12}\sigma_1\sigma_2 x_1 x_2 + \sigma_2^2 x_2^2 \tag{4$'$}$$

where:

　μ　expected value of terminal wealth
　σ^2　variance of terminal wealth

The budget constraint on the holdings of the two assets is:

$$x_1 + x_2 = W \tag{5}$$

where W is the individual's initial wealth and the prices of the two assets have been normalized at unity to avoid continual usage of the price symbols.

5.5.2 The opportunity locus for a riskless asset and a risky asset

Assume that the market offers a riskless asset C such that $\mu_C > 0$ and $\sigma_C = 0$, and a risky asset X_2 with $\mu_2 > \mu_1$ and $\sigma_2 > 0$. In this case, the opportunity locus for combinations with any risky asset would also be linear, as shown by the line CB in Figure 5.3. Intuitively, if the individual holds only C, his yield will be $\mu_C W$, with $\sigma = 0$. If he holds only X_2, his yield to the portfolio would be $\mu_2 W$, with a risk of $\sigma_2 W$. If he holds half his wealth in C and half in X_2, he would have $\mu = (\tfrac{1}{2}\mu_C W + \tfrac{1}{2}\mu_2 W)$ and $\sigma = \tfrac{1}{2}\sigma_2 W$.

If C also had a zero return – so that, $\mu_C = 0$ – then the opportunity locus would be from the origin to point B.

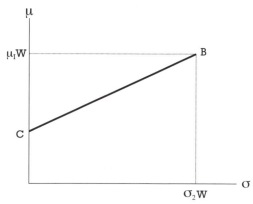

Figure 5.3

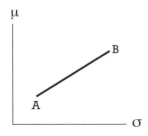

Figure 5.4a

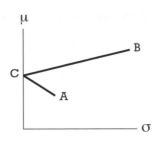

Figure 5.4b

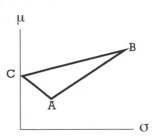

Figure 5.4c

5.5.3 The opportunity locus for risky assets

Suppose the market offers only the two risky assets X_1 and X_2, with $\sigma_1, \sigma_2 > 0$. Since $-1 \leq \rho_{ij} \leq +1$, the two extreme values of ρ substituted in equation (4″) provide the following two cases:

(i) Perfect positive correlation with $\rho_{12} = 1$

$$\sigma = \sigma_1 x_1 + \sigma_2 x_2 \tag{6'}$$

which along with (3′) and (5) gives a linear relationship between μ and σ. Such a relationship is shown by the line AB in Figure 5.4a, and its equation is established in the following derivations.

Derivation of the opportunity locus for the perfect positive correlation case

Define $x_1^* = x_1/W$ and $x_2^* = x_2/W = (1 - x_1^*)$, where x_1^* is the proportion of wealth held in the first asset. Therefore, for $\rho_{12} = 1$,

$$\mu = \mu_1 x_1^* + \mu_2(1 - x_1^*)$$

and

$$\sigma = \sigma_1 x_1^* + \sigma_2(1 - x_1^*)$$

Rewrite μ as:

$$\mu = \mu_2 + x_1^*(\mu_1 - \mu_2)$$
$$= \mu_2 + (\sigma_2 - \sigma_2)(\mu_1 - \mu_2)/(\sigma_1 - \sigma_2) + x_1^*(\sigma_1 - \sigma_2)(\mu_1 - \mu_2)/(\sigma_1 - \sigma_2)$$

Let $k_1 = (\mu_1 - \mu_2)/(\sigma_1 - \sigma_2)$, so that:

$$\mu = \mu_2 + (\sigma_2 - \sigma2)k_1 + (\sigma_1 - \sigma_2)k_1 x_1^*$$

Now let $k_2 = \mu_2 - \sigma_2 k_1$, with the result that:

$$\mu = k_2 + k_1\{\sigma_1 x_1^* + \sigma_2(1 - x_1^*)\} \tag{3''}$$

This is a general result for the expected return on the two-asset portfolio. For the special case where $\rho_{12} = +1$, $\{\sigma_1 x_1^* + \sigma_2(1 - x_1^*)\} = \sigma$. Hence,

$$\mu = k_2 + k_1\sigma \tag{3'''}$$

where k_1 and k_2 are constants for given values of the means and standard deviations of the assets. Therefore, in the case of perfect positive correlation between the two assets in the portfolio, the relationship between the portfolio's expected return μ and its standard deviation σ is linear, as shown by the line AB in Figure 5.4a.

For the end-point representing the whole portfolio consisting only of the first asset, we have $x_1^* = 1$ and $(1 - x_1^*) = 0$, so that the preceding equations imply that:

$$\mu = \mu_1 = k_2 + k_1\sigma_1$$

which, along with $\sigma = \sigma_1$, corresponds to the point A in Figure 5.4a.

For the end-point B representing the whole portfolio consisting only of the second asset, we have $x_1^* = 0$ and $x_2^* = (1 - x_1^*) = 1$, so that the preceding equations correspondingly imply that:

$$\mu = \mu_2 = k_2 + k_1\sigma_2$$

which, along with $\sigma = \sigma_2$, corresponds to the point B in Figure 5.4a.

(ii) Perfect negative correlation with $\rho_{12} = -1$

$$\sigma = \sigma_1 x_1 - \sigma_2 x_2 \tag{6''}$$

so that $\sigma = 0$ for $x_1/x_2 = \sigma_2/\sigma_1$.

In this case, we can define a riskless composite asset X_3 for which $\sigma_3 = 0$. It would combine X_1 and X_2 in the proportions given by $x_1/x_2 = \sigma_2/\sigma_1$, with $\mu_3 = \{(\mu_1\sigma_2 + \mu_2\sigma_1)W\}/(\sigma_1 + \sigma_2)$ and $\sigma_3 = 0$. Now suppose that we have these three assets (X_1, X_2, X_3) in the portfolio. Combinations of only X_1 and X_3 in the portfolio yield $\sigma(X_1, X_3) = 0$ and $\mu(X_1, X_3) = \mu_1 X_1 + \mu_3 X_3$, with the linear opportunity locus AC in Figure 5.4b.[12] Similarly, combinations of only X_2 and X_3 in the portfolio yield $\sigma(X_2, X_3) = 0$ and $\mu(X_2, X_3) = \mu_2 x_2 + \mu_3 x_3$, with the linear opportunity locus CB in Figure 5.4b.

Derivations of the opportunity locus for the perfect negative correlation case

In terms of the proportions x_1^* and $x_2^*(= 1 - x_1^*)$ of the portfolio invested in the two assets with $\rho_{12} = -1$, the standard deviation σ of the portfolio is given by:

$$\sigma = \sigma_1 x_1^* - \sigma_2(1 - x_1^*)$$

so that for $\sigma = 0$, we have:

$$x_1^* = \sigma_2/(\sigma_1 + \sigma_2) \tag{6'''}$$

Substituting (6''') in (3''), we get, for the portfolio with $\sigma = 0$,

$$\mu = c\left[\frac{2\sigma_1\sigma_2}{\sigma_1 + \sigma_2} - \sigma_2\right] + \mu_2$$

where

$$c = \frac{\mu_1 - \mu_2}{\sigma_1 - \sigma_2}$$

This value of μ and $\sigma = 0$ specify the point C in Figure 5.4b. Corresponding to this point, we can define a third asset X_3 such that

$$\sigma_3 = 0$$

$$\mu_3 = c\left[\frac{2\sigma_1\sigma_2}{\sigma_1 + \sigma_2} - \sigma_2\right] + \mu_2$$

$$= \frac{\mu_1\sigma_2 + \mu_2\sigma_1}{\sigma_1 + \sigma_2}$$

In Figure 5.4b, a portfolio consisting only of X_3 is represented by the point C. Combinations of X_1 and X_3 only in the portfolio would yield the opportunity locus AC and combinations of X_2 and X_3 only would yield the opportunity locus CB. ACB represents the opportunity locus given by the combinations of X_1 and X_2.

The opportunity locus for $-1 < \rho_{12} < +1$
In the common case where the two assets entail some risk and ρ_{12} lies between -1 and $+1$, the opportunity locus will be non-linear and will lie in the area enclosed by ACB in Figure 5.4c. The closer ρ_{12} is to $+1$, the closer will this locus be to the line AB. When ρ_{12} differs from $+1$, there exist economies in risk from holding a diversified portfolio and the opportunity locus moves towards ACB.[13]

5.5.4 The efficient opportunity locus

The risk averter is only concerned with the part of the (μ, σ) combinations called the *efficient opportunity locus*, which gives him the highest possible μ for a given value of σ. Thus, in Figure 5.5, looking at the opportunity locus ADB for combinations of X_1 and X_2, with $-1 < \rho_{12} < 1$, the points on the segment AD will be inefficient combinations of the two assets compared with those on the segment DB: for example, point b on DB gives a higher μ at the given σ_0 than the combination a on AD. Therefore, AD can be disregarded for risk averters and the efficient opportunity locus for risk averters is DB, which is non-convex to the origin.

The opportunity locus for three risky assets
Now assume that three risky assets X_1, X_2, X_3 are available. Combinations of X_1 and X_2 alone, of X_1 and X_3 alone and of X_2 and X_3 alone give the opportunity loci in Figure 5.6a as

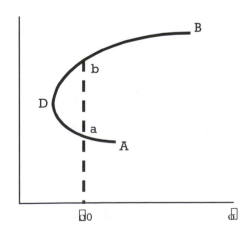

Figure 5.5

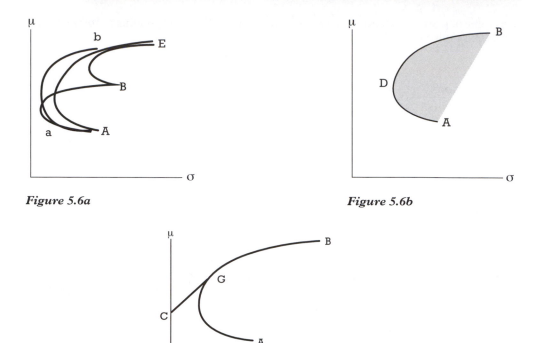

Figure 5.6a   Figure 5.6b

Figure 5.7

AB, *AE* and *BE* respectively. Further, consider combinations of the points *a* on *AB* and *b* on *BE*. These generate the locus *ab*. If we were similarly to take combinations of all the other points on *AB*, *AE* and *BE*, the opportunity locus will be the area enclosed by the curve *ADB* in Figure 5.6b. The opportunity locus in the general case with more than three risky assets would have a similar shape. However, the *efficient* opportunity locus will be the curved segment *DB*.

The opportunity locus for a riskless asset and several risky assets

Consider, further, the possibility that the individual will wish to hold combinations of a riskless asset and the two risky assets. The individual can hold various combinations of the risky assets only or hold a combination of the riskless asset with some combination of the risky assets. Assuming that the return to the portfolio, when the total wealth is put in the riskless asset only, is given by μ_0, the efficient opportunity locus is shown by *CGB* in Figure 5.7. This locus has two segments, *GB* and *CG*. If the individual chooses a point on *GB*, he will hold only the risky assets and his demand for the riskless asset will be zero. If the individual chooses a point on *CG*, he will hold a portfolio consisting of the riskless asset and some combination of the risky ones, with only the riskless asset held at the point *C*. As he diversifies and holds increasing amounts of the risky assets, he moves towards *G*, with *G* representing a combination of only the risky assets. Note that the movement from *C* towards *G* represents an increase in the amount of the investment in the bundle of assets represented by *G* without a change in the relative composition of this bundle.

Demand among several risky assets

The still more general case would have two riskless assets X_1 and X_2 having $\mu_1 > 0$, $\mu_2 > \mu_1$, and $\sigma_1 = \sigma_2 = 0$, and many risky assets. Since $\mu_2 > \mu_1$, and both assets have the same zero standard deviation, the rational individual would prefer holding X_2 to X_1, so that his demand for the asset X_1 with the lower return will be zero. To illustrate, if demand deposits and saving deposits in banks are both riskless but savings deposits pay a higher interest rate than demand deposits, as they normally do, the speculative demand for demand deposits – as well as currency – would be zero under this analysis. Similarly, if the money market mutual funds have higher expected return than savings deposits in banks, but can also be taken to be riskless because of their very short maturity, then the speculative demand for savings deposits would also be zero.

5.5.5 Optimal choice

The preceding two subsections analysed the risk averter's indifference curves and the opportunities open to him. Since such an individual prefers being on a higher indifference curve to being on a lower one, he will prefer being on the highest indifference curve that touches his opportunity locus. Such a curve will be that which is tangential to the efficient opportunity locus, and the individual's optimal combination of expected net worth and risk would be given by the point of tangency. Such points are shown by a and b in Figures 5.8 and 5.9.

The optimal point a in Figure 5.8 is a combination of riskless asset and the standard bundle of risky assets represented by point G.[14] The optimal point b in Figure 5.9 is a combination of the risky assets A and B only, while the riskless asset C is not held. A change in preferences that leaves the individual on the segment GB of the opportunity locus will change the relative demands for the risky assets A and B, but still without a positive demand for the riskless asset C. However, the individual whose initial optimal choice does not include the riskless asset may shift partly or wholly into the riskless asset, either because of an increase in his degree of risk aversion – which would shift the indifference curves – or because of an increase in the riskiness, or decrease in the expected net worth, of the risky assets – which would shift the efficient opportunity locus.

Periods of financial panic are likely to both increase the individual's cautiousness – that is, his degree of risk aversion – and increase the riskiness of the assets generally. Hence, there would be a drastic increase in the demand for the riskless asset in such periods. Such an increase in this demand may be self-reinforcing for a period since it is at the expense of the demand for risky assets, whose prices decline, causing a capital loss from the holdings of the risky assets. If this also causes the future expected net worth of the risky assets to fall and

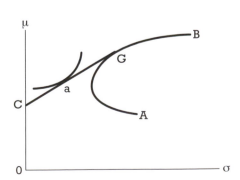

Figure 5.8

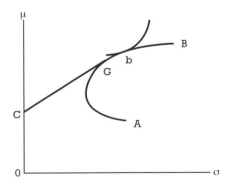

Figure 5.9

their expected riskiness to increase, the opportunity locus shifts further down and the optimal combination, with given preferences, will include still more of the riskless asset and even less of the risky assets. This process of declines in the net worth of risky assets and increased demand for the riskless asset could prove to be a *cumulative* one for some time.

In periods of optimism and a boom in asset prices, the opposite process whereby the demand for the riskless asset falls and that for the risky assets increases, along with their prices, could also prove to be a cumulative one over several periods.

5.6 TOBIN'S ANALYSIS OF THE DEMAND FOR A RISKLESS ASSET VERSUS A RISKY ONE

In an early form of the preceding analysis, James Tobin (1958, pp. 65–86)[15] analysed the demand for a riskless asset called *money* with a zero rate of return – that is, with a terminal value of unity and with zero standard deviation – as against a risky asset called *bonds*, with a positive return and a positive standard deviation. This analysis is presented in Figure 5.10, though with the difference that we will assume money to have a positive but still riskless rate of return. This figure has the expected value μ of terminal wealth on the vertical axis and the standard deviation σ of wealth on the horizontal one. If the individual invests his wealth wholly in money, he will be at the point M. If he invests only in bonds, he will at the point B. The efficient opportunity locus is MB. In the bottom part of this figure, designate any point on the vertical axis as 1. The distance from 0 to any point on the segment 01 measures the proportion of wealth invested in bonds. The line from the origin down to the point given by $(1, \sigma_B W)$ is $0X$.

If the individual chooses the point A, he will purchase σ_A, which implies, as shown in the bottom part of Figure 5.10, that he will place the proportion $0a$ in bonds and the proportion $a1$ in money.

We can use Figure 5.10 to investigate the effects of changes in the opportunity locus or the indifference curves. We consider three examples of the former.

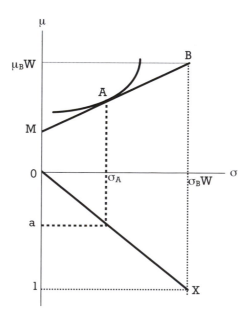

Figure 5.10

(i) This example considers a portfolio composed of a riskless asset with a positive return and a risky asset. Assume that the tax authorities impose a lump-sum tax on a positive return to the portfolio, *without* a loss offset for investors incurring losses, such that the opportunity locus shifts down in a parallel fashion, as shown by the shift from MB to $M'B'$ in Figure 5.11.[16] Under this assumption, the particular shape of the indifference curves drawn in Figure 5.11 leads to an increase in the optimal purchase of risk to $0\sigma_{a'}$, so that the proportion invested in bonds increases to $0a'$. This proportion is greater than the initial proportion $0a$.

With $M'B'$ parallel to MB, the marginal rate of substitution between the expected return and risk does not change. Hence, the substitution effect between them does not occur and the only effect in operation is the 'income effect' – really a wealth effect in the context of portfolio selection – which could go either way, so that the after-tax optimal demand for risk could be greater or smaller than the pre-tax proportion.[17]. At $\sigma_{a'}$, the net effect shown is an increase in the demand for risk. Since the riskiness of assets has not changed, the increased demand for risk translates into a higher demand for bonds. This is shown in the bottom half of Figure 5.11, which shows that the demand for bonds increases while that for the riskless asset falls. This example illustrates the behaviour of an individual who strongly wishes to maintain the amount of terminal wealth and with the decreased after-tax returns on the assets, has to purchase more bonds than before to do so.

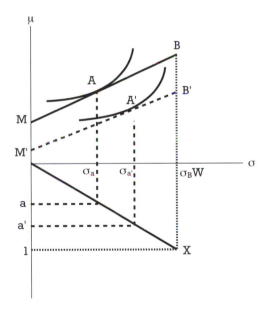

Figure 5.11

(ii) This example also deals with a portfolio composed of a riskless asset with a positive return and a risky asset. Assume that the tax authorities impose a 50% tax on a positive return and refund 50% of any negative return, so that the maximum amounts of μ and σ purchased through only holding bonds are cut down to those represented by the point B'' in Figure 5.12. The opportunity locus becomes MB'', while the relevant line in the bottom part of Figure 5.12 becomes $0X''$.

In Figure 5.12, assuming that the pre-tax optimal point was at A, the investor will stay at A in the post-tax situation in Figure 5.12. However, the amount $0\sigma_A$ of the risk bought now requires that he purchase the proportion $0a''$ of bonds, which is definitely greater than the pre-tax investment in bonds. Hence, although the tax reduced the after-tax return on bonds, the amount invested in bonds increased, seemingly contrary to intuition. In this example, the

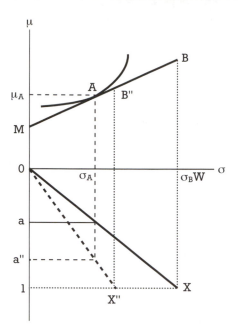

Figure 5.12

substitution effect is again zero since the slope of the opportunity locus at A did not change, so that the income effect alone determines the changes in the desired holdings of money and bonds. In the case shown in Figure 5.12, the individual maintains his initial purchases of (μ_A, σ_A) but this requires increased investments in bonds and a decrease in the demand for the riskless asset.

(iii) For the third example, assume, as in Tobin, that the riskless asset has a zero return. The relevant figure is now Figure 5.13, with the initial opportunity locus being $0B$. Further, assume that the tax authorities impose a 50% tax on the average rate of return on investments, without a loss offset for investors incurring losses, such that the post-tax opportunity locus becomes $0B'$. The optimal purchase of risk becomes $0\sigma_{a'}$, implying that the proportion invested in bonds falls to $0a'$. This proportion is less than the initial proportion $0a$, contrary to the situation shown in Figure 5.11. In this example, the nature of the indifference curves is such as to imply an increased demand for the riskless asset.

The difference between Figures 5.11 and 5.13 is that the slope $(\partial \mu / \partial \sigma)$ of the opportunity locus shifted in the latter but not in the former. In Figure 5.13, the imposition of the tax reduces the marginal return to risk-taking – measured as $\partial \mu / \partial \sigma$ – so that the substitution effect comes into play and will cause a reduction in the optimal amount of the risk bought through bond purchases. While the income effect could go either way, Figure 5.13 assumes that the two effects are in the same direction or that the substitution effect in favour of purchasing less risk dominates an opposing income effect. Since less risk is bought at A', and the riskiness of bonds has not changed, the bottom part of this figure shows that the individual will invest a smaller part of the portfolio in bonds.

Figures 5.11 to 5.13 illustrate the use of the general utility function for deriving the demand for money, assumed to be riskless with zero or positive return, and risky assets. This analysis is diagrammatic and implies that the demand for money will depend on the expected return and standard deviation, as well as on the wealth to be allocated. Shifts in the opportunity locus because of tax changes or, more generally, because of changes in the perceptions of the future risk and return – as occur periodically in the bond and stock markets – will alter the demand for money.

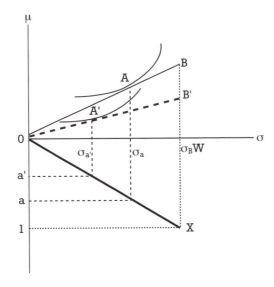

Figure 5.13

Since the preceding analysis has relied only upon indifference curves to represent preferences, its underlying utility function can be taken to be ordinal and need not be cardinal in the von Neumann–Morgenstern sense. Current portfolio analysis is usually mathematical and based on the expected utility hypothesis. It also tends to use specific utility functions. The next section presents this type of analysis.

5.7 THE EXPECTED UTILITY HYPOTHESIS (EUH) AND SPECIFIC FORMS OF THE UTILITY FUNCTION

5.7.1 The EUH and measures of risk aversion

Looking at the preceding indifference curve analysis, a suitable measure of risk aversion would seem to be $\partial\mu/\partial\sigma$. However, this measure does not directly relate to the form of the utility function that has wealth as its argument and we would like to have one that does so.

As shown above by the analysis of section 5.4 relating the slope of the utility function $U(W)$ to risk aversion, risk aversion is implied by the decrease in marginal utility so that one measure of risk aversion would be $U''(W)$, which is the change in the marginal utility of wealth. However, $U''(W)$ is not invariant to the admissible transformations of the utility function,[18] as we show in the next few paragraphs.

The cardinality of the von Neumann–Morgenstern (N–M) utility function

The *von Neumann–Morgenstern (N–M) utility function* is based on a set of axioms[19] which imply that, for an individual whose preferences obey the axioms, the utility function will be *'unique up to a linear transformation'*. That is, given a utility function $U(W)$ for such an individual, we can construct another utility function $V(W)$ where:

$$V(W) = a + bU(W) \quad b > 0 \tag{7}$$

In constructing $V(W)$ from $U(W)$, a and b can be given any arbitrary values as long as b is positive. $V(W)$ is an equally valid utility function for an individual having $U(W)$, and the indifference curves for both $U(W)$ and $V(W)$ are identical. However, their partial derivatives do differ in value, since,

$$V'(W) = bU'(W) \tag{8}$$

$$V''(W) = bU''(W) \tag{9}$$

where '' designates the first-order derivative and '''' designates the second-order one. Note that by the assumptions specifying a risk averter's preferences, U', $V' > 0$ and U'', $V'' < 0$. The above equations imply that:

$$V''(W)/V'(W) = U''(W)/U'(W) \tag{10}$$

Hence, U''/U' is not altered by admissible transformations of the N–M utility function. This property makes this ratio, as against U'' alone, appealing as a measure of the degree of risk aversion implied by the given utility function $U(W)$.

Measures of risk aversion

In (10), $U' > 0$, $U'' < 0$ and $U''/U' < 0$, so that the degree of risk aversion is usually measured by $[-U''/U']$, which gives a positive value. $[-U''/U']$ is called the *absolute degree of risk aversion*.

Since U' and U'' are unlikely to increase or decrease proportionately with wealth, $[-U''/U']$ will be affected by the amount of wealth. In order to ensure that the degree of risk aversion is independent of the level of wealth, another popular measure of the degree of risk aversion is $[-W \cdot U''/U']$. This measure is independent of the level of wealth as well as of the arbitrary constants a and b. $[-W \cdot U''/U']$ is called the *relative degree of risk aversion*.

The absolute and relative degrees of risk aversion can be calculated for any utility function. While there is no *a priori* reason to expect that either of these will be constant for any given individual's particular utility function, the utility functions for which such constancy holds are analytically convenient to use and are therefore popular in economic analysis. We examine these in turn, and will follow them with a presentation of the quadratic utility function which does not have the constancy of either the absolute or the relative degree of risk aversion but which is sometimes used in speculative demand analysis.

5.7.2 Constant absolute risk aversion (CARA)

Constant absolute risk aversion (CARA) requires that:

$$-U''(W)/U'(W) = \gamma \tag{11}$$

so that,

$$U''(W) = -\gamma U'(W) \tag{11'}$$

where $\gamma \geq 0$. Since $U''(W)$ is a second-order derivative, integrating both sides of (11') gives the utility function itself, though with two integrating constants, which would have been dropped in the differentiation process. The utility function given by integrating (11) twice[20] is:

$$U(W) = a - b \exp(-\gamma W) \tag{12}$$

Assuming that W is normally distributed with mean μ and standard deviation σ, as before, the expected value of this utility function is given by:

$$EU(W) = a - b[\exp(-\gamma\mu + \tfrac{1}{2}\gamma^2\sigma^2)] \tag{13}$$

Since $b > 0$ and $\gamma \geq 0$, maximizing the expected utility function (13) is equivalent to minimizing $[\exp(-\gamma\mu + \tfrac{1}{2}\gamma^2\sigma^2)]$ or maximizing:

$$(\mu - \tfrac{1}{2}\gamma\sigma^2) \tag{14}$$

In (14), substituting $\mu = \sum_i \mu_i x_i$ from (3) and $\sigma^2 = \sum_i \sum_j \rho_{ij}\sigma_i\sigma_j x_i x_j$ from (4) restates the decision problem as:

$$\text{Maximize} \quad \{\sum_i \mu_i x_i - \tfrac{1}{2}\gamma(\sum_i\sum_j \rho_{ij}\sigma_i\sigma_j x_i x_j)\} \quad i, j = 1, \ldots, n \tag{15}$$

$$\text{subject to:} \quad \sum_i x_i = W$$

Equation (15) represents one of the simplest decision frameworks in portfolio selection analysis and is the main reason for its usage in such analysis. Note its main assumptions: the degree of absolute risk aversion is constant, the frequency distribution of terminal wealth W is normal and the individual's preferences satisfy the N–M axioms. The following analysis applies (15) to the case of two risky assets.

CARA and choice between two risky assets

Assume in the context of (15) that the individual's choice is between different quantities of the two risky assets X_1 and X_2 so that $n = 2$. His decision problem can be stated as:

$$\text{Maximize} \quad (\mu_1 x_1 + \mu_2 x_2) - \{\tfrac{1}{2}\gamma(\sigma_{11}x_1^2 + 2\sigma_{12}x_1 x_2 + \sigma_{22}x_2^2)\}$$

$$\text{subject to:} \quad x_1 + x_2 = W \tag{16}$$

The Lagrangian function L for this problem is:

$$L = (\mu_1 x_1 + \mu_2 x_2) - \{\tfrac{1}{2}\gamma(\sigma_{11}x_1^2 + 2\sigma_{12}x_1 x_2 + \sigma_{22}x_2^2)\} + \lambda[x_1 + x_2 - W] \tag{17}$$

where λ is the Lagrangian multiplier. The first-order conditions for a maximum for this problem are:

$$\mu_1 - \gamma(\sigma_{11}x_1 + \sigma_{12}x_2) + \lambda = 0$$
$$\mu_2 - \gamma(\sigma_{22}x_2 + \sigma_{12}x_1) + \lambda = 0$$
$$x_1 + x_2 = W$$

These conditions yield the optimal holdings of the two assets as:

$$x_1 = k_1 + k_2 W \tag{18}$$

$$x_2 = -k_1 + (1 - k_2) W \tag{19}$$

where:

$$k_1 = (\mu_1 - \mu_2)/\gamma(\sigma_{11} - 2\sigma_{12} + \sigma_{22})$$
$$k_2 = (\sigma_{22} - \sigma_{12})/(\sigma_{11} - 2\sigma_{12} + \sigma_{22})$$

so that the demand for each asset increases with wealth but the proportions of the two assets in the portfolio change as initial wealth W increases. These demand functions depend upon the expected returns and the variances and covariances.

CARA especially lacks realism for deriving the demand function for riskless assets such as money. This is illustrated by the use of (15) in the next subsection.

CARA and the special case of riskless money

If X_1 were a *riskless* asset, money, with $\sigma_1 = 0$, while X_2 was still a risky asset, note that $\sigma_{11} = \sigma_{12} = 0$. Inserting these in the demand functions (18) and (19) implies that:

$$x_1 = W - (\mu_2 - \mu_1)/(\gamma\sigma_{22}) \tag{20}$$

$$x_2 = (\mu_2 - \mu_1)/(\gamma\sigma_{22}) \tag{21}$$

where x_2 is independent of initial wealth, so that any increases in the initial wealth will be used to add only to money holdings – that is, to the riskless asset. The amount of wealth held in the risky asset will stay unchanged as wealth increases beyond the amount specified by (21), so that as the investor becomes wealthier, the proportion of his optimal portfolio allocated to the riskless asset (money) will increase. This is far from the behaviour pattern of most investors who increase their holdings of the risky assets as their wealth increases. Therefore, while CARA is analytically very convenient, it is not very realistic for portfolio selection behaviour in the presence of a riskless asset. This makes CARA especially unsuitable for the speculative demand for nominal balances since money in nominal terms is a riskless asset.

The limitation of CARA as a utility function for portfolio selection

On a more general note, CARA assumes that the investor becomes increasingly reluctant to take risks as he gets richer and invests in increasing proportions of the *less* risky assets. Intuitive knowledge of investor behaviour indicates the opposite: investors tend to be rather more cautious with limited wealth and become more willing to take chances as their wealth increases. Hence, CARA cannot be taken to be plausible for the choice among assets and its use in this sphere is mainly due to its analytical convenience. Constant relative risk aversion (CRRA) is more realistic in this respect and we now turn to its analysis.

5.7.3 Constant relative risk aversion (CRRA)

Relative risk aversion (RRA) is specified by:

$$RRA = [-W \cdot U''/U'] \tag{22}$$

CRRA is the requirement that:

$$[-W \cdot U''/U'] = \beta \tag{23}$$

Integrating both sides of this equation twice leads to the utility function:

$$U(W) = a - bW^{1-\beta} \quad \text{if } \beta > 0, \beta \neq 1 \tag{24}$$

$$= \ln W \quad \text{if } \beta = 1 \tag{25}$$

where a and b are the constants of integration and $b > 0$.[21]

In (25), $U(W) = \ln W$ is analytically very tractable and is probably the most popular form of the von Neumann–Morgenstern utility function. Its degrees of absolute and relative risk aversion are:

$$ARA = 1/W$$

$$RRA = 1$$

so that the absolute degree of risk aversion decreases as the investor gets richer. This is also true of the general form of the CRRA utility function.

If there are only risky assets, maximizing the CRRA utility function subject to the budget constraint yields the demand function for the ith risky asset as:

$$x_i/W = k_i\mu \quad i = 1, 2, ..., n \tag{26}$$

where $k_i = k_i(\beta, \underline{\mu}, \underline{\sigma}, \underline{\sigma}_{ij})$.

The underlined variables indicate the vectors of the relevant variables (Cuthbertson, 1985, Ch. 3).

CRRA and the special case of riskless money

But if the first asset is riskless while the others are all risky ones, the demand function for the riskless asset is:

$$
\begin{aligned}
x_1/W &= 1 - \sum_i (x_i/W) \quad i = 2, ..., n \\
&= 1 - \sum_i k_i\mu_i
\end{aligned}
\tag{27}{}^{22}
$$

The asset demand functions (26) and (27) are homogeneous of degree one in W, so that the proportions of the riskless and each of the risky assets in the portfolio remain constant as the portfolio grows. Alternatively stated, the individual's portfolio demand for each asset has an elasticity of unity with respect to his wealth.

5.7.4 The quadratic utility function

Besides CARA and CRRA, the third type of utility function in common usage in portfolio selection theory is:

$$U(W) = a + bW - cW^2 \quad a, b, c > 0 \tag{28}$$

Hence,

$$EU(W) = a + b\mu - cE(W^2) \tag{29}$$

where, by the definition of σ^2,

$$
\begin{aligned}
\sigma^2 &= E(W - \mu)^2 = E(W^2 - 2W \cdot \mu + \mu^2) \\
&= EW^2 - 2EW \cdot \mu + \mu^2 = E(W^2) - 2\mu^2 + \mu^2 \\
&= (EW^2) - \mu^2
\end{aligned}
$$

Therefore,

$$E(W^2) = \mu^2 + \sigma^2 \tag{30}$$

so that from (29) and (30),

$$EU(W) = a + b\mu - c\mu^2 - c\sigma^2 \quad a, b, c > 0 \tag{31}$$

The individual maximizes (31) with respect to μ and σ.

To derive the asset demand functions, substitute the equations for μ and σ in (31) and maximize the resulting expected utility function with respect to the quantities of the assets.

Since the quadratic utility function does not possess the CRRA property, the proportions of the assets will not remain constant as wealth increases.

The quadratic utility function is a second degree polynomial in W. Such a polynomial transforms to an expected utility function in the first two moments of the probability distribution of returns. Polynomials of higher degrees can also be used as utility functions. These would bring into the expected utility function the other moments of the probability distribution, which is desirable, but they are usually quite difficult for analysis.

Limitations of the quadratic utility function

From (31),

$$\partial EU(W)/\partial\mu = b - 2c\mu$$

Since the individual prefers a higher mean return to a lower one at *all* levels of wealth, the above derivative must be positive. Hence in (28),

$$[b - 2c\mu] > 0$$

which requires that,

$$\mu < b/(2c)$$

where μ is the expected value of the portfolio and grows as wealth grows, so that the above condition can be very restrictive for applications of the quadratic utility function.

This restriction can also be specified as the requirement that $\partial U/\partial W = b - 2cW > 0$, which translates to $b > 2cW$, where the right-hand side of the inequality increases with W, thereby severely limiting the range over which the quadratic utility function is plausible.

Further, for the quadratic utility function in (28), the absolute degree of risk aversion (ARA) is given by:

$$ARA = -U''(W)/U'(W) = 2c/(b - 2cW)$$

which is positive since $(b - 2cW) > 0$ and increasing in W, so that as the investor gets wealthier, he becomes more risk averse.[23] This increase – rather than a decrease – makes the quadratic utility function even less appealing than the CARA, but, as seen above, the latter has its own limitations.

5.8 THE VOLATILITY OF MONEY DEMAND FUNCTIONS

Note that the speculative demand for money and the coefficients of its independent variables will depend upon the means, the standard deviations, and the correlation coefficients of the expected terminal values of the assets, for all of which the subjectively expected future and not the past actual values are the relevant ones. Keynes (1936, Ch. 13) had argued that the expected bond yields and equity prices depend on the mood of the market participants, their perceptions of the future based on very limited information, as well as herd instincts. These elements of the financial markets are as much in evidence today as in Keynes' day, as the day-by-day movements of the stock market indices clearly indicate.

These arguments imply that the demand functions for bonds and equities are constantly shifting, so that they could not be properly estimated, or, if estimated, would be worthless – unless the nature of the shift could be specified and the adjustments made for it. If we follow Keynes' analysis, presented in Chapter 2 above, of bulls and bears for the speculative demand for money, this demand function must also be similarly volatile. However, if we believe that the demand for money is a function of the market interest rate – rather than of the total yield including the expected changes in bond and equity prices, on bonds and equities – this function need not necessarily be volatile, since the volatility of bond and equity prices is thereby removed from consideration.

Empirical studies, reported in Chapter 9, do not generally estimate a speculative demand for money separately from the demand for real balances as a whole. While these studies sometimes show instability of the demand function for money as a whole over time, they do not show the sort of high volatility, due to sudden shifts in expectations, suggested by Keynes. Further, any shifts in the estimated functions are usually attributed to innovations in the transactions technology.

5.9 AN IMPORTANT CAUTION: IS THERE A POSITIVE DEMAND FOR SPECULATIVE BALANCES IN THE MODERN ECONOMY?

The modern economy with a well-developed financial sector has a plethora of financial assets which are as riskless as currency and demand deposits, or close enough in riskiness not to matter much to the individuals in the economy. Among these assets are: various types of savings deposits, term deposits, certificates of deposit (CDs) and very short-term money market instruments. Since they pay higher returns than M1 without an accompanying higher risk, M1 will not be part of the efficient opportunity locus and will not be demanded for speculative purposes. Similarly, there will only be a speculative demand for the savings deposits component of M2 as long as these deposits are not dominated in expected return by other riskless assets in the economy.

Consequently, in economies with a variety of riskless assets which are riskless in nominal terms but which do not directly circulate as a medium of exchange and are therefore not part of narrow money, the speculative demand for M1 (which is the medium of exchange but pays a lower rate of interest) would be non-existent or confined to those individuals who do not have access to other riskless assets at a low enough cost. Hence, the speculative demand model may be generally applicable – and the speculative demand for narrow money may be positive – in economies with poorly developed financial institutions and markets, where other riskless assets do not exist or do not dominate over money in their return. However, this model does not any longer seem to be applicable to the M1 holdings of the common households, firms and financial institutions in the modern developed economy. In such a context, while there may be a significant and large speculative demand for certain forms of savings deposits and for money market instruments, there need not be a significant one for currency and demand deposits.

In terms of the general evolution of the financial sectors in the Western economies, the increasing proliferation of banks, accompanied by a considerable increase in the ease of transfer from savings accounts to checking accounts, especially in the banks, since the 1950s have brought about an increasing dominance of the net return (over transfer costs) on savings deposits and a continuing increase in the proportion of savings to M1, with a corresponding increase in the M2/M1 ratio. The innovation of automatic tellers and their spread in the 1980s hastened this movement, so that M1 now tends to be quite small relative to M2 in economies with developed financial systems.

In more recent years in the North American and European economies, it has become possible to buy and sell almost without notice and without significant brokerage costs, various types of mutual funds through commercial banks. Among these, the money market funds, with investments in the Treasury bills of a month's or a few months' maturity, are virtually riskless and offer a higher yield than most savings deposits, often held in the same financial institution. The preceding analysis implies that the ratio of M2 (which excludes such money market funds) to a wider definition of money which includes such funds, would also decline.

CONCLUSIONS

Keynes had introduced the speculative demand function for money into the literature, and Friedman had embedded aspects of the demand for money as a temporary abode of purchasing power in the neoclassical money demand analysis. This role of money occupied centre stage in the analysis of the demand for money for several decades and was used to show the dependence of the demand for money on the rates of interest. The varieties of the analytical developments discussed in this chapter are testimony to the importance of the speculative motive in the literature on monetary economics.

The demand function for speculative balances derived in this chapter includes, among its arguments, wealth (rather than current income) and the expected yields (rather than actual ones) on the available assets. Such a function would be stable in an unchanging environment but could be unstable in periods of volatility in the bond and stock markets, changes in financial regulations, innovations in the characteristics of existing assets and the creation of new ones, and changes in the payments mechanisms. Of these, the volatility arising from changes in the expectations of future returns on bonds and equities had been of special concern to Keynes, since he considered such expectations to be volatile in practice.

Further, the applicability of this analysis to the demand for money in the modern economy needs to be carefully reconsidered. Keynes' analysis was based on only money – the only available liquid and riskless asset – and consols. In such a context, the uncertainty on the terminal value of consols would create a demand for money in the economy. But developed economies since Keynes' day have created a wide variety of riskless assets that pay positive rates of interest. In these, economic units with access to such assets would prefer holding them as temporary abodes of purchasing power for speculative purposes rather than holding currency and demand deposits, which do not pay interest or pay lower rates of interest than riskless savings accounts. Therefore, the demand for M1 – and even for wider definitions of money including savings deposits which now face competition from money market funds – must come from transactions and precautionary motives rather than from speculative motives. The transactions demand analysis was presented in Chapter 4 and the precautionary demand analysis will be presented in Chapter 6. A related topic is that of the buffer stock role of money which is also analysed in Chapter 6.

SUMMARY OF CRITICAL CONCLUSIONS

- The speculative demand for money is analysed for money balances as an asset when the yields on other assets are uncertain.
- Portfolio selection analysis requires a cardinal utility function, rather than the more general ordinal utility function. The most commonly used version of cardinal utility functions is the von Neumann–Morgenstern utility function.
- Investors maximize the expected utility of their terminal wealth, not the expected value of this wealth.
- Risk aversion requires decreasing marginal utility of wealth.
- The functional form of the utility function with constant absolute risk aversion is analytically convenient but has implausible implications for the wealth elasticity of money demand.
- The functional form of the utility function with constant relative risk aversion is analytically convenient and implies a unit wealth elasticity of money demand.
- The speculative demand for M1 and even M2 may be zero in the modern financially developed economy with alternative assets that are riskless but have higher yields.

review and discussion questions

1 Compare and contrast Keynes' theory of the speculative demand for money with Tobin's portfolio selection one utilizing the expected utility hypothesis.

2 Does Tobin's theory imply the potential for volatility that Keynes attributed to the speculative demand for money?

3 'The more volatile are the returns on bonds and stocks, the greater the demand for money.' Can you derive this proposition from Tobin's liquidity preference model? Does it apply to interest-bearing as well as non-interest-bearing money?

4 If the speculative demand for M1 is zero in the modern financially developed economy, is it also zero for some of the broader money aggregates? If not, what are the appropriate scale determinants of the speculative demand for M1 and the broader money aggregates.

5 Assuming a riskless asset called money and two risky assets, analyse the individual's asset demand for money. What will be the general form of the money demand function?

Further, assuming that the two assets have perfectly negatively correlated returns, derive the implied demand function for money. Use diagrams for your answer.

6 Assume that there are only two assets, money with $\mu_m = 0$ and $\sigma_m = 0$ and bonds with μ_b, $\sigma_b > 0$, and that the individual has a CARA utility function, so that he maximizes:

$$EU(W) = \mu_t - \tfrac{1}{2}\gamma_t \sigma_t^2$$

Now assume that γ fluctuates such that $\gamma_t = \gamma_0 + \eta_t$ and $\gamma_{t+1} = \gamma_0 - \eta_t$. Derive the individual's speculative demand functions M_t^{sp} and M_{t+1}^{sp}.

7 Again, assume that there are only two assets, money with $\mu_m = 0$ and $\sigma_m = 0$ and bonds with μ_b, $\sigma_b > 0$, and that the individual has a CARA utility function, so that he maximizes:

$$EU(W) = \mu_t - \tfrac{1}{2}\gamma_t \sigma_t^2$$

Now assume that σ fluctuates such that $\sigma_t = \sigma_0 + \epsilon_t$ and $\sigma_t + 1 = \sigma_0 - \epsilon_t$. Derive the individual's speculative demand functions M_t^{sp} and M_{t+1}^{sp}.

8 In the preceding two questions, what are likely to be the determinants of η and ϵ in your economy? How volatile are these shifts likely to be over the business cycle?

9 Use your answers to the above questions to discuss Keynes' assertion on the high volatility of the speculative demand for money. Is this assertion still valid? Discuss.

10 Consider a two-asset model with money paying the positive given interest rate r_m and the bonds paying the return r which has the expected value μ_b and the standard deviation σ_b. Show diagrammatically the effects of the following for the proportions held of the two assets:

(i) The government imposes a tax on the excess return $(r - r_m)$ on bonds, with a corresponding refund if the return is negative.

(ii) The government imposes a tax on a positive excess return $(r - r_m)$ on bonds, but without any refund if the return is negative.

(iii) Show the effects for the above cases if $r_m = 0$.

11 Consider a two-asset model with money paying the fixed interest rate r_m and the bonds paying the return r which has the expected value μ_b and the standard deviation σ_b. The government imposes a tax on the excess return $(r - r_m)$ on bonds, with a corresponding refund if the return is negative. What will be the effects of the following on bond purchases:

  (i) the tax revenues are not returned to the investors.
 (ii) the tax revenues are returned to the investors as a lump-sum transfer.

12 Does the existence of a speculative demand component increase or decrease the interest elasticity of the overall demand for money? When would broader monetary aggregates have higher interest elasticities than narrower ones, especially M1?

13 Does the existence of a speculative demand component increase or decrease the income elasticity of the overall demand for money? When would broader monetary aggregates have higher income elasticities than narrower ones, especially M1?

14 'The theory of portfolio choice has little to do with the demand for money in the modern economy.' Discuss.

15 'Liquidity preference as behaviour towards risk is a demand for short-term securities – not money.' Present Tobin's analysis of the demand for money.

    Use Tobin's analysis, or any other, to show the conditions under which the above (quoted) statement will apply. How will the accuracy of this statement modify the demand for money?

NOTES

1 Thus, even if all uncertainty with respect to the yields on assets were removed, a wide variety of assets with different characteristics and yields could continue to exist.

2 In experiments, the individual can always be made to refine his information so that the probability of occurrence that he attaches to any particular actual yield can be calculated as a unique number and not merely within a range. However, in the real world, this likelihood may be fudged and vague or refined depending upon the monetary stakes involved and the information at hand.

3 Note that in Keynes' analysis of the speculative demand for money, as set out above in Chapter 2, the individual had uni-valued expectations: he definitely expected a particular yield to occur so that his subjective probability attached to this yield was one. Further, this expected yield was taken to be independent of the actual one. That is, the individual was said to have 'inelastic expectations' of his expected yield with respect to changes in the actual rate of interest in the market.

4 'Terminal wealth' refers to the wealth attained at the end of the period for which the individual expects to hold the assets.

5 The St Petersburg paradox refers to the following gamble. Suppose an individual A tosses a coin until it comes up heads. If heads come up on the nth toss, he pays to B an amount equal to (2^{n-1}) dollars. The expected value (Ey) of the payoff y to B is infinitely great since:

$$Ey = \{(1/2) + (1/2)^2 \cdot 2 + (1/2)^3 \cdot 2^2 + (1/2)^n \cdot 2^{n-1} + \ldots\} \to \infty$$

Individuals are rarely, if ever, willing to offer very high prices for the opportunity to play as B in this game, thus refuting the expected wealth hypothesis.

While this paradox was historically used to establish and is still used to justify the EUH, note that the amounts usually offered to play B in experiments also tend to be far below the amounts which would be implied by the commonly used utility functions in the EUH, thereby also creating doubts about the empirical validity of these functions or of the EUH itself.

6 The same arguments apply against a theory that would *a priori* bar the individual from considering the third and fourth moments of the subjective distribution of yields in his decisions.

7 This hypothesis was first proposed by Daniel Bernoulli in the seventeenth century. The axioms for its modern version were first presented by von Neumann and Morgenstern in *The Theory of Games* (1946).

8 Economics has two major notions of the cardinality of the utility function. One of these – often called as the Marshallian one – was proposed by the early proponents – such as Menger, Jevons and Marshall – of the utility analysis in the late nineteenth century. It required the constancy of the marginal utility of income. The validity of such an assumption is doubtful and the notion of Marshallian cardinal utility had been discarded in utility analysis by the 1930s. The other notion of cardinal utility is the von Neumann–Morgenstern (N–M) one and is based on a set of axioms. In intuitive terms, they require the constancy of the marginal utility of the probability of an outcome.

9 Figure 5.1c shows a constant positive degree of risk aversion as risk increases. If there were risk indifference, which translates to a constant zero degree of risk aversion, the indifference curves would be horizontal.

10 An analysis based on the rate of return keeps constant the portfolio composition as the size of the portfolio changes. This may not be valid in all cases.

11 Therefore, a risk averter will be willing to buy insurance against the risks in his life and business – for example, against death, disability, job loss, etc. – and be willing to pay a maximum amount of premium implied by his utility function and the risk in question. If a firm is willing to insure him for the risk for less than this amount, he will buy the insurance; if the required premium is greater than this amount, he will not buy the insurance.

12 σ in $\sigma(X_1, X_3)$ and μ in $\mu(X_1, X_3)$ are being used as functional symbols, so that their arguments can clearly indicate which assets are in the portfolio. However, σ and μ retain their definitions as being respectively the standard deviation and the expected return to the portfolio.

13 This can be intuitively illustrated by the folklore that one should not put all one's eggs in one basket. It pays to divide one's eggs between two baskets as long as there is a possibility that when one of the baskets falls, the other one may not. If both baskets are guaranteed to fall simultaneously or not fall at all, for example, when bound together, there is no advantage to separating the eggs between the baskets: the same number of eggs will break whether they are separated or not. In our formal language, the correlation coefficient of the baskets falling is one and there are no economies. However, if it is guaranteed or certain that when one basket falls, the other will not – as when the baskets are at the opposite ends of a pole carried across one's shoulders – separating the eggs into the two baskets will ensure that some eggs will with certainty escape breakage. In this case, the correlation coefficient of the baskets falling is (−1). In the intervening cases, the eggs should be divided between the baskets, the exact division depending upon the probability that when one basket falls, the other will not – that is, upon the correlation coefficient between the baskets falling. Similarly, the individual investor must consider the correlation coefficient of net worth between the assets since he may be able to reduce his risk through the diversification of the portfolio between the assets.

14 A shift in the degree of risk aversion that changes the slope of the indifference curves in the neighbourhood of point *a* but leaves the optimal combination on the segment *CG*, will change the demand for the riskless asset and the risky bundle. It will, however, leave the composition of the risky bundle unchanged. Such a shift in preferences was termed by Hicks as a change in the degree of liquidity preference.

15 The part of Tobin's analysis that refers specifically to Keynes' arguments on the speculative demand was presented in Chapter 2.

16 This assumes that the tax does not change the standard deviation of terminal wealth.

17 It would be smaller if the indifference curve tangential to $M'B'$ were such that the optimal point were to the left – rather than right – of the point A.

18 For ordinal utility functions, even the sign of $U''(W)$ can change under admissible (increasing) transformations of the utility function, so that it does not make sense to talk of decreasing marginal utility for them. For cardinal functions, the sign remains invariant under admissible (linear) transformations but the magnitude can change.

19 These axioms are not presented in this book. They can be found in many intermediate and advanced microeconomics textbooks. An early version of them is in Friedman and Savage (1948).

20 CARA requires that:

$$U''(W) = -\gamma U'(W)$$

Hence, integrating both sides of this equation specifies that:

$$\ln U'(W) = k_1 - \gamma W$$

so that

$$U'(W) = \exp(k_1 - \gamma W)$$

Integrating again,

$$U(W) = k_2 - (1/\gamma) \exp(k_1 - \gamma W) = a - b \exp(-\gamma W)$$

where k_1 and k_2 are the constants of integration, $a = k_2$ and $b = (1/\gamma) \exp(k_1)$.

21 CRRA is often used in intertemporal consumption analysis, where the intertemporal and the period utility functions are specified as:

$$
\begin{aligned}
U(c_0, c_1, ..., c_T) &= \textstyle\sum_t u(c_t)/(1 - \partial)^{-t} \quad t = 0, 1, ..., T \\
u(c_t) &= (c_t^{(1-b)})/(1 - b) \quad \text{for } b > 0, b \neq 1 \\
&= \ln c_t \quad \text{for } b = 1
\end{aligned}
$$

For these functions, the elasticity of substitution between consumption in any two periods is constant and equal to $1/b$. The corresponding period utility function for CARA is:

$$u(c_t) = -(1/a) \exp(-ac_t) \quad a > 0$$

22 See Cuthbertson (1985, Ch. 3) for the derivations of this and the earlier results on the CRRA utility function.

23 It is commonly believed that the wealthier investors are, *ceteris paribus*, less risk averse.

REFERENCES

Arrow, Kenneth J. 'The Theory of Risk Aversion'. In Kenneth J. Arrow, *Essays in the Theory of Risk-Bearing*. Chicago: Markham Publishing Co., 1971.

Chang, Winston W., Daniel Hamberg and Junichi Hirata. 'Liquidity Preference as Behavior toward Risk is a Demand for Short-Term Securities – Not Money'. *American Economic Review*, 73, June 1983, pp. 420–27.

Cuthbertson, Keith. *The Supply and Demand for Money*. London: Basil Blackwell, 1985.

Friedman, Milton, and L. J. Savage. 'The Utility Analysis of Choices involving Risk'. *Journal of Political Economy*, 56, 1948, pp. 279–304.

Keynes, John Maynard. *The General Theory of Employment, Interest and Money*. London: Macmillan, 1936, Chs 13, 15.

Tobin, James. 'Liquidity Preference as Behaviour towards Risk'. *Review of Economic Studies*, 25, February 1958, pp. 65–86.

——. 'The Theory of Portfolio Selection'. In F. H. Hahn and F. P. R. Brechling, eds, *The Theory of Interest Rates*. London: Macmillan, 1965.

chapter six

THE PRECAUTIONARY AND BUFFER STOCK DEMAND FOR MONEY

This chapter has been included for completeness of the analysis on the demand for money and also in an attempt to present some of the newer ideas on this topic.

The introduction to this chapter presents a simplified analysis of the precautionary and buffer stock demands for money. It should definitely be covered as an adjunct to the treatment of the transactions demand in Chapter 4 and of the speculative demand in Chapter 5. The rest of the chapter presents a more advanced treatment of the precautionary and buffer stock reasons for holding money.

While this chapter only uses differential calculus, it is still mathematically more difficult than the other chapters in this book, and its main parts (other than the introduction) are intended for more advanced courses.

---

key concepts introduced in this chapter

- Uncertainty of consumption expenditures and income
- Precautionary demand for money
- Buffer stock demand for money
- Overdrafts and standby credit arrangements
- The dependence of the demand for money on money supply changes

---

The transactions demand for money was analysed in Chapter 4 under the assumptions of the certainty of the amounts and timing of all of the variables, including income receipts and expenditures. The speculative demand for money was analysed in Chapter 5 under the assumption of the uncertainty of the rates of return on the various assets but certainty of the amount of wealth to be allocated over the assets. Neither of these dealt with the uncertainty of income or the uncertainty of the need for expenditures in the future. Such uncertainty is pervasive in the economy, and the individual can respond to it through precautionary saving, some or all of which could be held in the form of precautionary money balances.

Precautionary saving is that part of income that is saved because of the uncertainty of future income and consumption needs. It would be zero if the future values of these variables were fully known. Precautionary wealth or savings are similarly the part of wealth held due to such uncertainty. Such wealth may be held in a variety of assets, one of which is money. Money balances held for such a reason constitute the precautionary demand for money.

Precautionary wealth is clearly affected by the economic and financial environment, as well as by the individual's own personal circumstances. The economic environment – which includes the possibility of being laid off or, if unemployed, of finding a job, the growth of incomes, the social welfare net etc. – is one of the determinants of the uncertainty of the individual's future income. The economy's financial structure provides for such devices as credit cards, overdrafts, trade credit, etc., which allow for payments for sudden expenditures to be postponed and reduce the need for the precautionary holdings of assets. The individual's personal circumstances affect his expenditure needs, the timing of expenditures and the possibility of delaying them, or temporarily meeting them through the use of credit cards and overdrafts etc. The precautionary demand for money depends upon the above factors and the relative liquidity and transactions costs of the various assets that can function as precautionary wealth.

In addition to the above, even if the individual's income and expenditures over a given period are known in advance, precautionary saving over the period would be zero but the precautionary demand for money would still be positive and would depend upon the uncertain timings of receipts and expenditures within the period. Saving and precautionary money balances are thus different concepts, with saving being the means of carrying purchasing power from one period to the next and precautionary money balances being the means of paying for unexpected expenditures during the period.

Since the focus of the speculative demand for money is on the uncertainty of the yields on the various assets, the precautionary demand for money is for simplicity analysed under the assumption that these yields are known – and therefore are not uncertain. Given this assumption, the analysis of the precautionary demand for money is an extension of the inventory analysis of the transactions demand to the case of the uncertainty of the amount and timing of income receipts and expenditures. This uncertainty of income is captured through the moments of the income distribution, with the analysis assuming a normal distribution and therefore considering only the mean and the variance of income during the period.

The inventory analysis of transactions demand in Chapter 4 had implied the general version of the demand function as:

$$m^{trd} = m^{trd}(b, r, y) \qquad (1)$$

where:

m^{trd} transactions demand for real balances
b real brokerage cost
r interest rate
y real income/expenditures

Under uncertainty, assuming a normal distribution of income, y is a function of its mean value and standard deviation. Hence, the modification of (1) to the case of precautionary demand (subsuming within it the transactions demand) for money, would be:

$$m^{prd} = m^{prd}(b, r, \mu_y, \sigma_y) \qquad (2)$$

where:

m^{prd} precautionary demand for money

μ_y mathematical expectation of income

σ_y standard deviation of income

In addition, under uncertainty, the degree of risk aversion and the available mechanisms and substitutes for coping with such uncertainty would also be among the relevant determinants of money demand. That is, (2) needs to be modified to:

$$m^{prd} = m^{prd}(b, r, \mu_y, \sigma_y, \rho, \Omega) \tag{3}$$

where:

ρ degree of risk aversion

Ω substitutes for precautionary money balances

Among the components of Ω would be credit cards, overdrafts at banks, trade credit, etc. In the limiting case in which the individual can pay for any precautionary needs by credit cards and pay the credit card balances on the date he receives income, his precautionary demand for money would be zero.

Note that in (3), if the individual was risk indifferent, $\rho = 0$ and (3) would simplify to:

$$m^{prd} = m^{prd}(b, r, \mu_y, \Omega) \tag{4}$$

The preceding arguments imply a *unique* value for the precautionary demand for money for given values of its determinants. Such models are presented in sections 6.1 to 6.3. Somewhat different from these models are those known as buffer stock models. In a *buffer stock model*, money is held as a 'buffer' or fallback because money has lower transactions costs than other assets, so that the receipt of income can be held in the form of money until a sufficiently large amount has accumulated for it to be worthwhile to adjust other assets or income–expenditure flows. The actual holdings of money would therefore exhibit 'short-run' fluctuations, implying that the short-run money demand function and velocity would be unstable, though within a specific range. There are two common patterns of such short-run fluctuations. One of these is fluctuations around a long-run desired level. Another is fluctuations within a band whose upper and lower limits are specified by longer-term factors.

This chapter presents in sections 6.1 to 6.3 the precautionary demand models, using the contributions of Whalen (1966) and Sprenkle and Miller (1980), which imply determinate levels of the precautionary demand for money rather than fluctuations around a desired level or in an optimal range. Sections 6.4 to 6.7 present some of the buffer stock models.

The economic agent can be the individual/household or firm, though some of the contributions in the literature refer specifically to the firm, some to the individual and some to the (economic) agent. We will use the terms individual, firm and agent interchangeably in the following, with the understanding that the analysis is to be applied as appropriate.

6.1 AN EXTENSION OF THE TRANSACTIONS DEMAND MODEL TO PRECAUTIONARY DEMAND

The following analysis for the precautionary demand for money is based on Whalen (1966). Assume as in the inventory model of transactions demand that the individual has a choice between holding money or bonds. Money is perfectly liquid and does not pay any interest. Bonds are illiquid and pay interest at the rate r. There is a brokerage cost of converting from money to bonds and vice versa. Further, as an item additional to those in the transactions demand model of Chapter 4, selling bonds at short notice to obtain money for unexpected transactions or having to postpone such transactions imposes an additional 'penalty' cost. Therefore, there are now three components of the cost of financing transactions: brokerage costs, interest income forgone and penalty costs. As in Chapter 4, the individual is assumed to withdraw an amount W from bonds at evenly spaced intervals.

The cost function associated with money usage is:

$$C = rM + B_0 Y/W + \beta p(N > M) \tag{5}$$

where:

C	nominal cost of holding precautionary (including transactions) balances
M	money balances held
B_0	nominal brokerage cost per withdrawal
Y	total (uncertain) nominal income/expenditures
W	amount withdrawn each time from interest-bearing bonds
N	net payments (expenditure less receipts)
$p(N > M)$	probability of $N > M$
β	nominal penalty cost of shortfall in money balances

Since the individual has an uncertain pattern of receipts and payments and needs to pay for any purchase in money, he suffers a loss ('penalty') whenever he is short of money to make an intended purchase. This loss can be that of having to unexpectedly sell 'bonds' to get the required money balances or having to postpone the purchase until he has enough money balances, so that this loss has monetary and non-monetary components. With p as the probability of $N > M$, (5) species the penalty cost of having inadequate balances by $\beta p(N > M)$.

Suppose that the individual holds money balances M equal to $k\sigma$, where σ is the standard deviation of net payments N, so that:

$$M = k\sigma \tag{6}$$

We need to know the probability $p(N > k\sigma)$ that the net payments N will exceed holdings $k\sigma$, so that the penalty will be incurred. By Chebyscheff's inequality, the probability p that a variable N will deviate from its mean – which is zero under our assumptions – by more than k times its standard deviation σ is specified by $p(-k\sigma > N > k\sigma) \leq 1/k^2$. Therefore, $p(N > M)$, where M equals $k\sigma$ is:

$$p(N > M) \leq 1/k^2 \quad k \geq 1^1 \tag{7}$$

where, from (6),

$$k = M/\sigma \tag{8}$$

Assume that the individual is sufficiently risk-averse to base his money holdings on the maximum value of $p(N > M)$. In this case,

$$p(N > M) = 1/(M/\sigma)^2 = \sigma^2/M^2 \tag{9}$$

Equations (5) and (9) imply that,

$$C = rM + B_0 Y/W + \beta\sigma^2/M^2$$

Therefore, since $M = \frac{1}{2}W$, as in Baumol's analysis,

$$C = rM + \frac{1}{2}B_0 Y/M + \beta\sigma^2/M^2 \tag{10}$$

Note that the first two terms of the above equation are as in Baumol's analysis. The third term arises because of the uncertainty of expenditures. To minimize the cost of holding money, set the partial derivative of C with respect to M equal to zero, as in:

$$\partial C/\partial M = r - \tfrac{1}{2}B_0\,Y/M^2 - 2\beta\sigma^2/M^3 = 0 \tag{11}$$

Multiplying by M^3,

$$rM^3 - \tfrac{1}{2}B_0 MY - 2\beta\sigma^2 = 0 \tag{12}$$

Equation (12) specifies a cubic function in M and is in general difficult to solve. To simplify further, we can make one of two possible simplifying assumptions:

(i) If there is no penalty cost to a shortfall in money holdings, $\beta = 0$, while if there is no risk of such a shortfall, $\sigma = 0$. For either $\beta = 0$ or $\sigma = 0$, (12) reduces to Baumol's demand function for transactions balances in Chapter 4. This was:

$$M^{tr} = (\tfrac{1}{2}B_0)^{1/2}Y^{1/2}r^{-1/2}$$

However, the simplifying assumption $\beta = 0$ or $\sigma = 0$ eliminates the precautionary demand elements, so that for precautionary demand analysis, we opt for the following simplification.

(ii) Assume that the brokerage cost is zero, so that $B_0 = 0$.[2] Making this assumption,

$$rM^{pr3} - 2\beta\sigma^2 = 0$$

so that:

$$M^{pr} = (2\beta)^{1/3}r^{-1/3}(\sigma^2)^{1/3} \tag{13}$$

The particular insight of (13) is that the precautionary demand for money will depend upon the variance σ^2 of net income, and not necessarily on the level of income itself. By comparison, the transactions demand for money in Baumol's analysis depended upon income or, in the present context, on the expected level of income. In (13), the average level of income/expenditures Y has dropped out of the money demand function because of the elimination of the brokerage cost term $(\tfrac{1}{2}B_0 Y/M)$ in the simplification in going from (12) to (13). This simplification, therefore, drops out of the transactions demand for money, which is related to the level of expenditures, so that (13) should be taken as specifying the precautionary demand – *exclusive* of the transactions one – for money. In keeping with this, the superscript *pr* has been added to the money symbol in (13).

From (13), the interest elasticity of the precautionary demand is $-1/3$, not $-1/2$.

Now assume that the time pattern of receipts and payments during the period does not change but their amounts vary proportionately with the total expenditures Y over the period. In this case, for a normal distribution of net payments, the variance of receipts and payments will increase proportionately with Y^2. Let this be represented by:

$$\sigma^2 = \alpha Y^2 \tag{14}$$

where α is a constant whose value depends on the given time frequency of receipts and payments. From (13) and (14), we get:

$$M^{pr} = (2\alpha\beta)^{1/3}r^{-1/3}Y^{2/3} \tag{15}$$

so that the elasticity of precautionary balances with respect to the amount of income/expenditures will be 2/3.

However, if the amounts of the payments and receipts do not change but their number increases proportionately with Y so that they become more frequent as Y increases, σ^2 will change proportionately with Y, such that $\sigma^2 = \alpha' Y$. The demand for money for this case would be:

$$M^{pr} = (2\alpha'\beta)^{1/3} r^{-1/3} Y^{1/3} \tag{16}$$

so that the income elasticity of precautionary balances is now only 1/3.

Since expenditures can change in the real world in either of the two ways envisaged in (15) and (16) or in other ways, the implied income elasticity of the precautionary money demand lies in the range from 2/3 to 1/3, depending upon how income and expenditures change. Further, note that since the transactions demand was dropped out of the model in simplifying from (12) to (13), (15) and (16) do not provide any information on the transactions demand elasticities, so that these equations only specify the demand for precautionary balances. If we had been able to solve (12) for M, such a solution would have provided a combined money demand for both transactions and precautionary purposes, but there is no guarantee that this solution would have an income elasticity of either 1/2, 1/3 or 2/3. Further, even for the precautionary demand alone, as in (15) and (16), the actual elasticity will not necessarily be 1/3 or 2/3 if the distribution of net payments is not normal or if the time pattern or the amount of individual transactions during the period both change simultaneously.[3] Empirically estimated *real income elasticities* of the demand for real balances of M1 (currency and demand deposits) in the economy tend to be somewhat below unity, but not as low as 1/3. The income elasticity of 1/3 in (16) is, therefore, quite unrealistic, which is not surprising since it excludes the transactions demand and also assumes that the amounts of the individual transactions do not change. However, its *interest elasticity* of $(-1/3)$ is closer to the empirically estimated values than its value of $(-1/2)$ in the transactions model.

To examine the elasticity of the demand for precautionary balances with respect to the price level, first note that β is the nominal penalty cost. Set it equal to $\beta'P$, where β^r is the real penalty cost and P is the price level. Also assume that the increase in the price level increases the magnitudes of all receipts and payments proportionately, while leaving their timing unchanged. Hence, with $Y = Py$, where Py is nominal expenditures and y is its real value, $\sigma^2 = \alpha P^2 y^2$, so that (15) becomes:

$$m^{pr} = M^{pr}/P = (\alpha\beta^r)^{1/3} r^{-1/3} y^{2/3} \tag{17}$$

so that the demand for real precautionary balances is homogeneous of degree zero in the price level. Such homogeneity of degree zero of real balances does not hold in the context of (16) which has a price elasticity of only 2/3 for nominal balances.

6.2 THE PRECAUTIONARY DEMAND FOR MONEY WITH OVERDRAFTS

The preceding model from Whalen assumes that the individual does not have automatic access to overdrafts. This is often not the case for large – and sometimes even for small – firms. It is also not the case for many individuals who have arranged overdraft/credit facilities with their banks or who can resort to credit cards, whose limits can be treated as overdraft limits. The analysis of this case and its variations in the following is from Sprenkle and Miller (S–M) (1980). These authors analyse three cases, with no-limit overdrafts, with overdraft limits and without overdrafts. These cases can apply to firms as well as households. However, S–M consider the no-limit overdraft case to be especially applicable to large firms and the no-overdraft case to be the most pertinent one for households.

S–M assume that the economic agent – which will be taken to be a firm for this case but could instead be a household – has an overdraft from a bank and wants to minimize the cost of holding precautionary balances. If it holds larger balances than needed, it foregoes the interest rate r from investing the funds in bonds; if it holds inadequate precautionary balances, it has to pay the interest rate ρ on overdrafts but earns the rate r on the balances held in bonds, so that the net loss in using overdrafts is only $(\rho - r)$.[4] We will assume that $\rho > r$. The cost C of holding precautionary balances is therefore:

$$C = r \int_{-\infty}^{A} (A - Z)f(Z)dZ + (\rho - r)\int_{A}^{\infty} (Z - A)f(Z)dZ \qquad (18)$$

where:

A   precautionary balances at the beginning of the period
Z   payments less receipts
$f(Z)$ probability distribution of Z, with $f(\infty) = 0$
r interest rate on bonds
ρ interest rate charged on overdrafts

S–M treat Z as a forecast error with $E(Z) = 0$ so that the payments and receipts over the period are equal. Equation (18) involves deciding on the amount A at the beginning of the period to cover the possibility of overdraft charges rather than the periodic withdrawals from bonds in the absence of overdrafts in Baumol's analysis of the transactions demand for money. Minimizing (18) with respect to A yields:

$$dC/dA = r \int_{-\infty}^{A} f(Z)dZ - (\rho - r) \int_{A}^{\infty} f(Z)dZ \qquad (19)$$

Designating $F(Z)$ as the cumulative probability distribution of Z, with $F(\infty) = 1$, (19) becomes:

$$dC/dA = r - \rho[1 - F(A)] = 0 \qquad (20)$$

so that,

$$F(A^*) = (\rho - r)/\rho \qquad (21)$$

where A^* is the optimal value of A and $F(A^*)$ is the cumulative probability that the optimal cash holdings will at least equal the need for cash.

To derive the optimal precautionary holdings, note that the precautionary balances will be zero when actual overdrafts are positive. Therefore, the precautionary balances M^{pr} only equal:

$$M^{pr} = \int_{-\infty}^{A^*} (A^* - Z)f(Z)dZ \qquad (22)$$

Assuming a normal distribution with zero mean,

$$M^{pr} = A^*F(A^*) + \sigma f(A^*) \qquad (23)$$

where σ is the standard deviation of Z. In the case of a normal distribution, the average amount borrowed through overdrafts (O) will be:

$$O = -A^*[1 - F(A^*)] + \sigma f(A^*) \qquad (24)$$

From (21) and (23),

$$\partial M^{pr}/\partial \rho = [\{1 - F(A^*)\}F(A^*)]/\rho f(A^*) > 0 \qquad (25)$$

$$\partial M^{pr}/\partial r = -F(A^*)/\rho f(A^*) < 0 \qquad (26)$$

so that M^{pr} decreases (and overdraft borrowings increase) when the bond rate r increases and the overdraft rate ρ decreases. These are intuitively plausible results since a rise in r and a decrease in ρ increase the opportunity cost of holding precautionary balances.

There is no easy way to derive the interest elasticity of the precautionary money demand for (23) unless the probability distributions $f(A)$ and $F(A)$ are first specified. What is clear from (23) is that this demand depends upon these distributions and therefore upon their moments. Assuming a normal distribution, this demand will depend upon the mean and variance of expenditures, as in section 6.1.

Equation (23) specifies the precautionary demand for money, and does not include the transactions demand. To compare the above analysis with that of Baumol's transactions demand under certainty, now add the assumption of certainty to the present analysis. The assumption for the uncertainty case was that $E(Z) = 0$. In the case of certainty, Z always has a known value. If $Z \le 0$ (that is, receipts exceed payments every time), C in (18) would be zero and so would be the demand for money derived from it. But, if payments exceed receipts at different points during the period so that $Z > 0$, the individual will prefer to start with enough transactions balances in order to avoid using the more costly overdrafts with $\rho > r$. Hence, under certainty, the precautionary demand for money (exclusive of transactions demand) in this analysis will be zero.

6.3 THE PRECAUTIONARY DEMAND FOR MONEY WITHOUT OVERDRAFTS

If the economic agent is not allowed overdrafts, the total cost consists of the interest lost on not holding bonds and the costs of being overdrawn, which is assumed for the time being to be equal to or less than the cost of having to postpone expenditures, so that:

$$C = r \int_{-\infty}^{A} (A - Z)f(Z)dZ + \beta \int_{A}^{\infty} f(Z)dZ \qquad (27)$$

where β is the penalty to being overdrawn and the second integral on the right-hand side is the probability of being overdrawn, so that the second term in (27) is the cost of being overdrawn. Minimizing (27) implies that:

$$F(A^*)/f(A^*) = \beta/r \qquad (28)$$

Since β is the penalty cost of holding inadequate balances, it can be compared with $(\rho - r)$ in the analysis of section 6.2, where ρ was the interest charged by the bank on overdraft balances. In the present analysis, if the banks want to discourage some customers from being overdrawn, they would set ρ and β fairly high, so that, for such customers, the operative value of β would become the penalty cost of finding funds elsewhere or of postponing expenditures.

The response of M1 to the interest rate r, where r is the cost of holding M1, was derived from (28) by S–M as,

$$\partial M1^{pr}/\partial r = \{F(A^*)^2\}/[rf(A^*) - \beta f'(A^*)] < 0 \qquad (29)[5]$$

where f' is the partial derivative of f with respect to A^* and money is M1 (which excludes the assets on which the interest rate r is paid). The above analysis is very similar to that of section 6.2 with the penalty rate β corresponding to the overdraft interest charge ρ.

If money is defined very broadly as M3 to include the closest substitutes for M1, and r_s is the interest rate on such substitutes, the S–M derivation showed that:

$$\partial M3^{pr}/\partial r_s = [F(A^*)\{1 - F(A^*)\}]/[\rho f(A^*) - \beta f'(A^*)] > 0 \qquad (30)$$

The difference in the signs of the partial derivatives in (29) and (30) occurs because r in (29) is the return on the alternative assets to M1 and therefore part of the cost of holding it, while r_s in (30) is the return on one of the (short-term) assets in M3.

The above two cases – with a no-limit overdraft and without an overdraft – illustrate the basic nature of the S–M analysis, so that their analysis of the intermediate case of a binding limit on the overdraft is not presented here. The two analyses imply that, under uncertainty of the timing of receipts and payments, there will be a positive precautionary demand for money. This demand has the general form:

$$M^{pr} = M^{pr}(r, \rho, \beta, f(z)) \tag{31}$$

The elasticity of precautionary balances with respect to the bond rate r is negative. However, it is not possible to derive the interest and income elasticities of M1 and M2 without further specification of the probability distribution of expenditures.[6]

6.4 BUFFER STOCK MODELS

The theoretical analysis of buffer stock models extends the inventory analysis of the trans-actions demand for money to the case of uncertainty of net payments (payments less receipts), as in the case of the precautionary demand models of sections 6.1 to 6.3. However, while this precautionary demand analysis had determined an optimal amount of precautionary balances, the buffer stock models allow short-run money balances to fluctuate within a band which has upper and lower limits, also known as thresholds, or fluctuate around a long-run desired money demand.

There are basically two versions of buffer stock models. In one of these, a 'policy decision' is *a priori* made by the individual that cash balances will be allowed to vary within an upper (M_{max}) and a lower limit (M_{min}). This case is depicted in Figure 6.1. When the autonomous – that is, independent of the decision to invest in bonds or disinvest from bonds – net receipts cause the accumulated cash balance to hit the upper limit (M_{max}), action is taken to invest a certain amount in other assets, say bonds, thereby reducing cash holdings suddenly by the corresponding amount. Whenever the autonomous net payments deplete the cash

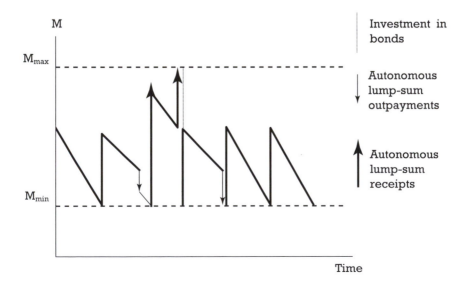

Figure 6.1

reserves sufficiently to reach the minimum permitted level (M_{min}), action is taken to rebuild them by selling some of the bonds. This lower limit can be zero or a positive amount, depending upon the institutional practices such as minimum required balances by banks etc. Such buffer stock models with a pre-set band belong to the (Z, z) – with Z as the upper limit and z as the lower one – type of inventory models and are called '*rule models*' where the rule specifies the adjustment made when the money balances hit either of the limits.

In such rule models, money balances can change because of positive or negative net payments or because of action taken by the agent to reduce them when they reach the upper limit or increase them when they reach the lower limit. The former can be designated as 'autonomous' or 'exogenous' changes and the latter as 'induced' changes in money balances. In the former, the change occurs even though the agent's objective is not to adjust his money holdings. In the latter, the agent's intention is to adjust the money balances since they have moved outside the designated band.

The second type of buffer stock models is '*smoothing or objective models*'. In these, the objective is to smooth movements in other variables such as consumption or expenditures and bond holdings. Unexpected increases in income receipts or decreases in payments would be added to money balances acting as the 'residual' inventory or temporary abode of purchasing power until the adjustments in expenditures and bond holdings can be made. Conversely, unexpected decreases in income receipts or increases in payments would be temporarily accommodated by running down money balances, rather than through an immediate cutback in expenditures or sales of bonds. The reason for thus treating money holdings as a residual repository of purchasing power is that the cost of small and continual adjustments in such balances is assumed to be lower than in either expenditures or payments, or in bond holdings, so that temporarily allowing such balances to change is the optimal strategy. In such smoothing models, actual balances fluctuate around their desired long-run demand, but there are no pre-set upper and lower limits, as in the case of the rule models. This case is illustrated in Figure 6.2. Note that the distinction between the autonomous and induced (causes of) changes in money balances applies in both smoothing and rule models.

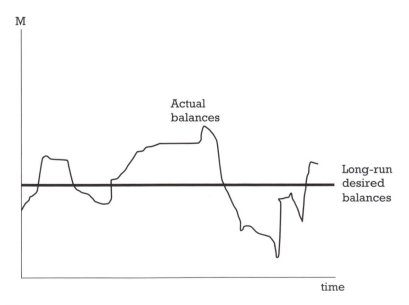

Figure 6.2

There can be quite a number of models of each variety. This chapter examines two models of each of the two versions of the buffer stock models. The models presented for the rule version are those by Akerlof and Milbourne (A–M) (1980) and Miller and Orr (M–O) (1966). The models presented for the smoothing version are Cuthbertson and Taylor (C–T) (1987) and Kanniainen and Tarkka (K–T) (1986).

6.5 BUFFER STOCK RULE MODELS

6.5.1 The rule model of Akerlof and Milbourne

We start the analysis of buffer stock models with the contribution of Akerlof and Milbourne (A–M) (1980). As in Baumol's transactions demand model, Akerlof and Milbourne[7] assume a lump-sum receipt of Y at the beginning of the period and expenditures of C at a constant rate through the period. However, in a departure from Baumol's model, Akerlof and Milbourne assume that $C \leq Y$, with saving $S = Y - C$. Saving during the period is added to money balances until the latter reach the set upper limit, at which time action is taken to decrease them to C through their partial investment in bonds, so that they are expected to be exhausted by the next period.

Designate the upper limit as Z and the lower one as z, with the latter taken to be zero for simplification. The agent wishes to start each period with the amount C. Therefore, the desired amount at the beginning of each period will be C. The actual amounts held at the beginning of the ith period equal $C + iS$, as long as $(C + iS) \leq Z$. If the upper limit is reached after n periods, we have:

$$C + nS \geq Z \geq C + (n-1)S \tag{32}$$

so that:

$$n \geq (Z - C)/S \geq (n - 1) \tag{33}$$

so that the maximum and minimum values of n are:

$$n_{max} = [(Z - C)/S] + 1 \tag{34}$$

$$n_{min} = [(Z - C)/S] \tag{35}$$

The amount C is spent evenly during the period so that the average amount of cash balances corresponding to it is $C/2$. When saving S is added to money balances in a period, this amount is held from the beginning of the period to its end, so that the average cash balances corresponding to it are S. Therefore, the sequence of money balances at the end of each period is:

$$\{C/2, \; C/2 + S, \; C/2 + 2S, \; ..., \; C/2 + (n-1)S\}$$

which equals:

$$(C/2)\{1, \; 1 + S, \; 1 + 2S, \; ..., \; 1 + (n-1)S\} \tag{36}$$

Let n be the number of periods before an induced transfer takes place. Then, over n periods, the average balance *between induced adjustments is*:

$$M^d = \frac{1}{n}\left[\frac{C}{2} + \left(\frac{C}{2} + S\right) + \left(\frac{C}{2} + 2S\right) + \cdots + \left\{\frac{C}{2} + (n-1)S\right\}\right]$$

$$= \frac{C}{2} + \frac{S(n-1)}{2} \tag{37}$$

Using (34) and (35) to eliminate n in (37) implies the minimum and maximum values of money balances as:

$$M_{max} = Z/2 \tag{38}$$

$$M_{min} = (Z - S)/2 \tag{39}$$

Hence, the average of the money balances held as a buffer stock, designated as $\underline{M}^b$, is:

$$\begin{aligned}\underline{M}^b &= (1/2)(M_{max} + M_{min}) \\ &= Z/2 - S/4 \end{aligned} \tag{40}$$

so that:

$$\partial \underline{M}^b/\partial Y \cong -(1/4)(\partial S/\partial Y) < 0 \tag{41}$$

where $\partial S/\partial Y$ is the marginal propensity to save, which is positive, so that $\partial \underline{M}^b/\partial Y$ is *negative*. This is a surprising result. Its intuitive explanation is that as income rises, the upper threshold is reached more quickly, so that the interval before the money holdings are run down by an induced adjustment, is shortened. As a result, the richer agents review their money and bond holdings more often than those with lower incomes, *ceteris paribus*, and will hold less balances on average.[8]

However, since the limits z and Z were assumed to be exogenously specified in the above model, the impact of increases in Y on them is not incorporated in (40). Transactions demand analysis implies that both of these limits would be positive functions of the level of expenditures.[9] Therefore, the impact of a rise in income would have a positive and a negative component, with the net impact of indeterminate sign unless a fuller model were specified. Another limitation of the above model is that it does not distinguish between the expected increases in income and the unexpected ones. The (z, Z) concept is more appropriate to the latter than the former.

Akerlof and Milbourne extend their preceding model to the case of the uncertainty of net payments by assuming that the agent buys and pays for durable goods at uncertain times, with p as the probability of making such a purchase. For this case, the Akerlof and Milbourne result, under their simplifying assumptions including $S = sY$ where s is the constant average propensity to save, is that:

$$\underline{M}^b \approx Z/2 - s(1 + p)(Y/4) < 0 \tag{42}$$

where p is the probability of payments (for a durable goods purchase). Equation (42) implies that:

$$\partial \underline{M}^b/\partial Y = -(s/4)[1 + p + Yp'(Y)] \tag{43}$$

where $p' = \partial p/\partial Y$. Assuming p' to be positive – that is, the probability of buying durable goods increases with income – (43) implies that the income elasticity of money balances is again *negative*.

The Akerlof and Milbourne model is meant to encompass both the transactions and precautionary demands. The agent's desire to finance an amount of transactions C out of income receipts Y creates his transactions demand, while the uncertainty of payments adds an additional precautionary demand. However, this framework does not properly capture the transactions demand since it ignores the dependence of (z, Z) on total expenditures and does not make a distinction between expected and unexpected changes in income. Its implication of a negative income elasticity of money demand must, therefore, be accepted as reflecting the influence of saving, and especially unexpected saving, on money demand, with consumption – and hence permanent income – being held constant. Some of the ideas behind these criticisms will become clearer from the theoretical and empirical models presented below.

6.5.2 The rule model of Miller and Orr

Miller and Orr (M–O) (1966) assume that net receipts – which would be net payments for a negative value – of x at any moment follow a random walk with a zero mean over each period (for example, a 'day').[10] Assume that in any time interval (for example, an 'hour') equalling $1/t$ ($t = 24$), x is generated as a sequence of independent Bernoulli trials. The individual believes with a subjective probability of p that he will have net receipts of x during each time interval (hour) or net payments of x with a probability of $(1 - p)$, so that, over an hour, the probability of an increase in money holdings by x is p and that of a decrease by x is $(1 - p)$.

Cash holdings over a decision period of T periods will have a mean and standard deviation given by:

$$\mu_T = Ttx(p - q) \tag{44}$$

$$\sigma_T^2 = 4Ttpqx^2 \tag{45}$$

where:

x net receipts per hour
μ_T mean cash holdings over T periods
σ_T standard deviation of cash holdings over T periods
p probability of positive net payments
q probability of negative net payments $(= 1 - p)$
t number of sub-intervals (hours) in each period (day)
T number of time periods up to the planning horizon

For simplification, p was assumed by M–O to be $1/2$,[11] so that:

$$\mu_T = 0 \tag{46}$$

$$\sigma_T^2 = Ttx^2 \tag{47}$$

With the variance of changes in cash holdings (σ_T^2) during T periods as Ttx^2, the variance σ^2 of daily changes in balances (over the day) is:

$$\sigma^2 = \sigma_T^2/T = tx^2 \tag{48}$$

The cost of holding and varying cash has two components: the interest cost of holding cash rather than bonds, and the brokerage cost of making deliberate changes in cash holdings. Per period (daily) expected cost is:

$$E(TC) = B_0\,E(N)/T + rM \tag{49}$$

where:

$E(TC)$ expected cost per period of holding and managing cash
M average daily cash balance
$E(N)$ expected number of transactions between money and bonds over T periods

B_0 brokerage cost per transaction
r interest rate per period (day) on bonds

The firm is taken to minimize (49) with respect to the upper limit Z and the lower limit z on cash balances.

M–O show that under certain specific assumptions,

$$E(N)/T \rightarrow 1/D(z, Z)$$

where D is the mean of the time intervals separating portfolio transfers between bonds and cash, and that:

$$D(z, Z) = z(Z - z)/tx^2 \tag{50}$$

Further, M–O show that the steady-state distribution of money balances during the day has a discrete triangular distribution for $p = 1/2$, so that the average balances M are given by:

$$M = (Z + z)/3 \tag{51}$$

Hence, using the maximum value of $E(N)/T$, (51) can be restated as:

$$E(TC) = B_0 tx^2/zw + r(w + 2z)/3 \tag{52}$$

where $w = Z - z$; w is thus the width of the band. Setting the partial derivatives of (52) with respect to z (with w constant) and w (with z constant) equal to zero, yields:

$$\partial E(TC)/\partial z = B_0 tx^2/z^2 w + 2r/3 = 0 \tag{53}$$

$$\partial E(TC)/\partial w = -B_0 tx^2/zw^2 + r/3 = 0 \tag{54}$$

which yield the optimal values z^* and w^* as:

$$z^* = (3B_0 tx^2/4r)^{1/3} \tag{55}$$

$$w^* = 2z^* \tag{56}$$

Since $w = Z - z$, (56) implies that the optimal upper limit Z^* will be:

$$Z^* = 3z^* \tag{57}$$

Equation (57) specified the *relative* width of the band between the upper and lower limits as:

$$(Z - z)/z = 2$$

which is independent of the interest rate and the brokerage cost, though, by (55) to (57), the *absolute* width of the band does depend upon these variables.

From (57), the mean buffer stock balances M^b under the assumptions of this model are given by:

$$M^b = (Z + z)/3 \tag{58}$$

Therefore, the average optimal buffer stock balances M^{b*} derived from (55), (57) and (58) are:

$$M^{b*} = \frac{4}{3}\left(\frac{3B_0 tx^2}{4r}\right)^{1/3} = \frac{4}{3}\left(\frac{3B_0 \sigma^2}{4r}\right)^{1/3} \tag{59}$$

since $\sigma^2 = tx^2$. In (59), the average demand for money depends upon the interest rate and the brokerage cost, as in the certainty version of the transactions demand analysis, and upon the variance of net payments, as in the precautionary demand analysis. The elasticity of the average demand for money with respect to the variance of income is 1/3, and with respect to interest rates is (–1/3), as in Whalen's (1966) analysis.

However, M–O pointed out that, since there does not exist a precise relationship between σ^2 and Y, there will not exist a precise income elasticity of M^b with respect to Y. To illustrate, if we are dealing with a firm's demand for money and Y is its income from sales, a proportionate increase in this income/sales due to a proportionate increase in all receipts and payments by it, with their frequency unchanged, will increase x proportionately, so that $\sigma^2 = tY^2$, implying from (59) an income elasticity of 2/3, as in Whalen. But if the amount of each receipt and payment does not change but their frequency is increased, so that t increases proportionately with Y such that $t = \alpha Y$, we have $\sigma^2 = \alpha Yx^2$, thereby implying from (59) an income elasticity of 1/3, again as in Whalen. The implied range for the income elasticity of the average buffer stock balances becomes even larger than from 1/3 to 2/3 if the amounts of the transactions increase while their frequency decreases.

The M–O model extends the analysis of the precautionary demand for money to the case where there are fluctuations within upper and lower limits, with these limits derived in an optimizing framework. The existence of a range for the income elasticity of the average buffer stock balances rather than a single value as for Baumol's transactions balances is another empirically appealing feature of the M–O model. These authors considered their model to be especially appealing in explaining the firms' demand for money.

6.6 BUFFER STOCK SMOOTHING OR OBJECTIVE MODELS

6.6.1 The smoothing model of Cuthbertson and Taylor

The basic partial adjustment model (PAM) in the context of a single period often assumes that the adjustment in money balances involves two kinds of costs. One of these is the cost of deviations of actual balances from their desired amount. The second element is the cost of changing the current level of balances from their amount in the preceding period. The one-period first-order PAM[12] assumes that the cost function is quadratic in its two elements, as in:

$$TC = a(M_t - M_t^*)^2 + b(M_t - M_t-1)^2 \tag{60}$$

where:

TC present discounted value of the total cost of adjusting balances
M actual money balances
M^* desired money balances

The buffer stock models (Carr and Darby, 1981; Cuthbertson, 1985; Cuthbertson and Taylor, 1987; and others) posit an *intertemporal* cost function rather than a one-period one and minimize the present expected value of this cost over the present and future periods. This implies taking account of both types of costs over the present as well as the future periods. Hence, for the first element of cost, the expected cost of the future deviations of actual from desired balances, in addition to the cost of a current deviation, is taken into account. This modification allows the agent to take account of the future levels of desired balances in determining the present amounts held. For the second element of cost, the justification for the intertemporal extension is as follows: just as last period's money holdings affect the cost of adjusting this period's money balances, so would this period's balances affect the cost of adjusting next period's balances, and so on, and these future costs attached to current money balances need to be taken into consideration in the current period. The resulting cost function is intertemporal and forward-looking.

The intertemporal extension of (60) for $i = 0, 1, \ldots, T$, is:

$$TC = \sum_i D^i \left[a(M_{t+i} - M_{t+i}^*)^2 + b(M_{t+i} - M_{t+i-1})^2 \right] \tag{61}$$

where:

D gross discount rate $(= 1/(1 + r))$
r interest rate

In equation (61), a is the cost of actual balances being different from desired balances and b is the cost of adjusting balances between periods. b can be the brokerage cost of selling bonds but, as we have seen in earlier discussions, can be more than just a monetary cost. The economic agent is assumed to minimize TC with respect to M_{t+i}, $i = 0, 1, \ldots, T$. Its Euler condition for the last period T is:

$$\partial TC/\partial M_{t+T} = 2a(M_{t+T} - M_{t+T}^*) + 2b(M_{t+T} - M_{t+T-1}) = 0$$

so that:

$$M_{t+T} = \frac{a}{a + b} M_{t+T}^* + \frac{b}{a + b} M_{t+T-1} \tag{62}$$

$$= A_1 M_{t+T}^* + B_1 M_{t+T-1}$$

where $A_1/(a + b)$ and $A_1 + B_1 = 1$. For $i < T$, the first-order cost minimizing conditions are:

$$\frac{\partial C}{\partial M_{t+i}} = 2a\left(M_{t+i} - M_{t+i}^*\right) + 2b\left(M_{t+i} - M_{t+i-1}\right) - 2b\left(M_{t+i+1} - M_{t+i}\right) = 0$$

$$M_{t+i} = \frac{a}{a + 2b} M_{t+i}^* + \frac{b}{a + 2b} M_{t+i-1} + \frac{b}{a + 2b} M_{t+i+1} \tag{63}$$

$$= A_2 M_{t+i}^* + B_2 M_{t+i-1} + B_2 M_{t+i+1}$$

where $A_2 + 2B_2 = 1$. In (63), both the future and past values of actual balances M, as well as the future values of M^*, affect the demand for money in each period. Equation (63) implies[13] that:

$$M_t = q_1 M_{t+i-1} + (a/b)q_1 \sum_i q_i^i M_{t+i}^* \tag{64}$$

where $q_1 + q_2 = (a/b) + 2$ and $q_1 q_2 = 1$. We need to specify the demand function for the desired money balances M^*. As derived in Chapters 2 and 3, assume it to be:

$$M_{t+i}^*/p_{t+i} = b_y y_{t+i} + b_r r_{t+i} \tag{65}$$

Further, in the context of uncertainty and using the expectations operator E_{t-1} for expectations held in $t-1$, let:

$$M_t = E_{t-1}M_t + M_t^u + \mu_t \tag{66}$$

where M_t^u has been introduced to take account of errors in the expected value of M^*_{t+i} due to unexpected changes in its determinants in (65). From (64) to (66),

$$M_t = q_1 M_{t-1} + (a/b)q_1 \sum_i q_i^i \{b_y y_{t+i} + b_r r_{t+i}\} p_t + M_t^u + \mu_t \tag{67}$$

In (66), the actual demand for money depends upon the future and current values of income and interest rates, showing the model to be a forward-looking one. It also depends upon the lagged value of money balances, thus incorporating a backward-looking element. The model is, therefore, a forward- *and* backward-looking model. Note that the estimation of (66) will require the prior specification of the mechanism for deriving the expected future values of y and r, and also of the mechanism for the estimation of M^u. The estimation procedures for these are discussed in Chapter 7.

6.6.2 The Kanniainen and Tarkka (1986) smoothing model

An alternative version of the intertemporal adjustment cost function (61), used by Kanniainen and Tarkka (K–T) (1986)[14] was:

$$TC = E_t \sum_i [D^i \{a(M_{t+i} - M^*_{t+i})^2 + b(z_{t+i})^2\}] \quad i = 0, 1, 2, \dots \tag{68}$$

where z_t are the 'induced' changes in money balances brought about by the agent's own actions and b is interpreted as the brokerage cost of converting bonds to money. The other variables are as defined earlier, with M being nominal balances, M^* being the steady-state desired balances, and D being the discount factor. The rationale for this specification of the cost function is that while the induced changes in money holdings impose a brokerage cost, the autonomous changes do not since they result from the actions of others. The adjustment in nominal balances over those in $t-1$ occurs due to autonomous and induced changes in t, so that:

$$M_t - M_{t-1} = z_t + x_t \tag{69}$$

where:

    z_t induced changes in money holdings
    x_t autonomous changes

Substitute (69) in (68) and, to minimize total cost, set the first-order partial derivatives of the resulting equation with respect to m_{t+i}, $i = 0, 1, 2, \dots$, equal to zero. This process yields the Euler equations as:

$$E_t M_{t+i+1} - \beta E_t M_{t+i} + (1+r)E_t M_{t+i-1} = -\alpha E_t M^*_{t+i} + E_{t+i+1} - (1+r)E_t x_{t+i} \tag{70}$$

where:

    α a/Db
    β $(1/D)\{(a/b) + D + 1\}$
    i $= 0, 1, 2, \dots$

Note that (70) represents a large number of equations and shows the extensive information requirements of such models. To determine money demand in period t, the agent must have expectations on next period's autonomous changes in money holdings and next period's $(t + 1)$ optimal money balances, with the latter requiring this information for period $(t + 2)$, and so on. With new information becoming available each period, the model will require recalculation each period.

Equation (70) is a stochastic second-order difference equation in $E_t M_{t+i}$. Its roots are:

$$\lambda_1, \lambda_2 = (1/2)[\beta \pm \{\beta^2 - 4(1 + r)\}^{1/2}]$$

with $\lambda_1 > 0$ being the stable root and $\lambda_2 < 0$ being the unstable one. The latter was ignored by K–T in order to exclude cyclical adjustment. Using the positive root λ_1, the Euler condition becomes,

$$E_t M_{t+1} = \lambda_1 M_t + [\lambda_1 \alpha/(1 + r - \lambda_1)]M_t^* - \sum_i [\lambda_1/(1 + r)]^i [E_t X_{t+i-1} - (1 + r)E_t X_{t+i} \qquad (71)$$

In (71), the impact of the autonomous adjustment x_t on money demand is given by λ_1, the stable root of (70). This impact is the same whether it was anticipated or not.[15] The impact of future autonomous shocks, on which expectations have to be formed, depends upon the rate of time preference. If this rate is high, these expectations will have to be formed for only some periods ahead. Further, changes in these expectations will shift the money demand function.

Substitute (71) into (70) and solve for M_t, noting that $E_t M_t^* = M_t^*$. This yields:

$$M_t = \lambda_1 M_{t-1} + \rho M_t^* + \lambda_1 x_t + z_t \qquad (72)$$

where $\rho = [\lambda_1(a/b)(1 + r)/(1 + r - \lambda_1)]$ and z_t^* represents the weighted sum of the future shocks to net receipts and payments. z_t^* is given by:

$$z_t^* = -(1 - \lambda_1)\sum i\{\lambda_1/(1 + r)\}^i E_t x_{t+j} \qquad (73)$$

The above model can be transformed into real terms by dividing (71) by the current price level p_t. The resulting equation based on (71)[16] is:

$$\ln m_t = a_0 + (1 - \lambda_1) \ln m_t^* + \lambda_1 \ln m_{t-1} + \gamma \ln p_t/p_{t-1} + \lambda_1 x_t/M_{t-1} + z_t/M_{t-1} \qquad (74)$$

where $m_t = M_t/p_t$ and $m_t^* = M_t^*/p_t$.

K–T specified the desired demand m_t^* as a log-linear function of y_t and r_t, such that:

$$m_t^* = \gamma y_t^\theta r_t^{\eta} \qquad (75)$$

The critical autonomous net payments variable x_t was defined as:

$$x_t = \Delta L_t + \Delta L_t^g + B_t \qquad (76)$$

where:

L domestic credit expansion
L^g government net borrowing from abroad
B surplus in the balance of payments on current account

On the future values of x_t, the following extrapolative model was assumed:

$$E_t x_{t+i} = x_t(1 + \theta)^i$$

where θ can be positive or negative or zero. Assuming z_{t+i} to be proportional to x_{t+i} such that $z_{t+i} = -\xi x_{t+i}$, K–T use (74) to specify the estimating equation as:

$$\ln m_t = a_0 + (1 - \lambda_1) \ln m_t^* + \lambda_1 \ln m_{t-1} + \gamma \ln p_t/p_{t-1} + (\lambda_1 - \xi)x_t/M_{t-1} + \mu t \qquad (77)$$

where μ is random noise. Note that the current autonomous injections of money increase current money holdings through the variable x_t.

The differences between (67), which is the estimating equation for Cuthbertson and Taylor, and (77), which is the estimating equation for Kanniainen and Tarkka, arise from their different cost functions. Equation (77) is derived from (68) which assumes that only induced changes in money balances impose adjustment costs, while (67) is derived from (61) which attaches such costs to the total difference between balances in periods $t + i$ and $t + i - 1$ and, as such, requires a wider notion of adjustment costs than merely brokerage ones. Both models are forward- (and backward-) looking models and require specification of the procedures for estimating the future values of the relevant variables. They also require specification of the estimation procedure for net payments and receipts. Part of these net payments and receipts can be anticipated ones and part unanticipated.

The two approaches of Cuthbertson and Taylor and of Kanniainen and Tarkka are similar in many ways. Both are examples of smoothing buffer stock models in which money holdings are free to vary from their desired levels. Such models illustrate some of the most common elements used for the specification of the buffer stock analysis of the demand for money. Their critical feature is that the autonomous injections of money supply in the economy are for some duration passively absorbed by the public in actual money holdings.

To give an indication at this stage of the empirical findings on the critical points in the above analysis, we here briefly mention Kanniainen and Tarkka's empirical results. They estimated their model for five industrialized economies (West Germany, Australia, the USA, Finland and Sweden) for the period 1960–82. The estimated coefficients of their model had the predicted signs and plausible magnitudes. The lagged money variable had a magnitude consistent with other studies. However, as indicated by their estimate of γ, the adjustment of money balances to changes in prices was found to be costly. Their buffer stock equation did better than the standard (non-buffer stock) money demand models: the coefficients of the injection variable x_{t+i} were positive and significant, thus supporting the buffer stock approach. These findings also support the hypothesis that the monetary injections from the different sources are first absorbed in nominal money holdings and then dissipated.

CONCLUSIONS

This chapter has presented three of the basic models of the precautionary demand for money. This demand arises because of the uncertainty of the timing of payments and receipts, so that a major determinant of such demand is the probability distribution of net payments. Whalen's analysis captured this by the variance of the distribution, under the assumptions that the distribution was normal and the individual wanted to keep balances equal to a specified proportion of the variance of the distribution. How much of this proportion is kept by a particular individual will depend upon his degree of risk aversion. This analysis shows that the elasticities of the precautionary demand with respect to interest rates and income are not 1/2, as were the elasticities for transactions demand under certainty of the timing of receipts and payments, but are likely to be lower for the former.

The precautionary demand analysis also brings in the interest rates on standby credit facilities such as overdrafts and trade credit, and the penalties to being caught short of a payments medium, into the determinants of the precautionary demand and through it into those of the total demand for money. Such facilities and penalties differ between households and firms, and between large and small firms. Further, they often also differ by industry, so that we should expect the demand functions for money to differ between sectors and industries.

Is the precautionary demand for money a significant part of the total money balances? The answer to this will depend upon the degree of uncertainty of income and expenditures, and the relative penalty costs of being caught short of funds. Some numerical calculations done by Sprenkle and Miller suggest that the precautionary balances can be about one-third or more of the transactions balances. Further, with the increasing availability of short-term assets which offer a higher return without a significantly higher risk than M1, the speculative demand for M1 would nowadays be insignificant, so that the precautionary demand could be greater than the speculative demand. Consequently, the study of the precautionary demand for money has become more prominent in recent years. On the negative side, the increasing availability of several close substitutes for M1 means that the precautionary needs of the individual could also be met by the holdings of such near-monies, so that the precautionary demand for M1 would also be small.

Since the precautionary demand for money reflects the influence of the uncertainty of incomes and expenditures, fluctuations in this degree of uncertainty over the business cycle would imply fluctuations in the precautionary balances over the cycle. Periods of high employment and low uncertainty of incomes in booms would mean a lower precautionary demand for money, for given income levels, than recessionary periods with greater uncertainty of losing one's job. A higher variance of the rate of inflation would imply a higher variance of net receipts, and therefore a higher precautionary demand for money.

The buffer stock approach constitutes a very significant innovation in money demand modelling and represents an extension of the notions behind the precautionary demand for money. However, the former goes further than the pure precautionary demand motive by recognizing that there are different costs of adjusting various types of flows and stocks, and that, for the individual, adjustment in money balances is often the least-cost immediate option for many types of shocks. The result is that money balances are increased and decreased as a buffer in response to many types of shocks, and are only adjusted to their long-run equilibrium levels as and when it becomes profitable to adjust other stocks and flows. Hence, a distinction has to be drawn not only between short-run desired money balances and long-run ones, but also between the former and the balances actually being held. The difference between these concepts is buffer stock balances. Actual balances will be larger than the short-run desired ones for positive (unanticipated) shocks to the money supply and to income, and smaller for negative shocks in the latter.

The divergence of actual balances from the short-run desired ones and of the latter from the long-run ones provides one explanation for the delayed response of nominal income and interest rates to monetary policy where the latter include unanticipated changes in money supply. Hence, in terms of the implications of the buffer stock models for monetary policy, these models imply that since part of the changes in the money supply are accommodated through passive money holdings, the impact of such changes on the market interest rates is correspondingly smaller and the full impact takes some time to occur. Correspondingly, the full impact of such money supply changes on nominal national income takes several periods and is larger than the short-term effect.

While the rule models with money balances fluctuating in a band with upper and lower limits inaugurated the buffer stock notion through the pioneering contribution of Miller and Orr, empirical work has tended to follow the ideas of the smoothing models. The empirical contributions on the buffer stock models are discussed in Chapter 9.

SUMMARY OF CRITICAL CONCLUSIONS

- Precautionary saving and precautionary money demand are different concepts, so that the latter could be zero even when the former is positive.

- Precautionary money demand arises because of the uncertainty of either income or expenditures.
- The analysis of the precautionary money demand is an extension of the inventory analysis of transactions money demand. The former implies that the demand for money will also depend on the variances of income and expenditures and the availability of overdraft facilities, as well as the penalty cost of a shortfall in money holdings.
- Buffer stock money demand arises because money has a lower cost of adjustment than commodities, or labour and leisure. Money acts as a passive short-term inventory of purchasing power until it is optimal to make adjustments in the latter set of variables.
- Rule models of the buffer stock money demand allow fluctuations in money demand in a range between pre-selected upper and lower limits.
- Smoothing models of the buffer stock money demand imply that actual money holdings will vary around their desired long-run level.
- The precautionary and buffer stock holdings of money depend on the degree of uncertainty of incomes and expenditures of the different types of economic agents in the economy. Such holdings will, therefore, vary with the phase, duration and amplitude of the business cycle. Such balances of the household will vary with the rate of unemployment in the economy.
- The precautionary and buffer stock holdings of money depend on the availability of overdraft facilities to the different types of economic agents in the economy. Such holdings will, therefore, depend on the stage of financial development of the economy.
- The precautionary and buffer stock holdings of money also depend on the availability of other highly liquid assets in the economy. In the presence of these, such holdings could be insignificant.

review and discussion questions

1 'Individuals hold money because of uncertainty over the timing of transactions. Therefore, the theory of the transactions demand for money must take account of this uncertainty.' Discuss this statement.

 How can this uncertainty be incorporated into a model utilizing the inventory analysis of the transactions demand for money? Present a model that does so.

2 What is the buffer stock demand for money and how does it differ from the precautionary money demand? Present at least one model of each that shows such a difference.

3 'Some recent empirical studies seem to show that the money demand function may not be independent of the money supply function.' Report on the methodology and the results of at least one such study.

4 If money demand is dependent on changes in the money supply in the short run, as the buffer stock models show, does the functional form of the money demand function remain the same or change? What are the arguments of the money demand function incorporating a buffer stock component? How would you estimate this function?

5 What is the justification for and what are the arguments against the buffer stock approaches to money demand?

6 To what extent is Baumol's inventory-theoretic approach with its assumption of certainty a satisfactory explanation of money demand?

 How does managing an inventory of money differ from managing inventories of goods? How do such differences affect the speed of adjustment of money demand to expected and unexpected changes in money supply?

7 Present at least one rule model and one smoothing model of the buffer stock demand for money. What are the major differences in their implied money demand functions?

NOTES

1 This assumption is being made to ensure that the maximum value of $p(N > M)$ is less than or equal to one.

2 Note that making the assumption that $B_0 = 0$ in Baumol's model would imply that the transactions demand for money is zero. Hence, this assumption eliminates the analysis of the transactions demand from the present model.

3 Whalen also presents in the appendix to his article two other variations of the model presented above.

4 In the presence of overdrafts, $(\rho - r)$ corresponds to Whalen's penalty cost of being caught short of funds to pay for expenditures.

5 For the derivation of (28) and (29) from (27), see Sprenkle and Miller (1980, p. 417).

6 Sprenkle and Miller use some numerical examples to provide guidance on the money demand given by the above analysis.

7 The model presented below is only the basic one from Akerlof and Milbourne. For its more complex forms and for numerical illustrations, see the original article.

8 This result does not hold if the upper limit X was defined relative to income Y as xY.

9 If we follow the pattern of Baumol's transactions analysis, suitably adapted to the present context, z and Z would be non-linear functions of Y.

10 Under this assumption, the pattern of net payments will possess stationarity and serial independence.

11 In this case, cash holdings follow a random walk without drift.

12 See Chapter 7 for the treatment of one-period partial adjustment models in the context of money demand functions.

13 For the derivation, see Cuthbertson (1985, pp. 137–38) and Cuthbertson and Taylor (1987, pp. 187–88). The following derivation is from Cuthbertson (1985, pp. 137–38). The steps are:

Multiply (63) by $(a + 2b)$ and rearrange to:

$$(a + 2b - bL - bL^{-1})M = aM*$$

where L^{-1} is the forward (as opposed to the lag) operator, so that $L^{-1}M_t = M_{t+1}$. Multiply by L and divide both sides by b. This gives:

$$\left[-L\left(\frac{a + 2b}{b} \right) + L^2 + 1 \right] M = -\frac{a}{b} M^*_{-1}$$

$$\left[-L\left(\frac{a + 2b}{b} \right) + L^2 + 1 \right] = \left(1 - q_1 L\right)\left(1 - q_2 L\right)$$

$$= 1 - \left(q_1 + q_2\right)L + q_1 q_2 L^2$$

where $q_1 + q_2 = (a/b) + 2$ and $q_1 q_2 = 1$. Assume $q_2 > 1$, so that $q_1 < 1$. Hence,

$$(1 - q_1 L)M = (1a/b)(1 - q_2 L)^{-1}M^*_{-1}$$
$$= (-a/b)(1 - q_1^{-1}L)^{-1}M^*_{-1}$$

Using the Taylor expansion, $(1 - \lambda L)^{-1} = -(\lambda L)^{-1} = -(\lambda L)^{-2} - \ldots$, we get:

$$M_t = q_1 M_{t+i-1} + (a/b)q_1 \sum_i q_i^i M_{t+i}^*$$

14   The following exposition is based on Kanniainen and Tarkka (1986) and Mizen (1994, pp. 50–51).

15   This conclusion differs from that of Carr and Darby (1981) and Santomero and Seater (1981).

16   The procedure is: subtracting M_{t-1} from both sides of (72) gives:

$$M_t - M_{t-1} = (1 - \lambda_1)[\rho/(1 - \lambda_1)M_t^* - M_{t-1}] + \lambda_1 x_t + z_t$$

Divide both sides of this equation by M_{t-1} and use the approximation $\ln(1 + n) \cong n$ for small values of n. This gives:

$$\ln M_t = \ln [\rho/(1 - \lambda_1)]^{1-\lambda_1} + (1 - \lambda_1) \ln M_t^* + \lambda_1 M_{t-1} + \lambda_1 x_t/M_{t-1} + z_t/M_{t-1}$$

Now subtract $\ln p_t$ from both sides and also add and subtract the term $\lambda_1 \ln p_{t-1}$. This will give (74) with $a_0 = \ln [\rho/(1 - \lambda_1)]^{1-\lambda_1}$. See K–T for the derivations of these equations and those reported in the text.

REFERENCES

Akerlof, George A., and Ross D. Milbourne. 'The Short-Run Demand for Money'. *Economic Journal*, 90, 1980, pp. 885–900.

Carr, Jack, and Michael R. Darby. 'The Role of Money Supply Shocks in the Short-Run Demand for Money'. *Journal of Monetary Economics*, 8, September 1981, pp. 181–99.

Cuthbertson, Keith. *The Supply and Demand for Money*. Oxford: Basil Blackwell, 1985, pp. 30–32, 35–39, 130–43.

——, and Mark P. Taylor. 'The Demand for Money: A Dynamic Rational Expectations Model'. *Economic Journal* 97, 1987, pp. 65–76.

Darby, Michael R. 'The Allocation of Transitory Income among Consumers' Assets'. *American Economic Review*, 62, December 1972, pp. 928–41.

Kanniainen, Vesa, and Juha Tarkka. 'On the Shock-Absorption View of Money: International Evidence from the 1960's and 1970's'. *Applied Economics*, 18, October 1986, pp. 1085–101.

Milbourne, Ross. 'Disequilibrium Buffer Stock Models: A Survey'. *Journal of Economic Surveys*, 2, 1988, pp. 187–208.

Miller, Merton H., and Daniel Orr. 'A Model of the Demand for Money by Firms'. *Quarterly Journal of Economics*, 80, August 1966, pp. 413–35.

Mizen, Paul. *Buffer Stock Models and the Demand for Money*. London: St Martin's Press, 1994, Chs 1–3.

Santomero, A. M., and J. J. Seater. 'Partial Adjustment in the Demand for Money: Theory and Empirics'. *American Economic Review*, 71, 1981, pp. 566–78.

Sprenkle, C. M., and M. H. Miller. 'The Precautionary Demand for Narrow and Broad Money'. *Economica*, 47, November 1980, pp. 407–21.

Whalen, Edward L. 'A Rationalization of the Precautionary Demand for Cash'. *Quarterly Journal of Economics*, 80, May 1966, pp. 314–24.

chapter seven

THE ESTIMATING FUNCTION FOR THE DEMAND FOR MONEY

A number of issues have to be resolved prior to econometric estimation of the demand for money. Among these are the estimation of expected and permanent income and the treatment of lags in money demand. The important modern concept of the rational expectations is introduced and applied to the measurement of expected income. Adaptive expectations are used for the measurement of permanent income.

A number of econometric problems that usually arise in the estimation of money demand are also introduced in this chapter. Their nature is explained at the conceptual level, leaving their proper treatment to econometrics textbooks.

This is the first of three chapters on the estimation of the demand function for money.

---

key concepts introduced in this chapter

- Permanent income
- Expected income
- Rational expectations
- Adaptive expectations
- Lucas supply rule
- Keynesian supply function
- Partial adjustment model
- Autoregressive distributive lag model
- Stationarity
- Identification
- Serial correlation

Chapter 2 examined the contributions of Keynes and Friedman on money demand, Chapter 3 presented the Walrasian analysis of money demand and Chapters 4, 5 and 6 presented the money demand arising from each of Keynes' motives. However, these theoretical contributions require several issues to be settled before the empirical estimation of money demand can be attempted. This chapter examines these issues,[1] while Chapter 9 will present the findings of the empirical studies in the literature.

Milton Friedman's money demand function presented in Chapter 2 had argued that permanent income is one of the determinants of the demand for money. Other studies assume that the individual's planned money balances are a function of his expected income during the period ahead. While the data on the actual past and present levels of national income is readily available, the data on the expected and permanent income are not observable. This data has to be either generated or proxied in estimating the demand function for money. This chapter considers the two common ways of doing so.

Further, while the theoretical analyses of Chapters 2 to 6 provided the general nature of the demand function for desired balances, there could be significant costs of reaching the desired levels in each period, so that the actual balances held may differ from the desired ones. Since our aim is to explain the actual balances held, this chapter examines some of the reasons for the differences between the desired and actual money holdings, and the procedures for handling the lags which occur in this process.

Furthermore, while the money demand analyses of the preceding chapters established the arguments of the money demand function, they did not specify its specific functional form. There are numerous possible functional forms, with some more convenient than others for estimation. Further, such estimation often raises econometric problems. This chapter introduces the reader to some of the more prominent of the functional forms and the problems encountered in money demand estimation, though at an elementary level, with the proper study of them left to the econometric textbooks.

Section 7.1 starts with the two basic money demand functions which will be used in this chapter. One of these specifies the demand for real balances as a linear function of the permanent income and the interest rate. The other specifies it as a linear function of the expected income and the interest rate. For the latter, section 7.2 presents the rational expectations hypothesis for estimating this expected income. Section 7.3 presents the adaptive expectations procedure for deriving permanent income and section 7.4 lists the regressive and extrapolative ones. Sections 7.5 to 7.8 present the partial adjustment model and the general autoregressive model. Sections 7.9 and 7.10 discuss some of the econometric problems that can arise with the data and the common functional forms for estimating the money demand function. Section 7.11 discusses some of the reasons for the shifts of the money demand function.

7.1 PERMANENT OR EXPECTED INCOME IN THE MONEY DEMAND FUNCTION

The analysis of the demand for money in the preceding chapters implied that this demand depends on an income variable, also called the 'scale variable', and on the rates of return or interest rates on alternative assets. Since these rates of return are closely related to each other – and including several of them in the same regression induces multicollinearity, discussed later in this chapter – estimation usually simplifies the estimating equation to include only one interest rate. With this simplification and using actual/current income as the scale variable, the money demand function is:

$$m_t^d = m^d(y_t, r_t)$$

where:

m_t^d demand for real balances in period t
y_t actual real income in period t
r_t interest rate in period t

The linear or log-linear form of this demand function for real balances is:

$$m_t^d = a_0 + a_y y_t + a_r r_t + \mu_t \quad a_0, a_y > 0, a_r < 0 \tag{1}$$

Permanent income as the scale variable

However, Friedman's (1956) theoretical analysis of the demand for money presented in Chapter 2 had implied that this demand depends upon wealth, rather than current income, and on interest rates. For Friedman's analysis, the general form of the demand function for real balances is:

$$m_t^d = m^d(w_t, r_t)$$

where w_t equals the present discounted value of the current and future income and is the sum of human and non-human wealth. Since reliable data on wealth is lacking, as it almost always is, Friedman replaced it by 'permanent income' – which can be interpreted as the average expected income over the future – by using the relationship:

$$y_t^p = \underline{r} w_t$$

where:

y_t^p (real) permanent income in t

$\underline{r}$ the average interest rate over the future

The simplified linear (or log-linear) form of this demand function for real balances is:

$$m_t^d = a_0 + a_y y_t^p + a_r r_t + \mu_t \quad a_0, a_y > 0, a_r < 0 \tag{2}$$

where μ_t is white noise. Since the data on the observed values of y_t^p also does not normally exist, it has to be constructed in some way or other. Friedman had used the adaptive expectations hypothesis for deriving permanent income, though the REH can be used as an alternative procedure for doing so. We will use adaptive expectations as a means of providing an illustration of this procedure. This is done in section 7.3.

Expected income as the scale variable

Another money demand function that is in common usage replaces current or permanent income by expected income. A demand function with expected income as its scale argument is:

$$m_t^d = a_0 + a_y y_t^e + a_r r_t + \mu_t \quad a_0, a_y > 0, a_r < 0 \tag{3}$$

In (3), at the *beginning* of the period, m_t^d are the planned real balances for the period ahead, y_t^e is the expected income for the period, and r_t is the actual interest rate during the period. While we could also have introduced the interest rate in terms of its expected value, this is rarely done, so that we will continue with (3). While we can use either the REH or adaptive expectations for approximating expected income, the REH is the more appropriate procedure and will be used as a means of illustrating the application of this procedure. This is done in section 7.2.

Note that the three scale variables in (1) to (3) are different, so that their estimation will yield different coefficients. Further, even their stability properties may also differ.

7.2 RATIONAL EXPECTATIONS

7.2.1 The theory of rational expectations

The rational expectations hypothesis (REH) is stated in various forms. One way of stating it is that the individual uses all the available information at *his* disposal in forming his expectations on the future values of a variable. Since individuals often have to – or choose to – operate with very limited information, the relevant information set is sometimes specified to be the profit-maximizing one. In any case, the available information set is assumed to include the knowledge of the *relevant theory*,[2] with the rationally expected value of the variable being its value as predicted by this theory. The REH asserts that the deviations of the actual from the theoretically predicted value will be randomly distributed with a zero mean and be uncorrelated with the available information and with the theoretically predicted value.

Note that the relevant theory will commonly determine the non-random prediction of a variable as a function of the parameters, the past values of the endogenous variables and the past, current and future values of the exogenous variables. Of these, the future values of the exogenous variables will not usually be known to the individual and their rational expectations values will also be needed, so that the relevant theory for them will also have to be specified. In practical terms, the REH can be restated as: the expected values of the endogenous variables will be those predicted by the relevant theory, given the data on the past values of the endogenous variables, those on the past and current values of the relevant exogenous variables and the rationally expected future values of the relevant exogenous variables.

In (3), designate the value of y_t^e predicted by the relevant theory as y_t^T, where the superscript T stands for the relevant theory. Since y_t^T takes account of all the information available to the individual, the REH asserts that the deviation of the actual value y_t from y_t^T will be random with a zero expected value and will be uncorrelated with the available information and, therefore, with y_t^T which is based on that information. The following incorporates the above statements in a set of simple equations to show the various assumptions and steps in deriving the rationally expected value y_t^{e*} of the variable y_t.

Since the rationally expected value y_t^{e*} – with superscript e^* standing for the rationally expected value – is assumed to be determined by the value y_t^T predicted by the relevant theory T, we have,

$$y_t^{e*} = y_t^T \tag{4}$$

Since the REH assumes that the actual value y_t differs from the prediction of the relevant theory T by an error which is random and not correlated with any available information, we have:

$$y_t = y_t^T + \eta_t \tag{5}$$

where:

$$E\eta_t = 0 \tag{6}$$

$$\rho(y_t^T, \eta_t) = 0 \tag{7}$$

y_t	actual income
y_t^e	expected income
y_t^{e*}	rationally expected value of income
y_t^T	expected income predicted by the relevant theory

$E\eta_t$ mathematical expectation of η_t

$\rho(y_t^T, \eta_t)$ correlation coefficient between y_t^T and η_t

Equations (4) and (5) imply that,

$$y_t = y_t^{e*} + \eta_t \tag{8}$$

Taking the mathematical expectation of (8), with $E\eta_t = 0$ from (6), and using (4) gives,

$$Ey_t^{e*} = Ey_t = Ey^T \tag{9}$$

If y_t^{e*} and y^T are assumed to be single valued, as they often are, (9) becomes,

$$y_t^{e*} = Ey_t = y^T \tag{10}$$

so that the rationally expected value y_t^{e*} can be obtained by estimating y_t by a function implied by the theory for its determination, and taking its expected value Ey_t. This procedure is illustrated below and will also be applied in Chapter 15 in a macroeconomics context.

The information requirements and validity of rational expectations

There is considerable dispute in the literature about the information requirements leading to (9) and (10).[3] The information available to any given individual varies considerably, *inter alia*, with his level of education and interest, the openness of the society and the operating technology of information, as well as the losses from basing actions on inadequate, vague and inaccurate information. The actual amount of the information at the disposal of the individual can vary from almost non-existent hard information[4] to extensive one. The REH is meant to apply to all cases, regardless of the availability of the relevant information.

Assessing the validity of the rational expectations hypothesis

Sceptics have argued that the REH requires that the possible future outcomes are well anticipated and that economic agents are assumed to be superior statisticians, capable of analysing the future general equilibrium of the economy (Arrow, 1978). However, the supporters of rational expectations reject such criticism and claim that:

> The implication that economic agents or economists are omniscient cannot fairly be drawn from Muth's profound insights. . . . Rational expectations are profit maximizing expectations. . . . If the past proves to be a very imperfect guide to the future, then theory and practice will be inaccurate. . . .'
>
> (Kantor, 1979, p. 1424)

> It is, however, incorrect to assume that rational expectations regards errors as insignificant or absent. The implication of rational expectations is that the forecast errors are not correlated with anything that could profitably be known when the forecast is made.
>
> (Kantor, 1979, p. 1432)

While this interpretation of rational expectations is correct, the *empirical issue* boils down to a question of the usefulness or profitability of *acting* on one's rational expectations. This usefulness can be extremely limited when – without knowledge of the relevant theory and without good reliable information on the past values of the endogenous and exogenous variables, and on the relevant future values of the exogenous variables – the known paucity of information indicates that the actual error in the rationally expected value of a variable can be large[5] relative to the mean expected value of the variable, so that acting on the basis of the rationally expected value of the variable may turn out not to be a prudent exercise.[6] Conversely, if the information available is quite complete and the subjective probabilities are known to approximate the objective ones, the rational expectations would be an appropriate basis for action.

Two applications of the REH for predicting expected income

Equation (4) can be used to construct the estimate of y_t^{e*}, by using the relevant theory to specify the determination of y_t^T. We illustrate this use of theory by incorporating two alternative theories on the relationship between output and the rate of increase in the money supply. The first one will be the Lucas supply rule and the second will be the Keynesian one.[7]

(i) The REH and the Lucas supply rule for predicting expected income

This rule assumes the macroeconomic IS–LM model, with the labour market being in equilibrium at full employment and with deviations in real national output from its full employment level y^f occurring only due to errors in predicting the actual level of the money supply. One form of the Lucas supply rule[8] is:

$$y_t^T = y_t^f + \gamma(M_t - M_t^e) \tag{11}$$

where:

y_t^f full employment level of output in t

M_t nominal money stock in t

M_t^e expected value of the nominal money stock in t

M_t^{e*} rational expectations of M_t, formed in $t-1$

so that the rational expectation of income, with the Lucas supply rule as the relevant theory for its determination, is:

$$y_t^{e*} = y_t^f + \gamma(M_t - M_t^{e*}) \tag{12}$$

Use of (12) for predicting expected income requires using the relevant theory to determine M_t^{e*}. The relevant theory depends upon the monetary regime being pursued by the monetary authority. In the context of an endogenous money supply, it would depend upon the monetary base, the behaviour of the public in holding currency and of the commercial banks in holding free reserves.[9] In the context of an exogenous money supply, the central bank controls the money supply and can determine the money supply in the economy on the basis of a 'rule' or function. Assume this case and that the central bank's money supply rule M^T is:

$$M_t^T = \Psi_0 + \Psi_1 u_{t-1} + \Psi_2 M_{t-1} \tag{13}$$

where μ_t is the unemployment rate in period t. Designating the random error in M_t as ξ_t, (13) leads to the specification of M_t as:

$$M_t = \Psi_0 + \Psi_1 u_{t-1} + \Psi_2 M_{t-1} + \xi_t \tag{14}$$

Estimating (14) will provide the estimated values of the coefficients Ψ_i, $i = 0, 1, 2$, as $\underline{\Psi}_i$, where the bar under a variable indicates its estimated value. These estimated coefficients can be used to estimate EM_t, which yields the rationally expected value M_t^{e*}, as:

$$M_t^{e*} = EM_t$$
$$= \underline{\Psi}_0 + \underline{\Psi}_1 u_{t-1} + \underline{\Psi}_2 M_{t-1} \tag{15}$$

Equations (12) and (15) imply that:

$$y_t^{e*} = y_t^f + \gamma[M_t - \underline{\Psi}_0 - \underline{\Psi}_1 u_{t-1} - \underline{\Psi}_2 M_{t-1}] \tag{16}$$

Since the REH implies that $y_t^{e*} = Ey_t$, and $y_t = Ey_t + \eta_t$, where η_t is a random term, (16) implies that:

$$y_t = y_t^f + \gamma[M_t - \underline{\Psi}_0 - \underline{\Psi}_1 u_{t-1} - \underline{\Psi}_2 M_{t-1}] + \eta_t \tag{17}$$

Alternatively, since $\underline{\xi}_t = M_t - \underline{\Psi}_0 - \underline{\Psi}_1 u_{t-1} - \underline{\Psi}_2 M_{t-1}$, where $\underline{\xi}_t$ is the estimated value of ξ_t, (17) can be restated as:

$$y_t = y_t^f + \gamma \underline{\xi}_t + \eta_t \tag{17'}$$

Estimates of either (17) or (17′) yield the estimated values $\underline{y}_t^f$, $\underline{\gamma}$ of the coefficients, so that the rationally estimated value y_t^{e*} of y_t^e required for (3) can now be derived as:

$$y_t^{e*} = \underline{y}_t^f + \underline{\gamma} \, \underline{\xi}_t \tag{17''}$$

Estimating the money demand function using the REH and the Lucas supply function

In this illustration of the REH, it was necessary to estimate the money supply function (14) to estimate the expected value of the money supply; then use this value in (17) to estimate the expected value of real output/income, followed by the use of this estimated value of real income in the regression for the money demand function (3). Hence, estimating the money demand function – using the REH and the Lucas supply rule – required estimation of at least three equations in a stepwise procedure. The reliability of its estimates of the money demand coefficients in (3) would, therefore, depend upon the proper specification of the model for y_t^T and of its subsidiary equations such as (13) for the money supply function – as well as of the reliability of the data and the estimating techniques used at the various stages. Clearly, there is considerable scope for possible errors in specification and estimation.

Keynesians believe that one of the sources of errors in the above estimation is the specification of the Lucas supply rule as the relevant theory for the determination of income. They believe that a Keynesian supply function is the appropriate theory. The following presents their approach.

(ii) The REH and the Keynesian supply function for predicting expected income

A Keynesian supply rule,[10] in a format which is really a take-off from the Lucas supply rule, is:

$$y_t^T = y_0 + \beta M_t \tag{18}$$

Equation (18) specifies that the real income/output depends upon the actual money supply, rather than on only the unanticipated change in the money supply. The stochastic form of this relationship is:

$$y_t = y_0 + \beta M_t + \eta_t \tag{19}$$

Equation (19) uses the actual value of M_t, on which data is available, as the regressor and therefore does not require the prior estimation of the coefficients of the money supply function. Consequently, (19) requires the estimation of only one equation rather than of two for estimating the expected value of income under the Lucas supply rule. Assuming the REH, using the estimated values from (19) of y_0 and β provides the rationally expected value y_t^e as:

$$y_t^{e*} = \underline{y}_0 + \underline{\beta} M_t \tag{20}$$

Compare (17″) and (20). Both represent the rationally expected values of income but under different theories as being the 'relevant' one.

Estimating the money demand function using the REH and the Keynesian supply function

Proceeding further with (20), its rationally expected value can now be inserted into the money demand function (3) to estimate the latter. Hence, the use of the Keynesian supply function and the REH required only a two-step procedure for the money demand estimation.

7.2.2 Rational expectations: problems and approximations

While rational expectations require that y_t^e be based on all available information, the information available to the economist is different from that available to the individual. Further, the economist generally deals with aggregates – for example, with aggregate national income – rather than with the income of any given individual, so that what the relevant information set should be is not always clear. Furthermore, there are disputes among economists as to the relevant theory, or at least to the theory held by the public.[11] Even when there is agreement among economists that the IS–LM framework is the relevant theory, there is disagreement on whether the data reflects the equilibrium values only or includes disequilibrium values also.[12] Moreover, economists rarely agree on the values of the coefficients of the model *and* on the *expected* values of the exogenous variables. Even the data on the lagged values of the endogenous variables is usually approximate and is subject to revision, sometimes for several years after the data period. These problems and disputes render rational expectations a blunt procedure at the estimation level – and its applications subject to doubt and disputes.

In view of the absence of direct quantitative data on expected income and problems with applying rational expectations at the empirical level, some researchers choose to proxy y_t^e in various ways. Two examples of this are:

(i) Use the actual income y_t as a proxy for y_t^e since the two differ only by a random term whose expected value is zero under rational expectations.

(ii) Use the autoregressive model:

$$y_t = \delta_0 + \delta_1 y_{t-1} + \delta_2 y_{t-2} + \ldots + \mu_t \tag{21}$$

and then use $y_t^e = E y_t$ and the estimated coefficients of (21) to estimate y_t^e. The justification for this approximation to the rational expectations one is that the past experience of income itself is likely to be the dominant part of the relevant information set of the individual and the public, and the past values of income are likely to be the most important determinant of current income in the relevant model.

While the REH at the conceptual level is very appealing, such approximations in empirical applications do reduce its distinctiveness from the rivals to the REH and are not recommended – unless there is no better choice.

7.3 ADAPTIVE EXPECTATIONS (GEOMETRIC DISTRIBUTED LAG) FOR THE DERIVATION OF PERMANENT INCOME

In order to illustrate the application of adaptive expectations in the money demand estimation, we will use (2) with permanent income as the income variable in the money demand function. The adaptive expectations model assumes that the individual bases his permanent income on his experience of current and past actual income, so that the general function for permanent income y_t^p would be:

$$y_t^p = f(y_t, y_{t-1}, y_{t-2}, \ldots) \tag{22}$$

A simple form of (22) which has proved to be convenient for manipulation and which was used by Friedman for deriving permanent income in his empirical work on consumption and money demand, is the *geometric distributed lag or adaptive expectations function*. It specifies the functional form as:

$$y_t^p = \theta y_t + \theta(1-\theta) y_{t-1} + \theta(1-\theta)^2 y_{t-2} + \ldots \tag{23}$$

where $0 \le \theta \le 1$. Permanent income is thus specified as a weighted average of current and past incomes, with higher weights attached to the more recent incomes. Note that if $\theta = 0.40$, a weight often cited as approximating reality for annual data, the weights decline in the pattern 0.4, 0.24, 0.144, 0.0864, ..., so that income more than four years earlier can be effectively ignored. If actual income becomes constant, permanent income will come to equal this constant level of actual income.

Lag (23) one period and multiply each term in it by $(1-\theta)$. This gives:

$$(1-\theta)y_{t-1}^p = \theta(1-\theta)y_{t-1} + \theta(1-\theta)^2 y_{t-2} + \theta(1-\theta)^3 y_{t-3} + \ldots \tag{24}$$

Subtracting (24) from (23) gives the equation,

$$y_t^p = \theta y_t + (1-\theta)y_{t-1}^p \tag{25}$$

Equation (25) is known as the *Koyck transformation*.

y_t^p from (25) can now be inserted in (2), which was:

$$m_t^d = a_0 + a_y y_t^p + a_r r_t + \mu_t \quad a_0, a_y > 0, a_r < 0 \tag{2}$$

Substituting (25) in (2) gives:

$$m_t^d = a_0 + a_y \theta y_t + a_y(1-\theta)y_{t-1}^p + a_r r_t + \mu_t \tag{26}$$

Lag each term in (2) by one period and multiply it by $(1-\theta)$. This gives:

$$(1-\theta)m_{t-1}^d = (1-\theta)a_0 + a_y(1-\theta)y_{t-1}^p + a_r(1-\theta)r_{t-1} + (1-\theta)\mu_{t-1} \tag{27}$$

Subtracting (27) from (26) to eliminate y^p_{t-1} gives,

$$m^d_t = a_0\theta + a_y\theta y_t + a_r r_t - a_r(1-\theta)r_{t-1} + (1-\theta)m^d_{t-1} + \{\mu_t - (1-\theta)\mu_{t-1}\} \tag{28}$$

where $a_y, a_r > 0$, and $0 \le \theta \le 1$. The objective in carrying out the above steps was to eliminate the variable y^p on which data is not available. Equation (28) achieves this.

The estimating form of (28) is:

$$m^d_t = \alpha_0 + \alpha_1 y_t + \alpha_2 r_t + \alpha_3 r_{t-1} + \alpha_4 m^d_{t-1} + \eta_t \tag{29}$$

where:

$$
\begin{aligned}
\alpha_0 &= a_0\theta \\
\alpha_1 &= a_y\theta \\
\alpha_2 &= a_r \\
\alpha_3 &= -a_r(1-\theta) \\
\alpha_4 &= (1-\theta) \\
\eta_t &= \{\mu_t - (1-\theta)\mu_{t-1}\}
\end{aligned}
$$

Note that (29) involves lagged terms in m and in r, but not in y. Further, the disturbance term in (29) is $\{\mu_t + (1-\theta)\mu_{t-1}\}$, which is a *moving average error*.

Assessing the validity of the adaptive expectations procedure

Comparing the rational and the adaptive expectations procedures for estimating the money demand function, the former requires the estimation of at least two (possibly, three, as in our illustration above) equations for the Lucas supply rule. However, it has the advantage that it allows better identification of the sources of shifts. Conversely, the adaptive expectations procedure has the disadvantage that if the parameters of the estimated money demand function shift, it is not clear whether the parameters of the money demand function or of the expected income equation had shifted. Further, in cases of monotonic increasing or decreasing income paths, adaptive expectations induce persistent and increasing errors in expected income relative to the actual one, so that the rational individuals will revise their procedure for forming expectations away from adaptive expectations. They also fail to take account of any information available to the individual about future changes in income, and are said to be (only) backward looking.

However, note that adaptive expectations, in spite of its name, really provides an average measure of income – rather than the expected value of current income – through its geometric distributed lag procedure. If the non-stochastic component of income is fluctuating and the appropriate scale variable is permanent or *average* expected income y^p_t, the geometric distributed lag would be a better representation of this average than the rationally expected value of current income y^{e*}_t.[13]

Adaptive expectations as the error learning model

The adaptive expectations procedure in the form given by (25) can also be stated in a form known as the *error learning model*. This form is:

$$(y^p_t - y^p_{t-1}) = \theta(y_t - y^p_{t-1}) \tag{30}$$

which specifies the *revision in permanent income* on the basis of the experienced difference or 'learned error' between the actual income in t and the permanent income for period $(t-1)$. From (25), if $\theta = 1$, permanent income remains unchanged relative to current income, and if $\theta = 0$, the estimate of permanent income is never revised on the basis of the experience of current income.

7.4 REGRESSIVE AND EXTRAPOLATIVE EXPECTATIONS

An alternative to adaptive expectations is the *regressive expectations* model. This specifies that:

$$y_t^e = y_{t-1} + \delta(y_{LR} - y_{t-1}) \tag{31}$$

where y_{LR} is the long-run level of income. Here, the expectation is that income will tend towards its long-run value.[14]

Another model of expectations is the *extrapolative expectations* one. It is that:

$$y_t^e - y_{t-1} = \delta(y_{t-1} - y_{t-2}) \tag{32}$$

This model assumes that income is expected to change as a proportion of the change in income in the preceding period. That is, recent *changes* – or the factors producing those changes – are expected to determine the pattern of future changes.

Whether the adaptive, regressive, extrapolative or rational expectations procedures are more appropriate, depends upon how the individual forms his expectations. The adaptive expectations model seems to be the most common one for modelling permanent income while the rational expectations procedure is the most common one for modelling expected income.

7.5 LAGS IN ADJUSTMENT AND THE COSTS OF CHANGING MONEY BALANCES

The first-order partial adjustment model

Lags often occur in the adjustment of a variable to its desired long-run value. One reason for such a lag can be the short-run cost of making changes in it. To investigate the relationship between such costs and the adjustment lag in money balances, let the individual's desired money balances be m_t^* and assume that the individual faces various types of costs of adjusting instantaneously to m_t^*. Examples of such costs are:

(i) the cost of being below or above m_t^*: for example, having inadequate balances can prevent carrying out purchases which require immediate payments in money; and
(ii) the cost to changing actual balances from m_{t-1} to m_t.

These costs can take various forms. A simple example of these is one where (i) has the proportional quadratic form $a(m_t - m_t^*)^2$ and (ii) has the proportional quadratic form $b(m_t - m_{t-1})^2$. Assuming these to be so, the total adjustment cost c of reaching desired balances in period t is given by:

$$c_t = a(m_t - m_t^*)^2 + b(m_t - m_{t-1})^2 \quad a, b > 0 \tag{33}$$

The individual is taken to minimize this cost. The first-order maximization condition is that:

$$\partial c_t / \partial m_t = 2a(m_t - m_t^*) + 2b(m_t - m_{t-1}) = 0 \tag{34}$$

which yields the actual balances m_t as:

$$m_t = \gamma m_t^* + (1 - \gamma)m_{t-1} \tag{35}$$

where $\gamma = a/(a + b)$. Equation (35) can be restated in a more intuitive form as:

$$m_t - m_{t-1} = \gamma(m_t^* - m_{t-1}) \tag{36}$$

Equations (35) and (36) constitute the *first-order partial adjustment model (PAM)*: the adjustment of money balances in period t is partial, linear and involves a one-period lag. This model suffers from the problem that if m_t^* has a positive or negative trend, the divergence of actual balances from the desired ones would increase over time. The individuals would find it profitable to avoid this by abandoning the first-order PAM and using some other adjustment mechanism.[15] Therefore, the first-order PAM is inappropriate where the desired or actual balances have a strong trend component.[16] A higher-level PAM would be more appropriate in such a case.[17]

The second-order partial adjustment model

Higher-order partial adjustment models result from more complicated specifications of the adjustment costs. The *second-order partial adjustment model* is given by the adjustment cost function:

$$c_t = a(m_t - m_t^*)^2 + b(m_t - m_{t-1})^2 + k(\Delta m_t - \Delta m_{t-1})^2 \quad a, b, k > 0 \tag{37}$$

$$= a(m_t - m_t^*)^2 + b(m_t - m_{t-1})^2 + k(m_t - 2m_{t-1} + m_{t-2})^2 \tag{38}$$

where $\Delta m_t = m_t - m_{t-1}$, and $k(\Delta m_t - \Delta m_{t-1})^2$ is additional to the adjustment costs (i) and (ii) and represents the cost of continual adjustments over time in balances. Minimizing (38) – that is, setting the partial derivative of c with respect to m equal to zero – and solving implies that:

$$m_t = \gamma_1 m_t^* + \gamma_2 m_{t-1} + (1 - \gamma_1 - \gamma_2) m_{t-2} \tag{39}$$

where:

$$\gamma_1 = a/(a + b + k)$$
$$\gamma_2 = (b + 2k)/(a + b + k)$$

Equation (39) is the second-order partial adjustment model and involves a two-period lag.

The error feedback model

A further elaboration of these models is obtained if, in addition to the earlier types of costs, the costs of continual adjustment were less when the actual changes Δm_t were in the same direction as the desired changes Δm_t^*. A specification of such a cost function would be:

$$c_t = a(m_t - m_t^*)^2 + b(m_t - m_{t-1})^2 - k \Delta m_t^*(m_t - m_{t-1}) \quad a, b, k > 0 \tag{40}$$

In this case, the demand for actual balances would be:

$$m_t = m_{t-1} + \gamma_1(m_t^* - m_{t-1}) + \gamma_2(m_t^* - m_{t-1}^*) \tag{41}$$

where $\gamma_1 = [a/(a + b)]$ and $\gamma_2 = [k/2(a + b)]$. Equation 41 is another form of PAM and is called the *error feedback model*.

Assessing the validity of partial adjustment models

The various types of the adjustment cost functions depend upon the notion that it is costly for the individual to change money balances. Note that these costs will differ for the different definitions of money. In practice, in the modern financially developed economies, the costs of converting to M1 from savings deposits and other near-money assets are virtually zero, so that there should not be any significant adjustment lags at the level of the individual. The costs for changing M2 can be similarly very small and seem to be of little consequence at the individual's level. This is especially so when such costs are compared with those of changing the individual's stock of commodities or labour supplied.[18] The costs of adjustment for monetary aggregates usually become significant only when such adjustment involves countervailing changes in non-financial variables or in illiquid financial assets. But this happens only for very broad definitions of money and not for M1 and M2, so that the practice of using PAM models for these definitions is of questionable value.

7.6 MONEY DEMAND WITH THE FIRST-ORDER PAM

If there exist adjustment costs in changing money holdings, these costs should properly be incorporated into the structure of the individual's decision processes and the demand for money holdings be derived after such incorporation. However, this can prove to be analytically intractable, so that the usual procedure is to derive the demand function separately from the adjustment function, and then combine them. This is the procedure followed here.

Assume that the individual has the demand function,

$$m_t^* = a_0 + a_y y_t + a_r r_t + \mu_t \quad a_0, a_y > 0, a_r < 0 \tag{42}$$

Note that (42) differs from (2) and (3) in that money demand now depends upon actual income rather than on permanent or expected income and m_t^* are the desired balances in the absence of adjustment costs.

Further, assume the first-order PAM (36), which was:

$$m_t - m_{t-1} = \gamma(m_t^* - m_{t-1}) \tag{36}$$

Substituting (36) into (42) to eliminate m_t^* gives:

$$m_t = a_0\gamma + a_y\gamma y_t + a_r\gamma r_t + (1-\gamma)m_{t-1} + \gamma\mu_t \tag{43}$$

where $a_0, a_y > 0$, $a_r < 0$ and $0 \le \gamma \le 1$. The estimating form of (43) is:

$$m_t^d = \beta_0 + \beta_1 y_t + \beta_2 r_t + \beta_3 m_{t-1} + \mu_t \tag{44}$$

where $\beta_0 = a_0\gamma$, $\beta_1 = a_y\gamma$, $\beta_2 = a_r\gamma$ and $\beta_3 = (1-\gamma)$.

The estimating equations (29) and (44) should be compared to see the effects of adaptive expectations versus those of the first-order PAM on the estimated money demand equation. Each introduces the lagged money balances m_{t-1} into this equation, but adaptive expectations also introduce the lagged interest rate r_{t-1}. The disturbance terms also have different properties.

7.7 MONEY DEMAND WITH THE FIRST-ORDER PAM AND ADAPTIVE EXPECTATIONS OF PERMANENT INCOME

Assume that our model now consists of:

$$m_t^* = a_0 + a_y y_t^p + a_r r_t + \mu_t \quad a_0, a_y > 0, a_r < 0 \tag{2}$$

$$y_t^p = \theta y_t + (1-\theta)y_{t-1}^p \tag{25}$$

$$m_t = \gamma m_t^* + (1-\gamma)m_{t-1} \tag{36}$$

where (36) can be restated as:

$$m_t^* = (1/\gamma)m_t - \{(1 - \gamma/\gamma\} m_{t-1} \tag{45}$$

This model implies the estimating equation:[19]

$$m_t = a_0\gamma + a_y\theta\gamma y_t + a_r\gamma r_t - a_r\gamma(1-\theta)r_{t-1} + (2-\gamma-\theta)m_{t-1}$$
$$- (1-\theta)(1-\gamma)m_{t-2} + \gamma\{\mu_t - (1-\theta)\mu_{t-1}\} \tag{46}$$

where $a_0, a_y > 0$, $a_r < 0$ and $0 \le \gamma, \theta \le 1$. The estimating form of (46) is:

$$m_t^d = \alpha_0 + \alpha_1 y_t + \alpha_2 r_t + \alpha_3 r_{t-1} + \alpha_4 m_{t-1} + \alpha_5 m_{t-2} + \eta_t \tag{47}$$

where:

$$\alpha_0 = a_0\theta\gamma$$
$$\alpha_1 = a_y\theta\gamma$$
$$\alpha_2 = a_r\gamma$$
$$\alpha_3 = -a_r\gamma(1-\theta)$$
$$\alpha_4 = (2-\gamma-\theta)$$
$$\alpha_5 = -(1-\theta)(1-\gamma)$$
$$\eta_t = \gamma\{\mu_t - (1-\theta)\mu_{t-1}\}$$

Equation (46) provides a more general estimating equation than either the PAM model or the adaptive expectations one. Therefore, these models are nested in (46), with the PAM one alone obtained when $\theta = 1$ and the adaptive expectations obtained when $\gamma = 1$. Hence, (46) provides a way of testing whether there exist both or either of these processes, and is preferable to using either (29) or (44) as the estimating equation unless it is known *a priori* that one or both of these processes is not applicable to the data. However, (46) is not necessarily preferable to the alternative estimation procedure using the PAM and rational expectations to estimate expected income.

The structural coefficients in (46) are: $a_0, a_y, a_r, \gamma, \theta$. The coefficients in the estimating equation (47) are: $\alpha_0, ..., \alpha_5$. Hence, there are only five structural coefficients compared with six coefficients in the estimated equation, so that appropriate non-linear restrictions have to be imposed on the α_i in the estimating equation (47).

The earlier criticisms of adaptive expectations from the rational expectations perspective also apply here. To reiterate, the criticism is that adaptive expectations are backward looking and ignore information that may be available to the individual about the future as well as on other variables. Further, if the expectations parameter θ shifts, the estimating equation (47) would shift, without it being transparent whether the shift is due to a shift in γ, in θ, or in the coefficients of the demand function. By comparison, using the rational expectations procedures to estimate y_t^e in the first step and then estimating the demand function with PAM, will more clearly disclose the source of the instability.

7.8 THE GENERAL AUTOREGRESSIVE DISTRIBUTED LAG MODEL

The general *autoregressive distributed lag (ADL) model* of money demand is:

$$m_t = a_0 y_t + a_1 y_{t-1} + a_2 y_{t-2} + ... + b_1 m_{t-1} + b_2 m_{t-2} + ... \tag{48}$$

where y_{t-i} can be specified as $L^i y_{t-i}$, with L^i as the lag operator which can be treated as a variable subject to mathematical manipulation in the following manner:

$$
\begin{aligned}
a_0 y_t + a_1 y_{t-1} + a_2 y_{t-2} + \ldots &= a_0 y_t + a_1 L y_t + a_2 L^2 y_t + \ldots \\
&= y_t (a_0 + a_1 L + a_2 L^2 + \ldots) \\
&= a(L) y_t
\end{aligned}
\tag{49}
$$

where $a(L)$ is the polynomial $(a_0 + a_1 L + a_2 L^2 + \ldots)$ in L. Hence, (48) can be rewritten as:

$$
m_t = a(L) y_t + b(L) m_t
\tag{50}
$$

where:

$$
\begin{aligned}
a(L) &= a_0 + a_1 L + a_2 L^2 + \ldots \\
b(L) &= b_1 L + b_2 L^2 + \ldots
\end{aligned}
$$

Therefore,

$$
\begin{aligned}
m_t - b(L) m_t &= a(L) y_t \\
m_t &= [\{1 - b(L)\}^{-1} \cdot a(L)] y_t
\end{aligned}
\tag{51}
$$

so that m_t is a function solely of y_t and its lagged terms. Equation (51) is the compact form of the ADL lag model.

As an illustration, consider the simplest example of (51) where $a(L) = a_0$ and $b(L) = b_1 L$. That is, (48) is simply:

$$
m_t = a_0 y_t + b_1 m_{t-1}
\tag{52}
$$

In this case, (48) simplifies to:

$$
m_t = \{1 - b_1 L\}^{-1} \cdot a_0 y_t
\tag{53}
$$

Expand $\{1 - b_1 L\}^{-1}$ in a *Taylor's series* around $E(b_1 L) = 0$ where $E(b_1 L)$ is the mean value of $b_1 L$. This gives:

$$
\{1 - b_1 L\}^{-1} = \{1 + b_1 L + b_2 L + \ldots\}
$$

Hence, (53) becomes,

$$
\begin{aligned}
m_t &= \{1 + b_1 L + b_2 L^2 + \ldots\} a_0 y_t \tag{54} \\
&= a_0 y_t + a_0 b_1 y_{t-1} + a_0 b_1 y_{t-2} + \ldots \tag{55}
\end{aligned}
$$

While both (52) and (55) are identical, the money demand function in the form of (55) does not contain the lagged value of the endogenous variable, although we started with equation (52) where it does so. Conversely, we could have started with (55) without the lagged money term and derived (52) as equivalent to it. Hence, a comparison of (52) and (55) – and of (51) with (48) for the general case – leads to the caution that it may not be possible to distinguish between a money demand equation which contains the lagged values of the endogenous variable and other independent variables, and one which contains only the current and lagged values of the independent variables.

The general ADL model with the suitable addition of disturbance terms is now in common usage in monetary analysis, and falls in the category of vector autoregression (VAR) models.[20]

7.9 *CAVEAT EMPTOR*: AN INTRODUCTION TO COMMON ECONOMETRIC LAPSES IN THE ESTIMATION OF MONEY DEMAND

This section is intended to show that the estimation of the money demand function is not a simple and straightforward matter, and that an application of the one-stage least squares regression technique to its estimation need not provide reliable estimates. This section is not meant to provide an in-depth or rigorous treatment of the econometric problems discussed, and also does not provide econometric solutions to them. The appropriate treatment of these problems and econometric methods is a broad topic, requires tools outside the scope of this book, and is left to econometrics textbooks.

Any empirical work on money demand needs to start with the implications of the theory for it. We, therefore, start with a brief review of the money demand function derived in Chapters 2 to 6, even though this does involve some repetition of material presented earlier.

7.9.1 Review of the implications of theory for the money demand function

The money demand function derived in Chapter 4 had established that an individual's *transactions demand for money balances* depends upon the return on other financial assets and on his current expenditures. The assets that the individual is most likely to consider for this role are those which can be liquidated or exchanged into money at short notice without significant loss. Such near-money assets are composed of various types of time deposits in banks, in near-banks and various types of short-term bonds such as Treasury bills.

The *portfolio approach* of Chapter 5 to the demand for assets established that these demands depend upon the rates of return on these assets and on the individual's total wealth to be allocated among these assets. In a wider context, these demands must depend upon the return to physical and human capital, since these are alternative forms of holding wealth. However, note that the demand for money in portfolio selection theory was the demand for money as a riskless asset. But, as noted in Chapter 5, for well-developed financial markets, money is relatively inefficient compared with some riskless near-money assets as a form of transferring wealth from the present to the future since these assets, as in the case of time deposits, yield a positive return and are also riskless.

If we assume that the *precautionary demand for money balances*, like the transactions demand, is related to the individual's expenditures rather than his wealth, or that the precautionary balances are held in near-money assets rather than in money, as is likely, the individual's demand for money balances depends upon the rates of return on other, mainly near-money, assets and upon his expenditures. This demand is in real terms. It does not, in a comparative statics framework, depend upon the rate of inflation; but since the real world is not a comparative statics one, the demand for money, from an empirical viewpoint, would also depend upon the rate of inflation.

The *partial equilibrium study* of the demand for money would only estimate the demand function for money and formulate this function as:

$$M^d/P = m^d = m(r_1, \ldots, r_m, \pi^e, y, w) \tag{56}$$

where:

- M nominal balances
- m real money balances
- P price level
- π^e expected rate of inflation
- r_i rate of return on ith near-money asset, $i = 1, \ldots, m$
- y real income/expenditures
- w real wealth

Equation (56) is similar to Friedman's money demand function presented in Chapter 2, though with the income variable specified as current income rather than permanent income. The following subsections consider some of the econometric issues which arise in the estimation of such a money demand function. Section 7.10 will consider some of the specific simple functional forms of this function.

7.9.2 Single equation versus simultaneous equations estimation

From a *general equilibrium* viewpoint, the rate of return on each of the near-money assets is influenced by the demand and supply of money and by the demands and supplies of risky assets as well. A general empirical study of the demand for money would then simultaneously estimate the demand and supply functions for all the financial assets, where the demand function for the ith asset is,

$$x_i = x_i(r_1, \ldots, r_m, r_{m+1}, \ldots, r_n, \pi, y, w) \tag{57}$$

where:

x_i real quantity of the ith monetary asset, $i = 1, \ldots, m$
r_j rate of return on the jth non-monetary asset, $j = m + 1, \ldots, n$

Note that from a rigorous general equilibrium viewpoint, each asset should be homogeneous. Thus, for example, even currency and demand deposits should be treated as separate assets rather than summed into M1.

A general equilibrium study, however, becomes an extremely large enterprise and poses its own econometric problems. Most studies of the demand for money have been partial and, for statistical and other reasons, have used various degrees of aggregation in defining money. They also often confine the explanatory variables to one rate of interest and either income or expenditures or wealth. However, whether one is estimating the demand functions for several assets simultaneously or not, it is important to consider the cross-equation restrictions that the relevant theory might imply for them. We illustrate these in the following for the case of the allocation of a portfolio between money and bonds, as analysed in Chapter 5 on the speculative demand for money.

7.9.3 Estimation restrictions on the portfolio demand functions for money and bonds

Chapter 5 had implied that the general form of the speculative demand functions for assets is:

$$x_i^d = x_i^d(\underline{\mu}, \underline{\sigma}, \underline{\rho}, W) \quad i = 1, \ldots, n - 1 \tag{58}$$

where μ, σ and ρ are respectively the vectors of the mean returns, the standard deviations and the correlation coefficients among the values of the assets. Equation (58) and the portfolio budget constraint imply that,

$$x_n = W - \sum_i x_i^d(\underline{\mu}, \underline{\sigma}, \underline{\rho}, W) \quad i = 1, \ldots, n - 1 \tag{59}$$

so that the demand function for one of the assets must be derived as a residual from the estimated demand function of the other assets. Alternatively, if the demand functions for all the assets are being estimated, the appropriate cross-equation restriction must be imposed on the estimating equations. As an illustration of this, the restrictions imposed by (59) for the two-asset case of money (M) and the composite bond (B) are set out below.

Suppose the estimating equations for M and B are linear and are specified as:

$$M = a_0 + a_1 r_m + a_2 r_b + a_3 W \tag{60}$$

$$B = b_0 + b_1 r_m + b_2 r_b + b_3 W \tag{61}$$

The budget constraint on M and B is:

$$M + B = W \tag{62}$$

Substituting (60) and (61) into (62) yields,

$$(a_0 + b_0) + (a_1 + b_1)r_m + (a_2 + b_2)r_b + (a_3 + b_3 - 1)W = 0 \tag{63}$$

To satisfy (63) for all possible values of the variables, we must have,

$$a_3 + b_3 = 1 \tag{64}$$

$$a_i + b_i = 0 \quad a_i = 0, 1, 2 \tag{65}$$

Failure to impose these restrictions on the estimated coefficients in simultaneous estimation of both demand functions will generally yield the estimated values of the coefficients that are not consistent with the budget constraint and, therefore, are not valid. In cases where a single demand function, say for money, is estimated, and its estimated coefficients seem to be quite plausible, the *implied* values of the coefficients for the bond equation may not prove to be accurate or even plausible. For example, if the estimated elasticity of the demand for money is much larger than one, this would in turn imply that the elasticity of the demand for all other financial assets is correspondingly less than one, which may not be plausible for the economy and the period in question, thereby leading to a rejection of the estimated money demand function. Therefore, if it is feasible, it would be better to estimate *simultaneously* the complete system of demand equations and impose the appropriate restrictions on the coefficients. However, this is not always feasible and often exceeds the researcher's interests, so that most studies tend to confine themselves to estimation of only the money demand function.

7.9.4 The potential volatility of the money demand function

Note that the coefficients a_i, $i = 0, 1, 2, 3$, in the money demand function (60) depend upon the means, the standard deviations, and the correlation coefficients of the expected terminal values of the assets, for all of which the subjectively – not objectively – expected future and not the past actual values are the relevant ones. If these characteristics of assets change, the implied coefficients will change and the demand functions will shift. In the real world, the subjective expectations on the returns and future values of the financial assets continuously shift for a variety of reasons, so that the subjectively-based characteristics of assets are constantly changing. In fact, Keynes (1936, Ch. 13) had argued that the expectations of asset returns and hence of these characteristics, are very volatile. This argument implies that the demand functions for money and other financial assets would be constantly shifting, so that they could not be properly estimated, or, if estimated, would be worthless – unless the nature of the shift could be specified and the adjustments made for it.

Further, adapting the Lucas critique[21] of estimated functions used for policy purposes, if a change in policy – for example, in the monetary regime, tax laws, banking and financial regulations, relevant political stance, etc. – shifts the characteristics of the returns to the assets, the demand functions would shift and the prior estimated forms would no longer be valid. Hence, specific forms of the demand functions will not hold across policy regimes.

These arguments caution that, since the money demand and supply functions, as well as other relevant policy functions, are constantly changing and definitely do so over decades, the validity of using data over long periods of time to estimate a demand function with constant coefficients should be extremely suspect. This is especially so in a period of financial innovation which keeps changing the characteristics of the existing assets and over time keeps adding newer ones in the market place.

7.9.5 Stationarity

Regression analysis used for deriving the money demand function assumes that the variables are *stationary*. However, many of the variables, such as income and the money stock, tend to have a trend term, so that the typical variables in the money demand function are not stationary. This can cause biased regression estimates of the coefficients of the independent variables. Detrending the data prior to its use in the regression analysis can introduce its own statistical problems, so that *cointegration analysis*, which does not involve prior detrending, is preferable.

7.9.6 The identification problem

Estimation of the demand function for money under any of its definitions also raises the *identification problem*, illustrated through Figures 7.1a to 7.1c. These figures display the relationship between the rates of return (or the prices of the assets) and the corresponding quantities bought/sold. D_1, D_2, ... represent the shifts in the demand curves, and S_1, S_2, ... represent the shifts in the supply curves; while the observed points are the intersection points relating the rates of return r to the equilibrium quantity Q which is demanded/supplied. The equilibrium points trace out the demand curve in Figure 7.1a and the supply curve in Figure 7.1b. But the equilibrium points in Figure 7.1c do not lie either on a single demand curve or on a single supply curve, so that if we were to connect them, we would not get either the demand curve or the supply curve. Most real-world situations are as depicted in Figure 7.1c with both the demand and supply curves shifting over time due to random changes. In such a context, a regression of the quantity bought/sold against the observed rate of return gives a biased estimate of the relationship between the quantity demanded and the rate of return. Hence, the researcher should ensure prior to estimation that the demand function will be identified.

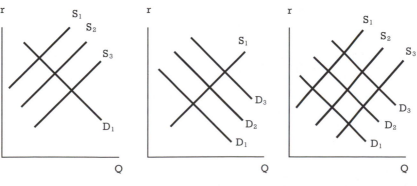

Figure 7.1a   *Figure 7.1b*   *Figure 7.1c*

7.9.7 Multicollinearity

Another statistical problem encountered in partial studies is the *multicollinearity problem*. Suppose that the demand for money is related to both income and wealth but that income and wealth are themselves highly correlated. The estimate of the relationship between money balances demanded and income is then influenced by the relationship between income and wealth and vice versa, so that the estimated relationship may not be an accurate measure of its actual value.

Similarly, the various rates of return are highly correlated, so that the estimates of the coefficients of the rates of return in the money demand function in the economy also tend to be biased and must be treated with caution.

If there is fairly close correlation among a set of variables, one solution to the multicollinearity problem is to use only one of the variables in the set and interpret its estimated coefficient as representing the collective effect of all the variables in the set. For instance, given the close correlation among the interest rates, most money demand functions include among the independent variables only one interest rate in order to avoid multicollinearity. This is usually a short-term rate, such as the Treasury bill rate. However, some studies include both a short-term and a long-term interest rate. As between current income and permanent income, while some studies include only current income, others include permanent income, with multicollinearity between these two variables preventing the simultaneous inclusion of both of them.

7.9.8 Serial correlation

Most regression techniques assume that the error terms are serially uncorrelated and have a constant variance. These should be checked for the estimated equation. If the estimated error does not satisfy these conditions, as it often proves not to be so, the estimated coefficients will be biased and the appropriate techniques which can ensure unbiased estimates have to be used. Among these techniques often used for correcting for serial correlation are estimating the money demand function in a first difference form or using a technique with a built-in correction for the relevant order of serial correlation.

7.10 THE FUNCTIONAL FORM OF THE MONEY DEMAND FUNCTION

Theory, as in equation (56), had implied the variables that determine money demand, but did not specify the particular form of the money demand function. There is no theoretical basis for assuming its form to be linear, log-linear or non-linear in some other way. However, for reasons of convenience in estimation, the linear and the log-linear functional forms are the most commonly used ones. This section compares these functional forms and points out the differences among them. It ignores, for simplification, the possibility of lags and expectations and assumes that money demand depends only upon income and the interest rate.

To start, consider the following simple specific forms of the money demand function, with μ as the random term. The subscript t has been omitted as being unnecessary for the discussion.

$$M/Y = a_0 + a_r r + \mu \tag{66}$$

$$M = a + a_r r + a_y y + a_P P + \mu \tag{67}$$

$$m = a + a_r r + a_y y + \mu \tag{68}$$

Equation (66) assumes that the elasticity of the demand for money with respect to nominal income – and hence with respect to both prices and real income – is unity. Equation (68) assumes that this elasticity is unity with respect to the price level but not necessarily so with respect to real income. Equation (67) does not make either assumption.

Equation (68) is the only one consistent with the discussion in earlier chapters that the individual's demand for money balances is in real rather than in nominal terms. Proceeding further with (68), money demand in a world where commodities and money are substitutes would also depend upon the expected rate of inflation π^e, so that (68) would be modified to:

$$m = a_0 + a_r r + a_y y + a_\pi \pi^e + \mu \tag{69}$$

Other variables, such as the expected exchange rate depreciation to take account of currency substitution etc., could be introduced in a similar manner on the right-hand side of (69).

The money demand functions are often presented in a log-linear form. The log-linear form corresponding to (68) would be:

$$\ln m = \ln a_0 + \alpha \ln r + \beta \ln y + 1n\mu \tag{70}$$

A variant of (70) replaces $\ln r$ by $\ln(1 + r)$ since r is often between 0 and 1, so that its logarithmic value would be a negative number, while $\ln(1 + r)$ would be positive. Equation (70) is identical, with:

$$m = a_0 r^\alpha y^\beta \mu \tag{71}$$

This functional form is the well-known *Cobb–Douglas* functional form. It was implied by the inventory analysis of the transactions demand for money, though not by the speculative or the precautionary demand analyses. In (71), the elasticity of the demand for real balances is α with respect to the rate of interest r and β with respect to income. A variant of (71) is:

$$\ln m = \ln a_0 + \alpha r + \beta \ln y + 1n\mu \tag{72}$$

Equation (72) does not require taking the log of the interest rate since this would yield negative values when the values of r lie between 0 and 1. However, note that (72) translates to:

$$m = a_0 e^{\alpha r} y^\beta \mu \tag{73}$$

Since (70) and (72) are different and are unlikely to perform equally well, the researcher has to choose between them. There is no theoretical basis for doing so, with the result that the one which is reported often depends upon their relative empirical performance.

CONCLUSIONS

This chapter has examined the form of the money demand function to be used for estimation purposes, as well as some of the issues that arise in estimation. Among these was the measurement of expected income, which is itself not observable except possibly through surveys, so that a procedure has to be adopted for its estimation. The two procedures considered for this were the adaptive expectations hypothesis and the REH. Of these, the adaptive expectations hypothesis is the older one. However, the REH is clearly the preferable one on theoretical grounds and should be used where feasible. In particular, adaptive expectations are backward looking and ignore information that may already be available on the future.

This chapter has also looked at the use of partial adjustment models. These models are based on the notion that there are various costs of adjusting money balances quickly and these imply the specific order of the PAM. The general autoregressive distributed lag model nests the PAM and the adaptive expectations models. An alternative to such a model would be a PAM model with a separate procedure for the rational expectations estimation of expected income.

The researcher estimating the demand for money must also watch out for such problems as the non-stationarity of the data, non-identification of the functions estimated, multi-collinearity, simultaneous equations bias, and be prepared for possible misspecification of the functional form used for estimating the money demand function. There is also the question of the particular monetary aggregate that should be used. This question is investigated in the next chapter.

We have in this chapter combined a Keynesian-type supply function with rational expectations. Many economists who view rational expectations as particular to the neoclassical or new classical models are likely to object to our doing so.[22] Some defence of our mix of the Keynesian models with rational expectations, here as in the other sections of this book, needs to be given. Leaving aside the historical origins of rational expectations, we view the rational expectations procedure as a tool which can be freely combined with any theory which requires the expected value of a variable. Our purpose in this free-form association of tools – that is, sub-theories – is meant to arrive at the most attractive theoretical framework for explaining the real world. From an historical perspective, the REH was not known until the 1970s, so that the lack of usage of it by Keynes and the Keynesians until the 1970s cannot be taken to imply that, had they known it, they would have rejected it. Further, Keynes' own treatment of expectations in *The General Theory* can be interpreted as implying the notion of rational expectations. In any case, combining the REH with the Keynesian aggregate demand and supply, as set out in Chapter 14, does not introduce any logical inconsistency into the combined model. Since it does not do so, the real issue is whether the Keynesian models *cum* the REH provide a better explanation of reality than other groupings of economic theories.

SUMMARY OF CRITICAL CONCLUSIONS

- The appropriate scale variable for the demand for money may be current income, expected income or permanent income.
- Rational expectations is more suitable than adaptive expectations for estimating expected income for the next period.
- Adaptive expectations is the more appropriate statistical method for estimating permanent income since this concept specifies the average expected income over the future.
- The unanticipated component of income is usually estimated as income less the statistical estimate of expected income.
- The partial adjustment model provides one way of capturing the lagged adjustment of actual to desired money demand.
- There are considerable theoretical and econometric problems in the accurate estimation of the money demand function. In particular, the relevant time series must be stationary. If they are not stationary, the appropriate technique is cointegration with an error correction model.

review and discussion questions

1 Are there significant costs in adjusting actual to desired money balances or in changing balances between periods? Or are any such costs relatively insignificant but the delay in the adjustment of actual to desired balances occurs as a consequence of the costs of adjusting commodities and other financial assets to their desired levels? Discuss.

2 Discuss the suitability of rational expectations for estimating permanent income for the next period.

3 Discuss the suitability of adaptive expectations for estimating expected income for the next period.

4 Starting with a cost function leading to a second-order partial adjustment model, and a money demand function with expected income as the scale variable, derive the appropriate form of the estimating equation for the demand for money.

5 Starting with a cost function leading to a second-order partial adjustment model, and a money demand function with permanent income as the scale variable, derive the appropriate form of the estimating equation for the demand for money.

6 Discuss the relevance of the Lucas critique for the estimating equations in the preceding two questions.

NOTES

1 Cuthbertson (1985, Ch. 3) is a good adjunct to this book for adjustment lags, expectations and several of the other topics dealt with in this chapter.

2 Note that the word 'relevant' is a loaded one. It means the *correct* theory for the economy or market in question. However, the correct theory is hardly ever known, as witnessed by the differing macroeconomic schools on the determination of national income and inflation, or by disagreements among the exponents of a given school on the actual values of the structural and reduced-form coefficients of the model.

3 This is called the *weak* version of the REH. A *strong* version of it is that $F(y_t^{e*}) = f(y_t)$, where F and f specify the respective frequency distributions. This version requires that the distribution of expected income is the same as that for actual income except for a random term.

4 For instance, in many underdeveloped or developing countries, there is hardly any reliable information published on national income and the rate of inflation. Even if it is published, most of the inhabitants in the rural and even the urban areas may never receive or bother to acquire this information.

5 This need not mean that their mean value is not zero. It is that they can take relatively large absolute values.

6 Acting on the basis of the same rational expected value of a variable may be very prudent behaviour when the information on which it is based is fairly complete and reliable. Acting on it may be foolhardy behaviour when the information is scanty and represents a shot in the dark rather than an adequate basis for action.

A distinction is drawn here between 'prudence' and 'profit maximizing' in the presence of an acute lack of information: I may know nothing about horse racing and about the horses entered in a race, yet I can on the basis of the available information – say on the pleasing and non-pleasing colours of horses – specify my subjective probabilities of the performance of the horses in the race and place my profit-maximizing bets on the basis of these probabilities.

Prudence may instead dictate that I recognize the vagueness and inadequacy of my information underlying my probabilities and that I not bet at all.

Another distinction is drawn between *holding* rational expectations and *acting* on those expectations. Rational expectations can always be held, as long as the required probabilities are subjective and not objective ones. However, experience may have taught the individual not to act on them or to act on them after due allowance and caution for a large margin of error.

7 See Chapters 12 to 15 for these models and rules.

8 The macroeconomics of the Lucas supply rule are covered in Chapters 13, 14 and 15.

9 See Chapter 10 for the money supply theories.

10 See Chapters 14 to 16 for the discussion and further use of this concept.

11 Evidence of this comes from the disputes among the classical and the Keynesian paradigms, and within each of these paradigms. The periodic switches that occurred between them in the 1930s and 1940s from the classical to the Keynesian paradigm, and then from the Keynesian to the classical one in the 1970s and 1980s, is historic testimony to the fact that economists do not know the true model of the economy – and, therefore, do not know the relevant model for determining national income or the rate of inflation, or other macro-economic variables. If the economists do not know the true model, the public can hardly be expected to form expectations on the basis of the 'relevant' model of the economy.

Further, the economists as a group are notorious for their forecasting failures.

12 For example, while the new classical school tends to assume continuous market clearing and hence continuous equilibrium in the economy, many neoclassical economists believe that the markets and the economy tend towards equilibrium, without equilibrium being a continuous state.

13 However, the rationally expected value of a permanent measure of future incomes would be better.

14 Keynes specified such a process for the interest rate expectations in the speculative demand for money: the individual expects the interest rate to move towards its long-run value.

15 From a rational expectations perspective, partial adjustment models are inappropriate since they are backward looking and do not take account of the available information on the expected future changes in desired balances. The individual may find it profitable to make changes in current balances to provide for future changes in desired balances.

16 The first-order PAM imposes the same response pattern to the changes in desired balances, irrespective of whether such a change is due to changes in income or in interest rates. In fact, the adjustment costs may differ depending on the source of the changes in the desired balances.

17 This is desirable to detrending the data and using the first-order PAM.

18 This idea was explored in Chapter 6 in the context of the buffer stock models of money.

19 The procedure is: lag each term in (2) by one period and multiply by $(1 - \theta)$. Call it (2′). Subtract (2′) from (2) and designate the resulting equation as (2″). Substitute (25) in (2″) to eliminate y_t^P. This will give $m_t^* - (1 - \theta)m_{t-1}^*$ on the left-hand side and terms in y_t rather than y_t^P on the right-hand side. Now use (36) to substitute for $m_t^* - (1 - \theta)m_{t-1}^*$ and rearrange it as (46).

20 In some of the VAR models used in the analysis of monetary policy, the disturbance terms are interpreted and modelled as policy initiatives, thereby allowing the dynamic intertemporal impact of various policy options to be derived. This use of the VAR models has made them fairly popular in the dynamic analysis of monetary policy.

21 The Lucas critique is explained in Chapter 15.

22 Note that the classical paradigm through most of its history during the nineteenth century and the first three-quarters of the twentieth, developed independently of the rational expectations hypothesis. In fact, in the 1960s and 1970s, the adaptive expectations technique tended to be associated with the neoclassical approach.

REFERENCES

Arrow, Kenneth. 'The Future and the Present in Economic Life'. *Economic Inquiry*, 16, April 1978, pp. 157–69.

Cuthbertson, Keith. *The Supply and Demand for Money*. London: Basil Blackwell, 1985, Ch. 3.

Kantor, Brian. 'Rational Expectations and Economic Thought'. *Journal of Economic Literature*, 17, December 1979, pp. 1422–41.

Mishkin, Frederic S. 'Are Market Forecasts Rational?' *American Economic Review*, 71, June 1981, pp. 295–306.

Muth, John F. 'Rational Expectations and the Theory of Price Movements'. *Econometrica*, 29, July 1961, pp. 315–35.

chapter eight

MONETARY AGGREGATION

One of the most persistent questions in monetary economics has been about the proper definition of money. In the nineteenth century, the disputes were about whether demand deposits, gradually increasing in usage, should be included in the definition of money or not. By the 1950s, their inclusion in money was beyond dispute but new questions had arisen about whether savings deposits should also be in the money measure. While savings deposits are now part of some of the commonly used definitions of money, a fresh set of questions has arisen about the inclusion of other financial assets in the monetary aggregates. This perpetual problem with the definition of money and the solutions proposed for it is the subject of this chapter.

---

key concepts introduced in this chapter

- Monetary aggregates
- Simple sum aggregation
- Friedman's criterion for defining money
- Weak separability
- Elasticity of substitution among monetary assets
- The variable elasticity of substitution function
- Divisia aggregation
- User cost of monetary assets
- Statistical causality
- The St Louis monetarist equation

The preceding chapters have discussed several definitions of money. Of these, the *narrow definition* (M1) is the currency in the hands of the public plus demand deposits of the public in commercial banks. The somewhat wider *Friedman definition of money* (M2) consists of M1 plus time and savings deposits of the public in commercial banks. The still wider definition (M3) includes M2 and adds deposits in near-banks.[1] There are also several variants of M1, M2 and M3, as well as still wider definitions of money. The wider definitions extend the range of assets to include other liquid assets held by the public. Examples of these assets are

Treasury bills, money market mutual funds, etc. The broader aggregates merge the concept of money in the concept of '*liquidity*'.

Given the possibility of the many definitions of money, the basis on which the definitions are arrived at and their relative validity and performance become essential to any empirical study on money. This basis can be purely theoretical, using the functions of money, and concentrating on its role as a medium of exchange and payments. However, as discussed in earlier chapters, this procedure does not normally provide a unique definition of money. Financial assets are created ones and close substitutes to currency and demand deposits can be easily created in an unregulated, free enterprise financial system. A plethora of them usually exists in the developed economies with unregulated financial markets, so that an empirical basis for including some of these in the definition of money and excluding others is needed. One of these procedures is provided by the *theory of aggregation* or composite goods, since any measure of money is an aggregate or composite of its component assets. Aggregation theory requires *weak separability* among the assets to be included in the monetary aggregate, so that a test for weak separability provides a mechanism for judging the validity of the assets to be included in the monetary aggregate.

Once the assets to be included in the definition of money have been selected, the *relative weight* to be attached to each of the component assets has to be determined. These weights can be arbitrarily set at unity for each of the assets, as in the definitions of M1, M2 and M3 – which are examples of *simple sum aggregates* – or they can be determined from the data itself. Among the procedures for the latter are the estimation of a *variable or constant elasticity of substitution function* and the *Divisia aggregates*. The various aggregates in turn have to be tested for their empirical usefulness. The commonly used tests for this purpose are presented later in this chapter.

There is a two-way relationship between the monetary aggregate used as the dependent variable and the form of the estimating equation. The appropriate money demand *function* and its arguments depend upon the monetary aggregate used as the dependent variable. Conversely, the appropriate definition of money depends upon the explanatory variables included in the demand function. For instance, the narrow definition of money M1 seems to be the most satisfactory one if the explanatory variables are current expenditures and the return on time deposits or on Treasury bills or some other measure of the short-term interest rate.

The aggregate M2 includes time deposits in commercial banks which, for many individuals, represent an alternative to risky assets as a form of holding wealth. Further, the return on time deposits is itself a form of the short-term interest rate. Therefore, the appropriate explanatory variables for M2 tend to be the long-term interest rate and wealth, rather than current expenditures. Still wider definitions submerge currency and demand deposits in other near-money assets, whose demand is more closely related to wealth, so that current expenditures as an explanatory variable do not seem to have the relevance that they do for the narrow definition of money.

A considerable number of empirical studies of the demand for money exist in the literature. They are too numerous to review in this book and, with the benefit of the hindsight of current econometric methodology, many early studies are out of date in terms of their econometric methodology, so that their findings are suspect. Further, there are also several reviews of such studies in the literature (Goldfeld, 1973; Feige and Pearce, 1977; Belongia, 1996). Therefore, this chapter will focus mostly on the overall pattern of the widely accepted empirical findings on the demand for money, though with more detail provided on a few selected studies on the buffer stock demand for money and those using cointegration analysis.

Section 8.1 points out the failure of monetary theory to provide a unique definition of money when there are several close but not perfect substitutes for currency and demand deposits, so that the rest of this chapter examines the empirical considerations which have been proposed for selecting among various empirical measures of money. Section 8.2

discusses Milton Friedman's criterion for empirically defining money. A more rigorous criterion for defining a composite variable such as money is provided by aggregation theory, whose weak separability criterion of aggregation is specified in section 8.3. The three competing modes of aggregation – simple sum aggregation, variable elasticity of substitution function and Divisia aggregates – are discussed in sections 8.4, 8.5 and 8.7. A moot question arises about the appropriate cost of holding and using money. If money is used for its liquidity services in financing transactions, the appropriate measure of this cost is the user cost of money. This is defined in section 8.6. Section 8.8 concludes with a presentation of the various criteria for judging among empirically derived monetary aggregates. Since the Divisia aggregates are among the newer measures and have many appealing features, the appendix to this chapter presents their derivation.

8.1 THE APPROPRIATE DEFINITION OF MONEY: THEORETICAL CONSIDERATIONS

As discussed in the earlier chapters and in the introduction to this chapter, there are several possible variants of 'money' and several possible ways of selecting a preferred version among them. One of these ways is the intuitive one of focusing on the functions of money and asserting that the medium of payments function is the pre-eminent characteristic of money, so that only assets which perform this function are entitled to be in the definition of money.[2] In the United States and Canada until about the 1970s, such a rule would have resulted in the definition of money as currency plus demand deposits (M1) since other assets did not directly perform this role to a significant degree at that time.[3] However, financial developments in the 1970s and 1980s led to the creation of various types of savings deposits on which cheques can be written and from which funds can be easily withdrawn as well as bills paid through automatic teller machines. For many such accounts, further developments in the 1990s have allowed transfers to demand deposit accounts or to third parties to be made on the telephone or through a remote computer terminal. Therefore, over the recent decades in developed economies, savings and several other types of accounts also have come to perform the medium of payments function to a more or less extent. Hence, the focus on the medium of payments to define money would now support the use of variants of M2 and M3, which not only include savings deposits besides M1, but often also include other types of liabilities of financial intermediaries.[4]

Therefore, the *a priori* theoretical specification of the definition of money does not provide a unique measure of money, and economists are forced to look for empirical measures of money. One of the earliest ones, proposed by Milton Friedman and his associates in the 1950s, is presented in the next section.

8.2 MONEY AS THE EXPLANATORY VARIABLE FOR NOMINAL NATIONAL INCOME

One of the empirical approaches to the definition of money has been concerned with the policy question: what is the monetary aggregate that can best explain or predict the relevant macroeconomic variables? In several studies in the 1950s and 1960s, Milton Friedman and his associates considered the relevant macroeconomic variable to be nominal national income or expenditures. They argued that the appropriate monetary aggregate is that which is more 'closely related' to nominal income than other such aggregates.

This relationship was usually examined by the linear or log-linear regressions of the form:

$$Y_t = \alpha_0 + \alpha_1 M_t + \mu_t \qquad (1)$$

where Y is nominal national income, M is a monetary aggregate and μ is the disturbance term. The 'best' predictor of Y was specified as that monetary aggregate which yields the highest R^2 and also possesses stability of the estimated coefficients. Under this criterion, Friedman and many other economists, in line with the quantity theory, took the relevant macroeconomic variable to be nominal national income. Their empirical findings for the 1950s and 1960s data showed that the 'proper' definition of money in many financially developed economies such as the USA, Canada and Britain was currency plus all time and savings deposits in commercial banks – that is, M2 rather than M1.

Keynesian theorists of the time and those emphasizing the asset approach often broadened the list of the relevant variables to include an interest rate or rates in addition to nominal national income. One application of this was to estimate a linear or log-linear equation of the form:

$$M_t/Y_t = a_0 + a_1 r_t + \mu_t \tag{2}$$

The definition of money arrived at through estimations of (2) usually differed from the Friedman criterion specified by (1), since the two criteria are different.

Further, even if nominal income is the only relevant variable to be explained, financial deregulation and technological innovations since the 1960s have led to shifts in the monetary aggregate which 'best' explains nominal national income, with the results depending upon the country, as well as the time period of the study. Consequently, there is no clear-cut unique measure of money which has consistently proved to be the 'best' one over time for any country or across countries. For instance, during the 1950s and 1960s, as Friedman showed, most studies indicated that for the USA and Canada, M2 was 'more closely' related to national income than M1 in terms of R^2 and the stability of the estimated relationships. But for the 1980s, M1 did better than M2 under this criterion.

8.3 WEAK SEPARABILITY

From a rigorous theoretical standpoint, an aggregate is a composite good and must satisfy the weak separability conditions required for aggregation. These are explained in the following.

Assume that we have n goods, $X_1, ..., X_m, X_{m+1}, ..., X_n$, related by the function $F(\cdot)$, as in:

$$x = F(x_1, ..., x_m, x_{m+1}, ..., x_n) \tag{3}$$

where:

x utility (or output)
x_i quantity or real value of the ith good
$F(\cdot)$ utility (or production) function

Equation (3) can be written as:

$$x = F(f(x_1, ..., x_m), x_{m+1}, ..., x_n) \tag{4}$$

if and only if F_i/F_j, $i, j = i = 1, ..., m$, is independent of $x_{m+1}, ..., x_n$. $F_i = \partial F/\partial x_i$ and F_i/F_j is the marginal rate of substitution (MRS) between X_i and X_j. This independence of the MRS between each pair of goods in a group from all other goods not in the group, is known as the *weak separability* of the group from other goods in the overall function. It ensures that a quantity index – of the composite good m – can be constructed from the quantities of the goods only in the group, and that changes in the quantities or the prices of the goods not in the group do not directly change the index for the composite good. To illustrate, if weak separability holds, a change in the price of one of the goods not in the group will not directly affect the demand for the goods in the group but only the total expenditure on the group and hence the budget line for the group.

If the condition of weak separability is met, (4) can be rewritten as:

$$x = F(m, x_{m+1}, ..., x_n)$$ (5)

where:

$$m = f(x_1, ..., x_m)$$ (6)

The aggregate m in (6) specifies a sub-utility function and can be used to construct the quantity or real value of the monetary aggregate. To derive the optimal values for $x_1, ..., x_m$, the sub-utility function $f(\cdot)$ can be maximized subject to the total expenditures allocated for m without reference to the prices or quantities bought of $x_{m+1}, ..., x_n$.

If the financial assets $X_1, ..., X_m$ are currency, demand deposits and near-money assets, m is a valid composite monetary aggregate. The demand for the component assets in m would depend only on the quantity index m and the prices of $X_1, ..., X_m$ but not directly upon the quantities or prices of the other goods $X_{m+1}, ..., X_n$. If $F(\cdot)$ is the individual's utility function over all goods, the remaining goods $X_{m+1}, ..., X_n$ will include among them other financial assets, consumption goods, leisure, and any other goods in the individual's utility function. If $F(\cdot)$ is the firm's production function and x is the firm's output, $X_{m+1}, ..., X_n$ will include among them the firm's other inputs such as labour, capital, other financial assets, etc.

The condition of weak separability may be satisfied by different groupings of goods, with some of these encompassing others. In such a case, the former would be a wider aggregate and would include the latter – narrower aggregates – as sub-categories of composite goods, just as M2 includes M1 as a component.

If a grouping $f(\cdot)$ of a set of goods does *not* satisfy the weak separability condition, changes in the quantities of the other, excluded, goods would change the marginal rates of substitution between the pairs of the included goods and hence the value of the sub-utility function $f(\cdot)$, so that $f(\cdot)$ and hence m will not be invariant to changes in the quantities or the prices of the other goods. In this case, if $F(\cdot)$ is the utility function and m is a monetary aggregate, shifts in the quantities bought of consumption, leisure and other excluded goods would mean a shift in the rates of substitution and therefore in the slopes of the indifference curves between the pairs of the monetary goods. Consequently, the value of the monetary aggregate will alter – not because of changes in the quantities of its components but because of changes in the non-monetary variables. But the construction of the monetary aggregate requires that its value depends only on the value of its own components. Further, if the marginal rates of substitution between the monetary assets shift because of changes in the quantities of the non-monetary assets, the demand functions for the monetary assets will shift.

For the appropriate monetary aggregate M to satisfy the weak separability condition, it will include the assets $X_1, ..., X_m$ and be specified by the *particular* form of $f(x_1, ..., x_m)$ given in equation (2). A misspecification in the form of the $f(\cdot)$ function would mean that the weak separability condition is violated in the context of the misspecified function. However, the form of $f(\cdot)$ is normally not known *a priori*, so that empirical work has used a variety of arbitrarily specified forms such as the simple sum aggregate, the variable elasticity of substitution function, the Cobb–Douglas function and more flexible functional forms.[5] Ideally, the functional form applied to the data should be as flexible as possible, so that the data could determine the specific functional form.[6]

Empirical evidence

Varian (1983) is a pioneering study on judging weak separability among goods using non-parametric econometric methods. Swofford and Whitney (1987) used Varian's technique for the United States data (from 1970 to 1985) on consumption goods, leisure and various monetary aggregates. Several definitions of money were found to be weakly separable from consumption goods and leisure, with the broadest measure doing so including currency, demand deposits, checkable deposits and small time deposits. Measures broad enough to include money market mutual funds were not weakly separable from consumption and leisure. Conversely, consumption goods and leisure together were weakly separable from monetary assets, but consumption goods alone were not. Our concern is only with the former result. It showed that M1 and M2 were acceptable monetary aggregates but broader measures than M2 were not. Hence, for the period of their study, the definitions or indices of money which include monetary assets beyond those in M2 – and, therefore, implicitly assume their weak separability from other goods in the economy – are misspecified.

Note that the assets that meet the weak separability criterion for inclusion in the monetary aggregate are likely to differ among countries and periods. Further, in view of the considerable degree of innovation and change in the moneyness of assets in the 1980s and 1990s, the admissible assets in the monetary aggregate have been changing and are likely to have increased beyond M2 for many countries.

Another study using weak separability is Belongia and Chalfant (1989). They started with the assumption that the monetary assets were weakly separable from consumption and only examined weak separability within this category. Using USA monthly data over the brief period from January 1983 to February 1986, they reported that several groups of assets were weakly separable from others. Among these groups were: (C, DD), $(C, DD, NOWS)$, $(C, DD, NOWS, MMMF)$, where C is currency balances, DD is demand deposits, $NOWS$ are negotiable orders of withdrawal,[7] and $MMMF$ are money market mutual funds. Hence, Belongia and Chalfant's results offered a choice among various levels of acceptable monetary aggregates for further analysis. This multiplicity of weakly separable groups is a common finding, so that other criteria, such as the Friedman one in section 8.2 and others discussed later in this chapter, are further needed to select the most useful aggregate among them.

8.4 SIMPLE SUM MONETARY AGGREGATES

We are at this point going to switch from the theory of aggregation specified in the preceding section to the practical construction of the usual monetary aggregates which are aggregations of the nominal values (X_i)[8] rather than the real values (x_i) of the assets. However, note that the assets included in any such aggregates must meet the separability criterion for aggregation.

In defining money, the most common *functional* form for the monetary aggregate is the *simple sum aggregate* given by:

$$M = X_1 + \Sigma_i a_i X_i \quad i = 2, 3, \ldots \tag{7}$$

where:

    M nominal value of the monetary aggregate
    X_1 M1 (currency in the hands of the public plus demand deposits in commercial banks)
    X_i nominal value of the ith liquid asset
    a_i (1, 0)

In Friedman's analysis, the term a_i took the value 1 if inclusion of the ith asset gave better results in explaining the level of national income than if it were excluded. However, the general functional form (7) was not exclusive to Friedman but was the most common form used in the 1950s and 1960s, and is still the most common monetary aggregation function in monetary economics.

A monetary aggregate given by (7) *a priori* assumes that:

(i) the coefficients a_i can take only the values zero or one so that all other values are excluded, and
(ii) an *infinite elasticity of substitution* exists among the assets with a non-zero coefficient, so that the included assets are perfect substitutes.

A generalization of (7) is a weighted sum aggregate that allows the coefficients a_i to take on any positive weights between zero and one. In this case, the monetary aggregate, designated as M', is given by:

$$M' = X_1 + \Sigma_i a_i X_i \quad i = 2, 3, \ldots \tag{8}$$

where, now, $0 \le a_i \le 1$. The weights a_i are sometimes called the *degree of moneyness* of asset i and can be specified *a priori* or on the basis of a statistical procedure. To illustrate the latter in line with Friedman's procedure for defining money, the values of the coefficients can be determined empirically by estimating the stochastic form of the equation:

$$a_0 + \Sigma_i a_i X_{it} = Y_t \quad i = 1, 2, \ldots \tag{9}$$

where Y is nominal national expenditure and $0 \le a_i \le 1$. Equation (9) still defines money as that variable which 'best' explains national expenditures and the weights a_i of the assets are derived by multiple regression. The coefficient of each additional asset should decrease as the definition of money is broadened to include assets in a decreasing order of the degree of moneyness. However, there are other criteria besides Friedman's for selecting among monetary aggregates and its extension to (9) is not common.

While (7) and (9) both specify simple sum aggregates, this term is usually associated with (7). It will henceforth be used in this sense. Many economists object to its underlying assumption that the elasticity of substitution must be either 0 (between an included and an excluded asset) or infinity (between any pair of the included assets). Two specifications of the monetary aggregate that use other elasticities are the variable elasticity of substitution function and the Divisia aggregates. These are presented in the next two sections.

8.5 THE VARIABLE ELASTICITY OF SUBSTITUTION AND NEAR-MONIES

The variable elasticity of substitution (VES) function for the nominal value of the monetary aggregate has the form,

$$M\left(X_1, \ldots, X_m\right) = \left(\sum_{i=1}^{m} a_i X_i^{1+v_i}\right) \Big/ \left(\qquad \right)^{1/(1+v_1)} \tag{10}[9]$$

If $v_i = v$ for all i, the above functional form becomes the constant elasticity of substitution (CES) function commonly used in the production analysis in microeconomics.[10] In this case, there would be an identical elasticity of substitution equal to $(-1/v)$ between each pair of the assets. This represents an unjustified constraint on the data since, in the general case, v_i is unlikely to be identical for all i, so that the elasticity of substitution would differ between the different pairs of assets and would vary over time for any given pair.

Equation (10) has the nature of a utility (or production) function over the various monetary assets. The first asset can be designated as M1, with the others being near-money or other liquid assets. The monetary aggregate defined by (10) is sometimes referred to as *moneyness* or *liquidity*. The partial elasticity of substitution[11] $\sigma_{i,j}$ has the general definition given in equations (11) and (12) below.

$$\sigma_{i,j} = \frac{d\ln\left(X_i/X_j\right)}{d\ln\left(M_i/M_j\right)} \tag{11}$$

$$= \frac{\left(M_i/M_j\right)}{\left(X_i/X_j\right)} \frac{d\left(X_i/X_j\right)}{d\left(M_i/M_j\right)} \tag{12}$$

where $M_i = \partial M/\partial X_i$. The partial elasticity of substitution varies along any given indifference curve (or isoquant), except for the case where $v_i = v$ for all i, and may differ between pairs of assets. It may be negative for any particular pair or pairs of assets, though substitution must dominate among all the assets taken together.

Therefore, in (10), $\sigma_{i,j}$ between asset 1 and i is:

$$\sigma_{i,1} = \frac{1}{-v_1 + \left(v_i - v_1\right)\Big/ \left[1 + \dfrac{a_i\left(1+v_i\right)\overline{X}_i^{1+v_i}}{a_1\left(1+v_1\right)\overline{X}_1^{1+v_1}}\right]} \tag{13}$$

which varies with the quantities of the assets and therefore with the period chosen. The average value of this elasticity is calculated using the average values of the quantities of the assets.

To derive the estimating equations, assume that the individual maximizes (10) subject to the budget constraint:

$$\Sigma_i p_i X_i = A \tag{14}$$

where:

p_i price of the ith asset
A expenditures to be allocated over M1 and the other monetary assets

Chetty (1969) proposed using the VES function for monetary aggregation and is associated with the preceding analysis.

Maximizing (10) subject to (14) gives the following first-order conditions, with λ as the Lagrangian multiplier:

$$M_i - \lambda p_i = 0 \quad M_i = \partial M/\partial X_i, i = 1, 2, \ldots, m \tag{15}$$

$$\Sigma_i p X_i = A$$

which yield for $i = 2, 3, \ldots$:

$$\frac{a_i\left(1+v_i\right)X_i^{v_i}}{a_1\left(1+v_1\right)X_1^{v_1}} = \frac{p_i}{p_1} \tag{16}$$

$$\ln X_i = \alpha_i + \frac{1}{v_i}\ln\frac{p_i}{p_1} + \frac{v_1}{v_i}\ln X_1 \tag{17}$$

where

$$\alpha_i = \frac{1}{v_i}\ln\frac{a_1\left(1+v_1\right)}{a_i\left(1+v_i\right)}$$

The stochastic form of (17) is the estimating equation for this procedure and can be easily estimated using single-equation regression techniques. It provides the estimated values of v and v_p from which the estimated values of the average partial elasticities of substitution can be calculated.

An important and rather complex question in the above estimation procedure is that of the measurement of the prices of financial assets. There are several possible ways of defining these prices, as we discuss later under the heading of user costs. Chetty defined the present price of an asset by the present discounted cost of purchasing one dollar of it at the end of the period, with the discount rate based on its own rate of return.[12] Designating the rate of return on the ith asset as r_i, Chetty's procedure specified p_i as:

$$p_i = 1/(1 + r_i) \tag{18}$$

Designating the non-interest-paying asset 1 as M1 with $r_1 = 0$, implies that $p_1 = 1$ and that:

$$p_i/p_1 = 1/(1 + r_i) \tag{19}$$

We use Chetty's study for the United States for the period 1945–66 to illustrate a set of findings based on (17) and (19). This study considered four assets, with $i = 1, \ldots, 4$, and used their nominal values to estimate the nominal value M' of the monetary aggregate. The four assets were:

X_1 currency plus demand deposits (M1) in commercial banks (M1)
X_2 time deposits in commercial banks (TD)
X_3 time deposits in mutual savings banks (TDM)
X_4 savings and loan associations shares (SLS)

Chetty's estimates of their elasticities of substitution, designated as $\sigma_{1,i}$, between money and the ith assets, were:

$$\sigma_{1,2} = \sigma_{M1,TD} = 30.864$$

$$\sigma_{1,3} = \sigma_{M1,TDM} = 35.461$$

$$\sigma_{1,4} = \sigma_{M1,SLS} = 23.310$$

Chetty interpreted these magnitudes as indicating that all the three near-money assets being considered were good substitutes for money. The estimated form of the monetary aggregate M was:

$$M = [X_1^{0.954} + 1.020X_2^{0.975} + 0.880X_3^{0.959} + 0.615X_4^{0.981}]^{1.026} \tag{20}$$

Since the exponents of the variables on the right-hand side of (20) were close to one, as is the coefficient of x_2, M was approximated by Chetty as:

$$M = X_1 + X_2 + 0.880X_3 + 0.615X_4 \tag{21}$$

The yield r_M on M can be calculated as a correspondingly weighted index of interest rates on the near-money assets, so that it was specified as:

$$r_M = (r_2 + 0.880r_3 + 0.615r_4)/(1 + 0.88 + 0.615) \tag{22}$$

Chetty's estimation of the elasticities of substitution, though limited in its usefulness by the form of the aggregation function specified *a priori* as (10) and by his use of the cost rather than the user cost of assets, is valuable for directly estimating the degree of substitution between money and near-money assets. His results basically confirmed the general perception by economists in the 1960s of the close substitution between money and several other financial assets, and supported the evidence derived from the estimates of the demand function for money. Note that the financial deregulation and the considerable technological innovation in the financial sector in the USA since the 1960s have changed the elasticities of substitution from those reported by Chetty and also created many new near-money assets, so that the monetary aggregate implied by estimating (19) would now be different from that derived by Chetty.

The VES (or CES) function estimates the elasticities of substitution which directly reflect the degree of substitution between money and near-money assets and are directly related to the debate on the appropriate definition of money, while the empirical studies of the *demand for money function* estimate the *own and the cross-interest elasticities of the demand for money*. The estimated values of the own and cross-price elasticities are usually less than one, which are of a different order of magnitude than the elasticities of substitution reported by Chetty, so that we need a procedure for comparing the two concepts.

The elasticities of substitution are not directly comparable with the price elasticities but are a component of the latter and the two are difficult to compare for the general case. However, Feige and Pearce (1977, p. 461) report the following relationship for the two-asset case:

$$\sigma_{1,2} = \left(\frac{1 + r_2}{r_2} \right) \left[E_{1,2} - E_{2,2} \right] \tag{23}$$

where:

$\sigma_{1,2}$ elasticity of substitution between asset 1 and asset 2
$E_{2,2}$ own-price elasticity of asset 2 (with respect to its own price)
$E_{1,2}$ cross-price elasticity of asset 1 with respect to the return on asset 2
r_2 return on asset 2

To illustrate the reconciliation between the estimated large elasticities of substitution and the less-than-one price elasticities, let $i = 1$ for M1 and $j = 2$ for a near-money asset. Then, if $E_{1,2} = -0.4$, $E_{2,2} = 1.0$ and $r_2 = 0.04$, (23) implies that $\sigma_{1,2} = 36.4$, which is close to the elasticities of substitution reported by Chetty (Feige and Pearce, 1977, p. 460). Hence, small values of own- and cross-price elasticities can be consistent with very large elasticities of substitution, so that Chetty's estimates of the latter are not necessarily inconsistent with the own- and cross-elasticities usually occurring in the estimated demand functions.

8.6 THE USER COST OF ASSETS

Chetty had specified a unit of the ith asset as having a *terminal* value of $1 at the end of the period and its current price – equal to its present discounted value – as $[1/(1 + r_i)]$ where r_i is the return on the ith asset itself. Similarly, the price per unit of the totally illiquid asset yielding R per period would be $[1/(1 + R)]$, so that the relative price of the ith asset to that of the illiquid one would be $[(1 + r_i)/(1 + R)]$.

However, the proper concept for the *usage* of a durable good is its user cost for the services provided by it during the period. Comparing the ith somewhat liquid asset with the illiquid asset, the cost of using the liquidity of the ith asset during the period would be the return forgone by holding it rather than the illiquid asset. This forgone return per dollar invested in the ith asset is $(R - r_i)$ at the end of the current period. Discounting this return to the present gives the nominal and real (per dollar) user costs of the ith asset as:

$$\gamma_{it} = \frac{p_{it}\left(R_t - r_{it}\right)}{1 + R_t} \qquad (24)$$

$$\gamma_{it}^* = \frac{\left(R_t - r_{it}\right)}{1 + R_t} \qquad (25)$$

where:

γ_{it} nominal user cost of ith asset in period t

γ_{it}^* real user cost per \$ of the ith asset in period t

p_{it} price of the ith asset in period t

r_{it} rate of return on the ith asset in period t

R_t rate of return on the totally illiquid asset

Further analysis in the body of this chapter assumes a zero tax rate, as in (24) and (25). The appendix to this chapter presents the corresponding equations if there is a tax on interest income.

Note that the above measures of the user cost of the liquidity services provided by assets assume that the differential in their interest rates arises only from their differences in liquidity services. This would not be accurate unless the rates are determined by the market under perfectly competitive conditions and there are no other implicit or explicit charges on them. Regulated rates do not satisfy this condition. Further, the market rates on assets may reflect differences in their associated services – such as investment advice, overdraft facilities etc. – other than their liquidity. Alternatively, some of the charges for these liquidity services may be through fixed charges and conditions – such as the requirements for minimum balances, payment of interest only on minimum monthly balances, set-up charges and monthly service charges etc. – in addition to the differential in interest rates. Further, for investors, there may also be portfolio adjustment costs for reallocations among assets or imperfect information about interest rates. These are not fully captured by the interest rate differentials.

Also note that the user cost functions defined by (24) or (25) can be used with Chetty's variable elasticity of substitution function since his definition of the relative cost of assets was only a subsidiary hypothesis to his main hypothesis – that is, using a VES function for the aggregator function – and is not an integral part of it.

8.7 INDEX NUMBER THEORY AND DIVISIA AGGREGATES

Another approach to monetary aggregation is derived from statistical index number theory and focuses on the quantity and price data, rather than on utility or production functions, and emphasizes the desirable properties of index numbers.[13] The simple sum aggregates do not meet several of these properties. One aggregate that meets more of these properties is the Divisia aggregate, first proposed by Francois Divisia in 1925. Among these properties is the statistically desired property that any changes in the prices of the components of the index only change the price index and any changes in the quantities of the components only change the quantity index, while the multiple of the price and the quantity indices thus computed equals the index of the expenditures on the services of the assets.

The Divisia aggregate $x_t(x_{1t}, \ldots, x_{nt})$ for the n monetary assets for the period t is given by:

$$x_t(x_{1t}, \ldots, x_{nt}) = \prod_{i=1}^{n} x_{it}^{sit} \qquad (26)$$

where:

x_t Divisia aggregate for period t
s_{it} share of the ith asset in the expenditure on liquidity services in period t
Π_1^n product from 1 to n

Equation (26) has the appealing log-linear form given by:

$$\ln x_t = \Sigma_i s_{it} \ln x_{it} \quad i = 1, \ldots, n \tag{27}$$

Further, (26) implies that:

$$\dot{x}_t = \sum_{i=1}^{n} s_{it} \dot{x}_{it} \tag{28}$$

where the dot on a variable indicates its growth rate. Equation (28) shows the very appealing feature of Divisia aggregates that the growth rate of the aggregate is the sum of the weighted growth rates of the individual assets, with the weights being the shares of the total expenditures on liquidity services. In (26) to (28), the expenditure shares s_{it} could be constant at s_i, or change over time as a result of the various types of innovations in the financial sector. These equations allow for such changes and, therefore, allow the resulting values of the Divisia aggregate to incorporate, at least to some extent, the impact of such innovations.

To examine the ith asset's share of the total expenditures, start with the nominal user cost of the ith asset as specified by (24). The nominal expenditure on the services of the ith asset is:

$$\gamma_{it} x_{it} = \frac{x_{it} p_{it} \left(R_t - r_{it} \right)}{\left(1 + R_t \right)} \tag{29}$$

and the share of the expenditure on the ith asset out of the total expenditures on all assets is:

$$s_{it} = \frac{x_{it} p_{it} \dfrac{\left(R_t - r_{it} \right)}{\left(1 + R_t \right)}}{\sum_{i=1}^{n} x_{it} p_{it} \dfrac{\left(R_t - r_{it} \right)}{\left(1 + R_t \right)}} \tag{30}$$

$$= \frac{x_{it} p_{it} \left(R_t - r_{it} \right)}{\sum_{i=1}^{n} x_{it} p_{it} \left(R_t - r_{it} \right)} \tag{31}$$

Returning to the general nature of the Divisia index, (26) and (27) specify the Divisia aggregate as a CES (constant elasticity of substitution) function where the elasticity of substitution is constant and identical at unity.[14] The functional form of the Divisia aggregate x_t as specified by (26) is the Cobb–Douglas one.

Among the appealing features of the Divisia aggregates is that the weighting used for each asset is its share of the total expenditures on the flow of liquidity services provided by it.[15] Another is that the growth rate of the aggregate is the sum of the similarly weighted growth rates of the individual assets. A third appealing feature is that the Divisia quantity aggregate is a quantity index and changes only if the quantities of the component assets change but its corresponding price index would similarly show a price change only if the prices of the component assets change, while the multiple of the quantity and price indices provides the index of the nominal value (total expenditures). These are among the statistical properties desired for index numbers, and make it tempting to select the Divisia aggregate as the appropriate aggregator function.[16] An additional appealing feature is that the weight assigned to each asset – its share in total expenditures – can be recomputed each period, so that the value of the resulting index – based on these changing weights over time – will incorporate the impact of the changes in these shares. While such revisions of weights can be cumbersome, the resulting index will capture the impact of innovations that alter the relative liquidity and demands for the component assets.

However, from an economic theoretic viewpoint, the appropriate form of the aggregation function is that which replicates actual economic behaviour. Theory does not prescribe this form, so that it has to be determined by the data itself. There is no *a priori* reason why the data need necessarily behave according to the Divisia format, which requires a constant unit elasticity of substitution between each pair of assets. On the basis of intuition, we expect the component assets of M1 and of M2, if not of wider aggregates, to possess high elasticities of substitution. This would make the Divisia aggregate a poor approximation to the actual aggregate underlying the data. One way around this criticism is to use a combination of simple sum aggregation and Divisia aggregation. In line with this, the Divisia aggregate is often *constructed to use M1 as its most liquid asset, where M1 is the simple sum aggregate* of currency in the hands of the public plus the demand deposits in commercial banks. The unit elasticity assumption is then imposed between M1 and each of the other distinct assets to construct the Divisia aggregate. This is an appealing construct in that it uses common sense to blend the various convenient forms of aggregation. However, we still cannot be sure that this construct rather than another alternative, possibly with a different elasticity of substitution than unity, is the most appropriate one for the given data set.[17] Therefore, we need to construct and use appropriate statistical tests to judge the relative usefulness of the various aggregates. Such tests are presented in the following sections.

8.8 JUDGING AMONG THE MONETARY AGGREGATES

While the economist can decide on the appropriate level of aggregation on an *a priori* basis, this is often not a satisfactory procedure for empirical applications since the empirical characteristics of assets vary over periods and economies. Therefore, monetary economics has a variety of empirical criteria for selecting among various aggregation procedures. Many of these are described in greater detail in other parts of this book and are only briefly described below. In the following, we assume that the weak separability tests were performed to determine the assets that have been included in the aggregate and the choice that has to be exercised is between the functional form of the aggregate.

8.8.1 Stability of the money demand function

If the estimated demand function for money is to be useful for prediction, it should be stable. If the function is not stable, its value for the predictability of money demand in future periods and for policy purposes is limited. While this requirement may not seem to be very stringent, it is not always satisfied and rejects many of the estimated demand functions. For instance, the money demand functions estimated for the 1980s and the 1990s show a high degree of instability for many countries.

8.8.2 Controllability of the monetary aggregate and policy instruments and targets

If the monetary aggregate is to be useful for policy purposes, the central bank must be able to control it through the policy instruments at its disposal. Assuming that the central bank can control the nominal monetary base B, it would be concerned with the relationship between B and the monetary aggregate M. A simple linear relationship between M and B is given by:

$$M = a_0 + a_1 B \tag{32}$$

where:

M nominal value of the monetary aggregate
B nominal value of the monetary base
a_1 marginal monetary base-money multiplier

The central bank can only control M through B if a_0 and a_1 are stable. Different monetary aggregates possess different values of these coefficients and different degrees of stability of these, with the preferred aggregate having stable values of the coefficients.

A related issue is whether there exists a monetary aggregate which can be used as a target or policy guide by the monetary authorities. Such a target should bear a predictable relationship with the *ultimate goals* that the monetary authority wants to pursue and should itself be predictable. While the latter requirement is for a stable demand function for the monetary aggregate, the former requires a stable functional relationship between the goal variable and the targeted variable. Taking real income to be the goal variable, the functional relationship could be as specified by the St Louis monetarist equation discussed later in subsection 8.8.5.

8.8.3 Causality from money to income

For a monetary aggregate M to be useful for controlling nominal national income Y, changes in the former should cause changes in the latter. The statistical procedure for determining causation between variables is the Granger–Sims test for causality. This procedure is a statistical determination of causality and judges (statistical) causality to go from a variable M to Y – that is, a change in M causes a change in Y – if the data on them shows a lag in the impact of M on Y. The impact of the expected future values of M on Y are ruled out.[18] That is, for this procedure to give valid results, lags are essential but leads must not exist. This procedure also does not work if there are no lags but only contemporaneous impact from M to Y.

Sims (1972), in an early application of Granger procedure for statistical causality to the relationship between money and income, defined *one-way statistical causality* as:

> If and only if causality runs one way from current and past values of some list of exogenous variables to a given endogenous variable, then in a regression of the endogenous variable on past, current, and future values of the exogenous variables, the future values of the exogenous variables should have zero coefficients.
>
> (Sims, 1972, p. 541)

This test relies on regression analysis to determine the pattern of lags among the variables. If nominal national income Y is the endogenous variable and the exogenous variables are the money supply M and other variables Z, the relevant regression equation is of the form:

$$Y_t = \Sigma_i a_i M_{t-i} + \Sigma_i b_i Z_{t-i} + \Sigma_i \gamma_i Y_{t-i} + \Sigma_j c_j M_{t+j} + \mu_t \tag{33}$$

where Z is the vector of variables other than M and Y and μ is the error term. Note that (33) includes not only the current and lagged values of M, Z and Y, but also some future values of M through the term $\Sigma_j c_j M_{t+j}$.

In (33), if the estimated coefficients of the lagged money supply terms are statistically different from zero but those for the future terms are zero, then one-way Granger causality is said to exist from M to Y. Usually a similar regression is also run with M as the dependent variable and Y among the independent ones. Such a regression would be of the form:

$$M_t = \Sigma_i \alpha_i Y_{t-i} + \Sigma_i \beta_i Z_{t-i} + \Sigma_i \lambda_i M_{t-i} + \Sigma_j k_j Y_{t+j} + \mu_t \tag{34}$$

For this regression with M on the left side, one-way causality from Y to M requires that the coefficients of the lagged values of Y be significantly different from zero, while those for its future values be zero.

Two-way causality from M to Y exists in (33) if both the lagged and the future terms in M have non-zero coefficients. This can be verified from (34) if both the lagged and future terms in Y have non-zero coefficients. We illustrate these remarks and the nature of the Granger causality test by a simple example where:

$$Y_t = a_1 M_t + a_2 M_{t-1} + a_3 M_{t+1} + \mu_t \tag{35}$$

In this procedure, M is taken to cause Y if $\hat{a}_2 \neq 0$. Suppose we rewrite (35) as:

$$M_{t-1} = (1/a_2) Y_t - (a_1/a_2) M_t - (a_3/a_2) M_{t+1} - (1/a_2) \mu_t \tag{36}$$

which can be rewritten as:

$$M_t = (1/a_2) Y_{t+1} - (a_1/a_2) M_{t+1} - (a_3/a_2) M_{t+2} - (1/a_2) \mu_{t+1} \tag{37}$$

where, assuming a_2 to be finite, $(1/a_2) \neq 0$. Hence, with M causing Y as assumed in (35), but with a regression of M_t – as the dependent variable – on the future value Y_{t+1}, the regression would yield a non-zero value of the coefficient of Y_{t+1}. Extending this argument to the general case shows that the non-zero coefficients of any of the future values of a variable indicate reverse causation from the dependent variable to that variable. Note also that, in (35), the coefficient of the contemporaneous term M_t does not provide any information on the direction of causality.[19]

Applying these arguments back to the estimation of (33), which is a regression of Y on M and Z, if the estimated values of any of the coefficients c_j (of the future values of the money supply) were non-zero, the implication would be that causation runs from Y to M. If the lagged values of M also had some non-zero coefficients a_i, the implication would be that causation runs from M to Y. For one-way causation from M to Y, some a_i should be non-zero while all c_j should be zero, but for one-way causation from Y to M, some c_j should be non-zero while all a_i should be zero. For two-way causation between Y and M, some of each set of coefficients should be non-zero.

Using causality tests to judge among monetary aggregates

The different monetary aggregates do not do equally well in terms of the one-way causality from money to nominal national income, so that the Granger–Sims test can be used as a selection device among them.

Note that the Granger–Sims test cannot be used if there are no leads or lags in the relationships among the variables, as would be the case where there is only a contemporaneous relationship. In such a context, the following test provides a useful criterion.

8.8.4 The information content of economic indicators

The information content of a stochastic variable relative to another is the expected uncertainty of – i.e., variation in – the former minus the uncertainty of (variation in) the former conditional on the second. For this, the stochastic linear model between nominal income Y and nominal balances M would be:

$$Y_t = a_0 + a_1 M_t + \mu_t \tag{38}$$

where μ_t is white noise. The expected information content of M with respect to Y is measured by:

$$I\left(Y \mid M\right) = \frac{1}{2}\ln\left[\frac{1}{\left(1 - R^2\right)}\right] \tag{39}$$

where R^2 is the coefficient of determination. Note that this test only uses the contemporaneous values of the variables. A higher value of $I(Y\mid M)$ indicates a higher information content for M, so that the monetary aggregate which has a higher value for this statistic would be preferable for explaining income.

8.8.5 The St Louis monetarist equation

The reduced-form equation from the short-run macroeconomic IS–LM models, as in Chapters 13 and 14, for the relationship between nominal national income Y and the money stock M is:

$$Y = f(\underline{M}, \underline{G}, \underline{Z}) \tag{40}$$

where:

   Y nominal national income
   $\underline{M}$ vector of the past and present nominal values of the appropriate monetary aggregate
   $\underline{G}$ vector of the past and present values of the appropriate fiscal variables
   $\underline{Z}$ vector of the other independent variables

The linear or log-linear stochastic form of the above equation popularized by the St Louis monetarist school (Anderson and Jordan, 1968) was:

$$Y_t = \Sigma_i a_i M_{t-i} + \Sigma_j c_j G_{t-j} + \Sigma_i b_i Z_{t-i} + \Sigma_i \gamma_i Y_{t-i} + \mu_t \tag{41}$$

Equation (41) is often called the St Louis equation and represents a popular method for determining the impact of the monetary and fiscal variables on nominal income. It is estimated with levels or first differences of the variables. There are many different ways of specifying the fiscal variable G. Among these is government expenditures and the fiscal deficit, or their values at full employment. The set of variables in Z also tends to vary between studies.

The monetary aggregate in (41) can be represented by one of its different forms. To make the choice among these forms for given versions of the Y, G and Z variables, (41) is estimated using different monetary aggregates. These estimates are examined for the signs, significance and stability of the coefficients. The monetary aggregate that performs 'better' – in terms of the coefficient of determination, the plausibility of the coefficients and their stability – is considered preferable to the alternative aggregates.

8.8.6 Comparing the evidence on Divisia versus simple sum aggregation

Theoretical considerations

As explained earlier in this chapter, in a fairly static context, simple sum aggregation between two monetary variables is relatively more appropriate – and therefore likely to do 'better' empirically – than their Divisia aggregate if the two are close substitutes and therefore possess a high elasticity of substitution. Their Divisia aggregate is relatively more appropriate – and likely to do better empirically – if the two assets have a relatively low degree of substitution and their elasticity of substitution is closer to 1. The wider the existing degree of aggregation, the more likely is an additional asset to fit into the latter case, so that the broader the definition of the monetary aggregate, the more likely is the Divisia aggregate to do better than its simple sum counterpart.[20]

Since the empirical findings depend upon the actual degree of the elasticity of substitution among assets, financial innovation that changes this elasticity could alter the results on the appropriate monetary aggregate. In fact, the past several decades have seen a considerable amount of innovation in financial intermediation and in the payments technology, causing shifts in the estimated demand functions for the monetary aggregates and therefore also in the relationships between money and national income. This process has been accompanied by increases in the liquidity of many assets that are not in M1 and even not in M2. Since Divisia aggregates weight each asset by the expenditures on it, the increasing liquidity can be accommodated through changes in these weights over time. Simple sum aggregates in their standard form have a fixed weight of one for each asset in the aggregate and zero for excluded assets, with the rigidity in weights being inappropriate in a period of changing liquidity patterns. Therefore, the expectation is that the simple sum aggregates are likely to do worse than the Divisia aggregates with time-variant weights for recent periods.

However, while Divisia aggregates are expected to perform better from a theoretical and statistical perspective in a changing environment, the simple sum aggregates retain their popularity for the public and the policy makers. The latter are easier to grasp and compute, while the former require intricate calculations. Further, if the Divisia aggregates are to be responsive to the changing liquidity patterns, they need recalculation of the user costs and expenditure shares for each period.

Empirical findings

We present below the results of just a few of the various empirical studies comparing simple sum aggregates (SM) with Divisia ones (DM). Among these is Barnett *et al.* (1984). They used quarterly USA data from 1959 to 1982 and conducted various tests related to money demand, velocity, and causality between money and income, and use in reduced form (St Louis) equations for income. They reported that neither the simple sum nor the Divisia aggregates did uniformly better than the other for all the criteria considered and no one aggregate was uniformly the best one. The Divisia aggregates performed better than the simple sum ones, except for M2, in causality tests. In the money demand functions and for its stability, the Divisia aggregates did better. But in the reduced-form equations for income, SM1 did better than DM1. Barnett *et al.* concluded that neither SM1 nor DM1 dominated the other under all criteria. However, the Divisia measures gave increasingly better results at higher levels of aggregation than the corresponding simple sum ones.

We have already mentioned Belongia and Chalfant (1989) in connection with weak separability tests. They tested the Divisia and simple sum versions of their weakly separable groups in St Louis equations and in equations relating the monetary aggregate to the monetary base to capture the degree of controllability, for USA quarterly data over 1976 to 1987. In the former test, there was a clear preference for M1 over broader measures. For the controllability tests, none of the measures did really well. Re-estimation for the period 1980 to 1987 led the authors to favour the Divisia over the simple sum version of M1A. Belongia (1996) tested the relationship between monetary aggregates and nominal income for the USA for the period 1980–1 to 1992–4 for the simple sum and the Divisia aggregates. His finding was that, for this relationship, the Divisia aggregates performed better than the simple sum ones and the instability of the money–income relationship is eliminated if the Divisia aggregates are used.

The above studies used standard estimation methods but not the cointegration techniques. Although these are explained in the next chapter, we do want to cite in this chapter some results based on these techniques. Chrystal and MacDonald (1994) compared the simple sum and Divisia aggregates for a number of countries, including the USA, the UK and Canada for various periods over the 1970s and 1980s. Their tests encompassed the St Louis equation and causality tests, and used cointegration. Note that the data for all the countries is contaminated by financial innovation over the sample period. We first examine their findings using the St Louis equation. For the USA, while M1 and M1A tended to do better than their Divisia versions, the latter did better for broader definitions of money. But DM2 – with D standing for 'Divisia' – did not sufficiently dominate SM2 – with S standing for 'simple sum' – for it to be clearly preferable. For the UK, the authors considered financial innovation to have sufficiently distorted the data to only include M0 – that is, the monetary base – and M4 in their estimations. While DM4 was clearly preferable to SM4, there was inadequate basis for choosing DM4 over M0. For Canada, while SM1 was slightly preferable to DM1, the broader Divisia aggregates were preferred to their simple sum versions.

For the causality tests, Chrystal and MacDonald considered it important to include an interest rate in their cointegration and error correction models. For the UK and Canada, both the Divisia and the simple sum aggregates showed little causal impact on real output. For the USA, the Divisia measures were significant but not the simple sum measures. The overall comparison based on both the St Louis equation and the causality tests did not, therefore, strongly favour one of the aggregates, though there was somewhat stronger support for the broad Divisia aggregates over the corresponding broad simple sum ones. For the USA, Chrystal and MacDonald found that this was especially so after 1980 when financial innovation occurred at a faster rate. By comparison, pre-1980 USA data did not favour the Divisia aggregates.[21]

To conclude, neither the simple sum nor the Divisia aggregates do better than the other for all levels of aggregation, all relevant tests and all periods. There is usually no clear dominance of DM1 over SM1, and the two measures have very similar growth rates. But, in general, the broader the aggregate, the more likely is the Divisia measure to do better. This is especially so in periods of financial innovation with increasing elasticities of substitution between M1 and other assets. As aggregation is broadened to include assets with very low substitution elasticities, further broadening of the Divisia aggregate makes little difference to the performance of the aggregate.

CONCLUSIONS

This chapter has examined several of the monetary aggregates used in the literature and the ways of evaluating their relative suitability. The starting point for any aggregation is establishing weak separability among the assets which are to be included in the aggregate. Once this has been established, the next choice is to construct a simple sum aggregate, a variable elasticity of substitution one, a Divisia one or some other aggregate. However, the usual comparison in the literature is between the simple sum aggregates and the Divisia aggregates, largely because of problems in reliable estimates of the variable elasticity of substitution.

Simple sum aggregation *a priori* assumes infinite elasticities of substitution between each pair of the component assets of the aggregate, and Divisia aggregation *a priori* assumes unit elasticity between each pair of the component assets of its aggregate. Intuitively, the former will tend to be the relevant one if the empirical elasticities of substitution are high and the latter if they are low. Thus, the public's currency balances and demand deposits in developed financial sectors tend to be almost perfect substitutes and their simple sum aggregate would be the more appropriate one. In fact, even the common constructs of the Divisia aggregates use the simple sum aggregate M1 for currency and demand deposits. However, in less developed economies with poor banking facilities in the rural areas and with high brokerage costs of banking, the rural public's currency balances and demand deposits are likely to have limited elasticity of substitution, so that their Divisia aggregation may be more appropriate in such a context.

For the financially developed economies, the simple sum M1 composed of currency in the hands of the public and demand deposits in commercial banks, is usually taken as one unified asset in constructing the broader Divisia aggregates. Further, since the return on M1 is usually taken to be zero, its rental cost would be higher than of any other asset with a positive rate of return, giving it a correspondingly higher weight in the Divisia aggregate.

While the Divisia aggregates are superior in terms of desirable index number properties, their *a priori* assumption of the unit elasticity of substitution limits their usefulness for aggregation over assets that are very close substitutes – and therefore have elasticities of substitution which are much greater than unity. It also prevents such aggregation over assets that are not substitutes – and therefore have a zero elasticity of substitution. Intuitive knowledge of the financial markets strongly indicates that there exist several near-monies[22] which are close substitutes for money and would have numerically very high elasticities of substitution. Chetty's estimates, though they have been called into question for various theoretical – especially in terms of their index number properties – and econometric reasons, indicate that many of the financial assets can have very high elasticities of substitution.

As the aggregation is broadened to bring in more and more assets into the aggregate, the additional assets are likely to have successively lower elasticities of substitution with currency balances and demand deposits, so that Divisia – as against simple sum – aggregation becomes correspondingly more relevant to the further broadening of the aggregate. In general, there is no *a priori* procedure for deciding which aggregation procedure is better over various groups of assets. One procedure may do better than the other over some groupings of assets and worse over others; further, the findings may differ among countries, and even over different periods for any given country.

In a dynamic context with innovation changing the liquidity weights, user costs and expenditure shares over time, the Divisia aggregates have the advantage that the relative weights of the assets can be changed and the computed index has a flexibility not available to simple sum aggregates. Therefore, the former are likely to perform better than the latter in a dynamic period of financial and technical innovation. However, they have not always done better than simple sum aggregates in different types of empirical tests; so that there is no convincing evidence that the former unambiguously dominate over the latter. Given this lack of convincing evidence and the familiarity and the ease of computation of simple sum aggregates, these aggregates continue to maintain their popularity for the policy makers, the public and much of the economics profession.

APPENDIX: DIVISIA AGGREGATION

The symbols in this appendix have the following meanings:

x Divisia index for the real value of the composite asset 'money'

x_i real value of asset X_i

s_i share of the expenditure on X_i

γ_i nominal user cost of X_i

γ_i^* real user cost of X_i

R maximum available yield – called the 'benchmark rate' – over the holding period

r_i pre-tax nominal yield on the ith asset

τ marginal tax rate

p_i price of asset i

Π product symbol

For Divisia price and quantity aggregates, we want to construct an overall index px where:

$$px = \Sigma_i p_i x_i \tag{8A.1}$$

The rate of change of px is given by:

$$\frac{dx}{x} + \frac{dp}{p} = \frac{\displaystyle\sum_{i=1}^{n}\left(x_i\, dp_i + p_i\, dx_i\right)}{\displaystyle\sum_{i=1}^{n} p_i x_i}$$

$$= \sum_{i=1}^{n} s_i \left[\frac{dp_i}{p_i} + \frac{dx_i}{x_i}\right] \tag{8A.2}$$

where

$$s_i = \frac{p_i x_i}{\displaystyle\sum_{i=1}^{n} p_i x_i} \tag{8A.3}$$

For the Divisia aggregates, we want to impose the conditions that the quantity index x in the overall index px change if and only if the quantities (but not the prices) of the component assets change and the price index p in the overall index change if and only if there is a change in the prices (but not in the quantities) of the component assets. Formally, the required conditions are that:

$$\frac{dx}{x} = \sum_{i=1}^{n} s_i \frac{dx_i}{x_i} \tag{8A.4}$$

$$\frac{dp}{p} = \sum_{i=1}^{n} s_i \frac{dp_i}{p_i} \tag{8A.5}$$

Integrating equations (8A.4) and (8A.5) and using the base period prices and quantities respectively designated as p_0 and x_0 as the constants of integration gives,

$$p_t = p_0 \exp\left[\int_0^t \sum_{i=1}^{n} s_i \frac{dp_i}{p}\right] \tag{8A.6}$$

$$x_t = x_0 \exp\left[\int_0^t \sum_{i=1}^{n} s_i \frac{dx_i}{x_i}\right] \tag{8A.7}$$

which yields the Divisia quantity index as:

$$x_t = \prod_{i=1}^{n} x_{it}^{s_{it}} \tag{8A.8}$$

$$\ln x_t = \sum_{i=1}^{n} s_{it} \ln x_{it} \tag{8A.8'}$$

and the Divisia price index as:

$$p_t = \prod_{i=1}^{n} p_{it}^{s_{it}} \tag{8A.9}$$

$$\ln p_t = \sum_{i=1}^{n} s_{it} \ln p_{it} \tag{8A.9'}$$

A comparison between two periods t and $t-1$, with $t-1$ treated as the base period for the index, changes equations (8A.6) and (8.7) to:

$$p_t = p_{t-1} \exp\left[\int_{t-1}^{t} \sum_{i=1}^{n} s_i \frac{dp_i}{p}\right]$$

$$x_t = x_{t-1} \exp\left[\int_{t-1}^{t} \sum_{i=1}^{n} s_i \frac{dx_i}{x}\right]$$

If we want to allow for the possibility that the expenditure on each asset is not constant over time so that s_{it} and s_{it-1} could differ, the equations corresponding to equations (8.A8) and (8.A9) can be approximated by:

$$p_t = p_{t-1} \prod_{i=1}^{n} \left[\frac{p_{it}}{p_{it}-1}\right]^{s_{it}^*} \tag{8A.10}$$

$$x_t = x_{t-1} \prod_{i=1}^{n} \left[\frac{x_{it}}{x_{it}-1}\right]^{s_{it}} \tag{8A.11}$$

where

$$s_{it}^* = \tfrac{1}{2}(s_{it} + s_{it-1}) \tag{8A.12}$$

The relevant weights now are s_{it}^*, the average share over time of the expenditure on the ith asset in period t. From (8A.10) and (8A.11), the rates of change in the Divisia price and quantity indices between periods t and $t-1$ are given by:

$$\ln p_t - \ln p_{t-1} = \Sigma_i s_{it}^* (\ln p_{it} - \ln p_{it-1}) \tag{8A.13}$$

$$\ln x_t - \ln x_{t-1} = \Sigma_i s_{it}^* (\ln x_{it} - \ln x_{it-1}) \tag{8A.14}$$

Returning to the general form of the Divisia index and focusing only on the Divisia quantity index, the before-tax nominal user cost γ_{it} and the real user cost γ_{it}^* of the ith asset in period t are:

$$\gamma_{it} = \frac{p_{it}\left(R_t - r_{it}\right)}{1 + R_t} \tag{8A.15}$$

$$\gamma_{it}^* = \frac{\left(R_t - r_t\right)}{1 + R_t} \tag{8A.16}$$

Equation (8A.15) specifies the present discounted value of the nominal user cost of holding the ith asset. As discussed in the body of the chapter, this user cost is defined for the flow of liquidity services provided by each asset, with these services assumed to be the only reason for the differences in their returns. The numerator $(R_t - r_{it})$ is the end-of-the-period *return forgone* from a dollar of the ith asset for its holding period;[23] R_t is the interest rate on the totally illiquid asset.[24] Therefore, the denominator $(1 + R_t)$ in (8A.15) is the discount factor to convert the end-of-the-period value to its present (beginning-of-the-period) value using the return R_t on the most illiquid asset.[25] Equation (8A.16) divides the nominal user cost by p_t to get the real user cost per dollar invested in the asset.

The corresponding nominal and real values of the expenditure shares on asset i are specified by:

$$s_{it} = \frac{x_{it} p_{it} \frac{\left(R_t - r_{it}\right)}{\left(1 + R_t\right)}}{\sum_{i=1}^{n} x_{it} p_{it} \frac{\left(R_t - r_{it}\right)}{\left(1 + R_t\right)}} \tag{8A.17}$$

$$= \frac{x_{it} p_{it} \left(R_t - r_{it}\right)}{\sum_{i=1}^{n} x_{it} p_{it} \left(R_t - r_{it}\right)} \tag{8A.18}$$

From (8A.8') and (8A.18), the Divisia quantity index is given by:

$$\ln x_t = \sum_{i=1}^{n} \ln x_{it} \left[\frac{x_{it} p_{it}\left(R_t - r_{it}\right)}{\sum_{i=1}^{n} x_{it} p_{it}\left(R_t - r_{it}\right)}\right] \tag{8A.19}$$

If the tax authorities levy a constant tax rate of τ_t in period t on interest income but not on liquidity services, the corresponding equations for user cost, shares of expenditures on each asset and the Divisia quantity index adjusted for this constant tax rate would be as in the following equations:

$$\gamma_{it} = \frac{p_{it}\left(R_t - r_{it}\right)\left(1 - \tau_t\right)}{1 + R_t\left(1 - \tau_t\right)} \tag{8A.20}$$

$$\gamma_{it}^* = \frac{\left(R_t - r_{it}\right)\left(1 - \tau_t\right)}{1 + R_t\left(1 - \tau_t\right)} \tag{8A.21}$$

$$s_{it} = \frac{x_{it}p_{it}\left(R_t - r_{it}\right)\left(1 - \tau\right)}{\sum_{i=1}^{n} x_{it}p_{it}\left(R_t - r_{it}\right)\left(1 - \tau\right)} \qquad (8A.22)$$

$$\ln x_t = \sum_{i=1}^{n} \ln x_{it}\left[\frac{x_{it}p_{it}\left(R_t - r_{it}\right)\left(1 - \tau_t\right)}{\sum_{i=1}^{n} x_{it}p_{it}\left(R_t - r_{it}\right)\left(1 - \tau_t\right)}\right] \qquad (8A.23)$$

SUMMARY OF CRITICAL CONCLUSIONS

- A simple sum aggregate assumes perfect substitution – that is, infinite elasticity of substitution – among its components.
- A Divisia aggregate assumes unit elasticity of substitution among its components.
- The variable elasticity of substitution (VES) monetary aggregate allows the elasticity of substitution to differ between pairs of its components and also does not *a priori* impose on each one a given elasticity of substitution. It allows the elasticity of substitution to lie in the range from zero to infinity.
- The Divisia aggregate weights each component by its share of expenditure out of the total expenditure on the aggregate.
- The appropriate cost of using a monetary asset is its user cost.
- There are several criteria for judging among monetary aggregates. Two of the most important of these are the stability of their demand function and their performance in explaining nominal national income.
- The empirical evidence tends to favour Divisia aggregation for broader monetary definitions while favouring simple sum aggregation for the narrower ones.
- Changes in the money stock do cause changes in nominal national income. However, there may also be a reverse causality, depending on the economy and the time period.

review and discussion questions

1 How would you define the liquidity of an asset, measure this liquidity and to what uses can your definition have relevance? Compare your definition with one other definition or measure of liquidity and its strong and weak points.
2 The definition of money is clear enough if we consider only the transactions demand for money, but the introduction of the asset demand for money makes any attempt to distinguish sharply between M1 and other monetary assets unsatisfactory. Discuss.
3 How would you test for the substitutability of different near-monies for M1? Present at least two different procedures that have been used in the literature for this purpose.

    How would you compare the estimates obtained from the two procedures?
4 Compare the *a priori* restrictions imposed on the elasticity of substitution by the following aggregation procedures:

    (i) simple sum aggregates;
    (ii) Divisia aggregates;
    (iii) VES (variable elasticity of substitution) aggregates.

Using your intuition on the likely elasticities of substitution in your country, with demand deposits as the base asset, in which aggregate would you place the following:

(a) saving deposits in commercial banks;
(b) saving deposits in other financial institutions (name these);
(c) money market mutual funds sold by banks to the public (if any);
(d) money market mutual funds sold by other institutions to the public (if any);
(e) Treasury bills;
(f) short-term bonds;
(g) shares of corporations.

5 Can evidence that the lagged values of the money stock are significant in equations forecasting nominal GDP help in establishing the claim that changes in the money stock cause changes in nominal GDP?

6 Can evidence that the future values of the money stock are significant in equations forecasting nominal GDP provide any information on the direction of causality between the changes in the money stock and nominal GDP?

7 Given two variables Y and M, specify the Granger–Sims test for the direction of causality between them. What did this test for the United States show?
How would you also test for the possibility that a third variable Z also causes one or both of Y and M?

8 Conduct the Granger–Sims test for the direction of causality between simple sum and Divisia monetary aggregates and income in your economy and interpret its results for the direction of causality and the choice among the monetary aggregates.

9 Specify the variable elasticity of substitution (VES) function for the monetary aggregate for your economy, derive its estimation equations and estimate the VES aggregate.

10 Specify the Divisia function for the monetary aggregate for your economy, derive its estimation equations and estimate the Divisia aggregate.
What tests would you use to select between your VES and Divisia estimates? Do at least two of them.

11 'Money demand functions have been shifting in ways that make them unsuitable for selecting the appropriate monetary aggregate for a given economy.' Report on some studies that have used the stability of the money demand function for judging among monetary aggregates but have arrived at conflicting results. In view of such conflicting findings, should we abandon 'data mining' for the 'best' monetary aggregate and stick to an *a priori* or theoretical definition of money?

NOTES

1 Beyond M1 and M2, there is no uniformity in defining M3 and M4 and so on, though the increase in digits does indicate the inclusion of progressively fewer liquid assets in the aggregate.

2 The other functions of money are: store of value, standard of deferred payments and unit of account.

3 In fact, at some of the earlier stages in financial development while the banks are non-existent or the costs of using demand deposits are very significant, demand deposits themselves do not serve as a medium of payments. In such stages, the medium of payments function would imply that only currency is money.

4 The history of monetary development is in a sense that of the extension of the list of assets

which function as the medium of payments. At the early stages, only currency performs this role; then currency and demand deposits; followed by currency, demand deposits and savings deposits; with still more additions of other assets further in the development process.

5 Among these are the translog form, the Gorman polar flexible functional form and the Fourier flexible functional form.

6 Weak separability is determined directly from the data on quantities (Varian, 1983). Another form of grouping can be based on the quasi-separability of prices. A set of variables is said to be *quasi-separable* if the expenditure on it is a function only of total utility and the prices of goods in the group, but not of the prices of other goods.

7 NOWs are essentially a type of checkable savings deposits which can be transferred by negotiable orders of withdrawal corresponding to cheques, so that NOWs are really a form of checkable deposits.

8 We use here the symbol X_i for the nominal value of the asset i even though it was used as the name of the asset in section 8.4.

9 The usual format of this equation can be obtained by setting $(1 + v_i)$ equal to $-\rho_i$.

10 Note that $v = -1$ turns the CES function into the Cobb–Douglas one, which is log-linear.

11 Note that the elasticity of substitution is different from the own-price elasticities of demand for the ith asset. The latter is defined as $\partial x_i/\partial p_i$. It is also different from the cross-price elasticity of demand for an asset i with respect to the price of another asset j, measured as $\partial x_i/\partial p_j$. The relationship between the elasticity of substitution and the own and cross-elasticities of demand is discussed later in this section.

12 This definition of the price of an asset is not based on its user or rental cost, discussed in section 8.6 below. More recent contributions in the literature have not used Chetty's specification of prices but have substituted a user cost definition in its place.

13 Irving Fisher had presented in the 1920s a detailed analysis of index number and their properties. Among the index numbers specified by him were the Laspeyres, the Paasche and Fisher's ideal index, with the last one as a geometric average of the former two.

14 A more specific functional form of the VES equation (10), for $v_i = v = 1$ for all i, is given by the Cobb–Douglas functional form.

15 Different assets provide different levels of liquidity services. Thus, currency and demand deposits are more liquid than long-term bonds. An aggregate measuring the total flow of these services should weight the holdings of the assets by a measure of the services provided by the respective asset, so that currency and demand deposits should have a higher weight than long-term bonds. The variable elasticity of substitution function and the Divisia aggregate do so, the simple sum aggregates do not.

16 Divisia aggregates are part of a class of statistical index numbers which are sometimes designated as 'superlative'.

17 For example, if the data is generated by a scenario where the elasticities of substitution are considerably in excess of unity for some pairs of assets and zero among others.

18 If economic theory implies such an impact, the following specification of this procedure will lead to erroneous conclusions on the direction of causality.

19 Note that the serial correlation of the error term in a regression would lead to spurious results. Such serial correlation can cause the estimated coefficients of the future terms to erroneously differ from zero.

20 Note that if the rates of return on both currency and demand deposits are zero and if their non-monetary costs are being ignored, the user cost of the two would be identical. This would impart a degree of similarity in their weighting in Divisia aggregation. Barnett *et al.* (1984) argue that since the return on currency and demand deposits move similarly, their simple sum aggregate M1 and its Divisia aggregate DM1 tend to perform similarly under the various criteria.

21 Serletis and Robb (1986) found a low degree of substitution among the monetary assets in Canada and little justification for M2 and broader aggregates. Their study favoured the Divisia aggregates over the simple sum ones.

22 For example, checkable savings deposits are now very close substitutes to demand deposits for most individuals.

23 Both interest rates should be over the holding period of the ith asset. However, r_i is usually over a shorter holding period than R, which would be the interest rate on a long-term bond. To adjust for the difference in the holding period, all rates have to be adjusted to the same maturity.

24 In practice, this asset is taken to be one with the highest interest rate, so that all other assets would have positive user costs.

25 Note that this designation (Barnett *et al.*, 1984) of the price or cost of the ith asset differs from that in Chetty (1969). In the present notation and assuming a zero tax rate, Chetty's measure of the current price of the asset would have been $\{1/(1 + r_{it})\}$. It is the present discounted value of \$1 obtained at the end of the period from the asset i, with the discount factor as $(1 + r_{it})$.

As against these two measures, Donovan (1978) defined the price of the ith asset as $(1 + r_{it})/(1 + R_t)$, where $(1 + r_{it})$ is the amount which one dollar invested in asset X_i in period t would yield at the end of the period; $(1 + r_{it})/(1 + R_t)$ is its present value.

There are thus different ways of defining the price or user cost of an asset. Equation (8.A16) seems preferable to the other measures because of its focus in the numerator on the return forgone from holding a liquid asset as against an illiquid one. It also uses the market discount rate on illiquid assets which would be the relevant one for loans to the individual.

REFERENCES

Anderson, Leonall C., and Jerry L. Jordan. 'Monetary and Fiscal Actions: A Test of their Relative Importance in Economic Stabilization'. *Federal Reserve Bank of St Louis Review*, November 1968, pp. 11–24.

Barnett, William A., Edward K. Offenbacher and Paul A. Spindt. 'The New Divisia Monetary Aggregates'. *Journal of Political Economy*, 92, December 1984, pp. 1049–85.

Belongia, Michael T. 'Measurement Matters: Recent Results from Monetary Economics Revisited'. *Journal of Political Economy*, 104, October 1996, pp. 1065–83.

———, and J. A. Chalfant. 'The Changing Empirical Definition of Money: Some Estimates from a Model of the Demand for Money Substitutes'. *Journal of Political Economy*, 97, April 1989, pp. 387–97.

———, and K. Alec Chrystal. 'An Admissible Monetary Aggregate for the UK'. *Review of Economics and Statistics*, 73, August 1991, pp. 497–503.

Chetty, V. Karuppan. 'On Measuring the Nearness of Near-Monies'. *American Economic Review*, 59, June 1969, pp. 270–81.

Chrystal, K. Alec, and Ronald MacDonald. 'Empirical Evidence on the Recent Behavior and Usefulness of Simple Sum and Weighted Measures of the Money Stock'. *Federal Reserve Bank of St Louis Review*, 76, March/April 1994, pp. 73–109.

Donovan, Donald J. 'Modeling the Demand for Liquid Assets: An Application to Canada'. *International Monetary Fund Staff Papers*, 25, December 1978, pp. 676–704.

Feige, Edgar L., and Douglas K. Pearce. 'The Substitutability of Money and Near-Monies: A Survey of the Time-Series Evidence'. *Journal of Economic Literature*, 15, June 1977, pp. 439–70.

Friedman, Benjamin, and Kenneth N. Kutner. 'Money, Income, Prices and Interest Rates'. *American Economic Review*, 82, June 1992, pp. 472–93.

Friedman, Milton, and Anna T. Schwartz. *A Monetary History of the United States 1870–1960*. Princeton, NJ: Princeton University Press, 1963.

———, and ———. 'Money and Business Cycles'. *Review of Economics and Statistics*, 45, 1963, Supp., pp. 32–64; Comments, pp. 64–78.

Goldfeld, Stephen M. 'The Demand for Money Revisited'. *Brookings Papers on Economic Activity*, 3, 1973, pp. 577–638.

Judd, John P., and John L. Scadding. 'The Search for a Stable Money Demand Function: A Survey of the Post-1973 Literature'. *Journal of Economic Literature*, 20, September 1982, pp. 993–1023.

Rotemberg, Julio J., John C. Driscoll and James M. Porterba. 'Money, Output and Prices: Evidence from a New Monetary Aggregate'. *Journal of Economic and Business Statistics*, 13, January 1995, pp. 67–83.

Serletis, Apostolos, and A. Leslie Robb. 'Divisia Aggregation and Substitutability among Monetary Assets'. *Journal of Money, Credit and Banking*, 18, November 1986, pp. 430–46.

Sims, Christopher. 'Money, Income and Causality'. *American Economic Review*, 62, September 1972, pp. 540–52.

Swofford, James L., and Gerald A. Whitney. 'Nonparametric Tests of Utility Maximization and Weak Separability for Consumption, Leisure and Money'. *Review of Economics and Statistics*, 69, August 1987, pp. 458–64.

Varian, Hal R. 'Nonparametric Tests of Consumer Behavior'. *Review of Economic Studies*, 50, January 1983, pp. 99–110.

chapter nine

THE DEMAND FUNCTION FOR MONEY: EMPIRICAL FINDINGS

This chapter presents a summary of the empirical findings on the demand for money. These are in addition to the empirical findings on monetary aggregation reported in the preceding chapter and on the precautionary and buffer stock demands reported in Chapter 6.

The empirical evidence clearly confirms the dependence of the demand for money on both a scale variable and an interest rate. The issue of which variable should be used – current income, permanent income or wealth – is not settled. Nor has any consensus emerged on the definition of the money variable to be used as the dependent variable, in spite of innumerable studies during the past half-century. In fact, we are compelled to conclude that this consensus will never be achieved.

An interesting new development is the attempt to determine the buffer stock demand for money. Another development is the application of cointegration techniques with error-correction modelling to the demand for money.

---

key concepts introduced in this chapter

- Shifts in the money demand function
- Buffer stock demand for money
- Shock absorption models of money demand
- Currency substitution
- Non-stationarity
- Unit roots
- Cointegration
- Error-correction model

Chapters 3 to 6 presented the theory of the demand for money for both the general case and from the perspective of each of the motives for holding money balances. Chapter 7 examined the issues of lags, expectations and the econometric problems commonly encountered in estimating the demand function for money. Chapter 8 looked into the questions of defining money for such functions. This chapter completes the treatment of the demand for money by a brief survey of the empirical findings on the more important of the issues raised by theory in Chapters 3 to 8.

There are a very large number of empirical studies on the money demand function. It would take up too much space to review even the more important of these studies, or to do justice to the ones from which we adopt the results. Among the many excellent reviews of these in the literature are Cuthbertson (1991), Goldfeld (1973), Feige and Pearce (1977), Judd and Scadding (1982), Goldfeld and Sichel (1990), and Miyao (1996). We will only present the generic findings on the more significant issues, especially those on the income and interest rate elasticities and the appropriate measure of the monetary aggregate. We intend to pay particular attention to the newer approaches of cointegration analysis and buffer stock money holdings.

Note that the empirical findings on monetary aggregation were reported in Chapter 8 and those on the buffer stock and precautionary demands were reported in Chapter 6. The empirical material in those chapters complements that in this one. In particular, the empirical findings concerning Divisia aggregates are to be found in Chapter 8 rather than this chapter.

Sections 9.1 and 9.2 present the basic findings on the dependence of money demand on income, wealth and interest rates. Section 9.3 looks at the liquidity trap, discussed earlier in Chapter 2. Section 9.4 examines the dependence of money demand on the rate of inflation, and section 9.5 deals with shifts in the money demand function due to innovations. Section 9.6 presents the findings on currency substitution. Section 9.7 presents a brief historical review of the estimation of money demand functions and their findings. Sections 9.8 and 9.9 present a brief treatment of the econometric techniques of cointegration and error-correction models and the findings of some empirical using these procedures. Section 9.10 presents some empirical studies on the buffer stock models presented in Chapter 6.

9.1 INCOME AND/OR WEALTH AS THE DETERMINANT OF MONEY DEMAND

What is the appropriate form of the income and wealth variables, and should there be only one of these as a regressor in the money demand function? In empirical studies, income is generally taken to be the net domestic product for the economy. Wealth has two components: non-human wealth, which is the aggregate value of assets in the economy, and human wealth, which is the present discounted value of current and future labour income. As discussed in Chapter 3, if data on either or both of these components is not available or cannot be reliably proxied, one recourse is to use the data on non-human wealth and use labour income as an additional variable, as in the life cycle consumption hypothesis. The alternative recourse is to use data on average expected or permanent income as a proxy for total wealth, as proposed by Milton Friedman for his permanent income hypothesis of consumption and discussed in Chapters 2 and 7 above. Under adaptive expectations, such a variable is specified as an exponentially weighted average of current and past levels of national income, constructed either in a study explaining consumption or directly estimated as part of the estimation of the demand for money. Alternatively, the rational expectations hypothesis, as discussed in Chapter 7, can be used for its construction.

For the data covering the 1950s and 1960s in the USA, regression analysis of the demand for money from equations containing both income and wealth, as well as from equations containing only one of these variables, showed that wealth provided a more stable demand function for money than current national income and that when both variables were included simultaneously the coefficient of the income variable was insignificant. Permanent income similarly did better than current income. These results held especially if money was defined as M2 or M3 but also held in some studies where the dependent variable was M1. Further, among functions using income, nonhuman wealth and permanent income, the empirical estimates showed that functions using a wealth concept gave more accurate predictions of the velocity of circulation of money broadly defined, and sometimes for M1, than did those containing income.

9.2 THE RELEVANT INTEREST RATE IN THE MONEY DEMAND FUNCTION

There are a number of interest rates in the economy, ranging from the return to time and savings deposits in banks and near-banks to those on short- and long-term bonds. Near-money assets such as savings deposits in commercial banks proved to be the closest substitutes for M1, so that their rate of return seems to be the most appropriate variable as the interest cost of using M1.

But if a broader definition of money were used, the interest rate on medium- or long-term bonds becomes more appropriate as the alternative to holding M2 or M3 is longer-term bonds, since the time and savings components of the broad definition of money themselves earn an interest rate close to the short-rate of interest.

The interest rates usually used in estimating money demand are: the interest rate paid on savings deposits in commercial banks, on those in credit unions (such as mutual savings banks and savings and loan associations in the USA, *caisses populaires* in Quebec, Canada); the yield on Treasury bills or on short-term prime commercial paper and the yield on longer-term – such as three-year to twenty-year – government or commercial bonds. Each of these interest rates seems to do fairly well, sometimes better and sometimes worse than others, in some study or other, and yields different coefficients.

A uniformly good performance, irrespective of which of the interest rates is included in the regression, is an indication that the various interest rates are related, moving up or down in a consistent pattern, so that it is immaterial which interest rate is included. One theory that points towards such consistency of pattern is the expectations hypothesis on the term structure of interest rates, i.e. on the yields on assets differing in maturity. Chapter 21 presents this hypothesis for the financially well-developed financial markets, pointing out that it has done remarkably well in explaining the differences in the yields of assets differing in maturity. A consequence of such a relationship among interest rates is that the inclusion of more than one interest rate results in multicollinearity and therefore in biased estimates of their coefficients, as discussed in Chapter 7.

However, while the relevant interest rates are closely related, they do not move so closely together that any of them will do equally well in estimation, so that usually one or two of them have to be chosen on empirical grounds for inclusion as regressors. On the wider question of whether the demand for money depends on interest rates or not, there is substantial evidence that the demand for money does depend negatively upon the rate of interest in financially developed economies. This is also the finding of many studies on the LDCs.

However, some studies on the LDCs do not find significant interest rate elasticities for a variety of reasons, including regulatory limits on the interest rates in the economy and inadequate access to banking and other financial facilities. In these cases, very often the rate of inflation rather than the published data on interest rates yields better empirical results. This occurs because the regulated interest rates usually do not accurately reflect the expected rate of inflation – as market-determined rates do in developed financial markets – so that land, inventories and other real assets – whose prices better reflect the rate of inflation – become more attractive alternatives to holding cash than bonds.

9.3 THE LIQUIDITY TRAP

One of the questions of interest, discussed in Chapter 2 above, in monetary theory since Keynes has been about the empirical existence of the liquidity trap. Keynes posited the possible existence of such a trap, though he also expressed the belief that he did not know of any case where it had existed.

One possible method of testing for the existence of the liquidity trap is to estimate the demand for money separately for periods with differing ranges of the prevailing interest rates. Estimates showing that the interest elasticity of demand tends to increase in periods with lower ranges of interest rates, and especially showing a substantial increase at very low interest rates, can be interpreted as raising a presumption that the liquidity trap could have existed empirically. However, empirical studies so far have not revealed such a pattern. Velocity functions estimated separately for each decade did not find any higher interest elasticity of the demand for money during the 1930s when interest rates were low than during other decades with higher interest rates. Further, regressions incorporating data from the 1930s did fairly well in predicting velocity during the subsequent decades, implying that the interest elasticities during the 1930s did not differ substantially from more normal conditions.

Therefore, the liquidity trap does not seem to have existed for any significant period, if at all, during the Great Depression of the 1930s and is even less likely as a possibility for other periods.

9.4 MONEY DEMAND AND THE EXPECTED RATE OF INFLATION

One of the alternatives to holding money is commodities, which have the (expected) rate of return equal to the expected rate of inflation less their storage and depreciation costs. Some of the commodities – as, for example, untaxed plots of land – have minimal storage and depreciation costs, so that the (expected) rate of return on commodities is usually taken to be proxied by the expected rate of inflation. Therefore, the expected rate of inflation is one of the arguments in the money demand function, in addition to interest rates, as Friedman's analysis of money demand in Chapter 2 had pointed out.

However, in perfect financial markets, the nominal and the real rates of interest are related by the equation:

$$r_t = r^r_t + \pi^e_t \tag{1}$$

where:

r rate of interest
r^r real rate of interest
π^e expected rate of inflation

The real rate r^r in practice has two components, a determinate one and a random one. In the modern classical approach with rational expectations, its determinate component is invariant with respect to changes in the money supply and in the past rates of inflation.[1] Further, at significant rates of inflation, variations in the real rate tend to be much smaller in magnitude than the expected rate of inflation, so that r_t and π^e_t will be closely correlated. Given this close correlation and that between π^e_t and the actual rate of inflation π_t, r and π are closely correlated in periods with significant inflation rates. Therefore, incorporating both r_t and π_t in the money demand equations often leads to multicollinearity and biased estimates of their coefficients. As a way round these statistical problems, π_t is often dropped in favour of r_t from the estimated money demand equations for developed economies with reliable data on r_t. However, economic theory implies its inclusion in addition to the inclusion of interest rates, so that its omission could result in a misspecified equation.

In economies, such as the LDCs, where the financial markets are not well developed, ceilings are often imposed on the rates of interest that can legally be paid and there could exist both an official interest rate and a free or black market rate. Further, reliable data on interest rates may not be available. In these cases, π^e_t should be retained in the estimating equation, in addition to – and sometimes even to the exclusion of – the interest rate. Note that the proper variable is π^e_t and that π_t is only one of the possible proxies to it.[2]

9.5 SHIFTS OF THE MONEY DEMAND FUNCTION

Financial innovation is a frequent occurrence in the economy. Some types of innovations change the liquidity characteristics of the existing assets or represent the creation of new assets. Other types of innovation are in the payments and banking technologies. Some of the innovations could also be due to the attempt of the financial industry to get around financial regulations. Another is the introduction of new techniques of financial management by firms, households and financial institutions. All of these occurred during the last three decades, probably collectively at a faster pace than in earlier decades.

Among the new types of assets, in the USA, interest-bearing checking accounts were first introduced as NOW (negotiable orders of withdrawal) and then as super-NOW accounts in the late 1970s and early 1980s. Commercial banks began to issue small certificates of deposit in the 1960s and money market mutual funds in the late 1970s. These were outside the traditional definition of M1. In the UK, commercial banks and building societies introduced checkable interest-bearing accounts in the 1980s. In each case, there was a learning period for the public and introduced shifts in the money demand function over many years.

If the innovations merely change the constant term or the coefficients of the independent variables in the money demand function, they can be relatively easy to capture in estimation through period splitting or the use of dummy constant and interactive variables. However, some of the resulting shifts of the money demand function are much more difficult to capture or cannot be captured, and the researcher ends up with the judgement that the money demand function has become unstable.

The desperate search for a stable money demand function

The last three decades have seen a remarkable number of innovations in the monetary sphere. These resulted in a breakdown of the estimated money demand functions and a large number of innovations by the researchers in their estimating equations and techniques. The attempts to find a stable demand function have included changes in the monetary aggregate used as the dependent variable (M1, M2, M3, or their Divisia counterparts). Other attempts centred around variations in the arguments of the function. These included the use of current income, permanent income, wage income or property income, etc., for the scale variable, and the use of short interest rates, long interest rates, the rate of inflation, or a composite index of interest rates, etc., for the interest rate variable.

Still other attempts changed the form of the estimating equation from linear to log-linear and semi-log-linear, or switched to non-linear functions or tried those with stochastic coefficients, or used transcendental functions, etc. Some other attempts focused on the proper specification of the dynamic adjustment of the actual to desired money balances. The econometric techniques have included the classical regression techniques and cointegration-error correction models, among others.

This prolific variety of attempts and deviations from the standard money demand equation almost gives one the impression of a field dominated by data mining and the *ad hoc* constructions of a profession desperate at finding a stable money demand function to back its theory. While this may sound a rather harsh assessment, it does serve as a reminder of the severe difficulties in finding a stable money demand function during the ongoing innovations of the recent decades.

For the USA, there appears to have been a downward shift in the demand function during the 1970s and an upward shift during the 1980s. In these decades, as in the 1990s, actual money holdings deviated remarkably from the predictions of most estimated money demand models. In terms of velocity, the velocity of M1 increased in the 1970s and decreased in the 1980s in a manner not predicted by these models.

9.6 CHANGES IN THE EXCHANGE RATE AND CURRENCY SUBSTITUTION IN THE MONEY DEMAND FUNCTION

Among the alternatives to holding domestic money are the currencies, bonds and other assets of foreign countries, so that, for open economies, the regressors of the domestic money demand should include not only the rates of return on domestic assets but also those on the foreign ones. Given this, some of the money demand studies pay special attention to the substitution between the domestic and foreign currencies, especially in the case of countries in which one or more foreign currencies circulate widely. Such substitution is called *currency substitution*.

Theories of currency substitution

For the study of currency substitution, the relevant alternative assets can be taken to be domestic and foreign currencies, and domestic and foreign bonds. There are enormous numbers of each of these. The relevant approaches to the degrees of substitution between pairs of them are the transactions approach and the asset approach.

Under the asset approach, the relevant theory would be the theory of portfolio selection, as set out in Chapter 5, to the choice among currencies and bonds. This theory would determine substitution between currencies on the basis of their expected yield and risk. Two currencies would, therefore, be perfect substitutes if they had identical returns. They would be poor substitutes if the return on one dominates that on the other. This dominance does not in general apply. Further, under flexible exchange rates, the returns on various currencies are expected to be equalized. Therefore, under the asset approach, various pairs of currencies are expected to be good substitutes for each other. This portfolio selection approach has so far dominated the literature on currency substitution.

Under the transactions approach, it is the general acceptance in daily exchanges and payments that would determine the degree of substitution between the alternative assets. Handa (1988) used this approach to designate the domestic currency as being 'the preferred habitat'[3] for medium of payments since it is the one which is most readily accepted in domestic transactions. Under this reasoning, since bonds do not serve as a medium of payments, they would have almost zero substitutability with the domestic currency. The degree of substitutability between the domestic currency and a given foreign one would depend on the latter's acceptance for payments in the domestic economy or the cost and ease of conversion from the latter into the former. In general, there is a very significant transactions cost in conversion of foreign currencies into the domestic one. These costs are in the spread between the purchase and sale conversion rates and in banks' commissions, and are usually quite significant for the size of the transactions of the representative household in the economy.

Consequently, the general presumption under the preferred habitat approach would be that foreign currencies will have low elasticities of substitution with the domestic one, except possibly in cases where a particular foreign currency is generally accepted in payments in the domestic economy. To illustrate, while the US dollars are sometimes accepted for payments in Canada, their usage and acceptance is not all that common so that, although there is some substitution with the Canadian dollar, it may not be a high one. However, the Canadian dollar finds almost no acceptance in the United States, so that they are poor substitutes in the US economy. Further, even in the Canadian economy, even if the Canadian and US dollars proved to be good substitutes, the British currency is not generally accepted and should be a poor substitute for the Canadian dollar. Therefore, under this preferred habitat hypothesis, we should in general find low or zero substitution between currencies, except in special cases.

Among these special cases of possibly high substitutability is the use of the local currency and the imperial one in the case of colonies during the colonial era. Another special case is the use of the euro and the national currencies within the member countries of the European

Union. The member countries started with their domestic currencies as the preferred habitat. As Europe integrates the euro into common transactions usage, the degree of substitutability between the domestic currency and the euro would increase. If there are no banking or other transactions charges between them, they would in the limit become perfect substitutes. Further, while the different national currencies continue to exist, the degree of substitutability among them would increase as there comes about easier conversion at zero transactions costs between the domestic and the foreign currencies, either directly or through the three-way conversion from the foreign ones to the euro and from the euro to the domestic one.

Estimation procedures and problems

There are two basic methods of estimating currency substitution. One is to estimate the Euler equations (first-order conditions) based on a constant or variable elasticity of substitution function, following Chetty's procedure explained in Chapter 8. In this procedure the domestic balances would be the dependent variable, and independent variables would include the foreign currency balances – or those of a designated foreign currency – held by the domestic residents.[4] Among the studies initiating this approach is Miles (1978).

The second estimation procedure is to expand the estimating money demand equation to include among its regressors the return on at least one foreign currency, as well as the returns on foreign bonds and physical assets. This is the more usual method for estimating currency substitution. It can be found in Bordo and Choudhri (1982), Bana and Handa (1987)[5] and Handa (1988). We elaborate on this approach in the following.

The returns on domestic and foreign currencies include both their non-monetary returns – that is, liquidity services and relative security, etc. – and the changes in their nominal values relative to each other. While the liquidity and other non-monetary services are often critical for the demand for foreign currencies, data on them is usually non-existent, so that they are almost always excluded from the analysis. This is a significant deficiency of the empirical studies on currency substitution. The return on foreign currencies is, therefore, measured only by the expected change in the value of the domestic currency in terms of the foreign one. This expected change in the relative nominal value is given by the expected rate of depreciation of the domestic currency *vis-à-vis* the given foreign currency.[6] Designate this return as $(\partial\rho/\partial t)^e$, where ρ is the exchange rate between currencies. $(\partial\rho/\partial t)^e$ is then the measure of the opportunity cost of holding the domestic currency rather than the foreign one.

In small open economies with perfect financial markets, the domestic and foreign interest rates are related by:[7]

$$r_t = r_t^f + (\partial\rho/\partial t)_t^e \tag{2}$$

where:

r_t	yield on domestic bonds (domestic rate of interest)
r_t^f	yield on foreign bonds (foreign rate of interest)
ρ	exchange rate (foreign currency per unit of the domestic one)
$(\partial\rho/\partial t)^e$	expected rate of depreciation of the domestic currency
t	holding period for currencies and bonds

In expanded money demand functions, since foreign bonds are among the alternatives to holding domestic money in open economies, r_t^f is also one of the opportunity costs of holding domestic money. Hence, r_t, r_t^f and $(\partial\rho/\partial t)^e$ are all arguments of the money demand function. Equations (1) and (2) imply that only two of these are independent variables so that any two of them, but not all three, should be included in the estimating money demand equation. The two variables so selected are usually the domestic rate of interest and the expected rate of exchange rate depreciation. However, this would make it difficult to capture the substitution between the domestic currency and foreign bonds, which is an element of capital mobility rather than of the substitution of the liquidity services of the foreign currency for the domestic one. Some authors would, therefore, include all three of these variables and designate the elasticity of domestic money demand with respect to $(\partial \rho / \partial t)^e$ as reflecting currency substitution while the elasticity with respect to r^f would reflect the substitution of domestic currency versus foreign bonds.

Note that the elasticity of domestic money demand with respect to $(\partial \rho / \partial t)^e$ is a 'price' elasticity and as such does not directly measure the elasticity of substitution between the domestic and the foreign currency. The relationship between the price elasticity and the elasticity of substitution has already been discussed in Chapter 8 in connection with Chetty's procedure.

The standard money demand function modified to take account of foreign currencies and foreign bonds as alternatives to domestic money is usually specified as:

$$m^d = a_0 + a_r r + a_y y + a_3 (\partial \rho / t)^e + a_4 r^f \tag{3}$$

where:

m^d domestic money balances
y domestic national income

Estimating (3) in a log-linear form would make a_3 the price elasticity with respect to the return on foreign currencies and therefore a measure of currency substitution. Similarly, a_4 would capture the substitution between the domestic currency and foreign bonds. As mentioned earlier, many studies set $a_4 = 0$. Equation (3) is often modified to incorporate a partial adjustment model and estimated by the ordinary regression techniques. It can, alternatively, be estimated using the cointegration and error-correction techniques, discussed later in this chapter.

Empirical findings on currency substitution

Giovannini and Turtelboom (1994) represent an excellent review of the theoretical and empirical literature on currency substitution.[8] Miles (1978), estimating the first-order conditions from a variable elasticity of substitution function, had reported high elasticities of substitution between the Canadian and US currencies under flexible exchange rates. This finding was questioned in re-estimations by other authors. Among the studies using the demand function approach,[9] as in equation (1), the 'price' elasticity measured has ranged between −0.2 and −0.5 for Canada. Evidence of more significant currency substitution has been reported for some of the Latin American countries, though usually with the return on foreign currencies being proxied not by $(\partial \rho / \partial t)^e$ but by other variables such as the differential between the domestic and foreign inflation rates or money growth rates.

Handa (1988), in a test of the preferred habitat for the medium of payments, reported that the degree of substitution between the Canadian and US currencies was virtually non-existent even for Canadian residents. Since the US dollar trades more commonly in Canada than most foreign currencies do outside their own countries, the above result has a wider application and suggests that we would in general not find significant substitution among most currencies.[10]

Whether direct currency substitution – that is, between the domestic and foreign currencies, rather than between the domestic currency and foreign bonds or between domestic and foreign bonds – is really significant and must be integrated in any estimations of the domestic money demand function for most economies remains a moot point. In practice, most such estimations do not incorporate it, so that the estimation of currency substitution remains a specialized and distinct topic within the money demand literature.

9.7 A BRIEF HISTORICAL REVIEW OF THE ESTIMATION OF MONEY DEMAND

By the end of the 1960s, the basic form of the money demand function had evolved as:

$$m^d = a_0 + a_r r + a_y x \tag{4}$$

where x is a scale variable. The stochastic form of this function was estimated in either a linear or log-linear form. During the 1960s, the main disputes were whether money should be defined as M1, M2 or by a still wider definition, whether the interest rate should be short term or long term, and whether the scale variable x should be income, permanent income or wealth. The data usually used for estimation was annual.

The period of the 1950s and early 1960s in many countries was one during which the regulatory authority did not allow interest to be paid on demand deposits. Further, the interest rates paid on savings deposits were subject to upper limits, savings deposits could not be drawn upon by cheque and a switch from savings deposits to demand deposits often required a personal visit to the relevant financial institutions. Under these conditions, the general finding among the empirical studies was that M2 did better than M1 and measures broader than M2. The explanatory variables that usually performed best with M2 as the dependent variable were medium or long interest rates, with wealth or permanent income as the scale variable. The estimating function was normally stable, the income elasticity was about 0.7 – definitely less than 1 – especially for M1 and the interest elasticity was definitely negative and significant and in the range -0.15 to -0.5.

The findings on the economies of scale were uneven. The studies using M1 as the dependent variable often found income elasticities to be less than one, typically around 0.7 or 0.8. Higher-income elasticities were usually reported for M2, with some in excess of unity. The reason for this divergence hinges on the inclusion of income earning savings deposits in M2. The demand for these savings deposits is likely to reflect more strongly a portfolio demand than for M1. This portfolio – rather than transactions – demand could make them a 'superior good' for households for whom bonds and equities are, in general, viable.

The 1970s were a period of the increasing deregulation of the financial system, with financial institutions offering a variety of interest-bearing checking accounts and checkable savings accounts. There was an increasing use of quarterly data in this decade, combined with a partial adjustment model, as discussed in Chapter 7, justifying the use of the lagged value of money among the explanatory variables, so that the linear or log-linear form of the commonly estimated money demand function was:

$$m^d_t = a_0 + a_r r_t + a_y y_t + (1-\gamma)m_{t-1} + \mu_t \tag{5}$$

where γ was the adjustment parameter and μ was a white noise disturbance term.

In an attempt to eliminate serial correlation in money demand functions, a common problem, or to incorporate a partial adjustment model, (5) was often estimated in its first-difference form. The empirical estimates still indicated the stability of the money demand function, but M1 now often, though not always, performed better than M2 and broader aggregates. The value of the adjustment parameter γ in (5) tended to be roughly between 0.20 and 0.5. The full adjustment to the long-run values occurred in about two to six quarters. There was a low impact (one-quarter) real income elasticity (about 0.2) and a long-run income elasticity less than 1 (often around 0.7), and a low-impact interest elasticity (about -0.02 or less) and a long-run interest elasticity roughly between -0.05 and -0.15.[11]

Table 9.1 Money demand estimates

Country	Sample	y	r_1	r_2	π	m_{-1}	Long-run elasticities	
							Income	Interest[c]
USA[a]	1952:3–1974:1	0.131	−0.016	−0.030	−0.771	0.788	0.62	−0.075
	1952:3–1979:3	0.039	−0.013	−0.002	−0.889	1.007	−0.57	1.857
	1974:2–1986:4	0.044	−0.018	0.100	−0.823	0.997	14.67	−6
Canada[b]	1962:1–1985:4	0.071	−0.004		−1.66	0.94	1.18	−0.067
U.K.[b]	1958:1–1986:1	0.118	−0.005		−0.69	0.44	0.21	−0.009

Source: Goldfeld and Sichel (1990), Tables 8.1 and 8.5, of which Table 8.5 is based on Fair (1987).

[a] All variables are in logs, except for the inflation rate π ($= \ln(P_t/P_{t-1})$). The dependent variable is real money balances m, measured by the real value of M1, and y is real GNP. r_1 is the commercial paper rate and r_2 is the passbook savings rate at commercial banks.

[b] All variables are in logs except the interest rate r_1 which is in levels. The dependent variable m is real balances per capita and the scale variable is income per capita. r_1 is a short-term rate. All variables are in logs except for the interest rate. The reported estimates are taken from Goldfeld and Sichel (1990), Table 8.5, calculated by them from Fair (1987).

[c] Based on the coefficient of r_1.

The empirical findings on the income and interest elasticities of money demand in Canada were roughly similar.

Table 9.1 provides an illustration of the estimates of money demand with a lagged dependent variable and is based on Goldfeld and Sichel (1990). Part of this table is based on Fair (1987), who presented the estimates of money demand for twenty-seven countries.

Income elasticities

In Table 9.1, the coefficient of the income variable y is the impact elasticity for the quarter and in the range 0.039 to 0.118. The long-run elasticity is obtained by dividing the impact elasticity by one minus the coefficient of the lagged dependent variable, m_{-1}. The computation of the long-run elasticity becomes extremely sensitive to small changes as this coefficient approaches one. In fact, if this coefficient is one or over one, the partial adjustment model leads to a misspecification in its adjustment mechanism. This is clearly so for the USA for 1952:3–1979:3, and almost so for 1974:2–1986:4. Therefore, the estimates for these periods cannot be relied upon, as a look at the long-run income and interest rate elasticities clearly shows.

Further, only two of the long-run income elasticities in Table 9.1 are plausible. These are 0.62 for the USA for 1952:3–1974:1 and 1.18 for Canada. The estimates of this elasticity for the other two periods for the USA are implausible and, as already argued in the preceding paragraph, the estimated equation as a whole for these periods is highly suspect. Further, Goldfeld and Sichel (1990) show that the estimates perform well in simulations only for the first period and that the money demand function shifts sufficiently after 1974 to lead to a breakdown of its estimation in the conventional form used for this table.

Interest rate elasticities

From column 3 of Table 9.1, the impact (first quarter) interest rate elasticities are −0.004 for Canada, −0.005 for the UK and −0.016 for the first period for the USA, ignoring the latter two periods for this country. The corresponding long-run interest elasticities are –0.066 for Canada, –0.009 for the UK and –0.075 for the USA. For comparison, for Canada for 1956:1–1978:4, Poloz (1980) had reported for M1 the impact and long-run interest rate elasticities of –0.054 and –0.18 respectively. His estimates of the corresponding income elasticities were 0.22 and 0.73. These are somewhat different from those reported in Table 9.1 for Canada and indicate that one should think in terms of the plausible ranges rather than precise magnitudes for elasticities.

This table also shows significant impact elasticities with respect to the inflation rate, in fact higher than the interest rate elasticities. Since the coefficient of the lagged dependent variable equals $(1 - \lambda)$, the adjustment during the first quarter was only 0.212 for the USA for the first period, 0.06 for Canada and 0.56 for the UK. We have already commented on the instability of the money demand function in the latter two periods for the USA. Fair found instability for thirteen out of the seventeen countries in his sample.

Income elasticities for M1 versus those for M2

On the long-run income elasticity, while many studies indicated the elasticity of M1 to be significantly less than unity and usually about 0.7, some studies reported the long-run income elasticity of M2 to be even greater than one. Others reported it as being less than for M1. The difference in the elasticities between M1 and M2 depends on the income elasticity of time deposits. The demand for time deposits is dominated by portfolio considerations while the demand for M1 is dominated by current transactions needs, so that the availability of other highly liquid and fairly safe financial assets in the economy very significantly affects the demand elasticities for time deposits. It can, therefore, vary considerably over time and among countries.

As between the partial adjustment model and adaptive expectations, Feige (1967) – on USA annual data for 1915-63 – used permanent income for the expected income and reported instantaneous adjustment and adaptive expectations on income. Goldfeld (1973) with quarterly US data found less than instantaneous adjustment. In general, quarterly data provided evidence of both adaptive expectations and partial adjustment.

Shifts in the money demand function

Much greater impact of financial deregulation was felt in the 1980s than had been permitted or achieved in the 1970s. Further, technological and product innovation in the financial sector was very rapid. Computers also came into general usage in firms and households, and permitted more efficient management of funds. By the end of the 1980s, automatic tellers for electronic transfer and withdrawal of funds from both demand and savings accounts had become common, and were more numerous than bank branches. Many new variants of demand and savings deposits had been created and the distinction between demand and savings deposits in terms of their liquidity became blurred almost to the point of disappearance, though savings deposits still paid higher interest but also imposed higher charges. Deregulation, innovation and technological change resulted in a failure of the quarterly specification for money demand, whether money was defined narrowly or broadly.

These developments in the 1980s led to the estimated demand functions doing poorly, with unstable money demand and with a highly variable velocity of circulation. The econometric tests also became much more sophisticated than in earlier periods. Among these, the econometric tests of the money and income time series showed that they were not stationary. To deal with this, cointegration analysis became one of the preferred techniques and showed that money and income were indeed cointegrated, and so were interest rates with them over many periods.

Velocity of circulation

We have not commented directly on the behaviour of the velocity of circulation. Velocity changes in the long run and fluctuates in the short run.

Velocity equals the ratio of nominal income to the money stock, which in equilibrium would equal money demand. Since the income elasticity of money demand is less than unity, an increase in income causes a rise in velocity. Further, with the interest elasticity of money demand as negative, an increase in interest rates decreases money demand which causes velocity to increase. Therefore, velocity increases with increases in both income and interest rates.

Changes in velocity occur also because of changes in the buffer stock holdings of money. An increase in the money supply temporarily held inactive until income changes, will decrease velocity. Velocity also changes as a result of innovations in the payments mechanisms, unusual delays in the payments mechanism such as postal strikes or bank holidays, special spending needs such as at Christmas, etc. Velocity is, therefore, not a constant, even in the short run, and fluctuates from quarter to quarter. The estimated range for the annual variation in velocity, even in a highly stable economy such as that of the USA, is about 3% to 4%.

9.8 THE BASICS OF UNIT ROOTS, COINTEGRATION AND ERROR-CORRECTION TECHNIQUES

This section is meant to provide a very brief and intuitive introduction to the topics of unit root, cointegration and error-correction models. The reader is referred to Davidson and Mackinnon (1993) and other references for a proper econometric treatment.

9.8.1 Non-stationarity

It is fairly common for time series to possess conditional means and variances that increase over time, so that the series are not stationary over time. Several of the variables in the money demand functions, especially the money stock and national income, have trends and are, therefore, non-stationary. Classical least squares regressions with non-stationary series can yield biased coefficients, spurious correlation and invalid statistical inferences. Therefore, econometric techniques that eliminate or handle non-stationarity are important for estimation. Among these, a simple technique is to detrend the data prior to its use in regressions. This will yield non-stationary data series for a variable if the non-stationarity is introduced by a trend term in the data-generating process. But it will not do so if the random term is serially correlated. If this serial correlation is of order one, one procedure that would render the series stationary is taking its first difference. This eliminates non-stationarity if the data-generating process for a variable x is:

$$x_t = a_0 + x_{t-1} + \mu_t \tag{6}$$

where μ_t is assumed to follow a stationary ARMA process. In this case, the first difference, Δx_t, follows a random walk with drift, and x_t is said to be integrated of order 1, or $I(1)$. An $I(1)$ series needs to be differenced once to make it stationary, while a series integrated of order p – that is, $I(p)$ – needs to be differenced p times to become stationary. However, regressions with even the first differences eliminates the relationship between the levels of the variables, so that the regressions do not provide estimates of the long-run relationship between the dependent and the independent variables in the estimating equation. Therefore, the use of differenced data is not a proper strategy for finding this relationship. In the context of the money demand function, the underlying theory implies an equilibrium relationship between the levels of the variables, so that using differenced data will not provide an estimate of this function.

9.8.2 Unit root tests

An autoregressive, non-stationary, data-generating process for a variable x is:

$$x_t = a_0 + a_1 t + a_2 x_{t-1} + \mu_t \tag{7}$$

where t is time and μ_t follows a stationary process. Subtracting x_{t-1} from both sides,

$$\Delta x_t = a_0 + a_1 t + (a_2 - 1)x_{t-1} + \mu_t \tag{8}$$

If $a_2 = 1$, x_t is $I(1)$. The test for $a_2 = 1$ as against $a_2 < 1$ is called a unit root test.

The most widely used tests for unit roots are referred to as the Dickey–Fuller (DF) and the augmented Dickey–Fuller (ADF) unit root tests.[12] The latter allows for higher-order autoregressive processes and is based on the estimation of the equation:

$$\Delta x_t = a_0 + a_1 t + \left(a_2 - 1\right)x_{t-1} + \sum_{j=1}^{n} b_{ij}\, \Delta x_{t-j} + \mu_t \tag{9}$$

which allows for n lags. The ADF unit root test is for the null hypothesis that $a_1 = 1$, against the alternative that $a_1 < 1$.[13] Failure to reject the null hypothesis implies non-stationarity of the series.

A stationary variable is denoted as being $I(0)$. A variable integrated of order p has to be differenced p times to induce stationarity. Therefore, an $I(1)$ has to be differenced only once to make it stationary.

If the ADF and other tests for the data series of the variables in a relationship, such as the money demand function (4), show that at least some of the series are $I(1)$ or $I(p)$, $p > 1$, the relationship has non-stationary variables and, as mentioned above, the classical regression techniques – such as ordinary least squares – do not provide unbiased and consistent estimates of the coefficients of the relationship. An appropriate technique would be cointegration.

9.8.3 Cointegration, an introduction

If the data series for a set of variables are non-stationary and are $I(1)$, they might possess a linear combination that is stationary. In this case, the series are said to be cointegrated. The vectors of the coefficients of these combinations are called the cointegrating vectors. The existence of such a combination is implied by the existence of an equilibrium relationship among the variables.

If the variables were linked by a long-run equilibrium relationship, then, while they could drift away from each other in the short run, the equilibrating forces would bring them back to their long-run relationship.[14] The cointegrating vector captures this long-run relationship. However, the variables could drift away from this relationship in the short run, so that, besides the long-run cointegrating vector, there would also exist a short-run dynamic relationship among the variables. We will look at this short-run relationship later under the concept of error-correction models.

Since a set of variables can be related by several equilibrium relationships, there could exist several cointegration vectors among them. For example, the IS–LM models imply several simultaneous structural relationships among money, income and the interest rate, so that there is likely to be more than one cointegrating vector among them. Where a set of variables has more than one cointegrating vector, a linear combination of these variables is also a cointegrating vector. This surfeit of cointegration vectors poses a problem in identifying a particular cointegration vector with a particular structural relationship in the theoretical model. Therefore, while cointegration techniques provide econometric evidence on the existence of long-run relationships among a set of variables, the identification or derivation of the structural coefficients of the model from the elements of the cointegration vectors can be quite problematical. This will be a significant problem for our purpose of estimating the money demand function. This is a structural equation and our objective is to estimate its coefficients, so that the income, interest rate and other elasticities of money demand can be derived. Our preceding remarks indicate that the cointegration techniques will not necessarily lead to reliable estimates of these elasticities.

The two main cointegration procedures are the Engle–Granger and the Johansen–Juselius ones (Johansen–Juselius, 1990; Johansen, 1991). The former uses a two-stage procedure, estimating the cointegrating vector for a given equation in the first stage, testing its residuals for stationarity, and then using the residuals, if stationary, to estimate the dynamic short-run response of the dependent variable in an error correction model. Our further focus will be on the Johansen–Juselius procedure, since it seems to have become the more common one in the literature and provides estimates of the cointegrating vectors and the error-correction model in one step.

Assuming further that the variables being considered are either $I(1)$ or $I(0)$, the Johansen–Juselius procedure takes all the $I(1)$ variables to be as if endogenous within a VAR structural model and determines a set of cointegrating vectors, among which a choice has to be made for the particular economic relationship being sought. This procedure is based on the maximum likelihood estimation of a vector autoregressive model. The number of cointegrating vectors is determined by the eigenvalue and trace tests.

As mentioned earlier, the Engle–Granger technique estimates the cointegration vector for a given set of variables in the first stage and uses it to estimate the error-correction model in a second stage. The Johansen–Juselius procedure provides the estimates for all the cointegrating vectors among the variables and the coefficients of the error-correction equation, for the specified dependent variable, simultaneously. A variety of diagnostic tests accompany this procedure in order to ensure that the assumptions – such as of normality, stationarity and serial independence of the residuals – for the cointegration analysis are satisfied. Other tests are for the stability of the short-run coefficients, that is, of the estimated error correction model.[15]

Applying the cointegration technique to money, income and interest rates

There is usually more than one long-run relationship among any given set of economic variables. For example, money demand depends upon national income and interest rates, while national income – as do interest rates – depends on the money supply, which equals money demand in equilibrium. Assuming these three variables to be all $I(1)$, such a simultaneous determination of economic variables implies the possible existence of a maximum of two cointegrating vectors among them. In general, for n variables, there could be $(n-1)$ cointegrating vectors. This poses a problem since the cointegration technique does not identify a given cointegrating vector with a specific economic relationship. For instance, suppose two cointegrating vectors are found among money, income and interest rates. The econometric estimation by itself does not make it clear which one of the cointegrating vectors specifies the money demand relationship. This has to be decided by the researcher on the basis of the signs imposed by economic theory on the coefficients of the money demand relationship and on the basis of the plausibility of the magnitudes of the elements in the cointegrating vectors. The elements of the selected cointegrating vector are then taken to specify the respective long-run coefficients of the linear (or log-linear) money demand function.

In some applications, it is found that the elements of none of the cointegration vectors possess signs consistent with the *a priori* expectations on the elasticities of the money demand function. Or these elements could be such as to imply implausible magnitudes of the elasticities. These problems could arise from the inaccuracy of the data, misspecification in the set of variables, breaks in the data, etc. But it is also possible to argue that, since a linear combination of the cointegrating vectors is also a cointegrating vector, one could try to find that linear combination of the cointegrating vectors such that the elements have the desired signs and magnitudes in a plausible range. However, there are objections to following this route.

9.8.4 The error-correction model

Even where economic theory posits a long-run equilibrium function for a variable, disequilibrium could exist in the short run. While the selected cointegrating vector captures the long-run relationship between the dependent variable and the independent ones, it does not capture the dynamic response of the former to changes in the latter. These are encompassed by an error-correction model (ECM), which is meant to capture the adjustment of the dependent variable to the long-run equilibrium specified by the cointegrating vector. It defines the deviation from the long-run value as the 'error' and measures it by the residual, i.e., difference between the actual value of the dependent variable and its estimated value based on the selected cointegrating vector. The ECM model specifies the first difference in the dependent variable as a function of this error lagged one period, the $I(0)$ variables and the first differences of the independent $I(1)$ variables.[16] Appropriate lags in the latter are introduced at this stage. Their coefficients measure the short-run movements in the dependent variable in response to fluctuations in the independent variables. The coefficient of the lagged residual is the error correction coefficient and measures the speed of adjustment of the dependent variable to its long-run value.

Application of the cointegration–ECM procedure to money demand

To illustrate this procedure, let the long-run relationship be specified as:

$$m_t^d = a_0 + a_r r_t + a_y y_t \tag{10}$$

Assume that the data series for m, r and y are all $I(1)$. Let their estimated cointegrating vector be $(1 - \hat{a}_r - \hat{a}_y)$ in which the second and third elements have the opposite sign to that of the respective coefficient on the right-hand side of the equation. Let the estimated value of m^d from this cointegrating vector be $\hat{m}^d$. That is,

$$\hat{m}_t^d = \hat{a}_r r_t + \hat{a}_y y_t$$

The error-correction model is then specified as:

$$\Delta m_t^d = \alpha z_t + \beta(m_{t-1}^d - \hat{m}_{t-1}^d) + \gamma \Delta x_t + \eta_t \tag{11}$$

where $(m_{t-1}^d - \hat{m}_{t-1}^d)$ is the lagged error, z is a vector which includes the constant term and any $I(0)$ variables and x is the vector of the independent variables which are $I(1)$ and included in the cointegrating vector. Under our assumptions on the money demand function, x would include r and y, which were assumed to be $I(1)$ and are in the theoretical demand function (4). Since there are no other independent variables in this function, z would consist only of the constant term.

But if only m and y were $I(1)$ while r was $I(0)$, the cointegration would be done only over m and y. If the estimated cointegrating vector met the theoretical restrictions for the money demand function and, therefore, was accepted as the long-run money demand function, the error-correction equation (11) would specify z by a constant term and r, while x would be specified by the single variable y.

To conclude this section, given that the data on the money stock and income – and possibly on other variables in the money demand function – are almost always at least $I(1)$, it is inappropriate to use the standard least squares regression methods. This has led to the popularity of the cointegration–ECM procedure for the estimation of money demand functions. An appealing feature of this procedure is the separation of the long-run money demand function from its dynamic short-run form but with the simultaneous econometric estimation of the two.

9.9 SOME COINTEGRATION STUDIES OF THE MONEY DEMAND FUNCTION

We examine a few recent studies using the cointegration–ECM for their findings. Among these, Baba *et al.* (1992) considered the standard money demand equation such as (4) to be misspecified for several reasons. They claimed that these include the omission of the inflation rate, inadequate inclusion of the yield on money itself, inadequate adjustment for financial innovation in the yields on alternative assets, exclusion of the risk and yield on long-term assets and, finally, improper dynamic specification. On the last item, they considered the partial adjustment model or the corrections made for serial correlation, such as the Cochrane–Orcutt technique, to be unacceptable for various reasons.

Baba *et al.*, therefore, estimated a more elaborate M1 demand function using the cointegration–ECM technique for the USA for 1960-88. They reported finding a stable cointegrating M1 demand function consistent with theory. Further, their finding was that the short-run money demand dynamics were adequately captured by the error-correction specification. They found a significant impact of inflation, apart from those of interest rates, on M1 demand. The inclusion of a long-term bond yield, adjusted for risk, was also significant and important for explaining the changes in velocity. However, their variable for the yield on alternative assets was a construct, which included adjustments for the changing availability of financial instruments and the time required in the learning process for these instruments to be fully adopted. They concluded that if the yield data is not suitably adjusted for these factors, the mere inclusion in the estimated equations of the own interest rates on financial assets will lead to the rejection of parameter constancy and stability.

These findings of the Baba *et al.* study point to the usefulness of the cointegration–ECM technique and the need to specify properly the variables in the money demand function. They also stressed that financial innovation had been significant. This leads to instability of the estimated function unless it is properly captured by the data.

Miller (1991) used the demand for nominal money balances as a function of real income, the nominal interest rate and the price level. His specification for money included M1, M1A, M2 and M3. The alternatives used for the interest rate were the four-to-six-month commercial paper rate and the dividend price ratio. The Engle–Granger cointegration–ECM technique was used on the USA quarterly data for 1959-87. Of the various monetary aggregates, only M2 was cointegrated with the other variables; none of the others were cointegrated.

Hafer and Jansen (1991) used the Johansen–Juselius procedure for USA quarterly data for 1915–88 and for 1953–88. In one part of their study, their variables were real money balances, real income and the commercial paper rate, which is a short-term interest rate. They found a cointegrating vector for M1 for 1915-88, though not for 1953-88, and found such vectors for M2 for both periods. For M1 for 1915-88, the long-run income elasticity was 0.89 and the long-run interest rate elasticity was -0.36. For M2, the former was 1.08 for 1915–88 and 1.06 for 1953–88. The long-run interest rate elasticity for M2 was -0.12 for 1915–88 and -0.03 for 1953–88, with both estimates being statistically significant. These estimates, especially the latter one, are much lower than the corresponding estimated elasticities in the range -0.15 to -0.5 in many other studies.

When Hafer and Jansen replaced the commercial paper rate by the corporate bond rate

– a long-term rate – there was still no cointegrating vector for M1 for 1953–88. There was also none for M2 for 1915–88, but there was one for 1953–88. The income elasticity for the latter was 1.13 and the interest rate was –0.09. Overall, the authors concluded in favour of using M2 over M1 in a long-term relationship with income and interest rates.

We examine one more study in this section. Miyao (1996) used M2 for his money variable and estimated a variety of linear functions involving income, an interest rate and the price level. His sample periods for USA quarterly data were 1959–88, 1959–90 and 1959–93. For the earlier periods, there were mixed results suggesting both cointegration and no co-integration, while there was no cointegrating vector at all for 1959–93. The author concluded that there were shifts in the data structure in the 1990s, so that an error-correction model was not appropriate for the 1990s. Further, his conclusion was that a stationary relationship between M2 and output disappeared in the 1990s, so that M2 was no longer a reliable indicator or target for policy purposes.

These differing results clearly indicate that the evidence on the cointegration of the variables in the money demand function is not unambiguous or robust for the United States for recent decades. Similar findings have been reported for the UK – see Cuthbertson (1991) for a review of some of these – and Canada. While the existence of such a vector cannot be rejected for some form of the monetary aggregate and for some definitions of the independent variables, such a finding is dependent on particular definitions and particular periods. Part of the reason for the conflicting findings is the sensitivity of the Johansen–Juselius cointegrating procedures to the sample size and its poor finite sample properties. But, from the perspective of economic theory, the problem can also stem from numerous shifts in the money demand function due to innovations of various types in recent decades. These shifts imply that there is no stable long-run money demand relationship over this period. Therefore, the cointegration techniques will not yield the appropriate cointegrating vector, unless the impact of the innovations is somehow first adequately captured in the measurement of the variables, as in the Baba *et al.* study cited above, and perhaps not even then, since the innovations have been of numerous types and their collective combination has itself been changing.

9.10 EMPIRICAL STUDIES ON THE BUFFER STOCK MODELS OF THE DEMAND FOR MONEY

Chapter 6 has analysed the precautionary and buffer stock models of the demand for money. While the transactions, speculative and precautionary models determined an optimal demand for money for each component, the buffer stock models allowed fluctuations in money holdings either in a band or around an optimal long-run path. As Chapter 6 showed, these models are forward- (and backward-) looking models and require specification of the procedures for estimating the future values of the relevant variables. They also require specification of the estimation procedure for net payments and receipts. Part of these net payments and receipts can be anticipated and part unanticipated. Another feature of the buffer stock models for estimation purposes is that the unanticipated injections of money supply in the economy are for some duration passively absorbed by the public.

There are two broad types of empirical studies of the buffer stock money demand. One of these distinguishes between a long-run (planned or permanent) desired money demand and a short-run (buffer stock or transitory) money demand, and estimates their sum by standard regression techniques. The empirical works of Darby (1972), Carr and Darby (1981) and Santomero and Seater (1981), among others, belong in this category. We will refer to this category as the shock-absorption money demand models. The second type of empirical studies uses cointegration techniques and error-correction modelling. Since the latter have already been discussed in the preceding section, this section only reports on the former type of studies.

The shock-absorption money demand models

Darby (1972) proposed and tested a version of the 'shock-absorption' model of money demand. In setting up his model, Darby argued that most of any positive transitory saving will be initially added to money balances and then gradually reallocated to other assets or be depleted by subsequent negative transitory saving – with money balances reverting to their long-run desired ('permanent') levels at the end of these adjustments. Therefore, money balances act to absorb shocks in income and saving. The Darby shock-absorber model is an early version of the buffer stock models of money and limits its shocks to innovations in income.

Darby separated money holdings into two categories, permanent and transitory, as in:

$$M_t = M_t^P + M_t^T \tag{12}$$

The demand for permanent money balances was assumed by Darby to be:

$$M_t^P = \alpha_0 + \alpha_y Y_t^P + \alpha_{RL} RL_t + \alpha_{RS} RS_t + \alpha_{RM} RM_t \tag{13}$$

where:

M^P	permanent real balances
M^T	transitory real balances
Y^P	permanent real income
Y^T	transitory real income
RL	long-term nominal interest rate
RS	short-term nominal interest rate
RM	nominal yield on money balances

Equation (6) specifies the dependence of permanent balances on permanent income and various interest rates.

For transitory balances M^T, Darby assumed that:

$$\Delta M_t^T = \beta_1 S_t^T + \beta_2 M_{t-1}^T \quad 0 > \beta_1 > 0, \beta_2 < 0 \tag{14}$$

where the proportion β_1 of transitory real saving S^T is added to transitory real balances during the period, but last period's transitory balances are run down or adjusted at the rate β_2.

Darby used Milton Friedman's ideas on permanent and transitory income in which,

$$Y_t = Y_t^P + Y_t^T \tag{15}$$

where permanent and transitory income are not correlated with each other and permanent income is generated by an adaptive expectations procedure. Further,

$$S_t^T = Y_t^T - C_t^T \tag{16}$$

where transitory consumption C^T is an independent random variable with a zero mean, so that Y_t^T was substituted for S_t^T in the estimating equation. As mentioned above, a proportion (β_1) of it is accumulated in transitory money balances during the period and eventually reallocated to other assets.

Equations (12) to (16) imply that:

$$M_t = \alpha_0(1 - \beta) + \beta_1 Y_t^T + \beta M_{t-1} + \alpha_Y Y_t^{P*} + \alpha_{RL} RL_t^* + \alpha_{RS} RS_t^* + \alpha_{RM} RM_t^* \tag{17}$$

where $\beta = (1 + \beta_2)$, $Y^{P*} = (1 - \beta)Y_t^P$, $RL_t^* = (1 - \beta)RL_t$, $RS_t^* = (1 - \beta)RS_t$ and $RM_t^* = (1 - \beta)RM_t$.

Darby's finding for the USA for the period 1947:1 to 1966:4 was that β_1 was about 40%, so that transitory income and saving had a strong effect on money balances and transitory balances increased by about 40% of transitory income. β_2, the induced reduction in transitory balances per quarter, was about 20%. These findings support the buffer stock approach where net income receipts are temporarily added to money balances and then gradually adjusted at periodic intervals. The estimated adjustment is relatively slow, though Darby also found that both β_1 and β_2 had increased since the 1940s. With the increasing innovation in the financial markets in recent decades, the increase is likely to have continued and be quite significant.

While the above model introduces the notion of transitory money balances arising from transitory income and saving into the analysis, it does not deal with the differing effects of anticipated and unanticipated changes in the money supply, and therefore does not deal with innovations in money supply. Carr and Darby (1981) argue that the anticipated changes in money supply are integrated by economic agents into their decisions on consumption etc. and are therefore already incorporated into the current price level, with real balances held being unaffected by the changes in the price level and in the anticipated money changes. However, the unanticipated money supply change alters the net receipts of the public, and can be treated as an element of transitory income. It may be wholly or partly added to buffer balances, is thereby not spent and is not reflected in the price level. Hence, the unanticipated money supply changes alter real balances while anticipated money supply changes do not.

To incorporate these arguments into the analysis, Carr and Darby (1981) assumed that:

$$M_t^s = M_t^{s*} + M_t^{su} \tag{18}$$

where:

M^s nominal money supply
M^{s*} anticipated nominal money supply
$M^{su} = M^s - M^{s*}$ = unanticipated nominal money supply

The short-run desired demand function was specified in real terms, with a partial adjustment model, as:

$$m_t^d - m_{t-1} = \lambda(m_t^* - m_{t-1}) \tag{19}$$

where:

m^d short-run desired demand for real balances, in logs
m^* long-run desired demand for real balances, in logs

so that the desired short-run demand for real balances is:

$$m_t^d = \lambda m_t^* + (1 - \lambda)m_{t-1} \tag{20}$$

where the short-run desired demand for real balances is a weighted average of the long-run demand and one-period lagged balances. The actual holdings of money balances are the sum of the short-run desired balances, transitory income and unanticipated money supply. Hence:

$$m_t = \lambda m_t^* + (1 - \lambda)m_{t-1} + \beta y_t^T + bM_t^{su} \tag{21}$$

The long-run desired demand is given by:

$$m_t^* = \gamma_0 + \gamma_1 y_t^P + \gamma_2 R_t \tag{22}$$

Therefore:

$$m_t = \lambda\gamma_0 + \lambda\gamma_1 y_t^P + \lambda\gamma_2 R_t + (1 - \lambda)m_{t-1} + \beta y_t^T + bM_t^{su} \tag{23}$$

Permanent and transitory income were measured as in the Darby model earlier: in calculating permanent income, the weight on the current quarterly income was set at 0.025%. In the present model, the demand for real balances depends upon transitory income and unanticipated money supply changes. The theoretical arguments require their coefficients to be positive.

Carr and Darby tested this model for eight industrial countries (the USA, the UK, Canada, France, Germany, Italy, Japan and the Netherlands) for the period 1957:1 to 1976:4 and reported that the coefficient b on unanticipated money supply was significant and between 0.7 and 1 for all countries for the GLS estimates. The coefficient β was significant and positive for the USA but was not significant for the other countries. To illustrate, using the generalized least squares (GLS) estimates for the coefficients, the estimated value of β (the coefficient for transitory income) was 0.090 while that of b (the coefficient for unanticipated money supply) was 0.803 for the USA; the corresponding estimate for Canada of β was 0.018 which was not significant, and of b was 0.922 which was significant. Hence, the transitory income influence on money balances was much weaker than of unanticipated money supply changes, with most of the latter added to money balances in the current quarter, so that the impact effect of such changes on the price level or economic activity will be minimal.

Santomero and Seater (1981) start with the Whalen (1966) model[17] and introduce elements of search theory into their buffer stock model. They assume that an individual with buffer balances in currency and demand deposits will search for alternative assets in a context of incomplete information on such assets – especially long assets and durable goods which are bought infrequently – but there is a cost to acquiring more information. Given this cost, the individual does not continuously perform the cost minimization decision to buy the alternative assets but only does so at discrete points in time, while holding buffer stocks in the intervals between decisions. The source of the shocks inducing a change in the pattern of assets held is among the determinants of this cost, as are interest rates, past shocks, variance of transactions, etc. Santomero and Seater show that, under their assumptions, excess money balances are run down gradually rather than completely at each decision point.

The empirical analysis of Santomero and Seater was as follows:

$$M_t = M_t^* + M_t^T \tag{24}$$

where:

M short-run desired real balances
M^* long-run (equilibrium) desired real balances
M^T transitory real balances

M^* was assumed to depend upon permanent income and the cost differential of holding money rather than other assets, in a Cobb–Douglas form, as:

$$M_t^* = \alpha Y_t^{P\beta} (r_{1t} - r_{Mt})^\rho \cdots (r_{mt} - r_{Mt})^\rho \tag{25}$$

The general determinants of transitory balances were specified as:

$$M_t^T = M^T(S_t, S_{t-1}, \ldots, (r_A - r_M), \beta_t) \tag{26}$$

where S_t was the shock to real balances in t, r_A was the nominal interest rate on alternative assets (savings deposits), r_M was the nominal interest rate on money and β was Whalen's penalty cost on holding inadequate balances. Equation (26) was given the more specific form that:

$$M_t^T = DM_t^* \tag{27}$$

where the disequilibrium factor D was a distributed lag function of past transitory shocks, and it was assumed that there were two sources of shocks, one to income and the other to the money supply. The specific form for D was:

$$D = \sum_{j=0}^{N} Z^j \left[\frac{\left(Y_{t-j} - Y_{t-j}^P\right) + \left(M_t^s - M_{t-1}^s\right)}{Y_{t-j}^P} \right] \tag{28}$$

where:

Y   current real income
Y^P permanent real income
M^s real money supply

Equation (28) assumes that all shocks, whether from income or money supply changes, have the same pattern of effects on transitory balances. Further, innovations in money demand are not considered, so that either they do not occur[18] or real balances adjust instantly to them. If the money demand function is unstable, (28) should be modified to include shifts in money demand.

The estimated demand function for short-run balances implied by (24) to (28) is of the form:

$$M_t^d = \alpha Y_t^{P\beta} \left(r_{1t} - r_{Mt}\right)^\gamma \cdots \left(r_{mt} - r_{Mt}\right)^\rho$$

$$\left[1 + \sum_{j=0}^{N} Z^j \left(\frac{\left(Y_{t-j} - Y_{t-j}^P\right) + \left(M_t^s - M_{t-1}^s\right)}{Y_{t-j}^P} \right) \right] \tag{29}$$

where $\alpha, \beta, \delta > 0$ and $\gamma, \rho < 0$, and r_i is the nominal rate of return on the ith asset.

The above model was estimated for M1 and M2 for the USA for the period 1952:2 to 1972:4, using the Cochrane–Orcutt technique to eliminate first-order serial correlation. It was assumed in the estimation process that equilibrium was achieved within each quarter between the money supply and the short-run money demand, so that the latter was proxied by the money supply. Only two interest rates – the commercial paper rate and the commercial passbook rate – were used. The estimate of the coefficient Z was significant and positive for both M1 and M2. Hence, both transitory income and changes in the money supply had a short-run positive impact on short-run money demand, thereby showing evidence of buffer holdings of money balances. Further, transitory balances did not increase proportionately with the magnitude of the shock, so that large shocks were corrected faster than smaller ones. M1 and M2 holdings adjusted within two to three quarters to their desired levels, implying a fairly fast rate of adjustment.

CONCLUSIONS

Empirical findings generally confirm the homogeneity of degree zero of the demand for real balances with respect to the price level – and the consequent homogeneity of degree one of the demand for nominal balances – as discussed in Chapter 3. The income elasticity of real M1 with respect to real income has been established as being less than one, even in the long run, though some studies show this elasticity for real M2 to be even slightly larger than unity. The latter is particularly so for developing economies, in which the bond and stock markets are not well developed, so that increases in savings are mostly held in savings deposits. Real balances do depend on interest rates, with a short-term rate being usually used in the estimation of M1 demand and a longer-term one being used for the estimation of M2 demand. The estimated interest rate elasticities usually fall in the range from -0.15 to -0.50. In the LDCs, the rate of inflation typically performs better in estimation than the rate of interest and is often used in lieu of the latter, with somewhat similar elasticities. While currency substitution is a theoretical possibility and some studies do confirm its existence for their data sets, empirical studies have not always found it to be so significant that the elimination of the return on foreign currencies from the money demand function leads to much worse results. Most money demand functions are, therefore, estimated without this variable. Not much support has been found for the liquidity trap and is now hardly ever investigated or even mentioned in empirical studies.

The velocity of circulation of M1 is not a constant in either the short or the long run. In the short run, its annual variation is quite significant even in stable economies without political and economic panics. It is about 3% to 4% for the USA, but can be much higher in less stable economies. Since the income elasticity of M1 is likely to be less than one in the long run, the long-run expectation for its velocity is that it will increase.

Innovations in the financial sector and in the usage of money by non-financial economic agents in the economy have been very rapid during the 1980s and 1990s. Consequently, the money demand functions estimated with data including this period are often not stable. Further, it is even rarer to find the estimated functions for both narrow and wide definitions of money to be stable for a given country over a given period.

The empirical contributions on the definition or measurement of money were covered in Chapter 8, so that they have not been presented in this chapter. However, note that the demand functions that are estimated can have simple sum, variable elasticity of substitution, or Divisia aggregates as their dependent variable. The estimated elasticities will therefore differ not only between narrow and broad definitions of money, but also between these measures of money.

Several of the variables crucial to money demand estimation are not stationary. This is especially likely to be so for the monetary aggregates themselves, as well as for the income and wealth variables. It may or may not also be so for the interest rates in the particular data set. Consequently, the classical regression techniques do not yield unbiased and consistent coefficients. Cointegration analysis is an appropriate procedure in this case and has become quite common in recent years for estimating money demand functions. Its combination with error-correction modelling has the further advantage that the estimation yields both the long-run and the short-run demand functions.

Cointegration procedures represent an attempt to capture the long-run equilibrium relationship and there should exist a cointegrating vector if such a relationship is stable over the sample period. However, when the long-run relationships are shifting due to innovations and the impact of the innovations has not been eliminated or somehow captured in the definition of the variables or the procedure used, the sample data would not incorporate a stable long-run relationship. In this case, the cointegration analysis should not give results indicative of the existence of a long-run vector. Where the instability is sufficiently limited, the analysis might improperly yield a cointegrating vector, indicating the existence of a stable long-run relationship when the data hides the shift, so that the elements of the cointegrating vector would be erroneous estimates of the true elasticities.

The money demand studies using cointegration techniques for data over the last few decades have provided a mixed bag of evidence about the existence of a cointegrating vector between money, income, interest rates and prices. The finding of such a vector has been culled from the data by using different definitions of money, different interest rates and different periods. The existence of a cointegrating vector with such culling cannot be said to be robust, nor can one be sure that the estimated functions are unbiased and consistent. We see this conclusion not as a criticism of the cointegration techniques but as part of their strength. The last few decades have seen a mixed bag of very significant innovations related to money demand, so that the long-run money demand function must have been shifting. Consequently, cointegration studies, just as earlier studies using the standard regression techniques, have not provided convincing evidence of the existence of a stable long-run money demand function for the last few decades for the UK, Canada and the USA.

In studies where acceptable cointegration vectors have been established, an error-correction model has usually also been estimated. These show, as expected, for quarterly data that the impact elasticities are relatively quite small and much smaller than the long-run ones, indicating that the adjustments of money demand to changes in the independent variables take at least several quarters.

Unlike the standard money demand models, the buffer stock models imply the dependence of money demand on the shocks to money supply, so that in the short run the money demand is not independent of money supply. These models imply that the money holdings can act as a buffer in response to many types of shocks, and may only be adjusted fully to their long-run equilibrium level as and when it becomes profitable to complete the adjustment of other stocks and flows. Hence, one has to differentiate not only between the short-run desired money balances and long-run ones, but also between the former and the balances actually being held. The latter are related to buffer stock balances, with actual balances being larger than the short-run desired ones for positive (unanticipated) shocks to the money supply and to income, and being smaller for negative shocks in the latter.

The divergence of actual balances from short-run desired ones and of the latter from long-run ones provides one explanation for the delayed response of nominal income and interest rates to monetary policy where the latter include unanticipated changes in money supply. Darby's estimates reported above showed that about half of the effect of money supply changes would occur in the three quarters after such a change. The distinction between permanent and nominal income was important: while both had positive effects on the demand for money, the two had different effects on the holdings of money – and of other assets. The empirical work of Carr and Darby provided comparison between the relative effects of income shocks and money supply shocks. The effect of the income shocks on money demand is weaker and for many countries insignificant while the effects of the money supply shocks are significant and substantially stronger. The latter represent a confirmation of the buffer stock hypothesis.

These findings imply that – since some part of the changes in the money supply result in passive money holdings, which are then gradually eliminated over time – the impact of such money supply changes on the market interest rates is correspondingly smaller and the full impact takes some time to occur. This has been confirmed in the findings from many error-correction models. Further, the full impact of the money supply changes on nominal national income will also take several quarters and the overall effect will be larger than the short-term one. This finding has relevance for the debate on the neutrality of money, discussed in Chapters 3 and 12 to 16. It is also related to the empirical findings of significant lags in the effects of money supply changes on nominal income, as in the St Louis model discussed in Chapter 8.

We have not differentiated between the demand functions estimated for the different segments of the economy, such as households, firms and financial institutions. There are numerous studies on these and the interested student is encouraged to explore them. There is a significant difference between the demand for money by households and firms, especially large ones. In general, the former tend to be relatively more predictable than the latter.

SUMMARY OF CRITICAL CONCLUSIONS

- The income elasticity of the demand for M1 is less than one.
- The income elasticity of M2 demand is higher than for M1 demand and is sometimes estimated to be greater than one.
- The negative interest elasticity of the demand for money, no matter how it is defined, is now beyond dispute.
- Incorporating more than one interest rate into the estimated money demand function or an interest rate and the expected inflation rate usually introduces multicollinearity which leads to biased estimates.
- Empirical studies do not show convincing evidence of the liquidity trap, even for data covering the 1930s.
- Financial innovations during the last three decades rendered the money demand function unstable for this period. Numerous attempts and innovative variations in estimation have not established a stable demand function, with a specific form and invariant coefficients, for out-of-sample data.
- M1 has done better than broader monetary aggregates during some periods and worse in others. Several recent studies have supported the use of M1 over M2 and broader aggregates.
- Empirical evidence shows very limited evidence of currency substitution.
- For the 1960s and 1970s, estimates based on a partial adjustment model often indicated a low-impact income elasticity for the first quarter but a long-run elasticity close to one, indicating a slow adjustment of money demand to its long-run level.
- Most of the variables relevant to the money demand function have proved to be non-stationary. Therefore, most empirical studies now use cointegration analysis with an error-correction model.
- Even the cointegration techniques have not provided estimates that are robust or that consistently favour one monetary aggregate over others.
- There is evidence of buffer stock holdings of money balances. Therefore, in the short run, money demand is not independent of money supply.

review and discussion questions

1 Empirical studies of the demand for money in the last two or three decades have raised serious doubts about the stability of the money demand function. What were the main causes of this instability?

   Was the finding of instability related to the particular monetary aggregate used or did it occur across all aggregates? What were the main modifications made in the estimating equations and in the definitions of the variables in order to reach a stable money demand function?

2 How would you formulate your money demand function for estimation in an empirical study? Comment on the *a priori* relationships that you expect between your independent variables and money. Compare your demand function with some roughly similar and some different ones estimated in the literature.

3 For a selected country and using quarterly data, specify and estimate the money demand function. Check and correct for shifts in this function during the period of your study. Try the following variations of the independent variables:

    (i) Expected income and permanent income for the scale variable.

    (ii) Two different interest rates, one a short-term one and the other a medium-term one.

    (iii) A proxy for the expected change in the exchange rate.

    (iv) Also do your estimations using the following techniques:

        (a) least squares estimation, with a first order PAM;

        (b) cointegration with an error-correction model.

    (v) Discuss your choice of the functional form of the money demand function and your choice of the variables and the econometric techniques used, as well as the data and econometric problems you encountered.

    (vi) Discuss your results, their plausibility and consistency with the theory, and their robustness.

4 Discuss: shifts in the estimated coefficients of the money demand function are as likely to be due to shifts in monetary policy (supply-side shifts) as about money demand behaviour.

5 What are the reasons requiring the use of cointegration techniques in money demand estimation? What would be the disadvantages of using ordinary least squares for such estimation? If you use both and obtain different estimates, which would you rely on and why?

6 Are there any conceptual problems with the application of the cointegration techniques to money demand functions or can the estimates from such techniques be relied upon? How can you make certain that the estimated cointegration vector is the money demand and not the money supply function or a reduced form relationship between money demand and money supply?

NOTES

1 See Chapters 13, 14 and 15 on this point.

2 If the real rate of interest were constant, the nominal rate of interest becomes the better proxy to π_t^e.

3 The preferred habitat theory is one of the approaches to explaining the substitution among government bonds of different maturities and has been offered by some economists as an explanation of the 'term structure of interest rates'. These issues are covered in Chapter 21.

4 These would properly include both currency and deposits, held by domestic residents at home or abroad. However, the data on foreign currency holdings is rarely available. Further, the data on the foreign demand deposits of domestic residents, held in foreign countries, is also often not available. These omissions can very significantly affect the empirical findings.

5 This study argued that the degree of currency substitution would differ between fixed and flexible exchange rates and found higher substitution under flexible rates.

6 The expected return is the expected rate of depreciation less the costs of holding foreign currencies. This cost can be very significant where it is illegal to hold and/or deal in foreign currencies, but is minimal in an unregulated free financial system.

7 See Chapters 18 and 19 on the open economy.

8 We draw upon their main findings on this issue, as reported by them, especially on their pages 417–18.

9 In an early application of this approach, Bordo and Choudhri (1982) did not find evidence of currency substitution between the Canadian and US currencies. This finding was, in turn, contradicted by other studies which found significant degrees of substitution between these

currencies and also among selected pairs of other, mainly European, currencies. However, the findings are often contradictory even between two given currencies.

10 As we have indicated above, the political and monetary integration in the European Union provide a special case, so that we expect the gradual emergence of a high degree of substitution between the euro and the national currencies within the European Union.

11 For a summary of the empirical findings on money demand, see Goldfeld and Sichel (1990) and Laidler (1990).

12 It is also necessary to supplement the ADF tests with other tests such as the Phillips–Perron test.

13 Note that a structural break in the data can sometimes be mistaken for a unit root, so that the appropriate checks and corrections for this possibility are needed.

14 Engle and Granger (1987) present a theorem showing that the cointegration between a set of variables implies short-run dynamics which return the variables to their long-run cointegrating relationship.

15 The above very brief and intuitive description of the cointegration–ECM procedure misses its assumptions, the econometric derivations and the numerous diagnostic tests that are usually conducted. It also does not address the doubts about the procedure and the problems that often come up in the estimation process. Among the latter are the use of seasonally adjusted data versus non-unadjusted data, shifts in the functions and the use of dummy variables, etc.

16 This model is only valid if the estimated error is stationary.

17 See Chapter 6 above.

18 Santomero and Seater assume that the money demand function is stable. In fact, empirical studies in recent decades have shown it to be unstable and therefore to generate transitory excess money holdings.

REFERENCES

Akerlof, George A., and Ross D. Milbourne. 'The Short-Run Demand for Money'. *Economic Journal*, 90, December 1980, pp. 885–900.

Baba, Yoshihisa, David F. Hendry and Ross M. Starr. 'The Demand for M1 in the USA, 1960–1988'. *Review of Economic Studies*, 59, 1992, pp. 25–61.

Bana, Ismail Mahomed, and Jagdish Handa. 'Currency Substitution: A Multi-Currency Study for Canada'. *International Economic Journal*, 1, Autumn 1987, pp. 71–86.

Belongia, Michael T. 'Measurement Matters: Recent Results from Monetary Economics Reexamined'. *Journal of Political Economy*, 104, October 1996, pp. 1065–83.

Belongia, Michael T., and James A. Chalfant. 'The Changing Empirical Definition of Money: Some Estimates from a Model of the Demand for Money Substitutes'. *Journal of Political Economy*, 97, April 1989, pp. 387–97.

Bordo, M. D., and E. U. Choudhri. 'Currency Substitution and the Demand for Money: Some Evidence for Canada'. *Journal of Money, Credit and Banking*, 14, February 1982, pp. 48–57.

Carr, Jack, and Michael R. Darby. 'The Role of Money Supply Shocks in the Short-Run Demand for Money'. *Journal of Monetary Economics*, 8, September 1981, pp. 183–99.

Cuthbertson Keith. 'Modelling the Demand for Money'. In Christopher J. Green and David T. Llewellyn, eds, *Surveys in Monetary Economics*, Vol. 2. Cambridge, MA: Blackwell, 1991.

———, and Mark P. Taylor. 'The Demand for Money: A Dynamic Rational Expectations Model'. *Economic Journal*, 97, Supplement 1987, pp. 65–76.

Darby, Michael R. 'The allocation of transitory income among consumers' assets'. *American Economic Review*, 62, December 1972, pp. 928–41.

Davidson, Russell, and James G. Mackinnon, *Estimation and Inference in Econometrics*. New York: Oxford University Press, 1993.

Engle, Robert F., and Clive W. J. Granger. 'Cointegration and Error-Correction: Representation, Estimation and Testing'. *Econometrica*, 55, March 1987, pp. 251–76.

Fair, Ray C. 'International Evidence on the Demand for Money'. *Review of Economics and Statistics*, 69, August 1987, pp. 473–90.

Feige, Edgar L. 'Expectations and Adjustments in the Monetary Sector'. *American Economic Review*, 57, May 1967, pp. 462–73.

——, and Douglas K. Pearce. 'The Substitutability of Money and Near-Monies: A Survey of the Time-Series Evidence'. *Journal of Economic Literature*, 15, June 1977, pp. 439–70.

Friend, I., and M. E. Blume. 'The Demand for Risky Assets'. *American Economic Review*, 65, December 1975, pp. 900–22.

Giovannini, Alberto, and Bart Turtelboom. 'Currency Substitution.' In Frederick van der Ploeg, ed., *The Handbook of International Macroeconomics*. Oxford: Blackwell, 1994, pp. 390–424.

Goldfeld, Stephen M. 'The Demand for Money Revisited'. *Brookings Papers on Economic Activity*, 3, 1973, pp. 576–638.

——, and Daniel E. Sichel. 'The Demand for Money'. In Benjamin M. Friedman and Frank H. Hahn, eds, *Handbook of Monetary Economics*. Amsterdam: North-Holland, 1990, Vol. 1, Ch. 8, pp. 299–356.

Hafer, R. W., and Dennis W. Jansen. 'The demand for Money in the United States: Evidence from Cointegration Tests'. *Journal of Money, Credit and Banking*, 23, May 1991, pp. 155–68.

Hamburger, Michael J. 'The Demand for Money by Households, Money Substitutes and Monetary Policy'. *Journal of Political Economy*, 74, December 1966, pp. 600–23.

Handa, Jagdish. 'Substitution among Currencies: A Preferred Habitat Hypothesis'. *International Economic Journal*, 2, Summer 1988, pp. 41–61.

Hendry, David F., and Ross M. Starr. 'The Demand for M1 in the USA, 1960–1988'. *Review of Economic Studies*, 59, 1991, pp. 25–61.

Johansen, Soren. 'Estimation and Hypothesis Testing of Cointegration Vectors in Gaussian Vector Autoregressive Models'. *Econometrica*, 59, November 1991, pp. 1551–80.

——, and Katarina Juselius. 'Maximum Likelihood Estimation and Inference on Cointegration – With Application to the Demand for Money'. *Oxford Bulletin of Economics and Statistics*, 52, May 1990, pp. 169–210.

Judd, John P., and John L. Scadding. 'The search for stable money demand function: A survey of the Post-1973 literature'. *Journal of Economic Literature*, 20, September 1982, pp. 993–1023.

Kanniainen, Vesa, and Juha Tarkka. 'On the Shock-Absorption View of Money: International Evidence from the 1960's and 1970's'. *Applied Economics*, 18, October 1986, pp. 1085–101.

Laidler, David. *The Demand for Money: Theories, Evidence, and Problems*. New York: HarperCollins, 1990, 3rd edn.

Milbourne, Ross. 'Disequilibrium Buffer Stock Models: A Survey'. *Journal of Economic Surveys*, 2, 1988, pp. 187–208.

Miles, M. A. 'Currency Substitution, Flexible Exchange Rates and Monetary Independence'. *American Economic Review*, 68, June 1978, pp. 428–36.

Miller, Stephen M. 'Money Dynamics: An Application of Cointegration and Error-Correction Modeling'. *Journal of Money, Credit and Banking*, 23, May 1991, pp. 139–54.

Miyao, Ryuzo. 'Does a Cointegrating M2 Demand Relation Really Exist in the United States?' *Journal of Money, Credit and Banking*, 28, August 1996, pp. 365–80.

Mizen, Paul. *Buffer Stock Models and the Demand for Money*. London: St Martin's Press, 1994, Chs 1–3.

Poloz, Stephen S. 'Simultaneity and the Demand for Money in Canada'. *Canadian Journal of Economics*, 13, August 1980, pp. 407–20.

Santomero, A. M., and Seater, J. J. 'Partial Adjustment in the Demand for Money: Theory and Empirics'. *American Economic Review*, 71, September 1981, pp. 566–78.

Whalen, Edward L. 'A Rationalization of the Precautionary Demand for Cash'. *Quarterly Journal of Economics*, 80, May 1966, pp. 314–24.

part four

MONEY SUPPLY AND CENTRAL BANKING

chapter
ten

THE MONEY SUPPLY PROCESS

This is the first of three interrelated chapters on the money supply and central banking.

This chapter explains the determination of the money supply from a theoretical perspective and also examines the empirical evidence on its determinants. While macroeconomic models tend to simplify by assuming that the money supply is exogenously determined, the private sector in the form of the banks, households and firms also influences the money supply.

The next two chapters will deal with central banks and their role in the money supply process.

---

key concepts introduced in this chapter

- The monetary base
- The currency ratio
- The demand deposit ratio
- The monetary base multiplier
- Free reserves
- Excess reserves
- Required reserves
- Discount/bank rate
- Mechanical theories of the money supply
- Behavioural theories of the money supply
- The interest elasticity of money supply

No matter how the money supply in the economy is defined or measured, several major participants are involved in its determination. If it is defined as M1 (the sum of currency in the hands of the public and the demand deposits of the public in commercial banks) or as M2 (M1 plus savings deposits of the public in commercial banks), or by a still broader measure, the three major participants in the determination of the money supply are:

(i) the central bank, which, among its other policies, determines the monetary base and the reserve requirements for the commercial banks, and sets its discount rate;

(ii) the public, which determines its currency holdings relative to its demand deposits; and

(iii) the commercial banks, which, for a given required reserve ratio, determine their actual demand for reserves as against their demand deposit liabilities.[1]

There is considerable interaction among the behaviour of the central bank, the public and the commercial banks in the money supply process. This interaction becomes of the greatest importance in studying the behaviour of the central bank which, as a policy-making body deciding on the total amount of money desirable for the economy, must take into account the responses of the public and the commercial banks to its own actions. Further, the behaviour of the central bank cannot be explained by a standard hypothesis such as the profit maximization one for firms or the utility maximization one for individuals. The behaviour of the central bank in the money supply process becomes a distinctive topic of study and is left to Chapters 11 and 12.

Some indication of the relative importance of the major contributors to changes in the money supply would be useful at this point. Phillip Cagan (1965) concluded that, in the USA, on average over the eighteen cycles during 1877 to 1954, the fluctuations in the currency ratio had a relatively large amplitude over the business cycle. They caused about half of the fluctuations in the growth rate of the money stock, while fluctuations in the monetary base and the reserve ratio accounted for roughly a quarter each. But from a secular perspective, by far the major cause of the long-term growth of the money stock was the growth in the monetary base.

A significant difference between the theories on the demand and supply of money lies in the variable each theory chooses as relevant. The theories of the demand for money choose, in general, their dependent variable as the demand for money in *real* terms. The theories of the supply of money invariably choose their dependent variable as the supply of money in *nominal* terms.

Section 10.1 briefly comments on the determination of the monetary base by the central bank. A more complete treatment of the control of the money supply by the central bank is left to Chapters 11 and 12 on the central bank. Section 10.2 presents the analysis of the demand for currency by the public while section 10.3 presents the behaviour of the commercial banks in determining their demand for free reserves. Sections 10.4 and 10.5 present two formats for the theory of the money supply. Section 10.6 derives the money supply function often used for estimation and section 10.7 gives a brief account of the empirical findings on the interest rate elasticities of the money supply function. Section 10.8 presents some findings from the application of cointegration and error-correction econometric techniques to the money supply function.

10.1 THE SUPPLY OF THE MONETARY BASE BY THE CENTRAL BANK

In an economy with a central bank monopoly of currency issue, the central bank controls the monetary base through its ability to increase the quantity of currency in the economy. Monetary economics makes one of the following alternative assumptions on the supply of the monetary base. These are:

(i) The supply of the monetary base is determined on an exogenous basis by the central bank.

(ii) The central bank ensures that the money supply in the economy is exogenous and determines the monetary base accordingly for the actual values of the currency and reserve ratios etc. using the appropriate money supply formula.

(iii) The money supply is endogenous to the economy but is determined by the central bank according to a money supply rule, and the monetary base is changed to achieve the money supply determined according to this rule.

(iv) The monetary base is endogenous but outside the control of the central bank, either because the central bank does not possess the power and/or ability to control it or does not wish to do so.

(v) The central bank sets its discount rate (also called the bank rate) to achieve a certain level of aggregate demand in the economy while the monetary base and the money supply adjust to support it.

Assumption (v) is the most commonly used operational technique, even where the central bank's intention is to focus on the monetary base or the money supply as the main determinant of aggregate demand. Under this procedure, the central bank sets the discount rate to achieve a certain level of aggregate demand in the economy and lets the financial sector determine the monetary base through borrowing or discounting bonds with it. Assumption (iv) is especially relevant for some of the LDCs with undeveloped financial systems and poor or lagged statistical information on monetary aggregates. Even if (iii) is applicable to these countries, the money supply rule may have the financing of the government deficit as its dominant element, with this element effectively outside the control of the central bank.

In any case, the central bank's behaviour is captured through the specification of the monetary base, no matter which of the above procedures is used. The next two chapters are on the central bank itself and examine these issues much more extensively. The money supply formulae presented in this chapter underlie all of the above possibilities.

10.2 THE DEMAND FOR CURRENCY BY THE PUBLIC

Fluctuations in the public's demand for currency relative to its holdings of demand deposits are a significant source of the fluctuations in the money supply. The closest substitute – and a fairly close one at that – to currency holdings (C) is demand deposits (D), so that most studies on the issue examine the determinants of the ratio C/D, or of the ratio of currency to the total money stock ($C/M1$), rather than directly the determinants of the demand for currency alone.

The C/D ratio varies considerably, with a procyclical pattern over the business cycle and over the long term. The desired C/D ratio depends upon the individual's preferences in the light of the costs and benefits of holding currency relative to demand deposits. Some of these costs and benefits are non-monetary and some are monetary.

The non-monetary costs and benefits are related to the non-monetary cost of holding and carrying currency compared with those of holding demand deposits and carrying cheques. They also take into account the general acceptability of coins and notes for making payments as against payments by other means. In financially less-developed economies, with few bank branches in the rural areas and with banking usually not open to or economically feasible for lower-income groups, even in the urban areas, currency has a clear advantage over cheques. However, even in financially advanced economies, cash is almost always accepted for smaller amounts while the use of cheques is restricted to payments where the issuer's creditworthiness can be established, or the delivery of goods can be delayed until after the clearance of the cheque through the banks. It is also more convenient to make very small payments in cash than by writing a cheque. These aspects of the non-monetary costs have changed substantially over time in favour of bank deposits with the expansion of the banking system and the modernization of its procedures, increasing urbanization, spread of banking machines, common usage of credit and debit cards, etc.

As against the greater convenience of currency over bank deposits for transactions, the possession of a significant amount of currency involves risks of theft and robbery, which impose not only its loss but also a risk of injury and trauma to the carrier. The fear of the latter is often sufficient to deter possession of large amounts in currency in societies where this kind of risk is significant. This is so in most countries, with the result that only small amounts of currency are carried by most individuals at one time or stored in their homes. By comparison, the demand for currency in Japan – a society with a very low rate of theft and robbery – is dominated by its convenience relative to bank deposits. Consequently, few individuals in Japan hold demand deposit accounts, cheques are not widely accepted in exchange even by firms or given by them for payment of salaries. Many transactions even of fairly large amounts are done in currency.

The monetary costs and benefits of holding currency relative to demand deposits really relate to the net nominal return on the latter since currency does not have an explicit monetary return or service charge while demand deposits often possesses one or both of these. In any case, even if demand deposits pay interest, there is usually a negative return on them since banks incur labour and capital costs in servicing them and must recoup these through a net charge on them.[2]

Chapter 4 presented the inventory analysis of the demand for money. This model is applicable to the demand for currency relative to demand deposits. This was done in Chapter 4. As pointed out there, the problem with an application of this analysis taking account only of the monetary cost of using currency versus demand deposits is that it ignores the non-monetary differences in their usage: acceptance in certain types of payments, risks of theft and robbery, etc. However, its central conclusion still holds: the optimal holdings of currency relative to demand deposits will depend on their relative costs and the amount of expenditures financed by them. Therefore, assuming both currency and demand deposits are 'normal goods', an increase in the net cost of holding demand deposits would increase the demand for currency and hence the C/D ratio.

However, in a time-series context, the major reasons for changes in this ratio have been the innovations in shopping, payments and banking practices which have made checking increasingly easier, and thereby lowered the C/D ratio. In addition, the significant possibility of theft and robbery – and the consequent risk to the person – with increases over time in such risks in many economies, have kept this ratio quite low or further reduced it. As indicated earlier, Japan with a low risk from such criminal activities is an exception to this rule and illustrates the greater convenience of using currency where a sufficiently wide range of denominations are made available in bank notes.

For the future, in financially developed economies, 'electronic purses' – also called 'smart cards' – are likely to become a close substitute for currency in many transactions which used to be settled in currency since these such cards may prove to be even more convenient than currency and yet no more susceptible to theft and robbery. Therefore, the demand for currency as a proportion of total expenditures or of M1 or M2 is likely to continue to decline in the future.

The above arguments imply that the demand function for currency can be written as:

$$C/D = c(\gamma_D, r^h, r_D, r_T, Y; \text{payments technology}) \tag{1}$$

where:

c currency-demand deposit ratio
γ_D charges on demand deposits
r^h average yield on the public's investments in bonds etc.
r_D interest rate on demand deposits
r_T interest rate on time deposits
Y nominal national income

$\partial c/\partial \gamma_D > 0$ and $\partial c/\partial r_D < 0$ for obvious reasons. We expect $\partial c/\partial Y > 0$, since an increase in Y increases transactions which are likely to increase the demand for currency proportionately more than for demand deposits. This implies that the currency ratio will increase in the upturns and decrease in the recessions. An increase in the return on both time deposits and bonds is likely to decrease the demand for both currency and demand deposits. Further, currency is needed for small everyday transactions that tend to be inelastic in response to changes in interest rates, while efficient cash management techniques allow reductions in demand deposits. Hence, the currency ratio will rise with increases in r^h and r_T, so that $\partial c/\partial r^h > 0$ and $\partial c/\partial r_T > 0$. This implies that an increase in the rate of inflation and/or in the nominal interest rates, as usually happens in the upturn of the business cycle, would increase the currency ratio. Conversely, this ratio will fall in a recession. Hence, we expect the currency ratio to be procyclical (rise in upturns and fall in downturns).

As stressed above, the currency ratio also depends upon the security environment and the availability of alternative modes of payment such as debit and credit cards. The impending innovations in creating smart cards that represent electronic purses are likely to reduce currency demand.

Households not only hold currency and demand deposits but also hold various forms of time deposits, including savings deposits, term deposits, certificates of deposit (CDs) and their variations. All of these pay interest and we can specify the arguments which would lead to the public's demand function for time deposits or for its desired ratio of time-to-demand deposits. The derivation of these functions is left to the reader.

10.3 COMMERCIAL BANKS: THE DEMAND FOR RESERVES

Commercial banks hold cash reserves against their deposits. A part of these reserves is normally held in cash (at the tills, in the automatic teller machines or in the bank's vault) and part is held in demand deposits with the central bank. The sum of these two parts constitutes the banks' cash reserves.

The central bank often requires the commercial banks to meet a certain minimum ratio – called the *required reserve ratio*[3] – of their reserves to their demand deposit liabilities.[4] Chapter 11 will present the required reserve ratios for several countries. In 1999, this ratio was zero in Canada and the United Kingdom. In the United States, it depended on the amount of deposits and varied between 3% and 9% for depository institutions.

Banks usually hold reserves in excess of those required to meet the required reserve ratio. Banks also borrow from other banks or the central bank. Reserves held in excess of the sum of required and borrowed reserves are referred to as '*free reserves*' – that is, at the bank's disposal for use if it so desires.

The free reserve hypothesis

Free reserves for the banking system as a whole are those in excess of the required reserves and the amount borrowed from the central bank. Free reserves must be distinguished from '*excess reserves*'. Excess reserves are actual holdings of cash reserves in excess of those desired by the bank and which the bank wants to eliminate either immediately or gradually. By comparison, free reserves are the reserves that the bank wants to hold under the existing economic circumstances.

The reserves that a bank wishes to hold in an economic sense – that is, its demand for reserves – must also not be confused with the reserves that it is required to hold. The two differ in general. The causes of the difference are studied in what is now often referred to as the *free reserve hypothesis*.

Both required reserves and free reserves for any bank vary over time. The former depends upon the required reserve ratio or differential ratios imposed by the central bank, discussed in Chapters 11 and 12 on central bank behaviour, and upon the total deposits in the bank. The computation of such required reserves is largely mechanical, according to a formula prescribed by the central bank.[5]

Each bank has to anticipate its deposit liabilities in making its decisions on its reserve holdings. Demand deposits may be withdrawn on demand at any time and individuals' demand deposits in any given bank fluctuate considerably over time as they make deposits and withdrawals. For any given bank over a given period, the total of new deposits and withdrawals is likely to cancel out to some extent, depending upon its size and the distribution of its depositors in occupations and between employees and employers. The degree of uncertainty as to the average levels of deposits in any bank is thus likely to vary between banks. It is likely to be higher for unit rather than branch banks, small rather than large banks, and banks with a smaller degree of monopoly than those with a greater one. The cancellation process is likely to be still greater for all the banks in the economy taken together, so that the overall amounts of demand deposits in the economy normally exhibit a great deal of stability.

The free reserve hypothesis assumes that, under certainty, banks act as profit maximizers in determining their demand for reserves. Profit maximization implies that they regard reserves as one type of asset in their portfolio, as against holdings of securities or loans, and hence that the demand for reserves depends upon the comparative cost of holding reserves rather than other assets. Reserves do not generally earn a monetary return while other assets do so and the demand for reserves depends upon the rates of return on these assets. This demand should, because of the substitution effect, fall as the rates of return on the other assets rise, and vice versa.

It has been pointed out earlier that banks face uncertainty as to the amounts of their deposits. Under uncertainty, the free reserve hypothesis assumes that banks maximize the expected utility of their terminal wealth, corresponding to the expected utility maximization by the individual investor presented in Chapter 5. Therefore, the theory of portfolio selection set out in Chapter 5 can be adapted to explain the bank's demand for free reserves. Assuming that the banks are risk-averters, disliking the prospect of ending up with less than the required reserves, they would always hold more than the required reserves. Part of these extra reserves could be borrowed, so that the demand for free reserves will depend upon the risks present, the response to risk, the cost of borrowing and the return on other assets in the bank's portfolio.

A significant element of the risk in falling short of the desired reserves depends on the structure of the banking system, the size of the bank in question and the diversity of its client base. Canadian and British banks tend to be large, with branches all over the country. They have a very diversified client base, so that the daily variance in their deposits is relatively low. The US banks in the smaller cities and rural areas are often small, have a limited number of branches and may be dependent on a particular segment of the economy. Consequently, they face higher daily variance in their deposits.

Another significant element of the risk in falling short of the desired reserves is related to the formula specified by the central bank for the minimum reserves that the banks should hold against their deposits.[6] In the UK, although the reserve requirement is zero, the banks are expected to meet it on a daily basis. This increases their risk, which to some extent is offset through their ability to borrow reserves in the overnight market from other financial institutions. Canada allows averaging of reserves and deposits over a four-to-five-week period and the United States allows this over two weeks, thereby implying less risk for their banks than for British banks.[7]

Borrowing by commercial banks from the central bank

Banks borrow reserves from a variety of sources. Banks frequently borrow reserves from each other bilaterally and often do so in the context of an organized overnight loan market such as the federal funds market in the USA and the overnight loan market in Canada. They can, depending on regulations, also borrow abroad to supplement their reserves. Borrowing by individual banks from other banks within the system does not change the monetary base and can, therefore, be ignored in the determination of the money supply. However, when the commercial banks as a whole increase their borrowing from the central bank or from abroad, the monetary base increases and the money supply expands.

In lending to the commercial banks as a whole, the central bank is said to act as the lender of last resort since the banking system as a whole cannot obtain additional funds from its own internal borrowing and lending. However, individual commercial banks sometimes treat the central bank as their lender of first resort rather than a lender of last resort. The terms on which it lends and the conditions under which its loans are made affect the amounts that the banks wish to borrow from it. In general, borrowing from the central bank can trigger greater oversight by the central bank into the borrowing bank's asset management and other practices. Since this is rarely desired, it acts as a disincentive to borrow.

In the USA, the discount rate – at which the Federal Reserve System lends to its member banks – is usually below the three-month Treasury bill rate, so that these banks stand to gain by borrowing from the Federal Reserve System. To limit the amounts and frequency of borrowing, the Federal Reserve Board imposes a variety of formal and informal rules on such borrowing. One of the latter is that borrowing from the Federal Reserve System is a *privilege*, extended by the Federal Reserve System to its member banks, rather than a right of the banks. This privilege can be curtailed or circumscribed by conditions if a bank tries to use it indiscriminately.

Canada has experimented with two different methods for setting the bank rate at which it lends to the chartered banks. Under a fixed bank rate regime adopted during 1956 to 1962 and 1980 to 1994, the bank rate was automatically set each week at 0.25% higher than the average Treasury bill rate that week. Since it was higher than the Treasury bill rate, the chartered banks incurred a loss if they financed their purchases of Treasury bills by borrowing from the Bank of Canada. Such a rate is said to be a 'penalty rate' and, by its nature, discourages borrowings. It does not, therefore, need the support of other restrictions on borrowings to the extent that the American discount rate requires. Since 1994, the Bank of Canada has placed its major focus on setting the overnight loan rate, with an operating band around it of 50 basis points. This rate is the rate at which the banks and other major participants in the money market make overnight loans to each other. Since 1996, the bank rate has been set at the upper limit of the operating range for the overnight loans, so that it is a floating rate and continues to be a penalty rate, irrespective of daily movements in the market rates. The Bank of Canada influences the bank rate by changes in its supply of funds to the overnight market or through its purchases or sales of Treasury bills.

In the United Kingdom, the Bank of England determines daily the rate at which it will lend to the banks. This allows it control over borrowings from it on a daily basis. It also allows close control over the interest rates that the banks charge their customers since these rates have base rates closely tied to the Bank of England's daily rate.

The banks' demand function for reserves

The free reserve hypothesis in attempting to explain the demand for free reserves, has to take these differing practices into account and would yield differing demand functions for different countries and periods. However, empirical studies[8] have confirmed its implication that the earnings on alternative assets influence the amount of reserves held and that the ratio of desired reserves to demand deposits cannot be taken as constant for purposes of monetary policy.

The preceding arguments imply that the demand function for desired free reserves can be expressed as:

$$R/D = f(r, r_R, r_{CB}) \tag{2}$$

where:

r average interest rate on banks' assets
r_R average return on banks' reserves
r_{CB} central bank's discount rate (for loans to the commercial banks)

In (2), $\partial f/\partial r < 0$, $\partial f/\partial r_R > 0$ and $\partial f/\partial r_{CB} > 0$. We have simplified this function by including average interest rates rather than the variety of interest rates that will need to be considered in practice.

Note that, in (2), r is an average of the return on Treasury bills, bonds of different maturities, mortgages and loans to the public, etc. Also note that r_R would be zero for reserves held in currency and would also be zero if the rest of the reserves are held in non-interest-paying deposits with the central bank. Banks will want to increase free reserves if the cost r_{CB} of covering a shortfall in reserves increases and decrease them if the return r from investing their funds rises. Free reserves would also increase if r_R were positive and were to increase.

10.4 MECHANICAL THEORIES OF THE MONEY SUPPLY: MONEY SUPPLY IDENTITIES

Mechanical theories of the money supply are so called because they use identities, rather than behavioural functions, to calculate the money supply. The resulting money supply equations in such an approach can be easily made more or less complex, depending upon the purpose of the analysis. We specify below several such equations, starting with the most elementary one.

(i) An elementary demand deposit equation

Assume that the ratio of reserves held by the banks against demand deposits is given by:

$$R = \rho D$$

where:

R reserves held by banks
D demand deposits in banks
ρ reserve ratio

If ρ equals the required reserve ratio, set by the central bank for the banking system, and R are the reserves exogenously supplied to it, profit-maximizing banks will create the amount of deposits given by:

$$D = (1/\rho)R \tag{3}$$

This equation is the elementary deposit creation formula for the creation of deposits by the banks on the basis of the reserves held by them. It suffers from a failure to take note of the behaviour of the banks and the public in the deposit expansion process, so that a more elaborate approach to the money supply is preferable.

(ii) A common money supply equation

Friedman and Schwartz (1963) used a money supply equation that not only takes account of the reserve/deposit ratio of banks but also of the ratio of currency to deposits desired by the public. Their ratio is derived simply from the accounting identities:

$$M = C + D \tag{4}$$

$$B = R + C \tag{5}$$

where

M money stock $= C + D$
C currency in the hands of the public
D demand deposits

R banks' reserves
B monetary base $= R + C$

The steps in the derivation are:

$$M = \frac{M}{B} B \tag{6}$$

$$= \frac{C + D}{R + C} B$$

$$= \frac{1 + D/C}{R/C + 1} B \tag{7}$$

$$= \frac{(1 + D/C)(D/R)}{(R/C + 1)(D/R)} B$$

$$= \frac{(1 + D/C)(D/R)}{(D/R + D/C)} B \tag{8}$$

Equation (8) separates the basic determinants of the money stock into changes in the monetary base and changes in the '*monetary base multiplier*', defined as $(\partial M/\partial B)$, for the monetary base. This multiplier is itself determined by D/R, the reserve ratio, and C/D, the currency ratio. Of these, the reserve ratio reflects the required reserve ratio and the banks' demand for free reserves. The currency ratio reflects the public's behaviour in its demand for currency. Hence, the three determinants of the money stock emphasized by (8) are the monetary base, and the currency and reserve ratios.

Another version of (8) is:

$$M = \frac{B}{\left[\dfrac{C}{M} + \dfrac{R}{D} - \left(\dfrac{C}{M} \dfrac{R}{D} \right) \right]} \tag{9}$$

Using this equation, Cagan (1965) examined the contributions of the three elements B, (C/M) and (R/D), to M2 over the business cycle and in the long term. He found that the dominant factor influencing the long-term growth in the money stock was the growth in the monetary base. Changes in the two ratios contributed little to the *secular* change in M2. However, for *cyclical* movements in the money stock, the changes in the C/M ratio were the most important element, while the reserve ratio had only a minor impact and changes in the monetary base exerted only an irregular influence.

The currency-demand deposit – and hence the currency–money – ratio is influenced strongly by changes in economic activity and especially by changes in the rate of consumer spending. As we have explained in earlier sections, this ratio varies in the same direction as nominal national income – hence, pro-cyclically – so that a rise in spending in cyclical upturns increases currency holdings, which lowers the money supply.

(iii) A more complex money supply equation

The preceding money supply equation does not differentiate deposits into various types such as demand deposits, time and savings deposits, and government deposits. A money supply equation that does so can be derived from the following identities:

$$M = C + D \tag{4}$$

$$B = R + C \tag{5}$$

$$R = \rho(D + T + G) \tag{10}$$

$$C = cD \tag{11}$$

$$T = tD \tag{12}$$

$$G = gD \tag{13}$$

where the new symbols are defined as:

ρ the average weighted reserve ratio, calculated by dividing total reserves by total deposits
T time deposits
G government deposits
c C/D
t T/D
g G/D

By substituting (10) and (11) into (5), we get:

$$B = \rho(D + T + G) + cD \tag{14}$$

Substituting (12) and (13) into (14) gives,

$$B = \rho(D + tD + gD) + cD$$
$$= [\rho(1 + t + g) + c] D \tag{15}$$

Hence,

$$D = \left[\frac{1}{\rho(1 + t + g) + c} \right] B \tag{16}$$

From (11) and (16), we have:

$$C = \left[\frac{C}{\rho(1 + t + g) + c} \right] B \tag{17}$$

Substituting (16) and (17) into (4) gives:

$$M = \left[\frac{1 + c}{\rho(1 + t + g) + c} \right] B \tag{18}$$

In (18), [·] measures the increase in the money supply following an increase of one dollar of the monetary base and can be labelled as the 'monetary base multiplier'. It is also sometimes called the 'money multiplier' but we believe the former term to be more accurate and appropriate. This multiplier, as stated in (18), has been refined to take account of the public's desired ratio of time deposits to demand deposits, as well as the proportion of government deposits in commercial banks to their total demand deposits. The former ratio depends upon the interest rates on time deposits and other short-term money market instruments. The latter ratio depends mainly upon the flow of fiscal receipts and expenditures of the government.

(iv) A still more elaborate money supply equation

The preceding money supply equation did not differentiate between the reserve ratios that each kind of deposit must meet. If this differentiation were made, (10) above would be modified to:

$$R = \rho_D D + \rho_T T + \rho_G G \qquad (19)$$

where:

    ρ_D the reserve ratio for demand deposits
    ρ_T the reserve ratio against time deposits
    ρ_G the reserve ratio against government deposits

Equation (19) modifies (18) to,

$$M = \left[\frac{1+c}{\rho_D + \rho_T t + \rho_G g + c}\right] B \qquad (20)$$

Equations (8), (9), (18) and (20) are all identities. Which one is used depends upon the rules and regulations about reserve ratios, the availability of statistical data and the further behavioural assumptions that are made. In practice, theories of the money supply go beyond these identities and embed the relevant identity in a behavioural theory.

10.5 A BEHAVIOURAL THEORY OF THE MONEY SUPPLY

A behavioural theory of the money supply process must take into account the behaviour of the participants in this process in order to determine the economic and non-economic determinants of the variables being studied. Such a theory studies such behaviour in terms of the main components of the preceding money supply formulae, such as the currency desired by the public, the reserves desired by the commercial banks, the amounts borrowed by them and the monetary base which the central bank wishes to provide, etc. It may, alternatively, focus on the ratios such as the currency ratio, the reserve ratio, etc. Either way can be used to build the supply function for money. Both ways represent a mixture of the above formulae approach and behavioural determinants of the main elements. On the behavioural elements, the basic analysis takes into account the sort of considerations that go into specifications of money demand functions, as discussed in Chapters 3 to 9.

Empirical studies following the behavioural approach to money supply determination usually postulate that the supply of M1 or M2 – depending upon the aggregate being studied – depend upon the public's income or wealth – or only monetary wealth defined as $(D + T + C)$ – as the scale variable, and other economic factors. The latter include various interest rates, costs of demand and time deposit accounts, and non-monetary wealth. The banks' demand for free reserves is assumed to depend upon total demand deposits, reserve requirements, cost of holding free reserves as reflected in various interest rates and the penalties from deficient reserve holdings. It is also often assumed that the monetary base B is exogenously given.

A simple form of the money supply function, say for M1, which takes the demand for currency, time deposits and bank reserves as given, specified in a linear form on this basis would be:

$$M1 = m_0 + m_1 B + m_2 C_0 + m_3 T_0 + m_4 R_0 \tag{21}$$

where the coefficients m_i, $i = 2, \ldots, 4$, are the relevant multipliers, measuring the impact of changes in the explanatory variables on the supply of M1 and are likely to differ in value. Equation (21) is a behavioural equation since its multipliers are determined by the data generated by the behaviour of the agents in the economy.

Equation (21) is a very simple form of the money supply equation in the behavioural approach. In countries where there are differential reserve requirements, varying either by types of deposits or types of financial institutions, account has to be taken of shifts of deposits among these categories. One way of doing this is to replace the monetary base term B by a modified term that specifies the 'effective' amount of the monetary base. An alternative would be to incorporate the various reserve requirements as explanatory variables on the right-hand side of (21).

Terms $m_2 C_0$, $m_3 T_0$ and $m_4 R_0$ in (21) represent the influence of economic factors other than those operating through m_1 and B. These terms in turn depend upon other economic variables, as discussed earlier. The government's demand deposits are not considered in equation (21) but can be introduced through additional terms.

Note that since C, T and R, as well as the multipliers, depend upon the rates of interest, a more elaborate form of the money supply function includes the rates of interest as variables. We bring these into the analysis in the next section.

10.6 THE GENERAL MONEY SUPPLY FUNCTION AND ITS EMPIRICAL ESTIMATES

The theoretical considerations in the preceding sections suggest that the general form of the money supply function is:

$$M^s = M^s(r_D, r_T, r_S, r_L, r_d, r_O, R, Y, B) \tag{22}$$

where:

M money supply
r_D charges on demand deposits
r_T interest rate on time deposits
r_S short-term interest rate
r_L long-term interest rate
r_d central bank rate for lending to the commercial banks
r_O overnight loan rate
R required reserve ratio
Y nominal national income
B monetary base

As argued in earlier sections, the money supply depends, among other variables, upon the free reserves desired by the banks and the currency desired by the public. Free reserves depend upon r_O, r_d, r_S and r_L since these determine the opportunity cost of holding free reserves. The public's demand for currency will similarly be a function of r_D and r_T. It also depends, as argued earlier, on the level of economic activity for which nominal national income Y is a proxy. Finally, the money supply depends upon the monetary base B.

As discussed in section 10.1, the monetary base is in the control of the monetary authorities which can operate it in such a way as to offset the effect of changes in the other variables on the money supply. Alternatively, they may only allow the changes in the other variables to affect the money supply in so far as the effect changes the money supply to a desired extent. Therefore, the monetary base is not necessarily a variable independent of the other explanatory variables in (22).

Now consider the directions of the effects that are likely to occur in the money supply function. An increase in the monetary base increases the money supply. An increase in national income increases the currency demand and lowers banks' reserves and, hence, decreases the money supply. An increase in the short-term market interest rate increases the profitability of assets which are close substitutes for free reserves and hence decreases the demand for free reserves, which increases the money supply. A cut in the discount rate has a somewhat similar effect. An increase in the yield on time deposits increases their demand by the public, which lowers the reserves available for demand deposits, so that demand deposits decrease.

In practice, the estimation of the money supply function is usually undertaken with a smaller number of variables than specified in (22). This is partly because of collinearity among the various interest rates.

Equation (22) specifies the money supply function and could be applied to the supply of either M1 or M2 or another monetary aggregate. However, note that the signs of the interest rate elasticities could differ among the aggregates. There are three main cases of difference:

(i)   If the interest rates on demand deposits increase, their demand will increase but this could be merely at the expense of time deposits, so that while M1 increases, M2 does not do so. Hence, the interest elasticity of demand deposits and M1 with respect to r_D is positive but that of M2 may be positive or zero.

(ii) Since time deposits are excluded from M1, they are part of the opportunity cost of holding M1. Hence, the elasticity of M1 with respect to the interest rate on time deposits, r_T, would be negative. These deposits are, however, part of M2 so that, when their interest rate increases, the desired amount of time deposits increases and so does M2. That is, the interest elasticity of M2 with respect to r_T is positive.

(iii) The interest elasticity of M1 would be negative with respective to the return r on bonds. But if the time deposits interest rates rise with this bond rate r, the respective interest elasticity of M2 is likely to be zero. However, if the time deposit rates do not increase when the bond rate r rises, the public will switch some time deposits to bonds, so that the elasticity of M2 with respect to r would be negative. Therefore, this interest elasticity depends upon the relationship between r_T and r.

Table 10.1 shows the pattern of interest rate elasticities for M1 and M2. This table also includes the elasticities of M1 and M2 with respect to the return on excess reserves and the central bank discount rate on borrowed reserves. Both are negative. The reasons for these, and the other signs shown in Table 10.1, have been explained above.

Table 10.1 Money supply elasticities

Interest rate on	M1	M2
Demand deposits	+	?
Time deposits	−	+
Bonds	−	?
Excess reserves	−	−
Central bank's discount rate	−	−

10.7 INTEREST RATE ELASTICITIES OF THE MONEY SUPPLY

The empirical studies on money supply are far fewer than on money demand. The following brief review of the empirical findings on the money supply function confines itself to reporting the elasticities' estimates for this function.

Rasche (1972) reports the impact and equilibrium elasticities calculated by him for the supply functions reported by DeLeeuw (1965) for the Brookings model, by Goldfeld (1966) for the Goldfeld model, and for the MPS model developed by the Federal Reserve–MIT–Pennsylvania econometric model project. These studies were for the USA using data up to the mid-1960s. Rasche's calculations of these elasticities were roughly in the ranges reported in Table 10.2.[9]

Table 10.2[a] Interest rate elasticities for the money supply function

	Impact[b]	Equilibrium
Currency demand		
Time deposit rate	−0.012 to −0.015	−0.136 to −0.14
Treasury bill rate	−0.008 to 0.0037	−0.07 to 0.026
Time deposit demand		
Treasury bill rate	−0.038 to −0.15	−0.374 to −1.4
Time deposit rate	0.070 to 0.3	0.683 to 2.9
Bank borrowings		
Treasury bill rate	0.134 to 0.88	0.50 to 2.625
Discount rate	−0.186 to −0.98	−0.70 to −2.926
Free reserves		
Treasury bill rate	−2.99 to −3.95	−6.42 to −8.47
Discount rate	3.23 to 3.48	6.93 to 7.46
Money supply, excluding time deposits[c]		
Treasury bill rate	0.214 (average over first six months)	
	0.267 (average over second six months)	
	0.2438 (average over third six months)	
Money supply, including time deposits[c]		
Treasury bill rate	0.219 (average over first six months)	
	0.278 (average over second six months)	
	0.258 (average over third six months)	

[a] Compiled from Rasche (1980), various tables.
[b] The impact elasticity is over the first quarter following a change in the interest rate.
[c] From Rasche (1980), Table 5.

Noting there have been many changes in the United States financial markets since the 1960s, the elasticity ranges reported in Table 10.2 are now mainly useful for pedagogical purposes. These elasticities indicated that the main components of the money supply – and the money supply itself – were not exogenous but functions of the interest rates in the economy. We conclude from Table 10.2 that:

(i)   Currency demand was negatively related to the time deposit rate, while time deposits were positively related.

(ii)   Time deposit holdings were positively related to their own interest rate and negatively to the Treasury bill rate.

(iii)   Banks increased their borrowing from the Federal Reserve as the Treasury bill rate rose and decreased them as the discount rate increased. Note that the discount rate is the cost of such borrowing and the Treasury bill rate represents the return on funds invested by the banks. Hence, an increase in the Treasury bill rate provides an incentive for the banks to increase their loans for a given monetary base, and also to increase their borrowing, given the discount rate, from the central bank. Both these factors imply a positive elasticity of the money supply with respect to the Treasury bill rate, as shown in Table 10.2.

(iv)   Conversely, while the banks' free reserves decreased as the Treasury bill rate increased, they increased with the discount rate. The Treasury bill rate represents the amount the banks lose by holding free reserves and is, therefore, their opportunity cost, so that they fall with the Treasury bill rate. However, these elasticities with respect to the discount rate are positive since the discount rate is the 'return' on free reserves, i.e., the banks escape having to borrow from the central bank and having to pay the discount rate if they hold adequate free reserves to meet withdrawals from them.

These reported elasticities are consistent with the analysis presented earlier in this chapter. Even though there have been numerous innovations in the financial markets since the 1960s – so that the magnitudes of the actual elasticities are likely to have changed – there is no reason to expect that the *signs* of elasticities have altered from those reported above.

Lags in the money supply function

The main findings on this show that:

(i)   The impact elasticities are significantly lower than the equilibrium ones, indicating that the adjustments take longer than one quarter.

(ii)   The money supply had positive interest elasticities each month through the first eighteen months for which the elasticities were reported.

These show that that financial sector did not adjust the money supply to its full equilibrium level within one quarter. In fact, (ii) points out that the money supply continues to change even after six quarters. This finding has been confirmed by many studies, so that the existence of lags in the response of the money supply to interest rate changes can be taken as well established.

Comparing money supply and money demand elasticities

Note that the estimated interest elasticities of money supply are positive, while the interest elasticities of money demand reported in Chapter 9 were negative. To illustrate this difference, note that an increase in the Treasury bill rate increases the money supply but decreases money demand. There are lags in both the money supply and money demand functions.

10.8 COINTEGRATION AND ERROR-CORRECTION MODELS OF THE MONEY SUPPLY

There are few cointegration studies on the money supply function and its major components. We draw the following findings from Baghestani and Mott (1997) to illustrate the nature of empirical findings on money supply and the problems with estimating this function when monetary policy shifts.

Baghestani and Mott performed cointegration tests on USA monthly data for three periods, 1971:04–1979:09, 1979:10–1982:09 and 1983:01–1990:06, using the Engle–Granger techniques. Their variables were log of M1, log of the monetary base (B) and an interest rate variable (r). The last was measured by the three-month commercial paper rate for the first two periods and by the differential between this rate and the deposit rate paid on super-NOWs (negotiable orders of withdrawal at banks) introduced in January 1983. Further, the discount rate was used as a deterministic trend variable, since it is constant over long periods. The data for the three periods was separated since the Federal Reserve changed its operating procedures among them.

Baghestani and Mott could not reject the null of no cointegration among the designated variables for 1971:04–1979:09. Further, for 1979:10–1982:09, while B and r possessed a unit root, M1 did not, so that the cointegration technique was not applied for this period. The only period which satisfied the requirement for cointegration and yielded a cointegration vector was 1983:01–1990:06. The error-correction model was also estimated for this period. The cointegration between the variables broke down when the period was extended beyond 1990:06. These results have to be treated with great caution. As indicated in Chapter 9 on the money demand estimation, cointegration is meant to reveal the long-run relationships and, for reliable results, requires data over a long period – rather than more frequent observations, as in monthly data, over a few years. The three periods used by Baghestani and Mott were each individually less than a decade.

For 1983:01–1990:06, Baghestani and Mott concluded from their cointegration–ECM results that the economy's adjustments to the long-run relationship occurred through changes in the money supply and the interest rate, rather than in the monetary base. Comparing their findings across their three periods, changes in the central bank policy regime, such as targeting monetary aggregates or interest rates, are extremely important in determining the money supply function in terms of both its coefficients and whether there even exists a long-run relationship. Further, even regulatory changes such as permitting, after 1980, the payment of interest on checkable deposits can shift the money supply function.

CONCLUSIONS

The supply of money in an economy is critical to its macroeconomic performance, so that most countries have allocated control of it to a central bank. Therefore, the theory of money supply for any given economy has to start with the knowledge of whether or not its central bank exogenously determines the money supply, thereby cancelling out any undesired changes in it induced by other factors in the economy. If it does so, the final determinant of the money supply is central bank behaviour. However, if it allows other factors some role in changing the money supply, a wider analysis of the money supply becomes applicable, and the behaviour of the public and of financial institutions also needs to be studied.

The theories of money supply can be specified as either mechanical or behavioural. In practice, most empirical studies combine both approaches in deriving their estimating equations. These studies show that, over time, changes in the monetary base are the main element in changes in the money supply. However, over the business cycle, changes in the currency and the reserve ratios also play a very significant role, with the result that their determinants also need to be incorporated into the estimating equations. These determinants include a variety of interest rates in the economy, as well as national income. The estimated money supply functions, especially for M1, usually show negative elasticities with respect to the central bank discount rate and positive ones with respect to the Treasury bill rate.

The monetary base multiplier is procyclical since the currency/demand deposit ratio rises in the upturns and falls in the downturns due to the influence on it of changes in national income and in interest rates.

The application of cointegration techniques to the money supply and its determinants is not as common as for the money demand function. Cointegration requires long runs of data for reliable results. Since the money supply depends critically upon central bank behaviour, periodic changes in the central bank's targets and money supply rules make it difficult to collect sufficient data for reliable cointegration results on the money supply function. However, the reported empirical studies on the money supply function usually yield signs consistent with the signs of the interest rate elasticities implied by the theory.

SUMMARY OF CRITICAL CONCLUSIONS

- The private sector affects the money supply, so that the central bank must be able to predict its responses if it is to offset them and control the money supply in the economy.
- The non-bank public influences the money supply through its demand for currency and various forms of its deposits with the banks.
- The commercial banks influence the money supply through changes in their demand for reserves.
- The central bank can influence the money supply through open market operations, through changes in the minimum reserve requirements, if any, imposed by it on the commercial banks, and through changes in its discount rate for loans to commercial banks. In some countries, it also does so by shifting government deposits between the commercial banks and itself.
- Monetary evolution, inducing changes in the currency or deposit ratios, can change the monetary base multiplier. In general, this has been increasing over time.
- Empirical studies support a behavioural approach to the money supply and indicate that the money supply depends on the interest rates in the economy.
- The estimated money supply functions are very sensitive to the monetary policy and target regimes.

---

review and discussion questions

1 'Macroeconomic models assume that the money supply is exogenously specified by the central bank. If this is so, there is no purpose to the specification and estimation of money supply functions.' Discuss this statement. How would you verify its validity?

2 What happens to the monetary base and the money supply if the government finances a fiscal deficit by:

  (a) selling bonds to the public;
  (b) selling bonds to the commercial banks;
  (c) selling bonds to the central bank;
  (d) selling bonds to foreigners.

  If any of these changes the money supply, what policies should the central bank adopt to offset these changes?

3 What happens to the monetary base and the money supply if:

  (a) the central bank lowers the discount rate;
  (b) the central bank lowers the discount rate and also sells bonds to the public;
  (c) the central bank forbids overnight loans and eliminates the overnight loan market.

4 Show what happens to the money supply if:

  (a) the economy enters a boom and interest rates rise;

(b) the underground economy with illegal holdings of currency is eliminated;

(c) firms give a significant discount for payment in cash rather than credit cards;

(d) credit cards are replaced totally by debit cards;

(e) both credit and debit cards are replaced by smart cards.

4 Does the central bank have tight control over the money supply? What are the factors that weaken the link between the central bank policies and the changes in the money supply?

5 Would a high (in the limit, 100%) reserve requirement imposed on banks strengthen central bank control over the money supply? If so, why do central banks never impose very high reserve requirements?

6 Discuss what will happen to the monetary base and the money supply if the central bank starts paying interest, say at the Treasury bill rate, on commercial bank deposits with it. If it does so, would the interest elasticity of money supply be higher or lower than it would be under a regime where interest was not paid on such deposits?

7 Specify the long-run and short-run money supply functions that capture the behaviour of the central bank, the public and the banks in the money supply process. Discuss the differences between the long-run and short-run functions.

8 How would you formulate your money supply function for estimation in an empirical study? What would be your definition of the money supply variable? What would be the arguments of your function, justifying each one? Comment on the *a priori* relationships that you expect between your independent variables and the money supply. Compare your supply function with some others estimated in the literature and comment on the differences.

9 For a selected country and using quarterly data, specify and estimate the money supply function. Among your independent variables, include at least two different interest rates, one being the discount/bank rate and the other a market-determined short-term one. Check and correct for shifts in the money supply function during the period of your study. Do your estimations using the following techniques:

(a) least squares estimation, with a first-order PAM;

(b) cointegration with an error-correction model.

Discuss your choice of the functional form of the money supply function and your choice of the variables and the econometric techniques used, as well as the data and econometric problems you encountered.

Discuss your results, their plausibility and consistency with the theory, and their robustness. Can you explain the estimated shifts in your function by reference to changes in the policies of the central bank?

10 What are the reasons requiring the use of cointegration techniques in money supply estimation? What would be the disadvantages of using ordinary least squares for such estimation? If you use both and obtain different estimates, which would you rely on and why?

11 Are there, in general, any problems with the application of cointegration techniques to money supply functions? Can the estimates from such techniques be relied upon? Discuss.

NOTES

1 These are not the only actors in the money supply process, and some of the others will be brought in at relevant points. In particular, in open economies, the balance-of-payments

surpluses (deficits) of a country can increase (decrease) its money supply. This relationship between the balance of payments and the money supply is discussed in Chapters 18 and 19.

2 One estimate of the average total cost of demand deposits in 1970 was about 2.4% of their dollar volume. The cost of time deposits was, by comparison, 0.6% if the interest costs were excluded and between 5.3% and 5.7% if the interest costs were included. Approximately 70% of the cost associated with demand deposits was the cost of processing cheques and involved wages, computer time costs, etc.

3 The next chapter on the central bank discusses required reserve ratios in greater detail. It is now close to zero in many Western countries excluding the United States where it is between 3% and 10%.

4 Some countries, including the United States, have different required ratios for different types of bank liabilities or for different financial institutions, depending on their size and nature.

5 The formulae for computing legally required reserves differ between countries, with significant impact on the behaviour of banks towards free reserves and hence towards monetary policy. A significant difference can be whether the reserves required to be held by a bank are computed as a proportion of its deposits in the current period or some past period, say a few weeks earlier. The former introduces uncertainty in the amount of required reserves, while the latter does not.

6 Information on these is given in Chapter 11, Table 11.1.

7 Another consideration is whether lagged reserve accounting is allowed, i.e., whether the banks can average their reserves and deposits over a specified past period only or have to include the current one. The former involves less risk.

8 For example, see DeLeeuw (1965), Goldfeld (1966) and Frost (1971).

9 These estimates cover different studies and different periods, and are reported for illustrative purposes only.

REFERENCES

Baghestani, Hamid, and Tracy Mott. 'A Cointegration Analysis of the US Money Supply Process'. *Journal of Macroeconomics*, 19, Spring 1997, pp. 269–83.

Brunner, Karl. 'Money Supply'. In *The New Palgrave Dictionary of Economics: Money*. New York: Macmillan, 1989.

———, and Meltzer, Allan H. 'Money Supply'. In Benjamin M. Friedman and Frank H. Hahn, eds, *Handbook of Monetary Economics*. Amsterdam: North-Holland, 1990, Volume 1, Ch. 9.

Cagan, Phillip. *Determinants and Effects of Changes in the Stock of Money, 1875–1960*. New York: Columbia University Press, 1965.

DeLeeuw, Frank. 'A Model of Financial Behavior'. In James S. Duesenberry *et al.*, *The Brookings Quarterly Econometric Model of the United States*. Chicago: Rand McNally, 1965, Ch. 13.

Friedman, Milton, and Anna Jacobson Schwartz. *A Monetary History of the United States, 1867–1960*. Princeton, NJ: National Bureau of Economic Research, 1963.

Frost, Peter A. 'Banks' Demand for Excess Reserves'. *Journal of Political Economy*, 79, July/August 1971, pp. 805–25.

Goldfeld, Stephen M. *Commercial Bank Behavior and Economic Activity*. Amsterdam: North-Holland, 1966.

———. 'An Extension of the Monetary Sector' In James S. Duesenberry *et al.*, *The Brookings Model: Some Further Results*. Chicago: Rand McNally, 1969, pp. 317–60.

———, and Edward J. Kane. 'The Determinants of Member-Bank Borrowing: An Econometric Study'. *Journal of Finance*, September 1966, pp. 499–514.

Papademos, Lucas, and Franco Modigliani. 'The Supply of Money and the Control of Nominal Income'. In Benjamin M. Friedman and Frank H. Hahn, eds, *Handbook of Monetary Economics*. Amsterdam: North-Holland, 1990, Vol. 1, Ch. 10.

Rasche, Robert H. 'A Review of Empirical Studies of the Money Supply Mechanism'. *The Federal Reserve Bank of St Louis Review*, 54, July 1972, pp. 11–19. Reprinted in Havrilesky, Thomas M., and John T. Boorman, eds, *Current Issues in Monetary Theory and Policy*, 2nd edn. Arlington Heights: AHM Publishing Co., 1980, pp. 296–312.

Sherman, Lawrence F., Case M. Sprenkle and Bryan E. Stanhouse. 'Reserve Requirements and Control of the Money Supply: A Note'. *Journal of Money, Credit and Banking*, 11, November 1979, pp. 486–93.

chapter eleven

THE CENTRAL BANK: GOALS, TOOLS AND GUIDES FOR MONETARY POLICY

This is the first of two chapters on central banks and their pursuit of monetary policy.

This chapter focuses on the institutional and historical aspects of the goals, instruments and targets of monetary policy as they have been actually pursued. The presentation is based on the history and practices of the central banks of the United States, Britain and Canada – with some material on the newly created European System of Central Banks. This material is intended to widen the discussion beyond the particularities of any one country and to provide some indication of the similarities and varieties of central bank practices in the pursuit of monetary policy.

The next chapter will focus on the theoretical aspects of the issues discussed in this chapter. Our main concern in these two chapters is with the general theory and practice of monetary policy, rather than with the particular laws, regulations and institutional arrangements concerning central banks in individual countries.

---

key concepts introduced in this chapter

- Central banks' mandates
- Objectives, instruments and guides of monetary policy
- The potential multiplicity of goals of Central banks
- Open market operations
- Required reserves
- Discount/bank rate
- Credit controls
- Moral suasion
- Selective controls
- Overnight loan interest rate
- Federal funds rate
- Administered interest rates
- Currency boards
- The competitive supply of money

Economic theory has long recognized the impact of the money supply changes and other monetary variables upon most of the important macroeconomic variables, such as output, employment, growth and prices.[1] The control of the money supply and the manipulation of interest rates, in so far as these are possible, is, therefore, in most countries, entrusted to the central bank, rather than left to market forces.[2] Exercise of this control requires an understanding of the process of choice among different goals, the nature and limitations of policy tools and the relationship between goals and tools, in conditions of both certainty and uncertainty. Important questions in this relationship relate to the lags that exist in the impact of the tools of monetary policy on national income and the structure of interest rates.

This chapter looks at the basic practical and institutional aspects of the goals and targets of central bank policies, and related issues such as the regulation of financial intermediaries. The institutional arrangements and practices are specified for the Federal Reserve System of the United States, the Bank of Canada, the monetary arrangements in Britain and the European System of Central Banks, which is the federated central bank for the European Union. The intention in presenting this material on several countries is to show the common elements as well as the diversity of monetary arrangements among a group of countries.

The next chapter is a companion one to this chapter and will extend the analysis of central bank policies to the choice among goals, guides and targets, as well as the conflicts among policy makers, the independence and credibility of central banks and the time consistency of policies. Chapters 15 and 16 will examine the theoretical aspects of the effectiveness of monetary policy in a macroeconomic context, while Chapters 18 and 19 will deal with the effectiveness of monetary policy in an open economy context.

Section 11.1 examines the historically multiple goals of central banks and section 11.2 investigates the evolution of these goals to the present ones, which is usually the sole one of price stability. Section 11.3 separates the goals into three levels: primary, intermediate and immediate. Section 11.4 reviews the instruments by which central banks conduct monetary policy. Sections 11.5 to 11.7 focus on the issues of competition and regulation of the financial sector and interest rates. Sections 11.8 to 11.11 present material on the central banks of the United States, Britain, Canada and the European Union. Section 11.12 appends a brief discussion of currency boards which represent an alternative institutional arrangement to central banks.

11.1 THE HISTORIC GOALS OF CENTRAL BANKS

The central banks of different countries usually have their own distinctive and somewhat different sets of goals in their mandates from their respective legislative authorities. However, as we shall see in this section, there is also a high degree of similarity in the goals, broadly defined, among them. Further, the mandate assigned to a given central bank is normally broad enough to allow it a great deal of latitude in the goals it chooses to pursue in practice. We illustrate the types of goals usually assigned to central banks by looking at those for the USA, Canada and the UK.

11.1.1 The original mandate of the Federal Reserve System in the USA

During the 1970s, the Federal Reserve System of the USA listed the broad objectives of the system as:

> To help counteract inflationary and deflationary movements, and to share in creating conditions favorable to sustained high employment, stable values, growth of the country, and a rising level of consumption.

It might have also added the additional objective of promoting a favourable balance of payments position. The list of economic goals in the mandates assigned until the 1980s to most central banks was very much similar to the above multiplicity of goals.

11.1.2 The original mandate of the Bank of Canada

The preamble to the Bank Act of 1934, setting up the Bank of Canada, had stated that the mandate of the Bank was to be:

> To regulate credit and currency in the best interests of the economic life of the nation, to control and protect the external value of the national monetary unit and to mitigate by its influence fluctuations in the general level of production, trade, prices and employment, so far as may be possible within the scope of monetary action, and generally to promote the economic and financial welfare of Canada.

This preamble required the Bank of Canada to use monetary policy – that is, the control of changes in credit and the money supply – to achieve its multiple goals. There was an implicit assumption behind the preamble that it was within the Bank's power to affect not only the rate of inflation and the exchange rate, but also to affect the real – and not merely the nominal – variables of output and employment. On the latter, the assumption was that the Bank could affect the short-run values of these real variables and thereby influence the fluctuations in them, so that these fluctuations were not solely real ones.

11.1.3 The evolution of the Bank of England and the goals of monetary policy in the United Kingdom

The Bank of England was founded as a private commercial bank in 1694.[3] Although a privately owned bank until 1946, it acted from the very beginning as the banker for the British government, under a business arrangement entered into in exchange for large loans made by the Bank to the British government through its purchase of government bonds. It was given the monopoly of (future) note issue in 1844, when it also withdrew from commercial banking. Its notes were made legal tender and convertible into gold at a fixed exchange rate. It evolved into a central bank through custom and practice in the eighteenth and nineteenth centuries, only gradually increasing its responsibility for maintaining orderly conditions in the money markets and influencing the policies and practices of the other commercial banks.

Given its origin as a private bank and its gradual evolution in practice into a central bank, there was no explicit legislated mandate for the Bank of England to pursue monetary policy in order to achieve specific national macroeconomic goals, even though it interacted closely with the government. Its primary goals through the eighteenth and nineteenth centuries seemed to be mainly related to its own profits and preserving its own solvency. This was consistent with the tenor of the traditional classical ideas which did not possess a theory of monetary policy for manipulating the economy and did not espouse an active monetary policy for the stabilization of the economy.

Since the Bank of England was nationalized in 1946, the relationship between the Bank and the government – represented by the Chancellor of the Exchequer, who is the government minister in charge of the Treasury – has gone through two distinct phases. From 1946 to 1997, the government had statutory power over not only the goals but also the use of instruments of monetary policy, though the day-to-day operations of the Bank and its normal business were left to the Bank. The Bank made recommendations to the Chancellor who had the final decision on the goals being pursued. The Bank implemented the policies defined by the Chancellor, though with some discretion over the timing of the implementation of decisions. Consequently, the goals pursued through monetary policy were ultimately those of the government for the economy and depended upon the preferences of the party in power. In 1997, the Bank was given operational independence in implementing monetary policy, but the power to set the ultimate goals of monetary policy was retained by the Chancellor and, therefore, the government.

Given this division of powers in Britain between the Bank of England and the government, it is appropriate to use the term 'monetary authority' to encompass both of them in their joint roles of setting the goals and pursuing the implementation of monetary policy. By comparison, in the United States and Canada, the monetary authority will simply be their respective central banks only.

In practice, the historic goals of the monetary authority in the UK were very similar to those of the central banks in the USA and Canada. From 1946 to the early 1980s, these policies were based on a wide set of goals, including lower unemployment, higher growth, lower inflation and the maintenance of the exchange rate, under the notion that it was possible to achieve several goals or at least trade-off among them through monetary policy.

11.1.4 Additional mandates of the central banks in the LDCs

Most LDCs are unable to raise the revenue internally to cover their fiscal operation, with the result that they continually incur large fiscal deficits. Some of these tend to be covered by foreign borrowing by the government, but very often there is still a remainder that needs to be financed. While such deficits in the richer and financially developed nations are normally covered through the government borrowing directly from the public through the issue of short- and long-term bonds, the financial markets in the LDCs are too thin to support much governmental borrowing. Given this constraint, many governments in the LDCs rely upon the central bank to directly finance the remaining deficit through increases in the monetary base, or do so indirectly by the sale of government bonds to the central bank.

Hence, while the LDCs have broadly similar mandates for their central banks as in the industrialized countries, an additional one in practice is that of financing the fiscal deficit. The justification sometimes given for this is that of national interest. In some cases, the deficit is related to massive development programmes, so that the central bank's financing of the deficit is further claimed to be a contribution to national economic development. However, such a practice makes monetary policy subservient to the fiscal one, and has implications for the independence of the central bank from the government and for its control of inflation. These issues are discussed later in this chapter.

11.2 THE EVOLUTION OF THE GOALS OF CENTRAL BANKS

11.2.1 The heritage of the multiplicity of goals and their evolution

As section 11.1 has indicated, the Federal Reserve System was set up in 1913 and the Bank of Canada was set up in 1934. For both of these central banks, the assigned mandate was to pursue a multiplicity of goals. In Britain, the monetary authorities (the Bank of England and the Chancellor of the Exchequer) also sought until the mid-1980s a similar multiplicity of goals. One broad category of goals related to the internal value (the price level) and the external value (the exchange rate) of the domestic currency. Another broad category was to improve on the performance of the real variables of unemployment, output, etc., and to reduce fluctuations among them.

These ultimate objectives assigned to the central banks were broadly consistent with the economic thinking and political philosophy of central banking of the time. Such broad consistency continued to exist to the mid-1980s, but then began to break down considerably. In the mid- and late 1980s, the Fed, the Bank of England, the Bank of Canada and many other central banks began to advocate and pursue the single goal of a low inflation rate, thereby abandoning the other goals listed in their mandates and previous practices, even when there were no legislative changes.[4]

Corresponding to the multiplicity of goals in the pre-1980 period was a multiplicity of instruments or tools of monetary policy. The ones generally advocated for use by the central banks, and used by them at various times, have been: open market operations, changes in required reserve ratios imposed on commercial banks, setting the bank/discount rates for lending to commercial banks, etc.

Both the goals and the tools used to achieve them have changed drastically in recent decades. For instance, the goals set for both the Federal Reserve System of the United States and the Bank of Canada had been influenced by the economic thinking and conditions in the first half of the twentieth century. This period had experienced several significant recessions and the decade of the 1930s was taken up by the Great Depression. It was clearly a period in which there was a dominant public realization of poor macroeconomic performance in many years, with massive declines in output and employment from their pre-Depression levels. In this period, it could hardly be claimed that the high unemployment levels were due to a shift in workers' preferences for more leisure since there was a clear macroeconomic dearth of jobs relative to the number of the unemployed workers looking for jobs. Such a macroeconomic failure was widely interpreted as requiring governmental action, and the central bank was clearly seen as one of the governmental authorities that should be made responsible for taking appropriate action to address this failure.

Keynes' *The General Theory* was published in 1936 in the midst of the Great Depression and served as the inauguration of the Keynesian School which favoured governmental intervention to prevent and correct macroeconomic failures. In particular, it espoused the elimination of major fluctuations in the real sectors of the economy. For about a couple of decades after 1936, Keynesians tended to downplay the effectiveness of using monetary supply changes to achieve these goals, especially expansionary ones, leaving it to fiscal policy to do so. However, by the 1960s, the Keynesians had come to include monetary policy, in addition to fiscal policy, as a major policy tool.

Part of this achievement was due to Milton Friedman, who had always tilted against the Keynesians and had made major contributions to establishing the short-run impact of money supply changes on the economy. The result was a sort of neoclassical–Keynesian synthesis during the 1960s and 1970s in the economics profession. A major tenet of this synthesis was that changes in the monetary aggregates do influence real output and employment, at least in the short run, and that the central bank could use monetary policy to reduce fluctuations in these variables, although there was a divergence of opinion on the central banks' ability to fine-tune these variables. The broad consensus seemed to be consistent with the practical experience with the Western economies during the 1960s, when several Western countries, including the USA, Canada and Britain, pursued expansionary monetary policies and experienced healthy increases in output and reductions in unemployment rates.

The Keynesian doctrines had been supplemented during the late 1950s by the Phillips curve which specified that the economy allowed the monetary authority a tradeoff between the rate of inflation and unemployment, so that the monetary authority was required to pursue the appropriate monetary policy to achieve its optimal combination of these variables. This belief in a potential tradeoff between inflation and unemployment was to be a significant feature of most central banks' policies, at least up to the mid-1970s.

While the 1970s were overall a period of stagflation in Western economies and there was beginning to be scepticism about the benefits of an expansionary monetary policy in a period of severe supply-side shocks – arising from the OPEC-led oil price increases – the main schools in economics were only just beginning to formalize their reasons for this scepticism. Monetary policy was still considered capable of helping to smoothen economic fluctuations, though not to the extent of 'fine-tuning' the economy but only roughly. This was the gist of the short-run economics of the monetarism of the 1970s, especially of the St Louis version of it. Consequently, while the long-run benefits of expansionary monetary policy were called into question, there was no major challenge, at least until the early 1970s, to the role of monetary policy in moderating economic fluctuations. Correspondingly, there was no major revision in practice of the multiplicity of goals embodied in the mandates of the central banks.

11.2.2 The revision in economic theory and the implied limitation on goals

The 1970s were a period of expansionary monetary policy but accompanied by stagflation in Western economies. This combination produced a period of increasing doubts about the relevancy and validity of Keynesian policy prescriptions, which, in turn, proved to be a fertile ground for the emergence and acceptance of the resurgent neoclassical theories. An early element in this resurgence was in the revision of the Phillips curve to the expectations augmented Phillips curve, often associated with Milton Friedman. The latter argued that there was a short-run tradeoff only between the unemployment rate and the deviation of the inflation rate from its expected level. But there was no long-run tradeoff between unemployment and inflation. Hence, monetary policy had a very limited ability to change the unemployment rate.

The 1970s also saw the introduction of the hypothesis of rational expectations. While Muth had proposed the basics of the rational expectations hypothesis in the 1960s, the work of Lucas, Barro, Sargent and Wallace, Kydland and Prescott and others in the 1970s and 1980s was to lay the foundations of the new version of the neoclassical theory – the modern classical school – with rational expectations and the neutrality of money as its core elements for policy analysis.[5]

Briefly, the traditional version of the neoclassical theory had implied that in equilibrium the labour market would clear and the deviation of the equilibrium level of employment from its full employment level would depend positively on the divergence of the expected price level from the actual price level. In the 1970s, Lucas, and Sargent and Wallace, among others, as discussed later in Chapters 15 and 16, modelled this divergence as an error in expectations arising from the failure of economic agents to distinguish correctly between the increase in relative prices and the increase in the general price level. The assumption of rational expectations implied that systematic errors would induce revision of the underlying model used by economic agents for forming their expectations and would lead to their elimination, so that eventually the remaining error would only be a random one. Focusing only on random errors – and without incorporating the time needed for any required revision of the underlying model, if such revision is required – employment would deviate from its full employment level due to random changes in demand, whether induced by money supply changes or other influences on aggregate demand. Systematic increases in money supply, under conditions of symmetric information between the monetary authority and the public, would be anticipated and would result in identical changes in both the expected price level and the actual one. Consequently, the monetary authority could not induce systematic errors in price expectations and could not bring about the deviation of employment from its equilibrium level.

In the 1980s, the impact of this theoretical revision in the scope of monetary policy was to persuade the central banks of the Western countries to abandon the multiplicity of goals in favour of a heavy and sometimes sole focus on controlling the rate of inflation. While the formal legislative revision of the traditional mandates of the central banks was rare, in practice there was a considerable reduction in the attempts to change the economy's unemployment rates and output through monetary policies. In some countries, the central bank totally abandoned these goals. The current practices of the central banks in the USA, Canada and New Zealand, and the monetary authorities in the United Kingdom, among others, provide examples of this evolution in the beliefs and practices on monetary policy.

11.2.3 The evolution of the goals of the monetary authorities in Britain

As discussed earlier, the British monetary authority from 1946 to the early 1980s possessed a multiplicity of goals. While the goal of price stability had been one of those goals and had received increasing emphasis by the end of the 1980s, the sole focus on it was made explicit in 1992 when the Chancellor of the Exchequer announced the adoption of explicit inflation targets (1% to 4%) aimed at achieving long-term price stability. This adoption of an explicit target for the inflation rate represented an explicit abandonment of other goals such as those on unemployment and output growth, exchange rate stability and business cycle stabilization.

The official inflation target was changed in 1995 by the Chancellor, with the agreement of the Bank of England, to a point target of 2.5%.

Hence, under the arrangements in force in 1999, the British government, through the Chancellor of the Exchequer, set the goals of the British monetary authority. Since the Chancellor is a cabinet minister, the inflation target can be changed by the government at any time and could, especially, change with a shift in the political party in power. Neither the Bank of England nor its Monetary Policy Committee has the independence to set the ultimate goal of monetary policy and its definition in terms of the target rate of inflation. This remains under the government's control, although the implementation of monetary policy, such as the setting of the bank rate, since 1997 has been left to the Bank and its Monetary Policy Committee.

11.2.4 The evolution of the goals of the Bank of Canada

In the late 1980s, in Canada, the Governor of the Bank of Canada publicly argued that the mandate of the Bank should be changed to focus only on price stability as its mandated goal. The proposal was considered in 1992 by a parliamentary committee which decided to leave the Bank's mandate as had been specified in the Bank of Canada Act of 1934, i.e., with a multiplicity of goals. However, several successive Governors of the Bank in the late 1980s and 1990s have advocated and in practice consistently focused solely or mainly on the goal of price stability. Since 1991, the Bank has announced explicit targets, in the range 1%–3%, for the rate of inflation consistent with price stability. These targets have been set jointly with the government of Canada. The Bank uses a monetary conditions index – a weighted sum of the interest rates and the exchange rate, explained later in this chapter – as an operational guide. It uses the overnight financing rate as its operational target, with a range of 50 basis points, and the bank rate – on loans to financial institutions – is now set at the upper limit of the target range.

11.2.5 The New Zealand experiment on the goal of price stability

After an extended period of double-digit inflation for much of the late 1970s and 1980s, as well as unsatisfactory growth, major legislative changes were made to the country's monetary arrangements in the mid-1980s and in 1990. Among these was the grant of a limited degree of independence to the central bank, the Reserve Bank of New Zealand, by the Reserve Bank of New Zealand Act of 1989: it assigned to the Bank the statutory obligation to formulate and implement monetary policy to maintain price stability. However, on the formulation of the goals of monetary policy, it required the Minister of Finance and the Governor to jointly establish the specific inflation target and the date by which it is to be achieved. This is set out in a Policy Targets Agreement (PTA), which is made public. The PTA also defines the range and the inflation index to be used for the target. These agreements are renegotiated at certain intervals, leaving, therefore, a measure of flexibility in meeting changing economic conditions. An illustration of this accommodation was the changes in the target range for inflation, 3%–5% from 1990–92, 0%–2% from 1992–96 and 0%–3% in 1996. The agreements specify permissible breaches of the established target in special circumstances, such as natural disasters, changes in indirect taxes and significant relative price shocks.

The Bank currently uses the *monetary conditions index*, a concept pioneered by the Bank of Canada. It is a weighted sum of an interest rate measure and the exchange rate, as a guide to its policies. It uses the interest rates and the banks' settlement balances with it as the operating targets.

In many ways, the New Zealand pattern is similar to that in Britain. Its central bank has operational independence but not total independence over the ultimate goals of monetary policy. The goal is limited to that of price stability by legislation and the legislation requires that the target range is set jointly with the government.[6]

11.2.6 The recent pattern of the goals of monetary policy in the United States

The pursuit of goals by the Federal Reserve System has changed in the 1980s and 1990s in a manner similar to that in the other countries discussed above from the pursuit of multiple goals during the pre-1980 period to that of price stability. One difference between the Fed and the British and Canadian monetary authorities is that the Fed does not set explicit targets for the rate of inflation, though its pursuit of a low rate of inflation consistent with price stability is not in doubt and is often asserted by the chairman of the Board of Governors of the Fed. There is also a similar abandonment or lack of emphasis on the Fed's other earlier goals related to unemployment and output.

The Fed is more genuinely independent of the United States' President and government than are the Bank of England or the Bank of New Zealand of their governments, both in terms of the formulation of its goals and their pursuit through its monetary policies. There is no question of the government issuing formal instructions to the Fed on the further pursuit of monetary goals or instruments, of requiring it to write open letters to the government explaining its actions or of penalties being imposed for a failure to achieve price stability.

11.2.7 Why the singular emphasis on price stability as the goal of monetary policy?

We have already discussed the evolution of economic theory from a Keynesian to a modern classical formulation that underlies the switch from multiple goals to the single one of price stability. This was supplemented by the experience of the central banks themselves during the 1970s and early 1980s when the pursuit of expansionary monetary policies produced higher rates of inflation without higher growth over a long or intermediate period.

It is worth noting that the goal of price stability is not meant to be an end in itself. It is followed in the belief that price stability fosters growth, so that a low target rate for inflation is meant to provide the monetary conditions that will produce the highest long-run growth of output and the lowest long-run unemployment for the economy. The target of price stability is also meant to remove or minimize the potential of monetary policy to destabilize the economy. It will clearly not remove all fluctuations from the economy, since fluctuations could still arise from supply shocks. But it is believed that a stable price and financial environment is still the best format for the economy to respond to such shocks.

In each of the above four countries, the targets or intentions on monetary policy for the period ahead are periodically communicated to the public and continuing efforts are made by each central bank to convey its assessment of economic conditions, the inflation outlook and expected outcomes. This openness and transparency of the central bank's thinking and decisions has substantially increased both the accountability of each of the central banks to the public and the credibility of its announced policies in the financial markets.[7]

11.3 LEVELS OF OBJECTIVES

The objectives of monetary policy may be divided into several levels or groups. These can be specified as:

- ultimate (or primary) objectives; these are the goals of monetary policy;
- intermediate objectives; and
- immediate objectives.

These three levels of objectives are clearly related, with the intermediate and immediate objectives as being a step in attaining the ultimate ones, which are usually taken to be the final goals of the central bank for the economy. The intermediate objectives are separated from the immediate objectives by taking the former as final objectives within the financial system, with the immediate ones being a step towards attaining these intermediate objectives.

The intermediate objectives of a central bank relate to the desirable levels and changes in the major monetary variables in order to achieve the desirable levels of the primary objectives. For example, the intermediate objectives of the central bank include achieving the desired levels of the money supply and overall credit and a certain structure of the interest rates in the economy.

The immediate objectives of a central bank are the operational targets it seeks to achieve directly through the policy tools at its disposal. They include the monetary base, the reserves held by the commercial banks, the discount rate or the bank rate charged on loans to the commercial banks, the Treasury bill rate and other selected market rates of interest, such as the Federal funds rate in the USA and the overnight loan rate in Canada.[8] Objectives tend to vary with circumstances, at this level no less than at other levels. For instance, at the intermediate level, the central bank may be concerned not with the monetary base as a whole, but with the overall amount of free reserves in the economy. Similarly, it may be concerned with the differential between the discount rate and the Treasury bill rate, rather than with their levels.

The appropriateness of the immediate and the intermediate objectives has to be examined in terms of their relationship to the ultimate objectives, which are usually those of full employment and a 'high' growth rate, in any given structure of the economy. Often, no one immediate or intermediate objective is equally satisfactory as an index to each of the primary objectives, or even an equally satisfactory index to any one objective under all phases of the business cycle. Further, imperfect information on the actual state of the economy and on the extent and timing of the impact of policies cautions against sole reliance on a single immediate goal. Therefore, reliance on a broad range of objectives at each of the two lower levels is often necessary. A simple formal analysis of these points is presented below in the section on the guides to monetary policy.

Further, an important policy question that has been the subject of considerable debate is the exact relevance of any one of the lower-level objectives to a given upper-level objective. Is the change in the money supply a good guide to changes in the price level? And if it is a good guide during inflationary periods, is it equally good during deflationary periods? Is it a better guide than the amount of credit outstanding in the economy? These questions – and others like them – are extremely important for achieving the primary objectives and the formulation of policy. Such a question cannot be answered without a theoretical frame of reference on the macroeconomic nature of the economy. The more theoretical aspects of these questions are, therefore, postponed to Chapters 15 and 16, which deal with monetary policy in the macroeconomy.

11.4 THE TOOLS OR INSTRUMENTS OF MONETARY POLICY

The central bank pursues its monetary policy through the use of one or more of the instruments at its disposal. The mix of the instruments used depends upon the structure of the economy, especially the financial system, and tends to depend on the stage of development of the bond and stock markets. The most common instrument among countries seems to be the change in interest rates, often supported by open market operations.

11.4.1 Open market operations

Open market operations are the purchase (or sale) by the central bank of securities in financial markets, and results in corresponding increases (decreases) in the monetary base. Countries with well-developed financial markets and extensive amounts of public debt traded in the financial markets usually rely on such operations to change the money supply as their main tool of monetary policy. They – along with the shifting of government deposits between the central bank and the commercial banks – are the most important tool of monetary policy in the USA, Canada and the UK. However, it does not hold a corresponding position among the countries around the world since its prominent position requires certain preconditions to be met. The most important of these are:

(i)   The financial structure of the economy should be well developed, with most of the borrowing and lending being done in the organized financial markets of the country itself.

(ii) There should be a relatively large amount of the securities of the kind that the monetary authorities are willing to purchase. These are often, though not always, government securities. A large public debt is thus generally essential.

(iii) The market-established priorities must broadly coincide with the politically acceptable priorities. This condition is not always met, as, for example, in a socialist country.

(iv) The financial system and markets of the country should be broadly independent of those of other countries. Very open economies with perfect capital flows and fixed exchange rates do not possess such independence. To take an extreme example, different states or regions within a country do not possess an independent financial system and cannot pursue a monetary policy independent of the country. Similarly, members of a currency or monetary bloc with fixed exchange rates among the member countries cannot pursue monetary policies independently of that of the bloc. An example of such a bloc is the implementation of the European Monetary Union with fixed exchange rates among the national currencies of the member countries. A less extreme case arises in the case of countries whose financial markets are closely tied to major financial centres outside the country.[9]

Financially underdeveloped economies generally fail to satisfy the first condition. Countries without a strong commitment to free enterprise and capitalism fail to satisfy the third condition. Countries in an economic and/or political union, such as the European Union, may not fully meet the fourth condition. In the past, this was also often true of the colonies of imperial countries. Many countries of the world fall into one or more of these categories. Even in the United States, they were rarely used prior to the Second World War. Most countries pursue other tools of monetary policy, to supplement – or as an alternative – to open market operations.

   While the central banks in the financially developed economies can, in general, directly rely on open market operations to alter the monetary base, this is more often the practice in the United States than in the United Kingdom and many other countries. In the latter, the operational instrument is more often an interest rate – the overnight market rate or discount or bank rate – set by the central bank, with the financial sector obtaining from it, through loans or sales of bonds, the monetary base that it needs at that rate.

Shifting government deposits between the central and the commercial banks

As we have seen above, the central bank almost always acts as the government's bank, keeping and managing the government's deposits. Increases in these deposits with the central bank through payments by the public to the government out of their deposits in their commercial banks, reduce the monetary base while decreases in such deposits because of increased payments by the government to the public increase the monetary base. One way of avoiding changes in the monetary base because of payments to the government or receipts from it, is for the government to hold accounts with the commercial banks and use them for its transactions with the public. The resulting increases and decreases in the government deposits with the commercial banks do not change the monetary base, while transfers of these deposits to the central bank reduce this base.

In Canada, the Bank of Canada manages the distribution of the government deposits between itself and the chartered banks in Canada as a way of manipulating the monetary base and therefore as a tool of monetary policy akin to open market operations. In current practice, such shifting of balances is more convenient and has become more important than open market operations for changing the monetary base over short periods.

11.4.2 Reserve requirements

The imposition of reserve requirements[10] has historically been a common tool of controlling monetary aggregates for a given monetary base. In cases where the markets are too thin for viable open market operations, or the monetary base cannot be controlled for some reason, the monetary authorities often attempt to limit the creation of reserves by the banking system through the imposition of, or changes in, reserve ratios against demand deposits and sometimes also against other types of deposits. These ratios can range from 0% to 100%, though they are often in the range of 0% to 20%, with changes in the required ratio being often of the order of 0.25% or 0.5%.

Until 1980, the USA had a complex system of reserve requirements for its banks, with different requirements for banks which were members of the Federal Reserve System and those which were not, between banks in large cities and others, etc. In 1980, the US Congress imposed much greater uniformity on the depository institutions, including banks, thrift institutions and credit unions. The Fed was given the power to set the reserve requirement between 8% and 14% on transactions deposits and raise it to 18% in special cases. The reserve requirements on personal time and savings deposits were eliminated. In 1998, the reserve requirement was 10% on checkable deposits if the bank had checkable deposits above a certain amount and 3% if these deposits were below this limit. There was no positive reserve requirement on non-checkable time deposits.

Canada had reserve requirements of 5% against demand deposits in chartered banks from 1935 to 1954, though the banks often kept much higher reserves (sometimes over 10%). From 1954 to 1967, the reserve requirement was 8%, with the Bank of Canada having the power to raise it to 12%, though this power was never used. By the Bank Act of 1967, the required ratio was raised to 12% against demand deposits, with 4% on notice deposits in Canadian dollars, but the power of the Bank to vary them was eliminated.[11] In 1980, the required reserve ratio against demand deposits was fixed at 10%, with lower ratios against other types of deposits. In early 1992, Canada, in an environment of a highly stable and well-developed financial system, abolished reserve requirements on its banks, leaving them to determine whatever amounts of reserves they want to hold. However, they have to maintain non-negative settlement balances with the Bank on a daily basis, with any negative balances being offset by overdrafts from the Bank at the bank rate. The average reserves held by the Canadian commercial banks are now usually less than 1% of demand deposits and sometimes fall as low as 0.1% or even lower.

In Britain, after 1945, the London clearing banks, which are the main clearing banks in Britain, adopted the practice of keeping a minimum reserve ratio of 8% of their deposits. Changes in it were never required as an instrument of monetary policy. After 1971, the banks agreed to keep an average of 1.5% of their eligible liabilities (mainly their sterling deposits) in non-interest-bearing deposits with the Bank of England. Even this requirement was eliminated in 1981, so that the reserve requirement in Britain became 0%. In 1999, the average ratio of the banks' non-interest-bearing deposits with the Bank of England to the sterling deposits placed with them was about 0.15%.

The difference between the reserve requirements in Britain and Canada versus those in the USA is illustrative. Part of the reason is historical patterns. But part is also due to the nature of the British and Canadian banks, which tend to be large and country-wide, with few failures in the past. Both countries display sufficient confidence in the solvency of their banks to eliminate positive reserve requirements. Although some of the US banks are among the largest in the world, many, if not most, of the USA banks are relatively small, confined to a state or a region, with a pattern of bank failures among such banks. Higher reserve requirements contribute to their solvency and the public's confidence in them.

Table 11.1 shows the reserve requirements in 1998 in the G7 countries, along with the length of the averaging period. As Table 11.1 shows, there are considerable variations in the reserve requirements among this group of countries. However, the countries with large oligopolistic banking systems tend to have very low, almost zero, reserve requirements. All countries allow some averaging period for meeting the reserve requirements, though it is only one day in the British case. Without averaging, or with averaging over only one day, the daily shocks to the banks' deposits and consequently their demand for liquidity result in sharp movements in the overnight interest rates, unless the central bank can manage to monitor these daily and to effectively offset the results of such shocks. Since it is not possible to do so on a daily basis in many countries, averaging over several weeks is the general pattern.

In the Western economies, changes in the required reserve ratios are now either no longer available as an instrument of monetary policy or not used in practice for this purpose.

11.4.3 The discount/bank rate[12]

In most countries, the monetary authority – normally the central bank – has the power to determine – directly or indirectly – the market interest rates in the economy.[13,14] Critical interest rates can be set directly, determined through instructions issued to the commercial banks, or influenced indirectly by the central bank varying the rate at which it lends to the commercial banks. In the more usual case in market-oriented economies, the market rates are influenced through the *discount rate* at which the central bank lends to the banks and other

Table 11.1 Reserve requirements, 1998

	UK	USA	Germany	France	Italy	Japan	Canada
Required ratio	zero	3–10%	1.5–2%	0.5–1%	15%	0.05–1.3%	zero
Length of averaging period	1 day	2 weeks	1 month	1 month	1 month	1 month	4–5 weeks

designated financial intermediaries. Canada, the UK and the USA have traditionally followed this method.

The use of interest rates as the major operating instrument of monetary policy occurs because interest rates play a pivotal intermediate role by which investment and therefore aggregate demand in the economy can be influenced. Further, it is argued by some economists that the economy has numerous substitutes for M1 and M2,[15] so that controlling these aggregates through open market operations or the reserve requirements of commercial banks only leads to substitution away from them, without a necessarily significant impact on investment and aggregate demand.[16] Further, in recent years, because of numerous financial innovations, the demand functions for money have proved to be unstable, so that many central banks prefer to target interest rates, and influence them through their discount rate, rather than to target monetary aggregates as the main operational tool of monetary policy.

The central bank, in setting or changing its discount rate, indicates its willingness to let the commercial banks determine the extent of the borrowing from it and thereby change the monetary base in the economy. Any announced change in this rate acts as an indicator of the Bank's future intentions about the interest rates that it will support through its open market operations and therefore serves as an indicator of the future stance of monetary policy. The commercial banks and other financial intermediaries usually, though not always, follow the lead given by the discount rate changes to alter their own interest rates – such as the prime rate, the personal loan rates and the mortgage rates – as well as in their purchases and sales of market instruments. This behavioural pattern results in a shift of the interest rates throughout the economy, while leaving the spread between any pair of rates to market forces. Conversely, the central bank's refusal to change this rate in the face of rising market rates serves to dampen the latter.

This discount rate is called the bank rate in Canada and the UK. In the UK, as explained earlier in this chapter, since 1997, the Bank of England, through the Monetary Policy Committee, has had the operational independence to set this rate. Until 1971, a sort of cartel arrangement among the British commercial banks linked the market interest rates on various types of bank deposits to the bank rate. The abolition of this cartel in 1971 made the market rates more responsive to market forces, though the bank rate set by the Bank of England continues to be the core rate for the financial markets and changes in it are the major operational instrument of monetary policy. Since the British banks as a whole need to achieve balance at the end of each day, the Bank of England can choose on a daily basis the interest rate at which it will provide additional funds to the banking system. Changes in this rate prompt the banks to change the base rates at which they lend to their customers, so that the changes in the Bank's own lending rate cascade through the various interest rates in Britain.

In Canada, the bank rate was set by the Bank of Canada until 1980. In the 1980s and the early 1990s, it was fixed at 0.25% above the ninety-one-day Treasury bill rate at its weekly auction of government bonds. Since it was above the Treasury Bill rate, it was considered to be a 'penalty' rate in the sense that it imposed a net loss on the borrowing bank, which had the option of obtaining the needed funds more cheaply by selling from its holdings of Treasury bills. The Bank influenced the Treasury bill rate through its own bids for Treasury bills. Since 1994, the Bank has been setting the overnight loan rate – that is, the rate on trades in reserves – with a band of 50 basis points, as an operational target. Since 1996, the bank rate has been set at the upper limit of the operating band specified for the overnight loan rate. Setting the bank rate at this upper limit makes borrowing from the Bank more expensive than in the commercial market for reserves and is meant to persuade commercial banks to meet their reserve needs through their borrowing of reserves in the private markets. However, borrowing from the Bank is treated as a right of the banks rather than a privilege. In any case, the Canadian banks consider borrowing from the Bank of Canada as sending out a signal that they have liquidity problems and have rarely resorted to such borrowing. Any advances are normally for only a few days and often overnight.

In the United States, the discount rate is frequently below the market short interest rates. Since banks can make a profit from borrowing from the Fed and then buying market instruments, keeping the discount rate below the market rates becomes an incentive for commercial banks to borrow from the Fed. However, the Fed treats borrowing from it as a privilege rather than a right. Frequent borrowing from the Fed can lead to its refusal to lend again and would invite closer scrutiny of the borrowing banks' accounts and policies.

Changes in the discount rate can serve an instrument of monetary policy in three respects:

(i)   It affects the amount of borrowing – which changes the monetary base and the money supply – from the central bank.

(ii) Changes in it – or lack of a change when one was expected – act as a signal to the private sector of the central bank's intentions about monetary policy.

(iii) The central bank's control over its discount rate provides it considerable control over the interest rates in the economy.

The latter two are now the relatively more important reasons for the use of the discount rate as an instrument of monetary policy.

The central bank as the lender of last resort

Borrowing from the central bank at the discount rate is associated with the notion of the central bank acting as the *lender of last resort* in the economy. While commercial banks with inadequate reserves can borrow from those with surpluses, a reserve shortage in the financial system as a whole cannot be met in this manner and could force the economy into a liquidity and credit crunch. The *discount window* – i.e., the ability to borrow from the central bank – is, therefore, a 'safety' valve for the economy.

The discount window also acts as a safety valve for an individual bank that needs reserves but is unable or unwilling to borrow from private financial institutions. However, in the United States, borrowing from the central bank invites the scrutiny of the central bank into the borrowing bank's management of its affairs and acts as a disincentive to frequent borrowing from the central bank as against borrowing in the market. Further, banks are not permitted to make chronic use of the discount window for meeting liquidity needs.[17]

The discount rate and interest rate differentials in the economy

The central bank's power to set its discount or Bank rate does not extend over the differentials or spreads among the various interest rates in the economy. In particular, the spreads between the commercial banks' deposit rates and the short-term market rates, such as on Treasury bills and money market mutual funds, are still outside the direct influence of the central bank and depend upon market forces.

From the perspective of monetary theory, the determinants of the demand for M1 and other monetary aggregates are critical for the impact of monetary policy. These demands would depend on both the levels and the differentials among interest rates. Since the latter are mainly outside the influence of the central bank, the impact of the changes in the discount rate on the demand for the monetary aggregates is correspondingly reduced.

11.4.4 Moral suasion

Moral 'suasion' – a rather out-of-date term for 'persuasion' – refers to the use of the influence of the central bank upon commercial banks to follow its suggestions, such as in exercising credit restraint or diverting loans to specified sectors of the economy. Such suggestions do not possess the force of law, although the threat of converting suggestions into legal orders, if necessary, often backs such suggestions. Moral suasion generally works well in countries with a very small number of large banks and with a long tradition of respect for the judgement and extra-legal authority of the central bank. Although both the UK and Canada are good examples of this, the Bank of England is especially known for its extensive use of moral suasion.

However, moral suasion is not generally appropriate for the large and diverse banking system of the United States, though it has been tried sometimes. An example of the latter occurred in 1965 when the President and the Federal Reserve laid down guidelines to limit foreign borrowing. This was fairly well adhered to by the member banks, but represented a rare usage of this tool in the USA. This term is also sometimes associated with the rules imposed by the Fed on banks that attempt to borrow too frequently from it and is, therefore, associated in the US with the use of the discount window.

11.4.5 Selective controls

Selective controls are those with impact on certain sectors rather than upon the overall economy. A common example of these is credit controls. The common reason for such controls is that social priorities may differ from private priorities. Thus, the government may wish to divert funds to exports, housing, agriculture, state and local governments, and to industries believed to be essential to national development. This can include giving special rediscounting privileges to private commercial export bills. Some central banks also favour housing and agriculture through favourable discount provision and direct credit controls, with such support given under the regulations and guidelines given by the central bank to the commercial banks. However, such support in the United States, Canada and the UK is generally fiscal, in the form of tax exemptions, subsidized loans from the government etc., rather than being an aspect of monetary policy.

Another reason for selective controls is to curb the destabilizing nature of certain sectors or to use the critical position of certain sectors for stabilization purposes. For example, on the former, the Federal Reserve limits the stock market credit extended by banks and brokers on the purchase of securities by setting minimum-margin requirements. These specify the minimum down payment at the time of purchase. This requirement was, for example, 70% in 1968 for stocks registered on national security exchanges, so that purchasers of such stocks could only borrow up to 30% of the purchase price from banks or brokers. The Federal Reserve can raise these requirements up to 100%.

Another example of such controls is those on consumer credit. These often specify, for designated durable consumer goods, the minimum down payment at the time of purchase and the length of time over which the balance has to be paid. Such controls are exercised in some countries and often go under the name of instalment-credit or hire-purchase controls. In the USA, the Fed was given the power to impose such controls in the Second World War, in the Korean War and briefly in 1948–49, but does not now possess such a power.

11.5 THE COMPETITIVE SUPPLY OF MONEY AND EFFICIENCY AND COMPETITION IN THE FINANCIAL SECTOR

11.5.1 The argument for the competitive supplies of private monies

It is a major contention of economic theory that production and exchange are at their most efficient in perfectly competitive markets. Hence, social welfare is maximized by having perfect competition in all sectors, including the financial one. Even if the actual markets cannot be made fully competitive, restrictions on competition are damaging to efficiency. These tenets are applicable not only to the markets for consumer and investment foods, but also to the financial markets. As a corollary, some economists have argued that the financial markets would be most conducive to maximizing the economy's output if they were free from administrative regulations on the products that financial institutions can supply and the prices they charge for these. The products supplied by the financial sector are essentially types of financial intermediation, and involve the holdings of assets and the issue of the liabilities by the financial intermediaries. The prices involved are interest rates in the financial markets and service charges etc. imposed by financial intermediaries. Hence, microeconomic theory implies that the various types of financial institutions should be allowed to compete with each other in the various financial markets, such as for demand deposits, savings and time deposits, mortgages, the purchase and sale of shares, mutual funds, trusts management, pension funds, insurance, etc.

Some economists extend this argument to the proposal that the issue of money should also be left unregulated and that there is no need for a central bank.[18] In fact, since the existence of such a bank with its issue of fiat money represents monopoly power over one aspect of money, its existence and supply of fiat money reduce social welfare. In line with this argument, it is proposed that private, competitive firms should be allowed to issue coins and notes. It is further argued that the power of commercial banks to create inside money in the form of demand deposits and other types of near-monies should not be limited by any imposition of reserve requirements. Nor should there be regulations on the interest rates charged, on ownership, limitations on the encroachment of banks on trust companies, insurance companies, etc., by limiting the products they can supply. As we have mentioned above, the basis for such proposals is application of principle of the Pareto optimality of perfect competition to the provision of monies and other financial products.

11.5.2 The arguments for the regulation of the money supply

While economists generally accept the propositions on the promotion of competition among the firms in the financial sector, few economists accept the proposals on the abolition of the central bank, on the elimination of its power to issue fiat money or on the elimination of its power to monitor and regulate the financial system to ensure its continued health etc. The basic reason for this stand is that the health and stability of the monetary sector is considered to be vital to the prosperity and functioning of the macroeconomy. Further, variations in the supply of money are taken to have a strong impact on the real sectors of the economy. While the analysis of this point is left to the macroeconomic chapters 13 to 16, we comment on some aspects of this debate in the following.

The commercial banking system is inherently fragile and based on trust by the depositors in the viability of the institutions in which they hold their deposits. A purely competitive and unregulated system is prone to fluctuations in the degree of this trust and, therefore, susceptible to runs by depositors concerned about the security of their deposits. Two basic reasons for this are the fractional reserve practices of banks and their policy of borrowing short and lending long. We have already used the former concept in the preceding chapter on the money supply process. Since banks keep reserves, in cash or in deposits with the central bank, equal to only a small fraction of their deposits, they cannot at short notice meet a sudden attempt by depositors to withdraw their deposits in cash. This is further exacerbated by the portfolio policies of banks under which large proportions of their assets are in bonds, mortgages, loans, etc., which are difficult to convert into cash at short notice or can only be cashed with significant losses. Individual banks may also be tempted to engage in high-risk investments, with a consequent possibility of losses which create a loss of confidence in the bank accompanied by a run to withdraw deposits from it.

Given this inherent fragility of a purely private competitive banking system, several measures are taken to ensure the continuation of a high level of confidence in the banking system. One of these is the insurance of individual deposits, usually to a pre-set limit, by a central deposit insurance agency. Another is having a central bank that attempts to anchor the supply of privately created inside money in the economy through its own issue of fiat money and attempts to control variations in the aggregate money supply in the national interest. In addition, the central bank tries to ensure confidence in the financial sector through its regulation and monitoring of financial intermediaries, especially commercial banks since they supply the most liquid financial assets in the economy and are the creators of inside money.

Focusing first on the supply of fiat money by the central bank, one reason for its issue by the central bank is to anchor the privately supplied demand and other types of deposits and therefore the money supply aggregates in the economy. Another concerns the seigniorage – that is, the revenue – emanating from the issue of money. The central bank is a national institution and its profits are added to the fiscal revenues, so that it seems to be the obvious recipient of such seigniorage. Further, in many low-income economies, seigniorage can be a significant proportion of national revenues and needed for financing government expenditures.

11.5.3 The regulation of banks in the interests of monetary policy

From the perspective of the central bank, an important aspect of its activities is its regulation of the financial institutions in the economy. Part of this regulation is aimed at the control of the money supply in the national macroeconomic interest. Another part is aimed at maintaining a sound financial system and encouraging, if necessary, its growth to fit the financial needs of the economy. This supervision often takes the form of regulations on the ownership of such institutions, forms of liabilities issued, the kind of assets held and the auditing of their accounts etc. Such supervision is only of minor interest from the standpoint of macroeconomics provided it is successful in maintaining a stable and adequate financial system. But it is often a substantial part of the activities of the central bank and its related agencies, and can be critical for the solvency and efficiency of the financial system of the country.

Monetary economics is closely concerned with those regulations of the monetary authorities that affect the liquidity of the economy, especially as reflected in the monetary aggregates. As discussed earlier, among these regulations, the central bank often specifies the minimum reserves that commercial banks must maintain against demand deposits. The interest rate at which commercial banks can borrow from the central bank is also set by the central bank rather than based purely on a market mechanism. There may also be other conditions imposed on such borrowing. The maximum interest rates that commercial banks may themselves pay on various kinds of deposits are also in some countries set by the central bank. There may be, and often are, other areas of regulation of commercial banks' behaviour.

The basic reason for the close regulation of commercial banks lies in the fact that they issue demand deposits that are a major part of the money supply, no matter how it is defined. Most of the regulations governing commercial banks are, in fact, aimed at regulating their creation of demand deposits, with the aim of bringing the total amount of demand deposits and hence the total money supply within the control of the central bank.

Historically, banking in the British tradition arose under a set of customary practices and imposed rules which restricted commercial banks to the issue of demand and saving deposit liabilities and the holding of short-term government bonds as assets. Banks were thereby confined to the highly liquid end of the spectrum of financial assets, leaving other specialized financial institutions to the markets for mortgages, insurance, trusts, pension funds, etc. In addition, there were also restrictions on bank ownership by non-bank corporations, as well as on the ownership of the latter by the banks.

This pattern began to change in the second half of the twentieth century both in the issue of bank liabilities and their portfolio of assets.[19] The changes became more pronounced during the 1980s and 1990s with the financial institutions increasingly being permitted to expand into other than their traditional financial markets, as well as their own or being closely associated with financial institutions in other markets. Among these changes were to allow commercial banks to issue mutual funds, act as investment brokers for the buying and selling of shares, sell insurance and manage pension funds – and conversely to allow firms formerly engaged in these markets to offer banking services. The result by the end of the twentieth century was a breakdown of the barriers in the USA, Canada and Britain between types of financial institutions, mergers and eventually larger sizes of the financial firms, as well as much more aggressive competition in the financial markets.

An aspect of the limitations on banks had been the regulation of the interest rates that banks could pay on the demand and savings deposits placed with them. Often this was an attempt to prevent too aggressive a competition for deposits and to ensure the solvency of banks. As example of this was Regulation Q in the USA during the 1950s and 1960s, under which ceilings were imposed by the Federal Reserve on the interest rates paid by its members on deposits, while many other financial institutions were not subject to such limits. In the interests of promoting competition and removing discriminatory restrictions on banks, such ceilings were first gradually raised and then eliminated in the 1970s and 1980s. The imposition of ceilings on interest rates paid by banks is now rare in financially developed economies, and such ceilings do not exist in Canada, the UK and USA. But they do exist in many countries, especially among the LDCs.

11.6 ADMINISTERED INTEREST RATES AND ECONOMIC PERFORMANCE

Manipulating interest rates as guides to monetary policy or as an aspect of short-term stabilization policies is quite different from setting them over long periods in order to achieve some long-run objectives. Among such objectives is that of attempting to increase the long-run growth rate of the economy.

Interest rates represent the cost of investment, which is the increase in the capital stock of the economy and an essential requirement for the growth of the economy's output capacity. Hence, it can be argued that low rates of interest imply higher investment and therefore higher growth rates for the economy. Many countries, especially LDCs, in the second half of the twentieth century, followed this reasoning to set interest rates in the organized markets of their economies below what would have been determined in unregulated markets. These rates were usually not adjusted to the rate of inflation, so that the interest rates that could be charged often fell below the rate of inflation, thereby implying a negative real rate of return on loans.

Interest rates are not only the cost of funds borrowed for investment, they also are the return on savings lent through the financial markets. Neoclassical theory posits a positive relationship between them, so that lower rates of interest imply lower saving. However, the empirical significance of this dependence of saving on interest rates is in considerable doubt. If saving in practice does not depend on interest rates, while investment does so, it could be argued that keeping the rates of interest low would promote growth of the economy on a net basis.

Interest rates, however, also play the role of allocating funds between the various projects and sectors of the economy. With interest rates below their levels for clearing the markets for loans, administrative mechanisms come into play to allocate the limited funds to the greater demand for them. Among these mechanisms are governmental or central bank regulations on the sectors, projects or firms which are to be given credit, rules of the banks themselves, or favouritism of bank managers etc. Corruption often becomes rife in such a context and becomes a basis for the granting of loans. The end result is the misallocation of funds to projects and firms, in which the most productive uses do not always or adequately get the funds. Such misallocation is detrimental to the growth of the economy. Conversely, leaving the interest rates to be determined in the open and competitive markets for loans promotes the efficient allocation of savings to the variety of investments and thereby increases the growth of the economy. This realization by many LDCs in the 1980s and 1990s led to the 'liberalization' of interest rates – a term for lifting ceilings or setting them free to be determined by market forces – in many of them. Such freeing of the interest rates from administrative control is very often part of the broader 'liberalization' of the economy, though deregulation and decontrol of exchange rates, imports and exports, production and investment, etc., and has resulted in many cases in increasing the growth rates of those economies.

While all economies have an informal financial sector in which borrowing and lending takes place other than through the established and regulated financial intermediaries, such a sector in the LDCs is larger and more significant relative to their formal financial sector. This sector is not only outside the purview of central bank control and policies, its spread between the deposit rates and the loan rates is usually much larger than in the formal sector. The low deposit rates discourage saving while the high loan rates discourage borrowing for productive investments. Therefore, while the informal sector is vital to the economies of the LDCs, policies which force savers and borrowers to the informal sector through restraints on the formal sector tend to reduce saving and investment in these economies. This implies a recommendation for the competitive and efficient expansion of the formal sector relative to the informal one, though not necessarily through statutory restrictions on the latter.

11.7 THE REGULATION OF BANKS RELATIVE TO OTHER FINANCIAL INTERMEDIARIES

Banks are financial intermediaries. Regulations placed on commercial banks when other intermediaries are exempt from them are discriminatory and unfair as between institutions. Economists are divided on the question of whether the special role of demand and time deposits as the most liquid of assets, along with currency, justifies such discriminatory regulation. The problem here is more one of equity among institutions rather than of monetary policy for macroeconomic purposes and we choose to ignore it henceforth.

The same issue can also be approached from an analytical point of view. M1 has several close substitutes among the liabilities of financial intermediaries. A decrease in the money supply could be compensated by an increase in these substitutes sufficient to negate the effect of the decreased supply of M1 on national income, prices and interest rates. Monetary policy by the central bank has been traditionally exercised through changes in the monetary base and M1. This policy would be rendered useless if such changes could be offset by appropriate counter-changes in the supply of monetary substitutes. Therefore, the extent of changes in the monetary substitutes brought about by the tightness or ease of monetary policy is a very important question and has elicited much discussion in recent decades.

To illustrate the arguments involved here, assume that the central bank has increased the reserve requirements against demand deposits. This decreases the supply of M1, raising interest rates in the economy and reducing the flow of bank credit to the securities and loan markets. Nonbank financial intermediaries, if not fully loaned up, can offset this effect by increasing their purchases of securities and loans to the public. Even if they are fully loaned up, the rise in interest rates is kept down by the existence of non-bank financial intermediaries for three reasons:

(i)   A given decrease in the demand for securities and loans by the banks has a larger influence on the interest rate if they are the only sources of funds than if they are one among many. This is partly a question of the amount of change *vis-à-vis* the size of the existing supply of funds and partly a question of borrowers shopping around for funds as interest rates rise.

(ii)   A rise in the interest rates on non-monetary assets, as part of the general rise in interest rates, may cause the public to switch from currency and demand deposits, which do not pay interest or pay relatively low rates, to the liabilities of the non-bank intermediaries. The latter do not keep significant amounts of reserves and lend out the additional funds, which return to the monetary stream without significant depletion but in the process having created additional monetary substitutes and lending capacity in the economy. Such creation of new liabilities and new lending capacity offset to some extent the impact of restrictive monetary policy on the economy. This argument implies imposing a reserve requirement on non-bank intermediaries somewhat similar to that on banks, though different in the percentages required.

(iii) The switch from currency and demand deposits to the liabilities of non-bank monetary assets leads to a net increase in liquidity in the economy. This depends upon the cash reserve ratios maintained by the intermediaries against their liabilities and the public against its assets. Take, for instance, an extreme case where the public's demand for currency – and the proportion of currency held to near-money assets – is zero. Assume also that the non-bank financial intermediaries do not keep any reserves against their liabilities, being able to meet withdrawals by enforcing due notice of withdrawals and liquidation of their short-term financial assets. A switch from demand deposits to time deposits and other near-money assets would increase the amounts of these assets. However, the extra funds thus made available to non-bank financial intermediaries are loaned out by them and eventually return in their entirety to the banking system in the form of demand deposits.

In the above process, extra near-money assets were created in the re-routing of financial flows and there is a net increase in liquidity in the process. This increase may partly or wholly offset the initial decrease in liquidity due to the decrease in the monetary base by the authorities. Therefore, the net effect of the existence and growth of financial intermediaries seems to be a dilution of the impact of monetary policy upon liquidity in the economy and a dilution of the impact of monetary policy upon nominal national income.

However, such dilution of the impact of monetary policy on the economy by the presence of non-bank financial intermediaries is not necessarily an adequate argument for extending reserve requirements and other controls to these intermediaries.[20] The cost of such control must be measured against the alternative of increasing the intensity of changes in the money supply to achieve any given impact on interest rates and expenditures. Changes in the reserve requirements against demand deposits or in the monetary base are virtually costless, involving a cost in terms of paper, ink and printing, so that a more intensive policy is not significantly more costly than a diluted one. Therefore, the presence of non-bank intermediaries does not necessarily require control over them, but does need recognition of their existence and behaviour for the proper formulation of monetary policy and its effects.

Another item of discussion in the literature has been about the wisdom of imposing reserve ratios and ceilings on interest rates on the banks themselves. A major objection to a policy of changing the required reserve ratio is that it is at best an inflexible and discriminatory tool for changes in the money supply. It is really a poor substitute for open market operations whose magnitude can be varied continuously and which have a generalized impact on the economy. Therefore, the extension of reserve ratio requirements to other intermediaries is hardly desirable.

The differential treatment of financial intermediaries in practice
It has already been mentioned above that, in Canada, the commercial banks have been required since 1994 to only maintain positive balances at the end of each day in their accounts at the Bank of Canada. This regulation applies equally to the other financial intermediaries which are members of the Canadian Payments Association. There is, therefore, now both the virtual absence of reserve requirements and the uniform treatment of financial intermediaries in Canada.

As noted earlier, in the United States, historically, there were a variety of reserve requirements for different categories of commercial banks. Uniform reserve requirements were introduced in 1980 for all financial institutions holding transactions deposits and, therefore, covering commercial banks, thrift institutions, credit unions, etc. The Fed is empowered to set reserve requirements between 8% and 14%. The reserve requirement in 1998 was 10%. There are no positive reserve requirements against time deposits.

On the question of the regulatory ceilings on interest rates, while such ceilings were common in the USA in the 1950s, they began to be relaxed in the 1960s and were generally eliminated in the 1970s and 1980s. They are no longer imposed nor are they envisaged as a tool to be pursued in the future. In fact, they have fallen out of favour in most countries. In the Canadian context, the Bank of Canada did not set interest rates or impose ceilings on interest rates paid by banks on deposits, but its small number of very large banks followed a common custom of not paying interest on demand deposits and of paying a low rate of interest on savings deposits for many decades prior to the 1960s.

With the advent of fairly uniform treatment of banks and other financial intermediaries in terms of reserve requirements and the abolition of interest rate ceilings, the debate related to banks versus other intermediaries has shifted to the areas in which each is allowed to operate versus areas from which they are excluded. For instance, in Canada, the United Kingdom and the United States, commercial banks were historically not allowed to act as brokers in the purchase and sale of stocks and bonds or of insurance, nor were the brokers in these fields allowed to accept demand deposits. In general, the trend has been towards allowing each institution to compete with the others in the various financial markets, so that the segmentation within the financial sector has already been considerably reduced. This trend towards greater competition and less segmentation is likely to continue.

11.8 THE FEDERAL RESERVE SYSTEM: OBJECTIVES, INSTRUMENTS AND GUIDES TO MONETARY POLICY

Section 11.1 has already discussed the original mandate of the Federal Reserve System, and the other parts of this chapter have referred to various aspects of the pursuit of monetary policy in the United States. This section brings together many of these points and adds to them to present a succinct overview of monetary policy in the USA.

The Fed has not explicitly endorsed stable prices or a low inflation rate as its target, though its pronouncements usually indicate such an aim. It also has not explicitly designated a particular variable as a target, let alone specify a desired range for it. As a consequence, its aims and targets have to be identified from summaries of policy-making meetings and other statements coming from the Fed. In the 1970s and 1980s, the main target of the Fed's policies was M1. The breakdown of a stable relationship between M1 and nominal GDP in the 1980s led to a switch to M2 as the main target. However, the long-run stability of the M2 velocity, and therefore of the relationship between M2 and GDP, is in doubt and has proved to be illusive.

The Fed currently favours, as a guide to monetary policy, the Federal funds rate on overnight loans of bank reserves by commercial banks in the Federal funds market. This rate is determined by the demand and supply of bank reserves, which can be manipulated by the Fed through changes in reserve requirements, the discount rate and open market operations. The last one is the most important and most often used instrument to affect changes in the supply of bank reserves in the market. This instrument is operated by the Federal Open Market Committee (FOMC), an operational element of the Federal Reserve System, which decides on the extent and timing of the open market operations to be carried out.

While numerous econometric and other studies are continually prepared by the Fed's staff, the Fed recognizes that the impact of its operations on the Federal funds rate, other interest rates and the economy depends on a variety of factors. These include business confidence, fluctuations in velocity, factors external to the US economy, and lags at various stages, etc. Hence, it is recognized that the proper pursuit of open market operations is not a simple technical matter but an art involving forecasting, experience and the exercise of judgement.

In the past, the Fed has used various targets for formulating its policy. It targeted non-borrowed reserves during 1979–82, borrowed reserves during 1983–87, and the Federal funds rate since 1994, with the degree of reserve pressure also being used as an additional target since 1983. The Federal funds rate is now the main guide and objective for the day-to-day operations of the Fed.

11.9 THE OBJECTIVES, INSTRUMENTS AND GUIDES TO MONETARY POLICY OF THE BRITISH MONETARY AUTHORITIES

The Bank of England, set up as a private commercial bank in 1694 and remaining a private bank until 1946, acted from the very beginning as the banker for the British government[21] and soon developed a special relationship with the government. Legislation in 1844 gave it the monopoly of (future) note issue in the same year, when it also withdrew from commercial banking, thereby taking on two of the major attributes of a central bank. Its notes were made legal tender and convertible into gold at a fixed exchange rate.[22] It also started the practice of fixing its discount rate – which soon came to be called the bank rate – for private bills of exchange on a weekly basis.[23] As the most secure and largest of the private banks, it gradually became the depository for the reserves of other commercial banks and then as a clearing-house for transactions among the latter and other financial institutions.

Therefore, during the course of the nineteenth century, the Bank of England gradually increased its responsibility for maintaining orderly conditions in the money markets and influencing the policies and practices of the other commercial banks. However, given its nature as a private bank, there was no explicit legislated mandate for the Bank of England to pursue monetary policy in order to achieve specific national macroeconomic goals. However, the Bank of England, because of its close relationship with the government, functioned in practice as a kind of central bank for Britain. Since Britain was in the forefront of both industrialization and financial development and the largest imperial power in the nineteenth century, the goals, policies and practices of the Bank of England strongly influenced central banking in the English-speaking countries as well as in many others. These were incorporated explicitly into the charters and mandates of many central banks set up in the early twentieth century. The mandates allocated to the Federal Reserve System in the United States (in 1913) and the Bank of Canada (in 1935) when they were set up in the twentieth century were roughly similar to the practices of the day of the Bank of England. Its degree of independence of the government in setting the bank rate and monetary policy was roughly similar. The major difference between the US and Canadian central banks and the Bank of England was that the latter was still privately owned, though more so in name than in terms of functions, until the end of the Second World War. Its ownership was nationalized in 1946.[24]

From nationalization in 1946 to 1997, the British government had statutory power over both the goals as well as the operational use of the instruments of monetary policy, though the day-to-day operations of the Bank and its normal business was left to the Bank. The Bank made recommendations to the Chancellor of the Exchequer who has the final decision on the bank rate, the main instrument of monetary policy in the UK, as well on other aspects of this policy. In practice, monetary policy was formulated through close consultation and periodic meetings between the Governor of the Bank and the Chancellor. The Bank implemented the policies defined by the Chancellor, though with some discretion over the timing of implementation of decisions.

From the mid-1980s onwards, monetary policy in the UK, as in many other countries, came to focus heavily on price stability. Part of this shift in the goals of monetary policy accompanied Britain's adherence to the European Exchange Rate Mechanism (ERM) from 1993 to 1995. It was also partly due to Britain's experience in the 1970s and 1980s with monetary policy and its impact on the growth of output and standards of living, as well as the deterioration of its exchange rate, relative to that of other countries such as Germany which had maintained their main focus on price stability. Some part of it was also due to the revision of the theory of monetary policy from the Keynesian to the modern classical approach. The former implied that monetary policy could affect unemployment and output, as well as the rate of inflation. The latter implied that systematic monetary policy could not change unemployment and output. In any case, the shift in the goals of monetary policy in Britain was similar to that which was occurring in the USA, Canada and many other countries at the end of the 1980s.

While the goal of price stability had existed in Britain for some years prior to 1992, the Chancellor of the Exchequer announced in 1992 the adoption of explicit inflation targets (1% to 4%) aimed at achieving long-term price stability. He also required the Bank of England to publish a quarterly *Inflation Report* assessing the extent to which the target was being met.[25] While this adoption of an explicit target did not represent a change in the fundamental objective of price stability, it meant the explicit abandonment of other goals such as those on unemployment and output growth. It also meant the abandonment of other targets such as monetary aggregates or exchange rates, though such variables continued to be monitored as a guide to future inflation. Note also that the inflation target was specified as a band, intended both to limit the freedom for counter-cyclical monetary policy and as an allowance for imperfect control.

The official inflation target was changed in 1995 by the Chancellor, with the agreement of the Bank of England, to a point target of 2.5% to be met on an ongoing basis. No other goal, such as that of exchange rate stability or business cycle stabilization, was explicitly acknowledged in this policy framework nor was there now an explicit commitment to a pre-specified range for the inflation rate. However, there implicitly seemed to be some short-run flexibility for unavoidable deviations from the specified target. The Chancellor still retained the right to specify the course of monetary policy in terms of the interest rates that were set.

In 1997, the Bank of England was given 'operational independence' of the government in its operation of monetary policy. An aspect of this operational independence was that the control of the base interest rate, to achieve the specified inflation target, was now assigned to the Bank. The inflation target continues to be set by the Chancellor, with the role of the Bank being that of consultation and advice, though usually its agreement would also be sought. Under an 'escape clause' the government retains the right to overrule the Bank's interest rate policy or its pursuit of the inflation rate target. Further, if the actual inflation rate deviated from this target by more than 1%, the Committee had to explain the deviation from 'the threshold' to the Chancellor in an open letter[26] and to outline the action being taken to eliminate the deviation. The Chancellor and, therefore, the government can change the target for the rate of inflation or specify other targets. This change can be expected to alter with a change in the political party in power since the main British political parties embody somewhat different economic philosophies. However, such changes did not occur on the replacement of the Conservative government by a Labour one in 1997.

Further, in 1997, the formulation of monetary policy was vested in a new broad-based committee, the Monetary Policy Committee. This is a broad-based committee, consisting of the Governor, two Deputy Governors, two other Bank Executive Directors and four members from the academic (usually economists) and financial sectors, appointed by the government, for three-year terms. Decisions on the bank rate are now made by the Monetary Policy Committee. Its decisions are announced immediately and its minutes are published, in an attempt to make the pursuit of monetary policy transparent and accountable to the public.

Hence, under the arrangements in force in 1999, the government defines the ultimate goals of monetary policy. These are currently defined solely as price stability, with its definition in terms of the target rate of inflation also being set by the government. The Bank of England and the Monetary Policy Committee formulate the implementation of monetary policy, such as in the setting of the bank rate.[27] This separation of goal independence and operational independence in Britain is clearly different from that in the United States and Canada, in each of which the central bank possesses both of these.

11.10 THE BANK OF CANADA: OBJECTIVES, INSTRUMENTS AND GUIDES TO MONETARY POLICY

The preceding sections of this chapter have already discussed the evolution of the Bank of Canada's objectives, and the instruments of policy used by it. Its main goal now is the achievement of price stability in the sense of a rate of inflation in the 1% to 3% range. It believes that such an inflation range is best for achieving full employment and long-term growth in the economy, as well as reducing economic fluctuations. Higher rates of inflation impose social and economic costs, and lead to the temptation for further increases in the inflation rate.

This section takes a brief look at the historical use of the interest rates and monetary aggregates as targets by the Bank, and also discusses its use of a composite variable, the monetary conditions index, as a target. Such an index is also being used by the central bank of New Zealand.

During the 1950s and 1960s, the Bank of Canada had emphasized short-term interest rates as its operational target. In the 1970s, the Monetarist School became more popular relative to the Keynesian one, whose policies seemed to be the cause of the stagflation of the 1970s. The monetarists claimed that real output had a more stable and predictable relationship with M2 than with interest rates, so that they recommended that M2, rather than interest rates, be used as the target for monetary policy. Further, in terms of experience during the 1970s, the rising rates of inflation were pushing up interest rates, so that the rise in interest rates was not really a proper indicator of monetary tightness in the economy. These factors led the Bank of Canada to shift its emphasis to monetary aggregates as a guide and intermediate target for its policies. From 1975 to 1982, the monetary aggregate used as the target for monetary policy was mainly M1, and the Bank announced its desired target range for the growth of M1. However, M1 proved to be unreliable as a target, partly because of extensive financial innovation that continuously reduced the demand for M1 and partly because its relationship with aggregate demand and the rate of inflation proved to be unstable. The use of M1 as a target was abandoned in 1982. The search for another suitable monetary aggregate for a target proved to be unsuccessful. In particular, M2 did not prove to be more desirable than M1.

Since the early 1980s, the Bank of Canada has held the view that the relationship between the monetary base and the monetary aggregates such as M1 and M2 is not stable. Therefore, the Bank policy on targets after 1982 has been that interest rates rather than monetary aggregates are more suitable as targets. This has led to a reliance on short-term interest rates as immediate targets, though with greater caution about their use and with closer attention paid to other indictors of the state of the economy, especially to the rate of inflation itself as the major objective variable for policy.

The monetary conditions index

In 1992, the Bank defined a *monetary conditions index*, labelled by it as MCI, which is a weighted average of short-term interest rates and the trade-weighted exchange rate of the Canadian dollar. Roughly, the change in the MCI[28] is specified as:

$$\Delta MCI = \Delta r + (\tfrac{1}{3})\, \Delta \rho$$

where r is the short-term interest rate, interpreted as the ninety-day commercial paper rate, and ρ is the effective exchange rate, interpreted as the exchange rate for the Canadian dollar against the ten major (G10) currencies. The reason for the one-third weighting of the exchange rate relative to the interest rate is the Bank of Canada's belief, based on empirical work done in it, that a change in interest rates by 1% has three times the impact of a corresponding change in exchange rates on aggregate demand in the Canadian economy. Given that the effect is in the same direction for both r and ρ, opposite changes in these variables offset each other's effects on the economy. Hence, if an increase in the exchange rate occurs and if the Bank considers the resulting increase in the MCI to be undesirable, the Bank responds by inducing a sufficient offsetting reduction in interest rates to keep the MCI unchanged. Alternatively, it can act to manipulate the exchange rate, though it normally does not do so.

The MCI is used as a guide for the Bank's policies. The Bank formulates its expectations on the state of the Canadian economy and those of its major trading partners, as well as decides on its desired rates of inflation and growth in aggregate demand, and determines the target values of MCI that would achieve these goals. Monetary aggregates, along with other macroeconomic variables, are used as information variables. The Bank does not specify a target path for the MCI, nor set a target path for the exchange rate, nor try to ensure that its actions result in the specific ratio of one-third in interest rate and exchange rate changes. The MCI is used as an operational guide but the main focus is on its goals defined in terms of aggregate demand and price stability.

The Bank sets the overnight loan rate, with a range of 50 basis points, as its operational target to achieve its desired value of the MCI. It allows the financial institutions and the markets to determine the actual amounts of the monetary aggregates on the basis of the targeted overnight loan rate. Its money market operations are used to hold the overnight rate in the specified range. Movements in the overnight rate in turn induce changes in the other interest rates and the exchange rate.

The Bank of Canada tries to influence the overnight rate through changes in the settlement balances[29] held with it by the direct clearers, mainly the commercial banks, in the Canadian payments system. Positive amounts of these balances do not pay interest, but any negative amounts have to be covered by overdrafts at the bank rate. While such changes in settlement balances can be brought about by open market operations, the Bank usually relies upon daily transfers of government deposits between it and the direct clearers, making such transfers and the resulting supply of settlement balances as its main instrument for changing the monetary base and exercising control over the economy.

The Bank of Canada believes that uncertainty is inimical to the proper functioning of the financial markets and the efficiency of the economy, and that the uncertainty of monetary policy can adversely affect saving and investment in the economy. In an attempt to reduce such uncertainty, changes in the target range for the overnight rate are immediately made known to the public, and the intended course of the monetary policy of the Bank is continuously explained to the public through publications and speeches of the Governor of the Bank and its officials.

11.11 THE EUROPEAN SYSTEM OF CENTRAL BANKS (ESCB) AND THE EUROPEAN CENTRAL BANK (ECB)

The gradual bonding of the European countries during the postwar years and their eventual merger into the European Union in the 1990s has resulted in their monetary unification. The central element of this unification – also called the European Monetary Union[30] – is the European System of Central Banks (ESCB), established under the Maastricht Treaty of 1992. The ESCB consists of the European Central Bank (ECB), based in Frankfurt, and the national central banks of the member countries, and is federalist in structure. The central decision-making body on monetary policy is the ECB's Governing Council, composed of the national central bank governors[31] and the Executive Board[32] of the ECB. The Executive Board, besides running the day-to-day operations of the ECB, carries out the decisions of the Governing Council and coordinates their implementation by the national central banks in their respective countries.

Many aspects of the ESCB were modelled on the Deutsche Bundesbank – the German central bank – which is considered to have had the best record among the European and North American countries on inflation and growth since the 1950s and also has a federalist structure. In particular, the statutes of the ESCB were similar to those governing the Bundesbank in assigning the ESCB complete independence from political pressures and the primary objective of price stability. The former was ensured through setting relatively long periods of appointment for the members of the Governing Council. This structure makes the ESCB independent of the European governing structures and the European Parliament, as well as of the politics and pressures from the member states. A side-effect of this degree of independence is that it reduces the accountability of the ESCB. The extent of its accountability comes about mainly through the required publication of various reports at fixed intervals.

The functions assigned to the ESCB are similar to those of the central banks of other countries. It issues the European currency (the euro), sets and implements monetary policy, conducts foreign exchange operations and holds the foreign exchange reserves of the member countries, and promotes the smooth operation of the payment system.[33] The Maastricht Treaty set the primary goal of monetary policy as price stability, with the Governing Council of the ESCB setting the actual target for the rate of inflation. Its other functions are to be pursued without prejudice to the goal of price stability.

The allocation of the overriding goal of price stability to the ESCB partly reflected the acceptance of the dominant economic theory of the early 1990s and the general admiration for the economic record of Germany and of the Deutsche Bundesbank. On the former, as we have pointed out earlier, the dominant economic theory in the 1990s was the modern classical one. It argues that the central bank can control the price of money – that is, the rate of inflation – and not the real variables of output and unemployment. The central bank can only improve upon the latter by ensuring price stability. By comparison, the Federal Reserve System of the United States and the Bank of Canada were set up in the first half of the twentieth century, at a time when the achievement of multiple goals or of tradeoffs among them was considered possible through monetary policy.

The legislative specification of a single primary objective to the ESCB, rather than a tradeoff between goals, makes the success or failure of the ESCB in achieving its designated goal readily transparent to the public, thereby increasing its accountability and the public pressure to attain it. But this single-goal specification can become an unproductive limitation if the economy enters a state where a tradeoff between the inflation goal and other economic goals comes into being. The ESCB is expected to use changes in interest rates as the main operational tool of monetary policy.

The euro came into being for transactions among financial institutions on 1 January 1999. Its exchange rates against the national currencies of the member countries were fixed at that time by the European Commission, while its exchange rates against the US dollar and other currencies were to be determined by the markets. The European bond and stock markets switched from the national currencies to the euro as the unit of account, thereby eliminating the risk of currency fluctuations for transactions within the European Union. The euro as a currency in the form of notes and coins is expected to be issued in 2002 and is intended to replace national currencies in circulation.

11.12 CURRENCY BOARDS

Some countries, more so in the past but rarely nowadays, had currency boards instead of central banks.[34] With a currency board, the country maintains a fixed exchange rate against a designated foreign currency, and the monetary base – a liability of the currency board – is backed by its foreign exchange reserves. As these reserves increase – for example, through a balance of payments surplus – the currency board increases the monetary base, and the money supply in the economy increases. Conversely, as foreign exchange reserves fall, the monetary base and the money supply are decreased. Other than this, the currency board does not have discretion to change the money supply or manage interest rates and, therefore, cannot pursue domestic monetary policies.

Currency boards were common in the colonies of imperial countries – for example, the UK – during the first half of the twentieth century. They were a means of linking the currency and the economies of the colonies to those of the imperial country. Further, if the imperial currency was under the gold standard – that is, with its value fixed in terms of gold – the colonies also indirectly adhered to the gold standard. Such currency boards were usually replaced by central banks on independence. In other cases, countries, though independent, maintained currency boards with a strict adherence to the gold standard, implying a fixed value of the domestic currency in terms of gold.

Most of the aspects of this chapter, bearing on the goals, instruments and targets of monetary policy, do not apply to currency boards. The implications of their maintenance of fixed exchange rates are examined later in the open economy macroeconomic chapters.

CONCLUSIONS

The monetary sector is central to modern economies and its proper functioning is critical to the levels of employment, output and growth. As an illustration of this importance, it is now generally agreed that monetary failure caused, or was a major contributor to, the Great Depression of the 1930s (Friedman and Schwartz, 1963). The central bank is the custodian of the health, efficiency and performance of the financial sector.

Therefore, the monetary policy pursued by the central bank is fundamental to the performance of the economy. This chapter has shown that the goals of central banks have varied over time and differ among countries. Currently, the dominant belief of most central banks is that they can best promote output, employment and growth through the maintenance of the value of the money, i.e. through fairly stable prices. In particular, the belief is that continual or discretionary attempts to increase aggregate demand through monetary policy do not yield higher output or reduce business fluctuations over a significant number of years. Further, monetary policy acts on the economy with a sufficient lag so that, with the future course of the economy being difficult to predict accurately, the proper formulation of monetary policy is an art and, as such, potentially susceptible to error.

In the 1990s, the dominant goal pursued in the USA, Canada and the UK was that of price stability, usually interpreted as the achievement and maintenance of a low rate of inflation (about 1% to 3%). Given the long-run neutrality of money, this goal is sometimes conveyed as an ultimate goal and at other times as an intermediate goal towards improving the growth rates of output and employment in the economy. For the UK and Canada, the target for the inflation rate is explicitly announced, while the USA does not announce – and, therefore, does not give an explicit pre-commitment for – a pre-specified inflation target.

The use of interest rates as operational targets is to be distinguished from a policy of fixing them administratively for long periods and at relatively low levels, with the ostensible purpose of promoting growth. This was done in many LDCs during the 1970s and 1980s, although there is currently a trend away from this practice. Direct limitations on interest rates imposed by the central bank on commercial banks or all financial intermediaries are questionable for various reasons. The interest rate is the opportunity cost of loans and should, for the proper allocation of funds in the economy, be determined by competitive forces in the open markets. Setting them or setting artificially low ceilings on them by administrative action introduces inefficiencies into the financial structure of the economy, inimical to the optimal generation of savings, as well as their allocation by the financial institutions optimally to investment among the sectors of the economy.[35] LDCs are especially prone to setting artificially low interest rates on loans in the organized financial sector. Many economists believe that this results in both a lower level of domestically generated savings and their misallocation to investment projects in the economy, thereby reducing the growth rates of these countries.

SUMMARY OF CRITICAL CONCLUSIONS

- Historically, most central banks have had the mandate to pursue a number of macroeconomic goals, including price stability, low unemployment, high growth, etc. Achievement of multiple goals is only possible if the economy allows such a possibility and the policy maker has enough policy tools.
- In the 1960s and early 1970s, economic theory implied, and most central banks attempted to achieve, a tradeoff based on the Phillips curve between unemployment and inflation. This tradeoff proved to be unstable for policy and was abandoned by the 1980s.
- In the 1990s, many economists have recommended, and the central banks have generally followed, the goal of price stability – translated as a low rate of inflation – for monetary policy. There is a corresponding abandonment, or relegation to a subsidiary role, of the objective of maintaining a low unemployment rate.
- While the interest rate was historically the operating target of monetary policy, a diversion to monetary targeting occurred during the late 1970s under the impact of St Louis monetarism. This experiment was not considered to be a success in most countries, and the most common operational target again became interest rates.
- Most Western countries have reduced percentage reserve requirements on commercial banks to levels that are close to zero. Changes in these requirements have ceased to be a tool of monetary policy.
- In the 1990s, the most common tools of monetary policy in developed economies are change in interest rates and open market operations.

review and discussion questions

1 From your knowledge of the short-run performance of the economy you live in, is there sufficient justification for the central bank to concentrate solely on the goal of price stability? Discuss.

2 Should the United States and Canada follow the example of Britain in giving the government the power to set the ultimate goal or goals of monetary policy, while leaving the implementation of these to the central bank? Or should Britain follow the example of the United States and Canada on this issue? Discuss.

3 What are the tools available to the central bank for controlling the money supply? Discuss how manipulation of each of these tools will change the money supply and how reliable each tool is likely to be.

4 Why has the use of changes in reserve requirements as a tool of monetary policy been largely abandoned in Western economies? What were the reasons for the virtual elimination of reserve requirements? Is there a case for their revival and usage as a tool of monetary policy in the context of the country you live in? In LDCs?

5 How can central bank discounting cause procyclical movements in the money supply? How can the central bank eliminate such a movement? Discuss.

6 The pursuit of selective fiscal policies in the form of tax exemptions and subsidies is common in almost all countries, while the usage of monetary policy on a selective basis is rare in the financially developed economies. Why? Should the use of selective monetary policies also be abandoned for the LDCs?

7 Suppose that for a given economy the preconditions for the effective pursuit of open market conditions are not met. What monetary policy tools are likely to be the most effective ones for such an economy? Relate your recommended tools to the preconditions that are not met.

8 'The standard practice of governments whereby they define the monetary unit is unnecessary and undesirable. The private sector should be encouraged to choose its own standards in a free competitive market'. (Friedrich Hayek). Discuss.

9 What does financial intermediation mean? How would you classify the different financial intermediaries in your country and their liabilities as components of the monetary aggregates?

10 Suppose that instead of imposing reserve requirements on demand deposits in the commercial banks, the central bank does the following: require automobile owners to hold $500 of non-interest-bearing deposits with the central bank.

(i) How would the determination of the price level differ between the two arrangements?

(ii) How would the real consequences of the two arrangements differ?

(iii) Are there any special characteristics of demand deposits or any other reasons that make one of these arrangements preferable to the other?

NOTES

1 See Chapter 2 for the economic heritage on this, and Chapters 13 to 16 for a modern treatment.

2 However, there are economists, belonging to the New Monetary School, who espouse competitive issue of money by private institutions. Such issue of money, even bank notes, by private firms was common in most countries until the twentieth century.

3 Its ownership was nationalized in 1946.

4 In the late 1980s and early 1990s, the Bank of Canada campaigned vigorously for a change in the Act defining its mandate to narrow it down to that of maintaining price stability only, claiming that money supply changes could not affect the real variables. In 1991, it proposed to the government of Canada that the statutory mandate of the Bank should be changed to one of primarily maintaining price stability. The government refused to introduce legislation to this effect. However, the Bank reduced its goals in practice to focus only on that of price stability.

5 See Chapters 15 and 16 for this analysis.

6 What is distinctive about the New Zealand case is that the Governor of the Bank can be held responsible for failure to achieve the announced targets, and sanctions may be imposed for such failure.

7 The analysis of credibility is presented in the next chapter.

8 These are essentially interest rates on one-day loans among financial institutions.

9 These cases clearly refer to open economies. For the analysis relevant to them, see Chapters 18 and 19 below on open economy macroeconomics.

10 In most countries, the required reserves have to be held by the bank in currency or in deposits with the central bank. These deposits normally do not pay interest.

11 From 1967 to 1992, the banks also had to meet a secondary reserve requirement. The reserves for this purpose were defined as the excess of primary reserve requirements plus Treasury bills plus loans to investment dealers, to be held against Canadian dollar deposits plus foreign currency deposits of residents with banks in Canada. The secondary reserve requirement was abolished in June 1992.

12 Also see Chapter 10.

13 This power to determine the domestic interest rates varies between closed and open

economies and can be very limited for small open economies. The use of such a power is also more common in LDCs than in the developed economies.

14 Where the interest rates are directly set by the central bank, variations in them can be exercised as a general policy tool for all loans by the banks or as a selective tool with differential effect among the sectors of the economy. As a general policy tool, fixing the interest rates is an attempt to influence investment and saving and thereby control aggregate demand in the economy.

15 This claim is often associated with the Radcliffe Report in the United Kingdom in the late 1950s. It claimed that the economy was awash in liquidity, which included trade credit and short- and medium-term bonds, and money was only a small component of it. Restrictions in its supply merely led to its substitution by other liquid assets. This extreme version of the argument was abandoned since the money demand functions proved to be quite stable for the 1960s and 1970s but it can still be used in a milder form.

16 However, Milton Friedman and other monetarists had argued in the 1960s that the demand function for money was stable, and more stable than the investment multiplier, so that controlling the money supply rather than the interest rates (and through them, investment) was preferable. The experiment in using monetary aggregates as targets was briefly tried during the late 1980s but was not pursued because of the instability of the money demand function.

17 In Britain, *discount houses* usually act as intermediaries between the banks and the Bank of England. Banks which need funds can draw down their balances at the discount houses, sell securities to them or borrow from them. If the discount houses need funds, they can either borrow or sell securities to the Bank of England at the bank rate (also called the dealing rate). The latter method is now the more common one. The explanation for this indirect method of banks' borrowing from the Bank of England is that direct borrowing by a bank might be seen as a sign of liquidity problems and could reduce the public's confidence in the bank.

18 Selgin (1988) provides a spirited defence of a banking system free from regulation and dismisses the idea behind central bank control of the money supply that competitive commercial banks, free to issue banknotes, would overissue notes and deposits for private gain.

19 In Canada, the chartered banks were first permitted to hold mortgages in the 1950s.

20 The economics profession in the 1960s was divided on the issue of extending controls similar to those on the banks, to non-bank financial intermediaries. The demand for such extension reached its zenith in the early 1960s and then died down. A major reason for this was the easing of interest rate ceilings on the savings deposits of commercial banks along with somewhat lower reserve requirements in the 1960s. By the late 1960s, commercial banks had, as a result of these and other factors, recovered sufficiently to reverse the decline in their relative position in the economy *vis-à-vis* other financial intermediaries issuing near-monies.

21 This privilege and many others, such as that of the monopoly of note issue in 1844, were usually granted to it in return for large loans from it to the government.

22 The rate of exchange was £3 17s 6d per ounce of standard gold.

23 For historical interest and comparison with current discount rates, this rate was 2.5% until November 1845 when it was raised to 3.5%.

24 The Bank of England is run by a Governor, appointed for five years by the government, and a Board, whose members are appointed for four years.

25 The Bank of England's *Inflation Report*, just as the *Monetary Policy Report* by the Bank of Canada, reports on the performance of the economy, compares actual inflation rates to the forecast ones for the past and forecasts the inflation rate for the future. Both are prepared independently of the government. They are a part of the central banks' communications to the public on its past performance and intended future policies.

26 The purpose behind this letter being open is to enhance the transparency of monetary policy to parliament and the public and increase the Bank's accountability to them.

27   The government retains the power, in the national interest and presumably in extreme circumstances, to give instructions to the Bank on interest rates for a limited period.

28   The actual formula is:

$$MCI = (CP90 - 7.9) + (100/3) \, (\ln G10 - \ln 0.8676014)$$

CP90 is the ninety-day commercial paper rate and G10 is the Canadian dollar index against G10 currencies, with its base value for 1981 set at 1.

29   'Settlement balances' is the term being currently used to designate the deposits held by designated financial institutions, called the *direct clearers* with the Bank of Canada. In the absence of any legally required reserves, these deposits are held voluntarily by the direct clearers and are used to settle their daily imbalances in receipts and payments against each other. This settlement is done through their accounts at the Bank.

30   In January 1999, when the euro was introduced, eleven countries had opted for and met the conditions for membership of the European Monetary Union (EMU). Greece did not meet the conditions for immediate membership. The countries which are members of the European Union but opted out of the EMU were Britain, Denmark and Sweden. The British government declared in 1997, and repeated subsequently, its intention to join the EMU if there emerges a clear and unambiguous economic benefit to Britain from doing so. In any case, Britain has also declared its goal of making London as the international financial centre for the euro.

31   Each of them is appointed for a minimum term of five years and cannot be dismissed by their respective governments.

32   The Executive Board has a President and five members, appointed by the European Council for eight-year, non-renewable, terms.

33   The function of the lender of last resort was not assigned to the ESCB. Presumably, the national central banks will continue to perform it.

34   As of 1998, currency boards exist in Hong Kong, Argentina, Estonia and Lithuania and a few other countries.

35   The continual revision of such ceilings in the light of changes in the market interest rates, as done in some countries, does moderate this argument. But since there are invariably delays and rigidities in changing administered interest rates, administered interest rates almost always introduce some inefficiency in the financial sectors of the economy.

REFERENCES

Coats, W. L., and D. R. Khatkhate. *Money and Monetary Policy in Less Developed Countries*. Oxford: Pergamon Press, 1980.

Friedman, Benjamin M. 'Targets and Instruments of Monetary Policy'. In Benjamin M. Friedman, and Frank H. Hahn, eds, *Handbook of Monetary Economics*. Amsterdam: North-Holland, 1990, Vol. II.

———, and Frank H. Hahn, eds, *Handbook of Monetary Economics*. Amsterdam: North-Holland, 1990, Vol. 2, Part 8.

Friedman, Milton. 'The Role of Monetary Policy'. *American Economic Review*, 58, March 1968, pp. 1–17.

———. 'Nobel Prize Lecture: Inflation and Unemployment'. *Journal of Political Economy*, 85, June 1977, pp. 451–73.

———, and Anna J. Schwartz. *A Monetary History of the United States*. Princeton, NJ: Princeton University Press, 1963.

Goodhart, Charles A. E. 'Central Banking'. *The New Palgrave Dictionary of Economics: Money*. London: Macmillan, 1989.

———. 'The Conduct of Monetary Policy'. In Christopher J. Green and David T. Llewellyn, eds, *Surveys in Monetary Economics* (Vol. I: *Monetary Theory and Policy*). Cambridge, MA: Blackwell, 1991.

———. *The Central Bank and the Financial System*. Cambridge, MA: MIT Press, 1995.

Guiseppi, John. *The Bank of England*. Chicago: Henry Regnery Co., 1966.

Mayer, Thomas. *Monetary Policy in the United States*. New York: Random House, 1968.

Meulendyke, Ann-Marie. *US Monetary Policy and Financial Markets*. New York: Federal Reserve Bank of New York, 1998.

Mishkin, Frederic S., and Adam S. Posen. 'Inflation Targeting: Lessons from Four Countries'. In Federal Reserve Bank of New York, *Economic Policy Review*, 3, August 1997, pp. 9–110.

Page, Sheila, ed. *Monetary Policy in Developing Countries*. London: Routledge, 1993.

Selgin, George. *The Theory of Free Banking: Money Supply under Competitive Note Issue*. Totowa, NJ: Rowman & Littlefield, and the Cato Institute, 1988.

Sherman, Lawrence F., Case M. Sprenkle and Bryan E. Stanhouse. 'Reserve Requirements and Control of the Money Supply: A Note'. *Journal of Money, Credit and Banking*, 11, November 1979, pp. 486–93.

chapter twelve

THE CENTRAL BANK: TARGETS, CONFLICTS, INDEPENDENCE AND THE TIME CONSISTENCY OF POLICIES

The preceding chapter discussed the institutional practices of the monetary authorities concerning their goals and instruments, especially those in the United States, United Kingdom and Canada.

This chapter focuses on the analytical treatment of the issues related to central banks. Assuming a potential for tradeoffs among the policy targets, it examines the determination of choices among them and the potential for conflicts among the monetary and fiscal authorities. In addition, it considers the important topics of the independence of central banks from the government, their credibility among the public, and the dynamic consistency of the policies that are followed over time.

---

key concepts introduced in this chapter

- The relationship between goals, targets and guides
- Targeting inflation
- Targeting output and unemployment
- Interest rate targeting
- Nominal income targeting
- Preferences over goals
- Economy's constraints on the tradeoff among goals
- Conflicts in choosing the goal levels
- Central bank independence
- Credibility of policy
- Time consistency of policies

This is an analytical chapter on the central issues of monetary policy. It starts with the relationships among the goals, targets and guides to monetary policy and examines the theoretical justification as well as the implications of adopting different targets. It follows this by specifying the analysis of the choice among goals when there exist tradeoffs among the goals. This raises the possibility of conflicts between the monetary and fiscal authorities in the attainment of their desired targets.

In cases of conflicts between the monetary authorities and the government, the ability of the central bank to pursue its own choices becomes important and is discussed under the heading of the independence of the central bank.

Other major issues addressed in this chapter are the time consistency and credibility of policies. The time consistency of monetary policies deals with the question of whether the central bank should determine its policies for the future periods within its horizon and stick to them, or whether it should retain discretion to reformulate its policies as time passes. Related to this issue of the time consistency of policy is the important issue of maintaining the credibility of the central bank among the public and the consequences of a failure to maintain credibility.

Sections 12.1 and 12.2 present the links between the goals, targets and guides to monetary policy. Sections 12.3 to 12.8 examine in detail the targets of monetary policy commonly used by central banks and their justification from macroeconomic analysis.[1] Section 12.9 presents the optimizing framework for making choices among targets. This analysis follows the utility maximization approach, subject to the constraints on targets set by the economy. Section 12.10 considers the case of two policy makers, the central bank in charge of monetary policy and the government in charge of fiscal policy, and shows that there is considerable scope for conflicts in the pursuit of these policies. Section 12.11 illustrates the possibility and nature of conflicts between the central bank and the government from the past experiences of the United States, Canada and Britain.

Section 12.12 addresses the important issue of the independence of the central bank from the government. Section 12.13 presents the analysis of the time consistency of policies versus the potential time inconsistency of discretionary policies. Finally, section 12.14 examines the credibility of central bank policies and their effectiveness, as well as the impact on credibility of gradualist versus cold turkey attempts to lower the rate of inflation.

12.1 GUIDES TO MONETARY POLICY

An important question for the formulation of monetary policy by a central bank concerns the appropriate variables on which it can focus as indicators of the need for such a policy. Such variables provide information on the current and future state of the economy, especially of the goal variables, and are known as policy guides. A variable selected as a policy guide is also sometimes used as a target variable, i.e. one whose value the central bank seeks to influence or control directly by the use of the tools at its disposal. Since the guide variable reflects the state of the economy, its value must also change if a policy changes that state, so that the guides are directly or indirectly functions of the policy instruments.

The appropriateness of a variable as an indicator of the need for monetary policy depends upon the structure of the economy. Consequently, what are recognized as the guides to monetary policy depend upon the policy maker's perception of the structure of the economy. Thus, in a Keynesian framework, interest rates in the money market are a major determinant of spending and hence a major indicator of the condition of the economy. For instance, a fall in the short-term interest rates accompanied, as it is generally, by a fall in long-term interest rates is often interpreted as an indication that investment will be stimulated and aggregate spending rise. If the monetary authorities do not wish such spending to rise, they can act to decrease the money supply so as to restore the interest rates to their former levels. The monetarists of the 1970s did not view interest rates as particularly significant or infallible guides to the strength of aggregate demand and focused directly on one of the monetary aggregates.

A variable can only serve as a guide or operating target if it has a close and predictable relationship with the ultimate goal variable of the policy maker. As discussed in Chapter 11, such a goal can be the rate of growth of output in the economy, the rate of inflation, or the rate of growth of nominal national income or expenditures, etc. Taking, for example, the last-mentioned variable as the ultimate goal, the proper guide to policy could in principle be any variable that follows a time path from which the time path of nominal national income can be forecast and influenced by policy in a predictable manner. The greater the degree of error in forecasting, the less reliable will be the variable as a guide. Further, if the guide is also to serve as an operating target, it must be susceptible to change by the policy instruments and must bear a closely predictable relationship to the operational instruments. Therefore, a guide is an intermediate variable in the transmission process from policy instruments to the ultimate objectives, bearing a close relationship to both instruments and objectives.

12.2 THE RELATIONSHIP AMONG GOALS, TARGETS AND GUIDES TO POLICY, AND DIFFICULTIES IN THE PURSUIT OF MONETARY POLICY

A target variable is one whose value the policy maker wants to change. The targets can be ultimate ones (final goals), intermediate ones or operating ones. Since a given variable can fall into any one of these categories, there is no hard and clear-cut separation among these categories. An operating target is one on which the central bank can directly or almost directly operate through the instruments at its disposal.

Several issues arise in the selection and use of goals, guides and operating targets by the monetary authorities. Among these are:

(i) Can the central bank achieve the desired levels of the operating targets through the instruments at its disposal?
(ii) Are the relationships between the ultimate goal variable, the intermediate and operating targets and the policy instruments stable and predictable?
(iii) What are the lags in these relationships, and, if they are long, can the future course of the economy be reasonably well predicted?

To illustrate these points, let the relevant relationships be:

$$y = f(x; \Psi) \tag{1}$$

$$x = g(z; \theta) \tag{2}$$

where:

y ultimate goal variable
x intermediate target
z policy instrument or operating target
Ψ, θ sets of exogenous variables

The above equations imply that:

$$y = h(z; \Psi, \theta) \tag{3}$$

so that z can be used to achieve a desired value of y. However, this can only be done reliably if the functional forms f and g are known and these are stable univalued functions.[2] In practice, given the complex structure of the real world economies, as well as the existence of uncertainty and lags in the actual relationships, the precise forms of f, g and h are often only imperfectly known at the time the decisions are made. Further, the coefficients in these relationships may be subject to stochastic changes. In addition, given the lags in the economy, the policy maker also needs to predict the future values of the coefficients and the exogenous variables – again usually an imprecise art.

Hence, the precision and clarity implied by (3) for the formulation of monetary policy and its effects is misleading. In many, if not most, instances, the impact of a change in most of the potential operating variables on the ultimate goals is likely to be imprecise, difficult to predict and/or unstable. This makes the formulation of monetary policy an art rather than a science and cautions against attempts to use monetary policy as a precise control mechanism for 'fine-tuning' the goals of such policy.

Another common problem with most target variables is that they are endogenous and their values depend on both demand and supply factors, so that the exogenous shocks to them could come from either demand or supply shifts. The policy maker may want to offset the effect of changes in some of these factors but not in all cases, so that it needs to know the source of such changes before formulating its policy.

12.3 THE TARGETS OF MONETARY POLICY

It is important to distinguish between the usage of a variable for controlling the economy from its usage as an indicator, with both uses leading to its being called a target. Sometimes, the same variable will be used to perform both of these purposes, while in other cases different variables will be used to perform these distinct roles. An illustration of the latter is when a selected monetary aggregate is used as the indicator variable for determining the state of the economy while the interest rate is manipulated for changing that state. In such a context, the interest rate becomes an immediate objective and is the operational target, while the selected monetary aggregate is being used only as a guide. An illustration of the former case is where the monetary aggregate serves as both the indicator of the state of the economy and, as such, is an indicator of the need for changes in monetary policy, and is also as an operational target, pursued through open market operations. There can, therefore, be considerable mixing of the concepts of guides, indicators and targets.

12.3.1 The usual targets of monetary policy

The target variables usually suggested for monetary policy are:

- monetary or reserve aggregates;
- interest rates;
- the price level or the inflation rate;[3]
- nominal income;
- the deviation of output from its full employment level.

There are also other variables that are sometimes used as targets. Among these are the exchange rate for relatively open economies. This section and the next one briefly discuss the relative merits and demerits of the above bulleted variables. The main focus of the discussion is on the first four of the above-listed targets.

12.3.2 The theoretical analysis of monetary aggregates and interest rates as operating targets

The two main operating targets proposed for monetary policy are the money supply, or one of its related aggregates, and the interest rate. This section draws upon the students' prior knowledge of the IS–LM macroeconomic model (otherwise, see Chapter 13) to distinguish between the relative merits of targeting the money supply versus targeting interest rates.

Shocks arising from the commodity market (IS curve)

Figure 12.1a shows the IS–LM diagram with the aggregate real demand y on its horizontal axis and the real interest rate on its vertical one. The commodity market equilibrium is shown by the IS curve and the money market equilibrium is shown by the LM curve. Initial equilibrium is at the point a, which has (r_0, y_0). Assume that the central bank targets the money supply and holds it constant through open market operations or the use of some other instruments, including the interest rate. Random shocks to the IS curve[4] would then change both r and y. To illustrate, if a positive shock shifts the IS curve to IS_1, aggregate demand will increase from y_0 to y_1 and interest rates rise from r_0 to r_1. Similarly, a negative shock, occurring say in the following period, which shifts the IS curve to IS_2 will lower aggregate demand to y_2 and interest rates to r_2.

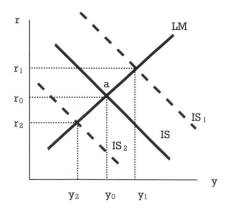

Figure 12.1a

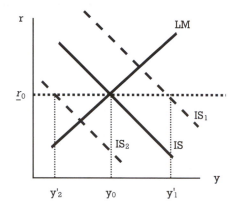

Figure 12.1b

Compare this with the impact of the same shock if the interest rate had been targeted. This is shown in Figure 12.1b where the interest rate is assumed to be held fixed by the authorities at the rate $\underline{r}_0$. The shifts in the IS curve first to IS_1 and then to IS_2 will produce movements in aggregate demand, first to y'_1 and then to y'_2. This fluctuation between y'_1 and y'_2 is clearly greater than between y_1 and y_2 in Figure 12.1b, so that targeting the interest rate produces greater fluctuations in aggregate demand than money supply targeting if the exogenous shocks emanate from the commodity market. Conversely, such shocks do not produce changes in the interest rate, since that is being held constant through monetary policy.

Shocks arising from the money market (LM curve)

Now assume that the exogenous shocks arise only in the money market, while there are no shocks in the commodity market, so that the IS curve does not shift. Such exogenous shocks can be to either money demand or money supply.

Money supply targeting would stabilize the money supply but not the money demand. Now suppose that the money demand decreases. Given the targeted money supply, the decrease in the money demand will shift the LM curve in Figure 12.2 to the right to LM_1 and increase aggregate demand from y_0 to y_1. Assume that the next period's shock to the money demand increases it and shifts the LM curve to LM_2, so that aggregate demand falls to y_2. The aggregate demand fluctuations are then from y_1 to y_2 and the interest rate fluctuations are from r_1 to r_2.

For interest rate targeting, assume that the interest rate had been targeted at $\underline{r}_0$, as shown in Figures 12.3 and 12.4. Figure 12.3 shows the initial demand curve for nominal balances as M^d and the initial supply curve as M^s, with the initial equilibrium interest rate as r_0 and the initial money stock as M_0. Now suppose that the money demand curve shifts to M_1^d. Since the interest rate is being maintained by the monetary authority at $\underline{r}_0$, the monetary authority will have to increase the money supplied to M_1. Therefore, the money stock adjusts

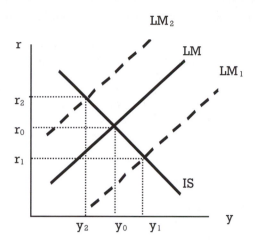

Figure 12.2

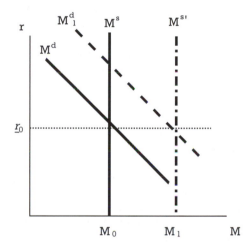

Figure 12.3

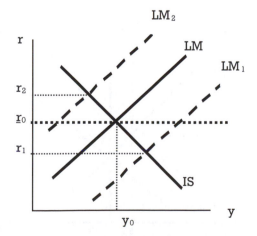

Figure 12.4

endogenously through an accommodative monetary policy to the changes in money demand.

In the IS–LM figure (Figure 12.4), a reduction in the money demand would shift the LM curve to the right to LM_1. However, given that the monetary authority maintains the interest rate at $\underline{r}_0$, the aggregate demand y_0 in this figure will be determined by the intersection of the IS curve and a horizontal line at the targeted interest rate $\underline{r}_0$. This is so because the exogenous shift in the LM curve to LM_1 produces an accommodative money supply increase which shifts this curve back to LM. Hence, in spite of any exogenous changes in money demand, aggregate demand would remain at y_0 (and the interest rate at $\underline{r}_0$). Hence, comparing the implications from Figures 12.2 and 12.4, monetary targeting will allow greater fluctuations in aggregate demand and interest rates than interest rate targeting when the exogenous shifts arise in the money market.

Therefore, the goal of minimizing fluctuations in aggregate demand recommends favouring monetary targeting if the fluctuations arise in the commodity market while favouring interest rate targeting if the fluctuations arise in the money market. This poses a problem for the policy maker since both types of shocks occur in the real world. Therefore, the monetary authority has to determine the potential source of the dominant shocks to the economy before making the choice between monetary and interest rate targeting. This is not easy to determine for the future, nor need the same pattern of shock necessarily hold over time. Further, since both types of shocks will occur, either target policy will reduce or eliminate the impact of some types of shocks while not of others.

While many central banks had for a few years during the late 1970s and sometimes in the early 1980s favoured monetary targeting, the common current practice is to set interest rates. In the context of the preceding analysis, this implies that the dominant sources of shocks are expected to be in the monetary sector.

12.3.3 The theoretical analysis of aggregate demand versus price stability as targets

Targeting aggregate demand through targeting monetary aggregates or interest rates

Figure 12.5 shows the aggregate demand (AD) and aggregate supply (AS) curves for the economy, using a short-run positively sloping AS curve as well as a long-run vertical AS curve. Assume now that the exogenous shocks are to aggregate demand, originating in the commodity or the money market. If we carry over the implications of monetary versus

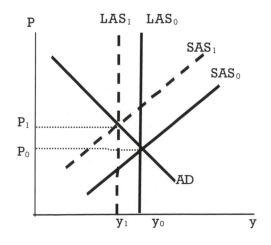

Figure 12.5

interest rate targeting from Figures 12.1 to 12.4, it is clear that minimizing the fluctuations in aggregate demand will mean minimizing the fluctuations in the price level and real output. Therefore, if the ultimate goal is that of relative price stability – or the relative stability of output – interest rate targeting will provide this better if the dominant shocks are from the monetary sector, while monetary targeting will provide it better if the dominant shocks are from the commodity sector.

However, note that neither of these forms of targeting will provide any leverage if the shocks are only from the real sectors of the economy and are permanent – that is, if the AD curve is stable but the LAS curve is shifted by the exogenous shocks. In this case, since there are, by assumption, no shocks from the monetary or commodity markets, neither monetary nor interest rate targeting will provide a permanent return to the original long-run level of output: while the supply shock will shift the LAS curve, the policy will not shift it. Therefore, in Figure 12.5, a negative supply-side shock from LAS_0 to LAS_1 will shift the economy from (P_0, y_0) to (P_1, y_1), without any monetary policy restoring y_0.

Targeting the price level

We now examine the case where the price level (or the inflation rate) is being targeted. Figure 12.6 also allows examination of the consequences of maintaining price stability when the shocks are from the demand rather than the supply side of the economy. Assume that there is an aggregate demand shock such that the AD curve shifts to AD_1. If the monetary authorities stabilize prices at P_0, output would remain unchanged at y_0. To achieve this, the monetary authority would pursue a compensatory decrease in the money supply to shift aggregate demand back to AD. The net effect of such a monetary policy would be the commendable one of stabilizing both the price level and output even though there are exogenous shocks from the money or commodity markets. Therefore, a goal of price stability is preferable to both monetary targeting and interest rate targeting when there are exogenous shocks to aggregate demand.

However, the exogenous shocks may come from the real sectors of the economy. Suppose that they are such that the aggregate supply decreases, so that, in Figure 12.7a, the short-run aggregate supply curve SAS curve shifts to SAS_1. This will produce an increase in the price level from P_0 to P_1 and a decrease in output from y_0 to y_1. Now, suppose the monetary authorities want to achieve price stability as their ultimate goal. Since the price level is not an operational variable under the direct control of the monetary authority, it would have to achieve price stability through changes in the money supply or in interest rates sufficient to offset the impact of supply shocks on prices. For instance, if the SAS curve had shifted to

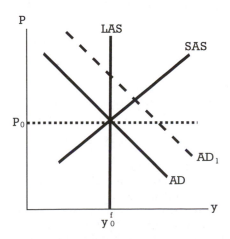

Figure 12.6

SAS_1, maintaining stable prices at $\underline{P}_0$ would require a reduction in aggregate demand – through a reduction in the money supply – such that AD is made to shift to AD′. This will, however, decrease output from y_0 at P_0 to y_1 at P_1 due to the supply shock and then to y_1', due to the reduction in the money supply and its implied shift of the AD curve to AD′. Hence, the monetary policy would have increased the fall in output over that which would have occurred if the monetary policy had not been pursued.

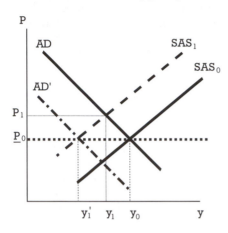

Figure 12.7a

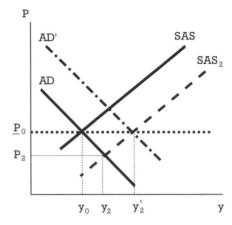

Figure 12.7b

Similarly, suppose that the aggregate supply shock had been a positive one, as shown in Figure 12.7b. This would shift SAS to SAS_2, resulting in the increase in output from y_0 to y_2 and the decrease in prices from P_0 to P_2. The monetary authority could change aggregate demand to stabilize the price level at $\underline{P}_0$ but this would mean an expansionary monetary policy which shifts the AD curve to AD′ and further increases output to y_2'. Price stabilization has, therefore, again increased the fluctuation in output.

Therefore, the pursuit of price stability in the face of supply-side fluctuations has the cost of increasing the instability of output – and, therefore, of unemployment – in the economy.

We have used positively sloped short-run aggregate curves in the above analysis. We leave it to the reader to adapt the arguments to the case of a vertical long-run supply curve.

12.4   MONETARY AND RESERVE AGGREGATES AS TARGETS

Intuitively, the most obvious target of monetary policy would seem to be one of the monetary aggregates or one of the concepts of reserves, and the 1970s monetarists recommended their use over other variables. The theoretical analysis within the IS–LM framework of targeting money supply has already been presented in section 12.3.2.

The monetary aggregates often suggested as targets are M1 or M2 – and M4 in Britain – though sometimes even broader targets are also considered. The reserve concepts often suggested for targeting are the monetary base, the reserves of the commercial banks, free reserves and borrowed reserves.

Monetary aggregates as targets

Milton Friedman and the 1970s monetarists, belonging to the St Louis School, had argued that because of the existence of both a direct and indirect transmission mechanism from the money supply to aggregate expenditures, the money supply rather than interest rates provided better control over the economy. Further, the Keynesian discretionary monetary policies of the early 1970s, using interest rates as the targets, had produced stagflation, so that there was a reaction against both discretionary monetary policy and the use of interest rates as targets. As a result, most countries – including the USA, Britain and Canada – switched to the targeting of monetary aggregates after the mid-1970s.

Monetary aggregate targeting was predicated in the belief that the relationship between such a target and aggregate demand was stable and had a short and predictable lag. This was certainly the finding of the studies done by the St Louis School. Monetary targets were pursued in the late 1970s and early 1980s by the monetary authorities in the USA, Canada and the UK. However, the functional relationships between the monetary variables and aggregate expenditures, let alone the rate of inflation, proved to be unstable, so that they had been abandoned by the 1990s in each of these countries. Among the reasons for this instability were financial innovations and changes in the payments technology occurring in recent decades.[5]

Targeting the monetary base or banks' reserves

The advantages and disadvantages of using the monetary base or one of the reserve concepts flow from their close relationship to the money supply. The advantage of using banks' reserves is that they are closely related to demand deposits and credit extended by banks, with changes in such reserves reflecting changes in the banks' capability to extend credit and create demand deposits. A related concept is that of bank reserves available to support 'private non-bank deposits'. This has the advantage of excluding reserves required for interbank and government deposits in the commercial banks. Free reserves have the advantage that they exclude required reserves, which are not available for lending in any case, and also exclude borrowed reserves against which banks tend to be reluctant to extend credit. Free reserves then represent the capacity of the banks to extend further credit.

In common with other targets, the reserve concepts share the disadvantage that their values are market-determined, so that their observed values change with demand and supply. We illustrate the nature of this problem by considering the use of free reserves as a guide. In this role, free reserves are taken to be an indicator of monetary tightness. As an endogenous variable, they depend on the discount rate, so that if the discount rate is lowered, banks find it more profitable to expand credit at the expense of their free reserve holdings. This reduced level of free reserves would indicate monetary tightness when, in fact, the reduction in the discount rate indicates relative monetary ease. As a variation on this example, suppose that the banks hold $100 million of free reserves at the prevailing rates of interest. Assume that the central bank views these as an indicator of monetary tightness and increases the monetary base by $50 million through open market operations, in an attempt to raise free reserves to a desirable level of $150 million. But banks only wish to hold $100 million of free reserves. They get rid of the excess by increasing their loans, thus increasing the money stock. If the central bank continues with its open market operations policy, the interest rates will eventually fall. Such a fall will make loans less profitable and induce banks to hold more free reserves. However, the desired increase in free reserves was brought about along with an expansion in the money supply that may not have been desired. Therefore, free reserves, in becoming a target of policy instead of merely being an indicator of market conditions, detract from the pursuit of the money supply as a target. Hence, the monetarists argue that the central bank should focus directly on the money supply or a reserve concept that is very closely related to the money supply. This suggests that it might be better to use the monetary base, the reserves of commercial banks and the private non-bank reserves of commercial banks as a target.

Problems with the use of monetary (including reserve) aggregates as targets

Note that the monetary aggregates and their related reserve variables are strictly more appropriate than interest rates for a quantity theorist but not for a Keynesian theorist. The latter argue, as in the IS–LM model, that changes in the monetary aggregates only impact on the national incomes and expenditures by changing interest rates. Consequently, it would be better to target interest rates rather than a variable that is further removed from nominal income. Further, if the impact of the monetary aggregates is uncertain or unstable or has long lags, the policy maker can exercise better control on the economy by targeting interest rates. This is also the case if the demand function for money and velocity are unstable, as experienced in the 1980s and 1990s in many economies.

In terms of experience during the late 1970s and 1980s, direct targeting of monetary aggregates increased both the level and the volatility of interest rates considerably, with the latter considered by many economists to be destabilizing for the economy.

Attempts to control the monetary or reserve aggregates directly, as a way of controlling the economy, were abandoned by most central banks in the early 1980s in favour of interest rate targets as the control variable. This is not to say that the monetary aggregates are not monitored and the changes in them not considered in formulating monetary policy. They are still among the indicators of the economy, but have ceased to be the control targets.

12.5 INTEREST RATES AS TARGETS

As we discussed in Chapter 11, the interest rates are currently the favourite operating targets and instruments of many central banks. The relevant theoretical analysis was presented in section 12.3.2 above. There are several measures of interest rates that may be considered, with the usual selection being of short-term nominal, rather than long-term or real, rates of interest.

The interest rates have been historically the most common target of monetary policy. A measure commonly used for this purpose has been the Treasury bill rate. This rate is a reflection of other interest rates in the economy and is a proxy for the interest rate variable in the short-run macroeconomic models. It is also a proxy for interest rates that form a fundamental part of the indirect transmission mechanism in the Keynesian models.

As discussed in Chapter 11, more recently, the USA, UK and Canada have used an overnight loan rate as an operating target. These countries have well-developed markets for overnight loans among financial institutions, with this market serving as the market for the excess reserves of banks. These reserves are partly held at the central bank and do not bear interest. This market for reserves is known as the Federal funds market in the United States and is the overnight loan one in Canada and the UK.

Such a rate reflects the commercial banks' demand and supply conditions for reserves. The central bank's policy actions on the monetary base immediately affect the commercial banks' demand and supply of reserves, thereby changing the overnight interest rate and starting a chain of reactions on other interest rates, and through these on the borrowing and lending, investment and consumer spending, etc., in the economy. A higher rate means that banks are relatively loaned up and a lower rate means that banks have relatively large free reserves and could increase loans of their own volition.

Problems with the use of interest rates in managing the economy

There are two basic objections to the use of short-term nominal interest rates as the guides or intermediate targets of monetary policy. First, as in the case of free reserves discussed above, the observed interest rates are equilibrium rates so that changes in them could reflect either changes in demand or supply conditions or both. Therefore, a rise in the interest rates may be due to an increase in the demand for loanable funds or a decrease in their supply, but the central bank may wish to take offsetting action in only one of these cases. For example, interest rates rise in an upturn in the business cycle. The central bank may not wish the upturn to be curbed by a decreased supply of funds but also may not wish to offset the stabilization effect of interest rates due to an increase in their demand. But changes in the equilibrium interest rates do not by themselves provide adequate information as to the causes of their rise and therefore as to the policy actions that should be undertaken. Therefore, the central bank has to, and does in practice, supplement its information on interest rates with other information on the demand and supply conditions before making its policy decisions.

As in the case of the reserve variables, the second basic objection to the use of interest rates as guides to monetary policy arises from one's belief in the structure of the economy. From the viewpoint of the 1970s monetarists, the interest rates could not be sufficiently reliable indicators since they are not part of the transmission process from the money supply to aggregate spending. From their viewpoint, money supply or one of the monetary base measures are more appropriate and reliable indicators than interest rates. But, in the Keynesian and modern classical approaches, monetary policy acts through interest rates on spending, so that the interest rates are closer in the chain of influence on spending. Hence, they are more reliable and more appropriate indicators of the need for action than are the various measures of money supply and the monetary base. In line with this, in financially developed economies, such as those of the USA, Canada and the UK, the central banks believe that the interest rates are a major indicator of the performance of the economy and tend to use them as the preferred guide and operating target of monetary policy.[6]

A problem with using interest rates as an operational target is that the central bank can determine the general level of interest rates but not equally well the differentials among them. Examples of these differentials are the loan-deposit spread of commercial banks, and the spread between the deposit rates and mortgage rates, if the latter are variable. Spreads depend upon market forces and can be quite insensitive/invariant to the central bank's discount rate. Financial intermediation in the economy is more closely a function of such differentials than of the level of interest rates, so that the ability of the central bank to influence the degree of financial intermediation through its discount rate becomes diluted.

Among other problems is the lag in the impact of changes in interest rate on aggregate demand in the economy. Among the reasons for such lags are the costs of adjustment of economic variables such as the capital stock and planned consumption expenditures, and the indirect income effects of changes in interest rates. There are two aspects of this lag: the length and the variability. The former is often assessed at about six quarters to two years in the United States, Britain and Canada. While there is agreement that there is some variability in the length of the lag, there is no consensus on whether it is so long that changes in interest rates, intended to be stabilizing, can prove to be destabilizing.[7] Within the lag, the impact effect of interest rate changes on real aggregate demand is estimated to be low, while the long-run effect is now believed to be very significant.

The actual use of interest rates for stabilization has often been found to be 'too little, too late' – though this is usually a result of the uncertainty about the need for and the lags in the effects of monetary policy. This results in its cautious use, no matter what operational or indicator variable is used. Given the duration of lags and the uncertainty at any time about the position of the economy in the business cycle, past experience indicates that central banks often change the interest rates later and in smaller steps than really needed. An initial change is, therefore, often followed by many more in the same direction over several quarters.

Overall comparison between interest rate targeting and money supply targeting

Given the theoretical implications of the IS–LM analysis for the two types of targets, an interest rate target is to be preferred if the dominant source of shifts in aggregate demand is from money demand or supply shifts, while a monetary aggregate target is to be preferred if the dominant source of shifts is in the IS variables. Both types of shifts occur over the business cycle, so that any target has to be used cautiously and with an eye to the evolution of the goal variables, such as aggregate demand, output, the rate of inflation, or some combination of these. However, these are not variables on which the central bank can operate directly, so that interest rates usually remain as the operating targets of monetary policy, even when other variables are intended to be the intermediate targets.

There seems to be a perceptible difference in the operation of monetary policy between Britain with its greater emphasis on interest rates as the operational targets and the United States where open market operations tend to receive more emphasis, though monetary policy is also conducted through interest rates. This is probably a reflection of the greater acceptance of Keynesian economics in Britain and of the monetarist prescriptions in the United States, as well as a difference in the size and diversity of the two economies. On the latter point, Britain has a highly concentrated banking system in a smaller economy, while the United States has a very diverse financial system, with thousands of commercial depository institutions. Further, there is also some difference in the institutional structure and practices. In the UK, a change by the central bank of its bank rate percolates almost immediately through the various interest rates in the economy since their base component is usually tied to the bank rate. However, in the USA, the connection between the Fed's discount rate and market rates is much looser and depends on market forces.

12.6 THE PRICE LEVEL OR THE RATE OF INFLATION AS A TARGET

The theoretical IS–LM analysis of targeting the price level has already been presented in section 12.3.

Given the problems with the use of intermediate variables as targets, a popular procedure in the 1990s has been to target the rate of inflation directly. With stable prices as the goal, the desirable target for the rate of inflation has often been about 1% to 2%. This range is generally considered to be consistent with the stability of the price level in the presence of the improvements in products, introduction of new products, and other biases in the measurement of the actual rate of inflation.

A low rate of inflation is sometimes justified as the ultimate goal of monetary policy. For this, it is argued that money is neutral in the long run, so that the monetary authority cannot change the level and path of full employment output, nor should it attempt to do so since such an attempt will only produce inflation. Under the neutrality argument, what the monetary authority can do is to ensure a stable value of money, so that its target should be in terms of the price level or the rate of inflation.

Alternatively, a low rate of inflation is justified as an intermediate goal. For this, the argument is that a stable price level reduces uncertainty in the economy and promotes the formulation and realization of optimal saving and investment, which in turn increase output and employment. Further, according to the modern classical school, higher inflation has higher costs, such as 'menu' and 'shoe leather' ones, without a benefit in terms of lower unemployment so that a low target for the inflation rate is preferable.

The rate of inflation is not an operating target, since the monetary authority cannot directly change it. To maintain a target range for the rate of inflation, the central bank will have to operate on the monetary aggregates and/or interest rates. Its success or failure will depend on the predictability of the relationships between the rate of inflation and these variables.

Since, as we have mentioned several times, the central banks of many countries have pursued price stability as a goal in the 1990s, a considerable amount of evidence has accumulated on it. This evidence shows that the pursuit of price stability as a goal has, in general, resulted in a reduction in inflation rates. However, this is not a surprising finding given the single-minded pursuit of this goal. What is in dispute is the impact of this policy on the levels and fluctuations in real output. Section 12.3 has already shown that targeting the price level tends to cause increased fluctuations in output and unemployment. As against this disadvantage, the reduction in inflation in the 1990s has lowered the market rates of interest, as implied by the Fisher equation on interest rates.

12.7 NOMINAL NATIONAL INCOME AS A TARGET

With the shifts in the velocity of the monetary aggregates in the 1980s, the relationship between these aggregates and nominal income became unstable, so that such aggregates could not be reliably used as the targets of monetary policy. This led to the proposal that nominal national income itself should be used as the target of monetary policy. One form of this proposal was to target nominal GDP, with its growth rate set at the growth rate of potential or full employment real output of the economy. In this role, nominal income would be an intermediate rather than an operating target or ultimate goal. Its advantage over the monetary aggregates is that it incorporates the effects of shifts in velocity on the economy. In the short run, maintaining a given target level of nominal income would mean that the exogenous shocks to aggregate demand would be offset through monetary policy and, therefore, will not impact on either prices or output. With aggregate demand thus held constant at the targeted level, a positive supply shock will lead to an increase in real output and a proportionate decrease in the price level, and a negative supply shock will lead to a decrease in real output, with a proportionate increase in the price level.

Figure 12.8a presents the AD–AS analysis of using nominal income as a target when there are shocks to aggregate demand. The initial aggregate demand curve is shown as AD and the short-run aggregate supply curve is shown as SAS. Given the initial general equilibrium at y_0 and P_0, assume that the central bank wants to stabilize nominal income Y at Y^*, equal to P_0 times y_0. Note that Y^* is not on one of the axes and does not explicitly appear within this figure. With nominal aggregate demand set at Y^*, Figure 12.8a shows AD* as the locus of all points at which nominal income will be equal to Y^*. AD* has a 45° angle with each of the axes and may be flatter or steeper than the AD curve. Figure 12.8a draws AD as steeper than AD*. Assume that aggregate demand shifts to AD_1. Since aggregate demand will be stabilized at AD* by the appropriate contractionary monetary policy, the economy will still generate P_0 and y_0, so that the exogenous shift in aggregate demand will not produce any impact on the economy. However, note that an activist monetary policy had to be pursued in order to stabilize Y at Y^*.

Figure 12.8b shows the case of a short-run negative supply shock – i.e., to SAS but not to LAS – under monetary targeting. The shift from SAS to SAS_1 will move the economy from point a to point b without pursuit of any monetary policy and to point c on AD* under nominal income targeting. In general, there is no clear basis for preferring c to b. Both imply a fall in real output and a rise in the price level. Further, while Figure 12.8b shows a greater price rise for AD than AD* because of the greater slope of AD, a lesser slope of AD relative to AD* would have produced a smaller price increase if nominal income targeting was not being implemented.

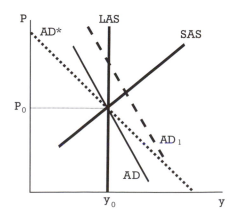

Figure 12.8a

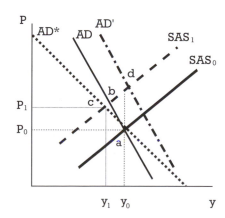

Figure 12.8b

Continuing with the case of shocks to the short-run aggregate supply curve, now compare the impact of nominal income targeting to the policy of targeting real output – i.e., in Figure 12.8a, stabilizing output at y_0. In Figure 12.8b, the latter policy would require using monetary policy to increase demand to AD′, which would yield a higher price level and constant output at point d. This would clearly produce a higher price level than targeting Y^* (which took the economy to point c). However, there is no general basis for preferring to be at c rather than at d, since the latter produces greater output at the cost of higher prices.

A better case can made for nominal income targeting versus real output targeting when there are long-run supply shocks. Their implications are shown in Figure 12.9. The initial equilibrium is again at point a. The adverse supply shock shifts the long-run aggregate supply curve from LAS to LAS_1 and the hands-off policy equilibrium to point b. Targeting Y^* takes the economy to point e. The policy of targeting real output would increase aggregate demand beyond AD in an attempt to stabilize output at y_0. This may be accomplished in the short run along an SAS curve, but, as Figure 12.9 shows, it cannot be achieved for the long run and will only set off a continuing inflation. Therefore, for long-run supply shocks, targeting nominal income is preferable to targeting real output but not necessarily to a hands-off monetary stance.

Therefore, the clear advantage of nominal income targeting is in stabilizing aggregate demand against shocks to it. Since shifts in the velocity of money and therefore in money demand change aggregate demand, targeting nominal income provides an escape from the instability resulting from a volatile velocity of money. However, since nominal income is not an operating target, its target level has to be achieved through changes in the monetary base or the interest rates. If the former is used, velocity is reintroduced in the link from the monetary aggregates to nominal income: if velocity is changing unpredictably, the impact of changes in the monetary or reserve aggregates on nominal income becomes unpredictable. An alternative would be to use interest rates as the operating target to achieve the pre-set nominal income target and to change these interest rates as required to offset the impact of the shifts in velocity and in aggregate demand.

Hence, while a nominal income target has the advantage of eliminating the impact of demand shocks on the economy, it does not necessarily provide a preferable solution when there are supply shocks. Further, nominal income targeting is normally an intermediate goal and not an ultimate goal so that it is itself a desirable procedure only if there is a stable and predictable relationship between nominal income and the final goal variables of stable prices and full employment output.

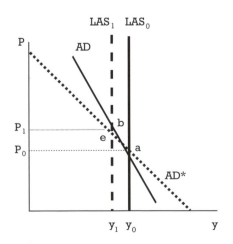

Figure 12.9

While the academic literature includes some support for nominal income targeting, central banks have stayed away from it.

12.8 TARGETING THE DEVIATION OF OUTPUT FROM FULL EMPLOYMENT

This is clearly a variable of concern to the policy makers. Keynesian economics implies that there can be significant deviations of output from its full employment level and these can occur for significant periods of time. The policy maker can, then, target a preferred level or range of deviation and use the monetary base and/or interest rates to achieve this target.

However, classical economists do not favour such a target in the belief that the economy tends to full employment on its own within a reasonable period. Alternatively, the classical economists believe that the actual deviations from full employment are caused by real shocks to the economy and cannot be ameliorated by monetary policy. A further problem with the pursuit of this target is the difficulty in measuring the full employment level, or its converse, the natural rate of unemployment. In any case, there currently seems to be little enthusiasm in the profession for such a target at a formal level. However, the deviation from full employment is definitely one of the variables figuring prominently in the discussions of the central bank policies.

12.9 CHOOSING AMONG MULTIPLE GOALS

As discussed in the last chapter, Keynesian economic theory and central bank beliefs prior to the 1980s had indicated that several goals could be addressed through monetary policy. For the analysis of such a possibility, this section assumes that the central bank has a multiplicity of goals at each level. Focusing only on the primary goals, the instruments available for achieving the multiple goals are severely limited in number and scope so that all the goals cannot be attained through the use of monetary policy. Therefore, the central bank has to make a choice among its desired goals or combinations of them.

Assume that the goal variables are quantifiable. Then the theory of choice, as among consumer goods in microeconomics, can be extended to the choices by a central bank over its goal variables. Assume that its choices over these variables are consistent and transitive. Therefore, its preferences can be stated in the form of an ordinal utility function over the goal variables. For diagrammatic analysis, the indifference curves between any given pair of these variables can be derived from this utility function.

Choosing between inflation and unemployment

To illustrate, assume that the goal variables are the rate of inflation and the unemployment rate. A lower value of each one of these variables is desirable to a higher one, so that the central bank's preferences over these variables can be encompassed in a preference or utility function,

$$U = U(\pi, u) \tag{4}$$

where π is the rate of inflation and u is the rate of unemployment, and U_π, $U_u < 0$. Hence, the indifference curves in the (π, u) space are negatively sloped. Further, it is reasonable to assume that the undesirability – that is, disutility – of each keeps on increasing, *ceteris paribus*, with higher levels of it, so that $U_{\pi\pi}$, $U_{uu} < 0$. Hence, as the rate of inflation rises, the central bank is willing to accept a higher marginal increase in the unemployment rate in order to prevent a further rise in the rate of inflation. Alternatively stated, the rate of substitution of the rate of inflation for marginal increases in the unemployment rate keeps on increasing. Indifference or tradeoff curves between the rates of inflation then have the usual convex shape, as shown in Figure 12.10 by the curves I^{CB} and I'^{CB}. A host of such curves exist, with a curve passing through every point in the quadrant. Note that since being on a lower curve is preferred to being on a higher one, the central bank will try to be on the lowest attainable indifference curve.

Choosing among the optimal values of the goals under a Phillips curve tradeoff

In achieving its preferences, assume that the central bank is subject to the constraint:

$$f(\pi, u) = 0 \quad d\pi/du < 0 \tag{5}$$

imposed by the economy on the tradeoffs that are achievable between these variables. Such a constraint is shown by the curve PC, with this notation standing for the 'Phillips curve', in Figure 12.10. In the context of inadequate or imperfect information on the structure of the economy, the tradeoff perceived by the central bank is likely to differ from the actual one. The former will be the relevant one in decision-making while the latter will be the relevant one for what actually gets achieved. For the time being, assume that there is sufficient information to make the perceived and actual constraints identical.

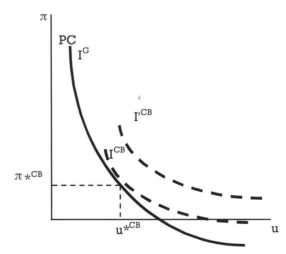

Figure 12.10

The general analysis of the choice among goals when the economy allows a tradeoff

This analysis can be generalized to the case of n variables, as in utility theory, with the basic results continuing to hold. The formal analysis of this general case assumes that the central bank maximizes a utility function:

$$U = U(x_1, \ldots, x_n) \tag{6}$$

subject to a constraint:

$$f(x_1, \ldots, x_n; \underline{z}, \underline{\Psi}) = 0 \tag{7}$$

where:

x_i ith goal variable
$\underline{z}$ vector of instruments available to the central bank
$\underline{\Psi}$ vector of exogenous variables

$U(\cdot)$ represents the central bank's preferences over its goals. These depend upon the organizational structure of the central bank, the interactions between the policy makers, their perceptions of society's goals, the structure of the economy and of what is achievable, political pressures, etc. Equation (7) specifies the constraint as it is perceived by the policy makers: it is specified by their perception of the structure of the economy and the political and social environment. As mentioned earlier, under imperfect information on the economy, this perceived constraint is not necessarily or even usually the actual one imposed by the economy.[8] The central bank maximizes (6) subject to (7) in order to determine its optimal choices among the goals.

The basic objections to the use of a preference function are to its requirements of consistency and transitivity in making choices. The central bank's decisions are made by a host of individuals and its major choices, if consciously made, are by a group. Such group decisions in a democratic framework need not necessarily be consistent and transitive, even at a point in time, let alone over time. Further, the policy makers in the central bank change over time, so that its preferences could shift over time as the decision makers change. Hence, one must be cautious in explaining the choices among goals made by the central bank within a static utility function and its implied set of indifference relationships.

In spite of these objections, the preceding analysis furnishes considerable insights into the problem of choice among alternative goals. Empirical and descriptive studies using data up to the 1980s indicate considerable validity for this analysis and show that the central banks often manipulated their policy instruments such as the monetary base[9] and interest rates in a systematic fashion to address their chosen goal levels.

Choices under a vertical Phillips curve

The modern classical school argues that unemployment can only be made to deviate from its natural rate through unanticipated inflation and, given rational expectations, this requires a random monetary policy. Hence, the long-run Phillips curve between unemployment and systematic changes in the inflation rate is vertical. Therefore, there is no tradeoff between these variables which systematic monetary policy by the central bank can exploit, so that the recommendation is that the central bank should adopt the target of price stability.

As discussed in the preceding chapter, many central banks adopted this economic framework in the 1990s and now believe that price stability or a low rate of inflation should be their only goal variable. In such a case, the question of a tradeoff among two or more goal variables does not arise. The central bank's utility function would be only over the rate of inflation. Further, in the 1990s, many central banks have believed that higher rates of inflation have little to contribute in terms of higher output, while they could lead to escalating inflation and lower output. At the same time, negative rates of inflation are considered inimical to full employment because of their potential for causing a recession. Given these beliefs, the utility-maximizing goal rate of inflation would be zero, or positive but close to zero. This is not to say that the fiscal authorities may not want a looser monetary policy at times, as in a recession, and be willing to risk higher rates of inflation than the central bank, so that there could be conflicts over the desired or permissible rates of inflation.

The above arguments leave the monetary authority's utility function (4) unchanged. This function was:

$$U = U(\pi, u) \quad U_{\pi}, U_{u} < 0 \tag{8}$$

But they modify its constraint to the expectations augmented Phillips curve, specified as:

$$f(\pi - E\pi, u - u_{n}) = 0 \tag{9}$$

where $du/dE\pi = 0$ and the use of a systematic monetary policy by the central bank can only change $E\pi$. Assuming that the monetary authority cannot directly change unemployment but can only change $E\pi$ through its systematic policies, the optimal systematic rate of inflation for this problem is zero, since inflation has a negative marginal utility.

On fiscal policy, given the accumulation of high levels of debt, with their resulting interest payments imposing a drain on tax revenues, many governments came to the conclusion in the 1990s that the goal level of the fiscal deficit – either actual or in full employment terms – should be zero or close to zero.

Balanced budgets and low rates of inflation, in turn, imply that the nominal rates of interest would be lower than otherwise. As discussed earlier in this chapter, the rate of interest is often used as an intermediate target of monetary policy, and its usual desired level is a low one, close to the real rate of interest.

A procedure for estimating the policy maker's tradeoffs among multiple goals

In cases where the policy makers have several objective variables, they rarely make explicit their utility function among these variables, so that such a function has to be deduced from their announcements or the policies actually pursued. One way of doing so is to determine the shape of the policy maker's indifference curves or tradeoffs among goals. This requires estimating the weights attached to the policy makers' goal variables. Assuming that the policy maker has only one instrument for achieving its several goals, one estimation procedure is to regress the instrument variable – a dependent variable – upon the goal variables.

As an illustration, in the case of the monetary targeting, one form of the regression equation would be:

$$M_t = a_0 + a_1 y_t + a_2 u_t + a_3 BP_t + a_4 CPI_t + a_4 M_{t-1} + \mu_t \tag{10}$$

where:

M the monetary aggregate used as the intermediate target
y real GDP
u rate of unemployment
BP balance of payments deficit
CPI consumer price index
μ stochastic variable

Equation (10) assumes that the intermediate target variable is a monetary aggregate and the goal variables are those included on the right side. If the intermediate target is the rate of interest and there is sufficient variation in it, it would become the dependent variable in (10).

In cases where the data is not available on the goal variables or is not considered appropriate, one can use published policy statements emanating from the central bank to find the relative importance it attaches to various goals. Thus, for the USA, the directives issued by the Federal Open Market Committee (FOMC) to the manager of its trading desk in the Federal Reserve Bank of New York can be examined for its first priority goal. These directives show that the FOMC's major concerns were with growth and balance of payments in the first half of the 1960s but shifted to inflation and growth in the second half of the decade and in the 1970s. The main goals emphasized in these policy statements in the 1990s were inflation and, to some extent, the balance of payments.

12.10 THE CONFLICTS AMONG POLICY MAKERS: THEORETICAL ANALYSIS

Another application of the utility approach is to the choices exercised by several (at least two) policy makers over the same set of goal variables. Different policy-making bodies in the economy are likely to have different preference functions and hence different indifference curves between any given pair of variables. Therefore, the formal optimization analysis for two policy makers A and B would be:

1 For policy maker A:

$$\text{maximize} \quad U^A = U^A(x_1, \dots , x_n) \tag{11}$$

subject to A's perceived constraint:

$$f^A(x_1, \dots , x_n; \underline{z}, \underline{\Psi}) = 0 \tag{12}$$

2 For policy maker B:

$$\text{maximize} \quad U^B = U^B(x_1, \dots , x_n) \tag{13}$$

subject to B's perceived constraint:

$$f^B(x_1, \dots , x_n; \underline{z}, \underline{\Psi}) = 0 \tag{14}$$

where the superscripts A and B refer to the policy maker. Since both the utility functions and the perceived constraints can differ, the optimal values of the goals for $x_1^A, \dots , x_n^A$ will differ from $x_1^B, \dots , x_n^B$, so that working at cross-purposes can be a common phenomenon, rather than a rare occurrence, among policy makers in the economy. This possibility depends upon the differences in the utility functions, becoming reinforced by any differences in the policy makers' perceptions of the actual present and anticipated course of the economy. In most cases, such conflicts in the understanding of the economy and desirable tradeoffs among objectives by the fiscal and monetary authorities of a given country usually tend to be mild. However, they can erupt into open and sometimes acrimonious public debate in times of radical economic and political change and of differences in ideology.

The two principal tools for the control of the economy are monetary and fiscal policies. In a country with an independent central bank, the former is in the control of the central bank, while the latter is in the hands of the legislature and the executive branches of government. The latter depend on the public for electoral support and generally tend to attach greater undesirability to increases in unemployment than to increases in inflation, than does the central bank that is more vitally concerned with inflation. Formally, in terms of the marginal rates of substitution of the two policy makers, $(\partial \pi / \partial u)^{CB} < (\partial \pi / \partial u)^G$, where CB stands for the central bank and G for the fiscal authority, implying in Figure 12.11 that the indifference curves of the central bank are steeper than of the government. This implies that for a given constraint $f(\pi, u) = 0$, the central bank would adopt a monetary policy aimed at achieving a lower rate of inflation than the government. This is illustrated in Figure 12.11 in which the central bank's indifference curves are shown by I^{CB}, the government's by I^G, and the economy's (common) constraint is shown by PC. The central bank's optimal choice is for (π^{*CB}, u^{*CB}) and the government's is for (π^{*G}, u^{*G}), implying a more expansive stance by the government relative to that by the central bank for the economy. Therefore, there exists in this case a conflict between the central bank and the government on the desired rates of inflation and unemployment for the economy. If each tries to achieve its goals through the policy at its command, neither will achieve its goals.

Over time, the political process may bring about a narrow 'consensus range' within which the differences between the central bank and the government in the desired goals are mild and accommodation is made easily. But a sharp change in the course of the economy outside such a range or a sharp change in the objective functions of one of the parties to the process, as after an election that brings a new political party with a different ideology to power, may provoke an open conflict between the policy makers which takes time to resolve.

The potential for conflicts between two independent policy makers leads to strategic considerations where each 'player' tries to outsmart the other, with the theoretical analysis appropriate to such interactions belonging to game theory. Such analysis is outside the scope of this book. A review of it is provided in Blackburn and Christensen (1989).

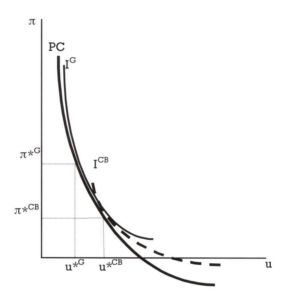

Figure 12.11

12.11 THE CONFLICTS AMONG POLICY MAKERS: EMPIRICAL ILLUSTRATIONS

12.11.1 An illustration from the USA

Conflicts, though of a minor character, are common between the monetary and fiscal authorities in the United States. Monetary policy in the United States is in the control of the Board of the Governors of the Federal Reserve System. Each member of this Board is appointed for fourteen years, an exceptionally lengthy appointment, which makes the Board virtually independent of any particular President or the Congress at any given time. Further, the legal framework makes the Federal Reserve Board of Governors independent of the President and Congress. The latter are in control of the budget and therefore of fiscal policy. Differences between the monetary and fiscal authorities in the choices among goals are, therefore, a distinct possibility at the best of times and can be acrimonious at the worst of times.

An example of the actual differences that can arise and their solution was the 1951 Accord between the Federal Reserve and the Treasury. The fundamental cause of the controversy lay in two long-run developments during the first half of the twentieth century. One of these was the massive growth in the public debt due to the heavy deficit financing during the two world wars and the Treasury's concern with keeping its interest cost as low as possible. The other factor was the setting up of the Federal Reserve System in 1913. It was charged by law with the responsibility for maintaining the stability of prices, which after 1935 was attempted through open market operations. Both the Treasury and the Fed were, therefore, operating in the market for government bonds. The aim of the Treasury was to maintain stable bond prices and a low rate of interest while that of the Fed attempted to restrain aggregate demand by restricting the money supply, an action that pushes up interest rates and increases the Treasury's costs of servicing the public debt.

The Federal Open Market Committee (FOMC), set up in 1935, declared in 1937 and 1938 that it was a part of its responsibility to ensure a fair degree of stability in the market prices of government securities. During the Second World War, this assumption of responsibility hardened into a compact with the Treasury for the maintenance of a fixed pattern of interest rates in order to ensure the financing of US war expenditures by borrowing at relatively low interest rates in the financial markets. These rates ranged from 0.375% on ninety-day Treasury bills to 2.5% for twenty-year bonds. During the war, there was a considerable increase in the public's and the banks' holdings of government securities, so that there was a drastic increase in liquidity in the economy and the prices of commodities had to be held in check by direct price controls. There was also continual upward pressure on market interest rates because of massive increases in the public debt. The Federal Reserve's commitment to a fixed pattern of interest rates on government securities meant that it could not drain the economy of its excess liquidity by selling bonds to the public at higher interest yields. Hence, the Federal Reserve had lost any power to influence the monetary base of the economy, leaving its determination to the discretion of the commercial banks.

At the end of the Second World War in 1945, the Federal Reserve sought to recapture its control over the monetary base and over interest rates in the economy by abandoning the established pattern of rates, restricting liquidity in the economy, and thereby forcing the market interest rates to rise. The Treasury, accustomed to the convenience of the established system and trying to minimize the very heavy interest payments on the then relatively large public debt, wanted to maintain the established pattern of low interest rates. The resulting conflict between the Federal Reserve and the Treasury became a matter of public knowledge and debate, with the President and Congress also brought into the open dispute, with the President taking the Treasury viewpoint. The dispute lasted till March 1951 when an accord was reached between the Treasury and the Federal Reserve which asserted the independence of the Federal Reserve to conduct its monetary operations, without having to maintain the par value of Treasury issues and the existing pattern of interest rates. However, prior consultations between the Treasury and the Federal Reserve were required for any changes of a major nature in debt management or credit policy. Monetary policy was thus effectively freed from the shackles of debt management policy, an independence which is still being maintained though minor conflicts still occur. In the 1970s, these often concerned the issue of controlling inflation by a tight monetary policy or by prices and incomes controls. However, a high degree of consultation between the authorities has limited the conflicts.

12.11.2 An illustration from Canada

An instructive case of conflict – and its mode of resolution – between the monetary and fiscal agencies arose in Canada in the late 1950s and early 1960s. Monetary policy in Canada is formulated by the Bank of Canada. Its chairman and chief executive officer is the Governor of the Bank. It has a board of directors, whose members are appointed for three-year terms and, subject to the approval of the Cabinet, choose the Governor and the Deputy Governor for seven-year terms. The latter terms are longer than those of the average duration of about four years between elections for Parliament, so that an incoming government or Prime Minister is not necessarily able to immediately appoint a new Governor of the Bank.

The Bank of Canada pursued a continuous policy of monetary restraint from mid-1955 to mid-1957 and from 1958 to 1961 in an attempt to keep inflationary pressures in check.

There was widespread public criticism of such policies in the face of what the politicians and the public considered to be unacceptably high rates of unemployment. The governments of the day dissociated themselves from the Bank's unpopular policies, claiming that the government had no power under existing legislation to give instructions to the Bank on the monetary policy to be pursued. The only power it possessed was one of appointment of the Bank's directors and, in the limiting case, of firing the Governor through the process of impeachment by Parliament. This view was supported by the then Governor of the Bank, J. E. Coyne, who argued that:

> The bank is not in the position of daily receiving instructions – or indeed receiving instructions at all – from the government in those matters which by statute are assigned to the responsibility of the management of the bank ...
>
> (Commons Committee on Banking and Commerce, Minutes, 1956, pp. 373–75)

Hence, Governor Coyne argued that the Bank did not have to pursue the monetary policy that the government wanted it to follow: the Bank was independent of the government in setting and pursuing the monetary policies that it considered to be the appropriate ones in the terms of its goals, its view of the state of the economy and its beliefs about the efficacy of monetary policies. Correspondingly, the government was responsible for fiscal and public debt policies and was free to pursue those as it thought fit.

The Bank's policies eventually proved so embarrassing for the government that it felt that it had to obtain Governor Coyne's resignation, even through the use of the politically costly process of impeachment. He did eventually resign under this threat of impeachment, but not without a serious political crisis for the government itself. The new Governor of the Bank, Louis Rasminsky, was agreeable to a compromise on the Bank's independence, as stated by him in:

> I do suggest a precise formula but have in mind two main principles to be established: (1) in the ordinary course of events, the Bank has the responsibility for monetary policy, and (2) if the government disapproves of the monetary policy being carried out by the Bank it has the right and the responsibility to direct the Bank as to the policy which the Bank is to carry out.
>
> The first principle is designed to ensure that the Bank has the degree of independence and responsibility necessary if it is, in the language of the Bank of Canada Act, 'to regulate credit and currency in the best interests of the economic life of the nation'. To discharge this duty the Bank must be sufficiently independent and responsible in its operations to be able to withstand day-to-day pressures from any source. But in the longer run, if there should develop a serious and persistent conflict between the views of the government and the views of the central bank with regard to monetary policy which, after prolonged and conscientious efforts on both sides, cannot be resolved, the Minister of Finance should be able formally to instruct the Bank what monetary policy it wishes carried out and the Bank should have the duty to comply with these instructions. The exercise of this authority by government would place on government direct responsibility for the monetary policy to be followed. If this policy, as communicated to the Bank, was one which the Governor felt he could not in good conscience carry out, his duty would be to resign and to make way for someone who took a different view.
>
> (Public statement by the Governor of the Bank of Canada, issued 1 August 1961)

This relationship was formalized in the Bank of Canada Act of 1967. Under it, in the case of a serious conflict and after consultation with the Bank, the Minister of Finance has the right to issue instructions to the Bank of Canada on monetary policy. This directive must be in specific terms and for a specific period. It must also be immediately published and be laid before Parliament, so that the government is publicly made to bear responsibility for its instructions. However, governments have been reluctant to bear the consequences of such an appropriation of monetary policy, which, among other effects, is likely to cause turmoil in the financial and foreign exchange markets, so that such instructions have never been given. As against the formal nature of such interference by the government in monetary policy, there is continual informal consultation between the Bank of Canada and the Department of Finance on monetary and macroeconomic conditions and policies. In fact, in recent years, both the Bank of Canada and the government have jointly agreed that the goal for monetary policy should be a low rate of inflation (in the range from 1% to 3%).

In practice, monetary policy in Canada remains under the sole jurisdiction of the Bank of Canada and the Bank is independent of the fiscal authorities, the government and Parliament in the formulation of its goals and targets, and in the use of policy instruments.

12.11.3 Conflicts in the UK

The Bank of England was a privately owned bank prior to 1946 and there were numerous instances in which the British government objected to the policies which the Bank had followed, sometimes resulting in calls for the nationalization of the Bank, which was done in 1946. From 1946 to 1997, the control of monetary policy both in terms of setting goals and their implementation was assigned to the Chancellor of the Exchequer, so that the potential for conflicts between the goals pursued by monetary policy and those by fiscal policy was minimized.

Since 1997, the Bank of England does not possess independence in setting the ultimate goal or goals of monetary policy but does possess operational independence in achieving the goals set by the government. Further, the Chancellor can, 'in extreme circumstances', give instructions to the Bank on interest rates for a specific period. Therefore, the possibility of an open conflict between the monetary policy as implemented by the Bank and the Monetary Policy Committee is likely to be much more limited in the British context.

12.12 THE INDEPENDENCE OF THE CENTRAL BANK

As shown by the preceding analysis and examples, potential conflicts are inherent in a situation where the central bank is free to formulate monetary policy independently of the government, which is in charge of the fiscal policies and the management of the public debt. This conflict can be about the ultimate goals of full employment and price stability. However, it is more often about intermediate targets, such as the desirable levels of the interest rates or exchange rates, or because of the introduction of other ancillary objectives such as the costs of servicing the public debt or financing fiscal deficits.

The potential for conflicts can be avoided by the subordination of the central bank to the government. As explained in section 12.11, this was done in the USA during the Second World War and till 1949 by a certain amount of the subordination in practice of the Fed to the Treasury. The Fed is now one of the most independent central banks in the world.

In Canada, the ostensible subordination of the Bank of Canada to the government was done, first through an understanding and then through legislation: the government can give directions to the Bank of Canada on monetary policy but only if it is publicly seen to have done so and after consultation with the Bank. It is likely that such a directive would trigger the resignation of the Governor of the Bank and lead to considerable turbulence in the financial markets and the value of the Canadian dollar. It has never been issued. In practice, the Bank of Canada has retained its independence, though there is close consultation between the Governor and the Minister of Finance on inflation targets and policy changes.

The British experiments with the independence have varied over time.[10] While the Bank of England was historically a quasi-private bank, independent of the government, the dominance of the government over the Bank of England was legislated by the Bank Act of 1946, which nationalized its ownership. It also allocated the choice over the goals and targets of monetary policy to the Chancellor of the Exchequer, representing the government, leaving the Bank of England with a consultative and implementation role. In 1997, the Bank of England and the Monetary Policy Committee were given operational independence towards the achievement of the inflation target set by the Chancellor. These arrangements were enacted into law by the Bank of England Act of 1998.

Under it, the Chancellor sets the goals of monetary policy – currently a target value of the inflation rate – and the Bank and the Monetary Policy Committee have the responsibility of formulating and implementing policies for their achievement.

Therefore, as of 1999, Britain allocates only operational but not goal independence to its central bank. At a formal level, this degree of independence differs from that of the central banks of Canada and the USA, both of which possess both goal and operational independence. The independence of the Bank of England is likely to be further truncated as and when Britain joins the European Monetary Union, in which case the Bank of England will become one of the national banks within the federal structure of the European System of Central Banks.

In many other countries, including many LDCs, the subordination of the central bank to the fiscal authorities is fairly common in practice, even if legally the central bank is independent.

Such lack of independence of the central bank in the formulation and pursuit of monetary policy represents a threat to the pursuit of appropriate monetary policies for price stability, a frequent objective of central banks, rather than those serving governmental or fiscal interests. Many empirical studies for the 1970s and 1980s have shown that countries that retained actual independence of the central bank tended to have lower rates of inflation; conversely, the lack of independence resulted in higher inflation rates (Alesina and Summers, 1993). A foremost example of the former is that of the German Bundesbank which has had complete independence for several decades and has maintained low rates of inflation.

Development strategies in LDCs, financing fiscal deficits and central bank independence

This issue takes on another dimension in countries that incur large and persistent deficits but do not possess adequate capital markets to finance these through new issues of public debt, and need the central bank to finance them through an expansion of the monetary base. This often happens during wars even in the developed economies, but has occurred most noticeably in recent decades in the LDCs.

LDCs tend to have low output per capita and are not able to raise adequate revenue for their desired levels of public expenditures. The latter are in many countries swollen by their plans for public development projects or the deficits of their public sector undertakings. Further, their domestic financial markets are underdeveloped and cannot support much, if any, government borrowing, and their ability to borrow abroad is also severely limited. As a result, many LDCs resort to increases in the monetary base either directly or indirectly through the compulsory sale of government bonds to the central bank. This process requires the subservience of the central bank and its policies to the needs of the fiscal authorities, and destroys the central bank's independent control over monetary policy.

Whether such an arrangement is advantageous to the economy is in considerable doubt. On the positive side is the financing of public projects that would otherwise not have been financed. On the negative side is the subordination of increases in the monetary base to budget deficits, with the consequent loss in control by the central bank over monetary policy and over aggregate demand and inflation in the economy. Another negative aspect of this arrangement is that the borrowing for the public projects thus financed is not done in competitive markets at market-determined rates. Hence, as argued earlier, allocative efficiency suffers and private projects that could be more efficient and could have been undertaken, are crowded out. These efficiency losses could be considerable and in the opinion of many economists have contributed to the low growth of those LDCs which, in the past, resorted heavily to the financing of governmental deficits by increases in the monetary base.

In any case, from the perspective of price stability, the loss of control of the monetary base by the central bank severely limits its capacity to control the rate of inflation in the economy. Many empirical studies have documented that countries with independent central banks, which are not obligated to necessarily finance the budget deficits, tend to have lower rates of inflation.

Central bank independence in practice

A country can have laws formally legislating the independence of its central bank from the government. However, its independence in practice will usually also depend on additional factors, such as the mode of appointment of the central bank directors, the duration and terms of appointment, their relationship with those in the legislature and the government, power politics, and how the spirit of the law is respected in the country in question. On this point, Cukierman *et al.* (1993) reported that while legal independence was an important determinant, with a negative coefficient, of inflation in the industrialized economies, the rate of inflation was strongly and positively related to the central bank governor's rate of turnover, rather than to legal independence, in the developing economies.

Hence, legal independence does not always ensure factual independence. In general, the factual independence of the central bank from the government of the day normally depends on its acceptance by the main political parties of the country and substantive support for it among the public. This acceptance, in turn, depends on the rule of law in the country, the belief in the integrity and commitment of the central bank directors and governors and the past record of the central bank, as well as the transparency of its policies and its accountability.[11]

Goodhart (1994) finds that central bank independence, if effective, is a way of making its commitment to price stability more credible and makes the achievement of low inflation more likely. But he finds no evidence that it lowers unemployment or the 'loss ratio' defined as 'the number of extra man-years of unemployment necessary to lower inflation by one per cent' (p. 68). Eijffinger and de Hahn (1996) from their review of the empirical studies concluded that the weight of empirical evidence supports the claim that the central bank independence of the government reduces inflation. However, central bank independence does not seem to have increased employment and growth. Further, there were higher rather than lower disinflation costs associated with independent central banks.

12.13 TIME-CONSISTENT POLICIES VERSUS DISCRETIONARY ONES, AND POLICY RULES

Adequate analysis of central bank policy requires consideration of its decision making over several periods. This section presents the theoretical analysis on whether the authorities should decide on an optimal policy rule once and for all and stick to it or whether they should retain discretion to reformulate their decision for each period when they reach it. Friedman's monetary rule is clearly of the former type, as are policy rules that operate with fixed values of the parameters across periods. Keynesians, in general, favour giving the monetary authorities discretion to change the rule (function and/or the values of its parameters) being pursued over time. To consider this issue, we need to define *consistent* and *discretionary* policies for an intertemporal context.

An intertemporal or time-consistent policy is defined as one that maintains the predetermined time pattern of policies. While the predetermined policies can vary over different periods, the set of such policies is determined at the beginning of the first period and adhered to subsequently. They represent an intertemporally fixed policy set. A discretionary policy set is one under which the policies pre-set for the future periods can be changed as time passes. In each case, we will assume that the policy pursued is the optimal one.

The time-consistent policy with a predetermined policy pattern over time involves the derivation of a policy set at the opening of period 1 under intertemporal optimization over *all* periods and its maintenance as time passes. Under such a policy, no currently anticipated future shocks to the economy will lead to deviations from these predetermined policies. By comparison, the discretionary policy involves the re-derivation of the optimal policy path each period from intertemporal optimization involving *only* the current and future periods, even if there are no unanticipated shocks. The latter procedure sheds past periods and information on them from successive optimization exercises as time passes. A compact way of differentiating between the two policies is that a time-consistent policy renders a once-for-all decision on the future policy *path* while a discretionary policy renders new policy paths as each period arrives. The intuitive presumption is that the latter procedure is preferable since it maintains continuous policy flexibility and since, with re-optimization at the beginning of each period, it ignores from decision making what is gone and past. However, this intuitive presumption has been called into question. This section examines whether time-consistent or discretionary policies are preferable for a given intertemporal structure of the economy, using the contribution of Kydland and Prescott (1977) for our theoretical framework.

Assume a two-period horizon and let the objective function of the policy maker over the two periods be:

$$U = U(x_1, x_2, \pi_1, \pi_2) \tag{15}$$

where:

    U policy maker's preference function over policies
    x_t economic agents' decision variable for time t, $t = 1, 2$
    π_t policy variable for period t

Economic agents are assumed to take account of the policies pursued in making their decisions on x_t so that:

$$x_1 = x_1(\pi_1, \pi_2) \tag{16}$$

$$x_2 = x_2(x_1, \pi_1, \pi_2) \tag{17}$$

Note that since we have not allowed for uncertainty, the future values of the variables are known at the beginning of period 1. We assume that there are no other constraints to be taken into consideration.

For the intertemporal optimization for the consistent policy path, both the policy decisions π_1, π_2 are made in period 1. To derive these decisions, substitute (16) and (17) in (15). This gives:

$$U(\cdot) = U(x_1(\pi_1, \pi_2), x_2(x_1(\pi_1, \pi_2), \pi_1, \pi_2), \pi_1, \pi_2) \tag{18}$$

For the optimal values of π_1 and π_2, the policy maker maximizes $U(.)$ in (18) with respect to π_1 and π_2, so that the two Euler conditions can be solved for the optimal values π_1^* and π_2^*. However, for the argument below, we need only to consider the first-order condition with respect to π_2, which is:

$$\left[\frac{\partial U}{\partial x_1} \cdot \frac{\partial x_1}{\partial \pi_2} + \frac{\partial U}{\partial x_2} \cdot \frac{\partial x_2}{\partial x_1} \cdot \frac{\partial x_1}{\partial \pi_2} \right] + \left[\frac{\partial U}{\partial x_2} \cdot \frac{\partial x_2}{\partial \pi_2} + \frac{\partial U}{\partial \pi_2} \right] = 0 \tag{19}$$

This simplifies to:

$$\frac{\partial U}{\partial x_2} \cdot \frac{\partial x_2}{\partial \pi_2} + \frac{\partial U}{\partial \pi_2} + \frac{\partial x_1}{\partial \pi_2}\left[\frac{\partial U}{\partial x_1} + \frac{\partial U}{\partial x_2} \cdot \frac{\partial x_2}{\partial x_1}\right] = 0 \tag{20}$$

For the discretionary policy path, in period 1, the policy maker chooses π_1^* and π_2^*, as before. However, in period 2, π_1 and x_1 are in the past, and the decision made in period 2 is based on the maximization with respect to only π_2 of:

$$U = U(x_1, x_2, \pi_1, \pi_2) \tag{21}$$

subject to:

$$x_2 = x_2(x_1, \pi_1, \pi_2) \tag{22}$$

$$x_1 = \underline{x}_1 \tag{23}$$

and

$$\pi_1 = \underline{\pi}_1^* \tag{24}$$

where the underlining indicates given values and the constraint (16) is no longer relevant. Substituting (22) to (24) in (21) gives the optimization problem as the maximization of:

$$U(\cdot) = U(\underline{x}_1, x_2(\underline{x}_1, \underline{\pi}_1^*, \pi_2), \underline{\pi}_1^*, \pi_2) \tag{25}$$

The first-order maximization condition for (25) is:

$$\frac{\partial U}{\partial x_2} \cdot \frac{\partial x_2}{\partial \pi_2} + \frac{\partial U}{\partial \pi_2} = 0 \tag{26}$$

Let the solution to (26) be π_2^{**}. Equation (26) will differ from (20) unless:

$$\frac{\partial x_1}{\partial \pi_2}\left[\frac{\partial U}{\partial x_1} + \frac{\partial U}{\partial x_2} \cdot \frac{\partial x_2}{\partial x_1}\right] = 0 \tag{27}$$

If (27) is not satisfied, which it will not be for many forms of the $U(\cdot)$ and $x_2(\cdot)$ functions, π_2^{**} will differ from π_2^*. Since the consistent policy path (π_1^*, π_2^*) maximized intertemporal utility, (π_1^*, π_2^{**}) will yield a lower utility level. Hence, the discretionary policies will not be intertemporally optimal from the *a priori* viewpoint. This suboptimality of discretionary policies does not arise because of myopia – i.e., the failure to recognize future effects – since each decision is based on *current* and *future* effects. The reason for this suboptimality is that the discretionary policies adopted in period 2 will ignore the impact of such policies, had they been known in advance, on *past* decisions on π_1 and x_1.

Hence, for the policy maker to pursue intertemporally consistent optimal policies, it must stick to π_2^* in period 2, even though reoptimization would now yield a different policy π_2^{**}. In practice, economic agents could know π_2^* and π_2^{**}, and some would find it to their advantage to have the latter rather than the former pursued, thereby leading to pressure on the policy maker to pursue π_2^{**}. However, for intertemporal optimization, the policy maker must resist such pressure. And if the economic agents are not to count on being able to pressure the policy maker into π_2^{**}, the policy maker must have a credible reputation for sticking to its pre-announced policies.

Some illustrations of time-consistent versus discretionary policies

Kydland and Prescott illustrated the above analysis by some examples. Consider one from patent policy. Suppose that economic agents will not invest in research and no innovations will occur unless the innovators can patent them and earn monopoly profits from them. Social welfare will be maximized if the innovations do occur, so that the optimal policy will be to allow patenting and to maintain this policy over time. However, once the inventions have already occurred in period 1 and been granted patents for both periods 1 and 2, the optimal policy in period 2, under a discretionary policy regime for social welfare maximization, will be to cancel past patents, even though such a policy of repudiation of patents granted in period 1 would not have been optimal *ex ante*.

Further, once we eliminate the assumption that there are only two periods and recognize that there is a continuing sequence of periods, the credibility of the policy maker for the future becomes relevant. If the patent protection is removed in period 2, investors would no longer allocate resources to innovating and society would be worse off without these innovations. If the policy makers realize this in period 3 and announce a renewal of patent protection, their experience with the removal of patent protection in period 2 would make them doubt whether such protection will not again be removed. With such scepticism about the continuance of a patent protection policy, investors will not allocate resources to innovations and they would not occur in period 3, even though patent protection is being offered. Therefore, once the credibility of policy is brought into the analysis, the social welfare maximizing policy even for period 2 is to stick to the *ex ante* optimal policies and to have the reputation of doing so.

We now illustrate the relevance of the time-consistency analysis to monetary policy. Suppose the central bank had announced and insisted that it was determined to follow for the future a counter-inflationary policy, and the public had made its economic decisions on investment, etc., accordingly. However, once short-term pressures mount, from the government facing an election or from supply shock to the economy, the central bank would be tempted to adopt an expansionary monetary policy. If it did so, the ensuing inflation would cause the public to doubt the central bank's commitment to the anti-inflationary policies and disdain any further rhetoric about it. As a result, investment and growth are likely to be lower and inflation higher than if the central bank had stayed with its original commitment.

Therefore, the monetary authority should announce clearly specified policies for the future and stick to them. Changes in the announced policies over time under conditions that were anticipated would be suboptimal.

Qualifications to the conclusions on the time consistency of policies

Note that the above conclusion on the superiority of consistent/fixed policy paths to discretionary ones holds only for anticipated events. They apply in the static environment with known objective probabilities of all potential outcomes. If these are not known or the subjective probabilities which are the ones which enter into the decision are not identical with the objectives ones, or if there are unanticipated shifts in them, as emphasized by Keynesians, then the above analysis does not properly apply.

To illustrate this limitation of the above analysis, it assumes that there will be no unanticipated shifts in the policy maker's preference function and the economy's constraints over time. Consequently, one limitation of the above analysis is that it does not take into account the likelihood of unanticipated non-transitory/non-random shifts in the economy. In the above model, if there are no such changes, the intertemporally fixed policy will be the optimal one from an *ex ante* viewpoint. However, if such formerly unanticipated shifts happen to occur at the beginning of period 2 and policy can thenceforth take account of them, then the *ex post* optimal policy will be the one that revises the second period's policy on that basis. Further, if it is already known that there is a good possibility that there will be unanticipated shifts (whose nature is not known in advance and which, if they occur, will change the structure of the economy in a non-transient manner), then the rational policy maker should keep his options open for the future. In fact, the change may be such that, with re-optimization, the intertemporal utility level attained would be higher than the *ex ante* anticipated intertemporal utility level without reoptimization.

The implication of these arguments is that, in order to maximize social welfare, the authorities should stick to a pre-announced policy path unless the economy changes in an unanticipated manner. Further, the authorities should not deliberately induce unanticipated inflation, for example, in order to take advantage of a tradeoff between unanticipated inflation and unemployment.[12]

Feedback policies

Feedback policies are those where the policy pursued depends upon the state of the economy, so that the actual monetary policy can change as the economic conditions alter. An example of such a feedback policy is one where the monetary base supplied by the central bank to the economy increases with increases in unemployment and falls with increases in the rate of inflation. Feedback policies can be consistent or discretionary. Consistent feedback policies would pre-specify the monetary base as a specific function of the rate of inflation and unemployment, with predetermined parameters. By comparison, a discretionary feedback policy would allow the central bank to deviate from the consistent policy function and change the parameters in the relationship as it judges best.

Policy rules

Therefore, consistent policies can be a fairly simple policy rule or be very complex functions, in either case with the possibility of allowing feedback from the economy. However, the *credibility* of policy usually requires that the policy function be a simple and transparent rule so that the public can easily judge the policy maker's adherence to or deviations from it. Among such simple rules are those that set the money supply growth rate at a constant level or prescribe it as a specific function of the unemployment and inflation rates during the period in question. The former does not leave any scope for feedback from the economy's actual performance while the latter does so.

Differences between the economy's short run and long run constraints

As we have discussed above at various places, and as Chapters 13 to 16 later point out, the economy's tradeoff between the rates of unemployment and inflation often differs between the short run and the long run. It is now generally believed that in the long run the rate of unemployment is independent of the rate of inflation. However, in the short run, there does exist a negative tradeoff. In the 1960s and 1970s, the Keynesians believed this tradeoff to be between the rate of inflation and the rate of unemployment as embodied in the Phillips curve. The modern classical economists believe this tradeoff to be between the unanticipated rate of inflation and the deviations of the actual rate of unemployment from the natural rate, as encompassed in the expectations augmented Phillips curve and the Lucas supply rule.[13]

The policy to be pursued in each period, say over a quarter or a year, would be a short-run one so that such policies, based on intertemporal optimization subject to the set of the economy's short-run constraints, would allow for the variation in economic conditions. This variation in the policies actually pursued among periods can occur under time-consistent policies if the economy's constraints differ among periods. This procedure could allow variations in the rate of growth of the money supply or the rate of inflation between recessions and booms.

By comparison, if the economy's short-run constraints were ignored and the optimization was made subject to the long-run constraint only, the optimal policy among periods would be identical. An example of this would be a constant money growth rate or a constant inflation rate, irrespective of whether the economy is in a recession or a boom. Such a policy, therefore, does not allow period-by-period variations in economic conditions to be taken into account.

The analysis of the time consistency of policies does not directly bear on this issue of whether the central bank's optimization should be based on the set of period constraints or only on the long-run constraint. The proper procedure would seem to be the former. However, doing so can impose period-by-period policies whose average in some sense is different from the policy based on the long-run constraint. For example, in a context where the economies are more often in recession than in booms, the growth of the money supply – expansionary in recessions and contractionary in booms – could prove to be more inflationary than if the long-run constraint held as the short-run one in each period. The stance of monetary policy would then be inflationary. There is also the danger that the pursuit of short-run-based policies could be interpreted by the public as opportunistic, and with an inflationary bias, as well as being perceived as time-inconsistent ones – even when they are time consistent. Such a perception would adversely affect the credibility and effectiveness of the central bank.

12.14 THE CREDIBILITY OF MONETARY POLICY

A credible policy is one in which the public has faith. That is, the public expects it to be maintained and believes that it will attain its declared objectives.

Therefore, the credibility of policies can be broadly defined as the extent to which the public's expectations about the future pursuit of policies are consistent with the policy maker's declarations on its future pursuit of these policies. The credibility of targets is correspondingly defined by the extent to which the public's expectations about the future paths of policy targets are consistent with the policy maker's declarations on its intended achievement of those targets. The former – i.e., credibility of policies – depends upon the expectations of whether the policy maker will deviate in its policies from the announced ones, whether of its own volition, under pressure from the public, or a shift in the economy's performance. The credibility of targets depends upon the credibility of policy and whether the economy has a structure (including the public's responses) that will deliver the intended target values of the announced policies. The latter depend upon the accurate knowledge of the current state of the economy and the proper formulation of policies given this knowledge, neither of which can be taken for granted even in the developed economies, let alone the LDCs.

The credibility of both policies and targets also depends upon the public's responses, which depend on the manner in which the public formulates its expectations of policies, targets and related variables. The current literature assumes that this will be done according to the rational expectations hypothesis, taking all past, current and anticipations about the future into account. These expectations include the public's knowledge of the policy maker's record on actually sticking to its policies, which includes knowledge of the political system and the responsiveness of the government to public sentiments,[14] and the structure of the economy.

Further, in the interests of maintaining credibility, the preceding theoretical analysis on the time consistency of policies clearly underlines the need for the central bank to maintain, even commit, itself to a given policy regime over time.[15] If this procedure is not followed, the public will learn from the shifts in policy that the central bank is willing to or can be made, under pressure from interested groups, to deviate from the consistent policy path. If it had announced its intention to follow that path and then not stayed on it, the public would have reason to be sceptical of its commitment to its intended policies and its credibility for the future will suffer.

The 1990s started with the attempts of various countries to lower their rates of inflation. However, the public's previous experience was with the higher rates of inflation in the 1980s and the general failure of announcements by their central banks of lower inflation target rates. The credibility of such targets was low, with the consequence that the disinflation process resulted in recessions and the loss of output. Therefore, a pertinent issue for monetary economics was whether or not establishing credibility could be beneficial by itself and what losses flow from the lack of credibility. The following parts of this section explore these issues.

12.14.1 Credibility and the costs of disinflation

The expected rate of inflation is one of the determinants of the actual rate of inflation and real output of the economy. This is apparent from the Lucas supply rule and the expectations augmented Phillips curve, discussed earlier at various points (also see Chapters 13 to 16). The conclusion of these supply functions is that the actual rate of inflation is positively related to its expected rate while real output is negatively related to the expected rate of inflation. Let this aggregate supply relationship for the economy be:

$$y_t = y^f + \alpha(\pi - \pi^e) \quad \alpha > 0 \tag{28}$$

where:

   y output
   y^f full employment (equilibrium) output
   π actual rate of inflation
   π^e rate of inflation expected by the public

Equation (28) implies that if $\pi^e > \pi$, $y < y^f$. That is, if the monetary authority is not able to reduce the expected rate of inflation below the actual one, as under a disinflationary policy, there will be a loss of output for the economy.

To illustrate the issue of the credibility of monetary policy in the context of (28), assume that the present state of the economy has identical high actual and expected rates of inflation, and the central bank has now decided to lower the actual rate of inflation. To achieve this, it decreases the money supply, and announces its new policy and the lower rate of inflation supported by that policy. One can imagine several scenarios. In the best of these, the public believes the central bank and immediately lowers its expected inflation rate to the now lower actual inflation rate. The last term in (28) stays at zero and the economy continues to enjoy full employment.

But, as an alternative scenario, if the central bank has gone along this route before but not, in the public's experience, delivered the lower money supply and the announced lower rate of inflation, the public would not find the announcement credible and would not lower its expected inflation rate correspondingly. Consequently, if the central bank does in fact deliver the lower announced actual rate of inflation, the expected rate would exceed the actual one and, by virtue of (28), output will fall below the full employment level. The lack of credibility was the cause of this fall. By extension, greater rather than lesser credibility of the central bank would mean a lower shortfall in output. This argument is sometimes used to assert that inflation – and possibly even hyperinflation – can be eliminated from an economy without severe reductions in output and employment provided that the credibility of the central bank is first established by the appointment of appropriate central bank governors with an established and tough reputation for espousing and establishing price stability.

Consequently, the poor credibility of the central bank implies that its restrictive monetary policy will affect the real variables of the economy. If the central bank continues its restrictive monetary policy, the public would eventually come to lower its expected rate of inflation. However, the poor credibility of the central bank would have induced a lag in the full impact of monetary policy on the economy, and required the implementation of stronger policies than would have been otherwise necessary in the interim. Hence, the lack of credibility of the central bank dilutes the impact of its policies on the expected rate of inflation and induces lags in the impact of this policy, with the extent of dilution and the length of the lag dependent on the 'extent of credibility' in the central bank's policies.

12.14.2 Sources of credibility problems

Among the sources of credibility problems are:

(i)   The potential time inconsistency of discretionary policies, as analysed earlier from the work of Kydland and Prescott.
(ii) The pursuit of conflicting policies by the monetary and fiscal authorities, with neither being able to achieve its announced targets. The possibility of such conflicts was discussed in section 12.3.
(iii) The responses of the public to policies. Assuming that the different segments of the public pursue their own self-interest, their responses and the pressures they exert would support or undermine the policy maker's declared objectives. In the latter case, the policy maker could demonstrate its commitment to its targets by not yielding to such pressure and by sticking to, or even strengthening, its policies in pursuit of its targets. These issues of the interaction, conflicts and conflict resolution both between the policy makers and between a policy maker and the public, can, to some extent, be analysed by the application of game theory to them.[16]
(iv) The structure of the economy and the extent of the policy maker's and the public's knowledge of it.
(v)   The nature of the political system and the political climate at the time. Among these, note that the interests of the policy makers can differ from the 'national interest'. For example, democratically elected governments have an incentive to manipulate economic policies for electoral gain, so that the strong interest of incumbent governments to win re-election would persuade them to pursue expansionary policies which buoy the economic conditions just prior to an election, while counteracting them by deflationary policies more in accordance with the national interest soon after an election.[17] A truly independent central bank would be immune to such self-interest of incumbent governments, but the central banks of many countries are not, by law or in practice, immune to governmental pressures.

12.14.3 Credibility and gradualist versus cold turkey policies

Starting from a period of high inflation and low credibility, the restoration of credibility depends on the vigour with which the anti-inflationary policies are pursued. The two extreme alternative ways of curbing high inflation are 'gradualism' and 'cold turkey' policies. Gradualism is a policy of a relatively slow reduction in money growth and inflation rates in an attempt to keep the disruption to aggregate demand and output to a minimum during the adjustment to low growth rates. The economy is thereby not forced into a recession or rates of unemployment much higher than the natural one, but the inflation rate falls slowly and takes a longer period to reach an acceptably low level.

In the alternative scenario of the cold turkey policy, the money supply growth rate and aggregate demand are cut drastically, causing the economy to go into a recession and raising unemployment substantially. The inflation rate falls rapidly.

Of the two types of policies, the cold turkey solution is clearly the more forceful and drastic policy and its impact is often more effective in lowering the expected rate of inflation, as well as in creating credibility that the lower rates will be maintained. This faster reduction in the expected inflation rate means a faster reduction in the actual inflation rate and a reduced lag in the impact of the anti-inflationary policy, which in turn translate into an earlier return to full employment. As against these benefits, the cold turkey policy usually starts by creating a deeper recession and greater rise in unemployment than a gradualist policy. Countries tend to follow different combinations of these two policies at different times.

12.14.4 The gains from credibility

The credibility of the central bank's announced inflation rate can yield real gains to the economy, as we illustrate in the following model. This model has certainty and implicitly assumes that the monetary authority has the same utility function as society and that it will achieve the inflation rate that it chooses.

Assume that the monetary authority wants to choose the optimal values of y and π for its utility function U^M:

$$U^M = -\gamma\pi^2 - [y - ky^f]^2 \quad \gamma > 0, k > 1 \tag{29}$$

where the symbols are as defined earlier. Equation (29) specifies a loss in utility from inflation, as well as from deviations from the monetary authority's pre-specified target output ky^f, set in this equation as a *proportion* of the full employment output y^f. The marginal loss in utility from a unit increase in output deviation has been normalized at unity.

Let the economy's aggregate supply relationship be of the Lucas supply rule or expectations augmented Phillips curve type, as in (28). This specifies the constraint on the utility function as:

$$y = y^f + \alpha(\pi - \pi^e) \quad \alpha > 0 \tag{30}$$

Substituting (30) into (29) gives:

$$U^M = -\gamma\pi^2 - [(y^f + \alpha(\pi - \pi^e) - ky^f]^2 \quad \gamma > 0 \tag{31}$$

To find the gains from credibility, we compare the following two extreme cases.

(i) There is no credibility and the monetary authority has to assume the public's expected inflation rate π^e as exogenously given.

For this case, maximize (31) with respect to π for given π^e. This yields the monetary authority's choice of π as:

$$\pi = \frac{\alpha}{\alpha^2 + \gamma}\left(ky^f - y^f\right) + \frac{\alpha}{\alpha^2 + \gamma}\,\pi^e \tag{32}$$

so that the monetary authority sets its optimal inflation policy to be a function of the expected inflation rate, the full employment output and the target output. Hence, its inflation target will vary as these change over time. The inflation rate is positively related to both π^e and $(k-1)y^f$.

Substituting (32) in (30) yields:

$$y = \left\{1 - \frac{\alpha^2}{\alpha^2 + \gamma}\right\}y^f + \frac{\alpha^2}{\alpha^2 + \gamma}ky^f - \frac{\alpha\gamma}{\alpha^2 + \gamma}\,\pi^e \tag{33}$$

Hence, output will depend on the target factor k and the expected inflation rate. If $k \neq 1$, y will not equal y^f, even if $\pi^e = 0$. If $k = 1$ and $\pi^e = 0$, $y = y^f$. Further, output is lower for higher values of π^e. Output can differ from its full employment level but note that, even if the former is higher, there occurs a loss in utility because of the nature of the assumed utility function.

(ii) To see the relative gains from full credibility, now assume that the monetary authority announces the per-period rate of inflation that it intends to achieve *and* the public fully believes it. In this case, $\pi^e = \pi$.

For $\pi^e = \pi$, (30) implies that:

$$y = y^f \tag{34}$$

Therefore, there will not be a loss in output from a disinflationary policy or a gain from an inflationary one, so that there will not be deviations from full employment and their implied loss in utility.

Note also that $y = y^f$ whether the monetary authority's chosen inflation rate is zero or some positive number. Hence, the output gains from full credibility do not require a zero inflation rate, as long as it is a known and credible rate.

With $\pi^e = \pi$, the maximizing function (31) becomes,

$$U^M = -\gamma \pi^2 - [(y^f - ky^f)]^2 \quad \gamma > 0 \tag{35}$$

Maximizing (35) with respect to π yields the condition:

$$\partial U / \partial \pi = -2\gamma \pi^2 = 0$$

which gives the optimal rate of inflation π^* as zero. Therefore, for the above model, while the gains from credibility occur at any inflation rate, the optimal inflation policy under full credibility is that of zero inflation. A positive rate of inflation, even though it may be fully credible and maintain full employment output, will yield a lower utility than zero inflation.

Comparing (33) for the no-credibility case with $y = y^f$ under the fully credible policy, the monetary authority can produce higher output by having $k > 1$ and $\pi > \pi^e$. But such deviations from y^f imply a loss in utility. Further, inflation is positive if there is no credibility and zero if there is, with the former giving lower utility. Hence, full credibility yields higher utility, lower inflation and smaller deviations in output from the full employment level.

12.14.5 The analysis of credibility under supply shocks and rational expectations

For further exposition of the modelling on credibility, we modify and extend the preceding model to bring in supply shocks and rational expectations. The model used will be:

$$U^M = -\gamma \pi^2 - [y - (y^f + k)]^2 \quad \gamma, k > 0 \tag{36}[18]$$

$$y = y^f + \alpha(\pi - \pi^e) + \mu \quad \alpha > 0 \tag{37}$$

where μ is a random disturbance to aggregate supply. Note that the utility function (36) differs from that in (29): the output target level now enters the utility function through an *additive* rather than a proportional factor.[19]

We investigate three scenarios for this model.

(i) The monetary authority does not guarantee that the actual inflation rate will be zero but does pre-commit itself to the average inflation rate $\bar{\pi}$ being zero. The public believes it and bases its expectations on this average rate, so that $\pi^e = \bar{\pi} = 0$.

Incorporating this restriction into (37) yields:

$$y = y^f + \alpha\pi + \mu \tag{38}$$

The monetary authority chooses π to maximize (36) subject to (38), which gives:

$$\pi = -\beta\mu + \beta k \tag{39}$$

$$y = y^f + \alpha\beta k + (1 - \alpha\beta)\mu$$

where $\beta = \alpha/(\alpha^2 + \gamma)$. Hence:

$$y = y^f + \frac{\alpha^2}{\alpha^2 + \gamma} k + \frac{\gamma}{\alpha^2 + \gamma} \mu \tag{40}$$

However, from (39),

$$E\pi = \beta k > 0 \quad \text{for } k > 0$$

The monetary authority had given a commitment to $\bar{\pi} = 0$. To meet this commitment, it will have to make $k = 0$ or it would be attempting to fool the public and will not be able to maintain its credibility. We designate this credible case as (i′). Therefore:

(i′) $k = 0$ so that the target output level is y^f.

Note that the requirement of credibility imposes realism on the objectives of the monetary authority. For this credible policy, $k = 0$ so that:

$$y = y^f + \frac{\gamma}{\alpha^2 + \gamma} \mu \tag{41}$$

$$\pi = -\frac{\alpha}{\alpha^2 + \gamma} \mu \tag{42}$$

Note that for $k = 0$, only the rational expectation of inflation – which equals $E\pi$ – is zero, so that the public must be taken to accept that actual inflation will vary over time, but have its expected value as zero. Further, the expectation of output is stabilized at y^f, but its actual level will fluctuate with the actual inflation rate.

(ii) The monetary authority guarantees that the actual (rather than the average) inflation rate will be zero. The public believes it and bases its expectations on it, so that $\pi^e = \pi = 0$.

Incorporating this expectations formation into (37) yields:

$$y = y^f + \mu \tag{43}$$

which implies that the monetary authority cannot achieve $k > 0$. It must, therefore, either give up its target of output greater than the full employment level, or its commitment to a zero inflation rate.

Further, substituting (43) into the utility function (36) gives:

$$U^M = -\gamma\pi^2 - (\mu + k)^2 \quad \gamma, k > 0$$

Maximizing this function with respect to π gives,

$$\partial U^M/\partial\pi = -2\gamma\pi = 0$$

so that:

$$\pi = 0 \tag{44}$$

Hence, the optimal inflation rate is zero. However, there may be problems in achieving it since the model includes random supply shocks which are unpredictable and the monetary authority may not be able to implement the policies that will counter their impact on the inflation rate. If the monetary authority can, in fact, achieve this rate, its optimal inflation policy will be consistent with its commitment to zero inflation.

(iii) The monetary authority takes π^e as given for its decisions while the public forms its expectations rationally.

For given π^e, maximizing (36) with respect to π and subject to (37) yields:

$$\pi = \beta(\alpha\pi^e + k - \mu) \tag{45}$$

where $\beta = \alpha/(\alpha^2 + \gamma)$. Assuming rational expectations, so that $\pi^e = E\pi$,

$$\pi^e = (\alpha/\gamma)k \tag{46}$$

Equations (45) and (46) imply that:

$$\pi = \frac{\alpha}{\gamma}k - \frac{\alpha}{\alpha^2 + \gamma}\mu \tag{47}$$

which implies that $E\pi = (\alpha/\gamma)k$ so that $E\pi > 0$ for $k > 0$. Therefore, the equilibrium level of output under rational expectations will be:

$$y = y^f + \frac{\gamma}{\alpha^2 + \gamma}\mu \tag{48}$$

We can now compare the inflation and output for the three cases. For this comparison, we will use for (i) not the general case ($k \geq 0$) but (i′) which has a credible commitment to the zero average inflation ($k = 0$). Ey is identical among them. The fluctuations in y are also identical between (i′) and (iii). A similar identity of implications also holds for the inflation rate. This is an interesting result into the nature of rational expectations. In (i′), there is a pre-commitment to a credible zero inflation on average. In (iii), there is no pre-commitment to any particular rate of inflation but the public, because of rational expectations, knows and bases its expected rate on the expected value of the inflation rate adopted by the policy maker. The identity of results between (i′) and (iii) shows that rational expectations acts as if there was a credible pre-commitment to an average inflation rate, so that it replaces the need for a pre-commitment. As a corollary, to achieve the benefits of zero inflation, the policy maker does not have to give a pre-commitment as long as it sticks with a systematic zero inflation policy.

Another result from this analysis has been that a credible policy is more than just informing the public of the intended policy. It has to be realistic or it will soon cease to be credible. This requirement imposes limitations on the monetary authority's objectives, which in (i') ensured that the target output was the full employment output itself, rather than a higher amount.

Comparing (i') and (iii) with (ii), the expected values of both inflation and output are the same in all cases but their fluctuations differ. Since $\gamma/(\alpha^2 + \gamma) < 1$, output fluctuates less and inflation more under (i') and (iii) than under (ii). Hence, rational expectations reduce the variability of output compared with a policy of zero inflation per period.

Finally, some caveats to the above conclusions. Some of the conclusions are specific to the assumptions of the above models. Note especially two of these assumptions. One, the utility function attributes negative utility to even positive deviations of output from its full employment level.[20] Intuitively, one considers higher output to be more desirable so that such positive deviations should have been assigned positive utility. Two, the economy's constraint has been assumed to have the form of the Lucas supply function or the expectations augmented Phillips curve. These belong in the classical paradigm, while the Keynesian paradigm has a different form. We will leave this differentiation to a couple of the questions at the end of this chapter and to Chapter 15.

CONCLUSIONS

This chapter has examined the implications of adopting different operational targets for monetary policy. For most central banks, the direct target is no longer a reserve aggregate such as borrowed or non-borrowed reserves, the monetary base or a monetary aggregate (M1, M2, M3 or M4), since these proved to have an unstable relationship with nominal GDP in the 1980s and 1990s. The main reason for this instability has been financial innovation leading to changes in the velocity of circulation, new monetary assets and increased substitutability between demand deposits and other financial assets. This instability has led to calls for the construction of new types of monetary aggregates. The foremost among them is Divisia aggregates. Their specification and relative performance were presented in Chapter 8 on monetary aggregation.

Among other target variables proposed for monetary policy are nominal income and the rate of inflation. The former has been recommended as a tradeoff between the price level and real output but has not been explicitly adopted. The latter has been adopted in several countries, including Canada and the UK. For the USA, while the Federal Reserve has not proclaimed it as an explicit target of monetary policy, with a pre-announced level or range, a low rate of inflation is among the goals of monetary policy in the USA. However, it cannot be an operating target since it is not directly under the control of the central bank, so that the central bank has to attempt to achieve its inflation goals through its manipulation of interest rates and monetary aggregates.

The achievement of specific goals through other operating targets and instruments requires the stability and predictability of the relationship between goals, intermediate variables, operating ones and the policy instruments at the central banks' disposal. These relationships are rarely so stable and predictable that the success of the policies pursued can be taken for granted in the developed economies, and even less so in many developing ones. Further, in most economies, changes in the central bank instruments have lags of one to two years in their impact on the ultimate goal variables, so that monetary policy has to anticipate the future course of the economy. As a corollary, current monetary policy cannot be formulated or judged by reference to the current state of the economy. The proper formulation and pursuit of monetary policy is, therefore, an art. One cannot be sanguine, in any country of the world, that inappropriate policies will not be formulated, or that the policies which appeared to be well considered, with wide support, at the time of their implementation, will not in retrospect prove to be undesirable and damaging to the economy.

At the level of the goals themselves, there exists a potential for conflicts among the desired goal levels or the tradeoff among them between two or several independent decision makers. This potential for conflict tends to be greater when the economy is displaying both high rates of inflation and unemployment and tends to be low when the economy has low rates of both these variables. Such conflicts among the central banks and the governments were more evident during the stagflation of the 1970s and 1980s, than they have been in the 1990s, partly because of the realization that there is no long-run benefit from high rates of inflation.

One procedure for reducing the possibility of conflicts between the monetary and fiscal authorities is to place one policy maker under the authority of the other one. This is usually achieved by placing the central bank under the jurisdiction of the government's Minister of Finance or requiring the former to obtain approval from the latter for its policies. However, this represents a loss of independence of the central bank, while empirical studies have shown that economies with effectively independent central banks tend to have lower rates of inflation. Therefore, economies with low rates of inflation as a societal objective should maintain the independence of their central banks. However, as the preceding chapter noted, societies tend to have a variety of macroeconomic objectives and these are reflected in the mandates assigned to the central banks.

From an *a priori* perspective in an intertemporal context, consistent policies – pre-announced and maintained over time – are superior to discretionary policies which allow the policy maker to re-optimize each period and deviate from the pre-announced policies. However, this is not necessarily so when there are shifts in information – other than the realization of prior probability distributions – and unanticipated shifts as time passes in the structure of the economy. Policies incorporating knowledge of such shifts are clearly likely to be more responsive to emerging events, and be more desirable. The choice between a pre-announced consistent policy path and discretionary ones must, therefore, depend upon the availability of information and the likelihood of unanticipated shifts in knowledge and in the structure of the economy.

However, no matter what policy is pursued, it is important that the central bank maintain credibility for its policies. Sticking to pre-announced consistent policies enhances this credibility and the effectiveness of the policies pursued. Frequent shifts in policy reduce this credibility, reduce the effectiveness of the policies and also introduce longer lags in the achievement of the central bank's targets. The importance of credibility becomes even greater if the public formulates its expectations according to the rational expectations hypothesis, which leads it to incorporate into its responses its expectations on the potential future policy revisions and possible failures to achieve announced targets. These are likely to depend on the structure of the economy, the ambitiousness (and lack of realism) of goals, the political system and the power of pressure groups etc. In order to achieve and maintain credibility, the central bank has to take all these factors into account in formulating a policy that it will stick to and be able to achieve. Its payoff for doing so is that its credibility, once established, makes its policies for the future more effective, as well as reducing the lags in their impact.

Both the time consistency and the credibility of policies require that the central bank not induce surprises, aimed at fooling the public, into the economy, such as in the form of sudden shifts in its monetary policy. While there might be short-term benefits of such a policy, such surprises would not be welfare optimizing in the intertemporal context and would also be detrimental to the bank's credibility. Another limitation imposed by credibility is that the monetary authority must pursue realistic objectives. If its goal is price stability, it has so announced it, and it operates in the context of a classical-type economy, its target output has to be the full employment output and not a higher one.

This chapter has brought out the close links between central bank independence, the time consistency of policies and credibility. Most of this discussion implicitly took the goal of price stability or a low inflation rate as society's objective. While empirical studies support the finding that central bank independence of the government tends to lower inflation, there is little evidence that it increases output growth or lowers unemployment. In fact, depending on the nature of shocks to the economy, a goal of price stability could increase fluctuations in output and unemployment.

One of the central concerns in this chapter has been about the macroeconomic structure of the economy and the tradeoffs that it allows among the goal variables, as well as the relationships between monetary policy, inflation, unemployment and output. These issues require knowledge of the macroeconomic models. As Chapter 1 explained, there are two main paradigms in macroeconomics. Of these, the models of the classical paradigm are presented in Chapter 13 and those of the Keynesian one in Chapter 14. Their policy implications and comparisons are carried over into Chapters 15, 16 and 17.

SUMMARY OF CRITICAL CONCLUSIONS

- If the economy does allow short-run tradeoffs among multiple goals, there is a high potential for periodic conflicts among policy makers in the goals attempted and the policies pursued.
- If the economy does not allow monetary policy to affect output and unemployment even in the short run – that is, money is neutral – the adoption of price stability as the single or dominant monetary policy goal becomes more clearly the optimal policy goal for the nation. It also reduces the potential for conflicts between monetary and fiscal policies.
- While adoption of the goal of price stability lowers the inflation rate and its variability, it also increases the fluctuations in output and unemployment under supply shocks.
- Successful interest rate targeting, in comparison with monetary targeting, increases the impact on aggregate demand of investment, net exports, fiscal deficits and other disturbances in the commodity markets while eliminating the impact of shocks emanating from the financial sectors.
- Monetary targeting eliminates the impact of fluctuations in the money supply induced by the private sector and moderates the impact of fluctuations emanating from the commodity market.
- Central bank independence has been found to reduce the rate of inflation.
- The credibility of the central bank is essential to the successful reduction of inflation rates by it. Credibility is also a factor in reducing the time lags in the adjustment of the expected inflation rate and of the actual inflation rate.
- The pursuit of time-consistent monetary policies buttresses the central bank's credibility. Whether such policies prove to be superior to discretionary ones depends on the nature of the shocks and whether they were anticipated.
- The credibility of a policy committed to keeping the price level stable imposes realism on the goals of monetary policy. In the analysis of this chapter, it requires that the central bank not try to achieve a target output higher than the full employment one.

review and discussion questions

1 Who should determine the economic policy goals for the nation: the government democratically elected by the public or a central bank whose directors (or governors) are not elected and cannot be made directly responsible to the public?

2 'If the monetary authority wants to control inflation, it should directly target the rate of inflation.' 'If the monetary authority wants to control inflation, it should use the rate of inflation as its *only* goal.' Discuss.

3 Discuss the following statement: if the money demand function has a high interest inelasticity, the case for a monetary target as against an interest rate target is strengthened, especially in an economy subject to stochastic shocks.

4 'The main instruments for controlling the money supply must be fiscal policy and interest rates.' Discuss the validity of this statement. Does it make any difference to your answer if the banking system is competitive and has a zero reserve requirement?

5 How do central banks manage interest rates in your country and one other country of your choice? What consequences can the central bank expect from targeting interest rates?

6 The monetary sector became increasingly unstable in recent years. Does this mean that the monetary authority should stay with interest rate targets and not try to pursue monetary targets?

7 Note that recessions seem to be caused by either reductions in aggregate demand or in aggregate supply or by the two acting in concert. What targets should the central bank adopt? Would the optimal choice of the target be the same for reductions in aggregate supply as for reductions in aggregate demand?

8 If the central bank cannot change output and unemployment through systematic money supply changes and its induced changes in the anticipated inflation rate, should it try to do so by causing changes in the unanticipated inflation rate? If such unanticipated inflation requires random changes in the money supply, how can the central bank achieve these? What will be the effect of such a random change on output and unemployment and what conclusions can be drawn on the advisability of such a monetary policy?

9 The time consistency of policy requires the specification of a policy plan for the future, say for the next five years, and sticking to it. Under what conditions – and shocks – is this a desirable policy? When is it not desirable? Discuss.

10 What is the relationship between rational expectations and the credibility of monetary policy? What do they imply for the relevance of credibility to the success of an anti-inflation programme? What do they imply for the choice between a gradualist versus a cold turkey approach to fighting inflation? Discuss.

11 'The time consistency literature suggests that it is always a good thing to have a tough central banker who cares about inflation and not at all about unemployment – even if society cares mainly about unemployment.' Discuss.

12 For pre-specified goals, it is easy for the academic economist to prescribe the course of monetary policy for the period ahead. But the devil is in the details: the limitations on the knowledge of the future course of the economy and its future response to policies, as well as in the implementation of the chosen policies. It is such details that make the successful pursuit of policies an art rather than a science. Discuss.

13 Each time the central bank changes its discount rate, there always seems to be plenty of criticism from many economists, some claiming that the change is not needed or too much while others claim that it is too little. Is this due to the disposition of economists as human beings, as the public seems to suspect, or due the nature of their discipline or are there other reasons? Discuss. Present the IS–LM analysis for the case of negative shifts in the vertical aggregate supply curve when the targets are (i) aggregate demand, (ii) price stability and (iii) output. Compare the output and interest rate fluctuations under these targets.

14 Assume that the monetary authority has the utility function:

$$U = -u^2 - 0.5\pi^2$$

where U is utility, u is unemployment and π is the inflation rate. Assume that the economy imposes a constraint in the form of the Phillips curve. Let this be:

$$u = 5 - 0.1\pi$$

Derive the optimal values of u and π. Compare these with their values under a credible pre-commitment to zero inflation.

15 Given the utility function in the preceding question, assume that the economy has an expectations augmented Phillips curve such that:

$$u - u_n = -0.1(\pi - \pi^e)$$

Derive the optimal values of u and π. Compare these with their values under a credible pre-commitment to zero inflation.

16 Suppose that the economy is such that a positive monetary shock reduces unemployment. Assume that the monetary authority likes a reduction in unemployment but dislikes an increase in inflation. The public forecasts money growth from the government's optimization problem. How are money growth and inflation determined in this context? If you so wish, you can answer this by specifying a model. What would be the implications of a commitment – a rule – binding the monetary authority to a future rate of money growth? Should it do so?

17 What advice would you give the central bank of your country on the appropriate monetary policy to follow at the present time? Your answer must specify your assessment of the current state of the economy, and the goals and targets you think the central bank should follow and how they agree with or deviate from those being followed by the central bank. You must present a detailed analysis of the impact of your suggested policy on output, inflation and interest rates.

18 'Due to fairly radical changes in the structure of the financial sector in recent decades, the importance of demand deposits has declined considerably and the role of commercial banks has changed dramatically. The mainstream of monetary theory and practice continues to be directed mainly at demand deposits and commercial banks as purveyors of checking accounts. But checking deposits are simply one kind of liquid asset and banks are simply one kind of intermediary. Therefore, to single out checking deposits and commercial banks for special analytical treatment is mistaken. Effective control of the economy by the central banks requires control over all types of liquid assets and over the liabilities of all financial intermediaries.' Discuss.

NOTES

1 This section requires some prior knowledge of the IS–LM model from macroeconomic courses. A review of this model is provided in Chapter 13.

2 See also Chapters 8, 15 and 16 for material relevant to this discussion.

3 Price stability is also sometimes designated as a primary policy goal. However, even in such a context, the justification given for it is that price stability promotes the achievement of full employment and output growth.

4 Shocks originating in the commodity market are to consumption, investment, exports and government expenditures. Of these, investment is considered to be the most volatile element.

5 These financial innovations included the payment of interest on checking accounts and the increasing degree of substitution between M1 and near-monies.

6 In this context, see the discussion in section 12.8 on the monetary conditions index used by the Bank of Canada.

7 This concern over the length and variability of the lag is shared with all monetary instruments and, in particular, with the monetary aggregates, as we discuss under the heading of 'lags in the effect of monetary policy' in Chapter 16.

8 Therefore, there is ample scope for wide differences among political parties, economists, political scientists and the public, etc., on what can be accomplished by any given set of policies.

9 However, note that the preponderant part of their operations on the monetary base is usually of a defensive nature, aimed at smoothing undesired variations in the monetary base.

10 Goodhart (1994) provides a compact statement of the issues related to central bank independence, time consistency and credibility, especially from the perspective of the British experience.

11 Eijffinger and de Hahn (1996) provide a thorough review of the issues and empirical studies on central bank independence.

12 For discussion of this tradeoff, see Chapters 13 and 14.

13 See the next section and Chapters 13 to 16 for these concepts and their analyses.

14 The credibility of policy is, therefore, affected by whether the country is a democracy, oligopoly or authoritarian, etc. It also depends on the existence and power of pressure groups.

15 Such a commitment can be qualified to allow for policy changes if there occur major unanticipated alterations in the economic environment.

16 Blackburn and Christensen (1989) discuss these applications.

17 Such policies can create cycles in the economy roughly synchronized with the dates of elections. Such cycles are called political business cycles.

18 To allow for a divergence of the monetary authority's utility function from the society's one, a possibility would be to define the monetary authority's utility function as $U^M = S - \gamma\pi^2 - [y - (y^f + k^M)]^2$, γ, $k^M > 0$, where S is, say, the remuneration of the governor of the central bank, and the society's utility function as $U^S = -\gamma\pi^2 - [y - (y^f + k^S)]^2$, γ, $k^S > 0$. Such divergence can be used to study performance contracts for central banks. If $k^M \neq k^S$, the monetary authority has a different output target from society and, therefore, a different 'agenda' (Waller, 1995).

19 The only justification for this change was the desire to present some variation in modelling. As an exercise, the student should derive the results for this section from (29).

20 This utility function is more in tune with the classical paradigm since it makes the desirable target of monetary policy the full employment level rather than some higher level. A Keynesian might prefer a utility function which allocates positive utility to positive deviations from full employment.

REFERENCES

Alesina, Alberto, and Lawrence H. Summers. 'Central Bank Independence and Macroeconomic Performance: Some Comparative Evidence'. *Journal of Money, Credit and Banking*, 25, 1993, pp. 151–62.

Blackburn, Keith, and Michael Christensen. 'Monetary Policy and Policy Credibility: Theories and Evidence'. *Journal of Economic Literature*, 27, March 1989, pp. 1–45.

Cukierman, Alex, Steven B. Webb and Bilin Neyapti. 'Measuring the Independence of Central Banks and its Effects on Policy Outcomes'. *The World Bank Research Review*, 6, 1993, pp. 353–98.

Eijffinger, Sylvester C. W., and Jakob de Hahn. *The Political Economy of Central Bank Independence*. Princeton University, Special Papers in International Economics, 19, May 1996.

Fischer, Stanley. 'Rules versus Discretion in Monetary Policy'. In Benjamin M. Friedman and Frank H. Hahn, eds, *Handbook of Monetary Economics*. Amsterdam: North-Holland, 1990, Vol. II.

Friedman, Benjamin M. 'Targets and Instruments of Monetary Policy'. In Benjamin M. Friedman and Frank H. Hahn, eds, *Handbook of Monetary Economics*. Amsterdam: North-Holland, 1990, Vol. II.

————, and Frank H. Hahn, eds. *Handbook of Monetary Economics*. Amsterdam: North-Holland, 1990, Vol. II, Part 8.

Friedman, Milton. 'The Role of Monetary Policy'. *American Economic Review*, 58, March 1968, pp. 1–17.

————. 'Nobel Prize Lecture: Inflation and Unemployment'. *Journal of Political Economy*, 85, June 1977, pp. 451–73.

Goodhart, Charles A. E. 'The Conduct of Monetary Policy'. In Christopher J. Green and David T. Llewellyn, *Surveys in Monetary Economics* (Vol. I: *Monetary Theory and Policy*). Cambridge, MA: Blackwell, 1991.

————. 'Central Bank Independence'. *Journal of International and Comparative Economics*, 3, 1994. Also in his *The Central Bank and the Financial System*. London: Macmillan, 1995.

————. *The Central Bank and the Financial System*. London: Macmillan, 1995.

Kydland, Finn E., and Edward C. Prescott. 'Rules Rather than Discretion: The Inconsistency of Optimal Rules'. *Journal of Political Economy*, 85, June 1977, pp. 473–93.

Mishkin, Frederic S., and Adam S. Posen. 'Inflation Targeting: Lessons from Four Countries'. In Federal Reserve Bank of New York, *Economic Policy Review*, 3, August 1997, pp. 9–110.

Waller, Christopher J. 'Performance Contracts for Central Bankers'. *Federal Reserve Bank of St Louis Review*, September/October 1995, pp. 3–14.

MONEY IN THE MACROECONOMY

chapter thirteen

THE CLASSICAL PARADIGM IN MACROECONOMICS: NEOCLASSICAL AND CLASSICAL MODELS

The most enduring tradition in short-run macroeconomics is represented by the classical paradigm. The microeconomic foundations of this paradigm lie in the Walrasian model, presented in Chapter 3 above. In equilibrium, the models of this paradigm imply full employment and full employment output in the economy, so that there is no need for the pursuit of fiscal or monetary policies to improve on the already perfect functioning of the economy. Further, money is usually neutral in the equilibrium states of these models, so that changes in the money supply by the central bank can have no real effects in equilibrium.

The main focus of the presentation in this chapter is that of the mainstream neoclassical macroeconomic model. This model is then varied to present the other major models in the classical paradigm. There is no scope for monetary policy in the general equilibrium states of these models. Their policy conclusions and recommendations for the short run depend on whether they allow disequilibrium in the short run or for significant periods within the short run.

---

key concepts introduced in this chapter

- The neoclassical model
- The IS relationship/curve
- The LM relationship/curve
- The employment–output relationship/curve
- The aggregate demand relationship/curve
- The long-run aggregate supply relationship/curve
- The short-run aggregate supply relationship/curve
- The natural rate of unemployment
- Economic liberalism
- *Laissez faire*
- The Great Depression

- Ricardian equivalence
- Monetarism
- The traditional classical approach/theory
- The modern classical approach/theory
- The new classical model

Chapter 1 presented a brief definition of the classical paradigm and its component models. They should be reviewed at this stage.

Microeconomics is concerned with the market for each individual good, including among them the various commodities produced, money, other financial assets and factors of production. Chapters 3 to 10 studied the demand and supply of money and represented a microeconomic study of monetary economics. Their core chapter for the microeconomic analysis of the demand and supply functions for commodities, money and labour, is Chapter 3, which should be reviewed before approaching the analysis of this chapter. Chapter 2 on the heritage of monetary theory is a prerequisite for the topics treated in this chapter.

A general study of the whole economy can be formulated in two distinct ways. One of these would be a Walrasian general equilibrium model, which includes a separate specification of the market for each good. This was the approach followed in Chapter 3. Such a system of simultaneous equations is a very detailed one, studying as it does the separate demand and supply and price of each good in the economy. It is, however, quite cumbersome for macroeconomic purposes, where the objective is to focus on a few macroeconomic variables only.

Another procedure for a study of the whole economy is to aggregate the very large number of goods in the economy into a small number of categories, thus reducing the number of relationships to be studied to a manageable level. Obviously, the degree of aggregation used must depend upon the intended use of the resulting model or framework. The analysis in the preceding chapters of this book has focused on four goods: commodities, money, bonds and labour. The macroeconomic models presented in this chapter and the next one analyse the markets for these goods and are basically those oriented towards the study of general fiscal and monetary policies and their implications for aggregate output, employment, interest rates and prices in the short run. These models are for the short run for a closed economy, defining the short run in this context as the period during which the capital stock of the economy is taken to be exogenously given. Two basic types of these models are those in the classical tradition and those in the Keynesian one. The former are presented in this chapter and the latter in the next one.

A major component of the classical paradigm is the neoclassical model. It is also useful for laying the foundations for the other current components, the modern classical model and the new classical model. We will, therefore, devote most of this chapter to the neoclassical model, and return to the other two models towards the end of the chapter.

13.1 THE EVOLUTION OF THE CLASSICAL PARADIGM

The principles of the classical paradigm evolved out of several rather disparate elements. The dominant one of these was the economic and political philosophy of liberalism in the first half of the nineteenth century. Its economic analysis was that of the individual markets for commodities, factors of production, money and bonds, with competition as the invisible hand guiding each of them to equilibrium through the adjustment of the relevant price. In this analysis, all prices were flexible and adjusted to bring each market into equilibrium, so that each market cleared at the trading price. Much of this analysis of individual markets was set out in the following rather separate categories.

(a) For the commodity markets, market clearance meant that the aggregate demand for
    commodities equalled their supply. Thus, David Ricardo, writing in the first decade of
    the nineteenth century, claimed that while the demand in any one commodity market
    could fall below its supply, the economy as a whole could not have deficient demand,
    i.e. inadequacy of aggregate demand relative to the aggregate supply, because all the
    income generated by the production of commodities has to be spent on some
    commodity or other. This statement on the impossibility of deficient demand
    eventually hardened into Say's law that the supply of commodities creates its own
    demand.[1]
(b) The labour market analysis was part of microeconomic theory and also took market
    clearance for granted, thereby implying full employment.
(c) The analysis of what we now call the bond market was presented in the loanable funds
    theory of interest rates, which determined the macroeconomic interest rate by the
    demand and supply of loanable funds. This theory has been already illustrated in
    Chapter 2 from the writings of David Hume, writing in the mid-eighteen century.[2]
(d) The price level was determined through the quantity theory, which had also been set
    out by David Hume and has been presented in Chapter 2.

These distinctive theories for the different types of goods nowhere appeared in a complete
format so that one cannot point to the work of any economist prior to Keynes' book *The
General Theory* (1936) for a statement of a complete macroeconomic theory or model. In
particular, there was no knowledge of the multiplier and no derivation of the consumption
and saving functions, which are central to the neoclassical analysis of the commodity
market. In fact, it can be argued that there was no theory of the commodity market as such
in the nineteenth century. But there was a theory of interest rates in the form of the loanable
funds theory (bond market analysis), a theory of the price level in the form of the quantity
theory (money market analysis) and a theory of the labour market. These are the elements of
what Keynes labelled in his Chapter 1 of *The General Theory* as the classical model, though
there did not exist in the literature at that time such an established and complete
macroeconomic model. We have labelled this pre-Keynesian model as the traditional
classical model, in comparison with a modern classical model popular in recent decades.

Keynes' *The General Theory* rejected the traditional classical labour market analysis with
its labour market clearance, and chose to give the foremost place in his model to the
commodity market, with an analysis incorporating the multiplier. Hicks in 1937 organized
Keynes' ideas on the different sectors into what he labelled the IS–LM framework, and cast
the traditional classical model in the same format to facilitate comparison. The traditional
classical model thus recast in the mould of the IS–LM framework, which had been proposed
to illuminate Keynes' ideas, came to be known as the neoclassical model. It was elaborated
and refined in the decades up to 1970. One part of this was its evolution into the Keynesian–
neoclassical synthesis of aggregate demand, arrived at by the 1960s. Other developments
included a more rigorous analysis of labour markets, especially its intertemporal analysis,
and the new doctrines of rational expectations and Ricardian equivalence.

Neoclassical economics with the addition of rational expectations, if there is uncertainty,
and an insistence on continuous labour market clearance, has again come to be known as
the classical model, though there are significant differences between this modern classical
model and the somewhat vague one of the nineteenth century.[3] We have labelled this
combination as the modern classical model. The combination of the modern classical model
with Ricardian equivalence is labelled as the new classical model. The exact differences
among these models will be presented towards the end of this chapter.

13.2 THE BOUNDARIES OF THE SHORT-RUN MACROECONOMIC MODELS

The basic orientation of the short-run macroeconomic models is towards a study of the impact of the general fiscal and monetary policies upon aggregate output and the general price level. There is no attempt to examine their impact upon the relative prices of commodities, so that these models operate as if in a single-commodity world. The study of the general price level – the average rate of exchange of commodities into money – necessitates the introduction of money as a separate good into the analysis and the study of interest rates necessitates the introduction of bonds, without, however, attempting to introduce the full structure of interest rates in the economy. This simplification to a single rate of interest in the macroeconomic model can become a source of confusion since the interest rate relevant to the investment demand for commodities is a long-term rate of interest and is likely to differ from the short-term interest rates relevant to the demand for money. However, while a more appropriate analysis would include at least two rates of interest, we will follow the standard versions of the macroeconomic models in assuming a single rate of interest. This interest rate is to be interpreted as the return on the non-monetary financial asset labelled as bonds, which will include real-world bonds of different durations as well as equities.

The output of commodities is assumed to require inputs of capital and labour. Since no attempt is being made to study the structure of wage rates, labour is treated as if it were a homogeneous input. It is also assumed that the existing capital stock is given and that while the purchase of commodities for additions to the capital stock – that is, investment – is made, the productive capacity of the stock does not change because of the gestation lags between purchases of equipment and its use for production. We are, therefore, left with only one variable input, labour, in the production process. The fixity of capital is the distinguishing characteristic of short-run versus long-run macroeconomic models. The latter will be covered in Chapters 25 and 26.

There are thus four types of goods in the closed economy: commodities, money, bonds and labour. Labour can be used as an input to produce commodities, whose purchase for consumption or investment is transacted with money as a medium of exchange. The demand for both commodities and real balances depends upon the income generated by production and the average interest rate on bonds. This is the underlying basis of our macroeconomic framework.

The basic classification of private economic units into households and firms can be carried over into the macroeconomic models, though it is not absolutely essential there. It does, however, put the discussion in more familiar terms as when we speak of consumers consuming, firms investing, labour supplying its services, etc. Besides the private economic agents, the model will have the government as the fiscal authority and the central bank as the monetary authority. The subsequent extension of the models to open economies in Chapters 18 and 19 will introduce imports and exports conducted with foreign economies.

Four basic goods have been assumed so far. A study of their markets and 'prices' requires specification of the demand and supply for each good. Their 'markets' are referred to as markets or sectors, the two terms being used interchangeably, though considering the degree of aggregation, the word 'sectors' seems more appropriate. The macroeconomic model thus has four sectors: the expenditure or product sector, or the market for commodities; the monetary sector, or the market for money; the financial sector, or the market for bonds; and the production–employment sector, composed of the market for labour and the production function, to specify output and employment in the economy. Each of these sectors is studied in turn.

The analysis throughout this chapter is a comparative statics one, focusing on equilibrium states but with some discussion of the out-of-equilibrium adjustments.

As in the earlier chapters, lower-case symbols will generally refer to the real values of the variables and upper-case symbols to their nominal values. The definitions of the symbols

Table 13.1 Symbols

y	aggregate output/national income
y^f	full-employment output
e	aggregate expenditures
c	consumption
c_0	autonomous consumption
s	saving
i	investment
i_0	autonomous investment
t	tax revenues
t_0	autonomous tax revenues
g	government expenditures
r	rate of interest
p	price level
π	rate of inflation
m^d	real demand for money
m^{trd}	real transactions demand for money
m^{spd}	real speculative demand for money
M^s	nominal money supply
n^d	demand for labour
n^s	supply of labour
n	employment
n^f	full employment
K	physical capital stock
w	real wage rate

frequently used in this chapter and subsequent ones on the short-run macroeconomic models are given in Table 13.1.

The capital (or upper-case) versions of the symbols in Table 13.1 will usually designate the corresponding nominal values, with K as a special exception to this rule.

The superscript d on a variable will indicate its demand and the superscript s will indicate its supply. The variable without either of these superscripts will be the equilibrium value at which its demand and supply are equal.

We will designate the change in a variable y by Δy, by $\partial y/\partial t$ or by y'; and the rate of growth of the variable by y''. Therefore, as appropriate, y'_t will equal $(y_t - y_{t-1})$ or $\partial y/\partial t$ while y''_t will equal $(y_t - y_{t-1})/y_t$ or $(\partial y/\partial t)(1/y)$.

13.3 THE DEFINITION OF THE SHORT RUN IN MACROECONOMIC MODELS

The short run is that analytical period in which some variable or other in the model is held fixed. Therefore, depending upon which variable is being held fixed, there can be many different designations of the short run.

In specifying the macroeconomic model to be a short-run rather than a long-run model, the variable being held constant is the physical capital stock. The usage here follows that initiated by the Keynesian models, where the focus had tended to be on variations on the demand side of the economy. This usage now applies to the short-run neoclassical models also. Note that investment in physical capital occurs in such models but the implicit assumption is that there is a sufficiently long gestation lag for such investment so as not to change the productive capacity of the economy. However, this investment does change aggregate demand in the economy during the short run. In contrast to the fixity of the physical capital stock in the short-run models, the long-run macroeconomic models assume that investment changes the physical capital stock. This change causes growth in the economy, so that the growth models are classified among long-run models.

Another type of fixity that occurs within the short run – that is, with a fixed capital stock – macroeconomic models is with respect to expectations and wage rates. The wage agreement between a firm and its workers normally specifies a nominal wage rate for a forthcoming contract period, while workers base their decisions to supply labour on the expected real wage rate over the contract period. This requires a theory on the formulation of the expected price level, with the possibility that the expected price would differ from the actual one over the contract period. The supply curves of labour and of output based on an expected price different from the actual one are called short-run models, as compared with long-run models which would exist if there were no errors in expectations. Such 'long-run' analysis – that is, with expected prices identical with the actual ones – of the economy is still within the context of the short-run macroeconomic model, with the latter assuming a fixed capital stock.

Also note that the terms 'short run' and 'long run' are different in meaning from their counterparts of 'short period' or 'short term' and 'long period' or 'long term'. The former are analytical constructs indicative of the forces allowed to work in the analysis, the latter are chronological ones and refer to a period of actual time. In the real world, both the analytical short run and long run coexist simultaneously at every moment of time in the economy, even though the latter would clearly be in the short period. To illustrate, the population and the capital stock are continuously changing, so that the analytical forces of the long-run growth models must be continuously operating in the economy.[4] At the same time, the analytical forces of the short-run macroeconomic models are also simultaneously operating in the economy.

13.4 THE COMMODITY SECTOR

Equilibrium in the commodity market

The output of commodities is produced by firms with the use of inputs. It is assumed that the total output produced by the firms is paid or credited as income to one or the other of their inputs, so that total output is always equal to the aggregate national income received by the inputs.

In the closed economy, the recipients of national income y may spend it on consumption c, pay it in taxes t or put it away as saving s. That is,

$$y = c + t + s \tag{1}$$

The demand for output originates as consumption expenditures c, as government expenditures g or as investment expenditures i. Designating the real aggregate expenditures on commodities as e,

$$e = c + g + i \tag{2}$$

National income y is the sum of the payments to inputs in the production process and is thus the aggregate cost of production in the economy. Aggregate expenditures e are the aggregate revenue from the sale of the output produced. Ongoing equilibrium in the production process requires that the aggregate costs and revenues be equal. If $e > y$, firms will find it profitable to increase production, and if $e < y$, firms will find it profitable to cut back on production. That is, in equilibrium in the commodities market,

$$y = e \tag{3}$$

Hence, in equilibrium:

$$c + t + s = c + g + i$$

so that,

$$t + s = g + i \tag{4}$$

When government expenditures and tax revenues are equal and the budget is balanced, $g = t$, and the equilibrium condition simplifies to:

$$s = i \tag{4'}$$

The equilibrium condition for the commodity sector is sometimes expressed as (4'), which requires the equality of saving and investment for equilibrium in the economy. However, since this condition requires a balanced budget, which does not always happen to be the case, it is preferable to specify the equilibrium condition as (4) rather than (4').

Saving is the residual of current output left over after consumption and payment in taxes. This residual may be directly committed for future production in the form of investment, lent to others in exchange for bonds or exchanged for money balances. Therefore, the overall demand for investment goods may not equal the supply of saving in an economy in which other goods, such as bonds and money, exist. Further, there is no reason to assume that the sum of saving and tax revenues would automatically and always equal the sum of investment and government expenditures, as (4) requires. Hence, equilibrium does not always exist in the commodity sector. When it does not, we need to examine the mechanisms that might take this sector towards equilibrium.

Equation (4) can be rewritten as an equation for the excess demand for – or its converse, excess supply of – commodities. Excess demand E_c^d for commodities is defined as their aggregate demand less their output, that is, as $(e - y)$. That is,

$$
\begin{aligned}
E_c^d &= e - y \\
&= c + g + i - c - t - s \\
&= (g - t) + (i - s) \tag{5}
\end{aligned}
$$

In equilibrium, excess demand is zero, so that:

$$(g - t) + (i - s) = 0$$

An economy in which aggregate demand is *always* equal to the output produced can conceivably exist in the real world. Such an economy would be a pure subsistence economy without exchange, or a barter economy without any goods other than commodities and labour. However, an economy in which other goods exist permits the demand for commodities to possibly differ from their supply, the excess demand (or excess supply) being reflected in a corresponding excess supply (or excess demand) for all other goods in the economy.[5] Such an excess demand or supply may be eliminated relatively soon or with a considerable time lag and depends upon the speed of adjustment towards equilibrium.

The behavioural functions of the commodity market

We develop (1) and (2) further by making simple assumptions about each of the variables involved. Assume that real consumption c depends linearly upon real disposable income $(y - t)$. That is,

$$c = c(y_d) = c(y-t)$$
$$= c_0 + c_y(y-t) \quad 0 \le c_y \le 1 \tag{6}$$

where the symbol c in $c(y)$ stands as a functional symbol, indicating the dependent variable, and c_0 and c_y are parametric symbols. c_0 is called 'autonomous consumption' – that is, that part of consumption which does not depend upon other variables – and c_y is called the marginal propensity to consume since it measures the change in consumption for a unit change in disposable income. Many neoclassical economists assume that consumption depends negatively on the rate of interest, so that (6) should have included another term $(-c_r r)$ on the right-hand side. The empirical dependence of consumption on the rate of interest, for the usual range of interest rates in the developed economies, is doubtful – and definitely much more doubtful than the dependence of investment on the rate of interest. Further, the impact of such a term within the macroeconomic model is identical with that of the dependence of investment on the rate of interest. Consequently, we have not included the rate of interest in the consumption function; by implication, the rate of interest will also not be in the saving function. In (6), y_d $(=y-t)$ is disposable income and t is tax payments.

Real investment i is similarly assumed to depend linearly upon the rate of interest, so that,

$$i = i(r)$$
$$= i_0 - i_r r \quad i_r \ge 0 \tag{7}$$

where i_0 is autonomous investment and i_r measures the interest sensitivity of investment.[6]

Government revenues t are assumed to be a linear function of real income y, as in

$$t = t_0 + t_y y \quad t_y \ge 0 \tag{8}$$

Government expenditures g are assumed to be exogenously determined at g_0, so that,

$$g = g_0 \tag{9}$$

A few points to note about the assumptions made so far: all variables have been assumed to be in real terms and independent of the aggregate price level. This assumption implies that consumers and firms are free of price illusion in their consumption and investment decisions. This assumption is a standard one in macroeconomic models and is valid under a strict interpretation of comparative statics.[7]

The IS relationship
Equations (2), (3) and (6) to (9) yield:

$$y = c_0 + c_y\left(y - \left(t_0 + t_y y\right)\right) + g_0 + i_0 - i_r r$$

$$= \left[\frac{1}{1 - c_y\left(1 - t_y\right)}\right]\left(c_0 + i_0 + g_0 - c_y t_0 - i_r r\right) \tag{10}$$

Equation (10) is derived from (3) and is therefore another form of the equilibrium relationship. It specifies the locus of values of y and r at which equilibrium exists in the commodity sector and is often called as the IS (investment–saving) relationship.[8]

Equation (10) implies that the equilibrium level of real income is a function of the rate of interest and not of the price level. This general statement remains valid even if consumption depended upon income *and* the rate of interest, and if investment depended upon the interest rate *and* income.[9] However, the parameters of (10) – and the multipliers (11) to (13) – would alter in such a case.

The commodity market (partial) multipliers
From (10), we have:

$$\frac{\partial y}{\partial i_0} = \left[\frac{1}{1 - c_y\left(1 - t_y\right)} \right] \tag{11}$$

$$\frac{\partial y}{\partial g} = \left[\frac{1}{1 - c_y\left(1 - t_y\right)} \right] \tag{12}$$

Equation (11) specifies the *investment multiplier* and (12) specifies the *government expenditures multiplier*: the increase in national income for a unit increase in investment or government expenditures. Correspondingly, the *autonomous tax multiplier* is specified by:

$$\frac{\partial y}{\partial t_0} = -c_y \left[\frac{1}{1 - c_y\left(1 - t_y\right)} \right] \tag{13}$$

Note that while we have derived the investment and fiscal multipliers in (11) and (12), they are deceptive and even erroneous for a monetary economy. The reason for presenting them is partly by way of an exercise in the illustration of multipliers and partly out of an attempt at uniformity of treatment with most textbooks in macroeconomics. They are based on the commodity market, which is a very limited part of the economy, and ignore the monetary sector, which is also needed for determining aggregate demand in the economy. Further, they ignore the supply side of the economy. The appropriate multipliers are those derived after a general analysis of all the sectors of the whole economy.[10] The usefulness of the above multipliers is only in studying the determinants of the shifts of the IS curve.

The IS curve
Equation (10) is plotted in Figure 13.1 as the IS curve. It has a negative slope since r has a negative coefficient in (10). Macroeconomics textbooks usually present its diagrammatic

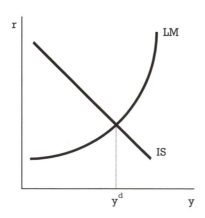

Figure 13.1

derivation but we have not done so under our assumption that the student either knows it or can access it from a macroeconomics textbook, or can rely on (10) for its understanding.[11]

The intuitive explanation for the negative slope of the IS curves is as follows. An increase in income y, along the horizontal axis, increases both consumption and saving, as well as increasing tax revenues. Equilibrium requires that investment must also increase by the combined increases in saving and tax revenues. But this can only occur if the rate of interest falls. Hence, an increase in income must be accompanied by a decline in the interest rate if equilibrium is to be maintained in the expenditure sector.

13.5 THE MONETARY SECTOR

Earlier chapters on the demand for money established that the demand for money should be studied in real rather than nominal terms and that, in its simplest form, the demand for real balances m^d is a function of real income y and the nominal interest rate r. Assuming a linear relationship for simplification, the demand for real balances is specified by:

$$m^d = m^d(y, r)$$
$$= m_y y - m_r r \quad 0 < m_y, m_r < \infty \tag{14}$$

The dependence of money demand on the rate of interest arises from several sources, such as the transactions demand in Chapter 4, the speculative demand in Chapter 5 and the precautionary and buffer stock demand in Chapter 6. However, for traditional reasons related to Keynes' treatment of money demand, the term $(-m_r r)$ is often referred to as the speculative demand element.[12] We will mostly refer to it as the interest-sensitive money demand.

The examination of the money supply process showed that the supply function for money should be specified in nominal terms and that if the monetary authorities allowed the economy to determine it, it would include the interest rate and real income among its arguments. Alternatively, the monetary authorities could set its level exogenously and achieve it through their control over the reserve base. In line with the latter assumption, we simplify the money supply function to:

$$M^s = M \tag{15}$$

where M is the exogenously determined money stock.

Equilibrium in the monetary sector requires that,

$$M = P m^d \tag{16}$$

Hence, the equilibrium condition in terms of real balances, from (14) to (16), is:

$$M/P = m_y y - m_r r \tag{17}$$

From (17), note that while the nominal stock of money is exogenously given and in the control of the monetary authorities, the real value of that stock, (M^d/P), depends upon the equilibrium price level P in the economy and incorporates choices made by the public, including those on its demand for money.

The LM relationship and the LM curve

Equation (17) specifies those combinations of y and r which maintain equilibrium in the monetary market. It is called the LM relationship – where L stands for liquidity preference and M stands for the money supply.

The LM relationship can also be rewritten as:

$$y = \frac{1}{m_y}\left[\frac{M}{P}\right] + \frac{m_r}{m_y}\,r \tag{18}$$

where $1/m_y$ is the real balances multiplier: an increase in real balances by one unit increases real income by $1/m_y$.

Equation (18) is plotted in Figure 13.1 as the LM curve. Since $\partial y/\partial r > 0$ in (18), the LM curve has a positive slope. The intuitive explanation for this slope is: an increase in y along the horizontal axis increases the transactions component of the demand for money, requiring the public to reduce its speculative component $(m_r r)$, which the public will only do at a higher rate of interest. That is, an increase in real income must be accompanied by an increase in the rate of interest for equilibrium to be preserved in the monetary sector.

13.6 THE COMMODITY AND MONETARY SECTORS COMBINED: THE AGGREGATE DEMAND FOR COMMODITIES

Separate treatment of the commodity and monetary sectors separates the influences operating on the aggregate nominal demand for commodities into its two distinct categories. This has its uses but it can also convey a distorted picture of a monetary economy. One can form the impression from it that because the expenditures on commodities are treated in real terms in the commodity sector and are not a function of prices there, the aggregate demand for the output of commodities is therefore not a function of the price level in the overall economy and can be determined solely from the commodity sector equilibrium. This impression is incorrect since the product market makes the demand for output a function of the rate of interest, which is jointly determined with the price level in the monetary sector, so that the IS and LM curves jointly determine the demand for commodities as a function of the price level. Further, if one focuses on the commodity and monetary sectors only, the IS and LM curves in the (y, r) space convey the impression that they are enough to determine real income and the rate of interest. This is again incorrect. *What is being determined by these sectors and curves is merely the demand for output*. This demand has to be set against the supply of output to determine actual real income or output in the economy and the price level at which this output will be traded. To proceed along this route, we have to first derive from the IS–LM analysis the demand for output as a function of the price level.

To derive the demand y^d for output as a function of the price level P, combine the IS and LM equations (10) and (17): the procedure is to solve the LM equation (17) for r in terms of y and P, and substitute this value of r in the IS equation (10). The resulting equation is:

$$y^d = \left[\frac{1}{1 - c_y\left(1 - t_y\right) + i_r m_y/m_r}\right]\left(c_0 + i_0 + g_0 - c_y t_0 + \frac{i_r M}{m_r P}\right) \tag{19}$$

Equation (19) specifies the aggregate demand for commodities. This demand clearly depends upon the price level P and is inversely related to the latter. Equation (19) specifies those combinations of (y, P) which simultaneously maintain equilibrium in the expenditure and monetary sectors.

The multipliers for aggregate demand

The investment and government expenditures multipliers *for aggregate demand* now become:

$$\frac{\partial y^d}{\partial i_0} = \frac{\partial y^d}{\partial g_0} = \left[\frac{1}{1 - c_y\left(1 - t_y\right) + i_r m_y / m_r} \right]$$

$$= \left[\frac{m_r}{m_r - c_y\left(1 - t_y\right)m_r + i_r m_y} \right] \qquad (20)$$

These multipliers are now smaller than given by (10) for the expenditure sector alone. The intuitive explanation for this change is that a given increase in autonomous investment (i_0) increases income through the multiplier, which increases the transactions demand for money. The decreased supply of money balances left for speculative purposes increases interest rates, which forces a reduction in induced investment $(i_r r)$. Total investment therefore rises by less than the initial increase in autonomous investment. Note that these multipliers becomes zero if there are no money balances which can be released from the speculative to the transactions purposes, as would be the case if m_r were zero. Fiscal policy would then have no effect on aggregate demand.

The money multiplier – the increase in aggregate demand for a unit real increase in the real balances supply – is given by:

$$\frac{\partial y^d}{\partial\left(M/P\right)} = \left[\frac{1}{1 - c_y\left(1 - t_y\right) + i_r m_y / m_r} \right] \left(\frac{i_r}{m_r} \right)$$

$$= \left[\frac{i_r}{m_r - m_r c_y\left(1 - t_y\right) + i_r m_y} \right] \qquad (21)$$

The money multiplier may be smaller or larger than the investment multiplier, depending upon the relative magnitudes of i_r – the interest sensitivity of investment – and of m_r – the interest sensitivity of money demand. If $m_r = 0$, the money multiplier is simply $1/m_y$ and if $i_r = 0$, the money multiplier is zero. Thus, an increase in the money supply could only affect aggregate demand if investment were sensitive to the rate of interest, irrespective of whether the demand for money itself is sensitive or is not sensitive to the rate of interest. Monetary policy also cannot increase demand if $m_r \rightarrow \infty$ – that is, any increase in the money supply is absorbed by the infinitely elastic demand for money at the existing interest rates. This case of an infinitely elastic demand for money at the existing interest rate is that of the *liquidity trap*.[13]

The effectiveness of fiscal policy in increasing aggregate demand thus depends not only upon the parameters of the commodity sector but upon those of the monetary sector as well. In particular, fiscal policy cannot affect aggregate demand if $m_r = 0$ – that is, the demand for money (just as its supply) – is insensitive to the rate of interest. Monetary policy cannot affect aggregate demand if investment is insensitive to the rate of interest. Further, monetary policy cannot affect aggregate demand in the liquidity trap.

Figure 13.2 plots equation (19) in the (y, P) space. Designate this curve as the AD (aggregate demand) curve. It has a negative slope.

13.7 THE SUPPLY SIDE OF THE NEOCLASSICAL MODEL

The production function

The counterpart of the aggregate demand for output is the aggregate supply of output. In industrialized economies, capital and labour are the dominant inputs in production, while

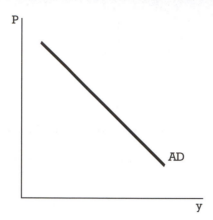

Figure 13.2

land plays only a minor role and is normally not included in macroeconomic analysis. With this assumption, the production of commodities uses only labour and capital as inputs. The production function for the economy – as represented by that for a single firm – can then be written as:

$$y = y(n, K) \quad y_n, y_K > 0; y_{nn}, y_{KK} < 0 \tag{22}$$

where:

- y output
- K capital stock
- n labour employed

The physical stock of capital has already been assumed to be constant in the short-run macroeconomic context of our analysis, so that $K = \underline{K}$, where the underlining indicates 'constancy' or 'exogeneity'. Hence, we have:

$$y = y(n, \underline{K}) \quad y_n > 0, y_{nn} < 0 \tag{23}$$

With this modification, labour is left as the only variable input, with a positive relationship between output and employment. The assumption of $y_n > 0$ and $y_{nn} < 0$ is that the marginal productivity of labour is positive but diminishing: successive increments of labour yield smaller and smaller increments of output.

The labour market

The specification of the labour market requires specification of the demand and supply functions of labour. The demand function for labour is derived from profit maximization by firms and the supply function for labour is derived from the utility analysis of households/workers. These were presented above in Chapter 3 along with the demand and supply functions for commodities and money. We here present the simplified functions used in standard neoclassical macroeconomic models. These assume that the demand and supply of labour depend only on the real wage rate.

It is assumed that firms maximize profits. Hence, they employ labour until its marginal revenue product equals its nominal wage rate. Using the price level to divide both of these variables, in perfect competition and in the aggregate, profit maximization requires that firms employ labour up to the point where the real value of its marginal product equals its real wage rate. That is,

$$y_n(n, \underline{K}) = w \qquad\qquad (24)$$

where:

y_n marginal product of labour
w real wage rate

Solving (24) for employment n, and designating this value as the demand for labour n^d by firms,

$$n^d = n^d(w) \quad \partial n^d/\partial w < 0 \qquad\qquad (25)$$

Chapter 3 had derived the supply function of labour from utility maximization. Its simple version in a single commodity world is:

$$n^s = n^s(w) \quad \partial n^s/\partial w > 0 \qquad\qquad (26)$$

where n^s is the supply of labour. Note that (26) specifies that the supply of labour depends upon the real rather than the nominal wage. Hence, workers are free from *price illusion* – the distortion caused when money wage rates and the prices of commodities rise by identical proportions but the workers, looking at the rising nominal wage rates, believe that they are better off, although the purchasing power of wages has remained unchanged.

The equilibrium levels of employment and output

Equilibrium in the labour market requires that,

$$n^d(w) = n^s(w) = n \qquad\qquad (27)$$

where n is employment. Since (27) is an equation in only one variable, w, solving it would yield the equilibrium wage rate w^*. This wage rate, substituted in either the demand or supply function, yields the equilibrium level of employment n^*. This level of employment substituted in the production function (23) would yield the equilibrium level of output y^* for the economy.

Note that n^* equals both the demand and supply of labour at the equilibrium wage. Therefore, at n^*, all the workers who want jobs at the existing wage rate are employed and the firms can get all the workers that they want to employ. This is the definition of full employment[14] so that the equilibrium level of employment n^* represents full employment and, to emphasize this property, can be designated as n^f. Its corresponding equilibrium output level y^* is the full employment level of output y^f.

These conclusions on the labour market equilibrium are that:

$$n = n^* = n^f \qquad\qquad (28)$$

From (23) and (28), we have:

$$y = y^* = y^f \qquad\qquad (29)$$

Diagrammatic analysis of output and employment in the neoclassical model

Figure 13.3a plots the demand and supply functions of labour, with the usual slopes for demand and supply curves. Equilibrium occurs at (n^*, w^*). Figure 13.3b plots the production function: it plots output y against employment n and is labelled as y (output).

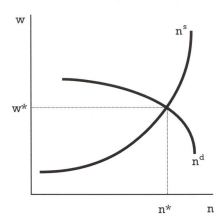

Figure 13.3a

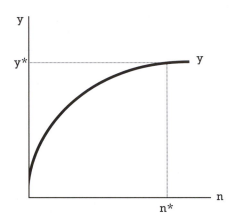

Figure 13.3b

This curve has a positive slope and is concave, representing the assumption of the diminishing marginal productivity of labour. The equilibrium level of employment n^* determined in Figure 13.3a is carried over into Figure 13.3b and implies the equilibrium – and profit maximizing – output y^*.

From (27) to (29) – and as shown in Figures 13.3a and 13.3b – the equilibrium levels of the real wage rate, employment and output do not depend upon the price level. They are determined uniquely and, in particular, are independent of the demand for output. The factors that will change these equilibrium values w^*, n^* and y^* are shifts in the production function – with implied shifts in the demand for labour – and in the supply of labour. Other shocks to the economy which do not bring about these shifts will not alter the equilibrium values of w, n and y. Among these shocks are changes in the policy variables, such as the money supply and fiscal deficits, which are in the overall macroeconomic model but do not appear as arguments of the production function and the supply function of labour. This is a very strong implication for the equilibrium states of the neoclassical model. It implies that the aggregate demand policies such as monetary and fiscal policies cannot affect the equilibrium levels of wages, employment and output in the economy. This implication will be discussed below at greater length.

The implications of full employment equilibrium for the impact of aggregate demand on output and employment

Since the equilibrium level of output is independent of the demand side of the economy, the preceding analysis has the implicit assumption that the economy has adequate and sufficiently fast reacting equilibrating mechanisms to force aggregate demand y^d into equality with y^f continuously or in a short enough period for the deficit or excess of demand not to affect the production and employment decisions of firms and/or the consumption demand and labour supply decisions of households. This is quite a strong assumption and not all economies in all possible stages of development or of the business cycle meet it.[15]

The neoclassical model assumes that the above assumption is met. In it, the equilibrating forces adjusting aggregate demand to the aggregate supply determined in the production–employment sector bring about appropriate changes in interest rates and the price level – but not in real output. *If these adjustments always occur and keep the economy at full employment output, we might caricature the adjustment process as: 'the equilibrium level of supply creates its own demand'[16] through the equilibrating variations in prices, wages and interest rates.*

13.8 GENERAL EQUILIBRIUM: AGGREGATE DEMAND AND SUPPLY ANALYSIS

We have now specified the markets for commodities, money and labour. We have not specified the market for bonds – defined as non-monetary financial assets – even though it is one of the four goods in the macroeconomic model. This omission is justified by Walras' law, which specifies that in a four-good economy, if three of the goods markets are in equilibrium, the market for the fourth good must also be in equilibrium. Therefore, at the general equilibrium (y^*, r^*, P^*) in the preceding analysis, the bond market will also be in equilibrium and can be omitted from explicit consideration.

A full view of the economy requires simultaneous consideration of all markets and general equilibrium in the economy implies a simultaneous solution to the equilibrium equations for all three sectors. We consider this in two alternate ways, the demand–supply analysis and the IS–LM analysis.

Demand–supply analysis

Equations (29) and (19) incorporate information on all the sectors and are respectively the aggregate supply and demand equations. They were:

Aggregate supply:

$$y^s = y^* = y^f \tag{29}$$

Aggregate demand:

$$y^d = \left[\frac{1}{1 - c_y\left(1 - t_y\right) + i_r m_y/m_r} \right] \left(c_0 + i_0 + g_0 - c_y t_0 + \frac{i_r M}{m_r P} \right) \tag{19}$$

In equilibrium, $y^d = y^s = y$, so that we have:

$$y = \left[\frac{1}{1 - c_y\left(1 - t_y\right) + i_r m_y/m_r} \right] \left(c_0 + i_0 + g_0 - c_y t_0 + \frac{i_r M}{m_r P} \right) \tag{30}$$

Equations (29) and (30) have two endogenous variables: y and P. Of these two equations, (29) clearly determines y, even without reference to (19) or (30), as being equal to y^*. Therefore, the aggregate demand equation (19) can only determine P, with y on its left side being set equal to y^*.

Aggregate demand and supply curves

The above conclusion is illustrated in Figure 13.4. Equation (29) specifies the equilibrium – often called the *long run* – aggregate supply curve LAS, and (19) specifies the aggregate demand curve AD. An examination of this figure clearly shows that shifts in the aggregate demand curve will not change the equilibrium output but only change the price level, while changes in the aggregate supply will change both output and the price level. This is a very strong conclusion and is, as we shall see later in this and the next three chapters, at the heart of the debate on the ineffectiveness of monetary and fiscal policies for the equilibrium states of the neoclassical model and its related modern classical and new classical models.

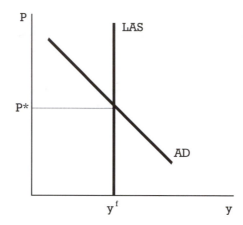

Figure 13.4

Equilibrium output and prices

Equations (29) and (30) imply the equilibrium values of y and P as:

$$y = y^f$$

$$P = \frac{\alpha i_r M_0}{m_r \left[y^f - \alpha \left(c_0 + i_0 + g_0 - c_y t_0 \right) \right]} \tag{31}$$

where

$$\alpha = \frac{1}{1 - c_y \left(1 - t_y \right) + i_r m_y / m_r}$$

13.9 COMPARATIVE STATIC POLICY EFFECTS

Demand shifts

In terms of the general equilibrium neoclassical model, (29) determines output and (31) determines the price level. These equations imply the monetary and fiscal multipliers on output as:

$$\partial y / \partial g = 0 \tag{32}$$

$$\partial y / \partial M = 0 \tag{33}$$

which clearly indicates that the equilibrium level of output is not responsive to monetary and fiscal policies. The elasticities of output and prices with respect to the policy variables of M and g are:

$$E_{y \cdot M} = \frac{M}{y} \frac{\partial y}{\partial M} = 0 \tag{34}$$

$$E_{P \cdot M} = \frac{M}{P} \frac{\partial P}{\partial M} = 1 \tag{35}$$

$$E_{y \cdot g} = \frac{g}{y} \frac{\partial y}{\partial g} = 0 \tag{36}$$

$$E_{P \cdot g} = \frac{g}{P} \frac{\partial P}{\partial g} = \frac{\alpha g}{\left[y - \alpha \left(c_0 + i_0 + g - c_y t_0 \right) \right]} \tag{37}$$

where $E_{i \cdot j}$ is the elasticity of i with respect to j. From (34) to (37), neither the monetary nor the fiscal policy variables of M and g can change the equilibrium level of output but both change the price level: increases in the money supply and/or increases in the fiscal deficit increase the price level. The relative magnitude of the effects of fiscal and monetary policies on the price level is given by:

$$\frac{\partial P}{\partial g} \bigg/ \frac{\partial P}{\partial M} = \frac{\alpha m_r M}{m_r \left[y - \alpha \left(c_0 + i_0 + g - c_y t_0 \right) \right]}$$

$$= \frac{m_r}{i_r} P \tag{38}$$

Equation (38) shows that the relative effects of money supply changes and those in government expenditures depend upon the interest-sensitivity of investment and the demand for money. In the extreme cases, if $m_r = 0$, fiscal policy does not change the price level and if $i_r = 0$, monetary policy does not do so.[17]

Supply shifts

In the real world, output is hardly ever static. Suppose the production function or the supply of labour shift such as to increase y^f, while the money supply is held constant. From (31), the impact of this increase in y on the price level is:

$$\frac{\partial P}{\partial y} = \frac{-\alpha i_r M}{m_r \left[y - \alpha \left(c_0 + i_0 + g - c_y t_0 \right) \right]^2} < 0 \tag{39}$$

The reason for the negative sign of (39) is that an increase in output raises the transactions demand for money which has to be offset by lower prices. Now consider the case where both output and the money supply simultaneously increase over *time*. Then,

$$\dot{P} = \frac{1}{P}\frac{\partial P}{\partial y} = \frac{1}{P}\frac{\partial P}{\partial M}\frac{\partial M}{\partial t} + \frac{1}{P}\frac{\partial P}{\partial y}\frac{\partial y}{\partial t}$$

$$= \dot{M} - \left[\frac{1}{y - \alpha\left(c_0 + i_0 + g - c_y t_0\right)}\right]\frac{\partial y}{\partial t} \tag{40}$$

where t is time and a dot on a variable indicates its rate of growth. From (31), $m_r = 0$ implies that $\alpha = 0$, so that in this case,

$$\dot{P} = \dot{M} - \dot{y} \tag{41}$$

From (41) when $m_r = 0$ – so that the interest sensitivity of money is zero and the velocity of money is constant with respect to changes in the rate of interest – the rate of inflation will equal the rate of growth of money less that of output.

But if $m_r > 0$, so that velocity can change, (41) will not hold. Note that if $m_r > 0$, the term $\alpha(\cdot)$ in the denominator of (40) is positive, so that the rate of inflation would be less than if $m_r = 0$. Thus the existence of the negative interest sensitivity of money demand reduces the rate of inflation for given rates of growth in the money supply and output. The reason for this is that the increase in the money supply reduces the rate of interest, which increases speculative holdings and so reduces the amount available for transactions.

13.10 THE ITERATIVE STRUCTURE OF THE NEOCLASSICAL MODEL

Another procedure for studying simultaneous equilibrium in all sectors of the economy emerges if the final *equilibrium* equations for the monetary and commodity sectors are examined separately in the overall problem. Equations (10), (17) and (29) incorporate information on all the sectors and were:

Production–employment sector:

$$y = y^f \tag{29}$$

Expenditure sector:

$$y = \left[\frac{1}{1 - c_y\left(1 - t_y\right)}\right]\left(c_0 - c_y t_0 + i_0 + g_0 - i_r r\right) \tag{10}$$

Monetary sector:

$$M/P = m_y y - m_r r \tag{17}$$

From the employment–output sector equilibrium given by (29), we know the level of equilibrium output. Substitute this equilibrium level of output y^* into the IS relationship (10). This yields the equilibrium rate of interest r^* as,

$$r^* = \frac{1}{i_r}\left(c_0 - c_y t_0 + i_0 + g_0\right) - \left[\frac{1 - c_y\left(1 - t_y\right)}{i_r}\right]y^f$$

so that we know the equilibrium level of the interest rates, even without introducing the money supply. Hence, the quantity of money supply is irrelevant to the determination of the equilibrium value of the rate of interest. Substituting the equilibrium levels of income y^* and interest rate r^* in (17) yields the equilibrium price level in (31) above as:

$$P = \frac{\alpha i_r M_0}{m_r \left[y^f - \alpha \left(c_0 + i_0 + g_0 - c_y t_0 \right) \right]} \tag{31}$$

where:

$$\alpha = \frac{1}{1 - c_y \left(1 - t_y \right) + i_r m_y / m_r} $$

Consider the nature of this procedure. The production–employment sector alone determined the full employment output in (29), without any reference to the interest rate and the price level; the expenditure sector then determined the interest rate, without any reference to the price level or the monetary sector; but the price level was determined by reference to all the sectors of the economy.

As a special (the classical) case, if $m_r = 0$, the monetary sector condition with $y = y^f$ simplifies to:

$$M/P = m_y y^f$$

which can be rearranged as:

$$P = \left(\frac{1}{m_y y^f} \right) M \tag{42}$$

which does not include r as a variable, so that we only need to know the equilibrium rate of output to determine the price level. Therefore, the dependence of the price level upon the interest rate gets eliminated if the interest sensitivity of money demand was zero and the demand for money was independent of the rate of interest.

This iterative structure of the economy in equilibrium comes into sharper focus by rewriting the above equations in their general form as:

Production–employment sector:

$$y = y^f \tag{29}$$

Expenditure sector:

$$\phi(r; y^f; g, t) = 0 \tag{43}$$

Monetary sector:

$$\Omega(P; y^f, r^*; M) \tag{44}$$

As discussed already, (29) determines output as y^f, which substituted in (43) – for given values of g and t – determines r as r^*. In turn, y^f and r^* substituted in (44) – for a given value of M – determine P as P^*. If r is not a variable in (44) – that is, $m_r = 0$ – then we can go straight from (29) to (44) and determine P without reference to r^* – and hence without reference to the fiscal variables of g and t.

Policy implications: the ineffectiveness of monetary and fiscal policies in changing output and employment

Important policy implications follow from the iterative nature in equilibrium of the neoclassical model. Fiscal policy enters in (43) through g and t and can affect the equilibrium interest rate r^*. In the general case, since r enters in (44), fiscal policy can also affect the price level P. Monetary policy through M enters in (44) only and can only affect the equilibrium price level P^* but cannot affect the equilibrium interest rate. Neither monetary nor fiscal policy can affect equilibrium output, since neither appears in (29).

Hence, since the equilibrium level of output cannot be increased through monetary and fiscal policies, these policies are useless for increasing the equilibrium levels of employment and reducing the equilibrium level of unemployment. However, with the economy in equilibrium, these policies are not only useless, they are also not needed since equilibrium employment in this model is at full employment. *There is thus no need or scope for the authorities to pursue policies to increase employment or output, which are both at their full employment levels. Any such attempt will be ineffective.* The qualifications to this can occur if the economy is not neoclassical in nature, as discussed in Chapter 14 on the Keynesian models, or if it is neoclassical but is out of equilibrium for some time.

The rate of unemployment and the natural rate of unemployment

The level of unemployment is defined as:

$$U = L - n \tag{45}$$

where:

    U level of unemployment
    L labour force

Since $n \leq L$, unemployment is always non-negative. If L can be assumed to be exogenously given as $\underline{L}$ so that it does not vary with the real wage, the labour force will be the sum total of workers who are able and willing to work at *any* wage, so that it represents the maximum amount of potential employment in the economy. But if $L = L(w)$, it is likely that the number of workers willing to work increases as the real wages rise, so that $L' \geq 0$. For our fairly basic analysis at this point, we will make the former assumption.

The natural rate of unemployment

The *equilibrium level* of unemployment U^* is:

$$U^* = L - n^* \tag{46}$$

The *equilibrium rate* of unemployment u is:

$$u^* = U^*/L = 1 - n^*/L \tag{47}$$

From (28) and (47), we have:

$$\partial u^*/\partial M = \partial u^*/\partial g = 0$$

that is, in the neoclassical model, since n^* is independent of the demand side of the economy and L is exogenous, the *equilibrium* rate of unemployment u^* is also independent of changes in aggregate demand and therefore of monetary and fiscal policies. This property of the equilibrium rate of unemployment u^* generated by the neoclassical model has led to its being designated as the *natural rate of unemployment*, so that we can henceforth use the symbol u_n for it. This rate is also called *the full employment rate of unemployment*, so that another symbol for it will be u^f.

Note that $u_n > 0$ by virtue of structural, frictional, search and seasonal unemployment in the economy, which prevent the employment of all members of the labour force since some would have inappropriate skills and education, be in inappropriate locations or require wages in excess of their marginal productivity in the current state of the economy.

On the characteristics of the natural rate of unemployment in the neoclassical model, this rate cannot be changed by monetary or fiscal policy. It does, however, depend upon the supply structure – the labour market relationships and the production function – of the economy and will change as the supply structure changes. Technical change and changes in educational and skill requirements, the level of education of the labour force, the availability of information on jobs and workers, the location of industry, etc., are thus likely to change the natural rate of unemployment. This rate is therefore itself a variable, though not one that can be changed by demand shifts in the economy, including the pursuit of monetary and fiscal policies. Shifts in the supply side of the economy can change the natural rate. Among these shifts is technical change and shifts in the industrial structure due, among other things, to shifts in the structure of demand among the sectors of the economy.

The natural rate of unemployment rises during a transition from one industrial and agricultural structure of the economy to a different one. Suppose that industry A is declining and laying off workers while industry B is expanding its labour force. The process of transfer of workers involves searching for new jobs by the laid-off workers, so that search unemployment increases during the transition. Further, some of the laid-off workers may possess skills not needed in industry B and may become permanently unemployed. This increases structural unemployment in the economy. That is, the shift in the economy's industrial structure induces a *transitional* increase in the natural rate of unemployment, but it can also imply a long-run shift in that rate.

The actual rate of unemployment

If the labour market is not in equilibrium, then,

$$u = \left(u - u_n\right) + u_n \tag{48}$$

$$\frac{\partial u}{\partial t} = \frac{\partial\left(u - u_n\right)}{\partial t} + \frac{\partial u_n}{\partial t} \tag{49}$$

so that the actual rate of unemployment will change over time – and over the business cycle – due to fluctuations in the disequilibrium rate of unemployment and in the natural rate of unemployment. The equilibrium assumption for the neoclassical theory sets the former equal to zero, while the disequilibrium version of the neoclassical theory and the Keynesian theory, set out in the next chapter, does not do so.

13.11 THE COMPARATIVE STATICS OF THE NEOCLASSICAL MODEL IN A DIAGRAMMATIC FORM

Figure 13.5 brings together the information incorporated in Figures 13.1 and 13.2 for each of the sectors of the economy and represented in equations (10), (17) and (29), with the y–n curve being specified by (29). This curve is called the output–employment curve and is the aggregate supply curve in the (y, n) space. It is vertical since y does not depend upon r, according to (29). Equilibrium in all the sectors of the economy exists at the point (r^*, y^*) which lies at the common intersection of the three curves.[18]

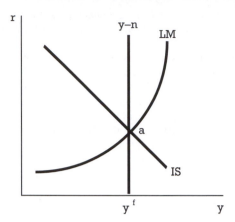

Figure 13.5

The only endogenous change that shifts at least one of the curves in the IS–LM Figure 13.5 is the price level. However, it is not a variable in the functional relationships for the expenditure and the output–employment sectors, and therefore cannot affect the IS and y–n curves. But it is a variable in the monetary sector and therefore in the LM equation (17) so that, since P is not on the axes, a change in P must cause a shift in the LM curve. The reason for this is that a rise in P decreases the supply of real balances which must be offset, for any given rate of interest, by a decrease in transactions demand and therefore in real expenditures, thereby shifting the LM curve to the left. A fall in P would conversely shift the LM curve to the right.[19]

An expansionary monetary policy

We now give some examples of how Figure 13.5 can be manipulated for comparative static studies. This is done in Figure 13.6 for monetary policy. Suppose that the economy is initially in overall equilibrium at point a and the money supply increases, shifting the LM curve to LM'. The new equilibrium between the monetary and expenditure sectors is shown by point d and represents nominal aggregate demand. But output specified by the output–employment sector is at y^f. Since aggregate demand at d exceeds the supply of output y^f, prices rise. As P rises, the LM curve shifts to the left. However, the rise in P leaves the IS and y–n curves unchanged. Prices will then continue to rise as long as aggregate demand for output exceeds its supply. This will occur until the shifts in the LM curve due to

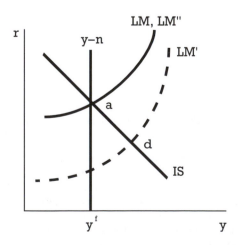

Figure 13.6

the price increases take it sufficiently back to pass through the initial equilibrium point a. In short, in terms of equilibrium states, an increase in the money supply increases aggregate demand, without affecting output, and raises prices to a new level, with the increase in the price level being proportionate to the increase in the money supply. The interest rate is unchanged between the old and the new equilibrium positions.

An expansionary fiscal policy

Now suppose that fiscal policy had become expansionary with an increase in government expenditures. This would have increased the real aggregate demand for commodities and shifted the IS curve to IS′ in Figure 13.7. Nominal aggregate demand at point d – at the intersection of the IS′ and LM curves – exceeds the output y^f. Prices rise, eventually lifting the LM curve to a new overall equilibrium at point b, with the final LM curve as LM′. Both prices and interest rates are higher in the new equilibrium position at b, than at the initial one at point a. Hence, increases in fiscal expenditures increase the equilibrium levels of interest rates and prices, but not of output.

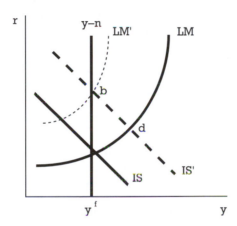

Figure 13.7

13.12 SPECIAL CASES OF THE IS–LM ANALYSIS AND THE NEOCLASSICAL–KEYNESIAN SYNTHESIS

The two special cases of historical interest in the monetary context have both been in connection with the interest sensitivity of money demand. To facilitate reference to these, note that the demand function for real balances used in the above analysis has been:

$$M^d = m_y y - m_r r \tag{17}$$

Our macroeconomic analysis has so far assumed that $0 < m_r < \infty$. The special cases arise when m_r is either (i) zero, or (ii) tends to infinity.

(i) The classical (quantity theory) range of the LM curve

In the case where $m_r = 0$, the overall demand for real balances is not responsive to interest rates. In this case, the condition for equilibrium in the monetary sector is:

$$M/P = m_y y \tag{50}$$

which specifies the LM curve to be vertical. The pre-Keynesian analysis of the demand for money – as in Pigou's version of the quantity theory – corresponds to this case, so that this case is called the *classical range* of the LM curve, though it was more truly the implication of the quantity theory for the shape of the LM curve. However, in the modern economy, there can be no doubt of the dependence of money demand on interest rates, so that (50) does not hold for such an economy. It might, however, be the case that at sufficiently high interest rates, the interest sensitivity of money demand becomes zero, so that the general LM curve would have a part that is vertical and has the properties of (50).

(ii) The liquidity trap

The second special case occurs where $m_r \to \infty$. Keynes drew attention to this case and labelled it as the *liquidity trap*.[20] In this case, bond holders would be willing to exchange their bond holdings for money at the existing rate of interest and the LM curve would be horizontal. If open market operations increase the supply of money, the increase in the money supply would be willingly held by the public as an asset in preference to bonds. Since the demand for bonds would not increase and their prices would not rise, the interest rates would not decline and investment would not increase. Consequently, the increase in the money supply would not induce any increase in expenditures in the economy. That is, increases in the money supply would not have any effects – including those on the price level – on the economy.

While there can undoubtedly be periods where the public becomes despondent about getting a positive net return in excess of brokerage costs from holding non-money financial assets,[21] such periods tend to be short lived in a normally functioning form of the modern economy. That is, the liquidity trap could exist for short periods but need not be of sufficient duration to have significant macroeconomic effects for such an economy.

The neoclassical–Keynesian synthesis on aggregate demand

Therefore, for the well-functioning modern economy, both the classical case and the liquidity trap are of historical interest, or are analytical curiosities, rather than because they are expected to be significant for the modern macroeconomy. The neoclassical–Keynesian synthesis on aggregate demand established by the early 1960s was based on the profession's acceptance that these two special cases were not relevant to the modern economy and, therefore, could be eliminated as sources of differences between the neoclassical and Keynesian schools of thought. We will, in general, ignore them from further discussion in this book.

13.13 THE FOUR FUNDAMENTAL ASSUMPTIONS FOR THE WALRASIAN EQUILIBRIUM OF THE NEOCLASSICAL MODEL

The preceding analysis has focused on the general equilibrium states of the model and is a succinct macroeconomic version of the Walrasian model. This equilibrium analysis makes four *fundamental assumptions*. These are that:

(I) Flexible prices and wages

The prices of all the goods in the economy are assumed to be flexible and adjust to equate demand and supply in the relevant market. They increase if there is excess demand and decrease if there is excess supply. These prices include wages, which is the price of labour.

(II) Continuous market clearance

Each market clears continuously, so that we can focus on the study of the general equilibrium in the economy and its properties, while largely ignoring the disequilibrium values of the variables.

(III) Transparency of equilibrium prices

All agents in making their demand and supply decisions assume that such market clearance will occur instantly after any disturbance and know/anticipate (or are informed by an agency such as a 'Walrasian auctioneer' or 'market coordinator') the prices at which it will occur. Further, all agents plan to produce, consume, demand money and supply labour at *only* these equilibrium prices.[22]

(IV) Notional demand and supply functions

All economic agents assume that they will be able to buy or sell as much as they want to at the equilibrium prices. The demand and supply functions derived under this assumption are known as *notional demand and supply functions*.

The neoclassical equilibrium analysis of the economy and its policy recommendations require the applicability of these fundamental assumptions: flexible prices and wages, continuous market clearance, transparency of equilibrium prices and notional demand and supply functions. Each assumption is related to the others but is still distinct. Any one or more of these assumptions may not be relevant to and valid for a particular stage or at a particular time in an economy.

   As shown above, money is neutral in the equilibrium states of the neoclassical model since changes in the money supply affect only the nominal but not the real variables. Hence, the neoclassical model implies that, in equilibrium, monetary policy cannot change output and employment in the economy. In fact, with the economy at full employment, there is also no need for the pursuit of monetary policy. Conversely, if the above assumptions hold, changes in the money supply also cannot be detrimental for output and employment in the economy. In particular, decreases in the money supply will not decrease output and employment and force the economy into a recession. Monetary policy is benign (harmless) in such a context.

13.14 DISEQUILIBRIUM IN THE NEOCLASSICAL MODEL AND THE NON-NEUTRALITY OF MONEY

Note that the neoclassical model does not assert that its equilibrium must always exist – as if it was an identity – so that it allows the possibility that the economy can be sometimes in disequilibrium. Further, for the study of disequilibrium to be a potentially useful exercise requires the belief that the economy will be away from its full employment equilibrium state for significant periods of time. Intuitively, continuous general equilibrium requires, for example, the belief that an increase in the money supply *immediately* causes a proportionate increase in the price level and that a decrease in it will not cause a recession in output and employment. There is considerable evidence to show that these requirements are not always, or most of the time, met in most real-world economies. Nor did the major proponents in the classical and neoclassical tradition claim that they did. Among those who allowed for the existence of disequilibrium for significant periods of time were Hume, Marshall, Fisher, Pigou and Friedman.

   However, when the classical economists allowed for disequilibrium, they maintained that any such state of disequilibrium incorporates certain forces that will force the economy to equilibrium. Among these forces were price changes and the Pigou effect, including the real balance effect. These were touched upon in Chapter 3 and will be explored more fully in Chapter 17. We explain them again, though briefly, in the following subsection as a reminder and for completeness of the neoclassical model.

13.14.1 The Pigou effect and the real balance effect

The Pigou effect is associated with the contributions of A. C. Pigou (at Cambridge University in England in the first half of the twentieth century) in the debate between the traditional Classical School and Keynes in the 1930s. The Pigou effect is another name for the wealth effect on consumption. Its working is as follows. A disequilibrum with deficient demand for commodities will cause a fall in their prices. Since the household's wealth includes financial assets, this fall in the price level will increase the household's wealth, which, in turn, will cause consumption to rise. The latter will bring about an increase in aggregate demand in the economy. This process will continue until the demand deficiency is eliminated – that is, until the economy returns to equilibrium.

The real balance effect is associated with the contributions of Don Patinkin in the 1940s and 1950s and represented a refinement of the neoclassical model for the analysis of disequilibrium. This effect represents the impact of changes in the price level on consumption through changes in the real value of money holdings. It works as follows. A price fall due to a demand deficiency will increase the real value of money holdings and thereby increase the household's wealth. This will lead to an increase in consumption and therefore in aggregate demand. The real balance effect will continue until the demand deficiency and its associated price-level decreases are eliminated.

Hence, the real balance effect and the Pigou effect are equilibrating mechanisms of the neoclassical model and require flexible prices. Their analytical relevance is significant and beyond dispute. However, they do not, *a priori*, provide any guidance on the time the neoclassical economy will need to return to equilibrium under their impetus. In particular, the real balance effect can be quite weak, so that the neoclassical economy could react to an exogenous fall in demand by a very slow movement towards equilibrium and, therefore, remain in disequilibrium for a significant period. Hence, it is important to analyse the disequilibrium properties of the neoclassical model and derive its policy implications.

13.14.2 An analysis of disequilibrium for the neoclassical model

The assumptions for disequilibrium analysis

The analysis of disequilibrium is tricky since there can be many possible disequilibrium patterns for the neoclassical model so that we should not expect a consensus on the particular pattern which will hold. In particular, the disequilibrium patterns depend on the specific assumptions made for behaviour in disequilibrium. To limit these patterns, we need to specify the source of deviations from equilibrium. For consistency with the neoclassical model and its spirit, we will maintain the assumptions of the rationality of economic behaviour by households and firms in the light of the information available to them, so that the rational expectations hypothesis will also be maintained. The first fundamental assumption on the flexibility of prices and wages will also be retained.

However, we will dispense with the other three fundamental assumptions above. Of these, (II) by definition is not consistent with the existence of disequilibrium. The invalidity of (III) follows from the absence of (II) and rational expectations: that is, if equilibrium is not instantly restored following a disturbance, rational economic agents will know this and will not rationally assume market clearance and, therefore, also may not know the equilibrium prices.

The invalidity of (IV) follows from the invalidity of (II) and (III) and rational behaviour. For example, the representative unemployed workers do not continue to consume on the basis of the income they would have received under a hypothetical state of being employed when the economy is in full employment equilibrium. Economic rationality requires them to cut their expenditures to suit their actual (and anticipated) income while unemployed, not to a hypothetical income. As another example, the representative firm in the modern economy, faced with a decline in the demand for its product due to a fall in aggregate demand in the economy and holding the belief, which often happens, that many months, possibly a few years, may lapse before recovery of its demand, usually finds it rational to reduce its production, besides any reduction in prices.

Therefore, disequilibrium analysis properly requires that we dispense with the fundamental assumptions (II) to (IV). We will do so for the following discussion of disequilibrium in the neoclassical model.

Sketching a plausible disequilibrium path

To start this analysis, take the economy to be initially in equilibrium. Now suppose that aggregate demand falls for some reason such as an exogenous decrease in consumption, investment, fiscal expenditures or money supply or an increase in taxes. Such a fall in aggregate demand is shown in Figure 13.8 by a shift from AD to AD'. We need to analyse plausible dynamic responses of the representative economic agents in the modern economy while maintaining the spirit of the neoclassical model.

First, consider the response pattern of the neoclassical model under its four fundamental assumptions of equilibrium analysis. Remember that the market is initially at (P_0, y^f), but is suddenly faced with the fall in demand to AD'. Under assumption (I) above, prices and wages will fall in response to the fall in demand. Under (II), the commodity market will clear; under (III), the agents will learn or be informed about the new market-clearing price P_1, and, under (IV), they will produce the output y^f at the price P_1, so that there will be no change in output. The dynamics of this analysis is that the economy would go instantly from P_0 to P_1, without changing output in the process.

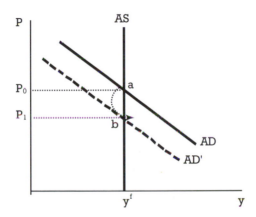

Figure 13.8

For comparison, consider the following components of an intuitively plausible dynamic scenario.

(a) As aggregate demand falls, the representative firm in the economy shares in this experience and finds that it cannot sell its former level of output, so that with production in advance of sales, it ends up unintentionally accumulating inventories. To run these down and to adjust to its reduced sales, its optimal response is to cut back on production, rather than wait for the economy's aggregative markets to clear, and possibly also to reduce the price for its products.[23,24] This reduction in output takes the economy below the equilibrium output y^f, with employment falling below full employment.

(b) This fall in employment results in a reduction in the purchasing power of workers, who then rationally decrease their consumption expenditures. Further, some of the employed workers find or believe their jobs to be at greater risk than normal at the full employment level, so that the employed workers on average will increase their precautionary saving and reduce their consumption expenditures. This process accentuates the initial decrease in aggregate demand, leading to further reductions in output and prices by the representative firm.

(c) Facing a fall in sales, the representative firm is also likely to be cutting back on its investment plans, thereby contributing further to the fall in aggregate demand.

Hence, the rational production responses of firms and consumption responses of households work in ways that do not make for an instant restoration of general equilibrium but could accentuate the departure from equilibrium for some time. Note that this scenario allowed prices and wages to be flexible, so that there is no assumed rigidity of prices and wages.[25]

Let us now assume that the economy eventually returns to equilibrium, as the neoclassical model maintains. However, our analysis implies that the economy would have spent some real time with less than full employment, so that, in Figure 13.8:

(a) the economy will not have gone from the initial equilibrium at (y^f, P_0) to the new equilibrium at (y^f, P_1) *instantly*; and
(b) output will loop from point *a* to *b*, with output in the loop falling for some period below the full employment level. These levels will be referred to as recessionary levels and are disequilibrium ones within the context of the neoclassical model.

13.14.3 Disequilibrium, flexible prices and wages and the absence of an instantaneous coordinating mechanism

The above scenario is not the only one that can be sketched but it does seem to capture the most common response patterns of actual firms, consumers and workers. Critical to this scenario is not any rigidity in prices and wages, for none has been assumed, nor the absence of an eventual return of the economy to equilibrium, but the absence of a mechanism for instantly restoring equilibrium. Note that the assumption of perfect competition does not *a priori* specify the chronological time needed by the 'invisible hand of competition' to return an economy, following a shock, to its full employment equilibrium.[26] Along with the absence of a mechanism for instantly restoring the full employment equilibrium, we have assumed that the competitive economy does not have an instantaneous mechanism operating in disequilibrium for computing the new price level and informing all firms and households of the new prices of the products. Further, we have assumed that there was no guarantee given to the firms that they could sell all they wanted at these prices, nor was there any guarantee that the workers will receive or recoup the incomes lost while they were unemployed. It seems that postulating these is less plausible for the modern capitalist economy than our sketchy scenario, which does allow for competitive market forces but without imposing instant adjustment to equilibrium following a disturbance. In this connection, note that the real balance and Pigou effects could be operating, but not fast enough and not with sufficient force to ensure instant restoration of full employment equilibrium.

In the absence of a fast and powerful equilibrating mechanism, can we plausibly take the firms and households to know, as under rational expectations, the new *equilibrium* price level? To do so, they need to know the notional forms of the aggregate demand and supply functions in the economy, not merely to observe their own actual demand and supply functions. The required information on the aggregates of the economy or notional functions is surely beyond the information available to any one firm, so that a scenario based on such extensive information seems less plausible than the alternative one sketched above. Therefore, it seems worthwhile to stick to the sketched scenario, even though it is admittedly one of many possible ones, as a reasonable one and proceed with further discussion on the disequilibrium state of the neoclassical model under it.

A caveat is necessary here. Many economists are likely to disagree with the preceding analysis of disequilibrium of the neoclassical model. Some would consider it to be an unwarranted departure from the neoclassical model and take the stand that the above three fundamental assumptions of the neoclassical model are an integral part of it. Such a stand rules out any analysis of the disequilibrium implications of the neoclassical model. Other economists could disagree with the above disequilibrium analysis because they may consider other scenarios to be more plausible.

13.14.4 Multipliers in the disequilibrium in the neoclassical model

Proceeding further with the results of our scenario, posited as a plausible one, our arguments imply under this scenario that the policy multipliers during disequilibrium are:

$$\text{For } y = y^d < y^f, \qquad \partial y/\partial M \; = \; \partial y/\partial g > 0 \tag{51}$$

$$\text{Similarly, for } u > n^f, \quad \partial u/\partial M \; = \; \partial u/\partial g < 0 \tag{52}$$

which differ from the zero values of these multipliers for the equilibrium version of the neoclassical model. Given these differences in the multiplier values between the equilibrium and the disequilibrium phases of the neoclassical model, a neoclassical policy maker has to be concerned with how long the economy will stay at recessionary levels, and what it can do to speed up the return to full employment.

To reiterate the gist of our arguments, suppose that the economy has entered the recessionary state with unemployment substantially in excess of the natural rate specified by the structural and frictional elements of the economy. Further, suppose that the experience is that the economy, if left to itself, is extremely slow to move to equilibrium. The policy prescriptions relevant to this disequilibrium state will not necessarily be those derived so far for the equilibrium states. In the posited recession, assuming that it is caused by a demand deficiency in the economy, an increase in the money supply would lower the rate of interest, stimulate investment and consumption, and through the multiplier, increase aggregate demand in the economy. Firms confronted with the increase in demand would increase output, employment and also possibly prices. Hence, money would not be neutral in the demand-deficient recession and increasing the money supply would be an appropriate – that is, output and employment increasing – policy to pursue.

13.14.5 The non-neutrality of money in disequilibrium in the neoclassical model

Therefore, since the neutrality of money – and the ineffectiveness of monetary policy – need not be a property of the disequilibrium states of the neoclassical model, the overriding question for policy becomes one of the determination of the actual existence of equilibrium or disequilibrium in a specific period – *even if the economy is inherently neoclassical in terms of its structural framework*. Unfortunately, there does not seem to be a convincing procedure for determining whether an economy at a particular point is in neoclassical equilibrium or not, so that there tend to be disputes on this issue and therefore on the effectiveness of monetary policy. Individual opinions of economists on this issue, even in a recession, often tend to have a large element of faith and psychological make-up rather than knowledge of the actual state of the economy, as must the actual policies followed by the central banks at such times.

On the deviations from the fourth fundamental assumption of neoclassical equilibrium, again assume that the economy is in a severe recession and has excess unemployment. The unemployed workers are not able to sell all the labour that they want to sell, so that their demand and supply functions for commodities, money and labour would not be the notional ones required for the neoclassical model. To illustrate, the involuntarily unemployed workers would not receive income for the labour they had wanted to sell, and must cut back on their purchases of commodities and on their demand for real balances. To align their production policies to this lower demand for commodities, firms would cut their output or their prices. An incentive to *increase* employment sufficiently to eliminate the excess unemployment need not emerge in this scenario. Therefore, the neoclassical model in its notional set-up and with the assumption of equilibrium or a strong tendency to it would not be relevant, nor would its implications on the neutrality of money and the ineffectiveness of monetary policy.

To summarize, the neoclassical model posits the potential for disequilibrium in the actual economy and its major proponents allowed for its existence for significant periods of time for their economies. But its policy conclusions and even the nature of its demand and supply functions derived from its equilibrium analysis need not apply in disequilibrium. If the economy has a strong tendency towards equilibrium, so that the actual economy can be expected to reach it in a short while, focusing the analysis and policy prescriptions on the equilibrium properties would be justified. However, economic theory and econometric tests provide some but not full guidance for determining this. Consequently, the policy makers are also forced to rely on their feel and perceptions on the state of the economy, making the pursuit of policy 'an art rather than a science'.

13.15 THE RELATIONSHIP BETWEEN THE MONEY SUPPLY AND THE PRICE LEVEL: THE HERITAGE OF IDEAS

The basic comparative static conclusions of the neoclassical macroeconomic model of this chapter were presented a couple of centuries ago. The following quote illustrates them from the writings of David Hume, one of the founders of classical economics:

> Money is nothing but the representation of labour and commodities, and serves only as a method of rating or estimating them. Where coin is in greater plenty – as a greater quantity of it is required to represent the same quantity of goods – it can have no effect, either good or bad, taking a nation within itself; any more than it would make an alteration in a merchant's books, if instead of the Arabian method of notation, which requires few characters, he should make use of the Roman, which requires a great many . . .

> (Hume, *Of Money*, 1752)

This quote is an assertion of the basic proposition of the quantity theory of money: an increase in the money supply causes a proportional increase in prices. Further, Hume asserts that changes in the supply of money do not change real output in the economy but correspond to a change in the unit of account. The quantity theory was presented in Chapter 2.

The conclusions of this theory on the proportionate relationship between the money stock and prices, and the inability of the monetary and fiscal authorities to control output and employment, apply in equilibrium. They do not necessarily apply in disequilibrium – the adjustment from one equilibrium to another. In fact, many supporters of this theory, in Hume's time and down to the present, have viewed changes in the money stock as exerting a powerful influence on output, employment and other variables in the adjustment process. Hume himself described this process as:

> Notwithstanding this conclusion, which must be allowed just, it is certain that since the discovery of the mines in America, industry has increased in all the nations of Europe, except in the possessors of those mines; and this may justly be ascribed, among other reasons, to the increase of gold and silver. Accordingly, we find that in every kingdom, into which money begins to flow in greater abundance than formerly, everything takes on a new face; labour and industry gain life; the merchant becomes more enterprising, and even the farmer follows his plough with greater alacrity and attention . . .

To account then for this phenomenon, we must consider, that though the high price of commodities be a necessary consequence of the increase of gold and silver, yet it follows not immediately upon that increase; but some time is required before the money circulates through the whole state, and makes its effect be felt on all ranks of people. At first, no alteration is perceived; by degrees the price rises, first of one commodity, then of another; till the whole at last reaches a just proportion with the new quantity of specie which is in the kingdom. In my opinion, it is only in this interval or intermediate situation, between the acquisition of money and the rise of prices, that the increasing quantity of gold and silver is favorable to industry.

(Hume, Of Money, 1752)

Hume's opinions on the disequilibrium path of adjustment serve as a note of caution against total reliance on the comparative static results.

Almost two centuries later, Pigou, a twentieth-century economist in the classical tradition, expressed similar ideas in the following excerpts from his book, *Money, A Veil* (1941).

Money – the institution of money – is an extremely valuable social instrument, making a large contribution to economic welfare . . . if there were no generally accepted money, many of these transactions would not be worth undertaking, and as a direct consequence the division of labour would be hampered and less services and goods would be produced. Thus not only would real income be allocated less satisfactorily, from the standpoint of economic welfare, among different sorts of goods, but it would also contain smaller amounts of many, if not of all sorts . . . Obviously then money is not merely a veil or a garment or a wrapper. Like the laws of property and contract, it constitutes at the least a very useful lubricant, enabling the economic machine to function continuously and smoothly . . .

So far everyone would be agreed. But now an important distinction must be drawn. The institution of money is, as we have seen, a powerful instrument promoting wealth and welfare. But the number of units of money embodied in that instrument is, in general, of no significance. It is all one whether the garment, or the veil, is thick or thin. I do not mean, of course, that it is immaterial whether the number of units of money is held constant, or is variable in one manner, or is variable in another manner in relation to other economic happenings. I mean that if, other things being equal, over a series of months or years the stock of money contains successively $m \times 1, m \times 2, m \times 3 \ldots$ units, it makes no difference what the value of m is. A doubled value of m throughout means simply doubled prices throughout of every type of goods – subject, of course, to the rate of interest not being reckoned for this purpose as a price – and all real happenings are exactly what they would have been with a value of m half as large. The reason for this is that, money being only useful because it exchanges for other things, a larger quantity does not, as with other things, carry more satisfaction on its back than a smaller quantity, but the same satisfaction.

(Pigou, 1941, Ch. 4)

13.16 THE CLASSICAL AND NEOCLASSICAL TRADITION, ECONOMIC LIBERALISM AND *LAISSEZ FAIRE*

The equilibrium analysis of the neoclassical model in this chapter implies that the economy functions at full employment, with full employment output, so that there is no scope for monetary and fiscal demand management policies for such an economy. Such a viewpoint is part of the classical philosophy of economic liberalism which can be broadly formulated as stating that the economy performs at its best by itself and that the state cannot improve on its performance. This is usually also supplemented by the proposition that any intervention by the state, even with the intention of improving upon the performance of the economy, worsens its performance. These propositions imply that the goods and input markets should be free and that free enterprise should be the desired standard. However, market imperfections such as imperfect competition, oligopoly, monopoly or monopsony could and often do exist in the actual economy. Advocates of the *strong form of economic liberalism* argue that, even in such cases, the economy should be left as it is and the state should not attempt to eliminate such imperfections: the imperfections are minor and even when they are not of minor significance, there is no guarantee that state intervention will achieve a net improvement since its intervention might eliminate some imperfections while introducing others. A *weaker version of economic liberalism* allows the state to intervene to eliminate market imperfections through selective policies, though without assigning a role to general monetary and fiscal policies.

To be credible, the general liberalism philosophy has its underpinnings in the nation's political, economic and social ideology, and in the public's perception and goals for the actual economic and social performance of the nation. In its general approach, the underlying philosophical basis of liberalism was provided by the utilitarianism approach of Jeremy Bentham and his followers in the first half of the nineteenth century. The main tenet of this approach was that economic agents (households and firms), working in their own best interests (utility and profit maximization), would ensure that social welfare was maximized. Consequently, the economy should be left alone by the government and regulatory agencies. This policy approach was summarized in the term *laissez faire*. In its economic aspects, the liberalism philosophy needed a theoretical economic model that could justify its economic policy recommendations. This model at the macroeconomic level was provided by the traditional classical approach in the pre-Keynesian period and is currently the neoclassical one – with the modern and new classical models among its versions.

The economic and social problems of nineteenth-century Britain, with rapid industrialization and urbanization, were sufficiently acute and transparent to lead to a gradual evolution of political and economic thought away from liberalism and *laissez faire* and towards some form of socialism, with support for some degree of state intervention in the economy. This evolution of ideas was widespread during the latter half of the nineteenth century and early twentieth century. The Great Depression of the 1930s destroyed the public's and economists' faith in *laissez faire*, so that Keynes' publication of *The General Theory* in 1936, with its encouragement to the state to use monetary and fiscal policies to improve on a poorly performing economy, proved to be timely and readily won acceptance from most economists and the public. Economic liberalism was eclipsed by Keynesianism for the decades from the 1930s to the 1970s. The Keynesian approach is the subject of the next chapter.

In economics, the traditional classical ideas were reformulated and rebottled in the form of the neoclassical theory during the decades of the 1940s to the 1970s. Since the 1970s, these ideas, in the form of the modern classical model and with the agenda of making microeconomics the foundation of macroeconomics, have again become the dominant approach in macroeconomics. Their return to this dominance detoured briefly through monetarism during the 1970s. They are currently supported by the new classical approach developed during the 1970s and 1980s.

Some major misconceptions about traditional classical and neoclassical approaches

A common misconception nowadays is that the traditional classical and neoclassical economists believed that the economy functioned well enough to maintain full employment most of the time or that it had a fast tendency to return to full employment following a disturbance and a decline in employment. In fact, many believed that 'the economic system is inherently unstable'. Another misconception nowadays is that the classical and neoclassical economists believed that money was neutral in practice and in theory or that velocity did not change. In fact, many believed that there could occur – and did occur – 'extreme alternations of hoarding and dishoarding' because of changes in expectations, and that the changes in the money supply and in its velocity were major sources of business fluctuations. Further, many of them believed that these fluctuations were 'exacerbated by the "perverse" behavior of the banking system, which expands credit in booms and contracts it in depressions'. Among the reasons for the real effects of money supply and velocity changes was that 'costs have a tendency to move more slowly than do the more flexible selling prices' – that is, firms' costs were sticky relative to their final prices and that 'sticky prices are peculiarly resistant to downward pressure' (Patinkin, 1969).[27]

To sum up, it was generally recognized that 'cycles and depressions [are] an inherent feature of "capitalism". Such a system must use money, and the circulation of money is not a phenomenon which naturally tends to establish and maintain an equilibrium level. Its equilibrium is vague and highly unstable'. In view of this, 'the government has an obligation to undertake a contracyclical policy. The guiding principle of this policy is to change M so as to offset changes in V, and thus generate the full employment level of aggregate demand MV' (Patinkin, 1969).

As the preceding quote shows, monetary policy was often envisaged and recommended as a stabilization tool. However, fiscal policy was usually not even considered a possibility nor was its analytical basis established by the pre-Keynesian economists. Its consideration and recommendation as a major stabilization tool was due to Keynes and the Keynesians, and needed as its basis the concept of the investment multiplier, first presented by Richard Kahn in the 1930s. As a counter-reformation, Barro's Ricardian equivalence theorem, presented in the next section, sought to again remove fiscal policy from the set of potential stabilization tools.

13.17 RICARDIAN EQUIVALENCE[28] AND THE RETURN TO CLASSICAL ORTHODOXY

While the theory of Ricardian equivalence is not directly relevant to the impact of monetary policy, it is relevant to the more recent modifications of the neoclassical model and the relevant impact of monetary versus fiscal policy on nominal income in the economy. Ricardian equivalence is the proposition that (debt-financed) fiscal deficits merely postpone taxation without changing the economy's aggregate demand in the current period, as well as in the future ones. This runs counter to some of the analysis of aggregate demand in this chapter, and to our results on the fiscal policy effects based on equation (19).

Ricardian equivalence rests on the propositions that in perfect capital markets, the tax liability[29] imposed by a bond-financed deficit equals the amount of the deficit itself,[30] and that the individual sets off the benefit to him from the deficit against its tax liability. For the formal analysis of Ricardian equivalence, assume an economy in which the government supplies exactly the goods that the consumers would have bought on their own, so that there is perfect substitutability – in both consumption and production – between government-supplied goods and privately demanded goods.[31] Consequently, the arguments of the consumer's utility function are not the privately bought goods but the sum of the privately bought and the government-provided goods. The consumers are assumed to have infinitely long lives or to possess an intergenerational utility function encompassing the utility from their own and their descendants' consumption. This intertemporal utility function can be stated as:

$$U(\cdot) = U((c^p + c^g)_1, (c^p + c^g)_2, \ldots, (c^p + c^g)_n) \tag{53}$$

where n can be made arbitrarily large to encompass the period by which the debt used to finance the current deficit is retired and where:

c^p privately bought consumer goods
c^g government-provided consumer goods

Equation (53) is maximized, given the assumptions of perfect foresight and perfect capital markets, subject to their intertemporal budget constraint. This intertemporal personal budget constraint has the form:

$$\sum_t \Psi_t c_t^p = \sum_t \Psi_t(y_t - T_t) \quad t = 1, \ldots, n \tag{54}$$

where:

T tax revenues
Ψ_t discount factor for period t ($= 1/(1 + r)^{t-1}$)

Equation (54) is the private budget constraint and is the usual statement that the present discounted value of the privately bought goods equals the present value of disposable income. We also need the government's intertemporal budget constraint, which is:

$$\sum_t \Psi_t c_t^g = \sum_t \Psi_t T_t \quad t = 1, \ldots, n \tag{55}$$

Equation (55) assumes that there is no outstanding debt at the end of period 0 and asserts that the government-provided goods have to be paid for through taxes over time. This rules out the monetary financing of deficits and indirectly incorporates their financing by the issuing of bonds. The implicit assumption that the discount factors are identical for the private sector in (54) and the government in (55) requires perfect, unregulated capital markets – as well as identical risk premiums for the private sector and the government. Defining the deficit in period t as $(c^g - T)_t$, since we have not imposed the requirement that $T_t = c_t^g$, the government can run a deficit or surplus, or neither, in any particular period i. If there is a deficit in period i, with $g_i > T_i$, it is covered by issuing bonds at the market rate of interest, so that higher taxes will have to be paid in the future to cover the interest on the bonds and their redemption in the future.[32]

Equations (54) and (55) imply that:

$$\sum_t \Psi_t (c^p + c^g)_t = \sum_t \Psi_t y_t \tag{56}$$

which does not include government surpluses and deficits as a variable.

The public's choice-theoretic problem can now be stated as: find the total consumption $(c_t^p + c_t^g)$ which maximizes (53) subject to (56). This will yield the optimal consumption pattern as:

$$(c^p + c^g)_t^* = f(\underline{\Psi}, PDW) \quad t = 1, 2, \ldots, n \tag{57}$$

where

$$PDW = \sum_t \Psi_t y_t \tag{58}$$

and $\underline{\Psi}$ is the vector of discount factors. Note that PDW is the present discounted value of total income y (rather than of disposable income) so that the optimal total consumption levels do not include tax revenues or tax rates among their determinants. Assuming an interior solution, if there is an increase (decrease) in the exogenous supply of government-provided goods in t, the private sector will reduce (increase) its own purchases of goods in t by exactly the same amount, leaving $(c^p + c^g)_t$ invariant to government-provided goods c_t^g, tax revenues, deficits and the government debt. That is,

$$\frac{\partial\left(c^p + c^g\right)_{t+i}}{\partial g_{t+j}} = 0 \quad \text{for all } i, j \tag{59}$$

where g can be government expenditures, tax revenues or deficits. This result is known as Ricardian equivalence.

Ricardian equivalence is usually stated as the proposition that national saving is invariant with respect to the fiscal deficit. National saving s^n, by definition, is:

$$s^n_t = y_t - (c^p + c^g)_t \tag{60}$$

with $(c^p + c^g)_t$ invariant to the size of fiscal deficits. Further, since the two types of consumption are assumed to be perfect substitutes, it is also assumed that a shift in production from one to the other type of good also has no impact on the aggregate output y. That is, $\partial y_t / \partial g_t = 0$. Therefore,

$$\frac{\partial s^n_{t+i}}{\partial g_{t+j}} = 0 \quad \text{for all } i, j \tag{61}$$

Hence, since national saving is the sum of private and public saving, where the latter equals the government budget surplus, private saving must fall (rise) by the amount of an increase in this surplus (deficit). This is another way of stating Ricardian equivalence.

The appendix to this chapter relates two of the common propositions of Ricardian equivalence to the evolution of the public debt.

Monetary and fiscal policies in the macroeconomic model with Ricardian equivalence

To incorporate Ricardian equivalence into the neoclassical model of this chapter, we need to modify its consumption function to accord with the Ricardian results. Designating $(c^p + c^g)_t$ by c'_t and dropping the time subscript t as a simplification for short-run comparative static analysis, the short-run Ricardian consumption function $c'(y)$ will be:

$$c' = c'(y) = c'_0 + c'_y y \tag{62}$$

Note that c' refers to the total of privately bought and government-provided goods, and depends on total income rather than merely on disposable income. Further, there is a change in the meanings of the parameters of the consumption function from those in the neoclassical model earlier in this chapter. In (62), $c'_y = \partial(c^p + c^g)/\partial y$, so that c'_y is the sum of the private and government marginal propensities to consume. Aggregate expenditures in the closed economy after the integration of government-provided goods into the preceding consumption function are now specified by:

$$e = c' + i \tag{63}$$

which no longer includes government expenditures, since these are now included in (57). In equilibrium, $e = y$, so that (62) and (63) modify the IS relationship to:

$$y = c'_0 + c'_y y + i_0 - i_r r$$

$$= \left[\frac{1}{1 - c'_y} \right] \left(c'_0 + i_0 - i_r r \right) \tag{64}$$

The aggregate demand function correspondingly changes to:

$$y^d = \left[\frac{1}{1 - c'_y + i_r m_y / m_r} \right] \left(c'_0 + i_0 + \frac{i_r M}{m_r P} \right) \tag{65}$$

Neither (64) nor (65) includes any of the fiscal variables, so that the changes in government expenditures, taxes and deficits will not shift the IS curve in the IS–LM figures or the AD curve in the AD–AS figures, and, therefore, will have no effects on the macroeconomy. That is, the fiscal variables cannot be used to change aggregate demand and nominal income in the economy, so that they do not provide a policy tool for macroeconomic stabilization.

Since the equations of the monetary sector in the neoclassical model are not affected by Ricardian equivalence, the only policy tool available for changing aggregate demand and nominal income under Ricardian equivalence is monetary policy. Ricardian equivalence, therefore, buttresses the importance of monetary policy in the economy.[33] From (65), Ricardian equivalence changes the money multiplier to:

$$\frac{\partial y^d}{\partial (M/P)} = \left[\frac{i_r}{m_r - c'_y m_r + i_r m_y} \right]$$

13.18 DEFINING AND DEMARCATING THE MODELS OF THE CLASSICAL PARADIGM

There can be considerable disputes about the proper delineation of these schools or models. We had introduced the following taxonomy in Chapter 1. We elaborate on it here, though at the risk of some repetition. No claim is being made to this taxonomy being a universal – or perhaps even as a majority – one. We have chosen it below for reasons of clarity in separating each model from the others, rather than leaving their differences ambiguous, while maintaining consistency with the writings and folklore in the history of economic thought.

All these schools share the common beliefs that the real-world economy under consideration – and not just the models – functions at full employment in the long run and that it does not get stuck in an *under-full employment equilibrium*. States with less than full employment are, therefore, states of disequilibrium during which the economy continues to adjust towards its full employment equilibrium – and not away from it. A major difference among these schools is whether the real-world economy adjusts so fast as to have continuous equilibrium, so that it will not show any evidence of disequilibrium, even though disequilibrium remains a hypothetical state within the model.[34] Further, one of the characteristics of the long-run equilibrium for all the schools is the independence of the real variables from the financial ones, so that money is neutral in the long-run equilibrium.

As explained earlier, the IS–LM (with *y–n* curve) and the AD–AS analytical techniques can be used – or not used, as one chooses – to analyse the models of each of these schools, so that their application or lack of application is not a distinguishing characteristic among these schools. The differences among them are in terms of assumptions and implications, not modes of analysis.

The traditional (or pre-Keynesian) classical model

This model is an attempt at the interpretation or distillation of the writings of the pre-Keynesian economists. However, their ideas were not expressed or formulated in terms of a compact model and the analysis of the expenditure sector (the IS curve) and the multiplier was not available to them. Their common belief was that the output and employment in the long-run equilibrium depended upon the real sector's relationships only and were independent of the monetary sector. The economy's interest rate was determined by the loanable funds theory. Further, the quantity theory for the determination of the price level applied in equilibrium. But outside this equilibrium, changes in the money supply could change output and employment. Not only could the money supply affect the real sector in this way, but the economy was considered to be very prone to fluctuations in output and employment. Many of these were attributed to money supply shocks or the response of the money supply to real shocks. In particular, most of the classical economists did not believe that the economy functioned so well that it always maintained full employment or that it did so most of the time. In fact, recessions and crises – many of them originating in the banking sector or financial speculation or occurring due to the response pattern of the financial sector to real shocks – were common – and widely recognized as such – during the nineteenth century. Hence, the traditional classical school did not assume continuous full employment.

The neoclassical model

This model was an attempt to bottle the main ideas of the pre-Keynesian classical economists into a compact modern macroeconomic model. This process was initiated by Hicks in 1937, who fashioned the IS–LM analysis for the presentation of Keynes' ideas and made it an integral part of the neoclassical model. The neoclassical model continued to have both equilibrium and disequilibrium aspects, and did not assume instant market clearance. In this, it represents the ideas of the pre-Keynesian classical economists more faithfully than does the modern classical model.[35]

The modern classical and new classical models

The certainty version of the modern classical model modifies the neoclassical model by adding the assumption of continuous market clearance, especially of the labour market at the full employment level. By doing so, it ignores the disequilibrium properties and multipliers of the neoclassical model as being irrelevant in practice. The uncertainty version of this model also adds in the rational expectations hypothesis.[36] Some economists would also add to this mix the assumption of Ricardian equivalence. However, our definition of the modern classical model excludes this assumption, but only makes it a part of the new classical model. This differentiation means that, under our definitions, fiscal policy would change aggregate demand in the modern classical model but not in the new classical model.

Hence, under our designations, the constituents of the *modern classical model* are:

(a) the neoclassical model, modified by the additions of:
(b) the rational expectations hypothesis; and
(c) continuous market clearance (especially of the labour market at full employment).

The constituents of the *new classical model* are:

(a) the modern classical model, modified by the addition of:
(b) Ricardian equivalence.

Note that both the modern classical and the new classical models do possess money supply changes as a policy tool for changing aggregate demand in the economy, but, of the two, only the modern classical model allows fiscal policy to change aggregate demand. Both these models imply the neutrality of money in their adoptive full employment state, so that the impact of the money supply and velocity changes can only be on the price level and not on real output and employment. Therefore, both imply that there is neither a need nor scope for systematic monetary policy for changing the levels of output and employment in the economy, so that such policies should not be pursued. These ideas are further explored in Chapters 15 and 16.

13.19 MILTON FRIEDMAN AND MONETARISM

Milton Friedman occupies a special place in the counter-reformation from Keynesian economics to the neoclassical and modern classical ones, though his ideas are, in many ways, closer to neoclassical economics of the 1960s and 1970s than to the modern classical ones. His major contributions from the 1940s to the 1970s laid the basis for challenging the then current versions and assumptions of the dominant Keynesian school. This school in the 1940s and 1950s had downplayed the impact of money supply changes on the economy and had a relative preference for fiscal over monetary policy.

In the 1950s, Friedman argued and showed through his theoretical and empirical contributions that 'money matters' – that is, changes in the money supply change nominal national expenditures and income – as against the then general view of the Keynesian school that changes in the money supply brought about through monetary policy did not significantly affect the economy or did so unpredictably.[37] On the latter, Friedman argued and tried to establish through empirical studies that the money-income multiplier was more stable than the investment-income multiplier, so that monetary policy was not less important or less predictable than fiscal policy in its impact on nominal national income.

Another aspect of Friedman's agenda to re-establish the doctrine that money matters was to set out in the 1950s and 1960s the theory – and establish empirically – that the demand function for money was stable, with the result that the velocity of money also had a stable function. We have already discussed some of these contributions in Chapter 2 in the context of Friedman's re-statement of the quantity theory of money. These arguments were accepted by the profession by the early 1960s, and contributed to the conversion of the Keynesian macroeconomics to a Keynesian–neoclassical synthesis expressed by the IS–LM model for the determination of aggregate demand.

On the relationship between the nominal variables and the real side of the economy, Keynesians in the late 1950s and 1960s had relied on the Phillips curve, which showed a negative tradeoff between the rate of inflation and the rate of unemployment. Friedman argued that the natural rate of unemployment – and, therefore, full employment output – was independent of the anticipated rate of inflation, so that the fluctuations in output and the rate of unemployment were related to the deviations in the inflation rate from its anticipated level. This relationship came to be known as Friedman's expectations augmented Phillips curve and incorporated his contributions on the natural rate of unemployment. The Phillips curve and its expectations augmented version will be discussed in greater detail in the next three chapters.

While Friedman brought the role of anticipations on the rate of inflation into discussions on the role and effectiveness of monetary policy in the economy, he did not have the theory of rational expectations. The rational expectations hypothesis had not yet entered the literature and Friedman had relied on adaptive expectations in his empirical studies. Consequently, for Friedman, the unanticipated rate of inflation – equal to the errors in inflationary expectations – was not random with a zero expected value. Further, since Barro's contribution on Ricardian equivalence had not yet been made, Friedman's writings did not incorporate this hypothesis. Hence, Friedman was a precursor of the modern classical school but not fully a member of it. Nor does this school follow all of his ideas.

However, Friedman was closer to the Keynesians in one important respect than to the later modern classical school. He believed, as did the Keynesians, that the economy does not always maintain full employment and full employment output – and does not always function at the natural rate of unemployment, even though this concept was central to his analysis. Hence, policy-induced changes in aggregate demand could induce short-term changes in output and employment. Therefore, money mattered even to the extent that changes in it could induce changes in employment and output, depending upon the particular stage of the business cycle. While this view was shared with the Keynesians, Friedman tilted against the Keynesians on the pursuit of discretionary monetary policy as a stabilization tool – especially for 'fine tuning' the economy – because of his belief that the impact of money supply changes on nominal income had a long and variable lag. He reported on the outside lag of monetary policy that:

The rate of change of the money supply shows well-marked cycles that match closely those in economic activity in general and precede the latter by a long interval. On the average, the rate of change of the money supply has reached its peak nearly 16 months before the peak in general business and has reached its trough over . . . 12 months before the trough in general business . . . Moreover, the timing varies considerably from cycle to cycle – since 1907 the shortest time span by which the money peak preceded the business peak was 13 months, the longest 24 months; the corresponding range at troughs is 5 months to 21 months.

(Friedman, 1958)

With such a long and variable lag between changes in the money supply and nominal income, the monetary authorities cannot be sure when a policy-induced increase in the money supply would have its impact on the economy. Such an increase in a recession may, in fact, increase aggregate demand in a following boom, thereby only increasing the rate of inflation at that time. Consequently, Friedman argued that discretionary monetary policy, intended to stabilize the economy, could turn out to be destabilizing. Friedman's recommendation on monetary policy was, therefore, that it should maintain a low constant rate of growth. This policy and its evaluation are further discussed in Chapter 16.

Therefore, while both Friedman and the modern classical economists are opposed to the pursuit of discretionary monetary policy, they arrive at this position for quite different reasons. For Friedman, money supply changes can change output and employment but the long and variable lags in this impact make a discretionary policy inadvisable. It could make the economy worse rather than better. For the modern classical economists, the economy maintains full employment, so that systematic policy changes in the money supply cannot change output and employment, but only change the price level. This joint stance against the pursuit of monetary policy hides a subtle difference. For Friedman, money matters for the real sectors of the economy, and changes in the money supply can alter output but are not advisable because of long and variable lags. For the modern classical economist, there are no lags in the impact of systematic money supply changes, and there is no impact on output, so that from the perspective of output and employment, it really does not matter what the money supply is.

On the transmission mechanism from money supply changes to income changes, Friedman supported Fisher's direct transmission mechanism – from money supply changes directly to expenditures changes – over the indirect one – from money supply to interest rates to investment – in Keynesian and IS–LM models. Neoclassical and modern classical models espouse the latter rather than the former.

Monetarists

Monetarism and monetarists have been defined in a variety of ways. In a very broad sense, monetarism is the proposition that money matters in the economy. In this sense, Friedman, and Keynes and the Keynesians, were all monetarists, while the modern classical school is less monetarist since it downplays the impact of money supply changes on the real variables of the economy. In a narrow sense, monetarism was associated with the St. Louis School in monetary and macroeconomics. We will define monetarism in this narrow sense. The St Louis School provided in the late 1960s and early 1970s an empirical procedure for estimating the relationship between nominal income and the money supply. This was the estimation of a reduced-form equation of the form:

$$Y_t = \alpha_0 + \sum_i a_i M_{t-i} + \sum_j b_j G_{t-j} + \sum_s c_s Z_{t-s} + \mu_t \qquad (66)$$

where:

Y nominal national income
M vector of the past and present nominal values of the appropriate monetary aggregate

G　vector of the past and present values of the appropriate fiscal variables
Z　vector of the other independent variables
μ　disturbance term

Equation (66) is called the St Louis equation and was presented earlier in Chapter 8. While its common form used nominal income as the dependent variable, the dependent variable can be changed, depending upon the researcher's interest, to real output, the rate of inflation or some other endogenous variable. In general, the St Louis equation is a reduced-form estimation equation of the short-run macro-models, with the monetary aggregates and the fiscal variables being taken as exogenous.

The St Louis equation has become a popular method for determining the impact of monetary and fiscal policies on nominal national income and other variables. Estimation of it by researchers at the Federal Reserve Bank of St Louis (Andersen and Jordan, 1968) showed that the money aggregates had a strong, positive and rapid impact on nominal income and this impact was more significant than of fiscal policy. The marginal money-income multiplier was about 5 over five quarters, while the marginal impact of fiscal policy was positive for the first year and then turned negative, with a multiplier of only about 0.05 over five quarters.[38] These findings were consistent with Friedman's stance, except that the estimations of the St Louis equation indicated a much shorter and more reliable lag than Friedman had found. Therefore, contrary to Friedman's recommendations and consistent with Keynesian ones, monetarism was consistent with the stance that monetary policy could be useful for short-term stabilization.

The St Louis monetarists also believed, as did Friedman and the Keynesians, that changes in the money supply have a significant and positive impact on real output in conditions of less than full employment. However, for monetarists, as with Friedman but not the Keynesians, the economy tended to full employment in the long-run, so that the long-run impact of money supply changes would only be on the price level.

On the transmission mechanism, the St Louis monetarists supported the direct transmission mechanism, though their estimation technique was not fine enough to separate the two types of mechanisms.

The St Louis monetarism represented a transitional stage in the transition from Keynesian ascendancy in economics in the decades before 1970 to the ascendancy of the neoclassical and modern classical schools in the 1980s and 1990s. In many ways, it was an amalgam of Keynesian and Friedman's ideas in macroeconomics, and led the way in the re-emergence of the classical doctrines.

CONCLUSIONS

The technique of analysis used in this chapter has been the usual one of grouping relationships in the IS–LM format or in the aggregate demand/supply analysis. These are not strictly models in their own right but merely techniques for deriving the implications from the assumptions of the model. As such, the use of these formats as analytical tools is not unique to the neoclassical model, but is shared with many expositions of the Keynesian model.

The traditional classical model, dominant through most of the nineteenth and early twentieth centuries, was a somewhat disorganized set of ideas, for which we can envisage full employment as the long-run equilibrium state but with the existence of disequilibrium being a distinct possibility. Changes in the money supply affected employment and output and caused business cycle fluctuations. The main components of the traditional classical analysis were the quantity theory of prices and the loanable funds theory of the rate of interest. There was no specific theory of employment and output, though there was a general belief that, after a monetary disturbance, the economy eventually returns to its full employment level, and there was no treatment of the product market with its concept of the investment multiplier. The neoclassical model re-organized the traditional classical analysis into a compact form, based on the IS–LM apparatus, and explicitly incorporated into it the analysis of the product market through the IS curve. It also replaced the quantity theory by a general equilibrium determination of the price level. In a departure from many other treatments of the neoclassical model, our version, presented in this chapter, emphasizes both its equilibrium – at the full employment level – and disequilibrium analyses. In particular, it does not assume that the latter can be ignored for applications to the real-world economies and in its policy recommendations.

In our definitions of the various schools which have evolved out of the neoclassical school, the addition of the assumptions of rational expectations and continuous full employment to the neoclassical model turns it into the modern classical model. Adding further the doctrine of Ricardian equivalence to the modern classical model defines the new classical model. While the neoclassical economists from the 1930s to the 1970s had not emphasized labour market clearance as a continuous phenomenon, thereby allowing the real-world economies to be below full employment in some periods, the modern classical and new classical schools tend to do it, or do it more vigorously. Given this assumption of continuous equilibrium at full employment in the labour market, the values of output and employment become independent of the money supply, thereby making monetary policy incapable of changing them.

The addition of the Ricardian equivalence hypothesis to the modern classical model (with continuous full employment and rational expectations) turns it into the new classical model, and changes the former's consumption function and investment and fiscal multipliers. This new classical model implies that fiscal deficits do not even affect the commodity market equilibrium or aggregate demand in the economy, so that the fiscal variables cannot be used as a policy tool. However, the money supply remains a policy tool for changing aggregate demand in the economy.

The implications drawn from the neoclassical model are usually for its full employment equilibrium states. For such states, output is also at the full employment level. Since the objective of policy is normally specified to be the maintenance of full employment, which occurs anyway in the equilibrium of this model, there is no need or role for systematic demand management policies in such a state. Further, since the neoclassical economists usually assume that equilibrium is restored within a reasonable or acceptable period of time, the neoclassical prescription even for the disequilibrium states is that the economy should be left alone to achieve equilibrium.

The main demand management policies are monetary and fiscal policies. The emphasis on full employment equilibrium and a relatively quick transition to it following a shock, translates into the recommendation that such policies should not be pursued. If pursued, they cannot affect the equilibrium real values of the macroeconomic variables, but would only change the nominal values.

Versions of the equilibrium part of the neoclassical model have provided in the last two decades the theoretical basis for the schools in political economy known as Reaganomics in the USA and Thatcherism in Britain. These political philosophies advocate the cessation of any attempts by the monetary and fiscal authorities to change real output and employment in the economy, and the restriction of monetary policy solely to the goal of price stabilization.

Not all economists believe that the economy always achieves full employment or remains reasonably close to it. In particular, the Keynesian school believes that the economy does not always perform at full employment for a variety of reasons. The models of this school are presented in the next chapter.

This chapter has presented the short-run analysis of the role of money in the economy. The analysis of money in long-run growth will be presented in Chapter 26. The analysis of money in the macroeconomy in the short run is continued in the next four chapters.

APPENDIX: THE PROPOSITIONS OF RICARDIAN EQUIVALENCE AND THE EVOLUTION OF THE PUBLIC DEBT

I. Define the amount of outstanding bonds, each with a real value of one unit of commodities, at the beginning of period i to be b_i, and assume $b_1 = 0$. The bonds issued in period i receive interest in $i + 1$. The evolution of the value of the public debt b_{i+1} is specified by,

$$b_{i+1} = \sum_{t=1}^{i} \phi_t \left(c_{i-t+1}^g - T_{i-t+1} \right) \tag{67}$$

where ϕ_t is the interest compounding factor ($= (1 + r)^t$) which multiplies the past deficits to arrive at their present value. Equation (67) specifies the evolution of the public debt over time under the assumption that there is no default.

To relate Ricardian equivalence to the public debt, we need to incorporate its assumption that any bonds issued by the government to finance current deficits are redeemed by some future date n which is within the representative individual's horizon[39] for consumption planning. Since all outstanding government bonds are redeemed at the end of period n, $b_{n+1} = 0$. Hence, setting $i = n$ in (67),

$$b_{n+1} = \sum_{t=1}^{n} \phi_t \left(c_{n-t+1}^g - T_{n-t+1} \right) = 0 \tag{68}$$

so that:

$$\sum_{t=1}^{n} \phi_t c_{n-t+1}^g = \sum_{t=1}^{n} \phi_t T_{n-t+1} \tag{69}$$

where $\phi_t = (1 + r)^t$. Multiplying both sides of (69) by $(1 + r)^{-n}$, we get:

$$\sum_{t=1}^{n} \frac{1}{(1+r)^{n-t}} c_{n-t+1}^g = \sum_{t=1}^{n} \frac{1}{(1+r)^{n-t}} T_{n-t+1} \tag{70}$$

which equals,[40]

$$\sum_{t=1}^{n} \frac{1}{(1+r)^{t-1}} c_t^g = \sum_{t=1}^{n} \frac{1}{(1+r)^{t-1}} T_t \tag{71}$$

which is identical with equation (55) for the government's intertemporal budget constraint, assumed earlier in this chapter for the derivation of Ricardian equivalence.

II. If the interest rate paid on bonds and the discount rate are identical, Ricardian equivalence incorporates the assertion that the present value of the future tax liability[41] imposed by the bonds issued to finance the deficit equals the deficit itself. To show this, let the deficit d be financed by the current issue of bonds b, so that $b = d$, and designate by PV_b the present value of the future tax liability. With the payment of the interest rb at the end of each period and the repayment of the principal b at the end of period n, PV_b is given by:

$$PV_b = \sum_{t=1}^{n} \frac{rb}{(1+r)^t} + \frac{b}{(1+r)^n}$$

$$= b \left(\sum_{t=1}^{n} \frac{r}{(1+r)^t} + \frac{1}{(1+r)^n} \right)$$

$$= b(1) = b \tag{72}[42]$$

Since $b = d$, $PV_b = d$, so that the present value of the future tax liabilities from a bond-financed deficit equals the deficit itself.

SUMMARY OF CRITICAL CONCLUSIONS

- In the Walrasian general equilibrium of the economy, the economy has full employment, full employment output and the natural rate of unemployment.
- In the Walrasian general equilibrium of the economy, the quantity of money is neutral and monetary policy cannot be used to increase or decrease the level of output or unemployment. It can only change the nominal value of aggregate demand, the price level and the rate of inflation.
- The Walrasian economy can at times be in disequilibrium and take time to return to general equilibrium with full employment. In this disequilibrium phase or state, money need not be neutral so that an appropriate monetary policy could speed the recovery to full employment equilibrium.
- While the traditional classical economists and the neoclassical approaches, as well as the 1970s monetarism, envisaged the possibility of the economy at times being in disequilibrium, the modern classical and the new classical approaches assume continuous full employment and Walrasian general equilibrium in the economy. While money is not always neutral in the former set of approaches, it is always neutral in the latter set. If there is uncertainty, then anticipated monetary policy is neutral.
- Whether the economy, especially when in recession, is in full employment equilibrium or not, is never certain, so that the particular monetary policy being followed by the monetary authority is usually in dispute among economists.

review and discussion questions

1 It is often asserted that there is a national income *identity*, so that in a closed economy without a government sector, there is an identity between saving and investment. Explore the implications of this statement by doing the following.

Given a closed economy without a government sector, modify the neoclassical model by the assumption that saving and investment are identical (i.e., equal under all circumstances and not merely in equilibrium). What are the levels of output and employment? Is the LM relationship required for their determination? Is any price level consistent with equilibrium in the commodity market?

Now suppose that the money market is in disequilibrium at the existing price level. Follow the transmission mechanism from this disequilibrium to the change in prices.

Now suppose that the money market was initially in equilibrium but the authorities double the money supply. Would this create an excess demand for (a) commodities, (b) labour? If it does not do so, what would cause prices and nominal wages to rise? What equilibrating mechanism, if any, exists in this model to determine the price level and nominal wages?

Now discuss the following statements: 'For purposes of a satisfactory theory of money supply and prices, the IS relationship must never be treated as an identity, so that there is only a national income equilibrium condition.' 'A satisfactory macroeconomic model must incorporate the potential for disequilibrium between saving and investment even in a closed economy without a government sector.'

2 Discuss: the Pigou effect ensures that a full employment equilibrium exists if prices and wages are flexible.

3 Suppose that the government wants to increase its expenditures g and has the options of financing it by higher taxes, bond issues or increases in the monetary

base. Further, when g is increased through bond or monetary financing, the central bank can also undertake offsetting open market operations. What combinations, if any, of financing methods and open market operations will allow the following goals to be met in the neoclassical model:

(i)   no change in the price level P;
(ii) no change in investment i;
(iii) no change in P and i.

4 Present the analysis of the statement that the effects of government deficits on the rate of inflation and real output and unemployment depend on the way in which the deficit is financed. Also analyse the above statement for the following cases:

(i)   The central bank is known to follow the rule of stabilizing the growth of the money supply.
(ii) Government debt (bonds) is only sold to the central bank.
(iii) The central bank is known to follow the rule of stabilizing the nominal rate of interest.

5 The monetary authority has decided to adopt for one of the following money supply rules:

(a) $M^s = kPy$

(b) $M^s = ky$

where $k > 0$. Show their implications for aggregate demand, prices and output in the context of (i) the neoclassical model and (ii) the neoclassical model with a zero speculative demand for money (i.e., $m_r = 0$). Is each one of these policies viable?

6 One of the banking innovations in the 1960s was the payment of interest on certain types of demand deposits. Assume that interest is paid on money at the rate r_m, which equals $(r - x)$, where x is exogenously determined in nominal terms by market structures and the cost of servicing deposits.

(i)   Use Baumol's transactions demand model to derive the demand function for money.
(ii) Generalizing the above demand function to $m^d(y, r, x)$, show the behaviour of the LM curve for shifts in x and P.
(iii) What is the effect of an increase in x on aggregate demand and the price level in the neoclassical model?
(iv) If both r and x always increase by the expected rate of inflation, do (ii) and (iii) again.

7 'For the economy to have a determinate price level and money to have a positive value, it is necessary that the economy have a demand for money and a mechanism for limiting its supply.' Discuss in the context of (a) the quantity theory, (b) neoclassical economics and (c) the views of the new monetary economics.

8 'In a closed economy, if the money stock is held constant by the central bank, an increase in the government deficit does not have either short-run or long-run effects on aggregate demand and the economy.' Discuss in the context of the neoclassical model and the new classical model (with rational expectations and Ricardian equivalence).

9 Discuss whether the existence of business cycles and the observed positive correlation between real and monetary variables mean that the modern classical models are neither valid nor relevant for policy purposes.

10 Specify a model that generates real business cycles only. Discuss whether this model allows for the observed cyclical correlation between money and output.

11 Present the new classical model (with rational expectations and Ricardian equivalence). Analyse the role of monetary policy in this model.
    How would this model explain the major recession in the early 1990s in most developed economies? What monetary policies – if any – are consistent with this model for moderating the effects of the recession on output and unemployment?

12 Discuss the proposition that a change in the rate of growth of the money supply will not affect output and unemployment in the short run, as well as in the long run, if wages and prices are fully flexible.

13 Explain 'debt neutrality' and 'ultra-rationality' and specify the assumptions needed for them.

14 'The rate of money growth is the sole determinant of the trend rate of inflation and the stance of fiscal policy is irrelevant to it.' Discuss.

15 Can monetary and fiscal policy be independent? If not, why is their independence postulated in the IS–LM analysis? Discuss.

16 What is the 'crowding out' hypothesis? Is it fully or partially valid in the IS–LM model? Can complete crowding out occur in the context of (a) a financially advanced economy, (b) a financially underdeveloped economy?

17 The 1970s monetarism and the new classical school are sometimes lumped under the same banner. How do these schools view the existence of short-run unemployment in the economy and what policies does each imply for curing it? What role do they assign to monetary policy in this respect?

18 What are the ways or reasons under which fiscal deficits can crowd out private expenditures? (In this discussion, do not forget the Ricardian equivalence theorem.) Which is most important in your country?

19 What are the main tenets of the modern classical school and how do they differ from those of the traditional classical one?
    Discuss critically the contributions of the modern classical school to our understanding of the role and limitations of monetary and fiscal policies for stabilization and compare these with those of the neoclassical model.

20 In the neoclassical model, how do:

    (a) the interest elasticity of money demand;
    (b) the interest elasticity of investment; and
    (c) the income elasticity of money demand;

    affect the relative efficacy of monetary and fiscal policies?

21 An empirical study tested for the Ricardian equivalence theorem by estimating the following equation:

$$\Delta A_t = a_0 + a_1 \Delta B_t + \mu_t$$

where A is the public's net real financial assets (excluding its holdings of government bonds), B is real public debt and μ is the random term. Does $\hat{a}_1 = 1$ confirm the Ricardian equivalence theorem? US aggregate time series tend to yield $\hat{a}_1 = 0$. What would this imply for the validity of the Ricardian equivalence theorem?
    Formulate some other estimation equations for testing the Ricardian equivalence theorem.

NOTES

1 See Chapter 17 for the treatment of Say's law.
2 This theory is presented in detail in Chapter 20.

3 Among these differences is the explicit commodity market analysis incorporating the multiplier concept, the interest sensitivity of money demand, the elimination of the direct transmission mechanism of money supply effects on nominal income, explicit analysis of government deficits and their implied future taxes, rational expectations, etc.

4 Note that Keynes' famous remark that 'in the long run we are all dead' is not valid under the above interpretation of the long run.

5 This is related to the concept of Walras' law, which is rigorously derived in Chapter 17.

6 If we believe that saving depends positively on the rate of interest, this can be easily incorporated into the model by redefining $(-i_r)$ to measure the decrease in investment plus the decrease in consumption (or less the increase in saving) induced by the marginal increase in the rate of interest.

7 It is not, however, supported by existing versions of those consumption and investment theories which permit substitution between present purchases of commodities for consumption or investment and those in the future as prices change over time.

8 It was given this name since it was originally derived for a model without a government sector. Hence it represented the equilibrium condition $i = s$, as in (4') above.

9 The general and linearized forms of these functions would then be: $c = c(y, r) = c_0 + c_y y - c_r r$ and $i = (r, y) = i_0 - i_r r + i_y y$, with the assumption that $c_y(1 - t_y) + i_y < 1$.

10 For the open economy, the appropriate multipliers are those from the open economy model which is presented in a later chapter.

11 We will follow this custom for the LM curve also.

12 To do so properly, the money demand function should be written as: $m^d = m_y y + (m_0 - m_r r)$, where $(m_0 - m_r r)$ is the speculative demand for money. However, as noted in the text, whether the money demand function is written in this form or as in (17), the interest-sensitive term in it can also arise even if the speculative demand is zero. This is especially important since Chapter 5 had argued that the modern economy with a variety of riskless assets may not have a positive demand for speculative balances.

13 The earlier treatment of this was in Chapter 2.

14 The definition of full employment is: it is the level of employment such that all the workers who want jobs at the going wage rate have a job, excluding those who are temporarily between jobs during the job search process.

15 If this assumption is not valid for an economy at any stage, then the equilibrium properties of the neoclassical model would not be applicable. The pertinent properties would be those of its disequilibrium analysis.

16 This sounds similar to but is really weaker than 'Say's law'. This law is discussed in Chapter 17.

17 Equation (35) establishes for the neoclassical model the quantity theory proposition that, in equilibrium, a change in the money supply causes a proportionate change in the price level, even though the neoclassical model encompasses the interest sensitivity of money demand – and, therefore, allows for a positive speculative demand for money.

18 The student can use Figure 13.5 to advantage for studying the comparative static effects of exogenous changes in the economy. To facilitate this, he must first make himself familiar with the exogenous changes that shift each of the curves and with the endogenous changes that also do so.

19 Note, however, that the price level is not an exogenous variable, so that a change in it must be determined and explained by reference to changes in some exogenous variables.

20 See Chapter 2 above for Keynes' definition and analysis of this concept.

21 Such periods would occur when there is a general expectation in the financial markets that the bond prices are going to fall, so that there is a widespread expectation of an imminent rise in interest rates by enough to imply a negative net expected return on bonds. This expectation can occur at high or low interest rates, so that the liquidity trap can exist at any rate of interest.

22 In particular, if there are delays in establishing these prices or communicating their

knowledge, it is assumed that all production and trade is put on hold during the delay and that any such delay does not impose costs on economic agents. This is known as recontracting.

23 In any case, there is no auctioneer to coordinate the economy-wide fall in prices to just the right levels.

24 This implicitly assumes monopolistic competition rather than perfect competition.

25 There has also been no assumption of money illusion by either firms or workers.

26 Because of this, the Walrasian and neoclassical models were buttressed with some *deus ex machina* such as the Walrasian auctioneer, *tâtonnement* and recontracting, which solved the problem analytically but represented an escape from answering the relevant question of how long does it take the real-world economies to return to equilibrium.

27 The various quotes are taken from Patinkin (1969), even though many of them are from passages quoted by him from other writers such as Henry Simons, Frank Knight and other economists at the University of Chicago in the second quarter of the twentieth century and presumably part of the Chicago tradition of classical economics.

28 While Ricardo had raised the main idea behind Ricardian equivalence, he had rejected its empirical significance. The modern version of this concept is due to Barro's contributions (Barro, 1974).

29 The tax liability imposed by a bond is defined as the present discounted value of the future interest payments and eventually of the principal at maturity, as specified by the bond.

30 The appendix to this chapter establishes this.

31 This assumption is usually not transparent in the standard presentations of Ricardian equivalence since they normally derive the effects of a deficit created through a reduction in taxes. However, deficits do often come into being through an increase in government expenditures. The more general analysis of deficits to cover both possibilities requires the above assumption.

32 Given the public's resentment over high tax rates and the commonly recognized dependence of labour supply and tax evasion on the marginal tax rate, we need to recognize – and evaluate the validity of – an implicit assumption on the labour supply function in establishing the Ricardian equivalence hypothesis. This assumption is that the labour supply over time is determined by the intertemporal maximization, so that the future labour supply is not a function of the future tax rate. Therefore, high current deficits resulting in high future tax rates do not reduce the future's labour supply.

33 This is consistent with the pre-Keynesian emphasis on monetary policy and a general neglect of fiscal deficits as a policy tool.

34 The empirical evidence on this issue is provided by the estimates of lags in the impact of monetary and fiscal policy. This evidence is discussed in Chapter 16. Our conclusion there is that there is incontrovertible evidence that changes in the money supply impact on aggregate demand and even real output with a lag extending over more than six quarters.

35 This modern classical model is also different from the traditional classical model in other ways. One of these relates to the existence of speculative balances in the modern classical model while the quantity theory component of the traditional classical model did not have such balances.

36 This hypothesis was discussed in Chapter 7 and will be introduced into the neoclassical model in Chapter 15.

37 See Chapter 2 for the elucidation of his 1956 article.

38 Numerous applications of the St Louis equation showed that the empirical findings from it differed among countries, periods and the definitions of the policy variables. However, their basic conclusion that the money supply changes have a strong short-term impact on the economy remained fairly robust.

39 This horizon can be further than the representative individual's expected date of death and will cover the lifetimes of his intended beneficiaries.

40 To see this, write out the preceding equation in its long form (without the summation sign).

41 That is, the interest payments prior to redemption and the payment of the principal on the redemption of the bonds.

42 If we let $D = 1/(1 + r)$, the proof uses the mathematical formula:

$$\sum_{t=1}^{n} D^t = \sum_{t=0}^{n} D^t - 1 = \frac{1 - D^{n+1}}{1 - D} - 1$$

REFERENCES

Andersen, Leonall C., and Jerry L. Jordan. 'Monetary and Fiscal Actions: A Test of their Relative Importance in Economic Stabilization'. *Federal Reserve Bank of St Louis Review*, 50, November 1968, pp. 11–24.

Barro, Robert. 'Are Government Bonds Net Wealth?' *Journal of Political Economy*, 82, December 1974, pp. 1095–118.

Friedman, Milton. 'A Monetary and Fiscal Framework for Economic Stability'. *American Economic Review*, 38, 1948, pp. 245–64.

——. 'The Supply of Money and Changes in Prices and Output' (1958). Reprinted in Milton Friedman, *The Optimum Quantity of Money and Other Essays*. Chicago: Aldine Publishing Co., 1969, pp. 171–88.

——. 'The Role of Monetary Policy'. *American Economic Review*, 58, 1968, pp. 1–17.

——. 'A Theoretical Framework for Monetary Analysis'. *Journal of Political Economy*, 78, February 1970, pp. 193–238.

——. 'Nobel Prize Lecture: Inflation and Unemployment'. *Journal of Political Economy*, 85, June 1977, pp. 451–73.

——, and David Meiselman. 'The Relative Stability of Monetary Velocity and the Investment Multiplier in the United States, 1897–1958'. In *Commission on Money and Credit, Stabilization Policies*. Englewood Cliffs, NJ: Prentice-Hall, 1963, pp. 165–268.

Hicks, John R. 'Mr Keynes and the Classics: A Suggested Interpretation'. *Econometrica*, 5, April 1937, pp. 147–59.

Hume, David. *Of Money*. 1752.

Keynes, John Maynard. *The General Theory of Employment, Interest and Money*. New York: Macmillan, 1936.

Patinkin, Don. *Money, Interest and Prices*, 2nd edn. New York: Harper & Row, 1965.

——. 'The Chicago Tradition, the Quantity Theory, and Friedman'. *Journal of Money, Credit and Banking*, 1, February 1969, pp. 46–70.

Pigou, A. C. *Money, A Veil*. 1941.

Sargent, Thomas J. *Macroeconomic Theory*. New York: Academic Press, 1979.

chapter fourteen

THE KEYNESIAN AND NEO-KEYNESIAN APPROACHES TO SHORT-RUN MACROECONOMICS

This Keynesian tradition differs from the classical one in not assuming that the economy is always in equilibrium with full employment or tends on its own to full employment within a reasonably short time. This was the core assertion of Keynes' The General Theory published in 1936 and remains at the core of all models within the Keynesian tradition. This assertion has the corollary that appropriate macroeconomic policies could improve on the functioning of the economy.

The Keynesian model has been evolving ever since its basis was laid in Keynes' contributions in 1936. It has gone through many versions, with different versions taking centre stage at different stages in its evolution and many coexisting simultaneously. From a policy perspective, their common element is their implication that monetary policy can have effects on real output and employment. Hence, the monetary authority should not take money to be neutral and should pursue the monetary policy appropriate to the state of the economy and the particular causes of its departure from full employment equilibrium.

---

key concepts introduced in this chapter

- Nominal wage contracts
- Involuntary unemployment
- Phillips curve
- Expectations augmented Phillips curve
- Macroeconomic coordinating mechanism
- Walrasian auctioneer and Walrasian *tâtonnement*
- Aggregate demand deficiency
- Quantity-constrained analysis
- Notional demand and supply functions
- Effective demand and supply functions
- Sticky prices
- Staggered wage contracts
- Implicit employment contracts
- Efficiency wages

This chapter is intended as a review of the Keynesian short-run macroeconomic ideas to derive the role of monetary policy in them, and assumes that the student is already familiar with Keynesian models from macroeconomic textbooks. It is also worth reviewing the material on the Keynesian paradigm in Chapter 1. That presentation had argued that the Keynesian paradigm was the study of the pathology of the macroeconomy. It focuses on the causes, implications and policy prescriptions for the deviations of the economy from a Walrasian general equilibrium. Since there can be many causes of such deviations, their appropriate study requires not one unified model but many, not all of which need be variations on a theme or even compatible with one another. This chapter provides a sample of their diversity.

Money is not neutral in the Keynesian tradition. Chapter 3 had presented the Walrasian general equilibrium analysis of the economy, established the conditions for money neutrality and discussed the 'departures' of the economy from these conditions. These departures provide the *raison d'être* for Keynesian analyses and are often their starting point. The reader is encouraged to review them at this stage.

There are several versions of the Keynesian approach. The original version of these was Keynes' own ideas as set out in *The General Theory*, followed by a number of evolving versions of the Keynesian framework,[1] with the current presentations being a broad and somewhat disparate set of ideas which are often classified as the neo-Keynesian approach. Keynesianism is a living tradition, evolving and refining its ideas over time, so that there is no single version of it.

However, the common strand in the Keynesian approaches broadly defined is the angst over the performance of the economy, and especially of the labour market. In particular, the Keynesian models assume that the labour markets do not perform well enough to ensure full employment as a continuous or almost continuous state for a variety of reasons. One of the basic reasons for this is that the labour markets cannot be taken to always clear at the current wage rate. They may do so, but not necessarily always, nor is there always a strong and rapid tendency for them to move from a disequilibrium state to the equilibrium one. The latter is related to the observation that the firms and the workers in the labour market do not even negotiate a real wage but rather negotiate and set a nominal wage. Further, there are very significant imperfections in the labour market for various reasons, including the fixity and firm-specificity of acquired skills, the differing geographical distributions of jobs and workers, and explicit and implicit contracts, etc.

Given the complexity of the functioning of the labour market, the Keynesian models have resorted to a *variety* of simplifying assumptions about it. At the risk of oversimplification, these were that:

(i) The nominal wage is fixed (1940s and early 1950s).
(ii) The nominal wage is variable but the supply of labour depends on the nominal and not the real wage (1950s and 1960s).
(iii) The structure of the labour market can be replaced by the Phillips curve (late 1950s and early 1960s) or the expectations augmented Phillips curve (late 1960s).
(iv) The demand and supply of labour depend on the expected real (not nominal) wage but that the expectations on prices, needed to derive the expected real wage from the negotiated nominal one, are subject to errors and asymmetric information between firms and workers (1970s and 1980s).
(v) The Keynesian analysis is that of states other than full employment, so that the notional demand and supply functions of Walrasian and neoclassical economics are not applicable. The applicable concepts are those of effective demand and supply and the equilibrium – or 'temporary equilibrium' as it is called by some writers – between them can occur at less than full employment and have different dynamic properties from those of neoclassical economics or its disequilibrium analysis. Such analysis is sometimes presented in the form of quantity-constrained models (1970s and 1980s).

(vi) The real wage is an efficiency wage which can be rigid in the short run while prices are sticky (1980s and 1990s).

The intention of this chapter is not to go through each of the various versions of the Keynesian approach but to show the general pattern of their implications for monetary and fiscal policies. The common theme among these versions of the Keynesian ideas is that money is not neutral in the short run. The models that will be used to show this are:

(a) Those which assume that the supply function of labour is different from the neoclassical one; in particular, the supply of labour depends in some way on the nominal wage and not merely on the real one.
(b) The labour market clears but the supply of labour depends on the expected real wage, and price expectations are subject to imperfect and asymmetric information. Since such a model involves uncertainty and expectations, its presentation has been postponed to the next chapter and is to be found under that chapter's analysis of the expectations augmented Phillips curve.
(c) The demand and supply functions are as in the neoclassical model but the labour market does not always clear in notional terms, with demand deficiency leading to involuntary unemployment in the economy.
(d) There are various aspects such as staggered contracts, implicit contracts, efficiency wages, menu costs, etc., affecting the functioning of the labour market. These are often grouped under the label of neo-Keynesian economics.

On the product, money and bond markets, most Keynesians seem willing to accept the IS and LM relationships and the aggregate demand analysis of the neoclassical model in Chapter 13. This acceptance within the main Keynesian approach is often labelled as the *Keynesian–neoclassical synthesis (of aggregate demand analysis)* – which evolved in the 1960s through the acceptance by both the neoclassical economists and the Keynesians of the IS and LM specifications for the demand structure of the economy. However, not all Keynesians go along with this acceptance, with some Keynesians – especially post-Keynesians – disputing the nature and/or the stability of the IS and LM curves and their accuracy in representing Keynes' own ideas in *The General Theory*.

In comparisons between the neoclassical and Keynesian schools, it is often contended that the distinguishing difference between them is that the former assumes the flexibility of nominal wages and/or prices while the latter assumes them to be rigid. As will be shown in this chapter, the rigidity of nominal wages and/or prices is not a necessary component of some of the Keynesian versions. If the analysis of a Keynesian model at any point requires such rigidity, it will be explicitly specified. This is not to say that the Keynesian models cannot be based on such an assumption; it is rather to assert that they do not necessarily require such an assumption and that the qualitatively distinct Keynesian policy results can be derived with flexible prices and nominal wages. Further, the Keynesian models do not necessarily need to rely upon irrational economic behaviour but can derive their distinctive conclusions under the rational demand and supply behaviour of economic agents, given the conditions that come about in the relevant markets.

Sections 14.1 to 14.4 present three of the main versions of the Keynesian model. Section 14.5 covers the main elements of the neo-Keynesian revision of the Keynesian model. Section 14.6 derives the reduced-form Keynesian relationship between output and the money supply. Section 14.7 introduces Barro's Ricardian equivalence theorem into the Keynesian framework and argues that this strengthens the role and need for monetary policy for stabilization. Section 14.8 compares the major economic philosophies of mercantilism and liberalism, and their relationship with the classical and Keynesian macroeconomic ideas.

14.1 KEYNESIAN MODEL I: THE NOMINAL WAGE MODEL

Keynes (1936) argued that, in a monetary economy, the worker is generally paid a wage rate that is not guaranteed in terms of its purchasing power but is paid a nominal wage rate. It is the nominal wage rate that is negotiated between an employee or his union and the employer. Once a nominal wage rate has been set in an explicit or implicit contract, under normal economic circumstances neither the employee nor his union seems willing to accept a cutback in the set wage rate. However, while workers are not willing to accept a cutback in nominal wage rates, they seem more willing to tolerate a reduction in the purchasing power of their nominal wage if this is brought about by changes in the purchasing power of money.[2] A simple version of this model in which the nominal wage rates are assumed to be rigid downwards was an early version of the Keynesian model. This was supplanted in the 1950s and 1960s by a model in which the nominal wage rate was flexible and the supply of labour depended on the nominal wage rate.[3] The following model is based on this assumption. Note that the assumptions of this model do not include the rigidity of nominal wages and prices, nor does it imply these.

The production–employment sector: the nominal-wage hypothesis

Assume that the supply of labour depends positively on the nominal wage rate. That is,

$$
\begin{aligned}
n^s &= n^s(W) \\
&= n^s(P \cdot w)
\end{aligned}
\tag{1}
$$

where:

n^s supply of labour
W nominal wage rate
w real wage rate
P price level

and $\partial n^s/\partial W > 0$, so that $\partial n^s/\partial w > 0$ and $\partial n^s/\partial P > 0$. The assumptions of the neoclassical model on the demand for labour are being retained in this model, so that from Chapter 13,

$$
n^d = n^d(w) \quad \partial n^d/\partial w < 0
\tag{2}
$$

In equilibrium:

$$
n^d = n^s = n
\tag{3}
$$

which translates to:

$$
n = n^d(w) = n^s(P \cdot w)
\tag{4}
$$

where n^d designates the demand for labour and n is employment. Expression (4) is an equation in two variables, P and w. We can solve it for the equilibrium real wage rate as a function of the price level.

An example: wages and employment for the nominal wage labour supply function

To confirm the preceding arguments in a simplified example, assume:

$$
n^s = b_1 wP \qquad b_1 > 0
\tag{1'}
$$

$$
n^d = a_0 - a_1 w \quad a_0, a_1 > 0
\tag{2'}
$$

In equilibrium,

$$a_0 - a_1 w = b_1 wP$$

so that:

$$w = a_0/(a_1 + b_1 P) \tag{5}$$

where $\partial w/\partial P < 0$. The equilibrium nominal wage is given by:

$$W = Pw = a_0/(a_1/P + b_1) \tag{5'}$$

where $\partial W/\partial P > 0$, but the elasticity of the nominal wage with respect to the price level is less than one, giving the earlier result that $\partial w/\partial P < 0$. Note that, in this analysis, the nominal wage is indeed flexible and determined in equilibrium by the demand and supply of labour.

Employment n in this example can be obtained by substituting (5) in (2'). This gives:

$$n = a_0 - \frac{a_1 a_0}{a_1 + b_1 P} \tag{6}$$

where $\partial n/\partial P > 0$. The reasoning behind this result is as follows. While nominal wages rise with the price level, they do not do so sufficiently so that the real wage falls. Consequently, labour becomes cheaper, making it profitable for firms to increase their employment.

To illustrate the impact of this increase in employment on output, assume a quadratic production function of the form:

$$y = \gamma n^2$$

so that,

$$y = \gamma \left[a_0 - \frac{a_1 a_0}{a_1 + b_1 P} \right]^2$$

where $\partial y/\partial P > 0$. Hence, the increase in the price level increases both employment and output in the nominal-wage model.

Diagrammatic analysis: output and employment with the nominal wage labour supply function

Returning to our general results for the Keynesian model with the nominal-wage labour supply function, we have:

$$w = f(P) \quad f' < 0 \tag{7}$$
$$n = g(P) \quad g' > 0 \tag{8}$$
$$y = y^s(P) \quad y^{s'} > 0 \tag{9}$$

Figure 14.1a presents the diagrammatic analysis of this labour market in the (w, n) space. The labour supply function is $n^s(W)$ but Figure 14.1a has the real wage w rather than the nominal wage W on the vertical axis. It is, therefore, preferable to rewrite the labour supply function as $n^s(Pw)$, so that, for purposes of Figure 14.1a, the labour supply depends on the two variables P and w. A change in w produces a movement along the labour supply curve while a change in P shifts this curve. Therefore, Figure 14.1a shows the labour supply curve as n^s for the price level P_0 and as $n^{s'}$ for the price level P_1.

To show the relationship between the two labour supply curves in Figure 14.1a, start with a given wage W_0 and assume that the price level increases from P_0 to P_1. For the nominal wage W_0, the labour supplied will remain the same whether the prices are at P_0 or P_1. Therefore, at prices P_0, the labour supplied is n_0 $[=n^s(W_0) = n(W_0 \mid P_0)]$ on the curve n^s. Given W_0, this quantity will be the same $[n_0 = n(W_0 \mid P_1)]$ for the curve $n^{s'}$ since the labour supply is a function only of the nominal wage and not the real wage. Therefore, the increase in the price level from P_0 to P_1 does not change the amount of *labour supplied* at a given nominal wage. But this price increase lowers the real wage from $w_0 = W_0 \mid P_0$ to $w'_0 = W_0 \mid P_1$, where $w'0 < w_0$. Hence, the labour supply curve in Figure 14.1a, with the real wage w on the vertical axis, shifts down from $n^s(W \mid P_0)$ – which passes through (w_0, n_0) – to $n^{s'}(W \mid P_1)$, which passes through (w'_0, n_0).

To examine changes to the equilibrium employment and wage levels, Figure 14.1a also specifies the demand curve $n^d(w)$. Since this depends on the real wage rate w, which is already on the vertical axis, the change in prices will not shift this curve. Hence, when prices change from P_0 to P_1, the equilibrium position shifts from a to b, with employment increasing from n_0 to n_1, while the real wage falls from w_0 to w_1. This increase in employment increases output in Figure 14.1b from y_0 to y_1. Intuitively, the reasoning is that an increase in the price level makes labour cheaper (in real terms) at the market-clearing nominal wage rate, thereby inducing increases in employment and output. In the shift from a to b, the real wage has fallen less than the increase in prices, so that the equilibrium real wage at b is greater than w'_0 and nominal wages rise from W_0 $(= P_1 w'_0)$ to $P_1 w_0$.

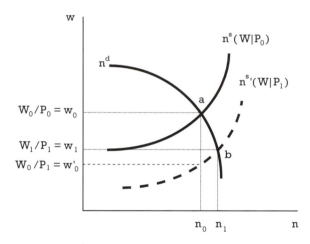

Figure 14.1a

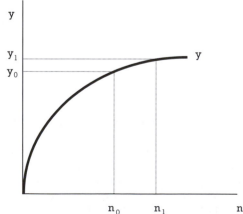

Figure 14.1b

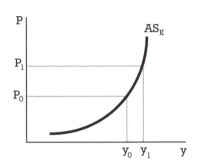

Figure 14.2a

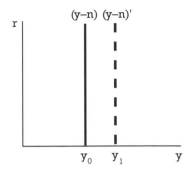

Figure 14.2b

This positive relationship of this model between output and the price level is shown by the Keynesian output supply curve AS_K in Figure 14.2a in the (y, P) space and by the y–n curve in Figure 14.2b in the (y, r) space. In Figure 14.2a, the positive relationship between P and y specifies a positive slope for the AS_K curve, with a change in P causing a movement along the AS_K curve. Therefore, this figure does not show a shift in the aggregate supply curve. The increase in prices from P_0 to P_1 increases output from y_0 to y_1. But, in Figure 14.2b, P is not on one of the axes so that the effect of an increase in P on y has to be expressed by a rightward shift in the y–n curve. Therefore, the increase in prices from P_0 to P_1 in Figures 14.1a and 14.1b produces in Figure 14.2b the shift in the y–n curve from y–n to $(y$–$n)'$.

The aggregate demand–supply analysis with a nominal-wage assumption

The assumptions made for the neoclassical model in Chapter 13 on the expenditure and monetary sectors are being retained, so that the complete model is now:

Aggregate supply:

$$y^s = y^s(P) \quad \partial y^s/\partial P > 0 \tag{10}$$

Aggregate demand:

$$y^d = \alpha\left(c_0 + i_0 - c_y t_0\right) + \alpha g + \alpha \, \frac{i_r}{m_r} \, \frac{M}{P} \tag{11}$$

where

$$\alpha = \left[\frac{1}{1 - c_y\left(1 - t_y\right) + i_r m_y / m_r} \right] > 0$$

and

$$\frac{\partial y^d}{\partial g} > 0; \quad \frac{\partial y^d}{\partial M} > 0; \quad \frac{\partial y^d}{\partial P} < 0$$

Equation (11) has the general form,

$$y^d = y^d(P; g, M) \tag{11'}$$

In equilibrium in the product market,

$$y = y^s = y^d \tag{12}$$

Equation (11) is the aggregate demand function from Chapter 13. Superscripts s and d have been placed on y to clearly indicate the relationship being considered. Given (12), (10) and (11) are two equations in the two variables y and P. We assume that they can be solved for the equilibrium levels of output and prices in the economy.

In Figure 14.3 in the (y, P) space, the general equilibrium given by (10) and (11) is shown at (y_0, P_0). If aggregate demand rises through an expansionary monetary or fiscal policy, the AD curve shifts to the right to AD', leading to higher levels of prices and output at (y_1, P_1). Similarly, an increase in aggregate supply through technical change would increase the equilibrium level of output – but would reduce that of prices.

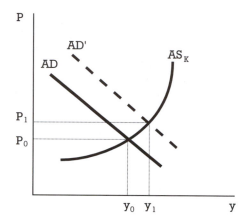

Figure 14.3

Taking the total differentials of (10) and (11) in terms of g, M and P, and incorporating the equilibrium condition by replacing y^s and y^d by y, we have:

$$dy = y^s_P \, dP \tag{13}$$

$$dy = \alpha dg + \left(\frac{\alpha i_r}{m_r P}\right) dM - \left(\frac{\alpha i_r}{m_r}\right)\left(\frac{M}{P^2}\right) dP \tag{14}$$

Substituting dP from (13) into (14),

$$dy = \alpha \, dg + \left(\frac{\alpha i_r}{m_r P}\right) dM - \left(\frac{\alpha i_r}{m_r P}\right)\left(\frac{M}{P}\right)\left(\frac{1}{y^s_P}\right) dy \tag{15}$$

Designate:

$$\beta = \left(\frac{\alpha i_r}{m_r P}\right) \geq 0$$

$$\gamma = 1 + \left(\frac{\alpha i_r}{m_r P}\right)\left(\frac{M}{P}\right)\left(\frac{1}{y^s_P}\right) \geq 0$$

so that (15) implies that:

$$dy = (\alpha/\gamma)dg + (\beta/\gamma)dM \tag{16}$$

where $(\alpha/\gamma) \geq 0$ and $(\beta/\gamma) \geq 0$, so that *real* output increases as fiscal expenditures and/or the money supply increase, with its fiscal multiplier as (α/γ) and the money multiplier as (β/γ).

The interesting point that emerges from (16) is that aggregate demand and output – and employment – are positively related: an increase in the former causes the latter to increase. This conclusion contrasts with that from the neoclassical real wage model for which aggregate demand was forced into equality with an output determined uniquely by the labour sector and the production function, with the result that an exogenous increase in aggregate demand was stifled through an increase in the interest rate or resulted only in a rise in prices.

Another point worth noting is that an increase in aggregate demand in the nominal wage model affects output only through a rise in the price level. If demand exceeds supply, prices rise; this lowers the real wage element of any given nominal wage rate, makes labour cheaper and induces firms to increase employment. Hence output rises. This is the cause of the contrast in the working of the classical real-wage and the Keynesian nominal-wage model. In the classical model, nominal wage rates are fully flexible so that a rise in prices cannot reduce real wages and make labour cheaper to employ; in the nominal wage model, nominal wages are flexible but do not rise proportionately with the price level, so that a rise in the price level makes labour cheaper and hence makes it profitable for firms to increase employment.

Focusing on the policy variables in (16), both fiscal and monetary policies can increase aggregate demand under normal conditions. If they can do so, the government can then indirectly influence output and employment in the economy.

The IS–LM analysis of the model with the nominal-wage labour supply function

Another method of assembling the overall picture of the economy is to specify the equilibrium relationship for each of the sectors. These are:

Commodity sector:

$$y = c_0 + c_y\left(y - \left(t_0 + t_y y\right)\right) + g_0 + i_0 - i_r r$$

$$= \left[\frac{1}{1 - c_y\left(1 - t_y\right)}\right]\left(c_0 + i_0 + g_0 - c_y t_0 - i_r r\right) \tag{17}$$

Monetary sector:

$$M/P = m_y y - m_r r \tag{18}$$

Production–employment sector:

$$y = y^s(P) \tag{19}$$

These are three equations in the three endogenous variables y, r, P. We assume that they can be solved for unique values of y, r, P. The interesting thing about these equations is that each equation contains at least two endogenous variables, in contrast with the real-wage model where the equation for the production–employment sector had only one endogenous variable y. Further, no set of two equations contains only two endogenous variables, enabling a solution for two variables independent of the third sector. Therefore, all equations must be solved simultaneously, so that the equilibrium values of y, P, r are interdependent and any exogenous changes affecting one of these variables would also affect the other two.

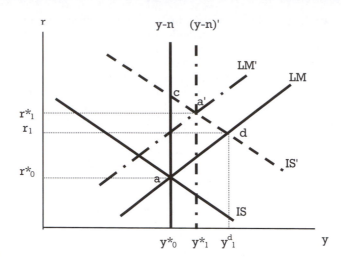

Figure 14.4a

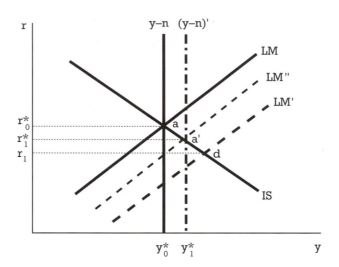

Figure 14.4b

The effect of an expansionary fiscal policy

Figure 14.4a presents diagrammatically the overall equilibrium in the economy. Initial equilibrium is at point a. For comparative static analysis, assume that government expenditures are increased. This increases aggregate demand for any given rate of interest and shifts the IS curve to the right (from the solid IS curve to the dashed IS' curve). Aggregate product demand is now given by point d – intersection of IS' and LM curves – while aggregate supply is still given by the $y-n$ curve as y_0^*. At d, since demand exceeds supply y_0^*, prices rise. As prices rise, the transactions demand for money increases and LM shifts left to LM'. Moreover, as prices rise, the real wage rate falls, so that employment and output increase. This shifts the $y-n$ curve to the right to $(y-n)'$. Prices continue to rise until overall equilibrium is restored by the shifting LM and $y-n$ curves, eventually intersecting at a common point on the IS' curve between c and d. This is shown as a'. Comparing the initial equilibrium point a with the new equilibrium point a', prices, output and interest rates are all *higher* at a' than at a. In contrast with the neoclassical model, the fiscal expansion did increase output in this Keynesian model.

The effect of an expansionary monetary policy

Figure 14.4b also shows the initial overall equilibrium to be at point a with (y_0, r_0). An increase in the money supply enables an increase in the output to be financed at any given rate of interest, so that LM shifts to the right to LM'. Excess demand at d (compared with the aggregate supply) causes prices to rise. The price rise causes the LM curve to shift leftwards and the $y-n$ curve to shift rightwards. A new overall equilibrium is shown at a', with a higher output at y_1, a higher price level P_1 and a *lower* rate of interest r_1. Therefore, the effect of the increase in the money supply is only partly on the price level so that the elasticity of the price level with respect to the money supply is less than one. In contrast with the neoclassical model, the money supply expansion does increase output in this Keynesian model.

Further, the difference between the effects of expansionary fiscal and monetary policies upon the *rate of interest*, compared with that upon prices and output implies that the two policies can be coordinated to yield an expansion in output, with a constant rate of interest or other combinations of output and the rate of interest. This is, however, not so with respect to output and the price level.

14.2 KEYNESIAN MODEL II: KEYNESIAN MODELS WITH THE PHILLIPS CURVE

The Phillips curve

In 1958, A. W. Phillips, on the basis of statistical observations for the UK, proposed a negative relationship between the rate of nominal wage growth and the rate of unemployment. This was subsequently extended to show a negative relationship between the rate of inflation and the rate of unemployment, with the name 'Phillips curve' being attached to both of these relationships. During the late 1950s and the 1960s, Keynesian economics came to embrace this curve, incorporating it in preference to a structural specification of the labour market, as incorporated in equations (1) to (3).

Phillips had plotted the rate of change of nominal wages against the rate of unemployment for the UK over several periods from 1861 to 1957, and found that the data showed a downward sloping curve. That is, the plotted relationship was of the form:

$$\overset{\circ}{W} = f(u) \tag{20}$$

where $\overset{\circ}{W}$ is the rate of increase of the nominal wage rate and $f' < 0$. One explanation for (20) is that unemployment represents the degree of labour market tightness, so that the higher the level of unemployment, the smaller will be the increase in the nominal wage.

Equation (20) soon evolved into its inverse and then into a relationship of the form:

$$u = g(\pi) \tag{21}$$

where $g' < 0$. This relationship is drawn as the curve PC in Figure 14.5a.

The transition from (20) to (21) comes from the link between the nominal wage rate and inflation: nominal wages represent the main element of the cost of production so that an increase in nominal wages will induce firms to increase their prices; alternatively, an increase in prices causes labour to ask for compensation in the form of wage increases. Hence, there is a positive relationship between $\overset{\circ}{W}$ and π, which, when substituted into (20), yields (21).

The estimated forms of the Phillips curve proved to be convex to the origin. To explain this curvature, it was argued that the response of nominal wages to excess demand was non-linear, and that decreases in unemployment caused successively greater increases in nominal wages. Further, a decrease in employment induces a smaller decline in wages than the increase in wages brought out by a corresponding increase in job vacancies, so that increases in employment in some industries with corresponding decreases in others will bring about a

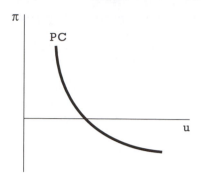

Figure 14.5a   **Figure 14.5b**

net increase in the average nominal wage rate. Hence, both the level of unemployment and its variance among industries together determined the Phillips curve relationship.

Numerous studies for many countries including Canada and the USA seemed to confirm the validity of (21). Even though the relationship seemed to shift between periods and countries, the general form of the relationship seemed to be valid for the 1950s and 1960s and became a mainstay for many Keynesian models, replacing the labour market structural relationships during the 1960s and 1970s. As a consequence, many Keynesian economists in the 1960s and early 1970s assumed the Phillips curve to be stable and recommended its use as a tradeoff between inflation and unemployment by the monetary and fiscal authorities, and called on them to use their policies to change aggregate demand to achieve the inflation rate specified by the Phillips curve as a concomitant of the desired rate of unemployment in the economy. In this sense, while (21) was a constraint on policy choices, it gave the authorities control over the unemployment rate in the economy, with the accompanying rate of inflation being an undesirable cost of the chosen unemployment rate. The Phillips curve was thus consistent with the economic philosophy of Keynesians that the authorities can manipulate employment and output in the economy and should attempt to do so to achieve better levels than the economy would generate on its own.

The expectations augmented Phillips curve[4]
The Phillips curve was challenged by Milton Friedman and the monetarists in the 1960s and 1970s. They argued that if inflation is perfectly anticipated, the labour contracts would reflect it so that the nominal wage would increase by the expected rate of inflation. Consequently, the expected rate of inflation would not affect the real wage rate, employment or output. Hence, at the expected rate of inflation, the rate of unemployment would be the natural rate so that only the unanticipated rate of inflation would cause deviations in the actual rate from the natural rate by reducing the real cost of labour and other inputs. That is, according to Friedman, the proper relationship between u and π is not (21) but has the form:

$$u - u_n = f(\pi - \pi^e) \tag{22}$$

with $f' < 0$ and $f(0) = 0$. In this limiting case of expectational equilibrium – an aspect of the 'long run' – $\pi = \pi^e$ and $u = u_n$. Equation (22) is known as the expectations augmented Phillips curve, as shown as the curve EAPC in Figure 14.5b. Its analysis and policy implications were presented in Chapter 13 in the discussion of the natural rate of unemployment. This relationship is again discussed in the next chapter in the context of the role of expectations in neoclassical and Keynesian models.

Empirical research and the widespread experience of stagflation in the mid and late 1970s in the industrialized economies seemed to show that (21) was unstable in a period of accelerating inflation. Further, (22) seemed to perform much better in such periods, especially at high and accelerating rates of inflation. Keynesian models after the 1970s tended to drop the Phillips curve as a primitive element of their models, though most such models can generate some form of it as an implication.

The next chapter resumes the discussion of the expected augmented Phillips curve, especially in the context of wage contracts and rational expectations.

14.3 KEYNESIAN MODEL III: KEYNESIAN MODELS WITHOUT LABOUR MARKET CLEARANCE

The assumption of labour supply depending on the nominal rather than the real wage as in (1) implies money illusion or myopia by labour, which is empirically not valid over any extended period of time. Many Keynesians and especially post-Keynesians have argued that Keynes' *The General Theory* did not make this assumption but agreed with the neoclassical assumption that workers would base the supply of labour on the purchasing power of the nominal wage, i.e. on the real wage rate. They also argue that Keynes assumed that the modern economy with numerous industries and firms and with decentralized wage negotiations, does not possess a mechanism which would ensure that the labour markets come into equilibrium at full employment with an equilibrium real wage. Hence, the claim being made is that the major distinction between the Keynesian and the neoclassical models is that while the neoclassical model makes the assumption of labour market equilibrium, Keynes did not do so. That is, Keynesian models following this pattern specify the labour market as:

$$n^d = n^d(w) \quad \partial n^d/\partial w < 0 \tag{23}$$

$$n^s = n^s(w) \quad \partial n^s/\partial w > 0 \tag{24}$$

These behavioural functions are identical with those in the neoclassical model. Since there is no assumption of labour market equilibrium in this type of Keynesian models and since firms are assumed to be able to hire the amount of labour that they demand, the market clearance condition ($n = n^f = n^d = n^s$) of the neoclassical model is replaced by:

$$n = n^d \leq n^s \tag{25}$$

Equation (25) does not assume that labour market equilibrium at full employment will never exist in the economy. This equation implicitly assumes that the modern capitalist economy does not possess sufficient mechanisms to ensure continuous full employment equilibrium or does not achieve it within a reasonable period of time. Further, an economy can get stuck at a level of employment below full employment, and these can also be equilibrium states.[5] That is, the Keynesian models allow the possibility of multiple macroeconomic equilibria, each with a different level of output and unemployment. One of these equilibria is the full employment one, so that we have to distinguish between the full employment equilibrium and other equilibria with less than full employment.

Defining the *full employment equilibrium* level of employment as n^f and the rate of unemployment consistent with it as u^f or u_n, (25) implies that:

$$u \geq u_n$$

and

$$u^i = u - u_n \geq 0 \tag{26}$$

where u^i is the rate of *involuntary unemployment*, while u_n is the natural or Walrasian (full employment) equilibrium rate of unemployment consistent with the structure of the economy, including any wage rigidities such as specific skills, minimum wage laws, labour unions and work preferences etc.; $u^i > 0$ is indicative of the failure of the economy to perform up to its potential. Neoclassical – and especially classical – economists believe that such a state would be a transient disequilibrium state, rapidly eliminated by the self-equilibrating mechanisms of the capitalist economy; while Keynesians believe that such a state can persist in the economy and the authorities should attempt to eliminate it by deliberate action.[6]

Therefore, Keynesians argue that the authorities should keep a close watch on the economy and when there is significant involuntary unemployment due to a deficiency in aggregate demand, they should use monetary and/or fiscal policies to increase demand by an appropriate amount. If they succeed, the economy will eliminate such involuntary unemployment and perform at its full employment potential, the state assumed by the neoclassical, classical and new classical economists.

The class of models which fit the preceding remarks are often called 'deficient demand models', though they allow the absence of deficient demand in the limiting case of full employment. The next section presents an example of a deficient demand analysis, noting that there can also be other versions that fall into this category.

14.4 KEYNESIAN MODEL IV: QUANTITY-CONSTRAINED ANALYSIS

Starting at the initial state of full employment equilibrium in the economy, assume that aggregate demand falls for some reason, thereby creating deficient demand relative to the full employment one. Following the ideas of the preceding section, assume that the labour market does not instantly clear, so that some of the workers become involuntarily unemployed because of the fall in aggregate demand. These workers will not receive the wage they would have got if they had been able to sell their labour according to their supply curve. Their lack of income forces them to reduce their demand for commodities and real balances below that specified by their Walrasian functions as derived in Chapter 3 and the neoclassical functions specified in Chapter 13. Hence, these latter functions are not 'effective' – that is, operational – in the state of involuntary unemployment. They can only be effective if there was full employment in the economy and workers could sell all the labour they wanted to at the existing wage rate.

Demand and supply functions derived under the assumption of the simultaneous clearance of all markets are called *notional functions*.[7] They are the ones derived in Walrasian analysis and used in neoclassical models. Since involuntary unemployment means that at least one of the markets does not clear, the use of notional functions to analyse the existence or non-existence of involuntary unemployment begs the question and is inappropriate. The more appropriate analysis would be to posit that the real world – that is, actual – demand and supply functions are approximated by effective functions, of which the limiting case is notional functions.

Effective functions for any market which take account of the non-clearance of other markets are also called *Clower or quantity-constrained functions* and the macroeconomic analysis based on them is similarly called quantity-constrained analysis. Such analysis clearly belongs among the Keynesian stable of macroeconomic models and became popular during the 1970s and 1980s. It lies outside the interests of this book and is therefore not presented in it.[8]

The quantity-constrained analysis can encompass the possibility that any or all of the four markets of the macroeconomic models need not clear instantaneously. However, Keynesian analysis focuses on non-clearance in the commodities[9] and labour markets. In particular, the main initial impulse of such models is a fall in the aggregate demand for commodities due to a fall in investment, in consumption or government expenditures, or in money supply. Firms respond to this demand deficiency by reducing output and employment, with the latter, in turn, reducing labour incomes and inducing a reduction in consumption demand. This reduction in consumption demand would come from unemployed workers without incomes; it could also come from the employed workers, a larger proportion of whom may come to believe that their jobs are at greater risk than normal (under full employment) and who, therefore, resort to increases in their precautionary saving to cover the increased possibility of job loss. This fallback in consumption demand exacerbates the demand deficiency in the commodity markets, which is likely to persuade firms to further reduce output and employment. While this process can occur in the disequilibrium phase of the neoclassical model, as discussed in section 13.10 of Chapter 13, with the neoclassical economy eventually returning to equilibrium, to the Keynesians this process can continue without necessarily restoring full employment to the economy, or do so after a sufficiently long time for the pursuit of expansionary demand policies to become optimal.

Neoclassical economists claim that as unemployment emerges, the real wage would fall to restore equilibrium in the labour market. The Keynesian response to such a suggestion is that the labour market does not possess a general mechanism for such a reduction in real wages, or, because the labour market is really a collection of very diverse markets in skills, occupations and locations, as well as with contracts, that they take too long for the required reduction in real wages. Moreover, the reduction in real wages would reduce labour incomes, which would further reduce consumption demand, worsen the demand deficiency in the economy and induce firms to further cut back on output and unemployment. Hence, while the reduction in real wages is viewed by the neoclassical economist as a critical market-equilibrating mechanism, the Keynesians view it as a possibly destabilizing mechanism that could worsen and prolong unemployment.

The dynamic analysis following a fall in aggregate demand

While the reader is referred to an appropriate macroeconomics book for a proper treatment of effective demand models, we pursue here Patinkin's (1965, Ch. 13) application of this analysis to the market for labour in order to derive the role of monetary policy in such models. Assume that the demand and supply functions for labour are the neoclassical notional ones as shown in Figure 14.6b and that initially the economy is at full employment n^f and full employment output y^f. Now assume that a shock reduces aggregate demand to y_0^d so that a demand deficiency emerges in the economy such that the firms are not able to sell the full employment output y^f at the existing price level.[10] The actual aggregate demand y_0^d can be supplied by the employment of n_0^d workers. In Figure 14.6b, the marginal product of labour for n_0^d workers is MPL_0, which is above the full employment wage of w^f. However, if firms were to employ more than n_0^d workers, they would not be able to sell the extra output so that their *marginal revenue product* would be zero. Hence, if aggregate demand falls to y_0^d, firms would cut employment to only n_0^d workers.[11]

Extending this argument to Figure 14.6b, these n_0^d workers can be paid nominal wage rates which can change, as can the price level, with the resultant real wage being anywhere in the range w_0' and w_0'', without a change in the firms' employment of n_0^d workers, so that real wage rates could drift up or down from the initial equilibrium level of w^f.[12] Hence, the decrease in employment (from n^f to n_0^d) can be accompanied by either an increase or a decrease in the real wage rate of the employed workers. Wages may, therefore, follow a pro-cyclical or counter-cyclical pattern: some recessions and some parts of a given recession could show wages falling while others show them to be rising. If wages rise, it could be claimed that the rise in wages is the cause of falling employment, when this rise is itself only an effect while the true cause was the initial fall in aggregate demand.

The above effects are only partial or initial ones. Since the unemployed workers do not receive any incomes, they cut back on their consumption demand. Further, if wages are cut below w^f, the lower incomes of the employed would also lead to a reduction in consumption.[13] The consequent fall in aggregate demand further reduces the effective demand for labour[14] and exacerbates the recessionary effects derived in the preceding paragraph.

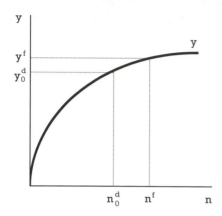

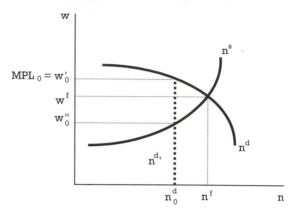

Figure 14.6a   **Figure 14.6b**

Comparing the analysis of demand deficiency in the Keynesian and neoclassical models

To compare the above effective demand analysis with the (full employment equilibrium) neoclassical one presented in Chapter 13, note that neither of them assumes that the nominal wage or the price level is rigid. The critical difference is that the neoclassical one requires firms to continue producing y^f output and employing n^f workers at a w^f wage rate, even when they observe the initial fall in demand. They are only likely to do so if they are, individually, convinced that the fall in demand is very temporary and will be reversed very soon, so that they would not be left with unsold output. However, there are many instances of reductions in aggregate demand which are not so transient or at least firms generally do not take them to be such, so that the actual response of firms would be to reduce output, thereby reducing employment and leading the economy into a recession. The policy cure for such recessionary tendencies is expansionary fiscal and monetary policies that would increase aggregate demand, and cause firms to respond to this by increasing output and employment. That is, real output, government expenditures and money supply will be positively related.

Note that the above Keynesian demand-deficient analysis:

(a) Is consistent with the *behavioural functions* of the neoclassical model, as well as with wage and price flexibility: the arguments did not assume that the labour supply function depends on nominal rather than real wages, nor was it assumed that the nominal wages or prices, or both, were rigid.

(b) Maintains the rationality of economic agents' behaviour in the demand-deficient conditions if they come about in the economy.

(c) Maintains that the industrial and market structures, including the speed at which competitive markets adjust to equilibrium, do not lead to instant market clearance in all markets, so that rational firms cannot assume this to be so, and must react in their production and labour-demand strategy to emerging demand conditions for their products as they see fit. In particular, firms faced with a fall in the demand for their product in the context of a general fall in aggregate demand, will not find it profit maximizing to maintain their output and employment unchanged while the market processes take their time to work themselves out to a new full employment equilibrium. This is not an assertion of the rigidity of prices, but of the dynamic response of firms to an emergent fall in demand and their past experience on the less than instantaneous movement of the economy from an initial equilibrium to a new one. Implicit in this is the assumption that firms react faster in their production strategy than the markets to the fall in aggregate demand. An alternative to (c) is that:

(d) The effective demand analysis maintains that there is no coordinating mechanism or coordinating agency (such as the Walrasian auctioneer with costless and open recontracting while adjustments to a new equilibrium are going on) in the economy which will work out the equilibrium wages, employment, output and prices, supply this data to the firms and workers, and that the firms and workers will wait to make – or suspend – their employment and output decisions until they can be informed of these equilibrium values and then base their decisions only on these values.

This lack of competitive market structures ensuring instantaneous adjustment to equilibrium or the lack of a coordinating mechanism or agency – with firms and workers not waiting out this process but responding faster than the markets to a fall in demand – is the critical reason in effective demand models why an economy in which a demand deficiency has emerged, need not rapidly move to the full employment levels.

Demand deficiency, wage and price rigidity, and rational behaviour

Since many textbooks associate the Keynesian models with price and/or wage rigidity, or irrationality in the form of money illusion in labour markets, further exposition of the effective demand analysis to justify our lack of reliance on these is presented in the rest of this section.

Assume that firms are rational, profit maximizing and operate in competition,[15] and that workers maximize utility subject to their budget constraints incorporating their actual wages and employment. To model the responses of the individual firm i to a macroeconomic demand deficiency, which has reduced the demand for its industry's output below the equilibrium level, let the firm's situation be as shown in Figures 14.6a and 14.6b, so that we now treat these figures as if they are for a single firm. The ith firm starts with its share of the equilibrium values of y^f, n^f, w^f, P^f, etc. Aggregate demand falls in the economy such that the demand for its industry's output falls correspondingly. The ith firm's share of this demand falls to y_0^d. Let its immediate response to this reduction in demand be to correspondingly reduce output[16] – so that the economy's output shrinks to meet the lower aggregate demand. Would each firm – and therefore the economy – adjust back to the initial full employment levels? Being in (monopolistic) competition,[17] a firm i can profitably produce and sell more, but, since its industry's demand is given by macroeconomic factors, the employment of an extra worker by firm i will not increase its demand by the amount of his output because he will purchase many different types of products and also save out of his wages. In fact, the demand for the ith firm in competition will increase by an imperceptible fraction of its increase in the additional worker's output, so that it can only sell the extra output if another firm in the same industry sells a correspondingly lesser amount.[18] But if each firm manages to keep its share, firm i will not have sold the extra worker's output, making a loss on his employment and therefore will not keep him. In fact, the rational firm, aware of the difficulty of increasing sales at the expense of other firms in a demand-deficient environment, need not attempt to increase its employment in the first place. Hence, the industry as a whole would not increase its output and employment.

By extension, no industry in the economy will increase its output, so that the economy's output, which had shrunk to meet the lower aggregate demand, does not increase to reach the full employment equilibrium, but stays unchanged at y_0^d. Given the lack of movement away from y_0^d, this level of output could become a static equilibrium level. However, since the now unemployed, but rational, workers do not receive any incomes, they will have to reduce their consumption expenditures, and some of the employed, becoming fearful of the possible loss of their own jobs, will also do so out of precautionary motives. This will mean a further fall in aggregate demand, so that the effective demand equilibrium could be less than y_0^d.

To compare this analysis with the neoclassical equilibrium one, suppose that the *markets* adjust to the new full employment equilibrium instantly. If this is so, the firms and workers will not need to change their production and labour demand and supply, so that the economy will continue at equilibrium, but with a lower price level. But if the markets are not that fast in establishing the new equilibrium prices instantly, as the real-world markets are not, the neoclassical analysis achieves the same result by assuming that the firms and workers respond to the fall in aggregate demand by maintaining their production and consumption *as if at their full employment levels* while the various markets take their time to adjust to their new equilibria consistent with full employment.

Alternatively, suppose there was a *coordinator* who could inform and persuade all firms that if they increased their output simultaneously by enough to ensure their share of full employment output y^*, the increased employment will generate additional demand for all firms. But, even if this could be achieved, this increase in demand will equal $c_y(y^* - y_0^d)$ which, for $c_y < 1$, will still leave a shortfall of aggregate demand by $(1 - c_y)(y^* - y_0^d)$, so that the firms collectively will be left with unsold output equal to this amount, making rational firms unwilling to increase their output in line with the coordinator's instructions. To persuade the firms to do so, the coordinator must ensure that *all* firms increase their output to attain y^*, *and* persuade the monetary and fiscal authorities to create new demand by $(1 - c_y)(y^* - y_0^d)$. Alternatively, for given fiscal expenditures and money supply, he must persuade the firms to increase their investment by this amount, so that he will also have to lower the economy's interest rates to an appropriate extent and persuade the firms to increase their investment fast enough.

The capitalist economies do not possess such a far-sighted and persuasive coordinator. Does the invisible hand of competition substitute for him? To do so, it must ensure that the numerous segments of the labour and commodity markets, as well as the financial markets, all instantly arrive at the new market-clearing prices, or, if they do not do so instantly, the economic agents continue to behave according to their notional and not their optimal effective functions.

Failing these ways of maintaining full employment after a fall in demand or returning demand to its initial level, the rational – and far-sighted – firms will not increase their output to achieve y^* but only produce to meet y_0^d. Hence, there will again be no tendency for output to change from this level, so that it will be an equilibrium level of output. We get the following conclusions from this discussion:

(i) Competition, flexible wages and prices, and economic rationality of firms and workers are not enough to ensure that the economy will revert to full employment after an aggregate demand shock.

(ii) The economy may behave in a manner which takes its output to a level below full employment, and leave it there, so that equilibrium could exist at less than full employment, with full employment as only one of the possible equilibrium states.

(iii) It is not enough for the economy to *eventually* bring nominal wage rates and prices to their equilibrium levels consistent with full employment, or for the coordinator to *eventually* arrive at these levels. These processes must occur fast enough – since, otherwise, the firms will act on the fall in their demand by cutting their employment. Further, the interest rates must also change appropriately and the increase in investment must occur adequately and fast enough.

(iv) The economy cannot be relied upon to act as the perfect coordinator. The likely reactions of competitive markets can include cutbacks in nominal wages and/or prices, which can be of a type which takes the economy back to full employment but they could, alternatively, be of the type which worsens the demand deficiency.

The distinction between the modern classical (equilibrium neoclassical) and Keynesian models

The dividing line between the neoclassical and some Keynesian analyses is, therefore, not necessarily on the behavioural functions of firms and households, or departures from the flexibility of nominal wages and prices, but rather on the dynamic responses – and the speed of adjustments – of the markets, firms and households constituting the economy. Critical to these dynamic responses are:

(a) Business confidence: will the economy revert to its full employment state of demand for the given firm's products and do so soon, so that it can afford to maintain production and employment in the interim, without piling up unsold output to a detrimental extent?
(b) Consumer confidence: will the economy return to full employment soon, so that the worker who lost his job has the belief that he will soon find another, and while he does not have a pay cheque in the interim, he will still have the confidence to maintain his consumption expenditures in the interim? And will those who are still employed but subjectively feel a higher risk of losing their jobs, not reduce their consumption?

In answer to these questions, it seems reasonable to posit that a very mild fall in aggregate demand in an overall time path of full employment can leave both business and consumer confidence intact and not produce a reduction in output and employment, while a more significant one and/or over a longer period, especially when backed by past experienced recessions, would produce a loss in such confidence and take the economy onto a dynamic path to involuntary unemployment levels. The irony of this remark is that the deliberative pursuit of aggressive Keynesian policies to maintain aggregate demand at the full employment level lead to a dynamic response by consumers and firms which maintains full employment; while a policy of leaving the economy alone, as the neoclassical economists recommend, brings into play dynamic responses which take the economy away from full employment. In support of this contention, the Western economies experienced very shallow and short recessions during the Keynesian period of the 1950s and 1960s, while the recessions lengthened and worsened with the resurgence of classical economics in the 1980s and 1990s.

These are issues of dynamic responses, rather than ones that can be handled through the comparative static solutions to the model's equations under the full employment assumption. Suppose we were to keep all the assumptions of the neoclassical model except for the full employment one (i.e., $n^d = n^s = n^f$), and in line with the dynamic considerations for the demand-deficient case above, impose other values of employment. The resulting system could be solved for other values of the endogenous variables just as easily as for the full employment ones – though with unemployment in the labour market. This system need not be stationary, but the economy could move from it sufficiently slowly for the optimal policy to seek a faster return to equilibrium.

The distinction between the disequilibrium analysis of the neoclassical model and the Keynesian demand-deficient analysis

The Keynesian demand-deficient analysis presented in this section sounds very similar to the disequilibrium analysis of the neoclassical model presented in Chapter 13. However, there is a fundamental difference between them. To show this difference, define 'equilibrium' as the state from which there is no inherent tendency to change. Keynesians claim that the economy can enter such an equilibrium at less than full employment, without inherent forces keeping it moving towards the latter. By comparison, the neoclassical economists claim that any such situation must be one of disequilibrium so that the economy's inherent forces or mechanisms will produce the changes required to keep it moving towards full employment. It is difficult to test empirically for this difference. In rough practical and intuitive terms, the difference can be taken to be that, following some disturbances, the Keynesian mechanism produces movements either away from full employment or very slowly – over, say, several years – towards full employment, while the neoclassical disequilibrium analysis produces a fairly rapid – over, say, a couple of quarters – move to full employment. Intermediate cases could fall in either analysis.

Optimal monetary policy in the Keynesian demand-deficient economy

To derive the optimal role and impact of monetary policy in such a context, assume that the economy is now at n_0^d of employment and y_0 of output in Figures 14.6a and 14.6b and suppose the monetary authorities increase the money supply. This increases aggregate demand in the economy, thereby shifting the n^d curve from $n^{d'}$ towards n^f, and increasing output beyond y_0^d. Since output increases in response to the increase in aggregate demand, prices may or may not increase. The increase in prices will depend on how deficient the earlier demand was and how large was the earlier excess capacity in the economy, but, in any case, prices will not rise in proportion to the increase in the money supply.[19] The expansionary monetary policy would have succeeded in increasing output in the economy. But once the economy has reached y^f – that is, there no longer exists any demand deficiency – further expansions in the money supply will not increase output but merely cause a proportionate increase in the price level. This limiting case of the demand-deficient analysis is, of course, the neoclassical full employment one, in accord with the Keynesians' claim that their analysis is the more general one and encompasses the neoclassical full employment and classical cases as a limiting case.

These arguments imply that there is no straightforward or linear relationship between the money supply increases and real output, or between the rate of inflation and the level of unemployment. These relationships depend upon the state of the economy and the extent of the monetary expansion. Further, the transmission of the impact of money supply increases on output does not always require or go through price level increases.

Asymmetry in the economy's responses to demand deficiencies and increases

We have so far considered the dynamics of demand declines from a full employment level. But suppose aggregate demand increases when there already exists full employment and the economy starts with the natural rate of employment. The dynamic response pattern of firms and workers should be basically consistent, though in opposite directions, in the two situations since these would be based on their rational response behaviour patterns, but the economy's constraints would be quite different between these cases. On the former, the individual firm seeing an increase in the demand for its product would tend to increase production through increases in employment, overtime worked and increased effort of employees and increases in efficiency. Each of these is feasible in the short run, with the increase in employment, beyond an initial full employment level, occurring through increased working hours of part-time workers, through students delaying resumption of studies and through increases in the overtime put in by employed workers, etc.[20] While such increases in employment and output above their full employment levels can occur, their scope is limited and constrained by the economy's short-run flexibility for these variables. Hence, while the increases in aggregate demand can increase output and employment in the short run beyond their full employment levels – and the economy can go below its natural rate of unemployment – the increase in prices is more likely and faster than the fall in prices in response to a decline in demand from the full employment level.

Therefore, there is a significant difference in the economy's constraints – or in their short-run flexibility – between increases in aggregate demand and decreases in it. Consequently, the dynamic response patterns are different between these cases. This asymmetry is vital to understanding the Keynesian policy recommendations on the stabilization role of monetary policy.

14.5 NEO-KEYNESIAN ECONOMICS

We will group under this heading the economic theories developed since the 1970s to provide a foundation for the Keynesian tenets that involuntary unemployment can exist in the economy and that changes in aggregate demand in the economy can affect output, at least in the short run. Another name often given to this group of theories is new Keynesian economics. These theories have in many ways supplanted the money-wage and the Phillips curve models presented in the earlier sections of this chapter. Their *raison d'être* is to present a rational basis for the rigidities of the nominal or the real wage and/or of the price level in the short run. We will present three of these theories. They are the efficiency wage theory leading to real wage rigidity, a theory of rigid or sticky prices based on sluggish price adjustments, and a theory of implicit contracts leading to labour hoarding. These are used as a set to derive the Keynesian conclusions that monetary policy, through aggregate demand, affects output and is not neutral in the short run, though it is neutral in the long run.

14.5.1 The efficiency wage theory

While the neoclassical and Keynesian theories presented so far in this book have taken the effort put in by each worker on the job to be constant, the efficiency wage model proposed by Akerlof (Yellen, 1984; Shapiro and Stiglitz, 1984) assumes that this effort is a function of the worker's wage. It can also be a function of other variables such as the unemployment rate and the unemployment benefits that also affect the opportunity cost of the job. In order to accommodate the concept of a variable effort on the part of workers, the firm's production function is modified from the usual one of:

$$y = f(n, \underline{K}) \quad f_n > 0, f_{nn} < 0$$

to:

$$y = f(e(w)n, \underline{K}) \quad f_e, f_n > 0, f_{ee}, f_{nn} < 0, e_w > 0, e_{ww} < 0 \tag{27}$$

where e designates 'effort', taking this to be a measurable variable. Equation (27) keeps the capital stock as constant for short-run analysis. Effort e is a function of the real wage rate w. Paying the workers more than the market clearing wage tends to increase their productivity by reducing shirking by workers, reducing turnover of workers, improving the average quality of job applicants and improving morale in the firm.

Focusing only on the shirking element, most jobs do not rigidly force the worker to work at a pre-set pace with a pre-specified productivity but allow the worker some leeway in their level of performance. Workers could, therefore, shirk on the job, thereby lowering their productivity or requiring the firm to prevent shirking through performance monitoring by inspectors, which imposes additional costs on the firm. If the worker is paid the market wage only, and is fired if caught shirking, he could obtain another job at the same wage and therefore would only lose by the extent of his search costs. But if he is paid a wage higher than the market wage, he has an incentive not to shirk and thereby lose a job with a better wage than he can get if he shirked and was fired for doing so. The absence of shirking, in turn, increases the worker's effort and productivity. Since a reduction in shirking increases the worker's effort and productivity, the firm has an incentive to pay its workers more than the market-clearing wage. For optimization, the wage paid will be that which yields the lowest labour cost per efficiency unit – that is with labour measured in terms of its efficiency. Designate this wage, known as the efficiency wage, as w^*. The profit-maximizing firm will then employ labour up to the point at which its marginal product equals its real wage. For the optimal efficiency wage w^*, employment is given by the condition:

$$e(w^*)f'(e(w^*)n, \underline{K}) = w^* \tag{28}$$

In equilibrium, all firms with the production function (27) would pay the real wage w^*, assuming it to be greater than labour's reservation wage.

The efficiency wage models assume the neoclassical labour demand and supply functions, with both demand and supply being functions of the real wage, so that the labour market is represented by Figure 14.7. At the wage w^*, higher than the market-clearing wage, $n_0^d < n^f < n_0^s$, so that employment at n^* is less than full employment and there exists involuntary unemployment equal to $(n^s - n^d)$. These unemployed workers are willing to accept the existing wage w^* or even somewhat lower wages but their competition for jobs will not reduce the market wage, since such a lower wage will be below the efficiency wage w^* and reduce the productivity of firms' existing employees and their profits. Consequently, the labour market will maintain involuntary unemployment equal to $(n^s - n^d)$ in the long run. Since such involuntary unemployment is a long-run feature of the labour market, it can be called as the long-run involuntary unemployment. Because of its long-run nature, some economists propose its incorporation into the notion of structural unemployment and redefine the natural rate to encompass it. However, since the determinants of structural unemployment and of such long-run involuntary unemployment are quite different, we prefer to keep them as separate concepts. Nor do we merge the latter into the classical concept of the natural rate of unemployment. In the efficiency wage context, the long-run rate of unemployment will, therefore, be the classical natural rate plus the efficiency-based long-run involuntary unemployment.

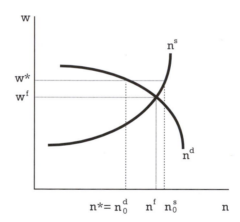

Figure 14.7

To explain the effects of a fall in demand on employment, rewrite (28) as:

$$p_i e(w^*) f'(e(w^*)n, \underline{K}) = Pw^* = W^* \tag{29}$$

where p_i is the price of the firm's product, P is the price level and W^* is the nominal wage equal to Pw^*, with w^* still as the efficiency real wage. Equation (29) can be rewritten as:

$$e(w^*)f'(e(w^*)n, \underline{K}) = (P/p_i)w^* \tag{30}$$

Now assume that there is a decline in the demand for the firm's product such that its relative price (p_i/P) falls. This will not change the firm's efficiency real wage w^*, but its demand curve for labour will shift down and its employment will fall. Conversely, an increase in the relative price of the firm's product will leave the efficiency real wage unchanged but increase its demand for labour and employment.

Now suppose that all product prices increase proportionately, so that we can use either (28) or (30). These imply that a change in the price level will not bring about a change in the efficiency wage w^* or the equilibrium values of employment n^* or involuntary unemployment u^{i*} in the economy. That is, this version of the efficiency wage theory does not imply that a change in aggregate demand – due to monetary or fiscal policy or other exogenous changes – will change aggregate employment and output. For this, we need to bring in the neo-Keynesian theories of price stickiness, presented in the next subsection.

Note that w^*, n^* and u^{i*} will change if the effort function $e(w)$ shifts or there is a shift in the production function. For instance, positive technical change which increases labour productivity will shift the labour demand curve outwards in Figure 14.7 and reduce the long-run involuntary unemployment for a given efficiency wage.[21] To study the effect of the business cycle on the efficiency wage, recessions have higher unemployment and pose greater difficulty and higher search costs of finding another job, so that workers have less incentive to shirk. Hence, the efficiency wage needed for minimizing labour cost per efficiency unit falls, so that the efficiency wage will fall in a recession. Conversely, it will rise in a boom with lower unemployment, so that efficiency wages behave pro-cyclically.

The efficiency wage theory implies long-run involuntary unemployment in the economy.[22] It can also be used to buttress the Keynesian claim that, following a fall in demand, the economy could settle into an equilibrium with a still higher level of un-employment. For this, it is preferable to modify the effort function to a more realistic one as $e = e(w, u)$, where $\partial e/\partial w \geq 0$ and $\partial e/\partial u \geq 0$, so that as unemployment rises, the firm can lower the efficiency wage necessary to get the maximum effort from the workers. In this case, a tradeoff will exist between the optimal efficiency wage and unemployment in the economy. A given fall in aggregate demand will, then, imply an equilibrium with a higher level of unemployment and a lower efficiency wage.

14.5.2 Price stickiness[23]

Neo-Keynesian theory assumes that while some goods in the economy are homogeneous and traded in perfectly competitive markets, many goods – especially at the retail level – are differentiated by firms in some characteristic or other. Such differentiation is often in the form of differences in colour, in packaging, in location, associated services or just established brand loyalty. Such differentiation in practice is usually not enough to create a monopoly for the firm but enables it to function in a monopolistically competitive manner. Profit maximization by a monopolistically competitive firm implies that it is not a price taker, as are firms under perfect competition, but a price setter with a downward sloping demand curve for its product. Consequently, increases in the price it sets do not reduce its sales to zero, nor do reductions in it allow it to capture the whole market for its industry. As a price setter, the firm sets the profit-maximizing price and supplies the output demanded at this price.

Changing the set price imposes a variety of costs, collectively known as *menu* costs. Examples of these are: reprinting price lists and catalogues, informing customers, re-marking the merchandise, etc. These costs, though often relatively small as a percentage of the price of the firm's product, can still be greater than the gain in revenue from a small price change. Further, even if there is a net gain from changing the price following an increase in demand, it may not be enough to persuade the firm to immediately raise its price since the inconvenience and costs to the firm's customers of frequent price changes are likely to be resented. Consequently, the firm may not find it optimal to respond to demand changes with price changes unless the demand changes imply large enough price changes. Over time, as demand increases occur, the optimal price change becomes large enough for the firm to be willing to incur the menu costs and change the actual price of its product.

These arguments imply that a monopolistically competitive firm will change its prices infrequently, but will respond to intervening changes in demand by changing its output at the existing price. In the long run, the price will adjust to demand and, even in the short run, if the demand increase is large enough, the price adjustment will occur. In the economy as a whole, an increase in aggregate demand will cause some sectors and firms, especially those with more competitive markets, to adjust their prices faster while others will not immediately do so but will respond to demand changes with supply changes. Consequently, an increase in the aggregate demand will be partly met with an increase in prices and partly by an increase in output.

The increase in aggregate output to meet an increase in aggregate demand requires an increase in employment. Even if the economy was initially in its long-run state, the efficiency wage theory, unlike the classical theory, implied that there would exist, in this long-run state, the involuntary unemployment of workers and these workers are willing to accept jobs at the existing real wage. Hence, the increase in aggregate demand will be accommodated through an increase in employment and output, without necessarily a change in real wages.

Conversely, a decrease in the demand for the products of the firm in monopolistic competition need not immediately cause it to lower its price unless the implied optimal price reduction was sufficiently large. Again, taking the economy to be a mix of firms in perfect competition and monopolistic competition, decreases in aggregate demand would partly result in a fall in the price level and partly a reduction in the output supplied. The latter will cause firms to reduce their employment. However, as the efficiency wage theory argued, this fall in employment will not lead to a competitive reduction in the real wage.

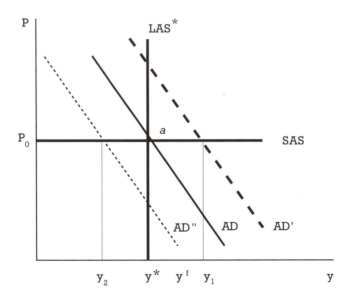

Figure 14.8

This analysis has provided a justification based on sticky prices for an upward-sloping short-run aggregate supply curve. This justification is different from that for the Phillips curve or its expectations augmented version, and is also different from that for the Lucas supply rule. Its extreme version is the simplification that no firms would change prices in response to demand changes, so that the aggregate price level can be taken as constant. In this version, shown in Figure 14.8, the price level is assumed to be constant at its initial level P_0 given by point a. The LAS* (with * designating its efficiency basis) shows the aggregate supply given by the efficiency wage model as y^*, while classical full employment is shown by the point y^f at a higher level of output. Prices are sticky at P_0, so that we can specify a short-run aggregate supply curve SAS which is horizontal at P_0. The increase in the aggregate demand from AD to AD' leads to the supply of output y_1 at the sticky price P_0. Conversely, the decrease in the aggregate demand from AD to AD'' leads to the supply of output y_2, but again without an accompanying change from the sticky price P_0. Transient and small changes in aggregate demand are, therefore, accommodated by the change in output, with an accompanying employment change. Cumulative changes in the same direction – or large aggregate demand changes – will, however, cause increases in prices, so that the long-run response to such changes is taken to be along the LAS* curve.

An economy with a mix of perfectly competitive and monopolistically competitive industries will have an SAS curve that is upward sloping rather than horizontal at the initial price level.

An implication of this menu cost approach to price stickiness is that prices will adjust faster the greater the increase in demand, so that the higher the inflation rate, the more quickly will prices adjust and the less will be the effect of aggregate demand increases on real output. Hence, at higher rates of inflation, nominal shocks will produce smaller real effects.

14.5.3 Implicit contracts and labour hoarding

The neo-Keynesians also argue that it is optimal for firms and workers to enter into long-term implicit and explicit employment contracts. Such contracts are optimal for the firm because of the cost of hiring and training workers and the firm specificity of skills acquired through training and learning on the job, so that the productivity of such a skilled worker will be greater than of new hires. The worker also benefits from this higher productivity through higher wages in his existing firm than if he was to quit and join other firms. This mutual benefit from continued employment implies that the firm would try to retain its skilled workers if it can do so through a period of reduced demand for its output, rather than laying them off immediately. The firm, therefore, finds it optimal to lay off fewer workers than justified by the fall in demand, leading to a form of labour hoarding during recessions. Such hoarded labour works less hard during recessions because there is less work to do or is often diverted to such tasks as maintenance etc. If a worker is laid off, the worker also has an incentive to wait to be recalled by his old employer rather than immediately accept a job with another firm in which his productivity and wage will be lower. Hence, reductions in aggregate demand in the short run partly lead to labour hoarding, with a consequent fall in average productivity, and partly to an increase in unemployment, with some of the laid-off workers being put on recall and voluntarily waiting to be recalled rather than actively searching for jobs.

Conversely, the implicit agreement between firms and workers also means that workers accommodate increases in the demand for the firm's output with increased effort, even in the absence of wage increases. Hence, output fluctuates more than employment over the business cycle, and the fact that the economy is in its long-run full employment state is not a barrier to short-run increases in output.

14.5.4 Monetary policy in the neo-Keynesian model

The neo-Keynesian model implies that changes in aggregate demand in the presence of sticky prices induce changes in output and employment in the same direction in the short run but not in the long run. Hence, since an expansion of the money supply increases aggregate demand and a contraction reduces it, monetary policy can be used to change output and employment in the economy for the short run but not for the long run. This implication for the short-run effects of monetary policy is shared with the other Keynesian models.

However, there are some distinctive implications of monetary policy in the neo-Keynesian model. Money is neutral in it in the long run while it is not so for the Phillips curve analysis, though it is for the expectations augmented Phillips curve. Further, in the short run, while an expansionary monetary policy induces an increase in output through a reduction in real wages (induced by the increase in the price level) in the Phillips curve model, it does not do so in the neo-Keynesian efficiency wage model, in which the efficiency real wage need not decline. Moreover, in the neo-Keynesian model, since the (sticky) price level does not rise in response to an increase in aggregate demand, the short-run increase in output occurs without a prior or accompanying increase in prices, so that the impact of monetary policy on output is not a function of the change in prices but rather of the change in the money supply itself. In fact, any increase in prices reduces the impact of monetary expansion on output. Therefore, the neo-Keynesian model runs counter to the Phillips curve model on the relationship between prices and output for a given monetary expansion, with the former implying a negative relationship and the latter a positive one. Furthermore, in the neo-Keynesian model, the relationship between output and money supply is non-linear since very rapid increases in the latter will induce more rapid price adjustment, with a consequently smaller increase in output.

The neo-Keynesian theory of sticky prices is supportive of the Keynesian dynamic analysis presented earlier. In this dynamic analysis, firms were taken to respond to an increase in their demand by increasing their output or by increasing both output and price but not by merely increasing their price only. However, the reasons given for the rationality of this behaviour were more than just menu costs, but included uncertainty about the duration and extent of the demand increase and the absence of a coordinating mechanism in the economy which limited trades to only the equilibrium of the notional demand and supply functions.

To sum up the neo-Keynesian implications for monetary policy, monetary policy is neutral in the long run but not in the short run. Further, higher rates of monetary expansion could evoke lower rather than higher increases in output. This impact of monetary policy does not require a reduction in real wages but can occur without a change in the real efficiency wage, which creates a long-run pool of involuntary unemployment.

Many economists see the neo-Keynesian model as replacing the earlier Keynesian ones. However, there are several distinctive elements in the earlier ones – for example, in the staggered labour contracts and errors in expectations behind the Phillips curve analysis and the lack of a coordinating mechanism in the dynamic analysis – which are not fully incorporated into the neo-Keynesian model but do have a strong plausible basis in reality. Further, some elements of the neo-Keynesian model, such as the short-run rigidity of real wages, are not consistent with Keynes' and Keynesian ideas. Therefore, the neo-Keynesian model should be taken to be a complement to – rather than a complete replacement of – the Keynesian group of models in explaining why money is not neutral in the short run.

14.6 THE REDUCED-FORM EQUATIONS FOR OUTPUT AND EMPLOYMENT IN THE KEYNESIAN AND NEOCLASSICAL APPROACHES

The fundamental implication of the various forms of Keynesian models is that in conditions of aggregate demand deficiency and less than full employment, aggregate output depends upon aggregate demand and therefore on the demand management policy variables of fiscal expenditures, taxation and the money supply. On the impact of monetary policy on real output, the Keynesian analyses imply that:

(i)   This impact will depend upon the existing demand deficiency in the economy, so that a linear relationship between real output and the money supply, with constant coefficients, is not a proper representation of the Keynesian implications.

(ii) Both the unanticipated *and* the anticipated values of the money supply m – as also of the fiscal variables – will affect output equally, as against the neoclassical assertion that only the unanticipated values do so.

The Keynesian reduced-form equations

A simple linear equation for capturing the dependence of output on the policy variables is:

$$dy = \lambda_g \, dg + \lambda_m \, dm \tag{31}$$

where λ_g, $\lambda_m \geq 0$. Note that, as we have shown in the preceding sections, λ_g and λ_m depend upon the existing demand deficiency in the economy and cannot be taken to be constants. Keynesian theory implies that they are essentially endogenous variables in the economy. In the demand-deficient cases, λ_g, λ_m will be positive, without being constant, while in the limiting case of full employment equilibrium, λ_g, $\lambda_m = 0$. In order to urge caution when using λ_g and λ_m, as if they were constants, we call (31) a pseudo-Keynesian relationship.

In a dynamic context, define $dy = y_t - y_{t-1}$, $dg = g_t - g_{t-1}$, $dm = m_t - m_{t-1}$, so that (31) becomes:

$$y_t = [y_{t-1} - (\lambda_g g_{t-1} + \lambda_m m_{t-1})] + \lambda_g g_t + \lambda_m m_t \tag{32}$$

In line with (31), an equation popular for empirically testing the Keynesian model is:

$$y_t = a_0 + \lambda_g g_t + \lambda_m m_t + \mu_t \tag{33}$$

where λ_g, $\lambda_m \geq 0$ under the Keynesian hypothesis, a_0 equals $[y_{t-1} - (\lambda_g g_{t-1} + \lambda_m m_{t-1})]$, μ_t is a random term, and all variables are in logs. a_0 is sometimes replaced by a term of the form αy_{t-1} to capture persistence patterns in output, and y_t and y_{t-1} are sometimes defined to be deviations in output from its full employment level. Equation (33), just like (32), is also a pseudo-Keynesian equation.

A more appropriate representation of the Keynesian equation is:

$$y_t = a_0 + \lambda_g(u_t - u_t^f)g_t + \lambda_m(u_t - u_t^f)m_t + \mu_t \tag{34}$$

where u is the unemployment rate and u^f is the natural (or full employment) rate of unemployment, so that λ_g and λ_m are to be treated as functional symbols. $\lambda_g(u_t - u_t^f)$ and $\lambda_m(u_t - u_t^f)$ need not be linear functions.

The neoclassical estimating equations

The neoclassical equation corresponding to (33) is:

$$y_t = y^* + b_g(g_t - g_t^e) + b_m(m_t - m_t^e) + \mu_t \tag{35}$$

where b_g, $b_m > 0$ and the superscript e indicates the expected value of the variable in question. In expectational equilibrium with $g_t = g_t^e$ and $m_t = m_t^e$, (35) becomes:

$$y_t = y^* + \mu_t \tag{36}$$

which states the neoclassical conclusion that if there are no errors in expectations, only random deviations around the full employment output can occur.

In the neoclassical model, since any impact of money supply increases and fiscal deficits on output must first cause an increase in individual prices or the price level, it is appropriate to estimate the neoclassical model by an equation of the form:

$$y_t = a_0 + \gamma_P P_t + \mu_t \tag{37}$$

or as:

$$y_t = a_0 + \gamma_\pi \pi_t + \mu_t \tag{38}$$

The equilibrium version of the neoclassical model implies that the estimated values of γ_P and γ_π will be zero, so that money supply changes will be neutral.

Keynesian price equations

Equations (37) and (38) are sometimes used for testing the Keynesian model. Estimated values of γ_p and γ_π greater than zero are taken as confirmation of this model.

However, note that (37) and (38) are not reduced-form equations, since they, like the Phillips curve to which (38) is related, relate an endogenous variable to another endogenous variable. While they emanate from the Keynesian nominal wage and the Phillips curve models, they are not good representations of the Keynesian deficient-demand model: in the latter, given deficient demand, an increase in the money supply raises aggregate demand which causes increases in output without necessarily causing increases in the price level or the inflation rate, but, in any case, without using the latter as a causal intermediate step. A corollary of this process is that, even if there are accompanying or coincidental price increases, the response of output to monetary increases will not be fully captured by a bivariate relationship between output and price. It is only the nominal wage and the Phillips curve models which necessarily rely upon price increases and inflation to lower the real wage, which in turn induces increases in employment and output. The deficient-demand models do not require decreases in real wages for a positive impact of money supply increases on employment and output. Hence, while a finding that $\gamma_p, \gamma_\pi > 0$ in (37) and (38) may serve as support for the nominal wage and Phillips curve models while $\gamma_p, \gamma_\pi = 0$ lead to their rejection, the latter do not serve as rejection for the deficient-demand models. Equations (37) and (38) are, therefore, not appropriate for tests of the Keynesian deficient-demand models. Consequently, the Phillips curve relationship, which is similar to (38), is not suitable for testing such models, even though both belong in the Keynesian stable of models.

14.7 KEYNESIAN ECONOMICS AND RICARDIAN EQUIVALENCE

The spirit and policy prescriptions of Keynesian economics are so different from those of Ricardian equivalence that the two are never integrated or even associated with each other: the former advocates governmental policies for improving on the economy's performance while the latter attempts to limit them. In spite of this, suppose we were to integrate the two. What modifications of the Keynesian models and their conclusions would follow from this mix?

The assumptions and equations of Ricardian equivalence were specified in Chapter 13. Ricardian equivalence had changed the equations for the IS relationship and the aggregate demand function. The IS relationship, modified by Ricardian equivalence, was:

$$y = c_0' + c_y'y + i_0 - i_r r$$

$$= \left[\frac{1}{1 - c_y'}\right]\left(c_0' + i_0 - i_r r\right) \tag{39}$$

The aggregate demand function correspondingly had changed to:

$$y^d = \left[\frac{1}{1 - c_y' + i_r m_y / m_r}\right]\left(c_0' + i_0 + \frac{i_r}{m_r}\frac{M}{P}\right) \tag{40}$$

where c_0' and c_y' include the government's purchases of commodities, so that these parameters will be larger than the corresponding ones (c_0 and c_y) for private consumption alone. None of these equations include fiscal variables, thereby eliminating the use of fiscal variables as policy variables for changing aggregate demand in the economy. However, the qualitative role of monetary policy is not changed. The money multiplier is now:

$$\frac{\partial y^d}{\partial (M/P)} = \left[\frac{1}{1 - c'_y + i_r m_y / m_r} \right] \left(\frac{i_r}{m_r} \right)$$

$$= \left[\frac{i_r}{m_r - m_r c'_y + i_r m_y} \right] \tag{41}$$

We can draw the following qualitative conclusions from the preceding discussion.

(i) The supply structure of the Keynesian model is not affected by the introduction of the Ricardian equivalence in it. Hence, the qualitative conclusions on the effectiveness of monetary policy in changing aggregate demand and real output in the economy are not altered by Ricardian equivalence, even though those on the impact of fiscal policy are drastically changed.

(ii) Ricardian equivalence has nothing to say on the existence of full employment or that of less than full employment in the economy, so that it does not preclude the Keynesian insistence on the possibility of less than full employment existing in real-world economies over significant periods of time. For such Keynesian cases, Ricardian equivalence strengthens the need and scope for monetary policy, and makes monetary policy the sole available instrument for offsetting demand deficiency in the economy.

14.8 MERCANTILISM, LIBERALISM, AND CLASSICAL AND KEYNESIAN ECONOMICS

The alternative to the philosophy of classical economic liberalism – which is nowadays associated with political and economic conservatism and is sometimes relabelled as neoliberalism – implied by the neoclassical and classical macroeconomic models, is an interventionist one which starts from the propositions that the economy left to itself under a *laissez faire* policy stance does not perform at the optimum level for its citizens, that its performance can be improved by appropriate state incursions, and that, in the international sphere, such incursions can improve the welfare of the country relative to that of other countries. An historic form of this philosophy, which often proposed detailed, general and selective controls over the economy, was *mercantilism*. Based on the desire to promote national economic interests, historically, mercantilism tended to be the dominant economic philosophy in most countries in the pre-industrial and development phases, with economic liberalism generally belonging to those periods in the history of a nation where it had a competitive advantage over other nations. Looking broadly over the last five centuries for examples, Britain favoured mercantilism until the Industrial Revolution in the late eighteenth century gave it such a competitive advantage; France followed the route to economic liberalism in the nineteenth century and the USA and Germany did so in the twentieth, each only doing so once they had acquired or were in a position to acquire an adequate competitive advantage. At any given time or stage of development, nations mostly try to pursue their national economic interests and often act as mercantilists in some sectors or others – i.e., promoting some sectors and protecting some others through a variety of policies and instruments – while leaving others to open-market competitive forces.

The origin of economics as a distinct area of study is often attributed to Adam Smith's *The Wealth of Nations*. It argued that the nation's wealth increases most when economic agents – individuals and firms – pursue their own self-interest in a free enterprise unregulated economy and that mercantilist policies were detrimental to the growth of trade, specialization and wealth of nations. This was a battle cry for a *laissez faire* economy, whose economic base was laid out and consolidated in the progress of economic analysis during the nineteenth century, and which became the basis for the liberal economic philosophy dominant in Britain until the beginning of the First World War. The inter-war years from 1918 to 1939 saw very extensive economic dislocation in many European countries, culminating in the Great Depression from 1930 to 1939, and causing a resurgence of state intervention and protectionism among the Western nations.

A very limited version of the interventionist philosophy, mainly confined to the macroeconomic level, was proposed in 1936 by Keynes who argued that the macroeconomy does not always perform at the full employment level and that state intervention through monetary and fiscal policies can improve on its performance. The model that justified this stance was originally provided by Keynes in *The General Theory* (1936) and, as we have seen in this chapter, has many versions under the general label of Keynesianism. It was essentially a call in the national interest for macroeconomic manipulation of the economy through monetary and fiscal policies. It was supported in the microeconomic sphere by the analysis of market imperfections – such as monopolistic competition, imperfect competition, oligopoly and monopoly – and production externalities, which were used to justify the regulation of firms and markets. Combined with the ideology of socialism, it brought about, in the decades from the 1930s to the 1970s, the nationalization of selected industries in several developed countries, including most European ones.

For several decades after 1945, with the independence of many countries from the imperial ones and with a nationalistic urge to improve their standards of living through economic development, the infant or 'national interest' industry argument was further used to justify extensive protection from foreign competitors through tariffs and quotas, while some industries were being subsidized to promote their growth or protect their survival. Such practices were more common in the developing rather than the developed economies, though the latter continue to have many examples of such protectionism.[24] The overall pattern of ideas was one which argued for a modernized version of mercantilism as a mode of promoting industrialization, and represented extensive state intervention in the economy. This pattern proved to be quite popular in many countries during the 1940s to the 1970s, but was called into question by the resurgence of classical economics during the 1970s and 1980s, the widespread failure of nationalized industries to deliver the expected growth rates, and, more dramatically, by the fall of communism in Eastern Europe in the early 1990s. The resultant resurgence of the liberal economic policies during the 1980s and 1990s has produced a widespread dismantling of the mercantilist type of policies – Keynesian at the macroeconomic level and regulatory and protectionist ones at the microeconomic level. The current trend is towards privatization of public sector enterprises, deregulation and promotion of competition by the elimination of inter-industry and inter-country barriers, and lowering of tariff walls, etc. The most noticeable examples of these have occurred in several of the formerly communist countries and the LDCs, but the process is also in evidence in the developed economies.

CONCLUSIONS

This chapter has presented three versions of the Keynesian model and a neo-Keynesian model. These attest to its evolutionary nature. It is also quite likely that the future will see additional contributions and versions of the general Keynesian stance that money is not neutral in the short run, while it could – and is likely to be – neutral in the long run.

We arrange the concluding comments for this chapter into various categories, as follows.

Keynes on the wage bargain and the rigidity of wages

A major point of disagreement between the classical and Keynesian ideas is on the nature of the labour market. Keynes himself considered his objections to the labour market assumptions of the classical model as being the most fundamental departures from it. He expressed his ideas on this as:

But the . . . more fundamental, objection [to the Classical model] . . . flows from our disputing the assumption that the general level of real wages is directly determined by the character of the wage bargain. In assuming that the wage bargain determines the real wage the classical school have slipped in an illicit assumption. For there may be no method available to labour as a whole whereby it can bring the wage-goods equivalent of the general level of money-wages into conformity with the marginal disutility of the current volume of employment. There may exist no expedient by which labour as a whole can reduce its real wage to a given figure by making revised money bargains with the entrepreneurs. . . .

Though the struggle over money-wages between individuals and groups is often believed to determine the general level of real wages, it is, in fact, concerned with a different object. Since there is imperfect mobility of labour, and wages do not tend to an exact equality of net advantage in different occupations, any individual or group of individuals, who consent to a reduction of money-wages relatively to others, will suffer a relative reduction in real wages, which is a sufficient justification for them to resist it. On the other hand it would be impracticable to resist every reduction of real wages, due to a change in the purchasing-power of money which affects all workers alike; and in fact reductions of real wages arising in this way are not, as a rule, resisted unless they proceed to an extreme degree. . . .

In other words, the struggle about money-wages primarily affects the distribution of the aggregate real wage between different labour-groups, and not its average amount per unit of employment, which depends, as we shall see, on a different set of forces. The effect of combination on the part of a group of workers is to protect their relative real wage. The general level of wages depends on the other forces of the economic system.

(Keynes, 1936, pp. 12–14)

The IS–LM analytical technique

The technique of analysis embodied in the IS–LM diagram was first set forth by Hicks in 1937 to explain the reasoning of Keynes in *The General Theory* to the economics profession and had become the dominant mode of exposition for both the neoclassical and Keynesian models by the 1960s. The Keynesian nominal wage model in terms of its assumptions and its exposition through the IS–LM framework eventually came under considerable attack from Keynes' followers, specially those in the post-Keynesian school, as being unrepresentative of Keynes' own ideas. Many of their views on this issue are now generally accepted, as shown by the following quotations from Leijonhufvud (1967).

Leijonhufvud on Keynes and Keynesian economics

One must be careful in applying the epithet 'Keynesian' nowadays. I propose to use it in the broadest sense possible and let 'Keynesian economics' be synonymous with the 'majority school' macroeconomics which has evolved out of the debates triggered by Keynes's *General Theory*. Keynesian economics, in this popular sense, is far from being a homogeneous doctrine. The common denominator . . . is the class of models generally used. The prototype of these models dates back to the famous paper by Hicks (1937). . . . This standard [IS–LM] model appears to me to be a singularly inadequate vehicle for the interpretation of Keynes's ideas. . . .

The emphasis on the 'rigidity' of wages, which one finds in the New Economics, reveals the judgement that wages did not fall enough in the early 1930s. Keynes, in contrast, judged that they declined too much by far. It has been noted before that, to Keynes, wage rigidity was a policy recommendation and not a behavioral assumption.

Keynes's theory was dynamic. His model was static. The method of trying to analyze dynamic processes with a comparative static analysis apparatus Keynes borrowed from Marshall. . . . The initial response to a decline in demand is a quantity adjustment. . . .

> The strong assumption of 'rigid' wages is not necessary to the explanation of such system behavior. It is sufficient only to give up the equally strong assumption of instantaneous price adjustments. . . .
>
> (Leijonhufvud, 1967, pp. 401–03)

Most of the points made in the preceding quote are now generally accepted. Thus, it is now accepted that Keynes did not assume that workers based their supply behaviour on nominal rather than real wages and did not assume that the nominal wages were rigid. Further, his analysis was not comparative static or equilibrium analysis, used in our exposition of the nominal wage model, based on the assumption of *price adjustments* in response to excess demand or supply. Keynes' analysis, in contrast, assumed *quantity adjustments* by firms in such situations and focused attention on the disequilibrium path of output and employment in this adjustment. If this adjustment towards equilibrium was a slow one, then in the classical or the Keynesian model, a shortfall in demand would result in a reduction in output and employment for periods of significant length. If the economy was beset by fresh disturbances arising frequently, such as through bouts of pessimism or optimism about the future among firms' managers, the disequilibrium state would be a persistent phenomenon, with varying levels of employment or output.

The distinctive nature of labour markets was a fundamental part of Keynes' ideas and is an essential component of current Keynesian and neoclassical research. One interpretation of those ideas led to the Phillips curve, as illustrated by the following quotations from James Tobin (1972), an eminent economist in the Keynesian tradition.

Tobin on wages and unemployment

> Unemployment is, in this model as in Keynes reinterpreted, a disequilibrium phenomenon. Money wages do not adjust rapidly enough to clear all labor markets every day. Excess supplies in labor markets take the form of unemployment, and excess demands the form of unfilled vacancies. At any moment, markets vary widely in excess demand or supply and the economy as a whole shows both vacancies and unemployment.
>
> The overall balance of vacancies and unemployment is determined by aggregate demand, and is therefore in principle subject to control by overall monetary and fiscal policy. Higher aggregate demand means fewer excess supply markets and more excess demand markets, accordingly less unemployment and more vacancies. . . .
>
> Workers will move from excess supply markets to excess demand markets, and from low wage to high wage markets. Unless they overshoot, these movements are equilibrating. The theory therefore requires that new disequilibria are always arising. Aggregate demands may be stable, but beneath its stability is never-ending flux: new products, new processes, new tastes and fashions, new developments of land and natural resources, obsolescent industries and declining areas. . . .
>
> (Tobin, 1972, pp. 9–10)

The critical role of dynamic analysis when aggregate demand falls

The introduction of demand deficiency in a dynamic context did away with the Keynesians' need to assume the rigidity of prices and nominal wages, or on the irrationality of the labour supply function based on nominal rather than real wages, and challenges neoclassical economics on its own grounds of rationality and price and wage flexibility. For such analysis, given a fall in aggregate demand, the central issue is the nature of the individual firm's response to a fall in the demand for its product and the nature of the worker's response who is laid off or whose job no longer seems to be secure, in a context where the numerous markets of the economy cannot realistically be assumed to come into macroeconomic equilibrium instantly. This is a shift in the debate from comparative static to dynamic analysis. There can be numerous plausible dynamic paths corresponding to any comparative static macroeconomic model, and not all necessarily lead to full employment or do so instantly. This implies a role for Keynesian demand-management policies depending upon the state of the economy and the speed at which it is expected to redress deficient demand or involuntary unemployment.

On the central issues in dispute from this perspective, Patinkin (1965) – an eminent neoclassical economist – wrote on effective demand analysis that:

> involuntary unemployment can have no meaning within the confines of static equilibrium analysis. Conversely, the essence of dynamic analysis is *involuntariness*: its domain consists only of positions off the [notional] demand or supply curves . . . [p. 323].
>
> First, we see that involuntary unemployment can exist in a system of perfect competition and wage and price flexibility. . . . Second, we see that a deficiency in commodity demand can generate a decrease in labour input without requiring a prior increase in the real wage rate . . . [pp. 323–24].
>
> And the assumption . . . that, granted flexibility, these [dynamic] forces will restore the economy to a state of full employment, is an assumption that . . . [a full employment] equilibrium position always exists and that the economy will always converge to it. More specifically, it is an assumption that just as the 'market' can solve the system of excess demand equations (of the neoclassical model), when the level of real income is held constant during the *tâtonnement*, so can it solve it when the level of real income (and hence employment) is also permitted to vary [p. 328).

(Patinkin, 1965)

Neo-Keynesian economics

Neo-Keynesian economics came into being in an attempt to rebuild the Keynesian framework after the decline of faith in the 1970s in the Keynesian models and their policy prescriptions, and the resurgence of classical economics in the 1980s and 1990s. The efficiency wage hypothesis of neo-Keynesian economics asserts the short-run rigidity of real wages, in contrast to that of nominal wages which had been a component of the earlier Keynesian ideas. But the neo-Keynesian theory does provide a new basis for the short-run rigidity of prices through its hypothesis of menu costs in monopolistic competition. Both the Keynesian and the neo-Keynesian theories agree that monetary policy is not neutral in the short run.

Keynesian versus neoclassical economics

The neoclassical and Keynesian schools represent different views of the self-adjusting dynamic nature of the capitalist economy. The former views it as being in full employment equilibrium or close to it, with the dynamic forces providing a strong tendency to return to full employment after any deviation. The Keynesian schools allow the possible existence of full employment but are concerned that the economy does not always or most of the time perform at full employment. Further, a demand deficiency for output can generate dynamic forces creating involuntary unemployment which could subsist for extensive periods because there is no adequate and rapid equilibrating mechanism, or the likely mechanisms are destabilizing. From the perspective of monetary policy, it does not matter whether the economy away from full employment is described as being in disequilibrium, in temporary equilibrium or in equilibrium, or even whether there do exist mechanisms, such as the real balance effect or wage and price adjustments which will eventually bring the economy to full employment. If the economy left on its own can stay away from full employment for some time, the appropriate question for monetary policy is whether it is optimal for such policy to hasten the economy's return to full employment. On this issue, the neoclassical, and especially classical and new classical, economists claim that it is better to leave the economy alone, no matter what its state happens to be, while the Keynesians claim that monetary policy does have a positive optimal role in certain states of the economy.

Historically, faith in these positions has tended to vary considerably. The Great Depression of the 1930s in industrial economies destroyed faith in the classical and neoclassical belief in a self-regulating economy; the fairly stable macroeconomic performance of such economies in the 1950s and 1960s, though with active Keynesian demand-management policies, produced shallow and short-lived recessions, led to a slow revival first of neoclassical economics – under the rubric of the Keynesian–neoclassical synthesis – and this, followed by the Keynesian policy errors in the 1970s, tended to restore faith in the general neoclassical position. The currently dominant school is the latter one, but there is no guarantee that the Keynesian doctrines, rejuvenated in a newer form, will not return one day to reclaim that dominance. The dragged-out recession of the early 1990s and the rise of the rate of unemployment to double digits in many industrialized countries in the early 1990s was widely blamed on the restrictive monetary policies pursued in these years to reduce the rates of inflation, followed or accompanied by deficit-cutting strategies. The length of the recession and the tempered recovery following it seem to indicate that the monetary and fiscal policies do affect real output and employment for significant periods, as the Keynesians claim.

And finally, what are we to believe?

The economics profession does not possess convincing empirical evidence for all economists to accept one school and reject the other, and many economists keep an open mind, applying their overall knowledge depending upon the state of the economy. Most economists also maintain a fair degree of scepticism. We illustrate this eclecticism and scepticism from a Presidential Address given to the American Economic Association by the Nobel prize-winner Robert Solow in 1980:

> Some of us see the Smithian virtues as a needle in a haystack, as an island of measure zero in a sea of imperfections. Others see all the potential sources of market failures as so many fleas on the thick hide of an ox, requiring only an occasional flick of the tail to be brushed away. A hopeless eclectic . . . like me, has a terrible time of it. . . . I need only listen to Milton Friedman talk for a minute and my mind floods with thoughts of increasing returns to scale, oligopolistic interdependence, consumer ignorance, environmental pollution, inter-generational inequity, and on and on. There is no cure for it, except to listen to John Kenneth Galbraith,[25] in which case all I can think of are the discipline of competition, the large number of substitutes for any commodity, the stupidities of regulation, the Pareto optimality of Walrasian equilibrium, the importance of decentralizing decision making to where the knowledge is, and on and on.
>
> (Solow, 1980, p. 2)

Given this schizophrenic attitude to the impact of monetary policy on the economy, our mode of presentation has been to discuss in Chapters 13 and 14 the views of each school as their proponents might present them. We follow this same 'putting the best foot forward' pattern in the next two chapters, leaving the conclusions of these chapters, and especially to those of Chapter 16, for a summation of where we believe the empirical evidence leads. An impatient reader who wants to know this without further ado – and thereby also find out this author's viewpoints – can, of course, immediately proceed to those conclusions.

SUMMARY OF CRITICAL CONCLUSIONS

- Early (1940s and 1950s) Keynesian models were based on nominal wage rigidity or price illusion by labour.
- In the 1960s and 1970s, Keynesian models were often based on the Phillips curve.

- More modern versions of such models rely on staggered wage contracts with price expectations and the possibility of expectational errors.
- An abiding theme in Keynesian models, originating with Keynes' *The General Theory*, is the failure of the economy to attain Walrasian general equilibrium. This is attributed to the absence in the real world of an adequate coordinating mechanism such as *tâtonnement*, auctioneer or recontracting, and the imperfect functioning of the competitive mechanisms that do exist in the modern economy. The Keynesian approach asserts that this failure is especially symptomatic of the labour market, so that involuntary unemployment is a common occurrence in the real-world economies.
- The Keynesian model based on this deficiency in the macroeconomic environment is the demand-deficient model. This approach posits that the rational dynamic responses by firms and households to conditions of inadequate demand and involuntary unemployment do not always take the economy to full employment or do so within an acceptable period.
- The demand-deficient models imply that the responses of output and unemployment with respect to changes in the money supply during periods of demand deficiency are not properly captured in the Phillips curve or the Lucas supply curve relationships.
- The neo-Keynesian theories rely on rational long-run behaviour resulting in implicit contracts, staggered wage contracts, sticky prices and menu costs, etc.
- There is no logical inconsistency between the Keynesian approach and rational expectations. Further, Keynes' *The General Theory* argued strongly for the adequate consideration of both short-run and long-run expectations in macroeconomic analysis. The Keynesian models can quite legitimately incorporate rational expectations, provided they are defined in a manner consistent with the economy's effective state – which need not necessarily be the general equilibrium one.
- There is no logical inconsistency between the Keynesian approach and Ricardian equivalence. While incorporation of Ricardian equivalence into the Keynesian models renders fiscal policy ineffective, it enhances the role of monetary policy in stabilizing the economy.
- However, the spirit both of Keynes' *The General Theory* and of Keynesian analyses, as well as their policy conclusions, runs counter to Ricardian equivalence. Therefore, while the Keynesian models can be modified to incorporate Ricardian equivalence, doing so is not consistent with the spirit of the Keynesian tradition.

review and discussion questions[26]

1 Discuss in the context of the different Keynesian models: excluding dynamic effects, an increase in the stock of money and a fall in nominal wages have essentially the same effects at a time of unemployment.
2 Discuss in the context of the neo-Keynesian models: excluding dynamic effects, an increase in the stock of money and a fall in nominal wages have essentially the same effects at a time of unemployment.
3 (a) Describe a simple fixed-price short-run macroeconomic model (with flexible nominal wages) and compare it with a conventional market-clearing model. Compare their predictions for the effectiveness of monetary and fiscal policies.
(b) Describe a simple short-run macroeconomic model with flexible prices but fixed nominal wages and compare it with a conventional market-clearing model (with flexible nominal wages). Compare their predictions for the effectiveness of monetary and fiscal policies.
(c) Describe a simple short-run macroeconomic model with a fixed price and fixed nominal wages and compare it with a conventional market-clearing model. Compare their predictions for the effectiveness of monetary and fiscal policies.

4 You are given the following fixed-price, closed economy, IS–LM model:

   IS: $y = c[(1-t_1)(y+b/r), M+b/r] + i(r,y) + g$

   LM: $M = m^d(r, y, M+b/r)$

The government's budget constraint is:

   $dM + db/r = g - t_1(y+b/r)$

where b is the number of consols, each paying \$1 per period in perpetuity. P is normalized to unity. Wealth is held only in money and bonds.

(a) Explain the differences between its IS and the LM relationships and those used in the text.
(b) Explain the government budget constraint.
(c) Using the IS–LM diagrams, derive the short-run and long-run equilibrium effects on output of a permanent increase in g financed by (a) money creation, or (ii) bond creation. Under what conditions are these policies stable?
(d) How are your results affected if bonds are not part of net wealth?
(e) Does this model explain some of the differences between the monetarists and the Keynesians on the relative efficacy of monetary versus fiscal policies?

5 Suppose that business pessimism reduces investment such that aggregate demand becomes less than full employment income at all *non-negative* rates of interest. Use the IS–LM analysis to answer the following:

(a) Are there positive equilibrium levels of y, r and P in the neoclassical model?
(b) Are there positive equilibrium levels of y, r and P in the Keynesian fixed-price model? In the Keynesian nominal wage model (without fixed prices)?

What processes will take the economy to these levels?

6 'From the time of Say and Ricardo the classical economists have taught us that the supply creates its own demand . . . [and] that an individual act of abstaining from consumption necessarily leads to . . . the commodities thus released . . . to be invested . . . so that an act of individual saving inevitably leads to a parallel act of investment. . . . Those who think this way are deceived. They are fallaciously supposing that there is a nexus which unites decisions to abstain from consumption with decisions to provide for future consumption, whereas the motives which determine the latter are not linked with the motives which determine the former' (Keynes, 1936, pp. 18–21). Explain this statement.

   If investment and saving depend on different determinants, what are these determinants and how is the equality of saving and investment in the economy ensured. Or does it also become an identity? If it is not an identity, outline the possible scenario of the likely adjustment pattern in the economy following an exogenous decrease in consumption.

7 Suppose the central bank pegs the price level by using money supply changes through open market operations. Present the IS–LM analysis incorporating this money supply rule and show the implications for the money supply, aggregate demand and output of an exogenous increase in autonomous consumption. Is the effect on interest rates less or greater under this money supply rule than if the money supply was held exogenous?

8 Start with the neoclassical model and assume that its equilibrium solution is (y^f, n^f, r^*, P^*). Suppose a reduction in investment reduces aggregate demand. Discuss the following:

(a) Within the context of the *neoclassical* model, analyse the behaviour of firms if they face imperfect competition and are hit with a fall in the demand for their products. If this analysis shows that employment is reduced below n^f, present the likely consumption response of households. If these responses of firms and households imply a movement away from (y^f, n^f, r^*, P^*), what equilibrating mechanisms will come into play to bring the economy back to (y^f, n^f, r^*, P^*). Which do you think is more powerful and has a faster response: the economy's equilibrating mechanisms or the (contrary) responses of firms and households which worked to take the economy away from (y^f, n^f, r^*, P^*)?

(b) For the context of a *Keynesian* model with nominal wage contracting, redo the questions in (a).

(c) Within the context of a *neo-Keynesian* model, redo the questions in (a).

9 'The *classical theory* dominates the economic thought, both practical and theoretical, of the governing and academic classes of this generation, as it has for a hundred years past. . . . [But it is] applicable to a special case only and not to a general case, the situation it assumes being a limiting point of the possible positions of equilibrium' (Keynes, 1936, p. 3).

(a) What are the traditional classical (also neoclassical and modern classical) and Keynesian definitions of equilibrium? How are they related? Can there exist an underemployment equilibrium in their models under each of these definitions?

(b) If you adopt the Keynesian definition of equilibrium, was the traditional classical model a special case of any of the Keynesian models? Of the neo-Keynesian model?

(c) Are the neoclassical and modern classical models also special cases of any of the Keynesian models?

10 Keynes argued that an economy could be in equilibrium with a substantial amount of involuntary unemployment, but other economists took the stand that an equilibrium in which an important market does not clear is a contradiction in terms. Explain the notions of equilibrium involved, Keynes' justification for his position, and his opponents' justification for theirs.

11 Distinguish between the Keynesian unemployment caused by an aggregate demand deficiency and classical unemployment due to real wages being above the full employment level. What can monetary policy do to reduce each of these?

12 One way of ensuring the indexation of nominal wages is by specifying the wage contract as:

$$W - W_0 = \alpha(P - P_0) \qquad 0 < \alpha \le 1$$

where W_0 and P_0 are the nominal wage and price level at the time of the negotiation of the wage contract and all variables are in logs. $\alpha = 1$ indicates full indexation.

Compare the aggregate supply curve when W is indexed to P with $\alpha < 1$ with those in the fixed nominal wage Keynesian model and in the flexible nominal wage neoclassical model. What are the implications of $\alpha = 1$ for the responsiveness of output and the price level to (a) aggregate demand shocks, (b) aggregate supply shocks? In this case, would the aggregate supply curve differ from the aggregate supply curve with a flexible nominal wage?

Show that real output is less sensitive and the price level is more sensitive to changes in the money supply if α is greater.

13 J. R. Hicks, in the 1937 article in which he proposed the IS–LM analysis, argued that Keynes' *General Theory* did not represent a major break with the classical tradition. In particular, he maintained that the main insight it contained was into the conditions existing during a depression or a deep recession. Was this claim valid?

Has Keynesianism contributed anything further since Keynes' *General Theory*? Does the above claim apply to the various Keynesian models?

Does the modern classical approach provide an adequate analysis of the economic conditions in recessions and depressions or does the profession still need the Keynesian approaches for their analysis?

14 'Keynes argued that wage stickiness was probably a good thing, that wage and price flexibility could easily be destructive of real economic stability. His reasoning went like this. In a monetary economy, the nominal interest rate cannot be negative. Hence the real interest rate must be at least equal to the rate of deflation. . . . If wages and prices were to fall freely after a contractionary shock, the real interest rate would become very large at just the wrong time, with adverse effects on investment. The induced secondary contraction would only worsen the situation' (Solow, 1980). Discuss the validity of these arguments. Do they apply also in the modern classical model.

15 Keynes (1936) had argued that, from a policy perspective, everything that can be achieved by a nominal wage could be more effectively achieved through an appropriate monetary policy.

(a) Does this statement hold in the deficient-demand Keynesian model?
(b) Discuss the validity of this statement for a negative shock to (i) aggregate demand and (ii) aggregate productivity.

16 'Keynesianism and neo-Keynesianism are fundamentally inconsistent in so far as their wage hypotheses are concerned. Keynesianism asserts nominal wage rigidity while neo-Keynesianism asserts real wage rigidity. In fact, in the 1930s, real wage rigidity – as proposed by Pigou, among others – was the explanation offered by the traditional classical economists for unemployment above its natural rate.' Discuss.

17 One frequently reads comments these days that Keynesian economics give little or even wrong prescriptions for dealing with the current economic problems in the United States (or British or Canadian) economy. What justifies such comments? What are your views on this issue and how would you justify them?

NOTES

1 There is considerable dispute as to whether any of the Keynesian models represents Keynes' own work or not. A close reading of Chapters 2 and 3 of *The General Theory* shows that they do not. It is therefore appropriate to make a distinction between the Keynesian models and Keynes' own analysis, though the former arose out of interpretations of the latter.

2 This is, however, a short-term phenomenon in the modern industrialized economy. Workers and their unions are nowadays sufficiently sophisticated to realize the losses in real income due to inflation and try to base the negotiated wage on the expected rate of inflation. If the actual inflation rate is higher than the expected one, workers try to get compensation for it at the next round of wage negotiations, so that in the long run labour supply will be effectively based on the real wage rather than on nominal wages. We will return to these considerations at a later stage in this chapter.

3 The above is clearly a rather simplified picture of the wage bargain. A somewhat better picture emerges if it were assumed that workers supply labour on the basis of the expected real wage rate and the expectations are explicitly modelled. This is particularly so when nominal wage rates and prices are rising and it is difficult for workers to perceive the actual change in the real wage rate. This specification is discussed in a later section.

4 The formal derivation of this curve is presented in Chapter 15, which discusses uncertainty and expectations.

5 The term 'equilibrium' is being defined here as a state from which there is no inherent

tendency to change. It specifies the values of the endogenous variables implied by the model for a specified set of values of the exogenous variables in the model.

6 In terms of empirical experience, long booms with low rates of unemployment interrupted by shallow and short recessions often increase faith in the neoclassical paradigm while deep recessions or mild upturns with fairly high rates of unemployment often weaken it.

7 See Chapter 17 on Walras' law for additional exposition on these.

8 Among its textbook expositions are Branson (1989, Ch. 18).

9 Such inequality of demand and supply occurs in notional terms, while for the commodity market the equality of the actual or effective demand and supply would still occur and determine prices. For the labour market, such non-clearance means that the notional supply of labour exceeds the notional demand.

10 Neoclassical reasoning at this point would be that the aggregate price level would fall, creating a real balance effect which shifts the LM curve to the right, thereby increasing incomes and inducing an increase in consumption spending, so that the fall in aggregate demand would be reversed. Keynesians claim that this process does not work or is too slow for many reasons: uncertainty of whether the fall in demand is transitory or longer lasting, firms may find it optimal not to change their price lists immediately, the real balance effect is quite ineffective and extremely slow in increasing demand, etc. Hence, Keynesians tend to assume that for analytical realism, it is better to assume constant prices rather than falling prices, so that the response of firms to the fall in demand is to adjust the quantity produce rather than a reduction in prices. The following analysis follows this Keynesian procedure.

11 As against this dynamic reaction, neoclassical economics claims that firms will cut prices, not output, in response to a fall in aggregate demand; or that markets will act fast enough to deliver the lower prices for all commodities sufficient to allow firms to sell all they want before individual firms react by cutting their production. Intuitive knowledge of the economy tends to favour the Keynesian response pattern.

12 Real wages will rise if the price level falls faster than nominal wages; they will fall if the price level falls more slowly than nominal wages, and will stay constant if both prices and wages fall in the same proportion.

13 The fall in employment usually increases among the employed workers the subjective risk of staying employed, so that such workers also tend to cut back on consumption in order to increase precautionary saving to provide for the eventuality of becoming unemployed.

14 The new demand curve is not the neoclassical notional one n^d but an effective one, and one cannot proceed with analysis using n^d.

15 Keynesians would here rely on imperfect or monopolistic competition in which there is competition but each firm would not be able to sell more except by lowering its price relative to its competitors.

16 This is a common way in which firms respond to declines in the demand for their output. Such a response is not excluded by the rationality assumption.

17 Take this competition to be of the sort that would actually exist in highly competitive economies, though slightly removed from the perfect competition assumptions.

18 This process may lead to a price war or just a tacit arrangement in which each firm does not encroach on other firms' market share, or it may lead to a price war, without necessarily increasing the industry demand.

19 The real wage may rise or fall, depending upon where it was earlier in relation to w^f.

20 However, they cannot be sustained over time (e.g., workers get tired of putting in undesired overtime etc.) and such increases in employment cannot be assumed for the long run.

21 However, this will not happen if shirking and effort are a function of the deviation of the wage paid from the market-clearing one, rather than of the wage itself.

22 It also explains the existence of dual markets, wage distributions among workers with identical skills and certain types of wage and job discrimination.

23 For an exposition of this approach, see Ball *et al.* (1988).

24 Agriculture, textiles and defence industries tend to be notorious examples of this. In Canada,

a confederation more than a federation, such protectionism even leads to inter-provincial barriers for certain industries. Mercantilist policies are rampant in the area of labour flows which are strictly regulated through immigration laws.

25 Milton Friedman is a neoclassical economist who favours free and unregulated markets because of his belief that they rather than government action yield the best overall economic state. John Kenneth Galbraith is a Keynesian who questions the ability of unregulated markets to deliver results in the public or national interest and therefore supports governmental intervention in the economy.

26 Unless a symbol is specifically defined in a question, its definition is as in the text.

REFERENCES

Ball, Laurence, N. Gregory Mankiw and David Romer. 'The New Keynesian Economics and the Output-Inflation Trade-off.' *Brookings Papers on Economic Activity*, 19, 1988, pp. 1–65.

Branson, William H. *Macroeconomic Theory and Policy*, 3rd edn. New York: Harper & Row, 1989.

Clower, Robert. 'The Keynesian Counter-Revolution: A Theoretical Appraisal'. In F. H. Hahn and F. P. R. Brechling, eds, *The Theory of Interest Rates*. London: Macmillan, 1965.

Hicks, John R. 'Mr Keynes and the Classics: A Suggested Interpretation'. *Econometrica*, 5, April 1937, pp. 147–59.

Keynes, John Maynard. *The General Theory of Employment, Interest and Money*. New York: Macmillan, 1936.

Leijonhufvud, Axel. 'Keynes and the Keynesians'. *American Economic Review, Papers and Proceedings*, 57, May 1967, pp. 401–10.

——. *On Keynesian Economics and the Economics of Keynes*. New York: Oxford University Press, 1968.

Patinkin, Don. *Money, Interest and Prices*. New York: Harper & Row, 1965.

Phillips, A. W. 'The Relation between Unemployment and the Rate of Change of the Money Wage Rates in the UK, 1861–1957'. *Economica*, 25, 1958, pp. 283–99.

Sargent, Thomas J. *Macroeconomic Theory*. New York: Academic Press, 1979.

——, and Wallace, Neil. 'Rational Expectations and the Theory of Economic Policy'. *Journal of Monetary Economics*, 2, April 1976, pp. 169–83.

Shapiro, Carl, and Joseph E. Stiglitz. 'Equilibrium Unemployment as a Worker Discipline Device'. *American Economic Review*, 74, June 1984, pp. 433–44.

Solow, Robert. 'On Theories of Unemployment'. *American Economic Review*, 70, March 1980, pp. 1–11.

Tobin, James. 'Inflation and Unemployment'. *American Economic Review*, 62, March 1972, pp. 1–18.

Yellen, Janet L. 'Efficiency Wage Models of Unemployment'. *American Economic Review*, 74, May 1984, pp. 200–05.

chapter fifteen

EXPECTATIONS IN MACROECONOMICS AND MONETARY POLICY

Since the economy faces a great deal of uncertainty, the public's expectations play a critical role in the impact of monetary policy on the economy, so that the macroeconomic models must incorporate uncertainty and expectations into their assumptions and analyses. This chapter and the next one do so and extend the policy analyses of the classical and Keynesian approaches presented in the preceding two chapters.

The major focus of this chapter is on the role and treatment of expectations – especially rational ones – in monetary economics and the policy implications that flow from the introduction of expectations into the classical and Keynesian models. In particular, the impact of anticipated monetary policy and the rate of inflation differ significantly from that of their unanticipated counterparts.

---

key concepts introduced in this chapter

- Risk and uncertainty
- The expectations augmented Phillips curve
- Rational expectations
- Expectational errors
- Expectational equilibrium
- The Lucas critique
- Estimating the unanticipated money supply
- Estimating the unanticipated rate of inflation

The short-run macroeconomic models of the previous two chapters assumed certainty or perfect foresight. However, the real world is beset with uncertainty. Under uncertainty, economic agents form expectations about the future values of the relevant economic variables and these expectations affect their behaviour and that of the macroeconomy. This chapter considers the nature of the uncertainty affecting economic variables and behaviour, and examines the hypotheses formulated to model this behaviour in macroeconomics.

Section 15.1 specifies the distinction between the traditional definitions of risk, in which agents act on the basis of objective probabilities and all possible outcomes are anticipated, and uncertainty, in which the objective probabilities are not known. Section 15.2 refers to the adaptive and rational procedures, specified in Chapter 7, for modelling expectations, and chooses the latter as the basis for modelling expectations in this chapter. Section 15.3 presents analysis based on the expectations augmented Phillips curve and derives the Friedman supply rule, and section 15.4 presents the Lucas model.[1] Section 15.5 focuses on the neutrality and the rational expectations assumptions of the Lucas and Keynesian models, and discusses the empirical evidence on the effects of anticipated and unanticipated money supply changes on output.

Chapters 15 and 16 in many ways form a single unit and present a continuum of analysis on expectations, neutrality and the effectiveness of monetary policy.

15.1 THE NATURE OF RISK, UNCERTAINTY AND EXPECTATIONS IN ECONOMICS

Events whose outcomes are not known at the moment of decision making used to be classified in economics in the first half of the twentieth century into risky ones or uncertain ones. The difference between these terms was that an event involves risk if the objective probabilities of its outcomes exist and are known, while an event involves uncertainty if the objective probabilities of its outcomes do not exist or are not known. Because of the nature of economic events and/or because of the pervasive imperfection of knowledge involving future outcomes, few economic decisions involve known objective probabilities, so that the standard case in economics is one of uncertainty. However, probability theory finds it unmanageable to include many of the elements of uncertainty such as the vagueness and imperfection of information that distinguish uncertainty from risk. As a consequence, neoclassical economics often abandons the above distinction between risk and uncertainty, and treats the latter as if it was really a case of risk, while Keynesian – and especially post-Keynesian – economics often makes a strong distinction between them.

For uncertain events, economists cannot validly assume that the decisions will be based on objective probabilities since these will usually not be known by the economic agent. However, it can be validly postulated that the individual does form subjective probabilities of the anticipated outcomes, with such probabilities being based on whatever knowledge the individual possesses or considers profitable to acquire. Such knowledge can be highly inadequate and imperfect and even the range of anticipated outcomes can differ from the possible ones, so that the subjective probabilities held can be highly erroneous, volatile[2] and would also differ among individuals. In general, neoclassical economics ignores these problems with subjective probabilities and assumes that the subjective probabilities follow the rules of probability theory.

The dominant hypothesis – though not the only one – in neoclassical economics for decision making under uncertainty – or rather risk – is the expected utility hypothesis, with its underlying basis being the von Neumann–Morgenstern axioms.[3] This hypothesis was utilized in Chapter 5 for analysing the speculative demand for money and we will also apply it in this chapter. Further, in order to be consistent with the usage of the terms *uncertainty* and *risk* in the expected utility hypothesis and the literature relevant to this chapter, we will use the word *uncertainty* as if it was synonymous with *risk*.

15.2 EXPECTATIONS HYPOTHESES

The two major hypotheses in economics for constructing the expected value of a variable are the adaptive expectations hypothesis and the rational expectations hypothesis (REH). The former is a statistical procedure, while the latter represents an economic theory of expectations. Both of these approaches were used in Chapter 7 to estimate expected income for the demand for money function, and should be reviewed at this stage. Their usage in this chapter will be to estimate the expected rate of inflation, the expected money supply or the expected level of aggregate demand for the determination of real output in the economy. In particular, our concern is with modelling expectations for the expectations augmented Phillips curve or the Lucas supply rule.

A preliminary issue before applying the adaptive expectations or the rational expectations hypotheses in macroeconomics is whether either or both of these are consistent with the neoclassical and the Keynesian hypotheses.

15.2.1 Rational expectations and the classical and neoclassical approaches

Adaptive expectations was popularized by Milton Friedman in macroeconomics in the 1950s and 1960s. It had also been used by Irving Fisher early in the twentieth century, so that the adaptive expectations procedure for modelling expectations was in many ways associated with the traditional classical and neoclassical schools.

Rational expectations was proposed by Muth and popularized by Lucas, Sargent and Wallace, and Barro in macroeconomics in the 1970s. These economists were in the classical and Walrasian tradition, so that their contributions on expectations became associated with the classical and neoclassical approaches. The notion of rationality and the emphasis on an expectational equilibrium in this hypothesis also seemed to be an extension of the rationality and equilibrium assumptions underlying the Walrasian model, which underpins the neoclassical and classical approaches. The result was not only the incorporation of the rational expectations hypothesis as a fundamental part of the neoclassical and modern classical approaches, but also the attempt to appropriate it in a way that would deny its incorporation in the Keynesian approaches.

15.2.2 Rational expectations and the Keynesian approach

Keynes, much more than the traditional classical economists, had emphasized the role of expectations in macroeconomics and the Keynesians have always attached great importance to taking account of them in policy decisions. However, neither Keynes nor the Keynesians came up with a satisfactory theoretical procedure for modelling expectations. For simplification, they often used static expectations or flirted with adaptive expectations. Many economists have, in fact, speculated that had the rational expectations hypothesis been available in Keynes' days, he would have incorporated it into his work.

Neither adaptive expectations nor rational expectations as procedures are *per se* logically inconsistent with Keynesian economics and can be incorporated into the Keynesian models at the will of the researcher. This eclecticism in the association of the available techniques for modelling expectations with macroeconomic approaches is in some ways similar to the usage of the IS–LM modelling technique with neoclassical and classical approaches. This technique initially arose as a way of modelling Keynes' ideas and was first offered in 1937 by John Richard Hicks, one of the foremost Keynesians.

In advocating this kind of eclecticism, we are suggesting a separation of the tools, techniques of analysis and the peripheral hypotheses from the core assumptions and economic philosophy of the macroeconomic schools. Some economists would definitely dispute this separation of the expectations modelling techniques – to us, a peripheral hypothesis – from the macroeconomic approaches, with the former to be associated at will and as needed with the latter. As we have argued above, there is adequate historical precedent for this from the incorporation of the IS–LM analysis into neoclassical and modern classical models.

15.2.3 Differences in the applications of rational expectations in the classical and Keynesian models

While the concept of rational expectations is logically consistent with both the classical and the Keynesian paradigms, there are vital differences in its applications to their models. For the classical models – which assume that the economy will either stay in equilibrium or soon revert to it – the expected levels of output, unemployment and prices, as of all other endogenous variables, are the full employment equilibrium levels. Their value can, therefore, be derived from the full employment solution of the model.

This procedure is not valid for the Keynesian paradigm since it can have many potential equilibria. In any case, the rationally expected values of the variables for the period ahead are those which will hold in the economy, whether that state is one of equilibrium or disequilibrium. It is, therefore, much more difficult for the theorist to specify the rationally expected values of the variables for the Keynesian than for the classical type of economy, without knowing the actual dynamic stage of the economy in the next period.

In terms of econometric work, if the data is quarterly or even annual, there is little reason to assume that the full employment values of all the variables would be precisely the ones shown in the data. Therefore, for such data, basing expectations on the full employment equilibrium values of the classical model can hardly be realistic or consistent with the rational expectations of actual consumers and firms. To reiterate the central notion of rational expectations, these expectations are those based on all available information. If this information is that in the next period (quarter or year) the economy will have levels of employment higher than the full employment one, the expectations derived by postulating the full employment state for the period ahead will not be rational – or realistic.

15.3 EXPECTATIONS AND THE LABOUR MARKET: THE EXPECTATIONS AUGMENTED PHILLIPS CURVE

15.3.1 Output and employment in the context of wage contracts

In industrialized economies, the nominal wage between a firm and its workers is established – whether explicitly negotiated or arrived at by implicit arrangement – ahead of the production and employment decisions by the firm and therefore before the actual price level is known. In arriving at this wage in the absence of 'money illusion', the firms and workers must base their agreement on the *expected* real wage – that is, the nominal wage divided by the expected price level – rather than the *a priori* unknown *actual* real wage which will apply at the time of employment and production. However, firms can continue to adjust their employment as the price level changes, so that their decisions on employment, as determined by their demand function for labour, will depend on the actual real wage – equal to the established nominal wage divided by the actual price level. This section modifies the neoclassical and Keynesian labour market analyses to incorporate these ideas.

To start, consider the household utility maximization as in Chapter 3, but now with the addition of uncertainty about the future price level and with labour forming expectations on it. Let the household's expected price level for the period ahead be P^{eh}. Utility maximization would then imply that the supply function of labour is:

$$n^s = n^s(w^{eh})$$
$$= n^s(W/P^{eh}) \quad n^{s\prime} > 0 \tag{1}$$

where:

n^s labour supply function
w^{eh} expected real wage – as expected by labour

W actual nominal wage
P^{eh} price level expected by households/workers for the duration of the labour contract

Designate the inverse of $n^s(\cdot)$ as $h(n)$, so that inverting (1) and rearranging yields:

$$W^d = P^{eh} \cdot h(n^s) \quad h' > 0 \tag{2}$$

where W^d is the wage demanded by workers in negotiations. Designate the representative firm producing the ith product – and being in the ith market – as the ith firm. From the theory of the firm, as in Chapter 3, the demand for labour by the profit-maximizing ith firm in perfect competition – and prior to the production period – would equate its marginal product of labour to the expected real wage measured in terms of the firm's expected product price, so that:

$$\begin{aligned} n_i^d &= n_i^d(w_i^{ef}) \\ &= n_i^d(W/p_i^{ef}) \qquad n_i^{d'} < 0 \end{aligned} \tag{3}$$

where:

w_i^{ef} expected real wage, based on the ith firm's expectations of its product price
p_i^{ef} expected product price, as expected by the ith firm

Aggregating over all firms, let P^{ef} be the average expected price for all firms and n^d the aggregate demand for labour. The aggregated demand for labour is given by:

$$n^d = n^d(W/p^{ef}) \quad n^{d'} < 0 \tag{4}$$

Designating the inverse of $n^d(\cdot)$ as $f(n^d)$, the nominal wage W^o offered in the wage negotiations by the firms is:

$$W^o = P^{ef} \cdot f(n^d) \quad f' < 0 \tag{5}$$

Assuming that the market-clearing (that is, with $n^d = n^s = n$) nominal wage is negotiated, the wage process based on (2) and (5) would yield the equilibrium nominal wage W^c as:

$$W^c = P^{eh} \cdot h(n) = P^{ef} \cdot f(n) \tag{6}$$

where the superscript c indicates the contractual nature of the wage.[4] W^c can be obtained by directly solving (1) and (4) and has the general functional form,

$$W^c = g(P^{ef}, P^{eh}) \quad \partial g/\partial P^{ef},\ \partial g/\partial P^{eh} > 0 \tag{7}$$

The explanation for the signs of the derivatives is: an increase in the firm's expected price level increases its willingness to agree to higher nominal wages, and an increase in the household's expected price level makes workers demand higher nominal wages, so that a higher nominal wage will be set in the wage contracts.[5] It is further assumed that this W^c is set for the duration of the labour contract and that workers will supply any amount of labour demanded by firms at W^c. That is, for the duration of the wage contract, the *ex ante* labour supply curve is to be temporarily ignored in the analysis and the ostensible labour supply is horizontal, in the neighbourhood of the equilibrium, at W^c in the (W, n) space.

While the firms negotiated the nominal wage on the basis of their expected price level, profit maximization by the ith firm implies, as shown by (4), that its employment and production decision depends only on its own expected price p_i^{ef} rather than on the price level P or the expected price level, so that its employment depends upon W^c and p_i. During the production process, the ith firm would know the actual price of its own product as a joint element of its production and pricing decision, so that actual employment will be based on the actual prices of the firms' products, rather than on the prices which had previously been expected by firms. The average of the former is the actual price level, so that the actual aggregate employment n by firms is based on the actual real wage w. In the wage contracts context, this actual real wage is given by the contracted nominal wage W^c divided by the actual price level P.[6] That is,

$$n = n^d = n^d(W^c/P) \quad n^{d'} < 0 \tag{8}$$

Since W^c depends upon P^{ef} and P^{eh}, we have:

$$n = \Theta(W^c(P^{ef}, P^{eh})/P) \tag{9}$$

where $\partial n/\partial P > 0$, $\partial n/\partial P^{ef} < 0$ and $\partial n/\partial P^{eh} < 0$. The explanation for these signs is as follows. As discussed earlier, increases in the firm's expected price level and/or the household's expected price level establish a higher contractual nominal wage during wage negotiations. This, *ceteris paribus*, – i.e., without an accompanying change in the price level – increases the real wage, which reduces employment. But, for the given contractual nominal wage, an increase in the actual price level lowers the real wage and raises employment. However, Θ is homogeneous of degree zero in P^{ef}, P^{eh} and P, so that a proportionate increase in the expected and actual price levels will not change employment, even though the nominal wage will rise proportionately.

Employment will thus depend upon the duration of the wage contract, upon the expected price levels by firms and households during wage negotiations, and upon the actual price level when employment occurs.

From (9) and the production function $y = y(n)$ with $y_n > 0$, we have:

$$y = \phi(P^{ef}, P^{eh}, P) \tag{10}$$

where $\partial y/\partial P > 0$, $\partial y/\partial P^{ef} < 0$ and $\partial y/\partial P^{eh} < 0$.

Therefore, for a given contractual nominal wage conditional on expectations, we have the critical results that,

$$\partial n/\partial P > 0, \ \partial y/\partial P > 0$$

However, note that both n and P are homogeneous of degree zero in P^{ef}, P^{eh} and P.

Diagrammatic analysis

Figure 15.1a presents the labour demand $n^d(W/P^{ef})$ and the labour supply $n^s(W/P^{eh})$ curves. Note that the vertical axis in this figure is the nominal wage rate W. The negotiated nominal wage will be set at the equilibrium level W_0^c, and has the expected employment level of n_0^e. An increase in P^{ef} will shift the labour demand curve to the right and a rise in P^{eh} will shift the labour supply curve to the left, so that each will raise the nominal wage. However, the former will increase the expected employment level and the latter will decrease it. If both P^{ef} and P^{eh} increase proportionately, the two curves will shift proportionately and the nominal wage will increase in the same proportion, without a change in the expected employment level.

Actual employment is determined not in Figure 15.1a but in Figure 15.1b, now with the actual real wage w – equal to W/P – on the vertical axis. For the contracted nominal wage W_0^c from Figure 15.1a, and a given price level P_0, employment is n_0. With the contracted

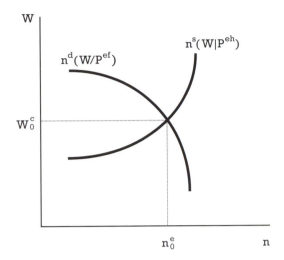

Figure 15.1a

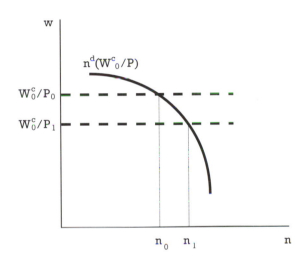

Figure 15.1b

nominal wage still at W_0^c, a higher price P_1, $P_1 > P_0$, will lower the actual real value of the contracted nominal wage to W_0^c/P_1 and increase employment to n_1 with $n_1 > n_0$. The implicit labour supply curve is horizontal at W_0^c/P in this figure.

If there were no errors in expectations – that is, if $P^{ef} = P^{eh} = P$, actual employment n will equal n_0^e, as determined in Figure 15.1a, so that we can take this to be the full employment level n^f or the 'expectational equilibrium' level n^*. If P is higher than both P^{ef} and P^{eh}, $n > n_0^e$, and vice versa. Therefore, the deviation in employment from its expected level n^e in Figure 15.1a is positively related to the errors $(P - P^e)$ in expectations.

Errors in price expectations, the duration of the wage contract and cost-of-living clauses

This deviation in employment from its expected level n^e will only occur during the duration of the wage contract since the past errors in expectations will be eliminated when the wage contract is renegotiated. This is usually done through the 'catch-up' cost-of-living clauses in labour contracts. Therefore, continuously new errors will be needed to maintain employment above n^e. While this can occur for some time – the 'people can be fooled some of the time' syndrome – it cannot continue indefinitely – 'they cannot be fooled all the time'. The former usually has to take the form of accelerating inflation rates. The latter usually occurs in two ways. One is for the future expectations of inflation to 'jump' beyond the past – experienced – inflation rates in an attempt to capture the potential future acceleration in inflation. The other is to reduce or eliminate the loss in purchasing power through inflation by reducing the duration of wage contracts or by building cost-of-living clauses in them. Therefore, while the errors in expectations can induce increases in employment – and do so during accelerating inflation – such increases can only be short term and not a long-term phenomenon in practice. These increases cannot be relied upon to occur over lengthy periods or at very high rates of inflation.

An example

Assume the labour market functions at the time of wage negotiations to be:

$$n^s = b_1 W/P^{eh} \quad b_1 > 0$$

$$n^d = a_0 - a_1 W/P^{ef} \quad a_0, a_1 > 0$$

In equilibrium,

$$a_0 - a_1 W/P^{ef} = b_1 W/P^{eh}$$

so that the contractual nominal wage will be,

$$W^c = a_0 \left[\frac{P^{ef} P^{eh}}{a_1 P^{eh} + b_1 P^{ef}} \right]$$

so that $\partial W^c/\partial P^{eh}$, $\partial W^c/\partial P^{ef} > 0$ and a proportionate increase in both expectations increases the nominal wage rate in the same proportion. The expected level of employment obtained by substituting this equation in the labour supply function is given by:

$$n^e = a_0 b_1 \left[\frac{P^{ef}}{a_1 P^{eh} + b_1 P^{ef}} \right]$$

so that a proportionate increase in both expectations does not change n^e. Note that the employment level is not set in the wage contract and can deviate from n^e.

At the time of production, with the nominal wage set by the wage contract at W^c, the actual real wage and employment will be:

$$w = a_0 \left[\frac{P^{ef} P^{eh}}{a_1 P^{eh} + b_1 P^{ef}} \right] \left(\frac{1}{P} \right)$$

$$n = n^d = a_0 - a_1 a_0 \left[\frac{P^{ef} P^{eh}}{a_1 P^{eh} + b_1 P^{ef}} \right] \left(\frac{1}{P} \right)$$

Both w and n are homogeneous of degree zero in P, P^{eh} and P^{ef}. If P exceeds both of its expectations, the real wage will turn out to be less than its expectation in the wage contract and n will be greater than n^e – and vice versa. If there are no errors in expectations, $P = P^{ef} = P^{eh}$, so that $n = n^f = a_0 - a_0a_1/(a_1 + b_1)$. This expectational equilibrium level of employment is independent of the price level and is, therefore, the classical full employment level. Note that expectational errors can induce actual employment to be less than or greater than this full employment level.

15.3.2 The Friedman supply rule

Some studies assume that:

$$P^{ef} = P \tag{11}$$

This assumption is often justified by the argument that, for profit maximization, *each* firm only needs to know the price of its own product – on which it possesses a great deal of information – and its own factor costs, represented by the contractual nominal wage, but does not need to know the prices of all the commodities in the economy. Since the average price level P in (10) is only a proxy for the average of the individual commodity prices, each of which is set by the firm supplying the commodity, the firms on average can be expected to fairly accurately predict P.

By comparison, utility maximization by a household requires knowledge of the general price level in order to calculate the purchasing power of the nominal wage. To know the price level requires knowledge of all the commodity prices, which is a degree of knowledge that each household rarely, if ever, possesses. Hence, it is assumed that households individually and on average in the aggregate cannot predict the price level with sufficient accuracy, so that P^{eh} can differ from P.

With these assumptions, (10) can be restated in the more specific form:

$$y = \phi(P/P^{eh}) \quad y' > 0, \partial y/\partial P > 0, \partial y/\partial P^{eh} < 0 \tag{12}$$

If $P > P^{eh}$, $w < w^e$, so that labour will prove to be unexpectedly cheaper and the firms will employ more than they had expected to employ. Hence, $y' > 0$, $\partial y/\partial P > 0$ and $\partial y/\partial P^{eh} < 0$. Equation (12) is homogeneous of degree zero in P and P^{eh}.

15.3.3 The expectations augmented employment and output functions

We choose to proceed further with (10) rather than (12). Starting with (10), since the expectations of both firms and households are negatively related to y, we can simplify the notation by replacing them by the single variable P^e. That is, rewrite (10) as:

$$y = y(P/P^e) \quad \partial y/\partial P > 0, \partial y/\partial P^e < 0 \tag{13}$$

where P^e is now the expected price level for both firms and households. There will not be any errors in expectations when:

$$P^e = P \tag{14}$$

Designate the respective levels of employment and output when there are no errors in household's price expectations as n^* (or n^f) and y^* (or y^f), consistent with the analysis of the neoclassical model in Chapter 13 in which there was perfect foresight so that there were no errors in price expectations. These employment and output values were designated in Chapter 13 as the natural levels of employment and output.

The *log-linear* form of (13) is:

$$\ln y = \ln y^* + \beta(\ln P - \ln P^e) \quad \beta > 0 \tag{15}$$

Equation (15) is the *expectations augmented output function* or *Friedman's supply function*. Correspondingly, we have for the level of employment,

$$\ln n = \ln n^* + \alpha(\ln P - \ln P^e) \quad \alpha > 0 \tag{16}$$

Equation (16) is the *expectations augmented employment function*.

Note that the price expectations in these equations refer to those incorporated in wage contracts, and the economy deviates from its full employment level due to errors in these expectations: compared with the full employment level, output is greater if $P > P^e$ and lower if $P < P^e$. In the former case, real wages are lower than the full employment real wage, making it attractive to hire more labour than in the error-free equilibrium; while the opposite holds in the latter case.

Define *expectational equilibrium* as the state where there are no errors in expectations. That is, it requires that:

$$P^e = P \tag{17}$$

From (15) and (16), in the expectational equilibrium:

$$n = n^* \tag{18}$$

$$y = y^* \tag{19}$$

which assert that, in expectational equilibrium, the levels of employment and output are the full employment levels and are independent of the price level. Equations (15) to (19) assert that the deviations from these levels occur because of expectational errors, with positive errors $(P - P^e > 0)$ causing an increase in output and employment, and negative errors $(P - P^e < 0)$ causing a decrease.

15.3.4 The actual rate of unemployment and Friedman's expectations augmented Phillips curve

Unemployment U equals $(L - n)$ and the rate of unemployment u equals U/L $(=1 - n/L)$. Therefore, the approximation for the relationship between the log values of u, L and n is:

$$\ln u = \ln L - \ln n \tag{20}$$

From (16) and (20),

$$\ln u = \ln u_n - \alpha(\ln P - \ln P^e) \quad \alpha > 0 \tag{21}$$

where $\ln u_n$ $(=\ln u^* = \ln L - \ln n^*)$ is the natural – synonymous with the full employment equilibrium – rate of unemployment. Equation (21) is the *expectations augmented Phillips curve*, proposed by Milton Friedman as a correction of the Phillips curve. Note that several assumptions were needed for deriving it. Among these was the assumption of market clearance in the labour and commodity markets, an assumption that many Keynesians would not accept. Also note that (21) places the burden of all possible deviations from the natural rate of unemployment on errors in price-level expectations over the duration of the wage contract. This has two implications:

(a) Any other sources of deviations from the natural rate are ruled out. In particular, the numerous sources of deviations considered by the Keynesians are not captured.[7] Among these is the failure of the labour market to clear on a continuous basis, such as in recessions, as well as the possibility of persistent underemployment equilibria in certain rare circumstances such as in the Great Depression of the 1930s.

(b) *If* the expectational errors are insignificant in magnitude or are not relevant because of a very short duration of labour contracts,[8] any fluctuations in unemployment over time would have to be explained by a theory of fluctuations in the natural rate of unemployment.

Given the experience of considerable cross-section and business cycle variations in unemployment rates in the real-world economies, the classical theory supplements its theory of expectational errors with a theory of fluctuations in the natural rate of unemployment over time and across countries. In particular, if this theory is to explain the experienced rates of unemployment, it cannot assume that the natural rate is a constant, so that the explanation of the long-run variations in the unemployment rate will require a long-run theory of changes in the natural rate, while the explanation of the cyclical variations in unemployment will require a theory of the cyclical variations in the natural rate.

These arguments lead to two competing sets of theories of unemployment. These are:

(i) the classical theories with fluctuations in the natural rate itself both over the business cycle and the long run, accompanied by continuous labour market clearance but with expectational errors to explain deviations of the actual rate of unemployment from the natural rate; and

(ii) the Keynesian theories of unemployment, which also allow – but do not require – changes in the natural rate, but emphasize deviations of the actual rate of unemployment from the natural one due to fluctuations in the demand for commodities and labour, especially in the presence of expectational errors, contractual rigidities, sticky prices, efficiency wages, etc.

15.4 PRICE EXPECTATIONS AND COMMODITY MARKETS: THE LUCAS SUPPLY FUNCTION

The preceding section introduced expectations and the possibility of expectational errors in the labour market. This emphasis on the labour market is in some ways more consistent with the Keynesian aggregative analysis, though the expectations augmented Phillips curve is associated with Milton Friedman. Neoclassical analysis focuses more on the markets for commodities and its microeconomic Walrasian basis, as in Chapter 3, shows that the output of each commodity depends upon its relative price. Lucas (1972, 1973) and Sargent and Wallace (1975) modified the certainty version of the microeconomic model by introducing into it uncertainty and firms' expectations on relative product prices. This section presents a version of their analysis.

The Lucas supply function or rule

Assume as in the preceding section that firm i produces good X_i, with the quantity produced as x_i and sold at the price p_i. The firm buys inputs, of which labour is taken to be the only variable input. Given the nominal wage W, the profit maximization by the firm in perfect competition implies that its supply function is given by:

$$x_i = x_i(p_i/W) \quad x_i' > 0 \tag{22'}$$

While the firm is not directly concerned with the price level P, Lucas's analysis assumes that the nominal wages change proportionately with the price level, so that P can be used as an index of labour cost.[9] Profit maximization yields:

$$x_i = x_i(p_i/P) \quad x_i' > 0 \tag{22'}$$

Firms in the ith market are assumed to be competitive, with p_i determined in market i. Both increases in the general price level and in the firms' relative product price can occur at any time, with the 'local price' of the ith product – that is, the product price p_i – incorporating changes in both the price level and its relative price. The ith firm is assumed to know the price of its own product but not know the price level, which it estimates conditional on the information available to it. Given such uncertainty, respecify $(22')$ as:

$$x_{it} = x_i(p_{it}/E(P_t^e \mid I_t(i)) \quad x_i' > 0 \tag{23}$$

where:

x_{it} output in market i in period t

$E(P_t^e \mid I_t(i))$ mean of the price level expected for period t by firms in market i, conditional on $I_t(i)$

$I_t(i)$ information available in market i in period t

Specify the log-linear form of (23) as:

$$x_{it} = x_{it}^* + \gamma[p_{it} - E(P_t^e \mid I_t(i))] \quad \gamma > 0 \tag{24}$$

where *all the variables are now in logs* and x_{it}^* is the ith firm's output under perfect certainty or if there are no expectational errors.

Lucas (1972, 1973) provides a specific procedure for determining the expected relative prices. Firms use the available information on aggregate demand and supply movements, and on local and general prices to form their expectations on the distribution of local and general prices in the present period.[10] That is, at the beginning of the current period, firms possess a prior distribution for the expected price level P^e, with mean $\underline{P}$ and constant variance σ^2, and with this distribution being formed prior to the observation of the current value of the local prices. For simplification, it is assumed that the price p_i in market i deviates in percentage terms from P by an amount z_i which is normally distributed, independent of P and has a zero expected value and variance η^2. That is,

$$p_{it} = P_t + z_{it} \tag{25}$$

Firms use (25), knowledge of $\underline{P}$, σ^2, η^2 and the observed local prices p_{it} to calculate the distribution of the expected price level P_t. The expected value of this distribution is:

$$E(P_t^e \mid I_t(i)) = \underline{P}_t + [\sigma^2/(\eta^2 + \sigma^2)][p_{it} - \underline{P}_t] \tag{26}$$

where:

$\underline{P}_t$ mean of the prior distribution of expected prices

σ^2 expected variance of the price level

η^2 expected variance of z_i

$\sigma^2 + \eta^2$ total variation in p_i (local price variance)

The second term on the right of (26) is the correction made to the expected price level on the basis of the observed local price p_{it}.

Equation (26) was justified on the basis of information available in the ith market when the price level is not directly observed. This view of the nature of information was couched by Lucas (1972) in what has come to be known as the *island parable*. This parable envisions the workers and firms as distributed spatially over islands (or isolated points). The firms do not know about activity (prices and output) on other islands but must forecast the price level on the other islands in order to formulate their labour demand and output supply decisions. To forecast the price level, they use the historic variability of their island price relative to overall variability to forecast the shift of the price level from a prior expected one, and do so as specified in (26).

Equation (26) can be rewritten as:

$$E(P_t^e \mid I_t(i)) = \alpha \underline{P}_t + (1 - \alpha)p_{it} \tag{27}$$

where $\alpha = \eta^2/(\eta^2 + \sigma^2) \geq 0$.

Substituting (27) in (24), we have:

$$x_{it} = x_{it}^* + \alpha\gamma[p_{it} - \underline{P}_t] \tag{28}$$

Integrating (28) over all markets i, with total output supply designated as y^s and replacing the known local price p_{it} by the actual aggregate price level P_t,

$$y_t^s = y_t^* + \alpha\gamma[P_t - \underline{P}_t] \tag{29}$$

which is the *aggregate supply function* based on firms' expectations about the variations in local and general prices. Equation (29) is known as the *Lucas supply function or rule*. If $\eta = 0$, $\alpha = 0$, so that relative prices are expected to be stable, (29) becomes:

$$y_t^s = y_t^* \tag{30}$$

In this case with $\eta = 0$, aggregate supply will not respond to absolute price changes and hence to changes in aggregate demand, with the result that the aggregate supply function will be vertical in the (y, P) space. But if $\sigma \to 0$ – that is, the price level is expected to be stable, so that the change in local price is taken to be wholly a relative price change – the aggregate supply function will have the positive slope γ.

Another explanation of the Lucas supply function

Equation (29) was based on price misperceptions. It is to be distinguished from a somewhat similar equation, also attributed to Lucas, which can be derived from the intertemporal substitution of work in household decisions. In this model of intertemporal utility maximization, for given nominal wages in each period and a given current price level P_t, if the expected price level (P_{t+1}^e) rises, it will decrease the expected future real wage for the given nominal wage while the current real wage is unaffected. Hence, from utility maximization, workers will substitute work in the current period (i.e., increase n_t^s) for work in future periods (i.e., decrease n_{t+1}^s but increase leisure in $t + 1$), Conversely, they would work – and produce – less in the present if the expected future price is lower and the expected real wage higher. Such behaviour would produce recessions in output in the latter case and booms in the former, thus causing real business cycles. However, the empirical significance of such a model is limited since the observed intertemporal substitution of work in labour supply decisions is too low to imply the larger observed variations in output over the business cycle, so that we will ignore it further in this chapter.

Comparing the Friedman and the Lucas supply functions

We are, therefore, left with two types of expectations-based Phillips curve relationships. One of these is Friedman's expectations augmented Phillips curve which is based on errors in expectations in labour market analysis and contractual rigidities; and the other is the Lucas supply function which is based on errors in the expectations of relative prices in commodity markets. The former is sometimes claimed to be an example of the latter under the argument that nominal wages are the 'local' price of workers as suppliers of labour and the observed increases in it are used by the workers in forming their expectations on the price level and the real wage (the 'relative price' of labour). However, the theoretical and empirical bases of the two are quite different,[11] so that it is preferable to keep them separate.

15.5 THE RELATIONSHIP BETWEEN OUTPUT, PRICES AND CHANGES IN AGGREGATE DEMAND IN THE LUCAS MODEL

On the *aggregate demand function*, Lucas assumed that:

$$Y_t^d = Y_{t-1}^d + \delta + \mu_t \tag{31}$$

where:

Y^d nominal aggregate expenditures/demand
∂ systematic (known) increase in demand
μ random shift in demand, with $E\mu = 0$.

Further, from the definition of nominal expenditures and noting that all variables are in logs,

$$Y_t = y_t + P_t \tag{32}$$

Assuming equilibrium in the commodity market with $y^d = y^s = y$ and $Y^d = Y^s = Y$, eliminate y_t from (29), (31) and (32). Then, using $Ey_t = y^*_t$ and $\underline{P} = EP_t$, we get:

$$P_t = \frac{\alpha\gamma\delta}{1 + \alpha\gamma} + \frac{1}{1 + \alpha\gamma} Y_t + \frac{\alpha\gamma}{1 + \alpha\gamma} Y_{t-1} - y_t^* \quad \alpha \geq 0, \gamma > 0 \tag{33}$$

Starting from (32), substitute (31) for Y_t, and (33) for P_t. This yields,

$$y_t = y_t^* - \frac{\alpha\gamma\delta}{1 + \alpha\gamma} + \frac{\alpha\gamma}{1 + \alpha\gamma} \left(Y_t - Y_{t-1} \right) \quad \alpha \geq 0, \gamma > 0 \tag{34}$$

which, using (31), simplifies in equilibrium to:

$$y_t = y_t^* + \frac{\alpha\gamma}{1 + \alpha\gamma} \mu_t \quad \alpha \geq 0, \gamma > 0 \tag{35}$$

If firms believe that all the variation in prices is in the general price level and none in the relative one, $\eta = 0$, so that $\alpha = 0$ and (35) yields the error-free output as y_t^*. That is:

$$y_t = y_t^* \quad \text{for } \eta = 0$$

so that $\partial y_t / \partial\delta = \partial y_t / \partial\mu = 0$. Therefore, (35) implies that, if firms do not expect any changes in relative prices, both systematic and random shifts in aggregate demand will not cause deviations in output from its full employment level under certainty. But if relative prices are expected to change, $\eta > 0$, so that $\alpha > 0$ and random – but not systematic – shifts in demand can have real effects, since from (35),

$$\partial y_t / \partial \delta = 0 \quad \text{for } \eta > 0 \tag{36}$$

while:

$$\frac{\partial y_t}{\partial \mu_t} = \frac{\alpha \gamma}{1 + \alpha \gamma} = \frac{\eta^2 \gamma}{\sigma^2 + \eta^2 (1 + \gamma)} > 0 \quad \text{for } \eta > 0 \tag{37}$$

Note from (37) that even the *random* shifts in aggregate demand cause changes in output only if firms misinterpret its impact on the price level and believe that some part of the resulting increase in prices is a relative price increase. In conditions of hyperinflation where the likelihood and magnitude of general price increases dominate over relative price increases, the public's expectation is likely to be $\eta = 0$, so that even random changes in aggregate demand will not have any output effects. In this context, neither systematic nor random demand increases will change output. Therefore, for hyperinflations, money is likely to be neutral for both systematic and random increases in the money supply. The general conclusion that can be drawn from this is that even the random increases in the money supply will not always induce increases in output and employment.

Asymmetric information and the impact of systematic demand increases on output

Equation (36) states that the systematic demand increases by the policy makers will not change real output. But, suppose that the policy makers systematically do increase demand but in such a way that the firms interpret it as a random one – a case of asymmetric information between the policy maker and the public. This 'disguised or misinterpreted' nature of the systematic demand increase will allow it to increase real output through the 'random multiplier' $\partial y / \partial \mu$, whose value is specified by (37). However, the systematic nature of the demand increase will, sooner or later, be observed by firms, leading to two types of changes. First, firms will find it optimal to acquire better information so that their likelihood of correctly perceiving a systematic demand increase as being systematic – rather than erroneously as random – will increase. For this correctly perceived systematic demand increase, there will be no change in output. Second, firms faced with repeated increases in the general price level will modify their expectations on prices by increasing the value of σ^2 relative to η^2, so that $\partial y / \partial \mu$ will decrease. In the limiting case, if there were only systematically induced increases in the price level, firms would adjust their expectations such that $\eta^2 / (\sigma^2 + \eta^2) \to 0$, so that $\partial y / \partial \mu$ will go to zero, and so would $\partial n / \partial \mu$. That is, the systematic demand increases, disguised or misinterpreted as being random ones, will eventually lose their efficacy.

The implications of the Lucas model for unemployment

To examine the response of unemployment to changes in aggregate demand, start with the definition of unemployment as being $(L - n)$ and use the production function $y = y(n)$, $y'(n) > 0$, to go from y to u. Then, (35) implies that employment n is a function of the random demand term μ_t but not of the systematic demand term δ. With all variables being in logs, and assuming a log-linear relationship, (35) implies that:

$$u_t = u^* - \beta \mu_t \quad \beta \geq 0 \tag{38}$$

where β is a positive function of $\alpha \gamma / 1 + \alpha \gamma$ such that $\beta = 0$ if $\alpha = 0$. First, note that δ is not in (38), just as it was not in (35), so that $\partial u_t / \partial \delta = 0$. Second, note that α is in (38) through β, just as it was in (35), and that $\beta > 0$ for $\alpha > 0$ and $\gamma > 0$. For $\beta > 0$, unemployment decreases if there is a random increase in aggregate demand, since the latter would persuade individual firms that the relative demand and the relative price of their product have increased. That is, for $\beta > 0$, (38) implies a negatively sloped curve in the (y^d, u) space, which looks like a Phillips curve – but is not the Phillips curve[12] – and can be called the 'Lucas–Phillips' Curve'. Hence, there is a seeming tradeoff – for *given* expectations on general versus relative price increases – between price level increases and output increases in the short run.

However, there is a vital difference between (38) and the standard Phillips curve. While the latter was envisaged by the Keynesians as a durable tradeoff between (both anticipated and unanticipated) price increases and unemployment, (38) cannot be used as a durable tradeoff for policy purposes. Meaningful policy increases in demand cannot be random but must be systematic, such as by a constant δ in (31) above or according to some established rule, and, under the Lucas analysis, any systematic demand changes cannot change real output. Further, as argued above, any systematic demand or price increases, disguised or mis-interpreted as being random ones, will sooner or later lose their efficacy as their systematic nature becomes understood.

Hence, according to (38), the policy makers cannot rely upon systematic aggregate demand increases to induce firms to increase output. Correctly anticipated inflation – such as would be the case if the inflation rate was constant or steadily increasing – has a vertical Lucas–Phillips curve, thereby not providing a durable negative tradeoff. While such a tradeoff might be observed for short runs of data due to temporary misinterpretations of the nature of inflation, a durable tradeoff, as asserted by the Keynesians, must rest on theoretical foundations and empirical factors not encompassed in Lucas's analysis.

The Lucas critique of estimated equations as a policy tool
Suppose the economic researcher was to use (34) to set up an estimating equation of the form:

$$y_t = a_0 + a_1 \Delta Y_t + \xi_t, \quad a_1 \geq 0 \tag{39}$$

where ξ is white noise, and found the estimated value of a_1 as $\hat{a}_1 > 0$. As argued above, if the policy maker increased aggregate demand by more than experienced during the estimation period, a_1 would shift, so that $\hat{a}_1$ would no longer be the relevant magnitude under the revised demand policy. Hence, a maintained shift in the expansion of demand does not leave the estimated parameters constant. This is known as the *Lucas critique* of estimated functions of the Lucas–Phillips curve type: if the underlying model of the economy is as set out by Lucas, the parameters of functions such as (39) are not invariant with respect to policy shifts.

Lucas (1973) estimated a variant of (39) for a cross-section of countries and found that countries with low rates of inflation (such as the USA in the 1950s and 1960s) showed evidence of a positive relationship between output and demand increases, while those with hyperinflation (such as Argentina in the 1950s and 1960s) did not, thereby concluding that this relationship shifts as inflation increases, and that the Phillips curve tradeoff does not hold at high and persistent rates of inflation.

Similarly, an estimating equation with unemployment as the dependent variable would be:

$$u_t = b_0 + b_1 \Delta Y_t + \xi_t, \quad b_1 \leq 0 \tag{39'}$$

Note that an estimated function such as (39') does not distinguish between the expectations augmented Phillips curve based on errors in price-level expectations in labour markets and the Lucas supply rule based on errors in relative commodity prices, so that the estimated coefficients would reflect the influence of both types of errors.

Equations such as (39) with output as the dependent variable or (39') with unemployment as the dependent variable have been estimated for a variety of countries and for a variety of time periods. Lucas's conclusion that such functions are often not stable under demand policy shifts is now well established. However, another of Lucas's conclusions was that the systematic price increases or systematic demand increases do not change real output and unemployment. This has not always been supported in empirical studies. This issue will be examined in the next section of this chapter.

Another aspect of the preceding discussion and of the Lucas critique is that economic agents learn from experience so that their expectations shift. This brings us back to the question of the expectations hypotheses and the role of learning in them. A number of learning mechanisms have been proposed and the speed at which expectational errors are eliminated, derived for them. However, they go beyond the concerns of this book and are not examined in it.

15.6 TESTING THE NEOCLASSICAL AND KEYNESIAN HYPOTHESES ON THE EFFECTIVENESS OF MONETARY POLICY: ESTIMATES BASED ON THE LUCAS MODEL

The Lucas supply function can be stated with output, employment, unemployment or another real variable such as the real rate of interest as the dependent variable, and with the expectational errors in absolute prices, in aggregate demand or with just money supply as the independent variable. From a monetary policy perspective, the form of the Lucas supply function that is usually tested is:

$$y_t = a_0 + a_1(M_t - M_t^e) + \sum_j a_j' z_{jt} + \mu_t \tag{40}$$

where:

M nominal money supply
M^e expected nominal money supply
z_j other exogenous variables
μ random term

Equation (40) focuses on money supply as the sole policy variable determining aggregate demand. We will call (40) by its more general name as the *neoclassical hypothesis*.

The *pseudo-Keynesian* equation corresponding to (40), as discussed in the last section of Chapter 14, is:

$$y_t = b_0 + b_1 M_t + \sum_j a_j' z_{jt} + \mu_t \tag{41}$$

Equation (41) was labelled as pseudo-Keynesian since it is strictly not in line with Keynesian ideas which imply that the money supply multiplier b_1 on output will not be a constant, as assumed in (41), but varies with the state of the economy. In particular, if the economy has involuntary unemployment, there would be a positive impact of the monetary expansion on output, while if there is already full employment, this effect would be much smaller or even zero. Hence, the coefficient of the money supply would vary over the business cycle and estimating it as a constant over both booms and recessions would provide inappropriate estimates: they are too low for the recessions and too high for the booms. Hence, the main justification for using (41) is that it is similar in structure to (40).

The distinction between (40) and (41) is that anticipated (or expected) changes in the money supply can affect real output in the pseudo-Keynesian function (41) but not in the neoclassical one (40). Unanticipated money supply changes can affect output in both hypotheses. Tests of this issue require estimation of the unobservable anticipated and un-anticipated money supply by the use of an expectations hypothesis. They can be estimated using either the adaptive expectations hypothesis or the rational expectations hypothesis. We will further proceed with the latter one since it is theoretically preferable.

A procedure for segmenting the money supply changes into their anticipated and unanticipated components

To estimate (40), we need the value of M_t^e as specified by the rational expectations hypothesis (REH). This value would be a function of the information available to the economic agent. Since the central bank in modern economies controls the national money supply, the relevant knowledge would be that of the public on central bank behaviour and on the policy rule that the central bank follows. Assume that this rule gives the money supply function as:

$$M_t = \sum_i \alpha_i x_{it} + \eta_t \tag{42}$$

where x_t is a set of exogenous and predetermined variables and the money supply rule is:

$$M_t = \sum_i \alpha_i x_{it} \tag{43}$$

Under the REH, the public is assumed to know (42) and use the estimated values $\hat{\alpha}_i$ to calculate the estimated value of $\hat{M}_t$ as:

$$\hat{M}_t = \sum_i \hat{\alpha}_i x_{it} \tag{44}$$

$\hat{M}_t$ is the rational expectations' proxy for the anticipated money supply, so that:

$$\hat{\eta}_t = M_t - \hat{M}_t \tag{45}$$

is the proxy, under the rational expectations hypothesis, for the unanticipated money supply.

The nested form of the Lucas model

The nested form of (40) and (41) specifies the linear (or log-linear) estimating equation as:

$$y_t = \beta_0 + \beta_1 \hat{M}_t + \beta_2 \hat{\eta}_t + \sum_j \gamma_j z_{jt} + \mu_t \tag{46}$$

If $\hat{\beta}_1 = 0$, the anticipated values of money supply do not affect real output, consistent with the neoclassical hypothesis but not with the pseudo-Keynesian one, but if $\hat{\beta}_1 > 0$, the Keynesian hypothesis is supported and the neoclassical one is rejected.[13, 14] Further, for the Keynesian case, $\hat{\beta}_1 = \hat{\beta}_2$.

Barro's test of the Lucas model: a joint test of neutrality and rational expectations

Barro (1977), in one of the earliest articles applying the REH to the Lucas supply rule, used a two-step OLS procedure to test jointly for rational expectations and neutrality. In the first stage, he estimated by OLS a forecasting equation for the money supply. Under the assumption of rational expectations, the calculated value of the money supply from this estimation was used as the proxy for its anticipated value and the residual as the unanticipated value. The impact of these on the dependent real variable – in his case, unemployment – was then estimated in a second equation. Using this procedure, Barro (1977) reported the following estimated functions using annual data for the USA for 1946–73:

$$\ln [U/(1-U)]_t = -3.07 - 5.8DMR_t - 12.1DMR_{t-1} - 4.2DMR_{t-2} - 4.7MIL_t + 0.95MINW_t \tag{47}$$

$$D\hat{M}_t = 0.087 + 0.24DM_{t-1} + 0.35DM_{t-2} + 0.082 \ln FEDV_t + 0.027 \ln [U/(1-U)]_{t-1} \tag{48}$$

where:

DM   growth rate of money supply
DMR   unanticipated money growth rate ($=DM_{-DM}$)
MIL   military size
MINW   minimum wage
FEDV   federal government expenditure relative to normal
U   unemployment rate

Equation (47) is a version of the Lucas supply rule and (48) is a money supply rule. Barro's estimates showed that unanticipated money growth was significant in explaining current unemployment. They also showed that when the total money supply, current and with two lags, replaced the unanticipated money supply terms in (47), their coefficients were not significant. Barro concluded that his study supported the neoclassical hypothesis and not the Keynesian one.

Mishkin's test of the Lucas model: separating neutrality from rational expectations

Mishkin (1982) objected to Barro's estimation procedure since it only provides a test of the joint hypotheses of the neutrality of money and rational expectations, without providing separate results on each of these hypotheses.[15] To understand Mishkin's objection, note that Barro's estimation system was of the form:

$$M_t = \sum_i \alpha_i x_{it} + \eta_t \tag{49}$$

$$y_t = \beta_0 + \sum_{j=0}^{n} \beta j \left(M_{t-j} - \sum_i \alpha_i x_{it-j} \right) + \mu_t \tag{50}$$

where x_{it} were a set of exogenous or predetermined variables for money supply determination. The output equation (50) embodies neutrality and rational expectations and allows for lags in the impact of the unanticipated money supply. Determinants other than the money supply of output have been left out of this equation for simplification. Equation (49) is the same as (42) while (50) has been obtained by substituting the estimate of M_t from (42) in (40). This system imposes rational expectations since α_i in the money equation (49) also appears in the output equation (50). The neutrality property is imposed in (50) since the coefficients on EM_t are constrained to be zero.

To test for rational expectations and neutrality separately, the estimation system should be:

$$M_t = \sum_i \alpha_i x_{it} + \eta_t \tag{51}$$

$$y_t = \beta_0 + \sum_{j=0}^{n} \beta j \left(M_{t-j} - \sum_i \alpha_i^* x_{it-j} \right) + \sum_{j=0}^{n} \gamma_j \alpha_{i,t-j}^* x_{i,t-j} + \mu_t \tag{52}$$

where (52) is the nested equation (46). Rational expectations requires $\alpha_i^* = \alpha_i$, while neutrality requires $\gamma_j = 0$.

Therefore, maintaining the rational expectations hypothesis – that is, setting $\alpha_i = \alpha_i^*$ – while relaxing the neutrality assumption implies testing the system:

$$M_t = \sum_i \alpha_i x_{it} + \eta_t \tag{53}$$

$$y_t = \beta_0 + \sum_{j=0}^{n} \beta j \left(M_{t-j} - \sum_i \alpha_i x_{it-j} \right) + \sum_{j=0}^{n} \gamma_j \alpha_{i,t-j} x_{i,t-j} + \mu_t \tag{54}$$

The null hypothesis of neutrality – that is, $\gamma_j = 0$ – can be tested by comparing the estimates of systems (53) and (54) with those from (49) and (50).

Maintaining the neutrality hypothesis – that is, setting $\gamma_j = 0$ – while testing for rational expectations requires estimating:

$$M_t = \sum_i \alpha_i x_{it} + \eta_t \tag{55}$$

$$y_t = \beta_0 + \sum_{j=0}^{n} \beta j \left(M_{t-j} - \sum_i \alpha_i^* x_{it-j} \right) + \mu_t \tag{56}$$

The null hypothesis of $\alpha_i^* = \alpha_i$ is tested by comparing the estimates from (55) and (56) against those from (49) and (50).

Mishkin's tests for the USA (quarterly data for 1954–76) used unemployment and output as the dependent variables, and nominal GNP and the rate of inflation among the independent variables. He reported that while the REH was not rejected by the data, neutrality was. Further, the estimated coefficients of the anticipated and unanticipated demand variables were very similar in magnitude. Therefore, Mishkin's results supported the Keynesian hypothesis and rejected the modern classical one on the key issue of the neutrality of anticipated aggregate demand and of demand management policies. These results did not reject the REH, which is merely a procedure for modelling expectations, and, as noted earlier, is not *a priori* inconsistent with either the Keynesian or the neoclassical theories.

15.7 DISTINGUISHING BETWEEN THE IMPACT OF POSITIVE AND NEGATIVE MONEY SUPPLY SHOCKS

It is sometimes argued that decreases in the money supply are likely to have stronger impact than increases in it. There can be several reasons for this. Among these are:

(i)   A decrease in the money supply represents a decrease in credit in the economy, so that the borrowers are forced to curtail their economic activities, and this reduces output in the economy. By comparison, an increase in the money supply means a greater willingness by the financial intermediaries to lend, which does not result in the same urgency to borrow as a decrease in loans to repay.[16]
(ii) The contractionary policies are likely to be pursued during booms with full employment and a high demand for investment and additional borrowing, while the expansionary policies are likely to be pursued during recessions when the firms generally face inadequate demand for their products and do not have enough incentive to increase their investment and borrowing for it. That is, the impact of the two types of policies also depends on the phase of the business cycle with which the two are associated.
(iii) The economy is likely to possess some downward rigidity in prices and nominal wages while it possesses a higher degree of flexibility for increases in them. Decreases in the money supply run into this downward rigidity and are more likely to have real effects, while most or all of the impact of the money supply increases could be only on prices and the nominal but not the real value of output.

The Barro and Mishkin tests can be modified to test for this differential impact. We illustrate this by modifying (40) to:

$$y_t = a_0 + a_1^+ M_t^u + \sum_j a_j' z_{jt} + \mu_t \tag{57}$$

and its nested form (46) to:

$$y_t = a_0 + a_1^+ M_t^{u+} + a_1^- M_t^{u-} + \beta_1^+ M_t^{e+} + \beta_1^- M_t^{e-} + \sum_j \alpha_j z_{jt} + \mu_t \tag{58}$$

where:

M^{u+} unanticipated increases in the money supply
M^{u-} unanticipated decrease in the money supply
M^{e+} expected (anticipated) increase in the money supply
M^{e-} expected (anticipated) decrease in the money supply

and z_j are the other variables in the determination of output. The other aspects of the estimation procedures of Barro and Mishkin remain as specified above. Empirical studies have found evidence of the asymmetrical effects – and non-neutrality – of monetary policy for the United States and Japan.[17]

15.8 TESTING THE NEOCLASSICAL AND KEYNESIAN HYPOTHESES ON THE EFFECTIVENESS OF MONETARY POLICY: ESTIMATES FROM A KEYNESIAN MODEL WITH A PHILLIPS CURVE

We have argued above that the impact of the money supply changes on output in the Keynesian model depends on the deviation of output and employment from their equilibrium – or full employment – levels. This can be captured through a Phillips curve relationship. To properly modify the Lucas–Sargent–Wallace model for such a Keynesian version would mean replacing its Lucas supply rule by a Phillips curve equation. One format of such a Keynesian model, used by Gali (1992), was:

IS equation:

$$y = \mu_t^s + \alpha - \sigma(r_t - E\,\Delta p_{t-1}) + \mu_t^{IS} \tag{59}$$

LM equation:

$$m_t - p_t = \phi y_t - \lambda r_t + \mu_t^{md} \tag{60}$$

Money supply process:

$$\Delta m_t = \mu_t^{ms} \tag{61}$$

Phillips curve:

$$\Delta p_t = \Delta p_{t-1} + \beta(y_t - \mu_t^s) \tag{62}$$

where the symbols designate the logs of the relevant variables, except for r which stands for the level of the nominal interest rate. μ^s, μ^{IS}, μ^{md} and μ^{ms} are the stochastic processes for output supply, expenditures, money demand and money supply, respectively. The IS and LM equations are essentially similar to those in the Lucas model, except that they provide greater detail. The major difference between this – IS–LM–Keynesian – model and the Lucas one lies in the specification of output supply. The former specifies it by the Phillips curve so that changes in the inflation rate between periods determine the variations in output from its equilibrium level μ^s. The latter model uses relative price misperceptions to explain such deviations.

In the above specification, output can change due to supply shocks through μ^s, or demand shocks due to μ^{IS}, μ^{md} or μ^{ms}. Positive demand shocks increase both output and prices while positive supply shocks increase output and decrease prices. Monetary shocks are transmitted to the real sector only through changes in the interest rate.

The segregation of the experienced shocks into four different types requires special assumptions on their origin or impact. Supply shocks were separated from the demand shocks by the assumption that the former have long-run effects on output while the latter do not. The IS shocks were separated from the money market shocks by the assumption that the latter do not have contemporaneous impact on aggregate demand in the same quarter, since their impact occurs through the changes in interest rates impinging on investment. The money demand and supply shocks were separated under three alternative assumptions, which we do not report here.

Gali's data was quarterly for the USA for 1955:I to 1987:IV. The monetary aggregate used was M1 and the interest rate was represented by the three-month Treasury bill rate. The findings supported the Keynesian claim that demand shocks do cause output changes while rejecting its claim that they, rather than supply shocks, were the dominant source of fluctuations. Supply shocks had a substantial deflationary impact and accounted for about 70% of output variability over the business cycle. However, their impact on the nominal interest rate was small.

Increases in M1 increased output, reaching a peak in about four quarters, accompanied by increases in inflation and nominal interest rates, but decreases in the real rate. While the money supply shocks accounted for most of the short-run variability of the nominal and real interest rates and for some variability in output over the business cycle, there was no long-run effect on output or the real rate – though this result really emanates from the built-in assumptions – but only on the inflation rate. Money demand shifts had a much faster impact on prices than money supply shifts and significant impact on real balances but little influence on output variability or the real rate.

The impact of the IS shocks on output started within the same quarter as the shock – clearly just a result of the assumptions made – reached a peak two quarters after the shock but almost vanished after four quarters. However, such shocks had permanent effects on money growth, inflation and the nominal rate. While they increased the nominal rate, they first increased the real rate but, because of their impact on inflation, soon led to a decline in the real rate, which returned to its initial level about two years after the shock. IS shocks accounted for a substantial part of the business fluctuations.

Gali's findings, therefore, support the Keynesian conclusions that demand shocks do cause variations in output. Further, money supply variations had a longer-lasting impact on output than IS shocks. However, the major source of the variations in output was supply rather than demand shocks. Demand shocks did not have long-run effects on output and the real rate of interest.[18] While Gali's model did not distinguish between the positive and negative money supply shocks and test for the asymmetry in their effects, it can clearly be modified to do so.

In another study, for a large number of countries, Bullard and Keating (1995) used vector autoregression to investigate the impact of inflation on output. In their procedure, they identified the permanent component of inflation as being due to permanent changes in the money growth rate while the exogenous shocks to output were taken to only cause transitory shocks to inflation. Their finding was that the permanent shocks to inflation did not *permanently* increase the level of output for most of the countries but did do so for certain low-inflation countries. In general, the estimated effects were positive for low-inflation countries, and low or negative for high-inflation countries. Money is not neutral under these findings. This pattern of the effects of inflation on output seems to reflect the opinion of most monetary economists.

15.9 TESTING THE NEOCLASSICAL AND KEYNESIAN HYPOTHESES ON THE EFFECTIVENESS OF MONETARY POLICY: THE RESULTS OF OTHER TESTING PROCEDURES

The empirical findings in numerous empirical studies have ranged back and forth against the neutrality assumption. We do not intend to review many more studies but do consider the findings of a different type of study to be worth mentioning. As against the use of compact (small) reduced-form models reported above from the works of Barro, Mishkin, Gali, and Bullard and Keating, Mosser (1992) based her findings on four large structural macroeconometric models, well established in the late 1980s and 1990s.[19] These were used to generate the elasticities of real output, real interest rates and various other real variables with respect to monetary variables such as M1 and non-borrowed reserves held by banks. The estimated elasticities were significant not only for the first four quarters but were significant for periods longer than twelve quarters for many of the real variables. For real output, the elasticities were positive and continued to increase up to twelve quarters, and were significant (either positive or negative) even at forty quarters. Hence, not only were the monetary variables not neutral, the estimated lags were very long.

15.10 SUMMING UP THE EMPIRICAL EVIDENCE ON MONETARY NEUTRALITY AND RATIONAL EXPECTATIONS

The results reported from Mishkin (1982), Gali (1992) and Mosser (1992), as against Barro's (1977), supported the Keynesian theory and rejected the neoclassical one on the critical difference between them on the neutrality of anticipated money supply changes and the continual clearance of all markets. This implies rejection of the Lucas supply rule, which incorporates the neutrality of anticipated money supply changes.

Another aspect of the neutrality modelling worth noting is that their supply functions embody either neutrality or non-neutrality. However, empirical evidence suggests that money can be neutral in some cases and non-neutral in other cases, and that the 'degree of non-neutrality' can be variant in intermediate cases, though it is *a priori* difficult to separate these cases.[20] These results need not come as a big surprise: the various theories presented in Chapters 13 and 14 indicate that there can be different causes of non-neutrality in the economy: contracts and the lagged adjustment of nominal wages to prices; disequilibrium factors in the neoclassical model; deficient demand in the Keynesian one; relative price errors in a Lucas-type model; sticky prices in certain markets, pensions and other predetermined sources of incomes; etc. Consequently, if our estimating equation only allows the black/white scenario of neutrality versus non-neutrality, when part of the data is from a neutral sample and part is from a non-neutral one, we are likely to get a mixed bag of empirical results, varying with the relative weights of the two types of data in our sample.

Overall, while there is by now a mixed bag of empirical studies favouring one or the other of these hypotheses, the empirical evidence seems more often to favour the non-neutrality of money rather than its neutrality. The evidence also seems to favour the finding that there is a distinction between the effects of anticipated *money supply* changes and those of anticipated *price* changes.

The empirical evidence on the rationality of expectations does not, in general, reject it.

CONCLUSIONS

Both rational expectations and adaptive expectations techniques are by now well-established approaches to modelling expectations, and tend to be used when appropriate and convenient. The former tends to dominate in theoretical modelling, while the latter continues to be used in some empirical studies, though with a general preference for the former. Their validity is no longer an issue in judging between neoclassical and Keynesian economics, since the latter school can also incorporate rational expectations, though both originally had used adaptive expectations. Rather, the critical distinction between these schools is that of the neutrality of money and continual market clearance, with neoclassical models embodying them while Keynesian economics generally deny them.

Empirical evidence has often rejected the Phillips curve and shows that this curve shifts with the experienced rate of inflation, raising the presumption that this curve is vertical in the limit, thereby providing justification for the concept of the natural rate of unemployment.

However, recent contributions no longer view the natural rate for an economy as invariable over time in response to supply and even to some demand shifts in the economy. Overall, the empirical evidence tends to favour the expectations augmented Phillips curve over the Phillips curve, but does not support the constancy of the natural rate of unemployment or the neutrality of money.

On a slightly separate but related issue, the empirical evidence favours the Lucas critique, so that significant shifts in monetary policy shift the multipliers and elasticities of the real variables with respect to the monetary ones. Hence, the private sector does incorporate information on the policy stance into its expectations. That is, the appropriate theory on expectations is that of rational rather than static or adaptive expectations.

The emphasis on the errors in relative prices as the main source of the real effects of monetary disturbances is too narrow. The real effects are also likely to occur – perhaps, mainly – through other types of mechanisms. Among these are those arising from the failure of certain markets – with labour as one of these markets – to clear continuously, and from various types of rigidities and imperfections in the economy. That is, if there are effects of unanticipated monetary changes on the real variables, they are more in the nature of an expectations augmented Phillips curve, derived from the labour market analysis, than coming from the Lucas supply rule, derived from firms' errors in interpreting the source of the observed local price increases. However, both could coexist and there could be also other channels for such effects.

In tests of models using the Lucas supply rule, unanticipated errors in the rate of inflation have been found to affect real output and other real variables, as have been unanticipated changes in monetary aggregates. However, the distinction between the neoclassical and Keynesian economics is not this effect, for it occurs in both approaches, but whether the anticipated changes in the monetary variables affect the real variables. Further, in estimation, the empirical tests must separate the hypothesis of rational expectations from that of the neutrality of money. While the evidence on the whole tends to support the former as against its alternatives, there is considerable evidence that the industrialized economies do not possess the neutrality of money. That is, changes in the monetary aggregates affect output, employment and unemployment, as well as other real variables, thereby rejecting the Lucas supply analysis. Some of the evidence even shows lags lasting over several years for the full impact of monetary expansions, with the evidence in favour of lags of several years usually coming from large structural models rather than reduced-form ones, but even the latter show lags lasting over a year.[21]

The rejection of the neutrality of anticipated changes in the money supply rejects the Lucas supply model in favour of the Keynesian implication of the non-neutrality of money and of the disequilibrium properties of the neoclassical model. However, the rejection of the Phillips curve implies rejection of the Keynesian nominal wage model of Chapter 14 and of other Keynesian models with heavy reliance on the rigidity – or rigidity relative to prices – of nominal wages. But these rejections do not necessarily imply a rejection of the Keynesian deficient-demand model (see sections 14.3 and 14.4 of Chapter 14). Nor do they necessarily imply a rejection of the neoclassical model if disequilibrium is a common phenomenon (see section 13.10 of Chapter 13) and if, under quantity adjustments, output responds to aggregate demand increases, so that output and employment increase, whether or not prices are also being raised. Both of these allow for output and employment to be away from their full employment levels for very significant periods of time, thereby allowing non-neutrality during these periods.

Overall, the above mixed bag of findings for the industrialized economies poses a dilemma for the policy maker. While the Phillips curve is not supported, its converse as the neutrality of money is also not supported by the evidence. While the expectations augmented Phillips curve and the Lucas critique are supported, the neutrality of anticipated monetary aggregates and the Lucas supply rule are rejected. While the latter findings seem to support the use of expansionary monetary policy to increase real output, the former strongly cautions against it. These results compel the monetary authority to be cautious in its pursuit of expansionary policies to improve on the real performance of the economy.

This discussion of the real nature of the economy and of the role of monetary policy is pursued further in the next chapter. Just as Chapters 15 and 16 are closely related, with Chapter 16 being an extension of this chapter, similarly the conclusions to Chapter 16 represent an extension of the conclusions of this chapter, and the reader can choose to read them at this point.

SUMMARY OF CRITICAL CONCLUSIONS

- Nominal wage contracts allow the impact of the errors in the expected rate of inflation on the real wage, unemployment and output. This effect is captured in the expectations augmented Phillips curve, which is a relationship between the deviation of unemployment from its natural rate and the unanticipated rate of inflation.
- The Friedman supply rule for output is based on the errors in the expectations – of households and firms – embodied in nominal wage contracts.
- The Lucas supply rule for output is based on the errors made by firms in their expectations of the relative prices of their commodities.
- The Lucas critique is important for the formulation of policy and implies that the relationship in the data on inflation and unemployment (or output) cannot be properly used as a tradeoff by the policy maker: it will not be invariant to a change in the policy.
- The critical distinction between the Keynesian and modern classical approaches to monetary policy is not on the effects of the unanticipated monetary policy changes, but rather on the effects of the anticipated monetary policy. The Keynesians imply a positive impact, at least in the demand deficient states, of the anticipated money supply changes on output and unemployment, while the modern classical model – and the Friedman and Lucas supply rules – do not do so. The latter represent the neutrality of the anticipated – which is based on knowledge of the systematic component of – monetary policy.
- Empirical studies generally seem to validate rational expectations but not the neutrality of the anticipated/systematic monetary policy.

review and discussion questions

1 Discuss the following: the rational expectations hypothesis, although unrealistic, should still be adopted as the best available method for modelling expectations in macroeconomics. Also discuss the potentially different applications of this hypothesis to the modern classical and Keynesian models.

2 Discuss the following: under rational expectations, the Phillips curve is vertical in the short run as well as the long run. While it is not vertical under adaptive expectations, it is steep.

3 Define the Phillips curve and the expectations augmented Phillips curve. What is the justification for each one? Show their relationship to the modern classical and Keynesian models and analyse their implications for monetary policy.

4 Explain the Lucas supply rule and its basis in the behaviour of economic agents in decentralized markets. Does it capture any part of – or totally ignore – staggered wage contracts and their implications for changes in output? Is there any relationship between this rule and the expectations augmented Phillips curve?

5 Discuss the following: the rational expectations hypothesis is logically and in spirit consistent with Keynesian economics. Moreover, Keynes had placed heavy emphasis on the role of expectations in macroeconomics, more so than the traditional classical economists had done.

6 What are the policy implications of price stickiness under rational expectations?

7 Discuss the following: involuntary unemployment can exist in the presence of rational expectations.

8 Discuss: monetary policies cannot stabilize unemployment below its natural rate or output above its full employment level in rational expectations models.

9 Discuss: active stabilization policies work only if private agents are differentially informed across markets.

10 For an economy with the Lucas supply rule and rational expectations:

   (a) Show that systematic monetary policy cannot affect the level of output.

   (b) Show how an appropriate monetary policy can be used to stabilize output when (i) the government and the public have different information or (ii) the unanticipated money supply changes enter non-linearly into the money supply function.

   (c) Can a 'Tobin effect' occur in such an economy? Would this refute the money neutrality proposition?

11 Discuss the following:

   (a) If private expectations are rational, monetary policy is ineffective.

   (b) If the monetary authorities react faster than economic agents to new information, discretionary monetary policy is as useful in rational expectations models as in Keynesian ones.

12 Determine the effects of a current unanticipated reduction in the money supply in the Sargent–Wallace model with the Lucas supply rule? What is the impact effect of an unanticipated announcement of a future monetary contraction? Compare these effects with those for Keynesian models.

13 Given rational expectations, a short-run tradeoff between the price level and unemployment can only exist if economic agents cannot distinguish monetary from real shocks. Discuss.

14 Discuss the significance of the Lucas critique for the formulation of economic policy. Give some examples.

15 Discuss the statement: reduced-form models are useless for policy formulation or evaluation. Give one example where such a model is useless and one where it is not. Given a reduced-form model, how would you judge which category it belongs to.

16 Write an essay explaining the following propositions: (a) long and variable lags in the impact of monetary policy on output (a finding by Milton Friedman) and (b) rational expectations. Are these two propositions conceptually consistent with each other? How would you test which of the two, or both, are valid? What are the implications of each one, and of both together, for monetary policy?

17 For the relevant models, prove the following statements:

   (a) The Lucas supply rule and rational expectations imply that only unanticipated money supply changes have real effects, while even anticipated ones can have real effects in Keynesian models with rational expectations.

   (b) Given the Lucas supply rule and rational expectations, money is neutral if changes in the money supply are anticipated, but not neutral if the growth of the money supply is anticipated and money supply depends on the rate of inflation.

18 Consider the following macroeconomic model:

Aggregate demand:

$$Y_t = a_p P_t + a_g G_t + a_m M_t + a_z Z_t + \mu_t$$

Aggregate supply:

$$y_t = y_t^f + \gamma(P_t - P_t^e) + \eta_t$$

where the symbols have the usual meanings and are in logs. Note that $Y \equiv Py$; G, M and Z are exogenous variables and μ and η are random errors. Further, assume rational expectation so that:

$$P_t^e = E(P_t \mid I_{t-1})$$

I_{t-1} (Private sector's information set in t

$$E(\mu_t \mid I_{t-1}) = E(\eta_t \mid I_{t-1}) = 0 \quad \text{for all } t$$

(i)   Solve for the reduced form for P_t (in terms of y_t^f, G_t, M_t, Z_t, μ_t and η_t).
(ii) Find the equation for $(P_t - P_t^e)$ in terms of the exogenous variables and their conditional expectations.
(iii) Can any type of monetary and fiscal policies affect y_t?
(iv) Can effective demand failures in the sense of Leijonhufvud (see Chapter 14) occur in a context of rational expectations? Can economic agents formulate and hold rational expectations in the context of effective demand failures? Discuss these statements.
(v)   Note that the above model incorporates the Lucas supply function. Now suppose that an effective demand failure occurs and that prices do not clear the commodity market. Will the Lucas supply function continue to hold? What will be the form of the supply function under the effective demand failure? Can rational expectations apply to this supply function?

19 Consider an economy with the following structure:

Aggregate demand:

$$y_t = M_t - P_t + \mu_t \quad \text{(A quantity theory-type equation)}$$

Aggregate supply:

$$y_t = y_t^f + \gamma(P_t - P_t^e) + \eta_t$$

Rational expectations:

$$P_t^e = E_{t-1} P_t$$

where the symbols have the usual meanings and are in logs; μ and η are random errors. The central bank knows the above structure. However, the private agents in the economy erroneously believe the supply function to be:

Erroneous supply function:

$$y_t = y_t^f + \beta(P_t - P_t^e) + \eta_t$$

where $\beta \neq \gamma$. In this case, the private agents do not know the true parameters and one of them is incorrect. What would then be the effects of anticipated monetary policy if the central bank supplies money on the basis of:

(i)   Constant money supply rule $M_t = \underline{M} + \epsilon_t$
(ii) Gradual adjustment rule $M_t = \underline{M} + \rho(M_{t-1} - \underline{M}) + \epsilon_t \quad 0 < \rho < 1$
(iii) Lagged feedback rule $M_t = \underline{M} + \alpha(y^f - y_{t-1}) + \epsilon_t$

where ϵ is a random error.

20 Suppose that the economy's structure is as in question 19, but that the private agents in the economy form their expectations on the basis of information two periods earlier (because the relevant information becomes available with a lag of one period), as in:

Rational expectations:

$$P_t^e = E_{t-2}P_t$$

so that the supply function becomes:

$$y_t = y_t^f + \gamma(P_t - E_{t-2}P_t) + \eta_t$$

In this case, the expectations are based on lagged information. What would now be the effects of anticipated monetary policy under each of the three money supply rules?

21 Consider an economy with flexible prices in which the demand for real balances is specified by the simple function:[22]

$$M_t^d - P_t = k - \alpha\pi_t^e \quad \alpha > 0$$

where M is the log of the nominal money stock and P is the log of the price level; π_t^e is the expected rate of inflation. Assume that the money supply is exogenously specified as M and that $M_t^d = M_t$. Let the expectations of inflation be formed rationally as:

$$\pi_t^e = E_t P_{t+1} - P_t$$

so that the expectations of inflation are conditional on information available at time t.

    Analyse the implications for prices, real balances and the inflation rate of the following:

(i) an unanticipated increase in the permanent rate of monetary growth;
(ii) an unanticipated increase in the temporary rate of monetary growth;
(iii) the announcement of a permanent increase in the rate of monetary growth, starting in period $(t + 1)$.

22 Given the information in question 21, now assume that the nominal money supply is stochastic and follows the autoregressive process:

$$M_t = \rho M_{t-1} + \epsilon_t \quad |\rho| < 1$$

where ϵ_t is independently identically distributed with mean zero and variance σ^2.

(i) Derive P_t as a function of M_t. Does the quantity theory hold in this case?
(ii) Assuming that the anticipations on the money stock are also formed rationally one period earlier, derive the anticipated change in P_t as a function of the anticipated change in M_t. Does the quantity theory hold in this case?
(iii) Derive the unanticipated change in P_t as a function of ϵ_t.

NOTES

1 For both of these, also see Chapter 14.
2 Keynes (1936) emphasized the volatility of expectations in financial markets, and, therefore, of the volatility of the speculative demand for money which is based on these expectations.

This volatility, in turn, affected the impact of monetary policy on the economy. The treatment of subjective probabilities as if they were objectives, tends to ignore the vagueness and volatility of the former.

3 There are also a number of other hypotheses for decision making under uncertainty. However, they are not often used in macroeconomic and monetary analysis.

4 Note that while the wage contract fixes the negotiated nominal wage, it does not fix the amount of employment so that the firm remains free to choose the amount of employment.

5 W^c will be homogeneous of degree one in P^{ef} and P^{eh}, but not in one of them.

6 Hence, there are two stages to the process being considered. In the first stage, the nominal wage is established; in the second stage occurring at a somewhat later date, the firm chooses the employment level based on the established nominal wage and its actual selling price of its product.

7 Among these sources of deviations are: lack of labour market clearance, coordination failures among goods markets, market inefficiencies such as adjustment lags, market imperfections such as firm and labour immobility, etc.

8 In periods of high and volatile inflation rates, labour tries to protect itself against positive errors in expectations by shortening the duration of the wage contract. Thus, during the 1950s with relative price stability, labour contracts of three years' duration were not uncommon. In the inflationary 1980s, three- and two-year contracts became rarer and one-year contracts or contracts with cost-of-living adjustments in the nominal wage became much more common. The result of such shortening of the contract duration was to reduce the impact of expectational errors and make the expectations augmented Phillips curve shift to a more vertical position.

9 For the price level to serve as an index of labour costs, the nominal wage rate must instantly adjust proportionately with the actual price level. Hence, there must be nominal wage flexibility and instant adjustment in nominal wages, without any rigidities introduced by labour contracts or money illusion in the labour supply function. Compare this with the expectations augmented Phillips curve, also in the neoclassical tradition, which assumes that nominal wages do not rise proportionately with the actual price level, but do so only with respect to the expected price level, so that real wages do change because of the unanticipated part of inflation.

10 This would include knowledge of past shifts in demand and supply and past variations in local and general prices, but can also include any available information about the future.

11 In particular, the expectations augmented Phillips curve requires contractual rigidities in (labour markers) while the Lucas supply rule does not have contractual rigidities.

12 It is not the Phillips curve because the Phillips curve is based on real wages falling as inflation occurs, while the Lucas version does not allow this. His curve emanates from the firm's belief that relative prices are increasing when they are not, so that the perceived inflation rate is below the actual one. Since, under our assumptions, nominal wages increase proportionately with the actual rate of inflation, the firm's relative price misperceptions imply that the firm perception is that the real wage is falling, even though it does not do so. This has the consequence that the firm's real profits fall even as it supplies more output – so that its output increase is likely to be short lived.

13 $\beta_1 < 0$ indicates that the money supply increases are detrimental for output in the economy, as when they increase the degree of uncertainty and reduce investment or otherwise lead to a diversion of resources to less efficient uses in the economy.

14 A simplified form of this system can give erroneous results, as Mishkin (1982) showed. Consider the following simple system:

$$y_t = a_1 \hat{M}_t + \sum_j g_j z_{jt} + \theta_t \tag{1}$$

$$M_t = b_1 y_{t-1} + \Psi_t \tag{2}$$

which imply that:

$$y_t = a_1 b_1 y_{t-1} + \sum_j g_j z_{jt} + \theta_t \tag{3}$$

where $\hat{M}_t$ does not occur as an explanatory variable in (3) so that it would appear that (3) rejects the Keynesian hypothesis when in fact this hypothesis was part of the initial model in the form of (1). This problematic result arose because (2) involved only the lagged terms of y as explanatory variables, so that (1) and (2) were not identified through the reduced form (3), thereby making it impossible to judge from (3) whether the anticipated part of the money supply affects real output or not. Hence, estimating (3) does not allow us to discriminate between the two hypotheses.

15 Mishkin also argued that while the two-step OLS estimation procedure will yield consistent parameter estimates, they do not generate valid F-test statistics, thereby resulting in inconsistent estimates of the standard errors of the parameters and test statistics, which do not follow the assumed F-distribution. He used the full information maximum likelihood (FIML) procedure for the non-linear joint estimation for his systems.

16 An analogy sometimes used is that one can pull on a string but not push on it.

17 A study which illustrates this procedure and presents the findings for Japan is Chu and Ratti (1997).

18 Note that these findings are affected by the assumptions made to segment the shocks to the economy, so that any errors in these assumptions could lead to erroneous results. For example, if the aggregate demand changes do cause long-run changes in output, such impact would have been erroneously attributed to supply factors.

19 These were: the Bureau of Economic Analysis Model, the Data Resources Inc. model, the Federal Reserve Board/MPS model, and the Wharton Econometric Forecasting Associates model.

20 Tests of a model embodying an expectations augmented Phillips curve allow such variation and are reported in the next chapter.

21 Chapter 16 extends this discussion on lags in a more intuitive manner.

22 This money demand function was used by Cagan (1956) in his study of hyperinflation.

REFERENCES

Akerlof, George A. 'The Case against Conservative Macroeconomics: An Inaugural Lecture'. *Economica*, 46, August 1979, pp. 219–37.

Arrow, Kenneth. 'The Future and the Present in Economic Life'. *Economic Inquiry*, 16, April 1978, pp. 157–69.

Barro, Robert J. 'Unanticipated Money Growth and Unemployment in the United States'. *American Economic Review*, 67, March 1977, pp. 101–15.

Bullard, James, and John W. Keating. 'The Long-Run Relationship between Inflation and Output in Postwar Economies'. *Journal of Monetary Economics*, 36, December 1995, pp. 477–96.

Cagan, Phillip. 'The Monetary Dynamics of Hyperinflation'. In Milton Friedman, ed., *Studies in the Quantity Theory of Money*, pp. 25–117. Chicago: University of Chicago Press, 1956.

Chu, Joonsuk, and Ronald A. Ratti. 'Effects of Unanticipated Monetary Policy on Aggregate Japanese Output'. *Canadian Journal of Economics*, 30, August 1997, pp. 722–41.

Friedman, Milton. 'The Role of Monetary Policy'. *American Economic Review*, 58, March 1968, pp. 1–17.

——. 'Nobel Prize Lecture: Inflation and Unemployment'. *Journal of Political Economy*, 85, June 1977, pp. 451–73.

Gali, Jordi. 'How Well Does the IS–LM Model Fit Postwar US Data'. *Quarterly Journal of Economics*, 107, May 1992, pp. 710–38.

Keynes, John Maynard. *The General Theory of Employment, Interest and Money.* New York: Macmillan, 1936.

Lucas, Robert E., Jr. 'Expectations and the Neutrality of Money'. *Journal of Economic Theory*, 4, April 1972, pp. 103–24.

——. 'Some International Evidence on Output–Inflation Tradeoffs'. *American Economic Review*, 63, June 1973, pp. 326–34.

Mishkin, Frederic S. 'Are Market Forecasts Rational?' *American Economic Review*, 71, June 1981, pp. 295–306.

——. 'Does Anticipated Aggregate Demand Policy Matter?' *American Economic Review*, 72, September 1982, pp. 788–802.

Mosser, Patricia. 'Changes in Monetary Policy Effectiveness: Evidence from Large Macroeconomic Models'. *Federal Reserve Board of New York Quarterly Review*, 17, Spring 1992, pp. 36–51.

Muth, J. F. 'Rational Expectations and the Theory of Price Movements'. *Econometrica*, 29, July 1961, pp. 315–35.

Sargent, Thomas J., and Neil Wallace. 'Rational Expectations, the Optimal Monetary Instrument, and the Optimal Money Supply Rule'. *Journal of Political Economy*, 83, April 1975, pp. 241–54.

——, and ——. 'Rational Expectations and the Theory of Economic Policy'. *Journal of Monetary Economics*, 2, April 1976, pp. 169–83.

chapter sixteen

MACRO MODELS, POLICY RULES AND PERSPECTIVES ON THE NEUTRALITY OF MONEY

This chapter continues the discussion of the effectiveness of monetary policy. It does so in the framework of the compact Lucas–Sargent–Wallace model, which is a popular platform for the modern classical approach. It also examines the following issues on monetary policy.

An important part of the debate on practical monetary policy has been about the advisability of using simple rules for the supply of money. The most famous of these is Friedman's money supply rule of a constant low growth rate in the money supply.

Among the problems that bedevil the practical pursuit of monetary policy is the existence of significant lags, often variable in duration, in the effects of monetary policy.

Economists' and central bankers' thinking on the relevance and impact of monetary policy is based not only on narrowly specified models but also on their intuition and practical experiences. What do they believe? This chapter illustrates their ideas on monetary policy through quotes from the writings of several famous economists and one banker.

---

key concepts introduced in this chapter

- Discretionary monetary policy versus simple rules
- The Lucas–Sargent–Wallace model
- The pseudo-Keynesian supply rule
- Optimal money supply rules
- Friedman's money supply rule
- Lags in the effect of monetary policy

A major issue in macroeconomics is whether it is better for the monetary authority to pursue a discretionary policy, adjusting the policy instrument to the emerging conditions, or to pursue a systematic policy according to a predetermined rule. The earlier debates on this issue in the 1950s and 1960s involved the Keynesian recommendation for discretionary rules as against Milton Friedman's recommendation that money supply should increase at a pre-set low growth rate. Among the latter are a zero growth rate and a rate equal to the growth rate of output, but the important element of Friedman's proposal was to eliminate variability and therefore uncertainty in the rate of growth of money. This debate widened in the 1970s with the contributions of Lucas (1972, 1973), Sargent and Wallace (1975, 1976) and others to include broader monetary policy rules. These issues have been discussed to some extent in Chapters 13 to 15. This chapter focuses more directly on them. A related issue is that of the optimality of the discretionary versus rule-based monetary policy. This was presented in Chapter 12 on the central bank.

Section 16.1 presents the debate on the role and effect of monetary policy on the economy. Section 16.2 analyses the effects of systematic and unanticipated money supply changes on output and prices in the context of the Lucas–Sargent–Wallace model. Section 16.3 shows the validity of the Lucas critique in this model. Section 16.4 analyses the Sargent–Wallace model with a Keynesian-type supply function. Section 16.5 presents the analysis of the optimal and other policy rules in the context of these models. The analysis of the effects of monetary policy cannot be complete without a discussion of the lags in these effects. Section 16.6, therefore, presents a discussion of these lags.

The conclusions of this chapter present a summing-up of our knowledge as reflected in the writings of some of the major protagonists on the neutrality debate.

16.1 DISCRETIONARY MONETARY POLICY VERSUS SIMPLE MONETARY POLICY RULES

An important issue in the debate on monetary policy is whether monetary policy should be allowed to be discretionary. A discretionary monetary policy is one where the monetary authorities have a broad degree of control over the money supply or the reserve base and can change them as they see fit. The need and scope for monetary policy depends upon whether:

(i)   Monetary policy has a significant impact on nominal national income.
(ii) It has a reasonably short lag in its impact.
(iii) The monetary authorities can be relied upon to possess adequate knowledge about the economy.
(iv) The monetary authorities can be relied upon to make the correct judgements on the policy to be pursued.
(v)   If the intention is to affect real variables, the additional required condition is that monetary policy should be able to change real output, employment and other real variables.

In the context of the developed economies, virtually all economists agree that the money supply has a significant impact on the nominal value of aggregate demand. A large number of economists now agree that there is a reasonably short lag in the impact effect of monetary policy and that most of its effects occur over six to eight quarters. Most economists would also agree that the authorities in the developed nations nowadays possess fairly adequate knowledge about the current course of their economies, with fairly sophisticated procedures for collecting data and high-speed computers for processing it. Agreement on point (iv) is partly a matter of faith in human judgement and partly a question of the record of past performance. While Keynesians[1] also accept point (v), the modern classical and the new classical schools do not do so, so that the latter groups do not support the use of discretionary monetary policy.

16.1.1 Keynesian monetary policies

The Keynesian models as set out in Chapters 14 and 15 imply that the economy need not consistently perform at its full employment level and that, when it does not do so, appropriate monetary and fiscal policy will increase output and employment in the economy. The impact of such a policy on these variables varies with their deviation from full employment levels. Consequently, the Keynesians support the use of discretionary monetary and fiscal policies to eliminate deviations from full employment.

The 1950s and 1960s were among the heyday of Keynesian influence on monetary policy and central banks tended to pursue such discretionary monetary policy.

16.1.2 Milton Friedman on monetary policy[2]

As against the Keynesian recommendations on discretionary monetary policy and their pursuit during the 1950s and 1960s, there was strong opposition to such policies by Milton Friedman and others in the classical tradition. Their position reflected their political and economic heritage as well as their perception of the nature of the economy. This heritage is one of nineteenth-century liberalism, with *laissez faire* in the economic sphere: the government should exercise only a minimum of control over the economy, and the economy works best when left to itself. This economic philosophy implies that while competition is to be promoted, the incursive techniques of monetary and fiscal policies are ruled out as discretionary tools for stabilization purposes.

Such an opinion can also be based upon empirical evidence, which refutes at least one out of the points (ii) to (v) above. Milton Friedman agreed that monetary policy has a strong impact on the economy. However, his early empirical work had shown this impact to have a long and variable lag, so that, since the course of the economy cannot be foreseen long in advance, a discretionary change in the money supply may have its impact at an unexpected or undesired time.[3] Hence, a discretionary monetary policy should be avoided. Friedman recommended that discretionary monetary policy should be abolished and that money supply should grow at a given constant percentage rate. This rate can be based on considerations of price stability or an optimal rate of inflation or deflation.[4]

Friedman's recommendations are summarized in:

> The stock of money [should] be increased at a fixed rate year-in and year-out without any variation in the rate of increase to meet cyclical needs. This rule could be adopted by the Reserve System itself. Alternatively, Congress could instruct the Reserve System to follow it. . . .
>
> The rate of increase should be chosen so that on the average it could be expected to correspond with a roughly stable long-run level of final product prices. For the concept of money just recommended, namely, currency plus all commercial bank deposits, this would have required a rate of growth of slightly over 4% per year on the average of the past 90 years – something over 3% to allow for growth in output and 1% to allow for a secular decrease in velocity, which is to say for the increase in the stock of money per unit of output that the public has wished to hold as its real per capita income rose. To judge from this evidence, a rate of increase of 3 to 5% per year might be expected to correspond with a roughly stable price level for this particular concept of money. . . .
>
> As with the definition, the particular rate of increase adopted seems to me less important than the adoption of a fixed rate provided only that the rate is somewhere in the range suggested and that it is adapted to the definition of money. A rate that turned out to be somewhat too high would mean a mild secular price fall. Neither, it seems to me, would be serious. What is seriously disturbing to economic stability are rapid and sizeable fluctuations in prices, not mild and steady secular movements in either direction. A fixed rate of increase in the stock of money would almost certainly rule out mild cyclical or secular fluctuations, and it would give a firm basis for long range planning on the part of the public.
>
> . . . There is little to be said in theory for the rule that the money supply should grow at a constant rate. The case for it is entirely that it would work in practice. There are persuasive theoretical grounds for desiring to vary the rate of growth to offset other

factors. The difficulty is that, in practice, we do not know when to do so and by how much. In practice, therefore, deviations from the simple rule have been destabilizing rather than the reverse.

(Friedman, 1959)[5]

16.1.3 The *laissez-faire* rule of the modern classical and new classical approaches[6]

The modern classical and the new classical schools with their assumptions of rational expectations and continuous clearing of all markets, including the labour market, argue that the labour market operates at full employment and the commodity market produces the full employment output. Therefore, there is never a scope or need for monetary policy. An expansion of the money supply could at best only increase prices and nominal national income but not real national income or employment. If there are any effects on output and employment, these are through misperceptions of price-level increases as relative price increases. But such errors in perceptions are short-lived so that the expansionary monetary policy will not produce any significant real benefits or not do so for a significant period of time. This conclusion also applies to fiscal policy. Hence, the modern classical and new classical schools argue that the authorities should leave the economy alone (*laissez faire*) as far as monetary and fiscal policies are concerned.

Further, many modern classical and new classical economists argue that since inflation increases uncertainty in the economy, which handicaps planning and investment for the future, the monetary authorities should aim at maintaining price stability. Therefore, they recommend that the major role of monetary policy should be to maintain a tight control over the money supply so that changes in it do not contribute to inflation. There is basically no other role assigned to monetary policy by this school. This economic philosophy won over many central banks in the late 1980s and 1990s.

16.2 THE LUCAS–SARGENT–WALLACE (LSW) MODEL

The Sargent–Wallace model (1976) and its variations represent the most commonly used format for deriving the implications of the neoclassical and modern classical models and testing them. It explicitly specifies the markets for commodities and money, with the assumption of equilibrium in these markets. However, the labour market is not explicitly modelled but is replaced, in conjunction with the production function, by the Lucas supply function. This model is presented in the following. Since it incorporates the Lucas supply function, we refer to it as the Lucas–Sargent–Wallace model.

16.2.1 The Lucas–Sargent–Wallace model with rational expectations

For our presentation of this model, we specify the change in the supply of output by stating the expectational error-based Lucas supply rule[7] as:

$$Dy_t^s = \alpha Dy_{t-1} + \beta(p_t - p_t^e) + \mu_t \quad \alpha, \beta > 0 \tag{1}$$

where all lower-case variables are in *logs*, the superscripts *s* and *d* stand, respectively, for supply and demand, and:

y output
y^f full employment output
Dy_t deviation of output in period t from its full employment level $(= y_t - y_t^f)$
p price level

p^e expected price level, with expectations formed one period earlier

μ random term

Note that Dy is the deviation from full employment output and not the previous period's output; μ and the other random terms in this chapter have a zero expected value and are independent of the other variables in the model. Equation (1) differs from the Lucas supply rule derived in Chapter 15 by including a lagged term in output, with $\alpha > 0$. This is done to capture the serial correlation of output over time in real-world economies. It can be explained by adducing adjustment costs for employment, so that the marginal product of labour depends on both current and last period's output.[8] Further, in (1), output can differ from its full employment level due to last period's lack of full employment. Equation (1) also allows the full employment output to change between periods. As seen in Chapter 15, the dependence of y_t^s on $(p_t - p_t^e)$ can be justified through the expectations augmented Phillips curve with nominal wages fixed for the duration of the labour contract or Lucas's island parable with nominal wages being fully flexible but with imperfect information about the price level and with expectational errors in perceived relative prices.[9]

The demand for output is specified as:

$$y_t^d = \theta(m_t - p_t) + \eta_t \quad \theta > 0 \tag{2}$$

where:

y^d aggregate demand

m nominal money supply

η random term

Equation (2) represents the aggregate demand function and is a reduced-form relationship derived from the IS–LM relationships. It ignores fiscal policy for one of two reasons. One is that the effects of monetary and fiscal expansions in the IS–LM models are similar, so that keeping only one policy variable simplifies the model. In this sense, fiscal policy does influence aggregate demand and its stance is proxied in (2) through the term in m_t. The alternative reason is that the new classical model with Barro's Ricardian equivalence theorem, as presented in Chapter 13 above, implies that fiscal deficits do not change aggregate demand. Only money supply increases do so, with the result that (2) becomes the accurate representation of the aggregate demand function, irrespective of the fiscal policy stance.

Equation (2) differs from the aggregate demand function in Lucas's model in Chapter 15 by making explicit the role of the nominal money supply in the determination of aggregate demand. But it also necessitates the specification of the money supply function, which is done by the monetary policy rule:

$$m_t = m_0 + \gamma Dy_{t-1} + \xi_t \quad \gamma < 0 \tag{3}$$

Equation (3) makes the plausible assumption that the monetary authority increases the money supply if $Dy_{t-1} < 0$, i.e. if output last period was below the full employment level.

The equilibrium condition for the commodity market is,

$$y_t = y_t^d = y_t^s \tag{4}$$

which also translates to:

$$Dy_t = Dy_t^d = Dy_t^s$$

The above model has to be supplemented by an expectations hypothesis. Assuming the rational expectations hypothesis (REH), we have:

$$p_t^e = Ep_t \tag{5}$$

where Ep_t represents the expected price conditional on information available in $t - 1$. In particular, p_{t-1} is part of this information set.

The complete LSW model consists of equations (1) to (5). It is:

$$Dy_t^s = \alpha Dy_{t-1} + \beta(p_t - p_t^e) + \mu_t, \quad \alpha, \beta > 0 \tag{1}$$

$$y_t^d = \theta(m_t - p_t) + \eta_t, \quad \theta > 0 \tag{2}$$

$$m_t = m_0 + \gamma Dy_{t-1} + \xi_t, \quad \gamma < 0 \tag{3}$$

$$y_t = y_t^d = y_t^s \tag{4}$$

$$p_t^e = Ep_t \tag{5}$$

The basic question we wish to investigate within this model is whether monetary policy can be manipulated to increase output. More explicitly, we want to investigate if there are particular values of m_0 and γ in (3) which optimize y_t. To answer this, we need to derive the reduced-form equation for y_t.

From (1), (4) and (5), and taking the expectation of y_t, we have:

$$\begin{aligned}
EDy_t &= \alpha EDy_{t-1} + \beta[Ep_t - E(Ep_t)] + E\mu_t \\
&= \alpha Dy_{t-1}
\end{aligned} \tag{6}$$

Substituting (4) in (2) and taking its expectation, with $E\eta_t = 0$, gives,

$$\begin{aligned}
Ey_t &= \theta(Em_t - Ep_t) + E\eta_t \\
&= \theta(Em_t - Ep_t)
\end{aligned} \tag{7}$$

Subtracting (7) from (2) yields:

$$y_t - Ey_t = \theta(m_t - Em_t) - \theta(p_t - Ep_t) + \eta_t \tag{8}$$

Subtracting y_t^f from both sides, we get:

$$Dy_t = EDy_t + \theta(m_t - Em_t) - \theta(p_t - Ep_t) + \eta_t \tag{8'}$$

where, from (3),

$$Em_t = m_0 + \gamma Dy_{t-1} \tag{9}$$

so that:

$$m_t - Em_t = \xi_t \tag{10}$$

From (1), (4) and (5),

$$p_t - Ep_t = (1/\beta)(Dy_t - \alpha Dy_{t-1}) - (1/\beta)\mu_t \tag{11}$$

In (8′), replacing the relevant terms on the right-hand side from (6), (10) and (11) gives,

$$Dy_t = \alpha Dy_{t-1} + \frac{\theta\mu_t + \beta\theta\xi_t + \beta\eta_t}{\beta + \theta} \tag{12}$$

$$= \alpha Dy_{t-1} + \psi_t$$

where:

$$\psi_t = \frac{\theta\mu_t + \beta\theta\xi_t + \beta\eta_t}{\beta + \theta} \tag{13}$$

The ineffectiveness proposition of the LSW model for monetary policy

Since neither of the systematic policy parameters m_0 and γ occur in (12), the authorities cannot use systematic monetary policy to change y_t. Since ξ_t is in (12), errors in predicting money supply do affect y_t but if the authorities were to increase such errors, it would only increase the variance of y_t, without constituting a sensible policy. There is, therefore, no optimal monetary policy in this model. Non-random policy does not have any long-run or even short-run effects on real output: it can neither cause nor improve nor worsen booms or recessions. These results are similar to those derived from the Lucas model in Chapter 15. The implication of the futility of systematic money supply changes to alter output – and, by implication, employment and unemployment – is known as the 'ineffectiveness of demand policies' or the 'demand policy irrelevance' result. Note that, just as systematic money supply changes can alter aggregate demand but not output and employment, systematic exogenous increases in investment, consumption, net exports, etc., also cannot change output and employment by virtue of their impact on aggregate demand. But their random components can do so.

The above model does not justify Keynesian policy recommendations on the use of monetary policy to reduce the deviations from full employment output. However, this is understandable since the model is not a Keynesian one to start with. In particular, its supply equation (1) is the Lucas supply rule which embodies, under rational expectations, the neutrality of systematic changes in the money supply.

The above model can also be used to evaluate Milton Friedman's recommendation of a constant money supply by setting $\gamma = 0$ in (3) for the money supply rule. Since γ does not occur in (12), such a policy is neither better nor worse than one with another value of γ. However, random and, therefore, unanticipated variations in the money supply produce random variations in output. This is consistent with Friedman's call for a constant and publicly known money growth rate, with the particular rate being less important than eliminating unanticipated variations in it.

The price level in the LSW model

The reduced form for p_t for this model is obtained by substituting (12)[10] in (2). This gives,

$$p_t = m_t - \frac{1}{\theta} y_t^f - \frac{\alpha}{\theta} Dy_{t-1} - \frac{1}{\theta} \psi_t + \frac{1}{\theta} \eta_t \tag{13}$$

Equation (13) implies that $\partial p_t/\partial m_t = 1$. Hence, since both variables are in logs, prices rise proportionately with the overall increase in the nominal money supply, whether it is due to the systematic factors γ and m_0 or the random component ξ_t.

To find p_t^e, since $p_t^e = E(p_t)$, taking the rational expectation of (13) implies that:

$$p_t^e = E(m_t) - (1/\theta)y_t^f - (\alpha/\theta)Dy_{t-1} \qquad (14)$$

From (14) and (9),

$$p_t^e = m_0 - (1/\theta)y_t^f + \{\gamma - (\alpha/\theta)\}Dy_{t-1} \qquad (14')$$

In (14) and (14'), $\partial p_t^e/\partial Em_t = 1$, so that the expected price level rises proportionately in the same period with the *systematic* component of the nominal money supply, and responds to the policy parameters γ and m_0 but not to the random part ξ_t of the money supply. Hence, systematic money supply increases and systematic demand increases proportionately change both the price level *and* the expected price level but do not cause an output change, while random changes in the money supply change the price level and output but not the expected price level.

The invariance of output to systematic monetary policy in this model should not come as a surprise: by equation (1), output can respond to demand changes only if there are errors in price expectations and the assumption of rational expectations in (5) rules out the possibility that systematic policy can induce such errors. Dispensing with either of these assumptions is likely to change the policy invariance result. We will examine the Keynesian form of (1) later.

The diagrammatic analysis of output and the price level in the LSW model

The diagrammatic representation of this model is shown in Figure 16.1. From (2), the aggregate demand curve AD has a negative slope and shifts to the right to AD' with a monetary expansion. From (1), the (short-run) aggregate supply curve SAS has a positive slope and shifts to the left to SAS' with an increase in the *expected* price level. Since the latter, from (14), increases proportionately with a policy-induced monetary expansion, such a monetary expansion results in proportionate shifts of both curves, and the economy goes directly from point *a* to point *c*, without an intermediate increase in output. However, a random increase in the money supply cannot be anticipated, so that the expected price level does not increase due to it and the supply curve does not shift from SAS. But the demand

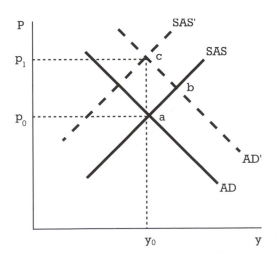

Figure 16.1

16.2.2 The LSW model with static expectations

To consider this model with a change from the REH to static expectations, let:

$$p_t^e = p_{t-1} \tag{15}$$

Substitute (15) in (1) to eliminate p_t^e. This brings p_{t-1} into the equation. Solve (2) for p_t and derive $(p_t - p_{t-1})$. Substitute the result in (1) and (12). Setting $\{1/(1 + \beta/\theta)$ equal to λ, we have:

$$Dy_t = -(\beta/\theta)\lambda(y_t^f - y_{t-1}^f) + (\alpha + \beta/\theta)\lambda Dy_{t-1} + \beta\lambda(m_t - m_{t-1}) + \beta\lambda/\theta(\eta_t - \eta_{t-1}) + \lambda\mu_t \tag{16}$$

Equations (16) and (3) yield the reduced form for y_t as:

$$Dy_t = -(\beta/\theta)\lambda(y_t^f - y_{t-1}^f) + (\alpha + \beta/\theta)\lambda Dy_{t-1} + \beta\lambda\gamma(Dy_{t-1} - Dy_{t-2})$$
$$+ \beta\lambda(\xi_t - \xi_{t-1}) + \beta\lambda/\theta(\eta_t - \eta_{t-1}) + \lambda\mu_t \tag{17}$$

where Dy_{t-2} occurs because lagged static expectations bring in p_{t-1} which depends on m_{t-1} which in turn depends on Dy_{t-2}. From (16), current output in the case of static expectations does depend on changes in the money supply. From (17), current output depends on the monetary policy parameter γ and upon the current and last period's random fluctuations in the demand and supply of commodities and in money supply.

In (17), since Dy_t depends upon the monetary policy parameter γ, the monetary authority can set the latter's value to achieve its objectives. To illustrate, if the objective is to set the systematic component of Dy_t in (17) at zero in order to eliminate the non-random variation in output, the policy would be to choose γ such that:

$$-(\beta/\theta)\lambda(y_t^f - y_{t-1}^f) + (\alpha + \beta/\theta)\lambda Dy_{t-1} + \beta\lambda\gamma(Dy_{t-1} - Dy_{t-2}) = 0$$

which would give the value of Dy_t as:

$$Dy_t = \beta\lambda(\xi_t - \xi_{t-1}) + \beta\lambda/\theta(\eta_t - \eta_{t-1}) + \lambda\mu_t \tag{18}$$

so that the effects of Dy_{t-1} and Dy_{t-2} on y_t will be eliminated by the optimal monetary policy and there would not occur *any* non-random changes in output.

16.2.3 A compact form of the LSW model

Since the price level is a function of the money supply and the expected price level is a function of the expected money supply, the above model with rational expectations is often replaced by the following more compact one.

Lucas supply rule:

$$Dy_t = \alpha Dy_{t-1} + \beta(m_t - m_t^e) + \mu_t \quad \alpha, \beta > 0 \tag{19}$$

Money supply rule:

$$m_t = m_0 + \gamma Dy_{t-1} + \xi_t, \quad \gamma < 0 \tag{20}$$

Rational expectations:

$$m_t^e = Em_t \tag{21}$$

Note that the assumption of equilibrium in the commodity market has already been incorporated in (19). From (20) and (21),

$$m_t - m_t^e = \xi_t \tag{22}$$

Hence, from (19) and (22),

$$Dy_t = \alpha Dy_{t-1} + \beta \xi_t + \mu_t \tag{23}$$

where Dy_t is again independent of the systematic monetary policy parameters m_0 and γ, so that changes in these parameters will not change y_t. Hence, the policy invariance result also holds in this model.

For another – though misleading – pattern of derivation in the above model, we have from (20) and (21),

$$Em_t = m_0 + \gamma Dy_{t-1} \tag{24}$$

so that from (19) and (24),

$$Dy_t = \alpha Dy_{t-1} + \beta m_t - \beta(m_0 + \gamma Dy_{t-1}) + \mu_t$$
$$= (\alpha - \beta\gamma)Dy_{t-1} - \beta m_0 + \beta m_t + \mu_t \tag{25}$$

In (25), Dy_t depends upon the policy parameters m_0 and γ, so that we get the impression that output will depend upon systematic monetary change. However, this would be erroneous since substituting (20) in (25) to eliminate m_t again gives (23) which establishes the policy irrelevance result.

16.3 THE LUCAS CRITIQUE IN THE LUCAS–SARGENT–WALLACE MODEL

16.3.1 The Lucas critique in the Lucas–Sargent–Wallace model with rational expectations

As explained in Chapter 15, the Lucas critique applies when the coefficients of an equation are not invariant to a change in policy. To check on its applicability in the model made up by equations (19) to (21), restate (25) compactly as:

$$y_t = a_0 + a_1 y_{t-1} + a_2 m_t + \mu_t \tag{26}$$

where $a_0 = y_t^f - (\alpha - \beta\gamma)y_{t-1}^f - \beta m_0$, $a_1 = (\alpha - \beta\gamma)$, $a_2 = \beta$. If (26) is estimated, it would yield the estimated values of a_1 and a_2 as $\hat{a}_1$ and $\hat{a}_2$. If $\hat{a}_2 > 0$, it would be tempting to conclude from (25) that the authorities could increase money supply to increase output. However, as we have shown earlier in section 16.2.1, this would not be a valid conclusion. A policy change in the money supply would mean a shift in the values of m_0 and/or γ. But as these shift, a_1 and a_2 in (26) would shift, as a glance at (25), of which (26) is only the compact form, shows. Hence, it cannot be assumed that a_1 and a_2 are invariant to a policy change and the Lucas critique applies to (26), so that (26) cannot be used as a tradeoff for policy formulation. Further, it cannot be used for regression estimates across policy regimes since such estimation assumes constant parameters.[12]

16.3.2 The Lucas critique in the LSW with static expectations

Suppose the model is made up of (19), (20) and static expectations such that:

$$m_t^e = m_{t-1} \tag{27}$$

Equations (19), (20) and (27) imply that:

$$Dy_t = \beta m_0 + (\alpha + \beta\gamma)Dy_{t-1} - \beta m_{t-1} + \beta\xi_t + \mu_t \tag{28}$$

where the constant term and the coefficient of Dy_{t-1} depend upon the policy parameters m_0 and γ, so that the Lucas critique will also apply to estimations of (28).

However, if we do not assume the money supply rule (20) but have a model composed only of (19) and (27), the implied equation is:

$$y_t = y_t^f - \alpha y_{t-1}^f + \alpha y_{t-1} + \beta m_t - \beta m_{t-1} + \mu_t \tag{29}$$

where the coefficients do not depend on the policy parameters m_0 and γ, so that the Lucas critique does not apply to estimates of (29). Hence, the Lucas critique does not always apply. Whether it applies or not to an estimating equation depends upon the underlying structural model: it will apply if the model is a Lucas–Sargent–Wallace one, including a money supply rule of the form (20), but may not necessarily apply in the context of other models.

Note that the constant term in (29) is $[y_t^f - \alpha y_{t-1}^f]$ which shifts with the supply factors of the economy.

16.4 POLICY IRRELEVANCE WITH A PSEUDO-KEYNESIAN SUPPLY FUNCTION AND THE LUCAS CRITIQUE

Adapting the Lucas supply function (19) to a pseudo-Keynesian format by replacing the unanticipated money supply $(m_t - m_t^e)$ by the total money supply m_t gives:

$$Dy_t = \alpha Dy_{t-1} + \beta m_t + \mu_t \quad \alpha, \beta > 0 \tag{30}$$

where the definitions of the symbols are as given earlier; β is the money multiplier for any changes in the money supply. As a reminder, note that the lower-case letters are logs of variables and D signifies the deviation from the full employment level and not a change from the previous period's level.

Equation (30) is a Keynesian form of the Lucas supply function since it allows both anticipated and unanticipated money supply changes to affect output. Note that, in the Keynesian context, the dependence of y_t on y_{t-1} occurs since Keynesian models allow for wage contracts longer than one period as well as the gradual adjustment of output to shocks. As argued in Chapter 14, the limitation of (30) to represent Keynesian ideas is that, for this school, the effect of money supply changes on output depends upon the state of the economy and the degree of involuntary unemployment, while the monetary expansion would be without any effect on output in the limiting case of full employment. β in true

Keynesian models would properly not be a constant but would be a function of the deviation of output from full employment level. However, Sargent and Wallace (1976) proposed (30) as the Keynesian reduced-form equation and it is frequently used as such. We will use it below for this reason, but have added, as in Chapters 14 and 15, the qualification 'pseudo' as a reminder to keep the above caveat in mind.

If we specify the complete model as (20) and (30), we find that:

$$Dy_t = (\alpha + \beta\gamma)Dy_{t-1} + \beta m_0 + \mu_t + \beta\xi_t \tag{31}$$

where Dy_t depends upon the policy parameters m_0 and γ, which can be used to achieve the desired objectives with respect to y_t, and upon the money multiplier β, as well as on the previous period's deviation from full employment output.

Equation (30) is not an appealing format for the Keynesian supply function. A better format seems to be one where the deviation of output from its full employment level depends not on the money supply but on its change. The supply function consistent with this is:

$$Dy_t = \alpha Dy_{t-1} + \beta(m_t - m_{t-1}) + \mu_t \quad \alpha, \beta > 0 \tag{30'}$$

The money supply rule (20) can be rewritten as:

$$m_t - m_{t-1} = \gamma(y_{t-1} - y_{t-2}) - \gamma(y_{t-1}^f - y_{t-2}^f) + (\xi_t - \xi_{t-1}) \quad \gamma < 0 \tag{20'}$$

where $\gamma < 0$, so that the monetary authority decreases the money supply if the actual output rose last period and increases it if there was a rise in the full employment output.

Equations (30') and (20') yield:

$$Dy_t = \alpha Dy_{t-1} + \beta\gamma(y_{t-1} - y_{t-2}) - \beta\gamma(y_{t-1}^f - y_{t-2}^f) + \mu_t + \beta(\xi_t - \xi_{t-1}) \quad \beta\gamma < 0 \tag{31'}$$

which implies that the monetary authority can change its policy parameter γ to affect output deviations from full employment.

Therefore, policy irrelevance does not occur in these pseudo-Keynesian models, irrespective of any assumption on the rationality of expectations. However, the Lucas critique will still apply since the coefficient of y_{t-1} in (31), and possibly its constant term as in (31'), will depend on the policy parameters.

Chapter 14 presented a Keynesian model with a Phillips curve instead of the Lucas supply function or its modified forms used above. Such a model would also maintain the relevance of monetary policy in changing output.

16.5 MONETARY POLICY RULES[13]

A monetary policy rule is one that forces the policy maker to follow the same specific function, with given values of the parameters, for setting the money supply in each period. Once the money supply function and its parameters are established, each period's money supply is determined by this function and the evolution of exogenous and predetermined variables in it, so that one could dispense with the monetary authority for the purposes of determining the money supply in each period. By comparison, discretionary policy would be one that does not bind the policy maker to abide by a pre-set money supply function.

An example of a *money supply rule* (3) is:

$$m_t = m_0 + \gamma y_{t-1} \tag{32}$$

Another example of it would be the simpler rule where $\gamma = 0$, so that $m_t = m_0$,[14] as suggested by Milton Friedman for an economy without growth. As compared with the Friedman rule,

(32) for $\gamma > 0$ implies that money supply would vary between periods. Some economists would consider this as a discretionary policy. However, since discretionary policy is associated with the Keynesian school and that school generally does not recommend that the monetary authority should be bound across periods by a set rule but have discretion in a broad sense, we define discretionary policy as one where the authorities can shift the money supply rule as they think fit. Under this definition, (32) – followed across periods – is not discretionary policy. Both it and Friedman's rules are examples of policy rules, with the latter being merely a simpler form.

Since policy irrelevance holds in the Lucas–Sargent–Wallace version of the neoclassical model, the issues of policy rules versus discretion cannot be properly examined in this model. Therefore, these issues will be examined in the context of the pseudo-Keynesian model using (30). For simplifications in this section, we will replace Dy by y in the output supply and money supply functions and assume, as in (32), that the monetary authority can control the money supply precisely, so that the random term is dropped from it.

We wish to examine optimal monetary policies. To define an optimal policy, we have to specify the policy maker's objectives. In the context of the Keynesian approach, the plausible objectives would be to get the expected value of output equal to full employment output y^f and to minimize the experienced variance of output. Taking the full employment output to be unchanged over time, the former is the requirement that $Ey_t = Ey_{t-1} = Ey = y^f$. These objectives make sense in the context of the Keynesian approach. However, if the model were the Lucas–Sargent–Wallace one, with output invariant to systematic monetary policy, the more plausible objectives would be to keep the expected change in the price level as zero and to minimize the variance of prices. This issue is not explored in this chapter and is left to the interested reader to pursue.

16.5.1 The optimal Keynesian policy rule with feedback

Let the complete structure of the economy and policy be specified by:

$$y_t = \alpha y_{t-1} + \beta m_t + \mu_t \quad \alpha, \beta > 0 \tag{30''}$$

$$m_t = m_0 + \gamma y_{t-1} \quad \gamma < 0 \tag{32}$$

Note the differences due to simplification between (30'') and (32) and the corresponding earlier functional forms (19) and (20). Equations (30'') and (32) imply that:

$$y_t = \beta m_0 + (\alpha + \beta\gamma)y_{t-1} + \mu_t \tag{33}$$

Further, assume that the monetary authority wants to follow an optimal policy rule of the feedback type as in (32) with m_0 and γ set optimally to achieve: (i) the expected value of y as y^f in each period; and (ii) to minimize the variance of output.

Taking the expectation of (33),

$$Ey_t = \beta m_0 + (\alpha + \beta\gamma)Ey_{t-1} + E\mu_t \tag{34}$$

Since $Ey_t = Ey_{t-1} = y^f$ and $E\mu_t = 0$ as a policy objective, (34) implies that:

$$E(y_t) = y^f = \beta m_0/(1 - \alpha - \beta\gamma) \tag{35}$$

From (33), since the variance of m_0 is zero and y_{t-1} and μ_t are independent of each other, the variance of output is given by:

$$\sigma_y^2 = (\alpha + \beta\gamma)^2\sigma_y^2 + \sigma_\mu^2 \tag{36}$$

where σ_j^2 is the variance of the subscripted variable j. Hence,

$$\sigma_y^2 = \sigma_\mu^2/[1 - (\alpha + \beta\gamma)^2] \tag{37}$$

For the policy maker to minimize (37) by choosing an appropriate value of the policy parameter γ, the first-order condition is that:

$$\partial\sigma_y^2/\partial\gamma = \sigma_\mu^2 [1 - (\alpha + \beta\gamma)^2]^{-2}\{-2(\alpha + \beta\gamma)\} \cdot \beta = 0 \tag{38}$$

which, for $\beta \neq 0$, requires that $\alpha + \beta\gamma = 0$, so that the optimal policy is to set:

$$\gamma = -\alpha/\beta \tag{39}$$

Substituting (39) in (34) gives,

$$y^f = \beta m_0 \tag{40}$$

which implies that,

$$m_0 = (1/\beta)y^f \tag{41}$$

Hence, the optimal Keynesian policy rule – the 'control rule' – from (32), (39) and (41) is:

$$m_t = (1/\beta)y^f - (\alpha/\beta)y_{t-1} \tag{42}$$

If this policy is followed, (30″) and (42) imply that output would be:

$$y_t = y^f + \mu_t \tag{43}$$

and its variance would be:

$$\sigma_y^2 = \sigma_\mu^2 \tag{44}$$

That is, the monetary authority will achieve y^f but with an uncontrollable random variance around it.

16.5.2 Milton Friedman's policy rules without feedback

As discussed earlier, Friedman's recommended policy rule for an economy without growth was to maintain a constant money supply. That is, the Friedman policy rule is to set:

$$m_t = m_0 \tag{45}$$

Equation (45) allows consideration of the two policy rules in (i) and (ii) below.

(i) Friedman's simple policy rule

In this case, m_0 is set at an *arbitrary* level, as Friedman had suggested. With m_t set arbitrarily at m_0, we have from (30) and (45),

$$y_t = \alpha y_{t-1} + \beta m_0 + \mu_t \tag{46}$$

which neither maximizes the expected level of output nor minimizes its variance, as (43) does, so that, in this model, Friedman's policy rule is inferior to an optimal policy control rule such as (39) and (41).

(ii) Friedman's optimal policy rule

In this case, m_t is to be set at an optimal level, given the objectives of the policy maker to achieve $Ey_t = y^f$ and to minimize σ_y^2. However, it cannot achieve both objectives, so that we will assume that m_t is set in order to achieve $Ey_t = y^f$ for all t. Hence, taking the expectation of (33) and setting $Ey_t = Ey_{t-1} = y^f$, with $E\mu_t = 0$, yields:

$$m_t = m_0 = [(1 - \alpha - \beta\gamma)/\beta]y^f \tag{47}$$

Substituting (47) in (33):

$$y_t = (1 - \alpha - \beta\gamma)y^f + (\alpha + \beta\gamma)y_{t-1} + \mu_t \tag{48}$$

Since the variance of y^f is zero, and y_{t-1} and μ_t are independent of each other, (48) implies that,

$$\sigma_y^2 = (\alpha + \beta\gamma)^2\sigma_y^2 + \sigma_\mu^2$$

so that,

$$\sigma_y^2 = (\sigma_\mu^2/[1 - (\alpha + \beta\gamma)^2] \quad 1 - (\alpha + \beta\gamma)^2 < 1 \tag{49}$$

$$> \sigma_\mu^2$$

Equation (47) specifies the optimal value of the money supply under an optimal Friedman policy and ensures that $Ey_t = y^f$. This level of output will be greater than that in (46) so that the optimal Friedman policy rule is preferable to the standard Friedman policy rule. However, comparing (44) for the optimal Keynesian policy rule and (49) for the Friedman optimal policy rule, the variance of output is greater under the latter since it does not provide a policy parameter to control this variance. Hence, even Friedman's optimal policy rule is inferior to the Keynesian one since the latter allows more control mechanisms (i.e., over both m_0 and γ) to the monetary authority.

In the preceding models, with the uncertainty of output and the normal distribution of the disturbance terms, there are two policy targets: expected value and variance. Friedman's optimal policy rule possesses at most only one policy instrument (m_0), while the control policy provides two instruments (m_0 and γ), to address the two targets, so that the former performs worse than the latter. We can extend this conclusion to adduce the general rule that more control mechanisms in the hands of the monetary authority for influencing the economy are preferable to less, especially under uncertainty. If any prove to be superfluous to the achievement of the authority's objectives, they need not be pursued.[15]

The preceding discussion implies that Friedman's recommendations on monetary policy are inferior to optimal policy rules. However, this implication is in the context of a model that does not represent Friedman's assessment of the relevant model of the economy. In particular, the former assumes in its supply function (26) that there does not exist a lag in the effect of money supply changes: all monetary effects in it are contemporaneous. Even if this model were modified to introduce a lag, such a modification would still not make it consistent with Friedman's notions of the relevant model. To Friedman, as shown in the next section, money supply changes had their impact on nominal income, let alone real output, with a long and variable lag. It is the length and variability of this lag that makes the pursuit of monetary policy hazardous, and justifies Friedman's recommended policy. The Lucas–Sargent–Wallace model does not incorporate such a lag pattern, so that its use to represent Friedman's model and policy prescriptions is not strictly appropriate. In order to derive policy prescriptions for the real world, it needs to be determined first whether or not there is a long and variable lag in the impact of money supply changes on real output. There is substantial consensus that this lag in many developed economies is often six quarters or more. There is also consensus that the length of this lag does vary over the cycle. But there is little consensus that its variability is so severe that the pursuit of monetary policy by central banks is more harmful than beneficial for the economy. However, most central banks do choose to pursue monetary policy, as the discussions in the chapters on the central bank have already shown.

The following section examines the duration of the lag in the effect of monetary policy.

16.6 LAGS IN THE EFFECTS OF MONETARY POLICY

The preceding models do not specify the duration of the period. Since they assume that monetary policy has its full impact on output and prices in the same period, the duration of the period must be such as to encompass all such effects within it. We cannot, therefore, arbitrarily take the duration to be a quarter or a year, but have to let the data for the given economy specify it. In particular, if there are long lags in the effect of the monetary policy on the economy, then the appropriate duration of the period in the Lucas–Sargent–Wallace model would be a long one, and the distinctiveness of its conclusions from those of the Keynesian school would become diluted. This section looks at the nature and the length of the lag in the effect of monetary policy on nominal national income.

The lags in the effect of monetary policy on national income can be classified into three types.[16]

(a) The inside lag

This is the lag from the time when corrective action is needed to the time when it is actually taken. It can be subdivided into a lag from the time when the need arose to the time when this need for corrective action was recognized and another lag from the time of recognition to the time when the corrective action is taken.

The inside lag operates because statistical data becomes available with a lag and because the economy is extremely diverse, with some sectors entering a cyclical decline while others are continuing to expand. There is in general no clear-cut moment of upturn or downturn in the economy so that any recognition of the need for action takes time. In developed economies, the inside lag is relatively short for monetary action, with average estimates of this lag ranging from no lag at all to a maximum one of six months. In any case, this lag is no longer for monetary than for fiscal policy.

(b) The intermediate lag

This lag operates from the time of action by the monetary authorities to the time when impact is felt on the money supply, interest rates and credit conditions in the economy.

In developed financial markets, the intermediate lag is likely to be very short for monetary policy since changes in the reserve base or reserve ratios have a rapid impact on the money supply and interest rates etc. The intermediate lag is likely to be quite long for fiscal policy.

(c) The outside lag

This lag operates from the time of impact on the intermediate variables to the time of impact on the target variables or goals.

The outside lag has been of major concern to economists as far as monetary policy is concerned. There is a considerable disagreement as to the length of this lag and a considerable amount of statistical work has been done on this topic.

Quantitative estimates of the outside lag of monetary policy were rare prior to 1960. Most economists took this lag to be reasonably short so that monetary policy could be effectively used for economic stabilization. The major challenge to this view came from the estimates of Friedman and Schwartz that showed that this lag was too long and variable for monetary policy to be useful for short-run stabilization. They pointed out that money stock changes precede the movements in national income so that the former must cause the latter and not the other way around. Consequently, they measured the outside lag as between the peaks and troughs in the rate of change of the money stock and that of national income, using the standard time-series data on *reference business cycles* published by the National Bureau of Economic Research (NBER). Friedman and Schwartz reported their findings for the USA as:

> We have found that, on the average of 18 cycles, peaks in the rate of change in the stock of money tend to precede peaks in general business by about 16 months and troughs in the rate of change in the stock of money precede troughs in general business by about 12 months. For individual cycles, the recorded lead has varied between 6 and 29 months at peaks and between 4 and 22 months at troughs.
>
> (Friedman, 1959, p. 87)

These findings ran counter to the intuitive judgement of most economists in the 1960s. They also implied that, given the average length of business cycles as approximately four years, an expansionary policy pursued in a recession would have its main impact in the following expansion and vice versa. Therefore, monetary policy would be destabilizing and should be avoided rather than pursued for stabilization purposes. The fact that these estimates fitted in conveniently with Friedman's general economic philosophy, which was opposed to discretionary monetary policy, provided another cause for scepticism about the Friedman and Schwartz findings.

Many economists, especially in the Keynesian tradition, questioned these findings on intuitive or statistical grounds. Among these was the moderation of the business cycles, and especially of recessions, during the 1950s and 1960s when contra-cyclical monetary and fiscal policies were being actively pursued, thereby implying a fairly fast rate of response of the economy to such policies.

Friedman and Schwartz had compared NBER turning points in national income with the turning points in the series for the *rate of growth* of the money stock. Their reason for this was that money is a stock while national income is a flow so that a uniformity of dimension requires comparison of the *rate of growth of money* (a flow), with *national income*, also a flow. Further, since the economy tends to anticipate the trend rate of growth in the money stock, only a change in its rate of growth should be compared with changes in national income.

However, economic theory generally relates the money supply directly to national income and Keynesian studies of the 1960s followed this procedure, rather than the Friedman and Schwartz one, of comparing either the *money supply variable* and *national income*, or their rates of change. Such comparison usually showed that the money supply and the level of aggregate output move more or less simultaneously over the business cycle, with a short lag of one or a few quarters.

The debate during the 1950s and 1960s was, therefore, between Friedman and his followers arguing for a *long and variable lag* and those in the Keynesian tradition arguing for a reasonably short lag. However, subsequent empirical evidence modified the earlier findings and generally reversed the position of the monetarists and the Keynesians on the question of the lag in monetary policy: the 1970s monetarists' findings from the reduced-form equations used by the St Louis School (Andersen and Jordan, 1968) showed the lag to be reasonably short, while the findings from large structural Keynesian models such as those of the Federal Reserve Board–MIT model showed a much longer lag.

Among the findings from the empirical studies during the 1960s and 1970s were that the estimates of the length of the lag in the effect of monetary policy depended significantly upon whether the model was estimated in a structural or a reduced form, and upon the specification of the monetary policy variable. In general, a structural model tends to give estimates with a longer lag than a reduced-form model. A structural model focuses on the paths and the intermediate variables through which monetary policy affects expenditures, so that the overall lag is broken down into a series of lags between the policy variables, the intermediate variables and the target variables. The sum total of such lags is often longer than the single lag estimated in a reduced-form model.

The average length of the estimated lag also depends significantly upon the monetary policy variable chosen. These are often chosen as either the money supply, the monetary base or as non-borrowed reserves. The 1970s monetarists preferred the first two of these variables on the grounds that they provided the most appropriate measures of the impact of monetary policy on the economy. Their critics contended that these variables were deficient because they reflected the effects of both policy and *non-policy* influences and hence did not provide reliable estimates of the monetary policy lag. The monetarists replied to this criticism that since the monetary authorities did have the power to offset the effects of all non-policy influences on the money supply or on the monetary base, it was the movements in the money supply and not the reasons for such movement that were important.[17]

During the 1980s, for the developed economies, the dominant view among monetary economists generally agreed with the shorter estimates of the lag: that monetary policy has most of its effect on national income within a year or five quarters. This view became common among both monetarists and Keynesians during the 1980s. However, some economists continued to subscribe to the view that the monetary policy lag was a relatively long one.

Finally, looking at the rational expectations view of the lags in the impact of monetary policy, this hypothesis is that any systematic policy is anticipated by the public. Therefore, there will not be a lag in the effects of a systematic monetary policy. A non-systematic or random policy cannot be anticipated and its impact could occur with a lag, but a rational policy maker would not pursue such a policy. Finally, if a shift in systematic policies induces errors in expectations, the shift in policy could impact with a lag but only until the nature of the shift is realized or the post-shift data becomes available. In general, the rational expectations adherents take this lag to be short in a developed economy with extensive and fast information on the monetary policy being actually pursued.

The variability over the business cycle of the length of the lag rarely gets tested, since using time-series data without differentiation over different cycles and between recessions and booms hides this information. Intuitively, the length of this lag would seem to depend upon the particular stage of the business cycle and past experience of monetary policy and inflation.

Most central banks believe that there does exist a very significant lag in the impact of changes in the monetary base on nominal income and this lag is longer than a year and possibly longer than even two years. Their pursuit of monetary policy in the presence of lags has already been discussed in Chapters 11 and 12.

16.7 LONG LAGS AND THE LUCAS–SARGENT–WALLACE MODEL

As discussed in the last section, few empirical studies have reported a lag of less than one year in the effect of monetary policy on aggregate nominal income, and many have reported much longer lags. Since the Lucas–Sargent–Wallace model assumes that this effect occurs within one period, this period has to be defined as being longer than a year, say six quarters. With this specification of the duration of the period, the Lucas–Sargent–Wallace model would not be able to generate any implications on the impact of systematic money supply on output within six quarters following a money supply change. But this is the period of most interest for the need and scope for active monetary policy in a demand-deficient economy, and is the sort of period for which Keynesians espouse the use of corrective discretionary monetary policy. This reasoning implies that the Keynesian analysis and recommendations are relevant for the impact or short-term analysis, while the classical one is relevant to a longer-term context in which all markets would have cleared. Unfortunately, empirical tests indicate that the validity of the rational expectations hypothesis – which is an integral part of the Lucas–Sargent–Wallace model – is more in the next one or two quarters than several quarters or years in the future. We are, therefore, left with plenty of scope for controversy on the impact of monetary policy, both at the theoretical and empirical levels, and also for plenty of scope for further theoretical and empirical research on this topic.

CONCLUSIONS

The real-world economy is beset with uncertainty. The objective probabilities of the possible outcomes in the future are not known and policy makers and economic analysts have serious differences of opinion on these probability distributions – including their mean and variance – for the next quarter, let alone a year or two hence. Further, there is considerable dispute even as to the underlying macroeconomic model of the economy: there are many schools of thought, with the classical and the Keynesians differing quite clearly even on the issue of whether anticipated money supply changes can alter real output, unemployment and other real variables in the economy. On the more specific question of the aggregate supply function for the economy, the classical propositions of the Lucas supply rule and the Friedman expectations augmented Phillips curve propose a relationship in which output is invariant to anticipated inflation and anticipated money supply, while the Keynesians assert its dependence on the latter in states with involuntary unemployment. Empirical studies have not resolved this issue, with many – both reduced-form and structural ones – supporting the Keynesian position. The monetary authorities even in the industrialized countries, let alone the developing economies, have to form their policies against this background of imperfect knowledge on the future of the economy and of the relevant economic model to apply to it.

The neutrality of money and rational expectations – the two main tenets of the modern classical or new classical macroeconomic analysis of the role of money in the economy – leave no scope for systematic monetary policy to influence output in the economy. Chapter 15 had already concluded in favour of rational expectations rather than static or adaptive expectations, so that the former was emphasized in this chapter, while the latter was only used for comparative purposes. However, Chapter 15 had also raised severe doubts about the validity of the neoclassical implication of the neutrality of money in the economy. These doubts were reflected in the analysis of this chapter by examining the scope for monetary policy in turn under the classical supply rule which asserts money neutrality, except with respect to expectational errors, and the pseudo-Keynesian supply rule, which does not do so.

This chapter's analysis using the Lucas supply rule showed that the monetary authorities cannot use systematic monetary policy to influence output and, by extension, any other real variables. Any use of such policy would only affect the price level and the nominal values of the real variables. It also reaffirmed the Lucas critique: with output as the dependent variable, the estimated coefficients of the monetary aggregates would shift as the money supply function shifts. It was also shown that in the model with the pseudo-Keynesian supply rule, money supply changes would affect real output and other variables, but the Lucas critique could still apply.

The Sargent–Wallace model with either the Lucas supply or the Keynesian one does not specify the duration of the period but assumes that the impact of any changes in the money supply on output and prices is completed within the 'period'. Therefore, the duration of this period cannot be specified arbitrarily but has to be specified by reference to the structure of the economy being studied. This duration is likely to differ between the developed and developing economies, as well as over the business cycle for any given economy, and will depend on the actual lag in the effect of monetary policy in the economy being studied.

This chapter has reviewed the ebb and flow of ideas over the past four decades on the length of the lag. However, this issue of the length of the lag in the effects of both anticipated and unanticipated monetary policies is still not settled. Rational expectations in the context of the developed economies with markets responding fast to news, implies that the lag should be short or virtually non-existent for systematic policies. However, most empirical studies do not confirm this. While reduced-form estimation tends to show lags of several (say two to six) quarters for this lag, structural model estimations tend to show lags lasting several years.[18] These lag lengths may have less to do with expectations than adjustment lags at various points occurring in the structure of the economy from the monetary base to the money supply and credit, to investments of various types, through the steps of the multiplier to aggregate demand and thence to the myriad prices and production of commodities. Each of these adjustment lags at each link in the chain may be short and optimal in terms of planning by the economic agents at that stage, yet consecutive or even overlapping lags can collectively add up to a considerable duration over the whole length of the chain. If the average length of the lag is long, its variability becomes an issue of concern. As we had concluded in Chapter 15, policy has to be forward-looking, anticipate future developments and take into account consumer and business confidence in the future state of the economy and therefore also upon the particular stage in the business cycle. This makes the pursuit of the appropriate policies problematical and the success of the actual policies followed at best uncertain and, at worst, destabilizing for the economy.

The profession's assessment on the neutrality of money and discretionary monetary policy

We leave the set of Chapters 13 to 16, the controversy on the neutrality of money and the advisability of pursuing discretionary monetary policy, with the following assessments from several distinguished economists.

In their summing up of the effect of monetary changes on output, Milton Friedman and Anna Schwartz (1963) wrote that:

On the non-neutrality of money:

> Three counterparts of such crucial experiments [of physical science] stand put in the monetary record since the establishment of the Federal Reserve System. On three occasions, the System deliberately took policy steps of major magnitude which cannot be regarded as necessary or inevitable economic consequences of contemporary changes in income and prices. Like the crucial experiments of the physical scientist, the results are so consistent and sharp as to leave little doubt about their interpretation. The dates are January–June 1920, October 1931, and July 1936–January 1937. These were three occasions . . . when the Reserve System engaged in acts of commission that were sharply restrictive . . . each was followed by sharp contractions in industrial production . . . declines within a twelve-month period of 30 per cent (1920), 24 per cent (1931), and 34 per cent (1937), respectively [pp. 688–89].

The magnitude of the real effects in these examples is remarkable. Lest it be thought that only monetary contractions have real effects, Friedman and Schwartz (1963, p. 690) also cited three cases where monetary expansions by the Federal Reserve System caused large increases in industrial production.

Laurence Ball and N. Gregory Mankiw (1994), two of the foremost Keynesians – or neo-Keynesians – at present, write:

On the non-neutrality of money:

> We believe that monetary policy affects real activity. The main reason for our belief is the evidence of history, especially the numerous episodes in which monetary contractions appear to cause recessions [p. 128]. . . . monetary contractions are a major source of U.S. business cycle [p. 129].

On the nineteenth-century classical model and Friedman's views on the neutrality of money:

The [pre-Keynes] classical economists never suggested that money was neutral in the short run [but did offer] the key insight . . . that money is neutral in the long run [p. 132]. [Further] Friedman and Schwartz's 1963 treatise, *A Monetary History of the United States*, identified a number of episodes in which the money supply contracted sharply. Economic activity declined after each of these shocks . . . [pp. 128–29]. Milton Friedman . . . was the economist who argued most forcefully [in 1974] that monetary policy is a frequent cause of economic fluctuations, and he never doubted that wages and prices adjust gradually [p. 132].

On the sources of the non-neutrality of money:

We believe that price stickiness is the best explanation for monetary non-neutrality . . . many prices change infrequently . . . [though] many [other] prices in the economy are quite flexible [p. 131]. Other economists, however, accept monetary non-neutrality but resist the assumption of sticky prices. They have been led to develop models of non-neutrality with flexible prices [pp. 134–35].

On the influence of monetary policy and the role of the central banks, Ball and Mankiw assert that:

The Fed is a powerful force for controlling the economy [p. 133]. Policymakers and the press believe that monetary policy can speed up or slow down real economic activity [p. 132].

How do these views of admitted Keynesians compare with those of Robert E. Lucas, Jr (1994), who is associated with the modern classical school and has been a major contributor to it?

On the variant neutrality and non-neutrality of money:

Sometimes, as in the U.S. Great Depression, reductions in money growth seem to have large effects on production and employment. Other times, as in the ends of the post-World War I European hyperinflations, large reductions in money growth seem to have been neutral, or nearly so. Observations like these seem to imply that a theoretical framework such as the Keynes–Hicks–Modigliani IS/LM model, in which a single multiplier is applied to all money movements regardless of their source or predictability, is inadequate for practical purposes [p. 153].

On the lack of adequate knowledge and absence of theories of the variant non-neutrality of money:

. . . little can be said to be firmly established about the importance and nature of the real effects of monetary instability, at least for the U.S. in the postwar period. Though it is widely agreed that we need economic theories that capture the non-neutral effects of money in an accurate and operational way, none of the many available candidates is without serious difficulties [1994, p. 153].

Macroeconomic models with realistic kinds of monetary non-neutralities do not yet exist [1994, pp. 153–54]. . . . anticipated and unanticipated changes in money growth have very different effects [1996, p. 679]. [However, on the models which attribute this non-neutrality to unanticipated or random changes in the price level, the evidence shows that] only small fractions of output variability can be accounted for by unexpected price movements. Though the evidence seems to show that monetary surprises have real effects, they do not seem to be transmitted through price increases, as in Lucas (1972). [1996, p. 679].

In the 'Nobel Lecture' (1996) on his receipt of the Nobel Prize in economics, Robert Lucas added that:

> In summary, the prediction that prices respond proportionately to changes in the long run, deduced by Hume in 1752 [and by many other theorists, by many different routes, since], has received ample – I would say decisive – confirmation, in data from many times and places. The observation that money changes induce output changes in the same direction receives confirmation in some data sets but is hard to see in others. Large-scale reductions in money growth can be associated with large-scale depressions or, if carried out in the form of a credible reform, with no depression at all [1996, p. 668].

Chapters 13 to 16 have mostly dealt with models that imply or embody either neutrality or non-neutrality of money, without implying neutrality under some conditions but not others, with the exception of the demand-deficient model. The latter model implies the neutrality of money for increases in the money supply in conditions of full employment but non-neutrality for decreases in it from this state, as well as non-neutrality for increases in the money supply in conditions of less than full employment. Further, this model implies that, when money is non-neutral, the monetary impact on output will not be linear. We can also agree with the views of Ball and Mankiw quoted above that there can be slow adjustment in prices and nominal wages for a variety of reasons, even though there may never be total rigidity, and accept that inflexibilities tend to gradually clear out over time. These inflexibilities may be more operative at some initial states of the economy than in others, under certain states of expectations than others and more for decreases in demand than for increases. We will add to these the dynamic response pattern posited by the Keynesians and discussed in Chapter 14. Given the variety of factors which introduce non-neutrality into the economy, the degree of monetary neutrality will depend upon the state of the economy and upon the expectations in it, so that we agree with Lucas's assessment that monetary non-neutrality can exist but will not always do so to the same degree and may not exist under certain circumstances.[19] Hence, the pursuit of monetary policy is at best an art rather than a science.

A central banker's opinions on the neutrality of money, lags and the art of monetary policy

What do central bankers who are the real-world practitioners of monetary policy in fact believe and do? In 1997, the central banks of both Canada and the USA had their declared objective as that of aggressively promoting price stability. Both used interest rates, rather than monetary aggregates, as their target and instrument variables. On the dynamics of their policies, a speech by the Governor of the Bank of Canada on 7 October 1997 expressed the stance of the Bank's policy as:

> To get the economy moving, the Bank has been pressing hard on the monetary accelerator. But once the economy picks up speed, just as with a car, you need to ease off gradually on the accelerator and steady your cruising speed at a safe level. If you press hard on the accelerator for too long, you will reach speeds that are unsafe. You risk losing control and getting into serious trouble. The same holds true for the economy. Too much monetary stimulus can lead to an exhilarating temporary burst of economic activity. But it will almost certainly also lead to inflation-related distortions that undermine both the expansion and the economy's efficiency over the longer term. The end-result, as we know

only too well from past experience, is high interest rates, punishing debt loads, recession, and higher unemployment.

A further complication is that it takes between a year to a year and a half for the economy to fully respond to changes in the degree of monetary stimulus . . . you want to look way ahead to see what is coming, and you want to take action early. . . . That is why monetary policy must focus on the future, rather than the present, and why the Bank must act in a forward-looking pre-emptive manner.

If we wait to act until the economy is going flat out and pressing hard on the limits of capacity to produce, we will have waited too long.

. . . it is the strength of the momentum of demand, and thus how quickly the economy approaches the limits of its capacity to meet that demand, that will determine the timing and extent of our [monetary stimulus].

(Gordon Thiessen, Governor of the Bank of Canada, 'Challenges Ahead for Monetary Policy'. *Remarks to the Vancouver Board of Trade*, 7 October 1997)

Several points in this account, by a central banker, of monetary policy and the perceptions about the Canadian economy are related to the material of this chapter. One is that the objective of price stability is really intended to achieve goals about real variables such as output, employment and economic efficiency. Another is that output and employment can be below the limits of the economy's capacity. A third point is that monetary policy can have real effects on the economy, so that the money supply is not neutral. A fourth one is the emphasis on the dynamics of the economy. On these dynamics, there are lags in the effects of monetary policy, and the period over which the effects occur is believed to be four to six quarters long, so that the appropriate policy has to look at least six quarters ahead. Further, while an expansion of the money supply will increase output and employment in conditions with unemployment significantly above its full employment level, a continued expansion of the money supply beyond the productive capacity of the economy can induce a future reduction in output and employment, so that the money multiplier for output over the business cycle is not constant, and not necessarily even non-negative.

Collectively, these assessments of economists from the Keynesian and classical traditions and of a central banker show a high degree of agreement that, in the short run, money can be non-neutral, and more likely to be non-neutral than neutral, except for anticipated monetary expansions in economies already at or over full employment. However, there is also broad agreement and substantial evidence that, in the long run, output growth is independent of money supply growth.[20] While these conclusions indicate much less divergence on the final conclusions than the formal models of the different schools convey, there is little agreement on the sources of the potential short-run non-neutrality. There can be several possible sources of non-neutrality, as discussed in the first part of these conclusions, and the reasons for and the extent of non-neutrality can differ at different times and in different countries.

SUMMARY OF CRITICAL CONCLUSIONS

- The Sargent–Wallace model incorporating the Lucas supply function and rational expectations, is often used as the compact form of the modern classical model for short-run macroeconomics. It implies the futility of systematic monetary policy to change output, unemployment, the real rate of interest and other real variables in the economy. Hence, its policy recommendation is that the central bank should not use changes in the money supply to attempt changes in output and unemployment in the economy.
- While a negative relationship between the rate of unemployment and the rate of inflation occurs in the Sargent–Wallace model, its coefficients are not invariant to a change in monetary policy. Therefore, while this relationship looks like a Phillips curve, it cannot be used as a tradeoff by the policy maker. The Lucas critique applies to it.

- The Sargent–Wallace model, with the Keynesian supply function replacing the Lucas supply function, does allow systematic monetary policy to change output and unemployment in the economy. The Lucas critique need not apply in this context.
- Friedman's rule for the growth rate of the money supply is sub-optimal in the context of the Sargent–Wallace model but this implication does not take account of Friedman's contention that the lags in the impact of monetary policy can be long and variable.
- Central bankers are convinced that the lags in the impact of monetary policy are quite long, often assessed as being six quarters to two years in length even in the developed economies.
- A great deal of controversy remains on the fundamental issues of monetary policy and especially on that of the neutrality of money.

review and discussion questions

1 Discuss the statement: allowing the central bank to pursue discretionary monetary policies is inferior to its being made to follow a pre-specified money supply rule.

2 What evidence would you need to establish whether or not money supply changes have been the main cause of changes in nominal income? What procedure can you use to determine the direction of causality between the changes in money and in income?

3 Specify the hypotheses on the natural rate of unemployment and the rational expectations hypothesis. Discuss the logical and historical relationship between them.

   Discuss for each concept whether disequilibrium in the economy is consistent with it or not. If it is, discuss the role and usefulness of monetary policy in this state.

4 Discuss the evolution of the 1970s monetarists' claim that 'only monetary policy is effective' to the doctrines of the modern classical school that 'no foreseen monetary policy is effective' and 'no systematic monetary policy is effective'. Would Friedman have subscribed to any of these propositions?

5 Inflation and unemployment are two crucial economic items of interest to the public. Is it possible to explain one without the other? Present at least one theory that explains each independently of the other and one theory that establishes their interdependence. Is there a genuine difference between these theories or do they merely represent a distinction between the impact and long-term effects of an exogenous change to their determinants?

6 Why do models with rational expectations have difficulty in explaining the persistence of output from its trend and unemployment from the natural rate? What are some of the reasons given for this persistence? If this persistence were incorporated in them, what would be their implications for the effectiveness of monetary policy: could activist monetary policy stabilize output and the unemployment rate? Discuss in the context of a specific model embodying such persistence.

7 Outline the development and current theoretical status of the tradeoff between the unemployment rate and the rate of inflation.

8 'It makes no difference whether government expenditures are financed by taxes or bonds.' Discuss a scenario in which this is valid and then provide at least two reasons why it may not hold.

9 Discuss the validity of the following statements: 'It makes no difference whether government expenditures are financed by money or bonds.' 'A fiscal deficit has a larger impact on aggregate demand if it is financed by money than if it is financed by bonds.'

10 'In the past seventy years, macroeconomic theory has come full circle. The classical view of the 1920s was discarded in the 1930s and 1940s by Keynes' theory but the latter, in turn, has been gradually eroded to the point that the dominant theory is again a form of the classical one.' Discuss.

11 Modern classical macroeconomics argues that anticipated monetary policy does not have real effects. The new classical macroeconomics argues that anticipated fiscal policy also does not have real effects. Adapt the Lucas–Sargent–Wallace model to explicitly incorporate both of these propositions. From this model, what would you conclude for the effects of (i) an anticipated bond-financed deficit, (ii) an anticipated money-financed deficit. Specify your procedure and estimating equations for testing the validity of your conclusions.

12 Consider an economy with the following structure:

Aggregate demand:

$$y_t = M_t - P_t + \mu_t \quad \text{(A quantity theory-type equation)}$$

Aggregate supply:

$$y_t = y_t^f + \gamma(P_t - P_t^e) + \eta_t$$

where the symbols have the usual meanings and are in logs; μ and η are random errors.

Expectations are formed in one of the following alternative ways:

(a) Rational expectations:

$$P_t^e = E_{t-1} P_t$$

(b) Adaptive expectations:

$$P_t^e - P_{t-1}^e = (1 - \lambda)(P_{t-1} - P_{t-1}^e)$$

(i) Given rational expectations, solve for P_t and y_t (in terms of the money supply and random shocks).

(ii) Given adaptive expectations, solve for P_t and y_t (in terms of the money supply, etc.).

(iii) For the two expectations hypotheses, derive the time patterns of the response of the price level to a unit change in the money supply.

(iv) For the two expectations hypotheses, derive the time pattern of the response of real output to a unit change in the money supply. Discuss the differences implied by the two hypotheses for the impact of monetary policy on both real output and prices.

13 Consider the following model:

Aggregate supply:

$$y_t = \gamma(P_t - E_{t-1} P_t) + \gamma(P_t - E_{t-2} P_t)$$

Aggregate demand:

$$y_t = M_t - P_t + \mu_t$$

$$\mu_t = \mu_{t-1} + \eta_t$$

where y, P and M have the usual meanings and are in logs; η is a serially uncorrelated error with mean zero and variance σ^2.

(i) How would you justify the above aggregate supply function and how does it differ from the Lucas one?

(ii) Suppose that the central bank can observe μ_{t-1} but not μ_t when it sets the money supply. Is there then a role for systematic monetary policy?

(iii) Given (ii), suppose that the central bank wants to set the money supply to minimize the variance $E_{t-1}(y_t - y^f)^2$ of output about its full employment level? What monetary policy would it follow?

(iv) If the policy in (iii) has always been followed, is there any way of using econometric evidence to differentiate between the pattern shown by this economy and one in which the economy had a Lucas supply function?

NOTES

1 The 1970s monetarists, as epitomized by the St Louis School, also accepted point (v) for the short run.

2 See also Chapters 2 and 13 on Friedman's related contributions.

3 To illustrate, take an extremely ill patient. Further, assume that the only available medicine is one which has a strong impact with an unknown lag, such that it will cure him if he is still ill at the moment of impact or kill him if he has already become well. In such circumstances, if the patient is expected to recover on his own, though after a debilitating and miserable experience, it may be better not to administer the medicine.

4 Price stability in the long run is often taken to require that the money supply grow at the same long-run growth rate as national output, though this assertion requires that the velocity of circulation of money remain constant. Under this assumption, a moderate degree of inflation, if considered desirable, would justify a slightly higher rate of growth in the money supply.

5 The above prescriptions for policy were repeated in Friedman (1968).

6 See Chapter 13 for our definitions of the modern classical and new classical schools.

7 We are subsuming the expectations augmented Phillips curve in the Lucas supply rule in this chapter.

8 Such a term is needed for neoclassical models since, in its absence, the deviations of output from full employment would depend only upon errors in expectations. Since the current neoclassical models also assume rational expectations in which the errors in expectations are random, (1) with rational expectations would imply that output variations over time would be only random, even though business cycles show serial correlation in output.

9 Lucas (1973) specifies that production takes place on isolated points called islands, the selling price on the island is known but prices on other islands are not known. The demand for labour is a function of the real wage rate in terms of the island price which on average in the aggregate for all islands equals the actual price, while the supply of labour is a function of the expected real wage in terms of the expected price level over all islands.

10 To do so, first replace Dy_t by $(y_t - y_t^f)$.

11 If we continue the story further, the unexpected increase in the current price level will have become anticipated in the following period, so that, barring new sources of shifts in aggregate demand and supply, the economy will be at point c after the current period. Therefore, the increase in output is likely to be short-lived. Its duration will depend upon the time it takes the public to correct for erroneous price expectations.

12 For consistent and unbiased estimates using data from a given policy regime – i.e., with constant true values of m_0 and γ – estimate (24) and (26). Since there are five reduced-form coefficients (a_0, a_1, a_2, m_0 and γ), while there are only four structural ones (m_0, γ, a, b), cross-equation restrictions implied by (25) will have to be imposed and a simultaneous estimation procedure used.

13 This section is also based on the contributions of Sargent and Wallace (1976).

14 Friedman's money supply rule was that the money supply should increase at a constant rate roughly equal to the long-run rate of output growth. Since long-run output growth is zero in the model under discussion, Friedman's rule implies a constant money supply.

15 As seen earlier, for a modern classical model with rational expectations, monetary policy rules cannot improve on the performance of the economy, so that all control mechanisms will be superfluous for it.

16 The following schema has the advantage that some estimates of the length of each kind of lag can be formed on the basis of intuitive knowledge of the economy.

17 Other studies showed that the most significant difference in the estimate of the lag arose not from the kind of model used but from the specification of the monetary policy variable. One study during the 1970s reported that if the money supply, the monetary base or total reserves were taken as the exogenous monetary variable, the total response of GNP to a change in policy was completed within four or five quarters. But if non-borrowed reserves were taken to be the appropriate monetary variable, less than 40% of the total response in GNP occurred in five quarters and the full effect was distributed over two and a half quarters.

18 Chapter 15 referred to the findings of Mosser (1992) from a simulation of four large econometric models. These showed that the money-output lags last more than three years.

19 In particular, it does not exist in hyperinflations for further increases in the inflation rates.

20 This does not imply that output growth is independent of innovations in the financial sector. For this analysis, see Chapter 26 below.

REFERENCES

Akerlof, George A. 'The Case against Conservative Macroeconomics: An Inaugural Lecture'. *Economica*, 46, August 1979, pp. 219–37.

Andersen, Leonall C., and Jerry L. Jordan. 'Monetary and Fiscal Actions: A Test of their Relative Importance in Economic Stabilization'. *Federal Reserve Bank of St Louis Review*, 50, November 1968, pp. 11–24.

Ball, Laurence, and N. Gregory Mankiw. 'A Sticky-Price Manifesto'. *Carnegie-Rochester Series on Public Policy*, 41, 1994, pp. 127–51.

Barro, Robert J. 'Unanticipated Money Growth and Unemployment in the United States'. *American Economic Review*, 67, March 1977, pp. 101–15.

Friedman, Milton. 'A Monetary and Fiscal Framework for Economic Stability'. *American Economic Review*, 38, 1948, pp. 245–64.

——. *A Program for Monetary Stability*. New York: Fordham University Press, 1959.

——. 'The Role of Monetary Policy'. *American Economic Review*, 58, March 1968, pp. 1–17.

——, and Anna Jacobson Schwartz. *A Monetary History of the United States, 1867–1960*. Princeton, NJ: Princeton University Press, 1963.

Lucas, Robert E., Jr. 'Expectations and the Neutrality of Money'. *Journal of Economic Theory*, 4, April 1972, pp. 103–24.

——. 'Some International Evidence on Output–Inflation Tradeoffs'. *American Economic Review*, 63, June 1973, pp. 326–34.

——. 'Comments on Ball and Mankiw'. *Carnegie-Rochester Series on Public Policy*, 41, 1994, pp. 153–55.

——. 'Nobel Lecture: Monetary Neutrality'. *Journal of Political Economy*, 104, August 1996, pp. 661–82.

Mishkin, Frederic S. 'Does Anticipated Aggregate Demand Policy Matter? Some Further Econometric Results'. *American Economic Review*, 72, September 1982, pp. 788–802.

Mosser, Patricia. 'Changes in Monetary Policy Effectiveness: Evidence from Large Macroeconomic Models'. *Federal Reserve Board of New York Quarterly Review*, 17, Spring 1992, pp. 36–51.

Sargent, Thomas J., and Neil Wallace. 'Rational Expectations, the Optimal Monetary Instrument, and the Optimal Money Supply Rule'. *Journal of Political Economy*, 83, April 1975, pp. 241–54.

——, and ——. 'Rational Expectations and the Theory of Economic Policy'. *Journal of Monetary Economics*, 2, April 1976, pp. 169–83.

chapter seventeen

WALRAS' LAW AND THE INTERACTION AMONG MARKETS

This is a theoretical chapter dealing with some of the doctrinal issues in monetary and macro-economic theory. It will be of special interest to students interested in the history of monetary economics and the divisions sometimes imposed between the real and the monetary sectors of the macroeconomy.

The concept of Walras' law is fundamental to short-run macroeconomic analysis. It underlies the presentation of the IS–LM model, which has four goods – commodities, money, bonds and labour – but has explicit analysis of only three of them. While Walras' law has been defined and used in various earlier chapters, its foundations are examined rigorously in this chapter. The somewhat related concept of Say's law is also defined, followed by the implications of assuming both Walras' law and Say's law as identities.

The real balance effect is the impact of changes in the supply of real balances on the demand for commodities and played a key role in doctrinal disputes on whether or not the economy can be in equilibrium below full employment. This chapter examines the existence of the real balance effect in the short run and the long run.

---

key concepts introduced in this chapter

- A law versus an equilibrium condition
- Walras' law
- Say's law
- The excess demand function for bonds in IS–LM analysis
- Dichotomy between the real and monetary sectors
- Real balance effect
- Notional demand and supply functions
- Effective demand and supply functions

There are very few propositions in economics that have been considered to be so far beyond dispute as to be labelled 'laws'.[1] Among these are Walras' law and Say's law. The former represents a constraint on all goods in the economy while the latter represents a constraint on the commodity market alone. This chapter will consider these laws for the closed economy, though the arguments can also be easily extended to the open economy.

A statement in economics worthy of being called a *law* must be more than a behavioural relationship or an equilibrium condition – which are not necessarily valid at a given time for a given economy – since, otherwise, there would not be a special reason for assigning it a distinctive term with the compelling connotation that the word 'law' has. Hence, while there can be several ways of defining what is to be a law in economics, we will define it as a statement that holds without exception under any conditions – and is therefore an identity – or, if one is willing to be more tolerant, it must be a statement that approximates this degree of applicability. There are very few statements of this nature in microeconomics, let alone in macroeconomics or monetary economics. Classical economics asserts that Walras' law is one of this extremely select group – though, as we discuss in section 17.8 below, there are disputes even about that. However, whether Say's law is also entitled to the designation of a law is highly doubtful.

Sections 17.1 to 17.4 present the derivation of Walras' law and its implications. Section 17.5 deals with Say's law and finds it inappropriate for monetary economies. Sections 17.6 and 17.7 discuss the implications of the joint assumption of Walras' law and Say's law for the neutrality of money and the dichotomy between the real and monetary sectors. Both these concepts have already been presented in Chapter 3 in the context of the Walrasian general equilibrium model of the economy. The present chapter derives them from Walras' law and Say's law.

Section 17.8 examines the conditions for the breakdown of Walras' law. This condition is the failure of some markets to clear *and* the derivation by economic agents of their demand and supply functions in other markets, based on their recognition of the constraints imposed by the non-clearing markets. The demands and supplies derived in the presence of such constraints are called *effective* ones, as against the *notional* ones in Walrasian analysis. These effective functions can be of the *Clower* or *Drèze* variety. These concepts are clarified in section 17.9.

17.1 WALRAS' LAW

Walras' law is the statement that for any economy over any given period of time, the sum of the market *values* of all the goods demanded must equal the sum of the market values of all the goods supplied. For the closed economy,[2] we define 'goods' in this chapter as in earlier chapters to refer to commodities, money, labour (or leisure) and non-monetary financial assets ('bonds').

To explain Walras' law intuitively for a pure exchange economy, first start with the constraint on the individual's demands for goods. Assume that the individual initially possesses some commodities, some money and some bonds,[3] and that their total nominal value at current market prices is his nominal wealth ψ. He will also want to supply some labour, with a nominal labour income at current wage rates being equal to Y. Assuming that he spends these amounts to acquire the commodities, money and bonds that he wants to hold or use in the current period,[4] the total value ψ of his initial holdings of goods plus his labour income Y must equal his total expenditures on commodities, money and bonds. Since the individual's total expenditures on his purchases of commodities, money and bonds must sum to $[\psi + Y]$, the demand for any one of these three goods can be derived by subtracting his expenditures for the other two goods from $[\psi + Y]$.

If we now sum over all the individuals in the economy, the aggregate initial holdings of goods (including labour) plus the current national output becomes their supply and the aggregate expenditures on them become the value of the quantities demanded. Further, the total value of all the goods demanded must equal the total value of all the goods supplied. This is Walras' law and is the aggregate counterpart of the individual's budget constraint. It is often simplified to the statement that *the supply of all goods in the economy must equal the demand for all goods in the economy.* Note that this statement is valid only in aggregate value terms.

One of the implications of Walras' law for an economy with K goods is that if the demand for any $K-1$ goods were to be each equal to their supply, the demand for the remaining Kth good must also equal its supply. That is, if the markets for any $K-1$ goods are in equilibrium – with demand equal to supply – the market for the Kth good must also be in equilibrium.

Deriving Walras' law for a five-good economy

We prove these statements for a closed economy with a government sector and for its *five* goods – commodities, money, bonds, equities and labour.[5] The assumption basic to Walras' law is that there is no 'free' disposal of goods so that the goods that are produced or inherited from the past are either consumed, demanded for some other reason (such as for carrying to the future) or exchanged. Assume that the closed economy has three economic agents – households, firms and the government (including the central bank) – so that there are several budget constraints to consider in the analysis. These constraints are:

Households' budget constraint:

$$p_c c^{dh} + p_c m^{dh} + p_b b^d + p_e e^d \equiv p_c \underline{c}^s + \underline{M}^h + p_b \underline{b}^s + p_e \underline{e}^s + W n^s + \pi^{dis} \tag{1}$$

Firms' budget constraints:

$$p_c(c^{sf} + i + g) + p_e(e^s - \underline{e}^s) + \underline{M}^f \equiv W n^d + p_c i + p_c m^{df} + \pi^{dis} \tag{2}$$

$$\pi \equiv \pi^{dis} + \pi^{und} \tag{3}$$

$$p_c i \equiv \pi^{und} + p_e (e^s - \underline{e}^s) \tag{4}$$

Government's budget constraint:

$$p_c (g - t) \equiv (M^s - \underline{M}^s) + p_b (b^s - \underline{b}^s) \tag{5}$$

where:

p_c	price of commodities
p_b	price of government bonds
p_e	price of equities
W	nominal wage rate = rental price of labour
c	quantity of commodities
m	real money balances
M	nominal money stock
b	quantity of bonds
e	quantity of equities
n	number of workers (labour)
$\underline{c}$	existing stocks of commodities
$\underline{M}$	existing nominal money stock
$\underline{b}$	existing stock of bonds, issued by the government
$\underline{e}$	existing stock of equities, issued by firms
g	real government expenditures on commodities
t	government's tax revenues
i	real investment by firms

π total nominal profits of firms

π^{dis} nominal distributed profits of firms

π^{und} nominal retained (undistributed) profits of firms

The superscripts d and s stand for demand and supply, respectively. The superscripts h and f stand for households and firms, respectively. Underlining indicates that the value of the variable is given exogenously or was inherited from the past.

Equation (1) specifies that the sum of the households' nominal demands for commodities, money, bonds and equities equals the value of their existing stocks of these goods, their labour income and the profits that they receive from firms. Equation (2) specifies that the firm's income from their supply of commodities from current production and from the sale of new equities plus their money holdings, equals their payout in wages, for investment goods, for money balances in the current period and in distributed profits. Note that the firms' current production is used for consumption, investment and for supplying commodities to the government. Equation (3) specifies that the total profits of firms are either distributed or undistributed. Equation (4) specifies that firms finance their nominal investment through their retained profits and the supply of new equities. Equation (5) specifies that fiscal deficits must be financed from issuing new money or new government bonds. It has been assumed in these equations that only the firms issue equities and that only the government issues bonds.

Note that (1) to (5) are all *identities*, under the assumption that nothing is just thrown away in this economy. Equations (1) to (5) imply that:

$$p_c\{(c^{dh} + i + g) - (\underline{c}^s + c^{sf})\} + (M^d - M^s) + p_b(b^d - b^s) + p_e(e^d - e^s) + W(n^d - n^s) \equiv 0 \qquad (6)$$

where the left-hand side is the sum of the nominal excess demands for commodities, money, bonds, equities and labour. Equation (6) is one of the ways of stating Walras' law: *the sum of the nominal excess demands for all goods in the economy must be zero*. Equation (6) restated in terms of excess demands is:

$$E_c^d + E_m^d + E_b^d + E_e^d + E_n^d \equiv 0 \qquad (7)$$

where E_k^d is the excess *nominal* demand for the kth good, $k = c, m, b, e, n$.

The usual statements of Walras' law in macroeconomics, in a model with four goods

We had differentiated between bonds and equities to capture the financial structure of the economy in a more realistic manner and to show that Walras' law will hold for this structure. We have in fact proved that it will hold for any economy no matter how its goods are categorized. Since macroeconomic theory usually treats firms' equities and government bonds as the composite good 'bonds', we will at this stage shorten (6) in line with this usage. Walras' law for this more compact *four*-good economy can be stated in the following two different ways.

(i) $E_c^d + E_m^d + E_b^d + E_n^d \equiv 0$ (8)

where b now represents all non-monetary financial assets in the economy. Equation (8) is the statement that *the sum of the excess demands for the four goods is identically zero*.

(ii)   Equation (8) can be rewritten as:

$$p_c c^d + M^d + p_b b^d + W n^d \equiv p_c c^s + M^s + p_b b^s + W n^s \qquad (9)$$

which is the statement that *the sum of the nominal demands for all goods identically equals the sum of the nominal supplies of all goods in the economy*. This is another way of stating Walras' law.

For the general case of K markets, (8) and (9) generalize to:

$$\Sigma_k E_k^d \equiv 0 \qquad k = 1, \ldots, K \tag{10}$$

$$\Sigma_k x_k^d = \Sigma_k x_k^s \quad k = 1, \ldots, K \tag{10'}$$

where x_k is the quantity of the kth good and there are K goods in the economy. Equation (10) or (10′) is the general statement of Walras' law.

Adjustment costs which slow the adjustment in the demands and/or supplies of goods so that their short-run values differ from their long-run ones do not change the derivation or applicability of Walras' law as long as the model assumes continuous equilibrium in all markets. However, the validity of Walras' law becomes questionable if some of the markets do not clear on a continuous basis. Sections 17.8 and 17.9 will examine this issue.

The implication of Walras' law for a specific market

Note that the above statements of Walras' law are quite different from a statement that the demand for a particular good i equals its supply or that the excess demand for good i is zero. This would be an assertion about equilibrium in the market for the ith good. Walras' law by itself does not assert equilibrium in each market or in any one specific market, but is a statement covering all markets in the economy. In order to assert equilibrium in a specific market (say the Kth one), we need two statements: Walras' law and the information that there is equilibrium in the other $K - 1$ markets.

Equation (10) implies that:

$$E_K^d \equiv -\Sigma_k E_k^d \quad k = 1, \ldots, K-1 \tag{11}$$

where:

E_k^d excess demand in the kth market, $k = 1, \ldots, K-1$

E_K^d excess demand in the Kth market

Equation (11) states that the excess nominal demand in the Kth market equals the sum of the excess nominal demands in the other $(K - 1)$ markets. Note that we can designate the market for any specific good as the Kth market. Equation (11) is also sometimes used as a way for stating Walras' law.

Equation (11) implies that:

$$\text{If } \Sigma_k E_k^d = 0, \text{ for } k = 1, \ldots, K-1, \text{ then } E_K^d = 0 \tag{12}$$

which implies the *conditional* statement that if there exists equilibrium in $K - 1$ markets, then there would also be equilibrium in the Kth market. For *comparative static analysis*, (10) to (12) allow the analysis to dispense with the explicit treatment of one of the markets in the economy. However, such an omitted market continues to exist and to function but its treatment is pushed into the implicit state.

17.2 THE APPLICATION OF WALRAS' LAW IN THE IS–LM MODELS: THE EXCESS DEMAND FOR BONDS

Walras' law in the form of (12) is an essential element in the usual specification of short-run macroeconomic models. These models generally assume the economy to consist of the four goods – commodities, money, bonds and labour – but choose to explicitly state the markets for only three goods. In the usual modern statement of macroeconomics, these three markets are the commodities, money and labour markets, so that the *bond market is eliminated from explicit treatment*. In view of Walras' law, if the other three markets are already specified, the specification of the bond market would have been superfluous.

Further, we can derive the excess demand function for bonds from the excess demand functions for commodities, money and bonds. We will use for illustrative purposes the behavioural assumptions of the closed-economy neoclassical model in Chapter 13 for the following analysis. The definitions of the symbols will also be as given in that chapter.

Starting with the assumptions for the commodity market in Chapter 13, specify the equilibrium condition for the commodity sector as:

$$y^s = y^d = y$$

where:

$$y^d = c + i + g - t$$

so that the nominal excess demand for commodities is given by:

$$
\begin{aligned}
E_c^d &= P\{(c + i + g - t) - y\} \\
&= P\{c(y - t) + i(r) + g - t(y) - y\}
\end{aligned}
\tag{13}
$$

Similarly, from the assumptions of Chapter 13, the nominal excess demand for money is:

$$
\begin{aligned}
E_m^d &= Pm^d - M^s \\
&= Pm^d(y, r) - M
\end{aligned}
\tag{14}
$$

Again from the assumptions of Chapter 13, the nominal excess demand for labour is:

$$
\begin{aligned}
E_n^d &= Pw(n^d - n^s) \\
&= Pw\{n^d(w) - n^s(w)\}
\end{aligned}
\tag{15}
$$

Therefore, Walras' law requires that the excess demand for bonds be specified as:

$$
\begin{aligned}
E_b^d &= -E_c^d - E_m^d - E_n^d \\
&= -P\{c(y - t) + i(r) + g - t(y) - y\} - P\{m^d(y, r) - M/P\} - Pw\{n^d(w) - n^s(w)\}
\end{aligned}
\tag{16}
$$

which specifies the general form of the *nominal* excess demand function for bonds as:

$$E_b^d = P\Phi(y, r, w; g, t, M/P) \tag{17}$$

so that the form of the *real* excess demand function for bonds would be:

$$E_b^d/p_b = (P/p_b)\Phi(y, r, w; g, t, M/P) \tag{18}$$

Equation (18) specifies the excess demand function for bonds in real terms, without any price illusion. Further, the fiscal and monetary policy variables, g, t and M, influence the excess demand for bonds. By (16), $\partial E_b^d/\partial g < 0$, $\partial E_b^d/\partial t > 0$ and $\partial E_b^d/\partial M > 0$. On the interactions between the labour and bond markets, note that the bond market is not independent of the labour market since a (positive) excess demand for labour implies an excess demand for bonds and vice versa.

The excess demand for bonds, wealth and Walras' law

From an empirical perspective, (16) and (18) are unlikely to be valid for most economies because of their failure to include wealth among the determinants of the excess demand for bonds, since wealth provides the constraint on the holdings of bonds and other assets, both at the individual's level and the aggregate level. However, Walras' law requires that wealth cannot be an argument in the excess demand function for bonds unless it is also an argument in one of the other excess demand functions. Hence, since we can plausibly take wealth to be among the determinants of the excess demand function for bonds, at least one of the other excess demand functions must also be misspecified. This is especially likely to be true of the excess demand function for money, which is also an asset, but it can also be true of the excess demand functions for commodities and labour under intertemporal (lifetime) optimization by consumers and workers, as in the life-cycle consumption hypothesis.

17.3 WALRAS' LAW AND THE SELECTION AMONG THE MARKETS FOR A MODEL

Walras' law permits the equilibrium conditions for any three out of the four goods in the model to be explicitly specified for the overall equilibrium of the economy. Therefore, the complete model can explicitly set out the equations for the commodities, bond and labour markets, or those for the bond, money and labour markets, or those for the commodities, money and labour markets. The last set was used by Keynes, and has become the standard pattern of the modern IS–LM macroeconomics.

However, the classical economists prior to Keynes had generally favoured the specification of the overall equilibrium in terms of the bond, money and labour markets, with the bond market determining the interest rate in the loanable funds theory, the market for money determining the price level, and the labour market determining employment and – through the production function – determining output. Walras' law implies that the classical and IS–LM approaches provide the same picture of the economy, with the same values of the endogenous variables, even though the explicitly specified three markets differ between these approaches.

However, while the different approaches may yield the same values of the variables, the general pattern of economic analysis identifies a 'price' variable with each market. Thus, the price level is the 'price' of commodities and microeconomic analysis identifies its determination with the demand and supply of commodities. The interest rate is similarly the one-period 'price' of loans – 'bonds' – and microeconomic analysis would identify its determination with the demand and supply of loans in the bond market. The wage rate is the rental price of labour and microeconomic analysis identifies its determination with the labour market. Hence, there is no 'price' left to identify as the price of money, so that there is no price variable that can be uniquely identified with the demand and supply of money. *There can, in fact, be no such unique variable in a monetary economy since money is itself the good in which the prices of other goods – commodities, bonds and labour – are measured.* Thus, $1/P$ is sometimes said to be the value of money (in commodity units) while, at other times, the interest rate r is said to be its opportunity cost, and many pre-Keynesian economists designated its value (in labour units) as $1/Pw$.

This reasoning suggests that, if our intended use of a model requires that the model mirror the functioning of the markets in the real world, the complete macroeconomic model should explicitly lay out the commodity market, the bond market and the labour market. That is, the market for money balances should be the one left out of the explicit analysis. However, both Keynesian and pre-Keynesian (classical) analyses incorporated the market for money balances, the former supplementing this with the commodity and the labour markets, and the latter with the bond and labour markets. If the intended use of the model is to study general equilibrium states, as comparative statics does, Walras' law ensures the general equilibrium values of the endogenous variables will be the same no matter which three markets are explicitly specified. Therefore, in comparative static analysis, the incorporation of the money market at the cost of the exclusion of another market is of no consequence for the determination of prices, wages and the interest rate.

For the analysis of the dynamic movements of prices, wages and the interest rate in real-world markets, we need to take account of the empirical reality that the price in a particular market responds *in the first instance* to the excess demand only in that market but does not respond to the excess demand in other markets unless that excess demand spills over into the excess demand for the good in question. Therefore, for dynamic analysis, the appropriate assumptions would be:

$$P = f(E_c^d)$$

$$r = f(E_b^d)$$

$$w = f(E_n^d)$$

These dynamic functions seem to be consistent with the common intuition and economic folklore on market adjustments. Several studies of the dynamic analysis of the price-level and the interest rate have in recent years followed this pattern: that is, making the price-level changes a function of the commodity market disequilibrium and in making the interest rate changes a function of the bond market disequilibrium.[6] Hence, for dynamic analysis, the preferred overall macroeconomic model specifies the expenditure and bond markets, to the exclusion of the market for money balances.[7]

17.4 TWO IMPLICATIONS OF WALRAS' LAW

17.4.1 Walras' law and the assumption of continuous full employment

If it is assumed that the labour market is continuously in equilibrium – so that $n^d = n^s = n^f$ – (8) becomes,

$$E_c^d + E_m^d + E_b^d \equiv 0 \qquad\qquad (19)$$

The underlying assumption behind (19) is that equilibrium exists on a continuous basis in the labour market – so that $E_n^d = 0$, by assumption – but does not do so in the commodities, money and bond markets. In fact, in economies with developed financial markets, the most plausible assumption would be that the money and bond markets adjust the fastest to clear any disequilibrium, and that as between the commodity and labour markets, the labour markets are the slowest to adjust since they are characterized by long-term explicit or implicit contracts between the firms and their employees. In fact, the major dispute dividing economists into the main groupings of Keynesians and modern classicists is precisely over the issue of whether the labour markets will or will not clear over a reasonably short period – let alone continuously.

Hence, the underlying assumption of (19) that the labour market continuously clears – while the commodity, money and bond markets do not do so – is highly questionable as a basis for macroeconomic analysis. However, while this assumption is of doubtful validity, it is often made, as in the modern classical model, specified in Chapter 13. It modifies Walras' law to its truncated form given in (19), so that the macroeconomic model can be set out only in terms of the commodities and money markets, as specified in the IS and LM curves. This would leave out the bond and the labour markets – the latter by taking output to be at its full employment level. Our arguments have rejected the validity of this procedure.

17.4.2 Walras' law and the efficiency of the money and bond markets

Suppose we follow the claim of many monetary economists that the money and bond markets are so efficient in the modern developed economies that they adjust on a daily basis and are continuously in equilibrium. That is, we can take $E_m^d = E_b^d = 0$ continuously. Hence, (8) implies that:

$$E_c^d + E_n^d = 0$$

so that:

$$E_c^d = -E_n^d$$

so that there must exist positive excess demand for commodities whenever there is excess supply of labour. The latter manifests itself in increases in unemployment during the recessions, so that $E_n^d < 0$. But this is also precisely the part of the business cycle in which firms claim that the demand for their products has fallen and there is not enough demand for them to maintain their employment at the pre-recession levels, so that $E_c^d < 0$. That is, the excess supply of labour and the excess supply of commodities occur concurrently in a recession, so that $E_c^d + E_n^d < 0$. But this evidence contradicts Walras' law, thereby not only casting doubt on its claim to be a law but also on its validity during recessions for economies with well-developed financial markets. This is a strong indictment of Walras' law and we will pursue its reasoning further in section 17.10 below.

17.4.3 Walras' law and the wealth constraint

Economic analysis sometimes includes a *wealth constraint* over money and bonds of the form:

$$p_c m^d + p_b b^d = \underline{M} + p_b \underline{b} \tag{20}$$

where money and bonds are the only *assets* in the economy. Equation (20) asserts that the demand for assets must equal pre-existing wealth and can be restated as:

$$E_m^d + E_b^d = 0 \tag{21}$$

Equations (20) and (21) cannot be treated as identities since positive or negative national saving in excess of the intended investment (in a closed economy) can change the amount of wealth to be allocated to money and bonds. That is, if we want an 'identity' corresponding to (20), its proper form – derived from Walras' law identity (8) under the assumption of continuous labour market clearance – would be:

$$p_c m^d + p_b b^d \equiv \underline{M} + p_b \underline{b} - E_c^d \tag{22}[8]$$

which converts to the equilibrium condition (20) or (21) only *if* equilibrium can be taken to exist in the commodity market so that $E_c^d = 0$. Therefore, (20) is *at best* only an equilibrium condition and not an identity. But, then, there is no reason to prefer it over the individual equilibrium conditions $E_m^d = 0$ and $E_b^d = 0$, which imply it and which provide more information. We will, therefore, not use (20) or (21), and prefer to use (8) or, as a second best, (22).

Note that, given (22) or Walras' law as (8), $E_m^d = 0$ does not imply that $E_b^d = 0$. In the context of (22), it would also require that E_c^d is always equal to zero. Hence, money market equilibrium does not necessarily imply bond market equilibrium – and vice versa.

Is the LM relationship the portfolio balance condition?

An implication of the above remarks is that it is not appropriate to call the LM relationship of $M^s/P = m^d(y, r)$ as the *asset market equilibrium* or *portfolio balance condition*, though many studies describe it as such, since the LM relationship only specifies the equilibrium in the market for real balances but does not imply, alone and by itself, either the nature of the excess demand function for bonds or that equilibrium will also necessarily exist in the bond market.

Similarly, the bond market equations – demand, supply and equilibrium condition – cannot be described as being the asset market equilibrium or portfolio balance condition.

17.5 SAY'S LAW

Say's law is attributed to the writings of Jean-Baptiste Say in the first quarter of the nineteenth century[9] and is considered to be one of the underpinnings of the traditional (pre-Keynesian) classical macroeconomic model. Its usual statement is that 'supply creates its own demand'.[10] Since this statement is meant to refer exclusively to commodities rather than to the other goods in the economy and is meant to apply only in the aggregate over all commodities, it can be more precisely formulated as: *the aggregate supply of commodities creates its own aggregate demand.*

Say's law was implicit in many of the expositions of the traditional classical model. It can be found in the writings of not only Say but also of Adam Smith[11] and David Ricardo. Its general implication was that there could not exist either excess demand or excess supply of commodities in the economy. Further, saving was converted into investment and not into money holdings since the former had a positive return while the latter did not. Money was merely an intermediary in the saving–investment process and in the exchange of commodities.

There are disputes about both the attribution of Say's law and how accurately it reflects the ideas of Say and other writers who expounded it. Our concern will not be with the historical attribution of this statement or whether or not it accurately reflects the ideas of Say or his contemporaries, but rather with it as a theory, whose implications and validity need to be examined.

The statement that the supply of commodities creates its own demand has two components to it. One is the causality from supply to demand and the other is their equality. On the former, the argument runs as follows: the supply of commodities creates income which the recipients must spend on commodities, so that any increase in the aggregate supply of commodities creates a corresponding increase in the aggregate demand for them. This argument is fallacious in the commodities–monetary–bonds economy since the increase in income could be partly or wholly spent to increase money or bond holdings, so that the increase in the aggregate supply of commodities would induce only a less than corresponding increase in their aggregate demand. Conversely, if the economic agents choose to increase their commodity demand by running down their money or bond holdings, an increase in the aggregate demand for commodities will come about without a corresponding prior increase in their supply. Hence, the causal argument behind Say's law is not valid in modern economies.

Since our concern in this chapter is with the comparison of this law with Walras' law, our focus will be on the second component of Say's law. This concerns the equality of the aggregate value of the demand for commodities c^d and the value of the aggregate supply of commodities c^s. In examining Say's law from this viewpoint, it is a moot question whether it should be viewed as an equilibrium condition or as an identity. Corresponding to these two possibilities, we can define the weak and the strong forms of Say's law, as in the following.

The weak form of Say's law: Say's law as an equilibrium condition

The weak form of Say's law defines it as merely an equilibrium condition: that is, *in equilibrium, the aggregate demand for commodities equals their aggregate supply*. This form is hardly very restrictive for the commodity market and becomes an element of the specification of the IS relationship in macroeconomic analysis. Further, if it is only an equilibrium condition, it will allow the possibility of disequilibrium where it will not hold. With disequilibrium in the commodity market, the economy will be off the IS curve – which means that the economy may sometimes – but not at other times – have the aggregate demand for commodities equal to their supply. Interpreted in this way, Say's law would hardly merit the designation of a 'law' since we do not give the equilibrium conditions for the money market, the bond market, the labour market or the foreign exchange markets – or for microeconomic markets such as those for apples – the designation of laws.

Baumol points out that Say and other writers recognized that Say's law may not hold for short periods due to a temporary desire to hoard money but they thought that the market will 'immediately' or quickly restore equilibrium. These comments make Say's law an equilibrium condition, with the added assertion that the economy will be almost continually in equilibrium. In this interpretation, Say's law becomes close to the views of the modern classical school which assumes continuous full employment and commodity market clearance.

Since the interpretation of Say's law as an equilibrium condition does not merit the designation of a 'law', we will henceforth interpret Say's law as an identity.

The strong form of Say's law: Say's law as an identity

The strong form of Say's law is that it is an *identity*, thereby asserting that: *the aggregate demand for commodities would always equal their supply, with causality taken to run from the latter to the former.*[12]

For a rudimentary (barter) economy in which the only traded goods are commodities, Walras' law simplifies to the statement that the aggregate expenditure on commodities must always equal the aggregate income from their sale. That is, for such an economy, Walras' law implies that the demand and supply of commodities are always equal, which is identical with Say's law. Therefore, for such a rudimentary economy, Say's law can be derived from the aggregate budget constraint for the economy, obtained from summing over the budget constraints of all its economic units. Note that financial assets are excluded by assumption from such an economy, so that substitution between commodities and either of the financial assets (money and bonds) is being excluded.

Conversely, Say's law is inapplicable to an economy in which both financial assets and commodities exist and some substitution can occur between them. Hence, Say's law cannot be validly applied to modern economies, all of which have money and bonds among their traded goods.[13]

Evaluation of Say's law

We have shown that the weak form of Say's law as an equilibrium condition is not a serious restriction on macroeconomic models in addition to that already embodied in the IS relationship. Its strong form – and the form in which Say's law is usually interpreted – is that supply will continuously create its own demand, so that there can never be disequilibrium in the commodity markets. We have interpreted Say's law in this strong form. In this form, the continuous equality of demand and supply is being asserted, as is the line of causation from supply to demand. It is also being implicitly asserted that aggregate commodity demand cannot change independently of its supply, so that no exogenous changes in demand such as due to changes in autonomous investment or fiscal policy etc. could occur.

Therefore, the strong version of Say's law is objectionable for two reasons. One reason, as argued in the preceding paragraphs, is that the identity of the supply and demand for commodities cannot exist in modern economies, which also possess money and bonds, so that economic agents can and do substitute among commodities, money and bonds at certain times and for certain values of prices and interest rates, so that the supply of commodities can differ from their demand for some time intervals. The second objection is that the strong version of Say's law denies the possibility of exogenous changes occurring in the demand for commodities and of some adjustment of their supply in response to the changes in their demand.

Some invalid implications of Say's law

Since Say's law is inapplicable to monetary economies, its application to such economies leads to conclusions that are objectionable and inappropriate for monetary economies. The following arguments present some of these.

(i) Assume a simple exchange economy with commodities and money but without bonds and labour. Walras' law applies to such an economy and states that:

$$E_c^d + E_m^d \equiv 0$$

Say's law, if also applied to such an economy, states that:

$$E_c^d \equiv 0$$

Therefore, the two laws applied together imply that:

$$E_m^d \equiv 0$$

That is, the demand for money must *always* equal its supply, so that there can never be disequilibrium in the money market. This is not valid for the monetary economy, so that it is inappropriate to apply both Walras' law and Say's law simultaneously to a monetary economy.

(ii) If the demand and the supply of commodities are *always* equal, as asserted by Say's law, they would also have to be equal irrespective of changes in the demand and supply of money. Hence, such changes in the monetary sector cannot increase or decrease the demand for commodities – since otherwise such a change would be independent of those in the supply of commodities – and therefore could not affect nominal national income and expenditures, which is contrary to the conclusion of macroeconomic theory and empirical evidence that the changes in the demand and supply of money can cause changes in nominal national income.

(iii) From Say's law, since the commodity sector is always in equilibrium irrespective of the price level of commodities, we have:

$$y^d(P_0) = y^s(P_0)$$

as well as:

$$y^d(\lambda P_0) = y^s(\lambda P_0)$$

for any $\lambda > 0$. Hence, the price level becomes indeterminate in so far as the commodity sector is concerned: at a price P_0, there is equilibrium and zero excess demand in the commodities market, as it is at any price λP_0. Therefore, additional information is necessary to determine the price level.[14]

(iv) Another aspect of a theory incorporating both Walras' law and Say's law is disquieting in the context of a commodities–money economy. Suppose the price level was at its equilibrium position, given by, say, the quantity theory. Say's law states that the aggregate demand for commodities always equals their aggregate supply, irrespective of the price level. The price level is thus not determined or even affected by forces operating in the commodity market. The two laws *together* imply that the demand for money also always equals its supply, irrespective of the price level, so that the price level is also not determined by any adjustments in the money market. Therefore, the two laws rule any forces that would take the price level to its equilibrium position. In fact, by ruling out the likelihood of possible disequilibrium in both the commodities and money markets, they rule out the specification of any adjustment process, since such a process requires disequilibrium in at least one market. Hence, Walras' law and Say's law together rule out any study of monetary disequilibrium conditions and, therefore, rule out any examination of the stability of an equilibrium price level.

(v) The strong form of Say's law on its own asserts that the supply and demand for commodities are always identical, irrespective of the interest rate and the level of income in the economy. Hence, in IS–LM models, the IS relationship (curve) would span the whole (r, y) space, rather be merely a negatively sloping curve.[15] There can be no meaningful IS–LM analysis under such a shape of the IS curve. In fact, much of modern macro-economic theory would be ruled out in such a context.

Therefore, there are many reasons for rejecting the strong form of Say's law – that is, Say's law as an identity – for monetary economies.

17.6 THE DICHOTOMY BETWEEN THE REAL AND MONETARY SECTORS

There is another disturbing aspect of a theory encompassing both Walras' law and Say's law. Say's law alone implies that the demand for commodities always equals their supply, irrespective of the quantity of money and the price level. The 'real' system of the economy, concerned with the demand and supply of commodities and their relative prices, is thus independent of the monetary phenomena in the economy. There is thus a dichotomy (separation) between the real and monetary sectors of such an economy. Such a dichotomy was also derived in Chapter 3 in the context of the general equilibrium version of the macroeconomic model, under the assumptions that the demand and supply functions were notional and possessed the homogeneity of degree zero in all prices, rather than doing so in all prices *and* initial endowments. The present derivation of the dichotomy is related to the earlier one but is from a different perspective, with Say's law embodying within it the homogeneity of degree zero of the demand and supply functions of commodities in all prices.

As Chapter 3 has shown, such a dichotomy does not exist in the modern monetary economies. Further, again as Chapter 3 has argued, the *real balance effect* shows that a change in the price level changes the real wealth of the individual and changes his demand for real money balances, as well as his demand for commodities. Similar effects occur if the price level was constant and the money supply was increased in such a way that the wealth of the individual and (the private part of) the economy changed. There is thus interaction between the commodities sector and monetary phenomena through the real balance effect, so that there does not exist a dichotomy between the real and the monetary sectors.

17.7 THE REAL BALANCE EFFECT

The real balance effect was defined in Chapter 3 as: *the change in the aggregate demand for commodities due to a change in the real balances held by the individual, with the latter due to a change in the price level or an exogenous change in the money stock.* Such a change in real balances is taken to be a change in the individual's wealth. The real balance effect is clearly one of the interactions that can occur between the commodity and the money market, and can be brought into play by aggregate demand falling below aggregate supply in the economy.[16] Its elaboration and refinement owed much to the work of Don Patinkin during the 1940s to the 1960s and its analysis can be found in Patinkin (1965).

This section looks more closely at the role of the real balance effect, which causes changes in the holding of real balances to affect the excess demand for commodities, at least in the short run. This interaction may work itself out in successive short runs and not be in evidence in a comparison of long-run equilibrium states of the economy. Whether this happens or not depends upon the nature of the economy and the economic behaviour of its agents, as we show in the following analysis.

Archibald and Lipsey (1958) and Patinkin (1965) considered this question in the context of an exchange economy in which commodities and money exist but bonds do not, so that the individual can only save in the form of money (which does not pay any interest). Further, the individual is assumed to have a *one*-period horizon. For such an economy, these writers showed that a dichotomy does not exist in the short run but will exist in the long-run equilibrium values of the real and monetary variables. The following presentation considers their assumptions and arguments briefly and in a simplified fashion.

Suppose we have an individual's demand functions for commodities and money, both goods are normal ones and the individual has a one-period horizon. These include the amount of his real balances as part of his initial endowments and, by the analysis in Chapter 3, is one of the determinants of his demands for goods. A gratuitous increase in his money balances will then increase his demand for both commodities and real balances because of the real balance effect. A new short-run equilibrium would come about at higher levels of consumption and holdings of real balances. But the higher consumption implies that some of the gratuitous increase in the individual's real balances gets spent and the next period benefits from only a portion of the initial gratuitous increase in real balances. Consumption and the demand for real balances in the second period would be higher than without any increase in real balances. But the increase would be less than in the first period. Subsequent periods would see a smaller and smaller increase until all of the initial gratuitous increase in real balances is spent. The individual's demand for commodities and real balances would eventually revert to their initial levels, as if real balances had never increased. The real balance effect is thus a short-run phenomenon and is dissipated through higher consumption in the successive short runs.

Archibald and Lipsey (1958) presented this analysis in a diagrammatic form, using a diagram similar to Figure 17.1, for a commodities–money economy. In this figure, the units of the composite commodity (excluding real balances) are represented by G on the horizontal axis and real balances are represented by H on the vertical axis. The initial budget line is yy with a slope of 135 degrees since a unit of commodities exchanges for a unit of real balances. The individual has endowments per period of Oc_0 of commodities and of initial real balances m_0 equal to $(y - c_0)$. In the initial long-run equilibrium, with the individual's indifference curve (not drawn) being tangent to the budget line, the individual will consume c_0 of commodities and hold m_0 of real balances, with this pattern unchanging over periods, so that m_0 would be his long-run wealth. Let his consumption path be specified by OE.

Now assume that at the beginning of the short period[17] 1, he receives a gift of real balances equal to $(y' - y)$, so that his optimal consumption in period 1 is given by the point a'. He will, therefore, spend an additional amount $(c' - c_0)$ on commodities, running down his real balances and wealth by this amount in period 1. He will start period 2 with m' of real balances and a new endowment of c_0 of commodities, so that, for period 2, his budget line will be $y''y''$. For this budget line, his optimal point will be a'', so that his consumption is given by c'' and his real balance by m'', where $m'' < m'$. He will start period 3 with m'' of real balances and a new endowment of commodities of Oc_0, and choose an optimal point a''' (not

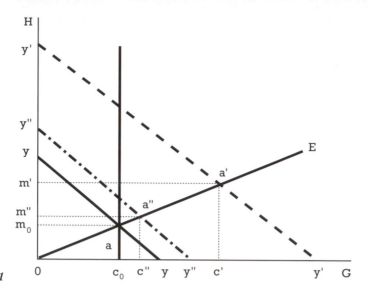

Figure 17.1

shown in Figure 17.1) which is closer to his long-run position at a than a'' or a' were. This process of decreasing real balances and wealth period by period will continue until the long-run position at a is achieved. Once this occurs, both the demand for commodities and real balances will have reverted to their initial long-run position. Therefore, following an increase in nominal balances (with prices held constant) or a decrease in the price level (with nominal balances held constant), the real balance effect will increase the demand for commodities and real balances in successive short periods until the long-run optimal pattern is restored. Hence, the latter is invariant with respect to an exogenous change in real balances and the real balance effect is only a short-run effect.

Since the real balance effect disappears in the long run for an individual with one-period horizons, it will disappear for all such individuals and the long-run position of the economy – in terms of its demand for commodities and real balances – will not change with a change in the aggregate real balances or their distribution. Hence, the long-run position of the economy is independent of the money stock and its distribution among economic agents, and a dichotomy exists between the real and monetary sectors in the long run but not in the short run.

This result is critically dependent upon the assumptions of an economy with money as the only asset and with a one-period horizon for the individual's decisions. If bonds were to exist and the individual had an infinite horizon, as in the permanent income hypothesis of consumption, he could allocate all of the gratuitous increase in his real balances to bonds, spending only their interest income in each period so that his consumption and demand for real balances would rise for all subsequent periods by the amount of the interest income. In this case, the real balance effect would not be merely a transitory phenomenon, confined to the short-run pattern. Hence, the dichotomy between the real and monetary sectors need not exist for an economy with bonds and with infinite horizon consumers.

The empirical importance of the real balance effect: outside versus inside money

The real balance effect operates through changes in the real value of the individual's wealth brought about by a change in the real value of his money holdings. To assess the magnitude of this effect, we need to distinguish between *inside money* and *outside money* in the economy. Outside money is a debt of the government (including the central bank), while it is an asset of the private sector. An increase in its value increases the wealth of the private sector and affects its expenditures through the income effect. This increase in value does not affect the expenditures of the public sector, since these are taken to be exogenously determined. Therefore, an increase in the real value of outside money induces a real balance effect. The empirical counterpart to outside money is the monetary base, so that the real balance applies to outside money.

Inside money is a debt of economic agents in the private sector as well as an asset held by them. An example of inside money is demand deposits in banks. These are an asset of the depositors and a liability of the banks and indirectly of the bank owners. Therefore, ignoring distribution effects, an increase in the real value of demand deposits does not change the real net worth of the private sector and does not induce a real balance effect. Hence, the real balance effect does not apply to inside money.

In the modern economy, the monetary base is a small proportion of M1 and an even smaller proportion of broader money aggregates. It is an almost insignificant proportion of total wealth in the economy. Therefore, increases in its real value are likely to be of minimal importance in terms of increasing total expenditures in the economy. Therefore, in practical terms, if the real balance effect was the only mechanism for taking an economy in recession with deficient demand to its full employment demand level, one could not put much faith in its efficacy in restoring full employment within a reasonable period. Its significance as a link from the monetary to the real sector is more analytical than empirical.

17.8 THE NEUTRALITY OF MONEY AND THE REAL BALANCE EFFECT

The preceding discussion on the dichotomy between the real and monetary sectors is part of a wider discussion on the necessary and sufficient conditions for the neutrality of money in the economy. As with the concept of dichotomy, the concept of neutrality and the conditions for its derivation were presented in Chapter 3. As defined in Chapter 3, money is said to be neutral – or a veil – if a change in its nominal amount does not alter the equilibrium values of the real variables – the demands, supplies, traded amounts and relative prices (including real wages) of commodities and labour – in the economy.

The existence of the real balance effect implies that the real sector is not independent of the monetary sector in the short run, so that money will not be neutral even in a simple exchange economy. However, if the individuals have one-period horizons, the Archibald and Lipsey analysis showed that the real balance effect exists only in the short-run equilibrium but disappears in the long-run equilibrium – so that the long-run equilibrium demands for commodities in such an economy are independent of the money supply: a change in the nominal money supply or in its real value due to a change in the price level has no effect on the long-run demand for commodities. Money is, therefore, neutral in the long-run equilibrium in the posited economy. But we also argued above that this long-run neutrality will operate only in a simple exchange economy with commodities and money but need not operate in a more complex economy with bonds in which consumers act according to the permanent income hypothesis of consumption.[18]

17.9 THE WEALTH EFFECT

A change in the real value of wealth induces a wealth effect on the demand for commodities. The Walrasian general equilibrium analysis of Chapter 3 had incorporated wealth in the form of initial endowments and studied the wealth effect as that from a change in the real value of initial endowments.

In the debates between Keynes and his critics, the wealth effect is associated with A. C. Pigou, who had argued that if aggregate demand was less than full employment output, prices will fall and increase the real value of wealth. This would in turn increase consumption, thereby increasing aggregate demand and moving the economy to equilibrium at its full employment level.

The real balance effect, associated with Don Patinkin's contributions, is merely one element of the wealth effect and takes account of only those changes in real wealth that arise because of changes in the real value of money balances. The wealth effect can also occur because of changes in the real values of non-monetary financial assets and physical assets. These can occur because of changes in the quantities of these assets or of their price relative to the price level, which is defined in terms of a bundle of currently produced goods – for example, the GDP deflator – or of currently consumed goods as in the case of the CPI.

Since the real values of bonds, stocks and physical assets rarely remain constant as the price level changes, changes in the price level do bring the wealth effect into play. It also comes into play if the current or future expected interest rates change. Since changes in the price level can be accompanied by or themselves induce changes in interest rates, there can be direct and indirect changes in wealth connected with changes in the money supply and the price level.

Short-run macroeconomic models properly should incorporate the wealth effect. However, stable and predictable relationships between the movements of the price level and those in the prices of bonds, equities and physical assets have not been established. The postulates used for such relationships are at best gross simplifications and reflect a severe deficiency of knowledge on this topic. In any case, the use of the standard consumption function – under which consumption expenditures depend on current income and not on wealth – in the IS–LM models avoids incorporation of the wealth effect altogether.

17.10 IS WALRAS' LAW REALLY A *LAW*: WHEN MIGHT IT NOT HOLD?

A *law* in economics has been interpreted in this chapter to be a statement that is true as an identity. It must hold under all states of the economy, from the most rudimentary to the most developed states, in recessions and in booms, in normal times and in chaotic conditions. For Walras' law to be a law, we should not be able to adduce any state of the economy, whether common or rare in the real world, which would not obey Walras' law. Walras' law was derived in section 17.1 from the agents' budgetary constraints. But what would happen if there are also other constraints? Would the particular form of the additional constraints vitiate Walras' law? The following subsection examines the implication of constraints imposed by the demand in the economy on the actual amounts of output that firms are able to sell and the actual amounts of labour that households can sell.

17.10.1 Two illustrations of the violation of Walras' law

To examine the validity and results of additional relevant constraints, consider the following two cases taken from the Keynesian and neo-Keynesian schools (Clower, 1969; Leijonhufvud, 1968, Ch. 2).

(i) For Leijonhufvud's arguments, assume an economy with efficient financial markets such that there exists continuous equilibrium in the money and bond markets. Under this assumption, (8) implies that:

$$E_c^d = -E_n^d \tag{23}$$

Now assume that there exists involuntary unemployment in the economy. Since this means that there is excess supply of labour with $E_n^s > 0$, Walras' law implies that there must be positive excess demand in the commodity market.

Let us now follow our intuition on the plausible and rational microeconomic behaviour of households and firms. Since the unemployed workers corresponding to E_n^s do not receive any income and, being rational, do not spend the income that they would have received only if they had been employed – but do not get since they are unemployed. Therefore, they reduce their expenditures below what would have occurred at full employment with the result that the commodity market will show less than the magnitude of the excess demand required by (23) and might even show excess supply. In this eventuality, we would have:

$$E_c^d < 0 \quad \text{and} \quad E_n^d < 0$$

so that:

$$E_c^d + E_n^d \neq 0$$

contrary to Walras' law under the assumptions that the money and bond markets adjust continuously. In this scenario, which we have argued above as being quite plausible, the economy displays excess supply of labour without a corresponding excess demand in any market. This violates Walras' law, under which the excess supply in any market must be balanced by an equal (but opposite in sign) excess demand in another market. Hence, Walras' law is not an identity and, therefore, not a law.

Further, the assumption required for the *reinstatement* of Walras' law is that the unemployed workers continue to base their expenditures on the incomes they would have been entitled to if they had, in fact, been employed. This posited behaviour for households is quite implausible and irrational. Alternatively, Walras' law would require that the firms continue to pay workers whom they have ceased to employ at their full employment wage rates. This posited behaviour for firms is also implausible and irrational.

We summarize this discussion in Table 17.1, compiled under the prior assumption of efficient money and bond markets so that they possess continuous zero excess demands.

Table 17.1

	E_n^d	E_c^d	E_m^d	E_b^d	$\Sigma_i E_i^d$
Walras' law	$< 0 \Rightarrow$	$= -E_n^d > 0$	0	0	0
Likely real-world and rational scenario	$< 0 \Rightarrow$	$\neq -E_n^d$	0	0	$\neq 0$

(ii) For the second case, this time from Patinkin (1965, Ch. 13), start with equilibrium in all markets. Assume that the money and bond markets stay in equilibrium but that a fall in investment reduces aggregate demand and creates excess supply in the commodity market. Firms respond to their unsold output by reducing production and unemployment, until the output of commodities becomes equal to their demand. While this adjustment by firms restores equilibrium in the commodity market through a reduction in their output to match the below full employment demand for commodities, it also reduces employment below full employment. There is no reason for firms to increase employment to its initial state of full employment, so that there continues to be excess supply of labour in the economy. Hence, the economy has excess supply in one market without a corresponding excess demand in any market. Again, Walras' law is violated – or the behavioural assumptions needed for its assertion are implausible and irrational at the microeconomic level.

Table 17.2 highlights this argument on the conflict between Walras' law and the plausible real-world scenario.

Table 17.2

	E_c^d	E_n^d	E_m^d	E_b^d	$\Sigma_i E_i^d$
Walras' law	$< 0 \Rightarrow$	$= -E_c^d > 0$	0	0	0
Likely real-world and rational scenario	$< 0 \Rightarrow$	$\neq -E_c^d$	0	0	$\neq 0$

Intuition

To put the information in Tables 17.1 and 17.2 in intuitive terms, consider a real-world economy in which a fall in investment or exports has reduced aggregate demand and caused a recession. Such a recession will have an excess supply of commodities. Walras' law tells us that there must be a corresponding excess demand for labour. But intuition and experience about real-world economies indicates that the excess supply (deficient demand) for commodities would be accompanied by an increase in unemployment (i.e., an excess supply of labour). That is, Walras' law is counter-intuitive in these circumstances.

17.10.2 The revision of the economic agents' constraints when some markets do not clear

In the two illustrations above, the violations of Walras' law occurred because of the particular dependence between the flow markets of commodities and labour: in the first case, labour cannot spend income that it does not receive, while, in the second case, firms do not employ workers whose output they cannot sell. Therefore, the violations of Walras' law must occur because the budget constraints of firms and workers, which were among the bases of Walras' law, are themselves violated. That is, for the examples used, the actual budget constraints must, in fact, be different from equation (1) (for the households) and equations (2) to (4) (for the firms).

To expand on these points, first consider the households' behaviour. This was:

$$p_c c^{dh} + p_c m^{dh} + p_b b^d + p_e e^d \equiv p_c \underline{c}^s + \underline{M}^h + p_b \underline{b}^s + p_e \underline{e}^s + W n^s + \pi^{dis} \tag{1}$$

We will now refer to this equation as the neoclassical version of the households' budget constraint. In this version, the income available for expenditures includes notional wage income $W n^s$, which the households will have to spend on commodities and other goods. If there exists involuntary unemployment (with $n < n^s$), households' actual labour income will be less than the notional one at $W n^s$, so that the right-hand side of (1) is incorrectly stated. However, (1) can be maintained if the unemployed workers determined their expenditures (the left side of (1)) *as if* they had the income which they would have received if they had succeeded in selling their labour (i.e., $W n^s$). This is neither rational nor plausible. Alternatively, (1) will be valid if the unemployed workers could continue to receive the income they would have got if they had been fully employed. But this is also not realistic since firms do not pay wages to laid-off workers at the full rate. Hence, the validity of (1) and of Walras' law requires actual labour market clearance.

Now consider the representative firms' behaviour and the violation of Walras' law in the second counter-example above. One of the firms' constraints was:

$$p_c (c^{sf} + i + g) + p_e (e^s - e^s) + \underline{M}^f \equiv W n^d + p_c i + p_c m^{df} + \pi^{dis} \tag{2}$$

which is neoclassical in nature and assumes that the left-hand side includes c^s, the amount of commodities that the firms want to sell if they can sell all that they want, rather than the amount that they will actually be able to sell or will want to produce under the existing aggregate demand conditions in the economy.

Firms demand labour to produce output and meet the demand for output. If the demand for output is at the full employment level, they will demand enough labour for full employment to occur, so that (2) would have the values of all its variables, including the demand for labour, consonant with full employment in the labour market. Alternatively, for (2) to be valid when there is inadequate aggregate demand for the full employment output, firms are required to act *as if* there was adequate demand forthcoming to sell the full employment output and to continue to supply output on that hypothetical basis. That is, firms must always act in the production and supply of output *as if* there was an output demand equal to the full employment level, *even* when it is not so. Such behaviour is not only hypothetical, it will in general be irrational, in the sense of not being profit maximizing under the actual demand conditions being experienced by the firm. Such hypothetical behaviour can also be subjected to empirical tests, and would be found not to be valid for the representative firm: since a firm producing to meet the full employment level of demand, when the actual one is less, follows a recipe that is not profit maximizing and could even end in its insolvency. Hence, the validity of Walras' law requires commodity market clearance at the full employment output level.

17.10.3 Notional demand and supply functions in neoclassical economics

For Walras' law to hold in the above two examples, there must be excess demand for output whenever there is excess supply of labour, and vice versa. Therefore, for Walras' law, we need the actual clearance of all markets, or, if some of them are not in equilibrium, we need the hypothetical behaviour pattern: *all agents continue to act as if all markets cleared even when they do not.* Walras' law requires this assumption to be an identity. As a consequence, Walras' law requires that the demand and supply functions in (1) to (5) be 'notional' functions, where a demand or supply function for a good i is said to be notional if economic agents act as if all *other* markets cleared. If this condition does not hold in practice, real-world functions could be different from the notional ones and Walras' law as specified so far would not apply in terms of these real-world functions. Hence, Walras' law would not be an identity for the real-world functions and strictly does not deserve the designation of a law.

17.10.4 Re-evaluating Walras' law

To wrap up this discussion, given the starting assumption of continuous bond and money market clearance, Walras' law requires the clearance of both the labour and commodity markets. When they do not clear, it assumes that one of the following two things must occur:

(i) firms continue to pay workers the full wage even after laying them off; or
(ii) households behave *as if* the labour market had cleared at full employment, even *if* it means spending incomes which were never received.

Both conditions are clearly hypothetical – and irrational in the sense of not being profit/utility maximizing under the actual constraints that apply to the firms and the households. Both can be empirically tested and in general would be found not to be valid for the representative consumer and firm. Hence, since these assumptions are unrealistic when the labour or commodity markets do not clear, the validity of Walras' law requires that we rule out the occurrence of such conditions from consideration, which in turn requires positing continuous commodity and labour market clearance. The new classical and modern classical schools follow this route. However, this rules out the proper analyses of some types of disequilibrium. Nevertheless, many studies in this tradition still base their disequilibrium analyses on notional demand and supply functions.

17. 11 REFORMULATING WALRAS' LAW: THE CLOWER AND DRÈZE EFFECTIVE DEMAND AND SUPPLY FUNCTIONS

17.11.1 Clower effective functions

Clower (1969) argued that in conditions where some markets fail to clear, the relevant demand and supply functions are not notional ones, but must take account of disequilibrium in other markets. For example, if some workers are unable to sell their labour supply and are thereby involuntarily unemployed, their constraints on the purchases of commodities, money and bonds must take into account their resulting lack of labour income, so that their actual demands for these goods would be less than their notional demands. That is, the relevant demand functions incorporate the *spillover effects* of disequilibrium in the labour market. However, the relevant supply function of labour is still the notional one since the workers can still buy as much as they like of other goods.

As another example, if firms face deficient demand for commodities – that is, they cannot sell all the output they wish to produce at full employment – they will have an effective demand for labour that is less than its notional demand. However, assuming that the firms do not face disequilibrium in markets other than for commodities, they would still operate with the notional supply function for commodities as their effective supply function. The demand and supply functions incorporating the impact of disequilibrium in *other* markets are called the *Clower effective demand and supply functions*. In microeconomic analysis, the effective demand/supply of an individual in market i is to be derived from the maximization of his utility function subject to his budget constraint *and* subject to the restrictions perceived by him in all other markets k, $k \neq i$. Similarly, the demand/supply of a firm in market i is derived from its profit maximization subject to its perceived constraints in markets k, $k \neq i$.

Clower and Leijonhufvud claimed legitimately that the Clower effective demand and supply functions – and not the notional ones – are the ones applicable to Keynesian analysis, while the notional ones are applicable in neoclassical analysis.[19]

Reformulating Walras' law for Clower effective functions

Assuming that a disturbance has led to a fall in employment below the full employment level, we have a constraint in the form $n = n^d < n^s$, which modifies equation (1) to the inequality:

$$p_c c^{dh} + p_c m^{dh} + p_b b^d + p_e e^d \leq p_c \underline{c}^s + \underline{M}^h + p_b \underline{b}^s + p_e \underline{e}^s + Wn^s + \pi^{dis} \tag{24}$$

which in combination with (2) to (5) yields the inequality:

$$E_c^d + E_m^d + E_b^d + E_e^d + E_n^d \leq 0 \tag{25}$$

so that Clower argued that the proper statement of Walras' law is (25): that is, the sum of all excess demands in the economy is *non-positive*. In this statement of Walras' law, in the context of our assumed involuntary unemployment, the excess demands for goods other than labour are effective ones while that for labour is notional. Correspondingly, note that if the perceived constraint by firms was that of the deficient demand for commodities – that is, $y^d < y^s$ – the excess demand for commodities will be notional while the others would be effective.

A consequence of (24) is that it cannot be used to derive the statement that equilibrium in $K-1$ markets implies equilibrium in the Kth one also, since the $K-1$ markets with demand equal to supply could be the markets with effective functions while the Kth one could be the one with the disequilibrium, with its disequilibrium being the inequality of its notional demand and supply.

17.11.2 Drèze effective functions and Walras' law

In the context of involuntary unemployment, Drèze (1975) proposed a reinstatement of Walras' law by equating the supply of labour to be the effective supply set by the smaller demand for labour. That is, set $n_D^s = \bar{n}^d$, where n_D^s is the Drèze supply of labour. The purpose is to impose *all* the constraints that operate in the economy. In the general case, this results in the Clower demand/supply functions for all markets i in which there are no perceived constraints, but with the Drèze demand/supply functions set by the constraints themselves in the constrained k markets. Equations (1) to (5) with demands and supplies redefined in this manner again imply Walras' law, but in a Drèze effective – and not a notional – sense. Excess demands would also be redefined in a corresponding manner and the sum of all such excess demands would again equal zero.

Note that we can speak of equilibrium in an unconstrained market in the sense of the equality between the Clower demand and supply in that market, and determine its price from such equality. However, we cannot consider the equality of Drèze demand and supply in a constrained market as representing equilibrium in it or use such equality as a basis for determining the price in it. Hence, both Clower's reformulation of Walras' law as an inequality and Drèze's reinstatement of it in terms of Drèze functions limit the usefulness of this concept.

CONCLUSIONS

Walras' law is a core underlying relationship in the specification of macroeconomic models and is used to eliminate the explicit treatment of one of the markets in them. By convention in neoclassical and Keynesian macroeconomic models, the market thus rendered implicit in the analysis is usually the bond market, though it could be any of the others. For a monetary economist interested in the nature of the bond market, it allows the derivation of the excess demand function for bonds, though not of its demand function or its supply function alone. This excess demand function could in turn be used to specify the dynamic path of interest rates using the loanable funds theory of the rate of interest.[20]

Say's law can be interpreted in a weak form as an equilibrium condition for the commodity market. However, this form does not impose any restrictions on the macroeconomy other than imposed through the use of the IS relationship in the IS–LM models and does not merit the designation of a law. It can be interpreted in a strong form as an identity between the supply and the demand for commodities. However, this form is not valid for a monetary economy, since such an economy allows substitution between real balances and commodities – and thereby possesses interaction, at least in the disequilibrium states, between the monetary and commodity sectors – while Say's law as an identity rules out any impact of a disequilibrium in the money market on the commodity market.

Walras' law and the strong form of Say's law imply the dichotomy between the real and monetary sectors and the neutrality of money. The dichotomy is not valid in a monetary economy. The validity of the neutrality of money in the short run depends upon the structure of the economy, since it requires wage and price flexibility, continuous market clearance and the absence of the real balance effect in equilibrium. While few economies would meet these stringent conditions in the short period, the disputes on the neutrality of money depend upon how relevant these departures from neutrality are in practice.

While Walras' law is an identity in the context of the notional demand and supply functions, it becomes an inequality with the Clower demand and supply functions. The use of Drèze functions reinstates its equality but at the cost of its usefulness. Keynesians claim that their macroeconomic analysis is based on the Clower effective functions, so that they question the validity of the IS–LM analysis, if it is based on notional behavioural functions.

If some markets fail to clear, the constrained demand and supply functions in other markets will not be notional but effective ones. The latter can be stated as Clower or Drèze functions. Walras' law does not hold if we work with Clower functions, but does hold for Drèze functions. The relevance of such functions is usually investigated in the context of a failure of either the labour market or the commodity market to clear. In the former case, there would be deviations from full employment and, in the latter case, there would exist aggregate demand deficiency or excess demand. Economists who see such macroeconomics failures as at best only a short-run phenomenon, would maintain the validity of Walras' law for the long run. The classical economists who believe in the continuous clearance of all markets – in particular, including the labour and commodity ones – maintain Walras' law also for the short run. Keynesians who deny such continuous market clearance – especially in the labour and commodity markets – also deny the short run validity of Walras' law in notional terms.

The real balance effect specifies the impact of changes in real balances occurring in the money market on the aggregate demand for commodities. It is, therefore, one of the elements interconnecting the commodity and money markets and played a critical historical part in discussions on the dichotomy between the sectors. It clearly exists in the short run but may or may not exist in the long run.

The real balance effect is the 'income' effect induced by changes in the real value of outside money – that is, of the monetary base – which is now only a very small proportion of M1 and an even smaller proportion of M2, M3 and M4, which are themselves small proportions of total wealth in the economy. Therefore, the percentage change in real wealth due to the likely magnitudes of the changes in the real value of the monetary base, is so small that its impact on the economy cannot be very significant. Hence, the real balance effect seems to be of greater theoretical importance than empirical relevance.

SUMMARY OF CRITICAL CONCLUSIONS

- Walras' law is based on the budget constraints of the various economic agents in the economy and is perhaps the closest we can get to an identity in economics.
- Say's law does not apply in monetary economies.
- Walras' law applies in monetary, as well as barter, economies provided that the various markets are in equilibrium or agents behave as if they are in equilibrium. Its application in demand-deficient recessions is in dispute.
- Walras' law can be used to derive the excess demand function for bonds, the asset which is in the macroeconomic framework even though its demand and supply functions are often left unspecified in the IS–LM analysis.
- The real balance effect is an important theoretical link between the money and the commodity markets. Its empirical importance in the modern economy is limited.
- Neoclassical and modern classical analyses use notional demand and supply functions and rely on Walras' law as an identity.
- Keynesian analysis of deficient demand and involuntary unemployment uses effective demand and supply functions, and modifies Walras' law to an inequality.

review and discussion questions

1 Walras' law is derived from the budget constraints of all the economic agents in the economy. Can Say's law be similarly derived from budget constraints? Use the relevant constraints and specify the additional assumptions needed for this derivation. Assess the validity of these assumptions.
2 What are the implications for monetary policy if both Walras' law and Say's law are imposed on the IS–LM model? Assess the likely validity of these implications. If they do not seem to be valid, which of these two laws should be discarded? Derive the implications for monetary policy of imposing the remaining law on the IS–LM model.
3 Do the modern classical and new classical schools effectively reinstate Say's law as one of their component doctrines? If so, should they state it explicitly?
4 Derive the implications of Walras' law and Say's law together for the determinacy of absolute and relative prices in a commodities–money (no bonds or labour)

economy. What role does the real balance effect (the short run and the long run) play in this determination?

5 Outline your understanding of the households' and firms' most likely responses to a fall in the aggregate demand for commodities. Does its perceived duration matter? If a downturn in the economy leads to a fall in demand that is perceived to be significant in magnitude and duration, discuss whether Walras' law will continue to hold. If it does not, what happens to the excess demand for commodities and for bonds in the IS–LM model?

    Does Walras' law hold in recessions?

6 In terms of your understanding and beliefs about the functioning of your economy, which of the four markets (commodities, money, bonds and labour) clear on a daily, weekly and monthly basis? Which may not do so at least within thirty days of a disturbance? Within six months? Within a year?

    If some of the markets do so while others do not, does this support Leijonhufvud's and Clower's contention that Walras' law is not an identity when there is disequilibrium in some markets?

7 For the magnitudes of the relevant variables in any of the past five years in your economy, try to assess the importance of the real balance effect for a 5 per cent fall in the price level.

8 What was the dichotomy between the real and the monetary sectors in classical macroeconomics? How would such a dichotomy arise in a Walrasian general equilibrium system?

    What was the contribution of Patinkin's real balance effect to this debate? Does the contribution of Archibald and Lipsey re-establish this dichotomy?

9 Does the dichotomy between the real and the monetary sectors hold in the modern classical approach? Is this dichotomy valid or not for the modern financially developed economy?

10 What were Keynes' arguments in his attacks on Say's law and the traditional classical dichotomy? In retrospect and especially in the light of the reversion (counter-reformation!) of macroeconomics to the (modern version of the) classical model, evaluate the success of these attacks.

11 Keynes argued that an economy could be in equilibrium with a substantial amount of involuntary unemployment, but other economists disagreed and argued that a state in which an important market does not clear is one of disequilibrium. Explain the notions of equilibrium and disequilibrium involved, Keynes' justification for his position, and his opponents' justification for theirs. Does the existence of the real balance effect or the wealth effect refute Keynes' position?

12 Discuss: 'the real balance effect provides a possible dynamic explanation of the adjustments in the economy in going from one equilibrium to another and is an effective answer to the assertion of a Keynesian under-full employment equilibrium. However, it is not really necessary for the comparative static propositions of the quantity theory or of neoclassical economics.'

13 Discuss: the derivation of the excess demand function for bonds using Walras' law provides both insights into its properties and also throws up some clearly invalid properties.

14 Robert Clower argued that 'either Walras' law is incompatible with Keynesian economics, or Keynes had nothing fundamentally new to add to orthodox economic theory'. Explain the basis for such a conclusion.

    Is Walras' law incompatible with the different Keynesian and neo-Keynesian models as they have evolved?

15 Define the notional, Clower and Drèze demand and supply functions. Prove whether or not Walras' law applies to each of these three types of functions and in what sense it does so.

NOTES

1 Another proposition which is sometimes referred to as a law is the 'law of one price', which in international trade translates to purchasing power parity between countries. However, Chapter 20 on the open economy shows that it is often rejected by empirical evidence so that it cannot be properly regarded as a law.

Another proposition often labelled as a law is that 'the demand curves for commodities slope downwards'. However, this is violated for many goods, such as those with snob appeal, which have an upward-sloping demand curve. Therefore, even this statement is not an identity and not really a law.

2 The open economy has an additional good in the form of foreign exchange held by the private and public sectors. The analysis for it is presented in Chapters 18 and 19.

3 Bond holdings can be positive (making the individual a net lender) or negative (making the individual a net borrower).

4 We have assumed here that the individual is a supplier of labour services; firms will be the buyers of such services.

5 We have included three financial goods (money, bonds and equities) in the following analysis in order to show that the separate treatment of equities does not destroy Walras' law. Note that in the rest of this book and in monetary economics generally, 'bonds' are defined to include all non-monetary assets and therefore would also include equities.

6 See Shaller (1983). Shaller's dynamic analysis of prices and interest rates specifies the changes in these in disequilibrium in terms of the commodity and bond market equations, rather than in the commodity and money market ones.

7 This point will be taken up again in Chapter 20 on the determination of the rate of interest.

8 Equation (22) is really not an identity since the assumption of continuous labour market clearance implicit in it is not an identity.

9 Baumol (1999) claims that the appellation 'Say's law' was given in the early twentieth century to ideas of which Say was an enunciator but that they did not originate with him. Further, Say and other writers espousing these ideas did not make claims to its being a 'law'.

10 Baumol (1999) attributes this mode of statement to Keynes and states that 'Keynes, at best, did not get it quite right' (p. 195).

11 For example, Adam Smith wrote that, 'What is annually saved is as regularly consumed as what is annually spent, and nearly in the same time too . . . saving . . . is immediately employed as capital either by himself or some other person. . . . The consumption is the same but the consumers are different' (Baumol, 1999, p. 200).

12 Baumol (1999) attributes the interpretation of Say's law as an identity to Oskar Lange (1942).

13 However, Say's law applied in some past periods when the economies were purely subsistence or barter ones. In these rudimentary economies, commodities were produced either for consumption or directly for exchange with other commodities. The supply of commodities as a whole was then necessarily equal to their demand, both for individuals and in the aggregate for the economy.

14 The classical model followed this procedure using the quantity theory to specify the price level. The model was supplemented by the equation $M = P \cdot m^d = P \cdot m_y y = m_y y$, where y was set at full employment. Hence, Walras' law, Say's law and the quantity theory can be logically consistent with each other, without such consistency implying their validity individually or as a set.

15 Further, if the economy was only a commodities–money one, then, as argued earlier, Walras' law and Say's law together would imply that the demand for money will also always equal its supply, irrespective of the interest rate and income. Hence, in this case, the LM curve will also span the (r, y) space.

16 The real balance effect is clearly relevant to the question of whether the economy can be in equilibrium below its full employment level. This effect was an element in the disputes between the neoclassical economists and Keynesians on the existence of an equilibrium

below full employment, with the neoclassical school arguing that such a state would be one of disequilibrium: prices would decline and changes in aggregate demand and output would occur because of the real balance effect.

17 Archibald and Lipsey (1958) used the term 'week' for it.

18 Chapters 13 to 16 had also argued that among other types of economic behaviour inimical to the short-run neutrality of money are adjustment lags, long-run relationships such as implicit labour contracts and the failure of markets to clear.

19 The two are identical if equilibrium exists in all markets.

20 This is specified in Chapter 20.

REFERENCES

Archibald, G. C., and R. G. Lipsey. 'Value and Monetary Theory: Temporary versus Full Equilibrium'. *Review of Economic Studies*, 26, October 1958, pp. 1–22.

Baumol, William J. 'Say's Law'. *Journal of Economic Perspectives*, 13, Winter 1999, pp. 195–204.

Clower, Robert. 'The Keynesian Counter-Revolution: A Theoretical Appraisal.' In F. H. Hahn and F. P. R. Brechling, eds, *The Theory of Interest Rates*. London: Macmillan, 1965. Also in Clower, Robert W., ed., *Monetary Theory, Selected Readings*. London: Penguin, 1969.

Drazen, A. 'Recent Developments in Macroeconomic Disequilibrium Theory'. *Econometrica*, 48, March 1980, pp. 283–306.

Drèze, Jacques H. 'Existence of an Exchange Equilibrium under Price Rigidities'. *International Economic Review*, 16, June 1975, pp. 301–20.

Keynes, John Maynard. *The General Theory of Employment, Interest and Money*. New York: Macmillan, 1936.

Lange, Oskar. 'Say's Law: A Restatement and Criticism'. *Studies in Mathematical Economics and Econometrics: In Memory of Henry Schultz*. Chicago: University of Chicago Press, 1942.

Leijonhufvud, Axel. 'Keynes and the Keynesians'. *American Economic Review Papers and Proceedings*, 57, May 1967, pp. 401–10.

——. *On Keynesian Economics and the Economics of Keynes*. New York: Oxford University Press, 1968.

Patinkin, Don. *Money, Interest and Prices*, 2nd edn. New York: Harper & Row, 1965.

Shaller, D. R. 'Working Capital Finance Considerations in National Income Theory'. *American Economic Review*, 73, March 1983, pp. 156–65.

part six

MONEY IN THE OPEN ECONOMY

chapter eighteen

THE OPEN ECONOMY: EXCHANGE RATES AND THE BALANCE OF PAYMENTS

This chapter and the next one present the macroeconomic and monetary analyses for the open economy. Their main focus is on the monetary aspects of the open economy and the role of monetary policy in it.

This chapter is an introductory and rather elementary one on the concepts and determinants of the foreign exchange markets and the balance of payments. It is meant to define the terms and lay the basis for the analysis of the open economy macroeconomics and the determination of the exchange rate, presented in the next chapter. Those familiar with the topics treated in this chapter can go directly to the next one.

---

key concepts introduced in this chapter

- Exchange rates: nominal, real and effective
- Balance of payments
- Foreign exchange reserves
- The demand and supply of foreign exchange
- Fixed, flexible and managed exchange rates
- Purchasing power parity
- Interest rate parity
- International Monetary Fund

This chapter presents introductory material on exchange rates, the balance of payments and related issues. The material is quite basic and the student is already likely to be quite familiar with it. It is presented as a review[1] and an introduction to the next chapter on the open economy macroeconomics.

The neoclassical and Keynesian macroeconomic analyses of a closed economy were presented in Chapters 13 and 14. In these, the economy was closed in the sense that there were no flows of commodities, money, bonds or factors of production between the domestic – or 'our' – economy and other economies. But every economy nowadays has considerable commodity and financial flows with other economies. These flows – mainly of commodities, currencies and financial capital, though sometimes also of people – between economies affect their domestic national income, employment, prices and other endogenous variables, as well as the scope and effectiveness of national monetary and fiscal policies.

The flows of factors of production other than physical capital[2] are minor and are generally ignored in macroeconomic analysis. Further, the short-run analysis of an open economy assumes that the physical capital stock is fixed so that any flows of such capital that occur are out of currently produced output and do not affect the productive capacity of any economy. In fact, there is a special use of the word 'capital' in the context of international trade. This is in its financial usage. Therefore, the international flows of 'capital' are to be understood as being only financial flows, that is, a flow of the currency and other financial assets of one country to another country in exchange for financial assets.[3] These flows have become quite considerable in the last few decades with the global integration of financial markets, and on a daily basis are larger than the values of commodity flows for many countries.

The open economy has one more good than the closed economy. This good is 'foreign exchange', which is the medium of payments between the domestic and foreign economies. This good consists of foreign currencies, gold and special drawing rights (SDRs) at the International Monetary Fund (IMF) which act as a kind of demand deposits of individual countries with the IMF. The price of the domestic currency against a foreign one is the exchange rate between the currencies. Since macroeconomic theory usually treats the rest of the world as a single unit, our analysis will be set out in terms of the composite category labelled 'foreign exchange' – meaning by it the foreign currencies of the rest of the world – and 'the exchange rate' between it and the domestic currency. Section 18.1 presents the basic concepts and analysis related to the exchange rate.

Flows of commodities and financial instruments occur between the domestic economy and the rest of the world. The former take the form of the exports and imports of commodities, with the net balance between them designated as net exports, and captured in the balance of trade and the balance of payments on current account. The flows of financial instruments are (financial) capital flows and are captured in the balance of payments on capital account. These are the subject of section 18.2. Section 18.3 presents the somewhat related concept of the accounting balance of payments.

Section 18.4 deals with the demand for and supply of foreign exchange, and the change in the foreign exchange reserves of the domestic economy. Countries have the choice of letting their exchange rate be determined competitively by the demand and supply of foreign exchange in the open markets, or fix a value for it, with the fixed value sometimes being identical with but often differing from the open market one. Section 18.5 deals with the case of the flexible exchange rates and section 18.6 with that of purchasing power parity (PPP). Section 18.7 presents the concept of interest rate parity (IRP) and section 18.8 describes fixed exchange rates. Section 18.9 briefly addresses the role of the International Monetary Fund in the foreign exchange markets and as a type of central bank for the world economy.

18.1 EXCHANGE RATES

18.1.1 Three concepts of exchange rates

Almost all countries have their own national currencies. The rate of exchange between a domestic currency and a foreign one is called the exchange rate between them. The exchange rates between currencies can be nominal, real or effective ones.

The nominal exchange rate

The *nominal exchange rate* is the rate at which a currency can be exchanged against another currency. This exchange rate between any two given currencies can be defined in two alternate ways. It can be defined as:

(i) the price per unit of a foreign currency – or of any other international mode of settling debts such as gold – in terms of the domestic currency. As an example, the price of British £ (pounds) was approximately \$2.10 in Canadian dollars (per £) in early 1996. The exchange rate (ρ) for the £ was thus \$2.10.

(ii) The price of the domestic currency (\$) in terms of a foreign currency (say £s). This measure of the exchange rate is clearly the reciprocal of the former measure, so that the exchange rate now would be specified by \$1 = £1/2.10 = £0.476.

The definition of ρ that would be appropriate to use obviously depends upon convenience and preferences. We prefer using the definition in (ii). That is, *the nominal exchange rate will be defined as the number of units of a foreign currency required to purchase one unit of the domestic currency.* Taking the dollar as the unit of the domestic currency and the £ as the generic symbol for a unit of the foreign currency, the nominal exchange rate will be the amount of £s per \$ in the foreign exchange markets. We will use the symbol ρ for the nominal exchange rate. The dimension of ρ is £/\$.

The real exchange rate

The *real exchange rate*, designated as ρ^r, is the amount of foreign commodities that can be exchanged for one unit of domestic commodities.[4] Its relationship with the nominal exchange rate is specified by:

$$\rho^r = \rho P/P^f \tag{1}$$

where:

ρ nominal exchange rate (units of foreign currency per unit of the domestic one)
ρ^r real exchange rate
P domestic price level
P^f foreign price level

Therefore, the real exchange rate is the nominal exchange rate adjusted for the relative price ratio between the countries. As mentioned above, the real exchange rate is a measure of the units of the foreign goods required to buy a unit of the domestic commodity. This measure requires a standardized composite commodity representative of the output of the countries in question. Such a standardized composite commodity does not exist. The closest we come to it in aggregate data is the price level. Hence, the relative price level (P/P^f) has been used to adjust the nominal exchange rate ρ in (1). Since the dimensions of ρ were £/\$ and of P/P^f are \$/£, the dimension of r^r are real ones (foreign commodities per domestic ones).

Since the standardized composite commodity on a worldwide basis does not exist, many economists trying to intuitively estimate the real exchange rate on their travels use the price of a standard commodity such as a McDonald's hamburger as they move from one country to another. Thus, a price of £1 per hamburger in the UK and \$1.20 in Canada, with a nominal exchange rate of £0.50 per \$, gives a real exchange rate of 0.60. Intuitively, in this example, it takes only 60 per cent of a British hamburger to buy a Canadian one: the British hamburgers are relatively expensive.

The effective exchange rate

There is obviously a different exchange rate for each foreign currency, even though economic analysis is formulated in terms of a single exchange rate for simplification purposes. Such a rate can be envisaged as an average exchange rate for all currencies, just as the 'price level' is an average of the prices of commodities in the economy. This average exchange rate between the domestic currency and all foreign currencies is called the *effective exchange rate.* As an average, the effective exchange rate is obtained by weighting the exchange rate against each foreign currency by the proportion of the amount traded with its country. Changes in this effective rate provide a measure of the average change in the value of a currency.

There can obviously be both a nominal and a real effective exchange rate. The effective rate is preferable for converting GDP, exports, imports, etc., from one currency to another for international comparisons.[5]

18.1.2 Purchasing power parity and the real exchange rates

For an internationally traded commodity i, which is traded in perfectly competitive markets and for which there are no transactions costs (such as for shipping, insurance, etc.) of movement across countries, the price in each country's domestic currency would be identical. In such a case, taking the McDonald's hamburger as our example, the hamburger should cost the same in real terms in the two countries. Extending this argument to all commodities, if there were perfect commodity flows between Canada and Britain for all goods in the economy, then in competitive markets and without transactions costs, the prices of all commodities would be the same and we would have ρ^r equal to unity. That is,

$$\rho^r = \rho P/P^f = 1 \tag{2}$$

Equation (2) is known as *purchasing power parity* (PPP), which is the condition that the purchasing power of different currencies after conversion by the exchange rate is the same across countries. ρ^r equal to one implies that:

$$\rho = P^f/P \tag{3}$$

The importance of focusing on the real rather than the nominal exchange rates is that since exports and imports depend on the relative prices of the goods at home and abroad, they depend on the real exchange rates and not the nominal ones. If $\rho^r > 1$, the same goods are relatively more expensive at home than in foreign countries. Conversely, if $\rho^r < 1$, then the goods are relatively cheaper in the domestic market.

The real exchange rate between countries rarely equals unity, partly because many of the goods (especially services) in each country are non-tradable across countries. If we assume that the real exchange rate has a particular value k and that this value does not change over the period in question, we have:

$$\rho^r = \rho P/P^f = k \tag{2'}$$

which implies a weaker form of (2) and (3) known as *relative purchasing power parity*. The *relative purchasing power parity condition*, derived from (2'), is that:

$$\rho'' = P^{f''} - P'' = \pi^f - \pi \tag{4}$$

where '''' stands for the rate of change in the accompanying variable and π is the rate of inflation.

18.1.3 Fixed, flexible and managed exchange rates

The market for foreign exchange can be allowed to determine the exchange rate or it can be set by the government. The former is known as the flexible exchange rate case and the latter as the fixed exchange rate case. In general, there are three exchange rate regimes: fixed, flexible or managed, with the last one covering the case where the government adjusts the exchange rate as economic conditions change.

Depreciation and appreciation of the domestic currency

If ρ decreases, say from £0.50 per \$ to £0.40 per \$, the domestic currency decreases in value relative to foreign currencies and there is a *depreciation* or *devaluation* of the domestic currency against other currencies. In this case, it would cost more in domestic currency to buy foreign goods and assets, and domestic goods and assets will become cheaper in foreign currencies. Conversely, if ρ increases, the domestic currency increases in value relative to foreign currencies and there is an *appreciation* or *revaluation* of the domestic currency against other currencies. In this case, foreign goods and assets will become cheaper in terms of the domestic currency, while the domestic goods and assets will become more expensive in foreign currencies.

18.2 THE BALANCE OF PAYMENTS

The balance of payments can be presented in an economic or accounting form. Economic analysis focuses mainly on its economic form. If the economic balance of payments were arranged in the form of a table, it would specify each of the sources of the inflows and outflows of funds from a country, and the difference between them. Defining the (economic) balance of payments by B, we have:

$$B = (X_c + Z_k + NR + NT) - (Z_c + X_k)$$
$$= (X_c - Z_c + NR + NT) - (X_k - Z_k) \tag{5}$$

where:

B	balance of payments
X_c	value of exports of commodities (goods and services)
X_k	value of capital exports
Z_c	value of imports of commodities (goods and services)
Z_k	value of capital imports
NR	net interest and dividend inflows
NT	net unilateral transfers (gifts and donations) to the domestic economy from abroad

Equation (5) defines the *overall balance of payments in an economic sense*. The balance of payments is thus a statement of the exports and imports of commodities and financial capital. Note that all of the magnitudes in (5) are in nominal form. $(X_c + Z_k + NR + NT)$ are the inflows of foreign exchange, with X_c as the inflows against the exports of commodities, Z_k as the inflows against the outflows of bonds (including stocks and shares and other claims to ownership), NR as the net inflows of interest and dividends from abroad and NT as the net inflows of gifts and remittances. NR and NT represent inflows of funds without a corresponding reverse flow of currently produced commodities or bonds. NR captures the payments of interest and dividends on foreign bonds held by the domestic residents or on domestic bonds held by foreigners, with such bond holdings representing past investments rather than being a current cross-border flow of bonds. NT captures cross-border remittances or gifts, which do not involve explicit future debt obligations. $(Z_c + X_k)$ is similarly the outflows of funds with a corresponding reverse flow of commodities or bonds against them.

Clearly, B in (5) need not equal zero. It could be positive, negative or zero. If $B > 0$, there is said to be a surplus in the balance of payments. If $B < 0$, there is said to be a deficit and if $B = 0$, the balance of payments is said to be in *equilibrium*. By comparison, if $B < 0$ or $B > 0$, the balance of payments is said to be in *disequilibrium*.

The balance of payments has three components:

(i) The balance of payments on current account (B^c):

$$B^c = (X_c - Z_c + NR + NT) \tag{6}$$

The balance of payments on current account has three components: net exports of goods and services (also known as *the balance of trade*), net interest and dividend income from foreign investments, and net unilateral transfers. If the sum of the *net* interest and dividend payments and net unilateral transfers were zero, the balance of payments on current account becomes identical with net exports, which is also known as the balance of trade. The common assumption on $(NR + NT)$ is that this sum is zero or that it can be taken as exogenous in short-run analysis.[6] We will mostly continue to retain this item in the following analysis, though we will at certain points simplify the notation and analysis by implicitly setting this sum as zero.

(ii) The balance of payments on capital account (B^k):

$$B^k = (X_k - Z_k) \tag{7}$$

This balance specifies the net exports of (financial) capital.

(iii) The official settlements balance (B^f):

$$B^f = -B \tag{8}$$

By convention, *the official settlements balance equals the negative of the balance of payments B*, so that $B + B^f = 0$.

Note that if the balance of payments is in equilibrium, $B = 0$ and $B^f = 0$, and also that,

$$(X_c - Z_c) + (NR + NT) = (X_k - Z_k) \tag{9}$$

That is, in the balance of payments equilibrium, a balance of payments deficit (surplus) on the current account is exactly matched by a surplus (deficit) in the balance of payments on capital account.

18.3 THE BALANCE OF PAYMENTS IN AN ACCOUNTING SENSE

The accounting balance of payments is given by:

$$(X_c - Z_c + NR + NT) - (X_k - Z_k) + B^f \equiv 0 \tag{10}$$

where '$\equiv$' indicates an identity.

The balance of payments accounts are a statement of the receipts and payments to foreigners in a given period of time, in a form such that the total receipts *always* equal total payments. In order to achieve this, the balance of payments in an accounting sense is related to the (economic) balance of payments by the identity:

$$B + B^f \equiv 0$$

An illustrative form of the balance of payments accounts is shown in Table 18.1. This table lists the flows by type of activity or function. While the items in this table are self-explanatory, a few comments would be useful. The interest and dividend payment flows are

Table 18.1 A stylized balance of payments accounts

Credits		Debits	

The balance of payments on current account

Credits		Debits	
Merchandise exports	150	Merchandise imports	125
Rent	0	Rent	5
Interest	80	Interest	25
Dividends	100	Dividends	10
Wages and salaries	25	Wages and salaries	35
Transportation	5		
		Donations to foreign countries	
		Private	10
		Government aid	20
Total for current account	*360*		*230*

The balance of payments on capital account

A. Private

Credits		Debits	
Sale of foreign equity	15	Purchase of foreign equity	40
Firms' long-term debt	10	Loans to foreign firms	20
Firms' short-term debt	20		
		Purchase of foreign government securities	10
Foreign demand deposits with local banks	5	Demand deposits with foreign banks	15
		Acquisition of foreign exchange by local banks	10

B. Government

		Long-term loans to foreign countries	100
Total for capital account	*50*		*195*

The balance of payments

Total	*410*		*425*

Official settlements balance

Net gold and foreign exchange outflows 15

the return to past flows of capital, and appear in the trade balance and the current account, while the current capital flows, through purchases and sales of bonds (including loans) and equities or deposits in foreign banks, are part of the capital account. High levels of net inflows (outflows) of capital over some years will imply increased outflows (inflows) for interest and dividends in subsequent years, creating a dynamic relationship between the present capital account and the future current account. The donations to foreign countries are unilateral flows and enter in the current account. While there is a large net surplus of 130 on current account, the deficit on the capital account of 145 because of net investments abroad result in a net deficit of 15 on the overall balance of payments. This deficit is settled by net sales of gold and foreign exchange worth 15 by the country, so that the official foreign exchange reserves decrease by 15.

The exports and imports of commodities and long-term capital assets occur virtually exclusively on the basis of the preferences of economic units (households, firms and governments) in the light of incomes, prices, interest rates, etc. Some of the short-term flows of capital and of foreign exchange, including gold, are also of such a nature. All such flows which are the result of economic preferences and are independent of equilibrium or disequilibrium in the balance of payments are known as *autonomous* flows. Only autonomous flows are considered in the balance of payments in an economic sense so that it is often known as the *autonomous balance of payments*.

However, some of the short-term capital flows and foreign exchange flows are not independent of the equilibrium in the autonomous balance of payments. For example, if $\Delta R^f > 0$, there is a net inflow of foreign exchange. The central bank or commercial banks receiving such 'residual' inflows often choose to convert some of these into short-term foreign bonds, holding the rest as an addition to their foreign exchange holdings.

Further, some of the short-term capital flows may be extremely sensitive to the balance in the (economic or autonomous) balance of payments. For example, if there was a large deficit in the balance of payments, it may lead to speculation about a possible devaluation of the domestic currency and heavy outflows of short-term funds seeking protection from such devaluation or trying to make a profit out of it. Funds whose flows among countries are very sensitive to expected exchange rate changes, interest rate fluctuations or security and convertibility considerations are known as *hot money*.

These considerations have led many economists to treat the inflows and outflows of foreign exchange and short-term capital as *induced flows*, that is, induced by the state of the autonomous balance of payments. They are usually never wholly so. Such flows are both an objective and a guide for national policy, since they affect the country's foreign exchange reserves and are an indication of the extent of disequilibrium in the balance of payments.

18.4 THE DEMAND AND SUPPLY OF FOREIGN EXCHANGE AND THE CHANGES IN FOREIGN EXCHANGE RESERVES

18.4.1 The demand and supply of foreign exchange

The closed economy models had four broad categories of goods in them. These were commodities, money, bonds and labour. An economy engaging in trade with other economies has an additional good labelled as *foreign exchange*, which is composed of all those assets that can act as media of exchange in international transactions. This category mainly includes gold, currencies of foreign countries and special drawing rights at the International Monetary Fund.[7] The analysis for an open economy requires that we also specify a market with a demand function and a supply function for foreign exchange.

The demand for foreign exchange by a country – designated as 'our', 'home' or 'domestic' country – has its converse in the supply of dollars by us to foreigners to act as an element of their foreign exchange balances. The supply of foreign exchange by foreigners is correspondingly the converse of the demand for dollars by foreigners from us. The market for foreign exchange, therefore, can be looked at from two different viewpoints: as the demand and supply of dollars in the foreign exchange market or as the demand and supply of foreign exchange. We will often find it convenient to switch from one to the other in the intuitive explanations of our analysis.

The demand for foreign exchange is the demand for international modes of payment, and arises because the residents of the domestic economy wish to purchase – that is, import – either commodities or financial assets from abroad.[8] The supply of foreign exchange to our economy arises because foreigners wish to purchase our commodities or financial assets, as well as make net payments of interest and dividends, and of net unilateral transfers. The difference between these inflows and outflows of foreign funds becomes the inflow or outflow of foreign exchange funds into our economy. The latter may be invested or held in the form of foreign currencies, gold, special drawing rights or short-term bonds of foreign countries. The sum total of these constitute the country's foreign exchange reserves.

Hence, the demand for foreign exchange (D^f) is the sum of our imports of commodities (Z_c), our imports of financial assets corresponding to our capital exports or outflows (X_k). Similarly, the supply of foreign exchange (S^f) is the sum of our exports of commodities (X_c) and our exports of financial assets corresponding to our capital imports or inflows (Z_k) plus net transfers of interest and dividends (NR) plus net unilateral transfers (NT). The difference between the supply and demand for foreign exchange equals the change in the nation's foreign exchange reserves and is designated as ΔR^f. Therefore:

$$D^f = Z_c + X_k \tag{11}$$

$$S^f = X_c + Z_k + NR + NT \tag{12}$$

where:

D^f demand for foreign exchange
S^f supply of foreign exchange

18.4.2 The change in foreign exchange reserves and the balance of payments

Equations (11) and (12) imply that,

$$
\begin{aligned}
\Delta R^f &= (X_c + Z_k) - (Z_c + X_k) + NR + NT \\
&= (X_c - Z_c) - (X_k - Z_k) + NR + NT
\end{aligned}
\tag{13}
$$

where R^f stands for the foreign exchange reserves. Comparing equations (5) and (13), we have $\Delta R^f = B$. Hence, the net change in our foreign exchange reserves is zero (that is, $\Delta R^f = 0$) if the balance of payments is in equilibrium. There is a net inflow of foreign exchange to the home country ($\Delta R^f > 0$) if the balance of payments is in surplus and a net outflow ($\Delta R^f < 0$) if the balance of payments is in deficit.

Countries hold reserves of foreign exchange with their central banks to meet the possibility of deficits in the balance of payments. These deficits draw down the reserves by a corresponding amount and the surpluses increase them by the size of the surplus. B is thus a measure of the change in the country's foreign exchange reserves.

The size of the foreign exchange reserves or changes in it are a matter of national policy, so that ΔR^f may be positive or negative for long periods. Thus, the United States had a deficit ($\Delta R^f < 0$) in its balance of payments virtually throughout the 1950s and the 1960s, and Germany and Japan have had surpluses in their balances of payments for some decades, with neither specially concerned about these for most of the period. The desired level of B should, therefore, be superimposed on (5) in further analysis. However, for pedagogical purposes, macroeconomic analysis usually assumes that the country desires equilibrium in its balance of payments. This corresponds to the assumption that the desired level of ΔR^f is zero. This is a simplification and further analysis can be carried out with any other desired value of ΔR^f. Note that if $\Delta R^f = 0$,

$$(X_c - Z_c) = (X_k - Z_k) - (NR + NT)$$

so that the net capital flows (less NR and NT) must exactly cover the net imports.

18.5 FLEXIBLE EXCHANGE RATES

18.5.1 The market for foreign exchange

Both the demand and supply of foreign exchange are functions of the exchange rate as well as of other variables. The exchange rate may be left unregulated by the national authorities to adjust to demand or supply pressures or its movements may be controlled rigidly or within certain specified limits. An uncontrolled exchange rate is said to be a *flexible* (or *floating*) exchange rate. A rigidly specified exchange rate is said to be a *fixed* (or *pegged*) exchange rate. There are many combinations of these two basic practices. Thus, the authorities may operate a system whereby the exchange rate is allowed to vary within wide limits or is altered at certain intervals.[9]

If the exchange rate is permitted to be completely flexible, it adjusts to equate the demand and supply of foreign exchange, as specified by (11) and (2). At this stage, it is convenient to view the demand for foreign exchange D^f in (11) as the supply $S^\$$ of our currency (dollars) in the foreign exchange markets and the supply of foreign exchange S^f as being the demand $D^\$$ for our currency in these markets. Therefore, from (11) and (12), we have:

$$S^\$ = Z_c(\rho^r, y) + X_k(r, r^f, \rho^r) \tag{14}$$

$$D^\$ = X_c(\rho^r, y^f) + Z_k(r, r^f, \rho^r) + NR + NT \tag{15}$$

where the determinants of the imports and exports have been inserted on the right-hand side. An appreciation in ρ means an increase in ρ^r, which makes our goods more expensive relative to foreign ones, so that X_c and $D^\$$ decrease, while Z_c and $S^\$$ increase.

Diagrammatic analysis

Figure 18.1a shows such a demand curve $D^\$$ and a supply curve $S^\$$, with the exchange rate ρ on the vertical axis and the quantity $Q^\$$ of dollars exchanged against foreign currencies. The equilibrium nominal exchange rate is shown as ρ^*. This rate is stable, for the slopes of the demand and supply curves shown in Figure 18.1a.

Figure 18.1a has several limitations. A major one of these is that it only focuses on the commodity flows, holding the interest rates and the expected future exchange rate constant under the *ceteris paribus* clause since these variables are not on one of the axes of the figure. As a consequence, this figure keeps capital flows constant and gives the impression that the commodity flows determine the movements in the exchange rate. But the foreign exchange markets are financial markets which adjust on a daily basis to the shifts in the demand and supply, and the shifts in the capital flows – under interest rate parity discussed in section 18.7 below – are the main short-run determinants of the exchange rate. This is particularly so since the responsiveness of imports and exports to exchange rate changes as shown in Figure 18.1a are subject to significant lags. Further, Figure 18.1a assumes that both the demand and supply of foreign exchange to the country are elastic.

18.5.2 Demand and supply elasticities

The slopes of the demand and supply curves shown in Figure 18.1a assume that our imports and exports are elastic – that is, possess an elasticity greater than unity – with respect to changes in the real (and nominal) exchange rate, so that, as the exchange rate depreciates and foreign goods become more expensive relative to ours, the *expenditures* (and not just the quantity) on our imports decrease and those on our exports increase. However, this need not be the case for all countries at all times and, even if it applies in the long run for a given country, it need not be the case in the short run while the buyers and suppliers make

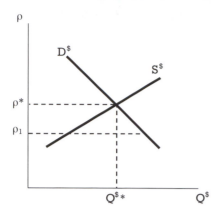

Figure 18.1a

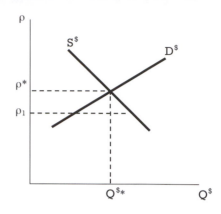

Figure 18.1b

adjustments to their purchasing and production patterns as a consequence of the changes in the exchange rate. Since our main concern is with the value of net exports rather than with the values of imports and exports separately, we can, therefore, posit the following two scenarios:

(i) an inelastic short-run pattern where the relative elasticities of imports and exports are such that the value of net exports decreases in response to a depreciation; and
(ii) an elastic long-run pattern in which the elasticities of imports and exports are both greater than one, so that the value of net exports increases in response to a depreciation.

Figure 18.1a shows the long-run pattern. An extreme version of the short-run pattern, with both imports and exports being inelastic, would have $D^\$$ sloping upwards and $S^\$$ sloping downwards. This case is shown in Figure 18.1b. To compare the stability of the exchange rate in these two figures, suppose a disturbance causes the exchange rate to fall to ρ_1 below ρ^* in Figure 18.1a. Excess demand exists at ρ_1. Making the neoclassical assumption that this market adjusts prices in response to a disequilibrium, the excess demand for dollars below ρ^* forces an increase in their value until equilibrium is restored at ρ^* through an exchange rate appreciation. These arguments can also be applied to Figure 18.1b to show that a fall in the exchange rate to ρ_1 will cause an excess supply of dollars, which will further lower their value – that is, cause a depreciation – so that the market adjustments will lead to a movement away from equilibrium. Conversely, in Figure 18.1b, an accidental exchange rate appreciation will cause a further appreciation, rather than a return to the equilibrium rate ρ^*. Hence, while the equilibrium exchange rate is stable in Figure 18.1a, it is unstable in Figure 18.1b and in the inelastic short-run case.

Therefore, a depreciation of the exchange rate can cause a decrease or increase in the supply of foreign exchange, depending upon the price elasticities of imports and exports. Note that the impact or short-run elasticities for many commodities are often lower for some time, say for a year or less, than their long-run ones, so that, depending upon the structures of demand and supply, the short-run elasticities of exports and imports can be less than unity on average for a given economy. In terms of net exports, if the elasticity of exports is less than that of imports in the short run, a depreciation will worsen the balance of payments in the short run, though this balance will eventually improve in the long run.

18.5.3 The J curve for net exports

The case where the elasticity of net exports is less than one for some time after a depreciation or devaluation but increases over time until it becomes greater than one, implies that the value of net exports will initially fall and then rise, generating a J-shaped curve for the net nominal – i.e. in terms of their value – exports over time. Such a curve is called a *J curve* and is applicable to many countries. The duration of the declining part of this curve depends upon the composition and nature of the country's exports and imports, their substitutes and upon the supply conditions.

Many developing countries have traditional exports with low elasticities of demand in foreign markets and low supply elasticities at home, while their imports tend to consist more of industrial goods with higher elasticities of demand, so that they face the possibility of net nominal exports worsening in response to a depreciation of their currency and doing so for a longer term than for the industrialized countries. Hence, for many of the developing economies, attempts to eliminate the net exports deficit and that in the balance of payments through a depreciation of the currency often increase, rather than decrease, these deficits, at least for a significant period, so that such actions have to be accompanied by other measures to support the balance of payments and the exchange rate.

18.5.4 The case for flexible versus fixed exchange rates

The preceding analysis in this section assumed that we can hold the interest rates, expected exchange rate changes and hence capital flows constant under the *ceteris paribus assumption* while the value of net commodity exports adjusts in response to disturbances in the exchange rate. But the former variables usually respond even faster to the exchange rate changes, which, among other things, can set up expectations of further exchange rate changes, which can, in turn, induce large capital flows. This faster pattern of dynamic capital market responses often dominates the slower commodity flow responses and turn a case of stability in the latter analysis into an actual case of instability in the overall market, at least for some time, and vice versa. These capital flows are even more likely to accentuate a case of the basic instability arising out of the commodity-induced foreign exchange flows. In such a context, the central banks are often tempted to intervene in the foreign exchange market by buying or selling, as required, foreign currencies to try to stabilize the exchange rate of their currency against what they perceive to be short-term destabilizing influences.

Whether a country has a stable or unstable foreign exchange market is an empirical question and generally one whose answer varies with the circumstances. Up to the late 1960s, the common belief in economics was that the foreign exchange markets tended to be unstable, so that it was in general preferable to have fixed exchange rates. This belief was embodied in the rules and recommendations of the IMF. However, many of the major industrialized economies, especially that of the USA, suffered systematic imbalances in their balance of payments towards the end of the 1960s. Given these imbalances, combined with the speculative runs on currencies, it proved impossible to maintain fixed exchange rates among currencies, and between the US dollar and gold, with the result that the economics profession and the IMF began to recommend flexible exchange rates. Eventually, the IMF and the USA became strong advocates of flexible exchange rates.

In the years since the early 1970s, most of the world's largest trading nations have had flexible exchange rates[10] and unhampered flows of financial capital, without seemingly excessive exchange rate volatility, though bouts of severe volatility have occurred for several emerging and transitional – mainly East European countries in the transition from communism to capitalism – economies. In general, this period has been one of very fast growth in the international flows of both commodities and capital, accompanied by very rapid technical change and shifts in the comparative advantage of countries. These changes constitute potential pressures for changes in the exchange rates. Such pressures have been accommodated well by the flexible exchange rate system, while a fixed exchange rate system would most likely have created severe imbalances in the balance of payments of countries, which, reinforced by speculative and chaotic runs on the exchange markets, would have forced periodic changes in the fixed exchange rates.[11] Consistent with this experience, many economists believe that the flexible exchange rates provide greater stability in practice, especially in periods of significant shifts in the underlying demand and supply of foreign exchange.[12]

However, the Latin American and Asian exchange crises during the 1990s seem to indicate a high degree of volatility in the currencies of individual countries. Part of the reason for this is that the extent of currency speculation that can potentially occur into or out of a currency can be a very significant proportion of the country's trading flows of foreign exchange and of its reserves. This is especially so for the smaller developing economies. In such cases, a speculative run into or out of the country's currency has the potential of creating large fluctuations in its exchange rate. Economic theory and evidence does not make it clear whether a flexible or a fixed exchange rate regime acts as a greater disincentive to such runs and/or contains them better.

Therefore, it seems that flexible exchange rates are better than fixed exchange rates at accommodating long-run changes in the foreign exchange markets related to changes in commodity flows – for example, from the differential developments of technologies, different inflation rates, etc. But they open the door to more frequent or more severe speculative runs into and out of individual currencies and these runs introduce a new element of volatility into exchange rates.

18.6 PURCHASING POWER PARITY (PPP)[13]

As explained earlier, purchasing power parity is the condition that a standardized commodity must cost the same in different countries. The assumptions required for this condition are that: the commodity is identical in different countries, there is perfect competition and there are no transactions costs (such as shipping, insurance, etc.) or information asymmetries among the countries. In the limiting case where all goods and services in the economy are of this type, the PPP as stated above was that:

$$P = P^f/\rho$$

so that $\rho = P^f/P$. All of the goods which exist in the economy do not meet the assumptions for PPP. Among the reasons for this are that many goods are not internationally tradable. Further, some of the inputs of even internationally tradable goods, such as the labour services in retailing or local transportation or the usage of immovables such as buildings and land, etc., have to be local ones. Therefore, even for the internationally traded goods, these transportation and local retailing costs drive a wedge between the domestic prices of goods and the prices in other countries. Hence, the conditions for PPP are not met for all or possibly most final goods in the economy, so that the absolute version of PPP will not apply in practice. To take account of the potential for the difference in prices among countries, rewrite (3) as:

$$P = k \cdot (P^f/\rho) \tag{16}$$

where k is the wedge between domestic and foreign prices and can be greater or less than unity. A constant degree of competitiveness for a given degree of comparative advantage between countries is consistent with a constant value of k, so that, taking k as a constant, we get the relative version of PPP defined in terms of the rates of change as:

$$\rho'' = \pi^f - \pi \tag{17}$$

Economists usually prefer using the relative version of the PPP as a guide to exchange rate determination and even then often as only a long-run – rather than as a daily or short-run – condition on exchange rate changes between countries.

On the question of whether PPP applies in the real world, we turn to the prices of hamburgers across countries as an intuitively appealing test. Pakko and Pollard (1996) compared the real exchange rates for McDonald's Big Mac in fifteen countries and found that its prices varied between 75 and 141 per cent of those in the United States. This evidence represents very significant deviations from PPP. Although the Big Mac is a standardized product, its local cost of production only partly depends upon internationally traded inputs, such as meat and flour, which should adhere to purchasing power parity. Its cost of production also depends on inputs, such as labour and buildings, which are not internationally traded and for which there need not be purchasing power parity. The degree of local competition for hamburgers could also differ, so that McDonald's may vary its profit margin among countries. These factors cause differences in its relative cost between countries. At the economy's level, most final products are similarly combinations of internationally traded and non-traded goods, and there are different degrees of competition for each country's goods. Therefore, PPP rarely applies to individual goods or to commodities as a whole.

18.7 INTEREST RATE PARITY (IRP)

Corresponding to the PPP for commodity flows, the interest rate parity condition is derived with reference to capital flows. In perfectly competitive markets with zero transactions costs, capital will flow to the country with the highest net rate of return after exchange rate changes. Designating the interest rates by r and r^f, the domestic return is r, while the net return (in the domestic currency) on foreign investments is r^f less any expected appreciation ρ''^e of the domestic currency – that is, plus any expected appreciation of the foreign one. If $r < r^f - \rho''^e$, investors will get a higher expected return from investing abroad and will only invest abroad, and if $r > r^f - \rho''^e$, investors (including foreigners) will invest only in the domestic economy. In equilibrium, the return must be the same from the two forms of investment, so that:

$$r = r^f - \rho''^e \qquad\qquad (18)^{14}$$

where ρ''^e is the expected rate of appreciation of the domestic currency and equals $(\rho^e - \rho)/\rho^e$.
   Equation (18) can be restated as:

$$r^f = r + \rho''^e \qquad\qquad (19)$$

There is said to exist *covered IRP* if the investors protect themselves against exchange rate fluctuations through forward contracts[15] and *uncovered IRP* if they do not do so. For covered IRP to exist in the foreign exchange markets, there must be forward markets with zero or relatively low transactions costs. While these normally exist to some extent in economies with well-developed financial markets, they do not usually exist for most of the LDCs which do not have organized and competitive forward markets for foreign currencies.
   International capital flows are nowadays potentially much larger than the value of commodity flows for developed economies with open capital markets, so that anticipated changes in interest rates can set up massive capital flows. These flows – entering on either the demand or supply side of the market for the foreign exchange of a country – dominate over other flows and determine the exchange rate – unless the governments have fixed the exchange rate or try to manage it through offsetting sales or purchases of foreign exchange from their reserves.[16]
   Further, since capital is extremely mobile and can be transferred between countries with well-developed financial markets at a few minutes' notice, IRP determines exchange rate changes on a continuous basis in free exchange markets, while, as we have already argued, PPP holds at best in a long-run context. In well-developed financial markets, IRP provides the short-run determination of the exchange rates while PPP or its relative version can only

be a long-run condition. Exchange rates determined through IRP can deviate from PPP for considerable periods.

18.8 FIXED EXCHANGE RATES

Countries sometimes fix – unilaterally or as part of an international agreement such as the International Monetary Fund rules (from 1945 to the early 1970s) – the exchange rates between their currency and those of other countries. This amounts to price fixing in the foreign exchange market for the country in question. If the exchange rate is fixed at a level lower than the equilibrium one at ρ^* and if the foreign exchange demand and supply curves are as shown for the stable case in Figure 18.1a, we have $\rho < \rho^*$, so that $B > 0$. In this case, the country experiences an excess demand for dollars in the foreign exchange markets and an excess supply of foreign exchange. If the exchange rate is above the equilibrium rate in Figure 18.1a, we have $\rho > \rho^*$, so that $B < 0$. That is, the country would face an excess demand for foreign exchange, implying an excess supply of dollars in the foreign exchange markets.

The excess demand and supply of foreign exchange can be handled easily if the authorities – usually the central banks – are willing to adjust their own official holdings (reserves) of foreign exchange by a corresponding amount. Countries hold such reserves, sometimes in substantial amounts relative to their imports, on the basis of considerations very similar to those which determine an individual's demand for money balances (for which see Chapters 3 to 6 above). The excess demand or supply in the foreign exchange market may be consistent with the authorities' desired change in such reserves, given their existing holdings. Even if it is inconsistent, it may be accommodated temporarily by offsetting changes in reserves before other adjustments are made to cut down on the excess demand or supply, as in the buffer stock models of the demand for money in Chapter 6, or if such excess demand or supply is expected to be a temporary phenomenon anyway.

A more serious adjustment problem arises if the authorities do not wish to accommodate the excess demand or supply out of their reserve holdings on a continuing basis. They may then switch to a flexible exchange rate. If they do not wish to resort to this, they could take other measures which would restore the excess demand or supply for reserves to its desired level. The measures that are feasible can be derived from the determinants of the demand and supply of foreign exchange.

Equation (13) defines the excess supply of foreign exchange. There would be excess supply if $\Delta R^f > 0$, with excess demand if $\Delta R^f < 0$. Of the components on the right-hand side of (13), $(X_c - Z_c)$ are net exports, which increase – that is, assuming an elasticity of net exports to be greater than unity – if domestic prices fall relative to foreign prices. Net exports also increase if domestic income falls and reduces imports. Another component of (13) is $(X_k - Z_k)$ – i.e., net capital exports – which depend upon domestic interest rates relative to foreign ones. Therefore, the domestic monetary and fiscal authorities can reduce the amount of excess supply B of foreign exchange by raising the domestic price and income levels and/or by lowering the interest rates. Conversely, in order to reduce an excess demand for foreign exchange, the authorities can lower the domestic price level and income and/or raise the domestic interest rates. The implications of such policies for the whole economy require a re-specification of our macroeconomic models for closed economies and are dealt with in the next chapter.

18.9 THE INTERNATIONAL MONETARY FUND (IMF)

National monetary policies have to be formulated in, and take account of, the existing environment of international financial system and arrangements. A core element of this system is the IMF. Our interest in its functioning and the constraints it imposes upon national monetary policy is rather limited, so that the following presentation primarily addresses its limited role as a world central bank.

The IMF was set up under arrangements made at Bretton Woods, New Hampshire, in 1945, and started functioning in 1947. Its main mandate was to be an international financial institution to oversee the member countries' payments arrangements and exchange rate policies, and to provide short-term financial assistance to members with balance of payments problems. In particular, among what came to be known as 'the Bretton Woods system', member countries were required to maintain fixed exchange rates and to devalue their currencies only in the case of a fundamental disequilibrium in their balance of payments and only after prior consultation in a specified manner with the IMF. The underlying support to this system of fixed exchange rates was provided by the decision of the United States to be on the gold exchange standard by maintaining a fixed exchange rate for its dollar against gold and convertibility of the dollar against gold. The turbulence in the exchange markets, in particular the speculative runs on the US dollar at the end of the 1960s and early 1970s, led the United States, in 1971, to abandon the gold exchange standard. The exchange rate between the US dollar and gold was allowed to float. In 1973, the European countries allowed their currencies to float against the US dollar. In 1974, the IMF adopted guidelines promoting managed floating exchange rates among its member countries. The encouragement and management of flexible exchange has since then been a central tenet of IMF policies.

Central to the IMF's role with respect to exchange rates is its mandate to exercise 'surveillance' over its members' exchange rate policies and their macroeconomic and related structural policies. Among these is the promotion of policies aimed at the elimination of balance of payments problems, the promotion of sound banking principles and efficient and solvent financial institutions, the collection and analysis of appropriate economic data, limiting fiscal deficits, etc.

The IMF is a strong supporter of the unhindered international flows of both goods and capital, taking these to be essential for continued economic growth and prosperity. It uses its influence and other powers to promote liberal trade practices and the free movement of capital among countries. Its clout becomes especially effective when a country runs into severe balance of payments problems and needs large borrowing from the IMF.

A core function of the IMF has been to provide short-term loans to its member countries with balance of payments problems, whether arising from shortfalls in net exports or capital outflows, and to help cushion the impact of adjustments to solve these. Such loans are often in the form of a 'stand-by arrangement' – that is, a line of credit – and are usually accompanied by concerted lending by other – creditor – countries. They are made subject to particular conditions, which, in certain cases, can include an explicit commitment by the borrowing country to take specific and quantitative remedial economic measures, including specific fiscal and money growth targets, to contain the balance of payments imbalances, and to repay the loan by specified dates. The policies and procedures governing the provision and use of these loans are known as 'conditionality'.

In providing short-term loans to cover foreign exchange shortages, the IMF performs a function similar to that of national central banks when they act as a lender – at times, as that of last resort – to their respective commercial banks. While such a role is needed and of considerable benefit to member countries facing severe shortages of foreign exchange, it also carries moral hazard. Moral hazard arises because the availability of an automatic or quasi-automatic borrowing facility reduces the compulsions and incentives for the member countries to contain their balance of payments deficits by appropriate policies. Conditionality is the instrument for containing moral hazard, since the loan will be made contingent on the pursuit of the economic adjustments required to enable it to repay the loan within a specified period – usually within three to five years. Another reason for conditionality is the protection of the value and quality of the IMF asset portfolio, which is mainly composed of loans to member countries. The required pursuit of policies under conditionality can have relatively minor consequences or, as in the case where the exchange crisis needs for its resolution major structural changes, have considerable economic, social and political repercussions, which the borrowing country may not wish to incur. In particular, in recent years, conditionality has had an underlying philosophy advocating free markets, competition and democratic political structures, which some countries have resisted. At the international level, conditionality has consistently taken the form of supporting the liberalization of import and export flows.

The original Articles of Agreement of the IMF signed in 1945 had allowed the use of controls by member countries on capital movements. Among the reasons for this was the aim of preserving for the member countries a degree of control over their monetary and fiscal policies. Many countries, including European ones, did maintain such controls for several decades. In recent decades, with the very considerable integration of the national markets for goods and services into the global economy, and in the current context of flexible exchange rates, the IMF has also strongly supported the liberalization of capital flows. Among the reasons for it is the belief that obstacles to capital flows reduce growth. However, unrestricted capital flows also pose a risk since a major part of them is highly liquid and susceptible to sudden reversals – giving their most liquid component the name of 'hot money'. These reversals can be related to the fundamental economic developments in the economy in question or be merely due to non-fundamental factors, such as shifts in the investors' perceptions of risk of investment in the country in question. But they can also occur because of international developments, such as the decisions of other countries to raise their interest rates or other countries or regions coming into 'fashion' as a new investment haven. With the considerable increase in the foreign investments, the role of the IMF as a lender of last resort has become of even greater importance than in earlier decades. A country faced with a capital account crisis usually requires relatively large financial support at a few days' or few weeks' notice. If this cure works, the loan can be repaid promptly; if it does not, there will be still greater demand for loans.

The liberalization and increase in the magnitude of world capital flows has clearly fostered world economic growth. But it has also increased the chances and scale of the potential systematic threats to the stability and soundness of the world economy and its various regions. The responsibility of the IMF to act as a lender at short notice and of last resort for the national central banks and governments is, consequently, now of vital importance to the stability and performance of the national and world economies.

Under the initial arrangements made in 1945, the IMF was not envisaged as a central bank with the power to issue its own currency. This changed in 1969 with the creation of the special drawing rights (SDRs) and their allocation to member countries. The SDRs are an international asset, which can be traded among member countries and used to settle payments imbalances among them. The IMF has increased the outstanding amount of SDRs at various times, allocating the increases among the members in proportion to their quotas in the IMF, as compared with the open market operations by which national central banks bring about increases in the monetary base. The total outstanding amount of SDRs is still a relatively small fraction (about 1.7 per cent in 1997) of the non-gold reserves of the member countries, so that increases in it do not significantly affect the world money supply and the world price level.

A unit of SDRs is a weighted average of five currencies, the US dollar, the Deutsche mark, the French franc, the Japanese yen and the British pound, with its value calculated daily. As a weighted average, its stability is more than of any of the individual currencies. Besides serving as a reserve asset for the member countries, it is also used as a unit of account in many international transactions and even for denominating private financial instruments. Countries can peg their currencies to the SDR, if they so wish, though, so far, few have done so. The SDRs are essentially a unit of account and their holdings are in the form of deposits. They do not have a physical existence and are not traded in national markets.

The interest rate charged by the IMF on its SDR loans is also a weighted average of the yields on specified short-term (mainly three-month Treasury bills) instruments of the five countries whose currencies are used for computing the value of the SDR.

Is the IMF a central banker for the world?

The IMF was not set up to function as a central bank for the world and has not yet fully evolved into this role. It is still much less than a world central bank since it is not able to control or change the world's liquidity, which national central banks can do for their economies. It does not issue a widely traded currency nor does it have much influence on the world money supply or the total reserves of foreign exchange held by its member countries. The IMF's main similarity with national central banks is in its role as a short-term lender to member countries, especially during exchange crises and also to provide them with liquidity while they tackle their balance of payments problems. This role is sometimes viewed as that of a lender of last resort for member countries, but is, in reality, somewhat different from and significantly less than the extent to which the national central banks can perform this function for their own commercial banks. While the IMF has acquired considerable respect for its recommendations and considerable leverage over the macroeconomic policies and financial practices of the countries that seek assistance from it, these still fall short of the powers exercised by national central banks over their financial sectors. Further, some of the member countries, especially the United States, exert greater influence on the world financial system and on short-term lending to countries with exchange crisis than the IMF does.

CONCLUSIONS

The world economy has experimented extensively with fixed, flexible and managed exchange rates. The post-Second World War period started with a strong belief in the greater benefits of fixed exchange rates over those of flexible ones, and over the belief that devaluations other than those for really fundamental imbalances in the balance of payments were to be discouraged. The modalities of this determination were embodied in the rules established in 1946 for the IMF whose permission was needed before member countries could devalue their currencies relative to others.

Another strong belief was in the desire to maintain some form of control over the world's money supply through some form of the gold standard. After 1946, this was done through setting a fixed exchange rate for the world's strongest currency, the US dollar, against gold at the rate of US$35 to an ounce of gold. The exchange rates for other currencies were set against the US dollar or against one of the world's other major currencies, such as the British pound or the French franc.

While the economies of the world recovered from their war-torn states and expanded extensively during the 1940s and 1950s, the relative strength of the economies and the relative competitiveness of their export sectors had changed markedly by the later 1960s from their status in 1945. In particular, there were persistent deficits in the US balance of payments, which caused persistent speculative runs on the US dollar, as well as on many other major currencies. The fixed exchange rate system came to be viewed as an undesirable and unmanageable constraint on needed adjustments and on world trade. Eventually, in a series of steps taken during the late 1960s and early 1970s, the twin pillars of the fixed price of gold in terms of US dollars and the fixed exchange rates among currencies were abandoned. The general pattern of exchange rates among countries since that period has been one of flexible exchange rates, with relatively fixed ones among the members of the emerging European Union.

Even though the trade in commodities has grown enormously in the second half of the twentieth century, that in capital flows has come to dominate the foreign exchange markets on a short-term basis. Consequently, the short-term behaviour of exchange rates, especially for countries with developed financial systems, is now explained by reference to the interest rate parity condition for the equality of rates of return among countries, while the application of the purchasing power parity, especially in its relative form, for the equality of the prices of commodities on world markets is reserved for the long-run movements in exchange rates. The actual foreign exchange markets also exhibit a great deal of randomness, so that the deviations from the exchange rates implied by the interest rate parity occur on a constant basis.

Expectations play a very significant role in the foreign exchange markets. To illustrate, the interest rate parity condition incorporates the difference between the expected rate and the spot foreign exchange rate. Speculation arising from differences in expectations and shifts in them can buffet currencies through speculative runs. This is especially so since the amounts of liquid assets at the disposal of the world's major financial institutions, big firms and even some individuals are extremely large, and shifts in them of even small percentages from a given currency to others can cause major changes in the demand and supply of foreign exchange for the given currency, and thereby in its exchange rates against other currencies.

In terms of the short-run macroeconomic models, taking account of the existence of foreign trade and capital flows modifies the assumptions of our earlier closed economy models, so that the specifications of the expenditure and monetary sectors for the open economy change. These are dealt with in the next chapter.

SUMMARY OF CRITICAL CONCLUSIONS

- The nominal exchange rate defines the value of a currency in terms of another currency.
- The real exchange rate defines the conversion rate between the commodities in one country and the commodities in other countries.
- Purchasing power parity occurs under perfect commodity flows without transactions costs and is the doctrine that the real exchange rate between countries will be unity. Relative purchasing power parity is the doctrine that the depreciation of the domestic currency in terms of another will equal the difference between the inflation rates of the relevant countries.
- Interest rate parity occurs under perfect capital flows and is the statement that, under fixed exchange rates, the domestic and foreign interest rates will be identical. Under flexible exchange rates, the domestic interest rate will (approximately) equal the foreign one less the expected rate of appreciation.
- While the accounting concept of the balance of payments is that the balance of payments will be always in balance, this is not so for the economic concept of the balance of payments, which can have a positive or negative value.
- While the original mandate of the IMF had been the promotion of fixed exchange rates except in cases of long-run imbalances in the balance of payments, its policies shifted in 1971 to the promotion of flexible exchange rates.

---

review and discussion questions

1 Using your own experiences, provide some examples of the differences in the prices of seemingly identical goods between stores (a) in the city centre and the suburbs, (b) in different parts of the country and (c) between countries. What factors account for these ostensible deviations from purchasing power parity? Are these factors likely to be stronger for (c) than for (a) and (b)?

2 Why do countries with flexible exchange rates continue to have deficits or surpluses on their (a) current account and (b) balance of payments?
    Why are deficits not always accompanied by depreciation and surpluses not accompanied by appreciation of the exchange rate?

3 Discuss the validity of the following statement for both the short and the long run: an economy with a flexible exchange rate can have an interest rate different from the world one only if its inflation rate differs from the world inflation rate.

4 In the light of the European experience and British policies, what are the costs and benefits to Canada and the USA if they were to (a) adopt a fixed exchange rate between their currencies, (b) set their exchange rate in a narrow band, or (c) adopt a single currency? Is it in the interest of either of them to adopt one of these options?

5 What is 'hot money'? To what extent can the long-term imposition of exchange controls be a satisfactory method for controlling speculative money flows? Will the imposition of controls when the country is already in the middle of an exchange rate crisis yield better results than not doing so? Are exchange controls consistent with a flexible exchange rate regime?

6 'The Asian Crisis of 1997 and 1998 shows that flexible exchange rates periodically cause highly unstable exchange rates.' Discuss.

7 'The basic cause of the Asian Crisis of 1997 and 1998 was that the exchange rates of the affected countries were fixed against some foreign currencies, even though not against all. If they had been truly flexible against all currencies, the crisis would never have happened.' Discuss.

8 Should the IMF evolve into a world central bank? If it were to do so, what new roles and powers would it need to adopt?

NOTES

1 This review can also be done from textbooks on international economics. Among these are Krugman and Obstfeld (1997), Husted and Melvin (1998) and Salvatore (1998).

2 The remaining flows are of immigrants and transient migrants. While these are not very significant for most economies, there are a few countries, especially in the Middle East, for which such workers can be a significant proportion of the labour force.

3 The flows of physical capital are counted in commodity imports or exports, rather than in international capital flows.

4 To illustrate this point, assume that we are comparing the price of an identical car that costs £10,000 in Britain and $2,400 in Canada, and the nominal exchange rate is £0.5 per $. Hence, for this car,

$$\rho^r = \rho P/P^f = 0.5 \times 24,000/10,000 = 1.2$$

The units of measurement of ρ^r are:

(£ per $ × $ per Canadian car)/(£ per British car) = British car per Canadian car

5 The purchasing power parity index would be an even better measure for certain purposes such as comparing standards of living across countries.

6 Such an assumption would be unrealistic for countries with large positive or negative values of either NR or NT. Among these are countries with a large externally held debt, as in the case of many developing economies, or large net remittances as in the case of some oil-rich countries on the Arabian Peninsula with a large number of foreign workers.

7 Special drawing rights are held by individual countries as a form of demand deposits, and are designated in a specified basket of the national currencies.

8 Note that capital equipment and services such as shipping, tourism, etc., are already included in the definition of commodities and are part of imports and exports.

9 For example, under the *Smithsonian Agreement* reached in August 1972, between the United States and nineteen other major trading nations which are members of the IMF, the exchange rates between the US $ and the currencies of certain specified countries were allowed to vary within ±2.25% of the designated exchange rates. It had fluctuated within a

band of ±1% of the designated rates earlier. In March 1973, the US dollar was set free to float against other currencies.

10 Over the last three decades, the European Union as a regional bloc, including several major trading countries, moved increasingly closer to a system of fixed exchange rates among its members, with flexible rates *vis-à-vis* other countries not in the Union. In the earlier part of this period, the national currencies were permitted a limited float in a pre-designated narrow band, known as a 'snake'

11 The substantial fall in the exchange rates of Thailand, Indonesia, Korea and some other Asian countries in the late 1990s is at first sight indicative of the volatility and instability of floating exchange rates. However, many of these exchange rates were not fully flexible but tied to the US dollar or the Japanese yen, and had become overvalued in effective terms against other currencies. The final assessment of whether this experience is indicative of the instability or not of flexible exchange rates is still pending.

12 The United States is the world's largest single trading nation and has enormous amounts of capital inflows and outflows. The currencies of most of the other major trading nations of the world had their exchange rates fixed directly or indirectly in terms of the dollar before March 1973. Some of the currencies, such as the Canadian dollar, however, had at that time a floating exchange rate against the dollar. The US dollar, therefore, faced a mixed case of fixed and flexible exchange rates. The US dollar was set free in March 1973 to float against gold. Most other industrialized countries also moved to flexible exchange rate regimes during the 1970s.

13 The treatment of this hypothesis in this section and the next (18.7) is meant to be introductory. Its implications and tests are more fully presented in Chapter 19.

14 This is an approximate formula that does fairly well at low values of the expected rate of change in the exchange rate but not very well at high values. It is only approximate since it does not incorporate for foreign investments, the conversion of the foreign interest rate back into the domestic currency. For accuracy, for foreign investments, proper account has to be taken of the conversions of the capital as well of the interest receipts.

The more accurate formula is derived as follows. Investment of $1 at home will yield $(1 + r)$. Investment of $1 abroad will be worth $£\rho$ in the foreign currency at the time of investment and, therefore, would yield $£(\rho + \rho r^f)$ in the foreign currency. The latter's expected value in the domestic currency will be $(\rho + \rho r^f)(1/\rho^e)$. This equals $(1 + r^f)(\rho/\rho^e)$. Therefore, the return from investments at home and abroad is the same if

$$(1 + r) = (1 + r^f)(\rho/\rho^e)$$

$$r = r^f(\rho/\rho^e) + (\rho/\rho^e) - 1$$

$$= r^f(\rho/\rho^e) - [(\rho^e - \rho)/\rho^e]$$

For small expected changes in the exchange rate, the difference between this formula and (18) is relatively small and is ignored for the sake of simplifying the presentation. It cannot be ignored for large expected changes.

15 A forward contract in the foreign exchange market is a contract for the purchase (or sale) of a designated amount of a foreign currency at a specified future date at a specific exchange rate, with the contract being agreed to at the present time. Designating the forward exchange rate as ρ^{for} and noting that the current value ρ of the exchange rate is the spot rate in foreign exchange markets, for covered IRP, replace the expected exchange rate ρ^e by ρ^{for} in (18) and (19) and ρ''^e by $(\rho^{for} - \rho)/\rho$.

16 The ability to do so depends upon the country's foreign exchange reserves (and other support it can arrange from other countries or the IMF) relative to the private capital flows. Since the latter can be potentially much larger than the former for most countries, countries now possess a very limited ability to manage exchange rates contrary to market forces.

REFERENCES

There are very few references to this chapter since it is basically standard textbook material for macroeconomics. If other sources of this material are needed, any textbook in international finance can be used. The references for the wider topic of open economy macroeconomics are provided at the end of the next chapter.

Husted, Steven, and Michael Melvin. *International Economics*, 4th edn. New York: Addison Wesley Longman, 1998.

Krugman, Paul R., and Maurice Obstfeld. *International Economics, Theory and Policy*. 3rd edn. New York: Addison Wesley Longman, 1997.

Pakko, Michael R., and Patricia S. Pollard. 'For Here or to Go? Purchasing Power Parity and the Big Mac'. *Federal Reserve Bank of St Louis Review*, January/February 1996, pp. 3–17.

Salvatore, Dominick. *International Economics*. Upper Saddle River, NJ: Prentice-Hall, 1998.

chapter nineteen

THE MACROECONOMIC MODEL FOR THE OPEN ECONOMY

This chapter extends the analysis of Chapters 13 to 16 for the closed economy to the open economy. The pattern of analysis is similar to the presentation of the closed economy analysis. The first part of it is the application of the IS–LM technique. This gives an intuitive understanding of the material, as well as a realization of the variety and complexity of the different scenarios that can occur in the real world. The second part of the analysis is based on the use of compact models of the open economy.

The open economy analysis shows that the roles of monetary and fiscal policies and their effectiveness differ significantly between the fixed and the flexible exchange rate cases. They also show that the pursuit of monetary policy is more complicated for the open than for the closed economy.

---

key concepts introduced in this chapter

- Small open economy
- Balance of payments curve
- Three gaps: saving gap, fiscal gap, external gap
- Active versus passive monetary policy
- Currency substitution
- World inflation rate
- Convergence of inflation rates under fixed exchange rates
- Overshooting of the exchange rate

The preceding chapter on exchange rates and the balance of payments has laid the foundation for this chapter by explaining the balance of payments and the market for foreign exchange. This chapter revises the closed economy short-run macroeconomic model to accommodate trade in commodities and assets with other countries. It will be assumed that the domestic – also called as 'our' – economy is small relative to the rest of the world so that changes in it do not induce changes in the values of the economic variables in other countries. That is, the rest of the world can be taken as exogenous to the domestic economy in question. The resulting model is known as the *small open economy macroeconomic model*. This chapter presents this model and examines its implications for the influence of the rest of the world on the domestic economy as well as the roles of monetary and fiscal policies in it.

The modelling of the open economy macroeconomics can be done in the format of the IS–LM framework or in the form of compact models. The former extends the closed economy macroeconomics of Chapters 13 and 14 to the open economy, and, as in those chapters, relies extensively on diagrammatic treatment for deriving its conclusions and insights. This approach is used in the first half of this chapter and is invaluable in showing the complexity of the issues to be considered and the difficulty in the formulation and successful pursuit of monetary policy for the open economy. The latter approach presents compact models based on purchasing power parity (PPP) and/or interest rate parity (IRP) and provides more clear-cut policy conclusions. However, since these two hypotheses have proved to be of doubtful empirical validity, these conclusions do not meet with general approval among economists.

Section 19.1 describes the versions of the IS–LM model to derive aggregate demand for the small open economy. The relevant model depends upon whether the country has a fixed or flexible exchange rate, and upon whether the central bank sterilizes the balance of payments surplus or not. Sections 19.2 to 19.4 analyse the roles of monetary and fiscal policies under fixed and flexible exchange rates. Section 19.5 integrates aggregate demand in the open economy with aggregate supply. Section 19.6 examines this model under the assumptions of interest rate parity and full employment. Section 19.7 examines the world rate of inflation under the assumption of purchasing power parity, and the convergence of the country rates of inflation to it. Section 19.8 re-examines the need and roles for monetary and fiscal policies when there is disequilibrium among the sectors of the economy. Section 19.9 presents the evaluation on the fundamental issue of whether a country should have a fixed or flexible exchange rate.

Sections 19.10 and 19.11 switch the presentation of the open economy macroeconomic analysis to compact models. Section 19.10 presents the monetary approach to exchange rates (MAER) while section 19.11 presents the Dornbusch approach. Sections 19.12 and 19.13 assess the empirical validity of the PPP and IRP hypotheses, respectively.

19.1 THE MACROECONOMIC MODEL FOR AN OPEN ECONOMY

Such a model has five goods: commodities, money, bonds, labour and foreign exchange, and therefore five markets. Of these, the bond market will again be the one omitted from explicit analysis by virtue of Walras' law, so that the analysis will proceed with the specification of the remaining four markets for commodities, money, labour and foreign exchange. We will start with the last one in the next subsection and then examine the modifications needed for each of the other markets for the small open economy.

The definitions of the symbols used in this chapter are as given in the last chapter and in Chapters 13 and 14, except when new symbols are introduced. The domestic country is again taken to be 'our' country, and the rest of the world is taken to be 'the world', 'foreign country' or 'foreign countries'.

19.1.1 The foreign exchange sector of the open economy and the balance of payments

Assume that the foreign exchange authorities desire equilibrium in the balance of payments so that $\Delta R^f = 0$. As Chapter 18 showed, this is the statement that:

$$\Delta R^f = (X_c - Z_c) - (X_k - Z_k) + NR + NT = 0 \qquad (1)$$

where the definitions of the symbols are as in Chapter 17.

We will henceforth simplify by assuming, unless otherwise explicitly specified, that both exports and imports have price elasticities greater than unity. Therefore, our nominal exports X_c increase as the real exchange rate ρ^r ($= \rho P/P^f$) falls (i.e., if domestic prices P fall, ρ falls and/or foreign prices P^f rise) since they would become relatively cheaper compared with foreign goods. They also increase with foreign income y^f. Our nominal imports Z_c similarly decrease if ρ^r falls or if domestic income y falls. Capital flows depend upon a range of factors, of which the rates of return on domestic and foreign assets are likely to be the most important ones. It will be assumed that capital exports X_k decrease, and capital imports Z_K increase, as domestic interest rates r rise or as foreign interest rates r^f fall.[1] Putting these ideas formally into (1), the equilibrium condition for the foreign exchange market becomes:

$$X_c(\rho P/P^f, y^f) - Z_c(\rho P/P^f, y) - X_k(r, r^f) + Z_k(r, r^f) + NR + NT = 0 \qquad (2)$$
$$\underset{-}{} \quad \underset{+}{} \qquad \underset{+}{} \quad \underset{+}{} \qquad \underset{-}{} \underset{+}{} \qquad \underset{+}{} \underset{-}{}$$

where y is domestic national income, y^f is foreign national income, and the signs under the variables indicate the signs of the respective partial derivatives. NR and NT have been assumed to be exogenous. To the extent that they are not exogenous, their influence can be captured in either commodity or capital flows.

We have assumed in the introduction that the domestic economy is *small* relative to the rest of the world: that is, the variables P^f, y^f and r^f would not be affected by changes in our exports and imports of commodities and capital and can be taken as exogenous for the analysis. Omitting the exogenous variables y^f and r^f from equation (2) and replacing $\rho P/P^f$ by ρ^r, we are left with the equation:

$$[X_c(\rho^r) - Z_c(\rho^r, y)] - [X_k(r) - Z_k(r)] + NR + NT = 0 \qquad (3)$$

There are three endogenous variables (ρ^r, r and y) in this equation. Each of the curves in Figures 19.1a to 19.1c shows the values of the two variables on the axes if equilibrium is maintained in the balance of payments and the third endogenous variable in equation (3) is held constant.[2]

The balance of payments (BB) equilibrium curve

An increase in the domestic income y increases imports, leaving exports unchanged. This increase in imports could be offset in the balance of payments by an additional net capital inflow induced by a rise in domestic interest rates. That is, equation (3) implies a positively sloping tradeoff curve BB between y and r, as shown in Figure 19.1a, if ρ^r is held constant. The student can easily find the reasons for the tradeoff shown in Figure 19.1b between P and y, and that shown in Figure 19.1c between P and r, in each case with ρ held constant. These curves would shift as the third variable not on one of the axes, changes. To illustrate,

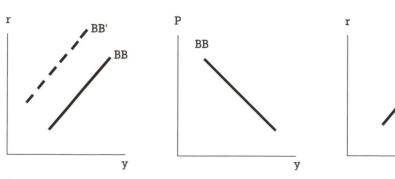

Figure 19.1a   *Figure 19.1b*   *Figure 19.1c*

in Figure 19.1a, if P rises, ρ^r would increase, causing net exports for given y to decline, so that a larger net capital inflow induced through a higher interest rate will be required to maintain equilibrium. The curve BB will, therefore, shift upwards, say to BB'.

If the nominal exchange rate is allowed to vary, as under a flexible exchange rate policy, to ensure continuous balance of payments equilibrium, then this equilibrium would occur through appropriate changes in the nominal exchange rate ρ for given values of r and y, so that we would not have a BB curve specifying particular combinations of r and y for balance of payments equilibrium. Hence, for the analysis of the fixed exchange rate case, we need to incorporate the BB curve into the IS–LM diagram, while this will not be done for the flexible exchange rate case.

19.1.2 The commodity sector (IS curve) of the open economy

Now consider the specification of the expenditure sector of the open economy. Real expenditures on the commodities produced in the economy and, therefore, the sales revenue of all the firms in the economy, are given by:

$$e = c + i + g + x_c \tag{4}$$

where all the variables are in real terms, x_c is the real value of exports and e is expenditures on domestic commodities.

National income can be spent by domestic residents in various ways as specified by:

$$y = c + s + t + (P^f/\rho P)z_c \tag{5}$$

where z_c is the quantity of imported goods bought at foreign prices P^f, converted into the domestic currency by dividing by the exchange rate ρ and then deflated into real terms at the domestic price P. Since:

$$\rho^r = \rho P/P^f$$

where ρ^r is the real exchange rate between foreign and domestic goods. Equation (5) can be more compactly stated as:

$$y = c + s + t + z_c/\rho^r$$

For equilibrium in the goods markets, we need:

$$e = y$$

as in the closed economy models, so that in equilibrium:

$$i + g + x_c = s + t + z_c/\rho^r \tag{6}$$

Three gaps: saving, fiscal and external

Equation (6) implies that:

$$(s - i) + (t - g) + [z_c/\rho^r - x_c] = 0 \tag{7}$$

where $(s - i)$ is the saving gap, $(t - g)$ is the fiscal gap and the last term $[\cdot]$ is the external trade gap. Note that (7) expresses a relationship among the three gaps, but without specifying a direction of causality. However, additional information on the exogeneity of any one of the gaps will insert causality from the exogenous gap to the endogenous ones. For example, if the above equation is rearranged as:

$$(z_c/\rho^r - x_c) - (i - s) = (g - t) \tag{7'}$$

and it is specified that $(g - t)$ is exogenous, the *exogenously created* fiscal deficit will induce either a saving gap and/or an external gap.

The open economy IS relationship

To derive the IS relationship, the assumptions made in Chapter 13 on c, i and g (for the closed economy) are maintained here. These were that:

$$s = y_d - c(y_d) = -c_0 + (1 - c_y)(y - t) \quad 0 \le c_y \le 1 \tag{8}$$

$$i = i(r) = i_0 - i_r r \qquad\qquad i_r \ge 0 \tag{9}$$

$$t = t_0 + t_y y \qquad\qquad 0 \le t_y \le 1 \tag{10}$$

where the symbols have the definitions given in Chapter 13 and government expenditures g are set exogenously. Further, for simplification, assume that for the small open economy, the export and import functions are linear and are:

Export function:

$$x_c = x_{c0} - x_{c\rho}\rho^r \quad x_{c0}, x_{c\rho} > 0 \tag{11}$$

Import function:

$$z_c = z_{c0} + z_{cy}y_d + z_{c\rho}\rho^r \quad z_{cy}, z_{c\rho} > 0 \tag{12}$$

Note that the coefficients in (11) and (12) will depend on the real exchange rate. Substituting (8) to (12) in (6) implies that the IS relationship is now:

$$y = \alpha[\{c_0 - c_y t_0 + i_0 - i_r r + g + x_{c0} + x_{c\rho}\rho^r\} + (1/\rho^r).\{-z_{c0} + z_{cy}t_0 + z_{c\rho}\rho^r\}] \tag{13}$$

where the multiplier α for this open economy is:

$$\alpha = \cfrac{1}{1 - c_y + c_y t_y + \left(1/\rho^r\right)z_{cy}\left(1 - t_y\right)} \tag{14}$$

Since z_{cy} is in the denominator, the autonomous investment multiplier α for an open economy with $z_{cy} > 0$, is smaller in value than its counterpart for a closed economy (with $z_{cy} = 0$), *ceteris paribus*.[3] Hence, for a given change in investment, national income will be more stable in the open than in the closed economy. However, it will also be less responsive to a given change in government expenditures. Therefore, *both the need for and the strength of stabilization policies will be less in an open economy.* The larger the marginal propensity to import, z_{cy}, the stronger will be this effect. As against this greater stability in response to domestic sources of disturbances, the fluctuations in imports and exports in the open economy will also affect domestic national income and may require offsetting stabilization policies.

The open economy IS curve

The slope of the IS curve for the open economy is given by:

$$\frac{\partial r}{\partial y} = -\frac{1}{\alpha i_r} \tag{15}$$

Since α is smaller in absolute value for the open economy than for the closed one, the slope of the IS curve is greater. Therefore, the IS curve will be *steeper* for an open than for a closed economy, though it will still have a negative slope.

The relationship between the IS curve and the changes in the exchange rate needs to be carefully specified and differs between the fixed exchange rate case and the flexible one. The nature of this difference can be seen from the general specification of the open economy IS curve as being:

$$y = f(r, \rho^r; g)$$

Under fixed exchange rates, the nominal exchange rate ρ is exogenously specified, so that if it is changed, the real exchange rate ρ^r would change. The effect of the latter on expenditures will shift the IS curve, which is drawn in the (y, r) space.

For the flexible exchange rate case, we need to consider the determinants of ρ. In this case, ρ is determined by the equilibrium condition (2) for the balance of payments, so that:

$$\rho = \rho(P/P^f, r, r^f)$$

Since the IS–LM diagram has r on the vertical axis, the impact of any change in it will produce a shift along the IS curve. The scenario for this is: an increase in r will induce capital inflows, so that ρ will rise to restore equilibrium in the balance of payments, but this rise will reduce net exports which, through the multiplier, will reduce income y in the economy. This reduction in y due to the increase in ρ caused by the increase in r is captured through a movement upward to the new level of interest rates on the existing IS curve.

However, an increase in P will increase ρ^r and cause net exports to fall, which will lead, through (12), to a decline in ρ. This depreciation will moderate the reduction in net exports in (13), still leaving some reduction in y from its original level.[4] Since P is not on the vertical axis of the IS–LM diagram, this reduction in y due to the increase in P is captured through a leftward shift in the IS curve, rather than through a movement along it. Similarly, increases in y induced by exogenous increases in P^f or in r^f will produce rightward shifts in the IS curve. In the mixed case, where the changes in the nominal exchange rate are produced by changes in both the domestic prices and domestic interest rates, there will be a shift in the IS curve as well as a movement along the curve.

19.1.3 The monetary sector of the open economy

Active versus passive monetary policy: foreign exchange flows and the money supply in the open economy

Now consider the specification of the money supply for the open economy. Suppose there is a surplus in the domestic country's balance of payments. Foreign exchange (i.e., foreign currencies and gold) in an amount equal to this surplus flow into the domestic economy. Most, if not all, of it is likely to be exchanged for the domestic currency (dollars) in the commercial banks, which cash it with the central bank. The payment of dollars by the central bank in exchange for the foreign exchange (in pounds sterling) increases the monetary base by a corresponding amount. The central bank has one of the following two alternatives before it:

(i) It could offset the increase in the monetary base by an appropriate sale of bonds. Such a step is called a *defensive open market operation*. A policy which aims at offsetting the impact of balance of payments surpluses or deficits on the money supply is called an *active monetary policy*.

(ii) Alternatively, the central bank could allow the increase in the monetary base, induced by the balance of payments surplus, to increase the money supply through the money–monetary base multiplier.[5] Such an inactive policy that does not seek to check or control the impact of the balance of payments surpluses and deficits on the money supply, is said to be a *passive monetary policy*.

The demand for money in the open economy and currency substitution

On the demand for money, an open economy introduces foreign currencies and bonds among the assets that can be held against the domestic currency. The substitution among the domestic and foreign currencies is known as *currency substitution*. As discussed in Chapter 9, while such substitution in theory seems significant, most empirical studies indicate a low rate of currency substitution. In view of this, we will assume that the demand for the domestic money is influenced in the present case of an open economy by the same variables – that is, domestic income and domestic interest rates – as in the case of a closed economy, so that the demand function for money will still have the form:

$$m^d = M^d/P = m_y y - m_r r \tag{16}$$

The LM relationship under an active monetary policy

An active monetary policy implies that the money supply can be taken as exogenous – that is, at the discretion of the central bank – instead of being influenced by the course of the economy or the balance of payments. That is, the money supply is exogenous. This is consistent with the assumption in the closed economy macroeconomic models of the earlier chapters. Under this assumption, the LM relationship for monetary equilibrium in an open economy with an active monetary policy – and zero currency substitution – is the same as that derived for the closed economy. Formally, the money supply M^s is given by:

$$M^s = M \tag{17}$$

where M is set exogenously by the central bank. Hence, the LM equation for the active monetary policy case is:

$$M/P = m_y y - m_r r \tag{18}$$

The LM relationship under a passive monetary policy

In the case of a *passive* monetary policy, the domestic money supply expands with a balance of payments surplus and decreases with a balance of payments deficit. In this case, the money supply M^s becomes a function of the size of the balance of payments disequilibrium B and hence of domestic income y, the domestic interest rate r and the real exchange rate ρ^r, among other variables. An increase in y or in ρ^r or a decrease in r decreases B, so that if B was initially zero, the money supply decreases. That is, for a *passive monetary policy*,

$$M^s = M^s(B(y, r, \rho^r)) \tag{19}$$

where B is the balance of payments surplus and depends upon y, r and ρ^r such that $\partial M^s/\partial B > 0$, $\partial B/\partial y < 0$, $\partial B/\partial r > 0$, $\partial B/\partial \rho^r < 0$. For simplification, assuming $B(y, r, \rho^r)$ to be linear, we have,

$$M^s = M^s(y, r, \rho^r)$$

$$= M_0 - a_1 y + a_2 r - a_3 \rho^r \quad a_1, a_2, a_3 \geq 0 \tag{20}$$

Equation (16) has assumed the demand function for money to be of the form:

$$m^d = M^d/P = m_y y - m_r r$$

In equilibrium, $M^d = M^s$, so that:

$$M_0 - a_1 y + a_2 r - a_3 \rho^r = m_y Py - m_r Pr \tag{21}$$

$$y(m_y P + a_1) = M_0 + (a_2 + m_r P)r - a_3 \rho^r$$

$$y = \theta M_0 + \theta(a_2 + m_2 P)r - \theta a_3 \rho^r \quad \theta = 1/(m_y P + a_1) > 0 \tag{22}$$

In (22), the coefficient of r is positive, so that an increase in r will increase y. Hence, the LM curve for such a case still has a positive slope in the (r, y) space. Taking $\partial y/\partial \rho^r$ to be negative, an increase in ρ^r decreases y, so that the LM curve shifts to the left as prices increase. This was also the case in the closed economy models.

In intuitive terms, if initially $B = \Delta R^f = 0$, an increase in y increases imports and brings about $B = \Delta R^f < 0$. As R^f decreases, the money supply falls. But an increase in y also increases the demand for money. Therefore, the excess demand for money, $(M^d - M^s)$, increases as y increases and at a more rapid rate than in a closed economy. However, an increase in r increases the net inflows of capital and also reduces the speculative demand for money. The excess demand for money, therefore, decreases with a rise in r and at a more rapid rate than in a closed economy. The effects of an increase in y could, therefore, be offset by an appropriate increase in r, so that the slope of the LM curve, with excess demand for money as zero, is positive. This slope may, however, be greater or less than for a closed economy.

Most central banks in the developed economies nowadays try to pursue an *active* monetary policy, allowing their money supply to change only when they so desire. We, therefore, pursue this case further, though the student could easily adapt the argument to the case of a *passive* money supply. The LM relationship for the open economy in the active monetary policy case is the same as that for a closed economy. It was analysed for the latter case in Chapters 13 and 14, and we will use it further in this chapter.

19.1.4 The labour sector and production in the open economy

We now come to the labour sector and the production function. The production function is:

$$y = y(n, \bar{K}) \tag{23}$$

where n is employment and $\bar{K}$ is the given capital stock. It has already been assumed that the openness of the economy in the short-run context consists only of commodity or financial capital flows but not of resource – labour or equipment – flows which can be immediately used in production. Further, since our analysis is short run, we assume that the capital stock and technology are constant.[6] Hence, the production function remains unchanged between the closed and the open economy. Therefore, the marginal productivity of labour and the demand for labour functions also remain the same.

Looking at the labour supply in the neoclassical model, the labour supply depends on the real wage rate and the labour force. Its function is:

$$n^s = n^s(w, \bar{L}) \tag{24}$$

where $\bar{L}$ is the exogenously specified labour force. While the cross-border flows of labour can be significant and endogenous for some countries – i.e., depend upon their unemployment rates and real wages – the annual inflows of labour to most developed economies are very small relative to their existing labour force, so that their labour force is not significantly affected by such movements in the short run. We will therefore assume that the labour force in the short run is exogenous even for the open economy model. Hence, (24) is restated as:

$$n^s = n^s(w) \quad n^s_w \geq 0 \tag{25}$$

Therefore, the analysis of the labour sector and the production function is unchanged from that for a closed economy. While (25) is a neoclassical relationship and we will work with it in this chapter, the reader is free to work with one of the forms of the Keynesian labour supply function specified in Chapter 14.

19.2 THE GENERAL EQUILIBRIUM IS–LM MODEL FOR THE OPEN ECONOMY

We have now all the building blocks for studying the complete macroeconomic model of the small open economy and bring them together in this section using the IS–LM diagrammatic framework. However, before drawing the curves in the IS–LM diagram, we need to specify the assumption on whether the nominal exchange rate is fixed or flexible. As explained in earlier sections, this difference will produce two differences between the IS–LM diagrams.

First, if the nominal exchange rate is fixed, there would exist a *BB* curve showing the (y, r) combinations for equilibrium in the balance of payments. But if it is flexible and adjusts to yield continuous equilibrium in the balance of payments, the balance of payments equilibrium can exist at any (y, r) combination, so that there will not be a separate *BB* curve. We have, therefore, two quite different versions of the IS–LM diagram, one with a *BB* curve for the fixed exchange rate case and the other without a *BB* curve for the flexible one.

Second, any exogenous shift in the fixed exchange rate will shift the IS curve. But, for the flexible exchange rate case, a change in the exchange rate due to a change in the domestic interest rate will not shift the IS curve since the slope of the IS curve will incorporate within it any impact of this on net exports and thereby on income.[7]

19.2.1 The IS–LM diagram for the flexible exchange rate case

This has the three curves, IS, LM and $(y\text{–}n)$, as in the case of the closed economy. While the LM and the $(y\text{–}n)$ curves are, under our assumptions, identical to those for the closed economy, the IS curve, as analysed earlier in subsection 19.1.2, incorporates the effect of changes in y and r on the nominal exchange rate and through it on exports and imports. It will be steeper than for a closed economy.

19.2.2 The IS–LM diagram for the fixed exchange rate case

This diagram has four curves in the (y, r) space: a negatively sloping IS curve, positively sloping *BB* and LM curves and a vertical $y\text{–}n$ curve. Since both the LM and the *BB* curves have positive slopes, we need a hypothesis to determine their relative slopes.

The relative slopes of the LM and *BB* curves

On the slope of the *BB* curve, we have two extreme hypotheses. One is that of the interest rate parity (IRP) discussed in Chapter 18. It implies that the capital flows are perfectly elastic and ensure that, for a small open economy with a fixed exchange rate, the domestic interest rate is set by the foreign interest rates. In this case, the *BB* curve for any given exchange rate is horizontal. But if the capital flows are zero or completely insensitive to the domestic interest rate, the *BB* curve for any given exchange rate would be vertical. Countries with their financial markets well integrated into the global ones would be closer to the former horizontal form, while developing economies with virtually non-existing or isolated financial markets would tend towards the vertical *BB* curve. We can therefore base further analysis on these extreme cases or on two slightly less extreme ones, one which assumes that the *BB* curve is flatter than the LM curve while the other assumes that it is steeper. The former would be more applicable to the developed economies and would be treated as the normal case for them. It would be called the *interest-sensitive capital flows case*, while the latter would be more applicable to some of the developing economies and would be called the *interest-insensitive capital inflows case*.

General equilibrium under fixed exchange rates, a diagrammatic treatment

Figure 19.2a shows general equilibrium for the developed economy in the fixed exchange rate case. All the curves intersect at the general equilibrium point *a*. To reiterate, the steeper slope of the LM curve compared with the *BB* curve assumes that the international capital flows are more sensitive to interest rate changes than the domestic money market,[8] so that an increase in *y* requires a larger increase in *r* to keep the monetary sector in equilibrium than that required to keep the balance of payments in equilibrium. Figure 19.2b shows what we referred to as the interest-insensitive capital inflows case. All the 'curves' are shown as straight lines.

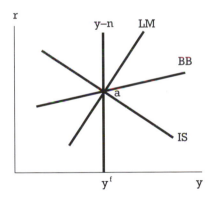

Figure 19.2a

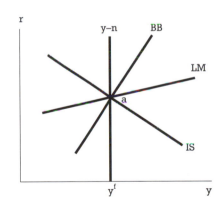

Figure 19.2b

In order to limit the number of cases that we have to analyse, we will further mainly analyse the developed economy case, mostly without even referring to it as such. That is, the default assumption in the rest of this chapter is that the *BB* curve for any given exchange rate has a steeper slope than the LM curve. However, some analysis for the interest-insensitive capital inflows case – relevant to many LDCs – will also be presented.

To analyse the roles of monetary and fiscal policies in the open economy, remember that these are demand-management policies. As such, the analysis of their role can be simplified by first focusing only on aggregate demand (AD) in the economy and only later studying the interaction between aggregate demand changes and supply responses. Further, the effects of monetary and fiscal policies on aggregate demand differ for the cases of flexible and fixed exchange rates, so that the following sections separate these cases.

19.3 MANAGING AGGREGATE DEMAND IN THE OPEN ECONOMY: MONETARY AND FISCAL POLICIES UNDER FLEXIBLE EXCHANGE RATES

Assume that the country in question has flexible exchange rates, initial general equilibrium as shown in Figure 19.2a and an expansionary fiscal policy is pursued. It raises interest rates and causes a surplus in the balance of payments at the initial exchange rate. The exchange rate rises so that domestic products become relatively more expensive than foreign ones. Imports rise and exports fall. These reduce aggregate demand in the economy. The expansionary impact of the fiscal policy is thus partly or wholly offset by the change in net exports.

Now consider the impact of an expansionary monetary policy. Such a policy lowers interest rates and causes a deficit in the balance of payments. Therefore, the exchange rate falls, making domestic goods relatively cheaper compared with foreign ones. Imports fall and exports rise. These have a further expansionary effect on the economy.

Therefore, in the case of flexible exchange rates, an expansionary monetary policy is effective in raising aggregate demand in the economy and its effect is reinforced by an increased amount of net exports. But an expansionary fiscal policy is not unambiguously effective in increasing such demand since its initial expansionary effect is partially or wholly offset by a decrease in net exports induced by the rise in exchange rates. Two limitations of this result should be noted.

The first limitation is related to the J curve discussed in Chapter 18: in this case, the short-term elasticity of net exports may be less than one in which case the short-term-induced effects through exchange rate changes and net exports on aggregate demand would be reversed: they would strengthen fiscal policy and weaken monetary policy effectiveness. If this adverse short-term effect lasts more than a year, but the policy makers were aiming at a more rapid increase in aggregate demand, fiscal policy would become preferable to monetary policy.

The second limitation arises from the inelasticity of capital flows. Assuming the extreme case of zero responsiveness of such flows to domestic interest rate changes, the secondary effects of interest rate changes on capital flows will not occur, so that the interest rate changes will not induce exchange rate changes and so will not induce the secondary effects on aggregate demand through changes in net exports. Consequently, expansionary monetary and fiscal policies will both have an initial expansionary impact on aggregate demand, but without any supporting or offsetting secondary effects occurring through capital flows and exchange rate changes. In the general application of this case, fiscal policy need not be less effective than monetary policy and might well be more effective. As mentioned earlier, this case is often the pertinent one for LDCs which, in addition, do not possess developed domestic financial markets and therefore may have insignificant responsiveness of domestic investment to domestic interest rates.

19.4 MANAGING AGGREGATE DEMAND IN THE OPEN ECONOMY: MONETARY AND FISCAL POLICIES UNDER FIXED EXCHANGE RATES

The basic difference between the fiscal and the monetary policies in the macroeconomic static models arises because an expansionary fiscal policy raises interest rates while an expansionary monetary policy lowers them. A rise in the domestic interest rate increases net capital inflows while a fall in this interest rate decreases such capital inflows. Therefore, if the balance of payments is initially in equilibrium, an expansionary fiscal policy creates a surplus ($\Delta R^f > 0$) by raising interest rates. But an expansionary monetary policy creates a deficit ($\Delta R^f < 0$) in the balance of payments.

Assume that the economy has a fixed exchange rate, has a flatter BB curve relative to the LM one, and is initially in overall equilibrium, as shown in Figure 19.3a.

The impact of an expansionary fiscal policy on aggregate demand

An *expansionary fiscal policy* will shift the IS curve to IS'. With aggregate demand thereby increased to d', this policy would raise interest rates and create a balance of payments surplus (since the interest rate at d' is higher than required for equilibrium in the balance of payments at d'') while increasing domestic demand, with further effects as follows:

(i) If the balance of payments is sterilized under an active monetary policy, the money supply will not expand but the domestic interest rate will stay above the foreign ones and the balance of payments surplus will continue, with a resultant increase in foreign exchange reserves, a result which many countries consider to be quite desirable.

(ii) If the balance of payments is not sterilized, as under a passive monetary policy, it will cause an expansion of the monetary base and hence of the money supply, thereby shifting LM rightwards. This will place downward pressure on interest rates, causing interest rates to fall towards their former level, while causing a further expansion of demand. Aggregate demand will eventually settle at d''', so that a fiscal expansion is supported by an induced expansion in the money supply.

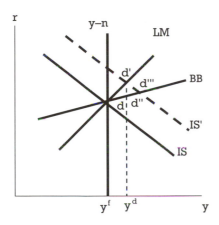

Figure 19.3a

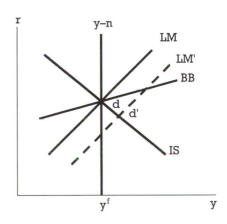

Figure 19.3b

The impact of an expansionary monetary policy on aggregate demand

Now consider an *expansionary monetary policy*. It shifts the LM curve from LM to LM' in Figure 19.3b, thereby increasing aggregate demand in the economy to d' while lowering interest rates. The latter reduce net capital inflows and cause a deficit in the balance of payments. This deficit would cause the money supply to fall unless this effect was offset by the monetary authorities through an active monetary policy. Hence, the two further scenarios are:

(i) If the balance of payments is sterilized, the money supply would remain at its new enlarged level and its expansionary impact upon the economy would continue. But so would the external deficit, with the result that the country must then run down its foreign exchange reserves by corresponding amounts. Such a policy clearly has a limit and can be pursued only up to the point where the reserves begin to fall to unacceptably low levels. The money supply will then have to be cut back to its initial level so that aggregate demand will also return to its initial level at d.

(ii) If the balance of payments deficit is not sterilized, the money supply will fall, shifting the LM curve to the left and thereby decreasing aggregate demand. This counteracts the initial monetary expansion. The balance of payments deficit will continue until the money supply has fallen to its initial amount and the LM curve has returned to its original position. That is, the expansion in the money supply would be offset through outflows of funds from the economy.

Therefore, for the developed economies' case with fixed exchange rates, an expansionary monetary policy is clearly circumscribed by the availability of foreign reserves to finance deficits while an expansionary fiscal policy is not thus circumscribed and can be pursued indefinitely. The latter is also reinforced by an induced expansion in the money supply in the case of a passive monetary policy. Hence, the pursuit of fiscal policy is preferable to that of monetary policy in the fixed exchange rate case.

The case of interest-insensitive capital flows

One limitation to the preceding analysis is that the capital inflows may be relatively insensitive to domestic interest rates, as in many LDCs, and the *BB* curve may be steeper than the LM one. This case is shown in Figures 19.4a and 19.4b.

For the expansionary fiscal policy analysis in Figure 19.4a, at the new level of interest rates given by point d′, there would be a balance of payments deficit, which causes a loss of foreign reserves. If it is not sterilized, the money supply will fall, with a contractionary effect running counter to the expansionary objective of fiscal policy, so that the desired expansion of aggregate demand will not be achieved. But if it is sterilized, the balance of payments deficit will continue and foreign reserves will continue to fall.

For the expansionary monetary policy analysis in Figure 19.4b, point d′ is still associated with a balance of payments deficit, so that the earlier analysis based on Figure 19.3b continues to apply, though the deficit will be even greater in Figure 19.4b.[9] As before, this balance of payments deficit, in the case when it is not sterilized, will result in a continuing reduction in the money supply until the original money supply is restored. If it is sterilized, there will be a continuing loss of reserves.

Hence, with fixed exchange rates in the interest-insensitive capital flows case, both expansionary fiscal and monetary policies will pose problems for the balance of payments deficits and loss of foreign exchange reserves. Further, in the passive money supply case, the expansionary fiscal policy will be accompanied by an induced contractionary rather than expansionary money supply, so that the desired expansion will not occur. An expansionary monetary policy will also cause balance of payments deficits and loss of foreign exchange

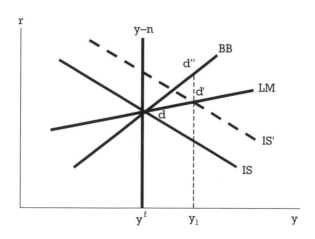

Figure 19.4a

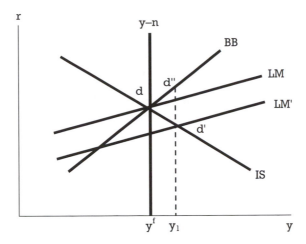

Figure 19.4b

reserves. Neither type of policy can be pursued for long unless the country has foreign exchange reserves whose depletion through deficits can be tolerated by the authorities. Since LDCs tend to have interest-insensitive capital flows, their pursuit of expansionary monetary and fiscal policies tends to pose relatively greater problems in terms of balance of payments deficits and loss of foreign exchange reserves, leading to an eventual reversal of such policies.

19.5 BRINGING AGGREGATE SUPPLY INTO THE ANALYSIS

The preceding sections have analysed the effectiveness of monetary and fiscal policies in changing aggregate demand. For the complete analysis, we now bring in aggregate supply, using the aggregate demand (AD) and aggregate supply (AS) curves in the (P, y) space. There is a long-run LAS curve and a short-run SAS curve, as in the closed economy case. This would give us an analysis similar to that for the closed economy case, except that AD is now susceptible to international influences through commodity and capital flows.

As for the closed economy, there are two different supply responses to an increase in AD depending on whether the economy is at full employment along the long-run aggregate supply curve (LAS) or off it and operating, as in the case of errors in price expectations or nominal wage contracts, along a short-run aggregate supply curve (SAS). Since the analysis for these cases is similar to that for the closed economy, as presented in Chapters 13 and 14, we do not present it in this chapter but leave it to the reader to pursue further.

However, there are two distinctive though extreme cases for the open economy with continuous full employment. These are provided by the assumptions of full employment and interest rate parity (IRP), and of full employment and purchasing power parity (PPP). We consider these briefly in the following sections.

19.6 MACROECONOMIC EQUILIBRIUM IN THE SMALL OPEN ECONOMY WITH FULL EMPLOYMENT AND IRP

If we assume IRP for the small economy, IRP determines the domestic interest rate under fixed exchange rates. Therefore, the domestic interest rate r is determined by:

$$r = r^f - \rho''^e \tag{26}[10]$$

where ρ is the nominal exchange rate defined as the units of the foreign currency per unit of the domestic currency, r^f is the foreign interest rate, the superscript e stands for 'expected' and '''' indicates the rate of change. The implications of IRP differ for the fixed and flexible exchange rate cases.

The fixed exchange rate case

Assume that the exchange rates are fixed and that the public also expects them to remain unchanged.[11] In this case, $\rho''^e = 0$, so that r is exogenously determined as $\underline{r}$ by r^f in (26).

Further, if we assume continuous labour market clearance, there would be full employment and output would be at y^f. Therefore, the IS–LM figure would be effectively as shown in Figure 19.5. Fiscal policy cannot alter this equilibrium since it cannot affect the exogenously determined interest rate or the full employment output, and must accommodate itself to $(\underline{r}, y^f)$. Hence, expansionary fiscal policy cannot be used to increase domestic output and interest rates. However, it will have an impact on the balance of payments on current account through the IS equilibrium condition derived earlier as:

$$\{x_c - (P^f/\rho P)z_c\} = -\{i(\underline{r}) - s(y^f)\} - \{(g - t(y^f)\} \tag{27}$$

Note that i and s are determined by r as $\underline{r}$ and y as y^f, so that, in (27), the only variable that can be affected by a fiscal deficit is the balance of payments on current account. Hence, from (27), a fiscal expansion, by decreasing the right-hand side, will in equilibrium decrease net exports.

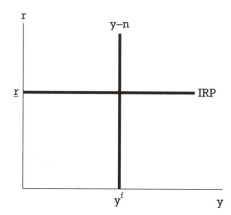

Figure 19.5

Under the assumptions underlying Figure 19.5, an expansion in the money supply also cannot change output or the interest rate. Hence, it cannot even alter the demand for real balances, since these are given by:

$$m^d = m^d(y^f, \underline{r}) \tag{28}$$

With the demand for real balances set by (28), the equilibrium domestic supply of real balances must adjust to this amount. The process by which this result is achieved is as follows. An attempted expansion of the nominal money supply would lower the interest rate, which leads to an outflow of capital, a balance of payments deficit and an outflow of the domestic currency by enough to maintain the interest rate at $\underline{r}$. Therefore, the amount of the domestic money supply will adjust to the unchanged domestic demand for real balances, making domestic monetary policy completely ineffective. Hence, the domestic money supply is endogenous to the fixed exchange rate, world interest rates and full employment output, only changing if these variables change.

Hence, with a fixed exchange rate, IRP and full employment, there is no role in equilibrium for monetary or fiscal policies. In fact, with output already at its full employment level, there is no scope or need for such policies.

The flexible exchange rate case

In the flexible exchange rate case, from (26), the expected change in the exchange rate is determined by:

$$\rho''^e = r^f - r \tag{29}$$

Since the domestic country can have an interest rate different from the world one, the IRP curve of Figure 19.5 for the fixed exchange rate case will not exist in the flexible exchange rate case.

The country is, therefore, free to pursue any domestic monetary and fiscal policies. However, as analysed above for the developed economy context, monetary policies will be relatively more effective than fiscal ones in changing aggregate demand. But this is of limited use under full employment, since changes in aggregate demand cannot change employment and output.

19.7 PPP, THE WORLD RATE OF INFLATION AND THE CONVERGENCE IN NATIONAL INFLATION RATES

The world rate of inflation in the fixed exchange rate case

Assume that all countries of the world have fixed exchange rates, so that we can treat the world as a single economy, with a world money supply defined by the weighted sum of the money supplies of the individual countries.

From the quantity equation, we have:

$$\pi^w \equiv M^{w''} + V^{w''} - y^{w''} \tag{30}$$

where the superscript w stands for the world, V is the velocity of circulation and '''' again indicates the rate of growth. Equation (30) implies that a general expansion of the money supplies among the countries will be a major source of world inflation. This occurred during the 1960s and 1970s when many countries simultaneously followed expansionary monetary policies in an attempt to increase their output and employment. The result was worldwide inflation. By the mid-1980s, most countries had abandoned such policies and were exercising much stricter controls on their money growth. As a consequence, the world rate of inflation in the 1990s fell drastically from its levels in the 1970s and 1980s.

If we also assume relative PPP, then the fixed exchange rate for the ith country implies that:

$$\pi_i = \pi^w \tag{31}$$

where π_i is the rate of inflation in country i. Equation (31) implies that the individual country inflation rates will be identical with the world one – or at least converge to it. Since the domestic inflation rate is determined by the exogenously specified world one, the equilibrium money supply of each country must adjust to accommodate this inflation rate and the money supplies of the individual countries become endogenous. While money supply growth and the price level in each country would then be closely related, note that causation runs from the world inflation rate to the country one to the country money supply, not from the country's money supply to its price level. However, at the world level, causation does run from the world money supply to the world price level.

Economic blocs, fixed exchange rates and the convergence in inflation rates

Equation (31) can be adapted to the case of a bloc of countries committed to a fixed exchange rate among its members. In the case of regional blocs such as the European Union with fixed exchange rates among its members, (31) implies that the member countries' inflation rates will converge to those of the bloc as a whole. This has been the experience of the European Union countries since the 1980s as the European Union has increasingly limited the permissible range of exchange rate variations among its member countries. Its long-term objective of a European Monetary Union with a European currency and fixed exchange rates among its members' national currencies and the European one would effectively impose (31) on the member countries and thereby limit their monetary independence.

Flexible exchange rates and convergence

We have seen above that in the long run the country inflation rates will converge to the world one under *fixed* exchange rates and purchasing power parity. Under *flexible* exchange rates and purchasing power parity, we have:

$$\rho'' = \pi^w - \pi_i \tag{32}$$

so that the exchange rate changes will accommodate the differences in the inflation rates across countries, and we would not expect long-run convergence in inflation rates. However, there would still be the relationship:

$$\rho'' + \pi_i = \pi^w \tag{33}$$

so that there would occur the long-run convergence of the composite variable $(\rho'' + \pi_i)$ to the world inflation rate.

19.8 DISEQUILIBRIUM IN THE DOMESTIC ECONOMY AND STABILIZATION THROUGH MONETARY AND FISCAL POLICIES

19.8.1 The fixed exchange rate case

The fixed exchange rate case with interest-sensitive capital flows

Figures 19.2a and 19.2b had shown the case of general equilibrium in the developed economy, with all the curves, including the output–employment y–n curve, intersecting at the same point a. Figure 19.6a shows the case corresponding to Figure 19.2a but for an economy with disequilibrium and therefore with several intersections. Assuming as before for analytical purposes that the commodity and the money markets adjust faster than the labour market and the balance of payments, the economy will be at point d (intersection of the IS and LM curves) in Figure 19.6a. At this point, the economy has deficient demand, relative to output y^f. There is also a balance of payments deficit, measured from point d to the BB curve: the interest rate at d is below that necessary to restore equilibrium in the balance of payments so that the capital inflows are inadequate for equilibrium. The deficient demand at d forces prices to fall so that the LM curve would shift downwards towards point b. While this movement will lower interest rates and worsen the balance of payments, the fall in prices will increase net exports. However, this increase need not be enough to ensure balance of payments equilibrium at full employment and is in any case going to be a longer-run rather than short-term solution. In the meantime, the country will lose foreign exchange reserves. Since the exchange rate is fixed, appropriate monetary and fiscal policies will be needed to bring the economy into overall equilibrium: this could, for instance, be done in Figure 19.6a by an expansionary fiscal policy and a contractionary monetary policy, so that the IS and LM curves shift to go through point a. Such a procedure will also avoid the need for price adjustments, in addition to avoiding balance of payments problems.

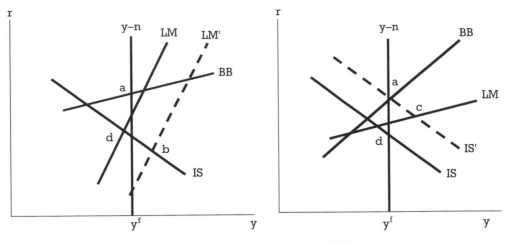

Figure 19.6a   *Figure 19.6b*

The fixed exchange rate case with interest-insensitive capital flows

In the interest-insensitive capital flows case shown in Figure 19.6b, there is initially deficient demand and balance of payments deficit at point *d*. An expansionary fiscal policy could shift the IS curve to IS′, passing through *c*. The excess demand at *c* would raise prices and shift the LM curve upwards towards point *a*. While this movement might fortuitously reduce the real money supply just by enough to take the LM curve through *a*, its likelihood is not encouraging. An appropriate expansionary fiscal policy and an appropriate contractionary monetary policy could (hopefully) ensure that all the curves intersect at the same point *a*, thereby obviating the need for domestic price-level changes and also eliminating the balance of payments deficit.

The preceding arguments have made the implicit assumption that the *BB*, IS and *y–n* curves do not shift as prices change. Our earlier arguments show that they do so. Thus, if we start again from point *d* in Figures 19.6a and 19.6b, as prices fall, the IS curve shifts to the right, the *BB* curve shifts downwards and the *y–n* curve shifts to the left (in the Keynesian case). It is unlikely that there would exist any fall in prices so fortuitous as to make all the curves intersect at the same point, so that one or more policy tools will still be necessary to restore equilibrium.

The scope for monetary and fiscal policies under fixed exchange rates

Suppose, in fact, that the authorities are willing to pursue both monetary and fiscal policies to restore equilibrium in Figures 19.6a and 19.6b. An expansionary fiscal policy could shift the IS curve to pass through point *a* and a deflationary monetary policy could shift the LM curve to also pass through this point. An expansionary fiscal policy and a deflationary monetary policy could, therefore, cure a deficient demand and a balance of payments deficit.

Now consider the case shown in Figure 19.6c. At point *d*, there is excess aggregate demand relative to output *y*^{f}. There is also a balance of payments surplus. A deflationary fiscal policy could shift the IS curve to pass through point *a*. An expansionary monetary policy could also shift the LM curve to pass through *a*. A deflationary fiscal policy and an expansionary monetary policy could thus cure a balance of payments surplus and excess demand in the context of Figure 19.6c.[12]

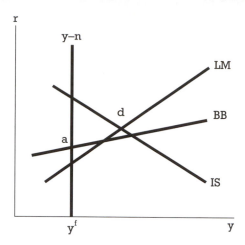

Figure 19.6c

The analysis of the above cases shows that the achievement of overall equilibrium in the context of fixed exchange rates is likely to require the use of fiscal and/or monetary policies. Alternatively stated, the economy with fixed exchange rates does not possess enough mechanisms that would automatically bring the economy into equilibrium so that appropriate policy actions are essential for maintaining equilibrium. Such a situation arises because one of the equilibrating price variables, the exchange rate, has been fixed.

A note of caution on the use of monetary and fiscal policies

A mix of monetary and fiscal policies can, therefore, restore equilibrium in the open economy with fixed exchange rates and obviates any need for adjustments in prices. However, a strong cautionary note on the pursuit of such policies must be added here. To pursue such a policy efficiently and with confidence that the wrong policies are not pursued, requires a great deal of knowledge about the interrelationships among the sectors. This knowledge may not exist or there may be shifts in these relationships because of the public's response to the policies pursued, so that the pursuit of discretionary stabilization policies can be risky: their outcome may make the economy worse rather than better. The impact of the policies attempted on the expectations of – and, therefore, speculation by – both domestic and foreign investors about the ability of the government to maintain its exchange rate must also be taken into account, and adds to the difficulty in deciding on the appropriate policies.

19.8.2 The flexible exchange rate with flexible domestic prices

Assume now that the country has flexible exchange rates and these ensure continuous equilibrium in the balance of payments. In this context, the *BB* curve is not relevant and any disequilibrium, as in Figures 19.6a and 19.6b, will emerge as disequilibrium between AD and AS and will be handled by the adjustments in domestic prices. Assuming that the economy has price-level flexibility, the price level will change to ensure equilibrium in the economy and monetary and fiscal policies will not be needed for this purpose. If the authorities do not want to rely upon changes in domestic prices for this purpose, they can try either monetary or fiscal policies, though monetary policies will be preferable since the economy has flexible exchange rates. Further, if the authorities wish to maintain interest rates different from the world ones, they can do so.

Exchange rate flexibility, therefore, provides the economy with a very useful equilibrating mechanism – that is, changes in the nominal exchange rate brought about by market forces

– for handling the balance of payments and reduces the need for policies to return the economy to general equilibrium. Exchange rate and domestic price flexibility eliminate this need, as long as the authorities are willing to give the economy enough time to make its own adjustments to equilibrium and are willing to put up with the possible reserve losses during the adjustment period.

19.9 THE CHOICE BETWEEN FIXED AND FLEXIBLE EXCHANGE RATE REGIMES

The preceding sections have considered some of the ways in which equilibrium in the balance of payments can be brought about or maintained in the face of disturbances. It could be done by market-determined changes in the exchange rate in a system of flexible exchange rates. But in a system of fixed exchange rates, equilibrium could only be maintained either by allowing induced changes in domestic income, prices and interest rates, etc., or by the appropriate use of the monetary and fiscal tools. It would, therefore, seem simpler for each country to allow its exchange rate to float rather than fix it, with all the constraints that the latter implies. However, there are several reasons why a country sometimes fixes its exchange rate against some or all foreign countries.

During the period from 1945 to the early 1970s, one of the reasons for a country to have a fixed exchange rate was its membership of the International Monetary Fund (IMF), which had been set up in 1944. Most of the nations of the world are such members. A basic rule of the IMF from its inception to the early 1970s was that the member countries would fix their exchange rates and change them only in cases of a 'fundamental disequilibrium' in the balance of payments.[13] This rule was adopted to limit the uncertainties affecting international trade and thus to promote such trade. It was also designed as a way of preventing manipulations (devaluations) in the exchange rate by any one country as a way of improving its own balance of trade with others, with the possibility of retaliatory changes in the exchange rates by other countries whose balance of trade worsens. Such a retaliatory war of devaluations creates a great deal of uncertainty in international trade and is usually accompanied by attempts by countries to curb their imports and promote their exports by other means such as tariffs, quotas, etc. The resulting reductions in exports and imports tend to substantially lower incomes and employment in the countries involved in such a 'war'.

Another reason for using a fixed exchange rate system is to avoid the possibility of instability in the foreign exchange markets, under the belief that flexible exchange rates promote such instability. This possibility has already been discussed above. However, its likelihood is now minimized by most economists.

A disadvantage of a country's adoption of a fixed exchange rate is that there sets in a great deal of reluctance for the country to change that rate even if a long-run disequilibrium occurs in the balance of payments. If the country has a surplus, which is sterilized and thus does not increase the money supply, it has no incentive to appreciate its currency since it could merely allow its reserves of foreign exchange to increase indefinitely. It might, however, face the jealousy of other nations and some international disapproval of its accumulation of reserves. In rare cases, it might even be faced with economic and political pressures from other countries to revalue. Thus, Germany and Japan, which had sizeable surpluses throughout the 1960s, came under strong pressures from 1971 to 1973 from the United States to revalue. Part of such pressure was a 10 per cent (surcharge) duty imposed on imports into the United States with a promise that it would be abolished after the appropriate revaluations had been made. Both Japan and Germany were forced to revalue in 1971 and again in 1973 under such pressure from the United States. But such explicit pressure tactics tend to be rare, are not always effective and anyway can be pursued by only a few powerful nations.

A country with a fixed exchange rate and a persistent deficit in its balance of payments could eliminate this deficit by devaluation. But devaluations tend to be unpopular with the electorate. They are often interpreted as a 'cheapening of our money' and mean a loss of national 'face' and prestige. Devaluations also increase the prices of imported goods, represent a worsening of the terms of trade and are often resented by the public. Therefore, deficit countries, such as Britain and the United States in the 1960s, often let their reserves fall or used restrictive monetary or fiscal policies at home, rather than devalue. Such policies usually prove to be palliative rather than cures of the underlying disequilibrium. Thus, the United States, after resisting devaluation through the 1960s, finally succumbed to the market pressures, reinforced by speculation, in March 1973, and allowed the dollar to float.

Other tools for handling balance of payments deficits

Countries also have at their disposal other tools to reduce deficits. These consist of direct measures to change exports and imports and capital flows. Imports can be hindered by the imposition of tariffs on their value or quantity, or by quota limitations on the quantity which can be imported, while exports can be encouraged by subsidies. These measures were formerly ruled out by the General Agreement on Tariffs and Trade (GATT) and now by the World Trade Organization, of which most Western nations are parties. This is because such actions by one country hinder the exports of other countries and invite retaliation. Overall, such actions reduce the gains in efficiency and welfare that come from free trade. However, countries do often try to get around such rules, often in the form of explicit or hidden subsidies to exporters and home producers.

Controls on the flows of capital can similarly consist of a 'tax' on capital inflows or outflows, administrative barriers or quota-type limitations. A country trying to reduce its capital outflow could impose a 'tax' on such outflows. The United States, for example, did so in 1964 when it imposed a 15 per cent 'interest equalization tax' on interest and dividend payments from foreign stocks and bonds bought after 1964. A country trying to reduce the capital inflows could similarly impose a tax on the inflows or the returns to them. Several European countries did so in 1973. An example of a quota on outflows of capital was the 'foreign credit restraint' programme instituted by the United States in 1965 and designed to limit the growth of US investments abroad. Quotas on the inflows of capital are commonly imposed by countries that are concerned about the foreign ownership of their real or financial assets. Japan has had some such controls through most of the post-1945 period. Most LDCs have experimented with such controls. There has been a marked worldwide trend during the decade of the 1990s towards the dismantling of such controls.

19.10 COMPACT MODELS FOR THE OPEN ECONOMY: THE MONETARY APPROACH TO EXCHANGE RATES (MAER)

19.10.1 The basic version of the monetary approach

A compact model of exchange rate determination under flexible exchange rates is provided by the monetary approach initiated in the 1970s at the IMF. This approach starts with the money market conditions for the domestic country and the foreign one (or the rest of the world) and imposes PPP on these. While the money demand functions have so far been specified as linear, we will assume for ease of exposition in further analysis that they are log-linear and *all variables will be measured in logs*. With these modifications, our assumptions are:

The money market equilibrium conditions:

$$M_t - P_t = m_y y^t - m_r r_t \tag{34}$$

$$M_t^* - P_t^* = m_y^* y_t^* - m_r^* r_t^* \tag{35}$$

where an asterisk indicates the foreign country, and all variables are in logs.

Purchasing power parity:

$$\rho_t = P_t^* - P_t \tag{36}$$

where ρ is now the log of the spot exchange rate. As a reminder, the exchange rate (£ per $) has been defined earlier as the units of the foreign currency (£) per unit of the domestic currency ($), so that $(E_t\rho_{t+1} - \rho_t)$ is the rate of appreciation of the domestic currency, while $-(E_t\rho_{t+1} - \rho_t)$ is its depreciation rate.

Equations (34) to (36) imply that:

$$\rho_t = (M_t^* - M_t) - (m_y^* y_t^* - m_y y_t) + (m_r^* r_t^* - m_r r_t) \tag{37}$$

Equation (37) specifies that the exchange rate is determined by the incomes and interest rates in the two countries and by their money supplies. Further, it implies that the changes in the exchange rates are positively related to those in domestic incomes, and negatively to domestic interest rates and changes in the domestic money supply. Therefore, an increase in the domestic money supply leads to a depreciation.

Some expositions of the MAER assume that $m_y = m_y^*$ and $m_r = m_r^*$. Under these assumptions, (37) reduces to:

$$\rho_t = (M_t^* - M_t) - m_y (y_t^* - y_t) + m_r (r_t^* - r_t) \tag{38}$$

This is quite a common simplification of the MAER equation, without changing the above conclusions.

If the domestic and foreign incomes and interest rates were constant over time, we would have:

$$\partial(\rho_{t+1} - \rho_t)/\partial(M_t^{*\prime} - M_t^\prime) = 1 \tag{39}$$

where ''' on a log value is the growth rate of the variable. In (39), the domestic currency appreciates if foreign money supply increases relatively faster than the domestic one, and vice versa. The intuition behind this result is as follows. If $M_t^\prime > M_t^{*\prime}$, this will induce higher inflation at home, so that our net exports will fall and create a balance of payments deficit, so that our currency will be in excess supply in the foreign exchange markets. With flexible exchange rates, our currency will have to depreciate to restore equilibrium in this market.

In general, incomes and interest rates do not remain constant, so that we will proceed further with the general equation (37). In this context, an exogenous increase in domestic real income will raise the domestic demand for money, lower the price level for a given money supply and raise net exports. This will cause our exchange rate to appreciate. But an exogenous increase in our interest rates will decrease the demand for money, increase the domestic price level and cause our currency to depreciate. Therefore, according to the MAER, higher growth of domestic incomes causes the exchange rate to appreciate while higher domestic interest rates or money growth cause it to depreciate.

Even if its assumptions are accepted, this basic version of the MAER suffers from several major shortcomings. First, it assumes that domestic and foreign incomes are independent of each other, while the evidence on the international business cycle shows a positive relationship. Second, it also assumes that the domestic and foreign interest rates are independent of each other, while the evidence shows that they are interrelated through capital flows. Third, it assumes each period to be isolated from its adjacent ones, so that the appreciation or depreciation of the exchange rate between periods has no implications for the endogenous variables of the model. The second and third shortcomings can be rectified simultaneously by taking account of the role of international capital flows in relating the domestic interest rates to the foreign ones. The following extension of the basic MAER does so by assuming perfect capital flows between countries.

19.10.2 The monetary approach with interest rate parity

The assumption of perfect capital flows between the domestic and the foreign economies adds the interest rate parity (IRP) condition to the assumptions of the basic MAER. We also assume rational expectations. Hence, the additional assumption is:

Interest rate parity

$$r_t - r_t^* = -(E_t \rho_{t+1} - \rho_t)$$ (40)[14]

Equation (40) is the arbitrage statement that the domestic return on investments equals the return abroad minus the expected rate of appreciation of the domestic currency. Equations (37) and (40) imply that:

$$\rho_t = \frac{m_r}{1 - m_r} E_t \rho_{t+1} + \frac{1}{1 - m_t}\left[\left(M_t^* - M_t\right) - \left(m_y^* y_t^* - m_y y_t\right) + \left(m_r^* - m_r\right)r_t^*\right]$$ (41)

so that the spot rate now depends on the next period's rate as well as on the money supplies, incomes and the foreign (but not the domestic) interest rates.[15] The equilibrating variables of this model are ρ for ensuring PPP for the commodity market and ρ' for ensuring IRP for capital flows.

Since $\partial \rho_t / \partial M_t < 0$ in (41), a jump in the current money supply – without a change in next period's – immediately lowers the spot rate ρ_t. Returning to next period's spot rate ρ_{t+1} will, therefore, mean an appreciation of the exchange rate during the period. The intuition behind this result is as follows. An increase in the domestic money supply raises the domestic price level which sets up a violation of PPP and causes an incipient deficit on current account. This requires the spot rate to fall to restore equilibrium. But the fall in this rate creates expected appreciation towards next period's rate and, therefore, creates arbitrage possibilities in favour of capital inflows, so that the interest rate falls. To maintain equilibrium in both the money market and the balance of payments, the fall in the exchange rate must be enough to induce the right amount of appreciation of the exchange rate for the domestic interest rate – which falls – to equilibrate the money market. Since the interest rate falls, the demand for real balances will rise in this process, so that $P_t' < M_t'$, unlike the basic version of the MAER in which P_t' always equals M_t'. The adjustments in response to the increase in the money supply are: P rises, ρ falls, $\rho' > 0$ and r falls, with $P_t' < M_t'$.

19.10.3 The monetary approach and exchange rates as a random walk

Rewrite (41) in the form:

$$\rho_t = \lambda E_t \rho_{t+1} + x_t$$ (42)

which specifies the relationship between the current and next period's spot rates as a function of the fundamental composite variable x_t, where x_t encompasses the effects of incomes, money supplies and foreign interest rates. Recursive forward substitution yields the particular (no bubbles) forward solution of (42) as:

$$\rho_t = \sum_{i=0}^{\infty} \lambda^i E_t x_{t+1}$$ (43)

Therefore, *if* the fundamental composite variable x_t did follow a martingale process,[16] then the spot rates will also follow a martingale process, so that:

$$E[\rho_{t+k} \mid \rho_t] = \rho_t, \quad k > 0 \tag{44}$$

Meese and Rogoff (1983) reported the finding that the spot exchange rate follows a martingale process among some pairs of currencies. Adler and Lehman (1983) failed to reject the hypothesis that the real exchange rates follow a random walk. Kim (1990) cannot reject it for the exchange rate against the US dollar of the Canadian dollar, the yen and the pound, if prices are measured by the CPI, while doing so for some other currencies.

19.11 COMPACT MODELS OF THE OPEN ECONOMY: THE DORNBUSCH MODEL

It is generally recognized in economics that PPP does not hold over short periods, so that several models, especially in the Keynesian tradition, do not assume it for the short run, though many still do so for the long run. One model that dispenses with it for the short run is the Dornbusch model. It assumes, instead, that prices adjust gradually to clear excess demand in the commodity market. Since the Dornbusch model does not assume PPP in the short run, it is sometimes also known as the 'sticky price' model, in comparison with the models that assume instant price adjustment and are known as the flexible price models of the exchange rate.

Compared with the slow adjustment of the commodity market to equilibrium, the Dornbusch model assumes that the asset markets[17] adjust instantly to equilibrium through adjustment of the interest rate, the spot rate and the expected appreciation or depreciation of the foreign exchange rate. On the latter, it assumes that the expected rate of change of the exchange rate is a function of the difference between its long-run value and its current one.

19.11.1 The Dornbusch model with fixed output

The assumptions of this model for the money market are:

The money market equilibrium condition:

$$M_t - P_t = m_y y_t - m_r r_t \tag{45}$$

Interest rate parity under rational expectations:

$$r_t - r_t^* = -(E_t \rho_{t+1} - \rho_t) \tag{46}$$

The expected rate of appreciation:

$$E_t \rho_{t+1} - \rho_t = E\rho_t' = \theta(\underline{\rho} - \rho_t) \tag{47}$$

where the line under a variable indicates its long-run stationary value.
Equations (45) and (46) imply that:

$$r_t - r_t^* = -\theta(\underline{\rho} - \rho_t) \tag{48}$$

Therefore, (45) and (48) imply that:

$$P_t = M_t - m_y y_t + m_r r_t^* - m_r \theta(\underline{\rho} - \rho_t) \tag{49}$$

In long-run (stationary) equilibrium, with $\rho_t = \underline{\rho}$ and $P_t = \underline{P}$, the long-run price level $\underline{P}$ is given by (49) as:

$$\underline{P} = \underline{M} - m_y \underline{y} + m_r r^* \tag{50}$$

Assume that $\underline{M} = M_t$, $\underline{y}_t = \underline{y}$ and $r_t^* = \underline{r}^*$, so that $\underline{P}$ is really the price level which equilibrates the money market for the long-run domestic money supply. This is held at the level of the current one, under the assumptions that the changes in the money supply and prices do not produce changes in domestic real output or foreign interest rates, which remain at their long-run levels. Subtracting (50) from (49) and solving for ρ_t implies that:

$$\rho_t - \underline{\rho} = \frac{1}{m_r \theta}\left(P_t - \underline{P}\right) \tag{51}$$

This appreciation is given by:

$$\frac{\partial \rho_t}{\partial P_t} = \frac{1}{m_r \theta} \geq 0 \quad \text{and} \quad \frac{\partial\left(-\rho_t\right)}{\partial P_t} = \frac{1}{m_r \theta} \leq 0 \tag{52}$$

The intuitive mechanics of the model so far are that an increase in the price level raises interest rates (by increasing money demand in the money market), which produces an 'incipient' capital inflow. This incipient inflow pushes up the exchange rate to a level from which the expected depreciation, as required by the arbitrage condition (47), exactly offsets the increase in the domestic interest rate. That is, the increase in P_t raises r_t and ρ_t (thereby lowering $-\rho_t$) and causes $\rho_t' < 0$.

Derivation of the time path of the price level

The assumption of the Dornbusch model for the aggregate demand for commodities is:

$$y_t^d = \delta(P_t^* - \rho_t - P_t) + \gamma y_t - \sigma r_t + \mu_t \tag{53}[18]$$

where, as before, all the variables are in logs; y^d is the (log of) the real demand for output and μ is a shift parameter. Aggregate demand increases with increases in the domestic income/output y and decreases in domestic interest rates, as in the standard IS–LM model. Consistent with the open economy IS–LM models, the aggregate demand for domestic output also increases with $(P_t^* - \rho_t - P_t)$, which is the rate of exchange ('price') of the domestic goods in terms of foreign commodities, so that a fall in the domestic price level or the spot rate makes the domestic goods more competitive and increases net exports.

Since P is the domestic price of commodities, the rate of increase in it is P'. Prices are assumed to adjust by a proportion of the excess demand (y^d/y), so that:

$$P_t' = \pi(y_t^d - y_t) = \pi[\delta(P_t^* - \rho_t - P_t) + (\gamma - 1)y_t - \sigma r_t + \mu_t] \tag{54}$$

Equilibrium in the commodity market requires $y_t^d - y_t = 0$, $P_t' = 0$, so that, for equilibrium:

$$[\delta (P_t^* - \rho_t - P_t) + (\gamma - 1)y_t - \sigma r_t + \mu_t] = 0 \tag{55}$$

In the long-run stationary state, $E_t \rho_t' = 0$ – so that, from (46), $r_t = r^*$. Further, in the long run, $P_t = \underline{P}$ and $P_t^* = \underline{P}^*$. Hence, the long-run exchange rate $\underline{\rho}$ is given by:

$$-\underline{\rho} = -\underline{P}^* + \underline{P} + (1/\delta)[(1 - \gamma)\underline{y}_t + \sigma \underline{r}^* - \mu_t] \tag{56}$$

Substituting (56) and (48) in (54) gives,

$$P'_t = -\pi \left[\frac{\delta + \sigma\theta}{\theta m_r} + \delta \right]\left(P_t - \underline{P} \right) \tag{57}$$

$$= -v \left(P_t - \underline{P} \right) \tag{58}$$

where:

$$v = \pi \left[\frac{\delta + \sigma\theta}{\theta m_r} + \delta \right] \geq 0 \tag{59}$$

Equation (58) is a first-order difference equation, whose solution is:

$$P_t = \underline{P} + (P_0 - \underline{P})\,\exp(-vt) \tag{60}$$

where $\exp(-vt) = 1/e^{vt}$ and $v \geq 0$. Therefore, for $v > 0$, the current price will converge to its long-run value at a speed determined by the value of v, as specified by (59). If $v = 0$, $P_t = P_0$ and the economy will not move towards $\underline{P}$. If $v \to \infty$, the economy will instantly adjust to $\underline{P}$. The larger is the value of v, the faster is the adjustment to the long-run value and the shorter the period of adjustment. In particular, the smaller is the interest sensitivity (m_r) of money demand, the shorter is the adjustment period. Further, the larger is the θ (the speed of adjustment of prices), σ (the responsiveness of aggregate demand to interest rates) and/or δ (the responsiveness of aggregate demand to prices), the shorter is the adjustment period.

Figure 19.7 shows the time path of P_t for $0 < v < \infty$. The economy starts with $\underline{P}_0$ at t_0, when the money supply is increased. The long-run price level increases proportionately to $\underline{P}_1$. The economy moves from $\underline{P}_0$ to $\underline{P}_1$ through a gradual price increase at the rate v.

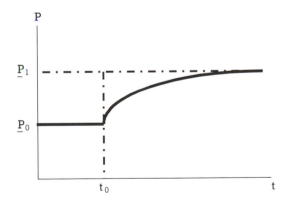

Figure 19.7

Derivation of the time path of the exchange rate

Substituting (60) in (51) yields:

$$\rho_t = \rho - \frac{1}{m_r\theta}\left(P_t - \underline{P} \right)\exp\left(-vt \right)$$

$$= \rho + \left(\rho_0 - \rho \right)\exp\left(-vt \right) \tag{61}$$

so that, for $v > 0$, the exchange rate will also converge to its long-run level. This rate will appreciate if prices are below their long-run level. If $v = 0$, the exchange rate will never adjust to its new long-run level. Figure 19.8 shows the time path of ρ_t for $0 < v < \infty$. The economy starts with $\underline{\rho}_0$ at t_0, when the money supply is increased. This causes a proportionate depreciation of the exchange rate to $\underline{\rho}_1$. The initial response of the economy is to push below $\underline{\rho}_1$ (overshooting). The exchange rate then appreciates gradually from ρ_0 to $\underline{\rho}_1$. The larger are π, θ or δ, or the smaller is m_r, the faster is the speed of adjustment and the shorter is the adjustment period.

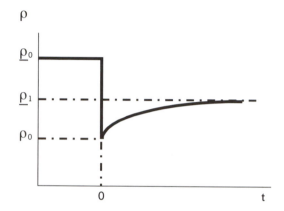

Figure 19.8

Diagrammatic analysis

Figure 19.9 draws the relationship between P and $(P^* - \rho)$, with P^* held constant at $\underline{P}^*$, specified by (51) as the curve QQ. At all points along this curve, the money market is in equilibrium and the IRP condition for the bond markets is satisfied. QQ has a negative slope, as required by (52). In long-run equilibrium in the commodity market, PPP implies that $P = P^* - \rho$, so that long-run PPP equilibrium requires $P = (P^* - \rho)$. This relationship is represented by the 45° line through the origin and is marked as PPP.

Long-run equilibrium, therefore, requires that the economy be at point A at the intersection of the QQ and PPP curves. At this point, $P_t = \underline{P}$ and $\rho_t = \rho$. Further, since the current spot rate equals its long-run values, the expected change in the exchange rate is zero and the domestic interest rate equals the foreign one. The commodity market is in equilibrium, so that the price level is constant.

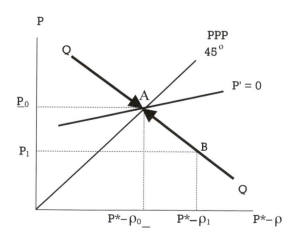

Figure 19.9

Equation (55) is represented by the curve $P' = 0$, so that points along it show the combinations of P and $(P^* - \rho)$ at which the money and commodity markets are in equilibrium. This curve has a positive slope, goes through A and, as Dornbusch argues, is flatter than the 45° line. At points above this curve, there is excess supply of commodities, causing prices to fall and move the economy towards this curve, and vice versa.

We now look at the dynamic movements in Figure 19.9. Start with a given price level, $P_1 < \underline{P}$. Since the exchange rate is assumed to adjust instantly through arbitrage to satisfy the IRP condition, the economy will always operate on the QQ curve, which also ensures money market equilibrium. Therefore, given current prices at P_1 below $\underline{P}$, the economy will be at point B on the QQ curve and have $(P^* - \rho_1)$, above its long-run value. At B, there exists excess demand for commodities, causing commodity prices to rise. This increase in the price level will reduce the real balances in the economy, thereby inducing an appreciation of the exchange rate. Hence, the economy will move along the QQ curve to the long-run position at A.

The distinctive aspects of the Dornbusch model as compared with the monetary approach

We illustrate the distinctive aspects of the Dornbusch model by comparing the effects in it of a permanent increase in the money supply with those in the basic MAER. Starting with the latter, an increase in the money supply causes an immediate and proportionate increase in the domestic price level, so that the real balances remain unchanged. The exchange rate also depreciates instantly, by the amount necessary to maintain PPP.

For the Dornbusch model, we rely on Figure 19.10. To maintain equilibrium in the asset markets, the increase in the money supply will have to be accompanied by a depreciation of the spot rate and/or raise prices, so that the QQ curve shifts outward to $Q'Q'$, with $Q'Q'$ parallel to QQ. The long-run equilibrium will now be at point C. Since the expected appreciation and the expected price increase will be zero at both A and C, the interest rate at A and C will be identical. Further, output has been held fixed. Therefore, the demand for real balances at A and C are identical, so that, in order to maintain market equilibrium, the price increase from A to C must be in proportion to the money supply increase. Further, since PPP holds along the 45° line, the exchange rate must fall by the rate of inflation, so that the fall in the spot rate from A to C must also be proportionate to the money supply increase.

For short-run dynamics, the Dornbusch model assumes that the interest and exchange rates adjust instantly to maintain equilibrium in the asset markets, the price level adjusts sluggishly. Therefore, in the current period, the increase in the price level is less than in

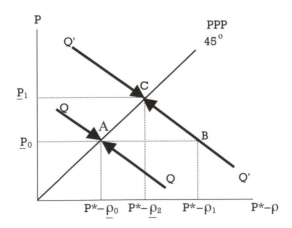

Figure 19.10

proportion to the increase in the money supply. Hence, real balances increase, so that, for given output, the interest rate falls. But lower domestic interest rates require, for equilibrium in the foreign exchange market, that the exchange rate must be expected to appreciate over time. For this to occur, the spot rate falls just sufficiently to satisfy the IRP condition between domestic and foreign bonds.

In terms of Figure 19.10, at the higher money supply but the current price level P_1, the economy moves to B on the $Q'Q'$ curve, and the exchange rate falls from ρ_0 to ρ_1. There exists excess demand for commodities at B, so that prices rise and the economy continues moving along the $Q'Q'$ curve to its long-run point C, with $\rho_2 > \rho_1$. Several points worth noting about this adjustment path are:

(i) For some time during the adjustment period, the economy overshoots the long-run exchange rate. This is a consequence of the sluggish adjustment of commodity prices. The extent of the overshooting will depend on the interest sensitivity m_r of money demand and expectations coefficient θ.

(ii) Excess demand occurs during adjustment for two reasons: the fall in the interest rate, which increases aggregate demand by increasing investment; and the fall in the exchange rate which increases aggregate demand by increasing net exports.[19]

(iii) Rising prices are accompanied by an appreciating exchange rate.

(iv) During the adjustment process, as the economy moves up from B along the $Q'Q'$ curve, prices rise and reduce the supply of real balances, so that the interest rate rises. However, given the too low exchange rate at B, the exchange rate appreciates to its long-run value. Hence, rising interest rates are accompanied by the expectation of an appreciating exchange rate. While this is often observed in practice, it runs counter to the implication of the static analysis, according to which the rise in domestic rates, for given foreign ones, should be accompanied by a decline in the exchange rate.

19.11.2 The Dornbusch model for endogenous output

The preceding analysis had assumed that the domestic output was exogenously set, say at the full employment level. For the case where output can vary, Dornbusch assumes that $y_t = y_t^d$, so that:

$$y_t = \delta(P_t^* - \rho_t - P_t) + \gamma y_t - \sigma r_t + \mu_t \tag{62}$$

Since output is thus determined by its demand, the excess demand for commodities is identically zero, so that a new price adjustment equation is needed. Dornbusch specifies this as:

$$P_t' = \pi(y_t - \underline{y}) \tag{63}$$

so that the rate of increase of prices is proportional to the 'output gap' – that is, the gap between current and long-run or potential (full employment) output. Dornbusch assumed that this long-run output $\underline{y}$ is invariant with respect to the money supply, prices, interest rates and exchange rates.

In the long-run equilibrium, since $P' = 0$ and output is constant at its potential level, the addition of (62) and (63) does not alter the earlier long-run analysis, so that the long-run analysis in Figures 19.9 and 19.10 will remain unchanged.

However, the short-run analysis does change. Since output can change in the short run, a fall in the spot rate due to the increase in the money supply will now increase aggregate demand and output. The latter increases money demand in equation (45). There are two possible scenarios beyond this point. In one, the increase in the supply of real balances is greater than the increase in their demand and the interest rate falls, so that, for IRP, there has to be expectation of the appreciation of the exchange rate from an 'overshot' level. This scenario corresponds to the one sketched out earlier for a constant output. The other scenario is that the demand for real balances is greater than the increase in their real supply, so that the interest rate rises. This causes, for IRP, the expectation of depreciation of the exchange rate towards its long-run level. In this case, the overshooting of the exchange rate does not occur. Therefore, the adjustment phase for the variable output model may or may not involve overshooting the exchange rate. It will, in any case, imply smaller fluctuations in the exchange rate than the fixed output model.

In the case where, following a monetary expansion, the interest rate does not fall, the increase in commodity demand during the adjustment phase will occur only through the fall in the exchange rates – that is, through the change in the terms of trade. Hence, the Mundell–Fleming channel will continue to operate, though not the interest rate one.

Dornbusch identifies the fixed output case with the 'very short run', so that overshooting will occur in this interval. He identifies the variable output analysis with the 'intermediate run', so that exchange rate changes will be relatively dampened and overshooting may not even occur.

As for the implications for monetary policy, the Dornbusch flexible output model implies that, even in the context of flexible exchange rates and capital mobility, the central bank can, for some duration, increase aggregate demand and output through an expansionary monetary policy. Conversely, a contractionary monetary policy will produce recessionary effects for some time. However, note that these will only occur during the adjustment phase but not in the long run, so that monetary policy will still be neutral in the long run.

19.11.3 Other models

There are numerous other models of exchange rate determination. Among very significant contributions that do not assume instantaneous PPP is Obstfeld and Rogoff (1995). Their paper assumes that firms are in monopolistic competition, have sticky prices and endogenous real output. These are to some extent also in the Dornbusch framework. Obstfeld and Rogoff, further, use an intertemporal analysis, with consumers maximizing lifetime utility. Their analysis shows that increases in the domestic money supply can increase real output *beyond* the period of price rigidity because of wealth effects. While this paper is an important and interesting contribution, it is not our intention to present its analysis since we want to bring to a close the presentation of the sticky price analysis.

19.12 EMPIRICAL EVIDENCE ON PPP

The simplest testable form of PPP, with all variables measured in logs, is:

$$\rho_t = a + P_t^* - P_t + \mu_t$$

where $a = 0$. This absolute version of PPP is a very restrictive hypothesis and is rarely found to be valid. In particular, it does not take account of non-traded goods and the non-traded inputs into the production and final sale of the traded goods. A weaker form of it is the relative PPP hypothesis, which is:

$$\rho_t' = \alpha + P_t^{*\prime} - P_t' + \mu_t$$

where $\alpha = 0$.

De Grauwe (1988) argued that the PPP hypothesis implies that the exchange rates should mirror the variability in the national price levels and that the real exchange rate should be independent of the nominal one. He found that the empirical evidence on the exchange rates between the yen, the Deutsche mark and the US dollar contradicted both of these implications.[20] Further, since the early 1970s, the real exchange rates, instead of tending to a constant, tended to move away from their PPP values.

A common explanation given for the deviation of exchange rates from PPP is the existence of goods that are not internationally traded. These do not adhere to PPP, only internationally traded ones are likely to do so, so that PPP may do poorly when applied to the overall price indices encompassing both goods of goods. Engel (1999) tested the validity of this argument for several developed economies, including the USA, UK and Canada. Using monthly data over thirty years and several alternative price indices, he found that the movements in the prices of non-traded goods were not significant in explaining the deviations from PPP.

Since P and P^* often prove to be non-stationary and PPP in either of its forms is considered to be a long-run relationship, its tests in recent years have favoured the use of cointegration analysis. An illustration of such tests is provided by Kugler and Lenz (1993). This study considered the exchange rates against the Deutsche mark of fifteen different currencies, using monthly data over the period 1973/1 to 1990/1. The use of the Johansen–Juselius technique gave the results that: for six countries, a cointegration vector exists and PPP is not rejected; for four countries, cointegration vectors are found but PPP is rejected; for the remaining currencies, the results depend on the lag length. In particular, PPP is rejected for the US and Canadian dollars, the Belgian franc and the Danish krone. It is even doubtful whether PPP holds between the Canadian and US dollars. The results are mixed for the Swiss franc, the French franc, the yen, the Dutch guilder and the Swedish krone. For the UK pound, PPP is not rejected.

The empirical evidence from the other, quite numerous, cointegration studies of PPP is also mixed. However, while some find support for it for particular pairs of currencies, most reject it. Given this mixed or preponderantly negative evidence, even between the currencies of countries with extensive trade and capital flows among them, embedding PPP in a model, even in the long run, becomes a potential source of the invalidity of its implications.

It is now also well established that it takes quite a long time for PPP to be restored after a deviation from it. As an illustration, Frankel (1986) reported this period to be as long as ten or more years. That is, exchange rates remain under- or overvalued relative to PPP for very long periods and balance of payments deficits and surpluses are persistent even under flexible exchange rates. The reversion of exchange rates to the PPP values is correspondingly very slow and in the estimation of some researchers, hardly significant. Bluntly put, the law of one price does not hold among countries (Dumas, 1994; De Vries, 1994). Among the reasons for this is that, even for traded goods, competition among firms producing similar goods but located in different countries is not perfect.

Some studies have even reported the specific finding that, over time, the real exchange rates follow a martingale or random process. Kim (1990), using cointegration analysis over very long data series (1900–87 or 1914–87), tested the hypothesis that the real exchange rates between the US dollar and selected currencies follow a random walk. They could not reject this hypothesis for the British pound, the Canadian dollar and the yen when the price level is represented by the CPI. It was rejected if the wholesale price index was used and it was rejected for France and Italy for both price indices. If the real exchange rate follows a random walk, there is no tendency for it to revert to a long-run equilibrium, such as implied by PPP.

Mark (1990) used the US, UK and Germany as the 'home' countries and examined their exchange rates against the currencies of eight OECD countries. Their finding was that the nominal exchange rate is mostly unrelated to relative price ratios between countries, both in the short run and the long run. Further, increases in nominal rates are related one-for-one to increases in the real rates, with the latter occurring in response to the former.

The weight of empirical evidence is, therefore, clearly that PPP does not hold over periods as long as thirty to fifty years. The deviations from PPP are more likely to occur if productivity growth is continual and differs among countries and if the price index used, such as the CPI, allocates a significant weight to non-traded goods while demand shifts between traded and non-traded goods. It is even likely to occur for traded goods if imperfect, rather than perfect, competition dominates across countries. Among the sources of deviations from PPP could be monetary factors, working through aggregate demand, and real ones, such as productivity changes.

The deviations of exchange rates from PPP also have the consequence that real interest rates could vary considerably among countries.

19.13 EMPIRICAL EVIDENCE ON INTEREST RATE PARITY

It is now generally accepted that most currencies do not possess uncovered interest rate parity with others, and that the deviations from it cannot be explained by risk premia. Part of the reason for this is that investors seem to possess strong home country preference with the result that the portfolios held are overwhelmingly composed of domestic stocks and bonds. Consequently, the correlation between domestic saving and investment is extremely high, contrary to the implications of perfect capital flows resulting in IRP. Part of the reason for the empirical failure of uncovered IRP is the investors' attribution of higher risk to assets, even portfolio ones, originating in foreign countries and the consequent requirement of risk premia (Dumas, 1994; De Vries, 1994). In any case, country-variant and asset-variant risk premia would mean departures from IRP and the assumption of perfect substitution among domestic and foreign bonds.

Looking at currencies as assets, empirical research has also shown the elasticity of currency substitution to be quite low. What is really surprising is that this elasticity is quite low even between the Canadian and the US currencies, even though their economies are quite integrated, accounts with financial institutions in Canada can be kept in US dollars and the US dollars are widely accepted in exchanges in Canada. Further, even in countries experiencing hyperinflation, the use of foreign currencies remains limited relative to that of the rapidly depreciating domestic currency.

CONCLUSIONS

The adaptations of the closed economy models to the open economy case introduced a great deal of complexity into the macroeconomic models. A new good, foreign exchange, was brought into the model. Its 'price' – the foreign exchange rate – could be flexible and determined by the supply and demand in the foreign exchange market, or managed by the central bank or the government or fixed by them. Our analysis showed that while monetary policy was less effective than fiscal policy in its impact on the domestic aggregate demand in the fixed exchange rate case, the reverse occurred in the flexible exchange rate case.

An aspect of the changes in the inter-country flows in recent decades has been the increasing dominance of financial capital flows over the values of the net exports of countries. The former are more volatile and more susceptible to speculative forces than the latter. The dominance in the magnitudes of the capital flows over the value of net commodity flows in perfect capital markets imposes interest rate parity among countries. This condition under flexible exchange rates implies that the exchange rate movements will be mainly determined, at least in the short run, by the interest rate differences among countries, rather than by purchasing power parity or by the differences in the rates of inflation among countries.

National economies have increasingly become more complex and more closely integrated into the world economy. Economists' opinions and national policies have gone from favouring fixed exchange rates among currencies – as in the years from the end of the Second World War to the early 1970s – to a strong recommendation for flexible exchange rates, since the latter are seen as more suited to ensure balance of payments equilibrium in the face of day-to-day and longer-term shifts in the commodity and capital flows among countries. In particular, the IMF now advocates flexible exchange rates. However, there continues to be concern that a flexible exchange rate regime can expose a currency to destabilizing speculative runs and thereby contribute to their volatility. This is especially likely to happen in smaller or poorer countries, with exchange reserves that are small relative to the potential inflows and outflows of financial capital.

Fixed exchange rates continue to dominate at the intra-national and intra-bloc levels, with flexible exchange rates being the common rule between countries and between blocs of countries. One of the most remarkable changes in this respect in the world economy is the evolution of the euro and the conversion of the national currencies of the European Union to a single one.

Open economies impose considerable limitations on the successful pursuit of monetary and fiscal policies. The complexity of the interactions among the various sectors is greater for the open than for the closed economy, making it more problematical to find which is the right policy to pursue. Further, the requirements of the purchasing power parity and the interest rate parity operate as constraints on the policies that can be successfully pursued. In the limiting case of the continuous clearing of the domestic labour markets at full employment and perfect capital flows, full employment and interest rate parity imply that while monetary and fiscal policies could change aggregate demand in the domestic economy, they could have no impact on domestic real output and employment.

While the general adoption of flexible exchange rates since the 1970s has mitigated the potential disruption from fundamental shifts in the competitive positions of countries and protected the domestic economies from the differences in the inflation rates among countries, flexible exchange rates do hold the potential of large speculative runs on the currencies of selected countries and of the depreciation of their currencies in excess of what is implied by the fundamental economic forces. Combined with the short-term inelasticity of net exports as encompassed in the J curve, these speculative episodes can become self-reinforcing and damaging for the affected domestic economy, as well as for its trading partners.

The two fundamental concepts relevant for the small open economy are PPP and IRP. These provide the underpinnings of the monetary approach to exchange rates. IRP is also an element of the Dornbusch short-run approach while both IRP and PPP are integrated in its long-run version. The distinctive aspect of the latter is that interest rates and exchange rates adjust instantly to ensure equilibrium in the money and bond markets, while commodity prices do so only in the long run. These lead to the implication that, following a change in the money supply, exchange rates overshoot their long-run equilibrium values.

The empirical evidence on both PPP and IRP seems to be preponderantly against their validity, though they have been supported for particular pairs of currencies over specific periods. In some cases, the evidence even seems to indicate that the spot exchange rates follow a random walk. Such evidence casts doubt on the empirical validity of the compact models based on PPP and IRP, so that their value lies in the insights that they provide, just as in the case of the IS–LM treatments of the open economy macroeconomics.

SUMMARY OF CRITICAL CONCLUSIONS

- The open economy macroeconomic model for the fixed exchange rate case differs significantly from that for the flexible exchange rate one. In particular, the equilibrium relationships for the commodity and the foreign exchange sector are different.
- Monetary policy is more effective in changing aggregate demand than fiscal policy if the exchange rates are flexible while fiscal policy is more effective in changing aggregate demand if the exchange rates are fixed. The appropriate monetary and fiscal policies differ between the two types of exchange rate regimes.
- A basic question for monetary policy in an economy with balance of payments deficits or surpluses is whether to neutralize their effects on the money supply and keep it 'exogenous' or let them affect the money supply and let it be 'endogenous'.

- Under a fixed exchange rate, with interest rate parity and continuous labour market clearance at full employment, there is no role for monetary and fiscal policies: they cannot change output or employment or interest rates.
- Under a flexible exchange rate, with covered interest rate parity and continuous labour market clearance at full employment, monetary policy can change aggregate demand, the price level and the interest rate as well as the exchange rate but not output or employment.
- Under purchasing power parity and a fixed exchange rate, the domestic price level is fully determined by the foreign one. The domestic inflation rates among countries will converge to the world inflation rate.
- Under purchasing power parity and a flexible exchange rate, the domestic rate of inflation can differ from the foreign one but the exchange rate will depreciate by the difference in the inflation rates. The domestic inflation rates plus exchange appreciation rates among countries will converge to the world inflation rate.
- Open economies increase the difficulties, the uncertainty and the limitations on the successful pursuit of monetary and fiscal policies.
- The assumptions and implications of the monetary approach to the exchange rate, based on continuous purchasing power parity, differ significantly from those of a sticky price model.
- If prices are sticky in the short run, the short-run adjustment of exchange rates can overshoot the magnitude required for long-run equilibrium.
- Empirical tests have called into question the validity of both continuous purchasing power parity and continuous interest rate parity.

review and discussion questions

1 In a world where wages and prices are perfectly flexible and there is perfect capital mobility, to what extent can a small open economy insulate itself from foreign disturbances by adopting a flexible exchange rate?

2 Given a small open economy with highly elastic capital flows and its goal of maintaining a stable price level, show the relative efficacy of monetary and fiscal policies under a regime of (a) fixed exchange rates, (b) flexible exchange rates. Which regime is best suited to the monetary authority's goal of price stability? Discuss the conditions under which the following statements are valid.

    (a) 'Given flexible exchange rates, monetary policy is likely to be more effective than fiscal policy in increasing the level of aggregate demand.'

    (b) 'Given fixed exchange rates, monetary policy is likely to be less effective than fiscal policy in increasing the level of aggregate demand.'

3 Given an economy with purchasing power parity and full employment equilibrium, analyse the effects of (a) a systematic increase in the money supply, (b) an unexpected increase in the money supply, (c) an increase in the discount/bank rate by the central bank.

4 'If all shocks are monetary in origin, a flexible exchange rate system will result in greater macroeconomic stability than will a fixed rate regime.' Discuss this statement for both the impact and the equilibrium effects of such shocks.

5 Given a small open economy with highly elastic capital flows and flexible exchange rates, what are the determinants of the domestic interest rates?

6 For a small open economy, can the monetary authority easily change the underlying domestic interest rate as an act of policy by changing its bank/discount rate? If it cannot do so, why do the monetary authorities use interest rates as an operational target? Are the changes in the bank/discount rate merely window dressing or even contrary to the dictates of economic theory and reality?

7 It is sometimes claimed that exchange rate volatility has more to do with the lack of flexibility in nominal wages and prices than excessive speculation in foreign exchange markets. Present the reasons given for this statement and discuss its validity.

8 Assume a small open economy with a flexible exchange rate, sluggish adjustment of prices and perfect capital mobility. Analyse the effects of the following on the exchange rate, nominal income and real output in the short run and the long run:

   (a) an unanticipated increase in the foreign demand for the country's exports;
   (b) an unanticipated increase in world interest rates.

    Suppose controls on capital flows were imposed at the time of the shock. How would your conclusions change? What is likely to be the response of the investors to the imposition of such controls?

9 Assume a small open economy with a fixed exchange rate and that it experiences an unexpected fall in foreign transfers to it. What are its policy options if it has (a) full wage and price flexibility and (b) downward nominal price and nominal wage rigidity?

10 Canada is a small open economy, next door to its dominant trading partner, the United States, which also has an open economy but not a small one. Under flexible exchange rates, how are macroeconomic predictions about the efficacy of monetary and fiscal policies affected for (a) the Canadian economy and (b) the US economy, by the 'openness' of the two economies?

11 Assuming that the central bank has adopted a zero inflation rate as its target and a managed exchange rate policy, how should it respond to an unexpected depreciation of its currency?

12 Discuss: while a gradualist policy pursued of reducing the money growth rate as a way of bringing down inflation has merit in a closed economy, it will be disruptive in a small open economy with perfect capital mobility and has few benefits over a one-time big drop in the money growth rate.

13 Under a fixed exchange rate regime, should the monetary authority try to manipulate the flows of commodities and capital to its own country? If so, what policies are appropriate for this purpose? Consider both the short run and the long run in your answer.

14 Under a flexible exchange rate regime, should the monetary authority try to manipulate the flows of commodities and capital to its own country? If so, how can it achieve this? Consider both the short run and the long run in your answer.

15 What are the advantages and disadvantages to the Canadian economy and the United States' economy of 'dollarization' (replacement of the Canadian dollar by the US one) versus a currency board system for Canada? Is there a way for Canada to capture the seigniorage involved?

16 What are the advantages and disadvantages to the British economy from the adoption of the euro as its currency? With this adoption, would the Bank of England become nothing more than a currency board? How can Britain capture the seigniorage involved in this step and what would be its probable share in the seigniorage of the European System of Central Banks.

17 In the light of the European plans for the European central bank, what are the benefits and costs to Canada and the USA of their setting up a unified central bank for the two countries?

18 'The best way to understand an exchange rate crisis is the simplest one: exchange rates are a monetary phenomenon. The currency does not decline in value because the country has a low productivity or exports decline or imports grow too fast. It declines in value because the country prints too much of it.' Discuss, using at least two different theories of the determination of the exchange rate.

19 Consider a small open economy (Canada) where the exchange rate is more flexible than the domestic price level and where wealth effects are negligible. Canada exports mainly to its giant neighbouring economy (USA), whose real income is y^*. At a certain time t, the United States government announces that it expects a permanent increase in US income from y^* at t to y^*_{t+1} at $t+1$. However, in $t+1$, it is found that real income is still at y^*. The US government revises its forecast and announces that it no longer expects a change in income. What are the effects of the two announcements on Canada's economy and exchange rate? (You can use any model that you like but do specify which one you are using.)

Suppose that the announcements had not been about real income but about the US money supply. What are the effects of these two announcements on Canada's economy and exchange rate?

20 You are given a small open economy with a flexible exchange rate and perfect capital mobility but sluggish adjustment of prices. Derive the effects on its exchange rate and economic activity in both the short and the long run of the following:

(a) an anticipated increase in the world interest rate;
(b) an unanticipated increase in the world interest rate;
(c) an anticipated decrease in the world demand for the exports of the country;
(d) an unanticipated decrease in the world demand for the exports of the country.

21 'A rise in the domestic rate of interest relative to the foreign one is likely to be accompanied by an appreciation of the currency in the foreign exchange market.' Discuss, using the monetary approach to the exchange rate and the Dornbusch model. Is this statement accurate in the light of the experience of your domestic currency during the last two decades?

22 Analyse the short-run and long-run effects in the Dornbusch model of an anticipated announcement of a future (next period) monetary expansion on the price level, the exchange rate, the interest rate and output.

23 Analyse the short-run and long-run effects in the Dornbusch model of an unanticipated announcement of a future (next period) monetary expansion on the price level, the exchange rate and the interest rate.

24 You are given the following model:

$$M_t - P_t = m_y y_t - m_r r_t$$

$$y_t = -\alpha r_t + \beta(\rho_t - P_t) + g_t$$

$$r_t - r^*_t = -(\rho_{t+1} - \rho_t) = -\rho'_t$$

$$P_{t+1} - P_t = P'_t = \varphi(y_t - y^f_t)$$

The symbols are as defined in the text and all the coefficients are positive.

(a) In this model, what are the responses of ρ, P, r and y to an unexpected permanent fall in the money stock M? What happens if the change in M was not unexpected but had been anticipated?

(b) Does this model imply that the exchange rate will appreciate on the publication of statistics showing that monetary growth proved to be faster than planned?

NOTES

1   It is also assumed that the other endogenous variables such as incomes, prices and exchange rates are not likely to significantly affect capital flows from the viewpoint of a purely comparative static analysis.

2   The relationships shown in Figures 19.1a to 19.1c have been assumed to be linear, though they need not be so in practice.

3   The *ceteris paribus* assumption is unlikely to hold. If an open economy were to somehow become closed, the consumers are likely to switch their former expenditures on imported goods to expenditures on domestic goods, so that the marginal propensity to consume domestic goods, c_y, will not be invariant to changes from an open economy to a closed one, or vice versa. Therefore, the multiplier will also not be invariant in such a comparison.

4   Unless purchasing power parity holds, in which case ρ will depreciate in proportion to the increase P and net exports will not change.

5   This multiplier is the increase in the money supply for a marginal increase in the monetary base.

6   Both these could be affected by international flows in an open economy in the long run.

7   However, as discussed earlier, changes in the domestic or foreign prices or foreign interest rates will shift the IS curve.

8   The international and domestic markets are different in nature: the former represents an exchange of domestic for foreign bonds while the latter represents exchanges between money and bonds and requires equilibrium in the market for money.

9   The size of the balance of payments deficit can be related to the interest gap between the one given by the intersection of the IS and LM curves and, for this level of aggregate demand, that given by the *BB* curve.

10   As the preceding chapter pointed out, this is an approximation.

11   The second assumption is sometimes violated when the authorities have fixed the exchange rate but the public believes that this exchange rate cannot be maintained. Suppose the public expects a devaluation. In such a case, there are usually speculative outflows of foreign exchange, which reduce the country's foreign exchange reserves and worsen the balance of payments, thereby putting pressure on the authorities to devalue in an attempt to stem the outflow of reserves.

12   These arguments involving shifts in several curves become quite complex when price changes are considered. The complexity arises basically from the dependence of the various sectors on domestic prices. It is, therefore, preferable to work directly with the equations derived earlier. If one wishes to stay with the diagrammatic form, it would be better to adapt the arguments to the (y, P) space while eliminating r as a variable through a combination of the expenditure and the monetary sectors and a combination of the foreign and the monetary sectors.

13   A fundamental disequilibrium is to be thought of as a long-run disequilibrium rather than a short-run – monthly or annual – disequilibrium.

14   As discussed earlier, this relationship is an approximation. It will be used for its analytical convenience.

15   Note that if $m_r^* = m_r$, the foreign interest rate drops out of the equation and does not affect the spot rate.

16   A variable x_t is a martingale if $x_{t+1} = x_t + \epsilon_{t+1}$ where $E\epsilon_t = 0$ and $E(|x_t|) < \infty$. In this case, $Ex_{t+1} = x_t$. A stronger assumption is that the ϵ_t is independently identically distributed, which implies the above restrictions and produces a random walk.

   If the variable in question is the exchange rate, we would have $E[\rho_{t+1} \mid \rho_t] = \rho_t$. That is, all the information on the future spot rate is contained in the current one.

17   These are the markets for money, domestic and foreign bonds – and implicitly involve the market for foreign exchange.

18   Dornbusch sets the foreign price level at unity, so that its log value, P^*, becomes zero and is left out of (57).

19 The latter is called the exchange rate channel and is identified with the Mundell–Fleming model. As such, it is also called the Mundell–Fleming channel.
20 However, the positive correlation between the nominal and the real exchange rates was less in periods of high inflation.

REFERENCES

Adler, Michael, and Bruce Lehman. 'Deviations from Purchasing Power Parity in the Long Run'. *Journal of Finance*, 38, December 1983, pp. 1471–87.

De Grauwe, Paul. 'The Long Swings in Real Exchange Rates – Do They Fit Our Theories?' *Bank of Japan Monetary and Economic Studies*, 6, May 1988, pp. 37–60.

De Vries, Caspar G. 'Stylized Facts of Nominal Exchange Rate Returns'. In *The Handbook of International Macroeconomics*, edited by Frederick Van Der Ploeg. Oxford: Blackwell, 1994.

Dornbusch, Rudiger. 'Expectations and Exchange Rate Dynamics'. *Journal of Political Economy*, 84, December 1976, pp. 1161–76.

Dumas, Bernard. 'Partial Equilibrium versus General Equilibrium Models of the International Capital Market'. In *The Handbook of International Macroeconomics*, edited by Frederick Van Der Ploeg. Oxford: Blackwell, 1994.

Engel, Charles. 'Accounting for US Real Exchange Rate Changes'. *Journal of Political Economy*, 107, June 1999, pp. 507–38.

Fleming, J. Marcus. 'Domestic Financial Policies Under Fixed and Under Floating Exchange Rates'. *IMF Staff Papers*, 9, November 1962, pp. 369–79.

Frankel, Jeffrey A. 'International Capital Mobility and Crowding-out in the US Economy: Imperfect Integration of Financial Markets or of Goods Markets'. In *How Open is the US Economy?*, edited by Ruth W. Hafer. Lexington, MA: Lexington, 1986.

Kim, Yoonbai. 'Purchasing Power Parity in the Long Run: A Cointegration Approach'. *Journal of Money, Credit and Banking*, 22, November 1990, pp. 491–503.

Kugler, Peter, and Carlos Lenz. 'Multivariate Cointegration Analysis and the Long-Run Validity of PPP'. *Review of Economics and Statistics*, 75, February 1993, pp. 180–84.

Mark, Nelson C. 'Real and Nominal Exchange Rates in the Long Run'. *Journal of International Economics*, 28, 1990, pp. 115–36.

Meese, R., and K. Rogoff. 'Empirical Exchange Rate Models of the Seventies: Do They Fit Out of the Sample?' *Journal of International Economics*, 14, 1983, pp. 3–24.

Mundell, Robert A. 'Capital Mobility and Stabilization Policy Under Fixed and Flexible Exchange Rates'. *Canadian Journal of Economics and Political Science*, 29, November 1963, pp. 475–85.

Obstfeld, Maurice, and Kenneth Rogoff. 'Exchange Rate Dynamics Redux'. *Journal of Political Economy*, 103, 1995, pp. 624–60.

part seven

THE RATES OF INTEREST IN THE ECONOMY

chapter twenty

THE MACROECONOMIC THEORY OF THE RATE OF INTEREST

The rate of interest is one of the endogenous variables in the Keynesian and classical models, so that its analysis is properly conducted as part of a complete version of those models. These were presented in Chapters 13 and 14.

This chapter singles out the competing views on the determination of the rate of interest and focuses on their differences and validity. It also highlights the very important difference between the comparative static and the dynamic determination of the rate of interest.

---

key concepts introduced in this chapter

- The Fisher equation of the nominal rate of interest
- Stocks versus flows of funds
- The loanable funds theory
- The liquidity preference theory
- The excess demand function for bonds
- The dynamics of interest rate determination
- The neutrality of money and inflation for the real rate of interest

---

Macroeconomics avoids the bewildering array of interest rates on the numerous assets in the market by focusing on one single rate of interest, without completely specifying which rate of interest it is, as for example in the IS–LM model of Chapters 13 and 14 and in most macroeconomic models. Among the macroeconomic theories that deal specifically with the determination of the rate of interest are the traditional classical loanable funds theory and the Keynesian liquidity preference theory. These are presented in this chapter.

Section 20.1 reviews the Fisher relationship between the real and nominal interest rates. Sections 20.2 and 20.3 look at the modern and historical versions of the loanable funds theory of the rate of interest. Section 20.4 presents the liquidity preference theory of interest. Section 20.5 compares the loanable funds and liquidity preference theories in the comparative statics context with the excess demand for bonds derived using Walras' law, and shows that the two yield identical comparative static implications for the rate of interest. Section 20.6 examines the dynamic applications of the two theories for changes in the rate of interest and shows that, in terms of dynamics, the two theories give different implications, so that a choice has to be made between the two. Section 20.7 derives the bond curve and relates it to the IS and LM curves and section 20.8 uses these curves to show the dynamic difference between the competing theories. Section 20.9 discusses the reasons for the selection of the loanable funds theory over the liquidity preference theory. Sections 20.10 and 20.11 discuss the neutrality of money for the real rate of interest and testing the Fisher equation of the nominal interest rate; section 20.12 presents the empirical findings of two studies to illustrate applications of the liquidity preference and loanable funds theories.

Given the common or underlying macroeconomic rate of interest as determined in this chapter, the next chapter will examine the time and the risk aspects of the interaction among the various interest rates in the economy. The main focus of that chapter will be on the term structure of interest rates.

20.1 NOMINAL AND REAL RATES OF INTEREST

The rate of interest that is charged on loans in the market is the *market* or *nominal rate of interest*. This has been designated by the symbol r. If the rational lender expects a rate of inflation π^e, he has to consider the real rate of interest that he would receive on his loan. In perfect capital markets, the real rate equals the nominal rate minus the expected loss of the purchasing power of money balances through inflation, so that the expected real rate of interest r^{re} equals:

$$r^{re} = r - \pi^e \tag{1}$$

Equation (1) was proposed by Irving Fisher and is known as the Fisher equation. The real value of the rate of return that the lender would actually – *ex post* – receive from his loan is the *actual real rate of interest* (r^r), which is given by:

$$r^r = r - \pi \tag{1'}$$

where:

- r nominal rate of interest
- r^r actual (*ex post*) real rate of interest
- r^{re} expected real rate of return
- π actual rate of inflation
- π^e expected rate of inflation

If the actual rate of inflation is imperfectly anticipated, then r^r would differ from r^{re} and may or may not be positive. However, the rational expectations hypothesis implies that the error in expectations would only be random and uncorrelated with information available at the time the expectations are formed.

In (1), on the interaction between the real rate of interest and the expected rate of inflation, Mundell (1963) argued that increases in the expected rate of inflation will cause a reduction in the demand for real balances, which will lower the real rate of interest, as can be seen through the use of the IS–LM analysis. Tobin (1965) argued that such a reduction in the demand for real balances will increase the demand for real capital and consequently lower its productivity and the real rate of interest. The impact of higher expected inflation on the real rate of interest is often called the Mundell–Tobin effect.

Many presentations of the short-run macroeconomic models of the IS–LM type do not distinguish between these differing concepts of the rate of interest. These models are comparative static ones for the analysis of a once-for-all price change: the equilibrium values of the variables are only compared before and after a price change, but not during the process in which inflation (rate of price change) is occurring. To encompass the effects of a non-zero expected rate of inflation, the IS–LM model can be modified to assume that the rate of interest relevant for saving and investment decisions is the expected real rate of interest, while the rate of interest relevant for a decision to hold money *vis-à-vis* bonds is the nominal rate of interest.

Note also the impact of changes in the money supply on the nominal rate through its impact on the real rate and the expected rate of inflation. An increase in the money supply lowers the real rate, as in the IS–LM analysis through a rightward shift of the LM curve, but it also causes inflation, which through the formation of expectations creates expected inflation and raises the nominal rates. At very low rates of expected inflation, the net effect of money creation is often to lower the nominal rate, at least for some time, but high and persistent rates of inflation are invariably accompanied by high nominal rates.

20.2 THE LOANABLE FUNDS THEORY OF THE RATE OF INTEREST

Using the concept of the user or rental cost of an asset, the rate of interest is the *rental cost of the funds* that are borrowed. Since it is a price, the familiar demand and supply analysis of the market for a good, in this case bonds, credit or 'loanable funds',[1] can be used to explain the determination of the rate of interest. Designating the nominal demand for loanable funds as $L^d(r, ...)$ and the nominal supply of loanable funds as $L^s(r, ...)$, equilibrium in the loanable funds market is given by:

$$L^d(r, ...) = L^s(r, ...) \tag{2}$$

where r is the rate of interest, and we have assumed that both the demand and supply of loanable funds depend on it. Each may also depend on other variables. Equation (2) yields the excess nominal demand for loanable funds as $E^d_b(r, ...)$ which can be compared with the excess (real) demand function for bonds derived in Chapter 17 in the context of the discussion on Walras' law.

Flows versus stocks

The demand and supply of funds in the loanable funds market can be interpreted in either flow or stock terms. In terms of the *flows over a specified period of time*, the supply of loanable funds is the amount flowing or coming onto the market for lending at the various rates of interest. Similarly, the demand for loanable funds comes from those wanting to borrow funds during the period.

However, the flow of funds which becomes available for loans over the current period is only a small fraction of the total amount of credit outstanding in the economy. This total amount is like a reservoir and is the *stock* of loanable funds. The stock of credit supplied at any point in time consists of all outstanding loans plus the net additional flow supply of loanable funds, specified for each rate of interest. In stock terms, the demand for credit is similarly the total amount already borrowed plus the net additional amounts that the borrowers wish to borrow at each rate of interest. In modern economies, a major part of this demand often comes from the existing public debt.

In perfect credit markets and with all the borrowers and lenders able and willing to renegotiate – that is, recontract – their loans each period at the prevailing rate of interest, the stock and the flow analysis yield the same equilibrium rate of interest. In imperfect markets, with long-term contracts and uncertainty, some of the borrowers and lenders are already committed to loans made at rates prevailing in the past. Therefore, the flow analysis of the credit market could yield a rate of interest different from that given by the stock analysis. This can be a common occurrence for those parts of the financial markets which tie up funds in long-term contracts, as in the case of mortgages, or in which there is unwillingness for some reason to re-arrange the portfolio every period.[2] In such a case, the proper market for determining the current rate of interest is that in terms of flows. The flow market is the actual operating market for credit in any given period, with borrowers entering it to borrow and lenders entering it to lend funds. However, note that the pre-committed stock of credit does exert a strong background influence on the flow demands and supplies since parts of it will be expected by borrowers and lenders to become uncommitted sooner or later and become flows available for renegotiation over time.

The *supply of the stock of credit* at any time has several sources. It includes loans made directly by the savers, often called the 'ultimate lenders' in the economy, to the firms, called the 'ultimate borrowers' in the economy. This is usually through the purchase by households of stocks and bonds issued by firms, and bonds issued by the government. In addition, there are the loans made by financial intermediaries. Part of the loans made by the ultimate lenders comes from past and current savings that are lent to others and not invested by the saver himself. But another part, likely to be a small part of the whole, could come from changes in the public's demand for real balances. For instance, a reduction in the demand for money to hold by consumers will release funds, with some of these being made available for loans to others while another part could be used to pay for additional consumption expenditures.

The *demand for the stock of credit* also comes from several sources. Part of it is by the firms, also called the 'ultimate borrowers' in the economy, who need it for financing investment. But part of this demand also comes from financial intermediaries, who use it in the financial intermediation process to make loans to firms and the government.

In practice, households seek specialized instruments such as demand and savings deposits, pension funds, mutual funds, etc., suited to their own needs, and channel most of their savings to the financial institutions that provide these. Correspondingly, firms which need funds approach specialized financial institutions such as investment banks to market their securities, with most of these securities being bought by financial institutions rather than households.

The determination of the rate of interest by flows of funds

The *flow supply of funds* can be interpreted as that part of the stock that has come up for renegotiation plus the additions being made currently. The net *new* supply of funds in any period t to the credit market comes from two sources:

(i) Current saving in the economy.
(ii) Excess supply of money made available for loans, with the excess supply resulting from changes in the public's desired balances or in the supply of money. The supply of money depends on the monetary base and the inside money created by financial intermediaries.

The supply of funds in period t is the net new supply from the above two sources plus:

(iii) Funds becoming available from loans which have matured in period t.

The *flow demand* for loans is from net new borrowers and those who wish to renew existing loans. The net *new demand* for loans comes from:

(iv) Current investment in the economy.
(v) Bond-financed government deficits.[3]

The flow demand for loans in period t is from (iv), (v) and

(vi) Demand for credit from those whose loans have matured.

Assuming (iii) and (vi) to be equal, the loanable funds theory in flow terms specifies the real demand and supply functions of loanable funds as:

$$f^s = s(r, \ldots) + (M^s/P - m^d(r, \ldots)) \tag{3}$$

$$f^d = i(r, \ldots) + (g - t) \tag{4}$$

where we have assumed the deficit $(g - t)$ to be wholly bond-financed. This theory then determines the interest rate by the loanable funds market equilibrium condition,

$$s(r, \ldots) + (M^s/P - m^d(r, \ldots)) = i(r, \ldots) + (g - t) \tag{5}$$

where:

f^s	real flow supply of loanable funds (bonds)
f^d	real flow demand for loanable funds (bonds)
s	real saving
i	real investment
g	real government expenditures
t	real government revenues
M^s	nominal money supply
m^d	demand for real balances
P	price level

The loanable funds theory states that the market rate of interest is determined by (5). Note that the left side of (5) represents the demand for bonds and the right side represents the supply of bonds. Equation (5) is the statement that the rate of interest is determined by the equilibrium in the flow part of the bond market.

Equation (5) specifies the determination of the interest rate in the short run. It shows that the rate of interest is not independent of the excess demand for money. Money supply and demand enter the determination of the rate of interest only if there is a disequilibrium in the money market. In disequilibrium, excess money demand raises the interest rate and excess money supply lowers it. The labour market does not appear explicitly in (5) but the determination of incomes in the labour market is clearly a determinant of saving in the economy, so that the labour market is implicitly included in the determination of the loanable funds interest rate.

The long-run and short-run determination of the interest rate

Equation (5) specifies the long-run determination of the rate of interest if the money market is in equilibrium. In this long-run case, the excess money demand term on the left side of (5) disappears, so that the long-run version of the loanable funds theory becomes:

$$s(r, \ldots) = i(r, \ldots) + (g - t) \tag{5'}$$

We can deduce from (5) that the economic agents who influence the loanable funds rate are the government, the public, the private financial sector and the central bank. The bond financing of a fiscal deficit increases the demand for loans and, therefore, raises the interest rate, just as an increase in private investment would do. The financial sector plays a long-run role in the determination of the interest rate not only by affecting the efficiency of the bond and money markets. It also plays a short-run role through changes in the excess demand for money brought about by changes in the commercial banks' reserve ratio. The public also plays a dual role: a long-run role through its saving and investment propensities and a short-run one through change in the excess demand for money brought about by changes in its currency ratio. Similarly, the central bank plays a dual role. It plays a long-run one through its regulations and management affecting the efficiency of the financial system and the channelling of saving into investment. It plays a short-run role through changes in the excess demand for money induced by changes in the monetary base.

20.3 A HISTORICAL INCURSION: THE TRADITIONAL CLASSICAL LOANABLE FUNDS THEORY OF THE RATE OF INTEREST

20.3.1 The traditional classical long-run theory of interest

The traditional (pre-Keynes) classical economists simplified their analysis of the credit market by ignoring financial intermediaries completely and assuming that governments do not incur deficits or surpluses. Under these assumptions, they formulated both a long-run and a short-run theory of interest, the former with equilibrium in the money market and the latter without it. In their long-run theory of interest, the flow demand for new loans was solely for investment purposes and the net increase in the supply of loanable funds was solely from new saving. Since full employment was an implication of their ideas on the labour market and became an assumption in their analysis of the credit market, this saving equalled the amount coming forth from full employment income. Hence, the rate of interest that would be determined by the long-run supply and demand for loanable funds in any period would be the same rate of interest as that determined by the equality of full employment saving and investment.

The traditional classical economists specified the fundamental determinant of saving as the public's 'time preference' – that is, a preference for present over future consumption.[4] They argued that people would only save – that is, postpone consumption – if induced to do so by a positive rate of interest. Thus, at an $r\%$ annual rate of interest, postponing consumption by $1 enables a saving of $1 which enables consumption next year of $(1 + r)$. The higher the rate of interest, the greater is the inducement to postpone consumption, so that saving is positively related to the rate of interest.[5] Note that in this analysis, the dependence of saving on income tended to be ignored since national income was assumed by the traditional classical economists to be at the full employment level in the long run.

The traditional classical economists specified the corresponding fundamental determinant of the demand for funds as arising from and being equal to investment. Such demand depends upon the productivity of investment which, in turn, depends upon the state of technical knowledge, the existing stock of capital and employment. The traditional classical economists equated investment to the change in the desired capital stock and determined the latter from the profit-maximizing condition that the marginal product of capital equal the real interest.

Hence, the rate of interest in this traditional classical long-run theory is determined by the equality of saving (the supply of loans) at full employment income y^f and investment (the demand for loans), modifying (3) and (4) to:

$$f^s = s(r; y^f) \tag{6}$$

$$f^d = i(r) \tag{7}$$

and the equilibrium condition (5) to:

$$s(r; y^f) = i(r) \tag{8}$$

With y^f set exogenously at the full employment level, (8) contains only one endogenous variable, r, and determines it as the rate that would exist at full employment. Equations (6) to (8) specify the long-run version of the traditional classical theory of interest: the rate of interest is determined in the long run solely by consumers' preferences on consumption over saving and by the marginal productivity of capital.[6]

20.3.2 The traditional classical short-run theory of interest

For a closed economy without a government[7] and with continuous full employment, (8) is identical with the equilibrium condition for the expenditure sector of the modern IS–LM macroeconomic model, so that the IS–LM model embodies the loanable funds theory. However, if there does not exist full employment, the IS–LM model implies that the rate of interest is also influenced by the excess supply for money: if the supply of money is greater than the demand for it, this excess supply will be used to buy bonds and become additions to the supply of loanable funds. Conversely, if the supply of money is less than its demand, the public will try to replenish its money holdings by selling bonds. The supply of loanable funds is, therefore, redefined in the general context of the IS–LM models to include both saving and the excess supply (positive or negative) of money. The latter is often called as the change in the hoarding (or dishoarding) of money balances.

In nominal terms, the IS–LM model with a government sector implies on the basis of Walras' law – for which, see Chapter 17 – that:

$$Pf^s = Ps(r, y; g, t) + [M^s - Pm^d(r; y)] \tag{9}$$

$$Pf^d = Pi(r) \tag{10}$$

Therefore, in real terms in equilibrium,

$$i(r) = s(r, y; g, t) + [M/P - m^d(r; y)] \tag{11}$$

so that:

$$r = \varphi(P, y; M, g, t) \tag{12}$$

The equilibrium condition (11) allows changes in the price level to affect the equilibrium rate of interest. Further, since this equation contains three endogenous variables, r, y and P, none of them can be determined uniquely from it.

The general IS–LM model in the form of (9) to (11) can be designated as the short-run version of the traditional classical theory of the rate of interest since the traditional classical economists were generally aware of the influence of hoarding or dishoarding of money balances on the flow of credit, and also did allow adjustment in economic activity during which the economy would not be at full employment. It comes out as such clearly in the work of Wicksell presented above in Chapter 2.

However, traditional classical writings often seemed to state that the price level was determined independently – as in the quantity theory – of the equations determining the rate of interest or the level of employment. For this to be so, (11) would either not possess P and y as variables or they would be set exogenously. These restrictions transform the short-run version (11) into the long-run traditional classical theory of the rate of interest given by (8), with the long-run rate of interest becoming independent of the price level.

The short-run theory also becomes the long-run one if the public never substitutes between money balances and loans on the basis of the rate of interest. To the traditional classical economists, the individual was a rational being who would never hold his savings in a monetary form when he could earn interest by lending them, so that all of his savings were made available by him for lending. Further, his money balances were always at the minimum necessary to finance his transactions, as in the pre-Keynesian versions of the quantity theory. If these balances increased for some reason and were greater than the desired amount, the individual would spend the excess on commodities, as embodied in Irving Fisher's version of the quantity theory. Therefore, the rate of interest was only influenced by saving and not directly by the demand for money. However, this line of reasoning was increasingly modified in the late nineteenth- and twentieth-century versions of the loanable funds theory to allow for substitution in the short run between money balances and bonds, thus leading to a separate short-run theory of the type specified by (9) to (11), and eventually to the modern IS–LM models.

20.3.3 David Hume on the rate of interest

David Hume occupies a special place in the macroeconomic theory of the rate of interest because he had specified the main elements of the preceding traditional classical theory at an early stage in its development. He expressed some of the basic elements of the traditional classical short- and long-run theories in his essay *On Interest*, published in 1752, as:

> High interest arises from three circumstances: a great demand for borrowing, little riches to supply that demand, and great profits arising from commerce: and the circumstances are a clear proof of the small advance of commerce and industry, not of the scarcity of gold and silver. Low interest, on the other hand, proceeds from the three opposite circumstances: a small demand for borrowing; great riches to supply that demand; and small profits arising from commerce: and these circumstances are all connected together, and proceed from the increase of industry and commerce, not of gold and silver.
>
> . . . For, suppose that, by miracle, every man in Great Britain should have five pounds slipped into his pocket in one night; this would much more than double the whole money that is at present in the kingdom; yet there would not next day, nor for some time, be any more lenders, nor any variation in the interest. And were there nothing but landlords and peasants in the state, this money, however abundant, could never gather into sums, and would only serve to increase the prices of everything, without any further consequence. The prodigal landlord dissipates it as fast as he receives it; and the beggarly peasant has no means, nor view, nor ambition of obtaining above a bare livelihood. The overplus of borrowers above that of lenders continuing still the same, there will follow no reduction of interest. That depends upon another principle; and must proceed from an increase of industry and frugality of arts and commerce.
>
> . . . the greater or less quantity of it [money] in a state has no influence on the interest. But it is evident that the greater or less stock of labour and commodities must have a great influence; since we really and in effect borrow these, when we take money upon interest.
>
> . . . Another reason of this popular mistake with regard to the cause of low interest, seems to be the instance of some nations, where, after a sudden acquisition of money, or of the precious metals by means of foreign conquest, the interest has fallen not only among them, but in all the neighbouring states, as soon as that money was dispersed, and had insinuated itself into every corner. Thus, interest in Spain fell near a half immediately after the discovery of the West Indies, as we are informed by Garcilasso de la Vega; and it has been ever since gradually sinking in every kingdom of Europe. Interest in Rome, after the conquest of Egypt, fell from 6 to 4 per cent, as we learn from Dion. The causes of the sinking of interest, upon such an event, seem different in the conquering country and in the neighbouring states; but in neither of them can we justly ascribe that effect merely to the increase of gold and silver. In the conquering country, it is natural to imagine that this new acquisition of money will fall into a few hands, and be gathered into large sums, which seek a secure revenue, either by the purchase of land or by interest; and consequently the same effect follows, for a little time, as if there had been a great accession of industry and commerce. The increase of lenders above the borrowers sinks the interest, and so much the faster if those who have acquired those large sums find no industry or commerce in the state, and no method of employing their money but by

lending it at interest. But after this new mass of gold and silver has been digested, and has circulated through the whole state, affairs will soon return to their former situation, while the landlords and new money-holders, living idly, squander above their income; and the former daily contract debt, and the latter encroach on their stock till its final extinction. The whole money may still be in the state, and make itself felt by the increase of prices; but not being now collected into any large masses or stocks, the disproportion between the borrowers and lenders is the same as formerly, and consequently the high interest returns. Accordingly we find in Rome, that, so early as Tiberius's time, interest had again amounted to 6 per cent, though no accident had happened to drain the empire of money. In Trajan's time, money lent on mortgages in Italy bore 6 per cent, on common securities in Bithynia 12; and if interest in Spain has not risen to its old pitch, this can be ascribed to nothing but the continuance of the same cause that sunk it, to wit, the large fortunes continually made in the Indies, which come over to Spain from time to time, and supply the demand of the borrowers. By this accidental and extraneous cause, more money is to be lent in Spain, that is, more money is collected into large sums, than would otherwise be found in a state, where there are so little commerce and industry.

   As to the reduction of interest which has followed in England, France, and other kingdoms of Europe that have no mines, it has been gradual, and has not proceeded from the increase of money, considered merely in itself, but from that of industry.

(Hume, On Interest, 1752)

The salient points in this quote can be summarized in modern terminology as:

(i)   The long-run equilibrium rate of interest is determined by the saving at full employment output and the productivity of investment.
(ii) The long-run rate of interest is invariant to changes in the money supply. A long-run decline of the rate of interest is brought about by a decline in the productivity of investment and not by increases in the money supply.
(iii) However, the disequilibrium rate of interest is affected by those changes in the money supply which change the supply of loanable funds in the economy, as occurs in the indirect transmission mechanism, but not by those which do not, as occurs in the direct transmission mechanism. The structure of the economy and the mode by which additional money balances are introduced into the economy determine which mechanism is the relevant one.
(iv) Increases in the money supply which increase the flow of loanable funds in the economy decrease the interest rate in disequilibrium and increase economic activity, that is, employment and output.

Note that Hume did not have Irving Fisher's equation relating the nominal rate of interest to the expected rate of inflation.

20.3.4 Adapting the traditional classical to the modern classical loanable funds theory of interest

The pre-Keynesian classical theories of the rate of interest were formulated under the assumptions of a closed economy without a government sector, without financial intermediaries but with a labour market possessing continuous market clearance. However, this existence of full employment cannot be taken for granted in modern economies. If the traditional classical short-run theory were to be modified to take account of the possibility of deviations from full employment at least in some disequilibrium states of the economy, this theory becomes, as argued in subsection 20.3.2, almost synonymous with the IS–LM macroeconomic models. In this case, for the neoclassical and modern classical models of Chapter 13, the equilibrium rate of interest is determined by the bond market alone if there exists full employment. But, for the Keynesian models of Chapter 14, the interest rate cannot be determined by the bond market alone but must involve the whole macroeconomic model in a joint determination of output, the interest rate and the price level.

The traditional classical theories were also formulated for an era in which the non-bank financial intermediaries were relatively insignificant. Until the Second World War, the market for credit was dominated by ultimate borrowers borrowing for investment and ultimate lenders lending out of savings, so that it was common for the role of financial intermediaries to be ignored or in any case not integrated into the theory of the rate of interest. Such an approach is inappropriate for the modern economy pervaded by financial intermediaries.

Taking account of these modifications to the traditional classical approach to fit the modern period involves generalizing the traditional classical theory to (11) which we have referred to as the modern version of the loanable funds theory of interest as implied by the IS–LM model. Rewrite (9) and (10) as:

$$Pf^s = Ps(r, y; g, t) + [\phi B - Pm^d(r; y)] \tag{13}$$

$$Pf^d = Pi(r) \tag{14}$$

where B is the monetary base and ϕ represents the influence of the activities of the financial intermediaries in determining the money supply as ϕB. Therefore, in equilibrium for the loanable funds market,

$$Pi(r) = Ps(r, y; g, t) + [\phi B - Pm^d(r; y)] \tag{15}$$

so that:

$$r = \varphi(P, y; g, t, B, \phi) \tag{16}$$

which indicates that the financial intermediaries through ϕ can also influence the short-run rate of interest, as can the monetary authorities through B and the fiscal authorities through g and t. The generalized version of the loanable funds theory represented by (15) and (16) takes account of the activities of financial intermediaries in the money markets and of the possible variations in income from its full employment level. It involves so many influences on both the demand and supply side of the credit market that the actual rate of interest may be widely different from one that would exist if saving was the sole source of supply and investment was the sole source of the demand for funds. The short-run rate of interest cannot then be regarded as being determined solely by the rate of time preference and/or by the marginal productivity of investment.

Further, saving is not directly lent to investors and therefore does not directly materialize as investment. Households usually keep much of their saving in the form of financial assets such as money and bonds, while firms borrow substantially from financial intermediaries towards the financing of their investments, so that the efficiency of financial intermediation in this process also affects the structure of interest rates. A less-developed financial system usually implies a greater differential between the interest rates paid to the savers/lenders and the interest rates charged to or paid by borrowers, as can be seen by comparing the structure of interest rates in the developed economies with those in the LDCs.

In recent years, the modern version of the classical school has reasserted market clearance for the labour markets, as for other markets, and with its assumption of rational expectations, has further asserted the possibility of disequilibrium in any market as at best a very transitory state. That is, with the labour and money markets clearing continuously, there would exist full employment in the economy and the excess demand in the money market would also be zero. Consequently, for the modern classical school, the theory of interest reverts to the long-run version of the traditional classical theory as set out in (6) to (8), with the difference that it is now intended to be not only the long-run theory but also the short-run theory of the rate of interest as far as systematic – and, therefore, anticipated – changes in the money supply are concerned.[8] The latter is a departure from the pre-Keynes classical economics, as a comparison of the doctrines of the modern classical school with the quotation from Hume in the preceding subsection clearly shows.

The modern classical version of the loanable funds theory, therefore, extends and differs from the traditional classical one in various ways. Among the differences are:

(i) The role of financial intermediaries, as discussed above.
(ii) The distinction in the modern version between the anticipated and unanticipated values of the relevant variables, among which are the money supply, the other determinants of aggregate demand, and the rate of inflation. Anticipated money supply increases cause anticipated inflation without changing the real rate of interest and, therefore, increase the nominal rate by the anticipated rate of inflation, as specified by the Fisher equation. Unanticipated money supply growth lowers the real rate and will lower the market rate of interest.
(iii) Ricardian equivalence, which makes national saving independent of the (anticipated) fiscal deficit and, therefore, removes such deficits from the determinants of the demand and supply of loanable funds. Hence, anticipated deficits do not affect the rate of interest.
(iv) In the short run, the traditional classical economists allowed deviations from full employment under the impact of money supply changes and the impact of these on saving. The modern classical economists allow such a deviation for only unanticipated money supply changes. Therefore, the short-run deviations of output from its full employment level under the impact of anticipated money supply changes could, in the short run, affect the rate of interest under the traditional version of the loanable funds theory but not its modern version.

Note that in the context of the short-run theory of interest represented by (15) and (16), the interest rate is not merely the reward for postponing consumption, it is also the return on lending, which is the act of parting with liquidity – that is, not holding money.

20.4 THE LIQUIDITY PREFERENCE THEORY OF INTEREST

Keynes' *General Theory* (1936) challenged the loanable funds theory, especially in what has been designated above as the traditional classical long-run form, on the grounds that the rate of interest was not the reward for saving but was rather an inducement to part with liquidity. He summarized his views in the statement:

> The psychological time-preferences of an individual require two distinct sets of decisions to carry them out completely. The first is concerned with that aspect of time-preference which I have called the propensity to consume, which . . . determines for each individual how much of his income he will consume and how much he will reserve in some form of command over future consumption.
>
> But this decision having been made, there is a further decision which awaits him, namely, in what form he will hold the command over future consumption which he has reserved, whether out of his current income or from previous savings. Does he want to hold it in the form of immediate, liquid command (i.e., in money or its equivalent)? Or is he prepared to part with immediate command for a specified or indefinite period. . . .
>
> It should be obvious that the rate of interest cannot be a return to saving or waiting as such. For if a man hoards his savings in cash, he earns no interest, though he saves just as much as before. On the contrary, . . . , the rate of interest is the reward for parting with liquidity for a specified period. . . .

Thus the rate of interest at any time, being the reward for parting with liquidity, is a measure of the unwillingness of those who possess money to part with their liquid control over it. The rate of interest is not the 'price' which brings into equilibrium the demand for resources to invest with the readiness to abstain from present consumption. It is the 'price' which equilibrates the desire to hold wealth in the form of cash with the available quantity of cash. . . . If this explanation is correct, the quantity of money is the other factor, which, in conjunction with liquidity preference, determines the actual rate of interest in given circumstances. Liquidity-preference is a potentiality or functional tendency, which fixes the quantity of money which the public will hold when the rate of interest is given; so that if r is the rate of interest, M the quantity of money and L the function of liquidity preference, we have $M = L(r)$. This is where, and how, the quantity of money enters into the economic scheme.

(Keynes, 1936, pp. 166–68)

First, consider Keynes' argument in terms of its general notion that the rate of interest is the reward for parting with liquidity. This is definitely true in a world with uncertainty. Savers have a choice as to the form in which to hold their savings. They may hold these in a monetary form or lend it. If the level of the rate of interest determines their division of savings into money balances versus loans, the rate of interest can be called the reward for parting with liquidity in the process of lending. However, if the rate of interest also influences the level of savings, then it may also be called a reward for postponing consumption. Both cases apply in the real world.[9]

Now consider Keynes' argument formally in terms of the equilibrium relationship of the monetary sector. In Chapter 2 above, Keynes' demand function for money was specified as:

$$M^d = kPy + L(r)$$

so that the equilibrium relationship for an exogenously given money supply M is

$$M = kPy + L(r) \tag{17}$$

as in Chapter 2 above. Equation (17) determines r *if* it is assumed that P and y are exogenously given to it. This is not true of the Keynesian model and is not true for Keynes' own ideas in general. In his theory, output, interest and prices were determined simultaneously so that r is not determined merely by (17): it is influenced by the saving and investment decisions of the expenditure sector as well as by the labour market structure. Hence, the interest rate is not merely the reward for parting with liquidity, even though that seems to be the most proximate or closely related cause.

20.5 THE LIQUIDITY PREFERENCE VERSUS THE LOANABLE FUNDS THEORIES OF INTEREST IN COMPARATIVE STATIC ANALYSIS

The traditional classical loanable funds theory of the rate of interest was clearly distinct from the Keynesian liquidity preference theory. This can be clearly seen by comparing (8) and (17) above. However, a lengthy controversy flared up in the 1950s and early 1960s as to whether the two theories were identical or different. In retrospect, the real difference between them proved not to lie in comparative static analysis, though the dispute between them had originally appeared in this context, but about their dynamic implications for the time path of the interest rate even in an otherwise identical comparative statics framework.

To illustrate this dispute, assume, as in Chapter 13, a linear demand function for money of the form:

$$M^d = Pm^d = P[m_y y - m_r r] \tag{18}$$

In equilibrium, the excess demand for money balances E_m would be zero. Therefore,

$$E_m = P[m_y y - m_r r] - M^s = 0 \tag{19}$$

Similarly, in equilibrium, the excess demand for goods E_c would also be zero. That is, in terms of a linearized version of the IS equation,

$$E_c = P[c_0 + c_y(y - t_0 - t_y y) + g_0 + i_0 - i_r r] - Py = 0 \tag{20}$$

where:

E_c	nominal excess demand for commodities
E_m	nominal excess demand for money
$c_0 + c_y(\cdot)$	consumption function
$t_0 + t_y y$	tax revenue function
$i_0 - i_r r$	investment function
g_0	exogenous government expenditures
$m_y y - m_r r$	demand for real balances

Assuming for the moment that we have a goods–money–bonds economy[10] and that we have output exogenously given to it, Walras' law implies that the excess demand for bonds E_b is given by:

$$E_b = -E_c - E_m \tag{21}$$

Hence, from (19) to (21), the equilibrium excess demand for bonds E_b implied by (19) and (20) is also zero. That is:

$$E_b = -E_c - E_m = 0 \tag{22}$$

$$= P[\, y(1 - c_y - c_y t_y) - c_0 - i_0 - g_0 + c_y t_0 + i_r r] - P[m_y y - m_r r - M^s/P] = 0 \tag{23}$$

Equations (19) to (21) for the assumed pure exchange economy contain only two independent equations. With y exogenously given in the exchange economy – or if the labour market is included, by a full employment assumption – the above equations contain only two endogenous variables r and P. Walras' law implies that any two out of these three equations imply the third one and can be used to find the comparative static solution for P and r. *The solution will be the same no matter which two equations are chosen.*

Keynes claimed that the demand and supply for money balances determined the rate of interest. This was his liquidity preference theory. That is, the rate of interest is determined by (19). But the loanable funds theory focuses attention on (21) for the bond/credit market for determining the rate of interest. In the strict and proper sense of general equilibrium analysis, neither (19) nor (21) determines the rate of interest since P is also a variable in these equations and the *general equilibrium* solution is the same whether (19) or (21) is considered along with (20). However, a difference seemingly exists if the analysis is limited to a *partial equilibrium* one, focusing on only one market. This difference comes out even more strongly if the analysis is a dynamic one.

Equation (21) was derived for a pure exchange economy with an exogenously given level of output. Assuming an exchange and production economy, with the four goods as commodities, money, bonds and labour, we also need to specify the labour market. Its specification from the neoclassical theory is that:

$$n^d = n^d(w)$$

$$n^s = n^s(w)$$

where n stands for labour (number of workers) and w for the real wage rate. In equilibrium,

$$E_n = n^d(w) - n^s(w) = 0 \tag{24}$$

As discussed in Chapter 17, by Walras' law for this four-good economy,

$$E_b = -E_c - E_m - E_n \tag{25}$$

Hence, from (19), (20), (24) and (25):

$$E_b = -E_c - E_m - E_n = 0 \tag{26}$$

$$= P[y(1 - c_y + c_y t_y) - c_0 - i_0 - g_0 + c_y t_0 + i_r r]$$

$$- P[m_y y - m_r r - M^s/P] - P[n^d(w) - n^s(w)] = 0 \tag{27}$$

which shows the dependence of the excess demand for bonds on variables coming not only from the commodity and money markets, but also upon the real wage rate.

The set of equations for a liquidity preference version of the macroeconomic model would include (19) (for money), (20) (for commodities) and (24) for labour. The set of markets appropriate for the emphasis on the loanable funds version would include (20) (for commodities), (27) (for bonds) and (24) for labour. Each set would give the *same* equilibrium values of all the endogenous variables, even though the two sets, *prima facie*, would seem to be quite different.

For comparative static analysis and estimation, since the interest rate is an endogenous variable among several in a fully specified macroeconomic model, the complete model needs to be specified and estimated. For the IS–LM analysis, this would mean estimating the structural equations of each of the sectors (except one, by Walras' law). The usual procedure here is to specify the equations – and do the estimation – for all sectors other than the bond one, and solve the estimated model for the rate of interest. However, as shown earlier, any one of the other sectors could have been omitted and the bond one included in the specification and estimation. The selection of the bond one for omission is partly due to the tradition set by Keynes in *The General Theory* and reinforced by Hicks in his interpretation of Keynes in the form of the IS–LM model, and partly because most countries do not publish adequate and reliable data on the amounts of bonds in the aggregate and for many types of bonds (and loans) in the economy. By comparison, the data on output, money, and employment – and their related variables – is usually made available in great detail and with more or less of an attempt at consistency over time.

20.6 THE LIQUIDITY PREFERENCE VERSUS THE LOANABLE FUNDS THEORIES OF INTEREST IN DYNAMIC ANALYSIS

If the estimation exercise is not a general equilibrium one but is a partial one, though still within a comparative statics framework, the selection of the one sector in which the rate of interest is determined becomes relevant. This is especially so if the analysis is a partial dynamic one to capture the movements in the interest rate over time. As we have discussed above, the sector that should be selected differs between the liquidity preference theory and the loanable funds theory. This is shown in the following analysis.

The dynamic version of the liquidity preference theory is that the changes in the rate of interest are determined by the excess demand for money, with a positive relationship. That is,

$$dr/dt = \Psi(E_{mt}) \quad \Psi' > 0$$

$$= \Psi(m_y y_t - m_r r_t - M_t^s/P_t) \tag{28}$$

The dynamic version of the loanable funds theory is that the changes in the rate of interest are determined by the excess demand for bonds, with an inverse relationship,

$$dr/dt = \phi(E_{bt}) \quad \phi' < 0$$

$$= \phi(P_t[y_t(1 - c_y + c_y t_y) - c_0 - i_0 - g_t + c_y t_0 + i_r r_t] - P_t[m_y y_t - m_r r_t - M_t^s/P_t]) \tag{29}$$

Equations (28) and (29) generate different paths for the interest rate. To illustrate, if the money market is in equilibrium but the bond market is not, the liquidity preference theory (28) would have $E_{mt} = 0$ and imply that the interest rates will not change, but the loanable funds theory (29) would have a non-zero excess demand for commodities and bonds, and would, therefore, imply changes in the rate of interest.

Further, the two theories would even imply different signs for changes in the rate of interest under certain states of the economy. To show this diagrammatically, we first need to draw the equilibrium relationship for the bond market in the (r, y) space. This is done in the next section.

20.7 THE BOND MARKET IN THE IS–LM DIAGRAM

Figure 20.1 shows the IS and LM curves and assumes for simplification an economy with continuous equilibrium in the labour market with full employment. Given this simplifying assumption, the equilibrium curve for the labour market has been omitted from this figure.

The *bb* curve in Figure 20.1 specifies the combinations of (r, y) which maintain equilibrium in the bond market, so that E_b is zero at all points along it. By Walras' law, the equilibrium in the commodity and money markets shown by the interaction of the IS and LM curves at point *a* also ensures that the bond market will also be in equilibrium at *a*. The three curves, therefore, all pass through the common point *a*.

Note that the *bb* curve in this chapter refers to the locus of points along which there is equilibrium in the bond market. This curve is to be distinguished from the *BB* curve in the open economy (see Chapter 19). The *BB* curve was the locus of points along which the balance of payments was in equilibrium. Since the current chapter is for a closed economy, the *BB* curve does not occur in its analysis.

In quadrant I, there exists excess demand for commodities, since, for a given income, interest rates are lower than those specified by the IS curve so that investment is higher than required for equilibrium. That is, $E_c > 0$. There is also excess demand for money, since the interest rate is lower than specified by the LM curve so that the speculative demand for money is too high compared with that in equilibrium. That is, $E_m > 0$. By Walras' law for our assumed economy, with $E_c > 0$ and $E_m > 0$, we must have $E_b < 0$. That is, there will exist excess supply of bonds at all points in this quadrant. Therefore, the *bb* curve (on which, by definition, $E_b = 0$ at every point) cannot pass through quadrant I.

By similar reasoning, it can be shown that in quadrant III, $E_c < 0$ and $E_m < 0$, so that by Walras' law, we must have $E_b > 0$. Hence, the *bb* curve also cannot pass through quadrant III.

To summarize, the excess demand functions for quadrants I and III are:

I $E_c > 0, E_m > 0, E_b < 0$

III $E_c < 0, E_m < 0, E_b > 0$

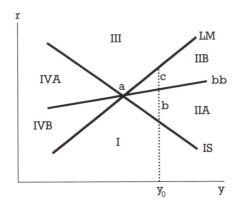

Figure 20.1

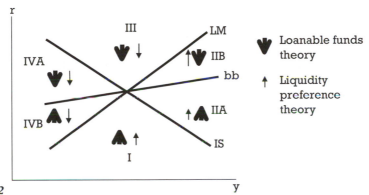

Figure 20.2

Since *bb* cannot pass through quadrants I and III, it must pass through quadrants II and IV. These quadrants are further divided into regions IIA and IIB, and IVA and IVB by the depicted position of the *bb* curve. To illustrate what happens in regions IIA and IIB, at point *b*, the interest rate is too low for equilibrium in the bond market, so that the existing bond prices are too high and there is inadequate demand (excess supply) for bonds at this lower-than-equilibrium interest rate. At point *c* in region IIB, the interest rate is too high and bond prices too low for equilibrium in the bond market, so that there would be too much demand (positive excess demand) for bonds at the higher-than-equilibrium interest rate. Similar reasoning can be used to separate regions IVA and IVB. The excess demand functions for regions II and IV are:

IIA $E_c < 0, E_m > 0$ and $E_b < 0$

IIB $E_c < 0, E_m > 0$ but $E_b > 0$

IVA $E_c > 0, E_m < 0$ and $E_b > 0$

IVB $E_c > 0, E_m < 0$ but $E_b < 0$

Since IIA has $E_b < 0$ while IIB has $E_b > 0$, the separating region between them must have $E_b = 0$. This is the requirement for points on the *bb* curve, so that the *bb* curve differentiates between two distinctive parts of region II. Similarly, IVA and IVB are separated by the locus of points at which $E_b = 0$. Hence, the bb curves passes through regions II and IV and not through I and III. This argument does not establish whether the bb curve will have a positive or a negative slope in the (r, y) space, though we have shown a positively sloping curve. The nature and magnitude of the slope will depend on the coefficients of the IS and LM equations, as can be seen from (23).

We can now examine the impact on the bb curve of changes in the exogenous variables and the parameters of the model. We do so explicitly only for the policy variables of the fiscal deficit and the money supply. Start with an increase in the fiscal deficit in Figure 20.1. We know from Chapter 13 that this would shift the IS curve to the right. With the LM curve taken to be independent of the fiscal deficit, by Walras' law, the bb curve must shift to pass through the intersection of the new IS and the initial LM curves. Hence, the bb curve will also shift to the right. The intuitive reason has to do with the bond financing of the deficit, which increases the supply of government bonds in the economy. These require either higher income or higher interest rates to generate a corresponding increase in demand.

But suppose, instead, that the money supply had increased. This would shift the LM curve to the right. Walras' law again implies that the bb curve must shift to pass through the new intersection of the initial IS curve and the new LM one. Hence, the bb curve shifts downwards. The intuitive reason for this is that the increased money supply is traded by the public for bonds, thereby increasing the demand for bonds. This raises bond prices and lowers the interest rate.

The dependence of the bb curve on shifts in both the IS and the LM curves is also apparent from equation (23), which shows that the excess demand for bonds depends on the fiscal deficit and the money supply. The bond market is thus the implicit link between the IS and the LM curves in the IS–LM model.

We derived the bb curve under the assumption of full employment and, therefore, for constant real output. If the labour market can also be in disequilibrium, Walras' law implies equation (26). However, in general equilibrium, the labour market would clear, so that the bb curve must still pass through the intersection of the IS and LM curves.

20.8 THE DIAGRAMMATIC ANALYSIS OF DYNAMIC CHANGES IN THE RATE OF INTEREST

Applying (28) and (29) to Figure 20.1, Figure 20.2 uses arrows to show the movements in the interest rate implied by the liquidity preference and the loanable funds theories. The movements implied by the former are shown by light arrows indicating the direction of movement, while those implied by the latter are shown by the heavy arrows. In quadrant I, both theories predict an increase in the interest rate, and in quadrant III both theories predict a decline in it. Further, in region IIA, both theories indicate a rise in the interest rate, and in region IVA both theories indicate a fall in it. However, note that the implied magnitude of the change in the interest rate could differ between the theories.

The especially interesting regions are IIB and IVB. Region IIB has $E_m > 0$ and $E_b > 0$. Therefore, the liquidity preference theory predicts a rise in the interest rates, while the loanable funds theory predicts a fall in it. In region IVB, $E_m < 0$ and $E_b < 0$, so that the liquidity preference theory predicts a fall in the interest rate and the loanable funds theory predicts a rise in it. Consequently, the dispute between these theories is not trivial even in terms of the sign of the movements in the interest rates in the economy.

The dispute is of importance even in quadrants I and III and regions IIA and IVA, where the two theories predict a similar direction of change in the interest rate since the dynamic speed of movements in it will be sensitive to the actual relationship and will differ between (28) and (29). Further, even the stability of the equilibrium interest rate could be affected. Since the explicit analysis of the dynamic paths would require solutions of difference or differential equations that are beyond the mathematical scope of this book, we do not pursue this line of analysis any further. However, enough has been shown to prove that the economist studying interest rates cannot dismiss the dispute between the theories as of no consequence. Hence, a choice has to be made between the two theories – for dynamic though not for comparative analysis.

20.9 INTUITION ON THE CHOICE BETWEEN THE LIQUIDITY PREFERENCE AND LOANABLE FUNDS THEORIES

We first illustrate the nature of our further arguments by starting with an illustration from the commodity markets. Suppose that equilibrium does not hold in a particular market, say for peanuts. Then there is an excess demand for peanuts; the price of peanuts is at a disequilibrium level and will change in response to the excess demand for peanuts. Further, in general, the larger is the excess demand, the faster will be the price change. This adjustment in the price of peanuts is, however, not *directly* influenced by the existence and extent of disequilibrium in the market for other products,[11] even though all markets are related by Walras' law. If there is disequilibrium in a market for a close substitute for peanuts, say potato crisps, this disequilibrium will flow into the demand for peanuts, creating disequilibrium in the market for peanuts and influencing the price of peanuts. But this change in the price of peanuts is not a direct effect of the disequilibrium in the market for crisps on the price of peanuts but rather an indirect effect occurring from the spillover, because of substitution, into the demand for peanuts and depends upon the small or large amount of that spillover. That is, the price of a good responds in a dynamic context directly to the excess demand for that good, with the state of excess demands for other goods being either irrelevant or indirectly relevant in so far as they first affect the excess demand for the good in question.

The rate of interest is a price. But what is the good with which it should be identified in a dynamic context? The liquidity preference approach would identify it with the good 'money', specifying dynamic changes in the rate of interest as a function of the excess demand for money, as given by (28) above. The loanable funds approach would define the relevant good as 'credit', 'loanable funds' or 'bonds', relating the dynamic changes in the rate of interest to the excess demand for bonds, as given by (29). As we have shown above, these two approaches yield different rates of change in the rate of interest.

At a practical level, the dispute between the traditional classical and Keynesian theories of the rate of interest comes down to which approach will do better empirically in a *dynamic* context. But there is no generally accepted empirical evidence on this issue, so that we should not ignore our intuition on it. Our intuition on the *operational* markets in the economy has already been specified in Chapter 17 and is along the following lines.

Commodities are always bought and sold at a price against a specific good that is labelled as money in a monetary economy. There are, therefore, operational markets for commodities (or an operational market for 'the commodity' in a single commodity model), so that the equilibrating variables are commodity prices in commodity markets. Loans are made, again always in a specific good that is money in a monetary economy, and the rate of interest is agreed between borrowers and lenders. It is then the 'price' of credit or loans. There is, therefore, an operational market for loanable funds (bonds), with the interest rate as the equilibrating variable.

Note that there is no real-world market where money is always bought and sold against *one* specific good. Individuals run down their money balances by either buying goods in the commodities markets or by making loans in the credit market. These arguments show that *the economists' market for money balances is an analytical construct without an operational real-world counterpart*. It is an 'image' provided by the merged reflection of two (or several) entities or figures (markets) standing in front of a mirror.[12] Looking at the composite reflection only provides a great deal of information – but not necessarily on the separate elements – about each of the figures (markets) facing the mirror, but is itself not independent of the existence and nature of the mirror – or of the figures (markets). The hypothetical market for money arises only because of Walras' law, a comparative statics concept, and is a composite of the bonds and commodity markets under equilibrium in the labour market. Therefore, the market for money balances can only be used for comparative statics analyses but not for dynamic analysis to determine the rate of interest in a dynamic disequilibrium context. Hence, in a dynamic context, the proper analysis of the rate of interest is as in the loanable funds theory and not as in the liquidity preference one.

The above arguments can be buttressed by the buffer stock role of money. As seen in Chapter 6 above, the buffer stock concept is based on the notion that the primary decisions are made as to when to change the purchases and sales of commodities and bonds. These decisions result in money holdings that are held passively. By contrast, the 'active' decision is not when to buy or sell 'money'.

20.10   THE NEUTRALITY OF MONEY FOR THE REAL RATE OF INTEREST

The real rate of interest is a real variable. As such, the modern classical analysis implies that in the general equilibrium without errors in price (or inflationary) expectations, the real rate of interest will be invariant to changes in the (nominal) money supply, since such changes in the money supply produce proportionate changes in the price level, without changing the real money supply. Hence, identifying this general equilibrium without expectational errors as the long run, changes in the money supply do not change the long-run real interest rate in the modern classical analysis.

We can capture this relationship in a Lucas-type function for the short-run real rate of interest, specified as:

$$r_t^r = f(M_t - EM_t)$$

$$= r^{r*} + \gamma(M_t - EM_t) \quad \gamma < 0$$

where r^{r*} is the long-run value of the real rate of interest.

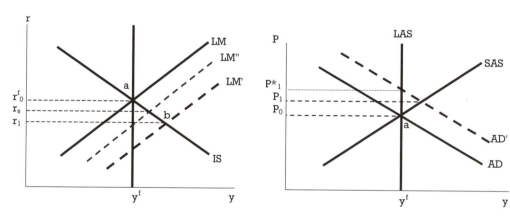

Figure 20.3a   *Figure 20.3b*

Diagrammatic analysis of the long-run and the short-run rate of interest

However, in the short run, if the economy is not at full employment, increases in the money supply through the indirect transmission mechanism will increase the supply of loanable funds and lower the real rate of interest. This impact is shown in Figures 20.3a and 20.3b. In Figure 20.3a, the long-run equilibrium rate of interest is r_0^f. An increase in the money supply will shift the LM curve out to LM', increasing demand to point b, thereby causing a long-run price increase (from P_0 to P_1^* in Figure 20.3b) which is sufficient to return the LM curve in Figure 20.3a back from LM' to LM and the general equilibrium real rate of interest back to r_0^f. The long-run equilibrium real interest rates and output are, therefore, invariant to the nominal money supply increase.

But, in the short run, assuming that the money market adjusts instantly while the commodity market is slower to adjust, the economy would initially lower the real interest rate to r_1. If the economy proceeds along a short-run supply curve SAS – either for Keynesian or modern classical reasons (with errors in relative price expectations) – the monetary expansion will shift the demand curve to AD' in Figure 20.3b, and lead to a price increase from P_0 to P_1 (rather than to P_1^*). This will mean in Figure 20.3a a shift in the LM curve up from LM' to only LM'' (rather than back to LM), and yield a short-run rate of interest r_s. Therefore, increases in the money supply can have both immediate (from r_0 to r_1) and short-run effects (from r_0 to r_s) on the interest rate in the economy, but not in the long run.

We now look at the factors that can change the long-run real rate of interest. Figure 20.4 shows the determination of the long-run real rate of interest r^f. This is given by the intersection of the IS curve and the long-run aggregate supply curve LAS. Shifts in either of these will change the long-run rate of interest in the economy. Therefore, productivity shifts in the economy as well as the saving and investment behaviour of the economy will shift the long-run real rate of interest. So will government expenditures and tax rates in the standard IS–LM model, since a deficit in this model shifts the IS curve to the right. This effect is shown in Figure 20.4 with a rightward shift in the IS curve to IS' due to a budget deficit, with a consequent increases the long-run rate of interest from r_0^f to r_1^f. That is, higher deficits produce higher real rates of interest, and eliminating them will lower the real rate of interest in the long run.

The LM curve is irrelevant to the determination of the long-run real rate of interest, so that it has not been drawn in Figure 20.4.

We conclude from Figure 20.4 that, for the closed economy, for a given production function, the long-run real interest rate is determined by the equality of investment and national saving where the latter equals private saving less the fiscal deficit. A decrease in national saving reduces the loanable funds available for investment and raises the real interest rate.

However, the addition of Ricardian equivalence to the IS–LM framework implies, as shown in Chapters 13 and 14, that private saving increases by the amount of the deficit, so

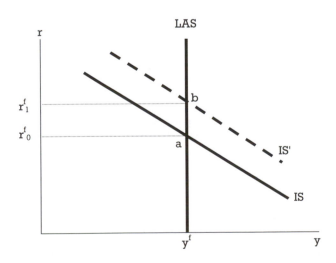

Figure 20.4

that national saving does not change as a result of a deficit being run. Therefore, budget deficits will not shift the IS curve, so that, in Figure 20.4, the long-run real rate of interest will remain at r^f irrespective of the deficit. Hence, given Ricardian equivalence, the long-run real rate of interest will be invariant to both fiscal and monetary policies. It will be determined in the closed economy context solely by the equality of national saving at full employment and investment, and will equal the marginal productivity of capital.

20.11 TESTING THE FISHER EQUATION OF THE NOMINAL INTEREST RATE

For tests of the Fisher equation of the nominal interest rate, note that an increase in the money supply lowers the short-run real interest rate, thereby tending to lower the nominal rate, while the resulting inflation, through anticipations, causes an increase in the nominal rate. Further, the Mundell–Tobin effect implies a negative impact of the expected inflation rate on the real rate of interest since the former is the opportunity cost of holding money and reduces the demand for real balances.

A test of the Fisher equation is provided by Crowder and Hoffman (1996). Since an increase in the interest rate due to inflation increases the tax payments on interest receipts, Crowder and Hoffman argue that the empirical estimates of the Fisher equation should have an estimated coefficient for the rate of inflation between about 1.3 and 1.5, rather than unity, as implied by the tax-free Fisher equation (1). By comparison, many studies find this coefficient to be less than unity. Since the data on nominal interest rates and inflation tends to be non-stationary, Crowder and Hoffman use the Johansen cointegration technique. Their estimating equation is based on a generalized form of the Fisher equation derived from intertemporal utility maximization subject to a budget constraint and is stated as:

$$r_t(1 - \tau_t) = r_t^r + E_t \Delta p_{t+1} + 0.5 \operatorname{var}_t \Delta p_{t+1} - \gamma \operatorname{cov}_t(\Delta c_{t+1}, \dots, \Delta p_{t+1}) \tag{30}$$

where p is the log of the price level, c is the log of consumption, E is the expectations operator conditional on information in t, r is the nominal rate and r^r the real one, τ is the tax rate and γ is the coefficient of relative risk aversion. In this study, the estimated coefficients for the expected rate of inflation were in the range from 1.34 to 1.37 and, when adjusted for the tax rates, in the range 0.97 to 1.01, so that their study supported the Fisher effect.

The Fisher effect incorporated into the theory of the term structure of interest rates allows the estimation of the expected rate of inflation from the yield curve. This derivation will be discussed in the next chapter.

20.12 TESTING THE LIQUIDITY PREFERENCE AND LOANABLE FUNDS THEORIES

Feldstein and Eckstein (1970) provided an application of the liquidity preference theory, combining it with the Fisher equation for the relationship between the nominal rate of interest and the expected rate of inflation. The liquidity preference theory implies that the rate of interest depends in the short run upon the excess demand for money. Since the demand for money depends upon income, the excess demand for money was represented through the use of the monetary base and national income among the explanatory variables, with the former capturing the effect of an increase in the money supply and having a negative expected coefficient and the latter increasing money demand and having a positive expected coefficient. The expected rate of inflation was proxied by a distributed lag autoregressive model. Among the results reported by these authors are:

$$r_t = -11.27 - 6.76 \ln B_t + 6.03 \ln y_t + 0.275\pi_t + \Sigma_j \alpha_j \pi_{t-j} \tag{31}$$

where $j = 1, 2, \dots, 23$, $\Sigma_j \alpha_j = 3.41$, with $\alpha_1 = 0.289$ and $\alpha_{23} = 0.020$, $R^2 = 0.982$.

In (31), r was a corporate bond rate (the yield on seasoned Moody's *Aaa* industrial bonds), B was the real per capita monetary base and y was real private GDP per capita. All the coefficients in (31) were significant and the mean lag for the impact of inflation on the interest rate was 8.14 quarters. These results are consistent with the liquidity preference theory.

Feldstein and Eckstein extended (31) to include privately held Federal government debt, and reported the estimates in:

$$r_t = -16.68 - 9.08 \ln B_t + 8.24 \ln y_t + 2.78 D_t + 0.27 \pi_t + \Sigma_j \alpha_j \pi_{t-j} \tag{32}$$

where $\Sigma_j \alpha_j = 3.93, j = 1, 2, \ldots, 23, R^2 = 0.985$, the mean lag for the inflation impact was 7.90 quarters and D was real per capita privately owned Federal government debt. In (32), the coefficient of government debt is positive, since, as explained by the loanable funds theory, an increase in the supply of bonds – that is, the demand for loanable funds – to the economy will raise the interest rate. In both (31) and (32), the mean lag for the impact of inflation on the rate of interest is about eight quarters and, therefore, quite long. Further, while the increase in the monetary base directly lowers the nominal interest rate, its indirect impact on inflation raises this rate. The reported coefficients imply that there does not exist short-run neutrality of money with respect to the real rate, at least not for periods up to eight quarters.

While (31) represents the liquidity preference theory, (32) combines elements of both the liquidity preference and loanable funds theories, the latter through its inclusion of government debt. Since the coefficients of both the monetary base and of government bonds are significant, the above estimates support the general version of the determination of the rate of interest as given by a broader commodities–money–bonds model with Walras' law, rather than providing a rejection of either of the rival theories.

The general conclusion of the Feldstein and Eckstein study was that the rise in the interest rate between 1954 and 1965 was more due to decreasing liquidity rather than inflation, but that inflation was more important from 1965 to 1969. The relatively slow growth of the public debt through the period held back the increase in the interest rate. Further, the direct impact of the changes in the monetary base and the government debt on the interest rate occurred within one quarter, so that there was not a significant lag in these effects, while the impact of inflation was over twenty-three quarters, with a mean lag of about eight quarters. It is not clear whether such a long lag arises from a lag in the adjustment of the nominal rate of interest to the expected rate of inflation or lags in the latter in adjusting to actual inflation rates. However, what is clear from this study is that Fisher's relationship between the interest rate and expected inflation must not be omitted in estimations of the nominal rate, even in studies based on the liquidity preference approach.

Sargent (1969), and Echols and Elliot (1976),[13] provided applications of the loanable funds theory. Sargent (1969) started with the identity:

$$r \equiv r^e + (r^r - r^e) + (r - r^r) \tag{33}[14]$$

where r is the nominal rate of interest (holding period yield on a bond). r^r is the real rate (the nominal rate less the expected rate of inflation over the holding period), and was called by Sargent as the market real rate of interest. r^e is the rate of interest that equates investment and saving and corresponds to the 'normal rate of interest' in Wicksell, as explained in Chapter 2 above. As in Wicksell's analysis, it was made a function of the excess of investment over saving. Its use by Sargent was meant to capture the loanable funds theory. $(r^r - r^e)$ is the deviation of the market real rate from the normal rate. As in Wicksell's analysis, this deviation depended upon the excess supply of money created through the bank's operations, and which increase the supply of loans over that through saving. From the Fisher equation, $(r - r^r)$ equalled the expected rate of inflation in commodity prices. Sargent represented expectations by a distributed lag model.

The normal rate r^e was specified as a function of the excess demand for loans, which was defined as desired real investment less desired real saving. Investment was specified as a function of this rate and ΔX, while saving was a function of this rate and X, where X is real output. Among the reported estimates[15] are the following ones for the *ten-year bond yield*:

$$r_t = 7.1338 + 0.0099\,\Delta X_t - 0.0456 X_t - 2.0151(\Delta m_t^*/m_{t-1}^*)$$

$$+ 3.8764\,\Sigma_i\,0.97^{i-1}\,(\Delta p_{t-i}/p_{t-i-1}) - 1.9849(0.97)^t \tag{34}$$

Adjusted $R^2 = 0.9298$, $i = 1, 2, \ldots, t-1$

where r was the ten-year bond yield, X was real GDP, m^* was real money supply and p was the commodity price index. All the coefficients were significant, except for ΔX_t and the signs were consistent with the assumed hypotheses. An increase in the real money supply reduced the real rate of interest, with a 10 per cent increase in the real money supply reducing the nominal interest rate by 20 basis points.

The estimated results for the *one-year bond yield* were:

$$r_t = 1.4396 + 0.0182\,\Delta X_t - 0.0405 X_t - 6.0260\,(\Delta m_t^*/m_{t-1}^*)$$

$$+ 6.4716\,\Sigma_i\,(0.98)^{i-1}\,(\Delta p_{t-i}/p_{t-i-1}) + 4.4933(0.98)^t \tag{35}$$

Adjusted $R^2 = 0.9298$, $i = 1, 2, \ldots, t-1$

In (35), the output level, changes in the money supply and the expectations variable were all significant and had the expected signs. The rate of change of output was insignificant in both (34) and (35). This variable was meant to capture the inclusion of the demand for loanable funds through investment.

Equations (34) and (35) show that both the money supply and the inflation rate have greater impact on the one-year rate than on the ten-year rate. Both indicate very long lags in the impact of inflation on the interest rate, possibly because of long lags in the process of expectations formation, though this result may have been due to the representation of expectations by a distributed lag function rather than by rational expectations.

Both equations include changes in the money supply, which is an element in the liquidity preference theory. Further, the inclusion of output could capture elements of money demand determination. Hence, it cannot be claimed that these equations exclude elements of liquidity preference. However, they also include elements of the traditional classical loanable funds theory. We tend to view them, as we did (31) and (32), as being consistent with the general macroeconomic model with Walras' law, and, therefore, with the interest rate moving in response to disequilibrium in both the money and bond markets.

CONCLUSIONS

This chapter has focused on the underlying rate of interest in the economy, while leaving the study of the term and risk structure of interest rates to the next chapter. There are two main theories of this underlying rate. The loanable funds theory is associated with traditional classical economics and asserts that the interest rate is determined in the market for loanable funds – designated as bonds or credit in modern macroeconomic models. The liquidity preference theory is associated with Keynes and Keynesian economics, and asserts that the interest rate is determined by the equilibrium in the market for money.

In a completely specified macroeconomic model, the money and bond markets are only two of the markets in the economy. The other markets are those for commodities and labour. An interdependent structure of such a model implies that the interest rate is jointly determined with the other endogenous variables – including output and the price level – of the model. For such a model, Walras' law implies that one of the markets can be omitted from explicit analysis. The loanable funds theory would omit the market for money while the liquidity preference theory would omit the market for bonds from explicit analysis, though both these choices would yield, *ceteris paribus*, the same equilibrium values of all the endogenous variables, including the interest rate. Hence, it does not matter for comparative static analysis which of these two theories is adopted in a given macroeconomic model.

Which theory is adopted does matter in a dynamic context. For analysing the dynamic movements in the interest rate, our preference has been for the theory based on the excess demand in the bond market.

However, empirical studies find support for the elements of both the excess demands for money and for bonds in explaining movement in the interest rate. An essential requirement for such empirical determination of the interest rate is the inclusion of the Fisher equation. While the empirical studies reported in this chapter used a distributed lag model for expectations, and found long lags, newer studies tend to use rational expectations. No matter which procedure for modelling expectations is used, most studies report that the increases in the money supply decrease the interest rate and that money is not neutral in the short run as far as the real interest is concerned.

SUMMARY OF CRITICAL CONCLUSIONS

- The traditional classical loanable funds theory stated that the real rate of interest is determined by the full employment saving and investment in the economy.
- Keynes argued that there is no direct nexus between saving and investment. His liquidity preference theory asserted that the rate of interest is determined by the demand and supply of money.
- The modern classical theory adapts the traditional classical loanable funds theory to the statement that the real rate of interest is determined by the demand and supply of bonds at full employment in the economy.
- The modern classical approach implies that the general equilibrium – also labelled as the long-run – real rate of interest is invariant to anticipated changes in the money supply and the rate of inflation. Therefore, for the real rate of interest, there is neutrality of anticipated changes in money and inflation.
- Under uncertainty and rational expectations, the modern classical approach implies that systematic monetary policy cannot change the real rate of interest.
- Walras' law implies that it is immaterial in general equilibrium whether the money or the bond market is taken to be the proximate determinant of the rate of interest: the rate of interest will be identical.
- However, dynamic analysis shows that it does matter for the magnitude, and in some cases also for the sign, of the change in the rate of interest whether this change is made a function of the excess demand for money or for bonds.
- In the modern financially developed economy, it seems that the more appropriate proximate determinant of changes in the rate of interest is the excess demand for bonds. Changes in the excess demand for money or bonds cause changes in the rate of interest by first changing the excess demand for bonds. Further, if there is disequilibrium in the commodities and the labour markets, the excess demand for bonds will not be identical with the excess supply – the negative of the excess demand – of money.
- The Fisher equation is the statement that in perfect financial markets, the nominal rate of interest will equal the real rate of interest plus the expected rate of inflation. Under rational expectations, the expected rate of inflation will only deviate from the actual rate of interest by a random component that cannot be manipulated by systematic monetary policy.

review and discussion questions

1 Explain how the monetary and real factors enter into the determination of the interest rates in the short run and in the long run.

2 Compare and contrast the liquidity preference and the loanable funds theories of the rate of interest. Discuss their implications for monetary policies intended to maintain full employment.

3 Keynes asserted that there is no such thing as a non-monetary theory of the rate of interest and that the rate of interest is uniquely determined by the demand and supply of money. Explain Keynes' reasons for this view. Compare this view with those of the traditional classical and modern classical schools.

4 Discuss the adjustment process likely to follow a change in (a) the money supply through open market operations, (b) a cut in the central bank's discount rate, leading to the eventual change in the interest rates in the economy.

5 Can the central bank change the interest rate in the economy through changes in its discount/bank rate? Present the analysis and theory relevant to your answer for the economy you live in.

6 Monetary theory implicitly assumes that the interest rates and the money stock are uniquely linked so that changes in one have a corresponding counterpart in the other, so that it does not matter whether the central bank chooses to change one or the other. What assumptions are needed for this assertion? Are they realistic enough for policy purposes?

7 This chapter has made the rather unusual assertion that in the real-world economies there is no explicit market for money. Instead, the money market is a reflection of the other markets. Do you agree or disagree? Give reasons for your answer. What does your answer imply for the theory relevant to the determination of the rate of interest if there is (a) general equilibrium in all markets, (b) disequilibrium in the economy?

8 The buffer stock analysis of the demand for money in Chapter 6 asserted that money acts as a buffer during periods in which economic agents need to adjust their stocks of other goods (commodities, bond and labour) to their optimal levels but that such adjustments are more costly in the short term than those in money balances. What does this imply for the determination of the rate of interest if there exists general equilibrium in all markets? What does it imply for the dynamic determination of the rate of interest while there are buffer stock holdings of money following a shock that changes the desired demands for other goods?

9 Is there some relationship between the assertions on (a) buffer stock money holdings and (b) that in the real-world economies there is no explicit market in the economy for money but that it is a reflection of the other markets? Discuss.

10 Dynamic adjustments occur in disequilibrium but Chapter 17 raised doubts about the applicability of Walras' law if there was disequilibrium in the commodities and labour markets. In this context, should the dynamic analysis of interest rates be conducted with notional or effective excess demand functions? Discuss, keeping in mind that the objective is to explain the dynamic, disequilibrium determination of the rate of interest.

11 'The assumption of the modern classical economics that there exists continuous labour market clearance at full employment means that we can confine the analysis of the real rate of interest to states of general equilibrium and ignore its properties for the disequilibrium states. Therefore, it does not matter whether the loanable funds theory or the liquidity preference theory was used: both imply the same rate of interest by virtue of Walras' law.' Discuss the various aspects of this assertion.

12 Do the existence and operations of financial intermediaries have any implications for the rate of interest? If so, are these adequately reflected in the short-run macroeconomic models and in what ways?

13 'The real rate of interest is a real variable. Under rational expectations, it is invariant to systematic changes in the money supply or the price level. However, unanticipated changes in these nominal variables can change the real rate of interest.' Discuss this in the context of the neoclassical model and specify the implied Lucas-type equation for the determination of the real rate of interest. What are its implications for the pursuit of monetary policy?

14 Is there a 'natural' rate of interest? What does it mean and what determines it? Is there a curve such as the Phillips curve for the real rate of interest? Discuss.

15 Why does the real rate of interest fluctuate over the business cycle? Can monetary factors change it? Discuss.

NOTES

1 The words 'loans', 'credit' and 'bonds' will be treated as synonyms in our exposition.

2 The difference in the stock versus flow determination of asset prices was used by some stock market analysts for explaining the high volatility during 1999 in the prices of the internet and computer-based corporations. These analysts pointed out that the major part of the stock of such corporations was tied up by mutual funds and other financial corporations and only a small proportion came up for trading. Therefore, small fluctuations in the demand, mainly from small investors, for such shares caused disproportionately large fluctuations in their prices.

3 This would be negative for a budget surplus.

4 This would now be treated in the context of an intertemporal utility function with a positive rate of time preference.

5 In the context of modern utility maximization analysis, this requires that future consumption not be an inferior good.

6 Knut Wicksell's analysis for the pure credit economy was presented briefly in Chapter 2. As discussed there, Wicksell's natural rate of interest was set by the marginal productivity of capital and his normal rate of interest was determined by the equality of saving and investment. Equilibrium in the economy required the equality of these two rates with the market rate set by the banks.

7 To adjust these models of the interest rate to an economy with a government sector, saving should be interpreted as national saving, which is private saving less the fiscal deficit.

8 The short-run theory could diverge from the long run because of random influences operating on the economy in the short run. These cannot be anticipated under rational expectations and would cause a divergence of the short-run rate of interest from its long-run level.

9 However, several empirical studies show the impact of interest rates on saving to be insignificant or of little importance.

10 Note that if there is a labour market, as in the modern economy, assuming a goods–money–bonds economy is tantamount to the assumption of a permanent state of full employment.

11 That is, the price of peanuts is not a function of the excess demands for other commodities, including say almonds; though the excess demand for peanuts could be a function of the excess demands for the other commodities. Since the change in the price of peanuts is a function of the former, it becomes indirectly a function of the latter.

12 Walras' law acts as the mirror.

13 The approach and results of this study will be examined in Chapter 21 in the context of the term structure of interest rates.

14 The symbols in this equation have been altered for consistency with our symbols in this chapter.

15 The Hildreth–Lu procedure was used to correct for serial correlation.

REFERENCES

Crowder, William J., and Dennis L. Hoffman. 'The Long-Run Relationship between Nominal Interest Rates and Inflation: The Fisher Equation Revisited'. *Journal of Money, Credit and Banking*, 28, February 1996, pp. 102–18.

Echols, Michael E., and Jan Walter Elliot. 'Rational Expectations in a Disequilibrium Model of the Term Structure'. *American Economic Review*, 66, March 1976, pp. 28–44.

Feldstein, Martin, and Otto Eckstein. 'The Fundamental Determinants of the Interest Rate'. *Review of Economics and Statistics*, 52, November 1970, pp. 363–75.

Johnson, Harry G. *Macroeconomics and Monetary Theory*. Chicago: Aldine Publishing Co., 1972.

Keynes, John Maynard. *The General Theory of Employment, Interest and Money*. New York: Macmillan, 1936.

Mundell, Robert A. 'Inflation and Real Interest'. *Journal of Political Economy*, 71, June 1963, pp. 280–83.

Patinkin, Don. *Money, Interest and Prices*, 2nd edn. New York: Harper & Row, 1965.

Sargent, Thomas J. 'Commodity Price Expectations and the Interest Rate'. *Quarterly Journal of Economics*, 83, February 1969, pp. 127–40.

———. *Macroeconomic Theory*. London: Academic Press, 1979.

Shaller, Douglas R. 'Working Capital Finance Considerations in National Income Theory'. *American Economic Review*, 73, March 1983, pp. 156–65.

Tobin, James. 'Money and Economic Growth'. *Econometrica*, 33, October 1965, pp. 671–84.

chapter twenty-one

THE STRUCTURE OF INTEREST RATES

This chapter extends the determination of the single macroeconomic rate of interest to the multitude of interest rates in the economy.

Two of the major reasons for the differences among interest rates are the differences in the term to maturity and the differences in risk. To explain the former, it is important that the riskiness of bonds be held constant across assets of different maturities. This is possible by confining the comparison to government bonds of different maturities and studying their yield curve. The main theory for explaining the term structure of interest rates is the expectations hypothesis.

Another reason for the differences among the yields on different assets is the differences in their riskiness. The major model for the study of the relationship between risk and return is the capital asset pricing model.

The empirical parts of this chapter are mainly meant for research-oriented courses.

---

key concepts introduced in this chapter

- The yield curve
- The short rate of interest
- The long rate of interest
- The expectations hypothesis
- The liquidity premium
- The segmented market hypothesis
- The preferred habitat hypothesis
- The random walk hypothesis
- The capital asset pricing model

The short-run macroeconomic models of Chapters 13 to 16 and 20 included a *single* rate of interest and analysed its determination. However, there is more than one interest rate and more than one asset in the economy. By definition, the economist's concept of the rate of interest (or yield) on any given asset is the rate of return, including the expected capital gains and losses, on that asset over a given period of time. Therefore, there is a rate of interest for each distinct type of asset in the economy.

Assets differ in various aspects or characteristics. Some of the more significant differences are those in their marketability, their risk and their term to maturity. Another classification of assets is often done on the basis of their '*liquidity*'. 'Liquidity' is not itself a unique or homogeneous property of assets but rather a compendium of characteristics. Keynes defined it in *The Treatise on Money* (1931) as: *one asset is more liquid than another if it is 'more certainly realizable at short notice without loss'* (1931, Vol. II, p. 67). Liquidity is thus partly a matter of the maturity of the asset (Treasury bills versus bonds), partly a matter of risk and partly a matter of the ease of dis-investment in the asset.

The rates of return on assets are likely to differ depending upon the extent to which they possess each characteristic or depending on their liquidity. These characteristics are not always objective, as shown by the discussion of subjective risk in the portfolio selection approach in Chapter 5. The subjective perceptions of asset characteristics may change and are sometimes volatile, changing the rates of return on assets even when there does not seem to be any objective change in the situation. Further, the market for each asset generally has a number of buyers with differing perceptions. Their estimates of the future price of any particular asset are often interdependent. Therefore, the characteristics of assets, individual psychology and mass behaviour are critical elements in the demands for assets and hence in their prices and rates of return.

The macroeconomic procedure of focusing on only one rate of interest is quite acceptable if all interest rates are related to each other in fixed proportions or fixed differences. They are so related to a considerable extent, though not completely. The relationship between the prices and rates of return on assets of differing maturities is brought out by the theories on the term structure of interest rates. These theories and the empirical work based on them are the focus of this chapter.

Section 21.1 defines the spot, forward and long rates of interest. Section 21.2 sets out the theories explaining the term structure of interest rates. Of these, the most significant one for developed financial markets is the expectations hypothesis, which is specified in subsection 21.2.2. Section 21.3 briefly touches on the relationship between asset prices and yields, and on tests based on the term structure of asset prices. Sections 21.4 and 21.5 report on some of the empirical work on the term structure of interest rates. Section 21.6 presents the random walk hypothesis. This hypothesis is related to the expectations hypothesis and uses the rational expectations hypothesis for the formation of expectations. Section 21.7 uses the term structure to derive estimates of the expected rate of inflation. Section 21.8 briefly introduces the variations in interest rates due to differences in the risks in the rates of return of the underlying assets.

While the relationship between the prices and yields of assets with different risks is usually not included in the textbooks on monetary economics, this topic is of considerable interest to students. It is also an extension of the speculative demand analysis covered in Chapter 5. We have, therefore, decided to provide an introduction to it in an optional section at the end of this chapter. The relationship between expected return and risk is usually explained by the capital asset pricing model proposed by Sharpe (1964) and based on the expected utility hypothesis developed in Chapter 5 above. This model is briefly discussed in section 21.8 below and presented more fully in the appendix to this chapter. However, note that the theories on the risk structure and the term structure of interest rates only explain the interest rate differentials due to differences in risk or the term to maturity, and do not explain the basic interest rate in the economy, which was the subject of Chapter 20.

Notation

The notation in this chapter is quite cumbersome, so that some explanation on its general pattern would be useful. The short (one-period) interest rates are designated by r. The current period is designated as t. Suppose that a contract is entered into in period $t + j$ for a one-period loan for period $t + i$ at an interest rate r. This will be written as $_{t+j}r_{t+i}$, where the left-hand-side subscript indicates the period in which the contract is made and the right-hand-side subscript indicates the period for which the loan is made. If future interest rates are expected ones, we would write the corresponding rate as $_{t+j}r^e_{t+i}$, whose rational expectations would be written as $E_{t+j}\,_{t+j}r_{t+i}$, where the expectations are based on information available in period $t + j$.

The long rates are designated by R. The contract for these is always assumed to be entered into in the current period t. $_tR_{t+i}$ will designate the long rate on a contract for a loan of i periods. Since this interest rate is known in the current period, it is an actual rather than an expected rate.

21.1 SOME OF THE CONCEPTS OF THE RATE OF INTEREST

The short-term markets for bonds have the spot, forward and long rates of interest. The meanings of these terms are as follows.

The current spot rate of interest

The *current spot rate* of interest $_tr_t$ – or written simply as r_t – is the annualized rate of return on a loan for the current period t, with the loan also being made at the beginning of period t.

The future (spot) rate of interest

The *future (spot) rate* of interest is the return on a one-period loan in a future period $(t + i)$, $i > 0$, with the loan made at the start of that period. It will be designated as $_{t+i}r_{t+i}$ or r_{t+i}.

The long rate of interest

The *long rate* of interest $_tR_{t+i}$, $i = 0, 1, \ldots, n$, is the annualized rate of return on a loan for $(i + 1)$ periods, the loan being made in period t and with repayment of the principal and accumulated interest after $(i + 1)$ periods.

The forward rate of interest

The *forward rate* of interest $_tr_{t+i}$ is the annualized rate of interest on a one-period loan for the $(t + i)$th period only, with the contract for the loan being made in period t. As such, it would differ from the *future spot* rate $_{t+i}r_{t+i}$, where the one-period loan for period $t + i$ is contracted in $t + i$. In incomplete financial markets, $_tr_{t+i}$ may not exist but $_{t+i}r_{t+i}$ would do so as long as there are spot markets. However, the former, if it exists, will be known in the current period t, while the latter is not likely to be known in t, though expectations on its value can be formed in t.

The current spot rate of interest $_tr_t$ and the one-period long rate of interest $_tR_t$ are identical. For simplicity of notation, $_tr_{t+i}$ will sometimes be written as r_i and $_tR_{t+i}$ will be written as R_i, with the subscript t being implicit or with the current period being treated as 0.

21.2 THE TERM STRUCTURE OF INTEREST RATES

21.2.1 The yield curve

The variation in the interest rates or yields on assets of different maturities (redemption dates) is known as the term structure of interest rates, with the assets being assumed to be identical in all respects except for their maturity. This requirement is generally fulfilled only by the bonds issued by the government, so that the yields on government bonds are examined to show the variation in yield with increasing maturity. This variation is shown graphically by plotting the nominal yield r on government bonds on the vertical axis and the time up to maturity on the horizontal axis, as in Figure 21.1. The curve thus plotted is known as the *yield curve*.

The yield curve is normally upward sloping from left to right, with the yield rising with the term to maturity, as shown by curve A in Figure 21.1. It can, however, possess any shape. In times of monetary stringency, short-term interest rates rise and move above the long-term ones, as shown by curve B. This can also happen when inflation is rampant in the economy but is expected to be a short-term problem so that the inflationary premium in nominal yields is greater for the shorter-term than for the longer-term bonds. In some cases, the curve may have a hump, as shown by curve C. In this case, some intermediate securities have the highest yield, usually because of the expectation that the highest rates of inflation will occur in the intermediate periods.

The two main determinants of the shape of the yield curve in practice are the time structure of the expected inflation rates and the current stage of the business cycle. On the former, Fisher's relationship between the nominal yields and the expected inflation rate is:

$$r_t = r_t^r + \pi_t^e$$

where r is the nominal yield, r^r is the real yield and π^e is the expected inflation rate. The higher the expected rate of inflation, the more will the time structure of expected inflation determine the shape of the yield curve.

The yield curve changes its shape over the business cycle. Long-term yields are usually higher than short-term yields mainly because long-term debt is less liquid and is subject to greater price uncertainty than short-term debt. However, the short-term yields are more volatile, rising faster and further than long yields during business expansions and falling more rapidly during recessions. Large swings in short-term rates, and to a lesser extent in intermediate rates, together with relatively narrow movements in long rates, cause a change in the shape of the yield curve over the course of a business cycle.

A sharp increase in short-term rates frequently occurs near the peak of a business expansion because of a combination of factors, most often including a strong demand for short-term credit, restrictive effects of monetary policies on the supply of credit, and changing investor expectations. Depending upon the intensity of these forces, the yield curve will be relatively flat, have a slight downward slope, or show a steep negative slope. As short rates fall absolutely and relative to long yields during the ensuing economic slowdown, the yield curve tends to regain its positive slope, acquiring its steepest slope near the cyclical trough. As the economy recovers and economic activity picks up, short rates again rise faster than long yields, and the yield curve tends to acquire a more moderate slope. Since the yield curve plots the nominal rather than the real rate of interest, and the former includes the

Yield

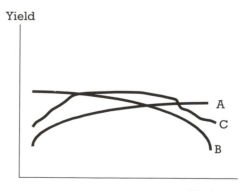

Figure 21.1   Time to maturity

expected rates of inflation, the dominant element of the shape and shifts in the yield curve are often the term structure of the expected rate of inflation.

The term structure of interest rates – the slope of the yield curve – is basically explained in the context of:

(i)   The expectations hypothesis first formulated by Irving Fisher.
(ii) The segmented markets theory, with Culbertson as its major proponent. The former theory is now the generally accepted one and is supported by a number of empirical studies.
(iii) The preferred habitat hypothesis.

21.2.2 The (pure) expectations hypothesis

Irving Fisher in *The Theory of Interest* (1930, pp. 399–451) considered the rate of return or yields on securities which differ only in terms of their maturity. His approach assumes that:

(i)   All borrowers and lenders have perfect foresight and know future interest rates and asset prices with certainty, so that there is no risk. An alternative assumption to this is that while there is uncertainty of yields, the borrowers and lenders are risk neutral and form rational expectations about the future short rates.
(ii) There are no transfer costs from money into securities and vice versa.
(iii) The financial markets are efficient.

A market is said to be *efficient* if it clears instantly and prices reflect all available information. In such a market, any opportunities for superior profits are instantly eliminated. By comparison, a *perfect* market assumes perfect competition *and* efficient markets. The above assumptions specify an efficient market, which need not be a perfect one.

Investors are assumed to maximize their expected utility so that under assumption (i), the investor will maximize the expected return to his portfolio. Under assumptions (i) and (ii), a lender wishing to make a loan for n periods will be indifferent between an n period loan or a succession of n one-period loans only if the overall return were the same in both cases. Under assumption (iii), with all investors acting on this basis, the market yields will be such as to ensure this indifference.

The expectations hypothesis, complete markets and forward rates

Assume that the financial sector has complete markets, so that there exist markets for long loans of all possible maturities as well as for spot and forward one-period loans. With the current period as t, the yield (per period) on an $(i + 1)$-*period* loan was designated as ${}_tR_{t+i}$, while that on a *one-period* loan for the $(i + 1)$th period was ${}_tr_{t+i}$, $i = 0, 1, \ldots, n$, where $n + 1$ is the longest maturity available in the market. Hence, ${}_tr_t$ is the (spot) yield on a loan for the first period; ${}_tr_{t+1}$ is the forward yield on a loan for the second period, and so on. An $(i + 1)$-period loan of \$1 will pay the lender $(1 + {}_tR_{t+i})^{i+1}$ at the end of the $(i + 1)$th period. The series of $(i + 1)$ loans starting with a principal of \$1 for one period at a time is expected to pay him $[(1 + {}_tr_t)(1 + {}_tr_{t+1}) \ldots (1 + {}_tr_{t+i})]$ at the end of the $(i + 1)$th period. Under the above three assumptions, the lender will be indifferent between the two types of loans if the total amount repaid to him after n periods is identical. With all investors exhibiting this behaviour, efficient markets under certainty ensure that:

$$(1 + {}_tR_{t+i})^{i+1} = (1 + {}_tr_t)(1 + {}_tr_{t+1})(1 + {}_tr_{t+2}) \ldots (1 + {}_tr_{t+i}) \tag{1}$$

This formula will hold for every i, $i = 0, \ldots, n$, where $n + 1$ is the longest maturity in the market, so that,

$$(1 + {}_tR_t) \quad = (1 + {}_tr_t)$$

$$(1 + {}_tR_{t+1})^2 = (1 + {}_tr_t)(1 + {}_tr_{t+1})$$

$$(1 + {}_tR_{t+2})^3 = (1 + {}_tr_t)(1 + {}_tr_{t+1})(1 + {}_tr_{t+2})$$

....

$$(1 + {}_tR_{t+n})^{n+1} = (1 + {}_tr_t)(1 + {}_tr_{t+1})(1 + {}_tr_{t+2}) \dots (1 + {}_tr_{t+n}) \qquad (2)$$

Under our assumption of complete markets, the forward rates are known – rather than merely expected – in period t. However, even well-developed financial markets do not have forward markets for all future periods, so that, in such a context, the investor's indifference in holding various combinations of long and forward bonds cannot be exercised in the form of (1) and (2).

The expectations hypothesis and future expected spot rates

Since there would always be spot markets over time, designate the spot rate expected in period t for the period $t + i$ as ${}_tr^e_{t+i}$. The investor would then have a choice of investing long for $t + i$ periods, with a known long rate ${}_tR_{t+i}$ and investing over time in a sequence of spot markets at the spot rates in those markets. In practice, since these future spot rates can differ from the actual ones, there is a risk in following the latter strategy. The investor will be indifferent between the two strategies if he is risk indifferent and if their expected return is identical. Hence, in terms of the expected future rates, the expectations hypothesis becomes:

$$(1 + {}_tR_{t+i})^{i+1} = (1 + {}_tr_t)(1 + {}_tr^e_{t+1})(1 + {}_tr^e_{t+2}) \dots (1 + {}_tr^e_{t+i}) \qquad (3)$$

Note that (3) differs from (1) since (3) involves expected future spot rates while (1) involves the corresponding forward rates, which are known in period t.

If a difference emerges in the markets between the left- and the right-hand sides of (1) and (3), profits can be made through arbitrage, which would occur to establish their equality. The rest of this chapter proceeds in terms of (3) rather than (1). While financial markets even in developed economies rarely have a large number of forward markets, they usually do have markets for government securities of many different maturities. The long rates of interest are quoted on these securities. These can be used to find the expected short rates of interest using the following iterative reformulation of (3):

$$(1 + {}_tr^e_{t+1}) = (1 + {}_tR_{t+1})^2/(1 + {}_tr_t)$$

$$(1 + {}_tr^e_{t+2}) = (1 + {}_tR_{t+2})^3/[(1 + {}_tr_t)(1 + {}_tr^e_{t+2})] \qquad (4)$$

and so on.

If the market forms its expectations in terms of the expected future short rates, the long rates will be determined from these short rates by the preceding equations. Some economists assume that the investors' expectations are formed in terms of a series of expected short rates for the future periods while others assume that investors are concerned with the prices of the assets currently in the market and that these prices can be used to calculate the long rates. Therefore, equation (3) can be used from right to left or left to right.

Long rates as geometric averages

According to equation (3), the long rates are geometric averages of the short rates of interest. This has the implications that:

(i) If the short interest rates are expected to be identical, the long rate will equal the short rate.

(ii) If the short interest rates are expected to rise, the long rates will lie above the current short rates.

(iii) If the short interest rates are expected to decline, the long rates will be less than the current short rate.

(iv) The long rate, being an average of the short rates, will fluctuate less than the short rate.

In principle, any pattern of expected future short rates is possible with the result that some long rates may be less and some greater than the current spot rate, so that the yield curve may have any shape whatever.

The assumptions of the expectations hypothesis may not always hold for all agents in the market which encompasses both households and firms. However, developed financial economies tend to be competitive and efficient. Therefore, the expectations hypothesis will hold if the credit markets have sufficient numbers of participants who behave according to the assumptions of perfect foresight (or rational expectations and risk indifference) and zero variable transfer costs between securities and money. These assumptions tend to be valid at least for large financial institutions operating in the developed economies. Hence, the expectations hypothesis should be more or less valid for developed financial markets.

Once the market has established a structure of short and long rates according to (1) or (3), the demand and supply functions for long and short bonds in the market would become indeterminate: an investor would be indifferent between a long bond maturing at the end of the ith period or various sequences of short and long bonds with a corresponding combined maturity.

21.2.3 The liquidity preference version of the expectations hypothesis

For many investors, the assumptions of the expectations hypothesis can be somewhat unrealistic. There is often both a transfer cost in and out of securities and a lack of perfect foresight (or risk indifference) about the future. The former implies that n one-period loans will involve a much greater expense and inconvenience than a single n-period loan. The latter implies that loans of different maturities involve different risks and, for risk averters, a higher risk has to be compensated for by a higher yield.

Note that both the n-period and a series of n one-period loans involve risks, though of different kinds. The n one-period loans involve the possibility that the future spot rates will turn out to be lower than the expected forward rates or the n-period long rate. This is an *income* loss. But the n-period loan – purchase of a bond maturing after n periods – involves the possibility that the lender may need his funds somewhat sooner and have to sell the bond before it matures. Such a sale may involve a *capital* loss, especially in the absence of a secondary market for loans. There is also the possibility that more profitable opportunities may turn up and have to be forgone if the funds are already loaned up for a long period.

It is likely that the possibility of a capital loss influences lenders' decisions more than that of the interest loss since the capital loss can certainly take on much greater magnitudes than the interest loss. Further, if the funds represent precautionary saving, the individual would prefer a more liquid (shorter maturity) to a less liquid (longer maturity) asset. Hicks (1946, pp. 151–52) suggested that lenders wish to avoid the risk of a capital loss by investing for shorter rather than longer periods. Therefore, they have to be compensated by a higher yield on longer-term loans. Conversely, borrowers – generally firms borrowing for long-term investments – prefer borrowing for a longer term than for a shorter term, which makes them willing to pay a premium on longer-term loans. Such risk avoidance behaviour on the part of both lenders and borrowers implies that the longer-term loans will carry a premium over shorter-term loans. Hence, the yield on bonds will increase with the term to maturity, so that equation (3) will be modified to:

$$(1 + {}_tR_{t+n})^{n+1} > (1 + {}_tr_t)(1 + {}_tr_{t+1}^e) \ldots (1 + {}_tr_{t+n}^e) \quad n \geq 1 \tag{5}$$

Equation (5) is known as the liquidity preference hypothesis of the yield curve. For a more specific hypothesis on liquidity preference, designating the *liquidity premium* as ${}_t\gamma_{t+n}$, we have:

$$(1 + {}_tR_{t+n})^{n+1} = (1 + {}_tr_t)(1 + {}_tr_{t+1}^e) \ldots (1 + {}_tr_{t+n}^e)\, {}_t\gamma_{t+n}(n;\rho) \quad n \geq 1 \tag{6}$$

where $\partial\gamma_n/\partial n \geq 0$ by virtue of the liquidity premium, and:

γ　liquidity premium
ρ　degree of risk aversion

We can distinguish between two versions of (6) on the basis of two alternative assumptions on the liquidity premium. These are as follows.

(i) The liquidity premium is constant per period such that ${}_t\gamma_{t+i} = i\gamma$, where γ is a constant. While there is no particular intuitive justification for making this assumption, it is analytically convenient and, as seen later in this chapter, is made in many empirical studies. It reduces (6) to:

$$(1 + {}_tR_{t+n})^{n+1} = (1 + {}_tr_t)(1 + {}_tr_{t+1}^e) \ldots (1 + {}_tr_{t+n}^e)n\gamma \quad n \geq 1 \tag{7}$$

Equation (7) with a constant per-period risk premium is sometimes called the *strong* form of the expectations hypothesis.

(ii) The per-period liquidity premium varies with the term to maturity and, moreover, may not be constant over time, for example, over the business cycle, so that (6) does not simplify to (7). This is sometimes called the *weak* form of the expectations hypothesis. Estimation of this form requires specification of the determinants of the liquidity premium.

Compared with these *weak* and *strong* forms of the expectations hypotheses, the original form (3) of this hypothesis without a liquidity premium is known as the *pure* form.

21.2.4　The segmented markets hypothesis

If the uncertainty in the loan market is extremely severe or if lenders and borrowers have extremely high risk aversion, each lender will attempt to lend for the exact period for which he has spare funds and each borrower will borrow for the exact period for which he needs funds. In this extreme case, the overall credit market will be split into a series of segments or separate markets based on the maturity of loans, without any substitution by either borrowers or lenders among the different markets. Therefore, the yields in any one market for a given maturity cannot influence the yields in another market for another maturity. Hence, there would not be any particular relationship such as (3) or (6) between the long and the short rates and the yield curve could have any shape whatever. This is the basic element of the segmented markets theory: the market is segmented into a set of independent markets. Culbertson (1957) stressed this possibility as a major, though not the only, determinant of the term structure of interest rates.

Culbertson also argued that the lender rarely knows in advance exactly when he will need his funds again and will prefer to make loans of shorter terms rather than longer ones, the former being the more liquid of the two. If the supply of short-term debt instruments is not sufficient to meet this demand for liquidity at a rate of interest equal to the long-term rate, the short-term rate will be less than the long-term rate. Further, the supply of short-term instruments is generally limited since lenders will not finance long-term investment with short-term borrowing. Therefore, the short-term yield will be less than the long-term one, *ceteris paribus*.

The segmented markets hypothesis is more likely to be applicable in the absence of developed financial markets, including secondary markets for securities, and sophisticated investors. It may therefore be more valid for developing rather than developed economies.

21.2.5 The preferred habitat hypothesis

The preferred habitat hypothesis was proposed by Modigliani and Sutch (1966, 1967), and represents a compromise between the expectations hypothesis of perfect substitutability and the segmented markets one of zero substitution between loans of different maturities. Modigliani and Sutch argued that lenders would prefer to lend for periods for which they can spare the funds and borrowers would prefer to borrow the funds for periods for which they need the funds. However, each would be willing to substitute other maturities depending upon their willingness to take risks and the opportunities provided by the market to easily transfer among different maturities. Bonds maturing close together would usually be fairly good substitutes and have similar risk premiums. This would be especially so for bonds at the longer end of the maturity spectrum. Therefore, in well-developed financial markets, a high degree of substitutability would exist among different maturities but without these necessarily becoming perfect substitutes. Hence, while the yields on different maturities would be interrelated to a considerable extent, there would also continue to exist some variation in yields among the different maturities.

21.2.6 The implications of the term structure hypotheses for monetary policy

The expectations theory and the segmented markets theory have significantly different implications for the management of the public debt and for the operation of monetary policy. The expectations theory implies that the market substitution between bonds of different maturities is so great that a shift from short-term to long-term borrowing by the government will not affect the shape of the yield curve. The segmented markets theory implies that a substantial purchase of short-term bonds will lower the short-term interest rates while a sale of long-term bonds will raise the long-term ones, so that such policies can alter the yield curve. The implications of the preferred habitat hypothesis lie between those of the expectations hypothesis and the segmented markets hypothesis, and are closer to one or the other depending upon the stage of development of the financial markets and the characteristics of the economic agents operating in them.

The empirical evidence for economies with well-developed financial markets has so far generally favoured the expectations theory or a version of the preferred habitat hypothesis close to the expectations hypothesis over the segmented markets hypothesis. Intuitively, the credit markets for such economies are not seriously segmented since borrowers and lenders do generally substitute extensively between assets of different maturities.[1] A number of studies for the USA and Canada have substantiated the expectations theory, though there also exist many empirical studies which reject the specific formulations of it. We discuss some of these in sections 21.5 and 21.6.

21.3 FINANCIAL ASSET PRICES

Financial assets are not generally held for their direct contribution to the individual's consumption. They are held for their yield, which is often uncertain, and the individual balances the expected yield against the risks involved. This is the basic approach of the theories of portfolio selection. These theories focus on the yields on assets rather than on the prices of assets, while the theory of the demand for consumer goods focuses on the prices of commodities.

The price of any asset is uniquely related to its yield and can be calculated from the following relationship. In any period t, for an asset j,

$$r_{jt} = ({}_tp^e_{jt+1} - p_{jt}) + x_{jt} \tag{8}$$

where:

    r_{jt} yield on the jth asset during period t
    p_{jt} jth asset's price in period t
    p^e_{jt+1} jth asset's (expected) price in period $t + 1$
    x_{jt} jth asset's coupon rate in period t

That is,

$${}_tp^e_{jt+1} = p_{jt} + r_{jt} - x_{jt} \tag{9}$$

Hence, a theory of the rate of interest is also a theory of the prices of financial assets. Alternatively, the yields on assets may be explained by a theory of asset prices. Such a theory at a microeconomic level would consider the market for each asset, and use the demand and supply functions for each asset to find the equilibrium price of the asset. At the macroeconomic level, the theory could focus on the average price of financial assets, with macroeconomic demand and supply functions. These demand and supply functions would have the prices of the assets as the relevant variables. The loanable funds theory as stated in the preceding chapter could then be reformulated to replace the demand and supply of funds (or securities) in terms of the rate of interest by the demand and supply of securities in terms of their prices, so that it would become a theory of asset prices.

21.4 EMPIRICAL ESTIMATION AND TESTS

The preceding sections suggest two basic estimation procedures for deriving the structure of short and long rates, and testing the various hypotheses relating them. These are as follows.

21.4.1 The structural approaches to estimation

This subsection drops the t subscripts and designates the current period as 0. It assumes that we are only considering bonds differing in maturity but being otherwise identical. There are three related estimation techniques for the structural approach.

(i) One version specifies the demands and supplies for the bonds of differing maturities, as being functions of the bond prices. The general form of these functions would be:

$$x^d_i = x^d_i(p_0, p_1, \dots, p_i, \dots, p_n, W) \quad i = 0, 1, \dots, n$$

$$x^s_i = x^s_i(p_0, p_1, \dots, p_i, \dots, p_n, x^{gs}_i) \quad i = 0, 1, \dots, n$$

where:

    x^d_i demand for bonds of maturity i
    x^s_i supply of bonds of maturity i
    x^{gs}_i supply of government bonds of maturity i

p_i price of bond of maturity i

W wealth constraint on bonds

Assuming market clearance:

$$x_i^d(p_0, p_1, \ldots, p_i, \ldots, p_n, W) = x_i^s(p_0, p_1, \ldots, p_i, \ldots, p_n, x_i^{gs}) \quad i = 0, 1, \ldots, n \tag{10}$$

Equation (10) is a set of $n + 1$ market conditions in $n + 1$ market prices, $p_0, p_1, \ldots, p_i, \ldots, p_n$ and we assume that a general equilibrium solution for them will provide the equilibrium values of the $n + 1$ bond prices as:

$$p_i = p_i(W, x_0^{gs}, \ldots, x_n^{gs}) \tag{11}$$

(ii) In the second version of the structural approach, since the price of the ith bond – defined as one with maturity i – is a function of the long yield R_i on it, the above functions for asset i can be rewritten as:

$$x_i^d = x_i^d(r_0, R_1, \ldots, R_i, \ldots, R_n, W) \tag{12}$$

$$x_i^s = x_i^s(r_0, R_1, \ldots, R_i, \ldots, R_n, x_i^{gs}) \tag{13}$$

Given market clearance:

$$x_i^d(r_0, R_1, \ldots, R_i, \ldots, R_n, W) = x_i^s(r_0, R_1, \ldots, R_i, \ldots, R_n, W, x_i^{gs}) \tag{14}$$

With $r_0 = R_0$, (14) is a set of $n + 1$ equations in $R_0, R_1, \ldots, R_i, \ldots, R_n$. Solving them would specify the reduced-form equations for the interest rates as:

$$R_i = R_i(W, x_0^{gs}, \ldots, x_n^{gs}) \quad i = 0, 1, 2, \ldots, n$$

Estimation of the stochastic forms of (12) and (13) and the solution of the resulting equilibrium conditions in (14) would provide the estimated values of $r_1, R_2, \ldots, R_i, \ldots, R_n$. These estimated values would depend upon the parameters and the exogenous variables in the demand and supply functions. Therefore, the expected returns as well as the variances and covariances of asset returns, along with the degree of risk aversion in the markets, transactions costs and market imperfections, will be among the determinants of the long yields. Further, the amounts and maturity structure of the government debt would also be among the determinants of asset prices and yields.

Equation (14), by itself, does not itself impose a particular pattern of relationships among the long yields. Barring further restrictions, the government could change the shape of the yield curve by changing the maturity structure of its debt. However, as we have seen earlier, the expectations and liquidity preference hypotheses impose severe restrictions on the interrelationships among the interest rates.

The above procedure does not directly provide estimates of the expected short interest rates. They can be obtained from the estimated long rates by adding a hypothesis such as, for example (4), on the term structure of interest rates, but doing so would not provide a test of these hypotheses. Further, this procedure will give different estimates for the short rates depending upon the hypothesis which is adopted.

(iii) A third estimation procedure integrates the term structure relationship between the long rates and short rates into the asset demand functions at the theoretical level prior to estimation. To do this, we assume that the investor can invest in (and borrowers can borrow through) an nth period bond or a sequence of short bonds, so that the demand and supply for the former would be a function of its long rate and the short rates up to n. The demand and supply functions for bonds can then be specified as:

$$x_i^d = x_i^d(R_i, r_0, r_1^e, r_2^e, \ldots, r_i^e, W) \quad i = 0, 1, \ldots, n \tag{15}$$

$$x_i^s = x_i^s(R_i, r_0, r_1^e, r_2^e, \ldots, r_i^e; x_i^{gs}) \quad i = 0, 1, \ldots, n \tag{16}$$

Equating demands and supplies for the ith period,

$$x_i^d(R_i, r_0, r_1^e, r_2^e, \ldots, r_i^e, W) = x_i^s(R_i, r_0, r_1^e, r_2^e, \ldots, r_i^e, x_i^{gs}) \quad i = 0, 1, \ldots, n \tag{17}$$

Solving for the long rates, we get:

$$R_i = R_i(r_0, r_1^e, r_2^e, \ldots, r_i^e, W, x_1^{gs}, \ldots, x_n^{gs}) \quad i = 0, 1, \ldots, n \tag{18}$$

Equation (18) allows estimation of the relationships between the long rates and the expected short rates, again without imposing a specific pattern on the relationship.

An example of such a structural approach to estimate the role of the determinants of the term structure of yields is Benjamin Friedman (1977). His study estimated the holdings of long-term government bonds by different institutional investors and concluded in favour of a structural model for the determination of long-term interest rates.

Another application of the structural approach is to estimate the spot or forward rates or the spread between rates of different maturities as functions of macroeconomic variables, including preferences for specific terms to maturity as in the preferred habitat hypothesis. The forward rates and the spread could also be tested for a liquidity premium as a function of macroeconomic variables. The economic variables used can be derived from the liquidity preference approach or the loanable funds approach or be a combination of the two. As reported in the preceding chapter, Feldstein and Eckstein (1970) emphasized the liquidity preference approach while Sargent (1969) followed the loanable funds one. Another study in the latter context is Echols and Elliot (1976). This extended Sargent's analysis and tested for the determinants of forward rates using real GNP, government deficit, net export balance, real money supply, stock of outstanding government bonds, bank funds and insurance company funds invested in government bonds – as well as inflationary expectations – among their explanatory variables. Their estimations of forward rates for USA data found the coefficients of the explanatory variables were significant, with signs consistent with the loanable funds approach. Among their results was the significance of the liquidity premium, as well as of the institutional (bank and insurance company) demands for bonds of different maturities and the supply of short versus long maturity supplies of government bonds, thereby supporting the preferred habitat hypothesis.[2] For example, an increase in the proportion of investment funds held relative to insurance companies lowered forward rates. However, these institutional holdings and supply factors did not prove to be significant in explaining the yield spread between twelve-year government bonds and Treasury bills, so that it is not clear that the government could shift the yield curve by debt management policy – for example, by increasing the issue of short-term government bonds relative to long-term ones.

21.4.2 Reduced-form approaches to the estimation of the term structure of yields

As shown earlier, the expectations hypothesis modified with the addition of a liquidity preference term implied (6), which was that:

$$(1 + {}_tR_{t+n})^{n+1} = [(1 + {}_tr_t) (1 + {}_tr_{t+1}^e) \ldots (1 + {}_tr_{t+n}^e)] \, {}_t\gamma_{t+n}(n; \rho) \quad n \geq 1 \tag{19}$$

where the current period is t, the expectations are those held in period t and γ represents the liquidity premium. Now, using the symbols R and r for the *logarithmic values of the gross returns* rather than the net returns, (19) becomes:

$${}_tR_{t+n} = \{1/(n+1)\}\,[{}_tr_t + {}_tr^e_{t+1} + \ldots + {}_tr^e_{t+n} + {}_t\gamma_{t+n}(n;\rho)] \quad n \geq 1 \tag{20}^3$$

where *all the return variables are now in logs and are gross rates of return.* We will follow this convention in the rest of this chapter.

In order to test (20), we need a hypothesis for generating the expected values of the forward short rates. Given the efficient markets assumptions, the natural complement of the expectations hypothesis is the rational expectations hypothesis (REH) presented in Chapters 7 and 15. This specifies that:

$${}_tr^e_{t+i} = E_t\,r_{t+i} \tag{21}$$

where $E_t\,{}_t r_{t+i}$ is the rational expectations value of r_{t+i} based on all the information available in t about period $t+i$. Among the information needed is that of the 'relevant theory' actually determining r_{t+i} and information on the values of its determinants. This throws us back to the demand and supply functions for assets for the $(t+i)$th period. Alternatively, if we can assume that this theory and the values of the explanatory variables are all known, we can estimate the stochastic form of (19). As an illustration of this point, assume that the 'relevant theory' is the simple autoregressive relationship:

$$r_{t+i+1} = a_1 r_{t+i} + a_2 r_{t+i-1} + \mu_{t+i+1} \quad i = 0, 1, 2, \ldots, n \tag{22}$$

where μ_t is a random error, with zero mean and constant variance. Under the REH,

$$E_t r_{t+i+1} = a_1 r_{t+i} + a_2 r_{t+i-1} \tag{23}$$

By iteration, $E_t\,{}_t r_{t+i}$ can be expressed as functions of r_t and r_{t-1}, where the values of these are already known in period t. These, along with the expectations hypothesis of the term structure, can be used to generate $E_t\,{}_t r_{t+i}$ for all i. As an example, (20) for $i = 2$ – that is, three periods – becomes,

$${}_tR_{t+2} = (1/3)\,[r_t + r^e_{t+1} + r^e_{t+2} + {}_t\gamma_{t+2}] \tag{24}$$

Combining (24) with the REH, we get:

$$E_t\,{}_tR_{t+2} = (1/3)\,[r_t + E_t r_{t+1} + E_t r_{t+2} + {}_t\gamma_{t+2}] \tag{25}$$

where $E_t\,{}_tR_{t+2}$ is the mathematical expectation in t of the long rate ${}_tR_{t+2}$ from t to $t+2$. From (25) and the 'relevant' theory (22), we have:

$$E_t\,{}_tR_{t+2} = (1/3)\,[r_t + (a_1 r_t + a_2 r_{t-1}) + (a_1^2 + a_2)\,r_t + a_1 a_2 r_{t-1}] + {}_t\gamma_{t+2}$$

$$= \alpha_1 r_t + \alpha_2\, r_{t-1} + (1/3)\, {}_t\gamma_{t+2} \tag{26}$$

where $\alpha_1 = (1/3)(1 + a_1 + a_2 + a_1^2)$ and $\alpha_2 = (1/3)(a_2 + a_1 a_2)$. Since the REH implies that,

$${}_tR_{t+2} = E_t\,{}_tR_{t+2} + \eta_t \tag{27}$$

where η is the stochastic disturbance, we have from (26) and (27) that,

$${}_tR_{t+2} = \alpha_1 r_t + \alpha_2 r_{t-1} + (1/3)\, {}_t\gamma_{t+2} + \eta_t \tag{28}$$

Equation (28) is the estimating equation given the expectations hypothesis, the REH and the assumed specification of the relevant theory as (22). Its general form is:

$$R_{t+i} = \alpha_1' r_t + \alpha_2' r_{t-1} + (1/3) \,_t \gamma_{t+i} + \eta_t \qquad\qquad (28')$$

for appropriate definitions of α_1' and α_2' in terms of a_i. Their estimated values would reflect the influence of the three underlying hypotheses. However, note that (28') requires data on $_t \gamma_{t+i}$ which is not observable so that a hypothesis on it will have to be specified before (28') can be estimated.

Two common hypotheses on the risk premium

The simplest possible hypotheses on the risk premium $_t \gamma_{t+i}$ are:

(i) $_t \gamma_{t+i}$ is constant per period such that $_t \gamma_{t+i} = i \gamma$, where the liquidity premium for $(i + 1)$ periods involves this premium for only i periods (after the current one). In this case, this term will become the constant in (28').

(ii) $_t \gamma_{t+i}$ is random such that $_t \gamma_{t+i} = \mu_{t+i}$. In this case, this term will become part of the random term in (28').

(i) is the more common assumption in the estimation of (28') and is used in the next section.

21.5 TESTS OF THE EXPECTATIONS HYPOTHESIS WITH A CONSTANT PREMIUM AND RATIONAL EXPECTATIONS

There is no particular basis for assuming that the liquidity premium is constant. However, making such an assumption facilitates the construction of empirical tests of the expectations hypothesis. The following two tests are based on this assumption. These tests use the implications of the expectations hypothesis that the expected (holding period) yields on the relevant bonds of different maturities will only differ by a constant representing the liquidity premium.

Define the difference between the actual long yield and the average one specified by the right-hand side of the expectations equation (1) as the excess yield on the long bond. From (20), the actual difference in the yields from holding a long versus a sequence of short bonds is the sum of the liquidity premium and expectational errors. Assuming the premium to be constant and assuming rational expectations, the remaining variations in the excess yields can then only be due to random fluctuations. This, in turn, implies that the difference between the excess yield and the premium will only be due to random errors in expectations and cannot be forecast with any information known at the time the expectations are formed.

21.5.1   The slope sensitivity test

Start with the assumption (20) of the expectations hypothesis and its following equation for the *two*-period long rate:

$$2 \,_t R_{t+1} = \,_t r_t + \,_{t+1} r_{t+1}^e + \,_t \gamma_{t+1} \quad t = 0, 1, \dots \qquad\qquad (29)$$

where, as a reminder, note that all the variables are in logs and the interest rate variables are gross rates. Assuming the constancy per period of the liquidity premium, and noting that a two-period loan involves a liquidity premium only for the second period, let:

$$_t \gamma_{t+i} = i \gamma \qquad\qquad (30)$$

Equation (29) can be restated as:

$$_{t+1} r_{t+1}^e - \,_t r_t = 2 [\,_t R_{t+1} - \,_t r_t] - \gamma \qquad\qquad (31)$$

Assuming the rational expectations hypothesis (REH),

$$_{t+1}r^e_{t+1} = E_{t\,t+1}r_{t+1} \tag{32}$$

and

$$_{t+1}r_{t+1} = E_{t\,t+1}r_{t+1} + \mu_{t+1} \tag{33}$$

where μ_t is a random error with $E_t(\mu_{t+1} \mid I_t) = 0$ and I_t is the information available in t. Hence, from (31) to (33),

$$_{t+1}r_{t+1} - {}_t r_t = \alpha + \beta(_t R_{t+1} - {}_t r_t) - \mu_{t+1} \tag{34}$$

where $\alpha = -\gamma$ and $\beta = 2$. Since each of the variables (except for the random term) in (34) is observable, it can be estimated by the appropriate regression techniques. This equation specifies that the change over time in the one-period spot rates from the current to the next period will depend upon the difference in the current two-period long rate and the current one-period spot rate, except for a constant term and a random term. New information appearing in the next period will do so randomly. If the regressions of the above equation yield estimates consistent with these restrictions on α, β and μ, the theory will not be rejected by the data.

This test is a joint test of three hypotheses: the expectations hypothesis, the REH and a constant liquidity premium per period. Since the test is that the estimated value of β does not significantly differ from 2, it is sometimes called the slope sensitivity test.

The slope sensitivity test is among the more common ones used for the expectations hypotheses. To illustrate this application, this test was used in Mankiw and Miron (1986), among others. They tested equation (34) for the United States using three-month and six-month data for five intervals during 1890–1979. The null hypothesis ($\beta = 2$) was rejected for all except the earliest period prior to the founding of the Federal Reserve System in 1915. That is, the spread between the short and the long rate was a good indicator of the path of interest rates prior to the commencement of the stabilization operations of the Fed, but not in the periods after it, with the spot rate following a random walk after 1915. Therefore, the authors concluded that a central bank policy of interest rate stabilization would make the spot rate follow a random walk and lead to a rejection of the expectations hypothesis. In general, there seems to be more empirical support for (34) when countries do not pursue interest rate stabilization policies.

21.5.2 The efficient and rational information usage test

Another test of the above joint hypothesis is based on the following restatement of (29):

$$_t\phi^e_{t+1} = 2\,_t R_{t+1} - {}_{t+1}r^e_{t+1} - {}_t r_t = \gamma \tag{35}$$

where $_t\phi^e_{t+1}$ is the excess yield over two periods, which under the constant liquidity premium version of the expectations hypothesis equals γ. Assuming REH,

$$E_{t\,t}\phi_{t+1} = 2\,_t R_{t+1} - E_{t\,t+1}r_{t+1} - {}_t r_t = \gamma \tag{36}$$

The stochastic form of this equation is:

$$_t\phi_{t+1} = 2\,_t R_{t+1} - {}_{t+1}r_{t+1} - {}_t r_t + \mu_{t+1}$$

$$= \gamma + \mu_{t+1} \tag{37}$$

where μ_{t+1} is again a random term with $E_t(\mu_{t+1} \mid I_t) = 0$ and I_t is the information available in t. Under the joint hypothesis, the excess yield would not be a function of information known in period t. If a regression of the excess yield on information known in t – such as on prices, output, unemployment, and other variables on which information is commonly available in t – yield significant coefficients for such variables, the joint hypothesis will be rejected by the data. From (37), the regression equation can be formulated as:

$$_t\phi_{t+1} = \alpha + \underline{b}\underline{X}_t + \mu_{t+1} \tag{38}$$

where $\alpha = \gamma$, $\underline{X}_t$ is a vector of commonly known variables in t, and $\underline{b}$ is the corresponding vector of coefficients. Among the $\underline{X}$ variables would be included the lagged values of the excess yield itself. The maintained hypothesis would be rejected if any of the estimated coefficients in $\underline{b}$ is significantly different from zero.

Alternatively, in (37), define:

$$_t\phi'_{t+1} = 2\,_tR_{t+1} - {}_{t+1}r^e_{t+1} \tag{39}$$

and specify the regression equation as:

$$_t\phi'_{t+1} = \alpha + \beta\,_t r_t + \underline{b}\underline{X}_t + \mu_{t+1} \tag{40}$$

where $\beta = 1$. The joint hypothesis would be rejected if the estimated value of β is significantly different from one and/or if any of the b coefficients are significantly different from zero.

Jones and Roley (1983) tested (40) for quarterly USA Treasury bill data. The coefficients of some of the X_t variables were significant, so that the joint hypothesis was rejected.

While many studies using the notion of already available information to test the joint hypothesis for changes in the term structure, tend to reject it, Pesando (1978) found support for it in Canadian data. This study is discussed in the next section. A rejection of the joint hypothesis could be due to rejection of the expectations hypothesis, of the assumption of a constant liquidity premium, of the REH, of the proxy used for the expected rate of inflation, or of any combination of them. Therefore, it is not clear whether the expectations theory itself is at fault, with the rejection of the joint hypothesis sometimes interpreted as a rejection of the assumption of a constant risk premium, sometimes of the REH and sometimes of the proxy used for the expected inflation rate.

The rejection of the assumption of the constancy of the liquidity premium per period implies that this premium can vary over time. This is not implausible for bonds of medium or long maturities, but there is no particular reason to assume that the liquidity premium would vary significantly over periods as short as a week or a few months. Since many of the rejections of the joint hypothesis occur for data using Treasury bill yields only, the rejection of the joint hypothesis may be due to that of the REH or the expectations one itself. Further, if the liquidity premia are not constant, then the theory needs to specify their determinants, which is difficult to do.

21.6 THE RANDOM WALK HYPOTHESIS OF THE LONG RATES OF INTEREST

Start with equation (20), which was:

$$_tR_{t+n} = (1/(n+1))[r_t + {}_tr^e_{t+1} + {}_tr^e_{t+2} + \ldots + {}_tr^e_{t+n}] + (1/(n+1))\,_t\gamma_{t+n}(n; \rho) \quad n \geq 1 \tag{41}$$

Lagging (41) by one period:

$$_{t-1}R_{t+n-1} = (1/(n+1))[r_{t-1} + {}_{t-1}r_t^e + {}_{t-1}r_{t+1}^e + \dots + {}_{t-1}r_{t+n-1}^e]) + (1/(n+1))\,{}_{t-1}\gamma_{t+n-1}(n;\rho) \quad (42)$$

Subtract (42) from (41). Applying the REH to the resulting equation gives,

$$_tR_{t+n} - {}_{t-1}R_{t+n-1} = (1/(n+1))[(r_t - E_{t-1\,t-1}r_t) + (E_t\,{}_tr_{t+1} - E_{t-1\,t-1}r_{t+1}) + \dots$$

$$+ (E_t\,{}_tr_{t+n-1} - E_{t-1\,t-1}r_{t+n-1})] + (1/(n+1))[(E_t\,{}_tr_{t+n} - r_{t-1})]$$

$$+ (1/(n+1))\,[{}_t\gamma_{t+n}(n;\rho) - {}_{t-1}\gamma_{t+n-1}(n,\rho)] \quad (43)$$

Assuming that no new information becomes available in period t – that is, $I_t = I_{t-1}$, where I_t is the information available in t – we have:

$$E_t\,{}_tr_{t+i} - E_{t-1\,t-1}r_{t+i} = \mu_{t+i} \quad i = 0, 1, \dots, n-1 \quad (44)$$

where μ_{t+i} are forecasting random errors, with a zero mean and are independently distributed. That is, the revisions to expectations are zero mean independent random variables.

Further, as $n \to \infty$,

$$(1/(n+1))[(E_t\,{}_tr_{t+n} - r_{t-1})] \to 0 \quad (45)$$

so that for large n, this term would be about 0 for the usually observed and expected range of values of the interest rate. Hence, if the liquidity premium term on the right-hand side was also a random term or if it equalled zero, $[{}_tR_{t+n} - {}_{t-1}R_{t+n-1}]$ would behave randomly. Noting that the last term on the right-hand side of (43) involves the difference between the n-period liquidity premiums in t and $t-1$, an assumption that the liquidity premium is time invariant – that is, does not change with new information – would make this term equal to zero. Alternatively, it can be assumed that, in the absence of any new information, the last term in (43) will also be randomly distributed.

Hence, under the above collection of assumptions, the right-hand side of (43) will be a random variable. Therefore, (43) can be rewritten as:

$$_tR_{t+n} = {}_{t-1}R_{t+n-1} + \epsilon_t \quad (46)$$

where ϵ_t is a random error, made up of the relevant set of random errors, with $E(\epsilon_t \mid I_{t-1}) = 0$. Equation (46) states that the long rates for large values of n will follow a random walk. This constitutes the random walk hypothesis (RWH) of the long interest rates. Note that it is expected to hold only for large values of n and if no new information becomes available between t and $t-1$.

Since systematic monetary policy followed in t will be anticipated in $t-1$, (46) implies that it cannot affect the change in the long rate between periods $t+n$ and $t+n-1$. Only unanticipated monetary policy – that is, policy shocks which change the value of ϵ – can shift this difference and shift the yield curve. Hence, the RWH of the long interest rates implies that systematic monetary policy cannot shift the yield curve, only an unanticipated one can do so.

However, since we needed (45) to arrive at (46), note that the RWH does not hold for low values of n. To illustrate the failure of the RWH of long interest rates for low values of n, assume a deterministic system so that $\mu_{t+i} = 0$ and that ${}_t\gamma_{t+i} = i\gamma$. Further, assume that there is a shift in fundamental factors – with the shift factor β already known in period $t-1$ – such that:

$$r_{t+1} = \dots = r_{t+n} = r_t + \beta \quad (47)$$

where β is the amount of the shift. Given these assumptions, (47) and (43), for $n = 1$, imply that the evolution of the long rate on two-period bonds would be given by:

$$_tR_{t+1} - _{t-1}R_t = (1/2)(r_t + \beta - r_t)$$

$$= (1/2)\beta \qquad (48)$$

We also have:

$$_tR_{t+2} - _{t-1}R_{t+1} = (1/3)\beta$$

and so on to:

$$_tR_{t+n} - _{t-1}R_{t+n-1} = (1/(n+1))\beta \qquad (49)$$

where the right-hand side goes to zero only as $n \to \infty$, so that the RWH must either be confined to very large values of n or must assume that there is no change ($\beta = 0$) in the fundamental or systematic determinants of the long rates.

Pesando (1978), tested (43) – with the assumption of a time-invariant liquidity premium term – in the form of the difference between the rationally expected long yield ($E_{t-1}\,_tR_{t+n} \mid I_{t-1}$) based on information in t – 1 and the long yield $_{t-1}R_{t+n-1}$. His dependent variable, therefore, was $[(E_{t-1}\,_tR_{t+n} \mid I_{t-1}) - _{t-1}R_{t+n-1}]$, which was implied by the joint hypothesis to be random and uncorrelated with information available at the beginning of the period. His regressions of this variable against a number of variables such as investment and saving, government deficit, deficit on the current account of the balance of payments,[4] real monetary base and real GNP and the current change in the monetary base.[5] Pesando's tests on Canadian ten-year bond yields for the periods 1961:1 to 1971:2 and 1961:1 to 1976:4 data showed insignificant and/or incorrectly signed coefficients for these variables, so that he could not reject the hypothesis that the current change in the long-term bond yield is a random variable and follows a martingale sequence. Pesando's tests of the models used by Sargent (1969), Echols and Elliot (1976) and Feldstein and Eckstein (1970) for his Canadian data set led to their rejection. These results also rejected the notion that the long yield includes a cyclical-term premium determined by these variables, thereby lending support to the hypothesis of a time-invariant premium. Further, his tests rejected the autoregressive procedure for modelling the expected inflation rate. Pesando also rejected the Modigliani and Sutch preferred habitat model since this model requires that the liquidity premium is not time invariant.

The alternative assumption to the above random walk hypothesis is that the changes in long yields depend on economic variables.

21.7 THE INFORMATION CONTENT OF THE TERM STRUCTURE FOR THE EXPECTED RATES OF INFLATION

Fisher's relationship between the nominal and real interest rates in efficient markets can be specified as:

$$_tr^e_{t+i} = _tr^{re}_{t+i} + _t\pi^e_{t+i} \qquad (50)$$

where:

$_tr^e_{t+i}$ expected market (nominal) rate of interest in period $t + i$

$_tr^{re}_{t+i}$ expected real rate of interest in period $t + i$

$_t\pi^e_{t+i}$ expected rate of inflation in period $t + i$

Restate (50) as:

$$_t\pi^e_{t+i} = {}_tr^e_{t+i} - {}_tr^{re}_{t+i} \tag{51}$$

Assume that there exist forward markets so that the known forward rates $_tr^f_{t+i}$ can be used to replace $_tr^e_{t+i}$ and use the REH to specify the following relationships:

$$_tr^{re}_{t+i} = E_t\,_tr^r_{t+i} = {}_tr^r_{t+i} - \eta_{t+i} \tag{52}$$

$$_t\pi^e_{t+i} = E_t\,\pi_{t+i} \tag{53}$$

Equation (51) can now be rewritten as:

$$E_t\,_t\pi_{t+i} = {}_tr^f_{t+i} - {}_tr^r_{t+i} + \eta_{t+i} \tag{54}$$

which can be restated as:

$$E_t\,_t\pi_{t+i} = {}_tr^f_{t+i} - E_t\,_tr^r_{t+i} \tag{55}$$

Equation (55) uses the information on the nominal forward and the rationally expected value of the real interest rates – assuming the latter to be known or already estimated – to derive the term structure of the expected inflation rates over future periods.

Common hypotheses on the real rate of interest

Equations (54) and (55) need data or estimates of r^r_{t+i}. The range of choices here is usually:

(i) Market data is available on it; for example, if there are an adequate variety of inflation-indexed bonds in the economy.

(ii) Market data on it is not available but it can be reasonably assumed to be constant, or that changes in it are very small relative to changes in the inflation rate.

(iii) The assumption of its constancy is not plausible but it is a function of a small number of determinants and this function can be estimated. For example, the loanable funds or the liquidity preference theory, as discussed in Chapter 20, or the more general IS–LM approach can be used to specify the determinants of this rate. Thus, the IS–LM approach implies that the real money supply and the real fiscal deficit are among the short-run determinants of the real interest rate. The appropriate function for it can be specified and estimated, and the estimated values then substituted in (54) or (55). Among the studies which use this approach to the real rate are Sargent (1969), Echols and Elliot (1976), Feldstein and Eckstein (1970) and Pesando (1978).

An illustration of the empirical results

Mishkin (1990) examined the rates of inflation implied by the yields on one- to five-year bonds in the United States. His data was monthly from 1953 to 1987. His estimation equation was:

$$_t\pi_{t+i} - {}_t\pi_t = \alpha_{t+i} + \beta_{t+i}(_tR_{t+i} - {}_tR_t) + \mu_{t+i} \tag{56}$$

where the difference ('inflation spread') in the average annual inflation rate over $t + i$ years was regressed on the spread between the corresponding nominal long rates. Mishkin argued that a rejection of $\beta_{t+i} = 0$ implies that the term structure contains information on the inflation spread, while a rejection of $\beta_{t+i} = 1$ implies that spread in the real rates is not constant over time, so that the nominal spread in interest rates provides information on the real spread. His estimates showed that, for the longer maturities, the spread in nominal interest rates contains substantial information about the inflation spread but little about the real interest rate spread. Contrary to the findings of many other studies, the converse was found for short maturities of six months or less. For these, the term structure did not contain any information on the future change in inflation but did imply a significant amount about the term structure of real rates of interest.

21.8 THE RISK STRUCTURE OF INTEREST RATES: THE CAPITAL ASSET PRICING MODEL

The rates of return on assets in the economy differ not only because of differences in the term structure of assets but also because of differences in the risk in holding various assets. These differences in risk are especially pertinent to privately issued bonds and stocks, but also occur for government bonds, since the coupons on these are usually designated in nominal, not real, terms and there is, in addition, the possibility of capital gains or losses over their holding period. While the analysis of the variations in returns due to the differences in the riskiness of assets is usually not covered in monetary economics textbooks, it is usually of considerable interest to students in the courses in monetary economics. The treament of this topic is also closely related to the portfolio selection theory used in the exposition of the speculative demand for money in Chapter 5. Further, monetary economists are increasingly familiar with the language of systematic and unsystematic risk in finance. We have, therefore, decided to include the following brief analysis on the relationship between risk and expected return in the economy.[6]

The starting proposition in the analysis of the risk premiums on risky assets is that since risk averters dominate the asset markets, the returns on assets increase with the riskiness of their return, *ceteris paribus*.

A popular model for explaining the variations in the expected returns due to the differences in risk is the capital asset pricing model (CAPM), first proposed by Sharpe (1964) and elaborated by Lintner, Fama and others. The CAPM is basically an extension of the individual investor's portfolio decision, as set out in Chapter 5 above, to the market for risky assets, with additional assumptions needed in going from the individual's subjective evaluations of expected returns and standard deviations to the market ones. These assumptions include an identical evaluation of the riskiness of each stock by all investors in the market, the specification of a riskless asset held by each investor and efficient markets. The CAPM shows that the return on an asset would include two kinds of premiums – one for systematic risk and the other for unsystematic risk – over the return on the riskless asset, with the systematic premium increasing with the riskiness of the asset in a specific manner.

Formally, the CAPM model specifies that the rate of return r_i on any asset i can be decomposed as in:

$$r_i = \alpha_i + \beta_i \gamma_S + e_i \tag{57}$$

where:

r_i rate of return on asset i
γ_S expected value of the market risk premium $[= (\mu_S - r_c)]$
μ_S expected rate of return on the market portfolio
r_c highest risk-free return available among the riskless assets
σ_S risk (= standard deviation) of the market portfolio

where α_i and β_i are constants and e_i is independent of r_S, with the symbols S (intuitively, 'stock market') standing for the market portfolio encompassing stocks, bonds and other (financial and non-financial) risky assets traded in the economy. The market portfolio is defined as consisting of *all* the *risky* assets in the market. In terms of the composition of the market portfolio, the proportion of each risky asset in the portfolio equals its value divided by the total value of all the risky assets in the market.

Equation (57) decomposes the return on an asset into three components: a constant term (α_i), a component $(\beta_i\gamma_S)$ which varies with the return on the market portfolio and a variable component (e_i) distinctive to the asset and not related to the variations in the market return. We discuss the nature of each of these components in turn.

To examine the nature of the constant term and holding the maturity period constant, assume that the market has several assets whose returns are constant (and, therefore, have zero standard deviation), with the *j*th riskless asset having the risk-free return r_j (and $\sigma_j = 0$). The constancy of this return implies for (57) that $r_j = \alpha_j$, and this asset's return is not correlated with the market return – so that $\beta_j = 0$ – and there is no individual variation in return – so that $e_j = 0$. The market can have many such riskless assets, especially in nominal terms. Examples of such assets include currency, demand deposits, savings deposits, money market mutual funds, etc., with each possessing somewhat different degrees of convenience and liquidity. These assets provide different returns because of differences in such (non-risk) characteristics even though they have the same degree (zero) of risk. Since the CAPM deals only with the choice among assets on the basis of their riskiness rather than these other characteristics, the appropriate risk-free return to include in (57) is the highest return among the available riskless assets for the given duration of the period of analysis.[7] Designate this return as r_c, where c or C stand for the riskless asset and the designating letter has been taken from the word 'cash'. Equation (57) can, then, be rewritten as: :

$$r_i = r_c + \beta_i\gamma_S + e_i$$

or as,

$$(r_i - r_c) = \beta_i\gamma_S + e_i \tag{58}$$

Equation (57) shows that the risky asset i pays a premium $(r_i - r_c)$ over the maximum available risk-free rate r_c.[8] This premium is related to two types of risks incurred in holding the ith asset, as we explain in the following paragraphs.

The second term in (57) specifies the variation in the return r_i with the market return. Of its two components, γ_S is the market premium and equals $(\mu_S - r_c)$. Its coefficient β_i is called the *beta* of the asset i and specifies the change in the return on asset i as the market premium changes. As the appendix to this chapter shows, the appropriate measure of β_i is $(\partial\sigma_S/\partial x_i)(1/\sigma_S)$ which equals σ_{iS}/σ_{SS}, where σ_{iS} $(\equiv \mathrm{cov}(r_i, r_S))$[9] is the covariance between the returns to asset i and to the market portfolio S, and σ_{SS} is the variance of the return to the market portfolio.[10] Intuitively, β_i – the beta of asset i – is the increase in the market (not in the individual portfolio) risk from marginally increasing the investment in this asset.[11]

The third component of (57) is e_i. This term is independent of the return on the market portfolio and captures all influences other than the market's return on the return to asset i. Examples of such influences are firm-specific technical change, strikes, etc.[12]

None of the terms on the right side of (58) depends on the utility functions of the investors. Therefore, an implication of (58) is that the individual utility functions of the investors are irrelevant to the determination of the equilibrium market returns on assets. Their relevance is only to the derivation of the individual's demand functions for the various assets.

For the market portfolio, $Ee_S = 0$, so that the expected return μ_S on the market portfolio is given by:

$$\mu_S = r_c + \beta_S\gamma_S \tag{59}$$

where $\beta_S = \sigma_{SS}/\sigma_{SS} = 1$. That is, the beta of the market portfolio is unity.

The individual's particular portfolio, of course, does not usually have the same composition as the market one. The rate of return to this portfolio, designated as r_P, can also be computed by applying (57) to the portfolio. This gives,

$$r_P = r_c + \beta_P \gamma_S + e_P \tag{60}$$

so that,

$$(\mu_P - \mu_S) = \beta_P \gamma_S + Ee_P \tag{61}$$

where μ_P is the expected return on the individual's portfolio. Therefore, the individual can obtain an expected return different from the expected return on the market portfolio by choosing a portfolio composition – that is, a different risk level, as reflected in the value of β_P – different from that of the latter.

Sharpe (1964, p. 425) concluded that the lender:

> may obtain a higher expected rate of return on his holdings only by incurring additional risk. In effect, the market presents him with two prices: *the price of time*, or the pure interest rate[13] . . . and *the price of risk*, the additional expected return per unit of risk borne. . . .
>
> (Sharpe, 1964, p. 425, italics added)

The determinants of *the price of time* have already been studied in the macroeconomic theories of the interest rate in Chapter 20 and in the theories of the term structure of interest rates in this chapter. This section has focused on *the price of risk*.

The appendix to this chapter presents the CAPM for explaining the differences in risk premiums across assets. Our concern with the risk premium and CAPM is a peripheral one, so that we do not present this model and the empirical evidence on it in detail. A good brief review is provided in Jagannathan and McGrattan (1995). As this review indicates, the empirical evidence on the CAPM is quite mixed. Their conclusion is that there is definitely some evidence supporting it[14] and, overall, there does not seem to be enough evidence in favour of an alternative to justify replacing the CAPM by another one for explaining the differences in risk premiums in the rates of return.

Therefore, while the empirical evidence on the CAPM has not always confirmed its validity, there seems to be enough empirical evidence and theoretical justification for it to remain the most popular basic model for explaining the differences in the rates of return on assets.

CONCLUSIONS

It seems clear that in well-established financial markets, the markets in the individual assets are closely interrelated. For such markets, while the risk premium may vary, possibly in a narrow range, the likelihood that the markets for government bonds of different maturities are very significantly segmented seems to be small. Hence, the expectations hypothesis of the term structure of interest rates is generally the maintained hypothesis for closely integrated markets. This assumes that there is very extensive substitution among the bonds of different maturities (with other characteristics such as risk held constant), the markets are efficient and the transactions costs are not significant, at least for the dominant economic agents in the financial markets.

The substitution among the securities of different maturities is likely to be limited where the markets are thin or not well developed, as in the less-developed economies. The degree of substitution existing in the markets is, therefore, primarily a function of the stage of economic and financial development of the country.

Empirical tests of the expectations theory are usually of a combined or joint hypothesis including the expectations theory, the assumption of a constant liquidity premium and the rational expectations hypothesis. These tests usually use reduced-form equations for the yield on different maturities or their spread. Most such studies prove to be unfavourable to the joint hypothesis, with some supporting it, but it is not clear whether the expectations hypothesis itself is at fault. The problem could lie with the assumption of a constant liquidity premium or the assumption of rational expectations.

Several of the tests of the joint hypothesis use Treasury bill rate data which is unlikely to incorporate much variation in the liquidity premia. Also, in general, tests on the rational expectations assumption do not provide unambiguous support for it.

Tests of the alternative hypothesis – that the markets are compartmentalized by the term to maturity – usually use structural systems of demand and supply equations. If this segmented markets or preferred habitat hypothesis were correct, the debt management policies of the government should be able to shift the yield curve. However, empirical studies do not report support for a significant shift in the yield curve brought about by changes in debt management policies.

Therefore, for the developed financial markets, while the more rigorous and detailed tests of the joint hypothesis often reject it, there is not sufficient evidence to individually support either significant variations in the liquidity premium or provide sufficient support for the alternative hypotheses of the segmented markets or preferred habitats. However, there may be some small possibility of these effects, which, along with small deviations in expectations from the rational ones, could be enough to reject the joint hypothesis. From the opposite perspective, there is a great deal of evidence that most of the variations in the long rates can be explained by variations in the expected future short rates. Since the latter are closely related to the expected rate of inflation for the relevant period, the long rates are often used as good (even though not perfect) predictors of the expected inflation rates.

APPENDIX: THE CAPITAL ASSET PRICING MODEL

The CAPM is based on the expected utility analysis of portfolio selection. It assumes that:

(a) All assets are perfectly divisible and traded in efficient and perfectly competitive markets. There are no transactions costs or taxes on asset returns.
(b) Each investor has the option of holding a non-zero amount (positive or negative) of a standard riskless asset at its risk-free rate of interest r_c. Alternatively, investors can borrow or lend any amount at the rate of interest r_c.
(c) All investors hold identical (subjective) values of the means, variances and covariances of the asset returns.
(d) Asset returns are normally distributed and the investors maximize the expected utility of the return to their portfolio. Alternatively, the investors maximize the expected value of their utility function over their portfolio mean and variance.

The individual's portfolio choice is shown in Figure 21.2, with the mean return μ to the portfolio on the vertical axis and its standard deviation σ on the horizontal one. The riskless asset has the rate of return r_c and is represented by point C. Combinations of the risky assets alone in the portfolio imply the opportunity locus ASB. The efficient opportunity locus combining the riskless and the risky assets, without borrowing, is CSB. The derivation of this locus was explained in Chapter 5.

In Figure 21.2, if the individual can borrow at the risk-free rate r_c and invest in the risky assets in the proportions specified by point S, his efficient opportunity locus becomes CSE. Since all investors have been assumed to hold the same estimates of the means, variances and covariances of the assets, the efficient opportunity locus for all investors would be identical and be CSE. The nature of the composite risky asset – labelled as asset S or the market portfolio – represented by the point S should be noted. It is that combination of the

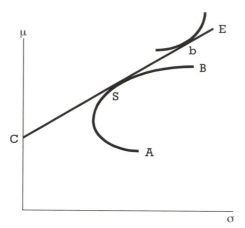

Figure 21.2

risky assets which offers the highest risk premium $(\mu - r_c)$ per unit of standard deviation. It is independent of the investor's preferences.

In Figure 21.2, each investor, to maximize his expected utility function, will choose the optimal (μ, σ) point as one at which his highest indifference curve is tangential to the efficient opportunity locus *CSE*. The two segments of the locus *CSE* are *CS* and *SE*. An optimal choice on the segment *CS* implies that the individual holds some amount of the riskless asset – and is, therefore, a net lender – and some of the risky asset *S*. An optimal choice on the segment *SE* means that the individual borrows at the risk-free rate r_c and is thereby able to invest more than his wealth in the risky asset *S*. Therefore, once the asset *S* has been determined, the investor's decision becomes simplified to a choice among the possible combinations of the riskless asset and the asset *S*. That is, the optimal composition of the risky assets is identical for all optimal portfolios and is produced by the market portfolio *S*.[15] Only the combinations of the riskless asset and the market portfolio vary among investors on the bases of their preferences.[16]

The locus *CSE* offers a linear tradeoff between expected return and risk. Since the locus *CSE* is linear and all optimal portfolios lie on *CME*, the expected return on any optimal portfolio *P* is specified by:

$$\mu_P = r_c + \lambda \sigma_P \tag{62}$$

where, as shown in Figure 21.2, the slope λ of the locus *CSE* equals $(\mu_S - r_c)/\sigma_S$, and is independent of the particular portfolio composition.

Let x_i be the fraction of the optimal portfolio invested in the ith risky asset, so that the fraction invested in the riskless asset is $(1 - \Sigma_i x_i)$. Then, the return to the optimal portfolio can be written as:

$$r_P = \Sigma_i x_i r_i + (1 - \Sigma_i x_i) r_c \tag{63}$$

Further, since the optimal portfolio *P* will lie on the line *CSE*, we have:

$$r_P = \alpha r_S + (1 - \alpha) r_c \tag{64}$$

where $r_S = \Sigma_i z_i r_i$ is the return on the market portfolio, $z_i = x_i / \Sigma_i x_i$ is the fraction of the market portfolio held in asset i and $\alpha = \Sigma x_i$. Therefore, α is the proportion of the portfolio held in risky assets and $(1 - \alpha)$ is the proportion held in the riskless asset.

Taking the expected values of (63) and (64) for the optimal amounts of the assets, the expected mean μ_P of the portfolio is given by:

$$\mu_P = \Sigma_i x_i \mu_i + (1 - \Sigma_i x_i) r_c$$

$$= \alpha \mu_S + (1 - \alpha) r_c \tag{65}$$

Further, from (65), noting that the standard deviation of r_c is zero, the standard deviation σ_P of the optimal portfolio is:

$$\sigma_P = \alpha \sigma_S \tag{66}$$

$$= \alpha [\Sigma_i \Sigma_j x_i x_j \sigma_{ij})]^{1/2} \tag{67}$$

We now examine the change in μ_P as the investor increases the amount x_i invested in the individual asset i by decreasing by a corresponding amount of his investment in the riskless asset. To derive this, differentiate the individual's utility function $U(\mu, \sigma)$ at the optimal point (μ_P, σ_P), so that:

$$dU = \frac{\partial U}{\partial \mu_P} \frac{\partial \mu_P}{\partial x_i} + \frac{\partial U}{\partial \sigma_P} \frac{\partial \sigma_P}{\partial x_i} \tag{68}$$

Since the change in utility at the optimal (μ_P, σ_P) point must be zero, setting $dU = 0$, we have:

$$\frac{\partial U}{\partial \mu_P} \frac{\partial \mu_P}{\partial x_i} + \frac{\partial U}{\partial \sigma_P} \frac{\partial \sigma_P}{\partial x_i} = 0 \tag{69}$$

so that:

$$\frac{\partial \mu_P}{\partial x_i} = \left[-\frac{\partial U}{\partial \sigma_P} \Big/ \frac{\partial U}{\partial \mu_P} \right] \frac{\partial \sigma_P}{\partial x_i} \tag{70}$$

where [·] is the slope of the individual's indifference curve, which, as shown in Figure 21.2, equals the slope λ of the efficient opportunity locus *CSE*. Therefore,

$$\frac{\partial \mu_P}{\partial x_i} = \lambda \frac{\partial \sigma_P}{\partial x_i} \tag{71}$$

From (65),

$$\frac{\partial \mu_P}{\partial x_i} = \mu_i - r_c \tag{72}$$

Substituting (71) in (72),

$$\mu_i = r_c + \lambda \frac{\partial \sigma_P}{\partial x_i} \tag{73}$$

so that the expected return on the ith asset exceeds the risk-free return by an amount related to the increase in the risk on the optimal portfolio as the investment in the ith asset marginally increases. Further, the definition of σ_P implies that, for the risky assets i and j in the market portfolio,

$$\frac{\partial \sigma_P}{\partial x_i} = \frac{\sum_j \sigma_{ij} x_j}{\sigma_P} = \frac{\text{cov}\left(r_i, \sum_j r_j x_j\right)}{\sigma_P} \tag{74}$$

Since $\sum_j r_j x_j = \alpha r_S$, where j refers only to the risky assets in the portfolio, (74) implies that:

$$\frac{\partial \sigma_P}{\partial x_i} = \frac{\alpha \, \text{cov}\left(r_i, r_s\right)}{\alpha \sigma_s} = \frac{\sigma_{is}}{\sigma_s} \tag{75}$$

so that (73) can be restated as:

$$\mu_i = r_c + \lambda \sigma_{iS}/\sigma_S \tag{76}$$

Therefore, the equilibrium expected return on the ith asset equals the risk-free return plus a risk premium equal to the market risk premium λ times the risk of the ith asset as measured by σ_{iS}/σ_S.[17] Since $\lambda = (\mu_S - r_c)/\sigma_S$, we can rewrite (76) in a more familiar form as:

$$\mu_i = r_c + (\mu_S - r_c)\beta_i \tag{77}$$

$$= r_c + \gamma_S \beta_i \tag{78}$$

where:

$$\gamma_S = \mu_S - r_c$$

$$\beta_i = \frac{\sigma_{iS}}{\sigma_{SS}} \tag{79}$$

The interpretation in the text of this chapter for the beta of asset i was based on this result. Equation (77) is often taken to represent the CAPM.

An implication of (78) is that the expected return on the ith asset is determined by measurable market parameters such as the risk-free rate, the expected return on the market portfolio and the variances and covariances of returns. It is independent of the preferences of the investors, the distribution of wealth among them, and their degrees of risk aversion.[18] The CAPM is, therefore, testable using market data.

Estimation

The estimating equation implied by (78) is:

$$\bar{r}_i = a_0 + a_1 b_i + e_i \tag{80}$$

In cross-section analyses of the returns to assets, $\bar{r}_i$ is the average return on asset i over the given period, and b_i is the estimate of β_i obtained, using time-series data, by regressing the ith asset's rate of return on a market index acting as a proxy for the market portfolio. e_i is the random error, with $Ee_S = 0$, though Ee_i need not be zero for individual assets during the period in question. $\text{Cov}(r_S, e_i) = 0$.[19] Estimates of (80) yield $\hat{a}_0$ and $\hat{a}_1$, which are compared with r_c and $(\bar{r}_S - r_c)$ respectively for the given period. In these comparisons, r_c is usually taken to be the yield on a government bond with maturity equal to the period under consideration and $\bar{r}_S$ is the average rate of return on the market index over the same period.

SUMMARY OF CRITICAL CONCLUSIONS

- While the yield curve can have any shape, its shape at zero current and expected inflation rates is usually upward sloping.
- Long rates are geometric averages of the current and forward short rates.
- The main theory of the yield curve is the expectations theory. It assumes that the bond markets are efficient and have zero transactions costs.
- Liquidity preference in the context of the term structure of interest rates asserts that bonds of longer maturities incorporate a premium over those of shorter maturities to compensate for their lesser liquidity.
- The segmented and preferred habitat hypotheses assume that there exist significant preferences among the borrowers and lenders for specific maturities, rather than indifference or a fairly weak preference for shorter over longer maturities.
- The expectations hypothesis and rational expectations imply, under certain other assumptions, the random walk hypothesis for changes in the long rates of interest.
- Under certain assumptions, the yield curve can be used to estimate the expected rates of inflation over future periods.
- The yield on financial assets differs not only because of differences in their term to maturity but also because of differences in their riskiness. The capital asset pricing model offers the most popular theory for capturing the latter.

review and discussion questions

1 The yield curve shows the relationship between the yields of high-grade securities that differ only in the term to maturity. Sometimes the curve rises, sometimes it falls and sometimes it is flat. Present the main reasons for these different shapes.

2 On the basis of recent empirical studies, the expectations hypothesis with efficient markets and rational expectations does not seem to explain the term structure of interest rates. Discuss.

3 Can the central bank change the shape of the yield curve through changes in (a) the term structure of government bonds and (b) variations over time in monetary aggregates? Discuss.

4 For your country, what is the current shape of the yield curve? Explain this shape.

5 Assuming that the expectations theory of the yield curve is correct, derive from your data on the yield curve the expected future spot rates for the next twelve months. If your economy has forward markets for this period, compare the forward short rates with your derived expected future spot rates, and explain the reasons for any differences.

6 Use your data on the yield curve to derive the expected rates of inflation monthly over the next twelve months and annually over the next five years. What assumptions were needed for this derivation? If the actual inflation rates turn out to differ from your computed ones, how would you explain the differences?

7 How does the inability to establish the yield curve on the real rate of interest affect the derivation of the future expected rates of inflation from the nominal interest rates? Does the existence of a term structure of liquidity premiums pose corresponding problems?

8 For the derivation of the expected future inflation rates from the yield curve, is it really valid to assume (a) a constant real rate of interest, (b) a constant liquidity premium per period? Cite some studies that have done so and report on their findings.

   What are the determinants of the real rate of interest and of the liquidity premium? Does the expected stance of monetary or fiscal policy affect these variables?

9 'The theory of portfolio selection has little relevance for explaining the demand for money. Its real relevance is to the theory of bond and equity returns and prices.' Discuss. Show how it can be used to explain these returns and prices.

10 For the two-period bonds, show that the expectations hypothesis approximately implies that:

$$R_2 = \tfrac{1}{2}r_1 + \tfrac{1}{2}r_1 r_2^e$$

where R and r are the logs of the relevant gross rates.

It is sometimes claimed that the long rates overreact to current short rates because financial markets are 'myopic'. Define what you mean by myopia in this context. How would you modify the above equation to allow for such myopia? How would you test the resulting hypothesis?

NOTES

1 An early study by Meiselman in 1962 had supported the expectations theory. He also found that there was not sufficient justification for the assumption of a liquidity premium.

2 The results of Echols and Elliot (1976) should be compared with those in Pesando (1978) discussed later in this chapter.

3 Some researchers have called (20) the '*fundamental equation*' of the term structure and bond pricing.

4 These variables were included in the Echols and Elliot (1976) study.

5 These variables are part of the liquidity preference approach and were included in the Feldstein and Eckstein (1970) study discussed in the preceding chapter.

6 This risk will be measured, as in Chapter 5 on the speculative demand for money, by the standard deviation of the distribution of the return on the asset.

7 Other riskless assets would offer a lower return because of their better characteristics.

8 The CAPM model assumes that the individual is able to borrow or lend at this rate.

9 σ_{iS} equals $\rho_{iS}\sigma_i\sigma_S$, where ρ_{iS} is the correlation between the returns to assets i and S, and σ is the standard deviation.

10 $\beta_i = 0$ means that the asset's return is uncorrelated with the market return; $\beta_i > 0$ means that the asset's return will move in the same direction as the market one and $\beta_i < 0$ means that the asset's return will move in the opposite direction.

11 The risk associated with holding asset i in the portfolio S is $\beta_i^2\sigma_S^2$ and is said to represent the *systematic risk* of holding the ith asset in the portfolio. $\beta_i\gamma_S$ is the market-determined expected return on the ith asset to compensate for this systematic risk.

12 e is assumed to be a random term with zero expected value for all assets – that is, $Ee_S = 0$. However, the dispersion of e is such that Ee_i can be non-zero for the ith asset, and differ among assets. The risk arising from this term is σ_e^2, which is called the *unsystematic or idiosyncratic risk* of the ith asset's return. e_i compensates for this risk.

13 This would equal the highest risk-free rate of return on the riskless assets with maturity equal to the duration of the period of analysis.

14 Jagannathan and McGrattan themselves find that while the CAPM did fairly well – that is, showed the positive linear relationship between the return and beta – over a very long period, it did not do well over short periods.

15 This implies that unless one has special or inside information on the individual stocks, for the risky assets, one should just hold the optimal amount of the asset representing the market index or hold stocks diversified to represent the market composition.

16 That is, each investor will hold the risky assets in the same proportions as other investors, but the proportions of the riskless asset and the market portfolio S composed of the risky ones

will vary among investors. This proportion will depend on each investor's expected utility function, and, hence, on his degree of risk aversion.

17 These results show that, even for an individual, the appropriate measure of risk from holding an asset is not the standard deviation or variance of the asset or in relation to his portfolio, but rather the covariance of the asset's return to the market portfolio. Appropriate diversification will eliminate most of the impact of the asset's own variance on the variance of the portfolio return but cannot eliminate the impact of the asset's covariance with the other assets in the portfolio.

18 However, as pointed out earlier, the individual's preferences do influence the allocation of his portfolio between the riskless asset and the market portfolio.

19 Hence, from (80), $\sigma_i^2 = b_i^2 \, \sigma_S^2 + \sigma_e^2$, so that the total risk on asset i can be partitioned into the systematic risk $(b_i^2 \sigma_S^2)$ and the unsystematic risk σ_e^2.

REFERENCES

Culbertson, J. M. 'The Term Structure of Interest Rates'. *Quarterly Journal of Economics*, 71, November 1957, pp. 485–517.

Cuthbertson, Keith. *The Supply and Demand for Money*. Oxford: Basil Blackwell, 1985.

Echols, Michael E., and Jan Walter Elliot. 'Rational Expectations in a Disequilibrium Model of the Term Structure'. *American Economic Review*, 66, March 1976, pp. 28–44.

Fisher, Irving. *The Theory of Interest*, New York: Macmillan, 1930.

Friedman, Benjamin M. 'Financial Flow Variables and the Short-Run Determination of Long-Term Interest Rates'. *Journal of Political Economy*, 85, August 1977, pp. 661–90.

Havrilesky, T. M., and J. T. Boorman, eds. *Current Issues in Monetary Theory and Policy*. Arlington Heights, IL: AHM Publishing, 1980, Part VII.

Hicks, John Richard. *Value and Capital*. Oxford University Press, 1946.

Jagannathan, Ravi, and Ellen R. McGrattan. 'The CAPM Debate'. *Federal Reserve Bank of Minneapolis Quarterly Review*, Fall 1995, pp. 2–17.

Jones, David S., and V. Vance Roley. 'Rational Expectations and the Expectations Model of the Term Structure: A Test Using Weekly Data'. *Journal of Monetary Economics*, 12, September 1983, pp. 453–65.

Keynes, John Maynard. *A Treatise on Money*. London: Macmillan, 1931.

Lutz, F. 'The Structure of Interest Rates'. In American Economic Association, *Readings in the Theory of Income Distribution*. New York: Irwin, 1951.

Mankiw, N. Gregory and Jeffrey A. Miron. 'The Changing Behaviour of the Term Structure of Interest Rates'. *Quarterly Journal of Economics*, 60, May 1986, pp. 211–28.

Meiselman, David. *The Term Structure of Interest Rates*. Englewood Cliffs, NJ: Prentice-Hall, 1962.

Mishkin, Frederic S. 'What Does the Term Structure Tell Us About Future Inflation?' *Quarterly Journal of Economics*, 105, August 1990, pp. 815–28.

Modigliani, F. and R. Sutch. 'Innovations in Interest Rate Policy'. *American Economic Review Papers and Proceedings*, 56, May 1966, pp. 178–97.

——, and ——. 'Debt Management and the Term Structure of Interest Rates: An Empirical Analysis of Recent Experience'. *Journal of Political Economy*, 75, August 1967, pp. 568–89.

Pesando, James E. 'On the Efficiency of the Bond Market: Some Canadian Evidence'. *Journal of Political Economy*, 86, December 1978, pp. 1057–76.

Sargent, Thomas J. 'Commodity Price Expectations and the Interest Rate'. *Quarterly Journal of Economics*, 83, February 1969, pp. 127–40.

——. *Macroeconomic Theory*. London: Academic Press, 1979, pp. 209–13; 291–92.

Sharpe, William F. 'Capital Asset Prices: A Theory of Market Equilibrium Under Conditions of Risk'. *Journal of Finance*, 19, September 1964, pp. 425–42.

part eight

OVERLAPPING GENERATIONS MODELS OF MONEY

chapter twenty-two

THE OVERLAPPING GENERATIONS MODEL OF FIAT MONEY

The OLG models of money have been proposed by some economists as an alternative to the money in the utility function (MIUF) and money in the production function (MIPF) models presented so far in this book. However, other economists do not consider the OLG models of money in their standard form to be valid or useful for modelling the actual role of money in the economy. Most textbooks on monetary economics skip their presentation.

This is the first of three chapters using the OLG framework to model the role of money in the economy. This chapter and the next one present the pure versions of the OLG models, while the third chapter attempts to integrate the concepts of MIUF and MIPF into the OLG format.

The three chapters on the OLG modelling of money are mainly meant for more advanced courses in monetary economics.

---

key concepts introduced in this chapter

- Fiat money
- Overlapping generations
- Intrinsically useless money
- Inconvertible fiat money
- Market fundamentals
- Sunspots
- Bubbles
- Bootstrap paths
- An individual's intertemporal budget constraint versus the economy's consumption frontier

---

The overlapping generations (OLG) model was introduced by Samuelson (1958),[1] with major extensions by Wallace (1980, 1981) and Sargent (1987), among others, for the analysis of money in the economy. The standard version of the OLG model assumes that the individuals in the economy live for two periods only – or for two lifestages 'young' and 'old', with each lifestage lasting one period – and that in each period the economy has two generations of individuals. One of these is the old generation of individuals who were born in the preceding period and the other is the young generation born at the beginning of the current period. The old of one generation and the young of the next one overlap in every period, so that the name given to the models using this framework is the overlapping generations models.

Fiat money: intrinsically useless and inconvertible

One of the applications of the OLG model is to an economy with fiat money. This literature attributes to fiat money two basic characteristics: (a) it is *intrinsically useless* – that is, it cannot be directly used in production or consumption[2] – and (b) it is *inconvertible*[3] – that is, the *issuer* does not give a commitment to redeem it into commodities. Further, it is assumed that fiat money is costless to produce, to store and to transfer, and does not pay interest to the holder. The common example of fiat money is bank notes issued by the central bank. In most modern economies, such notes do not carry a commitment by the central bank to redeem them into gold coins or gold bullion or into any other commodity.

One of the necessary conditions for fiat money to have a positive value is that its supply and that of its close substitutes be limited and strictly regulated. OLG models, therefore, assume that the supply of fiat money is limited, which requires, in turn, that it cannot be easily counterfeited and the counterfeit notes put into circulation to any significant extent,[4] and that the private sector cannot create close substitutes or near-monies.[5]

A positive value for fiat money

Given the intrinsic uselessness and inconvertibility of fiat money, it is a characteristic of all monetary models – whether OLG, MIUF or others – that fiat money will have value in exchange only if others are willing to accept it in exchange for commodities. Given the intergenerational emphasis of the OLG models, the OLG models narrow this condition to imply that fiat money will have value in exchange in any *given* period only if it is expected that the individuals in the *following* period will be willing to accept the fiat money in exchange for commodities. This requires that if the economy is currently to have a positive value of money, it must be expected to continue indefinitely into the future, so that the assumed model must not have a finite horizon.[6]

Further, while all monetary models imply that the expectations about the future value of the money are one of the determinants of its current value, the OLG models imply the stronger condition that if the next period has a zero value for money, its current value must also be zero. By extension, if fiat money is expected to be valueless in any period T in the future, it will also have a zero value in the current period and in all periods up to T. As against this conclusion of the OLG models, MIUF models do not require an infinite horizon, nor do they imply that money cannot have a positive value, determined by its usefulness in current exchanges, even if its value in some future period is zero.

Fiat money as the medium for holding savings

In OLG models, a necessary condition for fiat money to have a positive value in the current period is that there currently exist individuals who want to use it to carry purchasing power from the present to the future. This requires that they want to consume more in the future (when they are old) than their future receipts of commodities and that, to do this, they have saving – i.e., an excess of commodities over their consumption – in the young lifestage, and also that money is an attractive vehicle for saving. In order to ensure the former, the OLG models assume that the receipt of commodities in the first (or young) lifestage exceeds their optimal consumption, so that the individuals must have positive saving in the first lifestage to carry over for consumption in the second (or old) lifestage.

Saving could be done in the form of commodities. If the carryover of commodities were costless or consumption in the future could be financed at lower cost through some contrivance associated with commodities than with the use of fiat money, fiat money will not be used and again will not have positive value.[7] Therefore, the usual OLG models assume that fiat money does not have storage or transfer costs while commodities do so. In the limiting case, commodities are assumed to be perishable.

The essential assumptions and implications of the OLG models with fiat money

These are:

(i)   the fiat money must be preferable to commodities – and any other assets – as the medium for *saving*;
(ii) there is net saving in the first lifestage; and
(iii) future periods will not renounce the use of fiat money or pursue policies such that fiat money will become valueless.

Given these assumptions, the OLG models of fiat money explore the value of money for various growth rates of money versus commodities, growth of population, open market operations, etc.

As pointed out already, the OLG models generate a zero value of money in the current period if the expected value of money is expected to be zero in some future period. This is a characteristic of *bootstrap* or *bubble* paths which are paths along which the values of variables depend upon arbitrarily expected values in the future and change if the latter change. The numerous equilibria of this kind are among the *tenuous* kind. However, the usual focus of OLG models is not on such bootstrap or bubble paths. Rather, their implications are normally analysed for the stationary states of the economy, with expectations assumed to be identical with the stationary values or with those implied by the rational expectations hypothesis (REH).

Among the attractive features claimed for the OLG models are that, along certain paths, they establish a positive value for an intrinsically worthless fiat money which is not required by law to be convertible into commodities, and that time and the distinctiveness of the earning pattern over a lifetime are incorporated in an 'essential' manner.[8] Further, they allow for economic agents who are identical at birth – thus permitting the study of stationary states – while allowing for a degree of heterogeneity among the economic agents alive at any time in the economy, and also allow the economy to continue indefinitely into the future.

Sections 22.1 to 22.4 present the basic OLG model with money. Sections 22.5 and 22.6 show the inefficiency of monetary expansion in such models, even when such expansion is needed to ensure a stable price level. Sections 22.7 and 22.8 discuss money demand when there is a positive rate of time preference and when there are several fiat monies.

22.1 THE BASIC OLG MODEL

In the standard version of the OLG model, individuals live for two periods – that is, go through two lifestages – only. They are labelled as 'young' in their first lifestage and as 'old' in their second lifestage. The superscripts y and o will be used to indicate the individual's respective lifestages.

For the economy, the periods are $t + i$, $i = 0, 1, 2, \ldots$ The current period t is the initial period of the analysis and its old generation is called the 'initial old', whose members were born in period $t - 1$. Generations born in periods $0, 1, 2, \ldots$, will be called the 'future generations' and its members will be referred to merely as 'individuals'. The OLG model starts by endowing the initial old with the initial stock of money. Further, for the basic OLG model of this chapter, any increase in the money stock in any given period will be assumed to be gratuitously given as a lump-sum transfer to the old in that period. The next chapter examines the case where the seigniorage from money creation is used to buy up commodities that are then destroyed, resulting in a net decrease in the commodities left for consumption in the economy.

The number of individuals born in period t is N_t. In the early parts of the analysis of this chapter, this number is assumed to be constant at N over time. Under this assumption, in each period t, the population of $2N$ individuals consists of N young individuals and N old individuals.

Each individual is assumed to be given a commodity endowment of w^y in the young lifestage and w^o in the old lifestage. w^y and w^o are in units of the single consumption good, assumed in the basic model to be non-storable (perishable).[9] Some of the versions of the OLG models assume that w^o is zero, but such an assumption is not essential to the OLG framework. However, if fiat money is to have value, it is essential to assume that the optimal level of consumption in old age will exceed w^o.[10] This is usually guaranteed by an assumption that consumption will be the same in each lifestage and that $w^o < w^y$, so that the individual must save while young to provide for extra consumption in the second period.[11] This assumption will be implicit throughout this chapter.

22.1.1 Microeconomic behaviour: the individual's saving and the demand for money

The intertemporal budget constraint of the young

In the young lifestage, the representative individual can either consume c^y or hold money m out of his endowments of commodities. His budget constraint for the first lifestage is:

$$p_t c_t^y + m_t^y = p_t w_t^y \quad c_t^y < w_t^y \tag{1}[12]$$

At the beginning of period $t + 1$, the individual has the carryover money balances of m_t (which do not pay interest) and receives the endowment of commodities w_{t+1}^o, so that his old lifestage constraint is:

$$p_{t+1} c_{t+1}^o = p_{t+1} w_{t+1}^o + m_t^o \tag{2}[13]$$

where the money balances purchased when young, m_t^y, become the inheritance of the old as m_t^o, so that $m_t^y = m_t^o = m_t$. Note that there is no explicit interest rate in this model since the commodity is perishable and there are no interest-paying assets in the model. The only asset is money, which does not pay interest, so that the interest rate does not enter (2). Note also that the individuals are assumed to have perfect foresight over the future values of the variables. From (2),

$$m_t = p_{t+1} c_{t+1}^o - p_{t+1} w_{t+1}^o \tag{2'}$$

Substituting (2') in (1) gives the individual's lifetime budget constraint as:

$$p_t c_t^y + p_{t+1} c_{t+1}^o = p_t w_t^y + p_{t+1} w_{t+1}^o \tag{3}$$

Define the individual's real lifetime wealth W_t as:

$$W_t = w_t^y + (p_{t+1}/p_t) w_{t+1}^o$$

The symbols used so far and their definitions are:

c_t^y	consumption of the young in period t
c_t^o	consumption of the old in period t
p_t	price of goods in period t
w_t^y	exogenous income of the young in period t
w_t^o	exogenous income of the old in period t
W_t	lifetime wealth in period t
N_t	number of persons born in period t
$N_{t-1} + N_t$	population in period t
m_t	*per capita* demand for *nominal* balances by the young in t
m_t^o	initial money endowment of each old individual in period t
M_t	total amount of fiat money in period t $(= N_t^o m_t^o)$

Note that this chapter and Chapters 23 and 24 define m as nominal, not real, per capita balances, contrary to our usage in the rest of the book.

Since $c_t^y < w_t^y$ by assumption, the young want to transfer commodities to themselves in the future but the non-storable goods assumption of the model prevents them doing so directly – as if it were, through barter (via storage) between themselves when young and when old. Further, the auctioneer or other costless clearing mechanisms of the general Walrasian equilibrium models are excluded from the OLG models. So are state-enforced compulsory exchanges between generations. The OLG models only allow the trade of commodities over generations through the intermediation of money.

The general run of monetary models – and our analyses in Chapters 1 to 20 – allow the use of bonds which yield a higher positive return than fiat money and act as the intermediary instrument for exchanges of commodities over generations. However, the basic OLG model assumes that there are no other assets such as bonds that can act as a store of value with a rate of return higher than that on fiat money. Consequently, there is no private (or public) borrowing or lending in the basic model[14] and therefore no bonds and no explicit interest rate. The next chapter will present an OLG model with money and bonds.

Utility maximization by the young

The individual born in period t has an intertemporal utility function:

$$U(c_t^y, c_{t+1}^o)$$

where $U(\cdot)$ is assumed to be an ordinal neoclassical utility function with continuous first- and second-order partial derivatives. The young maximize this utility function subject to the budget constraint (3). That is, the young's optimization problem is:

$$\text{Maximize} \quad U(c_t^y, c_{t+1}^o) \tag{4}$$

$$\text{subject to} \quad p_t c_t^y + p_{t+1} c_{t+1}^o = p_t w_t^y + p_{t+1} w_{t+1}^o \tag{3}$$

implying the optimal consumption amounts c_t^y, c_{t+1}^o as:

$$c_t^y = c_t^y(p_{t+1}/p_t, w_t^y, w_{t+1}^o) \tag{5}$$

$$c_{t+1}^o = c_{t+1}^o(p_{t+1}/p_t, w_t^y, w_{t+1}^o) \tag{6}$$

By assumption,

$$c_t^y < w_t^y$$

$$c_{t+1}^o > w_{t+1}^o$$

The net dissaving in the old lifestage is accomplished by spending the money balances carried over from the young lifestage. Saving s_t^y in period t is:

$$s_t^y = w_t^y - c_t^y$$

$$= s_t^y(p_{t+1}/p_t, w_t^y, w_{t+1}^o) \tag{7}$$

and the demand for money, identical with that for nominal saving, is,

$$m_t^y = p_t s_t^y = p_t s_t^y(p_{t+1}/p_t, w_t^y, w_{t+1}^o) \tag{8}$$

In period t, the young individual receives more of the consumption good than he wants to consume but cannot store the excess since the consumption good is perishable. He sells it to the initial old for fiat money, provided that he expects to be able to exchange his holdings of fiat money for the consumption good in period $t + 1$.

Utility maximization by the initial old

From the perspective of the initial old in the initial period t, they receive some of the consumption good. Further, while they received fiat money, its utility in consumption is zero so that they are willing to exchange it for some amount of the consumption good. Formally, the utility function and budget constraint respectively of the initial old are:

$$U_t^o = U(c_t^o) \tag{9'}$$

$$p_t c_t^o = p_t w_t^o + m_t^o \tag{9''}$$

Each member of the initial old maximizes his utility by maximizing c_t^o which implies that he will try to trade m_t^o for the maximum amount that he can get of the consumption good.

22.1.2 Macroeconomic analysis: the price level and the value of money

There are only two goods, the commodity and money, in this model, so that the macroeconomic analysis has to take account of only the markets for money and the commodity. Further, by Walras' law, equilibrium in one of these markets ensures equilibrium in the other one. We choose to focus on the money market for further analysis.

The market for money and price-level determination

For the economy in period t, the aggregate demand for nominal balances M_t^d equals the value of the consumption good the young want to trade and is given by:

$$M_t^d = N_t[p_t(w_t^y - c_t^y)] \tag{10}$$

The amount of money supply M_t in the economy is given by the money balances held by the old (born in $t - 1$ with their number as N_{t-1}) and which they want to trade. It equals:

$$M_t = N_{t-1}[m_t^o] \tag{11}$$

so that money market clearance, with money demand equal to money supply, implies that,

$$N_t[p_t(w_t^y - c_t^y)] = N_{t-1}[m_t^o] \tag{12}$$

Hence:

$$p_t = M_t/[N_t(w_t^y - c_t^y)]$$

From (5), c_t^y on the right side of (12) depends on p_{t+1}/p_t, so that:

$$p_t = M_t/[N_t(w_t^y - c_t^y(p_{t+1}/p_t, w_t^y, w_{t+1}^o))] \tag{13}$$

In (13), the current price level depends on the intertemporal price ratio p_{t+1}/p_t. It varies proportionately with the money supply, which is a quantity theory result, for a given value of this ratio.

From (13), the value v_t per unit of money, which is equal to $1/p_t$, is given by:

$$\begin{aligned} v_t &= [(w_t^y - c_t^y)] \, N_t/(N_{t-1} \, m_t^o) \\ &= [(w_t^y - c_t^y)N_t]/M_t \end{aligned} \tag{14}$$

so that the value of money is positive and changes inversely with the money supply. It also varies proportionately with aggregate saving $[(w_t^y - c_t^y)N_t]$.

Note that since p_t and v_t are functions of c_t^y, which is specified by (5), they are also functions of the future expected price level p_{t+1}. Since the latter is a function of p_{t+2}, and so on, p_t and v_t are functions of the expected prices of the consumption good in future periods. The implications of this for price bubbles and the indeterminacy of prices will be analysed later.

The commodity market

Note that since there are only two goods – the commodity and money – in this model, money market clearance also implies commodity market clearance by Walras' law. Hence, the price level given by (13) also clears the commodity market, so that the derivations of the demand and supply functions in the commodity market are not needed.

22.1.3 The stationary state

If the model is stationary (with stationary population and endowments of commodities[15] – but with the endowment of money occurring only to the initial old) for all finite periods, all generations would want to trade in the above manner and fiat money will continue to have a positive value, as given by (14). In dealing with the stationary state, the subscript t on the variables can be omitted so that from (13) the trade between money and the commodity in each period is represented for the stationary state by:

$$N[p(w^y - c^y)] = N[m] = M \tag{15}$$

so that the stationary state price level is:

$$p = M/[N(w^y - c^y)] \tag{16}$$

Equation (16) yields a stationary state positive value v for money as:

$$v = 1/p = [N(w^y - c^y)]/M \qquad (17)$$

The rate of return on money balances

The gross rate of return on money,[16] r_t, is given by:

$$r_t = v_{t+1}/v_t = p_t/p_{t+1} \qquad (18)$$

so that in the stationary state,

$$r_t = r = 1$$

Hence, the net rate of return – that is, excluding the return of the principal amount lent – on real balances will be zero.

22.1.4 The indeterminacy of the price level and of the value of fiat money

The role of expectations

In equation (14), v_t is only one of the possible values of money in period t. From equations (14) and (5), this value depends upon the expected future value of money. That is, the value of money in the current period depends critically on the belief of the young that if they accept money in exchange for commodities in period t at the price p_t, they can exchange their money holdings for commodities when old in period $t + 1$ at p_{t+1}^e. Suppose the young of period $t + i$, for any i, develop the contrary belief[17] that they cannot exchange their money holdings for commodities in period $t + i + 1$ and that these holdings will become worthless. Hence, utility maximization implies that they will want to consume all of their $t + i$ period endowments in $t + i$ and will not be willing to accept money for commodities at any price in period $t + i$, implying that the fiat money will have a zero value in period $t + i$, without any exchanges in period $t + i$ between the young and the old through the intermediation of fiat money. By extension backwards, these results will also hold for all periods up to period $t + i$. This solution of the model without any exchanges between generations is known as the autarchic solution.

Now assume that the young in period $t + i$ expect a price p'_{t+i+1}, different from the price p_{t+i+1} determined by an appropriate version of equation (13) . This will determine the price p'_{t+i} in period $t + i$, which in turn will determine that in $t + i - 1$, and so on. There are, therefore, an infinite number of equilibrium prices between the expected future price p_{t+i} and zero – with the corresponding equilibrium values of money at which fiat money will be traded for commodities.

The fundamental solutions for prices, bubbles and tenuous equilibria

Designate the paths of the price and the value of money generated by the fundamentals of the system – i.e., preferences, endowments and money supply – as brought together by equation (13), as being the fundamental ones. The stationary state analysis belongs to this category.

There are two stationary solutions for the OLG model of fiat money. In one of these, the value of money is zero, money is not used and the individual does not trade with others. This is the no-trade or autarchic solution. The other stationary solution has a positive value of money; money is used and trade in commodities against money does take place. The focus of the OLG models of money is clearly on the latter.

Since the current price depends on the future prices, and these can change randomly, the deviation thus produced of prices from the fundamental ones is said to be a 'bubble' on the fundamental price path. This dependence of the current price on future prices in this argument – as incorporated in equations (13) and (5) – is known as 'bootstrapping': current prices are functions of the expected future prices; in the limit, if the latter were zero, the former would also be zero. This feature of the OLG models generates an infinite number of bootstrap paths – in which the path of the value of money depends on an arbitrarily specified expected value of money at a future date – with bubbles on the price level.

Given the bootstrap nature of the paths of the value of money in OLG models, none of these paths would be stable with respect to anticipated transitory shocks to the expected future value of money. This property merely reflects the essential nature of fiat money in OLG models that it is intrinsically useless and the amount an individual will pay for it in the current period depends critically upon the value that he expects to receive for it in the future. The indeterminacy and instability of monetary equilibria in OLG models lead to the monetary equilibria in these models being designated as *tenuous*.

In the non-stationary states, since the value of money need not necessarily be constant, the gross rate of return on it also need not be constant over time. However, any such state is unlikely to be stable and also would have a bootstrap path with bubbles on the price level. The studies on the OLG models do not usually investigate non-stationary states, even though the common observation in the real-world economies is that of non-stationary states with prices, the value of money and the rate of return on money varying constantly.

22.1.5   The competitive issue of money

Equation (13) implies that the equilibrium value of fiat money varies inversely with its quantity, so that this value will be positive only if the money supply is finite. Since such money – for example, bank notes – is costless to produce, the competitive issue of fiat money would drive this value to zero. Hence, for a positive valued equilibrium, OLG models rule out the competitive issue of fiat money by governments, as well as of privately issued perfect substitutes to it.

22.2   THE BASIC OLG MODEL WITH A GROWING POPULATION

To accommodate a growing population in the above OLG model, assume that:

$$N_{t+1}/N_t = n \tag{19}$$

where N_t is the number of persons born in t and n is the gross rate of increase in births. Therefore, the gross growth rate of population in this economy is given by:

$$[N_{t+2} + N_{t+1}]/[N_{t+1} + N_t] = [(n^2 + n)N_t]/[(n + 1)N_t] = n$$

so that the gross growth rate of the population is also n. Now assume that each young individual in this economy continues to receive at birth an *ex gratia* amount w^y of commodities,[18] so that the total amount received increases proportionally with the population. From (13), the price level in this economy for the given money supply equal to M_t is:

$$p_t = M_t/[N_t(w_t^y - c_t^y)] \tag{20}$$

so that, with the constant money supply ($m_t^o N_t$) in the economy, the price level will evolve as:

$$p_{t+1}/p_t = N_t/N_{t+1} = 1/n \tag{21}$$

Hence the price of commodities will fall over time.

The rate of return on nominal balances when population is increasing

Correspondingly, the gross rate of increase of the value of money will be:

$$v_{t+1}/v_t = N_{t+1}/N_t = n \tag{22}$$

so that the gross rate of return r on nominal balances is given by:

$$r = n$$

Hence, nominal balances will have a positive gross rate of return equal to n and a net rate $(n - 1)$, determined by the growth rate of the population. In other words, in the current context of the endowment economy without production, the rate of return or 'interest' – on the only asset, money, in the model – is determined by the biological growth rate.[19]

22.3 WELFARE IN THE BASIC OLG MODEL

Welfare of the initial old

There are two distinctive sets of individuals (the initial old and the young) in the OLG model, so that we have to examine the welfare of each one. The initial old were allocated the newly created fiat money and did not at any time have to part with any commodities to get money balances, but received them *ex gratia*. Trade with the contrivance of fiat money enables them to exchange it for commodities from the young. Therefore, there is a net benefit from trade with fiat money to the initial old.

Welfare of the young

Each young individual – including those born in period t and after t – also benefits from the trade with fiat money: it increases the overall utility that he can attain by being able to arrange a preferred consumption rather than having to consume the commodities according to the no-trade autarchic pattern. We prove this for the *stationary equilibrium* with a growing population, a given money stock and the price ratio given by the market and derived in equation (21).

The economy's constraint for each period is that the aggregate amount of the commodities consumed in the period cannot exceed the aggregate stock of commodities. That is, in period t,

$$N_t c_t^y + N_{t-1} c_t^o \leq N_t w_t^y + N_{t-1} w_t^o \tag{23}$$

Dividing through by N_t yields:

$$c_t^y + (1/n)c_t^o \leq w_t^y + (1/n)w_t^o \tag{24}$$

Dropping the subscript t for the stationary state and rewriting (24) as an equality to focus on the economy's feasible consumption frontier, we have:

$$c^y + (1/n)c^o = w^y + (1/n)w^o \tag{25}$$

Equation (25) is the per capita version of the economy's constraint and specifies the economy's exchange frontier or socially feasible consumption tradeoff between c^y and c^o in the stationary state. This is drawn as the line $W^y W^o$ in Figure 22.1. That is, with c^y on the horizontal axis, when c^o is zero, c^y will equal W^y, where

$$W^y = w^y + (1/n)w^o \tag{26}$$

Similarly, when $c^y = 0$, c^o will equal W^o, where:

$$W^o = n(w^y + (1/n)w^o) \tag{27}$$

From (25), the slope of the socially feasible tradeoff is:

$$\partial c^o / \partial c^y = -n \tag{28}$$

Now turning to the personal budget constraint of each individual in the young lifestage, this is:

$$c_t^y + (p_{t+1}/p_t)\, c_{t+1}^o = w_t^y + (p_{t+1}/p_t)w_{t+1}^o \tag{29}$$

From (21), the economy generates the price ratio $1/n$ for the case of stable money supply and population growth rate n. Hence, we have from (21) and (29),

$$c_t^y + (1/n)c_{t+1}^o = w_t^y + (1/n)w_{t+1}^o \tag{30}$$

In the stationary state, with $c_{t+1}^o = c_t^o$, and $w_{t+1}^o = w_t^o$, and dropping the time subscript, (30) becomes:

$$c^y + (1/n)c^o = w^y + (1/n)w^o \tag{31}$$

Equations (31) and (25) are identical, so that the young individual's budget constraint is identical with the economy's socially feasible tradeoff and is also given by the line $W^y W^o$ in Figure 22.1. The slope $(\partial c^o / \partial c^y)$ of this personal budget line $W^y W^o$ is $-n$, implying that since prices fall at the gross rate n, n units of the commodity can be purchased when old for one unit exchanged for money while young. Figure 22.1 also shows the individual's indifference curves I, I' and I'' as those specified by the individual's utility function (4). The young will maximize lifetime utility by being on the indifference curve which is tangent to the budget line $W^y W^o$. The optimal amounts consumed are given by point B and are c^{y*} when young and c^{o*} when old.

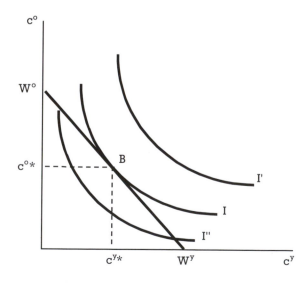

Figure 22.1

Since the budget line and the socially feasible tradeoff are identical, consumption at point B is feasible and maximizes the social welfare of the young generation. The level of utility at point B is higher than the level of utility obtained by the young from the autarchy (no trade) consumption of the original endowments w^y and w^o [20] and from the trade pattern associated with any other point on the socially feasible consumption tradeoff W^yW^o for the economy. Therefore, trade at the equilibrium value of money given by (22) maximizes the intertemporal utility function of the young of generation t – as well as those of each succeeding generation.[21] Hence, trade and consumption given by point B is Pareto optimal, with Pareto optimality being defined as the maximization of the intertemporal utility of all generations (except the initial old, which have a special utility function of their own).

22.4 THE BASIC OLG MODEL WITH A GROWING MONEY SUPPLY AND WITH A GROWING POPULATION

Assume that the money supply increases at the gross rate θ – with the net rate as $(\theta-1)$ – and population grows at the gross rate n. Therefore, the increase in the money supply is specified by:

$$M_t/M_{t-1} = \theta \tag{32}$$

The new money supply in each period is taken to be introduced into the economy by a free lump-sum gift of an identical amount to each of the old. Therefore, in each period, each old individual will have an amount which they had acquired in the preceding period through an exchange for commodities plus the lump-sum gift of newly created money. The latter equals:

$$[M_t - M_{t-1}]/N_t^o = (\theta - 1)M_{t-1}/N_{t-1}$$

$$= (\theta - 1)m_{t-1} \tag{33}$$

where the money balances per old person equal m_{t-1} and $(\theta - 1)$ is the net rate of growth of the money supply.

The determination of the commodity price

From (16), the equilibrium price levels in periods t and $t + 1$ respectively are:

$$p_t = M_t/[N_t(w_t^y - c_t^y)] \tag{34}$$

$$p_{t+1} = M_{t+1}/[N_{t+1}(w_{t+1}^y - c_{t+1}^y)] \tag{35}$$

In a stationary real equilibrium, $w_{t+1}^y = w_t^y$ and $c_{t+1}^y = c_t^y$, so that (35) can be rewritten as:

$$p_{t+1} = M_{t+1}/[N_{t+1}(w_t^y - c_t^y)] \tag{36}$$

Hence, from (32), (34) and (36), the gross rate of change of the price of the commodity is:

$$p_{t+1}/p_t = [M_{t+1}/M_t]/[N_{t+1}/N_t]$$

$$= \theta/n \tag{37}[22]$$

The rate of return on nominal balances in a growing economy with monetary expansion

From (37), the gross rate of change in the value of money is:

$$r_t = v_{t+1}/v_t = n/\theta \tag{38}$$

Hence, from (38), if $n = 1$ (zero growth in population) and $\theta > 1$ (monetary expansion), the population and the supply of the commodity, as well as saving, would be constant but the money stock will grow at the rate θ. The price level will increase at the gross rate θ, which is the same as the gross rate of increase θ in the money stock, implying that while the real value (per unit) of money will decline at the gross rate $1/\theta$, the real value of the aggregate money supply will remain unchanged over time.

If $\theta = n$, so that the money supply grows at the same gross rate as the population and the aggregate supply of commodities, the real value per unit of money will remain constant. In this case, the real value of the aggregate money supply will increase by θ.

If $\theta > n$, the rate of inflation will be $(\theta/n - 1)$ and the real value of the money supply will decline at the gross rate n/θ.

These conclusions are consistent with the quantity theory of money.

22.5 THE INEFFICIENCY OF MONETARY EXPANSION (MONEY TRANSFER CASE)

We have already examined in Figure 22.1 the efficiency of a constant money supply, with population growing at the rate n. The present section shows the inefficiency in the OLG models of money growth (or decline). Under the current assumptions, such money growth is achieved through a gratuitous lump-sum gift to members of the old generation, so that this case, as compared with others to be analysed later in Chapter 23, will be labelled as the *money transfer case*. The analysis in this section is again that of the stationary state.

The economy's availability of commodities is not affected by the creation of money, so that the socially feasible tradeoff (on a per capita basis) between c^o and c^y for the stationary state is not affected by the growth of the money supply and is as specified by equation (25). This was:

$$c^y + (1/n)c^o = w^y + (1/n)w^o$$

This tradeoff is shown by the line $W^y W^o$ in Figure 22.2, which is identical with the corresponding line in Figure 22.1.

Now assume that the money supply growth occurs over time at the gross rate θ, $\theta > 1$. The budget constraints of the individual of the first and second periods become:

$$p_t c_t^y + m_t = p_t w_t^y \tag{39}$$

$$p_{t+1} c_{t+1}^o = p_{t+1} w_{t+1}^o + m_t + [M_{t+1} - M_t]/N_{t+1}^o \tag{40}$$

where the second term, m_t, on the right-hand side is the amount of saving carried through in money balances by the individual, and the last term on the right-hand side is the receipt of a free lump-sum amount of newly created money in $(t + 1)$. Substituting (39) in (40) to eliminate m_t gives the individual's lifetime budget constraint as:

$$c_t^y + (p_{t+1}/p_t) c_{t+1}^o = w_t^y + (p_{t+1}/p_t) w_{t+1}^o + (1/p_t)[M_{t+1} - M_t]/N_{t+1}^o \tag{41}$$

In this economy, $M_{t+1}/M_t = \theta$, $N_{t+1}^o = N_t$, $M_t/N_t = m_t$ and, from (37), $p_{t+1}/p_t = \theta/n$. Hence, (41) can be restated as:

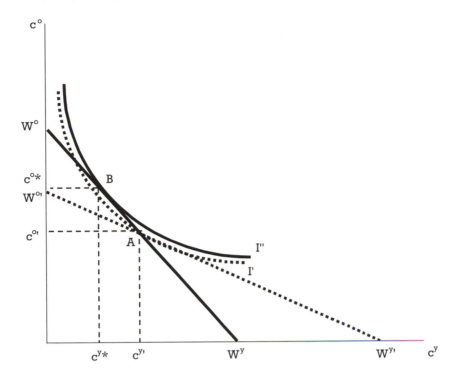

Figure 22.2

$$c_t^y + (\theta/n)\, c_{t+1}^o = w_t^y + (\theta/n)\, w_{t+1}^o + (1/p_t)[(\theta - 1)\,(M_t/N_t)]$$

$$= w_t^y + (\theta/n)\, w_{t+1}^o + (1/p_t)[(\theta - 1)m_t] \qquad (42)$$

In the stationary state, the intertemporal budget constraint (42) becomes:

$$c^y + (\theta/n)c^o = w^y + (\theta/n)w^o + (1/p)[(\theta - 1)m] \qquad (43)$$

Hence, the individual's intertemporal budget line in Figure 22.2 is $W^{y\prime}W^{o\prime}$, where:

$$W^{y\prime} = w^y + (\theta/n)w^o + (1/p)[(\theta - 1)m] \qquad (44)$$

$$W^{o\prime} = (n/\theta)[w^y + (\theta/n)w^o + (1/p)(\theta - 1)m] \qquad (45)$$

where $W^{y\prime}$ and $W^{o\prime}$ are the maximum amounts that can be consumed respectively in the young and old lifestages. Compared with the case when $\theta = 1$, the maximum possible consumption for $\theta > 1$ of the young increases because of the expected gratuitous receipt of money in old age while the maximum possible consumption in the old lifestage falls since the saving necessarily held in the form of money loses purchasing power through the rate of inflation caused by this receipt of newly created money.

From (43), the slope of the budget line $W^{y\prime}W^{o\prime}$ in Figure 22.2 is:

$$\partial c^o / \partial c^y = -n/\theta \qquad (46)$$

The economy's socially feasible tradeoff per capita (equation 25) defines the feasible combinations of c^o and c^y as $W^y W^o$ in Figure 22.2, with a slope of:

$$\partial c^o / \partial c^y = -n \qquad (47)$$

Hence, for $\theta > 1$, the socially feasible tradeoff is steeper than the budget line in Figure 22.2.

Let the intersection point between the budget line and the feasible set in Figure 22.2 be point A. The young's optimization requires choosing a point on the budget line at which it is tangential to his highest indifference curve. The young cannot on average choose a point on the segment $AW^{y\prime}$ (excluding point A itself) since all points on it are outside the feasible set and are therefore unattainable. The utility maximizing point can only be on the segment $AW^{o\prime}$ (inclusive of point A) which is feasible from the economy's standpoint.

Now consider the points on the segment $AW^{o\prime}$. All points on $AW^{o\prime}$ other than A itself are inferior to points on AW^o: more consumption can be obtained for both young and old along AW^o, so that choosing a point along $AW^{o\prime}$ involves a welfare loss.

If the utility maximizing point was at A itself, as shown by the tangency of the budget line to the indifference curve I' through A, the indifference curve would have a slope of $-n/\theta$. This slope is less than that of the socially feasible tradeoff W^yW^o so that I' must cut AW^o from below and there would be a higher indifference curve (say I'') which is tangential to W^yW^o (at B), and gives greater intertemporal utility to the young, whose indifference curves were drawn as I' and I''. B would be a point on the segment AW^o and yields a higher level of utility to the young. Comparing points A ($\theta > 1$) and B ($\theta = 1$), too much is consumed while young at A and too little is saved for old age.

Further, the initial old would also benefit from moving from any point on $AW^{o\prime}$ to AW^o, since they would receive a higher level of consumption.

Therefore, both the young and the old suffer a welfare loss because of the divergence between the budget line and the socially feasible tradeoff. We have shown this for $\theta > 1$ but it also occurs for $\theta < 1$. For the money deflation case with $\theta < 1$ (not shown diagrammatically), the budget line would be steeper than the socially feasible tradeoff, and by reasoning similar to that for $\theta > 1$, there will be a welfare loss compared with the stable money case. In this case, too little will be consumed while young and too much saved for old age, relative to $\theta = 1$.

The welfare losses from changes in the money supply

To summarize, if the money supply in the economy were constant, θ would be one. In this case, the budget line and the feasibility set would become identical and the individual's budget line would be the socially feasible tradeoff W^yW^o. The individual would maximize his utility at a point, say B, which is other than A and which lies on the segment AW^o, with B offering greater utility than A. Since the segment AW^o offers socially feasible consumption opportunities not available for $\theta > 1$, the individual would have a higher level of utility for $\theta = 1$ than for $\theta > 1$. The individual is, therefore, worse off with monetary expansion than with monetary stability.[23] Hence, monetary expansion – or contraction – implies a welfare loss for each individual and therefore for the economy as a whole.

Comparing intuitively the consumption bundles at points A and B in Figure 22.2 for $\theta > 1$, under monetary expansion, too much is consumed while young and too little is consumed while old. Consumption in the old lifestage is lower because its relative cost is higher than under monetary stability. This relative cost under monetary expansion is θ/n and under monetary stability is $1/n$.

From another perspective, monetary expansion brings about a difference between the social and private rates of exchange between c^y and c^o. The social rate of exchange between c^y and c^o from the socially feasible tradeoff is $1/n$. However, under monetary expansion, the private rate of exchange at which the individual is able to trade in the market is θ/n. The latter is higher since $\theta > 1$, so that the monetary expansion increases the private rate of exchange above the social one and makes the individual choose too little of old-age consumption and too much of consumption when young. It does this by depreciating the value of money holdings, which lose their value at the rate θ compared with the case of monetary stability.

Note that the total availability of commodities and therefore total consumption over both lifestages is held constant in this model. Therefore, the welfare loss of monetary expansion is not due to a decrease in total consumption but is due to an *inefficient* pattern of consumption. In the case of monetary expansion, too little is being consumed in old age because of the implied loss over time in the purchasing power of money which is required for increasing old-age consumption, but is not required for consumption while young.

The welfare loss from changes in the velocity of circulation

An alternative to monetary expansion is increases in the velocity of circulation of money. Velocity is constant at unity in this model, so that the innovations in the payments mechanism that would change this velocity are not allowed in it. But if money in the economy was public (government-supplied) fiat money M plus private fiat money M', with the latter say determined by $M' = \alpha M$, an increase in α would increase the velocity of fiat money. Since this corresponds to an increase in the monetary aggregate $(M + M')$, the increased velocity of public fiat money would imply a welfare loss.

22.6 THE INEFFICIENCY OF PRICE STABILITY WITH MONETARY EXPANSION AND POPULATION GROWTH

Given a population growth rate of n, price stability could be achieved by a money supply rule which sets θ equal to n. With such a rule, prices would be stable but the monetary expansion would still impose an allocative inefficiency and a welfare loss on the economy. To see this for the stationary state, again start with the per capita socially feasible tradeoff given by (25) for the money transfer case. This was:

$$c_t^y + (1/n)c_t^o = w_t^y + (1/n)w_t^o$$

The lifetime budget constraint from (43) with price stability ensured by $\theta = n$ would be:

$$c_t^y + c_t^o = w_t^y + w_{t+1}^o + (1/p)[(\theta - 1)m] \tag{48}$$

so that the budget line is again flatter than the socially feasible tradeoff. As argued earlier in similar analysis using Figure 22.2, the consumption pattern chosen by the young would be inefficient and would involve an allocative welfare loss for both the young and the old.

Therefore, the allocative inefficiency is that of monetary expansion (or contraction) rather than of inflation (or deflation). This inefficiency again flows from the divergence created by monetary expansion between the social rate of exchange between c^o and c^y and the private one. Population growth makes this rate as n – so that n units of c^y can be traded for one unit of c^o – while the money supply rule with $\theta = n$ makes it as 1.

22.7 MONEY DEMAND IN THE OLG MODEL WITH A POSITIVE RATE OF TIME PREFERENCE

We have so far not looked at the specification of the intertemporal utility function, though we derived in (46) the result that the individual's equilibrium intertemporal rate of substitution between c^y and c^o would be $-n/\theta$. This section extends the analysis to a specific time-separable utility function with a positive rate of time preference.

A common assumption on the form of the intertemporal utility function is that it is time separable in period utility functions and that period utility is the log of consumption in the period. That is,

$$U(c_t^y, c_{t+1}^o) = u(c_t^y) + \delta u(c_{t+1}^o) \tag{49}$$

$$= \ln c_t^y + \delta \ln c_{t+1}^o \tag{50}$$

where:

$U(\cdot)$ intertemporal utility function
$u(\cdot)$ period utility function
δ 1 over the gross rate of time preference (gross subjective discount factor)

The appropriate intertemporal budget constraint for the case of population growth at the rate n and monetary growth at the rate θ is given by (42) as:

$$c_t^y + (\theta/n)\, c_{t+1}^o = w_t^y + (\theta/n)\, w_{t+1}^o + (1/p_t)[(\theta - 1)m_t]$$

The right-hand side of this constraint can be designated as current wealth W_t, so that:

$$W_t = [w_t^y + (\theta/n)\, w_{t+1}^o + (1/p_t)(\theta - 1)m_t]$$

Maximizing (50) subject to (42) yields the optimal consumption pattern as:

$$c_t^y = [1/(1 + \delta)]\, W_t \tag{51}$$

$$c_{t+1}^o = (\delta n/\theta)c_t^y = [\delta n/(\theta(1 + \delta))]\, W_t \tag{52}$$

and the individual's saving in period t is:

$$s_t = w_t^y - c_t^y$$
$$= w_t^y - [1/(1 + \delta)]\, W_t \tag{53}$$

The demand for money

The individual's demand for real balances m_t^d/p_t is positive only in the young lifestage and occurs as a way of carrying forward his saving. It equals his saving and is given by:

$$m_t^d/p_t = w_t^y - [1/(1 + \delta)]\, W_t$$

or as,

$$m_t^d/p_t = w_t^y - [1/(1 + \delta)][w_t^y + (\theta/n)w_{t+1}^o + (1/p_t)(\theta - 1)\, m_t] \tag{54}$$

Note that the individual has zero saving and therefore zero money demand in his old lifestage. In the case of *price stability*, i.e., with $\theta = n$, we get:

$$c_{t+1}^o = \delta c_t^y \tag{55}$$

$$m_t^d/p_t = w_t^y - c_t^y = w_t^y - [1/(1 + \delta)]\, W_t \tag{56}$$

Hence, the demand for real balances – and saving – depends positively upon current income w_t^y and the gross subjective discount factor δ, but negatively upon the future income w_{t+1}^o.

22.8 SEVERAL FIAT MONIES

In the preceding version of the OLG model with a single type of fiat money, the individual used fiat money to transfer purchasing power between his lifestages. As shown above, fiat money had a gross rate of return n/θ for a population growth rate n and a monetary expansion rate θ. This return was in the form of a 'dividend' or 'tax' occurring through changes in the price level over time, even though the fiat money itself did not make an explicit interest payment.

If there are several fiat monies simultaneously available in the economy, and each one only offers the services of a store of value, the one with the highest return (coupon plus the rate of increase in real value) will be preferred by the savers and the fiat monies with the lower rates of return will not be held. Conversely, if several fiat monies offer the same rate of return, the savers will be indifferent among them and the relevant rate of monetary expansion will be that of all such fiat monies taken together.

Applying these results to the international context of many national currencies and open economies with zero transactions costs of exchange between currencies, either only one currency would possess a positive demand and positive value – in the absence of legal restrictions or frictions favouring the domestic currency – or all national currencies would be perfect substitutes for each other. In the latter case, with seigniorage from the national currencies going to their home nations, *profit-maximizing* governments would engage in a competitive issue of fiat monies until the value of all fiat monies goes to zero. Therefore, perfectly substitutable and competitively issued national fiat monies do not make sense in the context of frictionless OLG models. Alternatively, if many such monies exist in the real world and have a positive value, then the OLG models would not be valid for them or their demand will arise because of legal and other restrictions on the use of foreign currencies.

In the real world, national currencies usually remain the most commonly used fiat money in their own nation, even though they tend to have different rates of inflation and return from foreign currencies. The OLG models imply that this national usage must be due to legal restrictions or other frictions that prevent perfect substitutability between the national fiat money and foreign ones – and thereby create special niches or market segments in which each can dominate. The domestic demand for the national currency is to be determined by the nature and extent of frictions and restrictions, which are themselves often not specified or encompassed in the OLG models. To take a concrete example, consider the Canadian economy in which there do not exist any legal barriers to the use of the US currency relative to the Canadian one. Both circulate freely, payments at many stores can be made in either currency, deposits in banks can be held in either currency, etc., and, in the past several years, the expectation that the US dollar will appreciate relative to the Canadian one has often been held over several months. Yet, the Canadian currency, rather than disappearing from circulation, continues to be the dominant one in usage in Canada.

CONCLUSIONS

The OLG framework offers an alternative format to MIUF theories for modelling the demand for money. They are especially appealing to those who believe that since money cannot be directly consumed or used as a factor of production, it should not be entered as a variable in the utility and production functions. The OLG models do not do so, but still generate a demand and positive value for fiat money, even though it is intrinsically costless to create. However, to ensure a positive value of money, they must impose a restriction on the supply of money, so that the OLG models rule out the competitive supply of fiat money.

The OLG framework is a vehicle for the intertemporal reallocation of resources to the future by individuals with finite lifetimes but operating in an everlasting economy. It provides an attractive market mechanism as a substitute for an intergenerational social contract (to provide transfers of commodities to the elderly who are no longer productive but who, while young, made similar transfers). Limited elements of an implicit social contract continue to exist: the faith (or expectation) is firmly held that no future generation will make the fiat money inconvertible into commodities directly or indirectly by the substitution of a new currency while rendering the preceding one inconvertible into the new one.

Further, the current value of fiat money will depend upon what the future generations are expected to maintain, so that the OLG models show multiple equilibria for the value of fiat money. Of these, only two occur in the stationary state. These are the no-trade (autarchic) equilibrium and an equilibrium in which money has positive value.

Since the balances of fiat money are a durable or capital good, the value of such money in any period will depend upon its value in the next period, which will depend upon its value in the period after that, and so on. In the general case, an expected change in the future value of money in any future time period will change its value in all preceding periods. Therefore, the current value of money and the current price level in the economy are tenuous, and can involve a bubble on the value of money. While this is so for most intertemporal theories, including the MIUF one, the OLG models additionally assert that if any of these future values are expected to be zero, all preceding values would also be zero. This is not surprising since the fundamental assumptions of the OLG theory are that fiat money is intrinsically useless and inconvertible, and its single dimensional use is for carrying purchasing power to the future – a use that is totally eliminated if its expected future value is zero.

The OLG models with positively valued fiat money display sunspot activity, as can models of other durable assets and MIUF models of money. *Sunspots* are variables which are not among the fundamental variables of the economy but which can nevertheless affect the economy. Examples of the latter are endowments, preferences, technology and market structures. An example of a sunspot is the market expectation about the future values of a variable which influence its present value. As shown in this chapter, expectations play such a role with respect to the value of fiat money in the OLG models, so that the OLG models are very prone to sunspot activity. The limitation of the analysis of such models to stationary equilibrium states is a means of avoiding sunspots. In such stationary states, the value of money is determined by the fundamental determinants of the economy, with rational expectations specifying the expected value of money to be that prescribed only by the stationary state values.

A related concept to that of sunspots is that of *bubbles* in asset prices. A price bubble for an asset exists if its market value is different from the present discounted value of its expected dividends. The latter is designated as its *market fundamental*. Since fiat money in the OLG models does not yield any implicit (such as in utility) or explicit dividends to its holder, its market fundamental is zero. Since it can have a positive value in these models, its market price can differ from its market fundamental, so that there is a bubble on positively valued money. Such bubbles can be created by sunspots. Further, bubbles on an asset can have nominal and real consequences for other variables in the model. In the OLG models, the actual bubble on the value of fiat money has consequences for the consumption and saving path over time.

A major concern of this book, as of monetary economics, is the theoretical derivation of a money demand function which is empirically valid. As shown in this chapter, the demand for real balances in the basic OLG model is specified by saving. Such a function is empirically testable and is, without dispute, not valid for any real-world economy. This departure from the empirical money demand functions is so radical that it casts serious doubt on the OLG model as a satisfactory basis for monetary economics. This issue is discussed further in the next chapter.

SUMMARY OF CRITICAL CONCLUSIONS

- The OLG models incorporate a close relationship between the demand for money and saving, rather than between the demand for money and current consumption expenditures.
- The OLG models imply multiple equilibria for the price level and the return on money but only two stationary equilibria, one of which is the no-trade autarchic state in which money is not traded.
- A positive value of fiat money represents a bubble since fiat money is costless to create.
- Monetary expansion or contraction yields a less desirable allocation of consumption in the young and old lifestages relative to a constant money supply.
- While the inflation caused by monetary expansion – and disinflation caused by monetary

contraction – involves a welfare loss because it is the outcome of monetary expansion, the inflation caused by a fall in commodity endowments or population decrease, with a constant money supply, does not do so.

- In the presence of population growth, price stability achieved through monetary expansion is inefficient relative to a price decrease under a constant money supply.

review and discussion questions

1. For the OLG model, show and discuss the welfare implications of monetary expansion which ensures price stability with those of monetary stability which results in price deflation.

2. For the OLG model, you are given the utility function of the representative young as:

$$U(\cdot) = \ln c_t^y + \ln c_{t+1}^o$$

   For a given population and given endowments of the commodity in the two periods, derive the demand functions for the commodity, the price level and the rate of return on nominal balances in the stationary state.

3. In the OLG framework, assume that the economy has N persons born each period, each person lives two periods, each young person supplies one unit of labour and saves a constant proportion of income. The old do not supply labour nor do they save. Each period, the economy's saving can be held in physical capital, which can be bought at the end of the young lifestage and lasts only one period (i.e., during the old lifestage), or fiat money. The economy has the production function:

$$y = f(k) = Ak^\alpha \qquad 0 < \alpha < 1$$

   k is the capital/labour ratio. Derive the economy's steady-state output, saving, the capital stock and the demand for money functions. (Specify any additional assumptions that you need to make.) Is money neutral in this model?

4. Experience indicates that, in the real world, several fiat monies – for example, the Canadian and US dollars in Canada – can coexist in the economy with positive values even when there are no legal barriers to the use of each one. Further, each has its own determinate demand function, quite different from the other's. How do you reconcile this empirical fact with the analysis of the OLG model in this chapter or are they irreconcilable without fundamental alterations in the model?

5. For the fiat money in your country, what would be the arguments and signs of the partial derivatives of its demand function, according to: (a) the OLG model of this chapter, and (b) your knowledge of the economy and the empirical literature on it.

6. In the OLG framework, assume that the incomes in the (one-commodity) economy are paid to workers in the form of the commodity by the representative private firm, with full employment in the economy. Assume that each worker produces one unit of the commodity (without requiring physical capital). Specifying any other assumptions that you need to make, derive the implications for prices, the return on money, the efficiency of monetary expansion and the optimal rate of monetary expansion for the following cases:

   (i) a constant labour force;
   (ii) the labour force grows at the rate n;
   (iii) the labour force is constant, but its average productivity rises at a constant rate τ over time.

7. The assumption in many, if not most, macroeconomic models is that the firms do not save but borrow (through the issue of one-period bonds) each period the funds

they need for investment. Under this assumption, if fiat money is intrinsically useless for firms, its demand by firms will be zero under the rationale of the OLG models. How, then, can the usage of money by firms be generated and be positive in the OLG context?

8 Discuss the statement: money will have no value if there is a terminal date for the economy.

9 Discuss the statement: uniqueness of perfect foresight monetary equilibrium in the OLG model requires implausible conditions.

10 Discuss in the context of the OLG model the validity of Friedman's money supply rule: the best monetary policy is one that increases the money supply at a steady low rate.

NOTES

1 Samuelson presented a three-period (along with a simplified two-period) version of the OLG model, with his focus being on the rate of interest. In the three-period model, individuals worked and earned income in the first two periods and were retired in the third period. The problem was to allow positive consumption in the third period, when there was zero income and the commodities could not be stored over time. Samuelson also showed how the economy could achieve this pattern of consumption through the social contrivance of fiat money, with the latter bringing about a biological rate of interest.

2 It is not clear that 'intrinsically useless' concept is not an inherently flawed one for economic analysis since it is difficult, if not impossible, to define what is 'directly used in consumption or production' and what is not. For example, are diamonds – or other commodities with snob appeal – intrinsically useful? Is their value determined by their intrinsic usefulness? What does confer 'usefulness' at the margin of demand?

3 The validity of this concept for the individual is also of questionable merit. The individual does not care and usually does not even know whether the central bank – the issuer of fiat money – will ever redeem its notes into commodities, as long as others from whom he wants to buy commodities will do so. That is, the individual only requires convertibility of fiat money against commodities in the private markets.

4 Alternatively, the cost of counterfeiting a note must exceed the value of the note in exchange.

5 While modern economies allow the state to monopolize the creation of currency and make it illegal to counterfeit currency, the creation of near-monies is permitted and private financial intermediaries create a variety of substitutes for money. Other creations of the private sector allow an increase in the velocity of circulation of money. Among these have been the creation of credit cards, debit cards, automatic teller machines, electronic transfer of deposits, etc. These activities of the private sector limit the applicability of the standard OLG models.

6 With a finite horizon, money would be worthless at the end of the terminal period. To avoid a 100 per cent capital loss, individuals in the terminal period will not want to obtain and hold money, thereby rendering it worthless for individuals who would obtain it one period earlier and hold it to the terminal period, and so on for still earlier periods, thus making the demand for money zero in all periods.

7 Therefore, the return on commodities net of any premium for risk and depreciation from storage, must be less than on money. This is definitely the case if the commodity is assumed to be perishable, in which case the return on commodities is –100 per cent.

8 None of these properties is unique to the OLG models: the MIUF and other monetary models can be also formulated to possess them.

9 This assumption is relaxed in many versions of the OLG framework. It is maintained throughout this chapter, but not when presenting the Modigliani–Miller theorem on open market operations in OLG models in the next chapter.

10 An alternative – and common – set of assumptions in the literature is that: the individual supplies an amount n^s of labour in the young lifestage and none in the old one; consumption occurs only in the old lifestage and equals the amount c, the intertemporal utility function is $[u(c) - v(n)]$, and the production function has constant returns to scale, with one unit of labour producing one unit of the consumer good. The qualitative implications of these assumptions are similar to those where labour is supplied and consumption occurs in both periods, provided there is net saving in the first lifestage. The latter correspond to our assumptions in the text.

11 The endowments in the two periods can be considered as the ability to work and a corresponding job. In such an interpretation, the first lifestage would be interpreted as the individual's working life, with income from work, and the second as the retired stage, where there is no labour income but there could be some exogenous income from social security and other public sources.

12 We have specified this constraint as an equality for the rational young individual since he would either consume all his endowments or convert any saving into money m for possible usage in the future.

13 Since the individual derives no utility from unspent money balances or unconsumed commodities left over at the end of $t + 1$, utility maximization implies that the old lifestage constraint is an equality.

14 In the two lifestages models, private but non-negotiable borrowing (in IOUs or bonds) is excluded since any given borrower and lender can meet in only one period and never again, so that they can meet to arrange a loan but cannot meet to settle its repayment.

15 In the stationary state, the endowments of commodities are identical across generations, but are not identical over the two lifestages of any generation. In fact, it has been assumed that $w_t^y < w_{t+1}^o$.

16 The gross rate of return or interest over a period specifies the total amount (principal plus interest) that will be received at the end of the period from an investment of \$1 at the beginning of the period.

17 That is, contrary to the value implied by (13).

18 A corresponding assumption is that each worker supplies just one unit of labour, with a constant marginal product per worker, and there exists full employment, so that the output of commodities increases at the same rate as the population.

19 This rate of return is also called as the rate of interest, even though there are no loans in this model and this interest does not represent a distinct payment. Note that since the OLG models allow multiple solutions for the price-level path, they also imply multiple solutions for the rate of interest. In one of these, the barter state, the rate of interest would be zero. However, the biologically determined rate of interest will be optimal. The social contrivance of money allows this rate to be implemented through market exchanges (Samuelson, 1958).

20 If $p_{t+1} = 0$, the young will not find it worthwhile to hold and carry money to the next lifestage, so that we would have a socially feasible frontier consisting only of the points w^y and w^o.

21 Note that it does not maximize the utility of the old – in their old period – of any generation. Maximizing this utility means maximizing consumption in the old period, with their consumption while young being in the past and therefore without any tradeoff in consumption between the young and old lifestages.

22 Note that in (37), n is not only the rate of growth of population, it is also the rate of growth of output and saving. Hence, the rates of growth in saving of n and in nominal money – in which saving is held – of θ will increase prices at the rate θ/n.

23 The initial old who receive the increase in the money supply are also worse off, since they would be able to buy only $c^{o\prime}$ (at point A) of the commodity rather than c^{o*} (at point B) without monetary expansion.

REFERENCES

Aiyagari, S. Rao. 'Nonmonetary Steady States in Stationary Overlapping Generations Models with Long Lived Agents and Discounting: Multiplicity, Optimality and Consumption Smoothing'. *Journal of Economic Theory*, 45, June 1980, pp. 102–27.

Bullard, James. 'Samuelson's Model of Money with *n*-Period Lifetimes'. *Federal Reserve Bank of St Louis Review*, 74, May/June 1992, pp. 67–82.

Champ, Bruce, and Scott Freeman. *Modeling Monetary Economies*. New York: John Wiley, 1994, Chs 1–3, 5, 6.

Karekan, John H., and Neil Wallace, eds. *Models of Monetary Economics*. Federal Reserve Bank of Minneapolis, 1980.

McCandless, George T., Jr (with Neil Wallace). *Introduction to Dynamic Macroeconomic Theory: An Overlapping Generations Approach*. Cambridge, MA: Harvard University Press, 1991.

Samuelson, Paul A. 'An Exact Consumption–Loan Model of Interest With or Without the Social Contrivance of Money'. *Journal of Political Economy*, 66, December 1958, pp. 467–82.

Sargent, Thomas J. *Dynamic Economic Theory*. Boston, MA: Harvard University Press, 1987, Ch. 7.

Tobin, James. 'Discussion'. In Karekan and Wallace (1980, pp. 83–90).

Wallace, Neil. 'The Overlapping Generations Model of Fiat Money'. In Karekan and Wallace (1980, pp. 49–82).

——. 'A Modigliani–Miller Theorem for Open Market Operations'. *American Economic Review*, 71, June 1981, pp. 267–74.

chapter twenty-three

THE OLG MODEL: SEIGNIORAGE, BONDS AND THE NEUTRALITY OF FIAT MONEY

This chapter extends the analysis of the overlapping generations models of money to include bonds. It then examines various policy issues such as seigniorage, open market operations and money neutrality.

An important distinction between the different ways of increasing the money supply arises in the OLG models of this chapter: while open market operations have no impact on the economy, gratuitous increases in the money stock are not neutral.

This chapter also examines the empirical plausibility of important implications, especially for the demand for money, of the OLG models.

---

key concepts introduced in this chapter

- Seigniorage as a taxation device
- Open market operations in the OLG models
- The Wallace–Modigliani–Miller theorem on open market operations

---

This chapter continues the exposition of the various aspects of the OLG model. The assumptions of the model and the definitions of the symbols used are as in the preceding chapter. The present chapter has numerous references to the equations in Chapter 22, with such equations being cited as (22 . . .). This chapter starts with the consideration of the seigniorage from monetary expansion in section 23.1, with seigniorage as a taxation device. Section 23.2 introduces bonds into the OLG model and section 23.3 presents Wallace's version of the Modigliani–Miller theorem for open market operations in the OLG model. This theorem implies that changes in the supply of fiat money through open market operations will not have any impact on other economic variables, including the price level and nominal national income, let alone the real variables of output and unemployment. As such, this theorem is a somewhat different and much stronger statement than that of the neutrality of money considered in the earlier chapters of this book.

Section 23.4 presents an illustrative model of the economy to explore the determination of the capital stock, output, prices and the value of money. Money is not neutral in this model. Section 23.5 re-investigates the neutrality and non-neutrality of money in a slightly different model, and shows that neutrality or non-neutrality depends on the structure of the economy and the assumptions on how money is introduced into the economy.

The test for the acceptance or rejection of any theory in economics, viewing it as a positive science, is in its ability to explain observed behavioural relationships. A considerable part of this book dealt with the empirical estimates of the demand for money and with the implied velocity of money. Section 23.6 addresses the fundamental question of whether or not the OLG models with fiat money explain the estimated forms of the money demand function and other major facets of the monetary economy.

23.1 THE SEIGNIORAGE FROM FIAT MONEY AND ITS USES

The revenue from monetary expansion is termed as *seigniorage*. The nominal value of the seigniorage per person from monetary expansion at the rate θ in period t is:

$$G_t = [M_t - M_{t-1}]/N_t$$

$$G_t = (1 - 1/\theta) M_t/N_t \tag{1}$$

where G_t is the nominal value of seigniorage per person born in period t and $M_{t-1}/M_t = 1/\theta$; $(1 - 1/\theta)$ is viewed as the 'tax rate' and M_t/N_t as the per capita 'tax base'. Define g_t as G_t/p_t, so that g_t is the amount of real seigniorage per young person in the economy. The amount of commodities that can be bought with this amount is also g_t, where g_t is:

$$g_t = (1 - 1/\theta)M_t/(p_t N_t) = (1 - 1/\theta)m_t/p_t \tag{2}$$

In the stationary state, this amount would be constant.

The seigniorage received by the government can be allocated by it in various ways. Among these, two distinctive forms are:

(i) The seigniorage is distributed by the government to the old members of each generation in the form of money transfers and, therefore, as a unilateral transfer back from the public sector to the private one. This was the assumption used in Chapter 22.
(ii) The seigniorage is used by the government to purchase commodities in the open market from the private sector. This chapter makes this assumption.

Further, it is assumed that in each period *the government uses its seigniorage to buy commodities and destroys them* – or gives them away as a unilateral gift to foreigners (economic units outside the economy in question) – without producing any welfare for the economy through such action.[1] Such an assumption is of doubtful validity and is clearly irrational. Its purpose in such models is to isolate the effects of creating seigniorage from those arising from the distribution of the value of seigniorage either in the form of money transfers or commodity transfers to the population or some segment of it, and to compare these effects with those of lump-sum taxation as one of the alternatives to seigniorage.[2]

23.1.1 The value of money under seigniorage with destruction of government-purchased commodities

Under the above assumptions for this case, the economy on a per capita basis is left with g_t less of goods in period t. The economy's constraint (22.23) for the commodity market in period t is now modified to:

$$N_t c_t^y + N_{t-1} c_t^o = N_t w_t^y + N_{t-1} w_t^o - N_t g_t$$

where $N_t/N_{t-1} = n$, so that:

$$c_t^y + (1/n)c_t^o = w_t^y + (1/n)w_t^o - g_t \tag{3}$$

The demand for real balances in period t is determined by the saving out of the available supply of commodities to the private sector, so that the per capita demand for real balances, m^d/p_t, is now:

$$m_t^d/p_t = w_t^y - c_t^y - g^t \tag{4}$$

The nominal supply of money is:

$$M_t^s = M_t \tag{5}$$

Equilibrium in the money market specifies that:

$$p_t[N_t(w_t^y - c_t^y - g_t)] = M_t \tag{6}$$

so that:

$$p_t = M_t/[N_t(w_t^y - c_t^y - g_t)] \tag{7}$$

Equation (7) shows that prices increase as the seigniorage g rises.

Since w^y, c^y and g will be constant in the stationary state but M_t and N_t are growing, (7) implies that, in the stationary state,

$$p_{t+1}/p_t = \theta/n \tag{8}$$

From (7), the value of money is:

$$v_t = [N_t(w_t^y - c_t^y - g_t)]/M_t \tag{9}$$

and from (8) the rate of return on money is:

$$v_{t+1}/v_t = n/\theta \tag{10}$$

As (7) in comparison with (22.34) shows, the price level will be higher and the availability of commodities less in this case with the destruction of the government-acquired goods than with the money transfer case in the preceding sections. However, comparing (8) and (10) with (22.37) and (22.38) shows that the intertemporal price ratio and the rate of return remain the same in the two cases.

23.1.2 The inefficiency of monetary expansion with seigniorage as a taxation device

Remember that, in this case, the government is assumed to destroy commodities equal to the seigniorage. It is not transferred to the old, as under the money transfer case in Chapter 22. Since the commodity destruction reduces the amount of commodities available to the economy, social welfare under it must be lower than under the money transfer policy. Further, since the latter was inferior to the stable money case, monetary expansion with commodity destruction must also mean a welfare loss over the stable money case. We prove this formally in the following.

We want to derive at this point the personal budget constraint for the monetary expansion case with commodity destruction. In this case, since there is no money transfer to the individual, monetary creation does not affect his personal budget constraints for the two lifestages, nor does the destruction of the commodity obtained through seigniorage. These constraints remain identical to the ones without monetary expansion and are:

$$p_t c_t^y + m_t = p_t w_t^y \tag{11}$$

$$p_{t+1} c_{t+1}^o = p_{t+1} w_{t+1}^o + m_t \tag{12}^3$$

Substituting (11) in (12) to eliminate m_t gives the personal lifetime budget constraint as:

$$c_t^y + (p_{t+1}/p_t)c_{t+1}^o = w_t^y + (p_{t+1}/p_t)w_{t+1}^o \tag{13}$$

Since $p_{t+1}/p_t = \theta/n$, (13) becomes:

$$c_t^y + (\theta/n)c_{t+1}^o = w_t^y + (\theta/n)\, w_{t+1}^o \tag{14}$$

Therefore, in stationary equilibrium,

$$c^y + (\theta/n)c^o = w^y + (\theta/n)\, w^o \tag{15}$$

Hence, the individual's personal budget line in Figure 23.1 is $W^{y\prime\prime}W^{o\prime\prime}$, where:

$$W^{y\prime\prime} = w^y + (\theta/n)w^o$$

$$W^{o\prime\prime} = (n/\theta)[w^y + (\theta/n)]w^o \tag{16}$$

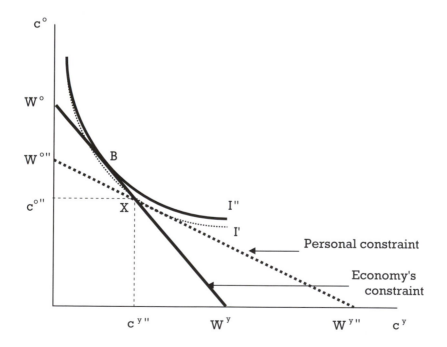

Figure 23.1

Since the seigniorage from monetary expansion is now no longer returned to the people, *the personal budget line from (15) lies inside the one from (22.43)* so that welfare is even lower in the commodity destruction case than in the money transfer case, though both have the same slope $(-n/\theta)$. Hence, a policy of commodity destruction is inferior to one with money or goods transfer back to the public.

Further, in Figure 23.1 for the choices made by the young, comparing the young's personal budget line $W^y{}''W^o{}''$ and the economy's per capita constraint W^yW^o, the former has a flatter slope equal to $(-n/\theta)$ than the latter whose slope from (3) equals $(-n)$. Let the intersection point between these lines be at X. Similar to our earlier arguments for the money transfer case, the segment $XW^y{}''$ (excluding point X) is not feasible since it lies outside the economy's constraint, so that the young's utility maximizing point will lie on the segment $XW^o{}''$ of the personal budget line. But, as shown in Figure 22.2 of Chapter 22, any point on this segment is inferior in utility to some points on the segment XW^o of the economy's constraint, with the latter offering more of both c^y and c^o. Since the segment XW^o is available to the young in the case of monetary stability, monetary expansion $(\theta > 1)$ decreases the welfare of the young. Further, the consumption and welfare of the old would also be higher if the young were to choose on the economy's constraint XW^o. Hence, there is a social welfare loss from the seigniorage as a taxation-*cum*-commodity destruction device.

Hence, monetary stability is preferable to monetary expansion with money transfer to the old, which is preferable to monetary expansion with destruction of the goods bought with seigniorage.

23.1.3 The change in seigniorage with the rate of monetary expansion

From (2), the real value of the seigniorage per person collected from the economy is:

$$g_t = (1 - \theta^{-1}) M_t/(p_t N_t) = (1 - \theta^{-1}) m_t/p_t \tag{17}$$

where M_t/p_t represents the real tax base – that is, the amount subject to taxation – and $(1 - \theta^{-1})$ represents the tax rate on the real value of the money holdings. Designate this tax rate as τ. From (11), m_t/p_t equals the saving $(w_t^y - c_t^y)$ in the young lifestage. Hence,

$$g_t = (1 - \theta^{-1})(w_t^y - c_t^y) \tag{18}$$

so that,

$$\partial g_t/\partial\theta = \{\theta^{-2}(w_t^y - c_t^y)\} + \{-(1 - \theta^{-1})\partial c_t^y/\partial\theta\} \tag{19}$$

Since $c_t^y = w_t^y - m_{t/pt}$ and $\partial(m_{t/pt})/\partial\theta < 0$ while $\partial w_t^y/\partial\theta = 0$, $\partial c_t^y/\partial\theta > 0$. For $\theta > 1$ and $c_t^y < w_t^y$, the first term on the right-hand side of (19) is positive and the second term is negative. Hence, the first term causes an increase in seigniorage as θ increases and the second term causes a decrease as the tax base shrinks through the reduction of the old lifestage consumption. If we assume that the second effect gradually becomes stronger as θ increases, the amount of seigniorage as a function of θ would first increase and then decrease.

23.1.4 Seigniorage from monetary expansion versus lump-sum taxation

To compare the relative merits of monetary expansion as a taxation device with lump-sum taxation in the preceding framework, assume for the latter case that a lump-sum tax[4] equal to g_t is imposed on each young individual[5] in period t, with the money supply now being held constant. Note the underlying assumption on the destruction of the commodity bought with the seigniorage from money or with the tax g_t. The economy's constraint in this case is as specified in (3). The lifetime personal budget constraint in this case is a modified version of (14) with $\theta = 1$ and with g_t being deducted from the available resources on the right-hand side of (14). That is, the personal budget constraint becomes:

$$c_t^y + (1/n)c_{t+1}^o = w_t^y + (1/n)w_{t+1}^o - g_t \qquad (20)$$

Equation (20) is identical with the economy's constraint (3), so that the consumption pattern (c^y, c^o) chosen by the individual is also welfare maximizing for the economy. Therefore, the lump-sum taxation is an efficient taxation device, while seigniorage from monetary expansion is not.

This comparison between the above two forms of revenue generation assumes that the costs of collection and administration between them are identical. This is almost never so in the real world. The cost of monetary expansion through the printing of more money is negligible and the economy through the money markets takes care of the administration of seigniorage through intertemporal price changes without direct collection costs to the government. By comparison, the bureaucracy needed for the collection of lump-sum taxes, their visibility as a tax on the public and the consequent public resentment at their payment reduce society's welfare and reduce the amounts actually collected on both a gross and net (of the cost of collection) basis. These costs can be high enough in certain economies, so that the monetary expansion may be preferable as the policy imposing the smallest possible welfare loss on the economy.[6] These considerations make the collection of revenue through seigniorage, in addition to direct and indirect taxes, tempting for governments in many countries. But, as against the advantages of seigniorage as a taxation device, monetary expansion and inflation have other costs – such as related to the variability of inflation under uncertainty, 'shoe leather costs' and 'menu costs', etc. – not captured in the preceding models.

As shown above, the real value of seigniorage to the government depends upon the rate of expansion of fiat money and the amount of fiat money in real terms. This amount for low rates of fiat money growth and inflation is likely to be a small percentage of the fiat balances held, which in turn are only a small fraction of M1 and even less of M2. Since M1 and M2 are themselves a small fraction of GDP in most economies, seigniorage from the creation of fiat money as a percentage of GDP will at most be only a few percentage points. This amount would be more substantial at monetary growth rates sufficient to cause hyperinflation, provided that such hyperinflation does not substantially decrease the real value of fiat money holdings, as it is likely to do.

We now leave the topic of seigniorage and its uses, and turn to the introduction of bonds in OLG models. One mode of this is given in the next section in the context of a pure OLG model, while an alternative one will be given in Chapter 24 in the context of an OLG model blended with a cash-in-advance constraint on the economy.

23.2 FIAT MONEY AND BONDS

Fiat money in the preceding OLG models functions merely as a store of value. This role could be equally well performed by bonds paying a positive rate of interest per period. For bonds to perform this role, we have to assume that the commodities can be *directly* exchanged against bonds, without the intermediation of money or brokerage or other transactions costs and without any lags in the transactions process. Under these assumptions, which also apply to fiat money, money and bonds would be perfect substitutes as a vehicle for saving except that bonds would have a higher rate of return. Hence, since the public would prefer the asset with the higher return, it would only use bonds and fiat money will not be traded. The value of fiat money will be zero.

In order to create a positive demand for fiat money in the presence of interest-bearing bonds, we have to create a mechanism for fiat money to pay interest at the same rate as bonds. We now lay out one scenario for this. Assume that the *commercial banks pay interest equal to that on bonds on all deposits of fiat money with them*, the public deposits its fiat money holdings with the commercial banks and the banks redeposit this fiat money with the central bank, which also pays the identical rate of interest on deposits with it. The banks will then function as purely pass-through financial intermediaries between the public and the central bank. The return-maximizing *public will deposit all the fiat money with the banks* and not hold any fiat money (or currency, in normal terminology). Instead, the public would carry out transactions between fiat money and commodities through the use of cheques drawn on their deposit accounts.

Since the bank deposits and the bonds will have the same rate of return, the public will be indifferent between them as a medium of saving, and they would be perfect substitutes. Hence, deposits (originating with fiat money) and bonds would be identical in their economic role. They would only differ superficially as accounts on the books of the banks (deposits) versus pieces of paper (bonds) held by the public. Since they are perfect substitutes, only their total quantity will be relevant for determining the price level and the values of money and bonds.

The determination of the price level when money and bonds are perfect substitutes

Note that with money and bonds as perfect substitutes, the demand for each is indeterminate and only their combined real demand can be determined. This will equal saving. Hence, the individual's – that is, the economy's per capita – joint demand for them is specified by:

$$(m_t^d + b_t^d)/p_t = s_t$$

where b_t^d is the per capita nominal value of bonds in the economy. Since $s_t = (w_t^y - c_t^y)$, the aggregate demand from (22.10) for these two assets is:

$$M_t^d + B_t^d = N_t[p_t(w_t^y - c_t^y)] \tag{21}$$

The aggregate supply of money and bonds in the economy is given by their amounts held by the old (born in $t-1$ with their number as N_{t-1}) and which they want to trade. It equals:

$$M_t^s + B_t^s = N_{t-1}[m_t^o + b_t^o] \tag{22}$$

so that market clearance, with the joint demand for financial assets equal to their supply, implies that,

$$N_t[p_t(w_t^y - c_t^y)] = N_{t-1}[m_t^o + b_t^o] \tag{23}$$

Hence:

$$p_t = (M_t + B_t)/[N_t(w_t^y - c_t^y)] \tag{24}$$

Since c_t^y on the right-hand side of (24) depends on p_{t+1}/p_t, we have:

$$p_t = (M_t + B_t)/[N_t(w_t^y - c_t^y(p_{t+1}/p_t, w_t^y, w_{t+1}^o))] \tag{24'}$$

Hence, the current price level depends on the intertemporal price ratio p_{t+1}/p_t and varies proportionately with the *combined* supply of money and bonds, *ceteris paribus*. Hence, an increase in the supply of bonds will raise the price level.

The inefficiency of changes in the supply of bonds in this model

The preceding chapter has shown the inefficiency of monetary growth. Since money and bonds are perfect substitutes in the preceding analysis, it can be shown by a similar argument that, for a given quantity of money, bond creation will also impose a welfare loss by introducing an allocative inefficiency in the intertemporal consumption pattern.

The distinctive roles of money and bonds in the real-world economies

The modern economy seems to have distinct roles for money (whether fiat money or deposits in banks) and bonds. In daily life, money functions as a medium of payments, while bonds do not, even though each can be a vehicle for holding savings. The preceding assumptions and analysis – and the standard OLG models – do not allow this differentiation and do not allow distinctive roles for money and bonds along the ways in which money and bonds function in the economy. The next chapter creates this differentiation in two different ways and explores the implications of this differentiation in the context of modified OLG models.

23.3 THE WALLACE–MODIGLIANI–MILLER (W–M–M) THEOREM ON OPEN MARKET OPERATIONS

The W–M–M theorem was first presented by Wallace (1981) and our treatment draws upon his presentation. Open market operations (OMO) are defined as the government purchase (or sale) of an asset with money, with government consumption held constant. To investigate open market operations in the OLG framework, we need to have money and another asset, both of which are simultaneously held by the public and can also be held by the government. This theorem states that *open market operations between money and another asset, with government consumption held constant, will not have any real effects (for example, on consumption and saving) or even change the price level and nominal values of the variables*. In the assumed scenario, since the individual will be indifferent between the proportions held of money and the alternative asset, policy-induced changes in their relative amounts in the hands of the public will have no consequences for the economy.

23.3.1 The W–M–M theorem on open market operations with commodity storage

We first present this theorem for the basic two lifestages model without bonds, modified to allow for the storage of the single commodity in the model. With this modification, both the commodity and money can act as a vehicle for saving, while bonds are, by assumption, now not available in this version of the OLG model. To create simultaneously a positive demand for both the stored commodity and money, Wallace assumed that storing the commodity in period t has a stochastic real gross return ρ_t, which has a stationary distribution with $E\rho_t > 1$ and positive variance. For some distributions of ρ_t, a risk-averse individual will be willing to hold part of his saving in money and part in the stored commodity, with $E(\rho_t - 1)$ just compensating for the riskiness of the yield on the stored commodity. If the return from the commodity storage is too favourable after taking account of its risk and the degree of risk aversion in the economy, such storage will dominate fiat money and fiat money will no longer be demanded.[7] The demand for money will thus be extremely sensitive to variations in the return distribution and the degree of risk aversion. Since we need to posit positive demands by the individual simultaneously for both fiat money and the stored commodity, we will assume – though it is admittedly highly unrealistic – that the return on commodity storage is *finely* balanced at the level – and stays at this level no matter how much endowments, consumption and saving, storage or supply of fiat money change – which ensures such positive demands.

The personal budget constraints are initially:

$$p_t s_t^y = m_t + p_t k_t \tag{25}$$

$$p_{t+1} c_{t+1}^o = p_{t+1} w_{t+1}^o + m_t + p_{t+1} \rho_t k_t \tag{26}$$

where:

k_t private real holdings of the stored commodity in t

ρ_t gross real rate of return on k_t and on k_t^g

Assume that the government undertakes a purchase of the stored commodity equal to dk_t from the individual and pays in exchange an amount of money dm_t equal to $p_t dk_t$. Further, in order to keep government stocks constant at k_t^g, *the government transfers the net return to the individual in $t+1$ as a lump-sum transfer* not associated with the individual's holdings of money or bonds. This net return is the growth of the commodity in storage less the loss from deflation (or plus the gain from inflation) in its price and is given by $(\rho_t - p_t/p_{t+1})$.

The open market operations modify (25) and (26) to:

$$p_t s_t^y = (m_t + dm_t) + p_t (k_t - dk_t) \quad m_t > 0, (k_t - dk_t) > 0 \tag{27}$$

$$p_{t+1} c_{t+1}^o = p_{t+1} w_{t+1}^o + (m_t + dm_t) + p_{t+1} \rho_t (k_t - dk_t) + p_{t+1} (\rho_t - p_t/p_{t+1}) dk_t^g \tag{28}$$

where k_t^g are the per capita governmental holdings of the stored commodity in t. The open market operation specifies the equation:

$$dm_t = p_t dk_t = p_t dk_t^g \tag{29}$$

Substitution of (29) into (27) and (28) yields equations identical to (25) and (26), so that there is no change in the period constraints and therefore also none in the intertemporal one. Since the open market operations also do not change the individual's utility function, the optimal consumption and saving paths are unchanged by the open market operations.

We have so far dealt with the change in the money supply. Now turning to the demand for money, from (27), the demand for real balances is given by the part of real saving that the individual wants to carry forward in the form of real balances. Let the per capita demand for and supply of nominal balances *after* the open market operations be designated respectively by m_t^{d*} and m_t^{s*} and those prior to the operations be shown without an asterisk. m_t^{d*} is given by:

$$m_t^{d*}/p_t = s_t^y - (k_t - dk_t) = (s_t^y - k_t) + dk_t \tag{30}$$

With $(s_t^y - k_t) = m_t^d/p_t$ from (21) and with $dk_t = dm_t/p_t$ from (29), (30) becomes,

$$m_t^{d*}/p_t = m_t^d/p_t + dm_t/p_t$$

$$m_t^{d*} = m_t^d + dm_t \tag{31}$$

Further,

$$m_t^{s*} = m_t^s + dm_t \tag{32}$$

so that the demand for money balances in both nominal and real terms increases by exactly the same amount as their supply at the existing prices. Therefore, the price level will also not be affected by the open market operations. Nor will the nominal income (endowments times prices) be changed by the open market operations.

Evaluating the W–M–M theorem in the context of the IS–LM analysis

Since this invariance of prices and nominal income in the W–M–M theorem is at odds with the conclusions of the macroeconomic models of Chapters 13 to 16, we illustrate its derivation in the context of the IS–LM analysis. In that analysis, an increase in the money supply resulting from the above open market operations will shift the LM curve to the right. But an increase in the money demand will shift it to the left. With the open market operations increasing money supply and money demand by exactly the same amounts, as shown by (31) and (32), the LM curve will not shift either way, nor will the IS and supply curves. Consequently, if the economy is initially in equilibrium at price level P_0, the open market operations will not change that price level.

Hence, we have the W–M–M theorem that the change through open market operations in the proportions held by the individual of the two assets – money and the stored commodity – has no effects on the individual's consumption and saving paths, or on the price level. The only change is in the proportion in which the individual will hold the two assets. The change in this proportion, due to the open market operation, is willingly held by the public at the existing prices.

This result is not surprising under the given assumptions. Since both money and the stored commodity only act as abodes of purchasing power, both have an identical degree of liquidity and both have the same return net of the risk premium,[8] the individual is indifferent between the actual amounts held of each at the current rate of return. The open market operations mechanism changes the amount of the commodity stored by the individual but without a change in his real lifetime endowment of the commodity and without a change in the consumption and saving paths. To compensate for this reduction in his stored commodity, the rational individual will want to carry forward the original amount of total saving by willingly holding the corresponding increase in real balances, without requiring any change in prices.[9]

23.3.2 The W–M–M theorem on open market operations in the money–bonds OLG model

To adapt the W–M–M theorem to an economy with bonds, consider an economy in which the central bank acts for the government and can store the commodity as efficiently as the public. It puts its liabilities in the form of fiat money and bonds into circulation by purchasing commodities and storing them. It earns the gross rate of return ρ on such storage, which it pays in interest on commercial banks' deposits with it and on bonds. Note that under these assumptions the rate of return is the same on bonds and on banks' deposits with the central bank. The public deposits its fiat money with banks, which pay the return ρ on it, and the banks place with the central bank the public's deposits with them. The public holds deposits and bonds and may or may not hold commodities. This scenario is an adaptation of that of section 23.3.1, except that the central bank now holds commodities on which it obtains a return ρ.

Since fiat money (or their equivalent deposits in banks) and bonds are equivalent in terms of being a medium of saving and pay the same rate of return, the public will be indifferent between them. The aggregate demand for money and bonds for carrying forward saving as against their aggregate supply will determine prices and the value of money. The composition of this aggregate is irrelevant in this determination. Therefore, an open market operation between fiat money and bonds would have no consequences for the price of commodities and for the value of money. Neither these nor the real variables of the economy will change because of the open market operations, so that the W–M–M theorem will also hold for this money–bonds economy. This can be established by repeating the analysis of the previous section, but replacing k by b in equations (25) to (29) – which we leave to the reader – or simply by modifying (24) to encompass market operations performed in t. These operations will increase the economy's money supply by dM_t and decrease its supply of bonds by dB_t, so that the equilibrium in the financial sector will imply the following version of (24):

$$p_t = (M_t + dM_t + B_t - dB_t)/[N_t(w_t^y - c_t^y)] \qquad (33)$$

where:

$$dM_t = dB_t \qquad (34)$$

so that (33) is identical with (24), and the open market operations will not change the price level and the value of money.

The W–M–M theorem, money neutrality and IS–LM analysis

Note that the W–M–M theorem for the economy with money, bonds and/or commodity storage is stronger than the concept of the neutrality of money. The latter is that the *real* values of the variables of the economy are invariant with respect to changes in the quantity of money, but the price level and the nominal values of the variables are affected by such changes. The W–M–M theorem states that both the real and the nominal values of the variables, including the price level, are invariant to money supply changes. This result runs counter to the fundamental implications of the IS–LM analysis and many other macroeconomic models, whether neoclassical, classical or Keynesian, that an increase in the money supply through open market operations will increase nominal national income and prices, and, in Keynesian models, might also increase real output. In these models, in contrast to the W–M–M set-up for bonds, bonds are illiquid, while money is liquid, so that an increase in the money supply, with an offsetting decrease in the quantity of bonds, increases liquidity in the economy. This increase in liquidity causes the increases in prices and nominal income. Therefore, the underlying assumptions on the nature of money and bonds are different between the IS–LM and the OLG models, and these yield the difference in the conclusions drawn from these models.

Differences in the liquidity of money and bonds – and the W–M–M theorem

What is the essential nature of bonds in the real-world economy and how does it differ from that of money? Money is the medium of exchange and the most liquid asset. While some types of bonds can be quite liquid, the medium- and long-term ones are not liquid enough to function as a medium of payments or as near-monies. If this empiricism is accepted, then bonds have to be modelled differently than done in the W–M–M model.

As we have shown, the reason for the W–M–M theorem is that money and bonds are *perfect* substitutes under its assumptions but the real world does not show such perfect substitution. The opposite scenario envisaging distinctive roles for money and bonds and with *limited* substitution between them occurs in the IS–LM models and can be incorporated into an extended OLG model adapted with cash-in-advance for purchases or with the indirect MIUF. The applicability of the W–M–M theorem in that context is re-examined in the next chapter.

23.4 AN ILLUSTRATION: AN OLG MODEL WITH MONEY, CAPITAL AND PRODUCTION

This section applies the analysis of this and the preceding chapter to a model with capital and specific utility and production functions in the OLG context.

Assumptions

Assume, as in earlier sections, that individuals live through two lifestages, each lasting one period. Each individual has an endowment of one unit of labour when young and none when old. This unit of labour can be rented to firms, in return for a real wage equal to the marginal product of labour, paid in commodities at the end of the young lifestage.

Saving can be held in either money or ownership of claims to the capital of firms, with capital being in the units of the commodity and equalling the stock of the commodity lent to the firms for use in further production. Money is fiat money and does not pay any interest. Capital borrowed in t pays in $t+1$ gross interest r_t^K equal to its gross marginal product in t. The young have neither endowments of money nor capital when they are born.

The production function of the economy is:

$$X_t = AL_t^\alpha K_t^\beta \quad \alpha + \beta = 1 \tag{35}$$

where X is output, L is the labour force and K is capital.

The utility function of each individual is:

$$U(c^y, c^o) = u(c^y) + \delta u(c^o) \tag{36}$$

where u is the period utility such that $u(c) = \ln c$.

Population in this economy grows at the rate n, with N_t born in period t, and the money supply M grows at the gross rate θ. The increase in the money supply is distributed as a gift to each of the old on a lump-sum per capita basis, so that the old start the second lifestage with per capita money balances equal to θm, where m, as before, is per capita money balances purchased during the young lifestage. We consider a number of issues for this economy.

Prices and the growth rate of the value of money

Since the individual has an income of w_t in period t and none in $t + 1$, and the increase in the money supply is distributed as a lump-sum gift to the old, the period constraints are:

$$p_t c_t^y + m_t + p_t k_t = p_t w_t^y \tag{37}$$

$$p_{t+1} c_{t+1}^o = r_t^K p_{t+1} k_t + m_t + (\theta - 1) M_t / N_t \tag{38}$$

where the lower-case letters, as before, designate per capita values of the variables. In (38), while m_t is the amount of balances carried over from period t, the last term is the lump-sum receipt of newly created money. In (37), the individual can carry forward his saving in the form of either nominal balances m_t or loans to firms equal to capital k_t. From (37), the per capita demand for real balances is given by:

$$m_t^d / p_t = w_t^y - c_t^y - k_t \tag{39}$$

The nominal supply of money in the economy is:

$$M_t^s = M_t \tag{40}$$

From (39) and (40), equilibrium in the money market requires that:

$$p_t [N_t (w_t^y - c_t^y - k_t)] = M_t \tag{41}$$

so that:

$$p_t = M_t / [N_t (w_t^y - c_t^y - k_t)] \tag{42}$$

Hence,

$$\frac{p_{t+i}}{p_t} = \frac{M_{t+j}}{M_t} \frac{N_t}{N_{t+i}} \cdot \frac{\left(w_t^y - c_t^y - K_t\right)}{\left(w_{t+i}^y - c_{t+i}^y - K_{t+i}\right)} \tag{43}$$

Since $M_{t+i} = \theta^i M_t$ and $N_{t+i} = n^i \cdot N_t$, in the stationary state with constant values of w^y, c^y, k, (43) implies that the price ratio is:

$$p_{t+i}/p_t = \theta^i/n^i \tag{44}$$

and the gross rate of growth of the value of money is,

$$v_{t+i}/v_t = p_t/p_{t+i} = n^i/\theta^i \tag{45}$$

Real wages and interest rates in the economy

The economy has the production technology,

$$X_t = AL_t^\alpha K_t^\beta \quad \alpha + \beta = 1 \tag{46}$$

Since the net interest rate $(r - 1)$ equals the net marginal product of capital X_K,

$$r_t^K - 1 = X_{Kt} = \beta AL_t^\alpha K_t^{\beta-1}$$

$$= \beta X_t/K_t \tag{47}$$

so that if an individual lends k_t to a firm at a net rate of return X_{Kt}, he will receive $(1 + X_{Kt})k_t$ in $t + 1$.

With real wages equal to the marginal product of labour X_L, and the (fully employed) labour force equal to N_t, the real wage rate is specified by:

$$w_t = X_{Lt} = \alpha \beta A N_t^{\alpha-1} K_t^\beta$$

$$= \alpha X_t/N_t \tag{48}$$

Conditions for the simultaneous positive demands for money and capital

A young individual is willing to simultaneously hold both money balances and capital if their return is identical. The gross return r^m on money is the increase in its value and is given by (45) as:

$$r_t^m = v_{t+1}/v_t = p_t/p_{t+1} = n/\theta$$

Both money and capital will be held if:

$$r_t^m = r_t^K$$

so that,

$$n/\theta = 1 + \beta X_t/K_t \tag{49}$$

which yields the required rate of price increase as:

$$p_{t+1}/p_t = [1 + \beta X_t/K_t]^{-1} \tag{50}$$

Equation (49) as the condition for the simultaneous demand for nominal balances and capital can also be derived in the following manner from the budget constraint.

Substituting (37) in (38) to eliminate the balances carried forward gives the personal lifetime budget constraint as:

$$c_t^y + (p_{t+1}/p_t)c_{t+1}^o = w_t^y + \{(p_{t+1}/p_t)r_t^K - 1\}k_t + (\theta - 1)m_t/p_t \tag{51}$$

Since $p_{t+1}/p_t = \theta/n$ from (44), (51) becomes:

$$c_t^y + (\theta/n)c_{t+1}^o = w_t^y + \{(\theta/n)r_t^K - 1\} k_t + (\theta - 1)m_t/p_t \tag{52}$$

where r_t^K is given by (47) and w_t by (48). Maximizing the utility function (36) subject to the budget constraint (51) or (52) yields the first-order condition:

$$U_t^y/U_{t+1}^o = p_t/p_{t+1} = n/\theta \tag{53}$$

where $U_t^y = \partial U/\partial c_t^y$ and $U_{t+1}^o = \partial U/\partial c_{t+1}^o$.

But if we had eliminated k_t in combining (37) and (38), the lifetime budget constraint would be stated as:

$$c_t^y + \frac{1}{r_t^K}c_{t+1}^o = w_t^y + \frac{m_t}{p_t} + \frac{1}{p_{t+1}r_t^K}\left(\theta - 1\right)m_t \tag{54}$$

so that utility maximization subject to (54) yields:

$$U_t^y/U_{t+1}^o = r_t^K \tag{55}$$

If both nominal balances and capital are held, from (53) and (55),

$$p_t/p_{t+1} = r_t^K \tag{56}$$

Hence, from (53), (56) and (47), we require (49) as the condition for indifference in holding nominal balances and capital. This was:

$$n/\theta = 1 + \beta X_t/K_t$$

Capital and output in the economy

Given θ and n, (49) specifies the amount of capital held in the economy as:

$$K_t = (n/\theta - 1)^{-1} \beta X_t \tag{57}$$

so that the representative individual's demand and holdings of capital equal to the per capita amount of capital held by the young are:

$$k_t = K_t/N_t = (n/\theta - 1)^{-1} \beta x_t \tag{58}$$

where $x = X/N$, so that the representative individual in t will carry forward nominal balances of m_t and real capital of k_t. Note that the amount of capital increases with the rate of money growth – which makes carrying forward money balances less attractive – and decreases with the rate of population growth, which makes carrying money balances more attractive.

With K_t specified by (57), output produced in the economy is given by (35) and (57) as:

$$X_t = AN_t^\alpha \{(n/\theta - 1)^{-1}\beta X_t\}^\beta$$

$$= [AN_t^\alpha \{(n/\theta - 1)^{-1}\beta\}^\beta]^{1/(1-\beta)} \tag{59}$$

where $\partial X_t/\partial\theta > 0$ and $\partial X_t/\partial n < 0$, so that output increases as the population growth rate decreases and the money growth increases. Hence, money growth is not neutral and has a positive impact on capital and output by making it less attractive to hold money balances.

The demand for capital or money for a linear production function

If, instead of (35), the production technology of the economy was a linear one of the form:

$$X_t = aL_t + bK_t \tag{60}$$

we would have $(r^K - 1) = X_{Kt} = b$, so that the condition for the equality of the return on money and capital would be $n/\theta = b$. If this condition is satisfied, neither the stock of capital – nor the output of the economy – will be uniquely determined. However, assuming the independent determination of θ, n and b, it would indeed be fortuitous if this condition is satisfied for any economy, let alone for most economies, and the more likely possibility will be that it will not be met. If it is not, and if $(n/\theta - 1) > b$, only money will be held. But if $(n/\theta - 1) < b$, only capital will be held.

Hence, this modification to our model also shows the money growth rate to be non-neutral, since for some values of θ, the equilibrium amount of capital will be zero, while it would be positive for other (higher) values of θ, so that output would be higher under the latter than the former.

Pareto dominance of the trade equilibrium with money over autarchy

In the case where money is used, maximizing the utility function (36) subject to the budget constraint (51) yields the optimal consumption pattern as:

$$c_{t+1}^o = (\delta n/\theta)c_t^y$$

and

$$c_t^y = (1 + \delta)^{-1}W_t$$

where W_t equals the right-hand side of (51). Let this optimal consumption pattern be c_t^{*y} and c_{t+1}^{*o}. Substitution of these in the utility function shows that these values will yield higher utility than the autarchic solution $c_t^{'y} = w_t = aX_t/L_t$ and $c_{t+1}^{'o} = 0$, and will be Pareto optimal.

23.5 THE NEUTRALITY AND NON-NEUTRALITY OF MONEY IN OLG MODELS[10]

The preceding section has shown that money need not be neutral in the OLG models. This section investigates this issue for a somewhat different structure of the economy.[11]

In the two lifestages OLG framework, assume a constant population and that each young person supplies h units of labour but does not consume in the young lifestage, while, when old, he consumes but has no labour to supply. The labour supply and consumption pair is (h^y, c^o). Let the lifetime preference function be $U(h^y, c^o) = -h^y + u(c^o)$, where labour has been assigned a negative utility and $u(\cdot)$ is the period utility function. Further, assume that one unit of labour yields one unit of the consumption good.

As in the earlier sections, assume that the money supply grows at a constant gross rate θ and the new money is distributed to the old as a lump-sum transfer.

For per capita consumption goods production of h while young, the lifetime budget constraint, incorporating the second lifestage's gratuitous receipt of the newly created money, is, as before, given by:

$$c^o_{t+1} = \{p_t h_t + (\theta - 1)m_t\}/p_{t+1} \tag{61}$$

so that the individual's lifetime utility function is:

$$U\left(h_t, c^o_{t+1}\right) = u\left(\frac{p_t h_t + \left(\theta - 1\right)m_t}{p_{t+1}}\right) - h_t \tag{62}$$

Maximizing (62) with respect to h_t gives the first-order condition as:

$$u'(\cdot)\,(p_t/p_{t+1}) - 1 = 0$$

which implies that,

$$u'\left(\frac{p_t h_t + \left(\theta - 1\right)m_t}{p_{t+1}}\right) = \frac{p_{t+1}}{p_t} \tag{63}$$

Assume that the solution to this equation is h^*. In the stationary state with h^*_t constant at h^* and a constant population, output will be stationary while the money supply increases at the gross rate θ. Consequently, prices will also increase at the gross rate θ, so that (63) implies that:

$$u'(\cdot) = \theta \tag{64}$$

Hence, h^* – and, therefore, production and saving – will be a *decreasing* function of the rate of inflation and monetary growth, with the result that the money growth rate is again non-neutral, as in the preceding section. However, while increases in the money growth rate increased output in the preceding section, they decrease output in this section. The reason for the latter is that the faster rate of money growth decreases the return to saving, which equals the income from labour supply, so that the former increases the inflation-based tax on labour supply and reduces it.

This tax is eliminated if the increase in the money supply is distributed, not as a lump sum, but in proportion to money holdings, which equal $p_t h_t$. In this case, the lifetime budget constraint becomes:

$$c^o_{t+1} = \{p_t h_t + (\theta - 1)p_t h_t\}/p_{t+1}$$

$$= h_t(\theta p_t/p_{t+1}) \tag{65}$$

With $(\theta p_t/p_{t+1}) = 1$ in the stationary state with a constant population, (65) becomes:

$$c^o_{t+1} = h_t \tag{66}$$

so that the individual's lifetime utility function is:

$$U(h_t^y, c_{t+1}^o) = -h_t + u(h_t) \tag{67}$$

Maximizing (67) with respect to h_t implies that:

$$u'(h_t) = 1 \tag{68}$$

so that the supply of labour – as well as output and saving – is independent of the rate of money growth, making money neutral – in comparison with (63) which implied its non-neutrality. Hence, the manner in which the seigniorage from the monetary creation is distributed matters for the neutrality of money.

While the above analysis shows the neutrality or non-neutrality with the negative effects of monetary growth, Lucas (1996) shows that further adaptations of the above model can also generate positive transitional effects of monetary growth. An example of the latter occurs if there are expectational errors of relative price changes, as in some of Lucas's other contributions.

Such neutrality or non-neutrality is at odds with the earlier W–M–M theorem that there would not be any impact of the increases in the money supply, even on prices or nominal variables. However, this theorem, unlike the current models, assumed the existence of bonds which are perfect substitutes for money and the increases in the money supply were assumed to occur through open market transfers, so that individual's wealth remained constant. The precise assumptions of the model and the mechanism for changes in the money supply are, therefore, critical to conclusions on the impact of money on the economy and to its neutrality.

23.6 DO THE OLG MODELS EXPLAIN THE MAJOR FACETS OF A MONETARY ECONOMY?

The major doubt or objection about the validity of the OLG framework as a way of modelling money in the monetary economy concerns the role of money as a medium of exchange. The fiat money in the standard versions of the OLG models clearly serves as a store of value or temporary abode of purchasing power. It trades against commodities and enables the multilateral exchange of commodities between members of different generations over time, so that its use increases allocative efficiency in the consumption of commodities over time. These properties seem to be aspects of a medium of exchange role and many proponents of the OLG models (e.g., Wallace, 1980, p. 77) have argued that money does function as a medium of payments in these models since its use is the only way the young and the old can trade in the simple OLG framework.[12] Further, the proponents of the OLG models argue that money does not properly belong in the utility function and such functions should not be introduced directly or indirectly into more elaborate forms of the OLG models.[13] The OLG paradigm is then proposed as an alternative to models with money in the utility function (MIUF) or to those with a cash-in-advance constraint, and is claimed by some of its proponents to be the best of the available paradigms for representing money in the modern economy (Wallace, 1980, p. 50).

The medium of exchange/payments role of money

The critics of the OLG framework respond that while money does act as a store of value in it, it does not really act as a medium of exchange in transactions in which no saving as an integral part of the transaction is intended by either party, and it is this role which is essential to the nature of money in the modern economy.[14] Its other role in facilitating multilateral exchanges across generations could be wholly performed by other assets that are clearly not media of exchange. To illustrate, if the return on the storage of commodities was higher than on fiat money, the latter would not be traded and the postponement of consumption from the young to the old lifestage would be accomplished directly by commodities, which clearly would not be acting as a medium of exchange. In fact, there would not be any exchanges in such an economy. Since the storage of commodities has been an option available in all economies and its return would have fluctuated with the commodity stored and the economic environment, the OLG models predict that the demand for fiat money would have fluctuated between zero and a positive amount in economies over time. Further, if the return on the storage of commodities varies sufficiently across individuals in an economy, depending upon their storage technologies, fiat money would be held by some and not by others. These predictions run counter to the observation that money holding is consistently a universal phenomenon across individuals and over time for the modern economies.

The simultaneous existence of money and bonds with different rates of return
Moreover, if bonds exist in the OLG economy and have the highest rate of return, then fiat money will again not be used. But the modern economy has many types of bonds with differing rates of return. Some of them (such as money market instruments) definitely possess a higher rate of return net of the risk premium than fiat money, yet fiat money continues to be traded in such an economy. The OLG models also fail to satisfactorily explain the demand for money under such conditions.

Note also that the actual usage of money as against that of bonds and stored commodities in OLG models does not provide any additional benefits other than the allocative efficiency made possible by the latter two assets. This runs counter to the generally recognized benefits of a monetary over a barter economy. The most important of these is that a monetary economy with given labour and capital inputs produces a substantially larger output of commodities than a barter one, *ceteris paribus*, in addition to the allocative efficiency of intertemporal exchanges done through the intermediation of bonds. The usage of money in current exchanges – as distinct from intertemporal exchanges over time – 'matters' vitally in a qualitative sense, providing a substantial increase in both output and social welfare in a monetary economy over that in the barter economy through a better allocation of output *and* a greater output.[15] This does not occur in the OLG models: beyond the increase in welfare due to the intertemporal allocative efficiency, the amount of the available commodities is not altered by the use of fiat money, so that their total amount would be the same in a monetary equilibrium and a barter one. This finding of the OLG models runs counter to one of the most widely accepted facts about the qualitative effects of money as a medium of exchange.

The continued usage of money in hyperinflations
Another well-established fact of monetary economies is the tenacity of the continued usage of money under conditions in which there are persistent and high rates of increases in the money supply, even under conditions in which (some types of) commodities can be easily stored and have a net increase in value over time, and even when there are also bonds with positive real rates of interest. The standard OLG models imply that the return on fiat money would be negative under such conditions and money would be inferior to commodities and bonds, so that it would not be demanded and used in such cases. This implication is clearly counterfactual. In fact, money continues to be traded even in hyperinflations though it is known to be rapidly losing its purchasing power. In other words, the usage of money in the economy is not tenuous, as the OLG models imply, nor do economies make periodic switches from monetary to non-monetary economies – autarchic, barter, or exchange economies with bonds but without non-interest-paying money – for the types of cases implied by the standard OLG models.

Does monetary expansion decrease welfare even with price stability?

A central implication of the OLG models is the inefficiency of monetary expansion relative to that of monetary stability, even when the monetary expansion ensures price stability. This runs counter to the purported belief of many central banks in Western countries that price stability or a low rate of inflation is preferable – in terms of increasing social welfare – to monetary stability. Further, as discussed in Chapters 11 and 12 on the central bank, central banks and economists generally believe that the ultimate objective of monetary policy should be formulated in terms of the desirable rate of inflation rather than of the rate of increase of the monetary aggregates, with the latter as intermediate targets in achieving the predetermined ultimate goals.

Money, velocity and innovations in the payments system

Monetary economies consistently show a velocity of circulation of fiat money greater than one. Among the reasons for this is the existence of near-monies, which are created privately and whose creation cannot be rigidly controlled by the state. Frequent innovation resulting in the creation of close substitutes for fiat money or otherwise economizing on the usage of such money is a common phenomenon. OLG models do not seem to be able to handle this process and impose rigid limitations on the role of the private creation of near-monies and innovations in the payments process, as well as on the evolution of velocity.

The OLG models with money, the short-run IS–LM model and business cycles

The money market of the monetary economy is handled in the standard IS–LM models through the concept of the LM curve, with changes in the real money supply due to open market operations (or price-level changes) shifting this curve. *Wallace's Modigliani–Miller theorem implies that such operations do not shift the LM curve and have no impact on the price level or the interest rate.* Neither the empirical studies on this topic nor the established wisdom as represented by the treatment of the LM curve and the views of central banks on this issue support this theorem.

Many monetary models, but especially OLG ones, assume full employment. However, this is not the universal state of all monetary economies, which also go through recessions and booms. Therefore, for the modern macroeconomy, a serious monetary model must also be able to present analyses of the disequilibrium states – with deviations from full employment in the form of involuntary unemployment or employment above the long-run equilibrium level – and the impact of alterations in the money supply on unemployment. In other words, any reasonably adequate monetary model must be able to deal with recessions and booms, as well as the consequences of money supply initiatives in such states. The current offerings of OLG models do not do so. It remains to be seen how they will be extended to the disequilibrium states and whether their implications will be consistent with the very considerable amount of data and empirical studies on the subject. However, there does seem to be some room for scepticism about this consistency.

In defence of the OLG models

It should be recognized that the OLG models with money have provided an interesting alternative to the existing MIUF and cash-in-advance paradigms and shown new insights into the role of money in the economy. Further, they are relatively new and there seems to be considerable room for their extensions and modifications. If we do not have to be purists, an attractive possibility would be to introduce elements of the medium of exchange role of money (as in the money directly or indirectly in the utility function or in the cash-in-advance models) into the OLG models. This is done in the next chapter.

CONCLUSIONS

In the stationary state of the OLG models with positive saving in the first lifestage, money has a positive demand, as long as its rate of return is not dominated by that on other stores of value. To create simultaneous demand for money and other assets, the ways in which other assets are introduced into the OLG model are sometimes such that the individual becomes indifferent between holding fiat money or the other assets – whether they be the storage of the commodity or bonds. Consequently, for certain sets of assumptions on the structure of the economy and the mode of injecting money supply increases into it, open market operations between such assets have no effects on the economy and lead to the Wallace–Modigliani–Miller theorem of open market operations. This leads to the surprising implication that the magnetization of the very considerable public debt of many countries will not change the price level in those countries. This runs counter to some of the most commonly held beliefs of economists and the policy makers – and historical experience with hyperinflations. From a purely analytical perspective, the Wallace–Modigliani–Miller theorem of OLG models runs counter to the analysis of price determination and the LM curve in IS–LM models, which are currently the most widely accepted of all macroeconomic models in economics. But other sets of assumptions on the structure of the economy and the manner in which increases in the money supply are introduced can yield an impact of the money supply increases on prices and nominal income, with such increases being neutral or non-neutral in their impact on real output and other real variables. However, each of the models presented above to derive these results still suffers from the assumption that money is no more and no less liquid than the other assets, and that the only role performed by money is to carry saving in whole or in part to the future.

In the developed monetary economy, current saving during, say, a month or a quarter, let alone a longer period, and accumulated wealth is rarely held totally in the form of money balances, whether designated as currency, demand deposits, M1 or M2. In the absence of transactions costs, most of one's wealth is converted to other financial assets paying higher rates of return. Conversely, depending upon uncertainty and expected market conditions, it is extremely rare that accumulated wealth is wholly or mostly held in the form of money. The OLG models do not properly capture such patterns of money and bond holdings, even though these patterns are central to the modern financial systems.

In less sophisticated financial systems, one can imagine developmental stages where marketable bonds do not exist, are not generally available or are too risky for the average consumer in the economy. Further, most of the economy's production in such a primitive developmental stage is likely to be of agricultural commodities with costly storage (through deterioration over time), so that the readily available commodities will also not be suitable for holding wealth from one year to the next or for more than a couple of years. In such circumstances, money would act as a store of value and be the vehicle for both saving and wealth. If the banking system is also poorly developed and inaccessible to the individual, currency – rather than demand deposits – would act as this medium for holding saving and wealth. Historically, in many economies without advanced financial systems, currency was used as the main temporary abode of saving, with gold being used for longer-term storage of wealth. There is, therefore, a closer relationship between money holdings and saving in such underdeveloped financial systems than in the modern economy.

The OLG models also do not satisfactorily explain the velocity of circulation of money in the modern economy with many near-monies and frequent innovations in the payments mechanism to economize on the use of money. Modern economies have many types of monies issued by private firms. These take the forms of demand and saving deposits, various types of liquid financial instruments such as money market funds, etc. There are also money-saving devices such as credit cards and debit cards. Privately issued electronic cards – also known as electronic 'purses' – are now coming into being. All these affect the velocity of fiat money, and must be accommodated in the OLG models if they are to explain the behaviour of velocity in a satisfactory manner.

The OLG models emphasize the use of current money acquisitions to obtain resources in the future. This is an intertemporal transfer of one's purchasing power and an aspect of the store-of-value role of money, rather than of its medium of exchange role. Any bond or storable commodity can perform this role. Further, the existence of money or its absence does not alter the flow of commodities in these models, even when they allow production, while we would expect that a monetary economy is superior to a non-monetary barter economy because the former yields higher output and more leisure.

As argued in this chapter, the standard OLG models of money do not do a satisfactory job of explaining the usage and effects of money as a medium of exchange in the monetary economy. To encompass this property of money in the OLG models seems to require the introduction into these of a cash-in-advance condition for exchange or an MIUF formulation. This is attempted in the next chapter.

From a wider perspective, fiat money is a social contrivance and there can be alternative contrivances that can substitute for its role of smoothing consumption. Among these would be social security arrangements to which individuals contribute voluntarily or through a tax scheme during their working years, and commodities are provided to them in their retirement. In a more common context, governmental schemes which reduce the need for precautionary or lifetime saving, such as social security schemes, national health care systems, unemployment insurance and welfare benefits, etc., also will reduce the demand for money in OLG models, and changes in such schemes will change this demand over time.

Economists are divided in their faith in the pure OLG models as *positive* theories capable of explaining and predicting the demand for money and the price level. Wallace (1980) claimed that the OLG model includes what is essential for a good theory of money and that it 'gives rise to the best available model of fiat money' (p. 50). Economists should recognize it as the best available and the [central bank] should not ignore its policy implications' (p. 2). However, many other economists reject the OLG models as being unsuitable for modelling money in the modern economy. This rejection has led to the claim that the overlapping generations framework 'should not be taken seriously as an explanation of the existence of money in human society' (Tobin, 1980, p. 83).

The final judgement on the usefulness of OLG models as against the cash-in-advance models and the MIUF models has to be based on the empirical applicability of the implications of these models to the modern economy with developed financial institutions. This criterion is basic to economics as a positive – rather than merely a normative – science. Under the positivist approach to economics, the basic questions relate to which of the theories better explains the demand function for money, the velocity function for fiat money, the short-run and long-run variations in the price level, and the impact of money on nominal and real output, etc. The standard OLG theory does not seem to be consistent with a great deal of empirical evidence on many of these issues. Among these are: its money demand function, with money demand a function of saving rather than of total income or expenditures; a velocity of circulation of one per period; no impact of open market operations on the price level, on interest rates, on nominal national income, and on real output and unemployment even in disequilibrium, etc. However, it must be said in favour of the OLG models that their presentation in this and the preceding chapters has been limited and basic, and that they are relative newcomers in monetary economics, so that their future developments will probably improve their usefulness for the explanation and prediction of the reality on the above issues.

As shown in this chapter, the Wallace–Modigliani–Miller theorem is not consistent with the modern classical and neoclassical analyses for either the short run or the long run, since these approaches imply that the price level and nominal national income are not invariant to open market operations. This difference in results should counter any impression that this theorem and the related OLG analysis of money in this and the preceding chapter are part of the modern classical, neoclassical or quantity theory approaches. Nevertheless, in their usual

OVERLAPPING GENERATIONS MODELS

formulations, they do possess an affinity with the classical rather than the Keynesian paradigm.

The focus of the OLG models on the investigation of the stationary states rather than of the non-stationary ones corresponds in some ways to the focus of the neoclassical and Walrasian models on the general competitive equilibrium of the economy. A Keynesian would object to such a focus, arguing that, in the short run at least, the real-world economies would not be in general equilibrium, let alone in a stationary state, so that their implications for monetary policy can have little validity for the states in which it is valid to examine the scope for monetary intervention. This issue can be put in the context of the distinction in Chapter 1 between the 'healthy' state of the economy and the 'diseased' state. The OLG models focus on the former and rarely look at the pathology of the economy. It would be interesting to adapt the OLG framework to study the latter.

We have shown that monetary growth in the OLG framework can be neutral or non-neutral, depending on the assumed structure of the economy and how monetary increases are introduced into it. The 'comparable alternatives'[16] to this OLG analysis are that of Chapter 3 for a Walrasian general equilibrium model with the MIUF and MIPF approaches and that of Chapter 26 on money in growth models. The former implied the neutrality of money under specific conditions. The latter implies the neutrality of the quantity of money in steady-state growth but non-neutrality outside the steady state. Chapter 26 distinguishes between the quantity of money and the efficiency and diversity of the financial sector. The OLG models confine themselves to the former and do not investigate the implication of changes in the latter.

SUMMARY OF CRITICAL CONCLUSIONS

- Seigniorage as a taxation device is inferior to lump-sum taxes, assuming no costs of collection.
- If money and commodities are perfect substitutes as a way of holding savings, open market operations between them do not have any impact on the economy, including its price level. This is the Wallace–Modigliani–Miller theorem.
- If money and bonds are perfect substitutes, the price level depends on their sum and not only on the quantity of money alone.
- If money and bonds are perfect substitutes, the Wallace–Modigliani–Miller theorem will also apply to open market operations between them.
- The Wallace–Modigliani–Miller theorem is a different statement than money neutrality.
- Depending on the specifications of the model, money neutrality need not hold in OLG models of money.
- Many of the implications of the OLG models of fiat money are rejected by the empirical evidence. In particular, the most significant scale variable for the demand for money is not saving, but rather expenditures on commodities.
- For OLG models to become more relevant to the modern economy, they must also include a private financial sector that creates close substitutes for money. Among these, demand deposits are in some ways at least as liquid as currency – the main component of fiat money held by households.
- Most of the fiat money in the modern economy is in the form of the deposits of the commercial banks with the central bank – and is, therefore, not directly held by the non-bank public. Its demand cannot be directly explained by the behaviour of the non-bank public.

review and discussion questions

1 What does M1 do in the real-world economies? What do bonds do? Why are they not perfect substitutes for the ordinary individual? Discuss some of the ways in which the OLG models might be modified to introduce bonds that are not perfect substitutes for M1 and capture the roles that you have attributed to M1 and bonds.

2 Compare the relationships between money, saving and wealth in the OLG model with that in the IS–LM model.

3 What is the impact in the OLG model of competitively created substitutes for fiat money by private commercial banks? What is the impact of innovations in the banking technology, such as that of ATMs?

4 For the production and utility functions specified in section 23.4 and zero population (equal to labour force) growth, examine the consequences of serious deflation for the average productivity of labour, employment and output. Is money neutral?

5 Given the information in the preceding question, would this economy always maintain full employment (at a positive real wage)? If not, derive the rate of unemployment as a function of the money growth rate.

6 Compare the assumptions and implications of the OLG models of this chapter with the neoclassical IS–LM model for (a) exogenously given endowments of commodities and without labour explicitly in the analysis, (b) the labour market and production functions of the type usually assumed in the IS–LM models.

7 Assuming full employment, does the Wallace–Modigliani–Miller theorem hold in the IS–LM model? Discuss.

NOTES

1 The usual usage of government-purchased goods and services is the provision of publicly provided goods to the economy. This is different from the assumption being made here.

2 Admittedly, the two are inextricably linked in this two-asset – commodity and money – economy, so that attempting to disentangle them through the assumption of the destruction of the commodity equal to seigniorage introduces a degree of irrationality and unrealism into the analysis.

3 Note the difference between (12) and (22.40), though both involve an identical monetary expansion.

4 A lump-sum tax is one that does not alter the relative price ratios in the economy. A common example of a lump-sum tax is a poll tax requiring the payment of a certain amount (g in the above context) by each person in the economy.

5 Imposing a lump-sum tax of g on each young and old person would mean a lifetime tax rate of $2g$. The alternative to a tax of g on the young would be a combination of lump-sum taxes on both the young and the old in each period, with a present value in the young lifestage equal to g.

6 This is also likely to apply to many other forms of direct and indirect taxation which need laws and a bureaucracy for collection. Further, such forms of taxation impose an additional welfare loss by modifying some of the relative prices in the economy.

7 Note that for any given distribution of returns to storage, if the individuals in the economy have different degrees of risk aversion, then some will demand fiat money and others will not.

8 After compensation for the riskiness of the return on the stored commodity, the gross return

on the stored commodity will equal p_t/p_{t+1}, which is the gross return on the riskless asset money.

9 An example from the microeconomic analysis of commodity markets can illustrate this point. Suppose an individual has bought ten red apples for his consumption. He is indifferent between red and green apples, which differ according to him only in colour, which to him is a totally superficial aspect. If another person were to force or ask him to exchange some of his red apples for green ones, he would remain indifferent and take no action, such as returning to the store to buy more red apples. Without such action, there would be no change in the demand and price of red apples.

10 This section is based on Lucas (1996).

11 The variation in models is being deliberately offered in an attempt to increase exposure to the types of models that can be used with the OLG framework.

12 Note that such a role is only a very limited part of the transactions' role of money in the real world, where most of the transactions between commodities and money are for current exchanges and do not involve any intended saving.

13 For example, Wallace (1980, p. 49) is critical of money-in-the-utility function approach, arguing that doing so 'begs too many questions [about which money appears in the utility function and why] . . . [and] theories that abandon intrinsic uselessness will be almost devoid of implications'.

14 Tobin (1980, p. 83) claims that 'The "consumption-loan" parable is valuable and instructive, but it should not be taken seriously as an explanation of the existence of money in human society. . . . One can call the fiat store of value of the model *money*, but it bears little resemblance to the money of common parlance or the money that economists and policy makers argue about.' Among his many other criticisms of the OLG models is 'isn't it ridiculous to identify as money the asset that the typical agent would hold for an average of 25 years, say, from age 40 to age 65? The average holding period of a dollar of demand deposits is about 2 days' (p. 84).

15 To allow the use of money to create a greater output, money balances must be an element of the production function or their usage must allow a saving of other inputs. The proponents of OLG models tend to shun both of these possibilities. They are considered in the next chapter in the context of a hybrid OLG model.

16 By comparable alternatives, we mean those which subscribe to the underlying assumptions of neoclassical economics rather than to Keynesian ones.

REFERENCES

Aiyagari, S. Rao. 'Nonmonetary Steady States in Stationary Overlapping Generations Models with Long Lived Agents and Discounting: Multiplicity, Optimality and Consumption Smoothing'. *Journal of Economic Theory*, 45, June 1980, pp. 102–27.

Bullard, James. 'Samuelson's Model of Money with *n*-Period Lifetimes'. *Federal Reserve Bank of St Louis Review*, 74, May/June 1992, pp. 67–82.

Champ, Bruce, and Scott Freeman. *Modeling Monetary Economies*. New York: John Wiley, 1994, Chs 1–3, 5, 6.

Lucas, Robert E. 'Nobel Lecture: Monetary Neutrality'. *Journal of Political Economy*, 104, August 1996, pp. 661–82.

McCandless, George T., Jr (with Neil Wallace). *Introduction to Dynamic Macroeconomic Theory: An Overlapping Generations Approach*. Cambridge, MA: Harvard University Press, 1991.

Samuelson, Paul A. 'An Exact Consumption–Loan Model of Interest With or Without the Social Contrivance of Money'. *Journal of Political Economy*, 66, December 1958, pp. 467–82.

Sargent, Thomas J. *Dynamic Economic Theory*. Boston, MA: Harvard University Press, 1987, Ch. 7.

Tobin, James. 'Discussion'. In John H. Karekan and Neil Wallace, eds, *Models of Monetary Economics*. Federal Reserve Bank of Minneapolis, 1980, pp. 83–90.

Wallace, Neil. 'The Overlapping Generations Model of Fiat Money'. In John H. Karekan and Neil Wallace, eds, *Models of Monetary Economics*. Federal Reserve Bank of Minneapolis, 1980, pp. 49–82.

——. 'A Modigliani–Miller Theorem for Open Market Operations'. *American Economic Review*, 71, June 1981, pp. 267–74.

chapter twenty-four

THE OLG MODEL OF MONEY: MAKING IT MORE REALISTIC

This chapter represents modifications and deviations away from the standard OLG models of money, even though the overall framework is still that of overlapping generations. This is done to make the OLG modelling of money more realistic in the way money actually functions in the economy and to derive implications which are closer to the empirical findings on the money demand function.

Each generation is now assumed to live for T-periods and in each period overlap with $(T-1)$ other generations.

In one of the modifications of the OLG model, cash-in-advance is required to pay for all purchases of commodities and bonds. In the second modification, money saves on transactions time in making purchases, so that it enters the utility and production functions in an indirect manner.

---

key concepts introduced in this chapter

- T-period ($T > 2$) lifetimes
- Cash-in-advance for transactions
- The relative liquidity of money and bonds in the context of the T-period OLG model
- Liquidity preference and the term structure of interest rates in the T-period OLG model
- The Wallace–Modigliani–Miller theorem for open market operations when money and bonds differ in liquidity
- The rationale for inserting money in the utility function
- The rationale for inserting money in the production function

---

The preceding two chapters presented the basic OLG model and its analysis. Many of its implications appeared to be implausible for the modern economy with well-developed financial systems. This chapter explores whether extending the OLG model from two to T-periods or blending it with the cash-in-advance concept or with the money in the utility function (MIUF) and money in the production function (MIPF) concepts would make it more applicable. Brock (1990) provides a good treatment of the relevant issues.

The OLG model arose as a contender to the traditional MIUF–MIPF approach to the role of money in the economy. It would, therefore, seem appropriate to first blend the OLG and cash-in-advance models to determine if their implications would offer an attractive alternative in terms of empirical applicability to the MIUF models. This blend in the context of a T-period model is presented in section 24.1. It is shown that it still has several implausible implications; for example, for the close relationship between saving and the demand for money, limitations on the velocity of money, etc. Therefore, we proceed to the alternative modification of the OLG models of money by introducing money in the utility function.

As discussed in Chapter 3, one justification for including money in an *indirect* utility function is that money balances reduce time in shopping and other transactions in a monetary economy. In such a context, while the *direct* utility function would only have consumption and leisure in it, the amount of leisure is reduced by the time spent in carrying out transactions, so that holding money increases leisure and therefore indirectly yields positive utility. Such justifications for the MIUF emphasize that, in a monetary economy, it is the *environment* that allows the individual to directly or indirectly attach utility to money balances.

Of the direct and indirect versions of the MIUF approach, the transactions time version seems to do less violence to the origins of the OLG model. It is, therefore, the version adopted in this chapter for blending with the OLG model. This is done in section 24.2.

However, while the holding of real balances in the context of the OLG model with the indirect MIUF increases leisure and labour supply in the monetary economy, it does not increase the output per hour of work unless money is also introduced into the production function. Here, again, there are the two possible variations of the money in the production function (MIPF) approach. The direct one puts real balances in the production function on the grounds that the greater the real balances held by the individual firm, the larger the output it produces and sells. The direct MIPF approach does not explicitly specify why money has the posited effect, but takes this effect to be a result of the environment given to the firm in a monetary economy.

The indirect MIPF approach starts with the assumptions that the firm's output depends on its use of labour and capital only, and that real balances are not in this production function. However, the firm needs to hire workers who have to be paid in a medium which they will accept, and the firm's output needs to be sold to consumers who are willing to pay in a medium the firm is willing to accept. Trying to evade or reduce the use of money forces the firm to use some workers and capital to the task of finding such workers and such consumers. In a monetary economy, the firm can reduce its costs for such labour and capital by the use of money in payments and receipts. This tradeoff brings real balances into the indirect production function and has the consequence of raising the firm's average productivity of labour, as well as increasing output in the economy as a whole. The specification of the indirect MIPF approach is given in section 24.3 and follows its presentation in Chapter 3.

Section 24.4 integrates the indirect MIUF and MIPF approaches into the basic two-lifestages version of the OLG model. Output in such an economy is greater than in the corresponding model without MIUF and MIPF for two reasons. One, a consequence of MIUF, is that the use of money by consumers/workers increases the labour supply to firms. The other, a consequence of MIPF, is that the use of money by the firm raises the average productivity per worker. Hence, the OLG monetary economy tends to yield more output than the non-monetary one. Further, the more advanced the financial system, the greater are these benefits.

Wallace's Modigliani–Miller theorem on open market operations between money and bonds or between money and a stored commodity ceases to hold in OLG models with the cash-in-advance or the direct and indirect MIUF and MIPF features. In particular, such operations can affect the price level. Further, the demand for real balances ceases to be closely related to saving.

Most of the symbols used in this chapter are carried over from the preceding ones on the OLG models and are defined there. Only the new ones are defined in this chapter.

24.1 A *T*-PERIOD CASH-IN-ADVANCE MONEY–BONDS MODEL

In order to create a positive demand and positive value for money in the presence of bonds that yield a higher return, we need to add assumptions that allow fiat money to possess a correspondingly higher liquidity than bonds. We sketch below one possible set of such assumptions. Assume that:

  (i)   the individual's lifetime is now divided into $T + 1$ ($T > 0$) lifestages from 0 to T;
  (ii) purchases of either commodities or bonds require the prior possession of money;
  (iii) bonds have a minimum maturity of one period and cannot be cashed before maturity;
  (iv) there is no resale market in bonds; and
  (v)   *only one transaction can be conducted between commodities and money, or bonds and money in a period.*

The distinction between money and bonds

The above assumptions imply that money is more liquid, in the sense of being usable for purchasing commodities *in* the period after its acquisition, while bonds cannot be so used: bonds cannot be cashed until the period after their acquisition and the funds thus obtained can only be used to buy commodities one period later. The requirement that individuals must pay in money (cash) for their purchases of commodities and bonds is known as the *cash-in-advance* or *Clower constraint*, and is a fundamental requirement of a monetary economy. Our method of its incorporation in the OLG framework is only one of the possible ways to do so, but this method does serve our purpose of introducing a liquidity difference between money and bonds in the economy.

The duration of *T*-periods and the magnitudes of the variables

Each individual in this extended model has been assumed to live for $T + 1$ periods from t to $t + T$ (inclusive). If a lifetime is taken to be 70 years, $T + 1$ would be 70 if each period equals a year; $T + 1$ would be 280 if each period is a quarter, and so on. By allowing T to become increasingly larger, the chronological equivalent of a period can be made very short. A given individual's lifetime would overlap with the lifetimes of T generations other than his own. The magnitudes of births, consumption, saving, interest rates and other flow variables would depend upon the duration of each period, each being smaller the shorter the period.

Saving in the extended model

It was a fundamental characteristic of the two-lifestages OLG model that there be (positive) saving in the young lifestage and dissaving in the old lifestage, with money being held as the vehicle for saving from the former to the latter. The extended model makes the corresponding assumption that there be saving and positive wealth accumulation in the early years of life, with dissaving in the latter years. If money is to be held in each year of life, there must be positive wealth from period 1 to period T, and there must be either saving or dissaving in each period. The latter is the statement that consumption must be different from the receipt of endowments in each period. In the absence of bequests, the amount of wealth remaining in period T is spent on commodities in that period.

In this extended model, money is assumed to be the only medium of exchange and payments. Bonds and commodities do not function as media of exchange and payments. That is, money is the medium of exchange and payments between commodities of different periods, between bonds of different periods and between commodities and bonds. Hence, saving out of the commodity endowments must be first exchanged for money and then for bonds. Similarly, bond holders receive money, not commodities, when bonds mature.

We have assumed that only one type of transaction can be performed in each period. That is, if money is received from the sale of either bonds or the commodity in a given period t, it cannot be exchanged for either commodities or bonds until the next period $(t + 1)$. If one-period bonds are then bought, they would have to be held for the period $(t + 1)$ and are cashed in period $(t + 2)$. The cash thus obtained cannot be used to pay for commodities or other bonds in period $(t + 2)$ but can be used for purchases in $(t + 3)$. Hence, while money can be used to buy either commodities or bonds in every period, bonds and commodities cannot, so that money is the only perfectly liquid (fungible) good in the model.

The term structure of bonds and the yields to maturity

There can be a variety of private or public bonds, each differing in the term to maturity from other bonds (and money), subject to the condition that the bonds must mature during the lifetime of the issuer. Since the minimum maturity is one period, there can be $T - 1$ types of bonds, each with its own coupon. Assuming Hicksian liquidity preference, as explained in Chapter 21, for shorter maturity by lenders and longer maturity by borrowers as in the expectations theory (incorporating liquidity preference) of the term structure of interest rates, there would be $T - 1$ coupon rates increasing in the term to maturity. Fiat money would have a zero coupon.

Starting with period 1, assume that the individual has positive saving in period 1 and negative saving in periods 2, 3 and 4.[1] He wishes to consume the period 1 saving in periods 2, 3 and 4. To finance the latter under our assumptions, he must hold the period 2 and 3 dissaving in money from period 1 onwards: if he wanted to invest in one-period bonds, he can only purchase them in period 2, hold them from period 2 to 3, cash them in period 3 and use the money for dissaving – that is, buying commodities – in period 4. Hence, a τ-year bond requires holding money equal to its initial value for one period and its maturity value for one period, and cannot be used for the postponement of consumption by less than $(\tau + 3)$ periods. This follows from the assumption that in a monetary economy, commodities exchange against money, not against bonds, and that bonds exchange against money, not commodities, and that there is only one exchange per period.

If the coupon rate is increasing in the term to maturity, a saver saving for τ periods – that is, with a net saving in a period $(t + i)$ followed by a corresponding amount of dissaving in period $(t + i + \tau + 1)$ – would prefer to buy $\tau - 2$ period bonds. He would not buy a sequence of shorter-term bonds since these would give him a smaller total return – with 'fallow' periods in which the non-interest-bearing money has to be held in going from one bond to another – so that even if the market yield curve were horizontal, the net return per period to the individual saving for τ periods would be higher by buying $\tau - 2$ period bonds than from any combination of shorter-term bonds. Hence, the effective rate of return for the individual would be increasing in the term to maturity even when the coupon payment per period is identical, and the markets in bonds would be segmented in the term to maturity. The effective yield curve would be upward sloping and concave.

While the preceding assumptions allow for the existence of a multitude of bonds differing in maturity in the OLG model, we will henceforth simplify by assuming that there exist only one period bonds and they can be rolled over instantly – that is, without a delay of one period which would occur if they were first converted into money. For the initial period as t, the individual will not be able to finance dissaving in $(t + 1)$ or $(t + 2)$ by holding bonds: his saving of commodities in period t is exchanged for money in t; if it is converted from money into bonds in $(t + 1)$, it would mature in $(t + 2)$ and be repaid in money in $(t + 2)$, which allows it to be spent on commodities in $(t + 3)$ but not in $(t + 2)$. Clearly, the OLG model with such a pattern must have at least four periods.

24.1.1 The analysis of the extended multiperiod OLG cash-in-advance money–bonds model

Assume that the individual lives for $T + 1$ periods from $t = 0, 1, \ldots, T$, so that he has $T + 1$ lifestages and receives some commodities in each lifestage. This endowment path is assumed to be concave as in the life cycle consumption theories, with income increasing in the early lifestages but eventually declining. There are zero endowments in the retirement lifestages. Peak 'income' from endowments occurs at some time prior to retirement. The essential assumptions are that saving be positive in the early lifestages and negative in the retirement lifestages, and that the accumulated wealth be positive at the end of every lifestage except the last one.

The assumptions on bonds are: there are only one-period bonds, each with a nominal value of \$1, and pay interest at the *gross* rate r per period. Money is the only medium of exchange so that commodities can only be traded against money and not bonds, and bonds can only be traded against money and not commodities. There is only one exchange per period, so that for net saving in t to be invested in bonds involves the conversion of commodities into money in t, holding money from t to $t + 1$ and then its conversion into bonds. The reverse process also requires two periods to convert from bonds into money and then from money into commodities. There are no transactions costs (other than the purchase price) in acquiring either bonds or commodities.

The symbols are as defined in Chapters 22 and 23. b is the number of bonds, each with a nominal value of \$1. Both m and b are in nominal terms so that their respective real values are m/p and b/p, while c is real consumption and s is real saving. We have assumed in the following that interest at the constant gross rate r on bonds is received in the form of money, which could be used to buy commodities in the period in which it is received.[2] The constraints on the individual as of the decision period t and with a life of $T + 1$ lifestages, are as follows:

For lifestage t:

$$p_t c_t + m_t = p_t w_t \tag{1}$$

For lifestage $t + 1$:

$$p_{t+1} c_{t+1} + m_{t+1} + b_{t+1} = p_{t+1} w_{t+1} + m_t \tag{2}$$

$$b_{t+1} \leq m_t \tag{3}$$

For lifestage $t + i$, $1 < i < T - 1$:

$$p_{t+i} c_{t+i} + m_{t+i} + b_{t+i} = p_{t+i} w_{t+i} + m_{t+i-1} + r b_{t+i-1} \tag{4}$$

$$p_{t+i} c_{t+i} \leq p_{t+i} w_{t+i} + m_{t+i-1} + (r - 1) b_{t+i-1} \tag{5}$$

$$b_{t+i} \leq r b_{t+i-1} + m_{t+i-1} \tag{6}$$

Now, moving to the last two lifestages, we have for lifestage $t + T - 1$:

$$p_{t+T-1} c_{t+T-1} + m_{t+T-1} = p_{t+T-1} w_{t+T-1} + m_{t+T-2} + r b_{t+T-2} \tag{7}$$

$$p_{t+T-1} c_{t+T-1} \leq p_{t+T-1} w_{t+T-1} + m_{t+T-2} + (r - 1) b_{t+T-2} \tag{8}$$

For lifestage T:

$$p_{t+T} c_{t+T} = p_{t+T} w_{t+T} + m_{t+T-1} \tag{9}$$

The demand functions for money and bonds

In the two lifestages OLG model, the demand for money was positive only in the young lifestage and equalled saving in that lifestage. This was also the amount of the intended dissaving in the following lifestage. In the $T + 1$ lifestages model, the demand for real balances is identical with positive saving only in the initial lifestage t (as in equation 1) and with the intended dissaving in the penultimate lifestage $(t + T - 1)$ (equation 8). In lifestage $t + i$, $1 < i < t + T - 1$, it will equal saving during the lifestage or the intended dissaving in the following lifestage $t + i + 1$. There is no demand for money or bonds in lifestage T.

For any lifestage $t + i$, the demand for real balances of any given individual will be the greater of (a) saving in the current lifestage in periods with positive saving, (b) expected dissaving in the next lifestage. That is:

$$m_{t+i}^d / p_{t+i} = \max(\mid s_{t+i} \mid, \mid s_{t+i+1} \mid) \quad s_{t+i} > 0, s_{t+i+1} < 0 \tag{10}$$

where s stands for saving. The demand for bonds in lifestage $t + i$ equals the individual's real accumulated assets a_{t+i} in lifestage $t + i$ less his demand for real balances. That is,

$$b_{t+i}^d / p_{t+i} = a_{t+i} - m_{t+i}^d / p_{t+i} \tag{11}$$

Leaving aside the 'ancillary' constraints – that is, other than the budget constraints – assume for analytical convenience that the desired consumption in any lifestage $t + i$ is always less than the sum of the endowments in $t + i$ and the accumulated savings by $t + i$, $i = 0, 1, \ldots, T - 1$. Under this assumption, the individual will always have positive net worth except in the last lifestage $t + T$, so that there would not be any need for the individual to borrow for dissaving, and he would not issue bonds. Consequently, if all individuals in the economy had positive net worth in all lifestages except the last one, there would not exist private bonds issued by households in such an economy. Bonds, like fiat money, would have to be exogenously created by the state – or by firms that could issue bonds to raise capital.

The life cycle consumption hypothesis (LCCH) implies that consumption will be a constant proportion of the present discounted value of lifetime endowments W_t and is specified by,

$$c_{t+i} = k(\cdot) W_t \tag{12}$$

where $k(\cdot)$ is the annuity rate (and kW_t is the income) from W_t, with W_t not being an argument in $k(\cdot)$. Hence, saving s_{t+i} would be:

$$s_{t+i} = w_{t+i} - k(\cdot) W_t \tag{13}$$

From (10) and (13),

$$m_{t+i}^d / p_{t+i} = \max(\mid w_{t+i} - k(\cdot) W_t \mid, \mid w_{t+i+1} - k(\cdot) W_t \mid) \quad s_{t+i} > 0, s_{t+i+1} < 0 \tag{14}$$

The *aggregate* demand for real balances in lifestage $t + i$ is the sum of the real balances demand of two groups, those with positive saving in $t + i$, with this saving being greater than the expected dissaving in $t + i + 1$, and those with higher expected dissaving in $t + i + 1$. This aggregate demand therefore depends on the time path of endowments over a lifetime, the age structure of the population, the distribution of each period's endowments in the population, the path of prices over time and the interest rate. Hence, the general form of the nominal aggregate demand function for money, M^d, in period $t + i$ would be:

$$M^d_{t+i}/p_{t+i} = m^d(p_t, p_{t+1}, \dots p_{t+T}, r, \omega_{t+i}, \eta_{t+i}) \tag{15}$$

where ω_{t+i} is the vector of past, present and future endowments of all individuals alive in the economy in period $t + i$ and η_{t+i} is the vector of the size of each cohort alive in period $t + i$. Equation (15) is homogeneous of degree zero in all prices.

The aggregate demand for bonds in period $t + i$ would be the accumulated wealth of the economy less the aggregate demand for real balances.

The coexistence of money and bonds

In the general case, the aggregate demand for both real balances and bonds would be positive for each period $t + i$, since some members of the population would be saving or expect dissaving in the following period, while others would be saving or carrying forward accumulated bonds for consumption several periods into the future. Both money and bonds would coexist in the economy, since money possesses liquidity and acts as a temporary abode of purchasing power, while bonds do not possess liquidity, are a longer-term store of value and yield a positive rate of interest. If bonds did not pay a positive rate of interest, money would dominate bonds by virtue of its liquidity; but if bonds possessed the same degree of liquidity as money – as when commodities could be directly exchanged for bonds or indirectly through the intermediation of money but otherwise simultaneously and without transactions costs – interest-bearing bonds would dominate money and money would not be held.

Given the above derivation of a positive money demand and a positive finite supply of money to the economy, the price of commodities would be non-zero and the value of money would be positive for each period $t + i$. It is not our intention to derive the specific demand and supply functions, and thereby derive the time path of the value of money for the extended model. The intention was to show – as has been done – the coexistence of money and bonds and a positive value of money for this general case.

Evaluating the implied money demand function

One defect of this extended $(T + 1)$ period OLG model, as of the two-period model, is the close relationship between saving/dissaving and the demand for money. Instead, in a realistic model, where money acts as the medium of payments, the model should show a close relationship between the demand for money and consumer purchases – that is, consumption.[3] Further, the close relationship between the demand for money and saving or dissaving in the OLG models is especially suspect for a financially advanced economy where savings can be held in a variety of marketable and highly liquid 'bonds' rather than in currency, demand deposits and savings deposits.

24.1.2 The Wallace–Modigliani–Miller (W–M–M) theorem in the extended OLG cash-in-advance money–bonds model

Wallace's Modigliani–Miller theorem was proved above in the context of a technology in which real balances and the stored commodity or bonds were *perfect substitutes* with *identical* rates of return. However, the extended $T + 1$ period model with money and bonds set out in the previous subsection assumes a technology at the other extreme: money can be traded against commodities while bonds cannot be directly traded against commodities, and there is only one trade per period. Hence, bonds cannot substitute for money in the individual's portfolio for the postponement of consumption by less than three periods. Further, for the postponement of consumption by more than three periods, an optimal diversified portfolio of money and bonds will be chosen, with this combination dominating in return over an exclusively money or a bond portfolio and over other combinations of money and bonds.[4] This optimal combination will depend upon the technology of exchange and the return on bonds relative to that on money.

To investigate the applicability of the W–M–M theorem in the context of our extended T-period model with money and bonds, we assume for this model that the commodity cannot be stored, or, if storable, has a rate of return less than on money and bonds, so that no one would use it for storage. Also add to this model the assumption that the central bank and the public can trade bonds against money in any period, so that the individual's purchase of bonds with money and the central bank's repurchase of some of these bonds from the individual can be accomplished in the same period.

The distinguishing aspect of the extended model was its cash-in-advance restriction so that the individual could not buy bonds in the first lifestage t of his life. In this model, his demand for bonds in lifestages $T-1$ and T was also zero. His demand for money equalled his saving or dissaving in lifestages t, $T-1$ and T. The individual could hold bonds in other lifestages, depending upon his saving and dissaving pattern. For the extended model, the central bank's open market transactions with this individual will be subject to these limitations.

To simplify the argument, assume that $t = 0$ and $T = 3$ – that is, with four lifestages from 0 to 3 – and that the net rate of return on bonds is positive while that on money is zero. Further, let there be net saving in lifestages 1, 2 and 3, with a corresponding amount of dissaving in lifestage 4. Bonds are then bought by the individual in lifestage 2 equal to the individual's saving in lifestage 1 and held from lifestage 2 to lifestage 3. Now assume that in lifestage 2 the central bank purchases some of these bonds – in the amount db_2 – from the individual against nominal balances of dm_2. To hold government consumption and the individual's lifetime income constant, also assume that the interest on these bonds while in the central bank's possession is returned as a lump-sum transfer to the individual at the maturity of the bonds in lifestage 3. Would the Wallace–Modigliani–Miller theorem hold in this context?

Let the symbols for the demands, supplies and prices prior to the open market operations be designated without an asterisk and with an asterisk after the operations. Since the operation is conducted in lifestage 2, our explicit analysis will be only with this lifestage. Under the above assumptions, the real demand for money and bonds in lifestage 2 is:[5]

$$b_2^d/p_1 = s_1 \tag{16}$$

$$m_2^d/p_2 = s_2 \tag{17}$$

Assuming initial equilibrium in the economy with the per capita demands and supplies of the money and bond holders equal to the above demands, we have:

$$b_2^s/p_1 = s_1 \tag{18}$$

$$m_2^s = p_2 s_2 \tag{19}$$

at the price level p_2 in period 2, with $p_2 = m_2^s/s_2$, where m_2^s is the exogenously given per capita supply of fiat money. The open market operation of the purchase of bonds from the individual changes these supplies to:

$$b_2^{s*} = b_2^s - db_2 \tag{20}$$

$$m_2^{s*} = m_2^s + dm_2 \tag{21}$$

where $\mid db_2 \mid = \mid dm_2 \mid$. These supplies become the individual's holdings of bonds and money. The question is whether the individual will continue to hold them willingly or seek to shed some amount of one asset for the other asset. For the following argument, note that the individual will receive the interest on db_2 as a lump-sum transfer in lifestage 3, but would not associate this as a return on the money increase, so that he does not perceive there to be any interest payment on his original money holdings or on the increase in them.

Since bonds pay interest and money does not, the individual will benefit by reinvesting dm_2 in bonds in the open market. That is, his demand functions for bonds and money in period 2 do not change. Hence:

$$b_2^{d*}/p_1 = s_1 \tag{16'}$$

$$m_2^{d*}/p_2^* = s_2 \tag{17'}$$

so that, for money market equilibrium in period 2, (21) and (17') imply that,

$$m_2^s + dm_2 = p_2^* s_2 \tag{22}$$

which implies that:

$$p_2^* = (m_2^s + dm_2)/s_2 \tag{23}$$

so that $p_2^* > p_2$ for $dm_2 > 0$. That is, since lifestage 2 has an unchanged real money demand set by saving but an increase in the money supply, the commodity price level will rise and the value of money will fall in lifestage 2. Comparing (16') and (20), since there is a decrease in the supply of bonds but an unchanged real demand, the price of bonds will rise in lifestage 2.[6] Hence, even without bothering to investigate the possible effects in the periods after period 2, we have shown that the W–M–M theorem does not hold in our extended cash-in-advance OLG model.

Hence, the W–M–M theorem of open market operations depends upon the specific assumptions introduced for the existence of an alternative asset to money. In this respect, the open market operations against bonds in our extended model seem more realistic in the modern economies than against the stored commodity or bonds in the standard OLG model without a cash-in-advance constraint. The divergence in the conclusions in the extended model from the W–M–M theorem depends on the former's cash-in-advance constraint – which, however, is not acceptable to many proponents of the OLG framework. Whether such a constraint should or should not be appended to the OLG models is a matter of dispute. But it does seem that the OLG models need to be made more realistic. An essential requirement in this process is that they must incorporate a liquidity differential between fiat money (or deposits in commercial banks) and bonds. This can be achieved through a cash-in-advance constraint, as was done above in the extended model, or through the introduction of the MIUF concept directly or indirectly in the utility functions of the OLG framework – as done in the next section. Either one of these modifications of the OLG framework would eliminate the W–M–M theorem from the modified model. Neither seems to be acceptable to many proponents of the OLG framework.

24.2 AN EXTENDED OLG MODEL WITH TRANSACTIONS TIME FOR CONSUMERS AND THE INDIRECT MIUF

The MIUF models emphasize the medium of exchange role of money, with its use as a repository for saving (temporary abode of purchasing power) as an ancillary role in the modern economy. These models and their justification were more elaborately laid out in Chapter 3. For purposes of review, we briefly repeat here some of the justifications for putting money in the utility function. The simplest one is that the individual's utility function includes any good of which more (less) is preferred to less (more). These preferences represent a subjective decision and take the macroeconomic, social, legal and other aspects of the environment as given. Further, the term 'utility' in preference theory does not mean 'satisfaction'. For a smoker, cigarettes (even though known to be harmful to health and without any objective benefits) are in the utility function. For a very polluted atmosphere in a city, clean air would be in the utility function of one who prefers cleaner air, but not in the utility functions of others. However, if the environment already has clean air, clean air need not explicitly appear in the utility function of any one. Similarly, knowing that fiat money balances can be exchanged with others for commodities, an individual who wants to trade prefers having more of money balances to less of them, *ceteris paribus*. They, along with cigarettes and clean air, would be in his utility function because of his own subjective factors operating in the context of his given economic and non-economic environment.

This raises the question: if money is intrinsically useless – that is, in terms of direct usage as a consumer good – as the OLG proponents contend, then how does it still yield utility? The above arguments based on the MIUF approach accept this intrinsic uselessness of money, as of many commodities with positive demands and prices in the real-world economies. This argument attributes utility to money by virtue of the economic environment[7] which makes it more convenient and pleasant to pay for purchases of commodities and bonds with money than with other commodities and bonds. This economic environment is part of the social setup, so that money is often called a social contrivance. This social setup is peculiar to each society and economy, so that some goods act as media of exchange while others do not.

The OLG model extended to incorporate money indirectly in the utility function

A major rationale given for the use of OLG models is that money does not directly yield consumption services to the individual and should not appear as an argument in the utility function. However, Chapter 3 had also proposed that even if money is not put directly in the utility function and therefore has no intrinsic usefulness, its usage in a monetary economy saves the consumer's time spent in shopping and payments for transactions in the context of the real-world heterogeneity of commodities and therefore increases the individual's available leisure, which has a positive utility for the individual. Using this proposal, as Chapter 3 showed, we can specify an indirect utility function with money as an argument. Since the direct and the indirect utility functions have very similar properties, we will here use the indirect utility function as a way of introducing the MIUF approach into the OLG framework.

This section reverts to the two lifestages version of the OLG framework and dispenses with the explicit use of the cash-in-advance constraint. It introduces into this OLG framework the notion introduced in Chapter 3 that the usage of money saves the individual's time in carrying out transactions and that the individual attaches positive utility to leisure. Further, it assumes that there exist one-period bonds with a positive gross coupon rate r with $r > 1$, while money has the gross rate of one.

A rather unrealistic assumption of our model in the preceding analysis was that there can be only one transaction among the commodity, money and bonds per period. We will now dispense with this assumption and assume instead that the commodity can be sold for money, which can then be used for buying bonds within the same period.

Under these assumptions, the individual's two lifestages intertemporal utility function would be:

$$U(\cdot) = U(c_t^y, h_t^{'y}, c_{t+1}^o, h_{t+1}^{'o}) \tag{24}$$

The *time constraint* for each lifestage is:

$$h'_{t+i} + n^{\sigma}_{t+i} = h_0 \quad i = 0, 1 \tag{25}[8]$$

where:

h' leisure

n^σ time required for carrying out transactions

h_0 exogenous constraint on available time (hours) per period

The justification for assuming that transactions require time and reduce leisure is obvious and also was given in Chapter 3. Further, the general form of the function for transactions time assumed in Chapter 3 was,

$$n^\sigma_{t+i} = n^\sigma(m_{t+i}/p_{t+i}, c_{t+i}) \tag{26}$$

where the partial derivative with respect to the first argument is negative and to the second one is positive. From (24) to (26),

$$U(\cdot) = U(c^y_t, h_0 - n^\sigma(m^y_t/p_t, c^y_t), c^o_{t+1}, h_0 - n^\sigma(m^o_{t+1}/p_t+1, c^o_{t+1})) \tag{27}$$

where (27) is the indirect intertemporal utility function. Money appears in the utility function for both lifestages. Since the individual dies at the end of the second lifestage and any money balances still held by him would have no value for him, we assume that he is able to rent the (usage of) money balances in the second lifestage. Since the alternative asset to money is the illiquid asset bonds with a gross coupon rate r, this rental rate of money in perfectly competitive and efficient markets would be $(r-1)$ per period. He could also rent the money balances during the first lifestage also,[9] but chooses to own them outright in this lifestage since he needs to carry over purchasing power through holding them to the second lifestage. Hence, money balances now perform both transactions and savings roles in all periods except the last one when they act only as a medium of exchange.

Therefore, the assumptions are that the saving in the first lifestage is greater than or equal to the demand for money in it and that the money balances in the first lifestage are owned outright, but are rented in the second lifestage. We also assume, as done earlier for the standard OLG model, that the first lifestage endowment exceeds its optimal consumption.

Since bonds can now be bought in period 1, the budget constraint for the first lifestage becomes:

$$p_t c^y_t + m^y_t + b^y_t = p_t w^y_t \tag{28}$$

The second lifestage budget constraint is:

$$p_{t+1} c^o_{t+1} + (r-1)m^o_{t+1} = p_{t+1} w^o_{t+1} + m^y_t + rb^y_t \tag{29}$$

where money is held in both lifestages but bonds are held only in the first lifestage. Further, money is owned outright in the first lifestage at a cost of unity but is rented in the second lifestage at a rental cost of $(r-1)$. From (29),

$$rb^y_t = p_{t+1} c^o_{t+1} + (r-1)m^o_{t+1} - p_{t+1} w^o_{t+1} - m^y_t \tag{30}$$

Substituting (30) in (28) gives the individual's lifetime budget constraint as:

$$p_t c^y_t + \{p_{t+1}/r\} c^o_{t+1} + (1-1/r)m^y_t + \{(r-1)/r\} m^o_{t+1} = p_t w^y_t + \{p_{t+1}/r\} w^o_{t+1} \tag{31}$$

The individual's real lifetime wealth W_t is now:

$$W_t = w^y_t + (p_{t+1}/rp_t)w^o_{t+1} \tag{32}$$

Intertemporal utility maximization with respect to c_t, c_{t+1}, m_t and m_{t+1} of (27) subject to (31) yields the per capita demand functions for real balances of the form:

$$m_{t+i}/p_{t+i} = \phi_{t+i}(p_t/p_{t+1}, r, W_t) \quad i = 0, 1 \tag{33}$$

The per capita demand for bonds would be:

$$b_t^y/p_t = p_t w_t^y - p_t c_t^y - m_t^y \tag{34}$$

$$= \Theta_t(p_t/p_{t+1}, r, W_t, w_t^y)$$

$$b_{t+1}^o = 0$$

Note that the demand for bonds, but not for money, in the second lifestage is zero in this two-lifestages model.

Saving in the two lifestages would be:

$$p_t s_t^y = p_t w_t^y - p_t c_t^y = m_t + b_t > 0 \tag{35}$$

$$s_{t+1}^o = 0$$

Hence, in the general case, there would be positive demands for real balances in both lifestages, a positive demand for bonds in the first one only and the demand for real balances would differ from that for saving. In particular, with $b_t^y > 0$, the demand for real balances would be less than saving in lifestage 1, and – with $m_{t+1}^o > 0$ but $s_t^y = 0$ – greater than saving in lifestage 2. This model is, therefore, somewhat more realistic than the basic OLG model in which money was merely a medium for saving, the demand for real balances had to be identical to saving, and in which money and bonds under the above assumptions could not simultaneously have a positive demand.

We do not carry this analysis further to investigate the value of money, the efficiency of monetary stability or that of monetary growth, etc., as had been done for the standard OLG model. However, it should be clear from a comparison of the above analysis in this section with that of the standard OLG model that the money demand functions are now dominated by the transactions role of money rather than by its medium-of-saving role, in which money is usually dominated by coupon-bearing bonds. Further, the demand for money is positive even when the individual's saving is zero – as in the second lifestage.

In the economy-wide context, the positive demand for money in each period for transactions implies that while the current value of money does depend on future prices, it would remain positive even if the value of money at some future date was expected to be zero. Hence, money would continue to be used even in extreme hyperinflations in monetary economies – since money continues to be required for the purchases of commodities.

An illustration

The above analysis can be illustrated by a time additive log-linear form of the intertemporal utility function. That is, let:

$$U(\cdot) = u_t^y + \delta u_{t+1}^o \tag{36}$$

Specify the period utility function as:

$$u_{t+i} = \ln c_{t+i}^\rho h'^\gamma_{t+i} \quad i = 0, 1$$

$$= \ln c_{t+i}^\rho \cdot (h_0 - n^\sigma (m_{t+i}/p_{t+i}, c_{t+i}))^\gamma \tag{37}$$

where:

$U(\cdot)$ intertemporal utility function
$u(\cdot)$ period utility function
δ 1 over the gross rate of time preference (gross subjective discount factor)

Assume for simplification that the technology of transactions is a Cobb–Douglas one and specifies the time available for leisure net of transactions time[10] as:

$$h_0 - n^\sigma(m_t^y/p_t, c_t) = k(m_t/p_t)^\alpha/c_t^\beta \quad k \geq 0 \tag{38}$$

Hence,

$$u_{t+i} = \ln[kc^{(\rho-\gamma\beta)}{}_{t+i} \cdot (m_{t+i}/p_{t+i})^{\gamma\alpha}] \quad i = 0, 1 \tag{39}$$

From (36) and (39),

$$U(\cdot) = \ln[kc_t^{(\rho-\gamma\beta)} \cdot (m_t/p_t)^{\gamma\alpha}] + \delta \ln[kc_{t+1}^{(\rho-\gamma\beta)} \cdot (m_{t+1}/p_{t+1})^{\gamma\alpha}]$$

which gives:

$$U(\cdot) = [\ln k + (\rho - \gamma\beta) \ln c_t + \gamma\alpha \ln(m_t/p_t)]$$
$$+ \delta [\ln k + (\rho - \gamma\beta) \ln c_{t+1} + \gamma\alpha \ln(m_{t+1}/p_{t+1})] \tag{40}$$

The individual is assumed to maximize (40), subject to the budget constraint (31), with respect to c_t, c_{t+1}, $m_t' (= m_t/p_t)$ and $m_{t+1}' (= m_{t+1}/p_{t+1})$, where m' signifies real balances held by the individual. Note that bonds are not a variable in this system, though they were in the period budget constraints (28) and (29), so that the optimal demands for bonds in each lifestage will be derived from these constraints for the derived optimal values of consumption and real balances.

The Lagrangian function for (40) subject to (31) is:

$$L = [\ln k + (\rho - \gamma\beta) \ln c_t + \gamma\alpha \ln(m_t')] + \delta[\ln k + (\rho - \gamma\beta) \ln c_{t+1} + \gamma\alpha \ln(m_{t+1}')]$$
$$- \lambda[c_t^y + \{p_{t+1}/p_t r\} c_{t+1}^o + (1 - 1/r)m_t' + \{(r-1)/r\} m_{t+1}' - w_t^y - \{p_{t+1}/p_t r\} w_{t+1}^o]$$

where λ is the Lagrangian multiplier λ. Maximization of this function with respect to c_t, c_{t+1}, m_t', m_{t+1}' and λ will yield the Euler conditions, which can be solved for the optimal values of these variables. We leave it to the interested reader to do so and show that these optimal values imply that:

$$m_t' < s_t$$

$$m_{t+1}' > s_{t+1}$$

Further, derive p_{t+i} and v_{t+i}, for $i = 1, 2$. It can also be shown that there can be a positive demand for real balances in each lifestage, though a zero demand for bonds in the (terminal) second lifestage. Since there can be a positive demand for money for transactions purposes in each period, its value in each period need not be zero even if its value in a future period is expected to be zero.

This model and its implied demand functions are closer to those that underlie the IS–LM macroeconomic model's demand functions for commodities, money and bonds. They can be modified to show that the use of money by households increases their labour supply and, therefore, the output produced in the economy by the increased labour force. But they will still not take account of the impact of the holdings of money on the firm's production of commodities. This is attempted in the next section.

24.3 AN EXTENDED OLG MODEL FOR FIRMS WITH MONEY INDIRECTLY IN THE PRODUCTION FUNCTION (MIPF)

24.3.1 The rationale for putting real balances in the production function

The preceding chapter claimed that it was a major defect of the standard OLG models that, while the introduction of money in them improved allocative efficiency in the consumption of a given path of endowments, it did not make for an increase in the output and availability of goods for consumption along that path. This runs against the dominant stylized facts of monetary economies that a monetary economy produces a greater output than a barter or autarchic one. One way of obtaining such a result from the OLG models is to introduce a production sector in them. This requires introducing profit-maximizing firms, with at least labour inputs in production.

For the simplest two lifestages OLG model with production, assume that each individual is endowed not with commodities but with labour time. He sells it to firms that produce commodities with it. Neither labour nor commodities can be stored. Firms use labour to produce commodities; there is no other input. In particular, the firm's real balances are not an input in this production function. Assuming a barter arrangement, the workers are paid their (real) wages in the form of the output of the commodities they helped to produce. If the worker's wage in the first lifestage exceeds his optimal consumption, then under the standard assumptions of the OLG models with money, any saving would be carried over to the second lifestage in the form of money.

Since the above scenario does not allow any benefits to the representative firm from the usage of money by it, it would not hold money nor would such balances increase its output. This is counterfactual and we need to modify the OLG model further for realism. It was also unrealistic in its assumption that firms pay their workers in the commodity they help to produce, without such a practice reducing the supply of labour to it, and its own employment and output.

Since the proponents of OLG models are generally against putting money directly in the consumer's utility function, they are also against inserting money directly into the firm's production function. The argument given for this is that fiat money is intrinsically useless and does not directly contribute as an input in production. Consistent with this standpoint, we have assumed above that money does not directly enter the production function. However, even if we accept this, in a monetary economy, while all input suppliers are willing to accept money in exchange for their supply of inputs and all consumers are willing to pay for their purchases from the firm in money, they are not all willing to do so against the commodities produced with their inputs. An 'island parable' to illustrate this would be as follows.

Assume that there are n commodities and each firm produces a particular commodity. Let the economy consist of n islands, each of which has a consumer/worker, with each worker demanding a particular commodity for consumption. If the firm is neither willing to pay wages in money nor is willing to accept payments for sales in money, its emissaries must search for islands with workers who would accept wages in its commodity – conversely, to look for islands with consumers who will pay for the purchase of its commodity with their labour. In each period, the firm sends out an emissary to look for workers. Let the possibilities of reaching the appropriate islands for effective exchange be randomly distributed. With n commodities and n islands, an emissary has a probability $1/n$ of hitting the right one in one day. If the firm sends out only one emissary per day, then, on the $(n-1)/n$ of the days that he is not successful, the firm does not get any inputs and does not produce any output. Further, the worker uncontacted but nevertheless appropriate on the appropriate island will not get to sell his labour services and does not receive any wage payment, which decreases his intertemporal consumption of commodities.

As against this scenario, consider an alternative one where all economic agents use money and stand willing to accept it in exchange for labour and commodities. An emissary in search of workers would be able to hire the required workers from the first island he reaches, promising to pay wages in money; an emissary with the commodity to sell would be able to sell them on the first island he reaches with the consumers paying in the form of money. The money brought back by the latter would be paid to the workers as wages at the end of the period, who would use it for purchasing their desired commodity in the next period and for saving. The firm would have its required workers in each period and therefore does not have to shut down for some of the periods. It would also be able to sell its output each period. Therefore, employment and output would be higher for the firm using money in addition to emissaries and for all firms in the monetary economy when compared with the expected value of employment and output in the non-monetary economy.

Now assume that the firm, without money holdings, tries to reduce its risks of shutting down or commodity spoilage by employing a larger number of emissaries. Two emissaries sent out in search of the appropriate workers reduce the possibility of shutdown for lack of workers to $(n-2)/n$. Three such emissaries reduce it to $(n-3)/n$ and so on. As against this benefit, there is the problem that multiple emissaries working independently could end up hiring more workers than can be utilized and the excess workers have to be paid even if they are not put to work, thereby involving losses for the firm.

24.3.2 Profit maximization and the demand for money by the firm

Clearly, the profit-maximizing firm in a monetary economy has a tradeoff between the amount of money it uses and the number of emissaries it has to keep. If it keeps more money balances, it needs to devote less labour for emissaries and the released labour can be used to produce a greater output. To incorporate this tradeoff into the analysis, assume a production technology with labour as the only input, of which n' of the representative worker's time is employed by the representative firm in production and n'' in exchange (as emissaries in search of workers who would accept the firm's commodity in exchange for their work). The firm's total employment of the worker's time in producing and selling output x is $n' + n''$. Assume that the firm's production function per worker is given by:

$$x = f(n') \quad \partial x/\partial n' > 0 \tag{41}$$

Further, assume that the payments technology for the monetary economy in which the firm operates is specified by:

$$n'' = \phi(m^f/p, x) \tag{42}$$

where $\partial n''/\partial(m^f/p) < 0$ and $\partial n''/\partial x > 0$, ϕ is the payments technology function and

x firm's output
n' time per worker used directly in production
n'' time per worker used as emissaries
m^f/p real balances per worker used by the firm

Let the firm's employment of the worker's time be $\underline{n}$. From (41) and (42),

$$x = f(\underline{n} - \phi(m^f/p, x)) \tag{43}$$

where $\phi x / \partial (m^f/p) = -(\partial f/\partial n')\{\partial \phi/\partial(m^f/p)\} > 0$, so that the firm's output is higher if it uses more real balances. Equation (43) is an indirect production function, with the real balances brought indirectly into it, and can be rewritten as:

$$x = x(\underline{n}, m^f/p)$$

which is the indirect production function.

The firm maximizes its profit π where π for given employment $\underline{n}$ is:

$$\pi = pf(\underline{n} - \phi(\cdot)) - W\underline{n} - \rho_m m \qquad (44)$$

ρ_m is the user cost of nominal balances and W is the nominal wage. (44) implies that the firm's supply function for output and its demand function for real balances are given by:

$$x^s = x^s(W/p, \rho_m; \underline{n}) \qquad (45)$$

$$m^{fd}/p = \psi(W/p, \rho_m; \underline{n}) \qquad (46)$$

The payments system is not static. An improvement in it makes the usage of real balances more efficient in carrying out transactions and therefore more attractive relative to the use of emissaries, so that it reduces n'' for given n, thereby increasing n' and increasing x. Hence, more advanced payments systems increase the economy's output for a given labour force.

If the firm's output also depends only on its capital stock used directly in production, but some also has to be used to support its emissaries (for example, as 'rowboats to go among islands'), the use of real balances will also allow a reduction in the latter usage of capital, leaving more capital – out of a given total amount – for direct usage in production, thereby contributing to an increase in the firm's output.

The preceding section had illustrated the incorporation of the indirect MIUF approach into the two lifestages OLG model by assuming Cobb–Douglas functions for the transactions technology. Such functions can also be used for illustrating the indirect MIPF and would assume a unit elasticity of substitution between labour, capital and real balances. The maximization by the firm of profits given such a production function would imply a positive (up to a point) but declining marginal productivity of real balances, so that the firm would have a positive demand for real balances. An economy with such firms would produce a higher output by having positive real balances facilitating the hiring of inputs and the sale of the output that is produced in the economy. We leave it to the reader to pursue the mathematics of this illustration.

24.3.3 Empirical evidence

Most economies have had well-established monetary exchanges for very long periods, so that it becomes easy to overlook the benefits from the intermediation of money in making exchanges. We offer empirical evidence in the form of descriptions of real-world cases where money was not available for making such exchanges or only gradually came into existence. One of these descriptions is provided by Radford (1945). Radford describes the economy of a prisoner-of-war camp during the Second World War. This was basically an exchange economy, with endowments in the form of prison rations and Red Cross packages and exchanges of a variety of consumer goods such as cigarettes, tinned milk, biscuits, clothing, etc. The pattern and extent of trading evolved in a number of stages, from direct trade based on barter, to the intermediation (and consequent use of the time) of intermediaries (itinerant arbitrageurs) who had to keep their cut, then to the use of cigarettes as money and eventually to the issue of paper currency (by the restaurant and shop in the camp). When cigarettes were used as a commodity money, although they could be consumed by the holder, even non-smokers began to accept them in exchange for their commodities with the expectation that they would be able to use them for buying other commodities, either immediately or later. Each stage in the transactions technology represented an increase in the welfare of those wanting to trade. There was, thus, both a transactions usage of money for obtaining a better consumption pattern than the exogenous endowment one, and a usage of money to change the intertemporal consumption pattern through holding savings in the form of money. OLG models of money capture the second usage of money but not the first one. In fact, Radford's article shows that the second usage would never have come into being if the first usage had not arisen, and that most trades were for the first type of usage. We can speculate that the usage of money for trading would have come into being even if money was only used for transactions during each day and at the end of each day returned to the issuer.

Prisoners were often transferred between camps, sometimes at short notice. Further, there was the general expectation in the camp that the war would end sooner or later and that all prisoners would then be released. Hence, this economy was fully expected to have a finite life. At the end of this life, the prison's paper money would become useless and have a zero value. The OLG models predict that, under these circumstances, paper money would have a zero value in all periods and would never have come into existence. This is contradicted by the evidence of the evolution and usage of paper money in the camp.[11]

Our second bit of descriptive evidence is given in Exhibit A. This provides a description of a context in which money becomes unavailable for transactions. This exhibit illustrates the payment and exchange practices of an economy in which money is no longer available for transactions between the firms and the workers, and between sellers and buyers, though the productions technology and the physical capital is constant, as required by the *ceteris paribus* clause of economic analysis.

The exhibit shows that when a firm pays its workers in the commodity produced, a great deal of the workers' (including their family members') time has to be diverted from labour supply and leisure to transactions activities. Consequently, the labour engaged in production – both market and home – is reduced and so is the economy's output. In addition, there is a very significant loss of utility from the reduction in leisure and in other ways (through being 'humiliated').

Further, even if we assume that the labour supply to the firm is held constant, this exhibit points out that the firm had trouble getting its raw materials because the suppliers wanted 'real money' – in the terminology used by one the factory's employees – and not the firm's output for barter. Without money to offer in exchange for the raw materials, the factory had to temporarily shut down, thereby reducing its output.

Hence, the conclusion from Exhibit A is that the use of money by firms and workers increases their production and utility. It is the environment – in this context, the need to trade with others – that creates the productivity of money and its utility. Their denial by the notion of the 'intrinsic uselessness of money' is irrelevant to the nature of the firm and the individual. This notion is unrealistically restricted, as is done in the OLG models, to the narrow context of the 'production function without trade' and the 'utility function without trade' and is counterfactual, as illustrated by exhibit A.

EXHIBIT A – AN EXPERIMENT IN REALITY[12]

Real-world experiments are rarely available to monetary economists for checking on their theories. The switch from the centralized system of the Soviet Union to the capitalist one of Russia provided many instances of the switch from a monetary system to a barter one. In these switches, the production technology and the physical system remained constant, at least for some time, but the mode of payment of workers and other inputs changed from payment in money to payment in kind. What were the consequences of this switch?

One of the instances of such a switch occurred in the context of a glass and crystal factory in Gus-Khurstalny in Russia in 1997. The factory used red lead as an input and had earlier obtained it from sources which were formerly in the Soviet Union but were now not in Russia. These suppliers wanted payment in money and refused to accept payment in the factory's products, or through some other multilateral barter arrangement. Since the factory did not have money to pay, it did not get adequate supplies of red lead and had to periodically shut down.

The workers were, however, willing to take their pay in glass and crystal – thereby agreeing to barter labour services for the factory's products – since other jobs were very scarce in the area. This meant that the workers had to bring adequate transport to the factory and had to make arrangements to sell their 'salary-in-kind' or barter it for the products that they needed.

Family members were often drafted to set up stalls by the roadside to try to 'market' the salary-in-kind. It was sometimes possible to barter some for fruit and vegetables. Some might be bartered for the products, such as linen and bathrobes, of other factories in the area. There could also be occasional sales to travellers with money who might stop to buy. But besides the considerable labour time involved, there were also many unpleasant elements. These included 'protection payments' to thugs, and the dust, discomfort, taunts and humiliation of being on such stalls.

With a shortage of money, the factory also had difficulty in making its payments in cash to the town, so that some form of barter arrangements had to be made. Under these arrangements, the town sent unemployed workers and others directly to the factory for the receipt of their benefits, paid in glass and crystal, which the recipients then had to sell or trade for the commodities they needed.

24.4 THE BASIC OLG MODEL WITH THE INDIRECT MIUF AND MIPF

To combine a technology based on the indirect MIUF and MIPF with the OLG model, note that each worker has been allocated an exogenous endowment h_0 of time in each period. Focusing on the net amount not taken up in leisure h', some of this time is used by the worker looking for work and in transactions n^σ, and the rest is offered to firms as labour supply n. But if the worker is paid for his labour by the firm in the firm's commodity, rather than in money, he has to spend part of his time (for example, on the 'roadside stand') in an attempt to exchange this commodity for those he needs for consumption, thereby reducing the labour time he sells to the firm. In fact, his productivity and real wage per hour is reduced by the time devoted on the roadside stand, which is a consequence of his employment in a barter economy. Although this is a very significant element, let us ignore this as a way of simplifying the argument.

Assuming full employment, n' out of n is used by the firm for emissaries and only the remainder n'' is available for production, so that $n = n' + n''$ and $h_0 = h' + n^\sigma + n' + n''$, where, as a reminder, h_0 is the total available time per worker, h' is leisure, n^σ is transactions time, n'' is used by the firm for facilitating transactions through emissaries and only n' is directly used in production. Introducing time subscripts for the two-period OLG model, n^σ_{t+i} depends on $(m^h/p)_{t+i}$, while n''_{t+i} depends on $(m^f/p)_{t+i}$, where m^h/p are the worker' own real transactions balances and m^f/p are the firm's real transactions balances.

Let the output produced by n'_{t+i} be w_{t+i} and assume that it is fully paid out in wages. Hence, the worker's income/output in the two lifestages will be:

$$w_t^y = \Psi(n_t'^y) = \Psi(h_0 - h_t'^y - n_t^{\sigma y} - n_t''^y)$$

$$= \Psi(h_0 - h_t'^y, m_t^{hy}/p_t, m_t^{fy}/p_t) \tag{47}$$

$$w_{t+1}^o = \Psi(n_{t+1}^{'y}) = \Psi(h_0 - h_{t+1}^{'y} - n_{t+1}^{\sigma y} - n_{t+1}^{''y})$$

$$= \Psi(h_0 - h_{t+1}^{'o}, m_{t+1}^{ho}/p_{t+1}, m_{t+1}^{fo}/p_{t+1}) \qquad (48)$$

where $\partial w_{t+i}/\partial(m_{t+i}^h/p_{t+i}) > 0$ and $\partial w_{t+i}/\partial(m_{t+i}^f/p_{t+i}) > 0$ for $i = 0, 1$. Consequently, an OLG economy with the indirect MIUF and MIPF produces more output in each period because the use of money by workers increases labour supply – by reducing transactions time – and employment, and the use of money by firms increases the amount of employed labour devoted to direct production.

In equilibrium, there will be an optimal amount of real balances held by both workers and firms, with the economy's per capita demand for nominal balances being given by:

$$m_{t+i}^d = m_{t+i}^h + m_{t+i}^f + f(p_{t+i}s_{t+i}) \qquad (49)$$

where $f(\cdot)$ is the medium of saving – i.e., store of value – demand for real balances in the OLG framework. This total demand for real balances, with some held by workers and some by firms, will not, except as a coincidence in special circumstances, be identical with saving in each period, thereby eliminating one of the undesirable implications of the basic OLG model. This was the close – usually identical – association between saving and the demand for real balances. In fact, according to (49), the transactions demand for real balances by both firms and households will be related to consumption and output, rather than saving, though there is also a component that is related to saving.

While a more advanced payments system may decrease or increase the demand for real balances, it will increase the time available for direct production by economizing on the use of workers' time in transactions and as emissaries, thereby increasing the output produced each period in the economy and the income of the workers in each lifestage. This will increase both the representative worker's welfare and social welfare.

As a corollary, saving and the demand for real balances by individuals and firms would depend upon the use of money, its cost and the stage of development of the payments system, and the desirability of holding saving in real balances. Further, with money performing a medium-of-payments role during each period – in addition to its store-of-value role across periods – and partly held for that purpose, while bonds are not, an open market operation between money and bonds will not yield Wallace's Modigliani–Miller theorem for fiat money in OLG models. Similarly, with money performing this medium-of-payments role while stored commodities cannot, an open market operation between money and the stored commodity will also not bear out this theorem. In particular, the price level will not be invariant with respect to such open market operations.

CONCLUSIONS

This chapter has amended the OLG framework by bringing into it either the cash-in-advance constraint or money indirectly in the utility and production functions. In the former case, fiat money can coexist with bonds paying a positive rate of interest if the bonds cannot be directly exchanged for commodities and there can be only one trade among commodities, money and bonds in any one period. Money is then needed for purchasing commodities and/or as the vehicle for saving or dissaving. Under our assumptions in the cash-in-advance OLG model, while bonds were one-period ones, their use did not allow the postponement of consumption by just one period, but the use of money could do so. Conversely, with bonds paying interest, money was not used for holding wealth unless it was required for buying commodities in the following period or because the endowments of commodities were in excess of their consumption in the current period. That is, money dominated bonds as a temporary abode (from one period to the next one) of purchasing power by virtue of its liquidity while bonds dominated money as a longer-term store of value.

The extended $(T + 1)$ lifestages OLG model with a cash-in-advance constraint implied that an individual's demand for money in any period i is identical with the larger of the saving in period i or the dissaving in period $i + 1$, in terms of their absolute values. Even this implication is unrealistic for the modern financially developed economy where there is rarely much of a correspondence between the quite different variables of real balances and saving.

The second extension of the OLG framework brought in the transactions time hypothesis in the context of a multiplicity of heterogeneous commodities. Money could now be used not only as a possible vehicle for saving but also for purchasing commodities within each period. This allowed the introduction of illiquid bonds which could not be exchanged for commodities directly but which could serve as a vehicle for savings and as such would earn a higher rate of return than money. The use of money for transactions allowed the individual to save transactions time and increase his leisure and utility in each period. Such usage also increased the social welfare for the economy. While the use of bonds was confined only to the longer-term carryover of savings, it allowed the individual to earn a higher rate of return than money and thereby allowed an increase in his welfare. The individual's demand for money in this context became distinct from the individual's saving and dissaving, and was determined by his liquidity needs. This is a more realistic implication than of the OLG models without the direct or the indirect MIUF.

This modified model with the indirect MIUF or with cash-in-advance can be further extended to allow a range of near-monies differing in the degree of liquidity. This would seem to require a T-period model, where each period is extremely short and where money can be used for payments at any time, but each near-money requires some delay in processing.

The addition of the indirect MIUF hypothesis to the OLG framework does not change the level of output per employed worker produced in the economy and therefore would not explain why monetary economies have higher output per worker than non-monetary ones. To explain this, we needed production in the model, with firms using money balances to economize on the labour which would otherwise be needed for transactions involving the purchase of their inputs and the sale of their output. The labour thus released from transactions purposes becomes utilized in production and increases the productive capacity of the economy as a whole. This led to the incorporation of the indirect MIPF in the OLG model.

While the 'merger' of the indirect MIUF and MIPF hypotheses with the OLG hypothesis yield much more plausible results, such 'merger' – or is it a 'takeover'? – is unlikely to be acceptable to many proponents of the standard OLG models with money. Further, the implications of this merger are very much similar to those of the MIUF and MIPF models, so that the distinctiveness of the OLG framework becomes severely diluted. This merger, however, is likely to be quite acceptable to those in the MIUF and MIPF traditions since they see the OLG framework as a way of extending the MIUF and MIPF notions to an intertemporal context.

SUMMARY OF CRITICAL CONCLUSIONS

- Cash-in-advance models of transactions impose a distinction between the liquidity of money and bonds, with money being the more liquid asset.
- The Wallace–Modigliani–Miller theorem does not hold in an economy with money and bonds that differ in liquidity.
- The use of money by consumers allows a reduction in the time devoted to the sale of their labour and their purchases of commodities, and implies an increase in their labour supply to firms.
- The use of money by firms reduces the labour and capital inputs that have to be allocated to the sale of their output and the hiring of their inputs, and, therefore, increases the proportion of their employees employed directly in production.

- At the economy's level, the use of money by consumers and firms increases the leisure time and labour supply of workers and the output produced in the economy. Therefore, the use of money in the economy increases both consumer welfare and profits of firms.
- The scale determinant of money demand in a period is not saving or dissaving in that period.
- Money continues to be used even in hyperinflations even though its holdings incur high negative rates of return.
- In the limiting case, money continues to maintain a positive value even if its value in some future period is expected to become zero.
- These facts are better explained by an OLG model incorporating MIUF and MIPF than by one with a savings role for money but without its usage in current payments.

review and discussion questions

1 Which of the following approaches to money demand do you prefer: (a) MIUF, (b) the indirect MIUF, (c) cash-in-advance or (d) OLG models? Why?

2 Some economists have claimed that the OLG model of fiat money includes what is essential for a good theory of money and that it should be recognized as the best available one. Draw up a list of (a) what you consider to be essential for a good theory of money, and (b) the policy implications of the OLG model. Assess how far (b) satisfies (a).

3 Given your list (a) of the preceding question, how far does the MIUF approach (i) without time and overlapping generations, (ii) with overlapping generations satisfy the items in your list (a)? In answering (i), you may, if you want, use the IS–LM framework as embodying the MIUF approach.

4 What is the meaning of utility in microeconomic theory? In answering this question, consider the following. Why are goods that seem to harm the individual's physical or mental well-being placed in the utility function? Why do goods with upward-sloping demand functions (i.e., with $\partial x_i^d/\partial p_i > 0$) due to snob appeal possess the marginal utility that they do? What is the significance of the environment (physical, economic, social, political, etc.) as an element in the determination of the preferences of the individual?

5 Why does the W–M–M theorem hold in the analysis of Chapter 23 but not in the analysis presented in this chapter? What is the critical difference in the assumptions that changed this finding and what is your own assessment of their plausibility?

   Does the W–M–M theorem hold or not hold in modern developed economies? Does it do so in the LDCs with poorly developed financial markets? Discuss.

6 If currency (a fiat money) is intrinsically useless for firms and households, are demand/checking deposits also intrinsically useless for them? Why, then, do they hold these when there are other highly liquid assets such as savings deposits and money market mutual funds that offer higher returns than demand deposits? If the only demand for checking deposits is for holding savings, as in the OLG models of money, why do banks offer such checking accounts and not confine themselves to savings and term deposit accounts?

7 Discuss the different parts of the following statement: 'For the modern economy, the theory of the speculative demand for money has come to the conclusion that there is no longer an asset demand for M1 and that any demand for it is only for facilitating current transactions. However, the OLG models have chosen to assert the asset demand for fiat money, and presumably for M1 also, to the exclusion of the transactions demand and the inventory models of the transactions demand. The OLG models of money, therefore, incorporate an out-of-date and currently non-existent motive for holding M1.'

NOTES

1 Period 1 is for $i = 0$; period 2 is for $i = 1$, and so on.

2 We could have alternatively assumed that this interest receipt could only be spent one period later. None of our results depend upon this assumption.

3 MIUF models do so. Another model which does so – even without MIUF – is the inventory model of the transactions demand in Chapter 3.

4 Assuming a gross rate of (riskless) return on bonds greater than on money, and for a desired i period postponement of consumption of one unit from period t to $t + i$, $i > 3$, the unit will be held in bonds from the $(t + 1)$th period up to (but not including) the $(t + i - 1)$th period, and in money for the t and $(t + i - 1)$ periods.

5 We have omitted the subscript t in the following, since it was an unnecessary appendage in this section.

6 Further, since the yield on bonds varies inversely with their price, it will fall in period 2 in response to the decreased supply of bonds brought about by the open market operations.

7 Many goods in the economy similarly belong in the subjective utility function by virtue of the social environment. For example, ladies' fashionable dresses of the 1890s would be in the utility function of the ladies in the 1890s but, being now out of fashion, are not likely to be in the utility function of the ladies of the 1990s. In the case of both fashionable clothes and money, the intrinsic usefulness or uselessness of goods in direct consumption is less relevant than the social and economic environment in determining whether or not a particular good is in the utility function or not. The emphasis on the intrinsic uselessness of money is, therefore, a red herring.

8 We have assumed here that none of the time is spent working. This is an unusual assumption but the introduction of the labour supplied would not change the results, but would require the introduction of a wage rate for it. This would be an unnecessary encumbrance at this point.

9 This assumption that the services of money are only rented is necessary only for the terminal period. In a T lifestage model, this assumption would be needed only for period T.

The alternatives of owning versus renting money are similar to those of owning versus renting a consumer durable good such as a refrigerator, with the user cost from owning equalling the rental rate in perfect markets.

10 Note that in this economy with endowments of commodities but no production and employment, leisure equals total available time less transactions time.

11 The paper money in the camp was supposed to be backed 100% by food held by the prison restaurant and shop, so that there could in principle be full redemption of the currency. We consider this to be a minor variation from the assumptions of fiat money, since no prisoner expected to be really concerned about redemption or non-redemption on the release day.

12 The following is based on an article that appeared in the *Montreal Gazette* (page D2), 7 February 1997.

REFERENCES

Brock, W. A. 'Overlapping Generations Models with Money and Transactions Costs'. In B. M. Friedman and F. H. Hahn, eds, *Handbook of Monetary Economics*, Vol. I. Amsterdam: North Holland, 1990.

Radford, R. A. 'The Economic Organisation of a POW Camp'. *Economica*, 12, 1945, pp. 189–201.

part
nine

MONEY AND FINANCIAL INSTITUTIONS IN GROWTH THEORY

chapter twenty-five

NEOCLASSICAL GROWTH THEORY WITHOUT MONEY

This is the first of two chapters on growth theory. This chapter sets out the neoclassical growth models without money, so that it is strictly inappropriate for a textbook in monetary economics and belongs in textbooks in macroeconomics. However, knowledge of the material in this chapter is a prerequisite for the growth analysis incorporating money. Students already familiar with the neoclassical growth theory and with the modern endogenous growth theories can either use this chapter for revision or skip it.

Modern growth theory has two distinct components. One of these was specified by Solow in the 1950s and was designated as the neoclassical or the Solow growth model. This model assumes that the shifts in the production function – also called technical change – are exogenous. The 1980s saw a major revision of growth theory to encompass endogenous technical change and growth.

---

key concepts introduced in this chapter

- The neoclassical growth model
- Steady-state level of output per capita
- Steady-state growth rate
- Convergence and divergence of growth rates among countries
- Exogenous technical change
- Innovations and inventions
- Endogenous technical change
- Endogenous growth theory
- Externalities generated by the creation of new knowledge
- International flows of knowledge

Our eventual objective in the study of growth theory is to present monetary growth theory, that is, growth theory that explicitly models the role of money in the economy. However, the basic building block of such a theory is the growth theory without money, so that the concepts and the foundation of the latter have to be first covered, even though selectively, as done in this chapter. The next chapter will extend this material to include money in the economy.

The critical assumption that separates growth theory from the short-run models of Chapters 13 to 16 is that the capital stock is taken to be a variable in the former and constant in the latter. Growth theory places also special emphasis on the steady state of the economy, where the steady state (SS) is defined as that long-run equilibrium of the economy in which the capital–labour ratio is constant. In terms of implications, our interest in the growth theories will focus on three issues:

(i)   The *SS level* of output per capita.
(ii) The *SS growth rate* of output per capita.
(iii) The growth rate of the economy in the long-run equilibrium outside the steady state. Since such analysis normally deals with the growth rates at capital–labour ratios below the steady-state one, we will denote it as the *pre-SS growth rate*.

Exogenous shifts which change per capita output are said to have *level effects*, while those which change the growth rate are said to have *growth effects*. While many expositions of growth theory often focus only on the SS growth effects, economic analysis and policy need to be concerned with all three types of effects, since (i) is related to the standard of living in the economy and (iii) is always of topical concern because economies are rarely, if ever, likely to be in the steady state and the attainment of the steady state could take many decades.

Much, if not most, of the growth theory in the literature is neoclassical in its assumptions and analysis, so that this chapter is based on the neoclassical format. However, there are also other approaches to growth theory. One of these is the Keynesian one, which emphasizes a role for investment, independent from that of saving, and seeks to integrate the divergence between the two into its long-run growth analysis, following the contributions of Roy Harrod and other economists, starting in the late 1930s. A more institutional approach, especially on the processes leading to technical change, is that of the Austrian School. These approaches have become less fashionable in modern economics and are not covered in this book.

The fundamental assumptions of neoclassical growth theory which distinguish it from the short-run neoclassical macroeconomic model studied in Chapter 13 are that, in the former:

(i)   all markets are taken to be in equilibrium; and
(ii) physical capital stock is variable.

Assumption (ii) clearly delineates the separate spheres of short-run models and growth theory, with the latter dealing with a long run in which the capital stock is no longer fixed but changes with investment. On (i), the *raison d'être* of short-run macroeconomic models is to examine the nature of the state or states of equilibrium in the markets and the consequences of deviations from these; growth theory, by assuming equilibrium in all markets, takes the equilibrium states of the short-run models for granted. As a consequence, the main items of interest in short-run models – such as the determination of prices, unemployment, fluctuation of output, monetary and fiscal policy effects, etc. – which depend on aggregate demand in the economy are not normally considered in growth theory.

The *basic* neoclassical growth model was specified by Solow (1956). Among its defining characteristics are constant returns to scale in production, diminishing returns to increases in each input (while holding other inputs constant), a constant average propensity to save, the lack of an independent investment function and the absence of money. This model also assumes that the pace of technical change is exogenous.

The new emphasis in growth theory in recent decades has been on endogenous growth, usually due to endogenous change in the knowledge of the techniques of production. While the earlier statements of neoclassical growth theory had assumed exogenous technical change, the notion of endogenous technical change is not inconsistent with neoclassical growth analysis and can be seen as its extension. There can exist different mechanisms that can lead to endogenous technical change. These are still not fully encompassed or understood in the literature, and their presentation in this chapter offers a very limited exposure to this topic.

Among the major contributions on endogenous technical change are those of Romer (1986, 1990) and Lucas (1988, 1993). There are two major alternative themes in the endogenous growth literature. One is that certain aspects of a firm's production create spillovers and externalities that also benefit other firms in the economy. One of these aspects is the generation of new knowledge through learning on the job, quality upgrading during production, through R&D expenditures and in other ways. Illustrations of such knowledge would be the blueprints drawn up in firms for new types of machines or products, or it could be just the knowledge of employees, even when no blueprints are produced.[1] Once created in a firm, the knowledge of new techniques and products can often be used by other firms, either without extra cost, or at relatively small cost or merely at the cost of buying some units of the equipment which embodies the new knowledge. Since the firm that creates the new knowledge does not necessarily benefit fully from its dissemination, the benefit to the economy as a whole from the creation of the new knowledge exceeds that to the firm creating it.

The alternative major theme in the endogenous growth literature focuses on the increase in new knowledge in the form of human capital. While the traditional approach to human capital was on the continuation of existing knowledge through schooling, the endogenous growth literature examines the generation of new knowledge as an outgrowth of the existing human capital.

At the international level, the emphasis on knowledge as a major contributor to growth increases the importance of learning from other, especially more technologically advanced, countries and therefore enhances the role of international trade and technology importation in the growth of countries. Economies that are relatively closed would be able to learn less from other countries and would tend to have slower growth.

Section 25.1 presents the basic concepts and assumptions of growth theory and their relationship to those of short-run macroeconomic models. Sections 25.2 and 25.3 present the basic neoclassical growth model of Solow (1956). This model assumes the diminishing marginal productivity of capital per worker and also assumes that technology and technical change are exogenous. Since it fails to explain in a satisfactory manner certain features of the experienced growth rates across countries, sections 25.4 to 25.6 modify the basic neoclassical model to introduce into it increasing returns to capital per worker and/or endogenous technical change. The importance of trade for growth is briefly discussed in section 25.7.

25.1 SETTING THE BOUNDARIES OF MACROECONOMIC GROWTH THEORY

The boundaries of the standard treatments of neoclassical growth theory analysis are set by:

(i) Standard neoclassical growth theory focuses on output growth as a consequence of labour force growth and growth in the capital stock. It ignores the growth in the stocks of money and bonds (including equities). In fact, many economists believe that the long-run growth of the economy is independent of the money stock and even of its growth rate. As a consequence, the inclusion of money in growth theory is left to the special topic of monetary growth theory. This will be set out in the next chapter.

(ii) Most treatments of growth theory ignore the government sector – thereby ignoring government expenditures, taxation and deficits.

(iii) Most presentations of growth theory also ignore the external sector – thereby ignoring imports, exports, the terms of trade, the balance of trade and the balance of payments.

(iv) Since neoclassical growth theory assumes short-run equilibrium in the labour market, it does not examine the determination of unemployment or changes in its rate in the short or even the long run. Therefore, it does not see a need to differentiate between employment and the labour force. Further, it usually assumes that the labour force grows at the same rate as population.

(v) As seen in Chapters 13 and 14, a critical assumption of short-run macroeconomic theory is that the saving and investment functions are distinct from each other. However, in fact, saving is done by households on the basis of utility maximization while investment is done by firms on the basis of profit maximization. Given a closed economy without a fiscal sector, short-run equilibrium requires the equality of saving and investment. Since growth theory starts by assuming such equilibrium, saving and investment become identical in growth theory. While this identity could be defined in terms of an exogenous investment function and accommodative saving, neoclassical growth theory assumes an exogenous saving function and accommodative investment. That is, neoclassical theory specifies the saving function on the basis of household behaviour and assumes that investment always equals saving – which is determined independently of investment – so that a separate investment function is not specified. Further, since such models assume continuous full employment, saving is the amount at full employment and investment is determined by and always equal to full employment saving.

Neoclassical growth theory focuses on the long-run equilibrium paths of the economy. A special state of such long-run growth paths is SS paths along which the growth rates of certain designated variables, particularly the capital–labour ratio, are constant. Quite clearly, the actual economy of any country at any particular time may not even be in long-run equilibrium, let alone in a steady state. However, many economists believe that economies tend towards the steady state and that its study reveals the long-run tendencies of the economy. Given this belief, the usual focus of neoclassical growth theory is on examining the existence and stability of steady states in long-run models. But, as mentioned in the introduction, the public and the policy makers do have a lively interest in the level of per capita output and the pre-SS growth rates, so that we will also examine the determinants of these variables.

25.2 THE BASIC (SOLOW'S) NEOCLASSICAL GROWTH MODEL

In setting out the basic version of neoclassical growth theory, Solow (1956) assumed a neoclassical production function of the form:

$$Y = F(K, L) \quad Y_K, Y_L > 0; Y_{KK}, Y_{LL} < 0, Y_{LK} > 0 \tag{1}$$

where:

  Y output[2]
  K capital stock
  L labour force

$F(\cdot)$ is assumed to have continuous second-order partial derivatives and constant returns to scale, so that:

$$\lambda Y = F(\lambda K, \lambda L) \quad \lambda > 0 \tag{2}$$

For $\lambda = 1/L$, (2) implies that:

$Y/L = F(K/L, 1)$

which can be rewritten simply as:

$y = f(k) \quad f_k > 0, f_{kk} < 0$ (3)

where:

  y output per worker/capita[3]
  k capital per worker/capita

The Solow model assumes that in the aggregate the average propensity to save is constant, so that the per capita saving function is:

$s = S/L = \sigma Y/L = \sigma y$ (4)

where:

  S aggregate saving
  s per capita saving
  σ average propensity to save (APS)

It is also assumed that the capital stock changes by the amount of investment and the latter equals saving, so that designating the change in a variable x over time as x' ($= \partial x/\partial t$):

$K' = \partial K/\partial t = \sigma Y$ (5)

Further, the labour force growth rate is assumed to be constant at n. Using our convention that the growth rate of a variable x is designated by x'', this assumption is:

$L'' = (\partial L/\partial t)(1/L) = L'/L = n$ (6)

Equations (1) to (6) constitute the basic assumptions of neoclassical growth theory. The analysis based on them is as follows. Since $k = K/L$, $k' = \partial K/\partial t$ and $k'' = k'/k$,

$k'' = k'/k = K'/K - L'/L$

so that:

$k' = K' \cdot (k/K) - nk$ (7)

where $K' = S$ and $k/K = 1/L$. Hence,

$k' = S/L - nk$ (8)

$\quad = \sigma Y/L - nk$

$\quad = \sigma f(k) - nk$ (9)

In the steady state with a constant capital/labour ratio, $k' = 0$, so that the steady-state requirement is that:

$$\sigma f(k) = nk \tag{10}$$

Figure 25.1a graphs equation (8) with k on the horizontal axis. Note that, just as for similar figures elsewhere in this chapter, we have not labelled the vertical axis of this figure. The measurement units for this axis are output units. The concave curve – representing $\sigma f(k)$ – measures saving per capita, while the linear line – representing nk – measures investment requirements for new workers to maintain the existing capital–labour ratio. We will follow this custom of not labelling the vertical axis for similar figures later in this and the next chapter.

In Figure 25.1, the curve marked $\sigma f(k)$ ($=S/L$) represents saving per capita. Since $f_k > 0$ and $f_{kk} < 0$, this curve is concave. Since n is a constant by assumption, nk is linear. Steady state occurs at k_0^*. To the left of k_0^* at k_1, saving is greater than required to equip new workers at the existing capital/labour ratio and capital per worker increases for all workers, causing a rightward movement towards k_0^*. To the right of this point, say at k_2, saving (i.e., new capital) is less than required to equip new workers at the existing capital/labour ratio. Since all workers have an identical amount of capital per worker, the capital provided to all workers will decrease, prompting a leftward movement to k_0^*.[4] Therefore, k_0^* is stable.

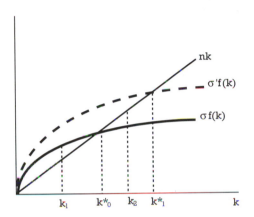

Figure 25.1a

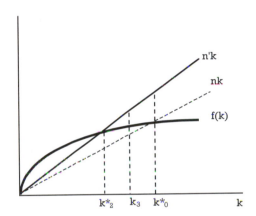

Figure 25.1b

In Figure 25.1a, at k_0^*, k – which equals K/L – is a constant, so that,

$$K'' = L'' = n \tag{11}$$

Further,

$$y^* = f(k_0^*) \tag{12}$$

so that y must also be a constant, say at y_0^*. That is, in steady state:

$$y''(k^*) = 0 \tag{13}$$

Given the constancy of y in steady state,

$$Y''(k^*) = n \tag{14}$$

That is, the steady-state growth rate of output is determined by, and equals, the growth rate of the labour force.

The impact of shifts in the saving rate and in the labour force growth rate

Note that by (11) and (14), Y'', just as K'', in the steady state depends only on the growth rate of labour and not on the saving rate. An increase in the APS from σ to σ' shifts the $\sigma f(k)$ curve in Figure 25.1a upwards to $\sigma' f(k)$ and establish a new SS rate at a higher value of k, say at k_1^* where $k_1^* > k_0^*$. At k_1^*, the output per worker – and therefore the standard of living – will be higher but the growth rate of output is still at the rate n specified by (14). However, it will rise above n during the *transition* from k_0^* to k_1^*: the growth rate is higher at k_2 than at k_0^* and k_1^*.

An increase in the labour force growth rate from n (to n') will raise the nk curve in Figure 25.1b to the $n'k$ curve. This decreases the SS values of k from k_0^* to k_2^*. This lower value of the SS output–capital ratio lowers the steady-state value y^*, thereby reducing the SS standard of living, even though, by (14), the higher labour force growth rate will increase the SS growth rate of output.

Hence, in terms of the standard of living, countries are better off with a higher σ and a lower n, even though variations in σ do not alter the SS per capita growth rates k'' and y'' while an increase in n increases the SS output growth rate Y''. Policy makers desirous of a higher standard of living for the population would want a higher saving rate and a lower labour force growth rate, even though the former does not change the steady-state growth rate while the latter reduces it.

Some implications of the above growth model versus empirical experience

We discuss here two implications of the Solow growth model which run contrary to empirical evidence, at least for some countries. These are as follows:

(i) If we assume that all countries have the same production function, but different values of σ and n, their SS growth rate would be set by their labour growth rate, which is exogenously given to the model. Hence, countries with higher population – and therefore higher labour force – growth rate should be observed to grow faster. This runs contrary to the general cross-country experience, since the industrialized countries with low population growth rates often have higher average growth rates than developing countries with higher population growth rates.

One possible explanation that might be adduced for this contrary observation would be that the countries are not in steady state, but are scattered along the k axis in Figure 25.1a, with the industrialized countries having higher values of k and being closer to k_0^*. However, starting from $k = 0$, as we move to higher values of k, y'' should be higher than at k_0^* and increasing for a good part of this range. This again does not appear to be consistent with the general growth experience across countries.

(ii) For the assumed production function, $\partial y_k / \partial k < 0$, where y_k $(=Y_K)$ is the marginal productivity of capital (MPK).[5] Since the real interest rate (excluding a risk premium) equals y_k, the model implies that the real interest rate would decline as a country moves to a higher value of k and therefore of y, which implies that countries with higher per capita output would have lower real rates of interest. Since investors prefer investing in countries with higher returns, capital would flow from developed to less developed countries. But, in reality, the poorest economies do not usually have higher rates of return to capital than more developed economies and capital sometimes flows on a net basis from the former to the latter.

An illustration

Assume a production function of the Cobb–Douglas form:

$$Y = AK^{\alpha'} L^{1-\alpha'} \quad 0 < \alpha' < 1 \tag{15}$$

so that,

$$y = Ak^{\alpha'} \tag{16}$$

The return to capital equals its marginal product, which can be derived as Y_K or as y_k since they are identical. The MPK is given by:

$$y_k = Y_K = \alpha' A k^{\alpha'-1} = \alpha' y/k \quad 0 < \alpha' < 1 \tag{17}$$

Since $(\alpha' - 1) < 0$, $y_{kk} = \alpha'(1 - \alpha')Ak^{\alpha'-2} < 0$, so that the return to capital falls as k increases. In perfectly competitive markets, this return specifies the real interest rate in the economy, so that, as argued earlier, this model predicts a decline in the real rate of interest as k increases in the pre-SS stage.

The labour force growth rate is still assumed to be n. That is, $L'' = n$. As in the earlier arguments, the average propensity to save is assumed to be constant at σ, so that $K' = \sigma Y$, and,

$$K'' = \sigma Y/K = \sigma y/k$$

From (15),

$$Y' = Y_K K' + Y_L L'$$

so that:

$$Y'' = Y'/Y = (Y_K K/Y)K'' + (Y_L L/Y)L''$$
$$= \alpha' K'' + (1 - \alpha')L' \tag{18}$$

which implies that:

$$y'' = \alpha'(K'' - L'')$$
$$= \alpha'\sigma y/k - \alpha'n$$
$$= \alpha'\sigma Ak^{\alpha'-1} - \alpha'n \tag{19}$$

Hence,

$$\partial y''/\partial k = \alpha'(\alpha' - 1)\sigma Ak^{\alpha'-2}$$

Since $(\alpha' - 1) < 0$, the growth rate of per capita output declines – and goes to zero[6] – as k increases. To derive the SS growth rate, rewrite (19) as:

$$y'' = (\sigma y - kn)\alpha' k^{-1} \tag{19'}$$

In steady state, $\sigma y = kn$, so that the SS value $y''* = 0$, where '*' indicates the SS value.

But, in the pre-SS stage, from (17) and (19), $\sigma y > kn$, so that $y'' > 0$. Further, with $\alpha' = y_k \cdot (K/Y)$,

$$y'' = y_k(\sigma - n(K/Y)) \tag{20}$$

so that, in the pre-SS stage, y'' depends positively on the saving rate and the marginal productivity of capital, but negatively on the labour force growth rate and the capital–output ratio.[7] Hence, countries with higher saving propensities (or better access to the savings of other countries) and a higher return to capital will have higher pre-SS growth rates of output and output per capita.

Suppose that, for some reason, the rate of return Y_K is reduced by τ_K. Such a reduction could be due to the imposition of taxes on dividends and capital gains or due to the inefficiencies resulting from regulations imposed on the capital or financial markets. This reduction will lower the return on capital from Y_K to $(1 - \tau)Y_K$. From (20), this lowers the pre-SS growth rate of output per capita to:

$$y'' = (1 - \tau_K)Y_K(\sigma - n(K/Y)) \quad 0 \le \tau_K < 1 \tag{21}$$

Therefore, taxing the return to capital is inimical to the growth in the standards of living and in the capital–labour ratio. Further, the slower growth of the latter will increase the time taken to reach the steady state.

25.3 GROWTH THEORY IF THERE IS INCREASING MARGINAL PRODUCTIVITY OF CAPITAL (MPK)

Solow's (1956) presentation of his growth model also included the possibility that, over a certain range, the production function had increasing rather than diminishing MPK. That is, in this range, the production function $f(k)$ in equation (3) has $f_k > 0$ and $f_{kk} > 0$ (rather than $f_{kk} < 0$).

25.3.1 The increasing MPK case

To investigate this possibility, assume that $f(k)$ has $f_{kk} > 0$. This implies in the context of Figure 25.2 that, in this range, the $\sigma f(k)$ curve would be convex, rather than concave. This implies in Figure 25.2 that there are two intersections between the $\sigma f(k)$ and nk curves and, therefore, two SS values of k, k_0^* and k_1^*, at each of which $\sigma f(k) = nk$. Of these, k_0^* is stable but k_1^* is unstable. This is shown by the following arguments:

(a) For $k > k_1^*$, saving per capita exceeds the capital requirement for new workers so that the capital–labour ratio k rises over time for all workers. The economy gradually moves further to the right of k_1^*. Consequently, for values of $k > k_1^*$, where k_1^* is an SS value, the growth rates of per capita capital and output will increase indefinitely rather than go to zero in the absence of technical change.
(b) For $k_0^* < k < k_1^*$, saving per capita is less than the capital requirement for new workers so that k decreases over time towards k_0^*.
(c) For $k < k_0^*$, saving per capita exceeds the capital requirement for new workers so that k increases towards k_0^*.

Since any deviation from k_0^* brings the economy back to it, it is a stable SS value. But since a deviation of k from k_1^* leads the economy away from it, k_1^* is an unstable SS value.

Even though k_1^* is unstable, it has the appealing empirical implication for economies with $k > k_1^*$ that the return to capital does not decrease as capital per worker increases nor do the growth rates of capital and output per capita go to zero, which seem to correspond to the experience of the developed economies. The objectionable implications of this case from the perspective of empirical validity are that:

(a) The growth rates of the economy will continue to increase *indefinitely*, which is highly doubtful.

(b) If the firm is assumed to possess a production function with this property of an indefinitely increasing MPK, the profit-maximizing firm will increase its K/L ratio indefinitely by reducing the employment of labour to minuscule amounts, so that the economy will end up with employing hardly any labour to all. This is not a realistic scenario.

Consequently, the case of the increasing MPK was discounted by the growth theorists, at least for the developed economies, so that, for several decades following Solow's (1956) contribution, the profession mainly opted for the standard neoclassical production function having $f_{kk} < 0$ and implying a stable steady state. There are two ways of incorporating some elements of the increasing MPK in growth theory while avoiding its above objectionable implications. These are:

(ii) assuming a more general production function to encompass increasing MPK over some range followed by decreasing MPK;
(ii) allowing only diminishing MPK at the firm's (or individual's) level but increasing MPK to physical or human capital for the economy.

Assumption (i) is attempted in the next subsection; (ii) is the approach of the endogenous growth theories examined in the later sections of this chapter.

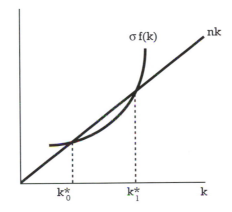

Figure 25.2

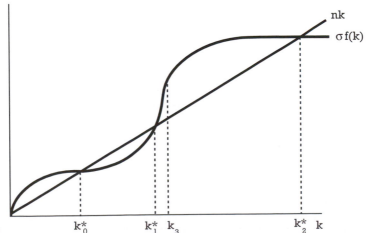

Figure 25.3

25.3.2 A more general production function for the firm

Another way of avoiding the preceding two implications is to assume that the region of increasing MPK is followed by one with diminishing MPK. To use a relatively attractive version of this possibility, assume that there exist two technologies along the continuum of the K/L ratio. The 'primitive' technology has diminishing MPK throughout (or with increasing MPK at a very low K/L ratios, which we choose to ignore) and is the optimal one at low levels of k, while beyond some value of k, an 'advanced' technology becomes the optimal one to use so that there occurs a switch in technologies. This advanced technology has initially increasing MPK, followed by diminishing ones. Assume that the combined production pattern $f(k)$ has the shape represented by that of the curve $\sigma f(k)$ in Figure 25.3.

Assuming again a constant growth rate of population, Figure 25.3 shows that such a production pattern generates an unstable SS at k_1^*, but stable ones at k_0^* and k_2^*, so that, in the long run, an economy to the left of k_1^* will decrease k and regress to the SS k_0^*, while if it somehow reaches to the right of the 'take-off' SS point k_1^*, it will progress to k_2^*.

This analysis can be generalized to one where new technologies open up as k increases, with each technology initially possessing a range in which there are increasing returns to scale followed by a range with decreasing returns to scale, with optimal switch points among technologies, thereby yielding an 'intertemporal production function' which is not the usual static production function but rather a compendium of the optimal ranges of each technology.[8] Such a function can yield several steady states, some of which would be stable. However, the movement between technologies would take time and investment, and also raises questions on what induces – and hastens – or slows such shifts. We will return to these questions later when we discuss endogenous technical change.

25.3.3 Convergence versus divergence in output per capita among countries

If all countries have:

(i) the same production function with a single technology possessing diminishing marginal productivity of capital;
(ii) the same saving propensity; and
(iii) the same population growth rate;

the Solow model implies that they would converge to the same steady-state output per capita. Empirical studies do not show a general worldwide tendency towards such convergence (Temple, 1999).

Further, the Solow model implies for the above assumptions that the SS growth rate of per capita output for all economies will converge to the same (zero) growth rate. Moreover, even if different countries have different production functions – though with diminishing MPK – and different saving rates, they would still converge to the same (zero) SS growth rate of per capita income. Such convergence has also not been observed in the real world.

Furthermore, the Solow model implies that, for countries having the same steady state, countries with lower values of y and k will grow faster than richer countries with higher values. The convergence of countries to the same steady state is sometimes indirectly tested for this implication.

Convergence to different SS levels of per capita income

Note that the neoclassical model does not *necessarily* imply convergence in the level of output per capita: it does not do so if the production functions are different, the saving propensities are different, or if the production function has intermediate segments with increasing MPK. In these cases, there would exist divergence in levels. Figure 25.3, embodying two or more technologies in sequence, shows the implications of the last point.

In Figure 25.3, the countries with lower values of k do not always have the higher growth rates, though some countries with intermediate capital–labour ratios (i.e., between k_1^* and k_3) will have the highest growth rates and the highest return to capital. Furthermore, this figure implies both a divergence and a convergence: divergence between the countries moving towards k_0^* and those tending to k_2^*, while there is convergence of the poorest countries to k_0^* and the richest ones to k_2^*.

This simple case of the two technologies occurring in sequence as a by-product of the change in technology over time is temptingly like the division of economies into three categories: the 'poorest' converging to k_0^* with very low values of k and y; the fast growing (intermediate) countries ('the economic tigers') moving rapidly through high growth rates towards the k and y values of the most developed economies; and the 'richest' industrialized countries converging to k_2^* with still higher values of k and y. In this scenario, the growth rates are higher for the economic tigers than for the other economies. Further, since the MPK is highest for the economic tigers, capital flows from the poorest and the richest countries to the economic tigers. There is divergence of living standards between the poorest countries and those over the take-off point (k_1^*) – that is, the economic tigers and the richest countries – while there is bipolar convergence, with that of the poorest countries to k_0^* and its implied low output per capita, while the economic tigers and the developed economies converge to k_2^* and its implied high output per capita.[9]

Looking at the implications of Figure 25.3 for the richest countries, there is still the unrealistic implication that y and k will become constant for the richest countries at the SS k_2^*, so that further increases in the standard of living will not occur. For these standards to continue improving in the SS analysis, one recourse is to modify Solow's model by the introduction of technical change into it. Such technical change can be assumed to be exogenous or endogenous. Before we consider these, we need an assessment of whether technical change is empirically significant or not. This is done in the next section.

25.4 ASSESSING THE IMPORTANCE OF TECHNICAL CHANGE IN THE BASIC NEOCLASSICAL MODEL

In order to encompass technical change, specify the production function as:

$$Y = F(K, L, T) \tag{22}$$

where T is the 'technology index', taking technology to be a measurable variable. Solow (1957) offered a procedure for the estimation of technical change under the assumption that (22) takes the specific form:

$$Y = A(T)f(L, K) \tag{23}$$

This pattern of technical change shifts the production function period by period even if there are no changes in labour and capital inputs. Since it affects the marginal productivities of labour and capital to the same extent, it is called *neutral technical change*.

Assuming, as before, constant returns to scale so that the income shares of labour and capital will sum to unity, (23) implies that:

$$Y'' = A''(T) + \alpha'K'' + (1 - \alpha')L'' \tag{24}$$

where:

α' share of capital in aggregate income
$(1 - \alpha')$ share of labour in aggregate income

Since $A''(T)$ is unobservable while all the other variables in (24) are observable, rewrite (24) as:

$$A''(T) = Y'' - \alpha'K'' - (1 - \alpha')L'' \tag{25}$$

Solow used (25) to calculate $A''(T)$ and found that historically the main increase in per capita output in the USA had been due to technical change rather than to increases in capital per worker, though there was considerable variation from year to year in the former. His conclusion for the period 1909–49 for the USA was that while output per capita almost doubled, about 87.5% of this increase was due to technical change and only about 12.5% was due to more capital per worker. While other studies for other countries or for different periods have arrived at somewhat different figures, there is no doubt about the preponderant effect of technical change on output per capita. Similar results indicating the importance of technical change in the growth of output per capita have been confirmed in many other studies on other countries. Given this importance, we need to incorporate technical change explicitly into the formal growth models and study its determinants. The former is done in the next section while the latter is left to the sections on endogenous technical change.

25.5 THE BASIC NEOCLASSICAL GROWTH MODEL WITH EXOGENOUS TECHNICAL CHANGE

In view of the above results on the importance of technical change, a major modification proposed to the basic neoclassical growth model was to introduce technical change into it. The easiest method of doing so is by assuming that technical change is such as to increase the average productivity of labour over time at the rate η, but not to do so for capital, *ceteris paribus*. Such technical change is labour-augmenting and of a different type from the neutral one used in (24). It leads to the specification of the production function as:

$$Y = F(K, \phi(L, T)) \tag{26}$$

For this form of the production technology, technical change is said to be *labour-augmenting* – as against being capital-augmenting or being neutral between the capital and labour inputs – since it increases the efficiency of labour. Let $\phi(L, T) = E$, where E can be viewed as the quantity of labour measured in constant efficiency units,[10] where $\partial E/\partial t = n + \eta$. That is, labour measured in constant productivity units would grow at the rate $n + \eta$. Hence, (26) becomes:

$$Y = F(K, E) \tag{27}$$

where $F(\cdot)$ is assumed to have the neoclassical properties of $F_K, F_E > 0$, $F_{KK}, F_{EE} < 0$. Now redefine k as K/E and y as Y/E. Without going into all the steps,[11] the capital growth equation (9) for the current model becomes:

$$k' = \sigma f(k) - (n + \eta)k \tag{28}$$

which implies that in the steady state of the current model,

$$y'' = k'' = \eta \tag{29}$$

$$Y'' = K'' = E'' = n + \eta \tag{30}$$

Hence, countries that innovate and increase labour productivity at a faster rate would have a higher rate of growth of output, and output per worker will continue to increase even in the steady state at the rate η.

The role of human capital

Labour-augmenting technical change in (26) can be viewed as a result of the increase in human capital, which represents the acquisition and use of skills relevant to production. The stock of human capital in the economy can increase in a variety of ways. Among these are:

(a) the allocation of labour and capital to impart the existing stock of knowledge in educational institutions and is labelled as 'schooling';
(b) the allocation of labour and capital to impart the existing stock of knowledge in firms through on-the-job training;
(c) exogenous changes in the stock of knowledge itself.

We will consider the accumulation of the stock of existing knowledge – as in (a) and (b) – at this point and changes in it in the sections on endogenous technical change.

The analysis of the accumulation – in the sense of duplication – of knowledge in the form of schooling and on-the-job training of new entrants to the labour force and its impact on growth is similar to that of physical capital in the above analysis. In fact, if we were to re-designate capital K as the total of human and non-human capital, while leaving labour L to designate the number of workers with a base period human capital per worker, the analysis would remain as is, and so would the conclusions. Among these is that the base stock and rate of accumulation of human capital, just as those of physical capital, do not alter the SS rate of growth of per capita output, but do change the SS per capita output itself.

SS growth versus level effects of exogenous shifts

Comparing the impact of shifts in the various exogenous variables and parameters, the Solow growth model makes a distinction between those shifts which shift the SS per capita growth rate and those which only change its SS level. Exogenous shifts in the production function, the stock of schooling, the saving propensity and population growth induce changes in the SS level, but not the SS growth rate of output per capita, while technical change also alters the SS growth rate.

Economies that want to grow faster in steady state must, therefore, find ways of increasing the rate of technical change. However, this rate is exogenous to the Solow growth model and is not affected by the accumulation of capital, labour and other aspects of the model itself.[12] In recent decades, economists have become convinced that the rate of technical change is not invariant with respect to these variables. Allowing for such effects, in general, makes the rate of technical change endogenous to the model. The following sections examine some of the sources of endogenous growth and the possibilities of increasing or decreasing growth rates by policy measures.

25.6 ENDOGENOUS GROWTH THEORIES

In the context of economic models, endogenous technical change can be defined as a shift or shifts in the production function which are determined within the model. In a more general way, endogenous technical change can be taken to be the outcome of decisions made by economic agents to change knowledge of the production technology. Examples of such decisions are those on the acquisition of new skills, research and development (R&D), investment in new or improved equipment. Through these decisions, the current state of the economy – and its existing levels of skills, capital–labour ratio, market and industrial structure, educational patterns, etc. – induces changes in its production technology. While this idea is not a new one in the literature, its formalization and incorporation into growth theory in the overall context of the neoclassical tradition mainly started in the 1980s.[13]

The modelling of endogenous technical change within the neoclassical context is still relatively new and imperfectly understood, so that there is no consensus around a single model. There are different ways of modelling endogenous technical change, leading to different versions of growth theory. The main popular approaches to endogenous technical change in recent years can be classified according to which input – capital, labour or knowledge – in production has constant or increasing returns at the economy's level. In all of these approaches, the usual pattern is to maintain the assumption of diminishing returns to each input at the level of the firm while somehow incorporating increasing returns to one of the inputs at the macroeconomic level. The latter is based on the externalities of the new knowledge generated by the individual workers and firms in the economy. This new knowledge can occur within a firm, costlessly from 'learning-by-doing' by workers or as a good produced through costly R&D expenditures, but the knowledge thus obtained is not only utilized in the originating firm but also becomes available to other firms and increases their productivity. This creates a wedge between the private and social returns to the creation of new knowledge.

If knowledge is specified as a separate input, the analysis incorporates knowledge both as an input in the production function and as a by-product of current production. If it is not treated as a separate input, it is taken to be embodied in either physical capital or workers' skills, but quite usually in both. Further, the acquisition of both capital and knowledge in endogenous growth theory occurs through economic decisions involving (physical or human or both) investments, which are undertaken for the sake of increasing personal incomes and profits. Given this similarity between the accumulation of capital and knowledge, the endogenous technical change approach usually combines the two and defines the term 'capital' in the production function to consist not only of physical capital but also to include human capital. For this new definition, the definitions of investment and saving are suitably modified to encompass those occurring in both physical and human capital. Among the latter are the amounts spent in formal education or otherwise on the acquisition of skills.

The externalities of new knowledge

The generation of new knowledge can be separated from its dissemination – 'spillover' to other firms – in the economy. The former usually occurs within firms, universities and research institutions. The latter is the process of its copying and adoption by other firms or by workers in other firms, and is an externality from the perspective of the firms and other units originating the new knowledge. The creation of new knowledge, therefore, possesses an externality, which gives it the nature of a public good in which other economic agents can share, without necessarily having to pay its full cost of production. These externalities can arise in many forms. Among these are the ability of firms to observe the types and quality of products, the methods of organization and the technology employed by other firms, and, if these are superior ones, to be able to replicate or adapt them to their own production.

Externalities in the economy can arise in other ways also. For example, as the output of some firms in an industry expands, the facilities for the transport of its raw materials, the training of workers appropriate to the industry and for marketing of output, etc., tend to improve and lower the relevant costs for all firms in the industry. Further, such an expansion of output and employment may also lead to an increased rate of innovation, which would further lower the cost of production of each firm. The latter represents an increase in the knowledge of production.

The externalities represent a public good, which is available to all firms, even to those that do not contribute to its creation. Access to it may, however, require some action and investment by the firm. For example, new investment may be required to buy the machines embodying the economy's new knowledge of production techniques, and therefore acts as the gateway to the firm's use of the increased knowledge. In some cases, the new machines may not be more capital intensive than the existing machines and may only involve replacement, which might be covered through depreciation over time.

New knowledge can have not only positive externalities but also negative ones for the economy. The incorporation of endogenous technical change into growth theory, in general, assumes that their net benefit is positive, that is, there is an increase in output for given levels of labour and capital in the economy. We will continue with this assumption, but will later include some mention of the negative externalities.

Innovations versus inventions as forms of technical change

Looking from the perspective of economic history, we can take technical change to be characterized by:

(a) 'Macroinventions' consisting of technological breakthroughs. Illustrative of these are the invention of the steam engine, cotton ginning, etc., during the Industrial Revolution in Great Britain during the seventeenth and eighteenth centuries, and the invention of the transistor and the computer chip in the second half of the twentieth century. Such breakthroughs are essentially unpredictable and can be taken to be exogenous.

(b) Innovations, consisting of refinements to the existing technology and usually occurring over a long period after the macroinventions or other inventions have been made. The innovations can themselves be major improvements in technology and, therefore, be difficult to distinguish from inventions. Among the constraining elements, particular to a country, on the pace and extent of such innovations are the smallness of markets, the weakness of scientific education, the protection of rights to the innovation such as through patenting, the willingness of labour to adapt its skills, etc.

Since macroinventions are rarely continuous, their eventual impact on the economy will peter out so that they cannot be made the main vehicle in a theory for *continuing* technical change even in the steady state. Therefore, the main emphasis for SS growth is usually placed on innovations. But, given the limitations on these and their long-run dependence on sporadic macroinventions, it cannot be taken for granted that they will result in SS growth in any given economy or in all economies. With the emphasis on innovations rather than inventions as the engine of continual technical change, the ability of a nation to generate or improve on imported ideas, its propagation mechanisms for knowledge spillovers among its industries and the learning capabilities of its workers become the main elements of its endogenous growth. Since governmental policies can affect these, the endogenous technical change theories imply that the long-run growth rate of the economy can be affected by such policies.

The modelling of endogenous technical change in the neoclassical framework

Romer (1986, 1990) and Lucas (1988, 1993) are among the founding contributions on endogenous growth theories. Romer (1986) assumed that the firm's production function includes the firm's knowledge and the economy's aggregate knowledge as arguments, in addition to labour and capital. From the social viewpoint, there are increasing returns with respect to the firm's *and* economy's knowledge – with labour and capital held constant – though each firm faces constant returns to scale in *its* knowledge, labour and capital, for a given amount of the economy's knowledge.

Given this production function, the firm maximizes its profits, taking the economy's knowledge as given. This knowledge is taken to be produced through R&D expenditures by individual firms. For the firm doing it, the production of knowledge through such expenditures is subject to diminishing returns. Consequently, each profit-maximizing R&D firm (or the research done by the production firm) would produce only a limited amount of it[14] since it will only get its private (and not the social) return to the new knowledge created by its R&D expenditures. However, this knowledge can be only partially kept secret or patented, so that there is a strong externality from its creation. While all firms could increase their profits if they were to collectively increase their research and therefore the economy's knowledge, such cooperation or collusion is ruled out by the usual incentives to shirk or cheat in the presence of externalities.

The theoretical model of Lucas (1993) emphasizes the role of human capital by making it the main engine of endogenous growth, with physical capital given a secondary or supporting role. The core element of this model is that the change in the stock of human capital is a function of the existing stock of human capital and the degree of effort – such as through labour time diverted to this activity and R&D expenditures – devoted to the acquisition of additional knowledge. Spillovers of new knowledge occur among firms and industries. Across countries, the growth of human capital in any one country depends on the local effort put into it, as well as on the worldwide knowledge (approximated by that of the most advanced countries). Consequently, the per capita incomes of countries with extensive exports and imports of commodities, factors and knowledge among them will tend to converge, but not necessarily those of countries without such exchanges. Therefore, as an illustration, the per capita incomes and growth rates of countries in the European Union in the coming decades are expected to converge but not necessarily those between the European and African countries.

While human capital is often measured by the amount of schooling, Lucas argues that the decision on the amount of schooling is like those on the amount of saving and investment in physical capital, so that increases in it will improve output per capita but not the SS growth rates, as we saw from Solow's model for shifts in the saving function. However, the quality of human capital is more than merely years of schooling and depends on learning on the job or from others' innovations by trading with them, etc. Such increases in human capital, therefore, depend on the existing and accessible stock of human knowledge and can increase even in the steady state, thereby causing growth in per capita output even in the steady state.

This emphasis on new knowledge leads to consideration of the intellectual ability to create new ideas or borrow and adapt them, and on the incentives for doing so. It is often contended that open, modern and capitalist economies give more scope to the creation and use of this 'intellectual capital' than closed, centralized and bureaucratic ones.[15]

As a cautionary note, the role of new physical capital must not be ignored. Innovation and new knowledge often enter production through new forms of equipment, so that physical capital, along with human capital, is the vehicle for endogenous capital change.

25.7 A SIMPLIFIED MODEL OF ENDOGENOUS GROWTH

As we have mentioned earlier, there are already several different ways of modelling endogenous technical change and more are likely to emerge as this field matures. Therefore, the two models that we offer below are rather basic ones and are mainly meant for illustrative purposes.

The first model, presented in this section, incorporates the core idea of Romer and others that while there are diminishing marginal returns to the originating *firm's* investment in new knowledge, the new knowledge, once created, also benefits other firms in the economy, so that the *economy* does not necessarily experience diminishing marginal returns to such investment. This distinction between the originating firm's and the economy's returns to the creation of new knowledge is fundamental to this type of model and to virtually all expositions of endogenous growth.

For this illustrative and basic model of endogenous growth, specify the *i*th firm's production function as:

$$y_{ij} = f_{ij}(k_{ij}, k_j, \phi_{ij}(k_{ij}, k_j, X(k_{max})_{-1})) \tag{31}$$

where:

y_{ij} output/labour ratio of the *i*th firm in country *j*

k_{ij} capital/labour ratio of the *i*th firm in country *j*

k_j *j*th economy's capital/labour ratio

k_{max} highest average capital/labour ratio among the world's countries

ϕ_{ij} stock of knowledge/techniques accessed by the ith firm of the jth country

X_{-1} stock of world knowledge of techniques of production lagged one period

To simplify the analysis, we have dispensed with the creation of new knowledge through R&D expenditures, and assumed that it is a costless by-product of production, such as through learning-by-doing by workers.[16] Further, as another simplification, the level of knowledge is assumed to be uniquely related to the capital per worker, which represents the existing technology and types of machines. Equation (31) incorporates two types of externalities from knowledge. One is through an increase in the country's knowledge and the other is from worldwide knowledge. The effects of the jth country's average capital–labour ratio k_j on the ith firm's output y_{ij} represent an externality of the country's general technological knowledge for firms within the jth country. This externality is assumed to lower the firm's cost of production and increase its output for a given value of k_{ij}. That is, $\partial y_{ij}/\partial k_j > 0$.

In (31), X represents the stock of world knowledge, assumed to depend upon the highest capital/labour ratio among the countries of the world, and ϕ_{ij} is the amount of this knowledge that is *accessed* by firm i in country j. This amount depends upon the jth country's average capital–labour ratio k_j, which captures the pool of knowledge made generally available to firms in the economy, and upon the firm's capital–labour ratio k_{ij}, which captures the extent to which the individual firm is in a position to take advantage of the known production techniques.

The dependence of ϕ_{ij} on k_{max} incorporates the idea that the countries with lower values of k have access to a large pool of knowledge, hitherto untapped by them.[17] But the country with $k = k_{max}$ can only benefit by truly new innovations in knowledge from a worldwide perspective:[18] as the country with the most advanced technology, there is no benefit to it from copying the inferior technology of countries with lower capital per worker.[19] We also incorporate in our analysis below the appealing notion that countries with too low a capital intensity cannot effectively imitate the advanced technologies and therefore cannot fully benefit from the knowledge developed in other countries.

25.7.1 A formal model of endogenous growth

We illustrate this discussion by specifying the form of the production function in (31) as:

$$y_{ij} = A_j k_{ij}^{\alpha'} k_j^{\alpha''} \phi_{ij}(\cdot) \quad 0 < \alpha', \alpha'' < 1 \tag{32}$$

The neoclassical theory of the firm assumes diminishing returns ($\partial^2 y_i/\partial k_{ij}^2 < 0$) to the capital per worker employed by the firm, so that $\alpha' < 1$. However, our concern is not with the individual firm but with the whole economy. For the representative firm of the economy and focusing only on economy-wide changes in k, the aggregate production function of the economy is of the form:

$$y_j = A_j k_j^{\alpha} \phi_j(k_j, k_{max}) \tag{33}$$

where $\alpha = \alpha' + \alpha''$.[20] Further, assume that:

$$\phi_j(\cdot) = k_j^{\psi(j)} \qquad 0 < \gamma_0 < \gamma < 1 \tag{34}$$

$$\psi(j) = \gamma_0 + \gamma(k_{max} - k_j)_{-1} \quad \text{for } (k_{max} - k_j) < \epsilon \tag{35}$$

$$= \gamma_0 \qquad\qquad\qquad \text{for } k_j = k_{max} \tag{35'}$$

$$= 0 \qquad\qquad\qquad\quad \text{for } (k_{max} - k_j) \geq \epsilon \tag{35''}$$

These functions assume away, as a simplification, the expenditure of effort and R&D expenditures usually required for the creation of new knowledge. From the perspective of the economy's production function, the main concern is with the overall exponent on k_j, which is $(\alpha + \psi(j))$. As (34) to (35) imply, the exponent can differ among countries and be less than unity for some countries while being greater than unity for others, with corresponding differences in the SS growth paths of countries. We distinguish between two broad cases.

(i) Equation (35″) incorporates the notion that countries at exceptionally low levels of capital intensity will not be able to access significantly the capital-intensive technologies developed by the advanced economies. To encompass this possibility, we have set $\psi(j) = 0$ for $(k_{max} - k_j)_{-1}$ greater than some ϵ, $\epsilon > 0$. Further, their own low-level technology may not generate adequate new knowledge or with sufficient externalities to ensure that $\alpha \geq 1$. With $\alpha < 1$, the country would have decreasing returns to capital intensity. The figure relevant for the growth analysis of such a country is Figure 25.1a above.

(ii) Countries with $\alpha > 1$ will definitely have increasing returns to capital intensity, while those with $\alpha < 1$ will also have increasing returns if $(\alpha + \psi(j)) > 1$. Figure 25.4, similar to Figure 25.2, is a representation of the latter case (i.e., with $\alpha < 1$ and $(\alpha + \psi(j)) > 1$). In this figure, the SS point at k_0^* is unstable, so that countries to the right of it (at k_2) will be on an ever-expanding path of output per worker. Countries (say, at k_1) with k less than k_0^* will be on a decreasing path of output per worker. Therefore, k_0^* represents a critical capital/labour ratio for the country and policy makers should ensure through their policies that their economy has a larger k than this critical one. Such a critical ratio is called a *takeoff* or *threshold* capital intensity, and a growth trap occurs from k_3^* to k_0^*.

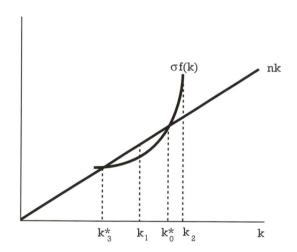

Figure 25.4

Looking across countries with differing values of k, since ϕ_j depends positively on $(k_{max} - k_j)_{-1}$, countries closer to k_{max} will have lower values of ϕ_j. In the limiting case, the jth country with $k_j = k_{max}$ will have ϕ_j equal to γ_0. While $\alpha + \gamma_0$ could be equal to or greater than 1, we will assume that $\alpha + \gamma_0 < 1$, so that the most advanced country (with k_{max}) has diminishing returns. This would occur even with the externalities from the expansion of its own knowledge, though such expansion of knowledge would moderate the extent to which the marginal product of capital diminishes. However, countries with $k_j < k_{max}$ but with $(k_{max} - k_j) < \epsilon$ have $\psi(j) = \gamma((k_{max} - k_j)$, and therefore could possibly have increasing returns with $(\alpha + \psi(j)) > 1$. But as $k \to k_{max}$, $\psi(j)$ decreases and the possibility of increasing returns falls so that eventually the country would have diminishing returns, as in the basic neoclassical model.

The above model implies that:

(i) The growth rates of countries are endogenous: they depend on the economy's capital intensity and its increase.

(ii) Over a certain range, an intermediate set of developing economies with lower existing values of k than k_{max} will experience a bigger impact on growth from any increase in their own capital intensity than more developed ones (with higher existing values of k).

(iii) The country with the highest value of k is already at the frontier of world technology and benefits only from the true innovations in its own – and therefore worldwide – knowledge while any other country (with $k_j < k_{max}$) will also benefit by copying techniques known to other countries but not yet adopted in it.

(iv) A country with an extremely low capital–labour ratio may not be able to take advantage of other countries' stock of knowledge. If its own ability to innovate is also absent, it could continue in a steady state with a static technology, diminishing MPK and low standards of living.

Diagrammatic analysis

Figure 25.5, similar to Figure 25.3, illustrates the general scenario for the case in which $(\alpha + \psi(j)) \gtreqless 1$ by curve $\sigma f(k)$.[21] Countries with a value of k in the neighbourhood of k_{max} would have $(\alpha + \psi(j)) < 1$ so that they would be on a concave segment of the curve $\sigma f(k)$ in the neighbourhood of the stable SS ratio k_2^*. The countries with a capital intensity inadequate for benefiting from the externalities of other countries' technical knowledge will have $\alpha < 1$ and be in the neighbourhood of the SS ratio k_0^*. By comparison, countries in the intermediate range of the capital–labour ratio will benefit from the externalities of the knowledge of the more advanced economies. Some of these will have increasing growth rates and increasing returns to capital. Such countries will be in the region k_1^* to k_3. However, these higher growth rate countries cannot increase or even maintain their high growth rates indefinitely: their higher growth rates of output and saving per worker takes them ever closer to k_{max} and lowers their growth rate. Eventually, as they reach their steady state with $k = k_{max}$, the growth rates converge to those at k_2^*. The countries with the lower SS rates of growth will be those with very low values of k, close to k_0^*, and those with very high values of k close to k_2^*.

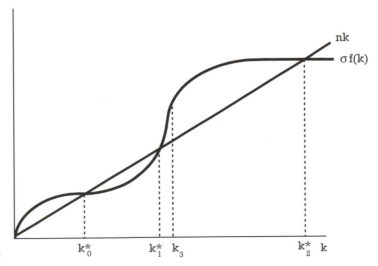

Figure 25.5

Among these lower-growth countries, the poorest countries (to the left of k_0^*) can stagnate at low values of capital intensity and low growth rates. These countries can be thought of as in a growth trap where they cannot even take advantage of the knowledge that already exists in the rest of the world. Further, such countries may themselves generate a lower degree of technical change because of their low-level technology than the countries with k_{max}, which lie at the other extreme. The latter also cannot benefit from other countries' knowledge but could have a greater internal generation of technical change by virtue of their higher capital intensities (including higher educational levels). Hence, it is very important for policy makers to push and position their economies along the k_j axis, and if they are LDCs with very low capital intensities, they must somehow exceed the threshold capital intensity.

Some studies in the endogenous growth literature assume that $\alpha \geq 1$, in which case even the country with the highest capital intensity and therefore the most advanced technology would not have diminishing returns. If this were so, then the other countries with $k_j < k_{max}$ will have an even stronger possibility of increasing returns.

25.7.2 The return to capital and the growth rate in the endogenous growth model

Rewrite the production function (33) as simply:

$$y_j = A_j k_j^{\alpha+\psi(j)} \quad \alpha > 0, \psi(j) \geq 0 \tag{36}$$

where $\psi(j)$ is specific to the jth country.

The rate of return to capital equals the marginal productivity of capital in equilibrium. The latter for the production function (36) is:

$$y_{kj} = \partial y_j/\partial k_j = (\alpha + \psi(j))A_j k_j^{\alpha+\psi(j)-1} \tag{37}$$

$$= (\alpha + \psi(j))y_j/k_j \tag{38}$$

which is decreasing in k_j if $(\alpha + \psi(j)) < 1$ and increasing in k_j if $\alpha + \psi(j) > 1$.

The growth rate of output per worker for the production function (36) subject to (5) for the constant saving propensity σ_j and (6) for the constant labour growth rate n is:

$$y_j'' = (\alpha + \psi(j))\sigma_j A k_j^{\alpha+\psi-1} - (\alpha + \psi(j))n_j \tag{39}[22]$$

$$= (\alpha + \psi(j))\sigma_j y_j/k_j - (\alpha + \psi(j))n_j$$

$$= \{\sigma_j - n_j (K/Y)_j\}y_{kj} \tag{40}[23]$$

Equation (40) shows the positive and very close relationship between the growth rate of output per worker and the marginal productivity of capital per worker. From (36) and (37), for the case of increasing returns to capital intensity – i.e., with $(\alpha + \psi(j)) > 1$ – growth is a path of continuous capital accumulation which increases the return to capital and the growth rate – and encourages further capital accumulation. However, to start on this path, the economy has to begin with a critical mass of capital and labour, as indicated by point k_1^* in Figure 25.5. Shocks (famines, civil and other wars, etc.) and policies (for example, those discriminating against capital accumulation) which shift the economy from the left of this point to the right are highly desirable, while those which do the reverse put the economy onto a path of ever decreasing standards of living. The danger is acute for an economy close to point k_1^*. This danger is minimal for the already developed economies, but can be acute for some developing economies.

Equation (40) for $\alpha + \psi(j) > 1$ implies that growth accelerates as k increases and the economy gets more developed. While this seems to be valid for certain stages in the development process, it does not seem to be true for the economies at the frontiers of world development. For example, the growth rates of the USA, Canada and Western European countries have been fairly stable or declining during the past few decades. The growth rates of Japan increased during its rapid development in the 1950s and 1960s, but decreased in the 1980s and 1990s. The growth rates of Korea, Taiwan and several other Asian countries increased in the 1980s and early 1990s as their pace of development picked up, though it remains to be seen if they will eventually also revert to a slower growth rate.[24] This slowdown and convergence to a common growth rate is implied by the above model as countries reach closer to k_{max}: once they reach k_{max}, they can no longer benefit from any hitherto unaccessed part of the existing store of world knowledge developed by other countries.

25.8 ANOTHER ENDOGENOUS GROWTH MODEL

The main elements of the endogenous growth model used in Lucas (1993) differ from the preceding one in that they do not create increasing returns to (physical) capital intensity in the production function. They focus on human capital or knowledge and rely on the international transmission of this knowledge. To illustrate Lucas's ideas, we compare two of his models.[25]

Model A for disparate growth rates

The production function

$$Y(t) = AK(t)^{\alpha}[uH(t)]^{1-\alpha} \tag{41}$$

Growth of physical capital

$$\partial K(t)/\partial t = \sigma Y(t) \tag{42}$$

Growth of 'human capital'[26]

$$\partial H(t)/\partial t = B(1-u)H(t) \tag{43}$$

where:

H	stock of human capital
u	given fraction of labour time spent on producing commodities
$(1-u)$	proportion of human capital used in the creation of new human capital

The production function (41) replaces the amount of labour in the production function used earlier in this chapter by the country's own stock of human capital H multiplied by its fraction u used in production. u is taken to be determined by the country's decisions on the proportions of the existing human capital to be allocated to the production of commodities and to the accumulation of human capital. With $0 < \alpha < 1$, there are diminishing returns to both physical and human capital in the production of commodities. In (42), the growth of physical capital is through saving, with the marginal propensity to save, σ, being constant, as in our earlier analysis. In (43), the proportion of human capital used in the creation of new human capital is $(1-u)$, and results in the increase in human capital given by (43).

For the steady state, the change in the ratio of physical to human capital is set at zero, and produces constant SS ratios of capital and output to human capital. For simplicity, if we assume the growth rate of workers and population to be zero, both physical capital and output per capita will grow in the steady state at the rate $\delta(1 - u)$, which can be treated as being the rate of technical change in the steady state. Note that this SS rate depends on $(1 - u)$. Hence, the SS growth of a country will depend on the economic decisions taken by its residents on the proportion of the human capital to be allocated to the creation of new human capital, so that different countries could have different SS growth rates.

Model B for convergent growth rates

This model assumes (41) and (42) but replaces (43) by the following equation for the growth path of human capital:

$$\partial H(t)/\partial t = B(1 - u)H(t)^{1-\theta}Z(t)^{\theta} \tag{44}$$

where Z is the world's average human capital and is defined as $(\sum_i u_i H_i)/(\sum_i u_i)$. The growth of the country's human capital depends not only on its own stock of human capital but also on the average world level of human capital. Lucas shows that, given (44), countries with below average stock will grow faster than those with above average human capital. However, each country's human capital will converge to the average world level, so that, in the overall model, *ceteris paribus*, output per capita and the growth rates of countries will also converge.

Model B is more appropriate among countries where there is a free flow and use of technical knowledge, which often, though not exclusively, occurs through trading in commodities and labour mobility, while model A is more appropriate to the opposite case where such flows are absent. The European Union provides an example of model B, so that we should expect standards of living among its member countries to converge. However, not all countries in the world have similarly high flows of technical knowledge or the capacity for the effective acquisition of others' knowledge, so that some countries may continue to diverge from others in their standards of living over long periods.

25.9 THE PROCESS OF ENDOGENOUS TECHNICAL CHANGE AND ITS NEGATIVE EXTERNALITIES

The pedagogical nature of neoclassical, and even Keynesian, economics does not focus on the institutions and processes that lead to technical change in the economy. As against these schools, the Austrian school in economics emphasizes the institutional structure. According to it, self-interest in competitive markets constantly drives firms – or entrepreneurs – to improve their products and to gain a competitive edge over others. The successful firms profit from such changes, and induce others to copy them, so that the production structure of the economy is in a state of flux and technical change is endemic. This Austrian notion that the firms and the technology of an economy are constantly in flux clearly differed from the reliance on the mainly static (or with exogenous technical change) production functions of the neoclassical economics and of its traditional growth models. The introduction of endogenous technical change in neoclassical growth models in recent years is in some ways a movement in such modelling to the Austrian view.

The above arguments on endogenous technical change suggest that the competitive capitalist economies are those in which the firms are constantly attempting to gain profits by making changes in the techniques of production. By comparison, the centrally planned or highly regulated economies do not provide sufficient market incentives for change, and do not innovate as fast.

An aspect of the struggle among firms to gain an advantage over other firms through innovation and invention is that some of these, possibly most, will not prove successful in the market, so that the investment in them will be wasted. Another is that technical change not only has positive externalities, it also causes negative externalities. The process of innovation usually leads to what Joseph Schumpeter, a prominent exponent of the Austrian school on this issue, called 'creative destruction', in which some firms will lose their market share and may even close. Further, some of the existing machines embodying the older technology will become obsolete while some will need investments to update them. The benefits from the new technology in terms of output have to be offset by the losses in production resulting from the obsolescence of existing capital and the failure of firms which can no longer compete. The net benefit is, therefore, reduced by these costs and may even become negative.

The innovative process also affects labour. The employees of firms that can no longer compete will be laid off and will need to find other jobs. Further, some of the workers even in the successful firms may be left with outdated skills and become unemployed. Such creative destruction by innovations would thereby increase unemployment in the economy, even while the innovations increase the average productivity of the employed workers.

Another source of the impact on employment arises from the substitution of capital for labour, or vice versa, in the shift from the old to the new technology. Whether this increases or decreases employment in the economy depends on the nature of technical change as being capital or labour intensive, the adaptability of labour to the new technology and the increase in labour demand due to the shift in the production function. It is often suggested that the overall effect of innovations is to raise the unemployment rate in the short run but not necessarily in the long run, but the latter is difficult to determine.

The impact of globalization and endogenous technical change

In the international context of free trade, if the innovating and expanding firms are abroad and the declining ones are domestic firms, an economy would suffer a net decrease in employment and output from endogenous technical change. Therefore, worldwide increases in knowledge do not necessarily benefit all countries equally and may be detrimental on a net basis for some countries, especially those lagging in innovations. Since poorer countries have limited resources to allocate to the creation of new knowledge and less absorptive capacity for innovations occurring in other countries, they are likely to be the laggards – and therefore, likely to be relative losers from the globalization of trade and knowledge.

25.10 IMPLICATIONS OF ENDOGENOUS GROWTH THEORIES FOR MACROECONOMIC POLICY

The traditional neoclassical model had assumed exogenous growth rates for labour and of technical change, so that there is no scope for policy in influencing the SS output per capita and the SS growth rate. However, note that even in such a model, an increase in the saving rate would have increased the pre-SS growth rate, so that there was some scope for policy to increase growth by increasing the saving rate in the economy. Since a particular economy may not reach its steady state for long numbers of years, the impact of increased saving rates on the growth rate would be observable over long periods even in the context of a strictly neoclassical economy without endogenous technical change.

The endogenous growth theories provide for much stronger policy effects on output per capita and its growth rate, depending on the success of policies undertaken to increase or decrease the growth rate of knowledge and human capital. Among such policies are those that promote R&D and other creative processes. But there are also other effects of macroeconomic policies on the long-run growth rates. We illustrate these by the possible effects of recessions on growth.

The Austrian notion of the creative destruction from technical change implies that recessions will serve to weed out firms that are not sufficiently innovative in finding new markets, new processes. Those that survive are more successful at this. Recessions, therefore, serve as a stick for innovations. Stabilization policies that eliminate or moderate recessions could, therefore, lower the rate of endogenous technical change. Conversely, sharp and unexpected recessions which reduce demand beyond the capacity of firms to protect themselves by innovating would also eliminate some firms which, had they survived, would have innovated. Similarly, the workers laid off in recessions do not acquire skills that occur by learning on the job and their previous skills may atrophy during the unemployment period. The resulting decrease in output – even if not in growth rates from a lower output base – will depend on the severity and duration of the recession. This is often labelled as a hysteresis effect.

The endogenous technical change theories also imply that governmental policies that affect the rate of technical change will affect output per capita over the long run, and not merely over the short run. In fact, the former effects could prove to be much more significant for the economy over time.

The role of policy can, therefore, be important in any economy but becomes much more critical for countries close to an unstable SS equilibrium, where the policy effects can push the economy to either side of the threshold. The following example illustrates such effects.

Suppose that the authorities in country j impose an income tax at the rate τ on the return y_{kj} to capital. In the context of (40), the growth rate of output becomes:

$$y_j'' = (1 - \tau)\sigma_j y_{kj} - (\alpha + \psi(j))n_j \tag{45}$$

so that a higher tax rate on the return to capital reduces the growth rate of the economy. Further, it also increases the threshold value of k_j, so that countries which were just past the threshold and therefore in a take-off stage, could fall back into the growth trap.

A tax on the return to capital is not the only policy with such effects. Any policies which lower the return to capital or reduce saving and thereby reduce the growth rates of physical and human capital would have similar effects. In the Lucas model presented earlier, part of the saving – and its investment – is represented by the allocation of human capital to the generation of new knowledge, so that governmental policies detrimental to R&D and innovation in general would lower the growth rate. Among other policies that could do so are excessive regulations, rampant corruption, hindrances to financial development, etc.

25.11 INTERNATIONAL LINKAGES AND GROWTH

The recognition of the role of knowledge as a very important ingredient for the growth of economies enhances the role which international trade and capital flows play. The benefits of trade can be classified as:

(i) static;
(ii) dynamic.

The static benefits derive from the ability of the country to take advantage of comparative advantage in relative factor intensities and from using its existing knowledge of production techniques. The dynamic ones derive from the new knowledge acquired through trade and capital flows and other contacts. New knowledge can include knowledge of the goods produced – and processes used – in other countries but not yet in one's own, with some of this knowledge leading to innovations in the country's production techniques. The importation or imitation of existing techniques and products promotes – or reduces the cost of – the search for new ones.[27]

Education abroad, personal travel and business contacts can contribute to increases in the country's knowledge of products and techniques. Direct investment by foreigners in the home country, transfer of technology agreements and even financial capital inflows which lead to consultation on production techniques also contribute to the country's knowledge. Conversely, barriers to foreign education, travel, trade and investment stem this flow of knowledge.

Therefore, from the perspective of economic growth, international flows, whether of products, capital or people, carry externalities in the form of knowledge flows. These knowledge flows are likely to be of greater benefit to those countries that lack the requisite knowledge than to those which already have it. They will also be of greater benefit for those that have the ability and production systems to use the knowledge of other countries than for those that cannot do so.[28] Hence, the developing economies are expected to be the greater beneficiaries of the international flows of knowledge, *provided* that they possess the openness, the absorptive capacity and the environment – consisting of the political, social and economic systems – to utilize them.

Historically, the openness of the economy and extensive international trade have been among the characteristics of rapidly growing economies. An illustration of this comes from the case of economies on the periphery (geographically, culturally and/or in terms of links and relationships) of the already industrialized economies. Presumably, those on the periphery have greater scope for learning from the industrialized economies than those further away, so that we would expect the former to grow faster than the latter, *ceteris paribus*.

Our discussion of the endogenous technical change also implies that opening the economy to the flow of foreign products and foreign firms need not always be to the home country's advantage. If the expansion of knowledge occurs mainly abroad while the creative destruction of productive capacity – through the inability of domestic firms to innovate at the rate attained by firms abroad – occurs at home, the domestic economy will end up with lower output. This is especially likely to occur in poorer countries with more limited resources for investments in R&D and in education. Whether this effect will be completely or more than offset by the inflows of investment and new knowledge is a moot point. Therefore, the endogenous growth theory does not imply that the liberalization of foreign trade will necessarily benefit all countries equally; in fact, some countries can be net losers – at least in the short term (Temple, 1999, p. 143). For the poorer countries, even if they are not net losers, the gains may be insufficient for their standards of living to converge to those in the richer countries. Consequently, a considerable dispersion of per capita incomes across countries, and especially across continents, can continue to persist, even while there may be convergence in the standards of living of other countries.[29]

CONCLUSIONS

The traditional neoclassical growth model had assumed constant returns to scale in labour and capital, diminishing returns to capital per worker, and exogenous technical change, as well as an absence of money in the economy. These assumptions imply that the growth rates of countries tend to the SS rate, in which per capita incomes grow at the rate of technical change. Per capita incomes do not grow endlessly unless there is technical change. Assuming identical production technology across countries, these models imply that the per capita growth rates of countries will converge to the same SS rate.

The traditional neoclassical growth models further imply that both the growth of the economy and the return to capital decrease as capital intensity increases. That is, the growth rates and the return to capital are higher in countries in which it is scarcer. In these models, while there is some impact of macroeconomic demand policies on growth, this impact is severely limited because the determinants of growth are exogenous. In the limiting case of the steady state, there is no impact of policy on the per capita growth rate, which is determined by the exogenous rate of technical change.

Some of these implications of the traditional neoclassical model seem to be contrary to the factual evidence. For example, Romer (1986) analysed the per capita growth rates for the USA and showed that these had a positive trend over the period 1800 to 1978, rather than the decline in the growth rate predicted by the traditional neoclassical theory. Further, for at least some of the middle-income countries in the world in the last couple of decades, the rates of growth have been increasing rather than decreasing over some periods. Among such countries were Korea, Taiwan, Singapore and Malaysia, before the Asian financial and exchange rate crisis started in 1997. Comparing the capital-intensive developed economies of North America and Europe with the least capital-intensive ones, mainly in Africa, the former economies have higher growth rates than the latter. Our analysis has shown that growth rates can be sensitive to macroeconomic policies and to the type of regime, such as a highly centralized bureaucratic one versus a decentralized capitalist one. However, the impact of macroeconomic policies on growth can take a long time to occur and be difficult to identify.

The endogenous technical change theories depart from the exogenous ones by adducing externalities that result from strategic complementarities between firms and countries. These externalities are aspects of the knowledge of production techniques, accumulation of human capital, a common geographical location, etc. All of these have at least the characteristic of a social good so that the return to a firm creating such a good is less than the social one. In these theories, a competitive equilibrium is ensured by assuming that the production and investment by a given firm is subject to diminishing private returns, even though their social returns may be constant or increasing. However, because of the existence of externalities or spillovers of new knowledge, the invisible hand of competition does not produce the optimal rate of R&D expenditures or other investments leading to invention and innovation and therefore will not yield the optimal long-run growth rate. Governmental policies that increase the acquisition and spread of new knowledge can increase this growth rate but, conversely, inappropriate policies can lower it.

While the human and physical capital intensities are not the only carriers of the factors – such as knowledge – with externalities, they are among the most important determinants. Consequently, simplified endogenous growth models often make such factors depend on one or both of these intensities, with some theories emphasizing physical capital intensity while others emphasize human capital intensity. In any case, both these intensities are usually highly correlated in practice.

The exogenous growth theory had implied that an increase in the saving rate can only increase the steady-state output but not its growth rate. By comparison, the endogenous growth theory implies that the increase in the saving rate, and therefore the rate of increase in capital intensity, can influence the pace of innovation and therefore the steady-state rate of growth of output. Hence, governmental policies that affect the saving rate and the rates of return to physical and human capital can have long-run growth effects.

Using physical and human capital intensities as the carriers for knowledge, some endogenous growth theories argue that there can exist constant or increasing returns to the capital/labour ratio of a country. With increasing returns, the return to capital and the growth rate of per capita income increase with capital intensity. This increase in the return to capital implies that, for open economies, capital would tend to flow from some of the poorer to the richer countries. Similarly, increases in the return to human capital could imply a 'brain drain' from the poorer to the richer countries.

Further, the endogenous growth theories imply that there would be divergence of growth rates so that, over time, the rich countries will get richer relative to poorer countries. This implication is moderated by the assumption that the former have to rely upon their own creation of new knowledge while other countries can also benefit by tapping more effectively into the existing knowledge and will therefore grow faster. This ability to tap into the existing stock of knowledge in the world becomes a major determinant of the growth rates of developing countries, making the endogenous growth theories especially relevant to them. As they catch up to the lead countries, their growth slows down, with eventual convergence in growth rates. However, not all poor countries will be able to effectively tap into the world stock of knowledge.

Endogenous growth theories posit that inventions and innovations are normally a result of economic decisions and require investments. As such, both the readiness of firms to invest in these activities and of workers to invest in their education, and the governmental support for these activities, play an important role in endogenous growth theories. Macroeconomic policies which promote physical and human capital growth increase the growth rate, and some may do so even in the steady state. Those that reduce the returns to these factors slow it down. Further, in the case where there is an unstable steady state with a take-off or threshold capital/labour ratio, policies that push the economy beyond this point become extremely important for the economic future of the country. Similarly, capital inflows would increase the domestic capital intensity and push up the country's growth rate. Patents and other exclusionary devices which close off access or make access to the knowledge of production techniques more costly will lower the growth rates of the countries denied such access.

Empirical studies indicate a large role for physical and human capital in explaining growth. However, even taking account of these and other purely economic determinants of growth, there is still a very significant unexplained residual in such studies. This raises the possibility that there are also non-economic elements such as the degree of openness of the economy, culture, ethnic divisions, political stability (or the lack of it), natural resource endowments, chance and luck, among the actual determinants of the growth of any given country.

A word of caution is needed at this point. The specific modelling of growth conveys the erroneous impression that growth is a smooth process over time. In reality, it is highly uneven, even precarious. Part of this is due to the uneven pattern of advances in knowledge and their incorporation into production, which can be major sources of fluctuations in the macroeconomy. Further, the shift of some countries to a development phase – that is, to long periods of high growth rates – has often come as a surprise and has enough fragility for the development process to be considered by many economists as a 'miracle'. Few miracles are sustained over very long periods, and definitely not without interruption or crises.

SUMMARY OF CRITICAL CONCLUSIONS

- The neoclassical growth model implies that in the steady state without technical change, output per capita will be constant, so that standards of living will be constant.
- In this neoclassical growth model, an increase in the saving rate does not alter the SS growth rate but will increase the SS output per capita.
- In this neoclassical growth model, countries will converge to the same SS output per capita.
- The neoclassical growth model with exogenous technical change produces the SS growth rate of output per capita equal to the rate of technical change in labour productivity.
- The endogenous growth theories emphasize the roles of inventions and innovations and their production. They introduce knowledge, whether in the form of human capital or embodied in physical capital, as an additional input in the production of final goods. The production of knowledge is subject to diminishing marginal productivity for the firm producing it so that its profit-maximizing production is limited. However, in its usage, such knowledge has an externality so that the social return to knowledge is greater than the private one.
- Endogenous growth theories can explain the convergence of the growth rates within groups of countries while allowing for the divergence of growth rates between groups of countries.
- Endogenous growth theories explain why the return to capital in the world economy need not decrease. They also provide a role for governmental policies in the promotion of long-run growth.

review and discussion questions

1 Why does neoclassical theory not assume, for the representative firm, a production function with increasing returns to scale or increasing marginal productivity of capital? For your answer:
   (i) assume that the ith firm has increasing returns to scale. Derive its optimal output.
   (ii) assume that the ith firm has decreasing returns to scale but increasing marginal productivity of capital. Derive its optimal capital–labour ratio.

2 Are either of the possibilities in question 1 consistent with perfect competition? Use your answer to comment on the importance of assuming diminishing marginal productivity of capital at the level of the firm for the existence of competition in the economy.

3 Assuming for the representative firm a Cobb–Douglas production function with constant marginal return to capital, without necessarily embodying decreasing returns to scale, show that the firm will do no investing at all, an infinite amount of investing or be entirely indifferent to how much it invests in physical capital.

4 It is often claimed that the population growth rate is negatively related to the standards of living. To investigate its implications in the Solow growth model, suppose that the population growth rate n is a function of the capital–labour ratio k and that n first increases and then decreases as k increases. Derive its implications for the steady states and their stability in the Solow model.

5 It is sometimes claimed that while a war destroys a great deal of the economy's capital, it also leads to very significant inventions and innovations that are incorporated into civilian production after the war. Present the diagrammatic analysis of this for the Solow type economy and compare the pre- and post-war steady-state output per capita.

6 How does endogenous growth theory accommodate the increasing marginal productivity of capital while maintaining the assumption of perfect competition among firms?

7 Which is more significant for growth: investment (without technical change) or innovation? How would you determine this?

8 What are the similarities and the distinctive elements between the engines of growth in Romer's and Lucas's endogenous growth theories?

9 Present a simple model of economic growth. Incorporate into this model technical change by including an industry called R&D with a production function and two inputs, capital (a stock) and labour (a flow). Show its steady-state properties under different assumptions about the private and social productivity of the output of the R&D industry.

NOTES

1 This knowledge (of how to produce or of the nature of a new product) is to be distinguished from the machines or products incorporating the new knowledge. The former is often a public good; the latter is not.

2 Contrary to our usage of capital symbols to designate the nominal values of the variables in the short-run models of Chapters 13–17, we will now use the capital symbols to designate the real values of the variables and the corresponding lower-case symbols to designate their per capita values.

3 We have made the assumption here and throughout our analysis of growth theory that the population and labour force can be taken to be identical for analytical purposes.

4 This incorporates an implicit assumption that capital is fungible and like putty, so that the adjustments to the implied capital/worker ratio can occur each period.

5 Note that y_k and Y_K are identical.

6 As k approaches its SS value, our earlier analysis implied that the SS growth rate y'' will go to zero, so that in the steady state, output will grow at the same rate as the labour force.

7 However, note that $Y'' = \sigma y_K + (1 - \alpha')n$, so that the growth rate of output will also increase with n.

8 Such a production function may not be of the neoclassical variety with continuous first- and second-order partial derivatives everywhere.

9 See Pritchett (1997) for the empirical evidence on this divergence and convergence.

10 Labour efficiency can be increased by the increase in skills and by education. The present model assumes that this increase is exogenous.

11 These steps are similar to those in the derivation of (10).

12 Further, while it represents the minimum to which the economy's growth rate converges under a stable steady state, actual economies often experience increasing rates of growth during some stages. The standard neoclassical growth model denies such a possibility.

13 However, the consideration of endogenous technical change and of the processes leading to it has a long history in economics. It was a core element of the economic analysis of economies by the Austrian school, and in that context is often associated with the work of Joseph Schumpeter. We refer to them briefly later in this chapter.

14 The profit-maximizing amount is given by the equality of the marginal cost and marginal revenue of new knowledge, treating it as an output of the production process.

15 This argument has been used in some explanations of the failure of centralized communist economies such as those of the Soviet Union and Eastern Europe prior to 1990 to generate economic growth rates comparable to those of the capitalist economies of North America and Western Europe, eventually leading to the collapse of communism in the former.

16 In one of the early studies, in 1962, Arrow had set out a growth model incorporating learning-by-doing on the job, so that the capital (physical and human) intensity also represented knowledge of the techniques of production.

17 Since we have made knowledge a function of capital intensity, it is worth reiterating that capital includes both human and non-human capital.

18 Romer (1986, p. 1008) phrased this as: 'Growth for a country that is not a leader will reflect at least in part the process of imitation and transmission of existing knowledge, where the growth rate of the leader gives some indication of growth at the frontier of knowledge.' He argued that the leader was the Netherlands during 1700–85 (with a growth rate of GDP per man-hour of –0.07%), the UK during 1785 to 1890 (with growth rates of 0.5% during 1785–1820 and 1.4% during 1820–90) and the USA since 1890 (with a growth rate of 2.3%). This evidence suggests that the leader can change over time and that the growth rates of the leading country have been increasing over time.

19 We have assumed the simplification that the value of k is identical across industries within each country. In reality, the capital intensity of industries varies across countries at about the same stage of development, being higher for some industries in one country while being lower for other industries, so that there is always some scope for copying from other countries.

20 Note that, while α was restricted to less than one in the basic neoclassical growth model, it can now be greater or less than one.

21 It has already been mentioned above that α need not always be below 1.

22 This corresponds to (19) above.

23 This corresponds to (20) above.

24 The long-run implications for growth of the crises in their exchange rates, stock markets and economies generally during the latter half of the 1990s have yet to be determined. The short-term impact of these crises has been to cut down their growth rates considerably.

25 For consistency with our use of symbols in this chapter, we have replaced Lucas's lower-case symbols with capital ones.

26 Lucas suggests 'technology' and 'knowledge capital' as alternatives for 'human capital' in this model, which can be viewed as the stock of technical knowledge.

27 Such importation may involve the payment of royalties to other countries or loss of control of domestic firms to foreign corporations. Imitation may initially mean the production of poor quality versions of foreign products.

28 The current state of knowledge is clearly an input into the generation and productivity of new innovations and inventions, with the greatest advantage being obtained by countries and firms which have the ability and means to understand and use the new knowledge.

29 Temple (1999) provides evidence of such experiences among countries. In particular, the per capita incomes of most countries in sub-Saharan Africa relative to the world average income have declined in recent decades.

REFERENCES

Lucas, Robert E. 'On the Mechanics of Economic Development'. *Journal of Monetary Economics*, 22, July 1988, pp. 3–42.

——. 'Making a Miracle'. *Econometrica*, 61, March 1993, pp. 251–72.

Mankiw, N. Gregory. 'The Growth of Nations'. *Brookings Papers on Economic Activity*, 1995, pp. 275–326.

Pritchett, Lant. 'Divergence, Big Time'. *Journal of Economic Perspectives*, 11, Summer 1997, pp. 3–18.

Romer, Paul M. 'Increasing Returns and Long-Run Growth'. *Journal of Political Economy*, 94, October 1986, pp. 1002–37.

——. 'Endogenous Technical Change'. *Journal of Political Economy*, 98, October 1990, pp. S71–S102.

Solow, Robert M. 'A Contribution to the Theory of Economic Growth'. *Quarterly Journal of Economics*, 70, February 1956, pp. 65–94.

——. 'Technical Change and the Aggregate Production Function'. *Review of Economics and Statistics*, 39, August 1957, pp. 312–20.

Temple, Jonathan. 'The New Growth Evidence'. *Journal of Economic Literature*, 37, March 1999, pp. 112–56.

chapter twenty-six

MONETARY GROWTH THEORY

It is vital for monetary growth analysis to distinguish between the quantity of money as currency and balances in banks from the financial institutions and the payments mechanism which back the use of money. This chapter shows that these two aspects of money lead to different implications for the economy's growth.

This chapter also attempts to apply the notions behind endogenous technical change to financial intermediation. This is a comparatively new topic. Its discussion in this chapter is a first step and illustrative rather than definitive.

This chapter, just as the discussions on this topic in the literature, does not provide definite conclusions on the significance of the role of money or financial intermediation to growth. However, there does exist some empirical evidence supporting financial development as a contributor to the economy's growth.

---

key concepts introduced in this chapter

- Commodity money
- Fiat money
- Inside money
- The steady-state rate of inflation
- The usage of money and the reduction of transactions time in exchanges
- Financial services as an intermediate good
- The use of money in exchange as a mechanism for using the services of financial intermediation
- Invention and innovation in the financial sector

The growth models of the preceding chapter do not include money or a financial sector. This chapter will first modify the neoclassical growth model in stages to incorporate money. Three types of money will be considered. The first one is a commodity-money and the second one is a costlessly supplied fiat money. The third type is inside money supplied by private financial intermediaries. The supply of inside money involves the use of labour and capital, so that in considering inside money, we shift the focus from nominal or real balances to financial intermediation as an industry, with real balances representing tokens to the use of the services of the financial sector (FS).

The economic literature on the importance of money to economic growth and development can be classified into several broad groups:

(A) those publications which consider the contribution of money to output per capita in the economy to be zero or minimal; and

(B) those publications which consider money and financial institutions to be vital to the prosperity of nations and therefore see these as having made substantial contributions to output per capita and its growth in the past;

(C) further to (B), in the steady state, the contribution of money and financial institutions to output per capita can be only a level effect, or there could also be a growth effect on output per capita; some studies, possibly a majority, advocate the former position of only level effects, while other studies adopt the latter one of both level and growth effects.

Approaches to money in growth theories

There are three main areas of differentiation in the approach to money in growth analyses. These involve:

(i) The consideration of money in terms of its nominal quantity, and especially of the nominal quantity of fiat money,[1] versus the consideration of this nominal quantity as 'claims' on the services of the financial sector, with the emphasis in the analysis of this sector being on its efficiency and innovation. The former view can be caricatured by treating money as a 'veil' which affects only the appearance but not the magnitudes of the real variables, such as national output and its growth rate. The latter view treats the financial sector as critical to the efficiency and performance of all production and exchange in the economy and, therefore, critical to output and growth in the economy.[2]

(ii) The consideration of the role of fiat money and financial institutions in a static economy or one with technical change only in the production of commodities, versus its role in a dynamic context, with interactive innovation, growth and development of the financial, production and exchange sectors of the economy.

(iii) The consideration of the role of an unregulated, competitive and efficient financial sector, compared with the costs imposed on the economy by regulation, inefficiency and lack of competition in the financial sector. This issue is particularly relevant in the discussions on why some countries develop faster than others even when they share the same knowledge of production techniques for commodities.

These differences lead to a dichotomy in the ways money is introduced into growth theory. On one side of this dichotomy is the introduction of money as only fiat money into the neoclassical growth theory presented in the preceding chapter, without an explicit consideration of the financial sector. This is done in sections 26.2 to 26.4 below. On the other side of the dichotomy is the focus on the financial sector as the user of inputs to provide services such as for the exchange of goods, the hiring and payments for inputs, mobilizing and allocating savings, the efficient funding of investment projects, etc., and often innovating in its provision of these services. The latter calls for the consideration of the financial sector, including the organized markets for trades in bonds and stocks, in the general context of the endogenous growth models. There is no generally accepted model or even framework for the latter, so that only an introduction to this approach is presented in sections 26.5 and 26.6.

Section 26.1 presents the basic model with one of the commodities serving as money. Sections 26.2 to 26.4 present in stages the modifications of the basic neoclassical growth model with exogenous technical change to incorporate fiat money. However, the main forms of money in the real-world economies are other than fiat money, and these – as well as many other liquid assets – are provided by financial intermediaries, which use labour and capital to provide monetary services. This role of financial institutions as intermediaries in the production–consumption process and financial intermediation as one of the industries in the economy is the subject of section 26.5. Section 26.6 draws upon the arguments in the endogenous technical change literature to analyse the contribution of money to income per capita and to growth in it.

The stylized empirical facts on the importance of money in output growth

As we will see from the models developed in this chapter, the neoclassical monetary growth models imply that monetary economies can have higher or lower output than corresponding barter (non-monetary) economies. In order to judge among these implications and use selectivity in not pursuing clearly counter-factual possibilities, we need to establish some stylized empirical facts about growth in monetary economies. We state two of these as:

(i)   The least controversial stylized fact about the contribution of money in the economy is that monetary economies have higher output per capita and per worker than barter ones.

(ii) Another stylized fact is that, for a given capital–labour ratio, monetary economies have higher growth rates than barter ones, though whether this higher growth rate also holds in steady state is more controversial.

The problem in interpreting and applying these statements is about the nature and domain of the *ceteris paribus* clause in them. Monetary economies over time develop production and exchange technologies which are drastically different from those of the barter economies which preceded them: monetary exchanges as against barter ones facilitate specialization in skills, commodity production, location, regional and international trade, etc. As an example of the drastic differences between the monetary and the barter economies, the modern large corporations could not really exist in a barter economy. In this sense, the usage of money has not merely proved to be a veil covering the surface of the real economy, it has shaped and altered the structure of the economy and increased its size.

Therefore, a realistic evaluation of the historical benefits of money over the long run has to allow for the resulting changes in the structure of production and the economy. The relevant analysis cannot include the resulting changes in technologies and organizational structures in the *ceteris paribus* clause (i.e., would not hold them constant in a comparison of the monetary economy with the barter one, and of a less financially developed one with a more advanced one). However, it is difficult to pin down exactly what parts of the changes in technology and exchange patterns are due to the use of money versus those that could have equally easily arisen in non-monetary and more primitive financial economies. The influence of the exchanges with money permeates the present-day economies and makes any decomposition of the existing economic structure and technology into that which could have existed without the usage of money and that due to its usage, impossible. Given this level of difficulty and the economists' limited analytical apparatus, the usual *ceteris paribus* clause – with its assumption of an unchanging technology even in the long run between the barter and monetary economies, and between economies with more primitive financial versus more advanced financial intermediation – is often imposed in modelling and colours many of the results derived from monetary growth models. Great care must, therefore, be used in applying the results based on such a *ceteris paribus* clause.

26.1 COMMODITY-MONEY, REAL BALANCES AND GROWTH THEORY

This section presents the basic neoclassical monetary growth model using the production technology of the Solow model of section 25.2 of Chapter 25, with one of the commodities serving as a medium of payments and thereby acting as money. It is assumed that there are no costs of using this commodity-money, that it is durable, and that it does not enter the utility and production functions. The overall scenario is really that of a barter economy just entering into multilateral exchanges by converting some of its output to usage as money, as against its usage in consumption or production.

Assume that the economy has per capita output y of commodities, which constitutes its per capita disposable income in each period. Its per capita consumption c and per capita saving s, as in Chapter 25, are assumed to be given by:

$$c = (1 - \sigma)y \tag{1}$$

$$s = \sigma y$$

Part of this saving is used to increase its real balances by m', with the remainder s_k used to increase its physical capital stock used in production, so that:

$$s_k = \sigma y - m' \tag{2}$$

where s_k is the change in per capita physical capital, m is the per capita real balances and m' is the change in m.

Assume that the demand for real balances of fiat money m^d is a proportion[3] λ of output y, so that:

$$m^d = \lambda y \tag{3}$$

Assuming equilibrium in the money market through instantaneous adjustment of the price level,

$$m = m^d = \lambda y \tag{4}$$

which implies that $m'' = y''$, where "''" designates the rate of growth, so that the increase m' in real balances per capita is:

$$m' = \lambda y'' y \tag{5}$$

Therefore, from (2) and (5),

$$s_k = \sigma y - \lambda y'' y \tag{6}$$

From Solow's growth theory presented in Chapter 25, we have the SS condition as:

$$k' = s_k - nk = 0 \tag{7}$$

where:

- k capital/labour (K/L) ratio
- k' change in k
- s_k per capita saving available for investment in physical capital ($=k'$)
- n growth rate of labour supply L
- nk capital per worker required to equip the increase in workers with the existing capital intensity

With $y = f(k)$ where $f(k)$ is the production function with $f' > 0$ and $f'' < 0$, we get from (6) and (7) that:

$$f(k) \, [\sigma - \lambda y''] - nk = 0 \qquad (8)$$

Therefore, the steady-state condition of the assumed economy is:

$$f(k)[\sigma - \lambda y''] = nk \qquad (9)$$

Equation (8) is graphed in Figure 26.1, with k on the horizontal axis.[4] This figure is similar to those used in Chapter 25 for Solow's growth theory without money. The curve for $f(k)[\sigma - \lambda y'']$ is shown as X'. This curve will be concave and lower than for $\sigma f(k)$, which is the curve relevant to the barter economy (with $m \equiv 0$). As Figure 26.1 shows, the SS value k_1^* for the monetary economy will be less than k_0^* for the barter economy. However, at k_1^*, k is constant, so that y is also constant. Hence, the SS growth rates of capital K and output Y are given by:

$$K'' = Y'' = n$$

which are identical to the growth rates in the absence of money. Hence, the commodity-money economy and the barter economy will have the same SS growth rates (y'' and Y'') in this model but the SS values y^* and k^* will be *lower* for the monetary economy which has, by assumption, the same production function as the barter economy. Therefore, the per capita incomes and standards of living will be lower in the commodity-money economy. Further, the introduction of commodity-money into the Solow model produces SS *level* but not SS *growth* effects.

However, in the pre-steady state, the commodity-money economy does produce a lower rate of growth for any given capital–labour ratio as shown by the following argument. Chapter 25 had derived the relationship between y'' and k'' for the production function $f(k)$ as:

$$y'' = \alpha'k''$$

where $\alpha' = y_k k/y$, so that α' is the output share of capital. Since k'' in the commodity-money economy is reduced by the need to provide some of the saving for increases in the real

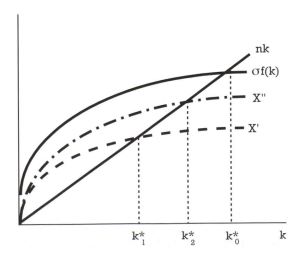

Figure 26.1

balances, k'' is less in the economy using a commodity as money than in the barter economy and so is y'' in the former.

The implications of the preceding analysis are:

(i) The SS per capita income y is lower in the commodity money economy than in the barter one.

(ii) The SS growth rates are the same.

Assumption (i) clearly contradicts our stylized facts.

26.2 REAL FIAT BALANCES IN DISPOSABLE INCOME, AND GROWTH

This section modifies the analysis of the preceding section by replacing commodity-money by fiat money, which represents a common historical pattern of monetary evolution. The model presented in this section is based on the analysis of Levhari and Patinkin (1968), who had incorporated and extended the analysis of Tobin (1965) and Johnson (1967). Money in this basic monetary model is fiat money issued by the government and is thus 'outside money'. It is assumed that there are no costs of producing and introducing into the economy, as well of using and holding this fiat money. Newly created fiat money is assumed to be transferred gratuitously and directly to the public. Alternatively, the seigniorage from its creation is used by the government to buy goods that are then provided free to the public. Under both these alternatives, the commodity income of the economy is not reduced by the introduction of fiat money into the economy. Hence, the disposable income of the public consists of the economy's output and the increase in real balances in the economy. That is,

$$y_d = y + m' \tag{10}$$

where y_d is disposable per capita real income. Hence, from (5) and (10),

$$y_d = y + \lambda y'' y \tag{10'}$$

Assuming as before that the average propensity to consume is constant at $(1 - \sigma)$,

$$c = (1 - \sigma)[y + \lambda y'' y] \tag{11}$$

Hence, per capita saving s out of per capita output y is:

$$s = y - c$$
$$= \sigma y - (1 - \sigma)\lambda y'' y$$
$$= y[\sigma - (1 - \sigma)\lambda y''] \tag{12}$$

Since fiat money does not use any commodities, all of s is used to increase the physical capital stock, so that $s_k = s$. Hence, the Solow growth equation becomes:

$$k' = f(k)[\sigma - (1 - \sigma)\lambda y''] - nk \tag{13}$$

Hence, in steady state,

$$f(k)[\sigma - (1 - \sigma)\lambda y''] = nk \tag{14}$$

The concave curve specified by the left-hand side of (14) is shown as X'' in Figure 26.1. X'' will lie $\sigma f(k)$ (i.e., for the barter economy). Hence, X'' implies a lower SS value of k^*, at k_2^* in the presence of fiat money, than k_0^* in the barter economy. But, comparing (9) and (14), since $0 < \sigma < 1$, X'' (for the fiat money case) will be above X' (for the commodity-money) case, so that $k_2^* > k_1^*$. This implies higher SS values of y^* and k^* for the fiat money case than for the commodity-money case, so that the economy becomes better off in level terms by the switch to fiat money from commodity-money, even though it is still worse off than the barter case. Note that the SS growth rates $y^{*''}$ and $k^{*''}$ are identical for all cases. Hence, the introduction of fiat money into the economy, just as for the commodity-money, produces only SS level but not SS growth effects.

However, in the pre-SS equilibrium for the fiat money case, the reduction in saving in the form of commodities because of the increase in the consumption of commodities, reduces k'', which implies that y'' also falls. That is, the pre-SS growth rate decreases. This decrease in the growth rate of output is lower than for the commodity-money case.

The steady-state rate of inflation

We have so far considered only the steady-state condition for capital. Since we now have another asset, real balances, in the model, its SS condition is:

$$m' = 0$$

where $m = M/PL$, so that:

$$m' = m''m = (M'' - P'' - L'')m \tag{15}$$

Therefore, the steady-state condition is

$$(M'' - P'' - L'')m = 0 \tag{16}$$

Let $M'' = \theta$, $P'' = \pi$ and $L'' = n$. Hence, for $m > 0$, (16) implies that:

$$\theta - \pi = n$$

and the SS rate of inflation π^* is given by:

$$\pi^* = \theta - n \tag{17}$$

Predictions of the model

Among the predictions for the real world, the preceding models imply that:

(i) SS output per capita and capital intensity in both the fiat money and commodity-money economies will be *lower* than in the corresponding barter economy;

(ii) growth rates will also be lower at given values of the capital–labour ratio outside the steady state;

(iii) SS growth rates will be the same.

These predictions indicate that the economy is better off without the use of money. This is counter-factual since rational economic agents will then prefer the barter economy to the money one and the barter economies will not evolve into monetary economies, which they have done. Further, our stylized facts argue that monetary economies invariably have higher output per capita than barter economies. Therefore, the preceding model misses important elements of the role of money in the economy and must be modified in order to derive more realistic implications. This will be attempted in the next section by introducing real balances into the production function.

26.3 REAL FIAT BALANCES IN THE STATIC PRODUCTION FUNCTION

We will take it as an established fact that the usage of money in the economy allows the economy to produce more with given levels of capital and labour. To ensure this, there are two routes for the modification of the above model. One is to redefine output to include in it the *services* of money in exchange and production.[5] The other is to assume that these services are captured by putting real balances in the production function and assuming that real balances have a positive marginal product (Levhari and Patinkin, 1968). We will proceed along the latter route.

To incorporate this suggestion into the fiat money model of the preceding section, redefine the production function of the representative firm as:

$$y = g(k, m^f) \quad g_k, g_m > 0; g_{kk}, g_{mm} < 0 \tag{18}$$

where m^f are the real balances held by the firm. With this modification, the SS condition corresponding to (14) becomes,

$$g(k, m^f) [\sigma - (1 - \sigma)\lambda y''] = nk \tag{19}$$

The left side of (19) is the saving available for investment in physical capital. By (18), for a given k, the presence of real balances increases the economy's output and therefore increases its saving. However, the transfer of seigniorage to the public increases disposable income and through the income effect increases consumption and reduces saving. The net effect of these opposing influences on the saving available for investment could go in either direction. Hence, if we were to show the left side of (19) by a curve X''' (not actually drawn) in Figure 26.1, X''' could lie above or below the curve σy for the barter economy. However, it would definitely lie above X' and X'', so that the SS value of k could be higher or lower than in the non-monetary economy, but definitely higher than if money was not in the production function.

Hence, the implications of this model are:

(i) SS output per worker could be higher or lower for the monetary than the non-monetary economy;
(ii) the SS growth rate would be the same at n for both economies.

However, we argued in the introduction to this chapter that the monetary economy produces substantially higher output than the non-monetary one. To obtain this result in equation (19) and Figure 26.1, we would have to add to our analysis the *ad hoc* postulate that the net effect of the use of money is an increase in saving in the monetary economy for the values of the real balances which are willingly held. There is no empirical basis for making this assumption as a general case so that we do not set out the analysis for such a shift in the saving propensity.

26.4 REFORMULATION OF THE NEOCLASSICAL MODEL WITH MONEY IN THE STATIC PRODUCTION AND UTILITY FUNCTIONS

Steady state with money in the utility function (MIUF) and the static production function (MIPF)

To determine the saving available for investment, we need to first derive the households' demand for real balances. One way of deriving it is to include real balances in the utility function. This is the money in the utility function (MIUF) approach of Chapter 3, and was proposed by Sidrauski (1967) for monetary growth theory. This approach assumes that:

$$U = U(c, m^h) \tag{20}^6$$

where:

$U(\cdot)$ household's utility function
c consumption per worker
m^h real balances per worker held by households

Sidrauski argued that, since the services of real balances yield utility, the imputed value of these services should be added to the output of commodities and the seigniorage from money creation in order to calculate the household's total income. In equilibrium, the real value of the services of a unit of real balances will equal the market rate of interest, which in turn equals the real rate of return r^r plus the rate of inflation π.[7] Hence, the per capita disposable income y_d of households is now modified to:

$$y_d = y + m' + r_m m^h \tag{21}$$

where $r_m = r^r + \pi$, so that,

$$
\begin{aligned}
y_d &= y + m' + (r^r + \pi)m^h \\
&= y + (\theta - \pi - n)m^h + (r^r + \pi)m^h
\end{aligned}
$$

where y is the real income from commodities, $[(\theta - \pi - n)m^h]$ is the increase in real balances, as in (16), and hence the real value of seigniorage, and $[(r^r + \pi)m^h]$ is the real value of the services from holding money. Simplify (21) to:

$$y_d = y + (\theta + r^r - n)m^h \tag{22}$$

Households maximize (20) with respect to c and m^h, subject to (22). Assuming, as before, a constant average propensity to consume at $(1 - \sigma)$,

$$c = y_d - s = (1 - \sigma)\{y + (\theta + r^r - n)m^h\} \tag{23}$$

where c is per capita consumption, of which $[(r^r + \pi)m]$ is spent on *using the services* of real balances and the rest – that is, $[c - (r^r + \pi)m^h]$ – is spent on commodity purchases. Per capita saving s_k available for investment in physical capital is:

$$s_k = y - \{c - (r^r + \pi)m^h\} \tag{24}$$

$$= y - [(1 - \sigma)\{y + (\theta + r^r - n)m\} - (r^r + \pi)m^h]$$

$$= \sigma y - (1 - \sigma)(\theta + r^r - n)m^h - (r^r + \pi)m^h \tag{25}$$

$$= \sigma y - \{(1 - \sigma)(\theta + r^r - n) - (r^r + \pi)\}m^h \tag{26}$$

where the impact of real balances m^h on s_k is ambiguous: s_k exceeds σy if the term $\{\cdot\}$ is negative but is less than σy if $\{\cdot\}$ is positive. The former is more likely the higher is θ relatively to π. Note that $\pi = \theta$ does not necessarily make s_k equal to or greater than σy.
    In steady state, $s_k = nk$, so that (26) implies the steady-state condition:

$$\sigma g(k, m^f) - \{(1 - \sigma)(\theta + r^r - n) - (r^r + \pi)\}m^h = nk \tag{27}$$

For the SS growth effects, since the steady state requires that $k' = 0$, the SS growth rates of capital and output in the present version of the model are still n. Hence, this introduction of money into the utility and production functions does not change the SS growth rate.

For the SS *level* effects, if we were to ignore the contribution of m^f in the production function, then, from the discussion following (26), s_k can increase or decrease as a consequence of the usage of real balances, so that the SS capital and output per worker in this monetary model could be higher or lower than in the corresponding barter model. To get a definitive increase in these variables for the monetary model, there must be large positive effects of the usage of money on output in the monetary economy. This points to the very significant role of m^f in the production function in (27).

For the pre-SS analysis with values of k less than the SS one, the rates of growth for any given value of k are greater after monetization if the left side of (27) exceeds $\sigma y(k)$ (for the barter economy), but are lower in the converse case. The latter implication highlights once again the critical role of money to the technology of production.

Real balances and inflation in the steady state

For the demand for real balances by households in the MIUF approach, utility maximization yields the households' demand for real balances m^{hd} as:

$$m^{hd} = m^{hd}(r^r + \pi, y_d) \tag{28}$$

For the holdings of real balances by firms in the MIPF approach, profit maximization by the firms implies that firms will be indifferent between holding capital or real balances if their net returns are the same. The net return on capital is its marginal product $g_k(k, m)$ while the net return on real balances is its marginal product less the rate of inflation, which is the loss due to inflation from holding real balances. Hence, the portfolio equilibrium condition for firms is:

$$g_m(k, m^f) - \pi = g_k(k, m^f) \tag{29}$$

where m^f are the real balances held by firms. Equation (29) yields the demand for real balances m^{fd} by firms as:

$$m^{fd} = m^{fd}(\pi, k) \tag{30}$$

Hence, the equilibrium condition for real balances, with m as the supply of real balances per capita, is:

$$m = m^d = m^{hd}(r^r + \pi) + m^{fd}(\pi, k) \tag{31}$$

To derive the SS growth rates of real balances and inflation, note that the steady state requires that $m' = 0$. That is, as in (16) for the steady state,

$$m' = (M'' - P'' - L'')m = (\theta - \pi - n)m = 0 \tag{32}$$

which implies for $m > 0$ that:

$$\theta - \pi = n$$

so that the SS rate of inflation π^*, again, is given by:

$$\pi^* = \theta - n \tag{33}$$

Hence, in the steady state, the real balances (M/P) grow at the growth rate n of labour while the SS inflation rate π^* becomes constant at $(\theta - n)$. Further, with the SS values of k and m^f being constant in the production function, the SS real rate of interest r^{r*} $(=f_k(k, m^f))$ would also be a constant. Furthermore, the SS nominal rate of interest r would be constant at $(r^r + \pi^*)$.

26.5 WHY AND HOW DOES MONEY CONTRIBUTE TO PER CAPITA OUTPUT AND ITS GROWTH RATE?

The failure of the preceding growth model to show an unambiguous increase in output per worker for the monetary economy over that in its barter counterpart, let alone an increase in its growth rate, is certainly disappointing. We consider this failure as evidence of this model's inappropriateness for the monetary economy because of its failure to provide a sufficiently realistic role for money in the economy.

We illustrate our views on the role of money in the economy by the following analogy. Consider, for example, the use of artificial (non-human and non-animal) energy, especially electrical, in the economy. There is a fundamental difference between the production structures and prosperity of economies using only human and animal energy in production and those heavily reliant on artificial energy. Yet the only way the latter's impact on the economy can be shown in models is through a shift or periodic shifts in the economy's commodity production function due to the innovation and evolution of the forms of artificial energy usage. As an intermediate good, the impact of electricity consists of two opposing forces: electricity generation uses some labour and capital, thereby reducing their amounts left over for usage in the production of final goods, while the usage of electricity as an intermediate good increases the output of the latter. Therefore, without knowing the actual shift in the production function of final output due to the use of electricity, it is not possible to determine *a priori* whether the switch to electricity will increase or decrease final output, and especially whether it will do so at the margin of existing usage.

From another perspective, the optimal production of electricity, and hence the optimal amount of the diversion of labour and capital to it, would be that which maximizes the output of the final commodities. Economic theory implies that in perfect competition, without externalities etc., the actual amount of electricity produced and used will be the optimal one, so that a competitive economy with a positive usage of electricity will clearly constitute evidence that the conversion to electricity did increase output per capita. However, note that this is an argument for a positive level effect, not one for a growth effect, of the invention and widespread usage of an intermediate good. There may also be a growth effect, but to show such an effect will require additional special arguments – for example, such as those showing greater technical change in this industry relative to the average one for the economy.

In our view, money, just like artificial energy, is an intermediate good in consumption and production. As in the case of energy, money's contribution to output per capita and output growth cannot be assessed without specifying the shifts and evolution of the economy's commodity production function under the impact of the innovation and evolution of money and financial intermediation. One implication of this argument is that the commodity production function is different in the pre- and post-versions of the innovation *and* widespread use of money, as it is in the pre- and post-versions of the innovation and extensive production of artificial energy. Hence, in our view, it is a mistake for growth theory to assume that the commodity production function in the barter economy would be the same as in the monetary economy, with the result that the monetary growth theory based on such an assumption is of doubtful value. Another implication is that monetary growth theory must include not only real balances in the commodity production function but also explicitly model the role of financial intermediation in the economy. This is attempted in the next section.

Further, the output of financial intermediation (FI), just as that of energy, need not be at the optimal level for commodity production. Note that the actual production of these sectors in any given economy can be non-optimal: either held below or induced to be above this optimal amount, depending upon the structure of the industry, externalities and rigidities, governmental policies and controls, the availability of investment funds, etc. However, in terms of the preceding monetary growth model, this model, in common with most such models, implicitly assumes that the financial sector, like any other sector, functions in a competitive and unregulated manner, and that the market for its services is continuously in equilibrium through price adjustments. But many countries regulate their financial sectors closely, sometimes over long periods, with some setting interest rates, credit allocations and imposing other restrictions. A common question asked in such cases – especially in the context of developing countries – is whether the liberalization and expansion of the financial sector would increase the standard of living and the growth rate of the economy. This is a different question, with a different perspective on money in the economy, from that considered so far in this chapter. We examine this issue as part of the broad consideration of FI in the next section.

26.6 HOW DOES THE USE OF MONEY CHANGE THE LABOUR SUPPLIED FOR PRODUCTION?

Chapter 3 introduced the concept of transactions time in the individual's utility function, so that the worker has to budget for the additional transactions time required to purchase the commodities bought with the income from the labour supplied. The required transactions time is an ancillary cost of labour supply (to earn income to pay for the shopping expenditures), so that the labour supply is a decreasing function of its ancillary transactions time. This transactions time is substantially less in a monetary economy than in a barter one without the double coincidence of wants.[8] In fact, the transition from a barter to a monetary economy represents a drastic reduction in the amount of labour used in exchange, accompanied by a large increase in the labour supply to both production for the market by firms and within the household. This is illustrated quite well by the quote in Chapter 24 on the breakdown of the monetary arrangements after the collapse of the Soviet Union showed. Following this breakdown, labour had to drastically increase the amount of time devoted to exchanges (for example, on roadside stands) at the cost of the time supplied to market and household production.

Therefore, going from a barter to a monetary economy results in a very drastic increase in the labour supply to production, at the expense of shopping and selling time. This increase in the labour supply, in turn, implies a substantial increase in the economy's output. There would also be additional effects, such as those of allowing specialization, increase in the size of the market, etc., which occur with the monetization of the economy.

To summarize, the production and labour supply functions in functioning monetary economies are likely to be significantly different from their counterparts in barter economies. Whether these shifts produce only level or also growth effects in steady state still remains to be discussed.

26.7 THE DISTINCTION BETWEEN INSIDE AND OUTSIDE MONEY

Inside money represents monetary assets that are also a liability of the individuals and firms, such as the banks, within the private sector. If the accounting procedure of summing over the assets and the liabilities of the private sector to calculate its net worth is followed, the assets represented by inside money are offset exactly by the liabilities represented by it, so that the net worth of the private sector does not include inside money. Demand and savings deposits are assets of the households and firms that hold them but are a liability of the banks in which they are held. Therefore, they are not part of the accounting calculation of the net worth of the private sector since banks are units within the private sector.[9]

Outside money is an asset of the private sector but a liability of the government sector, including the central bank. As such, the accounting calculation of the net worth of the private sector will include outside money. The monetary base is an asset held by the private sector including the banks but is not a liability of any units of the private sector. Therefore, the monetary base is part of the net worth of the private sector. As a liability of the government, it represents outside money.

Another distinction between inside and outside money is that the former requires the usage of capital and labour while the provision of the monetary base – which is fiat money – does not. This distinction – rather than whether one of them is part of the private sector's net worth and the other is not – is the one relevant to the rest of this chapter.

26.8 FINANCIAL INTERMEDIATION (FI) IN THE GROWTH AND DEVELOPMENT PROCESSES

The preceding mode of specifying monetary growth theory was based on the introduction of the real balances of fiat money at various points in neoclassical growth theory. These points were:

  (i)   the definition of disposable income;
 (ii) the allocation of saving to capital and to real balances; and
(iii) the insertion of real balances in the utility and production functions.

The concept of money in these models was that of fiat money, costlessly created without using any part of the economy's labour and capital in its production or usage. However, fiat money in circulation – which constitutes currency (notes and coins) in the hands of consumers and firms other than financial intermediaries – is a very small part of the actual moneyness or liquidity in the modern economy. Further, even the usage of currency imposes costs on the users: it has to be acquired, usually from financial intermediaries (by households) or from customers (by firms), with some expenditure of labour time and capital and its usage also involves labour and capital in the acts of safe keeping, counting and handing over to others. These costs are sufficiently significant for both households and firms to prefer various types of monies created by the private sector, even though these require the expenditure of labour and capital both for their creation and usage and, therefore, impose a user cost.

While the usage of real balances diverts some of the economy's savings to them, their excessive regulation can impose even higher costs on the consumption and production sectors of the economy. The basic reason for this is that it is much more efficient to consume or produce if all households and firms operate with money (as against a barter economy) and if the households and firms have adequate balances to perform their transactions properly. This argument adduces the benefits from the use of money to be akin to the benefits, say, from the use of electricity (or of automobiles). For all of these, when no one else in the economy uses them, the costs to a single firm or household using them are very high, and the benefits are very small, since both electrical stations (and car production plants and roads) would then be uneconomic to build and would not exist. There are, therefore, considerable externalities of economy-wide usage in these cases.

Further, comparing a restricted monetary system with a freer one, the household and production sectors need or can benefit considerably from customized monies – i.e., monies with specialized and customized characteristics – rather than with a strictly standardized money such as currency with a fixed set of characteristics. As an illustration of this, consider the severe disadvantages for consumers and firms of the following: only one standard size of shirt being made available to all consumers irrespective of their individual sizes; one standard material for all pipes in all kinds of different industries in the economy; and one standard automobile for all haulage and travel. In each of these examples, considerable efficiencies are to be gained from the competitive, free enterprise creation of alternatives. Similarly, considerable efficiencies are to be gained from the competitive creation of alternatives to fiat money, with consumers and firms selecting the particular one or the combination which best suits their needs. These arguments suggest that the focus of the appropriate treatment of money should be on the provision of, and access to, the services of financial intermediation (FI), along with the consideration of the labour and capital used in the FI sector. Banks are part of this sector, as are near-banks, investment brokers, insurance companies, pension funds, etc., with each providing a variety of differentiated products.

Banks, other financial intermediaries and financial development

Although the firms engaged in banking are a cornerstone of the financial sector, they are only one part of it. This sector also includes other institutions such as the stock and bond markets, brokerage firms, pension funds, insurance companies, mutual funds, etc. These institutions and markets are governed and supported by the rules, regulations and practices governing the financial system. These include the accounting and disclosure requirements, monitoring, certification and the public dissemination of information on firms, including financial intermediaries, as well as measures against fraud and inside trading, etc. These factors affect the extent to which firms can raise capital from external sources, and, in a competitive system, reduce the cost of such capital, whether directly in loans from banks and other financial institutions or through the public offerings of shares and bonds. Well-developed and efficient financial markets allow firms to rely on external sources of financing their investments and to do so in a competitive manner. For savers, the high degree of liquidity of the investment in these markets is attractive relative to the alternatives of hoarding and private illiquid investments.

Financial development is, therefore, often measured by the number and variety of financial intermediaries, the size and sophistication of the markets for bonds and stocks, and the efficiency of the rules, regulations and practices governing the financial practices of firms in the economy.

One can, therefore, distinguish between the contributions of banking and of the rest of the financial system to the growth of output. However, this is rarely done at the general level of our analysis and we will not do so in this chapter.[10]

Real balances and banking services

From the perspective of financial intermediation, the real balances of inside money may be viewed as tokens for the use of banking services. But the holdings and use of these tokens by the non-bank public require the banks to devote labour and capital, as can be witnessed by walking into any bank building (i.e., use of physical capital) and dealing with the bank employees (i.e., use of labour). Banks and other financial intermediaries can, therefore, be viewed as firms producing the services provided to owners of real balances, with these services being in the nature of intermediate rather than final goods, and charging the buyers for such services. Real balances are merely the tokens allowing access to banking services.

The basics of incorporating the financial sector into production in the economy

Therefore, an important approach to the contribution of FI to growth is to focus on the FI industry as a provider of services to consumers and to other industries. As noted above, these services are produced with the help of labour and capital, and sold in the market for a price. This picture differs substantially from that of a costlessly-provided and costlessly-used fiat money in the neoclassical growth theory of the preceding sections. We will now deviate from this theory and posit that while money and other financial assets are provided by either the government or the private sectors, they do not yield their services except through FI, which involves their production at a cost. These services are the products of financial intermediaries, who charge the users for such services.

Designate both the financial sector and its real output per worker by z, with Z standing for its total output. Note that even if the financial sector is defined as being synonymous with banks, its output will be different from the amount of real balances in the economy even when these are defined broadly to include all deposits with banks.

A simple neoclassical-type production function for the financial sector can be specified as:

$$z = z(k_z) \quad z_k > 0, z_{kk} < 0 \tag{34}$$

where:

  z real output per worker of the FI sector
  k_z capital/labour ratio of the FI sector

The neoclassical-type production function for the output of final commodities (excluding the services of the financial sector) can be similarly given the form:

$$x = x(k_x, z) \quad x_k, x_z > 0; x_{kk}, x_{zz} < 0 \tag{35}$$

where:

  x real output per worker of final commodities
  k_x capital/labour ratio in the commodity sector

We will add the plausible assumption that k_x and z are 'cooperative' in the sense that $x_{kz} > 0$ and $x_{zk} > 0$, so that an increase in financial services z increases the marginal product of capital, and vice versa. However, they are still substitutes in producing any given value of x.

In the real world, some of the output of the financial sector will be used as intermediate good in consumption and some in commodity production. As a simplification, assume that all of the FI services produced in the economy are used by the firms in the production of commodities so that all of the financial sector's output is used only as an intermediate good in production, and none is to be counted in the economy's final output. This final output is designated as Y, which equals $L_x x$, where L_x is the amount of labour employed in the production of commodities and x is the output of commodities per worker.

The nature of z in the commodity production function needs to be clarified. Equation (34) specifies the composite output z of financial services without specifying the actual assets which will provide it at least cost. Within this composite output, the production of different types of FI assets, with quantities z_i, would depend upon the technology of FI, the demand for z_i and the relative costs of producing z_i. For example, over time, the relative amounts of currency or demand deposits or savings deposits, etc., change with the amounts of output and capital per worker, depending upon the characteristics and relative costs of these assets, and upon the techniques of production such as the use of human tellers versus automatic teller machines.[11] In this sense, the services of FI are like those of the transport or the energy sectors, whose demand increases with production in the economy but the particular products which are bought to provide the required service can vary with the technology, the level of production, the capital/labour ratio and the costs of inputs.

The comparison of FI with the energy and transport sectors is also apt in another way. Limiting the production of the latter by regulation or through the introduction of inefficiencies in their production affects the output of virtually all the sectors in the economy, as well as forcing a change in the structure of the economy. The net effect is likely to be a change in the composition of aggregate output as well as a reduction in it. The same pattern of effects also applies to administratively-introduced inefficiencies in FI.[12] Conversely, an increase in the efficiency of FI causes it to provide its services to other sectors in greater variety and at lower cost, thereby inducing an increase in their production, so that the aggregate output in the economy would increase.

The economy benefits from FI if its existence – or, at the margin, its increase – for given amounts of labour and capital in the economy increases the aggregate output Y of commodities. This need not always be so since the output of the FI sector plays two opposing roles in the economy: from (34), it uses up some capital and labour in the production of the intermediate good but, as specified by (35), the use of this good in commodity production enhances the productivity of labour and capital in the latter. Hence, for a given level of labour and capital in the economy, the net effect of the expansion in the FI sector on the commodity output could go either way. However, economic agents are free to use financial services or not use them, and would do so only if it would be to their advantage. Further, as mentioned in the introduction to this chapter, the historical experience is that monetary economies generate much larger output per capita than corresponding barter economies. Therefore, a plausible assumption for long-run analysis is that an increase in the output of the financial sector in an efficient market economy causes a net increase in the economy's commodity output in the observed range of production of FI.[13] We will, therefore, assume that, in the long run, $\partial y/\partial z > 0$ and $\partial^2 y/\partial z^2 < 0$. Under these assumptions, an increase in the output of the financial sector would cause an increase in the economy's per capita output.

Another relevant question in the context of growth theory is whether such an increase in the efficiency and output of the FI sector also causes an increase in the *growth rate* of the economy and, further, whether it increases the *SS growth rate* of the economy. There is no consensus in the economics profession on these issues, though historical experience suggests that an efficient and growing FI sector does seem to be a requisite for the fast-growing economies.

A simple modification of (34) to encompass technical change in the production and financial sectors is:

$$z = z(\beta(t)k_z) \quad z_k > 0, z_{kk} < 0 \tag{36}$$

where $\beta(t)$ measures the efficiency of capital and labour in the production of financial services.

The corresponding simple modification of (35) to encompass technical change in the production and financial sectors is:

$$x = x(a(t)k_x, b(t)z) \quad x_k, x_z > 0; x_{kk}, x_{zz} < 0 \tag{37}$$

where $a(t)$ and $b(t)$ represent the efficiency of usage of the capital per worker and of the financial sector's output in the production of commodities. Changes in $b(t)$ can accrue because of innovations in the production sector or in the financial sector since the determinants of $b(t)$ include the diversity, liquidity and other characteristics of the latter's output. The financial development of the economy results in increases in either $\beta(t)$ or $b(t)$, or both.

The dispute on the role of financial development can now be framed as follows: are $\beta(t)$ and $b(t)$ caused wholly by $a(t)$ or can they occur independently to some extent at least? In the former case, financial development is wholly induced by technical change in the production sectors; in the latter, the independent elements of financial sector growth can induce greater output in the production sector than would occur otherwise. While both of these are theoretical possibilities, the dispute on the contribution of financial development to the economy's growth revolves around the real-world experience over long periods and can only be settled by empirical studies.

Equations (36) and (37) implicitly assume that technical change is exogenous and merely a function of time. But such change could also have endogenous elements. We consider this possibility in a subsequent section.

26.9 EMPIRICAL EVIDENCE ON THE IMPORTANCE OF MONEY AND THE FINANCIAL SECTOR TO GROWTH

We briefly and selectively consider some evidence on this issue from economic history and econometric studies. Corresponding to the pattern of the theoretical analyses in this chapter, we need to examine the empirical evidence on two separate issues: the effect of increases in the quantity of money, for a given financial structure, and those of the financial structure.

Empirical evidence on the quantity of money, inflation and growth

The effect of changes in the quantity of money on growth can be examined in one of two ways. It can be estimated directly by using the data on the money supply or indirectly, since the growth rate of the money supply is usually related to the rate of inflation, by examining the effect of inflation on the growth rate of output. The theoretical findings on these can be summarized as:

(a) the quantity of money is neutral in the long run;
(b) any deviations from neutrality emanating from the analysis in sections 26.1 to 26.3 are minor (of a second or third order of importance, which may not be visible in the data or not invariant among different periods or countries); and
(c) the long-run growth rate is independent of both the money supply growth rate and of the rate of inflation.

However, some of the inflation–growth literature claims that high inflation rates are inimical to growth because they introduce distortions and inefficiencies in the economy. This literature further claims that price stability enhances economic certainty and promotes investment, which is conducive to growth.[14] Hence, growth rates will be negatively related to the inflation rate.[15]

Among the studies which report that the growth rate is independent of the rate of monetary growth and the inflation rate is Lucas (1996). Lucas plots for 100 countries the bivariate relationship between thirty-year averages of the output growth rate and the M2 growth rate, and argues that the plots show the former as being independent of the latter.[16] His conclusion is that, in the long run, money is neutral for the output growth rate.

McCandless and Weber (1995) used time-series data for 110 countries and thirty-year geometric average rates of growth. Their finding was that there was no correlation between inflation and output growth. Further, in general, there was no correlation between the growth rate of money – measured by M0, M1 and M2 – and real output.[17] The exception to this was a subsample of OECD countries, with a positive correlation between these variables.

While some empirical studies have reported some sort of a correlation – some reporting a negative one[18] and others a positive one[19] – between the growth rate and the inflation rate (or the money growth rate), the estimated relationship is often weak and usually not robust to changes in the data set or the inclusion of other likely determinants of growth.[20] As a result, a vague sort of consensus continues to exist in monetary economics that output growth is independent of the inflation rate and the money growth rate.

Empirical evidence on the role of the financial sector in growth: some conclusions drawn from economic history

One form of the evidence on the relationship between the financial sector and growth comes from the economic history of the early stages of industrialization in countries noted for industrial innovation. Cameron's (1967) assessment on this was that:

financial innovation, after all, is not so very different from technical innovation. The former is frequently necessary for realization of the latter [p. 12].

Cameron's illustration of this point was based on the origin and expansion of commercial banking in Great Britain during and as an essential part of its Industrial Revolution. Further,

> while it is rare for banks to finance directly a period of experimentation with a completely novel production technique by a new, inexperienced businessman or inventor . . . it is quite common for bankers to finance the expansion of firms that have already introduced successful innovations, and also to finance the adoption of the innovation by imitators.
> (Cameron, 1967, p. 13)

The assessment by Schumpeter, an early proponent of the importance of technological change – in current terminology, of endogenous technical change – to development, was:

> The essential function of credit . . . consists in enabling the entrepreneur to withdraw the producer's goods which he needs from their previous employments, by exercising a demand for them, and thereby to force the economic system into new channels.
> (Schumpeter, 1933, p. 106).

These quotes point to the critical role of the financial sector in the innovation and restructuring processes which are elements of any technical change, including the endogenous one, and of economic development.[21]

Empirical evidence on the role of the financial sector in growth: recent empirical evidence

Chari *et al.* (1995) conduct a cross-section analysis of eighty-eight countries. They find that inflation by itself has negligible effects on the growth rate. However, there is a high correlation between the rate of inflation and the required reserve ratios, and there is a negative – and highly non-linear – relationship between these reserve ratios and the growth rates. They conclude that financial regulations and the interaction of inflation with regulation have substantial negative effects on growth. This evidence of the detrimental effects of financial regulation has the corollary that a more efficient and developed financial system is conducive to growth.

Support for the conclusions drawn above from economic history is provided by the empirical study by Rajan and Zingales (1998) who report from a cross-section econometric analysis of countries that industries which depend relatively more on external financing developed faster in countries with more developed financial sectors. The need for external financing varies among industries and depends on factors such as the initial project scale, the gestation duration, internal generation through retained earnings and the amounts needed for further investment, etc. Financial development reduces the cost of external financing and, therefore, promotes the growth of existing firms and industries dependent on such financing. It also promotes the establishment of new firms and industries, which usually account for a large part of new ideas, innovations and breakthroughs.[22] Financial development also reduces financial market imperfections, which usually favour internal financing and the growth of existing firms relative to that of new firms.[23] Therefore, the lower cost and easier access to external finance provides a mechanism through which financial development influences change and growth in the economy and, in the authors' view, is evidence of causality running from financial development to growth. They also argue that, at the country level, a country with a more developed financial market has a comparative advantage over others.

Levine and Zervos (1998) proceeded further and differentiated between banking development and stock market liquidity, where the latter was measured by 'turnover' defined as the values of trades of domestic shares on domestic stock exchanges divided by the value of listed domestic shares or by 'value traded' which was defined as the value of the above trades divided by the domestic GDP.[24] Stock market liquidity, therefore, refers to the ease with which domestic equities can be traded. Banking development was measured by the bank loans to private enterprises divided by GDP. Levine and Zervos reported from a cross-section country analysis of forty-seven countries over the 1976–93 period that the *initial* levels of both banking development and stock market liquidity were independently and positively related to *subsequent* growth rates, capital accumulation and productivity improvement.[25] The effects were very significant and indicated causality from financial development to economic growth. Further, they reported that the main impact of these variables on growth was through productivity increases rather than through capital accumulation (Levine and Zervos, 1998; Temple, 1999). On the latter, Levine and Zervos did not find a significant link between private saving and either of their financial development variables. Nor did domestic private saving prove to have a strong relationship with the international financial linkages.

A point worth noting – and one we have glossed over in this chapter – from the Levine and Zervos study is that banks provide different services from those provided by stock markets, and that each can have independent effects on economic growth. More broadly, the banking system is only a subset of a developed financial sector whose other segments are also vital to growth in the modern economy.

Another point worth noting from both the economic history findings and the econometric studies is that the contribution of the financial sector to growth rates is at least partly through the dynamics of the economy's industrial structure, especially in the external financing of new firms and new products. This ties in very well with the emphasis on innovation and change in the new theories of endogenous technical change.

26.10 A SIMPLIFIED GROWTH MODEL OF ENDOGENOUS TECHNICAL CHANGE INVOLVING THE FINANCIAL SECTOR[26]

One reason why an unregulated and efficient financial sector (FS) promotes growth in the economy as a *continuing process* can be seen from the endogenous growth theories. In these, the endogenous increases in knowledge and innovation are the vehicle for increases in the growth rate and for a positive growth rate of per capita output even in the steady state.

We now bring in the arguments on endogenous growth from the preceding chapter and adapt them to take account of our arguments in the preceding section. To incorporate the role of the FS in the economy, modify the corresponding commodity production function assumed in Chapter 25 to the form:

$$x_{ij} = [A^j k_{xij}^{\alpha'} k_{xj}^{\alpha''} \phi(k_j, \cdot)] z_{ij}^{\beta'} z_j^{\beta''} \quad 0 < \alpha', \alpha'', \beta', \beta'' < 1 \tag{38}$$

In (38), the subscript x refers to the commodity (final goods) sector, i to the firm and j to the country. $\phi(\cdot)$ is determined by the contribution to the firm's production from the differential in its knowledge and that associated with the highest capital intensity among the countries of the world.[27] $z_{ij}^{\beta'}$ represents the advantages to the ith firm from using real balances. The firm also benefits from the externality of economy-wide usage of real balances, as represented by the term $z_j^{\beta''}$, so that the social role of money in the production technology is thus explicitly recognized. For the per capita production function of the economy, assuming all firms to be identical, we have:

$$x_j = A_j k_{xj}^{\alpha} \phi(\cdot) z_j^{\beta} \tag{39}$$

where $\alpha = \alpha' + \alpha''$ and $\beta = \beta' + \beta''$; β can be less than or greater than unity. The productivity of capital is now:

$$\partial x_j / \partial k_{xj} = \alpha A_j k_{xj}^{\alpha-1} \phi(\cdot) z_j^{\beta} \tag{40}$$

so that the productivity of capital is higher in a monetary rather than a barter economy and is also higher if the FS has a greater output. Therefore, efficient FI encourages investment in physical capital in the commodity sector. Conversely, the marginal productivity of the services of the FS for firms in production is:

$$\partial x_j / \partial z_j = \beta A_j k_{xj}^{\alpha} \phi(\cdot) z_j^{\beta-1} \tag{41}$$

which is higher in the more capital-intensive economy, thereby providing an incentive for the more capital-intensive economies to use more FI than the less capital-intensive ones. It is also obvious from (38) to (41) that, within a given economy, a sector which has a higher capital–labour ratio or higher values of A and α – so that the productivity of labour and capital are higher in it – would have a higher productivity of real balances and a greater demand for it.

Equations (40) and (41) point to the importance of an efficient FS in the economy. The more relevant is FI to the needs of the production sector and the cheaper its provision, the greater will be the amount of it that will be used and the greater will be the return to capital, output per capita, as well as the pre-SS growth rate of output. Whether the SS growth rates will be higher or not is likely to depend upon whether β is less than one or not.[28]

26.11 INVESTMENT, FINANCIAL INTERMEDIATION AND ECONOMIC DEVELOPMENT

Most economies seem to show a special connection between the increases in capital and efficient FI, leading to higher investment in the commodity sector. We have seen this above in (38), which shows that the marginal productivity of capital increases with FI. But there also seems to be another connection. For this, we have to get away from the concept of *passive investment* – that is, investment responding passively to the saving available for the increase in physical capital – in neoclassical growth models.[29] In the real world, most firms do not possess enough capital through their own resources to finance all the equipment or all the investment that they want. Any investment requires additional funds, which can with difficulty and often at relatively high cost be obtained directly from the ultimate savers in the economy without going through some financial intermediary or other. A restraint on the FI process leads to blockages, reductions and inefficiencies in the flow of funds for investment and consequently to a reduction in investment.

For developing economies, McKinnon (1973), among others, has emphasized the importance of FI to the level and efficacy of investment. He argued that developing economies have fragmented markets with significant constraints on borrowing, which reduce the total amount invested and also channel the available funds into less productive uses, so that unregulated and efficient FI is vital to the growth of such economies. To pursue this argument, let,

$$i_x = i_x(s - s_z, z') \quad \partial i_x / \partial z' > 0 \tag{42}[30]$$

where:

i_x investment in the commodity sector
z' increase in z
s_z saving devoted to expansion of FI sector

In keeping with the emphasis of this section on the FS, z' is to be viewed not as the creation of new fiat money but as an expansion of the FS with the actual services changing as needed for the growing economy. An expansion of z directly encourages investment i_x so that $\partial i_x / \partial z' > 0$, but the saving devoted to the expansion of z reduces i_x. However, the efficient allocation of saving to investment projects and the sectors of the economy improves, so that the marginal productivity of investment and that of the capital stock in the production function improves, thereby increasing output per capita in the economy and providing higher growth rates.

Therefore, there are two types of effects of FI on capital. One is by increasing its marginal product, as in (40), for given levels of the aggregate capital stock. The other, as in (42), is the direct effect on the volume of investment of the expansion of the FI sector. Many economists believe that these effects imply higher per capita income and pre-SS growth rates for an economy with a more efficient and competitive financial sector relative to another, otherwise identical, economy. It is also likely that they also do so for the steady states of the two economies.

While these are persuasive arguments that an inefficient and overregulated FS can hold back per capita output and its pre-SS growth rate, such analysis does not provide any guidance on whether the expansion of an efficient and competitive FS will increase the SS growth rates of its economy. Monetary economics does not offer conclusive judgement on the latter issue.

CONCLUSIONS

The empirical regressions of output growth against the growth rate of money supply over very long periods do not show a significant – and robust – relationship among these variables, nor does the long-run data show a significant relationship between output growth and the rate of inflation. These findings imply the independence of the long-run growth rate of output from that of the money supply.

As against the above finding, it has been the contention of this chapter that monetary economies have substantially more capital and output per worker than barter ones. A secondary contention has been that more efficient financial intermediation further increases these. These contentions are not necessarily inconsistent with the empirical findings on the relationship between the growth rates of the money supply and output but rather highlight the way we should think of banking and financial intermediation in the context of growth theory. This is not in terms of the quantity of nominal money in the economy but rather of the real services provided by financial intermediation and of the interaction between this sector and the other sectors of the economy.

The standard neoclassical growth theory encompassing fiat money incorporates money only in terms of its nominal quantity and does not necessarily imply a positive impact of money on output, since the introduction of real balances in it reduces the saving available for the growth of physical capital. There are two reasons for this: the increase in real balances increases disposable income and thereby the consumption of commodities, and saving has to be partly allocated to this increase in real balances.

The essential requirement for more realistic effects of money on the economy requires the recognition of the basic fact that the production functions in a monetary economy are different from those in non-monetary economies: the former have higher marginal products of capital and labour. Money allows specialization, trade and expansion in the size of firms to an extent that can never occur under barter and in economies with rudimentary monetary systems. Further, with the shift in the transactions technology from barter to one with the use of money, the reduction in transactions time causes a shift/increase in the labour supply. In addition, an efficient financial sector allows the accumulation and more efficient allocation of savings to investment projects, and thereby promotes the growth of capital in the economy.

Monetary growth theory applicable to modern economies has to get away from its emphasis on fiat (outside) money and focus on the financial sector as a whole. This sector consists not only of the commercial banks, it also includes investment brokers and stock markets, insurance and mortgage companies, and pension funds, etc. Although the financial intermediaries use up some of the resources of the economy in intermediate production, the gains from the use of this intermediate good in final production are much more substantial. The optimal production and usage of financial services in the economy require the efficiency of the financial sector. Further, the technology of this sector evolves with that of the economy generally, with the proportions of the particular financial assets appropriate to the evolving technology of trade and production of the final goods changing with this technology. Hence, the amount of a given monetary asset does not invariably remain a good indicator of the final output of the financial sector.

Developing economies with evolving monetary systems provide a sort of laboratory for examining the effects of finance on production, trade, investment and capital intensity. There are a large number of empirical studies that support the conclusion that an efficient and evolving financial sector makes a major contribution to economic growth and development. This occurs through its very vital contributions to the efficiency of the production and exchange sectors of the economy, to the accumulation of savings and their efficient allocation among projects and sectors, and to the allocation of funds to innovation and risk taking, growth of capital, etc.[31] Consideration of these contributions suggests very significant deficiencies in the way the standard neoclassical growth theory has handled money in growth theory by considering it merely as fiat money balances or even in terms of aggregates such as M1 or M2. Such an approach does not, and possibly cannot, deal with the shifts in technology and labour supply due to the financial evolution of developing economies. Further, it assumes complete, competitive and efficient money markets while the financial sector in such economies is often a fractured, imperfect and controlled one. Development economists generally support the view that the latter characteristics imply lower output per capita and lower growth rates for economies than the former. Presumably, they would also imply lower SS growth rates, but this is not certain and can only be judged in the context of a specific model.

Returning to the discussion on the importance of complete, efficient and competitive FI, there is a two-way relationship between the FS and the other sectors of the economy. The efficiency of exchange and production in the latter depends on the former, innovation in which can exert an independent impact on the rest of the economy. But, conversely, the latter provides some of the inputs for the former, in the form of the types of capital equipment, knowledge and information technology, the education and skills of employees, etc. The efficiency of the financial sector is also dependent, as are the other sectors, on regulations, technological change and other aspects of the economic environment.

As a major sector whose services are needed and used by all the other sectors in the economy but which, in turn, uses the inputs and knowledge originating in other sectors, there is a symbiotic relationship between an efficient and competitive financial sector and the rest of the economy. This makes it difficult to assign causality on the questions of whether the efficiency of the financial sector emanate from the other sectors of the economy versus the contribution that an efficient financial sector makes to the efficiency of the latter. It also creates considerable differences of opinion in the profession on the dynamic contribution that the expansion of an already efficient financial sector can make to the growth – especially in the steady state – of the economy. Empirical evidence presented in this chapter indicates that financial development contributes to higher per capita growth rates, more so through productivity growth than through capital accumulation.

Empirical studies in recent years have begun to separate the relationship between the growth rates of output and the money supply (or inflation), and those between the growth of output and the efficiency and development of the financial sector. On the former set of variables, the usual finding is that there is no evidence of a relationship or the relationship is not robust or it is slightly negative. On the latter set of variables, the finding is usually that of a significant positive relationship. Therefore, the implication of these empirical findings for monetary policy is that it should support the greater efficiency and development of the financial sector.

SUMMARY OF CRITICAL CONCLUSIONS

- Monetary growth theory which focuses on the quantity of money rather than on monetary and other financial institutions, tends to assume that the commodity production function is the same in the monetary economy as in the barter one. Under its usual assumptions, this theory does not provide a clear implication that the use of money provides a higher steady-state standard of living than the non-monetary (barter) one. In fact, some versions of it imply a lower output per capita. In any case, the switch from the barter to the monetary economy is not a neutral one.
- For an existing monetary economy, this monetary growth theory implies that the quantity of money is neutral.
- The usage of money is an invention with remarkable externalities for the technology of commodity production and exchange: it increases the size of markets, promotes specialization and trade and shifts the commodity production frontier drastically. It also increases the supply of labour to firms.
- The primary usage of money in the monetary economy consists of the use of the liabilities of monetary institutions in the economy rather than of fiat money.
- The monetary sector in the modern economy should be seen as merely one component of the financial sector. The appropriate focus of monetary growth theory should be on the efficiency and structure of the financial sector rather than on variations in the quantity of money.
- The financial sector provides financial services as intermediate goods in the economy. The efficiency of its supply of these services, and their diversification, is a critical element in the determination of the commodity output per capita, including that in the steady state.
- Innovations in the financial sector contribute to the growth rate of output in the pre-SS stage and may also do so to the steady-state rate.

---

review and discussion questions

1. In the context of the traditional neoclassical growth theories with money, is the money growth rate neutral for the steady state and the pre-steady states of the economy? Explain your answer.
2. In the context of the endogenous growth theories with money, is the money growth rate neutral for the steady state and the pre-steady states of the economy? Explain your answer.
3. Is there room for considering changes in the structure and efficiency of the financial sector in the traditional neoclassical growth theories with money? If so, how would you modify the standard model to accommodate such changes and what implications would they have for the steady-state and the pre-steady-state growth rates of the economy?
4. 'Rapid increases in the money stock cause inflation and inflation raises interest rates, so that investment is reduced by the rapid increases in the money stock. Consequently, high rates of money growth reduce the growth rate of the economy.' Discuss this statement in the context of monetary growth theory. Is there any place for this line of reasoning in the traditional and the endogenous growth theories? Why or why not? If it is not, does it reflect a deficiency in monetary growth theory?

5 'Given that saving is positively related to the rate of interest and that an increase in the rate of inflation will increase the rate of interest, both saving and the growth rate of the economy will be positively related to the inflation rate and the money growth rate.' Discuss in the context of monetary growth theories.

6 'It is vital for understanding the contribution of money to growth that we distinguish between the quantity of money and the size and the efficiency of the financial sector.' Discuss.

7 Should a distinction be drawn between the growth rate of fiat money provided by the central bank and that of inside money provided by private commercial banks for the proper analysis of money in growth theory? Explain your answer.

8 What is the empirical evidence on the contribution of (a) the quantity of money, (b) the financial sector, to growth? Cite at least one study on each of these. Compare their findings and explain the reasons for any findings that may be different.

9 How would you test for the contribution of (a) the quantity of money, (b) the financial sector, to growth for a selected group of countries? Specify your variables, estimating equations and the frequency of data you would use. Perform this test and interpret your results.

10 LDCs have at times resorted to high money growth rates to finance their development efforts in an attempt to push up their growth rates. What is the theoretical analysis to support this policy? Was it misguided in retrospect and, if so, why?

11 'Banking inefficiency and the excessive regulation of the banking sector and interest rates in some of the LDCs have proved to be highly detrimental to their growth rates.' Can this be explained by monetary growth theories? Cite the relevant literature on this subject and relate it to the arguments of the monetary growth theories.

NOTES

1 The overlapping generations models of Chapters 22 and 33 fall into this pattern.

2 The role of money in the production function in Chapter 3 and the consideration of the financial sector in Chapter 24 fall into this pattern.

3 This proportion can be taken as a constant or as dependent upon the opportunity cost of holding real balances. This cost equals the real rate of return on physical capital (equal to the real rate of interest) plus the expected rate of inflation.

4 Note that, just as for similar figures in Chapter 25, we have not labelled the vertical axis of this figure. Its units are output units. The concave curves measure saving per capita while the linear nk line measures investment requirements for new workers to maintain the existing capital–labour ratio.

5 If money is not costlessly-supplied and costlessly-used fiat money but needs labour and capital to generate its services, its use will increase output only if there is a net gain in output from the reallocation of some capital and labour to the production of monetary services.

6 For a simpler analysis, we have used a timeless framework rather than the more elaborate intertemporal utility function of Sidrauski (1967).

7 We have assumed here that inflation is fully expected so that the expected rate of inflation equals the actual rate. This is really an assumption of certainty or perfect foresight. Such an assumption is common in growth theory and stronger than that of rational expectations under uncertainty.

8 In a barter economy, a good part of the available time of a producer would have to be devoted to the direct sale to the ultimate consumers of the former's output. Imagine him going around the farms with his produce (wheat, vegetables, implements, etc.) to find the

consumers for it and the time it takes to produce one unit of the good versus the time to sell it, especially if he wants to get in exchange something that he is going to use himself.

9 However, note that there are disputes in the literature on whether inside money should be included in the economic calculation of net worth and how to calculate this economic net worth.

10 A study which does so is Rajan and Zingales (1998). This empirical study finds that financial development enhances long-run growth.

11 For instance, currency seems to be the most convenient and least-cost asset for transactions at very low levels of output and capital per worker, yielding to demand deposits as the latter increase.

12 To continue with our analogy, restricting all transactions in the economy to the use of only currency and demand deposits could be akin to restricting all transport in the economy only to the use of one kind of car and one kind of lorry. Both would introduce considerable inefficiencies in transport and considerably reduce the output of the other sectors of the economy.

13 However, this need not be true in the short run.

14 However, this effect is not considered to be large.

15 It should also be kept in mind that the inflation rate and the growth rate of output are negatively related by virtue of the quantity equation, so that an observed negative relationship between them cannot be used as *prima facie* evidence of a causal link from inflation to growth.

16 Lucas further shows that the correlation – for 110 countries with thirty-year averages of the data – between the M2 growth and the rate of inflation is 0.95.

17 The correlation between the growth rate of money supply and inflation was 'almost unity'.

18 For example, Barro (1996) reported a negative and statistically significant relationship between the output growth rate and the inflation rate. The elasticity was –0.025, so that disinflation of 10% would increase the growth rate by 0.25%.

19 For example, McCandless and Weber (1995) reported a weak positive relationship for the OECD countries.

20 Levine and Renelt (1992).

21 As against these claims, Lucas (1988) claimed that economists 'badly over-stress' the role of the financial system. Other economists have argued that the financial sector responds passively to growth in the production sector.

22 In some cases, as much as two-thirds of the total growth of output in the economy comes from new firms, so that their number and development is a major element of growth. Rajan and Zingales show that the effect of financial development on the growth rate of new firms is almost double of that on existing firms.

23 Financial development also promotes higher accounting standards, which reduces the costs of obtaining external finance.

24 Levine and Zervos distinguished this variable from the size (in terms of the ratio of the value of the listed shares to GDP) of the stock market. This size did not prove to be a reliable predictor of growth. These authors also considered measures of international integration.

25 Their finding was that the significant variable for growth was stock market liquidity (i.e., ability to trade stocks) rather than stock market size (i.e., how many companies are listed). One reason for this is that the higher liquidity increases the willingness of investors to fund new long-term business ventures where there is a high risk and absence of dividends for many years but investors can sell their holdings, if they wish to do so, without incurring large costs.

26 This subsection is illustrative and is not designed to present a complete model.

27 Capital in this context of endogenous growth theories is defined to include both physical and human capital.

28 Note that, to analyse the actual growth rate of output, account will have to be taken of the production function and of the labour and capital used in FI.

29 For a Keynesian perspective on money and growth, see Tobin (1965).
30 Note that this function is a departure from the neoclassical assumption that investment is solely determined by the available saving.
31 See Levine (1997) for a review of these.

REFERENCES

Barro, R. 'Inflation and Economic Growth'. *Federal Reserve Bank of St Louis Review*, 78, May/June 1996, pp. 153–69.

Bruno, M., and W. Easterly. 'Inflation and Growth: In Search of a Stable Relationship'. *Federal Reserve Bank of St Louis Review*, 78, May/June 1996, pp. 139–51.

Cameron, Rondo. *Banking in the Early Stages of Industrialization*. New York: Oxford University Press, 1967.

Chari, V. V., Larry E. Jones and Rodolfo E. Manuelli. 'The Growth Effects of Monetary Policy'. *Federal Reserve Bank of Minneapolis Quarterly Review*, Fall 1995, pp. 18–32.

Dornbusch, Rudiger, and Alejandro Reynoso. 'Financial Factors in Economic Development'. *American Economic Review Papers and Proceedings*, 79, May 1989, pp. 204–09.

Fry, Maxwell, J. *Money, Interest and Banking in Economic Development*. Baltimore, MD: Johns Hopkins Press, 1988.

Johnson, Harry. 'Money in a Neoclassical One Sector Growth Model'. In his *Essays in Monetary Economics*. Cambridge, MA: Cambridge University Press, 1967.

Levhari, D., and Don Patinkin. 'The Role of Money in a Simple Growth Model'. *American Economic Review*, 55, September 1968, pp. 713–53.

Levine, Ross. 'Financial Development and Economic Growth: View and Agenda'. *Journal of Economic Literature*, 35, June 1997, pp. 688–726.

——, and David Renelt. 'A Sensitivity Analysis of Cross-Country Growth Regressions'. *American Economic Review*, 82, September 1992, pp. 942–63.

——, and Sara Zervos. 'Stock Markets, Banks and Economic Growth'. *American Economic Review*, 88, June 1998, pp. 537–58.

Lucas, Robert E., Jr. 'On the Mechanics of Economic Development'. *Journal of Monetary Economics*, 22, July 1988, pp. 3–42.

——. 'Nobel Lecture: Monetary Neutrality'. *Journal of Political Economy*, 104, August 1996, pp. 661–82.

McCandless, George T., Jr, and Warren E. Weber. 'Some Monetary Facts'. *Federal Reserve Bank of Minneapolis Quarterly Review*, 19, Summer 1995, pp. 2–11.

McKinnon, Ronald I. *Money and Capital in Economic Development*. Washington, DC: The Brookings Institution, 1973.

Metzler, Alan H. 'Money, Intermediation and Growth'. *Journal of Economic Literature*, 7, March 1969, pp. 27–56.

Page, Sheila, ed. *Monetary Policy in Developing Countries*. London: Routledge, 1993, Ch. 16.

Rajan, Raghuram G., and Luigi Zingales. 'Financial Dependence and Growth'. *American Economic Review*, 88, June 1998, pp. 559–86.

Schumpeter, Joseph A. *The Theory of Economic Development*. Cambridge, MA: Cambridge University Press, 1933.

Sidrauski, Miguel. 'Rational Growth and Patterns of Growth in a Monetary Economy'. *American Economic Review*, 57, May 1967, pp. 534–44.

Temple, Jonathan. 'The New Growth Evidence'. *Journal of Economic Literature*, 37, March 1999, pp. 112–56.

Tobin, James. 'Money and Economic Growth'. *Econometrica*, 33, October 1965, pp. 671–84.

Index